Professional
Java Server
Programming

**Danny Ayers, Hans Bergsten,
Michael Bogovich, Jason Diamond,
Matthew Ferris, Marc Fleury,
Ari Halberstadt, Paul Houle, Piroz Mohseni,
Andrew Patzer, Ron Phillips,
Sing Li, Krishna Vedati,
Mark Wilcox and Stefan Zeiger**

Wrox Press Ltd. ®

Professional Java Server Programming

First Published   August 1999
Reprinted   December 1999

Published by Wrox Press Ltd
Arden House, 1102 Warwick Road, Acock's Green, Birmingham B27 6BH, UK
Printed in USA
ISBN 1-861002-77-7

Trademark Acknowledgements

Wrox has endeavored to provide trademark information about all the companies and products mentioned in this book by the appropriate use of capitals. However, Wrox cannot guarantee the accuracy of this information.

Credits

Authors
Danny Ayers
Hans Bergsten
Michael Bogovich
Jason Diamond
Matthew Ferris
Marc Fleury
Ari Halberstadt
Paul Houle
Piroz Mohseni
Andrew Patzer
Ron Phillips
Sing Li
Krishna Vedati
Mark Wilcox
Stefan Zeiger

Additional Material
Tim Briggs
Louay Fatoohi
James Hart
Daniel Maharry

Editors
Jeremy Beacock
Tim Briggs
Paul Cooper
Louay Fatoohi
Andrew Froggatt
James Hart
Daniel Maharry
Richard Ollerenshaw
Robert F E Shaw

Technical Reviewers
Lee Ackerman
David Allen
Thomas Bishop
Michael Boerner
James Donelson
Joan Friedman
Brian Howell
Victoria Hudgson
Jim Johnson
Kito Mann
Benoît Marchal
Jacob Matthew
Tom Mitchell
Alexander Nakhimovsky
Simon Oliver
Stefan Osmont
Steven Pomerleau
Rick Stones

Design / Layout
Mark Burdett
Frances Olesch
Tom Bartlett
John McNulty

Illustrations
David Boyce

Cover Design
Chris Morris

Index
Martin Brooks

Cover Photographs

Left to right

Andrew Patzer (Expressly Portraits), Ari Halberstadt (Jerry Halberstadt), Paul Houle, Ron Phillips (Morrison Studios, Brookfield, WI), Piroz Mohseni (Dorn's, Red Bank, NJ), Krishna Vedati (Weaver Photography, Mountain View, CA), Mark Wilcox (Gary Dean Photography, The Picture House, Inc.), Danny Ayers, Sing Li, Marc Fleury, Hans Bergsten (Expressly Portraits), Stefan Zeiger

About the Authors

Danny Ayers

During the day, mild-mannered Danny Ayers tends the network at High Peak College (University of Derby), in the Derbyshire Peak District. At night he becomes a freelance writer and consultant Information Engineer. His interests include neural networks, woodcarving and drill'n'bass music. His first PC was a PET 2001 Series (8k). He may be contacted at danny_ayers@yahoo.com.

Thanks to Caroline.

Hans Bergsten

Hans has almost twenty years experience as a software developer. During seventeen years at Ericsson he developed software systems for everything from IBM mainframes, through DEC minicomputers and Unix workstations and servers, to PCs. He's worked with object-oriented concepts the last ten years, using Simula, Smalltalk, C/C++ and Java, developed database applications and network based applications since the late eighties, and started to study Java when it was first made public in 1995.

In 1997 Hans founded Gefion Software to further develop his ideas about network based, platform independent software systems. Gefion Software is a Java server-side technology leader with three popular Java servlet based products: a component suite for easy development of dynamic websites (*InstantOnline Basic*), a servlet engine for Netscape web servers (*WAICoolRunner*), and a Java web server with servlet support (*LiteWebServer*).

Hans is a member of the working groups for both the Servlet API and JavaServer Pages (JSP) specifications and is a frequent writer of articles for Java and web design related web sites.

Michael Bogovich

Michael S. Bogovich is a Consultant and Technical Manager with BALR Corporation in Oak Brook, Illinois, and has been working with object-oriented languages and relational databases for ten years. He is a member of the Chicagoland Java User Group.

My chapter is dedicated to my mother, who dedicated herself to my life journey, and to my new wife, Margaret, whom I've dedicated myself to.

Jason Diamond

Jason Diamond (jason@injektilo.org) is a software engineer and musician currently enjoying life in sunny Oceanside, CA. He doesn't write autobiographical notes very well but he does know how to dedicate this and everything else he does to his beautiful princess, Jill.

Matthew Ferris

Matthew E. Ferris is a consultant with BALR Corporation in Oak Brook, Illinois, and has been working with object-oriented software for the past 5 years. He is a Sun Certified Java Programmer, and president of the Chicagoland Java User Group.

Marc Fleury

Marc Fleury is an independent contractor based out of Foster City, CA in the Silicon Valley. Marc focuses on server side Java and e-commerce implementations. In a previous life he earned degrees in mathematics and theoretical physics, and topped off his long studies with a Ph.D. in Physics. He was reborn when the software bug bit him and bit him hard. Marc joined Sun Microsystems where he spent 3 years as a Java evangelist and an SAP expert, before going independent. In his spare time Marc likes to contribute to various open source projects including EJBoss, the EJB server for Linux, and is commited to seeing the WebOS become an open source reality before he dies. Marc is married and has a daughter, baby Elvira, to whom he dedicates his chapter.

Paul Houle

Paul recently got his Ph.D. in Physics from Cornell University and is now completing his post-doctoral research in Dresden, Germany. He likes Unix, Java and his two cats. He is moving into web consulting and is currently doing research on intelligent webcrawlers and content analysis of large hypertexts.

Piroz Mohseni

Piroz Mohseni is president of Bita Technologies focusing on business improvement through effective usage of technology. His areas of interest include enterprise Java, XML and business-to-business e-commerce applications. Prior to that he was a Member of Technical Staff and chief architect for a 100% pure Java application server at Lucent Technologies Bell Laboratories. Mr. Mohseni writes regularly for various Java publications and is an occasional speaker at conferences. He can be reached at pmohseni@iname.com.

To those who prefer dialogue over confrontation.

Andrew Patzer

Andrew Patzer is a Senior Consultant for New Resources Corporation as well as a Practice Manager in the company's e-business practice. He is a certified Java programmer and has been developing server-side Java applications for the past 2 years. Andrew has published white papers on distributed architectures and has given many presentations to user groups and conferences. In addition to Java, Andrew also enjoys working with the Linux operating system and playing around with Tcl/Tk and Python. Andrew resides in Oak Creek, Wisconsin USA with his wife Beth and daughters Ashley and Emily. He can be reached at apatzer@usa.net.

To my wife Beth and our daughters Ashley and Emily. Thank you for your patience and support. I am very blessed to have such a wonderful family.

Ron Phillips

Ron Phillips has been designing and developing commercial software tools for over ten years, with commercial 4GL environments, programming languages and software design tools to his credit. He is active in the IT community, and has spoken at several industry conferences in the USA and Europe. His current research efforts focus on distributed objects, n-tier systems and mobile agents.

Sing Li

First bitten by the computer bug in 1978, Sing has grown up with the microprocessor revolution. His first 'PC' was a $99 do-it-yourself COSMIC ELF computer with 256 bytes of memory and a 1 bit LED display. For two decades, Sing has been an active author, consultant, speaker, instructor, and entrepreneur. His wide-ranging experience spans distributed architectures, multi-tiered Internet/Intranet systems, computer telephony, call center technology, and embedded systems. Sing has participated in several Wrox projects in the past, and has been working with (and writing about) Java and Jini since their very first alpha release. He is an active participant in the Jini community.

To all Java enthusiasts, Jini hackers, and JavaSpace phreaks.

Krishna Vedati

Krishna Vedati is a senior software engineer at ValiCert, Inc. Prior to working at ValiCert, he was a senior software engineer at Rational Software Corporation, designing and developing load testing tools for X-windows and Web servers. Mr. Vedati also contributed to the Wrox Press book *Beginning Linux Programming*, and has taught introductory courses in Tcl and PGP for the Linux community. His technical areas of interest include Internet Security, Network Agents, Internet Protocols, Scripting Languages and Graphical User Interfaces. If he's not in front of the computer coding, he is out playing cricket. He can be reached at krishnav@valicert.com or kvedati@yahoo.com.

I would like to thank my friend JoAnne Chung for her encouragement and support through out the writing process. I would also like to thank Tim Briggs at Wrox Press for giving me the opportunity to be a part of this team. Finally I would like to thank my family: my parents Satya Narayana and Vara Lakshmi, and my brothers Subbiah, Nagender and Prasad for a their love, support and encouragement throughout out my life; without them I would not be who I am.

Mark Wilcox

Mark is the Web Administrator for the University of North Texas. He's also the author of *Implementing LDAP*, also published by Wrox Press, and is a regular columnist for Netscape's *ViewSource* magazine.

To my wife Jessica and to Dr. Kevin McKinney and Dr. Mitchel Kruger who made sure I was around to finish my chapter.

Stefan Zeiger

Stefan Zeiger has been working as a freelance Java programmer since 1997 and studying computer science at the Technical University of Darmstadt since 1996. He is the author of the *NetForge* web server software and the popular online servlet tutorial *Servlet Essentials*.

Summary of Contents

Table of Contents

Chapter 9: Connection Pools   185

Chapter 10: Servlet Chaining   213

Chapter 11: Servlet Communications   227

Chapter 12: Distributed Computing With Servlets   239

Chapter 15: Weeds of El Limon 2

Chapter 16: Bug Tracker Case Study   361

Chapter 17: Bug Tracker Case Study: Elaboration, Construction and Transition   381

Chapter 18: Moving from CGI to Servlets   445

Chapter 21: Server Programming with JNDI   515

Chapter 22: Using LDAP and Java   547

Chapter 24: Indexing and Searching   621

Chapter 25: Jini and JavaSpaces: Servers of the Future   661

Chapter 27: Coding a Jini-based Website 747

Appendix G: ServletRunner and Java Web Server Configuration

Appendix H: JRun Configuration

Introduction

Welcome

Welcome to Professional Java Server Programming. This book shows how Java Servlets and JavaServer Pages (JSP) can help you provide dynamic and customizable content to web clients in a portable, secure and well-designed way.

Because your web applications are only as good as the functionality they provide we also survey the Java Enterprise APIs that interface with Servlets and JSP. And to show the practice of programming Java applications, we present five case studies of servlets and JSP in action.

Who is this Book For?

Java, the language, needs no introduction. It's not been out of the news since it was released. What this book is about is not so much the language but the Java 2 platform, the class libraries that provide support and ready-built functionality for all manner of application domains, and how that affects programming for the Web.

The Java 2 platform is a fast-maturing way to program portable, object-oriented, secure, Internet-ready applications. Over the last two years, Java's support for applications has expanded enormously. You can now develop dynamic web server applications which

> ➤ Serve HTML, XML and GIFs
> ➤ Separate presentation, logic and data
> ➤ Track client sessions
> ➤ Scale better than CGI
> ➤ Interface to databases, other Java applications, CORBA, directory and mail services
> ➤ Make use of application server middleware to provide transactional support

The APIs in question have very broad industry support, having been developed by JavaSoft in wide consultation with expert partners. In consequence, the Java revolution of portable code and open APIs is married with an evolution in existing products (whether database, application, mail or web servers). The wide availability of products to run Java applications on the server has made this a fast-moving and very competitive market, but the essential compatibility through specifications, standard APIs and class libraries has held. This makes server-side Java a very exciting area.

This book is aimed at professional developers with some experience of programming for the Web. It also assumes familiarity with the Java language and the core APIs – through reading *Beginning Java 2* (Ivor Horton, ISBN 1-861002-23-8) or some other tutorial book that covers similar ground. We'll review key areas that crop up again and again in server-side programming.

What's Covered in this Book

In sketching out the contents of this book, we focussed on the idea that servlet and web programming are really just about input and output streams, requests and responses. The servlet is the communications bridge between any client that can talk over the HTTP protocol and any data or service that can be controlled through Java code. The diagram from the inside front cover is an attempt to show that.

The book has the following structure:

> A tutorial to servlet programming, showing the classes, the servlet lifecycle, error handling, sessions and the servlet context, and putting some simple examples together.

> An introduction to JSP, explaining how they relate to servlets, showing the tags and creating beans to encapsulate business logic and keep the page simple.

> Having covered the basics, the next few chapters look at integrating servlets into applications, with chapters on database access, connection pooling, working with mail, servlet-applet and servlet-servlet communication.

> The use of XML (Extensible Markup Language) on the Web is an upcoming but crucial part of these applications. We have an introduction to handling XML using Java and a case study of presenting XML data to a browser.

> There then follow chapters on designing for n-tier applications, internationalization, servlets that dynamically construct their runtime behavior from their input, naming and directory services accessed through JNDI, the design of EJBs and a case study of a servlet spider.

> Finally, as food for thought, we introduce Jini and JavaSpaces, and show something of the promise of these new technologies.

Appendices give programming refreshers, advice on installing several servlet engines and a detailed API reference to the enterprise classes and interfaces we use throughout the book.

What You Need to Use this Book

The code in this book was tested with the Java 2 Platform Standard Edition SDK (JDK 1.2.1).

For the extra downloads we needed, we used the following versions of the libraries:

> Servlets. We used the JSDK 2.1 and JSWDK 1.0 EA. The servlet engine included is fine for most software testing

> JSP 1.0 - We used the release version of the JSP 1.0 reference implementation from JavaSoft

> XML parsers - we used Sun's ProjectX classes (http://java.sun.com/xml)

- ➢ GIF encoder - available from http://www.acme.com
- ➢ Databases - any JDBC/ODBC compliant database. We used both Access and MySQL
- ➢ Mail server - any SMTP mail server in conjunction with JavaMail 1.1.2 and JAF 1.0.1
- ➢ JNDI / LDAP server - Netscape Directory Server, JNDI 1.2 Beta (1.1.2)
- ➢ International fonts
- ➢ Jini and JavaSpaces - we used version 1.0 of both kits
- ➢ Enterprise Java Beans 1.1
- ➢ Web Servers / Servlet Runners -We used Apache 1.3.6, Apache JServ 1.0, JRun 2.3, Servlet Exec and Java Web Server 2.0.

Most of the chapter code will work on a single machine, provided it is networked (that is, it can see http://localhost through the local browser). The Jini chapters really need three networked machines to put the code through its paces. Note also that you need UDP support for the Jini code, some Windows users may need an updated version of Winsock.

The complete source code from the book is available for download from:

http://www.wrox.com

Conventions

To help you get the most from the text and keep track of what's happening, we've used a number of conventions throughout the book.

For instance:

> These boxes hold important, not-to-be forgotten information which is directly relevant to the surrounding text.

While the background style is used for asides to the current discussion.

As for styles in the text:

- ➢ When we introduce them, we **highlight** important words.
- ➢ We show keyboard strokes like this: *Ctrl-A*.
- ➢ We show files and code like so: `doGet()`
- ➢ URLs and text on user interfaces is shown as http://www.wrox.com.

We present code in three different ways. Definitions from the Java class libraries are shown as follows:

```
protected void doGet(HttpServletRequest req, HttpServletResponse resp)
                    throws ServletException, IOException
```

In our code examples,

```
the code foreground style shows new, important, pertinent code
while code background shows code that's less important in the present context,
    or has been seen before.
```

Tell Us What You Think

We've worked hard to make this book as useful to you as possible, so we'd like to know what you think. We're always keen to know what it is you want and need to know.

We appreciate feedback on our efforts and take both criticism and praise on board in our future editorial efforts. If you've anything to say, let us know on:

feedback@wrox.com
or
http://www.wrox.com

Web Application Development

Over the past few years, we've witnessed some incredible changes in the way we think about computers. We are no longer bound by large and cumbersome applications on the desktop. With the introduction of the Internet and the World Wide Web, we can now access information, and even do business, from virtually anywhere. The challenge that we, as application developers, now face is that of raising the bar yet again. With these recent advances in technology also comes the demand for faster, lighter, and more robust applications that we can deliver across the Web.

Fortunately, we have some powerful tools to work with. In the past, if you wanted to deliver a database-driven application to customers over the Web, you were pretty much limited to writing CGI scripts to process form data and return some results. But in the last couple of years, a large number of technologies have appeared. The only trouble is trying to sort through the options and decide what is right for you and your organization.

CGI has served its purpose, of adding interactivity and dynamic content to the Web, well. The shortcomings of CGI, both in developing for it and in its scalability, have lead to the development of server-specific APIs like ISAPI and NSAPI. While these APIs are indeed more efficient than their CGI predecessor, they suffer from increased complexity. Scripting solutions like Active Server Pages (ASP) and PHP have helped simplify web application development. Such solutions have provided a web interface to components used to handle logic and communicate with data sources - integrating technology to create web applications.

To address the potential of these technologies and to offer a more extensible and portable server-side solution, Sun has developed a new technology called **servlets**. Java servlets are very efficient, due to an intuitive threading model in which each request is handled by a new lightweight thread. Servlets are also platform independent because they interface to a particular server architecture through a set of standard interfaces (that make the servlet engine) and a Java Virtual Machine. Lastly, Java servlets provide an object-oriented and highly extensible middle tier for web applications. Servlets can access all of the enterprise Java APIs like JNDI, JDBC, RMI, and Enterprise JavaBeans, to name a few.

This book will introduce and examine Java servlets and these related server-side Java technologies. We hope to show conclusively how server-side Java can act as the key to developing n-tier applications, with browser clients accessing business logic and data services through servlets.

We will see how to code servlets and how they can be used to extend the functionality of the web server. We will also use the newest server-side Java technology, called JavaServer Pages (JSP). JavaServer Pages give us a way to 'glue together' HTML, Java code and components by simply creating a special web page that the web server will dynamically compile into a servlet the first time it is called. These two technologies form the basis for an exploration of the various parts of the typical n-tier application we show on the inside front cover.

This chapter will cover the following:

> Give an overview of web development.

> Discuss server-side applications vs. client-side applications.

> Introduce server-side Java technologies.

> Look at the advantages of using Java on the server.

Web Architecture

Before we can begin to build server-side Java applications, we must first review some basics. For those of you with some experience with web applications, please feel free to skip ahead to the next section. For the rest of you, let's start by showing what happens behind the scenes when you request a web page by typing in a simple URL (Universal Resource Locator) in your web browser.

To open a web page in your browser, you usually either type in the URL or click an existing link to the URL. Once you submit this request and the web server receives it, the web server locates the web page and sends it back to the browser (see the figure below). The browser then displays the page. Each image in the page is also referenced by a URL and the browser requests each image URL from the server in the same way it requested the main HTML page.

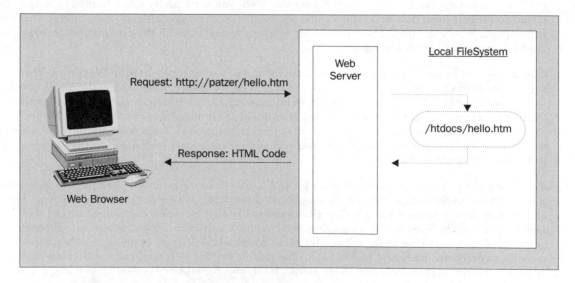

When developing applications for this architecture, it helps to have a good understanding of the role of both the web browser and the web server. As you'll soon discover, a thorough knowledge of each is essential to the overall success of your application.

The Web Browser

The web browser can be thought of as a universal user interface. Whether you're doing some simple web browsing or transacting online banking, the web browser's responsibilities are that of presenting web content, issuing requests to the web server, and handling any results generated by the request. The ubiquity of browsers, the generic HTML and Internet access is what makes this interesting.

In the past couple of years, we've seen considerable advances in the browser market. Both Microsoft and Netscape have continually raised the bar, giving us some incredible power on the client side. Both of the major browsers, Microsoft Internet Explorer and Netscape Communicator, have evolved into fully programmable document containers. Each has its own object model allowing for scripts, or objects, to manipulate the elements of the document itself. Scripting languages like VBScript or JavaScript can be used to perform client-side data validation, or provide some interactivity within the document.

Dynamic HTML (DHTML) is a combination of HTML, Cascading Style Sheets (CSS), the document object model, and scripting languages. Cascading Style Sheets are a better way of positioning and formatting your HTML elements. And since each property of the style sheet is made visible to the object model, you can use some script to manipulate and reposition your HTML elements. DHTML, as a whole, provides a greater level of interactivity within your pages. It also adds much more control over the presentation of them as well.

The latest must-have browser feature is Extensible Markup Language (XML) support. XML allows you to define your own tag set to characterize your data, and to construct documents and data structures using these tags. XML provides a way for structured data to be self-describing, and that means the data can be portable. Furthermore, with Extensible StyleSheets (XSL), you can select the data you want to see, and even change tag names, allowing you to transform XML tags to HTML, for instance. Exactly where you perform these translation steps depends on whether you can depend on XML support in your client browsers. In this book, because such browsers are by no means ubiquitous, we'll concentrate on making transformations to the XML on the server.

The web browser is also capable of executing applications within the same context as the document on view. The two most popular choices for client-side web applications are Microsoft's ActiveX technology and Java applets. ActiveX components are downloaded from the web server, registered with the Windows registry, and executed when called upon by other script elements. A Java applet is a small Java program also downloaded from the web server, and executed within the browser's own Java Virtual Machine (JVM). Both ActiveX objects and Java applets have full access to the browser's document object model and can exchange data between the browser and themselves.

Regardless of the way in which we make use of a browser, it will always serve the purpose of being our 'window to the world'. It serves as our primary user interface as we browse the web, conduct on-line business, or even play games.

The Web Server

At the heart of any web interaction is the web server. The web server is a program running on the server that listens for incoming requests and services those requests as they come in. Once the web server receives a request, it then springs into action. Depending on the type of request, the web server might look for a web page, or it might execute a program on the server. Either way, it will always return some kind of results to the web browser, even if its simply an error message saying that it couldn't process the request.

According to the Netcraft Web Server Survey (http://www.netcraft.com/survey), the leading web servers today are the Apache web server and Microsoft's Internet Information Server (see table below). The Apache web server has been developed as free software and has been contributed to by programmers around the world. Its power, flexibility, ease of use, and the availability for multiple platforms has contributed to its rise in popularity over the past few years. Microsoft's IIS, on the other hand, runs on the Windows NT operating system and is included as part of the Windows NT system. While Microsoft's IIS offers a wide range of features, its dependence on the Windows operating system may be holding it back. With the current rise in popularity that the Linux operating system has enjoyed, it is likely that the Apache web server (which comes packaged with most Linux distributions) will continue to gain ground on the competition.

Netcraft Web Server Survey (http://www.netcraft.com/survey)

Server	July 1999	Percent
Apache	3713470	56.28
Microsoft-IIS	1452333	22.01
Netscape-Enterprise	386927	5.86
CnG	147211	2.23
Rapidsite	113025	1.71
WebSitePro	87293	1.32
Stronghold	79580	1.21
Zeus	79206	1.20
thttpd	70414	1.07
WebSTAR	63347	0.96

The web server will play an important role in our server-side applications that we develop. Java servlets can be run using just about any web server. Since servlets can be run using a standalone servlet engine, the web server doesn't necessarily have to support servlets in order for you to make use of them. In this book we use the Java web development kit, but Apache JServ, JRun or the Java Web Server can all host the examples.

N-tier Applications

When discussing web application development, it is appropriate to introduce the concept of **n-tier architecture**. Typical client/server systems have fallen into the category of a two-tiered architecture. The application exists entirely on the client PC while the database sits out on a server somewhere in the organization. While this approach allows us to share data across the enterprise, it does have many drawbacks.

In a two-tiered application, the processing load is given to the PC while the more powerful server simply acts as a traffic controller between the application and the database. As a result, not only does the application performance suffers due to the limited resources of the PC, but the network traffic tends to increase as well. When the entire application is processed on a PC, the application is forced to make multiple requests for data before even presenting anything to the user. These multiple database requests can heavily tax the network.

Another problem with a two-tiered approach is that of maintenance. Even the smallest of changes to an application would involve a complete rollout to the entire user base. After a few rollouts, it may become hard to manage which versions exist where. Some users may not be ready for a full rollout and ignore the changes while another group insists on making the changes immediately. As a result, you now have two separate versions of the software to maintain.

To address these issues, the software community developed the notion of a three-tier architecture. The application is broken up into three separate logical layers, each with a well-defined set of interfaces. The first tier is referred to as the presentation layer and typically consists of a graphical user interface of some kind. The middle tier consists of the application logic and the third tier contains the data that is needed for the application.

The middle tier (application logic) is basically the code which the user calls upon (through the presentation layer) to retrieve the desired data. The presentation layer then receives the data and formats it for display. This separation of application logic from the user interface adds enormous flexibility to the design of the application. Multiple user interfaces can be built and deployed without ever changing the application logic, provided the application logic presents a clearly defined interface to the presentation layer.

The third tier contains the data that is needed for the application. This data can consist of any source of information, including an enterprise database like Oracle or Sybase, a set of XML documents (data that has been stored in a well-formed document conforming to the XML specification), or even a directory service like an LDAP server. The data for an application is not limited to just a relational database. There are many different sources of enterprise data that your applications can access.

By employing a three-tier architecture, the issues of performance, network traffic, and maintenance have all been addressed. This approach is almost where we would like it, but not quite yet. What it lacks is reusability and scalability. We could still end up with a series of "stovepipes" within an organization. We'd have dozens of applications that don't communicate with one another.

This is where n-tier architecture comes in. To turn a three-tier system into an n-tier system, we simply extend the middle tier by allowing for multiple application objects rather than just a single application (see figure below). These application objects must each have an interface which allows them to work together. An interface can be thought of as a contract. Each object states through its interface that it will accept certain parameters and return a specific set of results. Application objects communicate with each other using their interfaces.

With an n-tier architecture, we can now have multiple applications using a common set of business objects across an organization. This promotes the standardization of business practices by creating a single set of business functions for the entire organization to access. If a business rule changes, then changes have to be made to only the business object and, if necessary, its interface and subsequently any object that accesses the interface. It is important to note that when designing an object and its interface, it is a good idea to make the interface as generic as possible to avoid a lot of changes later on. Since other objects communicate with the interface and not the object itself, changes to the object, and not the interface, are relatively simple and quick.

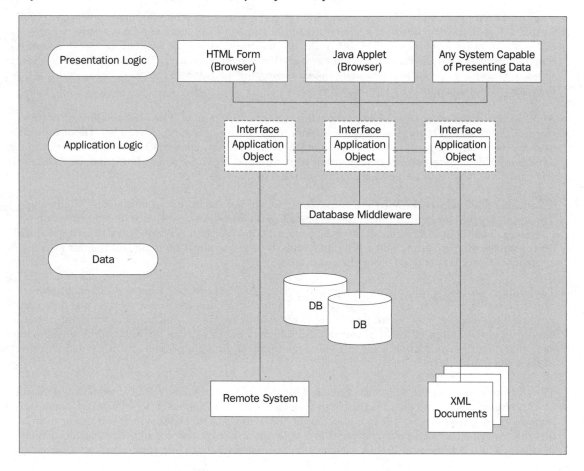

Web Application Architecture

A web application typically follows a three tiered model (see figure below). The first tier consists of the presentation layer which, in the case of a web application, includes not only the web browser but also the web server, which is responsible for assembling the data into a presentable format. The second tier is the application layer. It usually consists of some sort of script or program. Finally, the third tier provides the second tier with the data that it needs. A typical web application will collect data from the user (first tier), send a request to the web server, run the requested server program (second and third tiers), package up the data to be presented in the web browser, and send it back to the browser for display (first tier).

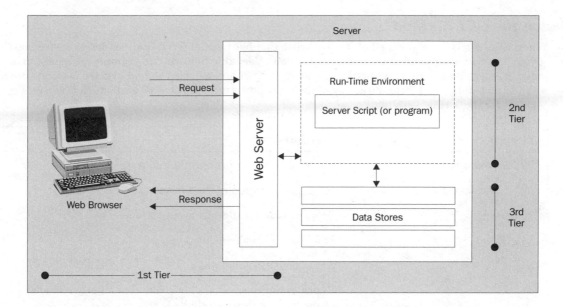

Collecting the Data

The first step of a web application usually, but not always, involves collecting some kind of data from the user. Traditionally, this was always handled using a simple HTML form. The user would type some information into some form fields, press a Submit button, and wait for the results. While this is still used today quite extensively, there is an alternative.

Since you're reading this book, I assume that you have some familiarity with a Java applet. Applets are Java programs that run inside a web page. Java applets can be used as a client to a server-side program by simply opening up a socket connection to the web server. This approach can help to move the majority of data formatting and validation off the server and onto the client. Remember that in a multi-tier architecture, we are not necessarily looking to move everything away from the client side. We are simply trying to put code where it belongs. While application logic doesn't belong on the client side, presentation logic might not always be appropriate on the server side. The main problem with applets remains the constrained bandwidth of most Internet access.

Sending the Web Server a Request

In order for the web server to 'spring into action' and execute a server program, the web browser needs to package up the user data and issue an HTTP request to the web server. An HTTP request consists of the URL for the page or script that the user wishes to access, form data (if entered), and any additional header info (browser information, length and type of request). A request is typically generated by the browser, but it's still important to understand how a request is constructed and used.

Each request must specify which method the request is to use. The three most commonly-used methods are HEAD, GET, and POST.

> ➢ The HEAD method simply retrieves information about a document and not the document itself.

> ➢ The GET and POST methods are the ones that you use to issue requests to execute a web program. While they both accomplish the same task, their methods of doing so are quite different.

13

Using the GET Method

When issuing a GET request, all of the form data that has been entered is appended to the request string. The data is appended using key=value pairs (see table below). For example, a request that looks like http://www.anyserver.com/cgi-bin/hello.cgi?name=Ashley would execute a script named hello.cgi in the cgi-bin directory of the www.anyserver.com server and pass it a value of 'Ashley' for the 'name' variable.

Element	Description
http://www.anyserver.com	The web server to process the request
/cgi-bin/hello.cgi	Name and location of the server resource
?	Separates the location from the data
key=value	Field names and associated values
&	Separates key=value pairs
+	Replaces the space character. Note that all other special characters are hex-encoded.

GET is used as the default method for all web requests. When a user makes a simple request for a web page, the browser issues the request as a GET request. Since a GET request packages all of the form data with the request string, the browser sees it as just another URL. If some previous results for the exact same request URL exist in the cache, then the older results might be displayed. Another potential problem with using the GET method is that the amount of data that can be passed is limited since it has to be appended to the request URL.

Using the POST Method

Requests that use the POST method also package up the form data as part of the request body. The server program will be able to read the contents of the input file and parse out the variable names and values. The POST method allows more data that can be passed and it will always send the request to the server (instead of looking to the cache directory).

Which Method Should You Use?

In most cases, it really won't matter which method that you use to issue a request to the web server. Ideally, a GET request should be used to retrieve information, that is, as it acts as a modified URL that issues instructions to the server. A POST request should be used if the request will actually modify the contents of a data store on the server. Along that line of thinking, a simple database search that returns a set of results should use a GET request and a timesheet entry program should use a POST request.

Executing the Server Script (or Program)

An important function of the web server is that of passing a request to a specific script, or program, to be processed. The web server first determines which type of operating environment it needs to load by looking at the extension of the requested file (or the directory the file is located in). This is done through mapping. When a web server is configured, it is told how to handle specific file types. For example, typically anything in the `cgi-bin` directory will be treated as a CGI script, or anything with a `.jsp` extension will be treated as a JavaServer Page.

Once the web server determines the type of the requested file, it then loads any required runtime environment for the file to be executed. For example, if a CGI program were written in Perl, the web server would create a new process and load the Perl interpreter into it. For some types of programs it is not necessary to load a separate runtime environment. This is dependent on the web server and the technology being used. Either way, the web server fulfills its responsibility by directing the request to the right place.

Returning the Results to the Browser

The final step in a web application is to make some kind of response to the operation and return that to the browser. Generally speaking, the server script specifies the content type and then writes the response to an output stream. When the web browser receives the response, it will first look at the response header and determine the mime type so that it knows how to render the data. The most common content type is `"text/html"`, but the server can return XML, unformatted text, GIFs and even streamed audio.

Developing Server Applications

A server-side web program is the same as any other program with a few important exceptions. To make a program accessible to a web server, it must possess the following characteristics:

- The program should be able to be invoked by the web server. When a user issues a request from a web browser, the web server has to be able to locate and execute the requested program.
- There must be a way in which the web server passes any form data to the program. When the web server invokes the program, it needs a way to pass in the HTTP request.
- Once the program is invoked, there has to be a standard entry point.
- After the program has processed the input data, it has to package up the results and send them back to the web server which will, in turn, send them back to the web browser. The exact division of responsibility may be blurred in some servers, but a web server in our sense just talks HTTP.

Server-Side Technologies

A few years back, the only real solution for bringing dynamic data to the web was something called the Common Gateway Interface (CGI). CGI programs provided a relatively simple way to create a web application that accepts user input, queries a database, and returns some results back to the browser. Both Microsoft and Netscape developed proprietary APIs that could be used to develop in-process code to service web requests. The latest server-side web technologies being offered are Active Server Pages (ASP) and Java Servlets and JSP. Each of these technologies are described and compared in more detail below.

Common Gateway Interface (CGI)

Being the most common of the server-side web technologies, just about every web server in existence today provides support for CGI programs. A CGI program can be written in just about any language, though the most popular language for CGI programming is Perl. Web servers implementing CGI act as a gateway between the user request and the data that it requires. It does this by first creating a new process in which the program will be run (see figure below). It will then load any required runtime environments as well as the program itself. Finally, it will pass in a request object and invoke the program. When the program is finished, the web server will read the response from `stdout`.

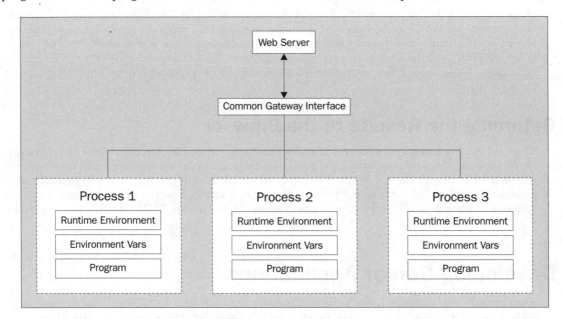

The biggest disadvantage to CGI programming is that it doesn't scale well. Each time a request is received by the web server, an entire new process is created. Each process consists of its own set of environment variables, a separate instance of whichever runtime environment is required, a copy of the program, and an allocation of memory for the program to use. It's not hard to imagine what might happen to a server when a large number of requests are received simultaneously. The resources of the server would be taxed very heavily, potentially causing the server to crash.

Technologies like FastCGI and Apache's `mod_perl` help here. They both address performance issues, FastCGI, by sharing single instances of each CGI program, and `mod_perl` by interpreting and executing Perl scripts within the Apache web server.

Proprietary Web Server API's (ISAPI, NSAPI)

Perhaps to answer the inefficiencies of CGI, Microsoft and Netscape each developed their own APIs to allow developers to write server applications as shared libraries. These libraries are designed to be loaded into the same process as the web server and are able to service multiple requests without creating a new process. They can either be loaded when the web server starts, or they can be loaded when they are needed. Once they have been idle for a set amount of time, the web server will unload them from memory.

While these in-process libraries do provide an efficient extension to the web server, they also have a few problems:

> Since these APIs are specific to a particular platform, any programs written using them can only be used on that platform. It would be a very difficult task to move these programs into a different environment.

> Since these libraries are accessed by multiple users simultaneously, they need to be thread-safe. This means that they need to be careful of how they access global and static variables.

> If a server program causes an access violation, since it is within the same process as the web server, it has the potential of crashing the entire web server.

Active Server Pages (ASP)

The latest web technology from Microsoft combines HTML, scripting, and server-side components in one file called an Active Server Page (ASP). When the server receives a request for an ASP file, it will first look for the compiled page and then execute it. If the page has not yet been compiled, the server will go ahead and compile and run it. The result of the ASP file is a finished web page returned to the browser.

An Active Server Page can be written using HTML, JScript, and VBScript. Through scripting, the Active Server Page can access server-side components. These components can be written in any language as long as it presents a COM (Microsoft's component specification) interface. An advantage to ASP files is that everything is executed on the server. This helps to ensure that the pages are browser-independent, limited only by what the server can do.

One real disadvantage to Active Server Pages is that they can only be used with a Microsoft web server (IIS, PWS) on a Microsoft operating system (Win9x, WinNT). There are ports to other platforms and web servers, but the lack of wide COM support reduces their effectiveness. The other problem is that the mix of script and HTML, basically two sets of information threaded together, can become a maintenance nightmare.

Java Servlets and JSPs

A few years ago, a new language and platform called Java was introduced. Java's main attraction is that it is platform-independent, secure, 100% object-oriented, extensible, and a relatively simple language to code (as compared to C++). This has made it very popular.

Unfortunately, in its early incarnations, quite a few people found it meant nothing more than an overly complex way to rotate a picture on their web page. Since then, however, the language and platform has matured a great deal. Recently, Sun has targeted the enterprise, introducing a series of new APIs that help connect your programs with enterprise services and data. The Java Servlet API is one of the cornerstones of these extensions to the Java platform, and provides a great way to create dynamic content and extend the functionality of a web server.

A Java servlet is a server-side program that services HTTP requests and returns results as HTTP responses. In that respect, it is very similar to CGI, but the comparison stops there. A good analogy for a servlet is as a non-visual applet that runs on the web server. It has a lifecycle similar to that of an applet and runs inside a Java Virtual Machine (JVM).

When a user issues a request for a specific servlet, that server will simply use a different thread and then process the individual request. This has a positive impact on performance, since multiple requests do not generate multiple processes as does a CGI program. Threads need fewer resources, so their use already gives them an advantage. Good server implementations will use thread pools to constrain the number of threads that can be used to service client requests, and prevent the machine grinding to a halt. Another benefit of using servlets is that since it runs inside a JVM, it can easily be ported to other platforms supporting Java. The Java language has various safety features that should keep failures from being catastrophic, like mandatory exception handling and type safety. And concerns over the interpreted nature of Java are being addressed through technologies like Sun's HotSpot and IBM's Jikes.

JavaServer Pages (JSP) is similar to Microsoft's Active Server Pages (ASP). A Java Server Page contains HTML, Java code, and JavaBean components. JSP provides a way to embed components in a page, and to have them do their work to generate the page that is eventually sent to the client. When a user requests a JSP file, the web server will first generate a corresponding servlet, unless one already exists. The web server then invokes the servlet and returns the resulting content to the web browser. Java Server Pages provide a powerful and dynamic page assembly mechanism that benefits from the many advantages of the Java platform.

Why Should You Use Java?

With so many choices for server-side development, you are probably wondering what makes Java such a great choice. Server-side Java technologies give you platform independence, efficiency, access to other enterprise Java API's, reusability, and modularity. Each of these are discussed below.

Platform Independence

Java servlets follow the same platform-independent model that the Java language does. The servlet code is compiled into bytecodes that are interpreted by a platform-specific Java Virtual Machine (JVM) on the web server. Since the servlets themselves are made up of platform-independent bytecodes, you can freely move your servlets to any other platform that supports Java.

Efficiency

As compared with the Common Gateway Interface (CGI), Java servlets provide a much more efficient method of handling user requests. Remember that a CGI program needs to create a separate process for each user request. When a servlet receives a user request, it simply spawns another thread within the same process and handles the request. This makes it possible for hundreds, and even thousands, of users to access the same servlet simultaneously without bringing down the server.

Access to Enterprise Java API's

Since servlets are an extension of the Java platform, they can access all of the Java APIs. A Java servlet can send and receive email, invoke methods of remote objects using RMI or CORBA, obtain directory information using the JNDI package, make use of an Enterprise JavaBean (EJB), or any other part of the Java platform.

Reusability

Code reuse is the holy grail of all programming. Creating component parts to an application is one way to achieve reuse, using object-orientation to encapsulate shared functionality is another. Java uses both. It is a completely object oriented language and, as such, provides mechanisms for reuse.

Modularity

When developing a complete server-side application, your programs can get large and complex in a hurry. It is always best to break down an application into discreet modules that are each responsible for a specific task. When you do this, it makes your application very easy to maintain and understand. Java servlets, JSPs and JavaBeans provide a way to modularize your application - breaking applications down into tiers and tasks.

Summary

Until now, there has not really been an all-encompassing technology with which to develop a server-side web application. Each technology offered some advantages, but not the whole solution. The Java Enterprise APIs provide a simple, efficient, platform-independent, object-oriented, flexible and extensible technology to handle the task of delivering dynamic data over the World Wide Web.

In the next chapter, we'll be introducing the Java Servlet Development Kit (JSDK), learn the servlet API, and build some simple servlets. This will be the first step in showing you the power and flexibility of the Java platform.

In this chapter, we learned the following:

> The World Wide Web (WWW) operates through web browsers issuing requests and web servers handling the requests and issuing responses, which are typically in the form of web pages.

> A web application consists of the web browser collecting user data, sending it to a web server to be processed, and finally receiving the results.

> An HTTP request is usually a GET request or a POST request. A GET request should be used to simply retrieve information and will send any form data along with the request URL string. A POST request should be used when the request will modify data on the server. All form data is packaged up and sent immediately following the request.

> A server program has the responsibility of receiving the request, processing it, and returning a response to the web server (which will then return it to the browser). The more popular server-side technologies include CGI, ISAPI and NSAPI, ASP, and Java servlets.

> Java servlets are platform-independent, efficient, and 100% object-oriented. They offer developers a way in which to extend the benefits of the Java platform to the web server.

Introduction to Servlets

One of the key tools we are going to be using throughout this book is the Java Servlet API. Servlets are the front line in Java web application development - they provide an easy way for our server side code to communicate with web-based clients. As such, they sit at the heart of server-side programming, and we'll be using servlets in many of the examples in this book. Over the next few chapters, we're going to look in depth at the way servlets work, and the different tools which the Servlet API provides - as well as building a few tools of our own.

The Servlet API provides a general model of a class which performs a service. At the most basic level, this is the definition of a server. In fact, true to their name, servlets are simply small, specialized servers.

To save servlet programmers from having to worry about the details of connecting to the network, catching requests, and producing correctly formatted responses, these tasks are all performed by a **servlet container**, also known as a **servlet engine**. The container translates requests from whatever protocol is being used into objects that servlets understand, and also gives the servlet an object that it can use to send a response. The container is also responsible for managing the lifecycle of the servlet, which we will also be discussing in this chapter.

Both the servlet API library and a servlet engine can be downloaded as part of the Java Servlet Development Kit (JSDK) located at http://java.sun.com/products/servlet/. For the code in this book, we have used version 2.1 of the JSDK, but because some servlet containers are only compatible with version 2.0, we have tried to give explanations of the changes which version 2.1 has introduced. For more information on the JSDK's ServletRunner, or for details of other servlet engines, see the appendices in the back of this book. We'll give a quick explanation of how to test servlets with Sun's ServletRunner later on in this chapter.

This chapter will cover the following:

> Explain the role of a servlet container.
> Discuss the fundamental classes and interfaces that make up the servlet API.
> Walk through the development of a simple servlet.
> Discuss some performance issues relating to servlets.
> Demonstrate form-handling techniques and HTML generation by building a servlet that acts as an SMTP mail client.

The Servlet Container

Servlet containers are responsible for handling client requests, passing the request on to a servlet, and returning the request to the client. The actual implementation of the container will vary from one program to another, but the interface between containers and servlets is specified by the Servlet API. This interface defines methods which the servlet container will call on the servlet, and classes of object which the servlet container will pass to the servlet.

Basically, the lifecycle of a servlet is as follows:

> The servlet container creates an instance of the servlet.
> The container calls the instance's `init()` method.
> If the container has a request for the servlet, it calls the instance's `service()` method.
> Before destroying the instance, the container calls its `destroy()` method.
> The instance is destroyed and marked for garbage collection.

And that's it. The interface guarantees that before the `service()` method is called, the servlet's `init()` method will be allowed to complete, and also that before the servlet is destroyed, its `destroy()` method will be called. There is nothing to stop a servlet container performing the entire servlet lifecycle each time a servlet is requested - although it is obviously not optimal, it is allowed by the interface. In practice, it makes sense for the servlet container to create an instance of the servlet when it is started up, or when the servlet is first called, and to keep that servlet instance in memory to service all the requests it receives. The container may decide at any time to remove the instance from memory, for example if the servlet has not been called for some time, or if the container is shutting down. If that happens, the container can easily do so, provided it calls the `destroy()` method first.

So in the typical model, the servlet container creates a single instance of each servlet (although there is no reason why the engine may not create more than one instance). However, we have not accounted for one more problem of server-side programming. What happens if the servlet's `service()` method is still running, when the servlet container receives another request? Well, the servlet container can wait until the `service()` method has completed before calling it again, or, as you probably guessed, it can create another program execution thread, and call the `service()` method from that. There is nothing in the specification to guarantee that the `service()` method can only be called from one thread at a time. So, when writing servlets, we will have to ensure that our code is threadsafe, and brush up on our Java `synchronized` commands.

In practice, it turns out that servlet containers do not generally create a new thread every time a request is received. Instead, the container uses a pool of threads to which incoming requests are dynamically allocated. But the effect, from the perspective of the servlet, is much the same. So, we can now build a picture of the way a typical servlet container works. This diagram shows a servlet being loaded, servicing two requests in quick succession, and then being unloaded when the server is shut down:

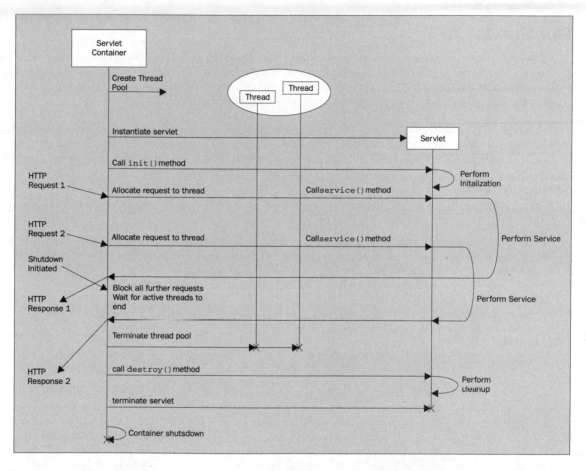

It is worth noting something about the nature of Servlet Containers here. Since they have to communicate directly with servlets, they are typically written in pure Java code. Unfortunately, the vast majority of web servers are written in other languages, such as C or C++. So while some 100% Pure Java web servers, such as Sun's Java Web Server and the ServletRunner supplied with the JSDK, have their own servlet container, other Servers such as Apache and Microsoft IIS need a separate Java program to actually run servlets. A plug-in or module is then typically required to handle communication between the web server itself and the Servlet Container. In the case of Apache JServ, for example, this communication is actually handled via a special Internet protocol called AJPv1.1, by which the web server makes a request for a servlet, and the servlet container passes the result back to the server. In this case, the container and the web server don't even need to be running on the same machine!

Since servlets work so closely with web servers, they can help to extend the capabilities of the web server a great deal. They can even be used to provide the most basic functionality: it's perfectly possible for a servlet to handle the standard web-server process of mapping a request URL to a filepath and returning an HTML file from the server. Sun's Java Web Server uses servlets to handle just about everything including CGI processing, Java Server Pages (JSP) execution, HTML templates, and Server Side Includes (SSI). It should be pretty clear that servlets can perform just about any task you want on a web server.

The Servlet API

So, we've looked at the world from the perspective of a servlet, now let's take a look at the details of the servlet interface. In order to develop servlets, you will need to obtain a copy of the Java Servlet Development Kit (JSDK). This contains all of the classes and interfaces needed to develop and run servlets, as well as a fully-fledged servlet container called ServletRunner.

The classes and interfaces form two Java packages: `javax.servlet`, and `javax.servlet.http`. The first provides the basic interface we discussed before, and the second provides classes derived from the generic servlet interface which provide specific tools for servicing HTTP requests.

Servlet Interface

```
public interface Servlet
```

The servlet lifecycle, as previously discussed, is defined by the `javax.servlet.Servlet` interface. When you write a servlet, you must either directly or indirectly implement this interface. You will most likely always implement the interface indirectly by extending either the `javax.servlet.GenericServlet` or `javax.servlet.http.HttpServlet` class.

When implementing the `Servlet` interface, the following five methods must be implemented:

init() method

```
public void init(ServletConfig config) throws ServletException
```

Once the servlet has been instantiated, the servlet container will call the `init()` method. The container will pass an object of type `ServletConfig` to the `init()` method so that engine-specific configuration data can be stored by that instance of the servlet for later use. The `init()` method throws a `ServletException` in the event of the `init()` method not completing normally. If a `ServletException` is thrown, the servlet will not be put into service and subsequent calls to the servlet will cause it to be reloaded by the container, and the `init()` method tried again. The interface guarantees that the `init()` method will be called exactly once on any given instance of the servlet, and that the `init()` method will be allowed to complete without throwing a `ServletException` before any requests are passed to the servlet.

service() method

```
public void service(ServletRequest req, ServletResponse res) throws
ServletException, IOException
```

Only after the servlet has been successfully initialized will the `service()` method be called to respond to incoming user requests. The `service()` method accepts two parameters, the `ServletRequest` and `ServletResponse` objects. The request object provides methods and fields to access the original request data, and the response object provides methods with which the servlet can build a response.

destroy() method

```
public void destroy()
```

At any given time, you must assume that the servlet container might decide to remove your servlet from service. This might occur if it needs to free some memory or the web server has been shut down. Before the servlet container calls this method, it will give the remaining `service()` threads time to finish executing (perhaps subject to some timeout period), so the interface guarantees that the `destroy()` method will not execute while a `service()` call is still underway.

getServletConfig() method

```
public ServletConfig getServletConfig()
```

As we know, during a servlet's initialization, a `ServletConfig` object passed in from the servlet engine is stored with the instance of the servlet. There are two things which the `ServletConfig` object allows you to access: **Init parameters** and the `ServletContext` object. Init parameters are usually specified in a file provided by the servlet container for the purpose, and allow the servlet to be passed deployment-specific information at runtime. The ServletContext object provides the servlet with the ability to discover information about the servlet container, and is discussed in Chapter 5. The `getServletConfig()` method allows the servlet to retrieve this object and obtain configuration information at any time.

getServletInfo() method

```
public String getServletInfo()
```

This method should return a String object containing information about the servlet (for example, author, creation date, description, etc.). This is available to the servlet container, should it wish to display, for example, a list of servlets installed together with descriptions.

GenericServlet Class

```
public abstract class GenericServlet implements Servlet, ServletConfig,
Serializable
```

The `GenericServlet` class provides a basic implementation of the `Servlet` interface. You'll notice that the class is declared as `abstract`. This is because the `service()` method is declared as `abstract`, meaning that if you extend this class you must implement the `service()` method yourself; remember that if one method is declared as `abstract`, then the class itself must also be declared as `abstract`. The other lifecycle methods are implemented as follows:

The `init(ServletConfig conf)` method stores the `ServletConfig` object in a `private transient` instance variable (called `config`), which the implemented `getServletConfig()` method accesses to return a reference to the object. Of course, this means that if you carelessly override the method, you won't be able to use `getServletConfig()` to retrieve the `ServletConfig` object. For this reason, you must remember to include a call to `super.config(conf)` if you do override it.

To get around this problem, version 2.1 of the API introduced an overloaded no-argument `init()` method to the `GenericServlet` class. Now, at the end of the `init(ServletConfig)` method, there is a call to `init()`, which in the `GenericServlet` is empty. By overriding `init()`, we can include initialization code without having to worry about calling `super.init(conf)`.

Something else new with version 2.1 of the API is that the `GenericServlet` class now implements the `ServletConfig` interface. This allows the servlet developer to call the `ServletConfig` methods directly without having to first obtain a `ServletConfig` object. These methods are `getInitParameter()`, `getInitParameterNames()`, and `getServletContext()`. Each of them simply calls the associated method of the stored `ServletConfig` object.

The `GenericServlet` class also includes two methods for writing to a servlet log, which in fact call the corresponding methods on the `ServletContext`. The first one, `log(String msg)`, will write the name of the servlet and the `msg` argument to the servlet container's log. The other method, `log(String msg, Throwable cause)`, includes an exception in addition to the servlet name and message. See Chapter 5 for more information about the `ServletContext`'s `log()` methods.

The following classes are contained within the `javax.servlet.http` package.

HttpServlet Class

The `HttpServlet` class extends the `GenericServlet` class and provides a more HTTP specific implementation of the `Servlet` interface. This will most likely be the class that all of your servlets will extend. It is possible to implement other classes extending `GenericServlet` that will provide a framework for handling other types of network services, but HTTP will likely be the most common protocol used with servlets.

service() method

```
protected void service(HttpServletRequest req, HttpServletResponse res) throws
ServletException, IOException
public void service(ServletRequest req, ServletResponse res) throws
ServletException, IOException
```

The `service()` method is implemented by the `HttpServlet` as a dispatcher of HTTP requests. This method should therefore never be overridden. When a request is made, the `service()` method will determine the type of request (GET, POST, HEAD, OPTIONS, DELETE, PUT, and TRACE - for more information on HTTP requests, see Appendix A) and dispatch it to the associated method (`doGet()`, `doPost()`, `doHead()`, `doOptions()`, `doDelete()`, `doPut()`, and `doTrace()`). The signature of each of these `doXxx()` methods is the same as the first service method above - an `HttpServletRequest` and an `HttpServletResponse` as arguments, and `throws` `ServletException` and `IOException`. In order to write a servlet which responds to a specific type of HTTP request, we just override the relevant `doXxx()` method. If a servlet receives a request for which you have not overridden to `doXxx()` method, it will return a standard HTTP error saying that that method is not valid for this resource.

getLastModified() method

```
protected long getLastModified(httpServletRequest req)
```

This method should return the time that the servlet was last modified in milliseconds since January 1, 1970 00:00:00GMT. The default implementation will return a negative number indicating that the time of modification is unknown. When servicing a GET request, this method can tell the server when this servlet was last modified and therefore let it conclude whether or not to pull the results from its cache.

HttpServletRequest Interface

```
public interface HttpServletRequest extends ServletRequest
```

To understand this interface, you will need to know a little about how HTTP allows data to be passed to the web server. HTTP allows you to submit parameters alongside your request. In a GET request, these parameters are added to the end of the request URL in the form of a **query string**. In a POST request, they are contained within the body of the request. In any case, they are pairs of strings referred to as **key/value pairs**. However, HTTP does not require that the keys are unique - so for some keys, there can be a list of values. This is because of the nature of HTML forms, which are typically the source for HTTP request parameters.

When you build an HTML form, you specify the controls using <INPUT> tags. Each control has a TYPE, such as CHECKBOX, TEXT, or SUBMIT, and can also have a NAME and/or a VALUE. The NAME attribute defines the key by which the value returned to the server will be known. The VALUE attribute has different effects on different controls. Obviously, if we give more than one <INPUT> tag the same name, we could have several key/value pairs with the same key as part of our request. The following table shows the value submitted to the server for different types of form control, and how the VALUE attribute affects them:

Control Type	Description	Value Returned
TEXT	Single line text input field, with VALUE attribute as default content	Text entered by user
PASSWORD	Single line password entry field (shows * instead of character entered)	Text entered by user
CHECKBOX	Standard checkbox	If checked: VALUE attribute (or "on" if not specified) If *not* checked: no key/value pair returned
RADIO	Standard radio button - all buttons with the same NAME form a button group, so only one can be selected.	VALUE attribute of selected radio button only
SUBMIT	Submit button, with VALUE attribute as button caption.	None, unless NAME attribute is supplied. Default for VALUE is "Submit"
HIDDEN	Form field which can't be modified by the client. See Chapter 4 for details of how this is used in web applications.	VALUE attribute

There are other controls, but these will do for now. The most common reason for having multiple controls with the same NAME, then, is to build radio button sets, and similarly to build sets of checkboxes. The radio button set will return the single selected VALUE, and the checkboxes will return all of the selected VALUEs.

Any object that implements the HttpServletRequest interface (such as the HTTP request object passed in from the servlet engine) will give the servlet access to all of the request data through its methods. The following is a listing of some of the basic methods you will need to use to retrieve form data. Other methods will be introduced later as they are needed.

getParameter() method

```
public String getParameter(String key)
```

This will attempt to locate a parameter with the given key in the query string and return its value. If there are multiple values for the given parameter, then the first value in the list will be returned.

getParameterValues() method

```
public String[] getParameterValues(String key)
```

If a parameter can return multiple values, such as a set of checkboxes, then you should use this method to retrieve all of the values for that parameter. Remember, this will return the VALUEs of all of the selected checkboxes. There is no way of discovering the VALUEs of unselected checkboxes.

getParameterNames() method

```
public Enumeration getParameterNames()
```

This method will return an Enumeration object with a list of all of the parameter names for the request.

There are many more methods provided by HttpServletResponse, to do with cookies, and discovering information about the client, but we will look at them later.

HttpServletResponse Interface

```
public interface HttpServletResponse extends ServletResponse
```

The servlet engine provides an object that implements this interface and passes it into the servlet through the service method. The servlet can modify response headers and return results through the HttpServletResponse object and its methods. The following are the two basic methods you will need to know when writing results back to the caller. Other methods will be introduced as they are needed.

setContentType() method

```
public void setContentType(String type)
```

Before writing a response back to the caller, this method needs to be called in order to set the MIME type of the HTTP response. This can be any valid MIME type, when we are writing HTML back to a browser, the type should be set to "text/html". We'll look at other MIME types in Chapter 13.

getWriter() method

```
public PrintWriter getWriter() throws IOException
```

This method will return a `PrintWriter` object that you can use to write the results of the servlet back to the caller as text. The PrintWriter automatically translates Java's internal UniCode characters into the correct encoding so that they can be read on the client machine. For information on how to change the encoding to deal with international character sets, see Chapter 19. Using the `PrintWriter` object returned, you would typically write data to the response object using the `println(String txt)` method.

getOutputStream() method

```
public ServletOutputStream getOutputStream() throws IOException
```

This method returns a `ServletOutputStream`, which is a subclass of `java.io.OutputStream`. This object can be used to send binary data back to the client. We will see how to use this in Chapter 6.

You may only retrieve one output object from an `HttpServletResponse` object. If you try to perform either of these methods when one has already been called, you will encounter an `IllegalStateException`.

setHeader() method

```
public void setHeader(String name String value)
```

This method can be used to set custom HTTP headers on the response you send to the client. There are several shortcut methods which allow you to make changes to certain commonly used headers, but in some circumstances you may want to use this method instead.

Anatomy of a Servlet

By now, I'm sure you'd like to see what one of these servlets actually looks like and how it works. So, without any further ado, let's build a servlet and learn how it works.

In order to compile the following code, you will need to obtain a copy of the JSDK at http://java.sun.com/products/servlet/. If you are using Java 2, then simply move the `servlet.jar` file from the `JSDK\LIB` location to the `JDK\JRE\LIB\EXT` folder. If you are using the JDK 1.1, then add `JSDK\LIB\SERVLET.JAR` to your `CLASSPATH` variable.

You can test the following example using any servlet engine you'd like. At the end of this book, you'll find information regarding the Java Web Server, the Apache Web Server, and the ServletRunner utility that comes with the JSDK.

For our first example, we will be building the time-honored 'Hello World' program. It may not be original, but it serves our purposes. First, let's look at the complete source-code:

```
//Import Servlet Libraries
import javax.servlet.*;
import javax.servlet.http.*;

//Import Java Libraries
import java.io.*;

public class HelloWorld extends HttpServlet
{

    public void doGet(HttpServletRequest req, HttpServletResponse res)
        throws ServletException, IOException
    {

        res.setContentType("text/html");
        PrintWriter out = res.getWriter();

        out.println("<HTML>");
        out.println("<HEAD>");
        out.println("<TITLE>Hello World Sample Servlet</TITLE>");
        out.println("</HEAD>");
        out.println("<BODY>");
        out.println("<CENTER><H1>Hello World!</H1></CENTER>");
        out.println("</BODY>");
        out.println("</HTML>");

        out.close();

    }
}
```

Now, since we've already explained the `javax.servlet` and `javax.servlet.http` packages, there shouldn't be any surprises here at all. Let's look at each part of the code.

Importing the Servlet Packages

The first thing that any servlet needs to do is include all of the necessary Java classes to support our servlet development. The servlet packages that we need to import are `javax.servlet` and `javax.servlet.http`. We also will have to import the `java.io` package to account for some possible `IOExceptions`.

```
//Import servlet libraries
import javax.servlet.*;
import javax.servlet.http.*;

//Import Java libraries
import java.io.*;
```

Class Declaration

All servlets have to implement the `Servlet` interface in order to function as a servlet. Fortunately for us, rather than having to implement the entire `Servlet` interface, we can just extend the `HttpServlet` class which implements the `Servlet` interface for us.

```
public class HelloWorld extends HttpServlet
{
.
.
.
}
```

Servlet Initialization

Keeping in mind the fact that the servlet is only loaded once initially and then services requests in multiple servlet container threads, there may be some type of initialization you will want to take place before requests are serviced. Initialization might include loading persistent data from file, or maybe creating database connections. No matter what initialization your servlet will need, the code belongs in the `init()` method of the servlet. For our example here, however, we do not require any initialization.

Servicing Requests with the doGet() Method

Whenever a request is made of our servlet, the servlet engine will spawn a new thread and execute the servlet's `service()` method. The service method will determine that the request is a GET request and pass the request and response objects on to the `doGet()` method to be executed. Through the request object, we can obtain all form parameters. For this example, we do not require anything from the request object.

```
public void doGet(HttpServletRequest req, HttpServletResponse res)
    Throws ServletException, IOException
{
.
.
.
}
```

Opening an Output Stream to the Browser

Using the response object, we can create a `PrintWriter` for us to send our results back to the browser. In our example here, we first set the content type of the response to "text/html". Then, we retrieve a `PrintWriter` object using the response object's `getWriter()` method. We use a `PrintWriter` to send the data back because we are sending formatted text. If we were sending binary data, we would have opened a stream using the `getOutputStream()` method of the response object.

```
res.setContentType("text/html");
PrintWriter out = res.getWriter();
```

Sending our Response

The last thing we need to do is actually send our response back to the browser through our output stream. We do this by making calls to the `PrintWriter`'s `println()` method. The `PrintWriter` encodes our output, but does not send it immediately. When we're finished with our response, we close the output stream using the `PrintWriter`'s `close()` method, and the response is committed.

```
out.println("<HTML>");
out.println("<HEAD>");
out.println("<TITLE>Hello World Sample Servlet</TITLE>");
out.println("</HEAD>");
out.println("<BODY>");
out.println("<CENTER><H1>Hello World!</H1></CENTER>");
out.println("</BODY>");
out.println("</HTML>");

out.close();
```

Deploying the HelloWorld Servlet

To get `HelloWorld` to work, you need to save it in a file called `HelloWorld.java`, and compile it, making sure that the JSDK files are in the classpath. If you're using the servlet container provided with the JSDK, ServletRunner, you need to move the class file to <JSDK Install Directory>/WebPages/WEB-INF/servlets and then use the provided `startserver.bat` file to get ServletRunner going. Now, by typing http://localhost:8080/servlet/HelloWorld into your browser's address box, you should succeed in calling the `HelloWorld` servlet. If your computer is attached to a network, you might want to try calling the servlet from another computer - just substitute your computer's hostname for localhost.

If you have problems accessing your servlet via localhost, you could try using the numeric IP address, 127.0.0.1, which is understood traditionally to map to the local machine.

You can find out more about configuring ServletRunner and deploying servlets with other servlet containers, in the appendices at the back of this book.

Simplifying HTML Generation

When developing servlets, it would be nice if you could just focus on the particular service being performed without worrying about how to format the response. To aid in the formatting of a response, it would be beneficial to have a predefined object to generate standard HTML markup through a few simple methods.

The object that we're going to use includes a few simple methods to generate simple HTML pages. Later on, in Chapter 6, we'll be adding a few more methods to this object to allow for a few different forms of table generation. For now, we need a method to create a header, add a line of HTML, and return the entire HTML string. Take a look at the following code fragments to see the difference when using the HTML object.

Without the HTML object:

```
out.println("<HTML>");
out.println("<HEAD>");
out.println("<TITLE>Hello World!</TITLE>");
out.println("</HEAD>");
out.println("<BODY>");
out.println("<H1>Hello World!</H1>");
out.println("</BODY>");
out.println("</HTML>");
```

With the HTML object:

```
HTML h = new HTML("Hello World");
h.add(HTML.HEADING, "Hello World", false);
out.println(h.getPage());
```

Obviously, the second piece of code is much simpler than the first. The first line creates a new HTML object and sets the title to "Hello World". Next, a heading line is added using the add method. This method takes three arguments. The first is the style. It can be NORMAL, HEADING, or LINE (for a horizontal rule). These styles can be added to the HTML class as needed. The second argument is the text to be added. Finally, the third argument tells the method whether or not to add a line break after the text. The last line of the code calls the getPage() method to return the complete HTML string. The following code defines the com.wrox.util.HTML object.

```
package com.wrox.util;

public class HTML
{
    public static final int NORMAL   = 0;
    public static final int HEADING  = 1;
    public static final int LINE     = 2;

    public StringBuffer buffer;

    public HTML(String title)
    {
        buffer = new StringBuffer(4096);
        this.buffer.append("<HTML><HEAD><TITLE>");
        this.buffer.append(title);
```

Continued on Following Page

```
            this.buffer.append("</TITLE></HEAD><BODY>");
    }

    public void add(int style, String text, boolean linebreak)
    {
        switch(style)
        {
            case NORMAL:
                this.buffer.append(text);
                break;
            case HEADING:
                this.buffer.append("<H1>");
                this.buffer.append(text);
                this.buffer.append("</H1>");
                break;
            case LINE:
                this.buffer.append("<HR>");
                break;
            default:
                break;
        }
        if(linebreak)
        {
            buffer.append("<BR>");
        }
    }

    public String getPage()
    {
        this.buffer.append("</BODY></HTML>");
        return this.buffer.toString();
    }
}
```

A Few Notes About Performance

When you consider the possible number of executions that a servlet might receive over time, it helps to pay attention to the efficiency and performance of the servlet. Since a servlet is instantiated once (presumably) and then executed several times, it is possible that even the smallest inefficiency could be magnified a great deal over time.

One thing to watch out for is the use of `String` objects in your code. When generating an HTML response, it is tempting to simply concatenate several strings together and then send it to the `PrintWriter`. The effect that this has is that it creates numerous `String` and `StringBuffer` objects to perform the concatenations, leaving more objects for the JVM to clean up through garbage collection.

There are two ways to get around this problem. One, you could simply write everything directly to the `PrintWriter`, line by line. The other option is to create a `StringBuffer` and use the `append()` method to add text to it. This has the effect of only creating a `StringBuffer` object, and not a series of `String` objects. This technique is used in the SMTP example presented later in this chapter, as well as in our `HTML` object.

Sometimes, regardless of how well you code your servlet, there are going to be some operations that will take a long time to complete. This may occur if the servlet has to perform a lengthy database operation or access a heavily used resource. When this happens, it would be nice to give the user something other than a blank screen to look at. If the user can at least see that something is happening, they will perceive a shorter execution time.

To give the user some of the servlet's output before execution has completed, you can use the `flush()` method of the `PrintWriter`. This will commit everything that has been written to the `PrintWriter` and send it to the browser. The following code illustrates the use of the flush method.

```
out.println("<H1>XYZ Corporation Company Directory</H1>");
out.println("<HR>");
for (int i = 0; i < recCount; i++)
{
  //  Retrieve record from directory server
  //  Add the record to the PrintWriter using out.println()

  out.flush();
}
out.close();
```

This code will effectively print each line of the directory as soon as it is retrieved from the directory server. If the retrieval process is very time consuming, then this will at least give the user something to look at rather than make them wait for the entire listing.

Processing Form Data and Sending Email

In this example, we will collect form data, send an email message containing the data, and then send a response to the browser acknowledging completion of the request. This is a very similar process to an extremely common function of CGI scripts, using the Sendmail program. To successfully test this servlet, you will need to have access to an SMTP server to actually send an email. If you do not have access to an SMTP server, you can replace the `SendMail()` code with some code to write the email message out to the browser. It's not quite the same, but at least you can experiment with gathering form data.

Setting up the HTML Form

For this example, we will be creating a technical support request form for a fictitious company called XYZ Corporation. You'll find that the concepts displayed in this example can be applied to numerous other forms. Simply replace the form fields as necessary and modify the servlet to account for the new fields.

```
<HTML>
<HEAD>
      <TITLE>XYZ Corporation IT Department</TITLE>
</HEAD>

<BODY>
<FORM ACTION="http://localhost:8080/servlet/TechSupport" METHOD="POST">
<CENTER>
```

Continued on Following Page

```
<H1>Technical Support Request</H1>
<HR>
<BR>

<TABLE ALIGN="center" WIDTH="100%" CELLSPACING="2" CELLPADDING="2">
<TR>
    <TD ALIGN="right">First Name:</TD>
    <TD><INPUT TYPE="Text" NAME="txtFirst" ALIGN="LEFT" SIZE="15"></TD>
    <TD ALIGN="right">Last Name:</TD>
    <TD><INPUT TYPE="Text" NAME="txtLast" ALIGN="LEFT" SIZE="15"></TD>
</TR>
<TR>
    <TD ALIGN="right">Email:</TD>
    <TD><INPUT TYPE="Text" NAME="txtEmail" ALIGN="LEFT" SIZE="25"></TD>
    <TD ALIGN="right">Phone:</TD>
    <TD><INPUT TYPE="Text" NAME="txtPhone" ALIGN="LEFT" SIZE="15"></TD>
</TR>
<TR>
    <TD ALIGN="right">Software:</TD>
    <TD>
            <SELECT NAME="ddlb_software" SIZE="1">
                    <OPTION VALUE="Word">Microsoft Word</OPTION>
                    <OPTION VALUE="Excel">Microsoft Excel</OPTION>
                    <OPTION VALUE="Access">Microsoft Access</OPTION>
            </SELECT>
    </TD>
    <TD ALIGN="right">Operating System:</TD>
    <TD>
            <SELECT NAME="ddlb_os" size="1">
                    <OPTION VALUE="95">Windows 95</OPTION>
                    <OPTION VALUE="98">Windows 98</OPTION>
                    <OPTION VALUE="NT">Windows NT</OPTION>
            </SELECT>
    </TD>
</TR>
</TABLE>
</CENTER>

<BR>Problem Description:
<BR><TEXTAREA NAME="txtProblem" COLS="50" ROWS="4"></TEXTAREA>

<HR>
<BR>
<CENTER>
     <INPUT TYPE="Submit" NAME="btnSubmit" VALUE="Submit Request">
</CENTER>

</FORM>
</BODY>
</HTML>
```

Writing the Servlet

The important lesson here is in how we gather form input. I've added the additional functionality of sending the mail using an SMTP server to make it interesting. I've already been asked a few times how to send mail from a servlet, so I'm assuming that this example should be quite useful to at least a few readers. Besides, this book is supposed to be teaching you useful web programming techniques - so let's start as we mean to go on.

Gathering Form Data

To collect the data that the user entered into the form, we use the `HttpServletRequest` object's `getParameter(String key)` method. The only argument to this method is a `String` specifying the name of the parameter we wish to extract a value from. You'll notice that we use a `StringBuffer` to build the message body. As mentioned previously, it is far more efficient to use `StringBuffer`s than `String`s when concatenating text together.

```
String message, msgFrom, msgTo, msgSubject;

private void getParameters(HttpServletRequest req)
    throws ServletException, IOException
{
    StringBuffer tempStringBuffer = new StringBuffer(1024);

    msgSubject = "Tech Support Request";
    msgTo = "tech@xyz.com";

    msgFrom = req.getParameter("txtEmail");
```

Continued on Following Page

```
        tempStringBuffer.append("From: ");
        tempStringBuffer.append(req.getParameter("txtFirst"));
        tempStringBuffer.append(" ");
        tempStringBuffer.append(req.getParameter("txtLast"));
        tempStringBuffer.append("\n");
        tempStringBuffer.append("Phone: ");
        tempStringBuffer.append(req.getParameter("txtPhone"));
        tempStringBuffer.append("\n");
        tempStringBuffer.append("Email: ");
        tempStringBuffer.append(req.getParameter("txtEmail"));
        tempStringBuffer.append("\n\n");
        tempStringBuffer.append("Software: ");
        tempStringBuffer.append(req.getParameter("ddlb_software"));
        tempStringBuffer.append("\n");
        tempStringBuffer.append("OS: ");
        tempStringBuffer.append(req.getParameter("ddlb_os"));
        tempStringBuffer.append("\n\n");
        tempStringBuffer.append("Problem: ");
        tempStringBuffer.append(req.getParameter("txtProblem"));
        tempStringBuffer.append("\n");

        message = tempStringBuffer.toString();
    }
```

As you can see, we put all of our form gathering code in a separate method called `getParameters()`. We pass the request object into this method from the service method. We could have included all of this code within the `doGet()` method, but as your servlets get larger and more complex, it pays to organize your code.

Sending Email Using SmtpClient

To send the gathered data in an email message, we use the `SmtpClient` class, which is part of the `sun.net.smtp` package included in the JDK. The basic process for using the `SmtpClient` class is to create an instance of the `SmtpClient` class, passing in a valid SMTP server name, and then, using a `PrintStream`, write the message to the `SmtpClient` object.

```
private boolean sendMail()
{

    PrintStream out;
    SmtpClient send;

    try
    {
        //  Replace the following with your outgoing mail server name
        send = new SmtpClient("mail.xyz.com");
        send.from(msgFrom);
        send.to(msgTo);

        out = send.startMessage();

        out.println("From: " + msgFrom);
        out.println("To: " + msgTo);
        out.println("Subject: " + msgSubject);

        out.println("\n----------------------\n");
```

```
            out.println(message);
            out.println("\r\n");
            out.println("\n----------------------\n");
            out.flush();
            out.close();
            send.closeServer();
        }
    catch (IOException e) {
            log("Error occurred while sending mail", e);
            return false;
        }
    return true
}
```

You'll notice that again we put this section of code in it's own method. Since we're dealing with a network operation (SMTP mail processing), we have to enclose our code within a try-catch block and account for an `IOException`. Also, you should note the format of the mail message. You need to follow this very closely for the `SmtpClient` to properly send the message. The SMTP server looks for messages in this specific format.

To test this servlet, you will need to replace `mail.xyz.com` with your particular SMTP mail server. If you do not have an available SMTP server, you can just comment out this method and write the message to the browser so that you can at least test the rest of the servlet.

The only thing left to do to complete this example is to send a response back to the browser acknowledging receipt of the request. Notice how we use the HTML object to generate a confirmation response and the `sendError` method to report an error if necessary. The `sendError` method will be discussed in greater detail in Chapter 4, but for now you can think of it as a way of passing an error code to the web server and letting it generate a standard error page for you.

Here's how we put all this code together:

```
//Import Servlet Libraries
import javax.servlet.*;
import javax.servlet.http.*;

//Import Java Libraries
import java.io.*;
import java.util.*;

//Import SMTP Class
import sun.net.smtp.SmtpClient;

//Import html helper class
import com.wrox.util.*;

public class techsupport extends HttpServlet
{

    String message, msgFrom, msgTo, msgSubject;

    public void doPost(HttpServletRequest req, HttpServletResponse res)
        throws ServletException, IOException
    {
res.setContentType("text/html");
        PrintWriter out = res.getWriter();
```

Continued on Following Page

```
            getParameters(req);

            if(!sendMail())
    {
                res.sendError(res.SC_INTERNAL_SERVER_ERROR,
                    "An error occurred while attempting to access the mail server.");
                return;
            }

            //Send acknowledgment to the browser
            HTML h = new HTML("XYZ Corporation IT Department");
            h.add(HTML.HEADING, "Your request has been submitted", false);
            out.println(h.getPage());
            out.close();
    }

    private void getParameters(HttpServletRequest req)
            throws ServletException, IOException
    {
        StringBuffer tempStringBuffer = new StringBuffer(1024);

        msgSubject = "Tech Support Request";
        msgTo = "tech@xyz.com";

        msgFrom = req.getParameter("txtEmail");

        tempStringBuffer.append("From: ");
        tempStringBuffer.append(req.getParameter("txtFirst"));
        tempStringBuffer.append(" ");
        tempStringBuffer.append(req.getParameter("txtLast"));
        tempStringBuffer.append("\n");
        tempStringBuffer.append("Phone: ");
        tempStringBuffer.append(req.getParameter("txtPhone"));
        tempStringBuffer.append("\n");
        tempStringBuffer.append("Email: ");
        tempStringBuffer.append(req.getParameter("txtEmail"));
        tempStringBuffer.append("\n\n");
        tempStringBuffer.append("Software: ");
        tempStringBuffer.append(req.getParameter("ddlb_software"));
        tempStringBuffer.append("\n");
        tempStringBuffer.append("OS: ");
        tempStringBuffer.append(req.getParameter("ddlb_os"));
        tempStringBuffer.append("\n\n");
        tempStringBuffer.append("Problem: ");
        tempStringBuffer.append(req.getParameter("txtProblem"));
        tempStringBuffer.append("\n");

        message = tempStringBuffer.toString();
    }

    private boolean sendMail()
    {

        PrintStream out;
        SmtpClient send;

        try
        {
            //  Replace the following with your outgoing mail server name
            send = new SmtpClient("mail.xyz.com");
            send.from(msgFrom);
            send.to(msgTo);
```

```
            out = send.startMessage();

            out.println("From: " + msgFrom);
            out.println("To: " + msgTo);
            out.println("Subject: " + msgSubject);

            out.println("\n----------------------\n");

            out.println(message);
            out.println("\r\n");
            out.println("\n----------------------\n");
            out.flush();
            out.close();
            send.closeServer();
        }
        catch (IOException e) {
            log("Error occurred while sending mail", e);
            return false;
        }
        return true
    }

}
```

Summary

The Java servlet API is both simple and powerful. It allows us to extend the functionality of any web server with just a few lines of code. Now that we have laid the groundwork for developing servlets, we're going to move on to cover the many different ways in which servlets can be used to enhance the functionality of a web server and extend the middle tier of your applications. Servlets will be a crucial component in almost all of our server side application development in this book.

In this chapter, we have learned the following:

> The servlet API is a set of classes and interfaces that allow a Java class to be loaded and instantiated as a servlet and then follow along a servlets lifecycle. A servlet engine is required to load a servlet and manage its lifecycle.

> When building a servlet, you need to implement the Servlet interface. You can do this by extending either the GenericServlet class or the HttpServlet class.

> The HttpServlet class extends the GenericServlet class and provides additional HTTP-specific functionality.

> To improve the performance of your servlets, try to reduce the number of objects that are created so that they don't need to be garbage collected. You can reduce the amount of objects created by using StringBuffers rather than Strings, or by writing output directly to the PrintWriter object.

Error Handling and Event Logging

When writing any kind of Java program, we should always keep Murphy's Law in mind: Anything that can go wrong, will go wrong. Java's error handling framework is based on precisely this pessimistic premise - and forces us to take account of all the exceptional situations which might arise while our program is executing. By forcing us to prepare for the worst, Java hopes to ensure that our code can survive every eventuality. When we write server-side code, it is doubly important to ensure that these circumstances are dealt with smoothly. Modern web sites should be available twenty-four hours a day, seven days a week - any failure on the server needs to be solved quickly, and with as little disruption to other services as possible. Server-side programs also have their own special circumstances: As well as informing the user that something has gone wrong and has prevented their request being fulfilled, we might want to inform the system administrator of the problem, or log the precise time and cause of the error. Alternatively, transient conditions may mean that a service is temporarily unavailable - in these cases, we need to ensure that our service is not called, and that the web server can inform the user of the temporary problem.

In this chapter we will do the following:

- ➢ Review the concept of Java exceptions.
- ➢ Learn how to handle exceptions within your servlet code.
- ➢ Demonstrate how it is possible to write errors to the client's browser and an error log with a single method call.
- ➢ Discuss the idea of logging events and how to send items to the event log from within your servlet.
- ➢ Demonstrate the use of two special exceptions that are handled by servlet engines, and show how to use them in your servlets.

Exceptions

As you should be aware if you have more than a little experience with Java, **exceptions** are the mechanism by which Java handles errors that arise during program execution. Before we look into the specifics of error handling on servlets, let's quickly go over the basics of exceptions one more time.

Run-time vs. Compile-time Errors

When there is an error in your Java code, the compiler will spot the mistake and force you to correct it before it will produce the expected class file. This kind of error is referred to as a **compile-time error**. These are errors in the structure of your code. You might misspell a variable name, assign a `String` value to an `int` variable, or maybe refer to a variable that is outside of the current scope. All of these errors need to be fixed to enable your program to function properly.

However, there are times when the compiler cannot know when it compiles the code whether a method call will succeed or not. For instance, you might have code which tries to access a database to retrieve some data, but the network connection that is used to access the database could be either up or down when the code is actually executed. The code might not work, but it is by no means an illegal operation that the compiler should force you to correct. If the connection operation does fail, a **run-time error** will occur.

Java provides a way to alert your program of these run-time errors as well as a way to handle them. When a run-time error occurs, an **exception** is **thrown** to your Java code. Exceptions are simply Java objects belonging to classes that extend `java.lang.Exception`. There are other classes of object which can be thrown during program execution, which are derived from the class `java.lang.Error`, but they are related to serious system failures and for the most part should not concern Java developers - typically, if they occur there's very little you can do to recover. Both the `Error` and `Exception` classes are derived from the `java.lang.Throwable` class, which is the root for all run-time error classes.

The Java compiler knows every single method that has the potential to cause a run-time error. It knows this because every method that performs an operation that may fail makes it known in its declaration. You have already seen an example of this in the `doGet()` method of your servlets:

```
public void doGet(HttpServletRequest req, HttpServletResponse res)
    throws ServletException, IOException {}
```

The `doGet()` method declares to the rest of the world that it can cause a `ServletException` or an `IOException`. The end result of throwing an exception is that it lets the compiler know that any code that calls a particular method must provide a way to handle such exceptions should they occur. When compiling your code, the compiler will not produce a class file until all such exceptions are handled.

There is a group of exceptions, derived from the class `java.lang.RunTimeException`, which do not need to be caught - these exceptions are **unchecked**. They will generally only arise if your code makes careless assumptions about the values contained in variables, and can easily be avoided if you write your code in a way that prevents them. For example, an `ArithmeticException` will be thrown if you divide a value by zero, and a `NullPointerException` will be thrown if you attempt to call a method or data member of an object variable containing `null`, rather than a reference to an instance of an object. It is possible to allow such errors to occur, and handle the `RuntimeException` just like any other, but it is considered better coding practice to avoid the exception altogether.

Handling Exceptions in Java

In order to understand exceptions, you need to understand the concept of the **call stack**. At any given point during program execution, the call stack is the sequence of method calls that has been followed to reach that point. During normal execution of the code, as a method is completed, it is removed from the top of the stack, and execution continues on the method which called it. If another method is called, that method is placed on top of the stack, and code execution continues on that method.

If at some point a method encounters a situation which it cannot resolve itself, it may be necessary for the method to abort execution and throw an exception. For example, a method may be written whose purpose is to connect to a remote server and return a connection object to the method that called it. In the event that the remote machine cannot be reached, the programmer might decide to throw an exception, and declare in the method definition that such an exception may be thrown. This exception will be passed up to the next method on the call stack, where it will either be handled, or the method will itself have declared that it throws that type of exception, and the exception will move on up the call stack. In most cases, your methods should immediately handle the exceptions that are thrown by methods they call.

As we have said before, except in the case of `RuntimeExceptions`, the Java compiler will ensure that you do not compile classes which make calls to methods which can throw exceptions, unless the exception is caught and handled, or declared in the definition of the method itself. This way, it ensures that all exceptions are handled at some level. How they are handled, however is up to the programmer, and careless handling is often the cause of `RuntimeExceptions`.

Let's look at how exceptions affect the flow of program execution:

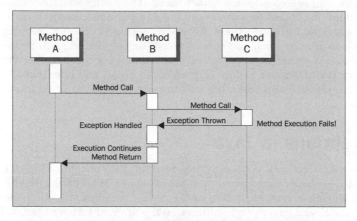

This diagram represents a short period during the execution of a program. The diagram begins with the program executing method A. At some point, A makes a call to method B, and during the course of this method, another call is made, this time to method C. However, while method C is executing, something goes wrong. The method fails, and an exception is created and thrown up the call stack. Method B is the method which called C, and in this example, B has been written to handle the exception. The exception handling code is executed, and program execution is able to continue on method B, which returns as normal to A. Method A is not affected by the exception, which has been resolved without its intervention.

In the following diagram, however, we take the same situation, but this time method B doesn't handle the exception. The exception is thrown on up the call stack to method A, which has to handle the exception itself.

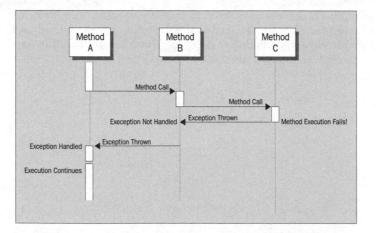

It should be obvious from these diagrams that it is usually better to handle exceptions lower down than let them propagate up to the high level code of your application. In the first case, method A was able to dispatch a request to method B without knowing or caring what could potentially go wrong. Such concerns are left to lower level methods. However, it is perfectly acceptable for a method to throw an exception if there is no way for the method to resolve the problem itself. If method B's entire purpose was compromised by method C's failure to complete, then there may be no other option than to throw the exception on up to method A.

So, now let's look at how we can actually deal with exceptions in our code. Exceptions are handled by placing the exception-causing code within a `try catch` block. The code which might throw an exception is placed in the `try` block, and the exception handling code is placed in a `catch` block immediately after the try block closes. There is no limit to the number of `catch` blocks that you use. Each `catch` block should catch the specific subclass of exception that your code may throw, such as `java.sql.SQLException` or `java.lang.NumberFormatException`. It is also possible to catch an exception class from which a number of specific exceptions are derived, and thus catch all of those exceptions with a single block of code. This can even be extended up so that you can catch a generic `Exception`, which will therefore catch any class of exception, since they are all derived from it. You should, however, have good reason for doing this, because it will be harder to establish the cause of the exception in the generic case. You should also beware when catching multiple exceptions to catch the highest level exceptions first, before catching more general exceptions, or the `Exception` class itself. The Java Virtual Machine will execute the code in the first `catch` block it finds which deals with the class of exception that's been thrown, and ignore all other blocks. Within the `catch` block, Java provides a neat way to access additional information about the exception which has been caught. The `catch` command takes the following form:

```
catch ([exception class] [variable name]) { [exception handling code] }
```

Within the handling code, we will now be able to access the `Exception` object which we have caught by calling methods and data members of the variable we have created. The most commonly used methods defined for exceptions are as follows:

- ➢ `String toString()` - typically returns the name of the exception plus the detailed error message.

- ➢ `void printStackTrace()` - prints the sequence of method calls which led to the exception to `System.out`. There are overloaded versions of this method which take either a `PrintWriter` or `PrintStream` object as an argument, to which the stack trace will be printed.

- ➢ `String getMessage()` - returns the detailed error message contained in the exception.

Some classes of exception may provide additional methods to provide further explanation of what went wrong.

So, putting what we've seen together, here is an example of a typical `try catch` block:

```
try
{
    .
    .
    //    code which could throw several types of exception,
    //    including a NumberFormatException
    .
    .
}
catch (NumberFormatException e)
{
    //    code to handle NumberFormatException goes here...
}
catch (Exception e)
{
    //    code to handle any other sort of exception goes here ...
}
```

Optionally, you can choose to add a `finally` block after all of the `catch` blocks. Any code that needs to be executed no matter what happens should be placed in here. Even if the program has reached a `break` or `return` statement during execution of the `try` or `catch` blocks, the code in the `finally` block will still be run. It is typically used to tidy up connections to databases, files, and so on, which need to be closed even if an exception was thrown.

If you can handle the exception in such a way that the program does not need to be terminated, then the program will continue as usual after the end of the last `catch` block, or after the `finally` block if it exists.

One problem to watch when writing exception-handling code is that of variable scope. Variables declared within each of the blocks will go out of scope as soon as the block finishes executing. If you want to access the contents of variables used within the `try` block from inside the `catch` or `finally` blocks, you will need to ensure that they are initialized before the `try` `catch` block is opened.

Handling Exceptions in Servlets

To demonstrate the use of exceptions, we will create a servlet that accepts a set of parameters, calculates a number, and returns it to the browser. Our example will calculate the number of months required to pay off a loan given the principal, interest, and monthly payment.

Building the HTML Interface

The HTML form used to input the data should capture the principal, interest, and payment parameters in text fields (see source listing below).

```
<HTML>
<HEAD>
  <TITLE>Loan Calculator</TITLE>
</HEAD>

<BODY>
  <CENTER>
    <H1>Please enter the following information:</H1>
    <HR>
    <FORM ACTION="http://localhost/servlets/LoanCalculator" METHOD="get">

      <TABLE CELLSPACING="2" CELLPADDING="2" BORDER="0">
        <TR>
          <TD ALIGN="right">Principal: $</TD>
          <TD ALIGN="left"><INPUT TYPE="text" NAME="principal"
                                   SIZE="10"></INPUT></TD>
        </TR>
        <TR>
          <TD ALIGN="right">Interest (0.nn): </TD>
          <TD ALIGN="left"><INPUT TYPE="text" NAME="interest"
                                   SIZE="10"></INPUT></TD>
        </TR>
        <TR>
          <TD ALIGN="right">Monthly Payment: $</TD>
          <TD ALIGN="left"><INPUT TYPE="text" NAME="payment"
                                   SIZE="10"></INPUT></TD>
        </TR>
        <TR>
          <TD COLSPAN="2" ALIGN="center"><INPUT TYPE="submit" NAME="cmdSubmit"
                                   VALUE="Calculate!"></TD>
```

```
        </TR>
      </TABLE>

      </FORM>
     </CENTER>
   </BODY>
 </HTML>
```

Processing the Request

There are two problems which might occur when the servlet attempts to process the request. The user could have entered a value into one of the fields that cannot be parsed into a number, or the user could enter a monthly repayment value which is too low to pay off the loan - the interest will keep mounting, and the balance will never reach zero. We're going to deal with these two situations by handling exceptions in the servlet. The actual exceptions will occur during the execution of public static methods in a helper class which we're going to build: com.wrox.util.LoanTools. LoanTools will contain two static methods, so we do not have to instantiate it to use them.

The first method is a basic helper which converts Strings into float values.

```
public static float stringToFloat(String inputString) throws NumberFormatException
  {
    Float f = new Float(inputString);
    return f.floatValue();
  }
```

If the String in inputString can't be parsed by the Float() constructor, the constructor throws a NumberFormatException. We can't handle this problem here, so we delegate it up the stack to the method which called stringToFloat().

The second method is the actual loan period calculator, which for the sake of simplicity here uses a very basic algorithm. In the course of performing this calculation, the method checks whether the balance on the loan is decreasing, or rising. If it is rising, rather than allowing the program to continue in an infinite loop, we throw an exception indicating that the values entered were invalid.

```
public static int calculateLoanPeriod(float principal, float interest,
                                                        float payment)
                throws IllegalArgumentException
{
    int months = 0;

    float balance = principal;
    //  quick and dirty loop to calculate the loan period
    while (balance > 0)
    {
        balance += ((balance * interest) / 12);  //  Add interest
        balance -= payment;                       //  Subtract payment
        months += 1;                              //  Increment months

        //  check to see if the repayments are working,
        //  or if the interest is pushing the balance up higher
        if (balance > principal)
        {
            throw new IllegalArgumentException("The values entered will not "
                    + "ever allow the loan to be paid off");
        }
    }
    return months;
}
```

It is perfectly possible for the servlet to perform this calculation itself, but it would be difficult to reuse the code in a different application. By moving this code out of the servlet and into a helper class, we are separating the business logic (calculating the loan repayment period) from the presentation logic (taking data from an HTML form, and returning data as an HTML page).

Next, we move on to designing the servlet. The basic process is simple:

> Collect the parameters we need from the `HttpServletRequest` object
> Use the helper class to translate the parameters into `float`s
> Use the helper class to calculate the repayment period
> If there was a problem, inform the client
> If the calculation succeeded, inform the client

If something does go wrong, regardless of which type of exception was thrown, we want to send the user an HTML page explaining the problem, so it makes sense to use a single piece of code to generate the error page. We can use the `getMessage()` method which all exceptions possess to pass information back to the user about the cause of the problem.

```
private void handleError(Exception e, HttpServletResponse res)
{
    res.setContentType("text/html");
    PrintWriter out = res.getWriter();

    HTML h = new HTML("Loan Calculator: Error");
    h.add(HTML.HEADING, "An error has occured...", false);
    h.add(HTML.LINE, "", false);
    h.add(HTML.NORMAL, e.getMessage(), false);
    out.println(h.getPage());
    out.close();
}
```

Now, we can simply use the same catch clause to trap both kinds of error, and call the `handleError()` method to notify the user. However, while our `IllegalArgumentException` has a friendly error message, it turns out that the error message contained in the `NumberFormatException` is simply the String which the `Float()` constructor was unable to parse. To ensure that the user gets a meaningful message, we need to treat the `NumberFormatException` as a special case. The code for the `doGet()` method, then, looks like this:

```java
public void doGet(HttpServletRequest req, HttpServletResponse res)
throws ServletException, IOException
{

    // retrieve parameter values as strings
    String principalAsString = req.getParameter("principal");
    String interestAsString = req.getParameter("interest");
    String paymentAsString = req.getParameter("payment");

    // initialize variables to hold floating point values
    float principal, interest, payment;

    // initialize a variable to hold the loan repayment period
    int months;

    try
    {
       // use the LoanTools class to obtain floating point values
       // stringToFloat throws a NumberFormatException,
       // so we'll have to catch it
       principal = LoanTools.stringToFloat(principalAsString);
       interest = LoanTools.stringToFloat(interestAsString);
       payment = LoanTools.stringToFloat(paymentAsString);

       // use the LoanTools class to calculate the loan period
       // the method throws an IllegalArgumentException,
       // so we'll have to catch it
       months = LoanTools.calculateLoanPeriod(principal, interest, payment);
    }

    // If a NumberFormatException was thrown, we want to
    // replace the error message with something more friendly
    catch (NumberFormatException e)
    {
       handleError(new NumberFormatException(
                   "Check that the values entered are numeric"), res);
       return;
    }

    // If any other kind of exception was thrown, we catch it here
    catch (Exception e)
    {
       handleError(e, res);
       return;
    }

    // If no exceptions were thrown, the code continues here
    // so we can send an acknowledgment to the browser

    res.setContentType("text/html");
    PrintWriter out = res.getWriter();
```

```
        HTML h = new HTML("Loan Calculator: Results");
        h.add(HTML.HEADING, "Loan Calculator Results", false);
        h.add(HTML.LINE, "", false);
        h.add(HTML.NORMAL, "Principal Amount: $", false);
        h.add(HTML.NORMAL, Float.toString(principal), true);
        h.add(HTML.NORMAL, "Interest:  ", false);
        h.add(HTML.NORMAL, Float.toString(interest), true);
        h.add(HTML.NORMAL, "Payment: $", false);
        h.add(HTML.NORMAL, Float.toString(payment), true);
        h.add(HTML.NORMAL, "Months Until Payoff: ", false);
        h.add(HTML.NORMAL, Integer.toString(months), true);
    out.println(h.getPage());
    out.close();
}
```

Test the program by putting in different values, and by putting in non-numeric values, and see what responses the server generates. If the program succeeds, you should see something like this:

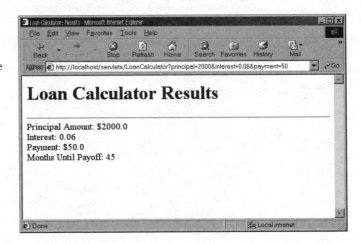

Invalid values, on the other hand, will result in the following:

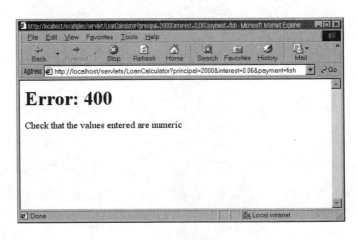

Sending HTTP Errors

In our previous example, when we encountered an exception, we assembled an HTML page and returned it to the browser to report the error to the user. The `HttpServletResponse` object provides an easier way in which to report errors back using one of the following `sendError()` methods.

```
public void sendError(int statusCode) throws IOException
public void sendError(int statusCode, String message) throws IOException
```

Both of these methods will set the HTTP response status code and commit the response. No further output should be written after executing the `sendError()` method. Once the error has been reported, the web server takes over. The server may send a special HTML page explaining the error to the browser, and will usually log the error in its standard log. The first of the above methods accepts a status code while the second one adds a user-defined message to further clarify the error to the user. Status codes can also be set without committing the response by using the `setStatus(int code)` method.

The following table describes some of the more useful HTTP codes you may encounter.

HTTP Status Codes

HTTP Code	HttpServletResponse Constant	Description
200	SC_OK	Request succeeded.
201	SC_CREATED	Request succeeded and created a new resource on the server.
202	SC_ACCEPTED	Request was accepted, but did not complete.
204	SC_NO_CONTENT	Request succeeded, but did not deliver any new content.
400	SC_BAD_REQUEST	The request was syntactically incorrect.
401	SC_UNAUTHORIZED	Indicates that the request requires HTTP authentication.
403	SC_FORBIDDEN	The server understood the request but refused to fulfill it.
404	SC_NOT_FOUND	The requested resource is unavailable.
500	SC_INTERNAL_SERVER_ERROR	An error within the HTTP server caused the request to fail.
501	SC_NOT_IMPLEMENTED	The HTTP server does not support the functionality needed to fulfill the request.
503	SC_SERVICE_UNAVAILABLE	The HTTP server is overloaded and cannot service the request.

There is a full explanation of HTTP status codes in Appendix A.

To illustrate the use of the `sendError()` method, we can modify our `handleError()` method to send a status code instead of our own HTML page. Notice that we pass on the `IOException` - this will be handled by the servlet container.

```
private void handleError(Exception e, HttpServletResponse res)
    throws IOException
{
    res.sendError(400, e.getMessage());
}
```

As you can see, we've cut down the amount of code required to handle the error, and in some ways we've actually increased the functionality. Depending on your servlet engine and web server, the browser may see an error page containing the plain text message you sent, or may see a special error screen generated by the server - but they will at least be told that the request was unsuccessful. Under Microsoft Internet Explorer 5, however, you may actually see an error screen generated by the browser, unless 'Show Friendly HTTP Error Messages' has been turned off in your Internet Options. You should also be able to find the error message in the server's error log, if it has one. In this case, the log will record that somebody entered inappropriate data to a form, which might seem annoying at first. However, if you analyze the data and discover that a lot of people are making the same mistake, you might want to redesign your web page to make the form requirements clearer. If the error message represents something more serious, you will almost certainly be interested in the details of the error, and want the event to be recorded. Similarly, there may be events which occur in the course of running your servlet which are not actually errors, but which need to be recorded. For that reason, the Servlet API provides methods which allow you to do just that.

Logging Events

Most web servers and servlet engines keep a set of logs that track information about the usage of the web server. In our previous example, we saw how using the `sendError()` method of the `HttpServletRequest` object wrote an error message to the web server's error log. There might be an instance, however, when you would like to record an event to a log that is not an error. These events can be logged to a file managed by your servlet engine. This makes it possible for a system administrator to monitor a system by simply looking at a log file, or to use additional programs to parse the log file and generate useful statistical data about the activity of the servlet.

You might recall that the `GenericServlet` class (as of JSDK 2.1) implements the `ServletConfig` interface. As part of the initialization of any servlet, a `ServletConfig` object is passed to the servlet from the servlet engine, which contains, amongst other information, a reference to a `ServletContext` object, which can be obtained by calling `ServletConfig`'s `getServletContext()` method. There's more about the features of the `ServletContext` in Chapter 5. For now, we'll just use the `ServletContext` object's `log()` method. The `log()` event has the following signatures:

```
public void log(String message)
public void log(String message, Throwable throwable)
```

The first of these methods accepts just a `String` object as a parameter. This `String` object will be written to the event log along with the time and date the event occured. The second of these methods adds the ability to pass an exception to the log file. If this method is called, the stack trace will also be included in the log.

To demonstrate the `log()` method, let's modify our `LoanCalculator` servlet so that it logs successful requests, as well as the unsuccessful ones we log already. All we need to do is add the following code to the end of the `doGet()` method:

```
ServletContext sc = getServletContext();
sc.log("Loan period calculated: " + Integer.toString(months));
```

Note that these log messages may not end up in the same log file as the error messages! Where the messages are logged is down to the individual servlet engine configuration.

Using The Servlet Exceptions

As we know, whenever we write a `doGet()`, `doPost()`, or other `doXxx()` method definition in one of our servlets, we always have to declare that it can throw an `IOException` or a `ServletException`. The `IOException` covers the various things that can go wrong when using a `PrintWriter` or `OutputStream`, which any servlet must do in order to produce output. A `ServletException`, on the other hand, is something new to us, and in fact is a tool we can make use of ourselves. Since `ServletException` is a checked exception, we can be sure that it is going to be caught by the servlet engine.

The Servlet API also provides a subclass of `ServletException` called an `UnavailableException`, which we can use to inform the servlet engine that something is currently preventing the servlet from functioning. But first, let's look at how we can use `ServletExceptions` in our code.

Throwing a ServletException

If we throw a `ServletException`, execution of the servlet will stop, and the exception will immediately be passed to the servlet engine. Generally, the result of this will be that the browser will be sent a **500 Internal Server Error** message, and the server will log the error. To create a `ServletException`, we have a choice of several constructors.

```
ServletException()
ServletException(java.lang.String message)
ServletException(java.lang.String message, java.lang.Throwable rootCause)
ServletException(java.lang.Throwable rootCause)
```

Two of these take a `Throwable` as an argument, which means that if we wish, we can catch an exception in our code, create a `ServletException` wrapper for it, and pass the exception on to the servlet engine. We also have the option of attaching a message to it.

So now we have a third option for reporting a problem executing our loan servlet - we could throw a `ServletException` in our `handleError()` method. However, we do have to remember to declare that the `handleError()` method throws a `ServletException`, or the code won't compile.

The UnavailableException

`UnavailableExceptions` come in two flavors - permanent and temporary. A servlet may consider itself temporarily unavailable if it is currently unable to fulfil its task, but is able to take action itself that will soon remedy the situation - for example, opening a database connection. On the other hand, if external assistance is required before the servlet will be able to function, it can declare itself permanently unavailable - for example if a database server has crashed.

The `UnavailableException` has two constructors:

```
UnavailableException(int seconds, Servlet servlet, java.lang.String message)
UnavailableException(Servlet servlet, java.lang.String message)
```

If no time period is specified, or a negative integer is supplied, then the servlet will be assumed to be unavailable permanently. If a positive time period is provided, then the servlet will not be contacted at least until that period has elapsed. However, the servlet specification does not demand that permanent and temporary availability be treated differently by servlet engines, so it is possible that the servlet will simply be treated as permanently unavailable.

Requests to unavailable servlets should be handled by the server, which should return a 404 Unavailable status page to browsers which request the servlet, together with the explanatory message provided by the constructor.

Summary

Errors are, we have seen, a fact of programming life. However, Java's exception handling mechanism allows us to see them as useful events which keep us informed, rather than evil traps to be afraid of. In Server-side applications, we must ensure that errors are handled correctly, so that a slight problem doesn't lead to the failure of the entire system. Happily, Java provides many ways for us to recover gracefully from such situations.

In this chapter, we learned the following:

- ➤ Errors that prevent your code from compiling are known as compile-time errors. These are errors with syntax and program structure.

- ➤ When an error occurs during program execution, an exception is thrown to your code.

- ➤ Exceptions can either be caught by use of `try catch` blocks, or passed on to be caught elsewhere.

- ➤ When an exception occurs, an error message can be sent to the browser, as well as be logged in the error log, using the `sendError()` method.

- ➤ During the course of a servlet's execution, a non-error event may occur that you would like to write to an event log. If this is the case, you can use the `log()` method to record an event to the servlet engine's log.

- ➤ The Servlet API provides two special exceptions, `ServletException` and `UnavailableException`, which can be used to inform the servlet engine of problems experienced by the servlet.

Sessions and Session Tracking

Internet Communication protocols are commonly divided into two types: **Stateless** and **Stateful**. The difference is in the nature of the connection they define between a client and a server. Telnet and FTP, for example, are stateful protocols - the client connects to the server, conducts a series of operations via that connection, and then disconnects. The server can associate all of the requests together, and knows that they all came from the same user. In Internet jargon, the server associates a **state** with the connection - it remembers who the user is, and what it is that they're doing. For example, when an FTP client requests a file for download, the FTP server can associate the request with previous ones and work out which directory the client was looking at, and therefore which file they requested.

HTTP, on the other hand, is a stateless protocol. It is concerned with requests and responses, which are simple, isolated transactions. This is perfect for simple web browsing, where each request typically results in a file (an HTML document or a GIF, perhaps) being sent back to the client. The server does not need to know whether a series of requests come from the same, or from different clients, or whether those requests are related or distinct. However, when writing Web applications, these are things that may well concern us. The problem facing us, then, is how to associate related requests together - how to maintain user state on the server.

The idea of maintaining state between requests to a Web application is known as **session tracking**. This basically means passing data generated from one request onward, so it can be associated with data generated from subsequent requests. When the Web application uses servlets to handle those requests, there are several approaches we can take. Sessions can be tracked by creating hidden form fields which contain the data, rewriting the URL to include data as extra parameters, using cookies, or using the session tracking tools which form part of the Servlet API.

This chapter will cover the following:

> ➤ Explain the idea of sessions and when we might need to use them.
> ➤ Show how to use URL rewriting and hidden form fields to track sessions.
> ➤ Learn how to track sessions using cookies.
> ➤ Introduce the `Session` object and other helpful session tracking tools in the Java Servlet API.
> ➤ Demonstrate session tracking using cookies and the `Session` object.

Sessions

A session can be defined as a series of related interactions between a single client and the web server which take place over a period of time. This session could be a series of transactions that a user makes while updating a stock portfolio, or the set of requests that are made to check an email account through a browser-based email service. The session may consist of multiple requests to the same servlet, or of requests to a variety of different resources on the same web site. Since HTTP is a stateless protocol, the web server does not automatically know which session a given request belongs to. There are two ways that we might get around this:

> ➤ We can get the client to identify itself each time it makes a request, and then store and retrieve data relating to that client from some store on the server.
> ➤ We can send the data to the client, and make the client send it back alongside each request it makes.

The client could provide the data we are referring to, by submitting forms, for example, or the server can generate it - for example, by recording requests the user has made. The source of the data is unimportant, however. What we have to work out is how we are going to share this data between the different requests which the user makes. The most basic (though not necessarily easiest) way to share session data is by either **URL Rewriting** or **Hidden Form Fields**. Basically, these techniques both write data into the HTML they send to the browser in a way which forces the browser to include it with its next request - either as additional data alongside a form, or as parameters appended to the end of a URL. It can also be transferred using **cookies**, which are short text strings stored on the client machine and sent by the browser to the server along with subsequent requests. When developing servlets, we have another option. Using methods provided by the Servlet API, we can create **session objects** and use them to store data which can be accessed by any servlets the user calls during the session. Each of these methods is discussed below.

Session Tracking Using Traditional Methods

Servlets may be new, but Web applications have been trying to get around the statelessness of HTTP for years. These techniques are exactly the same as those used by CGI Scripts - but there may well be times you'll want to use them yourself. In any situation where servlets are not the only server-side technology being used, these methods will prove invaluable.

URL Rewriting

As we've seen, an HTTP GET request is made up of the location of the server resource (URL) followed optionally by a query string containing pairs of parameters and values. An example of an HTTP GET request might be http://www.myserver.com/servlet/getSchedule?uid=apatzer &beg_period=3&end_period=6. In this example, the server is www.myserver.com, the server resource is servlet/getSchedule, and the query string is uid=apatzer&beg_period=3&end_period=6. These parameters are typically generated from an HTML form, where they represent the data entered by the user, but this need not be the case. The query string can simply be part of the URL referenced by an HTML hyperlink, as shown here:

```
<UL>
<LI><A HREF="http://www.myserver.com/servlet/usrmenu?uid=adp">User Prefs</A></LI>
<LI><A HREF="http://www.myserver.com/servlet/tsEntry?uid=adp">Time Sheets</A></LI>
<LI><A HREF="http://www.myserver.com/servlet/exEntry?uid=adp">Exp Form</A></LI>
</UL>
```

Now, when each of these menu options are chosen, the user ID is passed along with the request and will be made available to each resource. Each of the servlets referred to simply has to get the value of the 'uid' parameter from the `HttpServletRequest` object, then cross-reference user 'adp' to a database or file on the server to produce the relevant information. Naturally, this means that we have to dynamically generate each of the URLs from within a servlet - the web application will have to consist entirely of dynamic pages to pass the data on from one stage to the next. The data will also have to be URL Encoded, due to limitations inherent in HTTP as to which characters are allowed to be included in a URL string. See Chapter 6 for a full example using this method.

There are several disadvantages to URL rewriting. For large amounts of session data, the URL can get lengthy and out of control. You may also run into some environment limitations as to how long your URL can be. Another problem with this is privacy related. Often, you may not want the actual data you are tracking to be visible. By sending it along with the URL, it is exposed to the user, anyone looking over the user's shoulder, as well as anyone who may happen to intercept the request or view it in the browser's history window.

Hidden Form Fields

In a similar way, session data can also be tracked by storing it in hidden form fields and then retrieving it later using the `HttpServletRequest` object. We can pass the data on by including a field like this one in a dynamically generated HTML form:

```
<INPUT TYPE="HIDDEN" NAME="uid" VALUE="adp">
```

The same disadvantages apply as did with URL rewriting, with one exception. Since the values are stored as hidden form fields, an HTTP POST request would eliminate some of the privacy problems as well as the environment limitations present when appending fields to an HTTP GET request. However, anybody who is sufficiently curious can discover exactly what data you are tracking about him or her by viewing the HTML Source. This can create security holes, particularly if the data tracked relates to user identification, so this technique, like the previous one, should be used with care.

Cookies

Cookies have any number of uses for Web application developers, and one of them is to track user sessions. Cookies are small text files that store sets of key=value pairs. If you ever take a look at the temporary folder that your browser uses as a cache, you'll see a list of cookies (some browsers have them hidden away, while others display them in the cache folder).

Cookies originate on the server, where they are sent as instructions in the header of the HTTP response. The instruction tells the browser to create a cookie with a given name, which has a given value. If the browser already has a cookie with that name, from that server, the value will be changed to the new one. The browser will then send the cookie back with any requests it subsequently makes to that same server. Cookies can have expiry dates set, after which the browser will stop sending the cookie.

The Servlet API provides a class called `Cookie` which represents a cookie from the perspective of the servlet. The servlet can create a new cookie, set its name and value, set expiry dates and so on, and then put the cookie into the `HttpServletResponse` object to send back to the browser. Cookies can also be retrieved from the `HttpServletRequest` object, and their values read. This allows you to easily change the value held in a cookie on the client - simply retrieve it from the request object, change its value, and then pass it into the response object. You can learn more about cookies in Chapter 18, but for the purpose of our discussion, to create a cookie and store data in it, you would do the following:

```
// Create a new cookie with name and value arguments
Cookie c = new Cookie("userpref", "noframes");

// Set the life of the cookie
c.setMaxAge(2*24*60*60);        //Expires in 2 days

// Send the cookie to the browser to be stored on the client machine
response.addCookie(c);
```

The benefit of using cookies is that they are more intuitive than hiding data in a URL or a form. They don't involve us duping the browser into sending data back to us - the browser is participating deliberately in the process. But there are still problems when using cookies. Cookies can be used to track users over much longer periods of time than one short session - in fact, they can be used to track every request made to your site by a specific user. Some people worry that this means the administrators of web sites can gather too much information about which web pages they view, and so switch off the cookie function of their browsers. Older browsers may not even support cookies. If you rely solely on cookies to pass session data between requests, then your entire application could be rendered useless.

Session Tracking with the Java Servlet API

The Java Servlet API gives us another method of tracking session data that makes use of two different things, cookies and the `HttpSession` object. `HttpSession` objects are used to store session data in the current servlet context (see Chapter 5). Cookies are used to match a particular user with their associated session object by passing a session ID. So by sending a small amount of data to the client, we can associate each user with a large amount of data on the server. For browsers that don't allow cookies, you can employ URL rewriting to pass the session ID between requests, as described previously, and then use it to retrieve the correct session object.

Editor's Note: As of the Servlet API Specification 2.1, the methods used to retrieve a session by its session ID were deprecated for 'security reasons' without replacement. Instead, the session ID should be automatically passed as a URL extension if cookies are not supported. This should be transparent to the servlet programmer.

The `HttpSession` object is defined by the `HttpSession` interface and is obtained using the `getSession()` method of the `HttpServletRequest` object. The `HttpSession` object contains the following methods:

Method	Description
`long getCreationTime()`	Returns the time the session was created.
`String getID()`	Returns the session ID. This is useful when using URL rewriting to identify the session.
`long getLastAccessedTime()`	Returns the previous time a request was made that carried this particular session ID.
`void invalidate()`	Removes the current session.
`boolean isNew()`	Returns true if the session has been created by the server but has not yet been sent back to the browser.
`String[] getValueNames()`	Returns an array of all the value names that are stored for this session.
`Object getValue(String name)`	Returns the value stored for the given name.
`void putValue(String name, Object value)`	Adds an item to the session.
`void removeValue(String name)`	Removes an item from the session.
`int setMaxInactiveInterval(int interval)`	Sets the amount of time that the session will remain active between requests before expiring.
`int getMaxInactiveInterval()`	Returns the length of time that the session will remain active between requests before expiring.

When tracking sessions in your servlets, the first thing you need to do is obtain the session object. Then, once you have created a session object, you can read from or write to it. When you are finished, you can invalidate the session if you wish. If you do not invalidate the session, then it will stay alive until it expires. You may want to invalidate the session if it is defined by a particular transaction that has been completed. However, if the session is simply being used to track a user's actions or to store their preferences, then you will probably want to leave the session to expire on its own.

Obtaining a Session Object

When reading or writing session data, the session object must be obtained *before* writing any data to the servlet's output stream. This is done using the `getSession(boolean create)` method of the request object. The create argument tells the server whether or not it should create a new session object with this request if one does not exist already. If there is no current session, `getSession(false)` will return `null`.

Reading and Writing Session Data

The `HttpSession` object can now be used as a sort of bulletin board, to which servlets can post objects for other servlets to use, and from which servlets can take objects which they need. Any kind of object can be posted to an `HttpSession` - but not primitive data types. You'll have to use the object equivalents (`Integer` instead of `int`, `Long` instead of `long`, etc.) if you want to pass primitive data from one servlet to another using the `HttpSession`. When the object is posted, it is given a name, which is simply a string, by which other servlets can identify it. Naturally, the `HttpSession` can only contain one object with a given name.

Here is an example of how we write data to a session object:

```
/* Obtain a session object */
HttpSession session = request.getSession(true);

/* Add an item to the session */
Integer sessionItem = new Integer(2001);
session.putValue("mySessionItem", initValue);
```

And here is how we retrieve it:

```
/* Obtain a session object */
HttpSession session = request.getSession(true);

/* Read the session data and cast it to the appropriate object type */
Integer sessionItem = (Integer) session.getValue("mySessionItem");
int counter = sessionItem.intValue();
```

If the session item has not been set previously, the value returned from `session.getValue()` would be `null`, and we should account for this possibility in our code, by checking the value returned, or by catching a `NullPointerException`.

Invalidating a Session Object

Session objects will eventually be invalidated by the system and destroyed after a given time period has passed between user requests. The default time in most servlet engines that the server will wait until it destroys a session is 30 minutes. In some cases, you might wish to invalidate the session immediately after it has been used. For example, if the data you are tracking pertains to a particular transaction, you might want to invalidate the session so that the next time the user enters the transaction, a new session is created from scratch. To manually invalidate a session, we simply call the `invalidate()` method of the session object.

A Simple Shopping Cart Using Sessions

For our example, we will be using a session object to store and retrieve selected items for a simple shopping cart application. Shopping cart applications typically allow a user to select items from a catalog and place them in a virtual shopping cart. When the user is ready to purchase, or order, the selected items they 'check-out'. The shopping cart application then totals the items in the shopping cart, processes a payment, and places the order for the selected items. The user then waits for the items to either be shipped or downloaded.

In our example, when the user selects some items and presses the 'Add to Cart' button, the servlet will add the selected items to the session object and then retrieve all of the items currently in the session object and display them in the browser. At this point, the user would normally be presented with a 'Check-out' button to allow them to proceed with the transaction.

Building the HTML Form

The HTML form consists of a short list of items displayed in a table. Each item has a checkbox next to it for the user to select the item and add it to their shopping cart. Typically in a shopping cart program, the catalog pages are generated from a database. For our example, a static list will be sufficient.

```
<HTML>
<HEAD>
   <TITLE>Simple Shopping Cart Example</TITLE>
</HEAD>
<BODY>
<CENTER><H1>Programmers' Toy Shop</H1></CENTER>
<HR>
<FORM ACTION="http://localhost/servlets/ShoppingCart" METHOD="POST">
<TABLE CELLSPACING="5" CELLPADDING="5">
<TR>
   <TD ALIGN="center"><B>Add to Cart</B></TD>
   <TD ALIGN="center"></TD>
</TR>
<TR>
   <TD ALIGN="center"><INPUT TYPE="Checkbox" NAME="item" VALUE="JavaBeanie
Baby"></TD>
   <TD ALIGN="left">Item 1: JavaBeanie Baby<SUP><FONT SIZE="-
2">TM</FONT></SUP></TD>
</TR>
```

```
<TR>
   <TD ALIGN="center"><INPUT TYPE="Checkbox" NAME="item" VALUE="Cuddly Duke"></TD>
   <TD ALIGN="left">Item 2: Duke<SUP><FONT SIZE="-2">TM</FONT></SUP> Soft Toy</TD>
</TR>
<TR>
   <TD ALIGN="center"><INPUT TYPE="Checkbox" NAME="item" VALUE="Penguin"></TD>
   <TD ALIGN="left">Item 3: Barking Penguin Toy</TD>
</TR>
</TABLE>
<HR>
<INPUT TYPE="Submit" NAME="btn_submit" VALUE="Add to Cart">
</FORM>
</BODY>
</HTML>
```

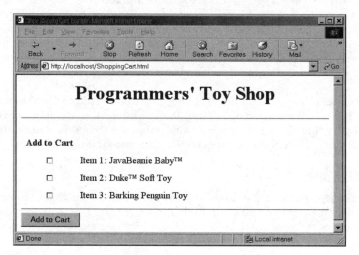

Building the ShoppingCart Servlet

The ShoppingCart Servlet is going to be called by a POST request from the browser when the user clicks on the 'Add to Cart' button of the form we've just built. So, all our code will go in the servlet's `doPost()` method.

The first thing we need to do is obtain a session object. Remember that this code has to be placed before any data is written to the output stream.

```
//   Get session object
     HttpSession session = req.getSession(true);
```

Sending the `getSession()` method a boolean `true` ensures that even if a session doesn't yet exist, one will be returned to us. Once we have a valid session object, we will need to retrieve the current number of items that are stored in the session object. The first time a user connects, the `itemCount` object won't be available, so we check if a value has been returned, and create one if it didn't exist.

```
//   Get item count from session object
     Integer itemCount = (Integer) session.getValue("itemCount");

     //   If the session is new, "itemCount" won't exist yet
     if (itemCount == null)
     {
         itemCount = new Integer(0);
     }
```

Next, we have to cycle through the form data and see if anything has been selected. If an item has been selected, then we increment the `itemCount` variable and write both the item and the new `itemCount` to the session object.

```
//   Retrieve Form Data
     String[] itemsSelected;
     String itemName;
     itemsSelected = req.getParameterValues("item");

     //   If there were items selected, add them to the session object
     if (itemsSelected != null)
     {
         //   Loop through all of the selected items
         for (int i=0 ; i < itemsSelected.length ; i++)
         {
             itemName = itemsSelected[i];
             itemCount = new Integer(itemCount.intValue() + 1);
             //   store the item under name 'ItemX'
             session.putValue("Item" + itemCount, itemName);
             //   store the increased itemCount
             session.putValue("itemCount", itemCount);
         }
     }.
```

Finally, we generate a page containing the current contents of the shopping basket. To do this, we retrieve all of the items that are currently in the session object.

```
//   Print Current Contents of Cart
     HTML h = new HTML("Shopping Cart Contents");
     h.add(HTML.HEADING, "Items currently in your cart", false);
     h.add(HTML.LINE, "", false);

     for(int i = 1; i <= itemCount.intValue(); i++)
     {
         //   retrieve the item called 'ItemX'
         String item = (String) session.getValue("Item" + i);
         h.add(HTML.NORMAL, item, true);
     }
```

Here is the full listing for the ShoppingCart class:

```java
import java.util.*;

//   Servlet Libraries
import javax.servlet.*;
import javax.servlet.http.*;
import java.io.*;

import com.wrox.util.*;

public class ShoppingCart extends HttpServlet
{
    public void doPost(HttpServletRequest req, HttpServletResponse res)
            throws ServletException, IOException
    {
        //   Get session object
        HttpSession session = req.getSession(true);

        //   Get item count from session object
        Integer itemCount = (Integer) session.getValue("itemCount");

        //   If the session is new, "itemCount" won't exist yet
        if (itemCount == null)
        {
            itemCount = new Integer(0);
        }

        PrintWriter out = res.getWriter();
        res.setContentType("text/html");

        //   Retrieve Form Data
        String[] itemsSelected;
        String itemName;
        itemsSelected = req.getParameterValues("item");

        //   If there were items selected, add them to the session object
        if (itemsSelected != null)
        {
            //   Loop through all of the selected items
            for (int i=0 ; i < itemsSelected.length ; i++)
            {
                itemName = itemsSelected[i];
                itemCount = new Integer(itemCount.intValue() + 1);

                //   store the item under name 'ItemX'
                session.putValue("Item" + itemCount, itemName);
                //   store the increased itemCount
                session.putValue("itemCount", itemCount);
            }
        }

        //   Print Current Contents of Cart
        HTML h = new HTML("Shopping Cart Contents");
        h.add(HTML.HEADING, "Items currently in your cart", false);
        h.add(HTML.LINE, "", false);
```

```
        for(int i = 1; i <= itemCount.intValue(); i++)
        {
           //  retrieve the item called 'ItemX'
           String item = (String) session.getValue("Item" + i);
           h.add(HTML.NORMAL, item, true);
        }

        //  add a link back to the shop to allow more items to be selected
        h.add(HTML.LINE, "", false);
        h.add(HTML.NORMAL,
                "<A HREF=\"../ShoppingCart.html\">Back to the shop</A>", true);

        out.println(h.getPage());
        out.close();
    }
}
```

You may need to change the URL referenced by the 'Back to the shop' hyperlink generated in the servlet to point back to the correct page. Make sure also that the `ACTION` property of the HTML page's `FORM` tag points to the URL of the servlet.

Which Method Should You Use?

Now that we've covered the different methods for tracking session data, let's take a look at when you might choose one method over another. When dealing with small sets of very public data, using cookies or URL rewriting can be an acceptable approach to session tracking. Use cookies when you can be sure that the users will have cookies enabled in their browsers. Also, use cookies if there may be some environment limitations regarding the URL query string.

When dealing with private data, or very large sets of data, the preferred method is to use the `HttpSession` object of the servlet API. This will allow the data to remain on the server, eliminating most privacy concerns as well as environment limitations. When you need to accommodate users without cookie support, use a combination of URL rewriting (to store the session ID) and the `HttpSession` object.

Summary

In this chapter, we learned the following:

> ➤ A session is defined as a series of related requests made by an individual user of a web application across a given period of time.

> ➤ Tracking application data throughout the life of a session can be useful when dealing with transactions that occur over more than one or two interfaces.

> ➤ Session data can be tracked using traditional methods like URL rewriting, hidden form fields, or cookies.

> ➤ Using the Java Servlet Session API, session data can be maintained on the server using the `HttpSession` object.

> ➤ The `HttpSession` object can be retrieved from the `HttpServletRequest` object using the `getSession(boolean create)` method.

> ➤ Once the application is finished with the current session, it can be destroyed using the `invalidate()` method, or it can leave the session to time out automatically.

Using the Servlet Context

In Chapter 4, we saw how we could use `Session` objects to maintain state relating to a single client on the server. But what do we do when we need to maintain a state for our web application, which is not specific to an individual user? The answer is, we use the **Servlet Context**. In this chapter, we'll see how.

The `ServletContext` object represents resources shared by a group of servlets. In the 1.0 and 2.0 versions of the Servlet API the `ServletContext` only provided access to information about the servlet's environment, such as the name of the server, MIME type mappings, etc., and a `log()` method for writing messages to the server's log file. Most implementations provided one servlet context for all servlets within a host, or per virtual host.

In the 2.1 version of the API the `ServletContext`'s role is extended to take on more of the responsibilities for a group of server resources that make up an application. It allows servlets in the same context to share information through context attributes, in a similar manner to the session attributes we have seen before. Most implementations support multiple contexts within the same host, each context representing an individual application. The introduction of application deployment descriptors planned for a future version of the Servlet API will make this application role even more pronounced.

In this chapter we will look at:

> how to configure servlet contexts to fit the needs of individual applications on the same server

> how to initialize a servlet context state from an application configuration file

> how individual servlets in an application can access the context state

> how context state changes made by one servlet are immediately available to the other parts of the application

We will develop a simple chat application to illustrate the features of the servlet context that help us keep the pieces of an application together.

Chat Application Overview

The chat application we will develop contains the following functions:

> Chat room administration, where new rooms can be defined and existing ones removed

> Chat room list, where a user can read the descriptions of all rooms and enter a room

> Chat room, where multiple users can chat with each other

As you will see this is a bare bones implementation, only intended to demonstrate the features of the `ServletContext`. Even though it works I'm sure you can come up with many ideas for how to improve it. For instance, you may want to apply what you will learn about JSP in Chapter 7 instead of generating HTML from hand-coded servlets.

The application contains two types of objects: data objects and user interface objects. Let's look at the data objects first:

> `RoomList`
> One instance of this class holds references to all `ChatRoom` objects. This object is kept as a `ServletContext` attribute so it can be accessed by all the servlets that make up the application.

> `ChatRoom`
> There's one `ChatRoom` object for each room, containing information about the room and a collection of all `ChatEntry` objects for the room.

> `ChatEntry`
> A `ChatEntry` object represents what someone says in a chat room. Each object contains the name of the person who said something and the actual message.

The application has a browser based user interface, implemented by the following servlets:

> `ChatAdminServlet`
> This servlet is loaded when the servlet engine is started and creates a `RoomList` object with all `ChatRoom` objects defined in an application configuration file. When the server is running it's used to define new rooms and to remove existing ones.

> `ListRoomsServlet`
> This servlet lists all available rooms and lets the user read about them and enter a room.

> `ChatRoomServlet`
> The `ChatRoomServlet` provides the user interface to a `ChatRoom`. Users can see what other people are saying and send their own messages.

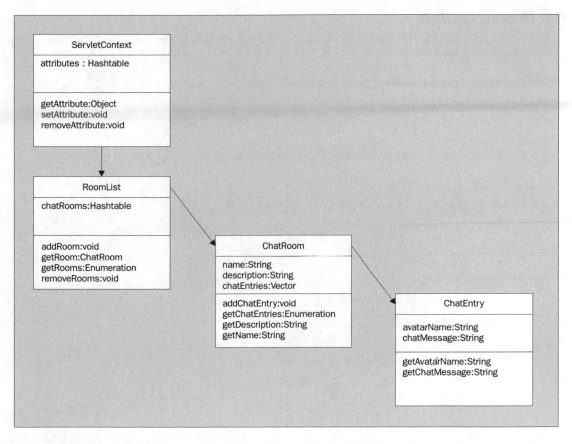

The class diagram above, using UML notation (see Appendix E), shows how the data objects are related: the RoomList contains a Hashtable with ChatRoom objects and each ChatRoom contains a Vector with ChatEntry objects. The RoomList object is the entry point to all the other objects, so a reference to the RoomList is stored as a ServletContext attribute.

Chat Room Data Objects

Together the data objects represent the application's state, accessible to all application servlets through the context's attributes. Before we get started with the servlets and all the details about the ServletContext API we'll therefore take a closer look at the classes for the data objects.

The RoomList Class

The RoomList class is the main data object that provides access to the individual ChatRoom objects available to the application.

```java
package com.wrox.context.chat;

import java.util.*;

public class RoomList
{
    private Hashtable chatRooms = new Hashtable();

    public void addRoom(ChatRoom room)
    {
        chatRooms.put(room.getName(), room);
    }

    public ChatRoom getRoom(String name)
    {
        return (ChatRoom) chatRooms.get(name);
    }

    public Enumeration getRooms()
    {
        return chatRooms.elements();
    }

    public void removeRooms(String[] rooms)
    {
        for (int i = 0; i < rooms.length; i++)
        {
            chatRooms.remove(rooms[i]);
        }
    }
}
```

As you can see it's a simple class that holds ChatRoom objects in a Hashtable. The name of the ChatRoom is used as the key in the Hashtable for easy access to a specific room.

Using the public methods, new rooms can be added, all rooms, or a specific room, can be accessed, and existing rooms can be removed.

The ChatRoom Class

An instance of the ChatRoom class represents an individual chat room, and each instance maintains all the messages for a specific room.

```java
package com.wrox.context.chat;

import java.util.*;

public class ChatRoom
{
    private static final int MAX_ENTRIES = 10;
    private String name;
    private String description;
    private Vector chatEntries = new Vector();
    public ChatRoom(String name, String description)
    {
        this.name = name;
        this.description = description;
    }

    public synchronized void addChatEntry(ChatEntry entry)
    {
        chatEntries.addElement(entry);
        if (chatEntries.size() > MAX_ENTRIES)
        {
            chatEntries.removeElementAt(0);
        }
    }

    public Enumeration getChatEntries()
    {
        return chatEntries.elements();
    }

    public String getDescription()
    {
        return description;
    }

    public String getName()
    {
        return name;
    }
}
```

A ChatRoom has a name and a description that are passed as parameters to the constructor when the room is created.

When a user says something in a chat room, the addChatEntry() method is used to add the message to the room. If the maximum number of cached entries has been reached the first cached entry is removed. This method is synchronized since it needs to complete all its actions as one atomic operation even when many users are talking at the same time.

The ChatEntry Class

A `ChatEntry` object represents a message in a chat room.

```java
package com.wrox.context.chat;

import java.util.*;

public class ChatEntry
{
    private String avatarName;
    private String chatMessage;

    public ChatEntry(String avatarName, String chatMessage)
    {
        this.avatarName = avatarName;
        this.chatMessage = chatMessage;
    }

    public String getAvatarName()
    {
        return avatarName;
    }

    public String getChatMessage()
    {
        return chatMessage;
    }
}
```

A `ChatEntry` contains the message itself and the avatar name of the person who sent it.

Avatar was originally a Sanskrit word meaning the incarnation of a god on earth, but it's also used, strangely, for the image or name you use to identify yourself in a chat room.

Servlet Context Configuration

Now you know how we will represent the chat rooms and what's being said in each room. It's time to take a look at the role played by the `ServletContext` in our application.

The `ServletContext` is used both to define URI-to-name mappings for an application and to let servlets in an application access shared information. In this section we'll look at the mappings, and in the following sections we'll look at access to the shared state.

Most servlet engines implementing the Servlet API 2.1 let you define multiple servlet contexts for the same server, with each context corresponding to one application. Typically you can define the following things for each servlet context:

> - the URI path prefix for the servlet context
> - names for servlet classes
> - initialization parameters for servlets
> - how request URIs map to servlets
> - session parameters
> - MIME types for static files

We'll look at most of these configuration options in this section. Exactly how a servlet context is configured varies between different servlet engines. So we'll look at *what* we can configure and what it means here and show an example of *how* to do it for a specific engine in the last section of this chapter.

A Unique URI Path Prefix for Each Servlet Context

An HTTP request always contains a Uniform Resource Identifier (URI), identifying the requested resource. The terms Uniform Resource Locator (URL) and Uniform Resource Identifier (URI) are unfortunately often used inconsistently in books, specifications and other documents. Here I use the terms as they are used in the Servlet 2.1 API specification, which is largely the same as their use in the HTTP specification.

> - A URI is any string used to identify an Internet resource.
> - A URL is such a string in a format for a specific protocol like HTTP – one with a scheme part (e.g. `http`), domain name of the server, a path, and possibly query string parameters.
> - Finally, a URI path is the part of the URL that identifies the resource within a specific server, i.e. just the path part. URL path might have been a better name, but URI path is the term used in the Servlet specification.

The URI path parts are used to first locate the correct servlet context responsible for the request and then to locate the servlet within the context to actually process the request.

So first of all each servlet context must be mapped to a unique URI path prefix, for instance `/chat`. The servlet engine uses the URI path prefix as the context identifier part of a URL.

As examples of URI path prefixes, we can configure a servlet engine for two servlet contexts like this:

```
/chat                A chat application context
/reservation         A hotel room reservation application context
```

When a servlet engine receives an HTTP request with a path starting with `/chat` it knows that the request shall be handled by the chat application, and that all requests starting with `/reservation` shall be handled by the room reservation application.

Servlet Names and URI Path Mappings for Each Servlet Context

We must then configure how requests are handled within a context. Let's start by defining names for our chat application servlets and a couple of other servlets:

```
chatAdmin        com.wrox.context.chat.ChatAdminServlet
listRooms        com.wrox.context.chat.ListRoomsServlet
chatRoom         com.wrox.context.chat.ChatRoomServlet
file             com.gefionsoftware.server.servlet.FileServlet
jsp              org.gjt.jsp.JSPServlet
```

This is just a mapping of short names to servlet class names. The short name allows us to refer to servlets more easily and also to replace the implementation class for a servlet without modifying the references to the servlet within the application. In addition to mapping the servlet class to a name, you can also define initialization parameters for the servlet and usually define that a servlet shall be loaded when the servlet engine starts.

Next we define how to map a URI path to the name of the servlet handling the requests:

```
/                file
/chatAdmin       chatAdmin
/listRooms       listRooms
/chatRoom        chatRoom
*.jsp            jsp
```

Path mappings are relative to the context's URI path prefix; the context URI path prefix is removed before the rules are evaluated. This means that a request for /chat/chatAdmin is first sent to the chat application context. The chat application context strips off the URI path prefix and compares the remainder of the path with the rules above to find out that the request will be handled by the servlet named chatAdmin. Similarly requests for files with a .jsp extension will be handled by the servlet named jsp in this context. Requests that do not match any of the specific mapping rules will be matched with the default rule, /, and handled by the servlet named file.

A request with a URL that starts with something other than /chat is handed to a context with a matching URI path prefix and the mapping rules specified for that context are applied to figure out how to handle the request.

Benefits

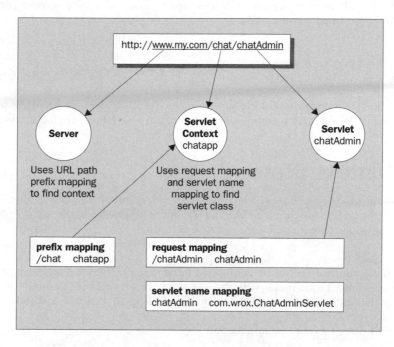

The diagram above illustrates how the different parts of a URL identify a server (with a servlet engine), a servlet context, and finally a servlet to process the request. The server uses a URI path prefix map to locate the correct servlet context. The servlet context uses the remainder of the URI path and a path map to find the name of the servlet to process the request, and a name-to-class map to locate the servlet class.

So what do we gain from all of this? Flexibility. Within the application all servlets use the servlet names to refer to each other, such as in the reference tags they generate or when they redirect to another servlet. If we want to replace one of the servlets with a different implementation, we just change the servlet name configuration:

```
chatAdmin         com.wrox.pssjp.context.chat.ChatAdminServlet
listRooms         com.wrox.pssjp.context.chat.ListRoomsServlet
chatRoom          com.wrox.pssjp.context.chat.EnhancedChatRoomServlet
file              com.gefionsoftware.server.servlet.FileServlet
jsp               org.gjt.jsp.JSPServlet
```

Since all URI paths within a context are relative to the context's root URI path, it's also easy to move the application to a different place in the servlet engine's name space. If we introduce a new version of the chat application and we want to use the /chat prefix for the new version, but still provide access to the old version at /oldchat, all we have to do is change the servlet engine's context mappings:

```
/chat             The new chat application context
/oldchat          The old chat application context
/reservation      A hotel room reservation application context
```

Separate mappings for each servlet context also prevent name collisions and let us use different default servlets for different applications. Part of the mapping rules for the room reservation application could for instance look like this:

```
/                       fancyFile
/listRooms              listAvailableRooms
*.jsp                   josper
```

In this application we use a different file servlet as the default servlet, another JSP processor and use the `/listRooms` URI path for a completely different purpose from our chat application.

Servlet Context State

In this section we will look at how servlets within a servlet context can access shared information. A servlet context's state information is held in its attributes. There are three `ServletContext` methods dealing with context attributes: `getAttribute`, `setAttribute`, and `removeAttribute`.

One servlet in the application can be configured to be loaded when the servlet engine is started so it can initialize the context's attributes with the `setAttribute` method. During operation all application servlets can read and modify the attributes using all attribute methods.

Let's see how it's done on our chat application.

Initializing the Servlet Context's State

As you saw above we use three data objects to represent the context's state in the chat application: one `RoomList` object with multiple `ChatRoom` objects, each containing multiple `ChatEntry` objects. The chat rooms are defined in an application configuration file. When the servlet engine starts, the `ChatAdminServlet` reads the configuration file, creates one `RoomList` object, and creates and adds the `ChatRoom` objects defined in the configuration file. It then sets a `ServletContext` attribute to reference the `RoomList` object so that all servlets in our application can access the shared information.

Let's look at this in detail.

The ChatAdminServlet Class

The `ChatAdminServlet` is defined to be loaded when the servlet engine starts so it can initialize the servlet context's state. When the servlet is loaded, its `init` method is invoked.

```
public void init() throws ServletException
{
    String propsFile = getInitParameter("chatprops");
    if (propsFile == null || propsFile.length() == 0)
    {
        throw new UnavailableException(this,
                "chatprops not set in servlet init parameters");
    }

    Properties props = new Properties();
```

```
    try
    {
        InputStream is = new FileInputStream(propsFile);
        props.load(is);
        is.close();
    }
    catch (Exception e)
    {
        throw new UnavailableException(this,
                        "Can't read the chatprops file " + propsFile);
    }

    RoomList roomList = createRooms(props);
    getServletContext().setAttribute("roomList", roomList);
}
```

We first ask the `ServletConfig` for the value of the `chatprops` initialization parameter. This parameter contains the file path for a configuration file in the format used by `java.util.Properties`. We then load the properties from the file, and use the `createRooms()` method to create the `ChatRoom` objects defined in the file and return a `RoomList` object containing all `ChatRoom` objects.

The `RoomList` object is our entry point to all shared application information. So we use the `getServletContext()` method to get a reference to the `ServletContext` and set the context attribute `roomList` to hold our `RoomList` object with the `setAttribute` method. Now all servlets in the application have access to the information they need.

That's all we do to initialize the context state, but let's take a brief look at how the `RoomList` object is created as well.

```
private RoomList createRooms(Properties props)
  {
      RoomList roomList = new RoomList();
      Enumeration propKeys = props.keys();
      while (propKeys.hasMoreElements())
      {
          String key = (String) propKeys.nextElement();
          if (key.endsWith(".description"))
          {
              String roomDescription = props.getProperty(key);
              String roomName = key.substring(0, key.lastIndexOf("."));
              roomName = StringUtils.replaceInString(roomName, "+", " ");
              roomList.addRoom(new ChatRoom(roomName, roomDescription));
          }
      }
      return roomList;
  }
```

The properties file contains one property per chat room, using the room name plus the string ".description" as the key name, and a description of the room as its value. Room names may contain spaces but spaces are not allowed in a property key name so we use plus signs for all spaces. After we have extracted the encoded room name from the key name we replace the plus signs with space characters using a utility method in a class named StringUtils. The source code for the StringUtils class is included with the source code for this book, which can be downloaded from http://www.wrox.com.

For each description property we find, we create a ChatRoom object, using the name and the description as constructor parameters. Each room is then added to the RoomList. We'll be coming back to the ChatAdminServlet later - for now, let's look at the other two servlets.

Accessing the Context's State

The ListRoomsServlet and the ChatRoomServlet classes implement the end-user interface. They both access the context's state through the roomList attribute set by the ChatAdminServlet. Before we dive into the code, let's look at the overall design.

The ListRoomServlet uses the RoomList object to get all ChatRoom objects and sends a list of them to the client. The user can select the room to enter, causing the ChatRoomServlet to be invoked.

The ChatRoomServlet first uses the RoomList object to get the ChatRoom object selected by the user, and then gets all ChatEntry objects from the ChatRoom. It sends a list of all chat entries to the client. This servlet is also invoked when the user sends a new message to the room. In this case it creates a new ChatEntry object and adds it to the selected ChatRoom.

Let's look at the servlets one by one.

The ListRoomServlet Class

A user of our application first invokes the ListRoomServlet. This servlet lists all available rooms and allows the user to choose an avatar name and enter a room.

The HTTP GET method is used to invoke the servlet, so we use the doGet() method to generate an HTML page with a form for the list, the avatar name field and an **Enter Room** button.

```
public void doGet(HttpServletRequest req, HttpServletResponse res)
            throws IOException
{
    res.setContentType("text/html");
    PrintWriter out = res.getWriter();

    String expand = req.getParameter("expand");
    HttpSession session = req.getSession(true);
    String avatarName = (String) session.getValue("avatarName");
    if (avatarName == null)
    {
        avatarName = "";
    }

    writePage(out, expand, avatarName);
    out.close();
}
```

We only use the context's state in the `writePage()` method, so that's really the interesting method. In `doGet()` we prepare ourselves by picking up a request parameter named `expand`, establishing a session if we didn't have one already, and trying to read the avatar name from the session. We'll look at the session data when we look at the `ChatRoomServlet` in the next section.

The `writePage()` method is quite long, so let's take it in pieces.

```
private void writePage(PrintWriter out, String expand, String avatarName)
{
    out.println("<HTML>");
    out.println("<HEAD><TITLE>Chat rooms</TITLE></HEAD>");
    out.println("<BODY>");
    out.println("<H1>Chat rooms</H1>");
    out.println("<FORM METHOD=POST ACTION=chatRoom>");
```

The first part just generates the HTML page header and the `<FORM>` tag. We use a `<FORM>` tag with the `ACTION` attribute set to the servlet name we defined for our `ChatRoomServlet`.

Note that we use a relative URL for the ACTION, in other words `chatRoom` as opposed to an absolute URL like `/chat/chatRoom`. A browser evaluates a relative URL based on the absolute URL for the current request. Since all our servlets are located on the same level in the web server's URL name space, a relative URL like this will always evaluate to the correct URL no matter what context URI path prefix we use. For instance, if we use a URI path prefix `/chat`, the absolute URL for this request is `/chat/listRooms`. When the browser sees our relative `chatRoom` URL, it will form an absolute URL `/chat/chatRoom`. If we instead used a URI path prefix `/oldchat`, the current absolute URL would be `/oldchat/listRooms` and the browser would interpret our relative URL as `/oldchat/chatRoom`.

Let's continue with the generation of the form.

```
        // Add radio boxes for selecting a room
        out.println("Select the room you would like to enter " +
            "or click on a name to see the description:<P>");
        RoomList roomList = (RoomList) getServletContext().getAttribute("roomList");
        Enumeration rooms = roomList.getRooms();
        boolean isFirst = true;
        while (rooms.hasMoreElements())
        {
            ChatRoom room = (ChatRoom) rooms.nextElement();
            String roomName = room.getName();
            out.println("<INPUT TYPE=RADIO NAME=roomName VALUE='" +
                roomName + "'" +
                (isFirst ? " CHECKED" : "") + ">" +
                "<A HREF=listRooms?expand=" +
                URLEncoder.encode(roomName) + ">" +
                roomName + "</A><BR>");
            isFirst = false;

            // Show description if requested
            if (expand != null && expand.equals(roomName))
            {
                out.println("<BLOCKQUOTE>");
                out.println(room.getDescription());
                out.println("</BLOCKQUOTE><BR>");
            }
        }
```

Next we get a reference to the `ServletContext` through the `getServletContext()` method and then a reference to the `RoomList` object by reading the `roomList` attribute with the `getAttribute()` method. We can now access the context's current state.

We're going to list all available rooms so we use the `getRooms()` method to get an `Enumeration` of all `ChatRoom` objects. For each `ChatRoom` we generate a radio button and a reference tag. The reference tag points back to this servlet and sets a query parameter named `expand` to the name of the chat room.

As a result, if a user clicks on a room name link, then this servlet is called again, but this time with the `expand` parameter set. We use the `expand` parameter in the code block above. If the `expand` parameter value matches the name of a room, we add the description of the room to the HTML page as well.

```
// Add a field for the avatar name
    out.println("<P>Enter your name: ");
    out.println("<INPUT NAME=avatarName VALUE='" +
        avatarName + "' SIZE=30>");

    // Add submit button
    out.println("<P><INPUT TYPE=SUBMIT VALUE='Enter'>");
    out.println("</FORM>");
    out.println("</BODY></HTML>");
}
```

In the last part of the `writePage()` method we generate a text field where the user can enter an avatar name. If the user has entered a name previously in the current session, we also show the current name in the text field.

The ChatRoomServlet class

As you saw above, the `ListRoomsServlet` generates a page with a FORM tag with the ACTION attribute set to the name of the `ChatRoomServlet`. The form contains a radio button control that holds the name of the selected room and a text field with the user's name, and it uses the POST method to invoke the `ChatRoomServlet`.

Let's look at what we do with the form information in the `doPost()` method.

```
public void doPost(HttpServletRequest req, HttpServletResponse res)
            throws IOException, ServletException
{
    res.setContentType("text/html");
    PrintWriter out = res.getWriter();

    ChatRoom room = getRoom(req, res);
    if (room == null)
    {
        return;
    }
    String avatarName = getAvatarName(req);
```

```
        // Save message if any
        String msg = req.getParameter("msg");
        if (msg != null && msg.length() != 0)
        {
            room.addChatEntry(new ChatEntry(avatarName, msg));
        }
        writeFrame(out, room);
        out.close();
    }
```

We use two private methods, getRoom() and getAvatarName(), to get the ChatRoom object corresponding to the chat room name selected in the form, and the avatar name of the user. We'll get back to these methods later.

There's also a request parameter named msg. It's not in the form produced by the ListRoomsServlet so where did it come from? As you'll see soon, the ChatRoomServlet also generates a form and uses the POST method to invoke itself again to send messages to the room. This form contains a field named msg.

If we find a message we create a ChatEntry with the message and the user's name and add it to the ChatRoom with the addChatEntry method. This is the interesting part: The ChatRoom object can be accessed through the RoomList object, and the RoomList object can be accessed through the ServletContext attribute listRoom. This means that as soon as we add the new ChatEntry to the ChatRoom, it's available to all other users of our application.

> **Changes to objects which have been passed to the ServletContext are instantly visible to any other servlet thread which accesses that same ServletContext.**

The ChatRoomServlet has to do two things:
> List all current messages in the chat room
> Allow the user to send new messages.

The list of messages should be updated as new messages are sent to the group. We can't actually tell every client browser when a new message has arrived, but we can accomplish a similar result using a "client-pull" model. This means that we ask the browser to reload the page with the list every 5 seconds by using an HTML META tag. If the user is in the middle of writing a message, automatically reloading the whole page clears the message text area. We don't want that to happen of course. A simple solution that works for most modern browsers is to use a frameset with one frame for the message list, automatically reloaded, and another static frame for sending messages. Sounds complicated? Don't worry, we'll take it step by step. First we generate the frame set. That's done by the writeFrame() method called from doPost().

```
private void writeFrame(PrintWriter out, ChatRoom room)
{
   out.println("<HTML>");
   out.println("<HEAD><TITLE>" + room.getName() + "</TITLE></HEAD>");
   out.println("<FRAMESET ROWS='60%,30%' BORDER=0 FRAMEBORDER=NO>");
   out.println("<FRAME SRC=chatRoom?list=true NAME=list SCROLLING=AUTO>");
   out.println("<FRAME SRC=chatRoom?list=false NAME=form SCROLLING=AUTO>");
   out.println("<NOFRAMES>");
   out.println("<BODY>");
   out.println("Viewing this page requires a browser" +
                         "capable of displaying frames.");
   out.println("</BODY>");
   out.println("</NOFRAMES>");
   out.println("</FRAMESET>");
   out.println("</HTML>");
}
```

We generate a complete HTML page containing a <FRAMESET> tag with two <FRAME> tags named list and form. Notice that the SRC attribute for both frames is the name of this servlet, but we use a parameter named list and the values true and false to distinguish between them.

A browser that supports the <FRAMESET> tag will use the GET method to request the URL specified by the SRC attribute. So let's see how we handle the requests in the doGet() method.

```
public void doGet(HttpServletRequest req, HttpServletResponse res)
               throws IOException, ServletException
{
   res.setContentType("text/html");
   PrintWriter out = res.getWriter();

   ChatRoom room = getRoom(req, res);
   if (room == null)
   {
      return;
   }

   // Check if it's a request for a message list or a form
   String listPar = req.getParameter("list");
   if (listPar != null && listPar.equals("true"))
   {
      writeMessages(out, room, getAvatarName(req));
   }
   else
   {
      writeForm(out);
   }
   out.close();
}
```

Here we use the getRoom() method again to get the current ChatRoom object. Then we use the list parameter to decide whether to generate the message list with the writeMessages() method or the form for sending messages to the room with the writeForm() method.

Let's look at writeMessages() first.

```
    private void writeMessages(PrintWriter out, ChatRoom room,
                String avatarName)
{

    out.println("<HTML>");
    out.println("<HEAD><META http-equiv=\"refresh\" content=\"5\"></HEAD>");
    out.println("<BODY>");
    out.println("<H1>You're in " + room.getName() + " as " +
        avatarName + "</H1>");

    // List all messages in the room
    Enumeration entries = room.getChatEntries();
    if (!entries.hasMoreElements())
    {
        out.println("<FONT COLOR=RED>There are no messages in this room
                                            yet</FONT>");
    }
    while (entries.hasMoreElements())
    {
        ChatEntry entry = (ChatEntry) entries.nextElement();
        String entryName = entry.getAvatarName();
        if (entryName.equals(avatarName))
        {
            out.print("<FONT COLOR=BLUE>");
        }
        out.println(entryName + " : " + entry.getChatMessage() + "<BR>");
        if (entryName.equals(avatarName))
        {
            out.print("</FONT>");
        }
    }
    out.println("</BODY></HTML>");
}
```

First we generate the HTML page header. Note that we use an HTML <META> tag to ask for this page to be reloaded (refreshed) every 5 seconds. This way new messages will show up in a reasonably timely fashion after they are sent to the room, but we won't be swamped with refresh requests all the time.

Next we get an Enumeration of all ChatEntry objects in the ChatRoom and add them to the HTML page one by one. If we find an entry sent by the current user, we highlight it by using a blue font. Again, remember that the ChatRoom object is part of the servlet's context state, shared by all servlets in the application and available to all users of those servlets. So no matter who sent the message to the room, we will be able to access it here and include it in our list.

Okay, so how do we send a message to the room? That's handled by the frame generated by the writeForm() method.

```
private void writeForm(PrintWriter out)
{
    out.println("<HTML>");
    out.println("<BODY>");
    out.println("<FORM METHOD=POST ACTION=chatRoom TARGET=_top>");

    // Add field for new message
    out.println("<P>Enter your message:<P>");
    out.println("<TEXTAREA NAME=msg COLS=50 ROWS=3 WRAP=HARD>");
    out.println("</TEXTAREA>");

    // Add submit button and hidden field with room name
    out.println("<P><INPUT TYPE=SUBMIT VALUE='Send Message'>");

    // Add an Exit button
    out.println("</FORM>");
    out.println("<FORM ACTION=listRooms METHOD=GET TARGET=_top>");
    out.println("<INPUT TYPE=SUBMIT VALUE=Exit>");
    out.println("</FORM>");

    out.println("</BODY></HTML>");
}
```

The form uses the POST method with the ACTION attribute set to the name of this servlet. So when the user clicks on the **Send Message** button, our doPost() method is invoked. The form also contains a text area named msg containing the message text. That's how we got the msg parameter you saw in the doPost() method above.

We only need two more methods to make this work. You have seen how the getRoom() and getAvatarName() methods are used above. These two methods allow us to keep the values for the current room and avatar name in the HttpSession object, while still accepting new values set in the forms generated by the application so the user can enter new rooms and use a different name in each room.

The first part of the getRoom() method looks like this.

```
private ChatRoom getRoom(HttpServletRequest req, HttpServletResponse res)
        throws IOException
{
    HttpSession session = req.getSession();
    PrintWriter out = res.getWriter();

    String roomName = (String) session.getValue("roomName");
    if (roomName == null)
    {
        // Just entered?
        roomName = req.getParameter("roomName");
        if (roomName == null || roomName.length() == 0)
        {
            writeError(out, "Room not specified");
            return null;
        }
        session.putValue("roomName", roomName);
    }
```

We try to get the room name from the session first. If there's no room name available in the session this is probably the first room the user has entered, so the room name should be available as a parameter value set by the form generated by RoomListServlet. We read the parameter value and put the value in the session for future reference. If the room name is neither in the session nor passed as a parameter then something is terribly wrong, so we inform the user about the problem.

```
        else
          {
            // Entered a new room?
            String newRoom = req.getParameter("roomName");
            if (newRoom != null && newRoom.length() > 0 &&
                !newRoom.equals(roomName))
            {
                roomName = newRoom;
                session.putValue("roomName", roomName);
            }
          }
```

Even when we find the room name in the session we must check if there's a parameter value as well. A room name that's different from the name we kept in the session means the user entered another room through the form generated by RoomListServlet. If so we put the new room name in the session.

```
        RoomList roomList =
            (RoomList) getServletContext().getAttribute("roomList");
        ChatRoom room = roomList.getRoom(roomName);
        if (room == null)
        {
            writeError(out, "Room " + roomName + " not found");
            return null;
        }
        return room;
      }
```

Finally we retrieve the RoomList object using our roomList servlet context attribute, get the ChatRoom object corresponding to the current room name and return it to the calling method.

The getAvatarName() method looks almost the same:

```
    private String getAvatarName(HttpServletRequest req)
      {
        HttpSession session = req.getSession();
        String avatarName = (String) session.getValue("avatarName");
        if (avatarName == null)
        {
            // Entered a room for the first time?
            avatarName = req.getParameter("avatarName");
            if (avatarName == null || avatarName.length() == 0)
            {
                avatarName = "A spineless spy";
            }
            session.putValue("avatarName", avatarName);
        }
```

Continued on Following Page

```
        else
        {
            // Entered a new room with a new name?
            String newName = req.getParameter("avatarName");
            if (newName != null && newName.length() > 0 &&
                    !newName.equals(avatarName))
            {
                avatarName = newName;
                session.putValue("avatarName", avatarName);
            }
        }
        return avatarName;
    }
```

The only notable difference is that if a user enters a room without giving us his or her name, we set the name to "A spineless spy". It's their own fault.

That's the bulk of the application, and now you have seen a practical example of how the servlet context attributes can be used to share information between all servlets in an application. As a recap of earlier chapters you have also seen how the HttpSession object can be used to keep track of information that's unique to one user of the application.

Next we will look at how we can change the context's state, or in other words its attribute values.

Changing the Context's State

In fact, we have already seen how a servlet can change the context's state. Remember how we added ChatEntry objects to a ChatRoom when a new message was sent to a room in the ChatRoomServlet? When we change an object that's accessible through a servlet context attribute, we're changing the context's state.

In this section we take a closer look at another example of changing the state. Besides initializing the servlet context's state at startup, the ChatAdminServlet can also be used to add and remove chat rooms while the application is in operation.

The doGet() method is used to generate a form where check-boxes are used to select rooms to be removed and a text field and a text area are used to add a new room.

```
public void doGet(HttpServletRequest req, HttpServletResponse res)
        throws IOException, ServletException
{
    res.setContentType("text/html");
    PrintWriter out = res.getWriter();
    writePage(out);
    out.close();
}
```

Actually, `doGet()` just calls `writePage()`, and that's where the interesting stuff takes place.

```java
private void writePage(PrintWriter out)
{
    out.println("<HTML>");
    out.println("<HEAD><TITLE>Chat room administration</TITLE></HEAD>");
    out.println("<BODY>");
    out.println("<H1>Chat room administration</H1>");
    out.println("<FORM METHOD=POST ACTION=chatAdmin>");

    // Add check boxes for removing rooms
    out.println("Check off the rooms you would like to remove:<P>");
    RoomList roomList =
                (RoomList) getServletContext().getAttribute("roomList");
    Enumeration rooms = roomList.getRooms();
    while (rooms.hasMoreElements())
    {
        ChatRoom room = (ChatRoom) rooms.nextElement();
        out.println("<INPUT TYPE=CHECKBOX NAME=remove VALUE='" +
                room.getName() + "'>" + room.getName() + "<BR>");
    }
    // Add fields for adding a room
    out.println("<P>Describe the room you would like to add:<P>");
    out.println("<TABLE>");
    out.println("<TR><TD>Name:</TD><TD>" +
                    "<INPUT NAME=roomname SIZE=50></TD></TR>");
    out.println("<TR><TD>Description:</TD>");
    out.println("<TD><TEXTAREA NAME=roomdescr COLS=50 ROWS=15>");
    out.println("</TEXTAREA></TD></TR>");
    out.println("</TABLE>");

    // Add submit button
    out.println("<P><INPUT TYPE=SUBMIT VALUE='Update List'>");

    out.println("</FORM>");
    out.println("</BODY></HTML>");
}
```

In this method we generate a form with the `ACTION` attribute set to the name of this servlet and the `METHOD` attribute set to `POST`. We get hold of the `RoomList` from the `ServletContext` and generate one check-box per `ChatRoom` and the text field and text area for adding a new room. The **Update List** button invokes this servlet's `doPost()` method.

```java
public void doPost(HttpServletRequest req, HttpServletResponse res)
        throws IOException, ServletException
{
    boolean isListModified = false;
    RoomList roomList =
        (RoomList) getServletContext().getAttribute("roomList");

    // Update the room list
    String[] removeList = req.getParameterValues("remove");
    if (removeList != null)
    {
        roomList.removeRooms(removeList);
        isListModified = true;
    }
```

Continued on Following Page

```
        String roomName = req.getParameter("roomname");
        String roomDescr = req.getParameter("roomdescr");
        if (roomName != null && roomName.length() > 0)
        {
            roomList.addRoom(new ChatRoom(roomName, roomDescr));
            isListModified = true;
        }

        if (isListModified)
        {
            saveList(roomList);
        }
        doGet(req, res);
    }
```

In doPost() we use the parameter values from the form. We used check-boxes and more than one can be checked so the remove parameter can contain the names of multiple rooms. We pass the array of room names to the removeRooms() method to remove them all in one shot.

If a new room name and description was specified, we create a new ChatRoom object with this information and add it to the RoomList with the addRoom() method.

The isListModified variable is set to true if we modify the RoomList in any way. So before we display the administration form again by calling doGet(), we save the updated list to the property file if isListModified is true. When the servlet engine is restarted, the latest configuration information is therefore always available in the property file.

What may be most important here is what we don't do: we never set the ServletContext roomList attribute after we're done updating the RoomList object. The attribute contains a reference to the RoomList object. We update the RoomList data but the *reference* is still the same; we didn't replace the RoomList object with another RoomList object. So setting the attribute to the same object reference again would be redundant.

Running the Chat Application

The chat application used in this example is primarily intended to illustrate how you can use the ServletContext, but that doesn't mean it's not a useful application. You may want to add some bells and whistles before you use it on a real site, but it works as is.

In this section we'll go through what you need to do to configure a servlet engine for the chat application and how to run it, step by step as a recap without too much fuss about how it really works.

> **If you haven't done so already, you need to download the file with all code for the classes described in this book from the Wrox Press web site, http://www.wrox.com, before you proceed.**

Configuring the Servlet Engine

First we need to configure a servlet context for the application. Exactly how this is done varies slightly between servlet engines. Most engines provide some form of administration tool for all configuration tasks, but also standard property files that can be edited manually.

We will use Gefion software's LiteWebServer (LWS) – a small, servlet-enabled, pure Java web server – in this section. You can download a free copy for non-commercial use at http://www.gefionsoftware.com.

If you want to use the chat application with another servlet engine you may have to adapt the instructions given here, but most servlet engines supporting the Servlet 2.1 API use the same or a very similar format for the configuration files.

In the LWS configuration directory there's a file named `server.properties`. That's where servlet contexts are defined. To define a context named `chatapp` mapped to the URI path prefix `/chat`, we add the following lines to the `server.properties` file:

```
context.chatapp.uriroot=/chat
context.chatapp.confdir=/usr/local/lws/config/chatapp
```

The first property is the URI path prefix mapping, the second specifies the configuration directory for the `chatapp` context. Replace the `confdir` value above with the path to an appropriate directory on your computer.

To make life simple, you can use forward slashes even on a Windows platform, for example `C:/lws/config/chatapp`. Copy the default `mime.properties`, `rules.properties` and `servlets.properties` files to this directory.

Next we define the servlet names and initialization parameters for our servlet classes. Add the following lines to the `servlets.properties` file in the context's configuration directory:

```
servlet.chatAdmin.code=com.wrox.pssjp.context.chat.ChatAdminServlet
servlet.chatAdmin.initArgs=chatprops=/usr/local/lws/config/chatapp/chat.properties
servlet.listRooms.code=com.wrox.pssjp.context.chat.ListRoomsServlet
servlet.chatRoom.code=com.wrox.pssjp.context.chat.ChatRoomServlet
```

Note that the second line sets the value of the `chatprops` initialization parameter for the `chatAdmin` servlet. You need to adjust this value so it points to an existing directory but you do not have to create the `chat.properties` file itself. We will use the `chatAdmin` servlet to add room properties instead.

You also need to specify that the `chatAdmin` servlet shall be loaded when the server is started - this ensures that as soon as the server is started up, the servlet's `init()` method is called, which sets up the chat rooms in the `ServletContext`. Until this happens, the other two servlets won't work. Locate the property named `servlets.startup` in the `servlets.properties` file and add the `chatAdmin` name to the list, e.g.:

```
servlets.startup=admin file invoker ssinclude chatAdmin
```

Finally we define the servlet mapping rules for this context. Add the following lines to the `rules.properties` file in the context's configuration directory:

```
/chatAdmin=chatAdmin
/chatRoom=chatRoom
/listRooms=listRooms
```

Be careful to ensure that the case of the paths you specify here matches the case you specified in your code.

The only thing left is to include the JAR file with all the chat application classes in the `CLASSPATH` for LWS. Edit the `lws` start script for your platform to add the JAR file you downloaded from the Wrox web site to the `CLASSPATH`. Then start LWS by running the updated script.

Adding Chat Rooms

Now we're ready to try out the application. We'll start by adding some chat rooms. Start a web browser and enter the following URL in the address field, assuming you're running LWS on the local machine using the default port number 9090:

```
http://localhost:9090/chat/chatAdmin
```

You should see a web page like the one below where you can enter information about a chat room and click Update List to add it.

Add a couple of rooms to play with.

Chatting

When you have defined a room or two, list all of them by entering a URL like this in the browser:

```
http://localhost:9090/chat/listRooms
```

You should see a page similar to this:

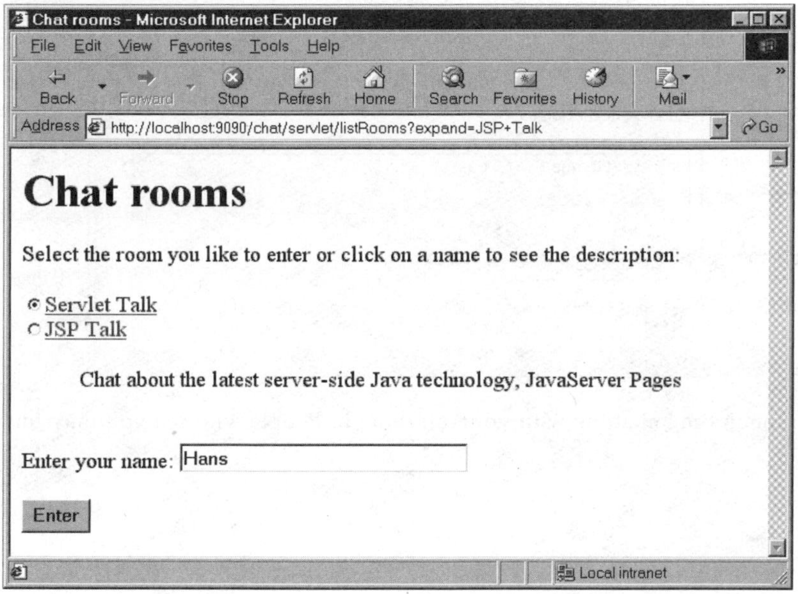

Select a room, write your name and click Enter. You're now looking at the page for the chat room you selected. All messages are listed in the top frame and you can send new messages in the bottom frame.

Don't spend too much time chatting with yourself though. People who see you may question your sanity.

Summary

In this chapter we developed a simple chat application to learn how the `ServletContext` can be used to represent a servlet application, by letting us

- ➢ Define a unique URI path prefix per servlet context
- ➢ Define rules for how request URIs are mapped to servlets within a context
- ➢ Initialize the servlet context state from an application configuration file using a servlet loaded at startup
- ➢ Give individual servlets in an application access to the shared state through context attributes

We also learned how context state changes made by one servlet are immediately available to the other parts of the application

Dynamic Content Generation

Now we have looked at the basic tools available to servlets, it's time to bring it all together and write a useful server application that does some real work. This will allow us to use what we've learnt about the request and response objects, error handling, and sessions, as well as learning about one part of the API we've been ignoring - delivering binary (non-textual) data from a servlet.

In this chapter, we will write a servlet which takes samples from a data set and generates an HTML page showing statistical values for the data set on the fly. Java servlets are not limited to returning text data like HTML or XML to a browser. Many other types of data can be created dynamically by a servlet. The most commonly used non-textual objects are images. Our servlet should be able to visualize the data not only as an HTML table but also as pie and bar charts which are created dynamically by the servlet.

The following topics are covered in detail in this chapter:

> **MIME Types:** How different data types are described by MIME content types and how a servlet works with different content types.

> **Image formats:** Which formats are commonly used on the World Wide Web and how they are represented as MIME content types.

> **Returning binary data to the client:** How does a servlet write a response that contains binary data as opposed to one containing text?

> **Creating a GIF image:** How are images represented in Java, what drawing tools are available for creating off-screen images and how does an image get encoded as as a GIF stream so that it can be displayed by a Web browser?

> **Returning mixed content:** How can a servlet return a response which contains an HTML page with embedded images which are all created on the fly?

In the process, we'll also have to tackle the following, more general problems:

> **Providing multiple services from one servlet:** Our servlet will be able to produce HTML code and images, depending on a request parameter.

> **Accessing the content of files on the server:** We'll be using files to store the data our servlet will need.

> **Using URL Encoding:** We'll be using URL rewriting to preserve the request state from one request to another. We'll need to encode arbitrary text data into URL query strings.

MIME Types

The format of any data returned by a servlet is classified by a **MIME content type** (Multipurpose Internet Mail Extensions), a universal and standardized name for a data format. As the name suggests, MIME was originally developed for the transmission of non-textual e-mail messages, but it can be applied to other domains like news articles and HTTP messages, where data is stored or transmitted together with meta-data headers as well. A content type is a string of the form `type/sub-type`. The following `image` sub-types are used for image formats which are of general interest for Web-based applications:

Image/jpeg

The JPEG/JFIF format (commonly referred to as "JPEG") is used to compress true-color or greyscale images. It uses a lossy compression algorithm which shows good results when compressing photographic images. JPEG images can be **progressive** which means that the image is separated into several scans of improving quality. When receiving a JPEG stream, a Web browser can display a low-quality preview of the image after a short time. The image quality improves until the image has been completely loaded.

Image/gif

The GIF format supports up to 256 colors or grayscales, one of which can be transparent. It uses a lossless compression algorithm. This format is commonly used for low-color images and images with sharp contrasts which need to be reproduced accurately. GIF images can be interlaced which means that instead of writing the lines of the image from top to bottom the image is written in two scans of alternating odd-numbered and even-numbered lines. This allows a Web browser receiving a GIF stream to display a half-resolution preview of the complete image after only the first half of the image data has been transmitted.

Image/png

The PNG (Portable Network Graphics) format was designed to replace GIF in the long run, although its adoption by browsers has not been as widespread as hoped. It uses a lossless compression algorithm which creates image that are usually a bit smaller than their GIF counterparts. PNG supports images with an alpha channel (a separate transparency setting in 256 steps for each pixel of the image) and can be used with low-color (256 colors or less), grayscale and true-color images.

Format	Suffix	Colors	Transparency
JPEG/JFIF	`.jpeg`	24 Bit True color	None
	`.jpg`	256 Grayscale	
GIF	`.gif`	Up to 256	One transparent color
PNG	`.png`	Low-color (up to 256 colors)	8 Bit alpha channel
		24 Bit True-Color	
		Grayscale	

The content type of HTTP data is specified in the `Content-Type` response header. A client may supply an `Accept` header with an HTTP request to provide a list of acceptable content types:

```
Accept: image/gif, image/jpeg, image/pjpeg, image/png, */*
```

This list indicates that the client will accept all data formats (`*/*`) but prefers the sub-types `gif`, `jpeg`, `pjpeg` and `png` for images. Note that the acceptance of all data formats does not imply that the client is actually capable of displaying them.

In this chapter, we will be using the widely accepted GIF format to return a bar or pie chart image from a servlet to the web browser. If a servlet intends to return data in a more exotic format, the `Accept` header should be checked to find out which format the client prefers.

Returning Binary Data

When returning text from a servlet, you generally use a `PrintWriter` object obtained by `ServletResponse.getWriter()` which automatically checks what character encodings are acceptable to the client, and converts the Unicode characters which are used internally by all Java applications to the best available encoding. This is a very convenient way for the programmer to handle text in different languages and character sets transparently (see Chapter 19). However, it is not acceptable for binary data which needs to be sent as-is from a servlet to the client. For that reason, `ServletResponse` offers the method `getOutputStream()` to return an `OutputStream` object which can be used to send bytes of data directly to the client without being re-encoded as text by the servlet engine.

Creating a GIF Image

Part of the Java core API is the **Abstract Windowing Toolkit** (AWT), a framework of classes to access the host system's windowing and graphics features, i.e. opening and closing windows, printing text into them, drawing figures, creating buttons and menus, handling mouse clicks, etc. While originally conceived for applets and interactive applications, the AWT can be put to good use in server-side applications as well. A servlet does not open windows on the server machine, though. Instead it creates off-screen images the same way applications with on-screen displays create off-screen images for double-buffering.

Creating an Off-Screen Image

In Java, images are represented by the `java.awt.Image` class. Image objects are relatively abstract. They do not need to represent actual pixel graphics. A straight-forward way of creating an image of pixels in the RGB color model is using a `java.awt.image.MemoryImageSource` object and creating an image for it with `java.awt.Toolkit`'s `createImage(ImageProducer)` method, using the default AWT Toolkit:

```
int width = 100, height = 100;
int[] pixels = new int[width * height];
ImageProducer source =
        new MemoryImageSource(width, height, pixels, 0, width);
Toolkit defaultToolkit = Toolkit.getDefaultToolkit();
Image img = defaultToolkit.createImage(source);
```

This creates an image that can be copied into AWT components and other images, but unfortunately it cannot be modified with AWT graphics methods but only by changing values directly in the `pixels` array. This is sometimes desirable because it allows the most direct control over the image. The chart servlet, however, can be implemented more easily with an image which can be drawn with the high-level graphics methods - lines, rectangles, even text. A little trick allows us to create such an `Image` object. A Frame (a decorated AWT window) is created and then connected to the host platform's AWT toolkit by calling its `addNotify()` method. Note that the frame is not actually displayed on the screen. The `Frame` object is merely a handle to a frame which could be displayed by calling `setVisible(true)`. The invisible frame can be used to obtain an off-screen image with full AWT drawing support:

```
int width = 100, height = 100;
Frame dummy = new Frame();
dummy.addNotify();
Image img = dummy.createImage(width, height);
```

There's another advantage to using the AWT graphics methods: The drawing code can be easily reused in other AWT applications. For example, the same method that draws a figure into an off-screen image in a servlet could be used to draw the figure into the visible area of an applet.

Using features of the AWT implementation requires access to the host machine's graphics system. In case of a Unix machine this is usually an X11 server, which is not available in standard server setups. It is therefore necessary to grant the servlet container access to an X11 server running somewhere in the network by setting up the right access restrictions on the X11 server and specifying the X11 server's name and display number in the `DISPLAY` variable of the servlet container's environment. Since we do not actually need to display anything on the X server, a virtual server which manages a framebuffer in memory but does not have a display will be enough. On Windows machines, you won't have to worry about this.

Encoding the Image

After an `Image` object has been created and filled with content, it should be sent to the browser. We therefore need to encode it as a binary stream in an image format which is understood by the browser. Image encoders are not part of the Java 1.2 core API, but there are free encoders available on the Internet. The ACME Java utilities contain a fast, stable, easy to use GIF encoder class, `Acme.JPM.Encoders.GifEncoder`. With this, it takes just a few lines of code to save an `Image` object to disk as a GIF image:

```
Image img = ...;
FileOutputStream out = new FileOutputStream("image.gif");
new GifEncoder(img, out, true).encode();
```

The `GifEncoder` class has the following constructors:

```
public GifEncoder(Image img, OutputStream out) throws IOException
```

`img` is the image to encode and `out` the `OutputStream` to write the encoded data to. The image will be written as a non-interlaced GIF89 image.

```
public GifEncoder(Image img, OutputStream out, boolean interlace) throws
IOException
```

`img` is the image to encode and `out` the `OutputStream` to write the encoded data to. The image will be written as an interlaced or non-interlaced GIF89 image, depending on the value of the `interlace` argument.

```
public GifEncoder(ImageProducer prod, OutputStream out) throws IOException
```

`prod` is an `ImageProducer` from which the image to encode will be obtained. `out` is the `OutputStream` to write the encoded data to. The image will be written as a non-interlaced GIF89 image.

```
public GifEncoder(ImageProducer prod, OutputStream out, boolean interlace) throws
IOException
```

`prod` is an ImageProducer from which the image to encode will be obtained. `out` is the `OutputStream` to write the encoded data to. The image will be written as an interlaced or non-interlaced GIF89 image, depending on the value of the `interlace` argument.

`GifEncoder` implements the `java.awt.image.ImageConsumer` interface and provides one additional public method:

```
public synchronized void encode() throws IOException
```

This method must be called after creating the `GifEncoder` to actually write out the GIF data.

To provide an abstraction from the `GifEncoder` we create an `ImageServlet` class which extends `javax.servlet.http.HttpServlet`, the base class of most servlets, and can be inherited by all servlets which should return images. Encoding and sending images from a servlet is implemented in the `sendImage` method:

```
protected void sendImage(HttpServletResponse res,
                         Image img) throws IOException
{
    res.setContentType("image/gif");
    OutputStream out = res.getOutputStream();
    new GifEncoder(img, out, true).encode();
    out.close();
}
```

Encapsulating the image encoding in the `ImageServlet` class makes it possible to change the encoding routines later without the need to change all image-creating servlets directly. Possible useful changes would include:

> **Using a different GIF encoder:** To support transparency, improve performance, etc.

> **Changing options of the GIF encoder:** To send non-interlaced GIFs, for example.

> **Dynamically selecting image formats:** For example, if the number of colors in an image exceeds 256 (the maximum allowed number of colors for GIF images), a JPEG encoder could be used instead.

> **Implementing content negotiation:** If a PNG encoder is available, the `Accept` header, if supplied by a Web browser with a request, could be checked to find out if the browser prefers GIF or PNG images.

All these changes would be transparent to `ImageServlet`'s sub-classes.

Creating images by asking an invisible frame for off-screen `Image` objects is also part of the `ImageServlet`. The invisible frame can be shared by all invocations of the servlet, so it is declared as a member variable:

```
private Component dummy;
```

The component gets initialized in the servlet's `init()` method. (note that this is a Servlet API 2.1 no-args `init()` method - you may need to make changes depending on your servlet container.)

```
public void init() throws ServletException
{
    dummy = new Frame();
    dummy.addNotify();
}
```

The `createImage()` method simply calls the corresponding method of the invisible frame:

```
protected Image createImage(int w, int h)
{
    return dummy.createImage(w,h);
}
```

The Statistics Chart Servlet

The main goal of this chapter is creating a servlet which draws pie and bar charts for statistical values. This `ChartServlet` should return images, so it extends our `ImageServlet` class instead of `javax.servlet.http.HttpServlet`.

Utility Classes

We a need a second auxiliary class called `Stats` whose instances contain sets of processed data which can be displayed as charts or tables. `Stats` contains a private array of `StatValue` objects. `StatValue` is a nested top-level class defined within `Stats` whose instances contain pairs of String names and int values:

```
    private static final class StatValue
    {
        int value;
        String name;

        StatValue()
        {
        }

        StatValue(String name, int value)
        {
            this.name = name;
            this.value = value;
        }
    }
```

The Stats class has a constructor that takes a single String argument which describes the data source. It is interpreted as the path to a text file relative to the Stats.class file which contains the raw data for the statistics. In a production environment you would probably get all data from a database instead, or parse files with a more complex structure. This is left out of the example servlet to keep it simple and easy to use. It can be adapted easily to retrieve the data from a different source by modifying only the Stats constructor.

The constructor can be divided into four parts:

➤ Getting an InputStream for the data source.

➤ Processing the data to compute the statistical values.

➤ Creating the StatValue array.

➤ Post-processing the values.

First, an input stream for the data source should be obtained. As you will see later, the source path comes directly from the requested servlet URL, so it needs to checked for validity:

```
public Stats(String source) throws IOException
{
    if(source == null || source.length() == 0)
        throw new IOException("No source specified");
```

For each Java class there is an object of type java.lang.Class which describes the class. It contains methods to access the class' constructors, methods, superclasses, etc. It also contains information about the origin of a class and can fetch other resources from the same source. This feature can be used to find a file whose path relative to a class file is known, no matter where that class file is actually stored. In a network application (e.g. an applet) it could even be retrieved on demand from an HTTP server. Servlets usually come from class files located in a special servlet directory on the local disk, so using a Class object makes it possible to load resources placed in the same directory without the need to set the path explicitly through an init parameter. The Stats class is also placed into the servlet directory, so a Stats object can simply ask for its own Class object and use the getResourceAsStream() method to retrieve the data file

```
    InputStream in = getClass().getResourceAsStream(source.substring(1));
    if(in == null)
        throw new IOException("Source not found");
```

Again, an `IOException` is thrown to abort the constructor (and thus also the `ChartServlet`'s `doGet()` method which passes the exception on to the servlet engine) if the data source was not found.

The data file is then read line by line with a `java.io.BufferedReader` object. Each line is expected to contain a single name. The following is a valid file - it's simply the subjects covered by the books on one shelf in my bookcase.

```
Languages
Languages
Languages
Languages
Languages
Languages
Languages
Languages
Languages
OOP
Languages
Languages
Languages
OOP
Languages
Compilers
Compilers
Compilers
X11
X11
Patterns
Patterns
Algorithms
Hardware
Math
Math
Math
Math
Math
Math
Math
Math
Math
```

A `java.util.Hashtable` object is used to store the names and current counts while the file is read to count all entries:

```
BufferedReader reader = new BufferedReader(new InputStreamReader(in));
Hashtable h = new Hashtable();
String line;
while((line = reader.readLine()) != null)
{
    int[] countWrapper = (int[])h.get(line);
    if(countWrapper == null)
        h.put(line, new int[] {1});
    else
```

```
            countWrapper[0]++;
    }
    reader.close();
```

The `HashTable` contains entries of the form *name:count*. The count value is of the primitive `int` type which can not be stored directly in a `Hashtable` object. Instead we need to convert it to a class type. The straight-forward choice would be the wrapper class `java.lang.Integer` but this would impose an unnecessary overhead for creating new `Integer` objects for each line that is read from the data file, since `Integer` objects are immutable. An `int` array with a single entry provides a simple mutable wrapper for an `int` value. For each data file entry we check if that entry is already in the `HashTable`. If it is not, a new new `int` array which contains a single "1" entry is put into the `HashTable` for that data file entry. It there is already such an array in the `HashTable`, the value of its only element is incremented by one.

When the file has been read and all values have been put into the `HashTable` (which is only used temporarily while reading the file) the values can be copied into their permanent storage, the `StatValue` array. A new array with the same size as the `HashTable` is created and then filled by enumerating through all `HashTable` elements and creating a `StatValue` object for each one.

```
values = new StatValue[h.size()];
Enumeration e = h.keys();
for(int i=0; i<values.length; i++)
{
    String key = (String)e.nextElement();
    int count = ((int[])h.get(key))[0];
    values[i] = new StatValue(key, count);
}

sort();
process();
```

Next, the `values` array is sorted with a simple bubble sort algorithm which is implemented in a separate method:

```
private void sort()
{
    for(int i=0; i<values.length; i++)
    {
        for(int j=i+1; j<values.length; j++)
        {
            if(values[i].value < values[j].value)
            {
                StatValue tmp = values[i];
                values[i] = values[j];
                values[j] = tmp;
            }
        }
    }
}
```

Finally, the `process()` method computes two values which will be useful later when drawing the pie and bar charts. `total` is the summed up total of all values in the `Stats` object and `max` is the highest of these values.

```
private void process()
{
    for(int i=0; i<values.length; i++)
    {
        total += values[i].value;
        if(values[i].value > max) max = values[i].value;
    }
}
```

The Servlet Itself

We start implementing the main `ChartServlet` class with a short `doGet()` method:

```
public void doGet(HttpServletRequest req, HttpServletResponse res)
                throws ServletException, IOException
{
    res.setHeader("Pragma", "no-cache");
    res.setHeader("Cache-Control", "no-cache");
    res.setDateHeader("Expires", 0);

    Stats stats = new Stats();

    Color fg = Color.black,
          bg = new Color(0xB2B2B2),
          fill = new Color(0xF0A0A0);

    sendImage(res, createPieChart(200, 200, stats, fg, bg, fill, false));
}
```

The servlet's response will change when the displayed data changes in the database (at least in a real-life application, where the data is not hardcoded like this), so it important to tell proxy-servers and browsers not to cache the response. This is done in the first three lines of code by creating the following HTTP response headers:

`Pragma: no-cache` is the HTTP/1.0 header for non-cachable resources. It is officially specified for request headers only, but it is commonly used for response headers as well. Using this header in a response tells all proxy servers between the Web server and the origin server that hosts the servlet not to store the response in a proxy cache. Subsequent requests for the same resource should always be forwarded to the origin server to get the most up to date response.

`Cache-Control: no-cache` is the official HTTP/1.1 header for non-cacheable resources. We use it in addition to the `Pragma` header because HTTP/1.0 software does not know `Cache-Control` and some HTTP/1.1 software may ignore `Pragma: no-cache` as a response header.

The `no-cache` headers should stop proxy servers from caching the Servlet's response but some browsers will ignore them and still display cached responses. The `Expires: Thu, 01 Jan 1970 00:00:00 GMT` header pre-expires the response as a last resort against browser caches. This may cause browsers to reload the resource even when only flipping through the history buffer or following a link to a resource which was already loaded in the current browser session. This may be inconvenient for the user, so you should use pre-expired responses with care. It is often enough to make responses partially or fully cacheable and tell users to reload the resource if they want an up to date version.

When the headers have been set, a `Stats` object and `java.awt.Color` objects for the foreground, background and fill color of the pie chart are created. The pie chart is drawn by a separate method, `createPieChart`, and sent with the `sendImage` method which is inherited from the `ImageServlet` superclass.

The Graphics Context

As we've seen, the `java.awt.Image` class provides a canvas to draw on. What we need now is the drawing tools. These are provided by a **Graphics Context**, represented by a `java.awt.Graphics` object, which can be obtained by calling an `Image`'s `getGraphics()` method. The graphics context provides the following basic drawing methods:

```
Color getColor()
void setColor(Color color)
```

Get/set the current color which is associated with the graphics context. This color is used for all drawing operations.

```
void drawLine(int x1, int x2, int y1, int y2)
```

Draw a line between the points (x1,y1) and (x2,y2). This method can also be used for drawing single pixels by making (x1,y2) and (x2,y2) the same point. There is no separate method for setting single pixels.

```
void drawOval(int x, int y, int width, int height)
void fillOval(int x, int y, int width, int height)
void drawArc(int x, int y, int width, int height, int startAngle, int arcAngle)
void fillArc(int x, int y, int width, int height, int startAngle, int arcAngle)
```

Draw an oval outline/filled oval that fills the specified rectangular area. The `Arc` methods draw only a segment of an oval starting at `startAngle` and extending to `startAngle+arcAngle`. Note that the outlines include the x+width and y+height borders at the lower and right side of the rectangles but the filled ovals don't.

```
drawRect(int x, int y, int width, int height)
fillRect(int x, int y, int width, int height)
draw3DRect(int x, int y, int width, int height, boolean raised)
fill3DRect(int x, int y, int width, int height, boolean raised)
drawRoundRect(int x, int y, int width, int height, int arcWidth, int arcHeight)
fillRoundRect(int x, int y, int width, int height, int arcWidth, int arcHeight)
```

This family of methods draws rectangular outlines and filled rectangles. The 3D methods draw rectangles with beveled borders whose colors are lighter and darker versions of the current color. The Round methods draw round corners with the specified arc sizes. As with the oval drawing methods the outlines include the borders at x+width and y+height but the filled rectangles don't.

```
drawPolygon(int[] xPoints, int[] yPoints, int nPoints)
drawPolygon(Polygon p)
fillPolygon(int[] xPoints, int[] yPoints, int nPoints)
fillPolygon(Polygon p)
drawPolyline(int[] xPoints, int[] yPoints, int nPoints)
```

Draw a polygon outline or a filled polygon. Polygons can be specified by a `Polygon` object or an array of coordinates from (xPoints[0],yPoints[0]) to (xPoints[nPoints-1],yPoints[nPoints-1]). The `drawPolyline` method does not automatically close the polygon if the first and last point are not identical.

111

Graphics context methods that deal with fonts and text are discussed later. The graphics context also offers some more advanced features like clipping regions and coordinate translation which are not covered in this chapter.

We can now make an important change to `ImageServlet`'s `createImage` method. The background color of newly created off-screen images is system dependent. Images created by `ImageServlet` subclasses will usually be embedded in HTML pages, so the images' background color should match the background color of the HTML pages. This can be achieved by filling all newly created images with a specified color which leads to the following improved `createImage()` method:

```
protected Image createImage(int w, int h, Color bg)
{
    Image img = dummy.createImage(w,h);
    Graphics g = img.getGraphics();
    g.setColor(bg);
    g.fillRect(0, 0, w, h);
    return img;
}
```

Creating the Colors

Another auxiliary method is required in the `ChartServlet` class to implement the main pie and bar chart methods. The values that will be drawn do not have specific colors associated with them (which would, however, be the case when drawing projection figures for an election, for example), so we need to assign colors automatically. Instead of hard-coding color values, we start with a single hard-coded fill color as shown in the `doGet()` method above, and rotate that color step by step through the color circle to create more colors. The `java.awt.Color` class uses an RGB (Red, Green, Blue) color representation, as does the pixel image that we're drawing on, but a `Color` object can also be converted to HSB (Hue, Saturation, Brightness) format and vice versa. In HSB space the color rotation can be performed easily by incrementing the color's Hue component, starting over at 0.0 when the maximum value of 1.0 has been reached. The result is a color with the same saturation and brightness, but a different hue, e.g. a pastel red would be repeatedly transformed into a pastel orange, yellow, green, and so on. This transformation is implemented in `ChartServlet`'s private `rotateColor()` method.

```
private Color rotateColor(Color c)
{
    float[] hsb = Color.RGBtoHSB(c.getRed(), c.getGreen(),
                                 c.getBlue(), null);
    hsb[0] += 0.095;
    if(hsb[0] > 1.0) hsb[0] -= 1.0;
    return new Color(Color.HSBtoRGB(hsb[0], hsb[1], hsb[2]));
}
```

In the context of the `ChartServlet` the fill color object could be reused in theory, but `java.awt.Color` objects are immutable, so a new object has to be created for each color. First, the old color is separated into the HSB components, then `hsb[0]` (the Hue component) is rotated. Finally, a new `Color` object is created from the modified `hsb` array. The `rotateColor()` method as shown above is sufficient for creating a few colors. If a great number of easily distinguishable colors are required, the method could be enhanced to also modify saturation and brightness levels within certain limits.

There is still one disadvantage to using the colors created by `rotateColor()`: They are not suitable for a grayscale display or black & white printing. When converting colors to grayscale, the hue and saturation components are dropped and only the brightness is left. Unfortunately the brightness is exactly the same for all rotated colors! We add a second method that creates colors by changing the brightness instead of the hue to overcome this problem.

```
private Color rotateBrightness(Color c)
{
    float[] hsb = Color.RGBtoHSB(c.getRed(), c.getGreen(), c.getBlue(), null);
    hsb[2] -= 0.085;
    if(hsb[2] > 1.0) hsb[2] -= 1.0;
    return new Color(Color.HSBtoRGB(hsb[0], hsb[1], hsb[2]));
}
```

This method is almost identical to `rotateColor()` except that `hsb[2]` (the brightness component) is decremented instead of incrementing `hsb[0]` (the hue component). We modify `doGet()` to read a `boolean` parameter (bw) to determine if the image should be drawn in color or black & white:

```
public void doGet(HttpServletRequest req, HttpServletResponse res)
            throws ServletException, IOException
{
    res.setHeader("Pragma", "no-cache");
    res.setHeader("Cache-Control", "no-cache");
    res.setDateHeader("Expires", 0);

    Stats stats = new Stats();

    boolean bw = Boolean.valueOf(req.getParameter("bw")).booleanValue();

    Color fg = Color.black, bg = new Color(0xB2B2B2), fill;
    if (bw)
        fill = new Color(0xFFFFFF);
    else
        fill = new Color(0xF0A0A0);

    sendImage(res, createPieChart(200, 200, stats, fg, bg, fill, bw));
}
```

Drawing the Pie-Chart

Now we have all the auxiliary methods and classes together to finally complete an image-generating servlet. Only the `createPieChart()` method is missing for a first version of the `ChartServlet`. The pie-chart which gets drawn by this method should look like this (for the sample data, in black & white mode)

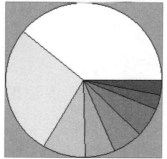

The `createPieChart()` method consists of three parts. First, an `Image` with the specified size is created and its graphics context is obtained.

```
private Image createPieChart(int w, int h, Stats stats,
                             Color fg, Color bg, Color fill,
                             boolean bw)
{
   Image img = createImage(w, h, bg);
   Graphics g = img.getGraphics();

   [...]

   return img;
}
```

Next, the segments of the circle are filled with the fill color, rotated for each segment. This is achieved by iterating through all entries of the `Stats` object and calculating the arc for each entry by scaling the summed-up total to 360 degrees (a full circle). Note that the absolute arcs are calculated directly from the original data instead of calculating arcs relative to the previous one. This distributes round-off errors evenly among all segments instead of letting them build up and falsify the final value. The filled segments are drawn with the graphics context's `fillArc()` method.

```
int done = 0, arc = 0;
for(int i=0; i<stats.size(); i++)
{
   done += stats.valueAt(i);
   int newArc = (done * 360) / stats.getTotal();
   g.setColor(fill);
   g.fillArc(0, 0, w-1, h-1, arc, newArc-arc);
   arc = newArc;
   if(bw) fill = rotateBrightness(fill);
   else fill = rotateColor(fill);
}
```

Finally, the borders are drawn with the foreground color. Unfortunately there is no method like `fillArc()` which draws only the outline of a segment (`drawArc()` draws a part of an oval outline but not the lines from the center of the oval to the end points of the arc). Instead we first draw a full circle with `drawOval()` and then manually calculate the end points for the lines which separate the segments by using the trigonometry functions of the `java.lang.Math` utility class:

```
g.setColor(fg);
g.drawOval(0, 0, w-1, h-1);
int done = 0;
if(stats.size() > 1)
{
   for(int i=0; i<stats.size(); i++)
   {
      int arc = (done * 360) / stats.getTotal();
      g.drawLine((w-1)/2,
                 (h-1)/2,
                 (w-1)/2 + (int)(w * Math.cos((arc*Math.PI) / 180) / 2),
                 (h-1)/2 - (int)(h * Math.sin((arc*Math.PI) / 180) / 2));
      done += stats.valueAt(i);
   }
}
```

The `sin()` and `cos()` methods operate on floating-point values of type `double`. It is important to convert the results back to `int` at the right time to avoid round-off errors which could render the results completely useless.

Drawing the Bar Chart

The `ChartServlet` should be able to produce pie or bar charts on request. So instead of always returning a pie chart we use the following code in the `doGet` method:

```
String img = req.getParameter("img");
if(img != null) // Return an image
{
  Color fg = Color.black, bg = new Color(0xB2B2B2), fill;
  if(bw) fill = new Color(0xFFFFFF);
  else fill = new Color(0xF0A0A0);

  if(img.equals("bar"))
    sendImage(res, createBarChart(200, stats, fg, bg, fill, bw));
  else if(img.equals("pie"))
    sendImage(res, createPieChart(200, 200, stats, fg, bg, fill, bw));
  else res.sendError(res.SC_BAD_REQUEST);
}
else
{
  [...]
}
```

To create an image with the new `ChartServlet` it needs to be invoked with the `img` option, e.g. http://localhost/servlet/ChartServlet?img=pie or http://localhost/servlet/ChartServlet?img=bar if the servlet is mounted as http://localhost/servlet/ChartServlet. If an illegal argument is given to the `img` option, the default "Bad Request" error response is returned. The second branch of the `if` clause will be discussed later in this chapter.

In addition to the drawing routines used for `createPieChart()` we will use some text routines to create a bar chart as shown in the following figure with labels and fitting bars

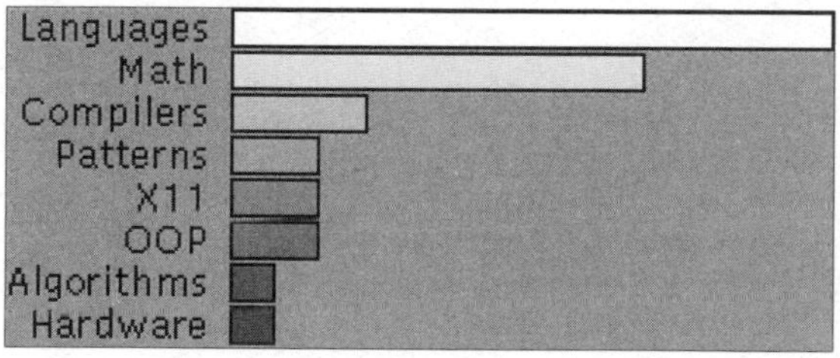

The `createBarChart()` method takes only one size argument called `baseWidth` instead of the width and height arguments of `createPieChart()`. The base width is the width of the bars without the labels. The real width and height are calculated automatically, taking into account the labels and the font size. In the AWT, fonts are represented by a `java.awt.Font` object. For each font there is also a `java.awt.FontMetrics` object which describes the size of characters in that font. The graphics context offers some methods for working with fonts and text:

```
Font getFont()
void setFont(Font font)
```

Get/set the current font which is associated with the graphics context. This font is used for all operations which print text.

```
FontMetrics getFontMetrics()
FontMetrics getFontMetrics(Font font)
```

Get the font metrics for the specified font. If no Font object is supplied, the graphics context's current font is used.

```
void drawString(String str, int x, int y)
void drawChars(char[] data, int offset, int length, int x, int y)
void drawBytes(byte[] data, int offset, int length, int x, int y)
```

Print a line of text. The text can be specified as a String object or a part of a byte or char array. The specified y coordinate is used for the baseline of the characters.

The graphics context's getFontMetrics() method could be used to get the right font metrics for calculating the size of the bar chart image, but it would be too late because the image must already exist to get a graphics context. Fortunately, similar methods for obtaining fonts and font metrics exist in java.awt.Component and thus in the invisible frame which is used by ImageServlet to create the off-screen images. Two additional methods need to be implemented in the ImageServlet class to provide access to these features:

```
protected FontMetrics getFontMetrics(Font f)
{
    return dummy.getFontMetrics(f);
}

protected Font getFont()
{
    return dummy.getFont();
}
```

We can now calculate the proper image size in the createBarChart method before creating an image.

```
private Image createBarChart(int baseWidth, Stats stats,
                             Color fg, Color bg, Color fill,
                             boolean bw)
{
    FontMetrics fm = getFontMetrics(getFont());
    int lh = fm.getHeight(), tw = 0, h = stats.size() * lh;
    for(int i=0; i<stats.size(); i++)
    {
        int lw = fm.stringWidth(stats.nameAt(i));
        if(lw > tw) tw = lw;
    }
    int w = tw + lh/2 + baseWidth;

    Image img = createImage(w, h, bg);
    Graphics g = img.getGraphics();

    [...]

    return img;
}
```

The font metrics method `getHeight()` returns the total height of any line of text, including line space. We get the image height by multiplying it with the number of entries in the `Stats` object. The image width is calculated as the base width, plus half the line height, for spacing, plus the width of the label area. The font metrics method `stringWidth()` is used to get the width of each label, the maximum of which is the width of the label area.

We can now draw the bar chart into the newly created `Image` object. The bars should be as high as normal upper-case letters. The font metrics methods `getAscent()` and `getDescent()` return the extent of such characters above and below the baseline. The vertical offset for the first label, from the top border of the image to the baseline, is returned by `getMaxAscent()`. The bars are drawn the same way as the segments of the pie-chart. First, a rectangle filled with the current fill color is drawn, then a rectangular outline of the foreground color. Here is the drawing code from `createBarChart()`:

```
int ascent = fm.getAscent(), descent = fm.getDescent();
int y = fm.getMaxAscent();
for(int i=0; i<stats.size(); i++)
{
   g.setColor(fill);
   g.fillRect(w-baseWidth, y-ascent,
                 ((baseWidth*stats.valueAt(i))/stats.getMax())-1,
                  ascent+descent-1);
   g.setColor(fg);
   g.drawString(stats.nameAt(i),
                 tw - fm.stringWidth(stats.nameAt(i)), y);
   g.drawRect(w-baseWidth, y-ascent,
                 ((baseWidth*stats.valueAt(i))/stats.getMax())-1,
                  ascent+descent-1);
   y += lh;
   if(bw) fill = rotateBrightness(fill);
   else fill = rotateColor(fill);
}
```

Creating an HTML Page With Embedded Images

One problem that arises frequently when writing a servlet which returns images is to make the servlet return both HTML text and images for a single request. e-mail messages and Usenet articles with mixed content can have bodies in a MIME multipart format, but this is not the kind of response a Web browser expects from a server. Instead of returning all text and image parts together in one response body, the servlet creates a response of type "text/html" which links back to the servlet for the embedded images. So what appears to the user to be a single entity consisting of text and images is actually created by several independent requests to the servlet.

We will now modify the `ChartServlet` to return an HTML page with a table containing the sample data and the pie and bar charts as embedded images. A naive solution would be to link back to the servlet name plus `?img=pie` or `?img=bar` for the embedded images. This, however, has two drawbacks when used in a real-life application which does not use hardcoded sample data: First, creating the data for the table and images is usually time-consuming, so it should not be done three times instead of just once. Second, the images are requested after the HTML page. In the mean time, the data source could have changed which would make the images inconsistent with the table (or even with each other). In order to avoid these problems we need a way to link the requests for the images to the request for the HTML page.

This can be done in several ways, and you should already be thinking back to Chapter 4's discussion of sessions for the solution:

The data which is required to create the images can be stored on the server side and referenced by a unique identification code which is passed to the client. This is how the session tracking mechanism which is built into the Servlet API works. If you are using sessions anyway, you can make the data for creating the images or even the images themselves part of the session's application layer data.

The session tracking mechanism will usually try to use cookies to store the session key on the Web browser before reverting to URL rewriting (where the session key is appended to all URLs which are returned by the servlet). This may be considered inconvenient if the user has configured the browser to ask for manual confirmation of each cookie. For embedded images, URL rewriting will work just as fine as cookies, so a natural solution would be to implement a separate session tracking mechanism which does not try to use cookies. However, this is a rather complex task compared to the other methods of linking embedded images to the surrounding HTML page.

If only a small amount of data is required to create the images, it can be stored entirely on the client side by appending it as parameters to the image URLs. The drawback of this method is that the data is transferred twice (from the server to the client and back) for each embedded image.

The images for the `ChartServlet` can be generated quickly from only a few name / value pairs, so we can safely use the third method without sacrificing too much bandwidth and processing time. Before writing the code that returns an HTML page we need a way to pack a `Stats` object into an option string and create a new `Stats` object from such an option string when it is passed back from the browser to the servlet. As you are no doubt aware, the root class, `java.lang.Object`, defines a method `toString()` which can be overridden in subclasses to return a string representation of an object. We will implement this method in the `Stats` class to return a `String` which contains all names and values of an object:

```
public String toString()
{
    StringBuffer b = new StringBuffer();
    b.append("num=").append(values.length);
    for(int i=0; i<values.length; i++)
    {
        b.append("&v").append(i).append('=');
        b.append(URLEncoder.encode(values[i].name+'|'+values[i].value));
    }
    return b.toString();
}
```

The result is an option string of the form `"num=2&v0=name%7cvalue&v1=name%7cvalue"` where `num` specifies the number of entries. The entries of the form `"name|value"` need to be url-encoded with the `java.net.URLEncoder` class because they contain special characters like the "|" separator (which gets encoded as "%7c") or whitespace in the names, which cannot form part of a URL query string.

A more direct way to create the options string would be to use the stats names directly as option names. This would lead to problems when decoding the option string because the Servlet API does not offer the options of a request in their original order, so we would have to implement our own option string parser. Simply sorting the values after they have been read in the wrong order does not work, either, because there can be several entries with the same value which would still come out in random order.

The `Stats` object gets reconstructed from the request options with a new constructor

```
public Stats(ServletRequest req) throws ServletException
{
    try
    {
        int num = Integer.parseInt(req.getParameter("num"));
        values = new StatValue[num];
        for(int i=0; i<values.length; i++)
        {
            String s = req.getParameter("v"+i);
            int sep = s.indexOf('|');
            values[i] = new StatValue(s.substring(0,sep),
                              Integer.parseInt(s.substring(sep+1)));
        }
    }
    catch(Exception e)
    {
        throw new ServletException("Error parsing chart values: "+ e.toString());
    }
    process();
}
```

First, the method reads the "num" option with the ServletRequest's getParameter method and creates the StatValue array for the actual data with the right size. Then all "v" options for the values are read from the servlet request in their original order. The servlet engine handles the decoding of the urlencoded values automatically. The option values are separated at the position of the "|" character. Everything before that position is made part of the name of a newly created StatValue object and everything after the separator becomes the value which is converted from the String representation back to an int value with method parseInt() of the java.lang.Integer wrapper class. This conversion can throw a java.lang.NumberFormatException (which needs to be caught) if the string is not a number. Some other operations in this constructor can throw runtime exceptions like java.lang.NullPointerException and java.lang.StringIndexOutOfBoundsException if the servlet was not called with the right parameters. All these exceptions should never occur because the option strings are always created directly by the Stats class itself. But, if we make a mistake changing this method, or the methods which write the query string, or a user tries to create the options for the servlet manually, we catch any exception that occurs and throw a ServletException. This aborts the work of the servlet and makes the servlet engine return an error message to the client. If all goes well, the process() method is called to recompute the missing variables max and total. We can now add the code which generates an HTML page to the ChartServlet's doGet() method.

```
public void doGet(HttpServletRequest req, HttpServletResponse res)
      throws ServletException, IOException
{
    [...]

    Stats stats;
    if(req.getParameter("num") != null) stats = new Stats(req);
    else stats = new Stats();

    boolean bw = Boolean.valueOf(req.getParameter("bw")).booleanValue();
```

Continued on Following Page

```
          String img = req.getParameter("img");
          if(img != null)
          {
              [...]
          }
          else
          {
              String statsString = stats.toString();
              res.setContentType("text/html");
              PrintWriter out = res.getWriter();

              out.println("<HTML><HEAD><TITLE>Statistics</TITLE></HEAD>");
              out.println("<BODY BGCOLOR=\"#B2B2B2\" TEXT=\"#000000\">");
              out.println("<H1>Statistics</H1>");
              out.println("<P><TABLE border=1 cellpadding=2>"+
                          "<TR><TH>Name</TH><TH>Count</TH><TH>%</TH></TR>");

              for(int i=0; i<stats.size(); i++)
              {
                  out.println("<TR><TD>"+stats.nameAt(i)+"</TD><TD>"+
                              stats.valueAt(i)+"</TD><TD>"+
                              stats.valueAt(i)*100/stats.getTotal()+"</TD></TR>");
              }
              out.println("<TR><TD>Total</TD><TD>"+stats.getTotal()+
                          "</TD></TR></TABLE>");
              out.println("</P><P><IMG src=\""+req.getRequestURI()+
                          "?img=pie&bw="+bw+"&"+statsString+"\">");
              out.println("<IMG src=\""+req.getRequestURI()+
                          "?img=bar&bw="+bw+"&"+statsString+"\"></P>");
              out.println("</BODY></HTML>");

              out.close();
          }
      }
```

The code for creating the `Stats` object has changed. If the request contains the "num" parameter the object is reconstructed from the request parameters. Otherwise a new object is created by processing the input data as before. The `else` branch is used to send the HTML page. The content type is set to "text/html" and the data is written with a `PrintWriter` returned by `ServletRequest`'s `getWriter()` method, to have the servlet engine automatically encode the text in a character encoding that the client understands. The page contains a table with the `Stats` object's contents which are obtained in the usual way.

The page also has two embedded images. Note how the source URLs for these images are constructed. The `getRequestURI()` method of the `javax.servlet.http.HttpServletRequest` class is invoked to find the URL with which this page was requested. The options (the final part of the URL following a question mark), if any, are stripped off. A new option part is appended. The option part starts with the "?" character, followed by the first option which is either "img=pie" or "img=bar" to request a pie or bar chart from the `ChartServlet`. Then an option separator "&" is appended, followed by the `bw` option as supplied with the request for the HTML page. Finally another separator and the options which describe the `Stats` object are appended.

Linking Back to the Page

The `ChartServlet` still lacks a way of requesting a color or black and white version without manually setting the `bw` parameter. We therefore add a link to the generated HTML page to switch to the other version.

```
if(bw)
{
    out.println("<A href=\""+req.getRequestURI()+"?bw=false&"+
                statsString+"\">[Color Version]</A>");
}
else
{
    out.println("<A href=\""+req.getRequestURI()+"?bw=true&"+
                statsString+"\">[Black & White Version]</A>");
}
```

The link is constructed in the same way as the URL for the embedded images. Of course, the `img` parameter is left out so that the servlet will return an HTML page when following the link. The data from the `Stats` object is appended to the URL as well to ensure that when switching between the color and the black and white version, the data does not change. Unfortunately, this also renders a web browser's "Refresh" button useless because reloading the page will always make it use the data from the URL. Instead another link is added to the HTML page which can be used to recreate the data from the data source:

```
out.println("<A href=\""+req.getRequestURI()+"?bw="+bw+
                "\">[Update]</A>");
```

The URL leads back to the servlet with the current `bw` setting but it does not include the data.

Summary

In this chapter, we have seen the real power of the Servlet API. Because servlets allow us access to every facet of the Java language, we can even make use of Java AWT graphics methods to generate images on the fly for download to a browser. The possibility exists of using the advanced tools of the Java 3D and 2D libraries, alongside the simple techniques we have explored here, to generate graphically rich, dynamic websites. We also showed how it is possible to get around some of the obvious difficulties which sending images from servlets can get us into, such as embedding dynamic images into pages with matching dynamic data. We learnt how to use URL Encoding to embed session data in the query string of a GET request, and we also showed how a single servlet can provide a wide range of services, depending on the options submitted.

Introducing JavaServer Pages

Based on servlet technology, and currently shaping up at breakneck speed, JavaServer Pages (JSP) is set to be one of the most important elements of Java server programming. It's by no means complete yet, but that will change as the Java 2 Enterprise Edition comes together.

So what are JavaServer Pages? Well, they combine markup (whether HTML or XML) with nuggets of Java code to produce a dynamic web page. Each page is automatically compiled to a servlet by the JSP engine, the first time it is requested, and then executed. JSP provides a variety of ways to talk to Java classes, servlets, applets and the web server. With it, you can split the functionality of your web applications into components with well-defined public interfaces glued together by a simple page.

This model allows tasks to be sub-divided - a developer builds custom components and the page designer assembles the application with a few judicious method calls. In this 'application assembly' model, the business logic is separated from the presentation of data.

To give you an idea of the future, this separation of logic and presentation may become yet more extreme with the use of custom tags slated for JSP 1.1.

JavaServer Pages is a specification that is already implemented by several web servers (for more details, see the JSP FAQ at http://www.esperanto.org.nz/jsp/jspfaq.html), on which your code will run without change, making it more portable and the server market more competitive than its rivals. Finally, it's nice and simple!

In this chapter, we will:

➤ Discuss the JavaServer Pages (JSP) architecture

➤ Look at the elements of a JSP file, and the tags used to represent them

➤ Encapsulate logic in a JavaBean component and integrate it with JSP

➤ Walk through a detailed example using JSP, showing a typical web application architecture

Architectural Overview

A JavaServer Page is a simple text file consisting of HTML or XML content along with JSP elements (a sort of shorthand for Java code). When a client requests a JSP page of the web server and it has not been run before, the page is first passed to a JSP engine which compiles the page to a servlet, runs it and returns the resulting content to the client. Thereafter, the web server's servlet engine will run the compiled page.

> *It should be no surprise, given the flexibility of the servlet model, that the current reference implementation of the JSP engine is itself a servlet.*

It is possible to view the finished servlet code that is generated by locating it within the directory structure of the servlet engine. For example, with JRun, you can find the source code for your JSP files (in servlet form) in the `jrun/jsm-default/services/jse/servlets/jsp` directory. This is very helpful when trying to debug your JSP files.

If you take a look in the source files for the `javax.servlet.jsp` package, you'll find the following classes:

➤ `JSPPage`
➤ `HttpJspPage`

They define the interface for the compiled JSP page - namely that it must have three methods. Not surprisingly they are:

➤ `jspInit()`
➤ `jspDestroy()`
➤ `_jspService(HttpServletRequest request, HttpServletResponse response)`

The first two methods can be defined by the JSP author (we'll see how in a moment), but the third is the compiled version of the JSP page, and its creation is the responsibility of the JSP engine.

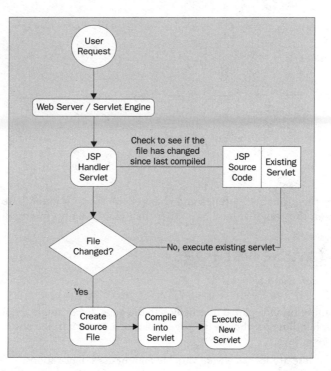

A Simple JavaServer Page

It's time we saw a JSP file:

```
<HTML>
<HEAD>
<TITLE>
Demo of a JSP page
</TITLE>
</HEAD>
<BODY>

<!-- Set global information for the page -->
<%@ page language="java" %>

<!-- Declare the character variable -->
<%! char c = 0; %>

<!-- Scriptlet - Java code -->
<%
   for (int i = 0; i < 26; i++)
   {
       for (int j = 0; j < 26, j++)
   {
           // Output capital letters of the alphabet, and change starting letter
           c = (char)(0x41 + (26 - i + j)%26);
%>
```

Continued on Following Page

```
<!-- Output the value of c.toString() to the HTML page -->
<%= c %>

<%
      }
%>
<BR>
<%
    }
%>

</BODY>
</HTML>
```

This page just outputs the alphabet 26 times and changes the starting letter. The HTML is self-explanatory and written the way it should be, rather than cluttering up methods of a servlet.

Elements of a JavaServer Page

The Java code in the page includes:

> ➤ Directives – these provide global information to the page, for example, import statements, the page for error handling or whether the page is part of a session. In the above example we set the script language to Java.

> ➤ Declaratives - these are for page-wide variable and method declarations.

> ➤ Scriptlets - the Java code embedded in the page.

> ➤ Expressions - formats the expression as a string for inclusion in the output of the page.

We will meet the last JSP element type, actions, soon. These elements follow an XML-like syntax, and perform a function behind the scenes. They provide the means to totally separate presentation from logic. A good example is `<jsp:useBean .../>` which finds or creates an instance of a bean with the given scope and name. With the tag extension mechanism to be introduced in JSP 1.1, you'll be able to define similar action tags and put their functionality in a tag library.

Now let's examine the basic elements of a JSP in a more complete fashion, before we code some more.

> *Something I've found very useful to have around while coding is the syntax crib sheet available at* http://java.sun.com/products/jsp/syntax.html *in PDF format. This has a concise summary of what we'll see here.*

JSP Directives

A JSP directive is a statement that gives the JSP engine information for the page that follows. The general syntax of a JSP directive is `<%@ directive { attribute="value" } %>`, where the directive may have a number of (optional) attributes. Each directive has an optional XML equivalent, but these are intended for future JSP tools, so we won't consider them here.

Possible directives in JSP 1.0 are:

> ➤ Page – information for that page
> ➤ Include – files to be included verbatim
> ➤ Taglib – the URI for a library of tags that you'll use in the page (unimplemented at the time of writing)

As is to be expected, the page directive has many possible attributes. Specifying these is optional, as the mandatory ones have default values.

Attribute and possible values	Description
`language="java"`	The `language` variable tells the server what language will be used in the file. Java is the only supported syntax for a JSP in the current specification. Support for other scripting languages is available at http://www.plenix.org/polyjsp and http://www.caucho.com (JavaScript).
`extends="package.class"`	The `extends` variable defines the parent class of the generated servlet. It isn't normally necessary to use anything other than the provided base classes.
`import="package.*,package.class"`	The `import` variable is similar to the first section of any Java program. As such, it should always be placed at the top of the JSP file. The value of the import variable should be a comma-separated list of the packages and classes that you wish to import.
`session="true|false"`	By default, the `session` variable is `true`, meaning that session data is available to a page.
`buffer="none|8kb|sizekb"`	Determines if the output stream is buffered. By default it is set to 8kb. Use with `autoFlush`
`autoFlush="true|false"`	If set to `true`, flushes the output buffer when it's full, rather than raising an exception.

Continued on Following Page

Attribute and possible values	Description
`isThreadSafe="true|false"`	By default this is set `true`, signaling to the JSP engine that that multiple client requests can be dealt with at once. It's the JSP author's job to synchronize shared state, so that the page really is thread safe.
	If `isThreadSafe` is set to `false`, the single thread model will be used, controlling client access to the page.
	This doesn't let you off the hook, however, as servers may, at their discretion, have multiple instances of the page running to deal with the client request load. And there's no guarantee that consecutive requests from the same client will be directed to the same instance of JSP page. Any resources or state that are shared between page requests must therefore be synchronized.
`info="text"`	Information on the page that can be accessed through the page's `Servlet.getServletInfo()` method.
`errorPage="pathToErrorPage"`	Gives the relative path to the JSP page that will handle unhandled exceptions. That JSP page will have `isErrorPage` set to true
`isErrorPage="true|false"`	Marks the page as an error page. We'll see this in action later.
`contentType="text/html; charset=ISO-8859-1"`	The mime type and character set of the JSP and the final page. This information must come early in the file, before any non-latin-1 characters appear in the file.

In the JSWDK-1.0-ea1 release there's a bug - the `import` statement needs to be `imports` to satisfy the JSP engine.

We'll see more of the `include` directive in a later example.

JSP Declarations

A JSP declaration can be thought of as the definition of class-level variables and methods that are to be used throughout the page. To define a declarative block, begin the block of code with <%! *declaration>*.

```
<%! String var1 = "x";
    int count = 0;

    private void incrementCount()
{
        count++;
    }
%>
```

Note that you put semi-colons after each variable declaration, just as if you were writing it in a class.

This is how you would define the optional `jspInit()` and `jspDestroy()` methods that we mentioned earlier.

JSP Scriptlets

Scriptlets are defined as any block of valid Java code that resides between <% and %> tags.

This code will be placed in the generated servlet's `_jspService()` method. Code that is defined within a scriptlet can access any variable and any beans that have been declared. There are also a host of implicit objects available to a scriptlet from the servlet environment.

Implicit Objects	Description
request	The client's request. This is usually a subclass of `HttpServletRequest`. This has the parameter list if there is one.
response	The JSP page's response, a subclass of `HttpServletResponse`.
pageContext	Page attributes and implicit objects (essentially what makes up the server environment in which the JSP runs) need to be accessible through a uniform API, to allow the JSP engine to compile pages. But each server will have specific implementations of these attributes and objects.
	The solution to this problem is for the JSP engine to compile in code that uses a factory class to return the server's implementation of the `PageContext` class. That `PageContext` class has been initialized with the `request` and `response` objects and some of the attributes from the page directive (`errorpage`, `session`, `buffer` and `autoflush`) and provides the other implicit objects for the page request. We'll see more on this in a moment.
session	The HTTP session object associated with the request.
application	The servlet context returned by a call to `getServletConfig().getContext()` (see Chapter 5).
out	The object representing the output stream.

Implicit Objects	Description
config	The `ServletConfig` object for the page.
page	The page's way of referring to itself (as an alternative to `this` in any Java code).
exception	The uncaught subclass of `Throwable` that is passed to the errorpage URL.

The following snippet shows both how to get a named parameter from the `request` object, and how to pass a string to the output stream for the page.

```
<%
    String var1 = request.getParameter("lname");
    out.println(var1);
%>
```

Having discussed implicit objects, we're in a better position to understand the code featured in the comment for the `PageContext` source from the JSP 1.0 reference implementation. This shows the code that the JSP 1.0 reference engine injects into the JSP page's `_jspService()` method.

```
public void _jspService(HttpServletRequest request,
                        HttpServletResponse response)
                        throws IOException, ServletException
{
    JspFactory factory = JspFactory.getDefaultFactory();
    PageContext pageContext = factory.getPageContext(
                        this,  // servlet
                        request,
                        response,
                        null,  // errorPageURL
                        false, // needsSession
                        JspWriter.DEFAULT_BUFFER,
                        true   // autoFlush
                    );

    // Initialize implicit variables for scripting environment
    HttpSession session = pageContext.getSession();
    JspWriter out = pageContext.getOut();
    Object page = this;

    try
    {
        // Body of translated JSP here...
    } catch (Exception e)
    {
        out.clear();
        pageContext.handlePageException(e);
    } finally
    {
        out.close();
        factory.releasePageContext(pageContext);
    }
}
```

`JspFactory` returns the `pageContext` implicit object, from which the other implicit objects are obtained for the duration of the `_jspService()` method.

JSP Expressions

A JSP expression is a very nice tool for embedding values within your HTML code. Anything between `<%=` and `%>` tags will be evaluated, converted to a string, and then displayed. Conversion from a primitive type to a string is handled automatically.

```
The current price of item A100 is <%= request.getParameter("price") %>
```

Something you'll want to note is that the expression doesn't end with a semi-colon. That's because the JSP engine will put the expression within an `out.println()` call for you.

JSP expressions allow you to essentially parameterize HTML (just as you would parameterize a SQL query that differs by only a couple of values). Again and again, your code will set up conditions and loops using a one-line JSP scriptlet and then include the HTML code directly beneath it. Simply enclose the beginning and the ending of the condition or loop in separate pairs of `<%` and `%>` tags:

```
<% for(int i = 0; i < 10; i++)
{ %>
   <BR>
   Counter value is <%= i %>
<% } %>
```

Coding JSP Pages

A big advantage in developing a JavaServer Page is that you can code the HTML without enclosing it in Java code, as you must do in a servlet. You can then take advantage of HTML editors to develop your content.

So from the drudgery of coding HTML output in servlets, we've arrived at the flexibility of coding Java snippets into the HTML page. But don't be dragged too far the other way. Heard of the people who can't fit their ASP files into Notepad? And if there's one problem with ASP and JSP, it's debugging the pages, making improvements to them, and untangling the meaning of that section you coded months back.

The "third way" is a mixture of presentation-based calls to a Bean or servlet, which components can be better tested, are well-encapsulated and good OOP citizens. This moves from embedding code to embedding components and action tags in the page.

> Note that the current reference JSP implementations don't automatically reload the new Bean if you recompile while the server is running. You'll need to restart the servlet engine.

Using JavaBeans Components with JSP

So, when setting up an application development architecture that involves JavaServer Pages, it is a good idea to try and put all of your business logic inside reusable components. These components can then be 'plugged' into any JavaServer Page that requires them.

What is a JavaBean?

The Java language has implemented the idea of a component as something called a JavaBean. A JavaBean is a Java class that fits the following criteria:

> ➢ Public class.

> ➢ Public constructor with no arguments.

> ➢ Public set and get methods to simulate properties. The get method has no arguments, unless it acts on an indexed property.

The JavaBeans architecture uses reflection to infer the public methods. But you can provide a `BeanInfo` *class, called* `BeanNameBeanInfo` *to give more explicit information.*

A bean can also be serialized and saved for later use. It does this by implementing the `Serializable` *interface. When a bean component is serialized, it saves its current state. The current state of a bean is defined by the current values of its public properties.*

Properties are always set and retrieved using a common naming convention. For each property, two methods must exist, a `getxxx()` and `setxxx()` method (where `xxx` is the name of the property).

Apart from that a bean is just like any other Java class. Typically, a bean component is imported into a program, its properties are set and its methods are called.

Most of the time beans are used to encapsulate visual and non-visual elements of a GUI. There's some snazzy stuff to link beans up, to implement drag-and-drop and to save the state of a bean between instances. The ultimate aim is to make them part of graphical application assembly tools. I found that once I stopped thinking about these graphical tools and concentrated on it just being a class that follows a few design patterns, things were easier to understand!

Because of this history, Beans don't sit obviously in JSP. Don't get me wrong - they work well. But it's not what they were originally designed for. If we think of them as components, simple encapsulations of Java code, then their purpose is clearer. Beans mean that your page isn't clogged with code.

Much of the business logic we're hinting at might be better placed in an Enterprise JavaBean, where the transactions and scaling issues are explicitly the problem of the container and not the bean. That kind of heavyweight use may be necessary sometimes but I think that beans will stay around for the lighter work we show here. And beans as graphical components of your final web page, for a richer user interface, will be another expression of their code- and complexity-wrapping role.

Letters from a Bean

To show how to use a simple bean, we're going to develop the alphabet example from earlier, and associate each letter with a color.

The presentation of the letters will remain the responsibility of the JSP page, but the color mapping will be the bean's job.

```java
package com.wrox.jspexamples;

import java.awt.Color;
import java.util.*;

public class AlphabetCode
{
    HashMap map;
    char c = 0;
    Integer colorNumber;
    static int FIRST_LETTER = 0x41;
    static int ALPHABET_LENGTH = 26;
    float s = 0.9f;
    float b = 0.9f;

    public AlphabetCode()
    {
        this.map = new HashMap(ALPHABET_LENGTH);

        for(int i = 0; i < ALPHABET_LENGTH; i++)
        {
            this.c = (char)(FIRST_LETTER + i);
            float h = (float)i/ALPHABET_LENGTH;
            this.map.put(new Character(c), Color.getHSBColor(h, s, b));
        }
    }

    public void setCharacter(String nextChar)
    {
        this.c = nextChar.charAt(0);
    }

    public String getCharacter()
    {
        return (new Character(this.c).toString());
    }

    public String getColor()
    {
        Color rgb = (Color)map.get(new Character(this.c));
        StringBuffer htmlColor = new StringBuffer(
                                    colorNumber.toHexString(rgb.getRGB()
                                                & 0x00ffffff));
        // toHexString() won't preserve leading zeros, so need to add them back in
        // if they've gone missing...
        if (htmlColor.length() != 6)
        {
            htmlColor.insert(0, "\"#00");
        } else
            htmlColor.insert(0, "\"#");

        htmlColor.append("\"");

        return htmlColor.toString();
    }
}
```

The bean things to note are the public class and constructor, and the set and get methods. The class sets up the color of each character in the constructor, and then returns the color of the current character as an HTML color.

The modified JSP page looks like:

```
<HTML>
<HEAD>
<TITLE>
Color demo I
</TITLE>
</HEAD>
<BODY>

<!-- This page generates a series of rainbow colored letters -->
<!-- It uses plain method calls to the Bean -->

<%@ page language="java" %>

<%! char c = 0; %>

<jsp:useBean id="letterColor" scope="application"
             class="com.wrox.jspexamples.AlphabetCode" />
<%
    for(int i = 0; i < 26; i++)
    {
        for(int j = 0; j < 26; j++)
        {
            c = (char)(0x41 + (26 - i + j)%26);
            Character thisChar = new Character(c);
            letterColor.setCharacter(thisChar.toString());
%>

<FONT COLOR=<%= letterColor.getColor() %> >
<%= letterColor.getCharacter() %>
</FONT>
<%
        }
%>
<BR>
<%
    }
%>
</BODY>
</HTML>
```

Giving the result:

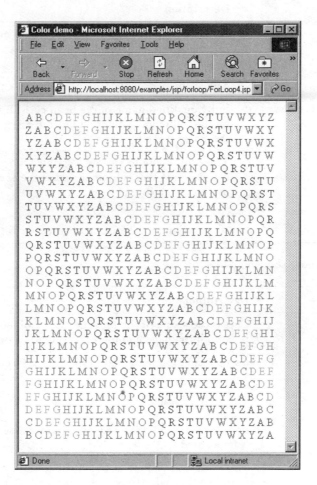

The JSP page uses straight method calls (setCharacter(), getCharacter() and getColor()) to the bean. The only new syntax is <jsp:useBean ... />, so let's look at that:

```
<jsp:useBean id="letterColor" scope="application"
          class="com.wrox.jspexamples.AlphabetCode" />
```

The jsp:useBean tag first searches for a bean instance that matches the scope and class. If it can't find one it instantiates the named class, using its public, no-args constructor. If there are any initialization time properties you need to set, you can place the appropriate tags between <jsp:useBean> and </jsp:useBean> - these are only executed when a new instance is created

In the JSP 1.0 reference implementation, the server looks for your packages in the CLASSPATH environment variable (on my machine, startserver includes jsp1.0/examples/WEB-INF/jsp/beans). Let's look at the attributes:

useBean Attributes	Description
id="name"	The name by which the instance of the bean can be referenced in the page. Other Bean tags use name to refer to it, so do note the difference.
scope="page"	The scope over which the bean can be called. More below.
class="package.class"	Fully qualified name of the bean class. Because this needs to be the full name, you don't need to import these classes in the page directive.
beanName="name"	This allows you to specify a serialized bean (.ser file) or a bean's name that can be passed to the instantiate() method from the java.beans.Beans. Needs an associated type tag rather than class.
type="package.class"	A synonym for class that is used for beanName.

Scope on a JSP page goes something like this:

Scope	Description
page	This is the scope of the PageContext object we saw earlier. It lasts until the page completes, and there is no storage of state.
	page wasn't implemented in the EA1 reference version of JSP 1.0.
request	The bean instance lasts for the client request. The named bean instance is available as an attribute of the ServletRequest object, so it follows the request to another servlet / JSP if control is forwarded.
session	The bean lasts as long as the client session. A reference is available through HttpSession.getValue(name).
	Don't use this scope level if you have declared the page directive session false.
application	The bean instance is created with the application and remains in use until the application ends. It's an attribute of the ServletContext object.

We're not finished in our tour of tags, though. With a couple of changes to our JSP code, we can show you two more - `jsp:getProperty` and `jsp:setProperty`:

```
<HTML>
<HEAD>
<TITLE>
Color demo
</TITLE>
</HEAD>
<BODY>
<!-- This page generates a series of rainbow colored letters -->
<!-- It uses the JSP property set and get tags -->
<%@ page language="java" %>
<%! char c = 0; %>
<jsp:useBean id="letterColor" scope="application"
            class="com.wrox.jspexamples.AlphabetCode" />
<%
   for(int i = 0; i < 26; i++)
   {
       for(int j = 0; j < 26; j++)
       {
           c = (char)(0x41 + (26 - i + j)%26);
           Character thisChar = new Character(c);
%>
<jsp:setProperty name="letterColor" property="character"
                 value="<%= thisChar.toString() %>" />

<FONT COLOR=<jsp:getProperty name="letterColor" property="Color" /> >
<jsp:getProperty name="letterColor" property="character" />
</FONT>

   ...
```

The `<jsp:setProperty ... />` needs the bean name, the property name and the value with which to set the property. Note that the property name is the `setCharacter()` method without the prefix. `<jsp:getProperty ... />` is self-explanatory.

We'll see an alternative version of the `jsp:setProperty` tag later.

A File Viewer

There's a little too much code in the page in the last example. It shows off the various JSP elements quite well, but it's not a particularly good design.

If we look at the MVC pattern, we see that the bean is the model, and the page is both the view and the controller (using the HTTP request). The question is how to prevent the control code taking over the page. Ideally, the page should be almost all presentation with simple JSP elements (methods and properties) to control the bean. Then the code to actually manipulate the model is in the bean, but the control rests with the page.

To show this simply, let's design a file viewer bean that will read a specific directory (C:\jdk1.2.1) and output the file and directory names, their size (if they're files) and their timestamp:

```
package com.wrox.jspexamples;

import java.io.File;
import java.util.Date;
import java.util.Iterator;
import java.util.Vector;

public class FileViewerBean
{
    File myDir;
    File[] contents;
    Vector vectorList;
    Iterator currentFileView;
    File currentFile;

    public FileViewerBean()
    {
        myDir = new File("C:\\jdk1.2.1");
        vectorList = new Vector();
    }

    public String getDirectory()
    {
        return myDir.getPath();
    }

    public void refreshList()
    {
        contents = myDir.listFiles();
        vectorList.clear();

        for (int i = 0; i < contents.length; i++)
            vectorList.add(contents[i]);

        currentFileView = vectorList.iterator();
    }

    public boolean nextFile()
    {
        while (currentFileView.hasNext())
        {
            currentFile = (File)currentFileView.next();
            return true;
        }
        return false;
    }

    public String getFileName()
    {
        return currentFile.getName();
    }

    public String getFileSize()
    {
        return new Long(currentFile.length()).toString();
    }
```

```
    public String getFileTimeStamp()
    {
       return new Date(currentFile.lastModified()).toString();
    }

    public boolean getFileType()
    {
       return currentFile.isDirectory();
    }
}
```

The idea here is to make the interface to the bean as simple as possible, so we need to support the different requirements of JSP pages. Therefore, a full-featured file viewer bean might have further methods to detail a file's attributes, order the vector by different criteria and so forth.

To put the bean to work, we have the `FileView.jsp` code:

```
<html>
<head>
<title>
A JSP file viewer
</title>
</head>
<body>

<!-- This page allows you to see files in selected parts of the drive -->

<%@ page language="java" %>

<jsp:useBean id="fileViewer" scope="session"
class="com.wrox.jspexamples.FileViewerBean" />

<hr>

<jsp:getProperty name="fileViewer" property="directory" />

<table>
<%
   fileViewer.refreshList();

   while(fileViewer.nextFile())
      {
%>
<tr>
<td>
<%= fileViewer.getFileName() %>
</td>
<td>
<%
   if (!fileViewer.getFileType()) {
%>
<%= fileViewer.getFileSize() %>
<%
   }
%>
</td>
<td>
<%= fileViewer.getFileTimeStamp() %>
</td>
</tr>
<% } %>

</table>
</body>
</html>
```

The page is much clearer here, with the bean almost acting as an iterator over the directory listing. The fine-grained properties simplify the page further.

Browsing and Querying Databases

To illustrate more functionality of JavaServer Pages, we will build an example that allows you to select from available databases, see their tables and column names, and query them. Our JSP application will make use of a bean to access the database.

I tried various architectures as I developed the application, as I saw how things panned out and learnt how to use more tags! The client's request should yield a `ResultSet` object, which has 22 `getXxx()` methods to work with. And I'm not interested in wrapping all that functionality in a bean when it's already available, so I've decided to handle it in the page.

This is where the tag extension mechanism will prove its worth - in that we'll be able to define actions that return `ResultSet` objects for the page to retrieve values from. Similar tags will enable JSPs to handle iterators.

Working backwards, let's look at the requirements:

> ➤ Consistent web interface across pages.
> ➤ Self-contained parts of the application each have their own JSP.
> ➤ Central error handling.
> ➤ Same bean code used for different client requests.

The parts of the project are:

> ➤ `DataList.jsp` - the main application page. It decodes GET requests and passes them to the relevant pages.
> ➤ `List1.jsp` - Presents the available databases. This is fixed by the sys-admin and is essentially HTML.
> ➤ `List2.jsp` - Shows the tables and their columns for the selected database.
> ➤ `List3.jsp` - Shows the result of a SQL query.
> ➤ `ErrorPage.jsp` - Where all the exceptions end up, their origin suitably noted.
> ➤ `Header.html` - The header for all the application pages.

Ask the Right Question

We want one page to coordinate the application, to receive all requests. We'll start `DataList.jsp` for the case where the client has just typed http://URL/DataList.jsp and needs the menu of databases.

```
<%@ page language="java" errorPage="ErrorPage.jsp" %>
<% if (request.getParameterNames().hasMoreElements() == false) { %>
<jsp:forward page="/jsp/data/List1.jsp" />
<% } %>
```

We have already sorted out an `errorpage` in the `page` directive for all error reporting. We'll repeat this code on each page.

The `request` object will have no parameters for the plain URL, so we can forward the work to the `List1.jsp` page. The `<jsp:forward ... />` needs the URL relative to the servlet context / application. In this case that's `/jsp/employee/List1.jsp`.

> Since `DataList.jsp` is only used for checking parameters and forwarding to the right page, you can use a regular servlet instead. You can mix and match servlets and JSPs depending which is most appropriate.

Now we'll code the `List1.jsp` page that shows the client what choice they have. From this they can formulate a query, or browse those databases:

```
<HTML>
<HEAD>
<TITLE>
Database Search
</TITLE>
</HEAD>
<BODY>
<%@ page language="java" errorPage="ErrorPage.jsp" %>
<%@ include file="Header.html" %>
Choose database:
<FORM METHOD="GET" ACTION="DataList.jsp">
Database URL:<SELECT NAME=DbURL SIZE=1>
<OPTION>jdbc:odbc:employee
<OPTION>jdbc:odbc:techlib
<OPTION>jdbc:odbc:this_should_break
</SELECT>
<P>
Database driver:<SELECT NAME=DbDriver SIZE=1>
<OPTION>sun.jdbc.odbc.JdbcOdbcDriver
<OPTION>com.imaginary.sql.msql.MsqlDriver
</SELECT>
```

Continued on Following Page

```
<P>
Input SQL if you know your query:
<P>
<INPUT TYPE=text NAME=inputSQL SIZE=40>
<P>
<INPUT TYPE=submit>
</FORM>
</BODY>
</HTML>
```

This is straightforward HTML for the most part. We've sorted out the consistent web interface for the application by using the `<%@ include %>` tag to include `Header.html`. I've put in databases and a driver I don't have, to test the error handling later.

It should be possible to make this a static HTML file, but the JSP engine complained mightily when I tried. I'm informed that support for forwards to a static page is a matter of interpretation of the specification at this time. Something for the future.

Finally, we have specified that `DataList.jsp` receives any submissions from this page.

> *To make this example a bit more realistic, we could let the main page (or servlet) create beans with all available databases and drivers and let this page use the bean to generate the database option lists.*

Querying a Database

Assuming all three sections of the `List1.jsp` form are filled in, `DataList.jsp` needs to forward the request to a page that can display the `ResultSet` of the query, or report why it didn't work.

The changes to `DataList.jsp` are the following:

```
<%@ page language="java" errorPage="ErrorPage.jsp" %>

<% if (request.getParameterNames().hasMoreElements() == false)
{ %>

<jsp:forward page="/jsp/data/List1.jsp" />

<% } else if ((request.getParameter("dbDriver") != null) &&
              (request.getParameter("dbURL") != null) &&
              (request.getParameter("inputSQL") != null))
{ %>
<jsp:forward page="/jsp/data/List3.jsp" />

<% } %>
```

Browsing our JDBC tutorials, we start to construct a bean that can connect to the specified database URL with the specified driver, query the database, and provide suitable methods to display the returned data. Plus if it all goes wrong the error handling needs to be informative.

```java
package com.wrox.jspexamples;

import java.sql.*;
import java.io.*;

public class DbBean
{
    String dbURL;
    String dbDriver = "sun.jdbc.odbc.JdbcOdbcDriver";
    private Connection dbCon;
public DbBean()
{
    super();
}
public boolean connect() throws ClassNotFoundException, SQLException
{
    Class.forName(this.getDbDriver());
    dbCon = DriverManager.getConnection(this.getDbURL());
    return true;
}
public void close() throws SQLException
{
    dbCon.close();
}
public ResultSet execSQL(String sql) throws SQLException
{
    Statement s = dbCon.createStatement();
    ResultSet r = s.executeQuery(sql);
    return (r == null) ? null : r;
}
public String getDbDriver()
{
    return this.dbDriver;
}
public void setDbDriver(String newValue)
{
    this.dbDriver = newValue;
}
public String getDbURL()
{
    return this.dbURL;
}
public void setDbURL(String newValue)
{
    this.dbURL = newValue;
}
}
```

Note that we've not wrapped the `ResultSet`, as it's the view of the data that the page will manipulate.

There's also no error handling in here, bar the mandatory declaration of `throws` clauses. The context of the error is better handled in the JSP where the call was made.

Let's write a test class to test out the methods and get the error handling sorted:

```java
import java.sql.*;
import com.wrox.jspexamples.DbBean;

public class TestDbBean
{

   public static void main(String[] argc)
{
      DbBean myDbBean = new DbBean();

      myDbBean.setDbDriver("sun.jdbc.odbc.JdbcOdbcDriver");
      myDbBean.setDbURL("jdbc:odbc:techlib");
int numColumns = 0;
      String sql = "select authid, lastname, firstname from authors";
ResultSet rs = null;
      ResultSetMetaData rsmd = null;
try {
         myDbBean.connect();
      } catch (ClassNotFoundException e)
{
         System.out.println("connect() ClassNotFoundException: " + e);
      } catch (SQLException e)
{
         System.out.println("connect() SQLException: " + e);
      }
try
{
         rs = myDbBean.execSQL(sql);
      } catch (SQLException e)
{
         System.out.println("execSQL() SQLException: " + e);
      }
try
{
         rsmd = rs.getMetaData();
         numColumns = rsmd.getColumnCount();
for (int column = 1; column <= numColumns; column++)
{
            System.out.println(rsmd.getColumnName(column));
         }
while (rs.next())
{
            for (int column = 1; column <= numColumns; column++)
{
               System.out.println(rs.getString(column));
            }
         }
         myDbBean.close();
      } catch (SQLException e)
{
         System.out.println("Problems with the database - SQLException: " + e);
      }
   }
}
```

Now we know it works, we can reuse the logic in the JSP file, and we've got the makings of the error handling. We want to tell the client what went wrong, and show them how to correct it if possible.

The possible errors are:

> The drivers for the database are unavailable (`ClassNotFoundException`) - which only a swift kick to the system administrator will remedy.

> The `DriverManager.getConnection()` fails because the `dbURL` is incorrect - another job for the sys admin.

> The call to `execSQL()` can throw a `SQLException` if the query is invalid - that's something that the user should be able to sort out.

> The rest are database or page errors, and should be shown as such.

Finally, we can code `List3.jsp`:

```
<HTML>
<HEAD>
<TITLE>
Database Search
</TITLE>
</HEAD>
<BODY>

<%@ page language="java" import="java.sql.*" errorPage="ErrorPage.jsp" %>

<%@ include file="Header.html" %>

<jsp:useBean id="db" scope="request" class="com.wrox.jspexamples.DbBean" />

<jsp:setProperty name="db" property="*" />

<%! int numColumns;
    ResultSet rs = null;
    ResultSetMetaData rsmd = null;
%>

<CENTER>
<H2>Results from</H2>
<H2><%= request.getParameter("inputSQL") %></H2>
<HR>
<BR><BR>
<TABLE BORDER="1" BGCOLOR="#cccc99" BORDERCOLOR="#003366">
<TR>

<%
    String sql = request.getParameter("inputSQL");

    try
    {
        db.connect();
    } catch (ClassNotFoundException e)
    {
        throw new ServletException("Database drivers not available", e);
    } catch (SQLException e)
    {
        throw new ServletException("Database URL is wrong", e);
    }
```

Continued on Following Page

```
    try
{
    rs = db.execSQL(sql);
} catch (SQLException e)
{
    throw new ServletException("Your query isn't working. " +
                               "Do you want to browse the database? " +
                               "If so, leave the SQL input empty", e);
}

    try
{
    rsmd = rs.getMetaData();
    numColumns = rsmd.getColumnCount();

    for (int column = 1; column <= numColumns; column++)
{
%>

<TH><%= rsmd.getColumnName(column) %></TH>

<%
    }
%>

</TR>

<%
    while (rs.next())
{
%>

<TR>

<%
        for (int column = 1; column <= numColumns; column++)
{
%>

<TD><%= rs.getString(column) %></TD>

<%        } %>
</TR>
<%    }
    rs.close();
    db.close();
} catch (SQLException e)
{
    throw new ServletException("Database error. The query worked, " +
                               "but the display didn't", e);
}
%>
</TABLE>
</CENTER>
<P>
<FORM METHOD="GET" ACTION="DataList.jsp">
<INPUT TYPE=hidden NAME=dbDriver VALUE=<%= request.getParameter("dbDriver") %>>
<INPUT TYPE=hidden NAME=dbURL VALUE=<%= request.getParameter("dbURL") %>>

Input SQL:<INPUT TYPE=text NAME=inputSQL SIZE=40>
```

```
<P>

<INPUT TYPE=submit>

</FORM>
</BODY>
</HTML>
```

There are a couple of noteworthy things in the code. First is the alternative use of `jsp:setProperty` tags.

```
<jsp:setProperty name="db" property="*" />
```

This matches request parameters with the property names of the `db` bean instance. `DbDriver` and `DbURL` will match, and so both these will be set with the values in the request.

This is a shorthand form of

```
<jsp:setProperty name="beanName" property="propertyName" param="parameterName" />
```

where *propertyName* and *parameterName* are identical.

In order that users can requery the database we have an input form that uses the current `DbURL` and `DbDriver` values as hidden input and takes a new SQL query.

The error handling is split into the connection, querying and display parts of the page, each throwing a different `ServletException` that the `ErrorPage.jsp` file will display.

The errorpage for the application must declare itself with the `isErrorPage` page directive set to `true`. Then we output the implicit `exception` object. And just to see where we came from and what we've brought with us, we cycle through the parameter and attribute names.

```
<HTML>
<TITLE>
DataList Error Page
</TITLE>
<BODY>

<%@ include file="Header.html" %>

<!-- Need an error page to handle the exception message -->
<!-- What error page does an error page use? -->
<%@ page language="java" isErrorPage="true" import="java.util.*, java.sql.*" %>

<BR>
<H4>Exception details:</H4>
<P>
<!-- The fully-qualified class that is the exception -->
<%= exception.toString() %>
<BR>
<!-- The exception's message to the world -->
<%= exception.getMessage() %>
<P>
```

Continued on Following Page

```
<A href="DataList.jsp">Want to try again?</A>

<P>

<%! Enumeration parameterList; %>
<%! Enumeration attributeList; %>

<P>
<H4>Parameter listing: </H4>
<P>

<%
   parameterList = request.getParameterNames();
   while (parameterList.hasMoreElements()) {
%>

<%=      parameterList.nextElement().toString() %> <BR>

<% } %>

<P>
<H4>Attribute listing: </H4>
<P>

<%
   Enumeration attributeList = request.getAttributeNames();
   while (attributeList.hasMoreElements()) {
%>

<%=      attributeList.nextElement().toString() %> <BR>

<% } %>

</BODY>
</HTML>
```

Browsing Databases

What if the user selects one of the available databases, and the driver, but doesn't enter an SQL query, because they don't have the table details. We need to decode that, and then show the user the database information they need to form a query.

First off, how do we look at the tables of a database? Reaching for Chapter 19 of Beginning Java 2, I see that you need the metadata of the connection - encapsulated in the `java.sql.DatabaseMetaData` object. The following code snippet shows this:

```
private DatabaseMetaData dbMetaData;
static String[] tableTypes = {"TABLES"};

...

dbMetaData.getTables(catalog, schema, tableName, tableTypes)
dbMetaData.getColumns(catalog, schema, tableName, columnName)
```

Here are the two new `DbBean` methods we need to return the appropriate `ResultSet`s to the JSP,

```
    public ResultSet getTables() throws SQLException
{
    dbMetaData = dbCon.getMetaData();
    return dbMetaData.getTables(null, null, null, tableTypes);
    }
public ResultSet getTable(String tableName) throws SQLException
{
    return dbMetaData.getColumns(null, null, tableName, null);
    }
```

with `tableTypes` and `dbMetaData` declared as above. Note how both methods can throw a `SQLException`.

Having added the declarations and methods to the `DbBean` class, here's the new code for the test bean:

```
        while (rs.next())
    {
            for (int column = 1; column <= numColumns; column++)
    {
                System.out.println(rs.getString(column));
            }
        }
        }
        catch (SQLException e)
    {
            System.out.println("Problems with the database - SQLException: " + e);
        }
// Test for List2.jsp
        ResultSet tables = null;
    try
    {
            tables = myDbBean.getTables();
        }
        catch (SQLException e)
    {
            System.out.println("getTables() SQLException: " + e);
        }
    try
    {
            while (tables.next())
    {
                String current_table = tables.getString("TABLE_NAME");
                System.out.println(current_table);
                System.out.println(" ");
ResultSet table = myDbBean.getTable(current_table);
                while (table.next())
    {
                    System.out.println(table.getString("COLUMN_NAME"));
                }
System.out.println(" ");
            }
myDbBean.close();
} catch (SQLException e) {
        System.out.println("Table listing failed: " + e);
        }
    }
}
```

149

From this, we can create the `List2.jsp` file. This will display every table in the database, plus the names of the columns in that table.

```
<HTML>
<HEAD>
<TITLE>
Database Details
</TITLE>
</HEAD>
<BODY>

<%@ page language="java" import="java.sql.*" errorPage="ErrorPage.jsp" %>

<%@ include file="Header.html" %>

<jsp:useBean id="db" scope="request" class="com.wrox.jspexamples.DbBean" />

<jsp:setProperty name="db" property="*" />

<%! int numColumns;
    String current_table;
%>

The database (<%= request.getParameter("dbURL") %>) you have selected has the
following tables:

<%
    try
    {
        db.connect();
    } catch (ClassNotFoundException e)
    {
        throw new ServletException("Database drivers not available", e);
    } catch (SQLException e)
    {
        throw new ServletException("Database URL is wrong", e);
    }

    try
    {
        ResultSet tables = db.getTables();
        while (tables.next())
        {
            current_table = tables.getString("TABLE_NAME");
%>
<P>
<H4><%= current_table %>    </H4>
<TABLE BORDER="1" BGCOLOR="#cccc99" BORDERCOLOR="#003366">
<TR>
<%
            ResultSet table = db.getTable(current_table);
            // Loop through columns and get their names and characteristics
            while (table.next())
            {
%>
<TD><%= table.getString("COLUMN_NAME") %></TD>
<%
            }
%>
```

```
        </TR>
        </TABLE>

        <%

                table.close();
            }
            tables.close();
            db.close();
        } catch (SQLException e)
        {

            throw new ServletException("Database problems", e);
        }
        %>

        <P>

        <FORM METHOD="GET" ACTION="DataList.jsp">

        <INPUT TYPE=hidden NAME=dbDriver VALUE=<%= request.getParameter("dbDriver") %>>
        <INPUT TYPE=hidden NAME=dbURL VALUE=<%= request.getParameter("dbURL") %>>

        Input SQL:<INPUT TYPE=text NAME=inputSQL SIZE=40>

        <P>

        <INPUT TYPE=submit>

        </FORM>
        </BODY>
        </HTML>
```

When you have a text field, the browser will always send a parameter with the same name as the text field element. The value is an empty string if the user has not entered anything, but it's hard to see if there are just a couple of space characters in the field. To check if inputSQL contains something that could be SQL, you need to check for a non-empty string that isn't all space characters. I've created a convenience method in DataList.jsp to do this. The code for the final DataList.jsp looks like:

```
<%@ page language="java" errorPage="ErrorPage.jsp" %>

<%! boolean emptySQL(String sql)
{
        if (sql != null)
{

            if (sql.trim().length() == 0)
                return true;
            else
                return false;
        }
        return true;
    }
%>

<% if (request.getParameterNames().hasMoreElements() == false)
{ %>
<jsp:forward page="/jsp/data/List1.jsp" />

<% } else if ((request.getParameter("dbDriver") != null) &&
                (request.getParameter("dbURL") != null) &&
                (emptySQL(request.getParameter("inputSQL"))))
{ %>
```

Continued on Following Page

```
<jsp:forward page="/jsp/data/List2.jsp" />

<% } else if ((request.getParameter("dbDriver") != null) &&
              (request.getParameter("dbURL") != null) &&
              (emptySQL(request.getParameter("inputSQL")) == false))
{ %>

<jsp:forward page="/jsp/data/List3.jsp" />

<% } %>
```

Mixing Servlets and JSPs

As we mentioned at the start of this example, it's very easy to mix JSP and servlets as and when the need arises. An ideal candidate is the `DataList.jsp` file which just forwards requests to the right JSP page.

To recast the code as a servlet, we need to use `RequestDispatcher` classes. We'll look at these in more detail in Chapter 11, but they are essentially the servlet equivalent of the `<jsp:forward ... />` and `<%@ include ... %>` tags we've used previously. We need one instance for each forward request.

> *Remember to change the `ListX.jsp` files to point to the servlet. I installed the servlet in* `examples\WEB-INF\servlets` *of the reference implementation and pointed my browser at* http://localhost:8080/examples/servlet/DataList.

```java
import java.io.*;
import javax.servlet.*;
import javax.servlet.http.*;

public class DataList extends HttpServlet
{

    public void doGet(HttpServletRequest request, HttpServletResponse response)
                    throws ServletException, IOException
{

        RequestDispatcher firstListRD = this.getServletContext().
getRequestDispatcher("/jsp/data/List1.jsp");
        RequestDispatcher secondListRD = this.getServletContext().
getRequestDispatcher("/jsp/data/List2.jsp");
        RequestDispatcher thirdListRD = this.getServletContext().
getRequestDispatcher("/jsp/data/List3.jsp");

        if (request.getParameterNames().hasMoreElements() == false)
{
            firstListRD.forward(request, response);
        } else if ((request.getParameter("DbDriver") != null) &&
                   (request.getParameter("DbURL") != null) &&
                   (emptySQL(request.getParameter("inputSQL"))))
{
            secondListRD.forward(request, response);
        } else if ((request.getParameter("dbDriver") != null) &&
                   (request.getParameter("dbURL") != null) &&
```

```
                      (emptySQL(request.getParameter("inputSQL")) == false))
    {
          thirdListRD.forward(request, response);
      }
    }

   boolean emptySQL(String sql)
   {
      if (sql != null)
   {
          if (sql.trim().length() == 0)
              return true;
          else
              return false;
      }
      return true;
   }
}
```

> Note that you can't forward the request if you have an open output stream or
> writer. This means that you can't include a file and then forward the request, and so
> the `DataList` servlet can't act as a template file.

Enhancing the User Interface with Applets and Beans

The `<jsp:plugin>` ... `</jsp:plugin>` tag included in JSP 1.0 (but not currently
implemented) allows you to specify an applet's or bean's place in the final page. For example:

```
<jsp:plugin type="applet" code="NervousText.class" codebase="/applets/NervousText"
            height="50" width="375" />

<params>
<param name=text value="<%= someObject.getWhackyText() %>" >
</params>
<fallback> <p>It's messed up - apologies</p> </fallback>

</jsp:plugin>
```

This holds out the potential of creating very rich, dynamic user interfaces within a web page.

Summary

JavaServer Pages technology brings together the power of Java Servlets and the ease of HTML coding to give developers a powerful method in which to create server-side web applications. It is currently one of the most exciting and fast-changing topics in the Java world.

In this chapter, we learned the following:

> ➤ A JavaServer Page file consists of standard markup tags, content, JSP directives, JSP declarations, JSP scriptlets and actions tags.

> ➤ The JSP engine performs a first-time compile on a JSP file which generates a new servlet with the desired content. If the file changes, then a new servlet is generated, otherwise the compiled version is used.

> ➤ JavaBeans can be used within a JSP file to help split presentation and logic into their component parts.

Connecting to Databases

To develop a truly useful servlet-based application, you are going to have to add database connectivity. Adding a database to a servlet is really no different from adding a database to an applet or application. This chapter will walk you through some common database functionality as well as introduce the concept of database pooling. Database pooling provides a mechanism for dynamically assigning connections to new requests as needed, rather than incurring the overhead of creating a new connection for each request.

This chapter will cover the following:

> Discuss the different options for adding database connectivity to your servlet application
> Explore the JDBC API and the various JDBC driver types
> Explain and demonstrate some common SQL functions implemented using servlets and JDBC
> Introduce the concept of database pooling and show how to implement it in your servlets

Adding Data to your Servlets

Servlets can access a variety of data sources including (but not limited to) relational databases, directory servers, proprietary fileformats, XML formatted documents and object databases. For most relational databases, your servlets will most likely use the Java database packages (`java.sql`, `java.text`) to access them, either through a straight JDBC connection, or through a JDBC to ODBC bridge if the data source requires an ODBC driver. Other data sources may require a vendor-specific API, or a Java extension library like the JNDI API (for directory services). Each of these access methods is described below.

Java Database Connectivity (JDBC)

Since the majority of data access occurs using relational databases, the focus of this chapter will be on the classes that make up the Java Database Connectivity (JDBC) API. The JDBC API is part of the Java 2 platform Standard Edition so there is no need to download anything additional or modify your classpath to use it. JDBC provides a way for Java programs to communicate with a variety of databases without having to write any platform specific code to do so.

JDBC abstracts the vendor-specific details and generalizes the most common database access functions. The result is a set of methods contained within the `java.sql` and `java.text` packages. These methods can be used on any database providing JDBC connectivity through a vendor-specific JDBC driver. If you decide to switch databases, you can keep the same code and just switch the JDBC driver.

A JDBC driver is what the Java Virtual Machine uses to translate the generalized JDBC calls into the vendor-specific database calls that the database will understand. These drivers are Java classes and are loaded at run time. This allows for maximum flexibility when deploying applications that may access databases from multiple vendors. JDBC drivers exist for all of the popular databases as well as most of the lesser known databases. Typically, the database vendor will supply the JDBC driver, but you can also find a variety of third-party JDBC drivers on the Internet.

JDBC Driver Types

All JDBC drivers fall into one of four categories. Each category of drivers has its own advantages and performance issues to consider. Review the following types of drivers and keep in mind the differences between them when selecting a JDBC driver to use for your application.

Type 1

This category of driver defines the JDBC to ODBC bridge that comes with the Java 2 platform. This driver translates standard JDBC calls to a corresponding ODBC call and sends it to an ODBC data source via the operating system's ODBC libraries (see the figure below). Using a bridge to an ODBC data source is not a preferred solution, but in some cases it might be the only solution. For instance, a Microsoft Access database can only be accessed using the JDBC-ODBC bridge.

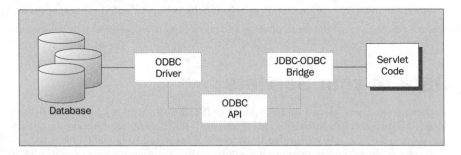

Accessing ODBC data sources using JDBC is a very inefficient and narrow solution. Not only does the system have to pass the database call through multiple layers, but it also limits the functionality of the JDBC code to whatever the ODBC driver can handle.

Type 2

A type 2 driver will use a Java driver to communicate with a vendor-specific API. It is similar in concept to a type 1 driver except it has one less layer to go through (no ODBC translation layer). When a database call is made using JDBC, the driver will translate the request into something that the vendor API will understand. The database will process the request and send its results back through the API, which will forward them back to the JDBC driver. The JDBC driver will format the results to conform to the JDBC standard and return them to the program.

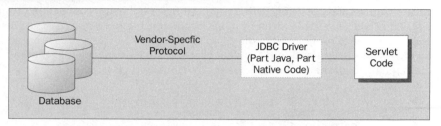

Type 3

Drivers that fall into this category make use of an all-Java driver and an all-Java middle tier to provide data access to your programs. The Java program sends a JDBC call through the JDBC driver and straight to the middle tier without translation. The middle tier then handles the request using another JDBC driver to complete the request. The only problem with this is that the middle tier may be using a type 1 or type 2 driver to talk to the database.

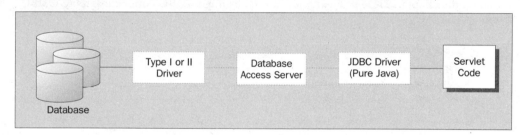

Type 4

A type 4 driver is an all-Java driver that issues requests directly to the database. This is definitely the most efficient method of accessing your database. It is also the simplest to deploy since there are no additional libraries or middleware to install. All of the major database vendors provide type 4 JDBC drivers for their databases. If yours didn't come with one, check the vendor's web site. Typically they can be downloaded for free.

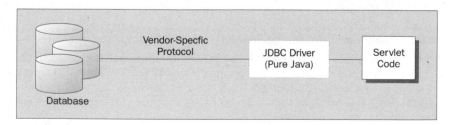

JDBC API

The JDBC API is made up of the classes and interfaces found in the `java.sql` and `java.text` packages. Both packages can be found within the core libraries of the Java 2 platform. Within these packages you will find a set of methods that allow you to connect to a database, retrieve information about the database, perform SQL queries and execute stored procedures.

Establishing a Connection

To communicate with a database using JDBC, you must first establish a connection through the appropriate JDBC driver. The JDBC driver can be specified using the `jdbc.drivers` system property, or it can be set at runtime using the `Class.forName(String drivername)` method. Assuming the driver has been listed in the system properties file or specified at runtime, the connection is made through the method of the `DriverManager` class.

```
public static synchronized Connection getConnection(String url,
    java.util.Properties info) throws SQLException
public static synchronized Connection getConnection(String url,
    String user, String pwd) throws SQLException
public static synchronized Connection getConnection(String url) throws
    SQLException
```

Using one of the above `getConnection()` methods of the `DriverManager` class, a `Connection` object is returned to the program. This `Connection` object is then used to perform all operations on the given database. The methods of the `Connection` object will be introduced as they are needed throughout the chapter. Here's an example of establishing a JDBC connection to an ODBC datasource:

```
Connection bdCon;

try {
    Class.forName("sun.jdbc.odbc.JdbcOdbcDriver");
    dbCon = DriverManager.getConnection("jdbc:odbc:employeedb");

    // Can enter database information here to catch possible SQL exceptions

} catch (ClassNotFoundException e) {
    //Catch error here
} catch (SQLException e) {
    //Catch error here
}
```

Remember that you have to catch two exceptions here. If the JDBC driver cannot be found, then the program will throw a `ClassNotFoundException`. If the connection cannot be made then a `SQLException` will be thrown.

Executing SQL Statements and Retrieving Results

All SQL statements are executed through the `Connection` object that is created by the `getConnection()` method of the `DriverManager` class. When issuing a SQL query to the database, we do it by first creating either a `Statement`, `PreparedStatement` or a `CallableStatement` using one of the methods of the `Connection` object. Once we have one of these statement objects, we then execute the statement and read the results through a `ResultSet` object (if the query returned any results). The following are the methods of the `Connection` object used to create a statement.

```
Statement createStatement() throws SQLException
Statement createStatement(int resultSetType, int resultSetConcurrency)
   throws SQLException
PreparedStatement prepareStatement(String sql) throws SQLException
PreparedStatement prepareStatement(String sql, int resultSetType, int
resultSetConcurrency)
   throws SQLException
CallableStatement prepareCall(String sql) throws SQLException
CallableStatement prepareCall(String sql, int resultSetType, int
resultSetConcurrency) throws SQLException
```

Each of these methods allow you to specify a couple of options. The result set type determines whether or not the result set can be scrolled backwards. The result set concurrency determines if the result set can be updated or not. The following constants from the `Connection` interface define the values which can be used for each of these methods.

```
int TYPE_FORWARD_ONLY = 1003;
int TYPE_SCROLL_INSENSITIVE = 1004;
int TYPE_SCROLL_SENSITIVE = 1005;

int CONCUR_READ_ONLY = 1007;
int CONCUR_UPDATEABLE = 1008;
```

Both the `prepareStatement()` and `prepareCall()` methods take a `String` parameter containing the SQL statement to be executed. This SQL string can contain one or more ? to mark placeholders for parameters. This is useful when a query is to be executed multiple times but with a different set of criteria each time. The `prepareCall()` method is similar to the `prepareStatement()` method except that it is used to execute stored procedures that already exist on the database.

The `createStatement()` method takes no arguments (except for type and concurrency if you wish) and returns a `Statement` object. The ultimate goal of a `Statement` object is to execute a SQL statement that may or may not return results. Although there are many different methods of the `Statement` object, the following methods will be most useful.

```
ResultSet executeQuery(String sql) throws SQLException
void executeUpdate(String sql) throws SQLException
```

The `executeUpdate()` method is used to execute SQL statements that do not return any results, for example `INSERT`, `UPDATE`, or `DELETE` statements. The `executeQuery()` method is used to perform a `SELECT` query on the database and retrieve a set of records in the form of a `ResultSet`. A `ResultSet` object can be navigated and updated using the following methods. The method used will vary according to the data type to be returned.

getAsciiStream()	getTimestamp()	getTime()	getBigDecimal()
getBoolean()	getBinaryStream()	getString()	getMetaData()
getDate()	getBytes()	getByte()	getClob()
getInt()	getFloat()	getDouble()	getWarnings()
getShort()	getObject()	getLong()	getBlob()

The two methods shown below provide two ways of identifying the column containing the data. The column can be selected by passing an index value for the column of type int, where the first column has the index value of 1, or by passing the SQL column name as a String argument. The column names are not case sensitive and so "LastName" is the same as "lastname".

```
boolean next() throws SQLException

String getString(int columnIndex) throws SQLException
String getString(String columnName) throws SQLException
void updateString() throws SQLException

void updateRow() throws SQLException
void deleteRow() throws SQLException
void refreshRow() throws SQLException
void cancelRowUpdates() throws SQLException
```

The ResultSet object contains something called a 'cursor', which you can manipulate to refer to any particular row in the resultset. This initially sets the cursor at a position preceding the first row. The next() method in the ResultSet object advances the cursor to the next position. Each time the next() method is called it returns true if there is a valid row and false if you fall off the end.

Processing a typical SQL SELECT statement might look something like this:

```
try {
    Statement s = db.createStatement();
    ResultSet rs = s.executeQuery("SELECT * FROM Employee WHERE status = 'ft'");
    while (rs.next()) {
        out.println(rs.getString("lname") + ", " + rs.getString("fname"));
    }
} catch (SQLException e) {
    //Handle errors here
}
```

Transaction Support

In some applications, you might like to group a series of statements together that need to either all succeed or all fail. For instance, if a banking application needs to transfer $100 from one account to another, then both the withdrawal from account A and the deposit to account B must succeed for the transaction to be completed. If either one of these actions should fail, the other action should be cancelled, returning the system to its previous state.

When a new Connection object is created, it is set to commit every transaction automatically. This means that every time a statement is executed, it is committed to the database and cannot be rolled back. The following methods in the Connection interface are used to group transactions and either rollback or commit them to the database.

```
void setAutoCommit(boolean autoCommit) throws SQLException
void commit() throws SQLException
void rollback() throws SQLException
```

Before doing anything, you must first call the `setAutoCommit()` method and set it to `false`. This will give you control over what gets committed and when. A call to the `commit()` method will commit everything that was done since the last commit was issued. Conversely, a `rollback()` call will undo everything that was done since the last commit. The following code fragment illustrates how this can be done.

```
try {
    db.setAutoCommit(false);
    Statement s = db.createStatement();
    ...
    s.executeUpdate("INSERT INTO glTable VALUES('1001', -100)");
    int tran1 = s.getUpdateCount();
    s.executeUpdate("INSERT INTO glTable VALUES('1002', 100)");
    int tran2 = s.getUpdateCount();
    if ((tran1 > 0) && (tran2 > 0)) {
        db.commit();
    } else {
        db.rollback();
    }
    ...
} catch (SQLException e) {
    //Handle errors here
}
```

Movie Database

In this example, we will build a web interface that will allow our users to retrieve a listing of movies from a movie database. Users will be able to query the database on one or more of the following criteria: Title, Lead Actor, Lead Actress, and Movie Type. The database we will use has been created using Microsoft Access and will be accessed using the JDBC-ODBC bridge that comes with the Java Development Kit. Feel free to use whatever database that you are comfortable with, provided it has a JDBC driver that you can use. The complete list of database fields in the titles table looks like this:

Field Name	Type
title (Key)	Text(20)
lead_actor	Text(20)
lead_actress	Text(20)
Type	Text(20)

In this example we will be calling the servlet `MovieQuery`.

Build the Query Interface

The first thing we're going to do is build our web interface using an HTML form. The following code and figure below shows the completed interface. Notice how we use the GET method for this request since we only retrieve data and don't update it.

```
<HTML>
<HEAD>
        <TITLE>Movie Database</TITLE>
</HEAD>
<BODY>

<!—The line below can be adjusted to your servlets position -->

<FORM ACTION="http://localhost:8080/servlet/MovieQuery" METHOD="GET">
<CENTER>
<H1>Enter Search Criteria</H1>
</CENTER>
<HR>
Enter search criteria in any of the fields below. For a complete listing of
movies, leave all of the fields blank.
<HR>
<TABLE ALIGN="center" CELLPADDING="5" CELLSPACING="5">
        <TR>
                <TD ALIGN="right">Movie Title:</TD>
                <TD><INPUT TYPE="Text" NAME="txt_title" SIZE="20"></TD>
        </TR>
        <TR>
                <td align="right">Lead Actor (Last name):</td>
                <td><input type="Text" name="txt_actor" size="20"></td>
        </TR>
        <TR>
                <TD ALIGN="right">Lead Actress (Last name):</TD>
                <TD><INPUT TYPE="Text" NAME="txt_actress" SIZE="20"></TD>
        </TR>
        <TR>
                <TD ALIGN="right">Movie Type:</TD>
                <TD>
                        <SELECT NAME="ddlb_type" SIZE="1">
                                <OPTION VALUE=""></OPTION>
                                <OPTION VALUE="action">Action</OPTION>
                                <OPTION VALUE="comedy">COMEDY</OPTION>
                                <OPTION VALUE="drama">DRAMA</OPTION>
                                <OPTION VALUE="gangster">Gangster</OPTION>
                        </SELECT>
                </TD>
        </TR>
        <TR>
                <TD COLSPAN="2" ALIGN="center">
                <INPUT TYPE="Submit" NAME="btn_Submit" VALUE="Submit Query"></TD>
        </TR>
</TABLE>
</FORM>
</BODY>
</HTML>
```

Connect to the Database

When connecting to a database, the biggest performance hit you will encounter is when you create a connection object and connect to the database. It makes the most sense to have this happen only one time when the servlet is first initiated. Later in this chapter, we will discuss connection pooling, which is a way to instantiate multiple connections at startup and dynamically assign connections as needed.

The following code retrieves the JDBC driver name and database URL from the initialization parameters that are set in the `servlets.properties` file (or wherever your web server stores initialization parameters). This allows us a great deal of flexibility when deploying this servlet with a different database. We could simply change the initialization parameters without having to recompile the servlet code.

```
Connection dbCon;

public void init() throws ServletException {
```

```
/* Connect to the database */
    try {
        String driver = getInitParameter("JdbcDriver");
        String dbURL = getInitParameter("dbURL");
        Class.forName(driver);
        dbCon = DriverManager.getConnection(dbURL);
    } catch(ClassNotFoundException e) {
        System.out.println("MovieQuery: Database driver could not be found.");
        System.out.println(e.toString());
        throw new UnavailableException(this, "JDBC driver class not found");
    } catch(SQLException e) {
        System.out.println("MovieQuery: Error connecting to the database.");
        System.out.println(e.toString());
        throw new UnavailableException(this, "Cannot connect to the
            database");
    }
}
```

Notice how we handle the different possible exceptions. If either the driver cannot be found or the connection cannot be made to the database, then we write the error to the system log and throw an `UnavailableException`. This lets the servlet engine know that the servlet is unavailable.

Gather Data from the Query Form

From this point forward, the rest of our code will go in the `doGet()` method since this is a GET request that we will be servicing. After declaring all of our variables and obtaining a `PrintWriter` from the `response` object, we gather the values of our form fields and assign them to a set of `String` variables using the `getParameter()` method of the request object.

```
/* Get form field values */
String title = req.getParameter("txt_title");
String actor = req.getParameter("txt_actor");
String actress = req.getParameter("txt_actress");
String type = req.getParameter("ddlb_type");
```

Build Query

To build our query, we start with a standard SELECT statement. We need to account for either no fields selected, one field selected or multiple fields selected. Remember, for performance reasons we use a `StringBuffer` rather than a `String` object to build the query string. We proceed to check each of the query fields to see if they contain any search criteria. If they do, we append a WHERE clause to the query. You'll notice the use of the '%' character as a wildcard in the LIKE statement. Some of you may know that Microsoft Access uses the '*' character as a wildcard. This is a good example of how your JDBC code is platform independent. The JDBC driver takes care of translating the calls to the vendor-specific protocol required by the database.

```
StringBuffer qry = new StringBuffer(1024);
int numCriteria = 0;

qry.append("SELECT * FROM titles WHERE");

if (title.length() > 0) {
   qry.append(" title LIKE '%");
   qry.append(title);
   qry.append("%' AND");
   numCriteria++;
}

if (actor.length() > 0) {
   qry.append(" lead_actor LIKE '%");
   qry.append(actor);
   qry.append("%' AND");
   numCriteria++;
}

if (actress.length() > 0) {
   qry.append(" lead_actress LIKE '%");
   qry.append(actress);
   qry.append("%*' AND");
   numCriteria++;
}

if (type.length() > 0) {
   qry.append(" type LIKE '%");
   qry.append(type);
   qry.append("%' AND");
   numCriteria++;
}
```

Now that the query string is built, we have to do a little bit of cleanup. If there were no selection criteria for the query, we need to strip off the WHERE that we initially added to the query string. If there were some criteria added to the string, then we need to strip off the final AND that was added. We accomplish both of these tasks with the following code:

```
if (numCriteria > 0) {
   qry.delete(qry.length() - 3, qry.length());      //Strip off AND
} else {
   qry.delete(qry.length() - 5, qry.length());      //Strip off WHERE
}
```

Send the Query to the Database

Once our query has been built, we can go ahead and send it to the database. First we create a Statement object using the Connection object's createStatement() method. Next, we create a ResultSet by calling the executeQuery() method of the Statement object with the query string as an argument. If the operation fails, then the exception is caught and an error is sent using the sendError() method of the response object.

```
try {
   stmt = dbCon.createStatement();
   rs = stmt.executeQuery(qry.toString());
} catch (SQLException e) {
   res.sendError(res.SC_ACCEPTED, "The request has been accepted, but it failed to
      complete due to a problem querying the database.");
   return;
}
```

Return Results to the Web Browser

In order to help us return the results of our database search, we're going to first add another method to our HTML helper class that we created back in Chapter 2. This method will take an array of column headings and a ResultSet object and add an HTML table to our HTML object. Here's the code for our new method:

```
public boolean addTable(String labels[], ResultSet rs) {
   int cols = labels.length;

   this.buffer.append("<TABLE WIDTH='100%'>");
   this.buffer.append("<TR>");
   for (int i = 0; i < cols; i++) {
      this.buffer.append("<TH ALIGN='left'>");
      this.buffer.append(labels[i]);
      this.buffer.append("</TH>");
   }
   this.buffer.append("</TR>");

   try {
      while (rs.next()) {
         this.buffer.append("<TR>");
            for (int i = 1; i <= cols; i++) {
               this.buffer.append("<TD>");
               this.buffer.append(rs.getString(i));
               this.buffer.append("</TD>");
            }
```

Continued on Following Page

```
            this.buffer.append("</TR>");
      }
   } catch (SQLException e) {
      return false;
   }
   this.buffer.append("</TABLE>");
   return true;
}
```

Getting back to our movie example, here's the code to output the results to the browser using the newly created helper `addTable()` method in the HTML class.

```
HTML h = new HTML("Search Results");
h.add(HTML.HEADING, "Selected Movies", true);
h.add(HTML.LINE, "", false);

String labels[] = {"Title","Lead Actor","Lead Actress","Type"};

if (!h.addTable(labels, rs)) {
   res.sendError(res.SC_ACCEPTED, "The request has been accepted, but it failed to
      complete due to a problem accessing the data.");
   return;
}
out.println(h.getPage());
```

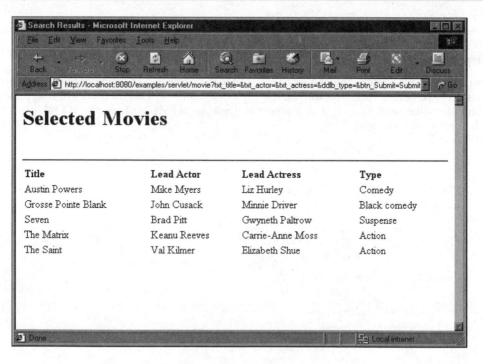

Close the Database Connection

Finally, in the `destroy()` method, we should go ahead and close down the database connection. This is important so that the object can be flagged for garbage collection and cleaned up. Also, if the database has a limited number of connections available (as most do), then it is even more important to close your connections as soon as they are no longer needed.

```
public void destroy() {

    /* Disconnect from the database */
    try {
        dbCon.close();
    } catch(Exception e) {
        System.out.println("MovieQuery: Database close failed");
        System.out.println(e.toString());
    }
}
```

Below is the full source code for the `MovieQuery` servlet.

```
import javax.servlet.*;
import javax.servlet.http.*;

import java.io.*;
import java.sql.*;

import com.wrox.util.*;

public class MovieQuery extends HttpServlet {

    Connection dbCon;

    public void init() throws ServletException {

        /* Connect to the database */
        try{
            String driver = getInitParameter("JdbcDriver");
            String dbURL = getInitParameter("dbURL");
            Class.forName(driver);
            dbCon = DriverManager.getConnection(dbURL);
        } catch(ClassNotFoundException e) {
            System.out.println("MovieQuery: Database driver could not be found.");
            System.out.println(e.toString());
            throw new UnavailableException(this, "Database driver class not found");
        } catch(SQLException e) {
            System.out.println("MovieQuery: Error connecting to the database.");
            System.out.println(e.toString());
            throw new UnavailableException(this, "Cannot connect to the database");
        }
    }

    public void doGet(HttpServletRequest req, HttpServletResponse res)
        throws ServletException, IOException {

        ResultSet rs;
        Statement stmt;
```

Continued on Following Page

```
StringBuffer qry = new StringBuffer(1024);
int numCriteria = 0;

res.setContentType("text/html");
PrintWriter out = res.getWriter();

/* Get form field values */

String title = req.getParameter("txt_title");
String actor = req.getParameter("txt_actor");
String actress = req.getParameter("txt_actress");
String type = req.getParameter("ddlb_type");

/* Build Query String */

qry.append("SELECT * FROM titles WHERE");

if (title.length() > 0) {
   qry.append(" title LIKE '%");
   qry.append(title);
   qry.append("%' AND");
   numCriteria++;
}

if (actor.length() > 0) {
   qry.append(" lead_actor LIKE '%");
   qry.append(actor);
   qry.append("%' AND");
   numCriteria++;
}

if (actress.length() > 0) {
   qry.append(" lead_actress LIKE '%");
   qry.append(actress);
   qry.append("%*' AND");
   numCriteria++;
}

if (type.length() > 0) {
   qry.append(" type LIKE '%");
   qry.append(type);
   qry.append("%' AND");
   numCriteria++;
}

if (numCriteria > 0) {
   qry.delete(qry.length() - 3, qry.length());  //Strip off AND
} else {
   qry.delete(qry.length() - 5, qry.length());  //Strip off WHERE
}

/* Execute Query */

try {
   stmt = dbCon.createStatement();
   rs = stmt.executeQuery(qry.toString());
} catch(SQLException e) {
   res.sendError(res.SC_ACCEPTED, "The request has been accepted, but it
      failed to complete due to a problem querying the database.");
   return;
}
```

```
        /* Output Results */

        HTML h = new HTML ("Search Results");
        h.add(HTML.HEADING, "Selected Movies", true);
        h.add(HTML.LINE, "", false);

        String labels[] = {"Title","Lead Actor","Lead Actress","Type"};
        if (!h.addTable(labels, rs)) {
            res.sendError(res.SC_ACCEPTED, "The request has been accepted, but it
            failed to complete due to a problem accessing the data.");
            return;
        }
        out.println(h.getPage());
        out.close();
    }

    public void destroy() {

        /* Disconnect from the database */
        try {
            dbCon.close();
        } catch(Exception e) {
            System.out.println("MovieQuery: Database close failed");
            System.out.println(e.toString());
        }
    }
}
```

Optimizing Performance with Prepared Statements

When issuing the same SQL statement repeatedly, it is more efficient to use a `PreparedStatement` rather than a `Statement` to execute the query. A `PreparedStatement` is precompiled before it is used. The precompiled version can also accept any number of parameters. When creating the `PreparedStatement` (using the `Connection` object's `prepareStatement()` method), you can insert a ? wherever you would like a parameter to be inserted later. The `PreparedStatement` object provides methods to set the values of each parameter. We will see how this is done in the following example.

Sales Update Interface

This example will process a set of sales results for each sales region of our make-believe widget manufacturer. The database used for this example is Microsoft Access. The field definitions for the daily sales table are listed below. Our servlet will read the form input, update the database using a `PreparedStatement` for each row of data, and then send back a confirmation message to the browser (or an error if one is encountered).

Field Name	Type
region	Text(7)
date	Date
QtySold	Long Integer
Revenue	Double

In this example we will be calling the servlet `Sales`.

Build the Sales Form

The form required to collect the sales data consists of a simple table with 3 columns - region, quantity, and revenue. Each row consists of a region (North, South, East, West, Central), a quantity input field and a revenue input field. The request that we will be making is a POST request since we are actually updating a server resource (the database) this time.

```html
<HTML>
<HEAD>
        <TITLE>Daily Widget Sales</TITLE>
</HEAD>
<BODY>

<!--The line below can be adjusted to your local servlet position -->

<FORM ACTION="http://localhost:8080/servlet/sales" METHOD="POST">

<CENTER><H1>Widget Sales</H1></CENTER>
<HR>
<TABLE ALIGN="center" CELLSPACING="2" CELLPADDING="2" WIDTH="75%">
<TR>
    <TH ALIGN="center">Region</TH>
    <TH ALIGN="center">Quantity</TH>
    <TH ALIGN="center">Revenue</TH>
</TR>
<TR>
    <TD>North</TD>
    <TD ALIGN="center"><INPUT TYPE="Text" NAME="qty_n" VALUE="0" SIZE="7"></TD>
    <TD ALIGN="center">$ <INPUT TYPE="Text" NAME="rev_n" VALUE="0" SIZE="7"></TD>
</TR>
<TR>
    <TD>South</TD>
    <TD ALIGN="center"><INPUT TYPE="Text" NAME="qty_s" VALUE="0" SIZE="7"></TD>
    <TD ALIGN="center">$ <INPUT TYPE="Text" NAME="rev_s" VALUE="0" SIZE="7"></TD>
</TR>
<TR>
    <TD>East</TD>
    <TD ALIGN="center"><INPUT TYPE="Text" NAME="qty_e" VALUE="0" SIZE="7"></TD>
    <TD ALIGN="center">$ <INPUT TYPE="Text" NAME="rev_e" VALUE="0" SIZE="7"></TD>
</TR>
<TR>
    <TD>West</TD>
    <TD ALIGN="center"><INPUT TYPE="Text" NAME="qty_w" VALUE="0" SIZE="7"></TD>
    <TD ALIGN="center">$ <INPUT TYPE="Text" NAME="rev_w" VALUE="0" SIZE="7"></TD>
</TR>
<TR>
    <TD>Central</TD>
    <TD ALIGN="center"><INPUT TYPE="Text" NAME="qty_c" VALUE="0" SIZE="7"></TD>
    <TD ALIGN="center">$ <INPUT TYPE="Text" NAME="rev_c" VALUE="0" SIZE="7"></TD>
</TR>
</TABLE>
<BR><BR>
<CENTER><INPUT TYPE="Submit" VALUE="Submit Figures"></CENTER>
</FORM>
</BODY>
</HTML>
```

Connect to the Database

Connecting to the database is the same process as in the previous example. We only have to change our initialization parameters to reflect a new ODBC datasource for the newly created sales database.

Retrieve the Form Data

From this point forward, all of our code will be put in the `doPost()` method of the servlet to handle a `POST` request from the browser. Our first task when handling a new request is to retrieve the form data. Since we would like to cycle through the records later on in the method, we will be storing the form fields in a two-dimensional array. The first dimension represents the sales region and the second dimension stores the data for each region.

```
String sales[][] = new String[5][3];

sales[0][0] = "North";
sales[0][1] = req.getParameter("qty_n");
sales[0][2] - req.getParameter("rev_n");

sales[1][0] = "South";
sales[1][1] = req.getParameter("qty_s");
sales[1][2] = req.getParameter("rev_s");

sales[2][0] = "East";
sales[2][1] = req.getParameter("qty_e");
sales[2][2] - req.getParameter("rev_e");

sales[3][0] = "West";
sales[3][1] = req.getParameter("qty_w");
sales[3][2] = req.getParameter("rev_w");

sales[4][0] = "Central";
sales[4][1] = req.getParameter("qty_c");
sales[4][2] = req.getParameter("rev_c");
```

173

Create the PreparedStatement

Enclosing the following fragment of code in a `try-catch` block, we first build our SQL statement and then, using the `Connection` object, `dbCon`, we create the `PreparedStatement`. The `?`s represent the parameters for the `INSERT` statement. When we actually execute the `PreparedStatement`, we will use a series of set methods to assign values to these parameter placeholders.

```
StringBuffer sql = new StringBuffer(512);
sql.append("INSERT INTO dailySales(region, [date], qtySold, revenue) ");
sql.append("VALUES(?,?,?,?)");
PreparedStatement stmt = dbCon.prepareStatement(sql.toString());
```

Insert the Records into the Database

Now, it's time to add the records to the database. Using a `for` loop, we'll cycle through each of the regions and insert the sales data for the day. First, we call the `clearParameters()` method to reset each of the parameters. Then, using some of the `setXxx()` methods of the `PreparedStatement` object, we set the parameters to their appropriate values. Finally, we call the `executeUpdate()` method to execute the precompiled statement.

```
for (int i = 0; i < 5; i++) {
    stmt.clearParameters();
    stmt.setString(1, sales[i][0]);
    stmt.setDate(2, new java.sql.Date(System.currentTimeMillis()));
    stmt.setInt(3, Integer.parseInt(sales[i][1]));
    stmt.setDouble(4, Double.parseDouble(sales[i][2]));
    stmt.executeUpdate();
}
```

Send a Confirmation Message

When all of the updating has completed, and if we haven't encountered an error, a confirmation message is sent back to the user letting them know that the updates took place. This is done using the HTML helper class that we created back in Chapter 2.

```
HTML h = new HTML("Widget Sales Update");
h.add(HTML.HEADING, "Sales figures have been updated.", false);
out.println(h.getPage());
```

Below is the full source code for the Sales servlet

```
import javax.servlet.*;
import javax.servlet.http.*;

import java.io.*;
import java.sql.*;


import com.wrox.util.*;

public class sales extends HttpServlet {

    Connection dbCon;
```

```
public void init() throws ServletException {

   /* Connect to the database */
   try {
      String driver = getInitParameter("JdbcDriver");
      String dbURL = getInitParameter("dbURL");
      Class.forName(driver);
      dbCon = DriverManager.getConnection(dbURL);
   } catch(ClassNotFoundException e) {
      System.out.println("sales: Database driver could not be found.");
      System.out.println(e.toString());
      throw new UnavailableException(this, "Database driver class not found");
   } catch(SQLException e) {
      System.out.println("sales: Error connecting to the database.");
      System.out.println(e.toString());
      throw new UnavailableException(this, "Cannot connect to the database");
   }
}

public void doPost(HttpServletRequest req, HttpServletResponse res)
   throws ServletException, IOException {

   res.setContentType("text/html");
   PrintWriter out = res.getWriter();

   String sales[][] = new String[5][3];

   sales[0][0] = "North";
   sales[0][1] = req.getParameter("qty_n");
   sales[0][2] = req.getParameter("rev_n");

   sales[1][0] = "South";
   sales[1][1] = req.getParameter("qty_s");
   sales[1][2] = req.getParameter("rev_s");

   sales[2][0] = "East";
   sales[2][1] = req.getParameter("qty_e");
   sales[2][2] = req.getParameter("rev_e");

   sales[3][0] = "West";
   sales[3][1] = req.getParameter("qty_w");
   sales[3][2] = req.getParameter("rev_w");

   sales[4][0] = "Central";
   sales[4][1] = req.getParameter("qty_c");
   sales[4][2] = req.getParameter("rev_c");

   try {
      StringBuffer sql = new StringBuffer(512);
      sql.append("INSERT INTO dailySales(region, [date], qtySold, revenue) ");
      sql.append("VALUES(?,?,?,?)");
      PreparedStatement stmt = dbCon.prepareStatement(sql.toString());
      for (int i = 0; i < 5; i++) {
         stmt.clearParameters();
         stmt.setString(1, sales[i][0]);
         stmt.setDate(2, new java.sql.Date(System.currentTimeMillis()));
         stmt.setInt(3, Integer.parseInt(sales[i][1]));
         stmt.setDouble(4, new Double(sales[i][2]));
         stmt.executeUpdate();
      }
```

Continued on Following Page

```
        } catch (SQLException e) {
            res.sendError(res.SC_ACCEPTED, "The request has been accepted, but it
                failed to complete due to an error updating the database.");
            System.out.println(e.toString());
            return;
        } catch (NumberFormatException e) {
            res.sendError(res.SC_BAD_REQUEST, "At least one of the input fields is
non-
                numeric. Please correct and try again.");
            System.out.println(e.toString());
            return;
        }

        HTML h = new HTML("Widget Sales Update");
        h.add(HTML.HEADING, "Sales figures have been updated.", false);
        out.println(h.getPage());
        out.close();
    }

    public void destroy() {

        /* Disconnect from the database */
        try {
            dbCon.close();
        } catch(Exception e) {
            System.out.println("Sales: Database close failed");
            System.out.println(e.toString());
        }
    }
}
```

Pooling Connection Objects

Perhaps the biggest concern for most end users is how well an application performs and, more specifically, how fast it responds. When speaking of web applications, there are certainly many areas where performance degradation can occur. It is our goal, as application developers, to try to smooth each of these potential speedbumps to the best of our abilities.

The slowest step in running a database-enabled Java Servlet is the initial connection to the database. In our previous examples, you can see that we are connecting to the database only once in the init() method. This causes us to take a performance hit only the first time the servlet is loaded. What do we do if we have a large number of users though? We're only creating one Connection object in these examples. For high-traffic systems, it would be very advantageous to create a larger number of connection objects during servlet initialization and then dynamically assign incoming requests to an open connection as needed. How many do you need? What if the number of users exceeds the number of connection objects? These questions can be answered with the simple, yet clever, concept of database pooling.

This section of the chapter covers the information required to create and run simple pooled connections. In Chapter 9 you will see more complex pooling solutions.

Database Pooling

This example is meant to simply illustrate the concept of database pooling. Once you learn how to implement this mechanism, you can apply it to whatever database application you like. In this example, we simply create a pool of connection objects, assign an open connection to each new request, perform some trivial database operation and return the results along with a user count and current user limit.

To properly test the following example, you will need to open up multiple browser windows, enter http://localhost:8080/servlet/DBPool into each of the URL boxes, and press enter in each of the windows. Chances are, the computer will process each request before the next one makes it to the server. I was able to send each request in succession quickly enough to see some results. You may want to add some more database code to slow things down a bit. What you should see, is that in each of the browser windows, the user count increases and the limit increases once you reach your maximum number of users.

To create and make use of a database pool, you will need to perform the following steps.

Set Your User Limit and Initialize the User Count

The user limit refers to the maximum number of concurrent users of the system. This will determine the number of database connections that are created during servlet initialization. This number could also be passed into the servlet as a parameter. We also would like to keep track of how many users are using the system at one time. Also, at this point, we need to declare a pair of Vector objects to keep track of our connection objects and the availability of each.

```
int limit = 2;          //Set initial limit to 2
int users = 0;          //Track user count with this variable

Vector db_v;            //Vector to manage connections
Vector db_status;       //Vector to keep track of open connections
```

Create All of the Connection Objects

This method will look very similar to the init() method of our previous examples. The only difference is that instead of creating just one connection object, we loop through and create multiple connection objects up to the predefined limit we set in the previous step. We add these Connection objects to a Vector object so that we can dynamically add connections to it as needed. At the same time, we also add an element to the db_status vector to indicate the status of the connection.

```
public void init() throws ServletException {

    /* Create initial pool of database connections */
    try {
        db_v = new Vector();
        db_status = new Vector();
        Class.forName(getInitParameter("JdbcDriver"));
        String dbURL = getInitParameter("dbURL");
        for (int i=0; i<limit; i++) {
            db_v.addElement(DriverManager.getConnection(dbURL));
            db_status.addElement("0"); // "0" - Available Connection
        }
    } catch (Exception e) {
        System.out.println("Database connect failed (init)");
        System.out.println(e.toString());
        return;
    }
}
```

Assign Connection Objects to New Requests

In the doGet() method, we assign an open connection object to the request. We first increment the user count and then check if it exceeds our preset limit. If it does, we add a connection object to our vector of connections in a method called addConnection(). We then loop through the db_status vector to find an open connection. Once we find one, we go ahead and assign a new connection object to it.

```
int limit = 2;          //Set initial limit to 2

/* If necessary, add a new connection */
users++;
if (users > limit) {
    if(!addConnection()) {
        res.sendError(res.SC_ACCEPTED, "The request has been accepted, but
        it failed to complete due to an error connecting to the database.");
        return;
    }
}

/* Assign to an open database connection object */
boolean found = false;
int i = 0;
String val = "";
while (!found) {
    val = (String)db_status.elementAt(i);
    if (val.equals("0")) {
        found = true;
    } else {
        i++;
    }
}
Connection dbCon = (Connection)db_vector.elementAt(i);
db_status.setElementAt("1", i);
```

The addConnection() method simply creates a new connection object, adds it to our vector object, sets the status of the connection in the db_status vector, and increments the limit variable.

```
public boolean addConnection() {
    /* Create another database connection */
    try {
        String dbURL = getInitParameter("dbURL");
        db_v.addElement(DriverManager.getConnection(dbURL));
        db_status.addElement("0"); // "0" - Available Connection
        limit++;
    } catch (Exception e) {
        System.out.println("Database connect failed (addConnection)");
        System.out.println(e.toString());
        return false;
    }
    return true;
}
```

Process Request and Decrement User Count

When we're finished processing the request, we need to decrement the user count and reset the status of the connection so that a future request can reuse it.

```
out.close();

/* Reset user count to free up connection object */
users--;
db_status.setElementAt("0", i);
```

Close all Database Connections

When the servlet is shut down, we need to close all of our open connections with the database. We can cycle through the Vector object by creating an iterator object and casting each of its elements to a connection object. We then call the close() method of each connection object to close the database connection.

```
public void destroy() {

    /* Close database connections */
    try {
       Iterator dbConnIterator = db_vector.iterator();
       while (dbConnIterator.hasNext()) {
          Connection dbCon = (Connection) dbConnIterator.next();
          dbCon.close();
       }
    } catch (Exception e) {
       System.out.println("Error closing database (destroy)");
       System.out.println(e.toString());
    }
}
```

Below is the full source code for the DBPool servlet.

```
//Import Servlet Libraries
import javax.servlet.*;
import javax.servlet.http.*;

//Import Java Libraries
import java.util.*;
import java.sql.*;
import java.io.*;

public class DBPool extends HttpServlet {
    int limit = 2;          //Set initial limit to 2
    int users = 0;          //Track user count with this variable

    Vector db_vector;       //Vector to manage connections
    Vector db_status;       //Vector to keep track of open connections

    public void init() throws ServletException {
       /* Create initial pool of database connections */
       try {
```

Continued on Following Page

```
        db_vector = new Vector();
        db_status = new Vector();
        Class.forName(getInitParameter("JdbcDriver"));
        String dbURL = getInitParameter("dbURL");
        for (int i=0; i<limit; i++) {
            db_vector.addElement(DriverManager.getConnection(dbURL));
            db_status.addElement("0"); // "0" - Available Connection
        }
    } catch (Exception e) {
        System.out.println("Database connect failed (init)");
        System.out.println(e.toString());
        return;
    }
}

public void doGet(HttpServletRequest req, HttpServletResponse res)
    throws ServletException, IOException {
    res.setContentType("text/html");
    PrintWriter out = res.getWriter();

    /* If necessary, add a new connection */
    users++;
    if (users > limit) {
        if(!addConnection()) {
            res.sendError(res.SC_ACCEPTED, "The request has been accepted, but it
                failed to complete due to an error connecting to the database.");
            return;
        }
    }

    /* Assign to an open database connection object */
    boolean found = false;
    int i = 0;
    String val = "";
    while (!found) {
        val = (String)db_status.elementAt(i);
        if (val.equals("0")) {
            found = true;
        } else {
            i++;
        }
    }
Connection dbCon = (Connection)db_vector.elementAt(i);
db_status.setElementAt("1", i);

/* Do some database stuff..... */
String count = "";
try {
    Statement s = dbCon.createStatement();
    ResultSet rs = s.executeQuery("select count(*) from dailySales");
    if (rs.next()) {
        count = rs.getString(1);
        Thread.sleep(500);  // Simulate a pause for testing purposes
    }
} catch (SQLException e) {
    res.sendError(res.SC_ACCEPTED, "The request has been accepted, but it failed
        to complete due to an error updating the database.");
    System.out.println(e.toString());
    return;
} catch (InterruptedException e) {
```

```
        // Necessary for testing purposes (Thread.sleep() method) }

        //Return some results.....

        out.println("<HTML>");
        out.println("<HEAD>");
        out.println("<TITLE>Database Pooling Test Results</TITLE>");
        out.println("<BODY>");
        out.println("Database Operation: Table Count - " + count + " records");
        out.println("<br>User Count: " + String.valueOf(users));
        out.println("<br>Threshhold: " + String.valueOf(limit));
        out.println("</BODY>");
        out.println("</HTML>");

        out.close();

        /* Reset user count to free up connection object */
        users--;
        db_status.setElementAt("0", i);
        }
    }
    public boolean addConnection() {
        /* Create another database connection */
        try {
            String dbURL = getInitParameter("dbURL");
            db_vector.addElement(DriverManager.getConnection(dbURL));
            db_status.addElement("0"); // "0" - Available Connection
            limit++;
        } catch (Exception e) {
            System.out.println("Database connect failed (addConnection)");
            System.out.println(e.toString());
            return false;
        }
        return true;
    }

    public void destroy() {
        /* Close database connections */
        try {
            Iterator dbConnIterator = db_vector.iterator();
            while (dbConnIterator.hasNext()) {
                Connection dbCon = (Connection) dbConnIterator.next();
                dbCon.close();
            }
        } catch (Exception e) {
            System.out.println("Error closing database (destroy)");
            System.out.println(e.toString());
        }
    }
}
```

Summary

As you can see, adding database interactions to your servlets isn't much different from what you're probably used to already with applets and applications. The dynamics of it are a bit different considering the potentially large number of concurrent users of a servlet-based application. Performance becomes an even more important issue than before. Remember that all processing is happening at the server. If you have 100 users trying to run the same servlet at the same time, poor database coding can bring a server to its knees. This is why it's important to explore techniques such as database pooling, `PreparedStatements`, and `CallableStatements`.

In this chapter, we learned the following:

> ➢ When connecting a servlet to a database, the options are pretty much the same as that of an applet or application. JDBC is the most popular and recommended option, while other options exist to access non-relational data sources such as an LDAP server or a set of XML documents.

> ➢ When developing servlets, it is important to consider the type of JDBC driver you will use. Each of the four types has its own unique advantages and pitfalls.

> ➢ If you need to issue the same SQL statement multiple times, consider using a `PreparedStatement` instead of a `Statement` object. A `PreparedStatement` is precompiled and can accept parameters.

> ➢ To increase the performance of your system, consider pooling your database connections during the servlet's initialization and then dynamically assigning open connections to each incoming request as needed.

Connection Pools

A server application, by definition, performs a service for a number of clients. As the number of clients increases, so too does the importance of serving the clients as efficiently as possible.

One powerful technique you can use to efficiently serve client requests is to reuse expensive resources as much as possible. There's always some overhead with creating an object; memory has to be allocated, the object must be initialized, and the JVM must keep track of the object so that it can be garbage collected when it's no longer needed. So in general it's a good idea to minimize the number of objects you create in your server code. But some objects are more expensive to create than others. If you can reuse such an object, instead of creating one for each request and then throwing it away, your server's performance can improve dramatically.

In this chapter we will

> ➢ look at the general benefits of a connection pool,
> ➢ look at the characteristics of an application that can take advantage of a connection pool,
> ➢ implement a classic connection pool,
> ➢ look at how JDBC 2.0 SE specifies connection pools,
> ➢ adapt our pool implementation to behave the same as a JDBC 2.0 SE pool.

Pooling Resources

Reusing a set of objects is often called **object pooling**. In this chapter we will study one example of pooling in detail, namely pooling of database connection objects. In JDBC, a Connection object represents a native database connection. Creating a Connection object is very time consuming since the database engine must allocate communication and memory resources as well as authenticate the user and set up a security context. The exact time varies, of course, but it's not unusual to see connection times of one or two seconds. As you can see, there's lots of time to gain here by sharing a set of already open connections between all clients.

A database connection pool benefits most server applications that access a database, but not all. Use a connection pool if these characteristics describe your application:

> ➢ Users access the database through a limited set of generic database user accounts, as opposed to a specific account per user.

> ➢ A database connection is only used for the duration of a single request, as opposed to the combined duration of multiple requests from the same client.

If the first criterion is not true, a connection pool will not buy you anything because a database connection is associated with one database user account; if each user needs a unique database account there are no connections to share. But since a connection pool can dramatically improve performance, you may want to analyze if your application can be redesigned to use a generic account instead of individual accounts. For instance, if the only way to access the database is through your application you can develop your own access control, using additional Access Control List (ACL) columns on the tables and new tables with user and group data, instead of relying on the database security. Whether this is a good idea or not depends on the specific requirements of your application.

The second criterion is more interesting. For instance, a typical e-commerce application lets users add items to a shopping cart at their leisure while they browse through your site. When they have found what they were looking for they bring the shopping cart to the checkout and pay for the contents. You can design this application in at least two ways:

> ➢ The shopping cart is a database table. When the user enters the site you get a database connection and keep it until the user checks-out or leaves. Each item added to the cart means adding a row to the table. If the user checks-out you commit the database transaction, and if the user leaves without buying you rollback the transaction. This model does not satisfy the criterion above.

> ➢ The shopping cart content is kept in a regular in-memory object associated with the user. In a servlet implementation this object can be kept in the `HttpSession`. Under other server models you could develop your own session object to hold the information - this technique is not exclusive to servlets. Each item added to the cart means adding the item to the in-memory object. If the user checks-out you get a database connection, add all items from the in-memory object as rows in a database table and commit the transaction. If the user leaves without buying you simply drop the in-memory object. This model satisfies the criterion above so you can use a connection pool.

You may argue that a connection pool is useful even with the first approach since you can keep the connection around until the user purchases your wares or leaves, and then return it to the pool where it can be picked up and used for another user. That's true, but if a connection is used for such a long time the pool must contain a lot more connections to handle the same number of users. You will therefore need more resources both in the server process and in the database to maintain all these connections.

Now you have a feeling for what a connection pool is and when you should use it, let's see how we can implement one.

The Classic Connection Pool

There are plenty of connection pool implementations described in other books and available on the net. Most of them implement the same model, the model I call the *classic* connection pool. This model works well so we'll look at it first and then compare it to the model described by the JDBC 2.0 Standard Extension.

With the classic model, an application

> ➢ gets a reference to the pool or an object managing many pools,
> ➢ gets a connection from a pool,
> ➢ uses the connection,
> ➢ returns the connection to the pool.

The application is fully aware that it's using a pooled connection, so it never closes the connection, just hands it back to the pool.

The implementation of the classic model we will describe here consists of a `PoolManager` class that manages multiple instances of a `ConnectionPool` class. Each `ConnectionPool` manages a pool of JDBC `Connection` objects.

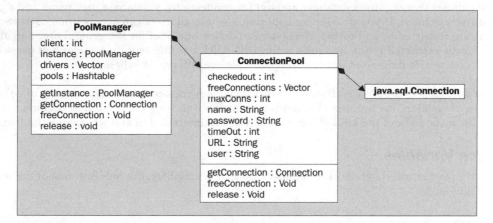

All pool clients interact with the `PoolManager`, and of course with the `Connection` object, but never directly with the `ConnectionPool`. As you can see in the UML diagram above, the `PoolManager` keeps a collection of named `ConnectionPool` objects in a `Hashtable`, each responsible for a unique JDBC URL and database account. The `PoolManager` `getConnection` and `freeConnection` methods both have a pool name attribute used by the `PoolManager` to relay the request to the correct `ConnectionPool` object. We will look at the implementation of this model in detail below.

Let's look at the `ConnectionPool` class first.

The ConnectionPool Class

The `ConnectionPool` provides methods to

- get an open connection from the pool,
- return a connection to the pool,
- release all resources and close all connections at shutdown.

It also handles connection failures, such as time-outs, communication failures, etc. and can create a number of initial connections and limit the number of connections in the pool to a predefined maximum value. We'll see how all of this is done below.

A `ConnectionPool` object has a name used by the clients and represents a pool of connections to one database. The database is identified with a JDBC URL. A JDBC URL consists of three parts: the protocol identifier (always `jdbc`), the driver identifier (e.g. `odbc`, `idb`, `oracle`, etc.) and the database identifier (the format is driver specific). For instance, `jdbc:odbc:demo`, is the JDBC URL for a database named demo accessed through the JDBC-ODBC bridge driver.

For databases that require a database account for connections, a database user name and a password can also be defined. If you develop an application where all users can access some database tables but others are restricted to authorized users, you can define one pool for the general user and another pool for the restricted group using the same JDBC URL but different user names and passwords. You can of course also define separate pools for completely different databases.

Other attributes of a `ConnectionPool` are a maximum connection limit, a number of connections to open at creation, the number of seconds a client can wait for a connection to become available, and information about the kind of log messages you're interested in and where to write them.

Instance Variables

The `ConnectionPool` class has a number of instance variables, but let's just look at the most important ones.

```
private int checkedOut;
private Vector freeConnections = new Vector();
```

The `ConnectionPool` needs to keep the JDBC `Connection` objects that are available for clients somewhere. It keeps them in a `Vector` named `freeConnections`.

It must also keep track of the total number of connections in the pool so it knows when it has reached the maximum connection limit. It uses a simple `int` variable named `checkedOut` for this purpose. The value of `checkedOut` plus the size of the `freeConnections Vector` is the total number of connections in the pool.

Constructor

The `ConnectionPool` constructor takes all the information described above as its parameters.

```
public ConnectionPool(String name, String URL, String user,
    String password, int maxConns, int initConns, int timeOut,
    PrintWriter pw, int logLevel)
    {

    this.name = name;
    this.URL = URL;
    this.user = user;
    this.password = password;
    this.maxConns = maxConns;
    this.timeOut = timeOut > 0 ? timeOut : 5;

    logWriter = new LogWriter(name, logLevel, pw);
    initPool(initConns);

    logWriter.log("New pool created", LogWriter.INFO);
    String lf = System.getProperty("line.separator");
    logWriter.log(lf +
                " url=" + URL + lf +
                " user=" + user + lf +
                " password=" + password + lf +
                " initconns=" + initConns + lf +
                " maxconns=" + maxConns + lf +
                " logintimeout=" + this.timeOut, LogWriter.DEBUG);
    logWriter.log(getStats(), LogWriter.DEBUG);
    }
```

The constructor saves most of the parameter values in instance variables and calls the `initPool()` method to open the specified number of initial connections.

It also creates a `LogWriter` using the `PrintWriter pw` and `int logLevel` parameters. You can read more about the `LogWriter` in Appendix D. Here, the only thing you need to know is that it's a class for writing log messages using a standard format. The constructor uses the `LogWriter` to write a message about the pool being created.

Opening the Initial Connections

The `initPool()` method opens the number of connections specified and adds them to the `freeConnections Vector`. Since `initPool()` is a private method which is called from the `ConnectionPool` constructor, you won't find it on the class diagram above.

```
private void initPool(int initConns)
{
    for (int i = 0; i < initConns; i++)
    {
        try
        {
            Connection pc = newConnection();
            freeConnections.addElement(pc);
        }
        catch (SQLException e)
        { }
    }
}
```

We ignore possible SQLException's here. One reason for a SQLException could be that the database engine is not running yet. We do not want to let that stop us, since by the time a client asks for a connection it may very well be up and running. The only drawback with ignoring the SQLException here then is that we were not able to create the initial connections, so we have to create them as clients ask for them instead. You can of course add a message to the log about the exception instead of just ignoring it, but there's no reason to stop the processing.

In case the SQLException signals a more serious problem, such as not being able to find a JDBC driver for the JDBC URL, we will deal with that later. When a client asks for a connection from the pool we will try to create a connection again, and this time the SQLException will be thrown back to the client.

Get a Connection From the Pool

The ConnectionPool class provides a public getConnection() method for checking out a connection. It does its best to return a Connection by calling an overloaded private method called getConnection() with the specified maximum wait time as a parameter.

The private getConnection() method throws a SQLException if a Connection can not be returned for some reason. In the public getConnection() method the SQLException is first logged and then thrown back to the client.

```java
public Connection getConnection() throws SQLException
{
    logWriter.log("Request for connection received", LogWriter.DEBUG);
    try
    {
        return getConnection(timeOut * 1000);
    }
    catch (SQLException e)
    {
        logWriter.log(e, "Exception getting connection",
                    LogWriter.ERROR);
        throw e;
    }
}
```

The private getConnection() method is more interesting.

```java
private synchronized Connection getConnection(long timeout)
throws SQLException
{

    // Get a pooled Connection from the cache or a new one.
    // Wait if all are checked out and the max limit has
    // been reached.
    long startTime = System.currentTimeMillis();
    long remaining = timeout;
    Connection conn = null;
    while ((conn = getPooledConnection()) == null)
    {
        try
        {
            logWriter.log("Waiting for connection. Timeout=" + remaining,
                        LogWriter.DEBUG);
            wait(remaining);
        }
```

```
        catch (InterruptedException e)
        { }
        remaining = timeout - (System.currentTimeMillis() - startTime);
        if (remaining <= 0)
        {
            // Timeout has expired
            logWriter.log("Time-out while waiting for connection",
                        LogWriter.DEBUG);
            throw new SQLException("getConnection() timed-out");
        }
    }

    // Check if the Connection is still OK
    if (!isConnectionOK(conn))
    {
        // It was bad. Try again with the remaining timeout
        logWriter.log("Removed selected bad connection from pool",
                    LogWriter.ERROR);
        return getConnection(remaining);
    }
    checkedOut++;
    logWriter.log("Delivered connection from pool", LogWriter.INFO);
    logWriter.log(getStats(), LogWriter.DEBUG);
    return conn;
}
```

In this method we return a `Connection` from the pool if one is available, or else create a new one if the maximum number of connections has not been reached yet. This is done by the call to the private `getPooledConnection()` method.

If no `Connection` is available and we have reached the limit, we wait for a `Connection` to be returned to the pool by another client running in a different thread. Books can be written about multi-threaded programming in Java. In fact, books *have* been written about multi-threaded programming in Java, so don't expect a detailed description about this intriguing subject here. It's sufficient to know that a call to the `wait` method blocks until one of two things happens:

> ➢   the specified time runs out,
>
> ➢   some other thread calls the `notify` or `notifyAll` method on the object we're waiting for, triggering an `InterruptedException`.

So when we return from the `wait` method we need to find out why the wait is over. First we check to see if the wait time has expired, and if so we throw a `SQLException` signaling a time-out and we are done.

Otherwise we must have returned from `wait` because another thread triggered the `InterruptedException`. As you will see later, this happens when a `Connection` is returned to the pool. So we go through the loop again and try to get a `Connection`. We may still not be successful, because there may have been other threads waiting for a `Connection` besides us and one of them may have snatched the returned `Connection` before we got a chance. So we wait in line again.

Eventually we get our `Connection`, unless we time-out, and need to check if it's still okay before we return it to the client. If it isn't, we call this method again recursively with the remaining wait time. But if the `Connection` is okay, we increment the number of checked out connections and return the `Connection` to the client.

I skipped a couple of details above: how do we determine that the `Connection` is okay, and how do we get a pooled `Connection`?

The `isConnectionOK()` method takes care of the first question.

```
private boolean isConnectionOK(Connection conn)
{
    Statement testStmt = null;
    try
    {
        if (!conn.isClosed())
        {
            // Try to createStatement to see if it's really alive
            testStmt = conn.createStatement();
            testStmt.close();
        }
        else
        {
            return false;
        }
    }
    catch (SQLException e)
    {
        if (testStmt != null)
        {
            try
            {
                testStmt.close();
            }
            catch (SQLException se)
            { }
        }
        logWriter.log(e, "Pooled Connection was not okay",
                         LogWriter.ERROR);
        return false;
    }
    return true;
}
```

The JDBC API specifies a `boolean Connection.isClosed()` method but it doesn't guarantee that a `true` result means everything is okay. It only means that the JDBC driver *believes* the connection is still open. If the connection has been closed from the database server end, for instance due to inactivity, the JDBC driver may not be aware of this and still return `true`.

Even so, we first use `isClosed()` to ask the driver if the connection is closed. If it is we know we can not use the `Connection` object and therefore return `false`.

But if `isClosed()` returns `false` we must still use an additional test to ensure the connection is really okay. One sure way to force the driver to talk to the database engine is to create a `Statement` object for the `Connection`. If it works we know the connection is fine and return `true`. If either the `isClosed()` or `createStatement()` methods throw a `SQLException`, we return `false`.

> Note that no matter what happens we must close the test statement if we get as far as creating it. The database allocates resources (often called cursors) for each statement; if we don't close the statement after this test we will eventually reach the upper resource limit and the database engine will refuse to create new statements.

The final piece of the puzzle is handled by two private methods: `getPooledConnection()` and `newConnection()`.

```
private Connection getPooledConnection() throws SQLException
{
    Connection conn = null;
    if (freeConnections.size() > 0)
    {
        // Pick the first Connection in the Vector
        // to get round-robin usage
        conn = (Connection) freeConnections.firstElement();
        freeConnections.removeElementAt(0);
    }
    else if (maxConns == 0 || checkedOut < maxConns)
    {
        conn = newConnection();
    }
    return conn;
}
```

The `getPooledConnection()` method is easy: if there's a `Connection` available, return it, otherwise call `newConnection()` to open a new `Connection` unless we have reached the maximum number of connections for the pool. The only thing to note here is that a `maxConns` value of zero represents a pool without an upper limit. It's usually a good idea to specify a limit even though your database may not have a hard limit on the number of open connections. Letting clients wait for a connection now and then may turn out to be more efficient than letting the server and database deal with a large number of connections.

The `newConnection()` method uses one of two flavors of the JDBC `DriverManager.getConnection()` method depending on whether a user name and password is defined for the pool or not.

```
private Connection newConnection() throws SQLException
{
    Connection conn = null;
    if (user == null) {
        conn = DriverManager.getConnection(URL);
    }
    else {
        conn = DriverManager.getConnection(URL, user, password);
    }
    logWriter.log("Opened a new connection", LogWriter.INFO);
    return conn;
}
```

That's it! We have implemented the hardest part of the connection pool, handling all the requirements for maximum connection limits and for letting multiple threads wait until a `Connection` is available.

Return a Connection to the Pool

Okay, so now we can deliver a `Connection` to a client who asks for it. But in order for a `Connection` to be reused we must also provide a way for the client to return the `Connection` to the pool when it's done. The `ConnectionPool` has a `freeConnection()` method for this purpose.

```
public synchronized void freeConnection(Connection conn)
{
   // Put the connection at the end of the Vector
   freeConnections.addElement(conn);
   checkedOut--;
   notifyAll();
   logWriter.log("Returned connection to pool", LogWriter.INFO);
   logWriter.log(getStats(), LogWriter.DEBUG);
}
```

This method adds the returned `Connection` to the end of the `freeConnections` `Vector` and decrements the number of checked out connections. As you may have noticed above, the `getPooledConnection()` method picks up `Connections` from the beginning of the `Vector`. Adding them to the end when they are returned ensures that all connections are being circulated and minimizes the risk of database time-outs.

`freeConnection()` also calls `notifyAll()` to alert other threads that may be waiting for a connection. This is what triggers the `InterruptedException` in the private `getConnection()` method we discussed earlier.

One addition you may want to do to this method is resetting the connection to its initial state. The `Connection` provides methods for setting properties like auto-commit, transaction isolation mode, etc. If the pool clients in your application modify these attributes you can reset them to their default values when the `Connection` is returned to the pool to ensure the next client gets the `Connection` in the default state.

Graceful Shutdown

Finally our `ConnectionPool` provides a method for gracefully releasing all pool resources. The `release()` method is called by the `PoolManager` when the last client announces that it's no longer interested in connection pool services, as you will see in the next section.

```
public synchronized void release()
{
   Enumeration allConnections = freeConnections.elements();
   while (allConnections.hasMoreElements())
   {
      Connection con = (Connection) allConnections.nextElement();
      try
      {
         con.close();
         logWriter.log("Closed connection", LogWriter.INFO);
      }
      catch (SQLException e)
      {
         logWriter.log(e, "Couldn't close connection", LogWriter.ERROR);
      }
   }
   freeConnections.removeAllElements();
}
```

The `release` method loops through the `freeConnections Vector` and calls the `close()` method on each `Connection`. When all `Connection` objects have been closed they are removed from the `Vector`.

The PoolManager Class

In the previous section we looked at the implementation of the `ConnectionPool` class. One `ConnectionPool` instance handles a pool of `Connection` objects for access to a database engine using the same JDBC URL and, optionally, database user account.

The `PoolManager` that we will implement next lets us use multiple connection pools. It provides the interface used by the client applications, and

> ➤ loads and registers all JDBC drivers,
> ➤ creates `ConnectionPool` objects based on properties defined in a properties file,
> ➤ maps connection pool names to `ConnectionPool` objects,
> ➤ relays client requests to a specific, named `ConnectionPool`,
> ➤ keeps track of connection pool clients to shut down all pools gracefully when the last client is done.

The `PoolManager` class is implemented according to the `Singleton` pattern described in many design books, such as *Design Patterns* by Erich Gamma, Richard Helm, Ralph Johnson and John Vlissides (Addison Wesley, 1995, ISBN 0-201-63361-2). A `Singleton` is a class with just one instance. Client objects get a reference to the single instance through a static method. In our case, the clients then ask for connections and return connections for any one of the `ConnectionPool` instances through the reference to the single `PoolManager` instance.

The `Singleton` pattern ensures there's only one instance of the class and it also makes it easy for clients of all kinds to get a reference to this single instance. If all clients are servlets within the same servlet context, you can let one of them create the instance and use a context attribute to provide access to the instance reference instead. This is mostly a matter of taste.

Pool properties

The `PoolManager` gets information about the JDBC drivers to use and the pools to create from a property file named `db.properties`. This file must be located in the CLASSPATH for the server process, as you will see below.

The `db.properties` file is a file in the Java Properties format containing key-value pairs that define the connection pools as well as properties shared by all pools. The following shared properties can be defined:

drivers	A space separated list of JDBC driver class names
logfile	The absolute path for a log file

Another set of properties is used to define each pool. The property name starts with the name of the corresponding connection pool:

`<poolname>.url`	The JDBC URL for the database
`<poolname>.user`	The database account user name for the pool
`<poolname>.password`	The password for the database account
`<poolname>.maxconns`	The maximum number of connections in the pool. 0 means no limit.
`<poolname>.initconns`	The number of initial connections to open for the pool.
`<poolname>.logintimeout`	The number of seconds to wait for a connection if none is available and the maximum limit is reached.
`<poolname>.loglevel`	The amount of information to log: none, error, info or debug

The `url` property is mandatory but all the others are optional. The user name and the matching password must be valid for the database defined by the URL.

Below is an example of a `db.properties` file for a Windows platform, with one pool for an InstantDB database and one pool for a database accessed through an ODBC Data Source Name (DSN) "demo".

```
drivers=sun.jdbc.odbc.JdbcOdbcDriver jdbc.idbDriver
logfile=D:/user/src/java/DBConnectionManager/log.txt

idb.url=jdbc:idb:c:/local/javawebserver1.1/db/db.prp
idb.maxconns=2
idb.loglevel=info

access.url=jdbc:odbc:demo
access.user=demo
access.password=demopw
access.initconns=5
access.maxconns=10
```

Note that the backslashes (\) in a Windows path would have to be written "\\", since a backslash in a properties file is also used as an escape character. In Java properties, you can use forward slashes instead, even on a Windows platform, as shown.

Instance Variables

Let's start by looking at how the `PoolManager` keeps track of things.

```
static private PoolManager instance;
static private int clients;
```

The `PoolManager` has two static (class) variables. The `instance` variable is used to hold the reference to the single instance of the class.

The `clients` variable is used to keep track of how many clients use the pools. By incrementing this variable every time a client calls `getInstance()` and decrementing it when they call `release()`, we know when no clients are interested in the pool resources so we can shut down all `ConnectionPool` objects gracefully. This is of course just one possible implementation. An alternative implementation could allow individual pools to be created and released dynamically. All you'd have to do is add a few methods to the `PoolManager`; the `ConnectionPool` implementation stays the same.

```
private Vector drivers = new Vector();
private Hashtable pools = new Hashtable();
```

The `drivers` and `pools` instance variables are used to keep track of the JDBC drivers and the `ConnectionPool` instances. Using a `Hashtable` for `pools` lets us access a pool by its name.

Constructor and getInstance()

The `PoolManager` constructor is private to prevent other objects from creating instances of the class.

```
private PoolManager()
{
    init();
}
```

Clients of the `PoolManager` call the static `getInstance()` method to get a reference to the single instance.

```
static synchronized public PoolManager getInstance()
{
    if (instance == null)
    {
        instance = new PoolManager();
    }
    clients++;
    return instance;
}
```

The single instance is created the first time this method is called and a reference is then kept in the static variable named `instance`. A counter for the number of `PoolManager` clients is incremented before the reference is returned. This counter is later used to coordinate the shutdown of the pools.

Initialization

The constructor calls a private method named `init()` to initialize the object.

```
private void init()
{
    // Log to System.err until we have read the logfile property
    pw = new PrintWriter(System.err, true);
    logWriter = new LogWriter("PoolManager", LogWriter.INFO, pw);
    InputStream is = getClass().getResourceAsStream("/db.properties");
    Properties dbProps = new Properties();
```

Continued on Following Page

```
    try
    {
        dbProps.load(is);
    }
    catch (Exception e)
    {
        logWriter.log("Can't read the properties file. " +
            "Make sure db.properties is in the CLASSPATH",
            LogWriter.ERROR);
        return;
    }
    String logFile = dbProps.getProperty("logfile");
    if (logFile != null)
    {
        try
        {
            pw = new PrintWriter(new FileWriter(logFile, true), true);
            logWriter.setPrintWriter(pw);
        }
        catch (IOException e)
        {
            logWriter.log("Can't open the log file: " + logFile +
                ". Using System.err instead", LogWriter.ERROR);
        }
    }
    loadDrivers(dbProps);
    createPools(dbProps);
}
```

The first thing we do is to set up a `LogWriter` that writes to `System.err` in case we run into trouble before we know if there's a log file specified.

Then we try to locate and read the `db.properties` file. The `getResourceAsStream()` method is a standard JDK method for locating an external file and opening it for input. How the file is located depends on the class loader but the standard class loader for local classes searches for the file in the CLASSPATH, starting in the directory where the class file is located. The `getResourceAsStream()` method is implemented by the class loader, but the `Class` class provides a relay method with the same name. We use `getClass()` to get a reference to the `Class` for this object. Next we create a `Properties` object, load the `db.properties` file and look for the `logfile` property. If a log file has been specified we try to use it with our `LogWriter`. If that fails, or a log file is not specified, we continue to write log messages to `System.err`.

The `loadDrivers()` method loads and registers all JDBC drivers specified by the `drivers` property.

```
private void loadDrivers(Properties props)
{
    String driverClasses = props.getProperty("drivers");
    StringTokenizer st = new StringTokenizer(driverClasses);
    while (st.hasMoreElements())
    {
        String driverClassName = st.nextToken().trim();
        try
        {
            Driver driver = (Driver)
                Class.forName(driverClassName).newInstance();
            DriverManager.registerDriver(driver);
```

```
        drivers.addElement(driver);
        logWriter.log("Registered JDBC driver " + driverClassName,
            LogWriter.INFO);
    }
    catch (Exception e)
    {
        logWriter.log(e, "Can't register JDBC driver: " +
            driverClassName, LogWriter.ERROR);
    }
  }
}
```

`loadDrivers()` uses a `StringTokenizer` to split the `drivers` property value into a `String` for each driver class name and then loops through all class names. It loads each class into the JVM, creates an instance, registers the instance with the JDBC `DriverManager` and adds it to the `drivers` Vector. The `drivers` `Vector` is used at shutdown to deregister all drivers from the `DriverManager`.

> *Explicit registration of a JDBC driver with the DriverManager is not really necessary since a compliant driver should register itself when it's instantiated. But some early JDBC 1.0 driver implementations are known to misbehave, so we do it anyway as a precaution.*

Next the `ConnectionPool` objects are created by the private `createPools()` method.

```
private void createPools(Properties props)
{
   Enumeration propNames = props.propertyNames();
   while (propNames.hasMoreElements())
   {
      String name = (String) propNames.nextElement();
      if (name.endsWith(".url"))
      {
         String poolName = name.substring(0, name.lastIndexOf("."));
         String url = props.getProperty(poolName + ".url");
         if (url == null)
         {
            logWriter.log("No URL specified for " + poolName,
               LogWriter.ERROR);
            continue;
         }
```

We create an `Enumeration` of all property names and look for property names ending with `.url`. When we find such a property, we extract the pool name and read the first property for the corresponding connection pool (the `url` property itself). Then we do the same for all the other properties.

```
        String user = props.getProperty(poolName + ".user");
        String password = props.getProperty(poolName + ".password");

        String maxConns = props.getProperty(poolName +
            ".maxconns", "0");
        int max;
        try
        {
```

Continued on Following Page

```
      max = Integer.valueOf(maxConns).intValue();
   }
   catch (NumberFormatException e)
   {
      logWriter.log("Invalid maxconns value " + maxConns +
                    " for " + poolName, LogWriter.ERROR);
      max = 0;
   }

   String initConns = props.getProperty(poolName +
                    ".initconns", "0");
   int init;
   try
   {
      init = Integer.valueOf(initConns).intValue();
   }
   catch (NumberFormatException e)
   {
      logWriter.log("Invalid initconns value " + initConns +
                    " for " + poolName, LogWriter.ERROR);
      init = 0;
   }

   String loginTimeOut = props.getProperty(poolName +
      ".logintimeout", "5");
   int timeOut;
   try
   {
      timeOut = Integer.valueOf(loginTimeOut).intValue();
   }
   catch (NumberFormatException e)
   {
      logWriter.log("Invalid logintimeout value " + loginTimeOut +
                    " for " + poolName, LogWriter.ERROR);
      timeOut = 5;
   }

   String logLevelProp = props.getProperty(poolName +
                    ".loglevel", String.valueOf(LogWriter.ERROR));
   int logLevel = LogWriter.INFO;
   if (logLevelProp.equalsIgnoreCase("none"))
   {
      logLevel = LogWriter.NONE;
   }
   else if (logLevelProp.equalsIgnoreCase("error"))
   {
      logLevel = LogWriter.ERROR;
   }
   else if (logLevelProp.equalsIgnoreCase("debug"))
   {
      logLevel = LogWriter.DEBUG;
   }
```

If a numeric property value is not a string representing a number we log an error message and use the default value instead, and we also parse the strings "none", "error", and "debug" into the relevant constants defined by LogWriter.

```
        ConnectionPool pool =
                    new ConnectionPool(poolName, url, user, password,
                                   max, init, timeOut, pw, logLevel);
        pools.put(poolName, pool);
      }
    }
  }
```

After verifying the property values we create a `ConnectionPool` object and add it to the `pools` `Hashtable`, using the pool name as the key and the `ConnectionPool` object as the value.

Get and Return a Connection

Clients use the `PoolManager` methods `getConnection()` and `freeConnection()`. Both methods take the pool name as a parameter and relay the call to the corresponding `ConnectionPool` object.

```
public Connection getConnection(String name)
{
    Connection conn = null;
    ConnectionPool pool = (ConnectionPool) pools.get(name);
    if (pool != null)
    {
        try
        {
            conn = pool.getConnection();
        }
        catch (SQLException e) {
            logWriter.log(e, "Exception getting connection from " +
                name, LogWriter.ERROR);
        }
    }
    return conn;
}

public void freeConnection(String name, Connection con)
{
    ConnectionPool pool = (ConnectionPool) pools.get(name);
    if (pool != null)
    {
        pool.freeConnection(con);
    }
}
```

Graceful Shutdown

Finally, the `PoolManager` has a method named `release()`. This method is used for graceful shutdown of the connection pools. Each `PoolManager` client calls the static `getInstance()` method to get a reference to the manager. As we discussed above, a client counter variable is used in this method to keep track of the number of clients. Each client must also call the `release()` method during server shutdown so that the client counter can be decremented. When the last client calls `release()`, the `PoolManager` calls `release()` on all `ConnectionPool` objects to close all connections.

```
public synchronized void release()
{
    // Wait until called by the last client
    if (--clients != 0)
    {
        return;
    }

    Enumeration allPools = pools.elements();
    while (allPools.hasMoreElements())
    {
        ConnectionPool pool = (ConnectionPool) allPools.nextElement();
        pool.release();
    }

    Enumeration allDrivers = drivers.elements();
    while (allDrivers.hasMoreElements())
    {
        Driver driver = (Driver) allDrivers.nextElement();
        try
        {
            DriverManager.deregisterDriver(driver);
            logWriter.log("Deregistered JDBC driver " +
                        driver.getClass().getName(), LogWriter.INFO);
        }
        catch (SQLException e)
        {
            logWriter.log(e, "Couldn't deregister JDBC driver: " +
                        driver.getClass().getName(), LogWriter.ERROR);
        }
    }
}
```

When all `ConnectionPool` objects have been released, all JDBC drivers are deregistered.

Example Client

The `PoolManager` and `ConnectionPool` classes described above can be used with any type of application that needs a connection pool. The source code available from the Wrox Press website (http://www.wrox.com) includes a stand-alone test client, `com.wrox.connectionpool.Test`, which can be used to test the functionality of the `ConnectionPool` and `PoolManager` classes, along with the source code for the `PoolManager` and `ConnectionPool` classes. But since a Java servlet is probably the most likely type of client, we'll look at a servlet example here.

A servlet using the connection pool typically performs the following actions in its life cycle methods:

➢ In `init()` it calls `PoolManager.getInstance()` and saves the reference in an instance variable.

➢ In `service()` (or in the extended `doXxx()` service method for an `HttpServlet`) it calls `PoolManager.getConnection()`, performs all database operations, and returns the `Connection` to the pool with `freeConnection()`.

➢ In `destroy()` it calls `PoolManager.release()` to release all resources and close all connections.

Here's an example of a simple servlet using the connection pool this way.

```java
import java.io.*;
import java.sql.*;
import javax.servlet.*;
import javax.servlet.http.*;
import com.wrox.connectionpool.*;

public class PoolTestServlet extends HttpServlet
{
    private PoolManager poolMgr;

    public void init() throws ServletException
    {
        poolMgr = PoolManager.getInstance();
    }
}
```

We get a reference to the `PoolManager` and save it as an instance variable in the `init()` method, in other words when the servlet is loaded.

```java
    public void doGet(HttpServletRequest req, HttpServletResponse res)
                    throws IOException, ServletException
    {

        res.setContentType("text/html");
        PrintWriter out = res.getWriter();
        Connection conn = poolMgr.getConnection("idb");
        if (conn == null)
        {
            out.println("Can't get connection");
            return;
        }
        ResultSet rs = null;
        ResultSetMetaData md = null;
        Statement stmt = null;
        try
        {
            stmt = conn.createStatement();
            rs = stmt.executeQuery("SELECT * FROM EMPLOYEE");
            md = rs.getMetaData();
            out.println("<H1>Employee data</H1>");
            while (rs.next())
            {
                out.println("<BR>");
                for (int i = 1; i < md.getColumnCount(); i++)
                {
                    out.print(rs.getString(i) + ", ");
                }
            }
            stmt.close();
            rs.close();
        }
        catch (SQLException e)
        {
            e.printStackTrace(out);
        }
        finally
        {
            poolMgr.freeConnection("idb", conn);
        }
    }
```

In the `doGet()` method we ask for a `Connection` from the pool, execute a SQL statement and return the `Connection` to the pool again. Note that we call `freeConnection()` in the `finally` clause. This way we are sure the `Connection` is returned to the pool even if an exception is thrown.

```
public void destroy()
{
    poolMgr.release();
    super.destroy();
}
}
```

Finally we call `release()` in the destroy method, telling the `PoolManager` we're no longer using the pool.

JDBC 2.0 Standard Extension Connection Pool

Together with the enhancements of the Core API in JDBC 2.0, a JDBC 2.0 Standard Extension (SE) API specification was released December 7, 1998. This set of APIs defines a number of additional concepts to make it easier for applications to use databases through JDBC.

At the time of writing this chapter, all major JDBC vendors have announced support for JDBC 2.0 but very few have actually released JDBC 2.0 compliant drivers, and even fewer offer implementations of the JDBC 2.0 SE. One exception is a company called Imaginary (http://www.imaginary.com/Java/). They offer both JDBC 2.0 Core and Standard Extension implementations for the mSQL database. Most likely more vendors will support JDBC 2.0 soon, including the Standard Extension, due to it's importance as part of the Java 2 Enterprise Edition (J2EE) announced at JavaOne '99 in June 1999.

Even though support is not there yet, the concepts defined by JDBC 2.0 SE are interesting. There will be more implementations available soon, so you may want to develop your application based on the JDBC 2.0 SE model now to take advantage of the driver vendors' implementations later.

In this section we will therefore take a look at the JDBC 2.0 SE concepts that are related to connection pooling. I recommend that you take a look at the other parts of the specification yourself, since many concepts can simplify other aspects of your application. The complete specification is available for download at http://java.sun.com/products/jdbc/.

In the last section of this chapter we will revisit the implementation of our classic connection pool and make a few minor adjustments to make it behave more like a JDBC 2.0 SE connection pool.

Main Concepts

JDBC 2.0 SE addresses a couple of concerns in a typical JDBC application:

> ➢ An application is often tied to a particular vendor's JDBC product and sometimes to the particular server name and port number where the database engine is running, as a consequence of code like this:

```
Class.forName("SomeJDBCDriverClassName");
Connection con =
DriverManager.getConnection("jdbc:vendorX_subprotocol:machineY:portZ");
```

> ➤ There's no standard API for accessing a connection pool, making it hard for JDBC driver vendors to support this feature in a portable way.

To resolve these issues JDBC 2.0 SE defines a number of new interfaces representing more abstract concepts than those provided by the Core API. This elegant design allows a greater flexibility, and means that the application no longer needs to be aware that it's using a connection pool; the application will work the same with both regular connections and pooled connections. Whether to use a pool or not becomes a simple configuration decision.

Let's take a look at the new interfaces:

> ➤ `javax.sql.DataSource`
> A `DataSource` object represents a database and creates connections for that database. Information needed to create the connections such as the database name, server name, port, user, password, etc. are represented as properties of the `DataSource` object. The properties are accessed through methods following the design pattern specified for JavaBeans.

> ➤ `javax.sql.ConnectionPoolDataSource`
> A `ConnectionPoolDataSource` object has a role very similar to the plain `DataSource` object. The only difference is that it creates `PooledConnection` objects instead of the regular `Connection` objects created by a `DataSource` object.

> ➤ `javax.sql.PooledConnection`
> A `PooledConnection` is associated with a regular `Connection` object. It provides access to the `Connection` through a simple wrapper that relays most of the methods to the `Connection` but overrides the `close` method so that instead of closing the `Connection` it's returned to the pool.

The `DataSource` objects are registered with a directory service accessed through the Java Naming and Directory Interface (JNDI) API, which is discussed in Chapter 21. An application can get hold of a `DataSource` reference and a regular `Connection` like this:

```
Context ctx = new InitialContext();
DataSource ds = (DataSource) ctx.lookup("jdbc/EmployeeDB");
Connection con = ds.getConnection();
```

When the application is done with the `Connection`, it closes it.

```
con.close();
```

`ConnectionPoolDataSource` objects are also registered and accessed through JNDI, but the methods in this interface are never used directly by an application. They are used by a `DataSource` object that provides pooling of `PooledConnection` objects, and we will look at this in more detail later. What's interesting here is how the application gets hold of a `Connection` from the pool, uses it and returns it.

```
Context ctx = new InitialContext();
DataSource ds = (DataSource) ctx.lookup("jdbc/EmployeeDB");
Connection con = ds.getConnection();
// Use the connection
con.close();
```

See, it's identical to how an application works with non-pooled connections! Next we'll take a look at how the `DataSource`, the `ConnectionPoolDataSource` and the `PooledConnection` cooperate to create this magic.

A DataSource With a Connection Pool

The JDBC 2.0 SE specification suggests that `ConnectionPoolDataSource` and `PooledConnection` implementations are to be provided by the JDBC driver vendors, and that middleware vendors will provide `DataSource` implementations that use the former implementations to deliver connection pool functionality. That's the model we will look at here, but note that there's nothing that stops a JDBC driver vendor from combining the roles of the `ConnectionPoolDataSource` and the `DataSource` and publish their own pool implementations.

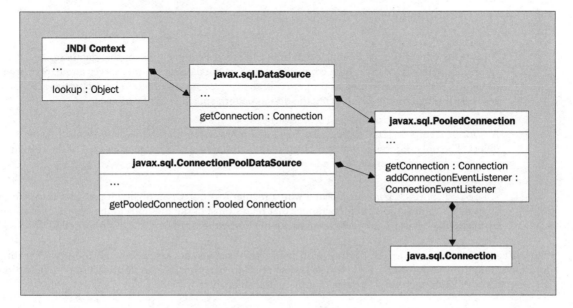

As we saw above, the `DataSource` interface contains a `getConnection()` method used by the application to get a `Connection` object. A `DataSource` that provides pooling capabilities can use an implementation of this method that's very similar to our implementation of the `getConnection()` method in the `ConnectionPool` class. To recap, our implementation

> ➢ returns an existing `Connection` if one is available,
> ➢ or creates a new `Connection` if the max number of connections has not been reached yet,
> ➢ or else it waits for a `Connection` to be returned to the pool by another client.

The only differences between our `ConnectionPool` class and the `DataSource` with pooling capabilities are:

> ➢ The `DataSource` pool contains `PooledConnection` objects instead of `Connection` objects.
> ➢ The `client` gets new `PooledConnection` objects from a `ConnectionPoolDataSource`, instead of `Connection` objects from the `DriverManager`.

The `getConnection` method must return a `Connection` object, not a `PooledConnection`, so the `DataSource` retrieves the `Connection` wrapper we talked about above from its `PooledConnection` and returns it to the client.

```
        return pc.getConnection();
```

When the `DataSource` needs a new `PooledConnection`, it gets one from the `ConnectionPoolDataSource`.

```
    Context ctx = new InitialContext();
    ConnectionPoolDataSource cpds =
        (ConnectionPoolDataSource) ctx.lookup("jdbc/EmployeeDB");
    PooledConnection pc = cpds.getPooledConnection();
    pc.addConnectionEventListener(this);
```

Note that the `DataSource` registers itself as an event listener for the new `PooledConnection` through the `addConnectionEventListener()` method. This way, it will be informed about what happens to the `Connection` wrapper. As a result, when the application calls `close()` on the `Connection` wrapper, the `PooledConnection` notifies the `DataSource` by calling its `connectionClosed()` event method. The `DataSource` can then put the `PooledConnection` back in the pool.

```
    public void connectionClosed(ConnectionEvent event)
    {
        PooledConnection pc = (PooledConnection) event.getSource();
        freeConnections.addElement(pc);
    }
```

Modifying Our Pool to Resemble JDBC 2.0 SE

Let's look at how we can modify our classic pool implementation so it resembles the model described by JDBC 2.0 SE.

First of all, our `PoolManager` already fills the role of JNDI when it comes to decoupling the application from the JDBC driver class name and URL so we will continue to use it as is. If you would rather follow the JDBC 2.0 SE model strictly, you can of course develop a solution where you create `ConnectionPool` objects and register them with a JNDI `directory` object. The application would then use the `Context.lookup` method to locate a `ConnectionPool` exactly as shown above.

The ConnectionWrapper Class

To be able to return a `Connection` to the pool when the application calls `close` instead of `freeConnection` we need to implement a `Connection` wrapper. That's easy.

```
    class ConnectionWrapper implements Connection
    {
        private Connection realConn;
        private ConnectionPool pool;
        private boolean isClosed = false;

        public ConnectionWrapper(Connection realConn, ConnectionPool pool)
        {
```

Continued on Following Page

```
      this.realConn = realConn;
      this.pool = pool;
   }

   public void close() throws SQLException
   {
      isClosed = true;
      pool.wrapperClosed(realConn);
   }

   public boolean isClosed() throws SQLException
   {
      return isClosed;
   }
}
```

The constructor gets a reference to the real `Connection` object and saves in an instance variable named `realConn`. It also gets a reference to the `ConnectionPool` that it saves in the pool variable.

The wrapper overrides the `close()` method to inform the `ConnectionPool` that the wrapper is closed, and the `isClosed()` method to use the wrapper's state instead of the real `Connection`'s state.

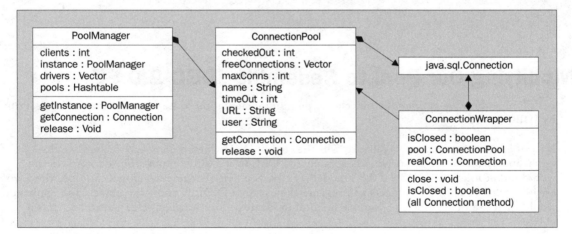

All other methods are just relayed to the real `Connection`, like so:

```
public void clearWarnings() throws SQLException
{
   if (isClosed)
   {
      throw new SQLException("Pooled connection is closed");
   }
   realConn.clearWarnings();
}
```

The complete source code available for this class on the Wrox Press web site includes relay implementations for all the other methods as well.

ConnectionPool Modifications

There's just one method we need to modify in the `ConnectionPool` class, plus one method to replace. We modify the public `getConnection()` method like this:

```
public Connection getConnection() throws SQLException {
    logWriter.log("Request for connection received", LogWriter.DEBUG);
    try
    {
        Connection conn = getConnection(timeOut * 1000);
        return new ConnectionWrapper(conn, this);
    }
    catch (SQLException e)
    {
        logWriter.log(e, "Exception getting connection",
            logWriter.ERROR);
        throw e;
    }
}
```

Instead of returning the pooled `Connection` we create a `ConnectionWrapper` that we return to the client application.

Then we replace the `freeConnection()` method with this `wrapperClosed()` method.

```
synchronized void wrapperClosed(Connection conn)
    {
    // Put the connection at the end of the Vector
    freeConnections.addElement(conn);
    checkedOut--;
    notifyAll();
    logWriter.log("Returned connection to pool", LogWriter.INFO);
    logWriter.log(getStats(), LogWriter.DEBUG);
    }
```

That's all we need to do. When the application calls `close()` on our `ConnectionWrapper` it calls `wrapperClosed()`, passing along the real `Connection` object as a parameter. We just put the `Connection` back in the pool, decrement the checked-out counter and notify possible waiting threads as before.

With these minor changes, applications can now use our pool the same way as they would use a JDBC 2.0 SE pool implementation. The only exception is that we use the `PoolManager.getConnection()` method instead of the JNDI `Context.lookup()` and `DataSource.getConnection()` methods to get a `Connection`.

The day you want to start using a connection pool from a vendor that follows the JDBC 2.0 SE specification you can modify the `PoolManager.getConnection()` method to use JNDI to locate the pool. Or, you can register your `ConnectionPool` objects with JNDI and let the applications use the `Context.lookup()` method from scratch as described above, so no changes are needed when you want to switch to a third party implementation.

Example Client

We will end this chapter with an example of how to use the modified pool implementation, using a similar sample servlet to the one we used earlier.

```java
import java.io.*;
import java.sql.*;
import javax.servlet.*;
import javax.servlet.http.*;
import com.wrox.pssjp.jdbc.pool1.*;

public class Pool2TestServlet extends HttpServlet
{
    private PoolManager poolMgr;

    public void init() throws ServletException
    {
        poolMgr = PoolManager.getInstance();
    }
```

We save a reference to the `PoolManager` in the `init()` method just as before.

```java
    public void service(HttpServletRequest req, HttpServletResponse res)
        throws IOException
    {

        res.setContentType("text/html");
        PrintWriter out = res.getWriter();
        Connection conn = poolMgr.getConnection("idb");
        if (conn == null)
        {
            out.println("Can't get connection");
            return;
        }
        ResultSet rs = null;
        ResultSetMetaData md = null;
        Statement stmt = null;
        try
        {
            stmt = conn.createStatement();
            rs = stmt.executeQuery("SELECT * FROM EMPLOYEE");
            md = rs.getMetaData();
            out.println("<H1>Employee data</H1>");
            while (rs.next())
            {
                out.println("<BR>");
                for (int i = 1; i < md.getColumnCount(); i++)
                {
                    out.print(rs.getString(i) + ", ");
                }
            }
            stmt.close();
            rs.close();
            conn.close();
        }
        catch (SQLException e)
        {
            e.printStackTrace(out);
        }
    }
```

We get a `Connection` from the `PoolManager`, the same as in the classic model. The only difference is that we no longer call `freeConnection()`; `close()` returns the `Connection` to the pool automatically.

```
public void destroy()
{
    poolMgr.release();
    super.destroy();
}
}
```

Finally, we call release in the `destroy()` method as we did in the classic model to tell the `PoolManager` we're done.

Summary

In this chapter we have studied connection pool implementations. More precisely, we have

> looked at the general benefits of a connection pool
> discussed the characteristics of an application that can take advantage of a connection pool
> implemented a classic connection pool
> looked at how JDBC 2.0 SE specifies connection pools
> adapted our classic pool implementation to behave the same way as a JDBC 2.0 SE pool

Servlet Chaining

Servlet chaining provides a way for us to specialize our servlets so that each one performs a singular task. When a single request is handled by a series of specialized servlets, the output of one servlet is the input to the next servlet in the chain. This way, each servlet can perform its task on the request object and pass it on for further processing. Eventually, the last servlet in the chain returns the final response to the browser. For those of you from the Unix world, this should resemble piping the output of one command to another.

There are two common methods for chaining the output of one servlet to another servlet. The first one that we will discuss is aliasing. This is done by describing a series of servlets to be executed when a specific name is called upon. The second method for chaining servlets is to define a new MIME-Type and associate a servlet as its handler. This method is often referred to as filtering.

This chapter will cover the following:

- ➢ Discuss servlet chaining using aliases.
- ➢ Learn how to configure a web server to perform servlet chaining using aliases.
- ➢ Discuss servlet chaining using MIME-Types.
- ➢ Learn how to configure a web server to perform servlet chaining, or filtering, using MIME-Types.

Chaining Servlets Using Aliases

A simple and straightforward way to chain servlets together is to specify a sequential list of servlets and associate them with an alias. When a request is made to this alias, the first servlet in the associated list is invoked. Once the first servlet has completed its processing, the output is sent to the next servlet in the list as a request object. This will continue until the last servlet in the list is reached. When this servlet finishes its processing, the output will be sent back to the browser that originated the request.

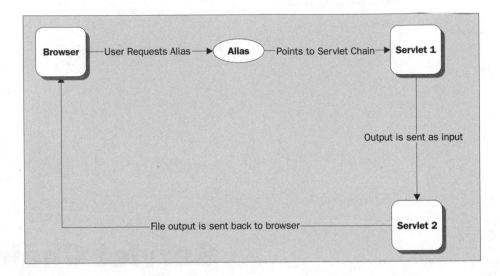

Configuring the Servlet Engine

To accomplish servlet chaining using aliases, some changes need to be made to the servlet engine. We will show what needs to be done to set up servlet chains using JRun from Live Software as well as the Java Web Server from Sun. For more information about the general setup and configuration of these products, refer to appendices H and E at the back of this book.

JRun (Live Software)

To configure JRun for servlet chaining, begin by starting the administrator interface. This is done by opening the JRun Service Manager and pressing the Start button underneath the Administrator section. The first screen you will see displays the list of JRun services available. The services listed are the JSE (JRun Servlet Engine), JCP (JRun Connector Proxy), JSEWEB (JRun Servlet Engine for the JRun Web Server), and the JWS (JRun Web Server). For servlet chaining, and most other servlet functionality, we will be configuring the JSE service.

Once the JSE service has been selected, press the Service Config button. The next screen you will see is the 'JSE Service Config' interface. Select the Mappings tab. This is where you can map a path or an extension to a particular servlet. To create a servlet chain, enter the name for the chain in the left column and a comma-separated list of servlets in the right column. The servlets entered should be in the order in which they should be called in the chain. The chain that has been set up in the figure below will be invoked if someone requests http://localhost:8080/servlet/CustService. The CustSvc servlet will be invoked first. Upon its completion, the results will then be piped into CustSvcResp for further processing. When CustSvcResp has finished processing the data, the results will be sent back to the browser.

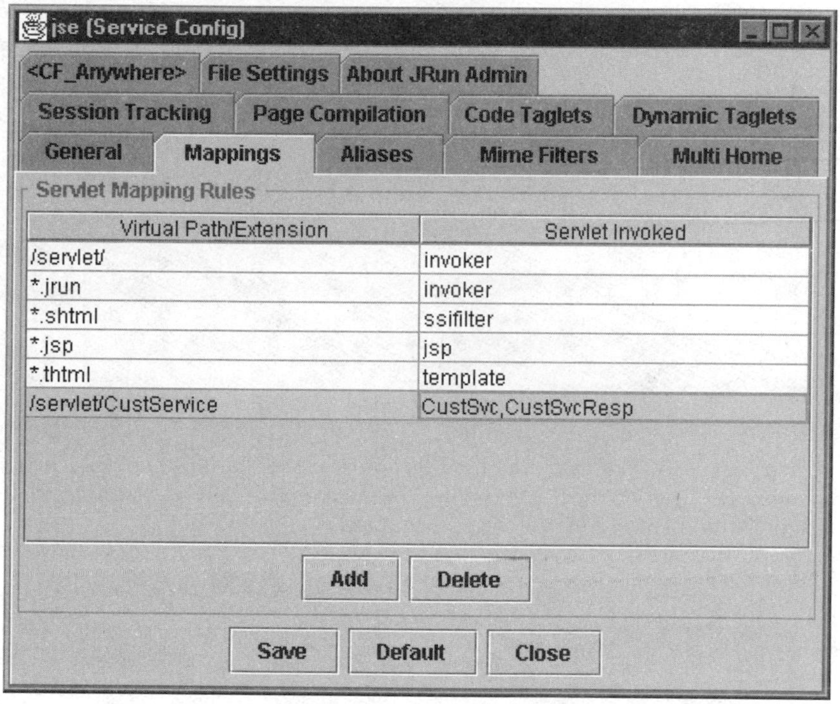

Java Web Server

As with JRun, to configure the Java Web Server for chaining using aliases, you must first open the administrator interface. This is done by pointing your browser to your local server hostname port 9090. Once you have successfully logged in to the administrator interface, you will be presented with a screen similar to the JRun services tab.

From this screen, select the Web Service listing and press the Manage button. Then select the Site listing and choose the Options tab. This is where we will enable servlet chaining in the web server. Find the Servlet Chains entry and switch it to Enabled.

Finally, we need to set up our servlet chain. Assuming the servlets have been added to the Java Web Server properly (see appendix E), the only thing left to do is to specify an alias for the servlet chain along with a comma-separated list of the servlets in the chain. From the same initial screen **Setup**, click on the **Servlet Aliases** selection in the list along the left hand side of the screen. On the right, there is a list of aliases and the servlet that is invoked for each. We set up the /CustService alias to invoke the CustSvc and CustSvcResp servlets. This is the servlet chain we will be using in the example.

Servlet Chaining Using Aliases

To illustrate the concept of servlet chaining, we will build a simple customer service request application. The user will enter a request into an HTML form and submit the data. This will invoke a servlet chain. The first servlet in the chain will log the request to the database and return the persons name. The second servlet will read in the name and return a personalized response to the web browser. The database table is named CustSvc and consists of the following fields:

Field Name	Type	Length
fname	text	30
lname	text	30
email	text	50
phone	text	20
request	text	255
status	text	50

Build the User Interface

The user interface consists of a simple HTML form. The important thing to note here is how we reference our servlet chain. Notice that we are referencing the alias we set up. Also note the method we are using. When using the Java Web Server, you can use either GET or POST. However, when using JRun, you must use the GET method when referencing a servlet chain.

```
<form action="http://localhost:8080/servlet/CustService" method="GET">
```

```
<HTML>
<HEAD>
      <TITLE>Customer Service Request</TITLE>
</HEAD>
<BODY>
<CENTER><H1>Customer Service Request</H1></CENTER>
<HR>
<BR>
<FORM ACTION="http://localhost:8080/servlet/CustService" METHOD="GET">
<CENTER>
<TABLE>
      <TR>
            <TD>First Name:</TD>
            <TD><INPUT TYPE="Text" NAME="txtFname" SIZE="30"></TD>
      </TR>
      <TR>
            <TD>Last Name:</TD>
            <TD><INPUT TYPE="Text" NAME="txtLname" SIZE="30"></TD>
      </TR>
      <TR>
            <TD>Email Address:</TD>
            <TD><INPUT TYPE="Text" NAME="txtEmail" SIZE="30"></TD>
      </TR>
      <TR>
            <TD>Phone Number:</TD>
            <TD><INPUT TYPE="Text" NAME="txtPhone" SIZE="30"></TD>
      </TR>
      <TR>
            <TD VALIGN="top">Request:</TD>
            <TD><TEXTAREA NAME="txtRequest" COLS="30" ROWS="10"></TEXTAREA></TD>
      </TR>
</TABLE>
<BR><INPUT TYPE="Submit" VALUE="Submit Request">
</CENTER>
</FORM>
</BODY>
</HTML>
```

Create the First Servlet in the Chain (Customer Service)

The first servlet acts to enter the data from the form into the database. The important thing to note is that the only thing it returns to the output stream is the user name field. This will be picked up by the next servlet in the chain.

```
//Import Servlet Libraries
import javax.servlet.*;
import javax.servlet.http.*;

//Import Java Libraries
import java.util.*;
import java.sql.*;
import java.io.*;

public class CustSvc extends HttpServlet {

   Connection dbCon;

   public void init() throws ServletException {

      try {
         String driverClassName = getInitParameter("JdbcDriver");
         String dbURL = getInitParameter("dbURL");
         Driver driver = (Driver) Class.forName(driverClassName).newInstance();
         DriverManager.registerDriver(driver);
         dbCon = DriverManager.getConnection(dbURL);
      } catch(ClassNotFoundException e) {
         System.out.println("CustSvc: Database driver could not be found.");
         System.out.println(e.toString());
         throw new UnavailableException(this, "Database driver class not found");
      } catch(SQLException e) {
         System.out.println("CustSvc: Error connecting to the database.");
         System.out.println(e.toString());
         throw new UnavailableException(this, "Cannot connect to the database");
      }
   }

   public void doGet(HttpServletRequest req, HttpServletResponse res)
      throws ServletException, IOException {

      PrintWriter out = res.getWriter();
      res.setContentType("text/html");

      String fname = req.getParameter("txtFname");
      String lname = req.getParameter("txtLname");
      String email = req.getParameter("txtEmail");
      String phone = req.getParameter("txtPhone");
      String request = req.getParameter("txtRequest");

      /* Log request in database */
      try {
         Statement s = dbCon.createStatement();
         s.executeUpdate("insert into CustSvc values('" + fname +
                   "','" + lname + "','" + email + "','" + phone +
                   "','" + request + "','open')");
      } catch (SQLException e) {
         System.out.println(e.toString());
         return;
      }

      /* Send name field to next servlet in the chain */
      out.println(fname + " " + lname);
      out.close();
   }

   public void destroy() {
```

Continued on Following Page

```
        /* Close database connection */
        try {
           dbCon.close();
        } catch (Exception e) {
           System.out.println("CustSvc: Error closing database (destroy)");
           System.out.println(e.toString());
        }
     }
   }
```

Create the Second Servlet in the Chain (Customer Service Response)

This is our final servlet of the chain; therefore it will be sending the results back to the browser. To read in the results of the previous servlet in the chain, simply open an input stream to the request object and read the data from the `InputStreamReader` object into the `BufferedReader` object. We can then use the `readline()` method to initialize the `String name`.

```
/* Get an input stream and read in the request */
BufferedReader br = new BufferedReader(new
InputStreamReader(req.getInputStream()));
String name = br.readLine();
br.close();
```

This is the source code for the `CustSvcResp` servlet.

```
//Import Servlet Libraries
import javax.servlet.*;
import javax.servlet.http.*;

//Import Java Libraries
import java.io.*;
import java.util.*;

//Import html helper class
import ap.servlets.*;

public class CustSvcResp extends HttpServlet {

   public void doGet(HttpServletRequest req, HttpServletResponse res)
      throws ServletException, IOException {

      PrintWriter out = res.getWriter();
      res.setContentType("text/html");

      /* Get an input stream and read in the request */
      BufferedReader br = new BufferedReader(new InputStreamReader
      (req.getInputStream()));
      String name = br.readLine();
      br.close();

      /*Send acknowledgment to the browser */
      html h = new html("Customer Service Response");
      h.add(html.HEADING, "Customer Service Request Received", false);
      h.add(html.LINE, "", false);
      h.add(html.NORMAL, "Thank you for your request, ", false);
      h.add(html.NORMAL, name, false);
      h.add(html.NORMAL, ". ", false);
      h.add(html.NORMAL, "It has been added to our database and will be ", false);
```

```
        h.add(html.NORMAL, "responded to within the next 3 days.", true);
        out.println(h.getPage());
        out.close();
    }
}
```

This is the HTML user interface that is used to enter the data. The CustSvc servlet will be run when the data is submitted.

This is the response that is sent back to the user when the CustSvcResp servlet runs. Notice the personalization of the return message.

Filtering Servlet Results Using MIME Types

Another popular way to move the results of one servlet into the input of another servlet is to configure a particular MIME-Type to be associated with a servlet or servlet chain. A MIME-Type describes the content that is being sent to the browser. By configuring the web server, or servlet engine, you can identify a servlet to handle the contents of any particular MIME-Type. A good example of this would be to associate the 'text/plain' MIME-Type with a servlet that would convert the contents to be displayed as all uppercase letters.

Configuring the Web Server

JRun (Live Software)

With JRun, associating MIME-Types with servlets is a very simple task. Once you have started the JRunAdmin interface and selected the 'jse' service config, go ahead and select the 'MIME Filters' tab. Type in a valid MIME-Type in the left column and the servlet to be invoked in the right column. We have set up the MIME filter so that whenever there is a response that is of type 'text/plain', the `ListFormat` servlet will handle the content, process and then send the output to the browser.

Java Web Server

Associating MIME-Types with servlets is a little bit less intuitive with the Java Web Server than with JRun. Instead of using a graphical administrative interface, you will need to edit the mimeservlets.properties file found in the `jws/properties/server/javawebserver/webpageservice` directory. Once open, simply add a line that maps a MIME-Type to a servlet.

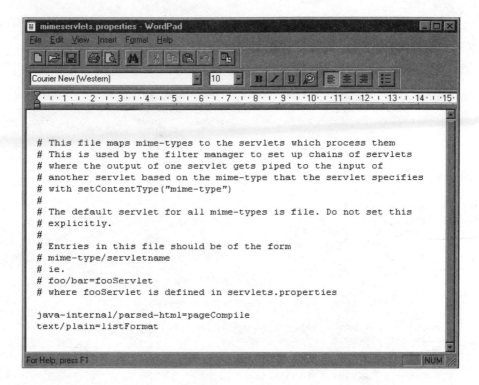

Filtering Content Using MIME-Types

This example will simply display a list of items that has a MIME-Type of 'text/plain'. The 'text/plain' MIME-Type should be associated with the `ListFormat` servlet that we will be creating in this example. The `ListFormat` servlet will read in the content and shade every other line before it outputs it. To invoke the demo, type `yourhostname/servlet/MimeDemo` into the URL box.

This is the source code for the `MimeDemo` servlet

```
//Import Servlet Libraries
import javax.servlet.*;
import javax.servlet.http.*;

//Import Java Libraries
import java.io.*;

public class MimeDemo extends HttpServlet {

    public void doGet(HttpServletRequest req, HttpServletResponse res)
        throws ServletException, IOException {

        PrintWriter out = res.getWriter();
        res.setContentType("text/plain");
```

Continued on Following Page

```
            /* Build arbitrary list of fruits for demo */
            out.println("Apple");
            out.println("Banana");
            out.println("Cherry");
            out.println("Grape");
            out.println("Pineapple");
            out.println("Tangerine");

            out.close();
    }
}
```

This is the source code for the `ListFormat` servlet

```
//Import Servlet Libraries
import javax.servlet.*;
import javax.servlet.http.*;

//Import Java Libraries
import java.io.*;
import java.util.*;

public class ListFormat extends HttpServlet {

    public void doGet(HttpServletRequest req, HttpServletResponse res)
        throws ServletException, IOException {

        PrintWriter out = res.getWriter();
        res.setContentType("text/html");

        out.println("<HTML><HEAD><TITLE>MIME Demo Results</TITLE></HEAD>");
        out.println("<BODY><TABLE>");

        /* Get an input stream and read in the request */
        BufferedReader br = new BufferedReader(new
        InputStreamReader(req.getInputStream()));
        String item = br.readLine();
        boolean lineState = false;
        while (item != null) {
        if (lineState) {
            out.println("<TR BGCOLOR='Gray'><TD>");
            lineState = false;
        } else {
            out.println("<TR><TD>");
            lineState = true;
        }
        out.println(item);
        out.println("</TD></TR>");
        item = br.readLine();
    }
    br.close();

    out.println("</TABLE></BODY></HTML>");
    out.close();
    }
}
```

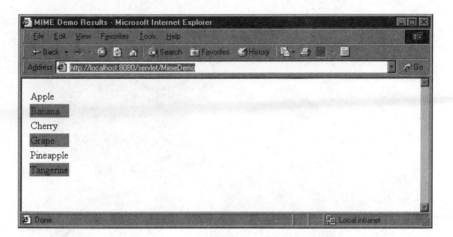

This is the result of the `ListFormat` servlets' action upon the text imputed by the `MimeDemo` servlet.

Summary

Chaining and filtering servlets add a new level of flexibility in designing our server-side applications. While chaining gives us a sophisticated way to spread a request across a series of distinct handlers, filtering allows us to extend the functionality of the web server by attaching handlers to common content types. We have seen how to accomplish both of these functions using JRun and the Java Web Server. The concepts are essentially the same across all other web servers and servlet engines and should not differ much from what we have seen here.

In this chapter, we learned the following:

> Servlets can be chained so that they send the output of one servlet to another servlet as input. Eventually, the last servlet in the chain will send the results back to the browser.

> A servlet chain can be invoked by associating an alias with a comma-separated list of servlets.

> Web content can be filtered through a servlet before being displayed by associating a particular MIME-Type with a servlet to process the content.

> MIME-Types can be handled by either a single servlet or a chain of servlets, in much the same way as servlet chaining with aliases.

Servlet Communications

There may be some instances where a simple HTML form might not satisfy the requirements for a user interface. When this is the case, a Java applet may be used to fill in the gaps that an HTML form leaves empty. HTML forms work well when the interaction between the user and the server can be met with a series of static requests. When building an applet for your interface, there's no need to lose your servlets. We'll show in this chapter how an applet can invoke a servlet and read its response.

Another area of servlet communications is introduced by a new interface in the servlet API, the RequestDispatcher. Using a RequestDispatcher object, a servlet's request and response objects can be either forwarded to another servlet, or they can be temporarily passed to another server resource to enable a programmatic server side include (SSI).

This chapter will cover the following:

> Show how to invoke a servlet from within a Java applet.

> Learn what a RequestDispatcher object can do.

> Demonstrate programmatic server-side includes using the RequestDispatcher interface.

Invoking a Servlet From an Applet

If we take a moment to step back and look at the fundamental model behind a web application, we find that the application is split up between the user interface (Web Browser), business logic (Servlets) and the data (Database). Until now we've developed our user interface layer using HTML forms. While HTML forms provide an easy to use and simple to code interface, they can be somewhat lacking in features. For instance, what if you wanted to do some simple validation of each of the form fields? You could have a servlet perform the validation, but this would be cumbersome for both the user and developer. The user would have to submit the form repeatedly until they had corrected all of the fields. An ideal solution would be to use a Java applet instead.

While a Java applet is ideal for a user interface, it is not necessarily the right choice for performing any serious processing or database interactions. The appropriate place to handle this is at the server. The only question that remains then, is how do we get our applet to talk to a servlet running on a web server? The figure below illustrates the steps that are necessary to perform applet to servlet communication. It is essentially a two-step process. First, the applet opens a `DataOutputStream` and sends an HTTP request to the server, invoking the servlet. Next, the applet opens an `InputStreamReader` to the server and retrieves the results of the servlet.

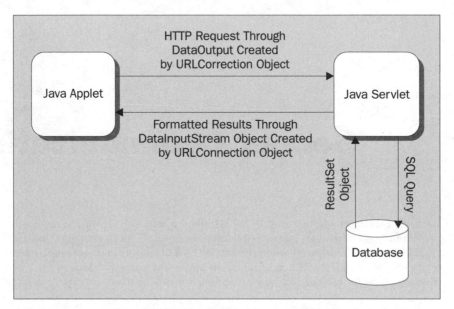

Applet to Servlet Communication

In this next example, we'll build an applet to act as the user interface and a servlet to handle the database interactions. The applet will allow the user to enter a simple SQL query and display the results in a text box below. Once the user enters the query and presses the button, the query will be passed to a servlet where the query will be executed. The applet will then retrieve the results from the servlet and display them in a text box.

This example assumes a single table exists in the database and processes it accordingly. To make this a more generic query interface, modify the servlet code to use the `ResultSetMetaData` interface to retrieve column names and column counts. Also, if you have trouble executing this applet, try using the Java plug-in from Sun. The plug-in circumvents some common security exceptions when trying to open a URL connection to the server.

Create the HTML Interface

Below is the code for the creation of the HTML page that will host the applet.

```
<HTML>
<HEAD>
     <TITLE>Database Query Interface</TITLE>
</HEAD>

<BODY>
<CENTER>
<H1>Database Query Interface</H1>
<HR>
<BR>
<!--"CONVERTED_APPLET"-->
<!-- CONVERTER VERSION 1.0 -->
<OBJECT classid="clsid:8AD9C840-044E-11D1-B3E9-00805F499D93"
WIDTH = "600" HEIGHT = "300" NAME = "DbApplet"
codebase="http://java.sun.com/products/plugin/1.1.1/jinstall-111-
win32.cab#Version=1,1,1,0">
<PARAM NAME = CODE VALUE = "DbApplet.class" >
<PARAM NAME - NAME VALUE = "DbApplet" >

<PARAM NAME="type" VALUE="application/x-java-applet;version=1.1">
<COMMENT>
<EMBED type="application/x-java-applet;version=1.1" java_CODE = "DbApplet.class"
NAME = "DbApplet" WIDTH = "600" HEIGHT = "300"
pluginspage="http://java.sun.com/products/plugin/1.1.1/plugin-install.html">
<NOEMBED></COMMENT>

</NOEMBED></EMBED>
</OBJECT>

<!--
<APPLET  CODE = "DbApplet.class" WIDTH = "600" HEIGHT = "300" NAME = "DbApplet" >

</APPLET>
-->
<!--"END_CONVERTED_APPLET"-->

</CENTER>
</BODY>
</HTML>
```

Create the User Interface (Applet)

Our applet consists of a text box to enter a query string, a button to execute the query, and a text area to display the results. This code uses the standard AWT components with a `FlowLayout` layout manager. You'll also notice that it implements the `ActionListener` interface. If you're using an older version of Netscape Communicator you may need to upgrade your browser or use the Java plug-in to utilize the JDK1.2 event handling model.

229

```
public class dbApplet extends Applet implements ActionListener {

    TextField tfQuery;
    TextArea taResults;
    Button btnExecute;

    public void init() {

        Panel p1 = new Panel();
        p1.setLayout(new FlowLayout(FlowLayout.LEFT));

        p1.add(new Label("Query String:"));

        tfQuery = new TextField("", 50);
        p1.add(tfQuery);

        btnExecute = new Button("Execute Query");
        btnExecute.addActionListener(this);
        p1.add(btnExecute);

        add("North", p1);

        taResults = new TextArea(10, 80);
        add("Center", taResults);
    }
    // Other methods....
}
```

Add Event Handling

Since our applet implements the `ActionListener` interface, we need to implement the `actionPerformed()` method so that when the user presses the button we can send the query to the server.

```
public void executeQuery() {
    // We'll fill in this code in the next section
}
```

```
public void actionPerformed(ActionEvent ae) {
    executeQuery();
}
```

Send the Query to the Servlet

Before we start talking to the servlet, we need to retrieve our query string. This is done using the standard `getText()` method of the text box.

```
String qryString = tfQuery.getText();
```

All of our code that will communicate with the servlet needs to be contained in a try-catch block and the exceptions `MalformedURLException` and `IOException` need to be caught. The first thing we'll do is create a URL connection object and open a connection to the servlet. At this point, we will also set a few flags to allow input and output, restrict the use of caches, and set the type of the request.

```
URL url = new URL("http://localhost:8080/servlet/dbServlet");

URLConnection uc = url.openConnection();
uc.setDoOutput(true);
uc.setDoInput(true);
uc.setUseCaches(false);
uc.setRequestProperty("Content-type", "application/x-www-form-urlencoded");
```

As you might recall from earlier chapters, HTTP requests are always encoded before they are sent to the server. This is done to account for spaces and special characters. When you put together a request for the server, you should always make use of the URLEncoder class and its static encode() method. Look at the following code to see how it is used.

```
String qry = URLEncoder.encode("qry") + "=" + URLEncoder.encode(qryString);
```

Finally we're ready to send our request to the server. We do this by opening a DataOutputStream through the URL connection object and writing our query string to it. To finish the operation, we flush the output stream and then close it.

```
DataOutputStream dos = new DataOutputStream(uc.getOutputStream());

dos.writeBytes(qry);
dos.flush();
dos.close();
```

Retrieve the Results from the Servlet

Within the same try-catch block from the previous section, we'll retrieve the results from the servlet and display them for the user. First create an InputStreamReader through the existing URLConnection object, then using the append() method, write to the String object in InputStreamReader, displaying the results.

```
InputStreamReader in = new InputStreamReader(uc.getInputStream());

int chr = in.read();
while (chr != -1) {
   taResults.append(String.valueOf((char) chr));
   chr = in.read;
}

in.close();
```

Code the Servlet

The servlet for this example is a simple one. It receives a query, sends it to the database and returns its results back to its caller. The database that is being used for this example was created in Microsoft Access and has a single table called project with the following definition.

Field Name	Data Type
proj_num (key)	text(3)
proj_name	text(30)
proj_desc	text(255)

The ODBC Datasource that we are going to create is called `projects`.

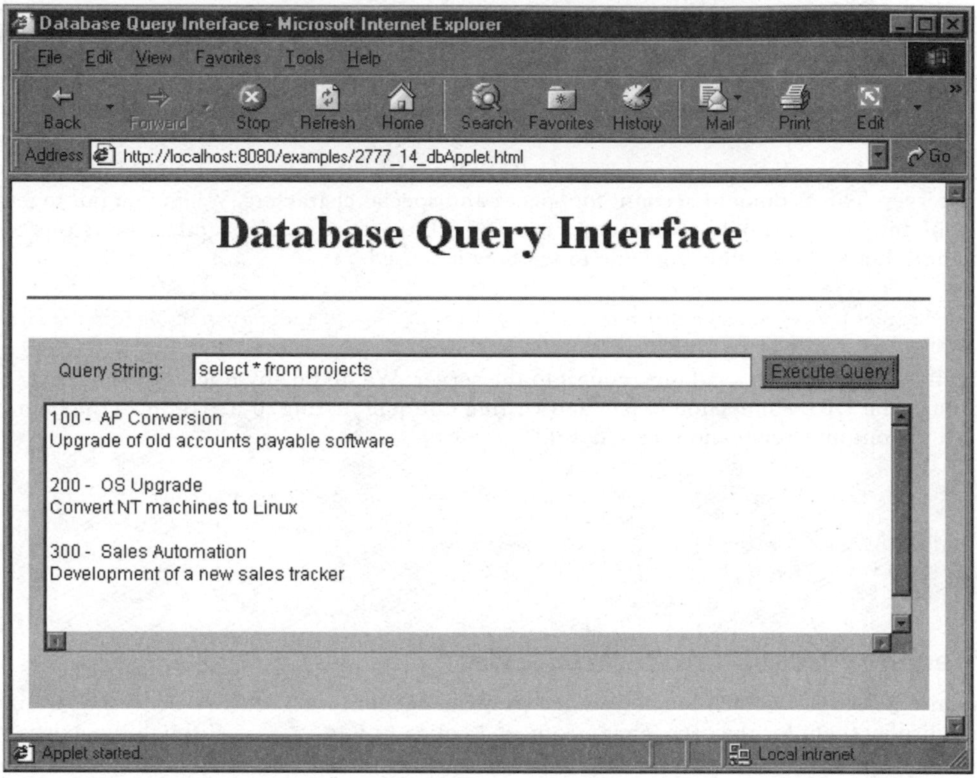

Below is the full source code for the `DbApplet` applet:

```java
import java.awt.*;
import java.applet.*;
import java.awt.event.*;
import java.io.*;
import java.net.*;

public class DbApplet extends Applet implements ActionListener {

    TextField tfQuery;
    TextArea taResults;
    Button btnExecute;

    public void init() {
```

```
        Panel p1 = new Panel();
        p1.setLayout(new FlowLayout(FlowLayout.LEFT));

        p1.add(new Label("Query String:"));

        tfQuery = new TextField("", 50);
        p1.add(tfQuery);

        btnExecute = new Button("Execute Query");
        btnExecute.addActionListener(this);
        p1.add(btnExecute);

        add("North", p1);

        taResults = new TextArea(10, 80);
        add("Center", taResults);
    }

    public void executeQuery() {

        String qryString = tfQuery.getText();

        try {
            /* The line below can be adjusted to your local servlet position */

            URL url = new URL("http://localhost:8080/servlet/DbServlet");
            String qry = URLEncoder.encode("qry") + "=" +
                            URLEncoder.encode(qryString);

            URLConnection uc = url.openConnection();
            uc.setDoOutput(true);
            uc.setDoInput(true);
            uc.setUseCaches(false);
            uc.setRequestProperty("Content-type",
                            "application/x-www-form-urlencoded");

            DataOutputStream dos = new DataOutputStream(uc.getOutputStream());
            dos.writeBytes(qry);
            dos.flush();
            dos.close();

            InputStreamReader in = new InputStreamReader(uc.getInputStream());

            int chr = in.read();
            while (chr != -1) {
                taResults.append(String.valueOf((char) chr));
                chr = in.read();
            }
            in.close();

        } catch(MalformedURLException e) {
            taResults.setText(e.toString());
        } catch(IOException e) {
            taResults.setText(e.toString());
        }
    }
    public void actionPerformed(ActionEvent ae) {
        executeQuery();
    }
}
```

Below is the full source code for the dbServlet servlet:

```java
//Import Servlet Libraries
import javax.servlet.*;
import javax.servlet.http.*;

//Import Java Libraries
import java.util.*;
import java.sql.*;
import java.io.*;

public class DbServlet extends HttpServlet {

    Connection dbCon;

    public void init() throws ServletException {

        try {
            Class.forName("sun.jdbc.odbc.JdbcOdbcDriver");
            String dbURL = "jdbc:odbc:projects";
            dbCon = DriverManager.getConnection(dbURL);
        } catch (Exception e) {
            System.out.println("Database connect failed (init)");
            System.out.println(e.toString());
            return;
        }
    }

    public void doGet(HttpServletRequest req, HttpServletResponse res)
        throws ServletException, IOException {

        PrintWriter out = res.getWriter();
        res.setContentType("text/html");

        String qry = req.getParameter("qry");

        try {
            Statement s = dbCon.createStatement();
            ResultSet rs = s.executeQuery(qry);
            while (rs.next()) {
                out.println(rs.getString(1) + " - " + rs.getString(2));
                out.println(rs.getString(3));
                out.println ("");
            }
        } catch (SQLException e) {
            System.out.println(e.toString());
            return;
        }
        out.println();
        out.close();
    }

    public void destroy() {

        /* Close database connection */
        try {
            dbCon.close();
        } catch (Exception e) {
            System.out.println("Error closing database (destroy)");
            System.out.println(e.toString());
        }
    }
}
```

The RequestDispatcher Interface

Version 2.1 of the servlet API took away our ability to directly invoke the methods of other servlets by deprecating the `getServlet()` method of the `ServletContext` interface. Fortunately, however, version 2.1 gave us something new that can be used to communicate with other servlets, the `RequestDispatcher` interface. It is used to pass the current request object to another servlet for further processing. This sounds a little bit like servlet chaining, but there are a few differences. A `RequestDispatcher` object can forward a request to any server resource, not just another servlet. Also, another servlet's output can be included within the current output, making it similar to a server-side include (SSI).

To obtain a `RequestDispatcher` object, you call the `getRequestDispatcher()` method of the `ServletContext` interface. Before doing this, we must first obtain a `ServletContext` object using the `getServletContext()` method of the `ServletConfig` interface. Recalling that `HttpServlet` implements the `ServletConfig` interface, the code would look like the following:

```
RequestDispatcher rd =
   this.getServletContext().getRequestDispatcher("/servlet/some_resource");
```

Once we have a `RequestDispatcher` object, we can do one of two things. We can forward the request on to another server resource, in a similar way to chaining, using the `forward()` method. Or, we can include the content of another servlet, or other server resource, using the `include()` method. Both methods have similar signatures:

```
public void forward(ServletRequest request, ServletReponse response)
throws ServletException, IOException;
```

```
public void include(ServletRequest request, ServletResponse response)
throws ServletException, IOException;
```

Programmatic SSI

A very common thing to do as a web site designer is to include the content of one HTML page inside another HTML page. This is known as a server-side include (SSI). The extension of the main page is usually `.shtml`. The web server is configured to handle an `.shtml` file appropriately and the content is included without the user ever knowing the difference.

As a web developer, you may find it useful to include either the content of an HTML page or the output of another servlet inside of your servlet. To do this, you would need to obtain a `RequestDispatcher` object and then invoke the `include()` method at the point in your code that you wish to include the other content. For our example, we will create two servlets, `SsiTest` and `SsiTest_include`. The first servlet will print the HTML headers along with a single line of text. It will then include the output of `SsiTest_include`. Finally, it will print out another line of text to demonstrate that control is returned to the calling servlet.

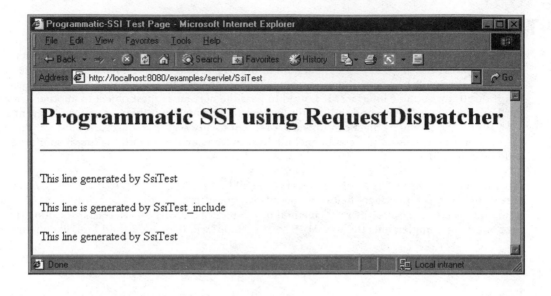

Below is the source code for the `SsiTest` servlet:

```java
//Import Servlet Libraries
import javax.servlet.*;
import javax.servlet.http.*;

//Import Java Libraries
import java.io.*;

public class SsiTest extends HttpServlet {

    public void doGet(HttpServletRequest req, HttpServletResponse res)
        throws ServletException, IOException {

        res.setContentType("text/html");
        PrintWriter out = res.getWriter();

        //Write header to the browser
        out.println("<HTML><HEAD><TITLE>Programmatic-SSI Test Page</TITLE>
        </HEAD><BODY>");
        out.println("<CENTER><H1>Programmatic SSI using RequestDispatcher</H1>
        </CENTER>");
        out.println("<HR>");
        out.println("<BR>This line generated by SsiTest<BR><BR>");

        //Pass the request on to fill in the next part
        RequestDispatcher rd = this.getServletContext().getRequestDispatcher
            ("/servlet/SsiTest_include");
        rd.include(req, res);

        out.println("<BR>This line generated by SsiTest");
        out.println("</BODY></HTML>");
        out.close();
    }
}
```

Below is the full source code for the `SsiTest_include` servlet:

```
//Import Servlet Libraries
import javax.servlet.*;
import javax.servlet.http.*;

//Import Java Libraries
import java.io.*;

public class SsiTest_include extends HttpServlet {

    public void doGet(HttpServletRequest req, HttpServletResponse res)
        throws ServletException, IOException {

        PrintWriter out = res.getWriter();
        out.println("This line generated by SsiTest_include<BR>");
    }
}
```

Summary

Servlet communications enable us to be more flexible in our design of server-side applications. It doesn't matter whether our user interface is an HTML form or a Java applet. We are also able to break up the servlets into smaller functional units by enabling them to pass a request object back and forth between them.

In this chapter, we learned the following:

> Using the `URLConnection` object, along with `DataInputStream` and `DataOutputStream`, we can use applets as a user interface and have them invoke servlets and read in their results.

> To communicate between servlets, the `RequestDispatcher` interface enables you to forward your request to another server resource.

> The `RequestDispatcher` interface also allows you to include the content of another servlet or server resource, like an image or HTML page, within your output.

Distributed Computing With Servlets

At the start of this book, we talked about building n-tiered applications. Well, we started off with simple client-server programs, and then we moved on to bring in a third tier with database access at the back-end. But in order to take the next step and build n-tiered applications, we're going to have to find ways for our servlet applications to talk to other servers. We need to extend the middle tier to include distributed objects – objects belonging to different applications. This will allow our applications to share both data and logic across the middle-tier, and will help us build truly distributed application solutions. We'll need to find a way for our application to discover at runtime other services it needs, on the same machine or across a network. And we'll need to manage communication between the applications, so that they can make use of remote business logic and data sources as if they were local. If we get it right, our server-side applications will be versatile, re-usable, and extensible.

Java provides us with a tool called **Remote Method Invocation**, which will provide us with one solution to this problem. **CORBA**, the **Common Object Request Broker Architecture**, is a solution which offers similar benefits, but which also allows our programs to interact with non-Java code. We'll look at using RMI here, and at CORBA in Chapter 17, where we'll build a five-tier application with CORBA as the glue.

In this chapter, we will do the following:

> Examine the process of invoking remote methods with RMI

> Learn the details of building an RMI server object

> Build a command line application that invokes methods of a remote server object

> Build a servlet that invokes methods of a remote server object

> Learn about the Java 2 security model and how it affects servlets and RMI

Remote Method Invocation

Java's RMI, and the Object Management Group's CORBA specification (http://www.omg.org) share several things in common, with the very important distinction that RMI is purely a Java-to-Java solution. In either system, we have a server, which makes an object available to receive remote method calls, and a client, which wants to use the object. The server registers the object with a naming service running somewhere on the network, so that clients can find the object using a name-lookup. In order to use the object, the client needs to know what interface the object presents. In RMI, naturally, this can be achieved with a Java interface, but CORBA uses a language neutral Interface Definition Language (IDL) to specify the interface.

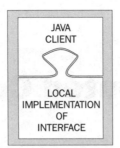

Here we see the normal way a client would interact with a service object on the local machine. The service object implements the well-known interface, which the client understands. All code is executed locally, and the results returned to the client.

To use a distributed object, the client uses a local proxy object, called a **stub**, which presents precisely the same interface to the client. Method calls can be passed over the network to the server object, where a special object called a **skeleton** reconstructs the method calls as local calls to the server object. Any results or exceptions produced by the method are handed back to the skeleton, which simply parcels them up and returns them to the stub, where either data is returned, or an exception is thrown. From the client's perspective, it's as if the method call was executed completely locally.

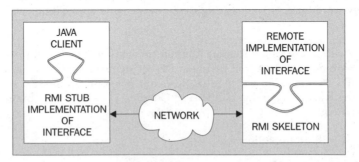

Java RMI follows precisely this pattern, and allows objects in one virtual machine to access the methods of objects that exist in other virtual machines. It does this by first locating the remote object, using a naming service called the **RMI Registry**, obtaining a stub to run in its own virtual machine by downloading it from a specified **CodeBase**, and then invoking a specific method on the stub. The stub communicates using a special protocol with a skeleton object in the server virtual machine, which makes the call on the remote object.

We'll now look at each of the participants in this interaction individually.

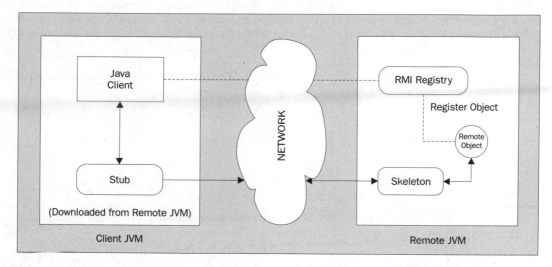

Remote Object

Any Java object can be considered a remote object as long as it implements a remote interface. A remote interface is a Java interface that extends the `java.rmi.Remote` interface and also defines all of the methods which you wish to make available to remote clients. All methods declared in the interface must declare that they throw a `java.rmi.RemoteException`. It is also important to note that any parameters or return values for these methods have to be `serializable` objects so that they can be serialized and transported between the different virtual machines - see appendix B for a refresher course on Java serialization. Most importantly, this means you can't use primitive data types as parameters or return values. Take a look at the following code that defines an interface for a remote object.

```
import java.rmi.Remote;
import java.rmi.RemoteException;

public interface SomeInterface extends Remote
{
    String someMethod(String val) throws RemoteException;
}
```

This interface declares that any object implementing it will be a remote object with one method that can be invoked remotely. The next step is to go ahead and implement the interface.

When implementing a remote interface, you need to always extend `UnicastRemoteObject` as well as implement your custom remote interface. You also need to include a no-argument constructor for the class. The only thing the constructor is required to have is a call to the superclass constructor. This will make the object available to accept incoming requests. So, your class declaration should look something like this:

```
import java.rmi.*;
import.java.rmi.server.*;

public class SomeServer extends UnicastRemoteObject implements SomeInterface
{
    public SomeServer() throws RemoteException
    {
        super();
    }
}
```

Our next step is to implement any remote methods that were declared in the interface. There's nothing special about this except that it may throw a `RemoteException`.

```
public String someMethod(String val) throws RemoteException
{
    // Do something and return a String value
}
```

The most important thing to do with our remote object is to register it with the RMI Registry. For a simple object like this, we can handle this in the object's own `main()` method. This is where all the magic happens. There are three important things that happen here. First, a security manager is installed. A security manager allows us to control the privileges which are granted to code. The `RMISecurityManager` restricts the code to simply class definition and basic access. Next, an instance of the object is created by calling its default constructor. Finally, we bind the object to the registry using the `java.rmi.Naming` interface.

```
public static void main(String[] args)
{
    System.setSecurityManager(new RMISecurityManager());
    try
    {
        SomeInterface si = new SomeServer();
        Naming.rebind("//localhost/myServer", si);
    }
    catch (Exception e)
    {
        //Exception handling...
    }
}
```

This will create an instance of the `SomeServer` object and register it as "myServer" on "localhost". Now, any client will be able to find the `SomeServer` object and obtain a reference to it.

Stub and Skeleton

Once the remote object has been created and compiled, the next step is to create a stub and a skeleton for the object. These are objects that serve as a proxy between the client and the remote object. Parameters and method calls are marshaled between these two objects rather than the calls going directly from the client to the remote object.

Marshalling is the term used in distributed computing to describe the process of serializing data and transferring it across a network.

When the client obtains a reference to the remote object, a stub is downloaded so that all method calls appear to be local rather than remote. The stub will relay any method calls (with parameters) to the remote skeleton. The remote skeleton will issue the method calls directly to the remote object. Return values will be returned to the client in much the same manner, with the values being passed first to the skeleton, then the stub, and finally the client.

Stubs and skeletons are generated using the rmic tool included with the JDK distribution in the /bin subdirectory. In our case, the command would be `rmic SomeServer`.

The client downloads the stub from a specified `codebase`. This can be an HTTP server, or it can be a local file system reference. In either case, the `codebase` is specified as a full URL.

RMI Registry

The RMI registry is a process that runs on the remote virtual machine and makes it possible for client applications to locate and obtain references to remote objects. We've already seen how the remote object binds itself to the registry in its main method. The client application will first locate the registry and then obtain a reference to the remote object.

The RMI registry must be started on the remote machine before anything else happens. This is done at the command line by typing either `start rmiregistry` (for Windows systems) or `rmiregistry &` (for Unix or Linux systems). The registry, by default, will start on port 1099. You can specify a different port by simply adding the port number to the end of the command.

Java Client

The Java client only has one RMI-specific job to do and that is to obtain a reference to the remote object. Once this has been done, then the object can be used as if it were local to the client application. The details of obtaining a stub, and of marshalling calls to the remote object, are hidden from the client.

The client has to import the `java.rmi` package as well as the remote interface. By importing the interface, our client knows how to talk to any class which implements it – such as the stub class downloaded from the `codebase`. So, when obtaining a reference to the remote object, you actually create a new instance of the stub, which you can store in a variable of the interface type. The remote interface is obtained using the `Naming.lookup(String server)` method. The value passed must match the host name and object name that was used when originally binding the remote object. Also, we have to remember to cast the reference returned to the interface type, as `lookup()` returns an `Object`. The code might look something like this:

```
import java.rmi.*;
import SomeInterface;

public class SomeClient
{
    public static void main(String[] args)
    {
        try
        {
        SomeInterface si = (SomeInterface) Naming.lookup("//localhost/myServer");
        String result = si.someMethod("foo");
        }
        catch (Exception e) {
            //Exception handling...
        }
    }
}
```

Summary of Steps to Implement RMI

To implement a RMI server and client, perform the following tasks:

> Develop the remote interface. This should extend `java.rmi.Remote` and also declare all of the methods that will be globally available to the public. Each method has to declare that it may throw a `java.rmi.RemoteException`.

> Implement the remote interface. Develop the remote object by implementing your remote interface and extending `UnicastRemoteObject`. In the `main()` method, install a security manager, create an instance of the object, and bind it to the registry.

> Compile the source files and generate the stub and skeleton. Once you have completed the interface and the remote object, first compile the interface and then the remote object. Then use the `rmic` tool to generate the stub and skeleton.

> Start the registry and activate the remote object. Start the registry as its own process. Then, run the remote object. The `main()` method will be executed, which will create an instance of the object and bind it to the registry.

> Develop the client application. In the client application, use the `Naming.lookup()` method to obtain a reference to the remote object, and cast it to the remote interface. This will make its methods available locally.

> Compile the client source files and run the application. Now you're ready to try it out. If you have trouble accessing the remote object, make sure that you are using the correct hostname and registry value.

Java2 Security

One of the big changes to get used to with the Java 2 SDK is that the security model has been entirely overhauled from its JDK1.1 predecessor. Prior to version 2, a Java object couldn't easily access anything outside the 'sandbox'. This security model is part of what made Java so attractive in the first place. However, it also made it somewhat restrictive in what it could do.

With the introduction of the Java 2 platform, you can now grant specific permissions to individual resources. This allows your code to interact with objects outside of its own virtual machine, including the local filesystem. This removes many of the previous limitations of the Java platform. Now, you can override the security mechanisms of the JVM. The new security model is quite complex, so we're just going to explore the area that we need to get our RMI code to work.

Policy Files

Code is granted permissions in what is called a policy file. If you look in the `[jdk home]/jre/lib/security` directory, you'll find the default policy file for your JVM named `java.policy`. This file can be edited either manually, or by using the `policytool` program found in the `[jdk home]/bin` directory. Either way, you need to grant access to your code using the following lines. These can be entered manually, but the same can be accomplished using the `policytool` program (see figure below).

```
grant {
   permission java.net.SocketPermission "*:1024-65535", "connect,accept";
   permission java.net.SocketPermission "*:80", "connect";
}
```

This will have the effect of granting programs running on ports 1024 and above (and port 80) access to the entire `codebase`. If you wish to limit these permissions to a more narrow `codebase`, you can specify a directory immediately after the grant statement before the first curly brace.

There is much more to the changes in security between 1.1 and 1.2 than we've covered here, but this should give you enough to implement a RMI solution. For more information on JDK security, refer to the Java web site for more documentation.

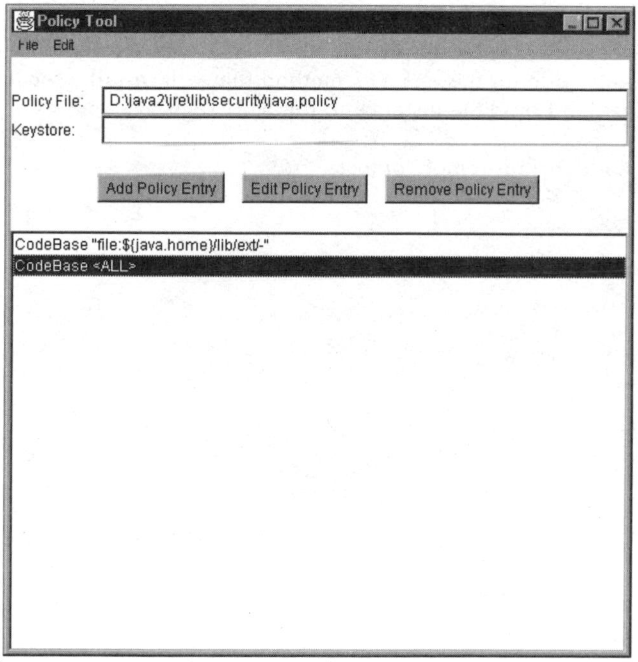

Building a Remote Object

In most cases, a remote object is built to perform a specific function or a related grouping of functions. By being made available as a remote object, the service can be used by clients on any machine on the network. The object we're going to build will provide a simple string manipulation service. It will accept a string parameter and return the reverse representation of it. We'll start by first building a remote interface.

Build the Remote Interface

Remember that the first step to building a remote object is to build an interface that declares the methods that will be made globally available. It also tells the virtual machine that any object implementing the interface is a remote object. For our remote object, the only method that we'll be creating is the method that performs the string manipulation to reverse the characters of a string parameter. Here's the code for our remote interface:

```
package com.wrox.rmi;

import java.rmi.Remote;
import java.rmi.RemoteException;

public interface ReverseInterface extends Remote
{
    String reverseString(String originalString) throws RemoteException;
}
```

Implement the Remote Interface

The next step in building our remote object is to actually implement the remote interface and all of its methods. In this case we need to implement the reverseString() method. The other thing we need to do is write our code for the main() method that will install a security manager, create an instance of the object, and bind the instance to the RMI registry.

Take a look at the code for our remote object:

```
package com.wrox.rmi;

import java.rmi.*;
import java.rmi.server.*;

public class Reverse extends UnicastRemoteObject implements ReverseInterface
{
    public Reverse() throws RemoteException
    {
        super();
    }

    public String reverseString(String originalString) throws RemoteException
    {
        int length = originalString.length();

        StringBuffer temp = new StringBuffer(length);
```

```
        for (int i = length ; i>0 ; i--)
        {
            temp.append(originalString.substring(i-1,i));
        }

        return temp.toString();
    }

    public static void main(String[] args)
    {
        if (System.getSecurityManager() == null)
        {
            System.setSecurityManager(new RMISecurityManager());
        }

        String name = "//localhost/com.wrox.rmi.Reverse";

        try
        {
            Reverse r = new Reverse();
            Naming.rebind(name,r);
            System.out.println("Reverse object bound");
        }
        catch (Exception e)
        {
            System.out.println("Error while binding Reverse object");
            System.out.println(e.toString());
        }
    }
}
```

Compiling and Running the Code

> **Compile the Interface**: At the command prompt, type in `javac ReverseInterface.java`.

> **Compile the Remote Object**: At the command prompt, type in `javac Reverse.java`.

> **Generate Stubs and Skeletons**: At the command prompt, type in `rmic Reverse`.

> **Start the RMI Registry**: At the command prompt, type in `start rmiregistry`. A new process will be created and the registry will be active and listening on port 1099 for incoming requests.

> **Execute the Remote Object**: At the command prompt, type in (on one line)

```
java -Djava.rmi.server.codebase=file:/d:\java\jdk1.2\rmi\
                -Djava.rmi.server.hostname-localhost reverse.
```

You need to specify the `hostname` and the `codebase` so that the registry can locate any bytecode that it may need to download to the client. If you were to use a custom policy file, you could specify that by adding `-Djava.security.policy=custom.policy`.

Building an RMI Client Application

The main goal of these examples is to demonstrate how to make a servlet an RMI client. However, before we do that, we can quickly and easily test out our RMI server with the following simple application.

```
import java.rmi.*;
import com.wrox.rmi.ReverseInterface;

public class Client
{

    public static void main(String[] args)
    {
        try
        {
            ReverseInterface ri = (ReverseInterface)
                    Naming.lookup("//jamesh:1099/com.wrox.rmi.Reverse");
            String result = ri.reverseString(args[0]);
            System.out.println("The reverse of " + args[0] + " is " + result);
        }
        catch (Exception e)
        {
            System.out.println("Error accessing remote object.");
            System.out.println(e.toString());
        }
    }
}
```

When you run the application, your results should look something like the figure below.

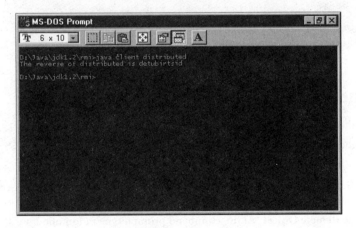

Building an RMI Client Servlet

With a few minor exceptions, you'll see that building a servlet that acts as a RMI client is really no different than building the previous application.

Install the Security Manager

Within the doGet() method, the first thing we need to do to invoke a remote object is to install the security manager. This is done with the following code:

```
if (System.getSecurityManager() == null)
    {
        System.setSecurityManager(new RMISecurityManager());
    }
```

Obtain a Reference to the Remote Interface

Inside of a `try{}catch{}` block, the next thing we do is obtain a reference to the remote object. This is done by looking up the object on the remote server and then casting it to the remote interface.

```
try
{
    ReverseInterface r = (ReverseInterface) Naming.lookup(
                            "//localhost:1099/Reverse");

    .
    .
}
catch (Exception e)
{
    out.println("Error executing remote method");
    out.println(e.toString());
}
```

Invoke the Remote Method

Finally, we invoke the remote method and display our output.

```
try
{
    .
    .
    out.println("The opposite of " + val + " is " +
                            r.reverseString(val) + ".");
}
catch (Exception e)
{
    out.println("Error executing remote method");
    out.println(e.toString());
}
```

When coding the servlet, it's important to remember to import the interface class. So that the error message returned is legible if the servlet fails, we also use `res.setContentType("Text/Plain")` to set the MIME type to plain, unformatted text, instead of HTML. Here is the rest of the code in context.

```
import java.rmi.*;
import java.rmi.registry.*;

import java.io.*;

import javax.servlet.*;
import javax.servlet.http.*;

import com.wrox.rmi.ReverseInterface;

public class RmiServlet extends HttpServlet
{

    public void doGet(HttpServletRequest req, HttpServletResponse res)
        throws IOException, ServletException
        {
```

Continued on Following Page

```
        res.setContentType("text/plain");
        PrintWriter out = res.getWriter();

        String val = req.getParameter("val");

        if (System.getSecurityManager() == null)
        {
            System.setSecurityManager(new RMISecurityManager());
        }

        try
        {
            ReverseInterface r = (ReverseInterface) Naming.lookup(
                                            "//localhost:1099/Reverse");
            out.println("The opposite of " + val + " is " + r.reverseString(val) +
                    ".");
        }
        catch (Exception e)
        {
            out.println("Error executing remote method");
            out.println(e.toString());
        }

        out.close();
    }
}
```

The results should be as follows (notice the val parameter on the address line):

Summary

Using RMI gives us the ability to extend our server applications to include remote objects regardless of their location. We can build applications which consist of several separate blocks, running on different machines if need be, with well defined interfaces between them. This will enhance the reusability and extensibility of our middle-tier. Implementing an RMI client as a servlet is the same as doing so in an application. By opening up our servlets in this manner, we can move our application from three-tiered to n-tiered.

In this chapter we learned the following:

> To implement a remote object using RMI, first develop the remote interface, then implement the interface, compile the source files, generate stub and skeleton objects, and finally start the RMI registry and run the object.

> Once a remote object has been implemented and activated, to invoke a method of the object, first install an `RMISecurityManager`, obtain a reference to the object, and finally invoke a method of the object as if it were local.

JavaMail and Servlets

Despite the immense popularity of the World Wide Web, the Internet's most used service is still, by far, electronic mail. Being able to send messages to colleagues, friends, and loved ones is practically, by definition, fundamental to being "on" the Net. Yet the details necessary for packaging, sending, and receiving messages are complex and involve a myriad of different protocols. It seems easy from within the typical email client but making the same functionality available programmatically would require learning multiple APIs and permanently coupling your application to the particular protocols those APIs exposed.

The JavaMail specification, however, provides a collection of abstract classes that define the common objects and their interfaces for any general messaging system. By defining the interfaces for messages, mail sessions, transports, and stores, Sun has given Java programmers a not only easy but extensible object-oriented view of the many existing protocols currently in use and even those that have yet to come.

While these interfaces are not directly usable, it's the JavaMail providers that implement the API that provide the concrete functionality needed to communicate using specific protocols. Sun's reference JavaMail implementation actually includes providers for some of the most essential protocols and specifications on the Net today including the Simple Mail Transfer Protocol (SMTP), the Internet Message Access Protocol (IMAP), and the Multipurpose Internet Mail Extensions (MIME). A provider for the Post Office Protocol 3 is available from Sun as well. Various other third-party providers can be obtained or even implemented yourself.

There are really two different types of protocols that providers can implement. Transport is Sun's term for a service that has the capability to send messages to its destination. The most commonly used transport type is the practically ubiquitous SMTP transport. A store, on the other hand, is a service you would connect to in order to retrieve messages that have been delivered to your mailbox through other user's transports. Most users should be familiar with the POP3 store although IMAP stores are starting to become increasingly popular as well.

Since both the POP3 and IMAP providers implement the same interface, any JavaMail enabled application can access a POP3 store in the exact same manner as an IMAP store as well as access any other store a provider might exist for (such as NNTP, P7, mbox, etc). Specific message transports such as SMTP and X.400, for example, can also be used virtually interchangeably.

Being able to interact with potentially any specific messaging system through the single JavaMail API is just one more benefit to coding dynamic web applications with Java servlets. To demonstrate the ease with which applications can make use of the JavaMail API we'll implement a servlet that can send MIME messages using SMTP and even potentially any other transport. We'll also develop a simple web-based email client that will allow users to view and reply to any messages stored on a remote store.

Installing JavaMail

JavaMail is not included in any standard distribution for the Java Runtime Environment or even the Java Developer's Kit. You'll need to download the reference implementation from Sun's JavaMail site at http://java.sun.com/products/javamail/, extract the archive's contents, and ensure the included `mail.jar` file is available to the Java virtual machine. This is usually accomplished by adding its path to the CLASSPATH environment variable or by specifying it on the command line using the – classpath option when invoking the interpreter.

Note that the reference implementation does include providers for SMTP and IMAP but Sun's POP3 provider will need to be downloaded separately from the same site and installed in a similar manner. Other POP3 providers by third parties do exist and Sun does maintain a list of third-party providers at their JavaMail site if you choose to use another.

JavaMail Messages depend on the Java Activation Framework being installed. You can retrieve the reference implementation from http://java.sun.com/beans/glasgow/jaf.html. Download, extract, and ensure the `activation.jar` file is in your classpath.

The Provider Registry

JavaMail was designed to be extensible so that when new protocols were developed, providers for those protocols could be added to a system and be usable by any of the pre-existing JavaMail enabled applications with no change. The way in which these applications detect which providers are available to them is done through the Provider Registry.

The registry is only a single file named `javamail.providers` which should be located in `java.home/lib`. If that file is missing, JavaMail will look in the META-INF directory under each directory or JAR in your classpath. Once it finds that file, it stops looking and then proceeds to look for a file named `javamail.default.providers` in the same manner and add it's entries to the previously found file, if any. The providers that came with Sun's JavaMail implementation are listed here. What this means to you is that you can add a single package containing any number of providers (as long as it includes a `javamail.providers` file in its META-INF directory--it should) without needing to create the "official" registry yourself. Adding another could possibly make your other providers disappear, depending on what order they appear in your classpath. For our examples, we'll only be using the default providers along with Sun's POP3 provider so we shouldn't need to worry about it.

Here's a program that can list the available providers on your system:

```
import javax.mail.*;

class ListProviders {
   public static void main(String[] args) {
       java.util.Properties properties = System.getProperties();
       Session session =
       Session.getInstance(properties, null);
       Provider[] providers = session.getProviders();

       for (int i = 0; i < providers.length; ++i) {
          System.out.println(providers[i]);
       }
   }
}
```

Using JavaMail

Before delving into how JavaMail works and how you can incorporate it into your own servlet code, let me give you a taste of what JavaMail programming is actually like. The following is a complete and functioning JavaMail application (albeit not very robust--all the necessary error checking was conveniently disregarded in the interest of clarity). It's designed to take in an SMTP hostname, from address, and to address as parameters on the command line and send a one-line message to the recipient.

```
import javax.mail.*;
import javax.mail.internet.*;

public class SendMailExample {

   public static void main(String[] args)
      throws MessagingException {
      if (args.length < 3) {
         System.out.println(
            "Usage: java SendMailExample smtpHost fromAddress " +"toAddress");
         System.exit(1);
      }

      String smtpHost = args[0];
      String from = args[1];
      String to = args[2];

      // Start a session
      java.util.Properties properties = System.getProperties();
      Session session = Session.getInstance(properties, null);

      // Construct a message
      MimeMessage message = new MimeMessage(session);
      message.setFrom(new InternetAddress(from));
      message.addRecipient(Message.RecipientType.TO,
      new InternetAddress(to));
      message.setSubject("JavaMail example");
      message.setText("Did it work?");
```

Continued on Following Page

```
        // Connect to the transport
        Transport transport = session.getTransport("smtp");
        transport.connect(smtpHost, "", "");

        // Send the message and close the connection
        transport.sendMessage(message, message.getAllRecipients());
        transport.close();
    }
}
```

Notice how sending the message involved only completing a few fairly self-explanatory steps:

- Start a JavaMail session
- Construct a message
- Connect to the transport
- Send the message through the transport

The actual JavaMail-specific code needed to accomplish the above only numbered about a dozen lines and could have been less (we'll see why in our coverage of the `Transport` objects). In the following sections, we'll go into more detail describing each of the steps listed above.

The JavaMail Session

The `Session` object is responsible for managing a user's mail configuration settings and handling authentication for the individual transports and stores used during the session. Not to be confused with a `javax.servlet.http.HttpSession` object, the JavaMail `Session` is simply a way to associate providers with a particular set of user properties and an authentication mechanism. No state information is maintained in this type of session. Your application will be retrieving the correct `Transport` and `Store` objects based on the current user's settings by interacting with the `Session`. Those transports and stores will retrieve any credentials needed to actually authenticate the user by asking the `Authenticator` object associated with the session.

Typically, an application obtains a `Session` object by calling the `Session.getInstance()` static method. The parameters to this method are a `Properties` object containing the user's configuration settings and an `Authenticator` object. The first two lines in the `SendMailExample` show how simple this usually is.

The actual properties passed to the `Session` object specify default settings for the current user. These include the user's email address (`mail.from`), the user's default `Transport` and `Store` protocols (`mail.transport.protocol` and `mail.store.protocol`), and specific settings for each of these protocols such as the host and user name (`mail.protocol.host` and `mail.protocol.user`). If we needed to specify the default server for a particular protocol we could add the setting to the properties object before creating the server.

```
Session createSession(String defaultSmtpHost) throws MessagingException {

    java.util.Properties properties = System.getProperties();
    properties.put("mail.smtp.host", defaultSmtpHost);
    Session session = Session.getInstance(properties, null);

    return session;
}
```

In our `SendMailExample` application, we specified the host we'd be connecting to when we called the `Transport.connect()` method so setting a default host wasn't required.

Authenticators are used by the session to request a username and password for a specific connection in an application specific manner. An authenticator for one application might prompt the user using an `AWT` or `Swing` dialog. Another might use text-based prompts in console applications. Yet another might retrieve the password from an encrypted database. Setting an authenticator gives individual transports and stores the ability to ask the session for the username and password, which would in turn ask the set authenticator for that session. Most transports, however, don't require a username or password and so we didn't bother creating an authenticator. Later on, in our `WebMail` servlet, we'll be requiring users to specify their username and password before connecting to their store and so won't need an interactive authenticator.

After the initial setup of a session, its primary use is for retrieving `Transport` and `Store` objects using the various `getTransport()` and `getStore()` methods, which you'll see shortly.

Constructing a Message

Messages are the focal point of the JavaMail API. `Message` is an abstract class. Subclasses of `Message` implement the concrete functionality needed for specific messaging systems. Sun's JavaMail implementation includes a `MimeMessage` class that not only implements the standard for Internet messages (as defined by RFC822) but also the Multipurpose Internet Mail Extensions (RFC2045-2049) saving us the tremendously complex task of having to write a class capable of parsing a MIME message ourselves.

Creating a message is a simple task. Simply construct an appropriate subclass of `Message`, set the necessary attributes (headers) to the appropriate values, and finally set the content. The following method shows a more detailed yet still incomplete method for creating a message:

```
public MimeMessage createMimeMessage(
    Session session,
    String from,
    String to,
    String cc,
    String bcc,
    String subject,
    String text)
    throws MessagingException {

MimeMessage message = new MimeMessage(session);

InternetAddress fromAddress = new InternetAddress(from);

message.setFrom(fromAddress);

InternetAddress[] toAddresses = InternetAddress.parse(to);
InternetAddress[] ccAddresses = InternetAddress.parse(cc);
InternetAddress[] bccAddresses = InternetAddress.parse(bcc);

message.setRecipients(Message.RecipientType.TO, toAddresses);
message.setRecipients(Message.RecipientType.CC, ccAddresses);
message.setRecipients(Message.RecipientType.BCC, bccAddresses);

message.setSubject(subject);

message.setText(text);

return message;
}
```

Notice how the `fromAddress` is constructed using `InternetAddress`'s standard constructor. The recipient addresses, on the other hand, use the `InternetAddress.parse()` static method. This method returns an array of `InternetAddress`es. The parameter to parse is a `String` containing comma-separated addresses in the form of user@host. Alternatively, we could have used the `addRecipient()` method like in the previous example if we were sure we only wanted to send the message to one address.

MIME messages are capable of containing content other than plain text. The `setText()` method is a convenience method that accepts a `String` object as the content and sets the content type to `text/plain`. JavaMail relies on the Java Activation Framework's `DataContentHandler`s for converting different content types to a byte stream format suitable for transfer inclusion in a MIME message. Unfortunately, the single `DataContentHandler` available with the standard JavaMail and JAF implementations only handles `text/plain` content types. Adding support for other types is beyond the scope of this chapter. Refer to the JAF specification for more information.

Transports

Sending a message is achieved using a `Transport`. Sun's JavaMail implementation comes with a fully functioning SMTP transport that might very well be the only transport provider you will ever need. You may be surprised to learn that `SendMailExample` sent a message the "hard" way. If we had set a default SMTP host when creating the session we could've used the `Transport.send()` static method. This method will, for each of the different Address types contained in the recipients list, instantiate the appropriate `Transport`, connect to the default host for that `Transport`'s protocol, send the message to the appropriate users, and then close the connection. This approach is actually more flexible than we need because we'll only be using the SMTP transport. Plus, connecting to a transport is really identical to connecting to a store so doing it the "hard" way (which wasn't really that hard, now, was it?) will make working with stores more familiar later on. The only difference is that most transports don't require a username or a password, which is why we passed empty strings above.

Services

The similarity between `Transport` and `Store` is by design. They both extend the `Service` class which defines the various `connect()` and `close()` methods. When connecting to a service, you're actually connecting to a possible remote server. This usually requires a hostname, port, username, and password. Invoking `Service`'s parameter-less `connect()` method will use the default hostname and username for that `Transport` or `Store` type and request a password using the `Authenticator` specified when initially starting the session. However, it is possible to use the other `connect()` methods and specify the hostname, port, username, and password yourself. This gives you a little more flexibility if you need to connect to more than one server for the same type of service. This is actually very necessary seeing as how most people these days have not one, but several, POP3 accounts and they often want to be able to check them all for new messages at once.

The SendMail Servlet

Now that we've seen how easy it is to send a message using JavaMail, let's try it within the context of a servlet. Did you ever wish you could send a message using your personal address while using someone else's computer? It's doubtful they would appreciate you changing their configuration. Or perhaps you're behind a firewall and can't even connect to an SMTP server but can access the web through your company's proxy. Using our `SendMail` servlet, you can send a message from any computer with only a browser. Simply visit the `SendMail` site, fill out the form, and click Send. The servlet will create the message with the email address you've specified and connect to the SMTP server for you to send it to the appropriate destination(s).

Interacting with the servlet could be accomplished with a front end similar to this:

Here's the HTML code that produced the above:

```
<HTML>
  <HEAD><TITLE>SendMail</TITLE></HEAD>
    <BODY>
      <H1>SendMail</H1>
        <form action='http://localhost:8080/servlet/SendMail' method='post'>
        <TABLE><tbody align='right'>
          <TR><TD>From:</TD><TD><input type='text' name='from' size='64'></TD>
          </TR><TR><TD>To:</TD><TD><input type='text' name='to' size='64'></TD></TR>
          <TR><TD>Cc:</TD><TD><input type='text' name='cc' size='64'></TD></TR>
          <TR><TD>Bcc:</TD><TD><input type='text' name='bcc' size='64'></TD></TR>
          <TR><TD>Subject:</TD><TD><input type='text' name='subject'
              size='64'></TD></TR>
          <TR><td colspan='2'><textarea name='text' rows='8'
              cols='64'></TEXTAREA></TD></TR>
          <TR><td colspan='2'><input type='submit' value='Send'> <input
              type='reset'></TD></TR>
        </TBODY></TABLE>
    </FORM>
  </BODY>
</HTML>
```

As you might have guessed from the form above, the `SendMail` servlet we're about to describe can take, as parameters, a single form address, a comma separated list, carbon copy and blind carbon copy addresses, a subject, and some text. The servlet also requires an SMTP host it can connect to in order to do the actual transmission. This could be either hard coded or specified as an `init` parameter passed to the servlet when first loaded by the server.

And now the `SendMail` servlet itself:

```
import javax.mail.*;
import javax.mail.internet.*;

import javax.servlet.*;
import javax.servlet.http.*;

public class SendMail extends HttpServlet {

    private String smtpHost;

    // Initialize the servlet with the hostname of the SMTP server
    // we'll be using the send the messages

    public void init(ServletConfig config)
    throws ServletException {
        super.init(config);

        smtpHost = config.getInitParameter("smtpHost");
    }

    public void doPost(
        HttpServletRequest request,
        HttpServletResponse response
    )
    throws ServletException, java.io.IOException {
        String from = request.getParameter("from");
        String to = request.getParameter("to");
        String cc = request.getParameter("cc");
        String bcc = request.getParameter("bcc");
        String subject = request.getParameter("subject");
        String text = request.getParameter("text");

        String status;

        try {
            // Create the JavaMail session
            java.util.Properties properties = System.getProperties();
            properties.put("mail.smtp.host", smtpHost);
            Session session =
            Session.getInstance(properties, null);

            // Construct the message
            MimeMessage message = new MimeMessage(session);

            // Set the from address
            Address fromAddress = new InternetAddress(from);
            message.setFrom(fromAddress);

            // Parse and set the recipient addresses
            Address[] toAddresses = InternetAddress.parse(to);
            message.setRecipients(Message.RecipientType.TO, toAddresses);
```

```
        Address[] ccAddresses = InternetAddress.parse(cc);
        message.setRecipients(Message.RecipientType.CC,ccAddresses);

        Address[] bccAddresses = InternetAddress.parse(bcc);
        message.setRecipients(Message.RecipientType.BCC,bccAddresses);

        // Set the subject and text
        message.setSubject(subject);
        message.setText(text);

        Transport.send(message);

        status = "Your message was sent.";

        } catch (AddressException e) {
            status = "There was an error parsing the addresses.";
        } catch (SendFailedException e) {
            status = "There was an error sending the message.";
        } catch (MessagingException e) {
        status = "There was an unexpected error.";
        }

    // Output a status message
    response.setContentType("text/html");

    java.io.PrintWriter writer = response.getWriter();

    writer.println("<html><head><title>Status</title></head>");
    writer.println("<body><p>" + status + "</p></body></html>");

    writer.close();
    }
}
```

Some possible useful extensions for the SendMail servlet could include adding support for HTML text and file attachments. While this would certainly increase the complexity of the code, notice that the required core functionality took little more than one page of Java code to implement.

Stores

Now that we've seen how easy it is to send messages using JavaMail, let's see how easy it is to connect to a store and list the messages stored there:

```
import javax.mail.*;
import javax.mail.internet.*;

public class ReadMailExample {
    public static void main(String[] args)
        throws MessagingException {

        if (args.length < 3) {
            System.out.println(
                "Usage: java ReadMailExample pop3Host user pass");
            System.exit(1);
        }
```

Continued on Following Page

```
          String pop3Host = args[0];
          String user = args[1];
          String pass = args[2];

          // Start the session
          java.util.Properties properties = System.getProperties();
          Session session =
          Session.getInstance(properties, null);

          // Connect to the store
          Store store = session.getStore("pop3");
          store.connect(pop3Host, user, pass);

          // Open the INBOX folder
          Folder folder = store.getFolder("INBOX");
          folder.open(Folder.READ_ONLY);

          // Get and list the messages
          Message[] messages = folder.getMessages();
          for (int i = 0; i < messages.length; ++i) {
            System.out.println(
            "From: " + messages[i].getFrom()[0] + "\n" +
            "Subject: " + messages[i].getSubject() + "\n");
          }

          // Close the folder and the store
          folder.close(false);
          store.close();
      }
  }
```

This code is almost identical in concept to sending a message. The only difference is the addition of the Folder class. Stores organize messages with folders--similar to the way in which we organize files on our hard drives. This may seem unnecessary since POP3 doesn't support any such notion of folders but the designers of JavaMail required the ability to utilize more advanced stores such as IMAP where folders did exist. Therefore, all store implementations are required to support the notion of at least one folder named INBOX. Folder-less store providers will grant access to messages only through this folder.

Lightweight Messages

Why did we wait until we were done with the messages before closing the folder and the connection to the store in the above example? Surely, listing a couple of message headers for each message did not take an inordinate amount of time. Since we had obtained the message objects with the getMessages() method, we could have possibly displayed them to the user, let the user choose which one they were interested in, and let them peruse it at their leisure. Trying to free resources by closing the connection immediately after the call to getMessages would cause an exception later on when trying to actually use the messages. The reason for this is that JavaMail requires instances of any specific Message class to be "lightweight." A lightweight message object means that it will only transfer the actual information from the store to the local machine when it is needed. The advantages to enforcing this can be seen when a message with an attachment several gigabytes in size was being stored on the server. Forcing an application to download the entire message just to display who the message was from and the subject would be a waste of time, space, bandwidth and money. This is easily accomplished with IMAP implementations but the ability to download only the attributes of a message and not the content is an optional command in POP3. Thankfully, most servers do implement this option letting Sun's provider take advantage of it.

The WebMail Servlet

The rise in popularity of mail portals such as Hotmail and Net@ddress has brought much attention to the fact that it's now possible to read and reply to your personal mail from any computer in the world provided it has access to the Internet and a Web browser. Not having to install and/or configure an email application to do such a simple task is a great boon to the average roaming Internet user.

Many users already possess at least one POP3 account, usually given to them by the Internet Service Provider they use for home access. Being able to check this account from behind the company firewall at work, for example, is usually impossible. A `WebMail` servlet, such as the one we'll be developing, not only makes this possible but rids the user of having to manage multiple email configurations. They simply surf to the site hosting the `WebMail` servlet, enter their store's hostname, username, and password, and are greeted with an HTML-ized view of their INBOX contents which they can then peruse and respond to at their leisure. It's also entirely possible for this servlet to be the focal point for multiple remote accounts. User's could "copy" messages from one store to this central store managed by the servlet and organize them into folders as they see fit. While a servlet of this magnitude is far beyond the scope of this chapter it's certainly not beyond the capabilities of any Java developer given the ease at which servlets and mail applications using JavaMail can be implemented.

A minimally complete `WebMail` servlet would include operations for logging in to the user's store, listing the messages, reading a message, replying to a message, and then logging out. This very simple example shows how this could be done with JavaMail. It's not really that complex at all. The output isn't pretty but it is functional although the code is far from bulletproof and currently will only allow one user to use the servlet at a time.

Here's the code for a simple HTML page that would let the user initiate a `WebMail` session:

```
<HTML>
<HEAD><TITLE>WebMail</title></HEAD>
<BODY>
<H1>WebMail</H1>
<form action='http://localhost:8080/servlet/WebMail' method='get'>
<input type='hidden' name='command' value='login'>
SMTP Server: <input type='text' name='smtp'><BR>
POP3 Server: <input type='text' name='pop3'><BR>
POP3 Username: <input type='text' name='user'><BR>
POP3 Password: <input type='text' name='pass'><BR>
<input type='submit'><input type='reset'>
</FORM>
</BODY>
</HTML>
```

Here, in the code for the servlet itself, we've broken up the logical parts of the `WebMail` application into six separate private methods. `doLogin()`, `doList()`, `doRead()`, `doReply()`, `doSend()`, `doLogout()` are all called from the servlet's main `doGet()` method. It's, in effect, six servlets in one. Each one takes different parameters and outputs a different HTML form as a result.

```
import java.io.*;
import java.util.*;

import javax.servlet.*;
import javax.servlet.http.*;
```

Continued on Following Page

```java
import javax.mail.*;
import javax.mail.internet.*;

public class WebMail extends HttpServlet {

    public void doGet(HttpServletRequest request,HttpServletResponse response)
        throws ServletException, IOException {

        String command = request.getParameter("command");

        try {
            if ("login".equalsIgnoreCase(command)) {
                doLogin(request, response);
            } else if ("list".equalsIgnoreCase(command)) {
                doList(request, response);
            } else if ("read".equalsIgnoreCase(command)) {
                doRead(request, response);
            } else if ("reply".equalsIgnoreCase(command)) {
                doReply(request, response);
            } else if ("send".equalsIgnoreCase(command)) {
                doSend(request, response);
            } else if ("logout".equalsIgnoreCase(command)) {
                doLogout(request, response);
            }
        } catch (MessagingException e) {
            throw new ServletException("MessagingException: " + e);
        }
    }

    private String defaultFrom;

    private Session session;
    private Store store;
    private Folder folder;

    private void doLogin(HttpServletRequest request,HttpServletResponse response)
        throws ServletException, IOException, MessagingException {
        String smtp = request.getParameter("smtp");
        String pop3 = request.getParameter("pop3");
        String user = request.getParameter("user");
        String pass = request.getParameter("pass");

        // Save a default From address
        defaultFrom = user + "@" + pop3;

        // Start the session
        java.util.Properties properties = System.getProperties();
        properties.put("mail.smtp.host", smtp);
        session = Session.getInstance(properties, null);

        // Connect to the store
        store = session.getStore("pop3");
        store.connect(pop3, user, pass);

        // Open the INBOX folder
        folder = store.getFolder("INBOX");
        folder.open(Folder.READ_ONLY);

        // List the messages
        doList(request, response);
    }
```

```java
    private Message[] messages = null;

    private void doList(HttpServletRequest request,HttpServletResponse response)
        throws ServletException, IOException, MessagingException {
        messages = folder.getMessages();

        response.setContentType("text/html");
        PrintWriter writer = response.getWriter();

        // Start a table and print the header
        writer.println(
        "<html><head><title>list</title></head>" +
        "<body><table border=\"1\">" +
        "<tr>" +
        "<th>Date</th>" +
        "<th>From</th>" +
        "<th>Subject</th>" +
        "</tr>");

        // Print each message
        for (int i = 0; i < messages.length; ++i) {
        writer.println(
        "<tr>" +
        "<td>" + messages[i].getSentDate() + "</td>" +
        "<td>" + messages[i].getFrom()[0] + "</td>" +
        "<td><a href='" + request.getRequestURI() +
        "?command=read&message=" + i + "'>" +
        messages[i].getSubject() + "</a></td>" +
        "</tr>");
        }

        // End the table
        writer.println("</table>");

        // Add a logout link
        writer.println("<p><a href='" + request.getRequestURI() +
        "?command=logout'>logout</a></p>");

        // End the page
        writer.println("</body></html>");

        writer.close();
    }

    private void doRead(HttpServletRequest request,HttpServletResponse response)
        throws ServletException, IOException, MessagingException {

        int num = Integer.parseInt(request.getParameter("message"));

        response.setContentType("text/html");
        PrintWriter writer = response.getWriter();

        MimeMessage message = (MimeMessage) messages[num];

        writer.println("<html><head><title>read: " +
        message.getSubject() +
        "</title></head><body>");
```

Continued on Following Page

```java
// Print some select headers
writer.println("<table border=\"1\">" +
"<tr><th>Date: </th><td>" +
message.getSentDate() +
"</td></tr><tr><th>From: </th><td>" +
message.getFrom()[0] +
"</td></tr><tr><th>To: </th><td>" +
message.getRecipients(
Message.RecipientType.TO)[0] +
"</td></tr><tr><th>Subject: </th><td>" +
message.getSubject() +
"</td></tr><tr><td colspan=\"2\"><p>");

ContentType ct = new ContentType(message.getContentType());

// If the text is in HTML, just print it
if ("text/html".equalsIgnoreCase(ct.getBaseType())) {
   BufferedReader reader =
   new BufferedReader(
   new InputStreamReader(
   message.getInputStream()));

   String s;

   while ((s = reader.readLine()) != null) {
      writer.println(s);
   }
} else {
   Object o = message.getContent();

   // If the text is plain, just print it
   if (o instanceof String) {
      writer.println("<pre>" + o + "</pre>");
   } else {
      // Print the content type
      writer.println(message.getContentType());

      // If it is a multipart, list the parts
      if (o instanceof MimeMultipart) {
         listParts((MimeMultipart) o, writer);
      }
   }
}

// End the message
writer.println("</p></td></tr></table>");

// Print a link to reply
writer.println("<p><a href='" +
request.getRequestURI() +
"?command=reply&message=" + num + "'>reply</a> ");


// Print a link to logout
writer.println("<a href='" +
request.getRequestURI() +
"?command=logout'>logout</a></p>");

// End the page
writer.println("</body></html>");
```

```java
        writer.close();
    }

    private void listParts(MimeMultipart mp, PrintWriter writer)
        throws MessagingException {

        writer.println("<ul>");

        for (int i = 0; i < mp.getCount(); ++i) {
            MimeBodyPart bp = (MimeBodyPart) mp.getBodyPart(i);
            writer.println("<li>" + bp.getContentType());
        }

        writer.println("</ul>");
    }

    private void doReply(HttpServletRequest request,HttpServletResponse response)
        throws ServletException, IOException, MessagingException {

        // Get the message we are replying to
        int num = Integer.parseInt(request.getParameter("message"));

        // Create a new messgage
        MimeMessage message = (MimeMessage) messages[num];

        String to = ((InternetAddress)message.getFrom()[0]).getAddress();

        String subject = "Re: " + message.getSubject();

        response.setContentType("text/html");
        PrintWriter writer = response.getWriter();
        writer.println("<html><head><title>reply</title></head><body>");
        writer.println("<form action='" + request.getRequestURI() +
        "?command=send' method='get'>");
        writer.println("<input type='hidden' name='command' value='send'>");
        writer.println("From: <input name='from' value='" +
        defaultFrom + "' type='text'><br>");
        writer.println("To: <input name='to' value='" + to +
        "' type='text'><br>");
        writer.println("Cc: <input name='cc' type='text'><br>");
        writer.println("Bcc: <input name='bcc' type='text'><br>");
        writer.println("Subject: <input name='subject' value='" +
        subject + "' type='text'><br>");
        writer.println("<textarea name='text' cols='32' rows='8'></textarea><br>");


        // Print the Submit and Reset buttons
        writer.println("<input type='submit'><input type='reset'>");

        // End the page
        writer.println("</body></html>");

        writer.close();
    }

    private void doSend(HttpServletRequest request,HttpServletResponse response)
        throws ServletException, IOException, MessagingException {
```

Continued on Following Page

```
        String from = request.getParameter("from");
        String to = request.getParameter("to");
        String cc = request.getParameter("cc");
        String bcc = request.getParameter("bcc");
        String subject = request.getParameter("subject");
        String text = request.getParameter("text");

        // Construct a message
        MimeMessage message = new MimeMessage(session);

        message.setFrom(new InternetAddress(from));

        message.setRecipients(Message.RecipientType.TO,
        InternetAddress.parse(to));
        message.setRecipients(Message.RecipientType.CC,
        InternetAddress.parse(cc));
        message.setRecipients(Message.RecipientType.BCC,
        InternetAddress.parse(bcc));

        message.setSubject(subject);

        message.setText(text);

        // Send the messge
        Transport.send(message);

        response.setContentType("text/html");
        PrintWriter writer = response.getWriter();

        writer.println("<html><head><title>send</title></head><body>");
        writer.println("<p>Your message was sent.</p>");
        writer.println("</body></html>");
        writer.close();
    }

    private void doLogout(HttpServletRequest request,HttpServletResponse response)
        throws ServletException, IOException, MessagingException {

        // Close the folder and store
        folder.close(false);
        store.close();

        // Say goodbye
        response.setContentType("text/html");
        PrintWriter writer = response.getWriter();

        writer.println("<html><head><title>logout</title></head>");
        writer.println("<body><p>Goodbye.</p></body></html>");

        writer.close();
    }
}
```

That's it. The code is rather straightforward. The only method that might need some explanation is `doRead()`. Since MIME messages are capable of containing virtually any type of content, we need to check what the content type of the message is before blindly outputting it to the user's browser. Since many email clients send text as HTML and since HTML is our delivery mechanism, we first check the content type for `text/html` and retrieve an `InputStream` to the text so that we can output it to the user. This is necessary since accessing content types for which no `DataContentHandler` exists can only be done through an `InputStream`. Otherwise, we could have used the `getContent()` method like we do when the content type isn't `text/html`.

After retrieving the actual content object (via the JAF--although that part is nicely hidden from us), we check to see if it's an instance of String. If so, we can just output the string to the client between <PRE></PRE> tags. If not, we simply print the content type with one extra check to see if the object is an instance of MimeMultipart and, if so, we list the parts by calling the listParts() method. A much more useful implementation would write the content to disk (by getting its InputStream) and displaying the file in the case of types like image/gif or letting the user click on a link to download the file to their local machine. This is left as an exercise for the reader.

Summary

I hope we've shown that using JavaMail gives programmers the ability to actually make use of messaging protocols like SMTP and POP3 without having to implement any of the low-level details of the protocols we normally would. In addition, adding support for an even more advanced and complex protocol such as IMAP to the WebMail servlet would be a breeze. Note that there's still a lot of work left to do not only to make the code robust but also to add all of the features users would most likely demand such as the ability to download content types that aren't displayable and the ability to display content types that are (other than text/plain and text/html).

What we have covered in this chapter:

> The installation of the JavaMail API and its usage.

> How to construct a message for use through JavaMail.

> Understanding the uses of transports and stores.

Introducing XML

Despite its relatively young age, XML (Extensible Markup Language) has had a deep impact on how the enterprise utilizes data. XML influences how we view, process, transport, and manage data. XML opens up many possibilities that simply were not available in the past. In this chapter, we introduce XML and some related standards. We then turn to how XML can be used in conjunction with an object-oriented programming language such as Java. We present two prevalent standards in dealing with XML documents programmatically. Finally, we turn to some architectural discussion where we combine XML and server-based Java to come up with some rather interesting results.

What is XML?

XML is another three-letter acronym to show the world that the computer industry is doing well and is still very much able to generate acronyms! On a more serious note, XML is a markup language. It is a simplified version of SGML (Standard Generalized Markup Language). SGML is used extensively in the document industry to facilitate management and markup of a variety of documents. The people who created XML wanted a more simplified version of SGML that could be used in the context of the Internet. XML is now a W3C standard and you can read the full specification at the following URL:

http://www.w3.org/TR/1998/REC-xml-19980210.html

One way to understand XML is to associate it with something you already know. If you think about it, you are already very familiar with a markup language: HTML. HTML is content marked up with some tags to specify its visual presentation. For example, the following is plain and simple content:

```
I love Pizza.
```

The following is the same plain and simple content marked up by HTML:

```
<H1> I love Pizza </H1>
```

Your browser knows how to interpret HTML tags. It knows how to separate content from markup. The instructions specified by the markup are used to create a visual presentation of the content that is what you end up seeing on your browser. A markup language is used to add some extra information to the content. In this case, the `<H1>` tag indicates the content is a Level 1 Header. You wouldn't have known that if you just looked at the plain and simple content.

Most HTML tags deal with presentation and layout of content. For example, the `<TABLE>` tag allows you to format some content in a tabular fashion. There is no question that when it comes to sharing information on the Web, HTML is currently the de facto standard. However, why should markup be limited to presentation and layout? Why can't content be marked up to provide additional information about the content itself and not just its layout? What happens if you like HTML, but wish you could add just one more tag to the specification so the page formatting will look just right? These questions show some of the limitations of HTML and lead us to XML.

XML is a bit different compared to other markup languages. XML is a language from which other markup languages can be created. These other markup languages are called XML applications. For example, the Chemical Markup Language (CML) is a markup language for the chemistry field and it is specified using XML. Efforts are under way to formally specify HTML using XML. If such standards are accepted within various industries, data exchange and communication will become much easier. Some XML applications that are either complete or under development are:

> Channel Definition Format (CDF) – introduced as part of IE 4.0 browser, CDF allows content to be pushed to browsers.

> Open Software Description (OSD) – a standard for specifying various parts of a software package. This information is useful for installation of the package under various environments.

> Open Financial Exchange (OFX) – a standard for exchange of financial information.

> Synchronized Multimedia Integration Language (SMIL) - a standard for sharing multimedia information.

> Mathematical Markup Language (MathML) – allows for markup of various mathematical entities and notations.

> Bioinformatic Sequence Markup Language (BSML) – a standard used for specifying biological characteristics such as DNA sequences.

> Resource Description Framework (RDF).

> vCard (Electronic Business Card) – a standard for specifying business card-like data.

> Tutorial Markup Language (TML) - a standard for marking up a tutorial.

> HTTP Distribution and Replication Protocol (DRP)- this protocol is to significantly improve the efficiency and reliability of data distribution over HTTP.

> Weather Observation Markup Format (OMF) – standard for weather related information.

> Java Speech Markup Language (JSML) – allows documents to include tags that will tie in with Java Speech API for pronunciation and document structures.

> Open Trading Protocol (OTP) - provides an interoperable framework for Internet commerce.

> Information and Content Exchange (ICE) – to facilitate content exchange among Web sites.

So why is XML different and what makes it useful? Experts from different backgrounds have different answers for the above question. Some of the main benefits of XML are that it is **extensible**, it is **structured** and it is **validating**. These points are discussed below.

Extensible

As the name of the language suggests, XML is extensible. With XML, you can create your own tags, which immediately opens up unlimited possibilities. You are no longer limited to tags dealing with presentation or layout. In fact, if you look at current XML applications you'll find markup languages dealing with mathematics, resumes, recipes, and many other fields. This extensibility also has a side effect of allowing the experts in a particular field to define the standard for that field. Many industries have already started efforts to define standards for their respective fields. Throughout this chapter we focus on the Pizza Markup Language (PML). We have just made up the tags and the markup language to show the extensibility of XML. Here is how we can describe a pizza using PML:

```
<pizza>
<topping extracheese="yes"> Pepperoni </topping>
<price> 12.99 </price>
<size> large </size>
</pizza>
```

Structured

Another important benefit of XML is that it adds structure to your data. If we strip out the XML tags from the above example, we have:

```
Pepperoni (extracheese)
12.99
large
```

As a human, you may look at the above and guess the context of each line and figure out its structure. You would guess that the first line is the topping, `12.99` is probably the price, and `large` is the size. However, a computer can't do what you just did. It needs some help and it likes structured data. XML not only provides meaningful tags to explain the data, but it also holds a certain structure. For example, we see a "containment" relationship where topping, price, and size are elements that are contained by pizza. As you will see later, the inherent structure of XML documents is very important when it comes to manipulation and interaction between a programming language and XML data.

Validation

Another benefit of XML is that it is validating. Using a **Document Type Definition** (which you will learn more about later), you can create a set of rules or grammar that will validate your documents. In order to make sure that everyone who uses the Pizza Markup Language plays by the rules, we must also provide a DTD for this markup language. This way, we can check a given document against the PML's DTD to make sure it satisfies all the specified rules. For example, we have decided that pizza must always contain a size (small, medium, or large). A pizza that has no size specification is not "valid" based on our markup language for pizza. This "rule" is specified via a DTD and there are programs that check a given document against a DTD.

The DTD helps in several ways. For one thing, it provides a standard mechanism to specify a grammar. That means, if a program can interpret a DTD it can interpret a wide variety of rules specified by it. The specification of XML rules via a DTD also means that a document that claims to be compliant to a specific XML application can easily be checked. This means that the program itself does not have to worry about validity of a given document. For example, if we write a program to handle orders at a pizza store, that program can expect every pizza to have a size, a price and a topping. That's because the DTD requires that. If someone creates an invalid pizza (say it is missing the topping), then our program would not even bother to look at it since it is not valid.

This is important since it guarantees data uniformity. Programs can be written so they focus on what the data is rather than what the data should be. If the data is verified before processing occurs, then the program has to deal less with exceptions and "special" cases. In actual fact, the DTD cannot capture every kind of rule, so the program must still do some error checking.

What Does XML Look Like?

All XML documents must satisfy a number of rules to be considered "well-formed". Programs only know how to deal with well-formed XML documents. Basically, a well-formed document is one that is properly tagged. Every tag must have a corresponding closing tag unless the tag is empty (and there is a short-hand notation for that). If a tag contains attributes, then the value of the attribute must be enclosed in quotations like this:

```
<topping extracheese="yes"> Pepperoni </topping>
```

Nesting is also important. That means the last opened tag must be the first to close. Here is a simple demonstration:

```
<header1>
    <header2>
         <header3>
         </header3>
    </header2>
</header1>
```

The indentation doesn't mean anything as far as XML is concerned. It is merely for enhancing readability by a human.

If a tag is empty (it contains nothing between the opening and closing tags), then XML allows a shorthand notation. The following:

```
<isfresh/>
```

is equivalent to:

```
<isfresh></isfresh>
```

For a complete description of all the rules for a "well-formed" XML document, you need to refer to the XML specification, but you already know the important pieces.

This XML stuff looks the same as HTML. What's up?

If you know HTML, the discussion we have had on XML so far is going to look very similar to HTML. XML, however, offers more and you have to read on to find out about other features of XML. HTML can be written as an application of XML (and there are efforts underway to do just that). However poor practice, along with forgiving browsers, has produced millions of HTML pages that do not satisfy the well-formedness requirement. For example, most people do not close the <p> tag in their HTML pages. That is one violation of the well-formedness criterion that requires every tag to have a corresponding closing tag. The fact that most browsers are forgiving of "poor" HTML programming practices aggravates the problem even more. HTML is close to being a well-formed XML, but is not quite there yet. In fairness, HTML is a markup language just like XML, but it is much more focused and limited. It has a defined set of tags and is focused on marking up content to be presented as Web pages. XML can be used to define tags in any domain and is extensible by its nature.

Parsing with Java

We are now going to change direction briefly and turn to Java. As you have seen, the rules for checking whether an XML document is well-formed or not are relatively simple. XML documents themselves are basically text files, so we should be able to write a program that checks a given XML file for well-formedness. The good news is that this program has already been written (by many different people) and is called an "XML parser". A parser takes an XML document and generates an event stream based on the tags it encounters. These event streams can also be translated to a data structure that represents the document. If the XML document is not well-formed, then the parser fails (as it should do). We are going to do a lot with parsers, but for now, we just want to introduce a simple parser and describe how to set up and use it.

A number of XML parsers have been written in a variety of languages. A partial listing is given below.

> XML Parser by IBM: (http://www.alphaworks.ibm.com)

> XML Parser by Sun: (http://java.sun.com/xml)

> XML Parser by DataChannel/Microsoft: (http://www.datachannel.com)

> Jim Clark's Parser: (http://www.jclark.com)

The parser we will use in this chapter is from Sun Microsystems. It is written in Java and is a core part of a suite of XML tools that Sun is working on. You will need a JDK 1.1 or higher compliant Java compiler and interpreter (JVM).

After installing the JDK, you need to download and install the parser from the following URL:

http://developer.java.sun.com/developer/earlyAccess/xml/index.html

Note that the above URL belongs to the Java Developer's Connection. You will need to register (it's free) before you can access the necessary files.

After installation, you should have a directory tree that looks like this:

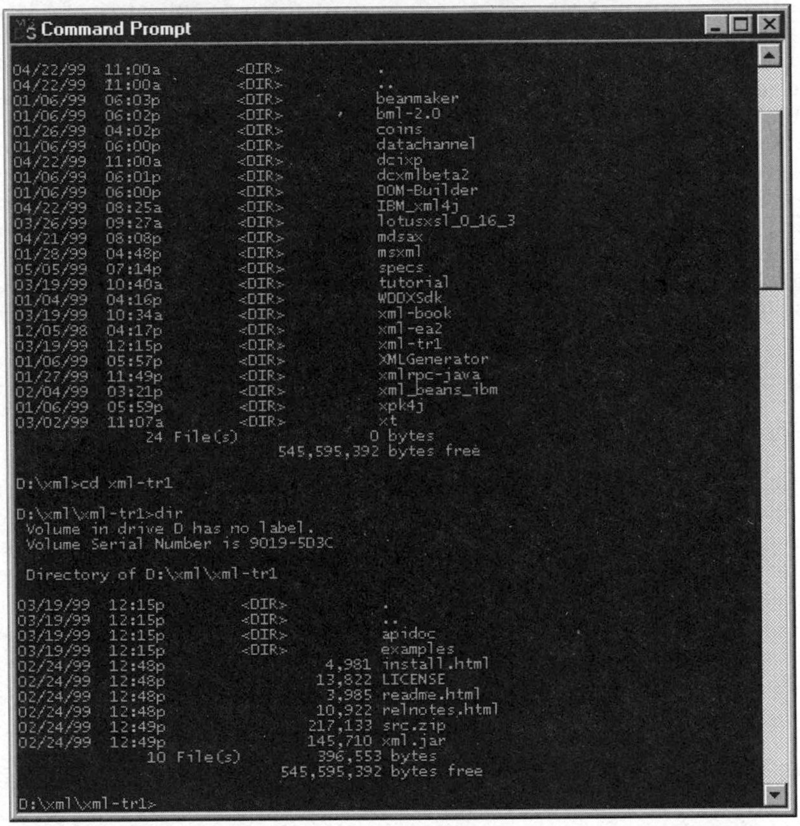

The file `xml.jar` contains all the classes related to the XML parser. You will need to include this file in your CLASSPATH in order to compile and run programs in this chapter. For now, let's take a look at a short program that takes an XML file as its input, parses it, and then writes the parsed version as its output. Should the XML file contain any errors, the parser will catch them and show an appropriate message. As you will see, the parser is your first tool when tackling XML documents. The code is shown here:

```
import java.io.File;
import com.sun.xml.parser.Resolver;
import com.sun.xml.tree.XmlDocument;
import org.xml.sax.InputSource;
import org.xml.sax.SAXException;
import org.xml.sax.SAXParseException;

public class Simpleparser
{
    public static void main (String argv [])
    {
        InputSource       input;
        XmlDocument       doc;
```

```
        if (argv.length != 1)
        {
            System.err.println("Usage: java Simpleparser [filename]");
            System.exit (1);
        }

        try
        {
            input = Resolver.createInputSource (new File(argv [0]));
            doc = XmlDocument.createXmlDocument (input, false);
            doc.getDocumentElement ().normalize ();
            doc.write (System.out);
        }
        catch (SAXParseException err)
        {
            System.out.println ("** Parsing                    error" + ", line " +
                            err.getLineNumber ()   +
                            ", uri " + err.getSystemId ());
            System.out.println("     " +    err.getMessage ());
        }
        catch (SAXException e)
        {
            e.printStackTrace();
        }
        catch (Throwable t)
        {
            t.printStackTrace();
        }
    }
}
```

Let's point out the highlights of the code shown above. The classes related to XML parsing are organized into a series of packages that need to be imported into each program. You see all the statements to do this at the beginning. We then create an instance of an `InputSource` and pass it to the `createXmlDocument()` method to create an instance of an `XmlDocument`. The second parameter passed to the `createXmlDocument()` method indicates whether the parser should only check for well-formedness or also for validity. Since we are just interested in the well-formedness of the XML document, we pass a `"false"` value there. The `createXmlDocument()` method is the line that actually invokes the XML parser. Different parser implementations invoke the parser in various ways. You should consult the documentation that comes with the parser to learn how it should be invoked from within a Java program.

Now we have our first Java program that does something with an XML document, let's create a quick XML document to experiment with. Note that our Java program will take any XML document as its input so you can use any XML files of your own. While the first line of the XML file may look unusual, it is actually a requirement for all XML files. It should be the first line of the file, indicating the version and the fact that the file is an XML file. Our simple XML file representing a pizza is:

```
<?xml version="1.0"?>
  <pizza>
    <topping extracheese="yes"> Pepperoni </topping>
    <price> 12.99 </price>
    <size> large </size>
  </pizza>
```

277

You should compile the Java program now (if you haven't done already). Make sure your CLASSPATH environmental variable contains the full path to the jar file xml.jar. You can then compile the program with

```
javac Simpleparser.java
```

and then you run the program giving the path to the pizza.xml file as a parameter on the command line, as in:

```
java Simpleparser pizza.xml
```

You should get the output:

```
<?xml version="1.0" encoding="UTF-8"?>

<pizza>

  <topping extracheese="yes"> Pepperoni </topping>

  <price> 12.99 </price>

  <size> large </size>

</pizza>
```

There is not much happening visibly, but behind the scenes some interesting things have happened. The XML parser was invoked and it processed the XML file, checking it for well-formedness. It then output the parsed file which, in this case, looks pretty much like the original file except that it has been reformatted.

Just so you believe that something is indeed happening and the program is not simply copying its input to the console, let's introduce an error in the input XML file and see what happens. For example, let's change the closing tag for <price> to </prices>. You know that a well-formed XML document must have a matching closing tag for each opening tag. With the introduction of the above error, we have violated that rule and hopefully the parser will catch it. Here is the output you should get if you try running the program with the erroneous file:

```
** Parsing                        error, line 4, uri file:/D:/data/wrox/pizza.xml
   Next character must be ">" terminating element "price".
```

Now that's not bad. The error message may not be very descriptive (which may not be a surprise), but it does point to the line in the XML file where the error occurred.

You now know how to access and parse an XML file from within a Java program. The parser will automatically check the XML file for well-formedness (that's a lot of code that you don't have to write). Parsing is going to be your first line of attack in most circumstances. It is through parsing that you can collect information about the structure and content of the XML document systematically and use it within your program. You will see later how this information can be captured, but before going there, we need to cover another kind of XML document commonly known as a valid XML document.

Valid XML Documents

So far we have only looked at well-formed XML documents. These documents offer many of the advantages of XML such as extensibility and adding structure to a set of data. If you recall, we mentioned that with XML you not only have the ability to create your own tags (for markup purposes), but you can also develop a grammar (rules) that can later validate your documents. A well-formed XML document that also complies with a Document Type Definition (DTD) is called a valid XML document. The DTD is where you specify the grammar for the markup language you have created. The distinction between a DTD and an XML document is important. Given a DTD, we can "verify" any XML document that claims to be compliant with that DTD and therefore the application will only end up dealing with XML documents that have been verified.

As you may have guessed, a parser is used to verify XML documents against a DTD. In fact, with a minor change, our `Simpleparser.java` program can become a valid parser. By definition, every valid XML document is also well-formed, but the reverse is not necessarily true.

There are several advantages of going the extra mile and creating a DTD for an XML document. With a DTD it is easier to maintain multiple documents or document sets and assure their compliance to a set of rules. Your applications will be assured of receiving a compliant XML document and this cuts out a lot of error checking on the part of the application. Also, you are using a standard (DTD) to write your rules which means the rules can be used by other programs.

What Does a DTD Look Like?

There are two things you need to be concerned with when dealing with a DTD. First, you have to create a DTD and second, you have to associate the DTD with an XML document. This association can be done in two ways: embedded and external. The DTD can be embedded right into the XML document, which gives you a single document containing both the rules and the content. This approach is usually used for smaller documents. A second way is to have an external file containing the DTD and have different XML documents pointing to it. You do that via the following line:

```
<!DOCTYPE doctype SYSTEM "foo.dtd">
```

where *doctype* refers to the parent tag of the document (the outmost tag) and *foo.dtd* is a file containing the actual DTD. The DTD can reside on a different machine across the Internet and in those cases, *foo.dtd* needs to be expanded to point to the URL of the file.

Here is our pizza XML with an embedded DTD:

```
<?xml version="1.0"?>

<!DOCTYPE pizza [
    <!ELEMENT pizza (topping, price, size)>
    <!ELEMENT topping (#PCDATA)>
    <!ELEMENT price (#PCDATA)>
    <!ELEMENT size (#PCDATA)>
    <!ATTLIST topping extracheese (yes|no) "no">
]>
```

Continued on Following Page

```
<pizza>
   <topping extracheese="yes"> Pepperoni </topping>
   <price> 12.99 </price>
   <size> large </size>
</pizza>
```

Let's go through the above code and then we'll cover in detail the various rules that can be specified via a DTD. The DTD is embedded within the `<!DOCTYPE>` tag. You can see that each element in the pizza file is represented in the DTD. The first element described is `<pizza>` and this tag must contain three other tags, namely `<topping>`, `<price>` and `<size>` in the order specified. So if we create a `<pizza>` tag that does not include a `<price>` tag, we have violated the first rule specified by the DTD and the parser would catch that violation. The other elements are said to contain `#PCDATA` which means Parsed Character Data. This is XML's way of saying they'll just contain text. The last rule deals with the attribute `extracheese`, which is part of the `<topping>` tag. The rule says this attribute can have two values, namely `yes` and `no`, and if the attribute is missing, the default is `no`. This should give you a feel for the type of rules that you can specify with a DTD.

A word of caution. Some people consider creating a DTD the boring part of XML, but the DTD is a very important part of developing an XML document. There are software packages that help you with this task, but most importantly you have to do your homework and have a good idea of the structure and the content of the XML document so you can create consistent and useful rules for checking those documents. In the next section, we will go through most of the different rules that can be specified by a DTD. You will soon find out that there are limits on what a DTD can check for, so again, a careful analysis of your XML document is crucial to developing a good, solid DTD for it.

Names

As we have seen, the tags that make up our document (elements) and the attributes all have names that most likely we have to make up. An XML document can contain almost any character from any language. The character encoding is specified in the header of an XML document. The limitation is what the application can support. The names that you make up are restricted by the following two rules:

> ➢ They can only contain four punctuation symbols – hyphens (-), underscores (_), colons (:), and periods (.). Any other punctuation characters are not acceptable in XML and will be rejected by the parser.

> ➢ They cannot begin with the character string "xml", "XML", or any capitalization variation. All "xml" variations are reserved for future use by XML standards.

This is not very restrictive, so you should have no trouble coming up with creative names to mark up your document. The next area addressed by DTD is the logical relationship between the elements such as who contains what, etc. DTDs use a system called **Extended Backus-Naur Format**, which gives you a method of specifying elements in XML documents, indicating how they relate and how they should be put together. The table below lists the Extended Backus-Naur operators and describes the function of each of them.

Operator	Description	Example
()	Enclose a sequence or group of choices	(topping, price, size)
,	Separate items in a list of required elements that must appear in order	(topping, price, size)
		Separate items in a list of choices	(yes|no)
?	Show that the element can occur 0 or 1 times	(topping?, price, size)
*	Show that the element can occur 0 or more times	(topping*, price, size)
+	Show that the element can occur 1 or more times	(topping+, price, size)

If you are familiar with wildcard operators in regular expressions, this should look familiar. Logically, you have to look at the element relationships and see which operator is most appropriate.

Data Types

Some of your tags are going to contain other tags. This is how the logical hierarchy of your XML document is determined. The containment hierarchy usually ends in elements that contain text. For example, in our pizza example, we have a simple hierarchy:

```
pizza
  |------->price
                |----->12.00
```

The `pizza` element contains `price`. `Price` could contain another tag, but in this case it does not. It contains some text (`12.00`) that indicates the price of the pizza. The most common way of specifying that an element contains some text is to specify its data type to be of `#PCDATA` (parsed character data). This means that the parser will actually parse the text and look for specific constructs. One such construct is an entity construct, which allows you to use a shorthand notation to specify a long text.

Sometimes, you don't want the element content to be parsed. You want it to be treated just as it is. One simple example is when your XML document is trying to provide instructions for coding XML. You don't want the instructions to be parsed (since they contain valid XML tags). You simply want the instructions to stay as they are and shown accordingly. In such cases you should use `CDATA` which stands for Character Data. The parser does not parse content that is marked as `CDATA` in the DTD. Here is an example of using `CDATA` in an attribute:

```
<!ATTLIST topping extracheese CDATA  #REQUIRED>
```

Now, instead of being limited to the two values of yes and no, any character data can be inserted as the value of the `extracheese` attribute.

Comments

You should include comments within your DTD so that others can follow its logic. This is a good practice since there are no standard ways of inheriting from a DTD, but many times you will discover that the DTD you want to create is just a modification of an existing DTD. With access to the DTD and its comments, the job of creating a subset DTD for your own needs becomes simpler.

The only restriction in using comments is that you must place them between tags (not inside them), and you must only use character data and not markup tags. The following code shows how you might include a comment within a DTD:

```
<!ELEMENT pizza (topping, prize, size)>
<!--Here are some comments-->
<!ELEMENT price (#PCDATA)>
```

Include/Ignore

Within a DTD you don't have conditional and looping structures, but there is the ability to include/exclude certain parts of the DTD. You typically utilize this feature when developing the DTD for optimization, debugging and restructuring. The syntax is simple as shown below:

```
<![IGNORE[
<!ELEMENT pizza (topping, price, size)>
]]>
<![INCLUDE[
<!ELEMENT pizza (topping, price, size, name)>
]]>
```

We have two declarations for the pizza element. The one we have used so far only includes `topping`, `price`, and `size` tags. Now we also want to include the name of the person who took the order. We refer to this tag as "name" and have modified the declaration of pizza accordingly. Everything between the `<![IGNORE[` and `]]>` is ignored by the parser. Typically, you put the part of the DTD that you know works in this part. Everything between the `<![INCLUDE[` and `]]>` is processed by the parser and usually contains the new things that you are testing out. You may not appreciate the include/ignore construct in our simple example, but for larger and more complex DTDs, this construct can prove very useful to systematically introduce changes in the document.

Processing Instructions

Processing instructions allow XML documents to contain instructions for the application using the XML document. You are already familiar with one processing instruction:

```
<?xml version="1.0"?>
```

This tells the XML parser that the document is an XML document and it is based on version 1.0 of the specification. The processing instructions take the form of:

```
<?ApplicationName [instruction]?>
```

The name xml is reserved for processing instructions specific to XML. Aside from the version number, you can specify whether the DTD is standalone or not like this:

```
<?xml version="1.0" standalone="no"?>
```

A declaration like this indicates that the DTD references other DTD's.

Another attribute that is specified in the xml processing instruction is the character encoding for the DTD and XML document. The default encoding is UTF-8, which includes all common ASCII characters in addition to most characters used in common Western languages. The following code adds the encoding attribute:

```
<?xml version="1.0" standalone="no" encoding="UTF-8"?>
```

Element Declarations

You should first think about what logical components your XML document requires. Once that is established, in most cases you can create a one-to-one mapping between the components you came up with and XML elements. For example, to represent a chapter in a book, you may come up with the following logical components:

Title
Number
Heading
Paragraph

In your DTD, you will most likely have a section that declares these elements:

```
<!ELEMENT Title …>
<!ELEMENT Number …>
<!ELEMENT Heading …>
<!ELEMENT Paragraph …>
```

The element name must match the tag names inside the document. The part that is noted by ... is what we'll focus on next. This is where you indicate *what* can be included within the element. The *what* can take several forms as listed below:

- Only specified elements can be included.
- Only data, such as words, numbers, or characters, can be included.
- Both specified elements and data can be included.
- Any element or data can be included.
- No elements or data can be included.

If an element contains other elements, you can specify what those "children" elements are. The most straightforward way is to list the "children" elements separated by commas (as we did for the pizza element). Another way is to use an OR operation. For example, a book chapter must have either a chapter title or a chapter number. This can be declared using the following:

```
<!ELEMENT chapter (title | number)>
```

With this declaration, both of the following are considered valid:

```
<chapter>
    <title> The chapter title </title>
</chapter>
```

```
<chapter>
    <number> 5 </number>
</chapter>
```

The following, however, is not valid since it contains both title and number:

```
<chapter>
    <title> The chapter title </title>
    <number> 5 </number>
</chapter>
```

An element may contain only data (not other elements). In that case, you use #PCDATA in the element declaration as we did before. This means that within the opening and closing tag for the element there can be any words, numbers and characters.

If you want to allow both elements and data to be included, then you use a notation like this:

```
<!ELEMENT chapter (#PCDATA | number)*>
```

Note that the order is important. The * at the end means that the mixture of data and elements can occur any number of times. The following XML code is consistent with the above DTD element declaration:

```
<chapter>
The best chapter in the book <number>5</number>
</chapter>
```

Sometimes you may want to remove any restrictions and allow anything and everything within an element. The keyword to use here is ANY, for example

```
<!ELEMENT chapter ANY>
```

This means that between the opening and closing tags for chapter you can have data, elements, characters – basically anything. You should have a good reason to use this declaration, since by allowing anything you lose one of the advantages of XML which is the structure of your data and the intended hierarchical relationship between the elements. Also, there is not much the parser can do as far as checking is concerned when the element declaration is ANY. The parser checks the rules that you specify in the DTD and makes sure that XML documents conform to it. The more rigid your rules are, the more effective the parser can be in verifying your documents.

The final case would be if you want to specify that nothing can be included within the tag. In other words the rule you want to specify is that the element is empty. That can be done using the following syntax:

```
<!ELEMENT chapter EMPTY>
```

The corresponding XML code would either look like

```
<chapter></chapter>
```

or the equivalent shorthand notation

```
<chapter/>
```

Note that this does not mean the element cannot have attributes. The following is still valid even though the element itself was declared to be empty:

```
<chapter title="My Chapter" number="4"></chapter>
```

Attribute Declarations

Just as HTML tags have attributes, XML elements can also have attributes and your rules can specify certain characteristics of these attributes. Such rules are specified using attribute declarations.

A simple rule would be to declare existence of an attribute. In our pizza DTD, extracheese was an attribute and it had two possible values: yes and no. The attribute declaration is shown here:

```
<!ATTLIST topping extracheese (yes|no) "no">
```

There are three ways you can limit the value of the attribute. Remember that extracheese is the attribute in the above example. One way is to allow any character data as the value of the attribute. Here is an example:

```
<!ATTLIST topping extracheese CDATA>
```

The following XML code fragments would satisfy the above rule:

```
<topping extracheese="yes">sausage</topping>
<topping extracheese="sure">sausage</topping>
<topping extracheese="lots of">sausage</topping>
```

This approach provides too much freedom to the author of the XML document as far as providing attribute values. It also makes it more difficult for the application since it has to be able to deal with a variety of attribute values.

A second approach would allow usage of enumerated values. This means that the possible valid values are listed (for example, yes and no) and the XML author would have to pick one of them. Here is an example:

```
<!ATTLIST topping extracheese (yes|no)>
```

Each attribute declaration can also have a setting. If the attribute and its value must be present, then the setting should be #REQUIRED, as in

```
<!ATTLIST topping  extracheese (yes|no)  #REQUIRED>
```

The #IMPLIED setting indicates the attribute's presence is optional (implied).

The third approach is used to indicate that the attribute always contains a fixed value and the fixed value is specified. Here is an example:

```
<!ATTLIST chapter heading (CDATA) #FIXED "A Day in the Dark">
```

When you used a fixed declaration, then the parser will reject all attribute values that do not match the fixed value specified (the string "A Day in the Dark" in the above example). By using this approach, you still keep the notation as an attribute but fix the value as a constant.

Entity Declarations

Everybody hates typing, especially typing long phrases. Macro-like substitutions are a part of most programming languages. The idea is that you type the long phrase once and give it a name. Throughout the rest of the program, you simply refer to the name and the "processor" will replace the name with the actual long phrase. In XML, entity declarations serve a similar purpose. Aside from saving you from retyping the same thing over and over again, by using an entity declaration you have a more rigid control over the content. You can change the declaration (in one place) and that change is immediately reflected throughout the entire document. There are three types of entity declarations. They are:

> ➤ General Entities
> ➤ Parameter Entities
> ➤ Character Entities

We'll discuss each one in turn.

General Entities

General entities allow you to make substitutions within an XML document. They are defined in the DTD, but the substitution is intended for the body of the XML document (not for the DTD itself).

Most pizza places have the same types of pizza, they just have a different store names. So we want our pizzamenu document to be generic and usable by different pizza parlors. This is where a general entity declaration would be helpful. If we store the pizza parlor's name using a general entity, then we only have to make the change once. The same XML document can be used to print menus for different pizza parlors. To do this, you need a line like this in the DTD:

```
<!ENTITY storename "Villa Pizza">
```

Inside your XML code, anytime you needed to reference the store name you would use `&storename;` like this:

```
<header>Welcome to &storename;</header>
```

The parser would transform the above line into:

```
<header>Welcome to Villa Pizza</header>
```

The above is an example of an *internal* entity. The definition is contained within one DTD and any XML document that uses that DTD can use the entity. There is another kind of entity called *external* entity where a reference is made to a different file. Suppose you have multiple DTDs and want to make a change that will be reflected across all DTDs. With the internal entity, you have to go and change each DTD individually. With an external entity, you make the change once, and since all DTDs pointed to an external file, they all inherit the change. Here is an external entity declaration example:

```
<!ENTITY storename SYSTEM "storename.txt">
```

The content of `storename.txt` is inserted wherever the entity `"storename"` is used.

Parameter Entities

While general entities focus mostly on the XML document, parameter entities focus on the DTD. Using parameter entities you can build and reuse DTDs more effectively by providing automatic substitution. Unlike general entities, the substitution and expansion happens in the DTD itself. Here is the general form of an internal parameter entity:

```
<!ENTITY % name definition>
```

Notice that this code begins with a percent sign (%) and follows with the entity name (`name`), then with the expansion text or definition of the entity (`definition`). The entity name must begin with a letter or an underscore (_), but you can use letters, numbers, dashes (-), underscores (_), periods (.), or colons (:) in the rest of the name.

If you have a set of elements in your current DTD that all have a common set of attributes (e.g., `UserName` and `ModifiedDate`), you could define those attributes one time at the top of the DTD, as shown here:

```
<!ENTITY % commonAttributes
"UserName CDATA #REQUIRED
 ModifiedDate CDATA #REQUIRED">
```

Then for each element that requires those two attributes, you can simply include the parameter entity `commonAttributes`, rather than the complete text. As an example, if we had the following code

```
<!ELEMENT report (#PCDATA | content )*>
<!ATTLIST report %commonAttributes;>
```

then a parser would expand the entity references to look like this:

```
<!ELEMENT report (#PCDATA | content )*>
<!ATTLIST report
 UserName CDATA #REQUIRED
 ModifiedDate CDATA #REQUIRED>
```

With the external parameter entity, you can change a set of DTDs at once. Again, remember that with parameter entities the change is happening in the DTD itself. Here is an example. You can have a master (reference) DTD with an entity definition like this:

```
<!ENTITY storename "Villa Pizza">
```

The rest of the DTDs in your collection would reference the master DTD as follows:

```
<!ENTITY % storename SYSTEM "http://www.pizza.com/storenameinfo.dtd" >
```

In this case, you could include the `storenameinfo.dtd` file in all DTDs that referenced it and apply all entities (and everything else) defined in the DTD to all documents referencing it.

Character Entities

Every language has some reserved words and characters and every language has a special provision for situations when you need to use those reserved words and characters in their regular context. XML is no exception. As you may have guessed, characters like < and " have special meanings in XML. Character entities allow you to include such characters in your document without treating them as special characters.

For example, instead of typing the character >, you would need to type > (note the semicolon at the end). The table below shows some of the built-in character entities:

Character Entity	Resulting Symbol
&amp;	&
&lt;	<
&gt;	>
&apos;	'
&quote;	"

You're not limited to using only these five built-in character entities. You should refer to the language set your XML document is using for other character entities and their corresponding notation. You can also create your own characters like this:

```
<!ENTITY sharp  "&#x266F;">
```

The above character entity is a musical notation. You use character entities like general entities inside the XML document like this:

```
<HINT>Musicians rely on the &sharp; symbol to make wonderful music.</HINT>
```

Notation Declarations

Notation declarations help applications to process non-XML data. The XML parser knows how to parse XML. It can resolve references to other XML documents that may exist in the parent XML file. It cannot, however, parse a GIF image and use some attributes of that image to complete parsing the entire document. Notation declarations allow you to specify how a non-XML document such as a GIF file may be processed:

```
<!NOTATION gif SYSTEM "gifview.exe">
```

The above notation suggests (but does not require) that the processing application use the program gifview.exe to process gif files. Note that this is not system independent as the program on a Unix platform most likely won't have the .exe extension.

Parsing Valid XML

With all the various rules in a DTD, you might think, "How am I going to check the XML document against the DTD?". Well, there are still a few things in this world that you don't have to worry about and one of them is existence of XML parsers that check for validity. In fact, the program you used to check for well-formedness can also be used to check for valid documents with a minor change. You simply have to pass a boolean true to the `createXmlDocument` method of the `XmlDocument` class. This will indicate that the parser must also check for validity in addition to well-formedness. Of course, if you are going to use this option, then you must make sure that a DTD exists to validate against, otherwise you will get an error. The listing below shows the `Validparser.java` program.

```java
import java.io.File;
import com.sun.xml.parser.Resolver;
import com.sun.xml.tree.XmlDocument;
import org.xml.sax.InputSource;
import org.xml.sax.SAXException;
import org.xml.sax.SAXParseException;

public class validParser
{
    public static void main (String argv [])
    {
        InputSource     input;
        XmlDocument     doc;

        if (argv.length != 1)
        {
            System.err.println ("Usage: cmd filename");
            System.exit (1);
        }

        try
        {
            input = Resolver.createInputSource (new File(argv [0]));
            doc  = XmlDocument.createXmlDocument (input, true);
            doc.getDocumentElement ().normalize ();
            doc.write (System.out);
        }
        catch (SAXParseException err)
        {
            System.out.println ("** Parsing                    error" + ", line " +
                            err.getLineNumber ()   +
                            ", uri " + err.getSystemId ());
            System.out.println("    " +   err.getMessage ());
        }
        catch (SAXException e)
        {
            Exception   x = e.getException ();
            ((x == null) ? e : x).printStackTrace ();
        }
        catch (Throwable t)
        {
            t.printStackTrace ();
        }
        System.exit (0);
    }
}
```

The next listing is the XML document with an embedded DTD that we will check.

```
<?xml version="1.0"?>

<!DOCTYPE pizza [
    <!ELEMENT pizza (topping, price, size)>
    <!ELEMENT topping (#PCDATA)>
    <!ELEMENT price (#PCDATA)>
    <!ELEMENT size (#PCDATA)>
    <!ATTLIST topping extracheese (yes|no) "no">
]>

<pizza>
    <topping extracheese="yes"> Pepperoni </topping>
    <price> 12.99 </price>
    <size> large </size>
</pizza>
```

You should now compile the program and then run it using the valid XML document as its input with

```
java Validparser pizza2.xml
```

Here is the output you should get:

```
<?xml version="1.0" encoding="UTF-8"?>

<!DOCTYPE pizza
[
<!ELEMENT pizza (topping, price, size)>
<!ELEMENT topping (#PCDATA)>
<!ELEMENT price (#PCDATA)>
<!ELEMENT size (#PCDATA)>
<!ATTLIST topping extracheese (yes|no) "no">
]>

<pizza>
  <topping extracheese="yes"> Pepperoni </topping>
  <price> 12.99 </price>
  <size> large </size>
</pizza>
```

Again, to convince ourselves that the parser is actually doing some checking, let's introduce an error and try running the program again. The attribute declaration limits the attribute values to the strings "yes" and "no". Let's use a different value and see what happens. We'll change the topping tag to read:

```
<topping extracheese="sure"> Pepperoni </topping>
```

Hopefully the parser will detect this rule violation and produce an error. When you run the program again, you should get the output

```
** Parsing                    error, line 11, uri file:/D:/data/wrox/pizza2.xml

Value "sure" is not one of the enumerated values for this attribute.
```

This time the error message is very clear and it is what we would have expected. You can experiment with the valid parser and examine various DTD constructs to see which XML documents conform and which don't conform to it.

More on Parsing

We have learned that the parser checks a given XML document for well-formedness and validity, but this is only one function of the parser. Through the parser, a program can also gain access to the content of an XML document (the data stored in XML). It is this avenue of access that is of interest to us when using Java to read/write and manipulate XML documents. After all, XML is a way to store (and describe) data and programs act on data. While the programming community has a good understanding of data manipulation through relational databases, similar operations on XML documents are not as mature yet.

There are two levels of data access commonly provided by parsers. To understand each one, let's take pictorial look at what the parser can do. The figure below shows two levels of abstraction for a parsed XML document.

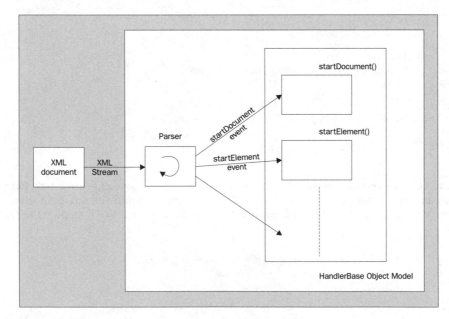

The parser reads an XML document line by line and fires events that contain information about the line that was just read. For example, when an opening tag is encountered, the parser fires an event.

Another event is fired when the closing tag is encountered. Other events are fired for attributes and so on. You can write a program that listens to particular events of interest and extracts the data from the XML document in that way. Although there is no standard approach to this, the most accepted method is to use **Simple API for XML (SAX)**. This is not a standard API, in the sense that it did not come from the W3C standard process. Rather it was developed by a group of developers on the xml e-mail list.

Your program may not be interested in all the events. The events contain information about the data. If one captures all the events, then collectively the information contained in all the events should be the same as the original document (if you were to put the events back together to reproduce the original document).

Aside from the "event-driven" model of processing an XML document, there is also an object model. Again, most parsers support this model as well and unlike SAX, the object model is a product of the W3C. The standard is called the **Document Object Model (DOM)**. The idea behind DOM is that the parser should capture all the events and build an object model of the document. This object represents the document in the form of a tree. The parent element is the tree node and all the other elements are children of the parent node preserving their containment hierarchy. The end application uses a set of standard APIs to access, read, write, and manipulate the XML data stored in the tree object. This should be familiar to most programmers since they are used to manipulating data via a data structure such as a vector or a tree.

These are the two common methods for a Java program to manipulate XML data: via an event model or an object model, each having pros and cons which are discussed a bit later. We'll take a look at each model and then develop a servlet example.

SAX

Although the event-driven approach to access an XML document may look primitive, it is still quite useful. SAX is especially useful when dealing with large documents. You should take a look at the documentation accompanying the parser you are using for the SAX API (we use the parser from JavaSoft, but you are free to use any SAX-compliant parser). There are four interfaces that are of interest:

- ➤ `EntityResolver`: basic interface for resolving entities
- ➤ `DTDHandler`: Receives notification of basic DTD-related events.
- ➤ `DocumentHandler`: Receives notification of general document events such as `startElement()` and `endElement()`.
- ➤ `ErrorHandler`: interface for handling parsing errors

Basic implementation for these interfaces is provided in a class called `org.xml.sax.HandlerBase`. You can extend this class and override the event handlers that you are interested in, or you can implement the interfaces yourself. We will take the first approach in this example.

We will develop an XML document containing several pizza types. We will then use SAX to extract the toppings information from that document. So, while the XML document contains more information about the different pizza types, our application is only interested in the topping element and the value it contains. The program will output a list of toppings.

The interface we are interested in to extract the information we need is the `DocumentHandler` interface. Here is a listing of its methods:

```
void characters(char[] ch, int start, int length)
void endDocument()
void endElement(java.lang.String name)
void ignorableWhitespace(char[] ch, int start, int length)
void processingInstructions(java.lang.String target, java.lang.String data)
void setDocumentLocator(Locator locator)
void startDocument()
void startElement(String name, AttributeList atts)
```

You should be able to guess which event triggers which method based on the method name. For example, when the closing tag for an element is encountered, the `endElement()` method is called.

For our application, we are interested in capturing the `startElement` event. We would then check and see if the event was triggered because of the topping element. If that is the case, we need to set a flag so the `character()` method knows to capture the character data it encounters (that is the value of the topping element). We continue this process until the `endDocument()` event is triggered which indicates we are done. We can then capture the vector that contains all the pizza toppings.

The next listing shows the XML document we will be using in this example.

```xml
<?xml version="1.0"?>

<!DOCTYPE pizzamenu [
    <!ELEMENT pizzamenu (pizza+)>
    <!ELEMENT pizza (topping, price, size)>
    <!ELEMENT topping (#PCDATA)>
    <!ELEMENT price (#PCDATA)>
    <!ELEMENT size (#PCDATA)>
    <!ATTLIST topping extracheese (yes|no) "no">
]>
<pizzamenu>

    <pizza>
        <topping extracheese="yes"> Pepperoni </topping>
        <price> 12.99 </price>
        <size> large </size>
    </pizza>

    <pizza>
        <topping extracheese="yes"> Cheese </topping>
        <price> 9.99 </price>
        <size> large </size>
    </pizza>

    <pizza>
        <topping extracheese="no"> Sausage </topping>
        <price> 11.99 </price>
        <size> small </size>
    </pizza>
```

```
    <pizza>
        <topping extracheese="no"> Mushroom </topping>
        <price> 12.99 </price>
        <size> medium </size>
    </pizza>

    <pizza>
        <topping extracheese="yes"> Green Peppers </topping>
        <price> 11.99 </price>
        <size> medium </size>
    </pizza>

    <pizza>
        <topping extracheese="no"> Onion </topping>
        <price> 13.99 </price>
        <size> large </size>
    </pizza>

</pizzamenu>
```

The next listing is the Java program that extracts the toppings from the pizza elements, puts them in a vector and then prints them out when the processing of the document is completed. Note that we have only provided methods that were related to our task. Also, the approach taken here (to use a flag as a way to inform other methods about a particular event) is a common technique in this sort of programming model. When you hit the beginning of the tag event, you don't know what the text between the opening and closing tag is until you hit another event. Unless you save data in a data structure, you don't have the ability to look back and forward.

```java
import java.io.*;
import org.w3c.dom.*;
import org.xml.sax.*;
import org.xml.sax.helpers.ParserFactory;
import org.xml.sax.helpers.AttributeListImpl;
import com.sun.xml.tree.*;
import com.sun.xml.parser.Resolver;


public class Pizzatopping
{

    static boolean toppingElement = false;
    static String toppings[] = new String[10];
    static int toppingsIdx = 0;

    public static void main(String argv []) throws IOException
    {
        InputSource input;

        if (argv.length != 1)
        {
            System.err.println("Usage: cmd filename");
            System.exit (1);
        }
        try
        {
```

Continued on Following Page

```
            input = Resolver.createInputSource(new File(argv [0]));
            Parser  parser;

            parser = ParserFactory.makeParser();
            parser.setDocumentHandler(new MyDocHandler());
            parser.setErrorHandler(new MyErrorHandler ());
            parser.parse(input);
        }
        catch(SAXParseException err)
        {
            System.out.println ("** Parsing error"
                        + ", line " + err.getLineNumber ()
                        + ", uri " + err.getSystemId ());
            System.out.println("    " + err.getMessage ());
        }
        catch(SAXException e)
        {
            Exception   x = e;
            if (e.getException() != null)
               x = e.getException();
            x.printStackTrace();
        }
        catch(Throwable t)
        {
            t.printStackTrace();
        }
        System.exit (0);
    }


    static class MyDocHandler extends HandlerBase
    {

        public void startElement(String name, AttributeList attributes)
                    throws SAXException
        {
            if (name.equals("topping"))
            {
                toppingElement = true;
            }
        }

        public void startDocument() throws SAXException
        {
            System.out.println("Document processing started...");
            toppingElement = true;
        }

        public void endDocument() throws SAXException
        {
            System.out.println("The toppings in the menu are:");

            for (int i=0; i<toppingsIdx; i++)
            {
                System.out.println(i+1 + ". " + toppings[i]);
            }
        }
```

```
      public void characters(char ch[], int start, int length)
      {
        String output = new String(ch, start, length);
        if (toppingElement)
        {
          toppings[toppingsIdx] = output;
          toppingsIdx++;
          toppingElement = false;
        }
      }

      public void warning(SAXParseException err)
          throws SAXParseException
      {
        System.out.println ("** Warning"
                   + ", line " + err.getLineNumber()
                   + ", uri " + err.getSystemId());
        System.out.println("    " + err.getMessage());
      }
  }

  static class MyErrorHandler extends HandlerBase
  {

      public void error(SAXParseException err)
          throws SAXParseException
      {
        System.out.println("** Error"
                   + ", line " + err.getLineNumber()
                   + ", uri " + err.getSystemId());
        System.out.println("    " + err.getMessage());
      }

          // dump warnings too
      public void warning(SAXParseException err)
          throws SAXParseException
      {
        System.out.println("** Warning"
                   + ", line " + err.getLineNumber()
                   + ", uri " + err.getSystemId());
        System.out.println("    " + err.getMessage());
      }
  }
}
```

Here is the output when you run this program:

```
Document processing started...
The toppings in the menu are:
1.  Pepperoni
2.  Cheese
3.  Sausage
4.  Mushroom
5.  Green Peppers
6.  Onion
```

DOM

You may be asking "Is there some other way to deal with XML documents that is more along the lines of OO programming?" There is indeed an object model that maps nicely into XML. The Document Object Model (DOM) is a W3C standard for dealing with XML documents. Hybrids of DOM have been used in Dynamic HTML where integration of scripting languages such as JavaScript and markup languages (HTML) is a necessity.

An object model is a representation of an entity. In the case of XML, that entity is a document. The document consists of a number of tags and some content plus items such as comments, processing instructions, and attributes. DOM specifies an interface via which you can access different parts of XML documents, navigate through them, and make changes to them.

At the heart of DOM is a tree representation of a document. Consider the following XML excerpt:

```
<name>
    <first> Jim </first>
    <last> Jones</last>
</name>
```

There is a hierarchical relationship inherent in the above code fragment. The two elements `first` and `last` are contained within the `name` element. The `name` element is a parent of `first` and `last`, and `first` and `last` are siblings at the same level. This sounds like tree talk from your Computer Science class, doesn't it? The figure below shows the tree object constructed from the above code fragment.

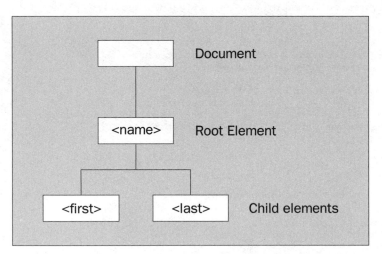

DOM is a specification. The interfaces are implemented by various parser creators. When you look at an XML tree, every branch is considered a "node." In fact, the Node interface is the primary datatype for the entire Document Object Model. The specification then extends Node and comes up with other specific node types such as Text, ProcessingInstruction, Comment, and Attr. You can traverse a tree by starting from the root node and navigate your way through using recursion. At each step, you have to determine what type of node you have landed on and take appropriate action. You can get a feel for how traversal works by looking at the methods in the Node interface. Other developers have created a lot of utility classes that makes dealing with "raw" DOM a bit less cumbersome.

To give you a better feel for DOM, let's take a look at an example. We are going to create an empty (blank) XML document in memory and use the DOM API to add elements to it. You can also do the reverse, that is start with an XML document and access the various elements and their values via DOM. The object model is bi-directional. In fact, one of the common uses of DOM is to get an object representation of a document, make changes to the object, and then write it back as an XML file. For making small changes, this is an effective technique. Where DOM fails to meet expectations, is when you are dealing with large documents. Since everything has to be parsed and loaded in memory, you are limited as to how large a document you can handle. The DOM example program is isted below.

```java
import java.io.*;
import com.sun.xml.tree.*;
import org.w3c.dom.*;

public class SampleDOM
{
    public static void main (String argc [])
            throws IOException, DOMException
    {
        XmlDocument xmlDoc = new XmlDocument();
        ElementNode name = (ElementNode) xmlDoc.createElement("name");
        ElementNode first = (ElementNode) xmlDoc.createElement("first");
        ElementNode last = (ElementNode) xmlDoc.createElement("last");

        Writer out = new OutputStreamWriter(System.out);

        out.write ("No tree exists yet\n");
        out.write ("\n");

        xmlDoc.appendChild(name);
        name.appendChild(first);
        first.appendChild(xmlDoc.createTextNode("\n John \n"));
        name.appendChild(last);
        last.appendChild(xmlDoc.createTextNode("\n Doe \n"));

        name.setAttribute("city", "New York");

        out.write ("DOCUMENT is:\n");
        xmlDoc.write (out);
        out.write ("\n");
        out.flush ();

        System.exit (0);
    }
}
```

We first create an `XmlDocument` that is empty. Next, we create three nodes called `name`, `first` and `last`. There is no relationship among the nodes yet. The following 5 lines build the relationship among the three nodes. We also add two extra nodes (text nodes) that contain the values for `first` and `last`.

```
xmlDoc.appendChild(name);
name.appendChild(first);
first.appendChild(xmlDoc.createTextNode("\n John \n"));
name.appendChild(last);
last.appendChild(xmlDoc.createTextNode("\n Doe \n"));
```

Note that `name` is first appended to the root node. We then append to `name` the element `first` and append a newly created `TextNode` to it. We go through similar steps for the element `last`. Finally, for fun, we add an attribute to the element `name` called `city` and set its value to `New York`.

Here is the output from the above program:

```
No tree exists yet

DOCUMENT is:
<?xml version="1.0" encoding="Cp1252"?>

<name city="New York">
  <first>
 John
</first>
  <last>
 Doe
</last>
</name>
```

The value shown for the encoding attribute may differ from above, depending on the default encoding on your system. If you are not familiar with object models, DOM may look a bit odd at first. Working with DOM takes some time, but once you get used to it, you'll find yourself climbing trees all over! For serious programming tasks, you should look into the utility and factory classes where the details of tree navigation are hidden from you for the most part.

Pizza Servlet

During the writing of this chapter, I consumed a lot of pizza late at night, so it should not come as any surprise that this section shows an example of a pizza ordering servlet that is based on XML. In this example, we rely on a number of XML files to describe various pizza types. We have already seen what a pizza XML file looks like:

```
<?xml version="1.0"?>
<pizza>
    <topping extracheese="no">Pepperoni</topping>
    <price>10.99</price>
    <size>small</size>
</pizza>
```

We will build a servlet that goes through a directory and parses all of the pizza files in there, translating them into a pizza object. A collection of pizza objects make up a pizza menu. The user can browse through the menu and order the pizza(s) he/she likes. Once they are ready to check out, they enter some contact information for delivery purposes. The end result is a pizza order expressed in XML.

The `Pizza` servlet consists of 6 files:

- ➢   Pizza.java
- ➢   PizzaMenu.java
- ➢   PizzaView.java
- ➢   PizzaDOMUtil.java
- ➢   PizzaHTMLUtil.java
- ➢   PizzaServlet.java

We will use Java Servlet Development Kit 2.0 for this example.

The first file is `Pizza.java`. This class contains attributes of a pizza as specified in the XML file such as topping, size, and price. The parser is used to parse the XML file and obtain the elements and their values. These are stored as member variables in the object. The variable `ordered` is a flag variable that indicates whether the pizza has been ordered or not. Note usage of the method `findNode()` to locate a particular node. Details of this method will be discussed later. The following shows the code for the `Pizza` class.

```
import java.io.*;
import java.net.*;
import java.util.*;
import org.w3c.dom.*;
// the following line is not needed for IBM Parser
import org.xml.sax.SAXException;

public class Pizza
{
    protected String filename;
    protected boolean ordered;
    protected String topping;
    protected String size;
    protected String price;

    public Pizza(String filename)
    {
        this.filename = filename;
```

Continued on Following Page

```
        try
        {
            Document document = PizzaDOMUtil.readDocument(filename);
            Node ntopping = PizzaDOMUtil.findNode(document, "topping");
            Node nprice = PizzaDOMUtil.findNode(document, "price");
            Node nsize = PizzaDOMUtil.findNode(document, "size");

            this.topping = ntopping.getFirstChild().getNodeValue();
            this.size = nsize.getFirstChild().getNodeValue();
            this.price = nprice.getFirstChild().getNodeValue();
        }
        catch (IOException e)
        {
            System.out.println("exception is " + e);
        }
        catch (SAXException e)
        {
            System.out.println ("exception is " + e);
        }
    }

    public String getTopping()
    {
        return topping;
    }

    public String getSize()
    {
        return size;
    }

    public String getPrice()
    {
        return price;
    }

    public void setOrdered()
    {
        this.ordered = true;
    }

    public boolean isOrdered()
    {
        if (ordered)
            return true;
        else
            return false;
    }
}
```

While `Pizza` represents a single pizza, `PizzaMenu` is a representation of all the pizza files in the specified directory. The class instantiates `Pizza` objects based on the XML files and stores them in a vector. The other important method is `getPizza()` which returns a `Pizza` object based on the index parameter. The next listing shows the code for the `PizzaMenu` class.

```java
import java.io.*;
import java.util.*;
import javax.servlet.*;
import javax.servlet.http.*;

public class PizzaMenu
{
   protected String path;
   protected Vector pizzas = new Vector();
   protected int NumOfPizza;
   public String name;
   public String phone;
   public String address;

   public PizzaMenu(String path)
   {
      this.path = path;
   }

   public void OrderIt(int index)
   {
      Pizza tmpPizza = (Pizza)pizzas.elementAt(index);
      tmpPizza.setOrdered();
   }

   public int getNumOfPizza()
   {
      return NumOfPizza;
   }

   public Pizza getPizza(int index)
   {
    if (index < 0 || index >= pizzas.size()) return null;
    return (Pizza)pizzas.elementAt(index);
   }

   private String[] getFileList()
   {
      File file = new File(path);
      String[] list = file.list();

      Vector vector = new Vector();
      for (int i = 0; i < list.length; i++)
      {
         if (list[i].toLowerCase().endsWith(".xml"))
         {
            vector.addElement(list[i].substring(
               0, list[i].length() - 4));
         }
      }
      int count = vector.size();
      list = new String[count];
      for (int i = 0; i < list.length; i++)
      {
         list[i] = (String)vector.elementAt(i);
      }
      return list;
   }
```

Continued on Following Page

303

```
public void buildPizzaMenu() throws IOException
{
    String[] list = getFileList();

    for (int i = 0; i < list.length; i++)
    {
        String fullPath = path + File.separator + list[i] + ".xml";
        pizzas.addElement(new Pizza(fullPath));
    }
    NumOfPizza = list.length;
}
}
```

We have placed all the code related to viewing a page in a class called `PizzaView`. The three methods are:

> `getPizzaPage(…)`
> `getPizzaOrderInfoPage(…)`
> `getPizzaOrderPage(…)`

The `getPizzaPage()` method prints out an HTML page that contains the attributes for the current Pizza item plus some buttons for navigation. We use a number of methods from another class called `PizzaHTMLUtil`. There are a few interesting implementations where HTML is treated as an object. So, for example, instead of writing out HTML code to create a table, you instantiate a "table" object and set all of its attributes. The object can then render itself into HTML. This approach is very useful in keeping things consistent, especially for larger projects. The same technique can be used to create objects that can render themselves in XML. For this example, we resort to the traditional writing out of the HTML code.

The `getPizzaOrderInfo()` page displays three input boxes where contact information for delivery of the pizza can be entered. Finally, the `getPizzaOrder()` page displays either an HTML or an XML version of the final order. The code for the `PizzaView` class is shown below.

```
import java.io.*;
import java.net.*;
import java.util.*;
import org.w3c.dom.*;

public class PizzaView
{
    public static void getPizzaPage(PrintWriter writer, String action,
                    int current, PizzaMenu pizzaMenu) throws IOException
    {

        PizzaHTMLUtil.writeDocumentHeader(writer, "temp title", action);
        PizzaHTMLUtil.writeInputField(writer, "HIDDEN", "CURRENT_PIZZA", ""
                                    + current);
        PizzaHTMLUtil.writeTableHeader(writer);
        Pizza tmpPizza = pizzaMenu.getPizza(current);

        PizzaHTMLUtil.writeTableCell(writer, "Topping ", tmpPizza.getTopping());
        PizzaHTMLUtil.writeTableCell(writer, "Price ", "$" + tmpPizza.getPrice());
        PizzaHTMLUtil.writeTableCell(writer, "Size ", tmpPizza.getSize());

        PizzaHTMLUtil.writeTableFooter(writer);
```

```
    if (tmpPizza.isOrdered())
    {
        PizzaHTMLUtil.writeInputField(writer, "CHECKBOX", "ORDER_IT", "" +
                    current, true);
    }
    else
    {
        PizzaHTMLUtil.writeInputField(writer, "CHECKBOX", "ORDER_IT", "" +
                    current);
    }

    PizzaHTMLUtil.writeText(writer, "Check box to order.<p>");

    if (current > 0)
    {
        PizzaHTMLUtil.writeInputField(writer, "SUBMIT", "PREV", "PREV");
    }
    if (current < pizzaMenu.getNumOfPizza()-1)
    {
        PizzaHTMLUtil.writeInputField(writer, "SUBMIT", "NEXT", "NEXT");
    }
    PizzaHTMLUtil.writeInputField(writer, "SUBMIT", "CHECKOUT", "CHECKOUT");

    PizzaHTMLUtil.writeDocumentFooter(writer);
    writer.flush();
}

public static void getOrderInfoPage(PrintWriter writer, String action)
    throws IOException
{

    PizzaHTMLUtil.writeDocumentHeader(writer,
                "Enter Order Information", action);

    PizzaHTMLUtil.writeText(writer, "Please provide the following
                information to complete your order<p>");

    PizzaHTMLUtil.writeText(writer, "Your Name: ");
    PizzaHTMLUtil.writeInputField(writer, "TEXT", "NAME", "");

    PizzaHTMLUtil.writeText(writer, "<p>Phone: ");
    PizzaHTMLUtil.writeInputField(writer, "TEXT", "PHONE", "");

    PizzaHTMLUtil.writeText(writer, "<p>Address: ");
    PizzaHTMLUtil.writeInputField(writer, "TEXT", "ADDRESS", "");

    PizzaHTMLUtil.writeText(writer, "<p>");
    PizzaHTMLUtil.writeInputField(writer, "SUBMIT", "FINISH", "FINISH");
    PizzaHTMLUtil.writeInputField(writer, "SUBMIT", "FINISHXML", "FINISHXML");

    PizzaHTMLUtil.writeDocumentFooter(writer);
    writer.flush();
}

public static void getOrderPage(PrintWriter writer, String action,
        PizzaMenu pizzaMenu, boolean doXML) throws IOException
{
```

Continued on Following Page

```
    if (!doXML)
    {
        PizzaHTMLUtil.writeText(writer, "<HTML><HEAD><TITLE> XML
                            Pizza Order</TITLE></HEAD>");
        PizzaHTMLUtil.writeText(writer, "<BODY><PRE>");
    }

    PizzaHTMLUtil.writeText(writer, "<?xml version=\"1.0\"?>\n");
    PizzaHTMLUtil.writeText(writer, "<pizzaorder>");
    PizzaHTMLUtil.writeText(writer, "<name>" + pizzaMenu.name + "</name>");
    PizzaHTMLUtil.writeText(writer, "<phone>" + pizzaMenu.phone + "</phone>");
    PizzaHTMLUtil.writeText(writer, "<address>" + pizzaMenu.address +
                "</address>");

    Pizza tmpPizza = null;
    for (int i=0; i< pizzaMenu.getNumOfPizza(); i++)
    {
        tmpPizza = pizzaMenu.getPizza(i);
        if (tmpPizza.isOrdered())
        {
            PizzaHTMLUtil.writeText(writer, "<pizza>");
            PizzaHTMLUtil.writeText(writer, "<topping>" + tmpPizza.getTopping() +
                                    "</topping>");
            PizzaHTMLUtil.writeText(writer, "<price>" + tmpPizza.getPrice() +
                                "</price>");
            PizzaHTMLUtil.writeText(writer, "<size>" + tmpPizza.getSize() +
                                "</size>");
            PizzaHTMLUtil.writeText(writer, "</pizza>");
        }
    }

    PizzaHTMLUtil.writeText(writer, "</pizzaorder>");

    if (!doXML)
    {
        PizzaHTMLUtil.writeText(writer, "</PRE></BODY></HTML>");
    }
    writer.flush();
    }
}
```

We have placed all of the code related to XML, parsing and DOM into a utility class called PizzaDOMUtil. I have commented out the lines that you would use if you were using the IBM parser, so it should be fairly easy to switch between the Sun and IBM parser. Look at the findNode() method, and notice how it goes through the children nodes one by one to find the node you are looking for. It uses a NodeList to traverse through the children nodes. We don't use the getNodeAttribute() method, but it is here for reference if you need to use it. We also don't use the printSubTree() method, but again, looking at the code helps you see how DOM tree navigation works. The code for our DOM utilities is shown here.

```java
import java.io.*;
import org.w3c.dom.*;
// the following line is for IBM parser
//import com.ibm.xml.parser.Parser;

// the following 4 lines are for Sun parser
import com.sun.xml.parser.Resolver;
import com.sun.xml.tree.XmlDocument;
import org.xml.sax.InputSource;
import org.xml.sax.SAXException;

public class PizzaDOMUtil
{
   public static Document readDocument(String filename)
         throws IOException, SAXException
   {

// if you are using the IBM parser, use the commented lines

//     Parser parser = new Parser(filename);
//     InputStream input = new FileInputStream(filename);
//     Document doc = parser.readStream(input);
//     input.close();
//     return doc;

// if you are using the Sun parser, use these lines
       InputSource input = Resolver.createInputSource(new File(filename));
       XmlDocument doc = XmlDocument.createXmlDocument(input, false);
       doc.getDocumentElement().normalize();
       return doc;

   }

   public static Node findNode(Node node, String name)
   {
      if (node.getNodeName().equals(name))
         return node;
      if (node.hasChildNodes())
      {
         NodeList list = node.getChildNodes();
         int size = list.getLength();
         for (int i = 0; i < size; i++)
         {
            Node found = findNode(list.item(i), name);
            if (found != null) return found;
         }
      }
      return null;
   }

   public static String getNodeAttribute(Node node, String name)
   {
      if (node instanceof Element)
      {
         Element element = (Element)node;
         return element.getAttribute(name);
      }
      return null;
   }
```

Continued on Following Page

307

```
    public static void printSubtree(PrintWriter writer, Node root, Node node)
    {
        if (node instanceof Element)
        {
            if (node != root)
                writer.print("\n<" + node.getNodeName() + ">");
            if (node.hasChildNodes())
            {
                NodeList list = node.getChildNodes();
                int size = list.getLength();
                for (int i = 0; i < size; i++)
                {
                    printSubtree(writer, root, list.item(i));
                }
            }
            if (node != root)
                writer.print("</" + node.getNodeName() + ">");
        }
        else if (node instanceof Text)
        {
            writer.print(node.getNodeValue().trim());
        }
    }
}
```

We have placed all HTML-related code in a class by itself called `PizzaHTMLUtil`. Rather than writing tedious HTML within the application, we have created common methods that take some parameters and write the HTML code. Again, this is a good technique to separate the HTML (presentation) from the logical code. It is also relatively easy to switch between XML and HTML since the methods can be overridden to write our XML tags. The `PizzaHTMLUtil` class is shown in the listing below.

```
import java.io.*;

public class PizzaHTMLUtil
{
    private static String formatAttr(String name, String value)
    {
        return " " + name + "=" + '"' + value + '"';
    }

    public static void writeDocumentHeader(PrintWriter writer,
            String title, String action)
    {
        writer.println("<HTML><HEAD>");
        writer.println("<TITLE>" + title + "</TITLE>");
        writer.println("</HEAD><BODY>");
        writer.println("<FORM" +
                        formatAttr("METHOD", "POST") +
                        formatAttr("ACTION", action) + ">");
    }

    public static void writeDocumentFooter(PrintWriter writer)
    {
        writer.println("</FORM></BODY></HTML>");
    }
```

```
    public static void writeTableHeader(PrintWriter writer)
    {
        writer.println("<TABLE" +
         formatAttr("BORDER", "0") +
         formatAttr("WIDTH", "100%") +
         formatAttr("CELLSPACING", "0") +
         formatAttr("CELLPADDING", "2") + ">");
    }

    public static void writeTableCell(PrintWriter writer,
                 String title, String cellContent)
    {
        writer.println("<TR><TD>");
        writer.println("<H1" +
        PizzaHTMLUtil.formatAttr("ALIGN", "center") +
           "><FONT COLOR=#008000>" + title + "</FONT></H1>");
        writer.println("</TD></TR>");
        writer.println("<TR><TD><H3 ALIGN=center>");
        writer.println(cellContent);
        writer.println("</TD></TR></H3>");
    }

    public static void writeTableFooter(PrintWriter writer)
    {
        writer.println("</TABLE><HR>");
    }

    public static void writeInputField(PrintWriter writer,
          String type, String name, String value)
    {
        writeInputField(writer, type, name, value, false);
    }

    public static void writeInputField(PrintWriter writer,
          String type, String name, String value, boolean check)
    {
        writer.println("<INPUT" +
         formatAttr("type", type) +
         formatAttr("name", name) +
         formatAttr("value", value) +
         (check ? formatAttr("checked", "true") : "") +
         ">");
    }

    public static void writeText(PrintWriter writer, String someText)
    {
        writer.println(someText);
    }
}
```

The final piece of the example is the actual servlet. We use the same servlet for all three pages (Pizza, PizzaOrderInfo, and PizzaOrder). Based on the value of the SUBMIT button, we determine which page to show and call the appropriate method from the `PizzaView` class. The `PizzaMenu` object is maintained as a session object. We recall that the menu holds a vector containing instances of all the pizzas and their order status.

```java
import java.io.*;
import java.util.*;
import javax.servlet.*;
import javax.servlet.http.*;

public class PizzaServlet extends HttpServlet
{
   public String getParameter(HttpServletRequest req, String name)
   {
      String[] values = req.getParameterValues(name);
      if (values == null) return null;
      return values[0];
   }

   public int getInteger(HttpServletRequest req, String name)
   {
      String value = getParameter(req, name);
      if (value == null) return -1;
      return Integer.parseInt(value);
   }

   public void exception(HttpServletResponse res,
         Exception exception)
   {
      try
      {
         res.setContentType("text/html");
         PrintWriter out = new PrintWriter(res.getOutputStream());
         out.println("<html><head>");
         out.println("<title>Servlet Exception</title>");
         out.println("</head><body>");
         out.println("<h1>Servlet Error</h1>");
         out.println("<code>");
         exception.printStackTrace(out);
         out.println("</code></body></html>");
      }
      catch (IOException e) {}
   }

   private PizzaMenu getPizzaMenu(HttpServletRequest req, PrintWriter out)
         throws IOException
   {
      HttpSession session = req.getSession(true);
      Object value = session.getValue("pizzamenu");
      PizzaMenu pizzaMenu = null;
      if (value instanceof PizzaMenu)
      {
         pizzaMenu = (PizzaMenu)value;
      }
      else
      {
         pizzaMenu = new
            PizzaMenu(getServletContext().getRealPath(getInitParameter("pizzas")));
         pizzaMenu.buildPizzaMenu();
         session.putValue("pizzamenu", pizzaMenu);
      }
      return pizzaMenu;
   }
```

```
    public void service(HttpServletRequest req, HttpServletResponse res)
        throws ServletException, IOException
{
    try
    {
        PrintWriter out = new PrintWriter(res.getOutputStream());
        PizzaMenu pizzaMenu = getPizzaMenu(req, out);

    //assume we are at the start point and then set current accordingly
        int current = 0;
        if (getInteger(req, "CURRENT_PIZZA") != -1)
        current = getInteger(req, "CURRENT_PIZZA");

    // if order checkbox was checked, then set the flag

        if (getParameter(req, "ORDER_IT") != null)
        pizzaMenu.OrderIt(current);

    // handle next and prev buttons
        if (getParameter(req, "NEXT") != null)
            current++;
        if (getParameter(req, "PREV") != null)
            current--;

        String path = req.getRequestURI();
        int pos = path.indexOf('?');
        if (pos > -1) path = path.substring(0, pos);
        String thisURL = "http://" + req.getServerName() + ":8080" + path;

     // if checkout was requested, print Info page
        if (getParameter(req, "CHECKOUT") != null)
        {
            res.setContentType("text/html");
            PizzaView.getOrderInfoPage(out, thisURL);
        }
    // if they are done, show the final order
        else if (getParameter(req, "FINISH") != null)
        {
            res.setContentType("text/html");
            pizzaMenu.name = getParameter(req, "NAME");
            pizzaMenu.address = getParameter(req, "ADDRESS");
            pizzaMenu.phone = getParameter(req, "PHONE");
            PizzaView.getOrderPage(out, thisURL, pizzaMenu, false);
        }
        else if (getParameter(req, "FINISHXML") != null)
        {
            res.setContentType("text/xml");
            pizzaMenu.name = getParameter(req, "NAME");
            pizzaMenu.address = getParameter(req, "ADDRESS");
            pizzaMenu.phone = getParameter(req, "PHONE");
            PizzaView.getOrderPage(out, thisURL, pizzaMenu, true);
        }
    // show another pizza
        else
        {
            res.setContentType("text/html");
            PizzaView.getPizzaPage(out, thisURL, current, pizzaMenu);
        }
        out.flush();
    }
```

Continued on Following Page

```
        catch (Exception e)
        {
            exception(res, e);
        }
    }
}
```

After compiling all the Java files, you should edit the `servlet.properites` file for your servlet engine. You will need to add the following lines:

```
#pizza servlet
servlet.PizzaServlet.code=PizzaServlet
servlet.PizzaServlet.preload=false
servlet.PizzaServlet.args=pizzas=/pizzas
servlet.PizzaServlet.initArgs=pizzas=/pizzas
```

The last line specifies the directory where all the Pizza XML files are located.

Also, make sure that your servlet engine has access to the XML parser class files (`xml.jar` for Sun's parser). With the JSDK, I set the CLASSPATH to the appropriate JAR file before I started the servlet engine. The figure below shows the page you should see when you first load the servlet.

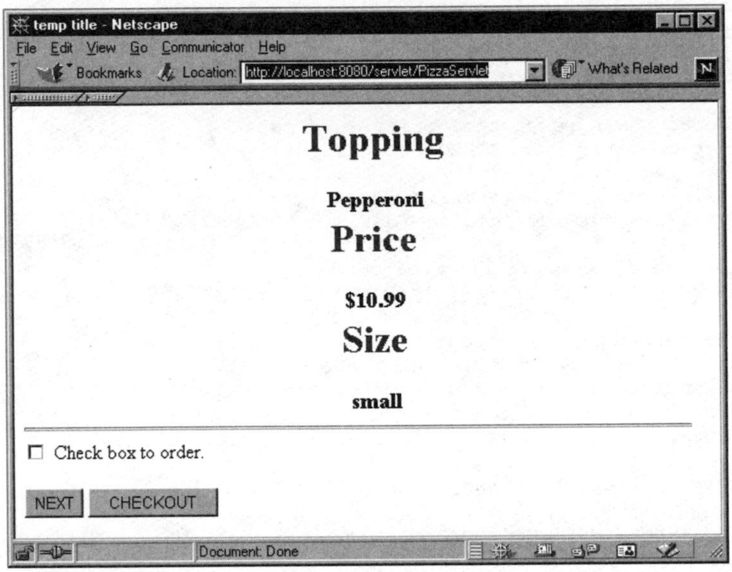

You can browse through the different pizza types. If you like any of them, check the checkbox as indicated. This changes the ordered flag to true in the corresponding pizza object. When you are ready to check out, click on the CHECK OUT button and you should see the following.

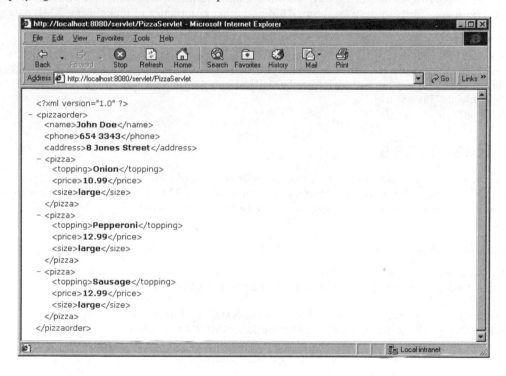

After you enter some contact information, click on FINISH to get an HTML version of the order or click on FINISHXML to get an XML version. At the time of writing, only IE 5.0 had support for displaying raw XML files. The XML output of the Pizza servlet is shown below.

Summary

This chapter has been an introduction to XML. XML is an exciting technology because it represents a set of self-describing data. With standards such as HTTP transport of such data is trivial. With standards such as DOM, access to the data in such documents is streamlined. There is a great match between Java and XML where Java uses its object oriented nature to do the processing and XML uses its document nature to act as data. They are also both platform-independent.

We introduced the basic syntax of XML and DTD where a set of rules for a given markup language can be specified. The current syntax of DTD is very different from XML and in the future, we may see another standard replacing DTD. Another area that is changing rapidly is the presentation of XML. With limited browser support for XML, practical applications must produce HTML for viewing purposes. Hopefully, in the future, a combination of XML and XSL can be used to further separate data and its presentation.

We also covered SAX and DOM and showed how your Java program can use these APIs to access and manipulate XML data. Most likely, we will see more intuitive access methods built on top of DOM. There are efforts underway at Sun, IBM and other companies to make using XML data easier for Java programmers.

XML is fun because it is relatively new and you can use your creative side to come up with interesting ways of using it in your applications. Challenges lie ahead and the technology and related standards will change. I hope this chapter has helped you gain a better understanding of XML and its usage within the Java world.

XML Resources

People turn to the internet to find information about all sorts of things. Given that XML is a true internet technology, there are a lot of resources that deal with XML and some of the other topics discussed in this chapter. Here is a partial collection to get you started:

XML and Java

"XML, Java and the Future of the Web." by Jon Bosak.
http://metalab.unc.edu/pub/sun-info/standards/xml/why/xmlapps.html

"Media-Independent Publishing: Four Myths about XML" by Jon Bosak
http://metalab.unc.edu/pub/sun-info/standards/xml/why/4myths.htm

Robin Cover's XML-SGML site (the bible of XML resources)
http://www.oasis-open.org/cover/

The W3C's XML resource page
http://www.w3.org/XML/

XML.com is a great source of news (XML news that is)
   http://www.xml.com

Textuality.com contains a lot of good material on XML.
   http://www.textuality.com/

The XML FAQ
   http://www.ucc.ie/xml/

IBM's XML Web site is an outstanding supplement to alphaWorks
   http://www.ibm.com/developer/xml/

Tutorials

The Mulberry Technologies Web site is a good resource for commercial training in XML
   http://www.mulberrytech.com

The Web Developer's Virtual Library Series on XML
   http://wdvl.com/Software/XML

ArborText's white paper, "XML for Managers,"
   http://www.arbortext.com/Think_Tank/XML_Resources/XML_for_Managers/xml_for_managers.html

Extensible Style Language (XSL)

W3C's CSS page to get you started on CSS (Cascading Stylesheets)
   http://www.w3.org/Style/CSS/

The W3C's XSL page
   http://www.w3.org/Style/XSL/

Microsoft's XML and XSL tutorial site
   http://msdn.microsoft.com/xml/

IBM's LotusXSL. A great tool for experimenting with XSL
   http://www.alphaworks.ibm.com/tech/LotusXSL

James Clark's XT XSL engine, another tool for experimenting with XSL
   http://www.jclark.com/xml/xt.html

Simple API for XML (SAX)

The definitive description of SAX
http://www.megginson.com/SAX/index.html

Document Object Model (DOM)

The W3C page for the Document Object Model
http://www.w3c.org/DOM/

W3C Recommendation for DOM Level 1
http://www.w3.org/TR/REC-DOM-Level-1/

The Java bindings for DOM, for both XML and HTML
http://www.w3.org/TR/REC-DOM-Level-1/java-language-binding.html

Software

IBM's alphaWorks
http://alphaworks.ibm.com

IBM's XML parser package, xml4j
http://www.alphaworks.ibm.com/tech/xml4j

IBM's Bean Markup Language project
http://www.alphaworks.ibm.com/tech/bml

Java XML parser written by James Clark
http://www.jclark.com/xml/xp/index.html

XEENA is IBM alphaWorks's DTD-guided XML editor
http://www.alphaworks.ibm.com/tech/xeena

Information about XML and CSS in Mozilla appears at
http://www.mozilla.org/rdf/doc/xml.html

Java Project X from Sun
http://developer.java.sun.com/developer/earlyAccess/xml/index.html

ArborText has a suite of sophisticated tools for editing SGML, XML, and XSL
http://www.arbortext.com/Products/products.html

Oracle's XML parser
http://technet.oracle.com/direct/3xml.htm

Microsoft's XML Notepad editor
http://msdn.microsoft.com/xml/notepad/download.asp

Vervet Logic XML <PRO>, a commercial XML editor
http://www.vervet.com/

Majix, to transform XML to HTML via XSL, is available at
http://www.tetrasix.com/

Weeds of El Limon 2

A little more than a year ago, we visited the village of El Limon in the Dominican Republic to help string power lines for a micro-hydroelectic generator. You can read about the project at http://www.career.cornell.edu/cresp/ecopartners/. When we got there, the money to buy the cable hadn't arrived, so we spent our time describing and making drawings of commonly occuring weeds. The villagers had a solar-powered laptop and would soon be getting a cellular Internet connection. If we converted our weed descriptions to HTML, they could access them, as could other users of the Web.

However, making the *Weeds of El Limon* site meant making 32 nearly identical web pages for 32 weeds. It seemed reasonable to write 32 pages once, but what if I decided I didn't like the look and I wanted to change it? The XML specification had just been approved, so I got the idea to write the weed descriptions in XML and write a program to convert them into attractive HTML. As an early application of XML, Weeds of El Limon, (http://www.honeylocust.com/limon/) attracted attention from the XML community and we wrote about it in Chapter 12 of *XML Applications* (ISBN 1-861001-52-5, Wrox Press).

A year later, we'd received e-mail from people interested in the weeds. Some had typed "prickle poppy" into a search engine and got our description, and we heard from a Peace Corps volunteer who was just about to visit the Dominican Republic. We asked ourselves, "How can we make our site more useful to people interested in plants?" Weeds of El Limon had problems: because we didn't take the right books with us and we weren't able to identify many of the plants, in particular the grasses. Also, our plants were numbered in the order in which we found them, not the conventional alphabetic ordering. We'd also got the rights to put a list of recommended street trees online, and improving Weeds of El Limon would be a way to test ideas for a more powerful publishing system.

To make the new site effective, we needed a clear mission. We thought about the Peace Corps volunteer who wrote to us, and, being able to find almost nothing else about tropical weeds online, decided that we could best help people by providing a brief introduction to weeds in the Caribbean. Our sampling procedure wasn't comprehensive or scientific; we just walked out of the schoolhouse where we were staying and dug up the first new weed we saw. This meant, however, that we observed and recorded ubiquitous species, the ones that you'd notice right after you stepped off the plane. Therefore, we bundled the 14 weeds we'd identified as common weeds of the Caribbean (http://www.tapir.org/weeds/), and redesigned the site to make it easier to use.

The Site

Common Weeds contains three kinds of database-generated page. Each plant has an individual page, and there are two index pages: an index by common name and a top page indexed by Latin name. When Common Weeds is completed, there will also be a few static pages with information about the authors, the software, and books about tropical weeds.

Common Weeds is a simpler site than the original Weeds of El Limon. In the original, with 32 weeds, I needed separate pages for indices by common name, Latin name, and by family. With just 14 weeds, it was practical to link to each weed from the top page, eliminating the need for separate indices. Since we put more information on the top page, the site is easier to use, since users need to click less.

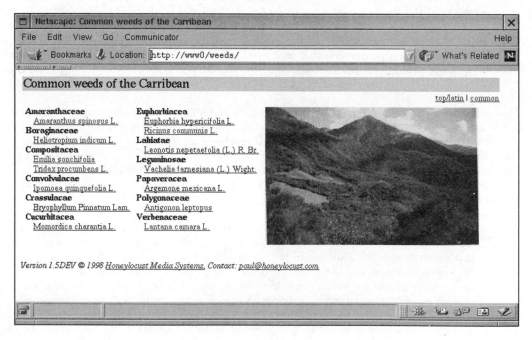

Beneath the surface, the HTML is simpler. In Weeds of El Limon, I used a table cell background to color the bar at the top of the page, making white letters on a black background. I first tried this with the BGCOLOR attribute of the <TD> tag and with <FONT COLOR>, but the result on Netscape 2, which doesn't support colored table cells, was disastrous: white letters on a white background are impossible to read. To solve this problem, I used cascading style sheets (CSS) to set the cell and text colors.

Since then, our staff artist has discovered just how bad the CSS implementations in Netscape 4 and IE 3 are, and that often it is much better to use old-fashioned, conservative HTML that works, even if it does make the W3C's blood boil. This time, to avoid trouble with table-cell backgrounds, I chose fail-safe colors. In a browser without table cell backgrounds, the pale green bar at the top is white - compatible with black text.

Like the top page, the common name index is information rich. For the roughly 80% of web users with screens 800x600 or greater, all of the names fit on one screen. Although I generate the page dynamically out of a database, I set the break points of the columns by hand to guarantee effective layout.

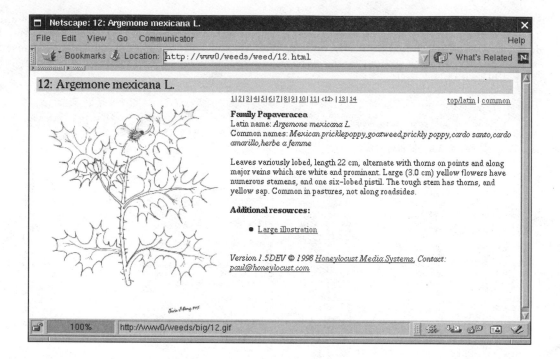

Compared to the indices, the changes to the individual weed pages were minor. Although some pundits think that page numbers are obsolete on the web, I decided to keep numbering the weeds. In the original, we numbered weeds by the order in which we found them. Now they're numbered in the order they appear in on the top page. I added a navigation widget that lets viewers jump to any number with a single click, to imitate the "feel" of a book.

How it Works

Weeds of El Limon was a simple filter: it took a collection of XML files as an input and created a set of static HTML files which I could put on my server. Afterwards, I built several database-driven sites and got hooked by their ability to provide multiple views of information stored in a database and the ability of two or more people to collaborate on maintaining a database driven site. For the first phase of Common Weeds, I took advantage of the existing XML format. Rather than building a system to interactively add and update weed descriptions in the database, I could simply import them in an XML format into the database. If I need to change the descriptions in the short term, I can edit the XML and reload the database. This way I could quickly develop a database-driven site, and in the future, I can add additional pages to edit the database directly. Since the original Weeds of El Limon software, WEEDS 1, was written in Java, it seemed natural to use servlets and JSP where I'd be able to reuse some of the software and design.

WEEDS 2, the software which generates Common Weeds, is a four-tier application because four separate processes are involved in each request: the web browser, the Apache web server, the Java virtual machine, and the MySQL database. Parts of WEEDS 2 run on the web server (URL rewriting rules), parts in the Java virtual machine (JSP and supporting classes) and parts run in MySQL (database queries.)

The output of WEEDS 2 is conservative HTML, roughly compliant with HTML 3.2, without style sheets, applets, or JavaScript. For any project, it's important to consider the audience when choosing which client-side features you use. Applets, for instance, can provide a sharp user interface for an intranet application, or a VRML world can draw an audience of thrill seekers, but, since fancy features aren't supported in old browsers and aren't completely compatible between new browsers, early adopters risk limiting their audience and greatly raising the cost of developing and maintaining their sites. It's often easier to add interactivity on the server side, where you can maintain a large database and be a center for communication between your users. On the server, you can maintain control over your platform, your tools, and not have to worry about supporting multiple versions of the software on which you depend.

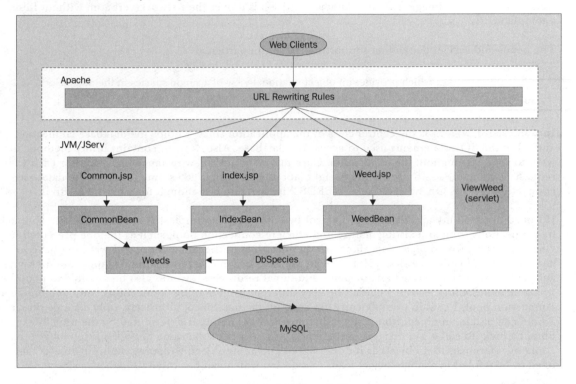

For each of the three page types, there exists a JavaServer Page and a JavaBean. For instance, to generate individual weed pages, WEEDS 2 uses `weed.jsp` and `WeedBean`. The JSP is, for the most part, an HTML template filled with information it gets from its corresponding Bean. There are a few advantages to this division. If I make a change in a Java class, I have to recompile the `.java` file, and, possibly, restart the servlet engine. (Some servlet engines, such as Apache JServ and JRun, can be configured to automatically reload class files that change. Others, such as Sun's Java Server Web Development Kit, cannot.) JSP files, however, are compiled into Java servlets by the JSP engine. So long as the JSP file stays the same, the JSP engine reuses the servlet. When you change the JSP file, the JSP engine detects this and recompiles. It's as easy to edit a JSP file on your server as it is to edit an HTML file. By defining the look of a page in a JSP, I can make simple changes without the hassle of recompiling. However, by hiding more complicated Java methods inside beans, the Java left inside the JSP is simple and stereotypical, generally of the form `<jsp:getProperty() ... />`, meaning that JSPs can be written and edited by people who know about graphic design and HTML while the complexities of Java, databases, and object-oriented design can be left to programmers.

A one-to-one mapping between JSPs and beans is only one possible design. You could, if you wanted, have multiple JSPs access the same bean, or, have a page incorporate more than one bean. JavaBeans can be used as reusable components across a site, to create navigation bars or to insert advertisements. In my case, there were some methods, for instance, those that display certain objects in HTML form, and properties, such as the copyright notice, that were common to all the pages. I could have used an additional bean shared by all the pages, but rather, I made IndexBean, CommonBean, and WeedBean subclasses of GeneralBean to share these functions.

WEEDS 2 contains images of the weeds. The images are stored in .gif format inside BLOB columns in the database, and are served by the ViewWeed servlet. I use a servlet here, because ViewWeed simply retrieves the image from the database and sends it over the network verbatim without filling in a template.

The beans and servlet depend on supporting classes, in particular:

> DBSpecies, which provides an object-relational view of a single species in the database
> Weeds, which is the gateway to the database

In some sense, Weeds is the central class of the application since it holds the database connection and all of the SQL statements used to access the database. Also, Weeds contains utility methods that I want to share throughout the application. Currently, I create a new instance of Weeds for each web request. Although Weeds itself is lightweight (about 32 bytes), it takes time to create the database connection. This is OK now, because WEEDS 2 is currently fast enough for what I do with it.

If I need to speed my application up, I've got two options. The simplest is to change Weeds so it gets its connections from an existing mature and efficient connection pool, such as the one presented in Chapter 9. This would be a snap, since Weeds encapsulates the connection, so I wouldn't have to change a line of code elsewhere. If, however, WEEDS becomes a more complex application - say, accesses more than one database, or pools additional resources, it would also be possible to pool the Weeds class. Pooling Weeds wouldn't be very different from pooling connections, although unlike a connection pool, I couldn't simply copy the code off the net. Since, ultimately, only a single thread at a time can obtain an object from a pool, the time cost of pooling is determined by the time it takes to obtain a lock (to call a synchronized method). Since it costs the same to pool a single object that contains references to n objects as it does to pool any other object, wrapping multiple objects that need to be pooled in a single object leads to a design which can be scaled to higher performance.

Locating all the SQL in the Weeds class has other consequences. There is the disadvantage that SQL statements are declared in a file far away from the places where they are used, which makes the code harder to read to a newcomer. Each SQL statement is wrapped in a method, and it's a pain to think up a good name for each statement! On the other hand, since all the SQL is in one place, all of the dependence on a particular database is in one place. Although SQL is supposed to be a standard, you'll discover many foibles in your database when you try to port an application from one database to another. If, for instance, I find the application doesn't work with database XYZ, I can make a subclass XYZWeeds which fixes the incompatibilities. This would also be a way to take advantage of special, non-portable features of a particular database, such as stored procedures, which could improve performance. With the SQL in one place, I can also change the names of columns and rows and make other changes in the structure of the database without affecting the rest of the program (I've already done this several times).

Organizing a server application in several layers makes your application more flexible for the future. Because the JSPs, beans, and supporting classes form three distinct layers, it is possible to move one of the layers onto another server using Java RMI or IIOP. For large business applications, Enterprise JavaBeans (EJB) provides a standard interface for application servers that provide services such as transaction management, security, distribution, and persistence. I'll talk about EJB more when I discuss the JavaBeans in this application.

The Unfriendly Net

I wish I could install the WEEDS 2 software and database on our web server in San Francisco and work on both the descriptions and the software from my computer at home. Unfortunately, in Germany, where I currently live, residential phone calls are charged by the minute. Between high costs, a busy modem pool, and a congested transatlantic cable, it's not practical to work online.

To cope with this problem, we keep a master copy of each of our web sites on our development server in Germany, each on a virtual host in our home LAN. We don't have a database or servlet engine in San Francisco, but instead, we create a static copy of the site (plain HTML and GIF files) on our machine in Germany and install the static copy on our web server. This technique can't be used for sites which process complicated queries (such as full-text search) or that can be modified by users (such as a site with a message board). However, our static site can be stored on a floppy and viewed on computers without a network connection.

There are two steps to copy our site to our server. First, on our machine in Germany, we make a static copy with a web crawler, specifically, pavuk (http://www.idata.sk/~ondrej/pavuk/). Pavuk crawls through a web site and makes a collection of directories and files that mirror the original site. Then, we mirror the static copy of our site to our web server using rsync (http://rsync.samba.org), a utility that brings two files or directories into sync by sending only the parts that are different.

To copy our dynamic site with a web crawler, we need to make it look, to web clients, like a static site. That is, there can't be any .jsp, .cgi, or .asp files, or cgi-bin directories. Also, we can't pass parameters via GET or POST methods (that is, no URLs that end like weed.html?id=7.) Although it's possible to write a servlet which pretends to be a directory, and reads the path after the servlet name (such as servlet/small/4.gif), JSPs can only read parameters via GET or POST. To get around this, I use Apache's mod_rewrite module to transform static URLs like weeds/weed/4.html into URLs with GET parameters, such as weeds/jsp/weed.jsp?id=4. URL rewriting is similar to servlet aliasing, but is much more powerful: mod_rewrite can

- ➤ Use external programs to transform URLs
- ➤ Use mod_proxy to pass a request to another web server (this was useful in early testing, when the only JSP 1.0 compatible engine didn't work with Apache)
- ➤ Distribute requests between multiple servers

There are other reasons to make a dynamic site look static. Major search engines and other robots often refuse to index sites that look dynamic, because some sites could send a crawler crawling through millions of dynamically generated pages, wasting the time and bandwidth of the crawler while overloading the dynamic site. Thus, many worthwhile dynamic sites lose the hits they could get by being indexed. If a finite subset of a database driven site is worth indexing, making it look static can increase your traffic and help people find a useful resource. Also, when you hide the mechanics of your site, you make it a little harder for hackers to take advantage of the published and unpublished weaknesses of your server software.

The Tools

Now I'll talk about the hardware and software that Common Weeds uses and how to set up a system to run it. Our development system is a 350 Mhz Pentium 2 with 64 Mb of RAM. It runs:

> - Debian Linux 2.0
> - Apache, with the optional `mod_rewrite` module compiled in (which is included with the Apache source but disabled by default), as well as Apache JServ
> - To add support for JSP, I use Sun's reference implementation
> - The shareware database MySQL (http://www.mysql.org/) and the `mm.mysql` JDBC driver (http://www.worldserver.com/mm.mysql/)

Configuration depends on your web server and servlet engine. After getting Apache, JServ and the JSP reference implementation working, I had to make two changes to run my application. First, I had to add the `mm.mysql` driver to the permanent classpath of the servlet engine. In `/usr/local/jserv/conf/jserv.properties`, add:

```
wrapper.classpath=/usr/local/jdk117_v1a/lib/mysql.jar
```

The Java class files (servlets, beans, and supporting files) are packaged in a `JAR` file, which I add as a JServ repository. Unlike classes in the permanent classpath, JServ monitors files in the repository and reloads them when they change so I can develop without restarting the servlet engine. So in `/usr/local/jserv/conf/zone.properties`, add:

```
repositories=/home/www0/weeds/weeds2.jar
```

XML, SQL and Java Objects

It's time to start development of the backend of the application. First we'll look at the existing XML descriptions of common weeds. Then from a discussion of the mapping of XML to SQL tables, we'll see how the descriptions are stored in MySQL before implementing a Java class to access the information for the application.

XML Files

The software that generated Weeds of El Limon was a filter that converted a collection of XML files into HTML files. Thus, I started WEEDS 2 with plant descriptions in XML form, a Document Type Definition (DTD) that defines the format of those files, and Java classes that transforms the document tree produced by an XML parser (MSXML) to a set of objects describing the weeds. Naturally, when adopting a database, I wanted to reuse as much of this work as possible. Here's the `limon.dtd` file:

```
<!ELEMENT plantdata ( species )+>
<!ELEMENT species ( family?,latin*,common*,text*,cite*) >
<!ATTLIST species id CDATA #REQUIRED>

<!ELEMENT family ( #PCDATA ) >
<!ELEMENT latin ( #PCDATA ) >
<!ELEMENT common ( #PCDATA ) >
<!ATTLIST common xml:lang CDATA "en">

<!ELEMENT text ( #PCDATA | A | cm | ref )* >
<!ATTLIST text type CDATA #REQUIRED>
<!ATTLIST text source CDATA #REQUIRED>
<!ATTLIST text xml:lang CDATA "en">

<!ELEMENT a (#PCDATA)>
<!ATTLIST a href CDATA #REQUIRED>
<!ATTLIST a xml:link CDATA #FIXED "simple">

<!ELEMENT cm (#PCDATA)>

<!ELEMENT ref EMPTY>
<!ATTLIST ref id CDATA #REQUIRED>

<!ELEMENT cite EMPTY >
<!ATTLIST cite source CDATA #REQUIRED>
<!ATTLIST cite page CDATA "">

<!ENTITY % ISOlat1 PUBLIC
    "ISO 8879-1986//ENTITIES Added Latin 1//EN//XML"
    "ISOlat1.pen" >
%ISOlat1;
```

No changes were needed in the DTD, or in the input XML files. To separate identified and unidentified weeds, I simply copied the identified weeds into a directory titled `identified-weeds/`. (`ISOlat1.pen` is a file that defines the entities such as `&aacute;` defined in HTML 4.0, included in the WEEDS2 package.) This DTD specifies a very rigid file format, in which there is little room for variation. The `<plantdata>` element, for instance, can contain only a list of `<species>` elements, which in turn contain `<family>`, `<latin>`, `<common>` and `<text>` elements in that order. A typical file, `19.xml`, looks like

```
<?XML VERSION="1.0"?>
<!DOCTYPE plantdata SYSTEM "limon.dtd">
<plantdata>
<species id="19">

<family>Labiatae</family>
<latin>Leonotis nepetaefolia (L.) R. Br.</latin>
<common>lion's ear</common>
<common xml:lang="es">cordon de fraile</common>
<common xml:lang="es">rubim de bolas</common>
<common xml:lang="es">cordao de frade</common>
<common xml:lang="es">boton de cadete</common>
<common xml:lang="es">molinillo</common>
<common xml:lang="es">quina de pasto</common>
```

Continued on Following Page

```
<text type="DESCRIPTION" source="Direnzo98">
Leaves are opposite, on long petioles, very soft, and coarsely toothed with round
teeth. Flowers occur in globes (<cm>2.5-3.4</cm>) slightly
prickly to touch with thin leaves immediately undeneath. Flowers are
orange and tubular with four stamens with white filaments, light
yellow anthers and one pistil. Stem is very rigid and square, plant
is taprooted. Common in fallow fields.
</text>
<cite source="Cardenas72" cite="181"/>
</species>
</plantdata>
```

Except for the contents of the `<text>` element, the structure is rigid, and, therefore, easy to map to a relational database.

Along with the DTD and XML files, WEEDS 2 also inherited a class, MSXMLSpeciesFactory. This converted XML plant descriptions into Java objects which implemented the interface Species:

```java
package tapir.weeds.representation;

public interface Species {
   public String getId();
   public LanguageString getFamily();
   public LanguageString[] getLatin();
   public LanguageString[] getCommon();
   public Text[] getTexts();
}
```

MSXMLSpeciesFactory creates an implementation of Species called SpeciesImpl, which simply stores information in Java fields:

```java
package tapir.weeds.representation;

import java.util.Vector;

class SpeciesImpl implements Species {

    String d_id;
    LanguageString d_family;
    LanguageString d_latin[];
    LanguageString d_common[];
    Text d_texts[];

    public String getId() {
       return d_id;
    };

    public LanguageString getFamily() {
       return d_family;
    };

    public LanguageString[] getLatin() {
       return (LanguageString[]) d_latin.clone();
    };

    public LanguageString[] getCommon() {
       return (LanguageString[]) d_common.clone();
    };
```

```
      public Text[] getTexts() {
         return (Text[]) d_texts.clone();
      };
   }
```

The methods are used to read the attributes of a species. There aren't any methods for setting attributes, because those are set directly by the MSXMLSpecies factory (which can see them because, like SpeciesImpl, it is a member of tapir.weeds.representation. These fields are available to the classes in tapir.weeds, where the beans and supporting classes are defined).

The tapir.weeds.representation package also contains several more classes, including LanguageString, an immutable object that contains both a string and the ISO digraph denoting the language of the string (we record common names in both English and Spanish) and Text, an object that describes the content of the <text> element.

Mapping XML to SQL

When we map XML objects to SQL tables, we're confronted with the differences between XML and the relational data model. Relational databases store information in a rigid and inflexible format. A database contains one or more tables, which are collection of rows (or records) composed of columns (or fields.) The rigid structure of relational databases is a good thing: it's the mathematical purity of the relational data model that makes it possible to build databases that scale into the stratosphere and meet the needs of global businesses.

XML, on the other hand, is much more flexible. Although some XML files, like 19.xml, can be divided into records (<species> elements) and fields (<latin>, <common>, etc.), XML can support complex, even recursive, hierarchies (such as WDDX, http://www.wddx.org/). Also, XML files can contain free-form text similar to HTML, such as the contents of the <text> element.

Another difference between XML and SQL, for the time being, is that SQL is typed and XML is untyped. A SQL database can understand, for instance, that some columns contain strings and other columns contain numbers, and thus, compare quantities correctly. You certainly can store data of a particular type inside an XML element or in an attribute, and write programs to process it any way you wish, but XML processing software cannot, yet, automatically determine the type of data inside an element or attribute. Some proposals have been made to replace the DTD with a more specific schema that contains type information. Examples include XML-Data (http://www.w3c.org/TR/1998/NOTE-XML-data) and DCD (http://www.w3c.org/TR/NOTE-dcd/). Both proposals are discussed in the book *XML Applications*.

Two kinds of products which help integrate XML and databases are on the cards: XML query languages and tools to automatically map XML documents and SQL tables. To be competitive with SQL, an XML query language will need a way to associate types with XML attributes and tags, and, likely, a feature similar to joins in SQL. Although the W3C has sponsored a conference on XML query languages, no standard has emerged. The closest thing to such a language in existence is the extensible stylesheets transformation language (XSLT, http://www.w3.org/Style/XSL/).

To use XSLT as a query language, think of relationships between XML elements and attributes as representing relationships between things in the world. To take an example, in 19.xml, the <common> element that contains the text "lion's ear" is a child of a <species> tag for which the ID attribute is 19. This means that "lion's ear" is a common name of plant 19. If we put all of our weed description in one big file, the following XSLT stylesheet selects out the common names of weed 19,

```
<xsl:stylesheet>
    <xsl:templace match='species
            [attribute(id)]=="19"/common'>
        <xsl:copy-of>
    <xsl:template>
<xsl:stylesheet/>
```

and gives the output:

```
<common>lion's ear</common>
<common xml:lang="es">cordon de fraile</common>
<common xml:lang="es">rubim de bolas</common>
<common xml:lang="es">cordao de frade</common>
<common xml:lang="es">boton de cadete</common>
<common xml:lang="es">molinillo</common>
<common xml:lang="es">quina de pasto</common>
```

SAXON (http://home.iclweb.com/icl2/mhkay/saxon.html) is an XSLT processor written in Java which can be extended by writing new XSL elements and new XSL functions in Java. SAXON, among other things, can insert data from XML documents into SQL databases. I've written a SAXON script to load the weed database from XML. However, I won't reproduce it here because SAXON is in rapid development and the current version probably won't work when you read this. Look for it at http://www.tapir.org/weeds/ if you're interested.

In WEEDS 2, I mapped XML to SQL with Java classes written by hand. Oracle, Microsoft, and other players in the database market are working on products to automate this process. As with query languages, with such tools you'll need to specify the types of elements and attributes, and how you'd like to map particular XML elements to particular SQL tables in either a GUI or a specialized programming language.

The first table in our database is `Species`, which holds the master record for each species. It contains the id, the primary key of the plant, and the only attribute of a plant which has a one-to-one relationship with the plant, its family name:

id	family
VARCHAR(32)	VARCHAR(32)
26	Labiatae

A species can have more than one Latin name. For instance, it might have been discovered independently in different parts of the world 100 years ago, or, at some point botanists might have argued about the classification of the plant. Since there is a one-to-many relationship between species and Latin names, I created a new table, `Latin`, for Latin names. Here, the column `species` is a foreign key that points to the `species` table. Each species is listed once on the top page. This is ensured by the `principal` column, which designates one name as the name which appears on the top page, the name for which `principal=1`.

species	name	principal
VARCHAR(32)	VARCHAR(64)	INT
19	Leonotis nepetaefolia (L.) R. Br.	1

I also map the `<common>` element to a table called `Common`, Each record contains the foreign key `species`, as well as the common name, in the `name` column, and the contents of the `xml:lang` attribute in the `lang` column.

species	name	lang
VARCHAR(32)	VARCHAR(64)	CHAR(2)
19	lion's ear	en
19	cordon de fraile	es
19	rubim de bolas	es
19	cordao de frade	es
19	boton de cadete	es
19	molinillo	es
19	quina de pasto	es

The `<text>` tag is more complex, partly because the `<text>` element has more attributes, but more importantly, because it contains free-formatted XML like `"is <cm>5</cm> tall, see also <a href='/foo/'/>"`. Here, we're not interested in questions like, "in what plants is there a measurement of a length greater than 5 cm?" or "how many pages contain hyperlinks to yahoo?" The contents of the `<text>` elements are text, not data, so I just copy them into the `text` column. Here's the `Text` table:

species	type	source	lang	text
VARCHAR(32)	VARCHAR(64)	VARCHAR(64)	CHAR(2)	TEXT
19	DESCRIPTION	Direnzo98	en	Leaves are opposite, on long...

Unfortunately, the content of the `text` column is not a well-formed XML document because a valid XML document must contain a single root element (plus processing instructions). For example,

```
<greeting>Hello!</greeting>
```

is a well-formed XML document, while the following is not:

```
This is <not/> a well-formed XML-document
```

This is acceptable, because to reconstitute a `<text>` element from the database, I add the `<text>` and `</text>` start and end tags and fill in the attributes of the element from the other columns in the row. I do this to avoid **denormalization**. Denormalization happens when a piece of information is stored in two different places in the database. For instance, suppose I stored the entire `<text>` element in the `text` column, and an application changed the type column, but forgot to change the type attribute of the `<text>` element in the `text` column. Later on, one application might use the value stored in the type column, and another might use the value stored in the `text` field - they don't agree, and this is a bug.

It's important to avoid accidental or unnecessary denormalization in database designs. Sometimes it's necessary to denormalize a database. Denormalization isn't itself a bug, it just invites bugs by making it possible for the database to hold inconsistent information. There are two limiting types of database application: online transaction processing (OLTP) and data warehousing.

Relational databases were invented for OLTP applications, such as airline reservation systems. In OLTP, a large number of clients are simultaneously reading and writing from the database and it's important that everybody share a consistent view of the database - the probability that two people get assigned the same airline seat should be close to zero.

In data warehousing, which is increasing in importance, the database is updated infrequently, and complex and time-consuming queries are run against it. In data warehousing, it's common to create summary tables containing redundant information. If updates are infrequent enough, it's adequate to rebuild the summary tables manually after an update, or triggers can be used to update the summary table automatically after an update.

The Cite table keeps track of references to literature that isn't online:

species	source	page
VARCHAR(32)	VARCHAR(64)	VARCHAR(8)
19	Cardenas72	181

Unlike the previous tables, the Images table is not loaded from the XML document, but rather from the collection of images accompanying them. After scanning the images, we reduced the number of colors in the images to conserve download time. We felt the best tradeoff was 32 colors, so images are stored in identified-weeds/32colors/. Images come in two sizes: small images that appear on the individual species pages, and large images for separate viewing. These were stored as 19half.gif and 19.gif respectively. I store .gif images in the BLOB field img. I also store information about the format of the image (its MIME type, as well as its width and height) so I can provide the correct attributes for the <IMG> tag.

By keeping meta-information on images, I could, for instance, store both a GIF and PNG version of an image, serving the PNG image only to browsers that support PNG. (This is one case where denormalization is justifiable. Even though the format, width, and height of an image can be determined by inspecting the BLOB, it would be a great deal of work. If the database supports user-defined functions, it might be possible to create a function which extracts the width and height from the img column, but it probably wouldn't be worth it.)

species	type	img	format	width	height
VARCHAR(32)	VARCHAR(64)	BLOB	VARCHAR(64)	INT	INT
19	big	0x3846494702...	Image/gif	555	781
19	small	0x3846494701...	Image/gif	277	359

In Weeds of El Limon, we numbered plants in the order we found them. To make Common Weeds more like most plant books, I sorted the weeds on the top page by family name, genus and species. Since users often navigate a site by editing URLs, and because I wanted page numbers in the printed version of Common Weeds, I had to renumber the weeds. I didn't want to throw the old plant numbers away, since I might someday want to look at an entry in my old notebooks. Keying the weeds by the new numbers rather than the old numbers would be a mistake, because if I ever added a new weed into the middle of the alphabetical order, I'd have to change the keys. It's safest, from the standpoint of database integrity, to sort the weeds every time I want to convert a new weed number to an old weed number, or vice versa. Although it's easy to sort the weeds using SQL,

```
SELECT species.id FROM species,latin WHERE latin.principal=1 AND
species.id=latin.species ORDER BY family,latin.name.
```

it seemed wasteful to resort the weeds on each query. Instead, I chose to sort the weeds and compute the mapping between new and old numbers just once, after loading the database. The table will be called `New_ordering`. Since the new numbers can be computed from the database, this is another case of denormalization, but it's acceptable if the database is changed infrequently. With a database that supports triggers, it would be possible to have the database reconstruct the `New_ordering` table whenever the database is updated, however, MySQL doesn't support triggers.

old_number	new_number
INT	INT
19	10

Storing XML Fragments in the Database

Now I'll discuss how I store the contents of the `<text>` element in the database. Consider the `<text>` element from `22.xml`:

```
<text type="DESCRIPTION" source="Direnzo98">
Tree-like plant, grows about 3m tall. Leaves are large (<cm>45-60</cm> wide),
deeply lobed with five to seven lobes, leaves are serrate with prominent veins.
Flowers occur in raceme with female flowers above male flowers. Fruits occur in
terminal clusters and are covered with soft spines. Fruits have three lobes with
three seeds inside; beans are dark brown with irregular white spots - seeds are
known to be poisonous. Pod length is about <cm>2.8</cm> and bean length about
<cm>1.3</cm>. Found growing in field by fence.
</text>
```

To avoid needless denormalization, I store the content of the `<text>` tag in the `text` columns of the `Text` table and the attributes in other columns. `<text>` elements are internally represented with instances of `tapir.representation.Text`. The `textToXML()` method of the `Weeds` class convert a `Text` object into the XML string, as stored in the `text` column.

```
public String textToXML(Text t) {

    StringBuffer sb = new StringBuffer();
    TextChunk[] chunks = t.getChunks();
    for (int i = 0; i < chunks.length; i++) {
        addChunk(sb,chunks[i]);
    }
```

```
            return sb.toString();
    }

    void addChunk(StringBuffer sb, TextChunk chunk) {
        if (chunk instanceof AnchorChunk) {
            addAnchorChunk(sb, (AnchorChunk) chunk);
        } else if (chunk instanceof RefChunk) {
            addRefChunk(sb, (RefChunk) chunk);
        } else if (chunk instanceof CMChunk) {
            addCMChunk(sb, (CMChunk) chunk);
        } else
            addPlainChunk(sb, (PlainChunk) chunk);
    }

    void addAnchorChunk(StringBuffer sb, AnchorChunk chunk) {
        sb.append("<A HREF='" + chunk.getHref() + "'>" + chunk.getText()
                + "</A>");
    }

    void addRefChunk(StringBuffer sb, RefChunk chunk) {
        sb.append("<REF ID='" + chunk.getId() + "'/>");
    }

    void addCMChunk(StringBuffer sb, CMChunk chunk) {
        sb.append("<CM>");
        sb.append(chunk.getText());
        sb.append("</CM>");
    }

    void addPlainChunk(StringBuffer sb, TextChunk chunk) {
        sb.append(chunk.getText());
    }
```

`Weeds.insertIntoText()` stores a `Text` in the database,

```
    private void insertIntoText(String id, Text t) throws SQLException {
        preparedStatement ps = prepareStatement("INSERT INTO text" +
                        " (species,type,source,lang,text) values (?,?,?,?,?)");
        ps.setString(1,id);
        ps.setString(2,t.getType());
        ps.setString(3,t.getSource());
        ps.setString(4,t.getLanguage());
        ps.setString(5,textToXML(t));
        ps.executeUpdate();
    }
```

It's straightforward to get `Text` objects out of the database. I didn't even need to rewrite `MSXMLSpeciesFactory`. By adding a synthetic `<!DOCTYPE>` tag, I tell MSXML to expect `<text>` as a root element rather than `<species>`. `MSXMLSpeciesFactory` has a hierarchical structure which reflects the structure of the XML document. An XML parser based on the document object model (DOM) returns a tree of `Element` objects. `MSXMLSpeciesFactory` contains methods to parse each element. For instance `Species parseSpecies(Element e)` parses a `<species>` tag and `Text parseText(Element e)` parses a `<text>` tag. The only change I had to make to `MSXMLSpeciesFactory` was to make the `parseText()` method of `MSXMLSpeciesFactory` `public`, so I could access it from other packages.

The method `DBSpecies.parseText()`, given type and source information and the contents of the `<text>` tag, wraps up the contents in start and end tags, feeds the resulting XML document into MSXML to produce a parse tree, and then uses `MSXMLSpeciesFactory` to convert the parse tree into a text object.

```
public static Text parseText(String type, String source,
                             String language, String xmlBody)
                        throws ParseException {
    StringBuffer xml=new StringBuffer();
    xml.append("<?XML VERSION=\"1.0\"?>\n");
    xml.append("<!DOCTYPE TEXT SYSTEM \"file:/home/paul/" +
               "identified-weeds/limon.dtd\">\n");
    xml.append("<TEXT TYPE=\"");
    xml.append(type);
    xml.append("\" SOURCE=\"");
    xml.append(source);
    xml.append("\" xml:lang=\"");
    xml.append(language);
    xml.append("\">\n");
    xml.append(xmlBody);
    xml.append("</text>");

    StringBufferInputStream feed = new
                        StringBufferInputStream(xml.toString());
    Document d = new Document();
    d.setLoadExternal(true);
    d.load(feed);

    Element root = d.getRoot();

    return MSXMLSpeciesFactory.parseText(root);
}
```

The Weeds Class

A number of system resources, such as the connection to the database, are the same in every page in the *Common Weeds* system. I concentrated these resources in a single class, named `Weeds`. Currently I create a new instance of `Weeds` with each request, but when I need to improve performance, I can pool instances of `Weeds` between requests, thus preserving database connections, prepared statements, and any other resources that should be preserved between requests.

Also, I decided to put all of the SQL statements in my application (except for those that create the database) in the `Weeds` class. Some authorities disapprove of this (such as web database pioneer and photographer Phillip Greenspun, at http://www.photo.net/) because it separates SQL code from the Java (or other language) code that uses it, thus making software harder to read. It's also annoying to think up a good name for each SQL statement. And, while writing about this project, I had to split up the `Weeds.java` file so I could show you methods from `Weeds` next to the methods of other classes that call them to make the code more understandable. However, I get a few benefits from this decision, as we discussed earlier in the chapter.

`Weeds` has a constructor, which simply creates a new database connection. Although `Weeds` classes could be pooled, `Weeds` could also be adapted to use the connection pool object from Chapter 9.

```
package tapir.weeds;

import java.io.*;
import java.sql.*;

import tapir.weeds.representation.*;

public class Weeds {

    public String d_dbname = "weeds";
    public Connection d_conn;

    public Weeds() throws ClassNotFoundException, SQLException {
        d_conn = getConnection(d_dbname);
    }
```

I provide `static` methods to get connections, so I can reuse them in both the `Weeds` class and in the `CreateDB` class which creates the weeds database. This way, when I switch databases, I only need to change one `getConnection()` method. `getRootConnection()` is used to create a connection to the database server before the weeds database exists, so we can create it. The two methods are:

```
public static Connection getConnection(String dbname)
                    throws ClassNotFoundException,SQLException {
    Class.forName("org.gjt.mm.mysql.Driver");
    return DriverManager.getConnection("jdbc:mysql://localhost/" +
                                    dbname, "root", "");
}

public static Connection getRootConnection()
                    throws ClassNotFoundException,SQLException {
    return getConnection("mysql");
}
```

JDBC provides three ways to execute SQL statements: with the `Statement` class, the `PreparedStatement` class, and the `CallableStatement` class. When you use plain statements, the database must recompile the statement for each use, which wastes time. Prepared statements are created inside an application which holds a database connection, and live as long as the database connection. They can't be reused between connections in the same application, or by another application. Callable, or stored, statements are compiled once and stored in the database. Callable statements can be used by multiple applications. Unfortunately, not all databases support stored statements (MySQL doesn't), and the procedure for storing statements in a database depends on the database.

In general, it's easier to use prepared and callable statements rather than plain statements in Java. For example, consider the `insertIntoText()` method of `Weeds`:

```
private void insertIntoText(String id, Text t) throws SQLException {
    PreparedStatement ps = prepareStatement("INSERT INTO text " +
                    "(species, type, source, lang, text) values (?,?,?,?,?)");
    ps.setString(1,id);
    ps.setString(2,t.getType());
    ps.setString(3,t.getSource());
    ps.setString(4,t.getLanguage());
    ps.setString(5,textToXML(t));
    ps.executeUpdate();
}
```

This class prepares a statement with a number of empty slots to fill, each marked with a question mark. It then fills in the blanks with the `setString()` method of `PreparedStatement`, and executes the statement. The `prepareStatement()` method looks like:

```
public PreparedStatement prepareStatement(String stmt) throws SQLException {
    return d_conn.prepareStatement(stmt);
}
```

This method is a hook - right now it simply calls the `prepareStatement()` on the database connection. However, because every call to `prepareStatement()` goes through it, it gives me the freedom to change the behavior later. For instance, if I want to save prepared statements between requests (once I'm pooling instances of `Weeds`) I could keep a `Hashtable` of prepared statements indexed by strings, and fetch them from the `Hashtable` rather than creating them in the database. This hook also provides a strategic place to take statistics on how often various queries are used.

Hypothetically, I could write the same method using the `Statement` class:

```
private void insertIntoText(String id, Text t) throws SQLException {
    Statement s = d_conn.getStatement();
    s.executeUpdate("INSERT INTO text (species, type, source, lang, text)" +
                    " values ('" + id + "','" + t.getType() + "','" +
                    t.getSource() + "','" + t.getLanguage() + "','" +
                    t.textToXML() + "')");
}
```

Although this contains fewer characters than the `PreparedStatement` version, it's the typing equivalent of a tongue-twister and, worse, it won't work all the time. If any of the strings, for instance, contained a single quote character, the database would think that the string ended and would return an error.

Or worse, some databases, such as Microsoft's SQL server, let you execute statements in batch mode - specifying several in the same call to `executeUpdate()`. If a hacker can feed your web application strings that fool it into feeding two queries to your database, they could possibly alter or destroy your database or extract confidential information. You can fix this by adding escape characters to your strings, putting a backslash before any backslashes, null characters, or single or double quotes.

> The `PreparedStatement` class automatically quotes strings and converts other types such as Java `Dates` to the appropriate type for the database. (Different databases use different date formats, and messing around with dates in string formats is what got us into the Year 2000 mess.)

`PreparedStatement` also lets you move chunks of data in and out of `BLOB` and `TEXT` fields through `InputStreams`. Other languages, such as Perl, have better syntax for manipulating strings, where you could do the above `INSERT` with just,

```
$self->{CONN}->do{"INSERT INTO text(species,type,source,lang,text) values
'$species', '$type','$source','$lang','$text'"}
```

but Java's weak string handling, combined with a strong `PreparedStatement` class make working with `PreparedStatements` preferable to working with `Statements`.

Mapping a Relational Database to Objects

WEEDS 1 had a package, `honeylocust.limon.representation`, which contained a set of classes to store information about weeds. Other than `MSXMLSpeciesFactory`, which reads `Species` objects out of XML files, the classes in this package only have accessor methods to let other classes read values from them. Sensing that someday I might want to change my representation for the weeds, say by storing them in a database, I used Java interfaces to separate the details of the representation layer from other packages that use it. When I first started writing WEEDS 2, I used the original classes out of the `honeylocust.limon.representation` classes - until I got tired of ugly warts in the original classes, moved them to `tapir.weeds.representation` and fixed them up.

The interface `Species` is implemented by classes that deliver information about weeds. It's an interface, so it can be implemented in different ways. WEEDS 2 contains two implementations of `Species`:

> `SpeciesImpl` (described previously, and carried over from WEEDS 1), which stores information about weeds in RAM

> `DBSpecies`, which only holds the ID number of a species in RAM and retrieves information about weeds directly from the database each time a method is called

`DBSpecies` is a drop-in replacement for `SpeciesImpl`. Any class that can handle an instance of `Species` can handle an instance of `DBSpecies`. Java's access protection hides the reality that `DBSpecies` is based on a different principle than `SpeciesImpl`:

```
package tapir.weeds;

import java.sql.*;
import java.io.*;
import java.util.Vector;

import tapir.weeds.representation.*;
import honeylocust.msxml.om.*;
import honeylocust.msxml.parser.*;

public class DBSpecies /* implements Species */ {
    public final Weeds d_w;
    public final String d_id;
    public final String d_oldId;
```

`DBSpecies` only contains a reference to the database (the `Weeds` class) and the ID of a weed: to get other information. `DBSpecies` queries the database and converts the results to the appropriate objects. The `DBSpecies` object is the place in the system where I translate the new ID numbers of the weeds, determined by their order on the top page to the old ID numbers used in the original XML data. I do it here because this minimizes the amount of code required.

I construct an instance of `DBSpecies` by passing in an instance of `Weeds`, and the ID of a weed:

```
public DBSpecies(Weeds w,String id) throws SQLException {
    d_w = w;
    d_id = id;
    d_oldId = w.getOldId(d_id);
}
```

The `Weeds.getOldId()` function looks up the old number in the `new_ordering` table. In this application, it's safe to store the old ID in `d_oldId` since I never update the database after loading. A few accessors just return the ID of the `Species` object,

```
public String getId() {
    return d_id;
}

public String getOldId() {
    return d_oldId;
}
```

A few methods retrieve their values from the database, by running SQL queries that are stored in the `Weeds` object, then converting the `ResultSet` returned by JDBC into the Java objects we used in the internal representation.

```
public LanguageString getFamily() throws SQLException {
    ResultSet rs = d_w.selectFromSpecies(d_oldId);
    return new LanguageString(rs.getString(1), "la");
}

public LanguageString[] getLatin() throws SQLException {
    ResultSet rs = d_w.selectFromLatin(d_oldId);
    Vector v = new Vector();
    while(rs.next()) {
        v.addElement(new LanguageString(rs.getString(1), "la"));
    }
    LanguageString names[] = new LanguageString[v.size()];
    v.copyInto(names);
    return names;
}
```

The `DBSpecies.getTexts()` method is trickier, since `Text` objects are stored in XML form inside a `TEXT` column of the `Text` table titled `text`! We fetch the columns out of the database, and then feed the columns into the method `DBSpecies.parseText()` which uses MSXML to construct a `Text` object. We talked about the `parseText()` method in the earlier section on SQL and XML.

```
public Text[] getTexts() throws SQLException, ParseException {
    ResultSet rs = d_w.selectFromTexts(d_oldId);
    Vector v = new Vector();
    while(rs.next()) {
        v.addElement(parseText(rs.getString(1), rs.getString(2),
                               rs.getString(3), rs.getString(4)));
    }

    Text texts[] = new Text[v.size()];
    v.copyInto(texts);
    return texts;
}
```

`DBSpecies` only scratches the surface of object-oriented design with relational databases. In this case, the `Species` class was designed to represent database-like information in the very beginning, so the mapping was easy. It's possible to create Java classes which reflect the structure of a SQL table, which is usually easy, or make SQL tables that reflect the structure of Java classes, which is generally harder. By adding an object-oriented layer over your database, you can distribute access to the database over RMI or IIOP, log access to the database, implement security policies, or work around the absence of triggers in some databases. Enterprise JavaBeans (EJB) has support for entity beans, which represent objects in a database or another persistent store.

When mapping a hierarchy of objects that inherit from each other, for instance, it's necessary to decide if you want to:

> ➢ Create a table for a superclass and additional tables to represent properties of subclasses
>
> ➢ Create a table for each class (without any special relationship between superclasses and subclasses)
>
> ➢ Create one big table that holds related classes and has a special column designating the type of the column (leaving columns not needed by a particular class `NULL`)

It can be faster to load all of the properties out of the database when an object is created, but sometimes we only need some of the properties, and any information stored in RAM runs the risk of becoming stale. Although it's possible to store serialized Java objects in `BLOB`s, (much like XML fragments can be stored in `TEXT`s), the database can treat them only as lumps of incomprehensible data. Since object-relational mappings try to hide the underlying database connections, it can be awkward to begin, commit, and roll back transactions, particularly if you're building systems that work with both RAM-based and database-backed objects. Finally, writing constructors for database-backed objects takes some thought, since there are two senses in which you might want to 'create' a database-backed object:

> ➢ Create a new instance of an object to represents an existing database record
>
> ➢ Create an entirely new object, including the database record. It helps here to create objects through factory methods.

Object databases, designed to work with OO languages, were a popular research topic in the early 80s. They have seen only limited commercial use because object databases are harder to query than relational databases, don't have a standard language as developed as SQL, and have historically had difficulty scaling beyond 4 GB databases. Java, multimedia, and the Internet are reviving interest in object databases, particularly Computer Associates' Jasmin (http://www.cai.com/products/jasmine.htm). Object-relational databases add features to relational databases to simplify mapping objects to tables: Ingres and the free PostgreSQL (http://www.postgresql.org/) databases are examples, although databases like Oracle now support object-relational extensions, which are addressed by the forthcoming SQL 3 standard.

A number of products automatically generate Java classes representing SQL tables:

> ➢ Sun's Java Blend (http://www.sun.com/software/javablend/)
>
> ➢ ObjectMatter's VBSF (http://www.objectmatter.com/)
>
> ➢ Thought Inc.'s CocoBase (http://www.thoughtinc.com/cocofree/doc/index.html)
>
> ➢ Jora (http://www.ispras.ru/~knizhnik/Jora-1.02/ReadMe.html)

Creating and Loading the Database

In MySQL, you can type the command `mysql` and then proceed to create a database and define tables. This is fun to do the first time you develop a database application, but it gets old fast - particularly when you need to make a backup copy or migrate your database to a new computer or DBMS. When you build a database application, you must also build a set of utilities for initializing and maintaining the database.

The CreateDB Class

The `CreateDB` class simply creates the `weeds` database, and the tables that make it up. Because we might want to make several databases for testing, `CreateDB` is a command line application which takes one argument: the name of the database we want to create.

```
package tapir.weeds;

import java.sql.*;

public class CreateDB {
    String d_dbname;

    public static void main(String argv[]) throws Exception {
        CreateDB self = new CreateDB(argv[0]);
        self.run();
    }

    public CreateDB(String dbname) {
        d_dbname = dbname;
    }
```

We face a problem when we wish to create a database. We need to connect to the database server, but we can't do that without the name of a valid database. In both MySQL and PostgresSQL, you can create a database when you're connected to any database, but you need to know the name of a database that exists on your system. MySQL uses a database called `mysql` to store access control lists, so you can always connect to the MySQL database through `mysql`. Note that the procedure varies on other databases. We use `getRootConnection()` to get a connection to create the new database with, then we open a connection to the new database with `getConnection()`.

```
public void run() throws Exception {
    Connection conn = Weeds.getRootConnection();

    Statement s = conn.createStatement();
    s.executeUpdate("CREATE DATABASE " + d_dbname);

    s.close();
    conn.close();

    conn = Weeds.getConnection(d_dbname);
    s = conn.createStatement();
```

Next we execute the SQL statements to set up the tables. The SQL isn't hidden away in the `Weeds` class because it runs before the database exists, when it would be impossible to create an instance of `Weeds`.

```
         s.executeUpdate("CREATE TABLE species (id varchar(32)," +
                         " family varchar(64))");
         s.executeUpdate("CREATE TABLE latin (species varchar(32)," +
                         "name varchar(64),principal int)");
         s.executeUpdate("CREATE TABLE common (species varchar(32)," +
                         "name varchar(64),lang char(2))");
         s.executeUpdate("CREATE TABLE text (species varchar(32)," +
                         "type varchar(64), source varchar(64), lang char(2)," +
                         "text text)");
         s.executeUpdate("CREATE TABLE cite (species varchar(32)," +
                         "source varchar(64),page varchar(8))");
         s.executeUpdate("CREATE TABLE images (species varchar(32)," +
                         "type varchar(64), img blob, format varchar(64)," +
                         "height int, width int)");
         s.executeUpdate("CREATE TABLE new_ordering (old_number int," +
                         "new_number int)");

         s.close();
         conn.close();
      }
   }
```

The InsertWeeds Class

With the database created, we're ready to fill it with information. `InsertWeeds`, given a list of XML files containing weed descriptions, inserts them into the database. I simply type:

```
% cd identified-weeds
% java tapir.weeds.InsertWeeds *.xml
```

The class is simple since most of the thinking is done by other classes.

```
package tapir.weeds;

import tapir.weeds.representation.*;

import java.io.File;
import java.util.Enumeration;
import java.util.Vector;

public class InsertWeeds {

   public static void main(String[] argv) throws Exception {

      Weeds w = new Weeds();

      Vector v = new Vector();
      for(int i = 0; i < argv.length; i++)
         MSXMLSpeciesFactory.parseLimon(v, new File(argv[i]));

      for(Enumeration e=v.elements();e.hasMoreElements();) {
         Species s = (Species) e.nextElement();
         w.insertWeed(s);
      }
      w.reorderWeeds();
   }
}
```

The `insertWeed()` method in the `Weeds` class has the following implementation:

```
public void insertWeed(Species s) throws SQLException {
    if (!s.identified())
        throw new IllegalArgumentException("Weed not identified");

    String id=s.getId();
    insertIntoSpecies(id, s.getFamily().toString());
    LanguageString l[] = s.getLatin();
    for (int i = 0; i < l.length; i++) {
        insertIntoLatin(id,l[i].toString(),i==0);
    }

    l=s.getCommon();
    for (int i = 0; i < l.length; i++) {
        insertIntoCommon(id, l[i]);
    }

    Text t[]=s.getTexts();
    for (int i = 0; i < t.length; i++) {
        insertIntoText(id, t[i]);
    }
}
```

which calls the method `insertIntoSpecies()`:

```
private void insertIntoSpecies(String id, String family)
                            throws SQLException {
    PreparedStatement ps=prepareStatement("INSERT INTO species (id, family)" +
                                "values (?,?)");
    ps.setString(1,id);
    ps.setString(2,family);
    ps.executeUpdate();
}
```

We discussed the other method `insertIntoText()` in the section on *XML and SQL*. It converts the `Text` object back into SQL before storing it in the relational database.

The last task `InsertWeeds` does is compute the new sort order of weeds: sorted first by family name and then by genus and species. Fortunately, you can get SQL to output results in almost any order you like. This is done as follows:

```
public void reorderWeeds() throws SQLException {
    Statement s = d_conn.createStatement();
    PreparedStatement ps = prepareStatement("INSERT INTO new_ordering" +
                                "(new_number, old_number) VALUES (?, ?)");
    ResultSet rs = s.executeQuery("SELECT species.id FROM species, latin" +
                                "WHERE latin.principal = 1" +
                                "AND species.id = latin.species" +
                                "ORDER BY family, latin.name");
    int i = 1;
    while (rs.next()) {
        // System.out.println(i + " " + rs.getInt(1));
        ps.setInt(1, i);
        ps.setInt(2, rs.getInt(1));
        ps.executeUpdate();
        i++;
    }
}
```

URL Rewriting and File Layout

WEEDS 2 uses Apache's URL rewriting to present a static appearance to a dynamic page. I do this because I want to make a static copy of my site with a web crawler, so every URL must be a file name that could exist on a static site.

How the Pages look to a Web Browser

To a web browser, the weeds/ directory has the following layout:

```
index.html
common.html
error.gif
mountains.jpg
weed/
    1.html
    2.html
...
big/
    1.gif
    2.gif
...
small/
    1.gif
    2.gif
...
```

For web clients, such as browsers, as well as web crawlers and cache programs, it's exactly like a static site, and we can use a web crawler to make an exact copy.

What's Really on the Server

The contents of the weeds/ directory on the server are entirely different from what the browser sees. None of the web documents exist in the weeds/ directory. Rather it looks like:

```
.htaccess
jsp/
    common.jsp
    copy.jsp
    error.jsp
    footer.jsp
    index.jsp
    weed.jsp
    error.gif
mountains.jpg
weeds2.jar
```

error.gif and mountains.jpg are the only files which get served to the client. The jsp/ directory contains our JavaServer Pages, but these URLs are never seen by the client. Client URLs are converted into server URLs by rewriting rules specified in the .htaccess file. The .htaccess file contains server configuration commands specific to a directory. Most of the directives that can be put in a httpd.conf file, to rewrite URLs, define new MIME types, or put a password on a directory, for example, can be put in an .htaccess file. When setting up security in the httpd.conf file you can use the AllowOverride directive to specify exactly what directives can be used in .htaccess files in particular directories and their subdirectories.

The .htaccess file is convenient, but if you're administering a web server with a large number of users who you don't completely trust, such as a departmental web server, it's only possible to exert central control on security policy if .htaccess is disabled or restricted.

The .htaccess file in weeds/ looks like:

```
RewriteEngine on
RewriteBase /weeds/

RewriteRule ^$ /weeds/jsp/index.jsp
RewriteRule ^index\.html /weeds/jsp/index.jsp
RewriteRule ^common\.html /weeds/jsp/common.jsp
RewriteRule ^weed/([0-9]+)\.html /weeds/jsp/weed.jsp?weed=$1
RewriteRule ^small/([0-9]+)\.gif /servlets/tapir.weeds.ViewWeed/small/$1.gif
RewriteRule ^big/([0-9]+)\.gif /servlets/tapir.weeds.ViewWeed/big/$1.gif

RewriteRule ^weeds2.jar /weeds/jsp/weeds2.jar [forbidden]
```

The first two lines turn on URL rewriting and tell the URL rewriting module what directory you want to have rewritten. The rest of the file consists of rewriting rules. The format of a rule is

```
ReWriteRule search replace [options]
```

The first argument, search is a regular expression. Most characters, such as letters and numbers, match themselves. Other characters have special meanings.

> ➢ ^ matches the beginning of a URL
> ➢ The period character matches any character
> ➢ [0-9] matches any digits
> ➢ * matches zero or more instances of the previous character
> ➢ + matches one or more instances of the previous character
> ➢ \ escapes the character that follows it, negating its special meaning (the following character matches itself)
> ➢ Parenthesis characters group several characters together.
> ➢ $ matches the end of the line

So,

```
RewriteRule ^$ /weeds/jsp/index.jsp
```

maps http://www0/weeds/ to http://www0/weeds/jsp/index.jsp and the rule,

```
RewriteRule ^index.html /weeds/jsp/index.jsp
```

matches http://earth/weeds/index.html so the web server instead serves the URL at http://earth/weeds/jsp/index.jsp. Unlike URL redirection, where the web browser is instructed to try a different URL, the web browser sees no sign that URL rewriting takes place - all processing takes place on the server. The next rule maps individual weed pages to the JSP page, taking the ID of the weed as a GET argument passed after the ? character.

```
RewriteRule ^weed/([0-9]+)\.html /weeds/jsp/weed.jsp?weed=$1
```

This rule matches URLs such as,

> http://earth/weeds/weed/5.html
> http://earth/weeds/6034.html

but doesn't match URLs such as:

> http://earth/weeds/.html
> http://earth/weeds/54a3.html

The parentheses in the rule group the digits together, so in the case of http://earth/weeds/6034.html, $1 equals 6034. This value is substituted into the *replace* string, so the URL http://earth/weeds/weed/5.html maps to http://earth/weeds/jsp/weeds.jsp?weed=5.

The next two rules map image URLs to the image servlet. For instance, they map http://earth/weeds/big/5.gif to http://earth/servlets/tapir.weeds.ViewWeed/big/5.gif. This points out a disadvantage of a JSP relative to servlets and CGI. A servlet, for example http://earth/servlets/tapir.weeds.ViewWeeds/, can have a path appended to it, like big/5.gif. This makes it possible for a single servlet (or CGI script) to serve an entire virtual directory tree underneath the servlet URL. Unfortunately, you can't do this with JSP, so you can only pass arguments as form elements, namely, weed=5.gif.

In the last rule, I use the forbidden option to prevent web users from accessing the weeds2.jar. In this case, I've got nothing to hide, but in general, web users should not be allowed to download server software from your server. Often, servlets, cgi-scripts, and other web programs contain passwords (for users to log in, or for a database) and other confidential information. And as Java class files can be decompiled, a hacker can get a head start at cracking your site by getting a copy of your server-side applications, so it's important to lock them down. I put weeds2.jar in the weeds/ directory so all of WEEDS 2 would be one convenient package for you to install. If I were feeling paranoid, I'd put it entirely outside the web server directory.

This is a bare introduction to URL rewriting. Many more features are supported, such as serving different pages to different web browsers, serving pages off other servers by proxy, and using external programs to decide which page to redirect to. Plus there are traps and pitfalls to avoid which you can read about in the online documentation at http://www.apache.org/docs/mod/mod_rewrite.html. In particular, URL rewriting is much faster when the directives are stored in the central httpd.conf file rather than in a per-directory .htaccess, but for our development system which doesn't get many hits, convenience wins over raw speed.

JSP and JavaBeans

In WEEDS 2, I use JavaServer Pages to define the look of my pages. These are filled with information obtained from JavaBeans. Systems that embed a programming language in HTML, such as JSP, Netscape's LiveWire and Microsoft's ASP, make it easy to separate the style and content of web pages. Many programmers feel it's easier to write web applications this way, compared to CGI scripts or Java Servlets, in which you must generate HTML inside your program and write a lot of repetitive code such as class and method declarations. With careful design, systems like JSP help divide the labor of constructing complex sites. The templates can be written by graphic designers with a good aesthetic sense, artistic ability, and knowledge of HTML. Implementing database-driven sites also requires skill in programming, software engineering, and data modeling. Although it takes a programmer to plan the architecture of a site, most of the tricky programming can be encapsulated in JavaBeans.

We met JavaBeans in Chapter 7. The JavaBeans specification describes a collection of standard design patterns to set and retrieve properties of Java objects, to pass events between objects, to create instances of objects, and to store objects using serialization. Also, the specification defines a format for storing meta-information about Java classes in a JAR file that allow visual GUI builders and other tools to import them and incorporate them automatically in projects. The JavaBeans specification is modular, so you can use parts of the specification you need for your application (such as getting and setting properties) without needing to implement everything, such as meta-information.

The aspect of beans most useful for web applications is properties. Properties are like variables or constants which can be set or retrieved through a standard interface. They are only like variables because the authors of Beans can implement them any way they like. A property could be stored in a variable, but could also be stored in a database, or computed by a lengthy calculation. When you set a property, Beans can make changes in other objects - a visual bean can redraw itself, for instance, if you change its appearance. Properties can be set and retrieved through two patterns called *accessor methods.* Suppose we have a bean named *pinto,* with a property called *weight* of type `double`. So other objects can set the property, it defines a method with the signature:

```
public void setWeight(double weight).
```

Other objects retrieve the property through the method:

```
public double getWeight().
```

In general, the name weight can be replaced by any other name, and the type `double` can be replaced by another type. You can use accessor methods by hand in other objects, and sophisticated programs such as GUI builders can automatically detect and use them via Java introspection.

There are two ways to use beans from JSP. The first is to use the `<jsp:useBean />` `<jsp:setProperty/>` and `<jsp:getProperty/>` tags. These make it possible to use beans without writing Java at all, and because they have a simple and limited function, they'll be useful for visual builder tools. However, it's still possible to access beans using the ordinary Java syntax. For instance, to insert the value of `pinto`'s weight property, we can either type,

```
<jsp:getProperty id="pinto" property="weight"/>
```

or,

347

```
<%= pinto.getWeight() %>.
```

In this project I've used the second approach, because the Java syntax is shorter and I'm already familiar with it. Also, more seriously, I find the `<jsp:useBean/>` tag is limited. Although it can automatically create Beans in different scopes, that is, create beans that exist for just one page, or that persist throughout a session or application, it can only create beans via an empty constructor, such as

```
pinto=new Pinto();
```

Unfortunately, this isn't flexible. My WeedBean corresponds to an entry in the database. It always corresponds to the same entry, so I pass the ID, the primary key of the weed, in its constructor:

```
weed=new Weed("12");
```

WeedBean plays a role similar to that of an Entity Bean in EJB - it represents an object held in persistent storage. Although I could provide a method in WeedBean to set its ID, say,

```
weed.setId("12");
```

this breaks my decision to make a particular instance of WeedBean correspond to a particular weed. (Suppose Object A and Object B held a copy of the same WeedBean and Object A changed the WeedBean's ID without telling Object B.)

Although Sun will add support for EJB in the next version of JSP, in the short term you have two choices to use EJBs or Beans with complicated constructors:

> ➤ Use Java expressions and scriplets
> ➤ Write a Bean with a simple constructor which wraps the complicated Bean

Index.jsp and Common.jsp

Let's take a look at the JSP file for the top page, `index.jsp`. We start out with a few definitions:

```
<HTML LANG="en">
<%@ page language="java" errorPage="error.jsp" %>
<%
    tapir.weeds.IndexBean b=new tapir.weeds.IndexBean();
    b.setBreak(8);
%>

<%@ include file="meta.jsp"%>
```

At the top, I declare an error handler - if `index.jsp` throws an exception, the JSP engine will execute and pass the exception to `error.jsp`. I'll talk about `error.jsp` in a moment. Next we create an instance of the IndexBean class. Next I configure the bean, setting the Break property. I could store the configuration of the bean in a database, or as a serialized object in a file, but since the Break property has to do with visual presentation, it makes sense to store its value in the JSP file, where most of the decisions about presentation are made.

Finally, I include the file `meta.jsp`, which is included by all the JSP pages in this project except `error.jsp`. It contains the HTML `<HEAD>` of the document, which contains HTML 4.0 meta-information tags which help search engines and other web robots:

```
<HEAD><TITLE><%= b.getTitle() %></TITLE>
<META NAME="ROBOTS" CONTENT="<%= b.getRobotInfo() %>">
<META NAME="Author" CONTENT="<%= b.getAuthor() %>">
<META NAME="Date" CONTENT="<%= b.getDate() %>">
<META NAME="Copyright" CONTENT="<%= b.getCopyright() %>">
<META NAME="Keywords" CONTENT="<%= b.getKeywords() %>">
<META NAME="Description" CONTENT="<%= b.getDescription() %>">
<META NAME="Version" CONTENT="<%= b.getVersion() %>">
</HEAD>
```

In `meta.jsp`, the `IndexBean` properties return plain text. This is, in general, good. If we wanted to write a GUI or command-line application that accesses the weeds database, we could easily use the `Author` property. Also, when bean properties return plain text, the JSP author (who isn't necessarily the same as the Bean author) has a great degree of choice. If, for instance, you want to print the title centered in bold, you can type:

```
<DIV ALIGN=CENTER><B><%= b.getTitle() %></B></DIV>
```

The JSP author can add more complicated scriptlets to the page, but it makes sense for a bean to return HTML which is included directly in the document. The next installment of the `index.jsp` file looks like:

```
<BODY BGCOLOR=#FFFFFF>
<TABLE CELLSPACING=0 WIDTH=100%><TR><TD BGCOLOR=#A0FFA0>
<FONT COLOR=#000000><FONT SIZE=+2><%= b.getTitle() %></FONT></FONT>
</TABLE>
<TABLE CELLPADDING=3>
<TR>
<TD VALIGN=TOP>
<%= b.getWeedList() %>
<TD VALIGN=TOP>
<IMG SRC="mountains.jpg" HEIGHT=201 WIDTH=310>
</TABLE>
```

The `WeedList` property is an HTML string that we insert into the middle of the document. It contains `<B>` tags to make the family headers bold, `<BR>` tags to mark the end of lines, and `<IMG>` tags pointing to single pixel `.gif`s for formatting, and a `<TD>` tag which breaks the table. As a result, the author of the JSP can make only limited changes in the appearance of the list: perhaps embed it in a `<FONT>` tag, make the family headers italic instead of bold, or change the indentation of the species tags isn't possible. I had some other choices here: I could have had the Bean return an array of species names and written a Java scriptlet, embedded in the JSP, to format the text. However, this would defeat the goal of confining Java code to the Bean.

If there were particular parameters that the JSP author would want to set, for instance, the indentation of the species names, the bean could expose properties to allow that. But how could I, as the bean author, imagine everything that a JSP author would want to change? Cascading style sheets (CSS) offer a ray of hope. If, for instance, `WeedList` marked text with logical meanings with the `<SPAN>` tag, a graphic designer could change the formatting of the page by changing the style sheet:

```
<SPAN CLASS="familyHeader">Amaranthaceae</SPAN>
<SPAN CLASS="species"><A HREF="weeds/1.html">
Amaranthus spinosus L.</A></SPAN>
```

I couldn't do that for this project, however, because *Common Weeds* is of interest to viewers who don't have the newest browsers.

Finally, at the bottom of the `index.jsp` page, I include the copyright message, stored in `copy.jsp`, and end the page:

```
<%@ include file="copy.jsp"%>
</BODY>
</HTML>
```

The common name index, `common.jsp`, is almost identical to `index.jsp`, except that it creates an instance of `CommonBean` rather than `IndexBean`, and has a more complicated method to give the computer a hint as to where to break the columns:

```
<%
    tapir.weeds.CommonBean b=new tapir.weeds.CommonBean();
    int[] breaks=new int[5];
    breaks[0]=22;
    breaks[1]=43;
    breaks[2]=61;
    breaks[3]=77;
    breaks[4]=100;
    b.setBreaks(breaks);
%>
```

Weed.jsp

The constructor of `WeedBean` takes a single argument, the ID number of the weed, and must therefore be created in a Java scriptlet:

```
<HTML LANG="en">
<%@ page errorPage="error.jsp" %>
<%
    tapir.weeds.WeedBean b=new tapir.weeds.WeedBean(request.getParameter("weed"));
%>
<%@ include file="meta.jsp"%>
```

The ID number of the weed is passed through the `weed` form parameter, which I retrieve through the `request` object, an instance of `javax.servlet.http.HttpServletRequest` which is automatically defined in any JavaServer Page.

```
<BODY BGCOLOR=#FFFFFF>
<TABLE CELLSPACING=0 WIDTH=100%><TR><TD BGCOLOR=#A0FFA0 COLSPAN=3>
<FONT COLOR=#000000><FONT SIZE=+2><%= b.getTitle() %></FONT></FONT>
<TR><TD WIDTH=<%= b.getSmallImageWidth() %> ROWSPAN=2>
<A HREF="<%= b.getBigImageURL() %>">
<IMG ALIGN=LEFT BORDER=0 ALT="[<%= b.getPrincipalLatin() %> illustration]"
HEIGHT=<%= b.getSmallImageHeight() %> WIDTH=<%= b.getSmallImageWidth() %>
    SRC="<%= b.getSmallImageURL() %>">
</A>
```

All of the Bean properties in the snippet above are plain text. I was careful in weed.jsp to avoid nested tables, because nested tables slow down the rendering of tables in web browsers. Many database-driven sites use complex table layouts to pack in a lot of information. That's good, but some browsers (particularly Netscape) won't draw tables until they've received enough information to lay them out correctly - a problem that synergises with overloaded servers, congested backbones, and slow modems. To avoid this, test your site over slow connections, avoid nested tables, and try breaking large tables into several tables.

```
<TD VALIGN=TOP>
<SMALL>
<%= b.getNumberNav() %>
</SMALL>
```

The NumberNav property of WeedBean is a block of HTML that draws a navigation bar that lets users seek out a page by number. Bean properties that return HTML can work like widgets in graphical user interfaces.

```
<TD VALIGN=TOP>
<DIV ALIGN=RIGHT>
<A HREF="../index.html">top/latin</A> |
<A HREF="../common.html">common</A>
</DIV>
<TR><TD COLSPAN=2 VALIGN=TOP>
<B>Family <%= b.getFamily() %></B>
<BR>Latin name: <I><%= b.toHtml(b.getPrincipalLatin()) %></I>
<BR>Common names: <I><%= b.toCommaList(b.toHtml(b.getCommon())) %></I>
<%= b.toHtml(b.getTexts()) %>

<P><B>Additional resources:</B>
<UL>
<LI><A HREF="<%= b.getBigImageURL() %>">Large illustration</A>
</UL>
<%@ include="copy.jsp"%>
</TABLE>

</BODY>
</HTML>
```

We then fill in the description of the weeds. A bean used in a JSP can provide useful functions, as well as properties. In this case, there are several toHtml() functions which convert types to HTML. For instance, getPrincipalLatin() returns a LanguageString which contains a string and the ISO digraph denoting the language of the string, which is "la" in the case of Latin. The toHtml(LanguageString l) method adds a SPAN tag which marks the language of the text,

```
<SPAN LANG="la">Ricinus communis L. </SPAN>
```

➤ toHtml(LanguageString l[]) converts an array of LanguageStrings into an array of Strings

➤ toCommaList(String s[]) inserts commas between the strings in a String array to produce a comma-separated list

➤ toHtml(Text t[]) uses toHtml(Text t) to convert the array of text objects produced by getTexts().

Another convenient way to define a library of utility functions for a collection of JSPs is to use the `<%@ page extends %>` directive to make them subclass a class you define. It takes some thought, however, to use subclassing well in Java, since Java does not support multiple inheritance and, therefore, a JSP, like any Java class, can only inherit from one other class.

Error.jsp

Many things can and will go wrong with a database-driven site. Not only will you encounter errors while prototyping, implementing, and debugging a site, but you'll probably have your database crash, administrators set incorrect settings, users incorrectly change URLs by hand, and other trouble when your site is in production. The default error pages provided by your web server and servlet engine are often ugly and uninformative. To make error messages useful, both to developers and end users, and to make your site have a consistent look, it's desirable to provide your own error pages when things go wrong.

JSP provides a simple method for handling errors. When an exception is thrown, and not caught inside a JSP, the JSP engine forwards the request to the page designated in the `<%@ page errorPage %>` directive. The error page must contain the `<%@ page isErrorPage="true" %>` directive, which ensures that, in addition to the usual `request` and `response` objects, an `exception` object is defined which is the exception thrown by the failed JSP. Our error page looks like:

```
<HTML LANG="en">
<%@ page isErrorPage="true" %>
<BODY BGCOLOR=#FFFFFF>
<TABLE CELLSPACING=0 WIDTH=100%><TR><TD BGCOLOR=#A0FFA0>
<FONT COLOR=#000000><FONT SIZE=+2>Common Weeds of the Carribean</FONT></FONT>
</TABLE>
<DIV ALIGN=RIGHT>
<A HREF="../index.html">top/latin</A> |
<A HREF="../common.html">common</A>
</DIV>
<IMG SRC="/weeds/error.gif" HEIGHT=300 WIDTH=276 ALIGN=RIGHT>
<FONT SIZE=+7>OOPS!</FONT>
<BR>
<FONT SIZE=+2>Either you punched in something invalid, or something went wrong
with our web server.
Try reloading. If that doesn't help
send a note to
<A HREF="mailto:paul@honeylocust.com">paul@honeylocust.com</A></FONT>
<BR CLEAR=ALL>
<B><U>Stack trace:</U></B>
<PRE>
<% exception.printStackTrace(new PrintWriter(out)) ;%>
</PRE>
</BODY>
</HTML>
```

Our error page is simple, with a look consistent with the rest of *Common Weeds* and the tapir.org site. The stack trace, generated by,

```
<% exception.printStackTrace(new PrintWriter(out)) ;%>
```

is useful for developers. For a more elaborate site, you should divide exceptions into two categories: expected and unexpected. Expected errors are those that can be identified to a specific problem which is the fault of the user or the server. For instance, if the user replaces the ID of the plant with something incorrect, or if the database crashes and you can't get a connection at all, these errors are to be expected and you can return a comprehensible error message. However, you can't predict everything that can go wrong (and a error handling system that's too complex is itself a source of bugs).

For the next version of *Common Weeds,* I will define an `Exception` called `WeedsException`, which will be thrown when expected errors occur. The detail message of `WeedsException` will be a user-friendly error message to replace the current vague message. When `error.jsp` receives a `WeedsException`, it will print the friendly message and omit the stack trace.

Note that you can put any Java code you like in an error handler, so you could have your error handler send a system administrator a mail with the JavaMail API, send a message to your system log, or store the details of the incident in a database.

The Beans

I created one bean for each JSP file. This way, the division of labor is clear. In some situations, it might be best to create one bean for several different pages, or use more than one bean in a page - for example, it would make sense to implement a navigation bar or advertising banner as a bean that is reused on multiple pages. Many of the same functions, such as site meta-information, are needed in all of the beans, so I use inheritance and put common code in `GeneralBean`. `IndexBean`, `CommonBean` and `WeedBean` all extend `GeneralBean`.

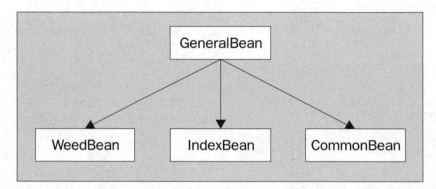

The `GeneralBean` class looks like this:

```
package tapir.weeds;

import tapir.weeds.representation.*;
import honeylocust.msxml.parser.ParseException;

import java.io.*;
import java.sql.*;
import java.util.*;

public class GeneralBean {

    Weeds d_weeds;

    public GeneralBean() throws ClassNotFoundException, SQLException {
        d_weeds=new Weeds();
    }
```

`d_weeds` is an instance of the class `Weeds`, which is the interface to the SQL database.

We next declare accessors for the meta-information fields accessed in `meta.jsp`. These values are inherited by beans that extend `GeneralBean`, but all can be overridden in subclasses if we wish.

```
    public String getRobotInfo() {
        return "ALL";
    }

    public String getAuthor() {
        return "Olivia S. Direnzo and Paul A. Houle";
    }
```

```
    public java.util.Date getDate() {
        return new java.util.Date();
    }

    public String getCopyright() {
        return "&copy; 1998 Honeylocust Media Systems" +
               "(http://www.honeylocust.com/)";
    }

    public String getDescription() {
        return "A collection of descriptions and illustrations of weeds " +
               "observed in El Limon, a small village in the " +
               "Dominican Republic during January 1998.";
    }

    public String getKeywords() throws SQLException {
        return "El Limon,Weeds,Botany,xml";
    }

    public String getLanguage() {
        return "en";
    }

    public String getVersion() {
        return "1.5DEV";
    }
```

After this, we have a few utility functions. `GetNumberNav()` for instance, generates the HTML code for the numbered navigation bar to navigate between individual weed pages by number:

```
    public String getNumberNav(int id) {
        StringBuffer out = new StringBuffer();
        for(int i = 1; i < 15; i++) {
            if (i != id) {
                out.append("<A HREF=\"" + i + ".html\">");
            } else
                out.append("&lt;");
            out.append(i);

            if (i != id) {
                out.append("</A>");
            } else
                out.append("&gt;");

            out.append(" | ");
        }
        return out.toString();
    }
```

`GeneralBean` also contains a utility function to convert objects of type `LanguageString` to HTML strings using HTML 4.0 language marking. This facility makes it possible for search engines and automatic web page translators to process your pages.

```
public String toHtml(LanguageString l) {
    if (l.getLanguage() == getLanguage()) {
        return l.toString();
    } else {
        return "<SPAN LANG=\"" + l.getLanguage() +
                "\">" + l.toString() + "</SPAN>";
    }
}
```

The next two methods are written in a functional style. When we make a list of plants by common name, which can be written in several languages such as Spanish, Portuguese, English, and French, we generate a comma separated list of names. First we convert an array of LanguageStrings into an array of HTML strings with toHtml(LanguageString l) and then use toCommaList(String[] s) to convert that array of HTML strings into a comma-separated list.

This style lets us write programs by composing existing functions such as toCommaList(toHtml(commonNames). If I invented a new kind of string, say a ColoredString, I just need to write a toHtml(ColoredString s[]) function. Java isn't quite as suitable for functional programming as more exotic languages such as LISP, but functional programming is often comfortable and fast in Java.

```
public String[] toHtml(LanguageString l[]) {
    int len = l.length;
    String[] x = new String[len];
    for (int i = 0; i < len; i++)
        x[i] = toHtml(l[i]);
    return x;
}

public String toCommaList(String s[]) {
    int len = s.length;
    StringBuffer out = new StringBuffer();
    for (int i = 0; i < len; i++) {
        if (i != 0)
            out.append(",");
        out.append(s[i]);
    }
    return out.toString();
}
```

Serving Images out of the Database

To serve images from the database, I use an ordinary Java servlet. JSP wouldn't help us here, since JSP uses Writers rather than OutputStreams, so it is limited to generating text documents. Other than that, serving images dynamically isn't much different from serving documents.

The ViewWeed Class

The ViewWeed servlet examines the path property of the request object - the part of the URL that comes after the name of the servlet. For example, in http://www0/servlets/tapir.org.ViewWeed/big/5.jpg, the path is "/big/5.jpg". I only need to implement the doGet() method of HttpServlet, since this servlet only handles GET requests. I catch all exceptions and display an error message containing the exception's stack trace to aid debugging.

```
public class ViewWeed extends HttpServlet {

    public void doGet(HttpServletRequest req, HttpServletResponse res)
                      throws ServletException, IOException {
        try {
            String path = req.getPathInfo().substring(1);
            if (path.endsWith("/")) {
                path = path.substring(0, path.length()-1);
            }

            if (path.length() > 6 && path.substring(0,6).equals("small/")) {
                serveImage(res,"small",path.substring(6));
            } else if (path.length() > 4 && path.substring(0,4).equals("big/")) {
                serveImage(res, "big", path.substring(4));
            } else {
                throw new Exception("Invalid path.");
            }
        } catch(Throwable e) {
            PrintWriter out = res.getWriter();
            out.println("<HEAD><TITLE>" +
                        "Exception processing ViewWeed" +
                        "</TITLE></HEAD>");
            out.println("<BODY><PRE>");
            e.printStackTrace(out);
            out.println("</PRE></BODY>");
        }
    }
}
```

Two things must be done to serve an image:

> Call `res.setContentType()` to specify the MIME type of the image

> Write the image data to the `OutputStream` obtained from `res.getOutputStream()`. I fetch the MIME type and the image, stored as a BLOB, out of the database.

```
public void serveImage(HttpServletResponse res, String type, String name)
                       throws Exception {
    Weeds w = new Weeds();
    int index = name.indexOf(".gif");
    if (index == -1)
        throw new Exception("bad filename <" + index + ">");

    String f = name.substring(0, index);
    String g = w.getOldId(f);

    ResultSet rs = w.selectFromImages(g, type);
    String mimeType = rs.getString(1);
    byte[] img = rs.getBytes(2);
    res.setContentType(mimeType);
    OutputStream os = res.getOutputStream();
    os.write(img);
    os.close();
}
}
```

The InsertImages Class

There is a separate program for inserting images in the database. As disk space is cheap, I load the images from all weeds, identified and unidentified, out of a directory containing all of them: I copied the GifInfo class wholesale from the old Weeds of El Limon

```
package tapir.weeds;

import tapir.weeds.representation.*;
import java.io.*;

public class InsertImages {

    public static void main(String[] argv) throws Exception {

        Weeds w = new Weeds();
        GifInfo g = new GifInfo();

        String dir = argv[0];
        for(int i = 1; i < 33; i++) {
            System.out.println(i);
            File f = new File(dir,i + ".gif");
            int x[] = g.getDimensions(f);
            w.insertImage(Integer.toString(i), "big", f, "image/gif", x[0], x[1]);
            f = new File(dir,i + "half.gif");
            x = g.getDimensions(f);
            w.insertImage(Integer.toString(i), "small", f,
                          "image/gif", x[0], x[1]);
        }
        System.exit(-1);
    }
}
```

If you need to put a lot of data in a TEXT or BLOB column, JDBC provides handy methods such as PreparedStatement.setBinaryStream() which copies text or binary data out of an InputStream and ResultSet.getBinaryStream() which provides an InputStream to read the column from. We use the former in the following helper methods in the Weeds class:

```
    public void insertImage(String species, String type, File file,
                            String format, int width, int height)
                            throws SQLException, FileNotFoundException {
        PreparedStatement ps = prepareStatement("INSERT INTO images" +
            (species, type, img, format, width, height) values (?,?,?,?,?,?)");
        ps.setString(1, species);
        ps.setString(2, type);
        storeFileInBlob(ps, 3, file);
        ps.setString(4, format);
        ps.setInt(5, width);
        ps.setInt(6, height);
        ps.executeUpdate();
    }

    public void storeFileInBlob(PreparedStatement ps, int slot, File f)
                            throws SQLException, FileNotFoundException {
        int length = (int) f.length();
        FileInputStream in = new FileInputStream(f);
        ps.setBinaryStream(slot, in, length);
    }
```

Summary

WEEDS 2, the software behind *Common Weeds of the Caribbean*, is a dynamic web application that uses JavaServer Pages and servlets on the Apache web server with the MySQL database.

For now, since I load the database with XML, I've eliminated the need to edit the database via the web. With a web crawler, I make a static copy of my dynamic site for final deployment on the web and on floppy disk. Although I've covered a lot of ground in this chapter, database-driven sites are a large topic. I ought to mention a few things that I haven't discussed:

> ➢ Since WEEDS 2 doesn't yet provide a web interface for changing the database, I haven't discussed how to safeguard the integrity of data when multiple users make changes simultaneously

> ➢ Nor have I looked at the design and implementation of web user interfaces for editing data

Maybe next time...

Bug Tracker Case Study

The next two chapters will put into motion many of the principals that have been discussed in the previous chapters. The focus of these two chapters will be the planning, design and construction of a software defect tracking system. We'll be examining construction of a distributed Java based software system, the design considerations that must be examined, and the activities of planning software design and development.

In this chapter, we'll be taking look at the software design planning process, as well as examining the primary use cases that the software system must accommodate. We'll build strategies for:

> Defining and identifying an appropriate development model
> Planning for change
> Developing a software development plan
> Software testing
> Identifying requirements through use cases
> Making architectural choices for Java-based distributed computing
> Selecting technologies to solve specific problems

Introduction to the Project

The first order of business is to review the scope of the software in question. This chapter and the next focus on a software system for a software vendor that allows customers to log defects, check on the status of reported defects, as well as supporting internal workflow for finding, reporting and closing software defects.

> Throughout this process, we'll be using the Unified Modeling Language (UML) notation to capture our knowledge about the system, requirements and design decisions. If you're familiar with UML, you'll have no trouble following along. If you've not yet learned a bit of the UML, you might want to read Appendix E in this book, which covers the basics of UML notation. You'll find it's quite easy and intuitive.

Birth of A Project

At this juncture, our specifications are a bit fuzzy – we don't yet know what we don't know, so we're going to take an incremental approach to design and development. I have received an email from the project sponsor at XYZ Software Corporation, who describes the system in fairly broad-brush terms. The details are sketchy, but his description provides an idea about the scope of the system that the company desires:

> Ron,
>
> I've talked with several of our department managers, and I've put together these notes that summarize the bug tracking system that you and I have talked about. I've asked the department managers to describe their specific requirements and assign relative priorities. I've assembled and consolidated those and have attached them to this email. Give me a shout if you have any questions, and let me know when next you'd like to meet.
>
> *Requirements:*
>
> Track the details of each reported defect
>
> Allow support engineers to enter defects and query the status of defects
>
> Allow triage team to assign defects to software engineers for resolution
>
> Allow software engineer to review assigned defects and update status of defects (for example, request more information, close as fixed, etc.)
>
> Allow sales engineers to enter defects, and query the status of defects on behalf of their clients.
>
> Allow product managers to get reports on the defects counts of a particular release
>
> Allow customers and outside sales to enter defects and query defects via the world wide web
>
> Allow support engineers to correlate incident records with reported defects (support incidents are currently tracked using a separate system that was developed in-house).
>
> [XYZ Software Corporation]

Because this study is intended to drive the design and development of a distributed application in Java, this study does not include a build-versus-buy analysis. Ordinarily this would be a fundamental exercise but is not considered here for obvious reasons.

Options for a Development Process

Before we get started, we need to lay out a plan of action that will define how best to gather the necessary information; plan, design and construct the software; and to test the software. Without this plan of action, we'll be flying by the seat of our pants and not have a good idea of where the project stands at any particular point in time.

There are many ways of structuring a software development process. There have been numerous books written on the topic. Some classical development processes include the waterfall model, spiral model, rapid application development and so forth. The development model shows and essentially dictates what the process is behind software development. For example, in a waterfall model, each phase of the project must be complete before proceeding on to the next phase. The requirements must be defined before any development can begin, development must be completed before testing can begin, and so forth.

For the project we are undertaking, we need to be more flexible than this. So far, all the information that we have about the project appears in a very short e-mail message. We can begin with this information, but we must also be prepared for significant course corrections along the way as we uncover more information through customer interviews and the process of developing software. In short, we will be discovering requirements and refining the system as we go along.

The Rational Unified Process

One development model that will accommodate our needs has been defined in the Rational Unified Process (RUP) from Rational Software. RUP provides a development process that is based from the notion of incremental development.

The goals of the Rational Unified Process are fairly straightforward. The process is designed to support software development, provide a means of managing requirements, support the use of component based architecture, control changes to software, and provide a means of verifying software quality.

RUP defines development as a series of phases and iterations. While each phase has a specific purpose, work activities within each phase often overlap. Each phase defines specific milestones and deliverable products that contribute to the completion of the project. These phases are the inception phase, elaboration phase, construction phase, and the transition phase. Each of these iterations are pretty well defined, and have specific milestones associated with them. Each phase includes, at its conclusion, a decision point where the relative success of the project is measured to determine if the project should continue to be funded or whether progress should be halted.

One of the most interesting things about RUP is that it can be tailored to accommodate projects of different sizes. For the bug tracker project, it's not necessary to plan and track the project as rigorously as a larger system with scores of designers and developers – this system simply isn't that big. Using a disciplined approach to the development plan, however, provides a better chance for successfully completing a product that will meet the needs of the end user. The four phases of RUP provide a logical sequence and framework for accomplishing the tasks of designing and building a software system, regardless of its size.

Let's take a closer look at the activities and end products of each of these phases. Please note that this overview highlights the basics of RUP but does not define it exhaustively. More detailed information is available directly from Rational's web site: http://www.rational.com.

Inception Phase

Overview

During the inception phase, our primary objectives are to define the business case for the software (that is, what makes us believe that building the software is a good idea) and put some bounds on the software by deciding what it is intended – and what is not intended – to do.

Objectives

The objectives of this phase are:

➢ Ensure that everyone involved in the project has a clear idea of the scope of the project under way, the estimated cost, and (most important) understands how the project will progress, be evaluated and re-estimated.

➢ Validity of primary use cases is verified by the sponsors of system and domain experts.

➢ Risks and estimates are defined and are realistic based on everything currently understood about the system to date.

Activities

This phase, like most, involves planning and work on both the product (the bug tracking system) and the process itself. Process-oriented activities include defining a business case for the software, taking first-pass estimates at required resources, defining the primary risks associated with the project, and defining the success criteria for the project – what needs to happen for us to consider our efforts and expenses worthwhile.

One of the most important activities in this phase is to define the primary **use cases** for the system. This involves identifying the external things (called **actor**s) that will interact with the system, and describing in fairly specific terms how they will interact with the system.

I like to keep a "top ten (or so) risks" lists throughout the project that identifies the top ten risks that could jeopardize the project. By updating my "top ten" list each week I can ensure that I'm paying attention to the right risks and am taking steps to mitigate those risks. This process has to begin right at the start of the project, so one of our tasks at this stage will be an initial risk assessment.

End Products

At the end of this phase, we should minimally have the following items:

➢ Vision document detailing what is planned, and the business case for building it.

➢ Initial use cases defined.

➢ Initial risks identified.

➢ Initial project plan outlined.

In addition, we may elect to build a prototype and construct a business model.

Elaboration Phase

Overview

During the elaboration phase, more analysis and research is performed to better understand the problem that is being addressed with the software. Because this phase entails a good deal of the heavy architectural and engineering work, it is a very important – and therefore high risk-phase of the project.

We will start putting together a "birds-eye" view of the overall system so that we can start putting together a logical architecture and have a broad understanding of the system. At this point, it's important to have a broad understanding of the overall system rather than to start delving into details.

Objectives

The objectives for this phase are to:

 ➢ Ensure that the vision for the software and the architecture defined during this phase are sensible and address the problem at hand.

 ➢ Ensure that the primary risks identified are being addressed directly.

 ➢ Ensure that the project team, sponsors and users understand the system as it is currently defined and agree that it still solves the targeted business problems.

Activities

The elaboration phase introduces many of the engineering design efforts. This phase will also require the involvement of an increasing number of participants from a broad range of skills.

The engineering efforts may involve some prototyping, technical risk assessments and requirements, and functional and design specifications. The use cases defined in the inception phase will be further detailed and expanded.

Project management and planning efforts will include fleshing out the project plan, revisiting risk assessment, and revising estimates and resources.

End Products

At the end of the elaboration phase, we should have the following items:

 ➢ Use case model   it should be considerably more detailed than at the end of the inception phase.

 ➢ Requirements, functional and preliminary design documents. Any requirements not explicitly captured by the use case model should be well documented.

 ➢ A document describing the software architecture.

 ➢ Revised project plan.

 ➢ Revised risks and estimates.

 ➢ Updated budget information (projected versus actual).

Construction Phase

Overview

The construction phase, as the name implies, involves the bulk of feature implementation and testing of the software. If the elaboration phase is compared to the architectural design of a building and the site preparation, the construction phase could be equally compared to the construction and finishing of the building itself.

Objectives

The ultimate objective of this phase is to get software that is ready to be delivered to the user. Accomplishing this goal requires:

➤ Specified features are implemented and integrated into the product.

➤ Overall product quality and stability has been verified.

➤ Documentation required to roll out software to users has been developed.

➤ The sponsors and end users of the system are prepared to take ownership of the system.

Activities

The primary engineering activities during this phase will include implementing the features as specified during the previous phases of the project, and performing the individual tests of each component prior to integration to ensure that its behavior complies with the specifications.

This phase also includes integrating the features into the product, and performing integration testing to ensure that features continue to work as they are added to the product.

From a management and planning perspective, this phase differs from the previous two in that the management focus changes from one of planning and forecasting to one of managing schedules and controlling quality and resources.

The measure of quality for many projects can be improved during this phase by rolling out early release of the product as "alpha" or "beta" cuts to end users. In general, "alpha" releases are functional releases that may not yet have all features integrated. "Beta" releases are generally considered to be feature-complete. An outside perspective on overall product quality is invaluable for finding software defects for projects of any complexity.

End Products

The primary end products from this phase are:

➤ The software product.

➤ The accompanying documentation.

➤ Updated budget information (projected versus actual).

Transition Phase

Overview

The transition phase moves the software from the hands of the developers into the hands of the end users. As the software is turned over, users will need to receive training, and the inevitable issues that crop up will need to be resolved. The purpose of this phase is to ensure a smooth turnover of the software from development to production.

Objectives

The primary objectives of the transition phase are:

➢   To ensure that the project sponsor and users are satisfied that the delivered product achieves the initial objectives.

➢   To ensure that the end-users can take ownership of the software with minimal intervention from the development team.

➢   To ensure that the software performs effectively and accurately within the deployment environment.

Activities

In order to achieve an effective transition, there are a number of activities that need to take place. The roll out effort may involve running the new system in parallel with an existing system (whether it be manual or automated) to ensure that the software produces the expected results. Also, where there was an existing automated system, there may be data conversions required to move legacy data to the new system. Finally, the recipients of the new system – whether they be end users or sales & marketing staff – need to be trained on the new software.

End Products

The end products of the transition phase are simple:

➢   The customer is satisfied with the delivered system.

➢   The actual cost of the system is acceptable.

Activities Within RUP

It is important to note that the activities detailed above are primary, but not sole, activities. Specific activities, such as requirements gathering and technical design, will frequently span iterations. The diagram below illustrates relative levels of engineering and management activities across the iterations as specified by the core workflows of RUP.

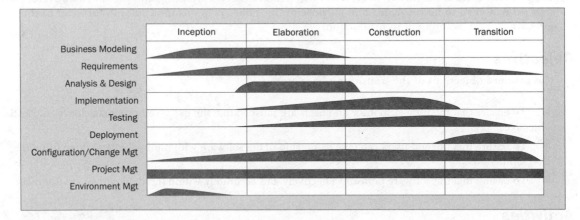

This reflects the incremental nature of RUP as a lifecycle model. Rather than taking a waterfall approach where all activities in a specific phase need to be complete before moving to the next phase, activities span across iterations. This approach plans for the inevitable changes in requirements, and therefore makes it much easier to accommodate changes throughout the project.

The incremental development process is ideal for the Bug Tracker project, because the project requirements are extremely sketchy and prone to change. We will be developing the requirements as we move forward and present prototypes to the client.

Bug Tracker Inception

The Bug Tracker inception phase addresses the following items:

- ➤ Vision statement
- ➤ Initial use cases
- ➤ Initial risks
- ➤ Development approach

Vision Statement

Bug Tracker Vision Statement

Purpose of Statement

This vision statement is intended to provide a high level view of the benefits anticipated for XYZ Sofware Corporation from the implementation and deployment of the Bug Tracker application, as well as to provide a high level outline of the features that are planned for the application.

Bug Tracker Vision

XYZ Software Corporation currently has only rudimentary tools for tracking defects reported against its software products. Developers currently use a shared spreadsheet for keeping track of bugs, but this practice is becoming unacceptable as the organization grows. Also, this does not allow technical support or customer support representatives to enter defect information or correlate defect reports to customer service incident reports created and maintained under XYZ's ERP packaged solution.

Successful deployment of the bug tracking system will enable broader access for reporting and reviewing the status of defects, thus eliminating the need to funnel bug reports and requests for status updates through the software developers. Automating this process will also help to streamline the process of prioritizing defects and assigning them to the developers who can resolve them.

Finally, by enabling customers to report defects and receive email notification when the defect has changed status, XYZ Software Corporation hopes to eliminate a common source of customer complaints relating to reported bugs "falling into the bit bucket."

Key Bug Tracker Features

Graphical user interface provides means of entering and editing defect information

Provides a means of tracking defect status to support a coordinated workflow from initial report to final disposition.

Provides programmatic interface allowing other software systems to interface with the bug tracker

Provides automatic transmission of emails when defect status changes. Notification can be specified at a per-defect basis.

Provides a browser-based interface that allows customers and staff to enter and query status of defects via the Internet.

Documentation Requirements

The documentation requirements for this application are modest, and will be limited to online HTML documents.

Limitations

This implementation does not fully address security issues, and as such the system sponsors have agreed that the system will be deployed in a manner that will physically isolate it from other operational systems in the business.

Use Cases

Use cases are a very expressive means of communicating how the software system will be used and how it interfaces with the outside world. Use case diagrams are very easy to create and comprehend, and are therefore a very useful means of expressing the external characteristics of the software to non-technical reviewers.

The initial use cases that have been assembled are presented in three categories: use cases internal to XYZ Software, use cases external to XYZ software, and automated interfaces. These have been developed through discussions and review with the project sponsor, and are considered accurate by the sponsor.

Internal Use Cases

This category is by far the most involved. The use case diagrams for internal use cases have been separated into multiple diagrams for clarity. These appear below, and are followed by descriptions of each use case.

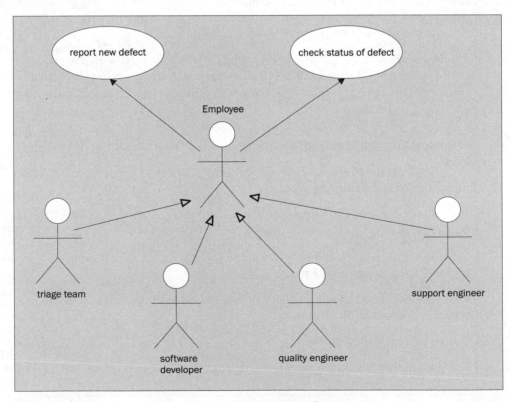

This diagram illustrates the base actor **employee**, with two associated use cases.

➤ `Report new defect` – any employee may report a defect, whether on behalf of a customer or one discovered through internal testing.

➤ `Check status of defect` – any employee may look up a defect in the bug tracker to check on its status.

This diagram also illustrates the following actors that are derived from **employee**:

➤ **Triage team** : one or more managers authorized to assess and assign reported defects.

➤ **Software developer** : an employee whose primary responsibility is developing, troubleshooting and fixing software products.

➤ **Quality engineer** : an employee whose primary responsibility is testing software, reporting discovered defects and verifying fixes to the software.

➤ **Support engineer** : an employee whose primary responsibility is to assist customers in determining solutions to their problems with the software products, and reporting software defects discovered in that process.

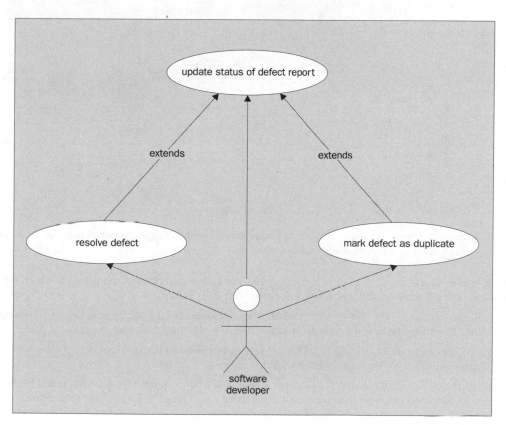

This diagram illustrates the use cases related to **software developer** actors.

➤ `Update status of defect report` – When the status of a defect changes (for example, when it is assigned, marked as fixed, etc.) the report is modified to indicate the new state. Note that this use case is associated with two other use cases by "*extends*" assocations, indicating that `Update status of defect report` is the basis of the other use cases.

➤ `Resolve defect` – When a software developer fixes a defect, the defect status is updated indicating that the defect has been fixed. In addition, the defect report is updated to indicate how the resolution was made.

➤ `Mark defect as duplicate` – Defects are frequently reported by more than one source. In these cases, it is most effective to keep only one report open until the defect is fixed. It is still useful, however to keep track of the duplicate defects in the tracking system to gauge how frequently problems are encountered. This use case involves changing the status of the duplicate defect, as well as adding a reference to the defect that it duplicates.

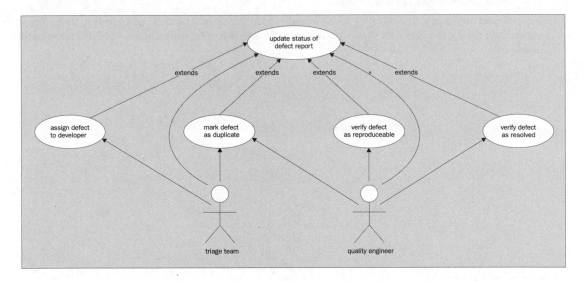

This diagram illustrates use cases related to **triage team** and **quality engineer** actors. Like the previous diagram, there are use cases that extend the `update status of defect report` use case.

➤ `Update status of defect report` - This use case is described in the previous paragraphs. Its inclusion here illustrates additional actors associated with this use case.

➤ `Assign defect to developer` - when a defect is reported it must be assigned to a **developer** for resolution. The **triage team** is the only actor authorized to make that change to the defect report.

➤ `Mark defect as duplicate` - This use case is described in the previous paragraphs. Its inclusion here illustrates additional actors associated with this use case.

➤ `Verify defect as reproduceable` - When a defect is reported by the field, it will be initially assigned to a support engineer to determine that it can be reproduced in-house. This step significantly reduces problems encountered due to misuse or miscommunication on the part of the original reporter, or where replicating the problem requires other software or specific procedures. Note that this use case extends the base use case `update status of defect report`.

➤ Verify defect as resolved - Although the **software developer** is allowed to mark a defect as resolved, it is up to a **quality engineer** to test the software and check that the resolution is effective, and hasn't broken anything else. Once again, this is an extension to the base use case, `update status of defect report`.

External Use Cases

These use cases reflect those that are associated with actors that are not employees – specifically, a **customer**.

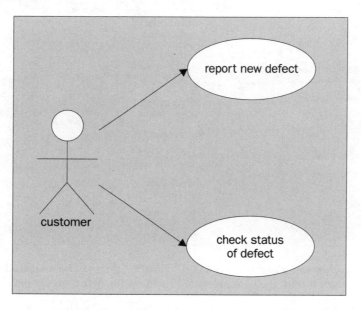

Two use cases that have already been described and associated with **employee** actors appear here : `report new defect` and `check status of defect`. Their inclusion indicates that customers will need to be provided with some means of access to the defect tracking system. The sponsor has already determined that the method of access should be through a Web browser connected to the Internet.

The sponsor requires some means of limiting access to defect information through this interface. The statistical information about defects (such as the total number, the find and close rates, and so on) are considered proprietary information, so customers should have access only to defect status for the defects they have reported.

Automated Interfaces

The bug tracker project includes some requirements that will provide automatic notification to customers and to other software system when a defect changes status.

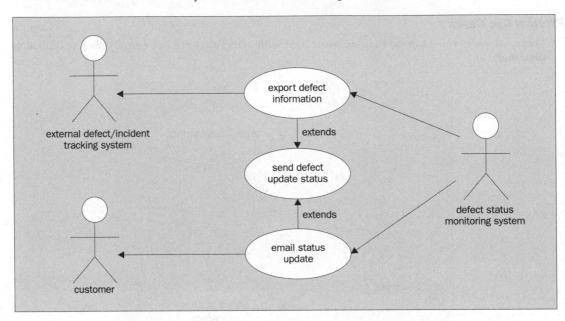

This requirement implies some sort of automated "daemon" that will be triggered when a defect changes status. For the present, this is represented by the actor **defect status monitoring system**.

Depending on the notification instructions in the defect report itself, the system may be required to send textual notification to a system user by email, or be required to export the defect information to an external system as a means of notification.

➢ `Send defect update status` – this is a generalized use case for collecting and assembling the notification information.

➢ `Email status update` – this use case, triggered by the **defect status monitoring system** actor, causes the defect status update information to be formatted into text and send to one or more Internet email addresses.

➢ `Export defect information` – this use case, also triggered by the **defect status monitoring system** actor, causes the system to update an external tracking system with the defect information. External systems may exist on a number of hardware/operating system platforms, and may be implemented in Java, C++ or other languages.

Initial Risks

The basic bug tracking system is not overly complex, and doesn't represent any major technical risks. No specific back end database requirements have been mandated, so the architecture effort is free to recommend best fit technology.

Risk: Interoperability

One item that does stand out as a risk is the requirement for automated updates of external systems. There is not a single application that has been targeted, and developing separate interfaces for multiple systems could quickly become unmanageable. More investigation is needed to see how best to provide system and data integration.

Mitigation strategy: Determine how this feature will be used and determine if scope can be narrowed.

Risk: Loose Requirements

Another potential risk is the looseness of the requirements so far. The project sponsor is eager for the system but does not have an exact vision for the end result.

Mitigation strategy: Build prototypes & models, review frequently with sponsor.

Development Approach

Based on the information assembled during the inception phase, I have put together a rough outline for the initial project plan.

The development approach is driven by the initial risks described above. In order to be successfully managed, these issues need to be addressed directly and early in the schedule. I've put the following outline of tasks that provide a framework for how to attack the elaboration, construction and transition phases of the bug tracker. The task area list is in sequential order, with the most pressing issues occurring earlier in the list.

Elaboration Phase

Engineering task areas	
Graphical User Interface Design	
➤ paper mockups	put together paper based "low fidelity" prototypes to test proposed user interface with sponsor, end users
➤ prototypes	refine user interface models in software prototypes to help solidify usability, functionality expectations
➤ application interface design	design the front end for the non-browser based (standalone application) version of the bug tracker
➤ browser-based interface design	design the front end for the browser based version of the bug tracker
Integration with external applications	
➤ refinement of actual requirements	higher granularity definition of the specific requirements for application integration
➤ application integration technology selection	determine the best candidate technologies for providing interoperability for distributed applications

Integration with external applications (*continued*)	
➤ information exchange technology	determine the best candidate technologies for data interchange between distributed applications
Architecture	
➤ high level design	create a high level roadmap of the application architecture by defining subsystems and the interfaces between subsystems
➤ application partitioning	based on the high level architectural model, begin specification of how application logic is divided and distributed
Object Model	
➤ logical model design	design the logical classes that comprise each subsystem
➤ component model design	map the logical model into the specific software components (e.g. Java classes)
➤ deployment model	define the physical aspects of the deployed system
Persistent storage	
➤ database technology selection	determine best fit database technologies for the bug tracker (e.g. object, relational, specific vendor products, etc.)
➤ persistence mechanism strategy	determine a consistent, reusable means of saving and restoring objects to and from persistent store
➤ database design	define the database schema and its mappings to the logical model
Process & Management task areas	
Testing strategy definition	
➤ unit testing procedures	define how individual components and collections of components will be tested to ensure readiness for integration and for regression testing
➤ integration testing procedures	define how the integrated builds of the bug tracker will be tested
➤ metrics	define how quality will be measured

Construction Phase

Engineering task areas	
➢ data access layer	construction of the data access components & database creation
➢ semantic layer	construction of business domain objects
➢ business rules	construction of objects supporting business rules
➢ user interface layer	construction of user interfaces
Process & Management task areas	
➢ quality metrics	collection and evaluation of quality metrics
➢ initial end user training	conduct initial training for end users
➢ beta testing	distribution of bug tracker to limited beta test sites, collect defect information

Transition Phase

➢ Bug tracker application rollout	initiate rollout of stand-alone bug tracker application to end users; provide required support & transition services
➢ Secondary end user training	conduct refresher training for end users
➢ Bug tracker application handoff	turn over support & maintenance of bug tracker to sponsor & end users
➢ Web-based bug tracker internal rollout	initiate rollout of web-based bug tracker for internal testing and verification
➢ Web-based bug tracker external rollout	initiate rollout of web-based bug tracker to external web site
➢ Web-based bug tracker handoff	turn over support & maintenance of web-based bug tracker to sponsor & end users
➢ Project post mortem	review project process and products; evaluate observations and lessons learned

Next Steps

In this chapter we've introduced the bug tracker project, outlined what the application will do, and mapped out a course for designing and building it. We've covered:

- The basic structure of the Rational Unified Process lifecycle
- The four iterations of RUP:
  - Inception
  - Elaboration
  - Construction
  - Transition
- The objectives, activities and end products of each of these iterations
- Finally, we've gone through the Inception phase to kick off the bug tracker project.

In the next chapter, we'll spend a good deal of the time covering the interesting engineering efforts of the elaboration phase. Technology selection figures prominently, as does architecture definition. Following that, we'll move into the construction phase and implement the subsystems using the Java JDK and other development tools.

Bug Tracker Case Study: Elaboration, Construction and Transition

Elaboration

During the elaboration phase, the design of the software will be expanded significantly. Functional decisions as well as technical decisions will be made, based on research, prototypes and the continual process of gathering information from the problem domain experts.

The specific goals for this project during the elaboration phase are:

➤ Solidify the application requirements for each user population, and discover user interface models that will be effective.

➤ Identify the specific requirements for achieving the objective for sharing information from the Bug Tracker with other applications, and identify the most applicable technology for doing so.

➤ Define the overall application architecture, and detail how the application will be partitioned throughout that architecture.

➤ Identify an effective persistence strategy for the application – that is, how the application will store data.

➤ Flesh out the object model for the system through the information gathered during this phase.

Prototyping

Prototyping can go a long way in helping to solidify the scope and functionality of the project. Just as a picture is worth 1,000 words, a mockup of the proposed software is invaluable to the sponsor and the developer of the system alike. It gives the sponsor an opportunity to verify that the system under construction does in fact move towards solving the business problems that have been identified. It gives the developer an opportunity to test his assertions of what the software should do, and allows the sponsor to provide immediate feedback earlier in the project lifecycle. Further, prototypes are helpful to test new technology that may be incorporated into the system.

Low Fidelity User Interface Protoyping

One of the most important issues to address in this phase of the project is to ensure that we are on the right track. The best way to do this is to have the project sponsor and the users directly experience our vision of what we're building (as we currently understand it). This provides a direct feedback loop so that designs and expectations can be adjusted accordingly.

One quick and easy way to accomplish this is a process called "low fidelity user interface prototyping." Low fidelity prototyping involves building paper models of the user interfaces, and allow the users to "work" the interfaces while the interface designer animates the interface. In essence, the designer acts as the computer, and makes the user interface model respond to the user actions. By observing which models work best for the users, and the information that the users seek to enter or retrieve, the system designer can quickly grasp of the needs of the user.

Designing the Application Interface

Through the process of low fidelity prototyping (and trial and error), some very important information has been discovered for the defect tracking system. First, each type of user is interested in a different slice of the defect information. For example, developers that resolve defects are interested in the detailed information describing the defect. Testers and configuration management types are interested in how the defect was resolved. Customer service types are interested in being able to notify the customer when a problem is resolved. By walking through the prototyping, we've been able to come up with a user interface that provides easy access to specific defect information instantly and without screen clutter. The design involves using multiple tabbed panes that allow the user to access categories of information. The sketch below illustrates the paper prototype that was constructed:

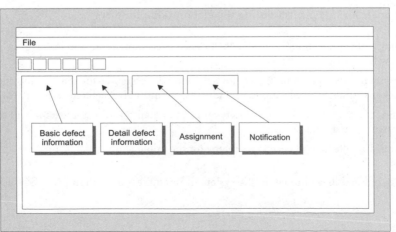

A similar process was used to frame the web-based user interfaces. The requirements for this group of users were far more modest than the other users (those that used the stand-alone application), which resulted in a much less complex user interface. Three primary user interfaces were discovered: navigation, defect retrieval and defect entry. The sketches below illustrate the basic layout:

Technology Selection – Information Export

Determining how the Bug Tracker applications work with the outside world is important to figure out early in the game. One of the primary requirements of this application is to allow other applications to get at the bug tracker data. This is a pretty broad requirement, since it's not really clear what other systems that the Bug Tracker needs to work with, so simple import/export to another database or application file format probably won't fulfil the general need.

As we have seen, the Extensible Markup Language (XML) provides a great means for exchanging data between applications. Rather than try to match a particular application's data and/or file format, XML enables developers to define a generic data format, and to export information into a document using that data format. Other applications that are given the defined data format (in the form of a DTD) can easily parse a document and extract the defect information.

The DTD is a sort of Rosetta Stone that other applications can use to understand the defect information that comes from the Bug Tracker applications. As with other aspects of the system that can affect other systems, the DTD for exporting defect information needs to be derived through studying the use cases, and defined early in the process. Once the DTD has been defined, it's a simple matter to make it available to developers and maintainers of other applications so that they can adapt their software to read in Bug Tracker defects.

Here is the DTD for the Bug Tracker Application. As you can see, this defines all of the information we will be able to track about a bug, so we need to make sure it is sufficiently flexible to allow us to include all of the data we might need:

```
<?xml version="1.0" ?>
<!ELEMENT bugreport (id, state, priority?, severity?, product, versionrep,
  subsystem?, summary, details+, reporter, assignedto?, resnotes*,
  changedmaillist?, resolvedmaillist?, versionres?, datereported,
  datelastchanged, externalid?)>

<!ELEMENT id (#PCDATA)>
<!ELEMENT state (#PCDATA)>
<!ELEMENT priority (#PCDATA)>
<!ELEMENT severity (#PCDATA)>
<!ELEMENT product (#PCDATA)>
<!ELEMENT versionrep (#PCDATA)>
<!ELEMENT subsystem (#PCDATA)>
<!ELEMENT summary (#PCDATA)>
<!ELEMENT details (#PCDATA)>
<!ELEMENT reporter (#PCDATA)>
<!ELEMENT assignedto (#PCDATA)>
<!ELEMENT resnotes (#PCDATA)>
<!ELEMENT changedmaillist (#PCDATA)>
<!ELEMENT resolvedmaillist (#PCDATA)>
<!ELEMENT versionres (#PCDATA)>
<!ELEMENT datereported (#PCDATA)>
<!ELEMENT datelastchanged (#PCDATA)>
<!ELEMENT externalid (#PCDATA)>
```

The first line of the DTD defines what sort of document this is. The second item (broken across several lines) defines the data from which the defect report is comprised. The DTD allows the document designer to indicate which elements are required, which are optional, etc. For the element `bugreport`, the fields that appear without any sort of decoration are mandatory. Those that are appended with a question mark, such as the `priority` member, are treated as optional, with either 0 or 1 elements of that flavor appearing in the document. Those that are appended with an asterisk, such as the `resnotes` member, can have 0 or more members.

The subsequent lines in the DTD define the data format for each of the `bugreport` elements. In this DTD, they are simply character data.

The actual bug report data that will be generated and exported by the Bug Tracker application will adhere to the rules of the DTD. Each element will be enclosed inside tags that are named according to the `bugreport` definition in the DTD, and mark the start and the end of each field's data.

An actual XML defect document is listed below so you can see how the exported data is formatted:

```
<?xml version = "1.0" standalone="no" ?>
<!DOCTYPE bugreport SYSTEM "defect.dtd">
<bugreport>
<id>1</id>
<state>NEW</state>
<severity>CRASH</severity>
<priority>CRITICAL</priority>
<versionrep>1.0</versionrep>
<subsystem>file.new</subsystem>
<summary>cannot create a new defect</summary>
```

```
<details>creating a new defect causes class not found exception</details>
<reporter>rkp</reporter>
<assignedto>rkp</assignedto>
<resnotes></resnotes>
<changedmaillist>rkp@acm.org</changedmaillist>
<resolvedmaillist>joejoe@xxx.com</resolvedmaillist>
<versionres></versionres>
<datereported>01-Apr-1999</datereported>
<datelastchanged>13-May-1999</datelastchanged>
<externalid>v12345</externalid>
</bugreport>
```

The first couple of lines of the XML document define what the document is. Notice on the second line of the DTD that the document format is specified. The remainder of the document contains the defect information. Notice that the `bugreport` element defined in the DTD appears here as start and end tags (`<bugreport>...</bugreport>`). Within those start and end tags are nested starting and ending tags for each field's information.

This step along the way defines how the Bug Tracker application uses XML for data export in a way that allows other application developers to know what to expect when the Bug Tracker application is completed. The actual implementation of the XML export will be done during the construction phase.

Note also that while the DTD has specified most of the data format, we still need to define some things outside the DTD. The date format, for example, and the separators between email addresses in the two notification lists, will also need to be agreed and specified before other programmers can go to work with the XML data.

Technology Selection - Object Distribution

One of the primary requirements of this application is that it be distributed. That is, the application components must be able to not only run on multiple computers, but act as if they're all running on a single computer. This has substantial implications for the scalability characteristics of the system. If the distribution of the application is poorly thought out, it will be very difficult to add to the system or provide more extensive operation over time. On the other hand, if the distributed model of the application is well thought out and executed, scalability becomes very feasible, and new functionality is much more easily incorporated.

There are a couple of options for the technical underpinnings of a distributed Java application, including RMI (Remote Method Invocation), CORBA (Common Object Request Broker Architecture), Jini, and distribution through Servlets, perhaps communicating via XML over HTTP. The requirements of this application drive the technology selection. Recall a couple of important requirements:

> ➢ The Bug Tracker must be available from other applications, including those not written in Java

> ➢ The Bug Tracker must be available as a stand-alone application and from a Web browser

> ➢ The Bug Tracker must be available over the Internet to permit customers and field staff to enter defects

The first requirement rules out RMI as an option, because it is fundamentally a Java feature. It's not impossible to make it work with non-Java applications, but it's more work than is really worthwhile.

The second and third options imply that applets, servlets, or some combination of the two are needed to drive a Web-based application. Because of the Internet requirement, an ultra-thin client with a servlet-based back end will perform well to satisfy the Web requirement, making us truly browser independent.

The servlet won't come into play with a stand-alone application, however, so we'll need a means of keeping the servlet pretty minimal and encapsulating the shared logic between the stand-alone application and the web-based application. This minimizes redundancy and shares a common body of business logic.

CORBA turns out to be a good choice for satisfying the overall criteria, with some help from a servlet-enabled web server. CORBA will, in fact, provide most of the logical glue that will connect all of the system components.

CORBA, if you are not familiar with it, is a specification for distributing objects across a network. CORBA provides an object distribution framework that allows you to invoke and manipulate objects on separate machines as if they were all living on the same machine.

The CORBA-based development tools provide the requisite infrastructure that gives us this location transparency. The client makes method calls into object "stubs". The ORB packages up those calls, sends them over the network, and invokes the corresponding methods at the remote machine. "Skeletons" on the server side provide the glue between the ORB and the remote objects:

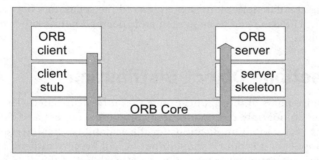

One of the most powerful aspects of CORBA is that it is language-neutral and operating-system neutral. That means that it's quite possible to have client applications written in one language, such as C++, and have servers that are written in a completely different language. The ORBs provide the magic that glues the different languages together. That is a primary motivation for using CORBA in the Bug Tracker application. We'll be able to provide bug tracking services to a broad range of client implementations on a number of different operating system platforms.

> Note: CORBA is a powerful and fascinating technology that certainly merits more
> exploration than is possible within these chapters. There are several web sites and
> books dedicated to the subject; the reader is encouraged to seek these out for more
> information. The Object Management Group - the body that developed and maintains
> the CORBA specification - has a web site (www.omg.org) that is a good starting point
> for finding out more about CORBA and the myriad resources surrounding it.
>
> It is important to recognize that CORBA is a specification and not a product. The
> CORBA specification from the OMG describes the interfaces and general behavior that
> CORBA-compliant products will have, but neither provides an ORB product nor
> enforces how ORB internals be implemented.

There are a number of commercial ORB products available (free and otherwise). Selecting which to use is an important part of technology selection. For the scope of this project, the ORB that is supplied with the JDK is quite sufficient, and is available to anyone working with the JDK 1.2 or later. This ORB may or may not, however, provide all of the features required for a large scale multi-application environment. Overall enterprise/departmental needs should drive the ORB selection.

If you've read the discussion of RMI in Chapter 12, you should notice some distinct similarities. Remember that to generate stub and skeleton classes in RMI, we first had to define an interface, then build a class which implemented it. The stub then was a special implementation of the interface, and the skeleton a special class which worked with that interface. In CORBA, we define the interface in a language-neutral **Interface Definition Language** (IDL), from which tools can be used to build stub and skeleton implementations in any language we choose. Thus our Java code can make method calls to a Java stub, which communicates with a C++ Skeleton to make method calls on a C++ object which implements the same interface. From the perspective of our Java code, it doesn't matter what language the object was written in, or where the code is running. We'll look at how this is achieved later on when we come to implement the CORBA interfaces.

Technology Selection – Messaging

The use cases created during the inception phase included the ability to automatically notify interested individuals when a defect is changed and when it has been resolved. It seems intuitively obvious to use Internet email for the notification, but it is very important to consider other options depending on the messaging requirements. A few very important considerations include:

- ➢ Is a delivery delay unacceptable?
- ➢ Is guaranteed delivery required?
- ➢ Is notification of receipt required?

If any of the above are answered with a "yes", then an alternative messaging mechanism ought to be explored. Other options might include Message Oriented Middleware (MOM) such as PeerLogic Pipes, IBM MQ Series, VeriQ VCOM and others. While incorporating MOM adds additional requirements to support client notification, it provides an extremely robust solution. If you're interested in learning more about message oriented middleware, the International Middle Ware Association maintains a web site (www.imwa.org) with good starting information and links to vendors' sites with additional resources.

In the case of this application, however, a "lazy and optimistic" messaging scheme is acceptable and quite convenient. The Bug Tracker will use Simple Mail Transfer Protocol (SMTP) to send a formatted mail message to the interested parties identified within the defect.

Defining the Application Architecture

Defining the application architecture is an important engineering step that's driven by a number of factors. These factors can include performance requirements, perceived need to scale the application later (that is, be able to easily modify it as more users access the system, or it's more broadly distributed across networks).

The application architecture also helps to define how the bits of the application will be partitioned, or split up, both in physical and logical terms. Physical partitioning defines how the software will be actually distributed and executed on one or more computers, and how those computers will be connected. Logical partitioning defines how the logic of the application is divided up into subsystems.

Physical Partitioning

The functional requirements and selected technology for this application drive the deployed architecture. Those decision points include:

- ➢ Web-based browser client
- ➢ "Stand alone" (not browser based) client
- ➢ CORBA-based object distribution
- ➢ Servlet-driven web interface

These ingredients combine to form an overall system picture that looks something like this:

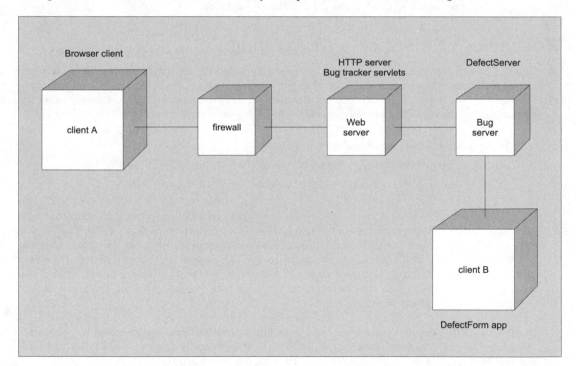

Each of the blocks in the diagram represents a processor. The two flavors of client are shown on the diagram. The processor running the Java application (which is a CORBA client) connects directly to the "bug server" - a processor running the CORBA-based `DefectServer` process. There is also a browser-based client processor that connects to a web server through a firewall. The web server executes the Bug Tracker servlets, which are really just proxies that provide a means of getting data from the browser client to the bug server and back. As you'll see through the balance of this chapter, the bug server provides a substantial part of the smarts of this application. The components that talk to the bug server are pretty lightweight and don't do much but draw stuff on the screen and collect data from the user.

Logical Partitioning

Logical partitioning deals with building layers of functionality that collaborate together through well defined interfaces, but don't really share a whole lot of internal knowledge about each other. This not only makes the structure and design of the application easier to understand; it also has scaling implications. When a software system is well structured with clearly defined subsystem boundaries, it is much easier to distribute those subsystems across multiple machines – even beyond the original distribution design.

If you've worked on client/server applications, you are no doubt familiar with three tier architecture, which is a strategy that divides the user interface, the business rules and the data access into distinct partitions.

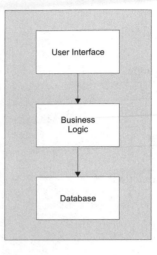

The advantage to this kind of division of labor is that since each layer communicates with the one below it using well-known interfaces, it's a simple matter to replace any one of the layers as long as the replacement presents an identical interface. As it turns out, the Bug Tracker application extends on the three tier model, and actually divides up system responsibilities into five tiers:

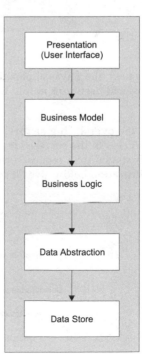

Presentation	The presentation layer is concerned only with providing a user interface that enables the user to view, add and update information.
Business model	The business model layer provides business objects – software representations of things that users deal with in the real world. The business model objects provide a means of interfacing the user interface (and by extension, the user) with the underlying business logic.
Business logic	The business logic layer provides the infrastructure in which the business model objects live, and enforces the rules for the creation, manipulation and destruction of the business model objects. Rules for the business are formally encoded into this layer.
Data abstraction	Data abstraction provides a means of coupling business model objects with the mechanism that allows them to persist beyond the invocation of the application. The data abstraction layer permits flexible options for how objects will be persisted.
Data store	The data store layer provides the actual storage and retrieval of data to and from disk.

As you might guess, the physical partitions fall on the logical partition boundaries. You'll see the logical and physical partitions unfold in Defect Server implementation as the source code is developed.

Based on this, the overall "big picture" is beginning to take shape. We need to have a defect server that provides access to the server-side resources that provide services. Clients to the defect server will connect to it first, and then request a reference to the other specific services hosted by the defect server. The illustration below gives a conceptual view of what that looks like:

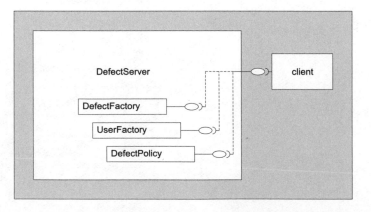

Note that while the service references are obtained from the defect server, they do not have to co-exist on the same machine as the defect server. As discussed in the previous section, the ORB makes it possible to work with objects without respect for or knowledge of where they reside.

Now that the application architecture is framed out, the next order of business is to expand the object model and design the object classes and interfaces that will populate the partitions that have just been defined.

Fleshing out the Object Model

Armed with the knowledge that has been garnered through the requirements gathering and prototyping process, it's time to model the classes and define the interfaces within the partitions that comprise the application architecture. Having defined the application architecture into logical partitions helps to divide the task of elaborating the object model into more manageable chunks.

UML diagrams have been used to capture the modeling decisions. Since the logical application architecture resulted in creating partitions that divide system responsibilities, we'll extend that partitioning into the object model itself. Like Java, UML provides the concept of **packages**, a means of organizing things with shared semantics into logical units. The object model will start with top-level packages that reflect the logical partitions (this doesn't include the data store partition, however. The data store will not be something that will be developed, but instead we'll use Java's built-in database connectivity layer. For that reason, it's been omitted from this diagram):

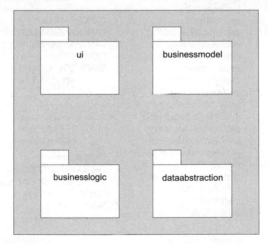

Defining Externals

We'll start with the things that are exposed by the application to the outside world, meaning any user interface or external application that wants to work with the Bug Tracker. This includes the business model classes that provide the software abstractions of real-world entities, and the interfaces by which those objects are manipulated:

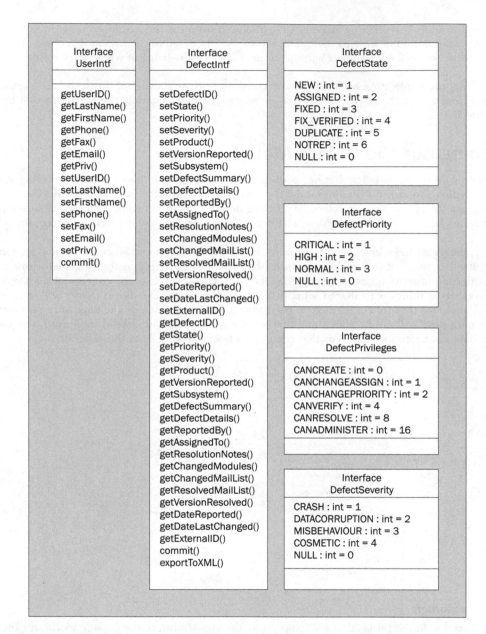

The `UserIntf` interface is the exposed interface for the User actor that was identified in the inception phase. The `DefectIntf` – no great surprise – defines the interface for a defect. Both of these interfaces have a number of accessor methods setting and getting the objects' values.

Additional interfaces in the diagram above identify the valid states, severity levels and priority levels for defects with constant identifiers. Finally, there is an interface that defines the privilege levels for users. Note that these components are placed in the `businessmodel` package.

Next, the interfaces for the **business logic** classes need to be defined. These provide the primary services for supporting the `businessmodel` objects. These interfaces are defined in the `businesslogic` package:

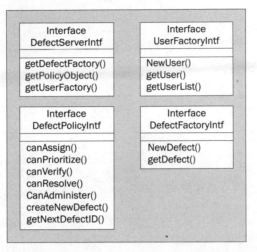

The `DefectServerIntf` interface is the "mother of all interfaces," at least as far as Bug Tracker is concerned. This interface provides a single point of entry for getting to the other server-based interfaces.

The `UserFactoryIntf` defines a factory object for creating and retrieving objects implementing the `UserIntf` interface defined above. The class that implements this interface is used by the classes that are responsible for enforcing user privileges.

The `DefectPolicyIntf` interface specifies a class that enforces the business rules associated with the creation and modification of defects within the system.

The `DefectFactoryIntf` defines another factory. In this case, the factory is responsible for the creation and retrieval of objects implementing the `DefectIntf` interface defined above.

The user interface components need to be modeled as well. The paper model that was constructed earlier in the process can be mapped directly into UML, with a main form that contains subordinate panels that contain the defect details:

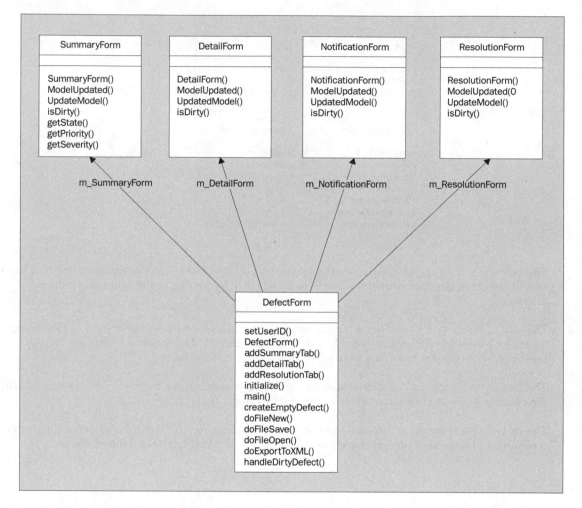

Hopefully the high level perspective of the external view of the system is beginning to emerge in your mind. The next step is to provide the implementing classes for the interfaces, as well as internal infrastructure to support the system.

Defining Internals

The primary internal elements we're concerned with span the entire system, from user interface on the client to the implementation of the server. This covers a lot of territory, so I am just going to walk through each of the packages defined above and identify primary components and things of special interest.

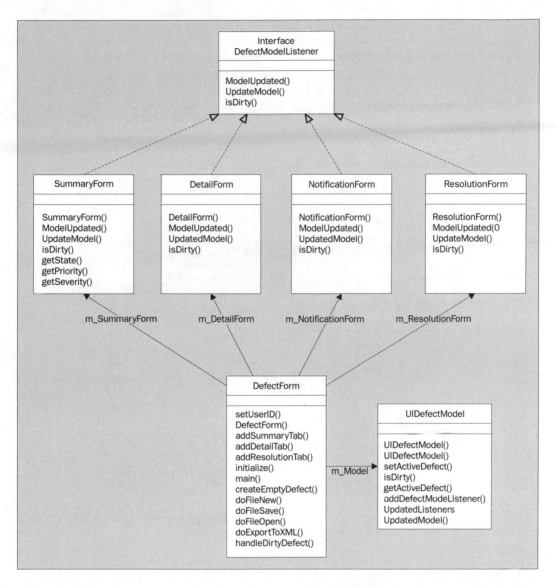

The UI package has been expanded here to show a couple of additional components. The multi-panel user interface approach requires a slightly more sophisticated approach than a simple form because there is more than one software component (each panel of the form) that is working with a `Defect` object at any time. This is a simple problem to solve, and has been addressed by using an `Observable` pattern. If you've worked with graphical interfaces, you've no doubt encountered Model-View-Controller (MVC), which essentially decouples the data model from the components that represent it on the screen. A `UIDefectModel` class has been introduced here to facilitate the separation. Its role is to encapsulate the `Defect` object, keep track of the user interface components that are interested in the model, and both update and get updates from the user interface as appropriate.

Each of the UI panels implement a `DefectModelListener` interface, and support methods that are called by the `UIDefectModel` to update the model from the UI and vice versa.

The `dataabstraction` package contains classes that handle how classes are made persistent. The `Persistent` interface serves the dual purpose of identifying that a class is a persistent one, but also defines the baseline methods that need to be supported for a `Persistent` object.

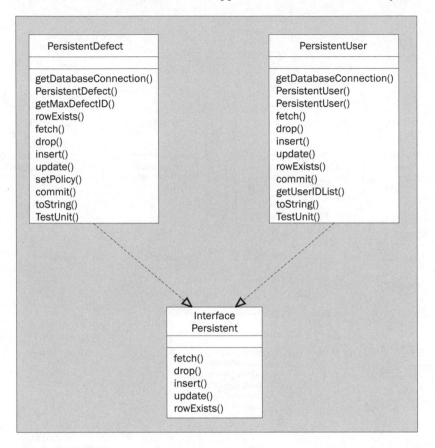

The two classes that implement `Persistent` are fairly straightforward – they implement the `Persistent` methods, constructors and housekeeping methods.

A reasonable designer might wonder why `Persistent` is an interface and not a base class from which to inherit. The primary reason behind this is simply that it ought to be feasible to support more than one persistence strategy in the application (this will be covered in more detail later in this chapter). By specifying only the external interfaces that need be supported, this becomes an easy thing to do. Were it designed with `Persistent` as a base class, however, the system would be engineered with the assumption that all persistent classes are implemented using a single storage strategy.

The `businessmodel` package contains the classes and interfaces that represent the things in the real world that we're modeling with software. We've already taken a look that the interfaces in this package that are exposed to the outside world. There are just a couple of items in this package left to examine.

The `UserIntf` and `DefectIntf` interfaces were already discussed. This package also includes two classes that will implement those two interfaces. It's important to note that conceptually, these classes realize their respective interfaces. In the actual implementation, that will get shuffled a bit. The implementation in Java is going to employ a delegation model, which I'll explain later. For now, we'll simply assume that the realized relationships between `UserIntf` and `User`, and `DefectIntf` and `Defect` are direct:

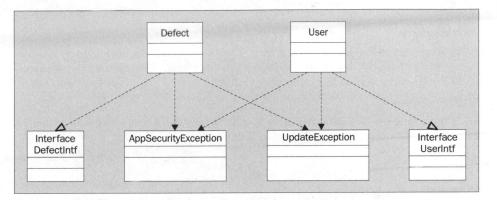

Two additional exception classes – `UpdateException` and `AppSecurityException` are included here; these classes are exceptions thrown by the `User` and `Defect` classes when exceptions occur when changing object state due to external errors and authorization problems, respectively.

The `businesslogic` package's internals are a bit more complex:

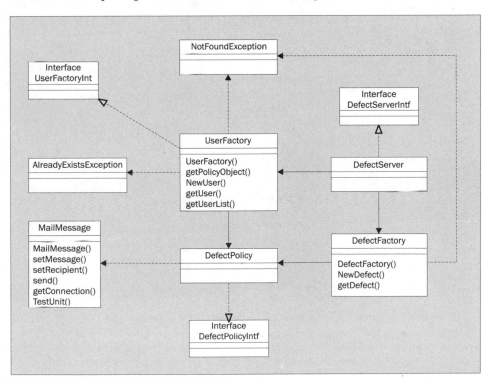

The interfaces on this diagram have already been introduced. Each of these interfaces is realized by a `businesslogic` class that implements the behavior specified by the interface. The `MailMessage` class provides an encapsulated means of sending an Internet mail message. The `DefectPolicy` class uses this class to send mail notifications when defects are modified and resolved. Finally, two exception classes – `NotFoundException` and `AlreadyExistsException` – are provided. These are thrown by the `UserFactory` and the `DefectFactory` methods when errors occur creating and finding objects.

Defining Collaborations

Looking at class diagrams (especially when they're static diagrams on paper) doesn't provide a complete picture of how the defect server classes work together. Let's take a look at the primary interactions between the classes that have been defined so far. This will provide some basic framework as we move towards implementing the BugTracker software.

There are a few sequence flows that will help to clarify how the BugTracker is intended to work. Let's first take a look at how the `DefectServer` initializes:

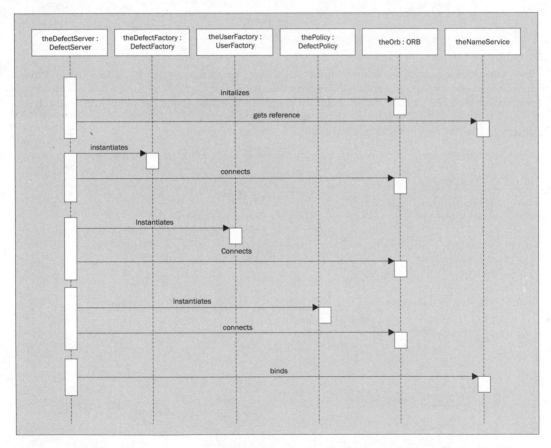

This sequence diagram illustrates the start-up sequence for the `DefectServer`. It first initializes the ORB. It then obtains a reference to the Name Service. It then creates `DefectFactory`, `UserFactory` and `DefectPolicy` objects (one of each) and connects them to the ORB. Once that has successfully completed, the `DefectServer` then binds its object reference to the Name Service by name.

Next, let's take a look at how the client BugTracker's DefectForm application initializes:

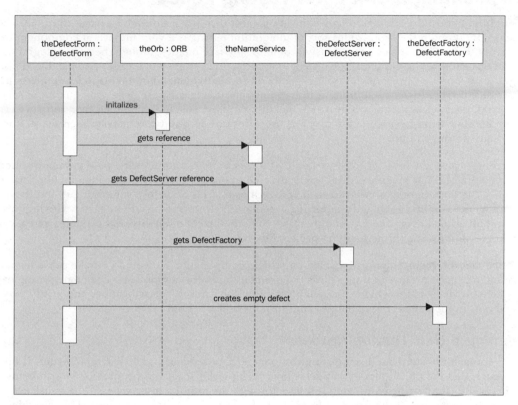

Like the `DefectServer`, it first initializes the ORB, and then obtains a reference to the Name Service. Then it asks the Name Service for the object reference to the `DefectServer` as it was registered by the initializing `DefectServer`. Once the `DefectForm` has obtained that reference, it asks the `DefectServer` for a reference to the `DefectFactory`. Once the reference to the `DefectFactory` is in hand, the `DefectForm` asks the `DefectFactory` for a new, blank object with which to fill the newly initialized form.

Subsequent operations to create, retrieve and store defects are trivial – once the `DefectFactory` reference is obtained, the application can retrieve existing and create new defects. The `Defect` objects themselves provide the methods necessary to modify the member data and store the changes to persistent store.

Quality Engineering

Before we get into the heads-down, hard core nuts and bolts of taking the information that's been gathered during the elaboration phase, it wouldn't hurt to ensure that a modicum of quality engineering is injected into the process.

Implementing a Unit-Level Testing Policy

Certainly, part of the strategy of any software project is to put it through its paces, find out where it breaks, fix it and test it again. This sort of integration testing is a very important component of an overall QE strategy. It's not an exclusive route to software quality, though, because integration testing is only as good as the ability of the testers to exercise the system from a user perspective. This puts a significant amount of responsibility for quality on the individual components that comprise the system. This is particularly important in building server-side software, when the quality of service expectations are significantly higher. It's one thing to have one user sidelined by a software error. It's quite another thing to sideline hundreds of users because of a software defect (been there, done that - it's really not much fun).

In order to raise the level of software quality for this project, a unit testing policy was instituted. This policy required that specific critical application components not only go through ad hoc unit testing (that is, the developer exercises the unit and verifies that it's ok before submitting it) but those components also be capable of supporting automated self tests to ensure integrity. Having this level of testing on critical components not only raises the initial level of quality, but provides an easy means for regression testing throughout the project lifecycle.

Notice that the requirement is imposed on critical components – it wouldn't make sense from a productivity perspective to impose this requirement on every component. The engineering team collectively determines which components fall into the "critical" classification, and justify why others need not. A good sense of judgement (and responsibility) is all it takes.

Designing a Unit Testing Harness

At first blush the automated-self-testing component requirement sounds like a tall order. It turns out, however, that the object model that gives Java such power in software construction also lends itself quite well to supporting automated self-tests through the use of a **test harness**. The construction of a test harness was one of the first and foremost tasks for the Bug Tracker project. This provided a standard means for implementing the unit testing policy.

The test harness is a little like a battery tester: it's essentially a shell that allows you to plug in a Java class, push a virtual button and instantly determine if the component is good or not. It can test a single unit at a time or be implemented like a "juke box" that tests multiple components in sequence.

The test harness is a remarkably useful tool, despite its simplicity. By implementing the `Testable` interface, it was possible to effectively test (and find a number of nasty bugs!) earlier in the construction phase – it wasn't necessary to have a large amount of the application infrastructure in place before these units could be tested.

The basic foundation of the test harness is a well defined interface that all testable components must implement in order to be tested by the harness. This provides the universal adapter that allows you to plug different classes into the same test harness. The source for the test harness interface for Bug Tracker components, `Testable`, is shown below:

```
package apputil;

public interface Testable
{

    public boolean TestUnit();

}
```

Any class that needs to be tested with the test harness must implement this interface. The interface provides dual functions. First, it identifies the implementing class as a Testable class, which allows the test harness to function without a whole lot of concern for the specific implementation details or semantics of the class. Secondly, it exposes a single method, TestUnit(), that provides the entry point called by the harness. The TestUnit() method must simply be implemented to return true if the unit passes the test, and false if it fails.

One important note that will become clear in the implementation of the test harness itself: the class that implements Testable must provide a default constructor (one which requires no arguments). That's because the test harness needs to instantiate an object of the class that's under test. If we needed the test harness to execute a non-default constructor, the test harness itself would have to know about the details of the class under test, which was far beyond the scope of this test harness.

The test harness itself does relatively little. It provides the carousel so that multiple classes can be tested, it instantiates the unit under test, calls its testing method and reports the results. The simplicity of the test harness is reflected in the implementation details:

```
package apputil;
import java.io.*;

public class TestHarness
{

    public static void main(String args[])
    {
        int numTests = args.length;

        int currentTestUnit = 0;
        Testable unitUnderTest;
        boolean[] results = new boolean[numTests];
        AppConfig test;

        try
        {
          test = new AppConfig("BUGTRACKER.PROPS");
         }
        catch (IOException ioe)
        {
            System.out.println("WARNING: Application " +
                        "properties not loaded!");
            System.exit(0);
        }

        for (int n = 0; n < numTests; n++)
        {
          try
          {
            Class unitClass = Class.forName(args[n]);
            unitUnderTest =
                  (apputil.Testable) unitClass.newInstance();

            results[n] = unitUnderTest.TestUnit();
            System.out.println("Unit " + args[n] + " : "
                + (results[n]?"passed":"failed"));
          }

          catch (InstantiationException inste)
          {
```

```
            System.out.println(args[n] +
                    " can't be instantiated!\n" +
                    "(did you include a default constructor?)");
        }

        catch (IllegalAccessException iae)
        {
            System.out.println("IllegalAccess exception loading " +
                                    args[n]);
        }
        catch (ClassCastException cce)
        {
            System.out.println(args[n] +
                        " can't be cast as Testable");
        }
        catch (ClassNotFoundException cnfe)
        {
            System.out.println(args[n] + " can't be loaded");
        }


        }
    }
}
```

This simple routine runs through the class names specified on the command line, and then

> Loads the class
> Instantiates a member of the class
> Calls the TestUnit() method of the Testable-implementing class
> Displays the results

You'll see that there is a mysterious `AppConfig` class that is instantiated by `TestHarness`. This is essentially a singleton object that is used throughout the Bug Tracker application for storing and retrieving application configuration information. This allows the test harness to more closely resemble the Bug Tracker application by performing the initialization of the singleton, rather than having each unit under test have to do so in its `TestUnit()` method.

The code in the class that implements the `Testable` interface can be as simple or as complex as necessary to sufficiently test the class. The code below illustrates a very simple `Testable` class with the requisite `TestUnit()` method that can be called by the test harness:

```
import apputil.*;

public class TestMe implements Testable
{

    boolean I_am_ok;

    public TestMe()
    {
        I_am_ok = true;
    }

    public boolean TestUnit()
    {
        return I_am_ok;
    }
}
```

To test this code with the test harness, simply execute the `TestHarness` and pass the name of the test class on the command line:

```
java apputil.TestHarness TestMe
Unit TestMe : passed
```

One significant advantage of having classes that are self-testing units is that it is much easier to keep the code and the automated test synchronized. As new functionality is incorporated, it is usually a simple matter to simply add the necessary code in the `TestUnit()` method to support the new feature.

Obviously, this test harness is pretty basic. To extend its functionality, you may wish to add the following:

> ❯ User interface that allows the user to select class to test

> ❯ Logging capabilities (allow units under test to log errors)

> ❯ More sophisticated handling of multiple test units

Construction

<table>
<tr><td>

Construction Requirements

If you want to build and test the Bug Tracker, you will need the following software tools:

- Java 2 compiler (JDK1.2 or higher)

- JavaIDL (provides IDL to Java compiler)

- Servlet SDK (JSDK 2.0 or higher)

- The JavaIDL executable `idltojava` must be on the search path

- The JSDK library (jsdk.jar) must be in your CLASSPATH

All of these tools are freely available for download from the JavaSoft website (http://www.javasoft.com).

</td></tr>
</table>

Finally, after all this, it's time to do the really fun stuff and start coding! The primary objective of the construction phase is to incorporate the design decisions made so far, implement them in software, and verify correct functionality.

As mentioned in the previous chapter, it's often helpful during the construction phase to have people outside the formal development and testing team to work with the product and provide feedback in the form of bug reports and suggestions. This outside alpha- and beta-testing can provide valuable information concerning how well the application holds up in the real world.

In short, the primary objective of the construction phase is to churn the specifications, prototypes and technology pilots into deployable software.

The following sections divide the application into logical groupings, and discuss the implementation strategy for each grouping.

Application Support Modules

There are a few support and utility modules that are part of the Bug Tracker application. You've already been introduced to the TestHarness, which provides automated unit testing for components. There are a few other support modules of interest:

TestHarness	The TestHarness class is described in the previous section. It provides a simple but powerful means for automated testing of individual classes of the application.
AppConfig	The AppConfig class was briefly described in the TestHarness discussion. This class provides a shared Properties object that is used for specifying and retrieving application-specific parameters. The AppConfig class is first instantiated by the application entry point, and is passed the filename of the application properties file in its constructor. Other methods in the running application can construct an AppConfig object using the default constructor, in which case the properties loaded in the application entry point will be used. This provides a very easy, generic and reusable means of sharing application properties.
Util	This class provides a handful of static methods for performing simple data conversion and manipulation. These are used throughout the application.

All of these classes are in the apputil package. The Util class is very rudimentary and doesn't really merit much discussion - the implementation is not really interesting to us. The only class left in this package to discuss in the AppConfig class.

The AppConfig class is basically a singleton object with a bit of wrapping. The purpose of the class is to provide a single strategy for storing and retrieving application configuration information that is used throughout the application.

Several methods are provided to get specific application parameters that are defined in a properties file. The properties file itself is read once when the first AppConfig object is instantiated. The constructor accepts a filename, which is then read into a Properties object:

```
public AppConfig(String configfilename) throws java.io.IOException
    {
        FileInputStream fis = new FileInputStream(configfilename);
        applicationProperties = new Properties();
        applicationProperties.load(fis);
    }
```

There is also a default constructor that does nothing. This is used by subordinate components that want to access the application properties that have already been loaded into the class Properties member. This simplifies things quite a bit - the main() method of each application component can create the first AppConfig object, since the main() method "knows" what properties file to use. Any other component can simply create an AppConfig object using the default constructor and use the application properties for free. Only one component need know what properties file to read, and it applies to all components in the application.

Using the Delegation Model

Before jumping into the other packages, some explanation of how the `idltojava` compiler generates code is in order. Due to the way that the IDL compiler generates Java classes, your servant classes normally have to inherit from `ImplBase` classes.

By default, the `idltojava` compiler generates classes and interfaces that define the methods that you've specified in your IDL file. For example, suppose that you've defined an interface called `SimpleService`. The `idltojava` compiler will generate the following classes illustrated below:

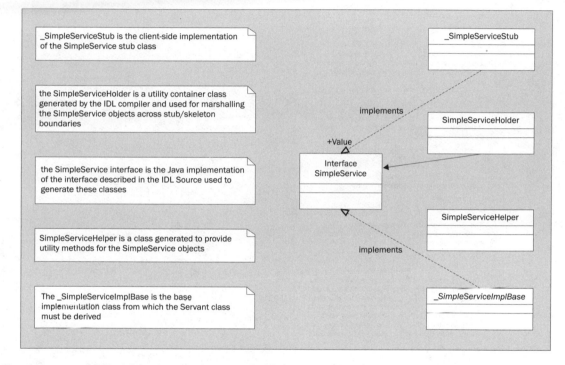

For this example, the class that implements the `SimpleService` server must extend the `_SimpleServiceImplBase` class. The interaction is pretty straightforward when a client ORB requests services from `SimpleService`:

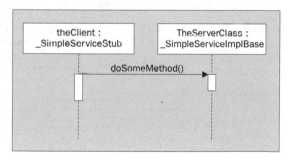

For trivial servers, that's ok, but if you are doing anything substantial, this creates a bit of a problem, since you may want to have the server's functionality derived from a different class. Java supports only single inheritance, so it's not possible to derive from both `ImplBase` *and* another class.

In order to facilitate this sort of practice, most ORB vendors provide a facility in their IDL compilers to generate **tie classes**, which provide a means of delegating server requests to another class. The concept is very simple but powerful – the IDL compiler generates an interface that defines the methods that must be implemented by the delegation class, and also generates a tie class that will receive method requests and then pass them to the specified delegation class. Again, assuming that the IDL defines a SimpleService interface, the idltojava compiler will generate the following classes and interfaces when the -ftie flag option is used on the idltojava command line :

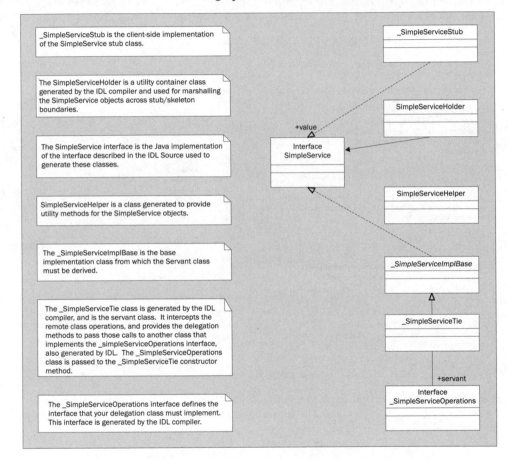

When delegation is used, the interaction is a bit more complex, but is extremely powerful in that you can plug in a delegation class that extends any other class without having to worry about extending the BaseImpl class - you can simply implement _SimpleServiceOperations. Here's the delegation interaction model:

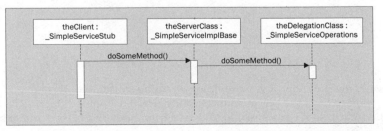

Defining Components Using IDL

The external interfaces defined in the `businessmodel` and `businesslogic` classes are important not only to the conceptual design of the Bug Tracker, but also important for generating the supporting Java code using the `idltojava` compiler. These interfaces are very straightforward, and the IDL code that defines them can be derived directly from the UML model of those interfaces. The file `businesslogic.idl` defines the exposed interfaces from the business logic layer. Note that these interfaces are primarily factory interfaces that supply `businessmodel` objects to the client. Let's take a look at what the IDL actually looks like:

```
#ifndef __BUSINESSLOGIC_DEFINED
#define __BUSINESSLOGIC_DEFINED

#include "businessmodel.idl"

module businesslogic
{

    exception NotFoundException{};
    exception AlreadyExistsException{};

    interface DefectPolicyIntf {

        boolean canAssign (in string userid);

        boolean canPrioritize (in string userid);

        boolean canVerify (in string userid);  .

        boolean canResolve (in string userid);

        boolean canAdminister(in string userid);

        businessmodel::DefectIntf createNewDefect (
            in string userid
        );

        long getNextDefectID();

    };

    interface DefectFactoryIntf {

        businessmodel::DefectIntf NewDefect (
            in string userid
        );

        businessmodel::DefectIntf getDefect(
            in long defectid
        )
        raises (NotFoundException);

    };

    typedef sequence<string>UserIDSeq;

    interface UserFactoryIntf {
```

```
    businessmodel::UserIntf NewUser (
        in string requestor, in string userid
    )
    raises (
        AlreadyExistsException,
        businessmodel::AppSecurityException
    );

    businessmodel::UserIntf getUser (
        in string requestor, in string userid
    )
    raises (
        NotFoundException,
        businessmodel::AppSecurityException
    );

    UserIDSeq getUserList();

};

interface DefectServerIntf {

    DefectFactoryIntf getDefectFactory ();

    DefectPolicyIntf getPolicyObject ();

    UserFactoryIntf getUserFactory();

};

};
#endif
```

You will notice several references to interfaces belonging to businessmodel. The IDL file businessmodel.idl, which you can find in the source code download, defines the exposed interfaces in the business model layer. It mostly consists of trivial getter and setter methods, as detailed in the UML diagram above, so we have not reproduced it here. The businessmodel interfaces represent the primary business objects (that is, objects which represent real world things, such as a defect) that the application and the user deal with in the problem domain. These are supplemented by the businesslogic interfaces, which provide the infrastructure, support and control for these business objects.

When the JavaIDL compiler is run against these interface definition files, it will generate a number of Java classes into the businessmodel and businesslogic packages. We'll use that code, along with our own, to frame out the application.

Constructing the Business Model Components

The businessmodel package contains a number of interesting classes. You've already been introduced to the concepts behind these in the elaboration phase discussion. There are a few details that merit some special discussion here.

The "remotable" objects have already had the infrastructure code generated from the IDL files, including the interfaces that the implementations of remotable objects must realize. Recall from earlier in this chapter that these interfaces have been built using the delegation model - that means that the implementations must implement the _[Interfacename]Operations interfaces generated by idltojava.

408

The remotable interfaces in this package that need to be realized are `_DefectIntfOperations` and `_UserIntfOperations`. These really are the equivalents of the `UserIntf` and `DefectIntf` interfaces that were covered in the discussion of external interfaces earlier. We'll create implementations directly from the logical model that we've already defined, and implement these as `User.java` and `Defect.java`.

These two classes contain the information about users and defects. `User` and `Defect` implement `_UserIntfOperations` and `_DefectIntfOperations`, respectively. They also implement the `Testable` interface so they can be exercised by the `TestHarness`.
Their methods are, for the most part, accessor (get and set) methods.

Both classes also implement a `commit()` method. This method is required to enable the remote clients of the object to indicate to the remote object that the changes made to the object are permanent.

One method in `Defect` that's a bit more interesting is the `exportToXML()` method in the `Defect` class. This method, as its name suggests, dumps the state of the object into a string that is formatted in XML according to the DTD that was described earlier in this chapter. There isn't much rocket science here, once you understand XML - it's just building a string that contains the necessary tags and values. You may find similar methods that dump the state of an object as XML to be a useful debugging aid. Here's the method's code:

```java
public String exportToXML()
    {

        String retval;

        retval = "<?xml version = \"1.0\" standalone=\"no\" ?>\n";
        retval = retval + "<!DOCTYPE bugreport SYSTEM \"defect.dtd\">\n";
        retval = retval + "<bugreport>\n";

        retval = retval + "<id>" + this.getDefectID();
        retval = retval + "</id>\n";

        retval = retval + "<state>" + DefectState.stateNames[this.getState()];
        retval = retval + "</state>\n";

        retval = retval + "<severity>" +
DefectSeverity.severityNames[this.getSeverity()];
        retval = retval + "</severity>\n";

        retval = retval + "<priority>" +
DefectPriority.priorityNames[this.getPriority()];
        retval = retval + "</priority>\n";

        retval = retval + "<versionrep>" + this.getVersionReported();
        retval = retval + "</versionrep>\n";

        retval = retval + "<subsystem>" + this.getSubsystem();
        retval = retval + "</subsystem>\n";

        retval = retval + "<summary>" + this.getDefectSummary();
        retval = retval + "</summary>\n";

        retval = retval + "<details>" + this.getDefectDetails();
        retval = retval + "</details>\n";
```

```
        retval = retval + "<reporter>" + this.getReportedBy();
        retval = retval + "</reporter>\n";

        retval = retval + "<assignedto>" + this.getAssignedTo();
        retval = retval + "</assignedto>\n";

        retval = retval + "<resnotes>" + this.getResolutionNotes();
        retval = retval + "</resnotes>\n";

        retval = retval + "<changedmaillist>" + this.getChangedMailList();
        retval = retval + "</changedmaillist>\n";

        retval = retval + "<resolvedmaillist>" + this.getResolvedMailList();
        retval = retval + "</resolvedmaillist>\n";

        retval = retval + "<versionres>" + this.getVersionResolved();
        retval = retval + "</versionres>\n";

        retval = retval + "<datereported>" +
        apputil.util.LongToDateString(this.getDateReported());
        retval = retval + "</datereported>\n";

        retval = retval + "<datelastchanged>" +
        apputil.util.LongToDateString(this.getDateLastChanged());
        retval = retval + "</datelastchanged>\n";

        retval = retval + "<externalid>" +    this.getExternalId();
        retval = retval + "</externalid>\n";

        retval = retval + "</bugreport>\n";

        return retval;
    }
```

If we were dealing with a more complex DTD, we may want to implement this method using an XML parser, as demonstrated in Chapter 14. However, our DTD is pretty trivial, so we can use this technique without too much difficulty.

There are a handful of interfaces that were defined in the logical model for this package that contain numeric values and names for defect priority, severity and state, and for user privileges. They are all patterned after a single model of providing symbolic names for values, and an array of names associated with those values. The code for the DefectPrivileges interface provides an example that is echoed by the other three interfaces:

```
public interface DefectPrivileges {
    public static final int CANCREATE = 0;
    public static final int CANCHANGEASSIGN = 1;
    public static final int CANCHANGEPRIORITY = 2;
    public static final int CANVERIFY = 4;
    public static final int CANRESOLVE = 8;
    public static final int CANADMINISTER = 16;
}
```

The DefectPrivileges interface values deserve a comment - these are the defined privileges that are governed by the DefectPolicy object discussed earlier. The values are designed as powers of 2, so they can be stored as a single integer by logically OR-ing privilege values, and tested by using bitwise AND operations.

Business Model Objects and Persistence

Before we move on, some discussion of persistence is necessary. Clearly if this application needs to track defects, it has to have some sort of mechanism for storing and retrieving information from disk.

Defining the Persistence Mechanism

We could simply use Java serialization to persist objects, which would be fine for applications with a small number of objects to track, or that did not require sophisticated searching capabilities. That doesn't really suit this application, however. We need to be able to manage a large number of defects, and be able to search them. For that reason, I've chosen to use a relational database as the persistence mechanism.

Using relational backing has several benefits. First, it opens up the data to a whole host of tools, and certainly makes it possible to access the data directly through Structured Query Language (SQL). Relational databases also lend themselves quite nicely to managing large numbers of entities, and handling complex queries through SQL.

The drawback is that there is an impedance mismatch between Java objects and relational databases. Recall the earlier discussion, however, of the multi-tiered approach to the BugTracker. One of the architectural choices was to introduce a data abstraction layer that would insulate the system from having to know anything about how the data storage mechanism was implemented. Thus, the `dataabstraction` package is introduced:

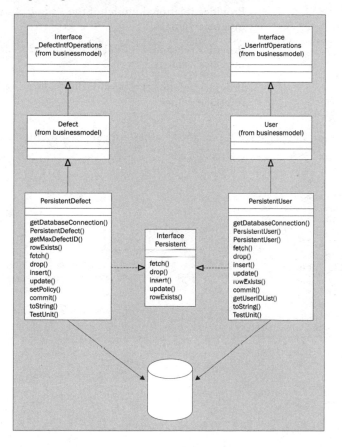

The classes in the `dataabstraction` package are all based upon (that is, they extend) classes in the `businessmodel` package. They inherit all the smarts that are embedded into the `businessmodel` objects, and simply provide the object-to-relational and relational-to-object mappings. From an application perspective, though, they look and act just like the `businessmodel` objects, but are persistent. The classes that implement the `Persistent` interface are the only classes that talk to the database.

The really nice thing about this arrangement is that since they extend the `businessmodel` objects, they can be accessed over the ORB - the ORB and the remote ORB clients neither know nor care that the objects are persisted in a relational database.

Designing the Relational Database

Designing the relational database is an exercise in mapping the object model into normalized form. Based on the classes that were defined and refined during elaboration, the following relational tables were defined:

`Users`	Stores the data for `PersistentUser` objects
`Defects`	Stores the data for `PersistentDefect` objects
`defect_priority`	Provides relational model of the `DefectPriority` interface values
`defect_severity`	Provides relational model of the `DefectSeverity` interface values
`defect_state`	Provides relational model of the `DefectState` interface values
`privilege_defs`	Provides relational model of the `DefectPrivilege` interface values

The SQL data definition language (DDL) for these tables appears below, and indicates the type mapping used:

```
CREATE TABLE users (
    userid char(8),
    lastname char(20),
    firstname char(20),
    phonenumber char(20),
    faxnumber char(20),
    emailaddress char(50),
    priv_levels integer)

CREATE TABLE defects (
    defectid integer,
    product char(30),
    versionreported char(8),
    subsystem char(20),
    defectsummary char(50),
    defectdetail memo,
    state integer,
    priority integer,
```

```
        severity integer,
        reportedby char(15),
        assignedto char(8),
        datereported date,
        datelastchanged date,
        resolutionnotes varchar(50),
        changedmodules varchar(50),
        changedmaillist varchar(50),
        resolvedmaillist varchar(50),
        versionresolved char(8),
        externalid varchar(25))

CREATE TABLE defect_priority (
        priority integer,
        pri_name char(15))

CREATE TABLE defect_severity (
        severity integer,
        sev_name char(15))

CREATE TABLE defect_state (
        state integer,
        state_name char(15))

CREATE TABLE privilege_defs (
        priv integer,
        priv_name char(25))
```

> Note: normalization of data puts it into a structure that conforms to relational
> database theory. This structuring is designed to avoid data inconsistencies and
> update anomalies in the database. If you are not familiar with relational databases
> and normal forms, you may want to check out *Instant SQL* by Joe Celko (ISBN 1-
> 874416-50-8, Wrox Press). *Beginning Java 2* by Ivor Horton (ISBN 1-861002-23-8,
> Wrox Press) broadly covers Java, with thorough discussions of interfacing
> relational databases to Java objects.

Building the Mapping Components

Now that the relational tables are defined, the `dataabstraction` package classes, which provide
the mapping, can be defined.

The `PersistentUser` and `PersistentDefect` classes follow the same pattern sketched out by
the `Persistent` interface. That interface defines methods that must be implemented by the realizing
class:

insert()	Create a new relational row using the object state
fetch()	Retrieves the stored object state from the table
drop()	Removes the table's row that stores this object's state
update()	Updates the row for this object with the object's current state
rowExists()	Tests to see if this object has a stored state

These methods are for the benefit of the server-side components. Client applications interact with the persistent object no differently than a non-persisted object. The client never explicitly tells the object to read its data from disk - it happens implicitly when the client obtains a `Defect` or `User` from the `DefectFactory` or `UserFactory`, respectively. The client application does need to tell the object when to make its current state permanent, though. Recall that the `UserIntf` and `DefectIntf` interfaces defined a `commit()` method that was described earlier as telling the object to make its state permanent - that's exactly what happens with the overridden `commit()` method in the `PersistentUser` and `PersistentDefect` classes. That method will cause the object to insert a new row in the table if it doesn't already exist, or update the row if it already exists.

So how do the objects know how to perform these operations? Since both of these classes follow the same pattern, we'll take a look at the simpler of the two, and start by looking at a fragment of the source that defines data members:

```
public class PersistentUser extends businessmodel.User
                implements Persistent, apputil.Testable
{

    static Connection databaseConnection = null;
    static String driverName;
    static String sourceURL;

    public static final String QUERYBYKEY =
            "select userid, lastname,firstname, " +
            "phonenumber, faxnumber, emailaddress, " +
            "priv_levels from users where userid = ?";

    public static final String DROPBYKEY =
            "delete from users where userid = ?";
    public static final String INSERTUSER =
            "insert into users (userid, lastname, " +
            "firstname, phonenumber, faxnumber, " +
            "emailaddress, priv_levels) values (?,?,?,?,?,?,?)";

    public static final String UPDATEUSER =
            "update users set lastname=?, firstname=?, " +
            "phonenumber=?, faxnumber=?, emailaddress=?, " +
            "priv_levels=? where userid = ?";

    .
    .
    .
}
```

The `PersistentUser` class, as indicated in the class diagram at the beginning of this section, extends the `User` class, so there's not much that this class needs to do in terms of User stuff. It implements the `Persistent` interface that was described above, as well as the `Testable` interface so it can be exercised by the `TestHarness`.

The class has a number of static members. There are class members that store specific JDBC-related information required to establish a connection to the database. This information is stored in the application properties file, and these values are obtained from an `AppConfig` object. The class members also include a JDBC `Connection` object. This allows a means of sharing a single connection to the database between multiple instances of this class. This eliminates a great deal of overhead. Since these objects are fairly short-lived, it would be extremely expensive to build and tear down a database connection for each object created.

Next, there are a number of static `String` members that contain SQL for reading an object's row in a table, deleting that row, inserting an object into a table, and updating the stored data from the object's state. These statements are used by the methods defined by `Persistent` and implemented by `PersistentUser`. We'll take a look at how a new object is inserted into a table, and how it is fetched from the table. The rest of the `Persistent` operations should make sense after that.

A new `PersistentUser` is created by the `UserFactory` on behalf of the requesting client. Note that in order to work with a `PersistentUser` object, new or existing, a unique identifier must be supplied. The following code snippet demonstrates:

```
public businessmodel.UserIntf createNewUser(
                              String requestor,
                              String userid)
            throws AlreadyExistsException, AppSecurityException
{
    PersistentUser pUser = new PersistentUser();
    pUser.setUserID(userid);
    if (pUser.rowExists())
    {   throw new AlreadyExistsException(); }
    pUser.setFirstName("Ron");
    pUser.setLastName("Phillips");
    pUser.commit(requestor);
}
```

This code first creates an instance of `PersistentUser`. The constructor for `PersistentUser` looks to see if there is an existing connection. If not, one is created. Next, the code sets the unique identifier by calling `setUserID()`, and checks to see if it exists. Assuming it doesn't, accessor methods are used to set the last name and first name, and then the `commit()` method is called to make the state permanent. Let's take a look to see what happens in the `commit()` method:

```
public void commit(String userid)
           throws UpdateException, AppSecurityException
{

    super.commit(userid);

    try
    {
        if (rowExists())
        {  update(); }
        else
        {  insert(); }
    }
    catch(SQLException sqle)
    {
        throw new UpdateException();
    }
}
```

This method is pretty simple - it calls the superclass' `commit` method, and then checks to see if the object has already been stored to disk or not. It then calls the `update()` or `insert()` method depending on whether the object's row exists or not, respectively. It needs to make that distinction (unlike writing a file to disk) because relational databases treat updates and inserts as very distinct activities.

Since we're creating a new PersistentUser, we'll trace the code path to the insert() method:

```
public void insert() throws java.sql.SQLException
{
    String theUserID = this.getUserID();

    if (theUserID == null)
    {  throw new SQLException("Cannot add user without id set"); }

    PreparedStatement pQuery =
         databaseConnection.prepareStatement(INSERTUSER);

    pQuery.setString(1, getUserID());
    pQuery.setString(2, getLastName());
    pQuery.setString(3, getFirstName());
    pQuery.setString(4, getPhone());
    pQuery.setString(5, getFax());
    pQuery.setString(6, getEmail());
    pQuery.setInt(7, getPriv());

    pQuery.executeUpdate();

}
```

Recall the SQL strings that are defined as static Strings for this class. The INSERTUSER string is designed to be used as the SQL for a prepared statement, which allows parameterization of elements in the SQL (much easier than building up a SQL string on the fly!). In the insert code, a PreparedStatement is created using the INSERTUSER SQL. The parameters for the SQL are set by obtaining the member values via accessor methods and calling setXxx() methods on the PreparedStatement object, as dictated by the data type of the member and its correlate SQL column. Finally, the row is inserted by calling the executeUpdate() method of the PreparedStatement (note that in this case, executeUpdate() is called because there is no returned result set as would be the case for a SQL select statement. There isn't an executeInsert() method that you have to use - the distinction between SQL insert and update occurs only within the SQL statements, not the JDBC methods!).

The fetch() method for PersistentUser works much the same way, except the data is read from the relational table and populates the object instead of the other way around:

```
public void fetch() throws java.sql.SQLException
{
    String theUserID = this.getUserID();

    if (theUserID == null)
    {
        throw new SQLException("Cannot fetch user without id set");
    }

    PreparedStatement pQuery =
         databaseConnection.prepareStatement(QUERYBYKEY);
    pQuery.setString(1, getUserID());

    ResultSet rs = pQuery.executeQuery();

    //any returns?
    if (rs.next())
    {
```

```
        String stringval;
        int intval;

        stringval = rs.getString("userid");
        setUserID(rs.wasNull()?"":stringval);

        stringval = rs.getString("lastname");
        setLastName(rs.wasNull()?"":stringval);

        stringval = rs.getString("firstname");
        setFirstName(rs.wasNull()?"":stringval);

        stringval = rs.getString("phonenumber");
        setPhone(rs.wasNull()?"":stringval);

        stringval = rs.getString("faxnumber");
        setFax(rs.wasNull()?"":stringval);

        stringval = rs.getString("emailaddress");
        setEmail(rs.wasNull()?"":stringval);

        intval = rs.getInt("priv_levels");
        setPriv(rs.wasNull()?0:intval);
        rs.close();
    }

    else
        throw new SQLException("No matching rows found!");

}
```

In the `fetch()` method, the `QUERYBYKEY` string is used to execute a SQL statement and find the row by using the unique identifier - again as a prepared statement with the `userID` as the single parameter. The statement is executed and a `ResultSet` object returned. The member values are then populated via the accessor methods. Note that the code tests to see if the value returned by the `ResultSet` was `null`. This method provides defaults in those cases - a zero length string for `String` types, and zero for numeric types. This step is necessary, or there would be exceptions thrown left, right and center as assignments are executed.

You should now have a pretty good handle on the basic patterns used within the `PersistentUser` class. The `PersistentDefect` class is quite nearly identical, with only the mapping elements (the SQL statements and the accessor method calls) being different. You can easily apply this pattern to other types of persistent objects you want to add to the application.

Constructing the Business Logic Components

The businesslogic classes provide the lion's share of the server-side functionality. The DefectServer class is the main class in this tier. We'll start by looking at the main() method of this class:

```
public static void main(String[] args)
{
    apputil.AppConfig config;

    System.out.println("java businesslogic.DefectServer " +
            "{<configfile> <orb opt 1> .... <orb opt n>}");

    try
    {
        if (args.length == 0)
        {   config = new apputil.AppConfig("BUGTRACKER.PROPS"); }
        else
        {   config = new apputil.AppConfig(args[0]); }

        // create and initialize the ORB
        ORB orb = ORB.init(args, null);

        // create the policy object
        DefectPolicy policyImpl = new DefectPolicy();
        policyImpl.setOrb(orb);

        _DefectPolicyIntfTie policyObj = new
        _DefectPolicyIntfTie(policyImpl);
        orb.connect(policyObj);

        System.out.println("Created policy object as " +
                    orb.object_to_string(policyObj));

        // create the defect factory object
        DefectFactory defectfactoryImpl = new DefectFactory(policyImpl);
        _DefectFactoryIntfTie defectfactoryObj =
                    new _DefectFactoryIntfTie(defectfactoryImpl);
        orb.connect(defectfactoryObj);

        System.out.println("Created defect factory object as " +
                orb.object_to_string(defectfactoryObj));

        // create the user factory object
        UserFactory userfactoryImpl = new UserFactory(policyImpl);
        _UserFactoryIntfTie userfactoryObj = new
        _UserFactoryIntfTie(userfactoryImpl);
        orb.connect(userfactoryObj);

        System.out.println("Created user factory object as " +
                orb.object_to_string(userfactoryObj));

        // create the server object; pass it factory and policy
        DefectServer serverImpl = new DefectServer(
                    defectfactoryObj, policyObj, userfactoryObj);
        _DefectServerIntfTie serverObj = new
        _DefectServerIntfTie(serverImpl);
        orb.connect(serverObj);
```

```
        System.out.println("Created server object as " +
                orb.object_to_string(serverObj));

        // get the root naming context
        org.omg.CORBA.Object objRef =
                orb.resolve_initial_references("NameService");
        System.out.println("Adding objects to naming service");

        NamingContext ncRef = NamingContextHelper.narrow(objRef);

        // bind the Object Reference in Naming

        NameComponent nc =
            new NameComponent(config.getBugServerServiceName(), "");
        NameComponent path[] = {nc};
        ncRef.rebind(path, serverObj);

        System.out.println("Defect service ready.");
        // wait for invocations from clients
        java.lang.Object sync = new java.lang.Object();
        synchronized (sync)
        {
            sync.wait();
        }

    }
    catch (Exception e)
    {
        System.err.println("ERROR: " + e);
        e.printStackTrace(System.out);
    }
}
```

The startup of the `DefectServer` should look pretty familiar - the interactions for initialization were described in detail in the section describing the `businesslogic` internals. The interesting things happening here include creating the `AppConfig` object with the specified (or default) properties file, creating the `DefectFactory`, `UserFactory` and `DefectPolicy` objects, registering them with the ORB and then binding itself with the CORBA name service.

This is really the bulk of what the `DefectServer` does. It provides accessor methods so the client can obtain the `DefectFactory`, `UserFactory` and `DefectPolicy` objects, but aside from that, once it's initialized it can kick back and let the `DefectFactory`, `UserFactory` and `DefectPolicy` objects do all of the work.

The `UserFactory` implements the `UserFactoryIntf` interface, which has already been discussed. It's really quite a simple bit of software - it will service a request to create a new user, find one that already exists, or get a list of user IDs. That's all it does. Here's the code for that:

```
public UserIntf NewUser(String requestor, String userid)
        throws AlreadyExistsException, AppSecurityException
{
    return m_DefectPolicy.createNewUser(requestor, userid);
}

public UserIntf getUser(String requestor, String userid)
        throws NotFoundException, AppSecurityException
{
```

```
    //  If the requestor doesn't have admin
    //  privileges, throw AppSecurityException
    if (!m_DefectPolicy.canAdminister(requestor))
    {  throw new AppSecurityException(); }

    try
    {
        businessmodel._UserIntfTie base;

        // need to assign a new uid to the defect
        PersistentUser theUser = new PersistentUser();
        theUser.setUserID(userid);
        theUser.fetch();

        //  create the tie object, bind it to the user,
        //  and let the policy object bind it to the orb
        base = new businessmodel._UserIntfTie(theUser);
        m_DefectPolicy.implConnect(base);

        return base;

    }
    catch(SQLException sqle)
    {
        throw new NotFoundException();
    }
}

public String[] getUserList()
{
    PersistentUser pUser = new PersistentUser();
    return pUser.getUserIDList();
}
```

As you can see, the Factory is really quite a lazy fellow - he foists much of his work onto the `businessmodel` and `dataabstraction` classes. The code for retrieving a user object should look pretty familiar – it's using the `PersistentUser` class that was described in the previous section

The `DefectFactory` is quite similar and follows the same patterns - no great surprise, as these are both factories for `businessmodel` objects that have very similar patterns.

You may also note that much of the work in these methods is done by the `DefectPolicy` objects. This is one of the more interesting classes in this package. It is tasked with the job of enforcing the business rules concerning how users deal with defects and how the lifecycle of the defect is managed. The business rules in the `DefectPolicy` object are pretty simple, but it's an easy matter to add more or make them more complex as needs dictate.

The methods supported by the `DefectPolicyIntf` interface (which we discussed earlier) are:

`canAssign()`	Determine if the specified user has rights to assign a defect
`canPrioritize()`	Determine if the specified user has rights to set or reassign the priority of a defect
`canVerify()`	Determine if the specified user has rights to verify that a defect has been adequately resolved
`canResolve()`	Determine if the specified user has rights to fix a defect

`canAdminister()`	Determine if the specified user has rights to perform administrative functions for the BugTracker application
`createNewDefect()`	Creates a new defect, checking that required privileges are held
`getNextDefectID()`	Get the next available numeric id for a defect

The first five methods use the privileges value stored for `PersistentUsers` to determine whether specific privileges are held or not. Let's look at `canAssign()` as an example - the remaining privilege level methods are nearly identical:

```
public boolean canAssign(String userid)
    {
    boolean retval = false;

    try
    {
        PersistentUser user = new PersistentUser(userid);
        user.fetch();
        int userpriv = user.getPriv();
        if (0 != (userpriv & DefectPrivileges.CANCHANGEASSIGN))
        {  retval = true; }
    }
    catch (SQLException sqle)
    {
        // do nothing - we'll just return false
    }

    return retval;

    }
```

The method is passed the unique identifier for the user. A `PersistentUser` object is created and assigned that ID. The `fetch` method is called, the user privilege value obtained and that value is then bitwise ANDed with the `CANCHANGEASSIGN` value defined in the `DefectPrivileges` interface.

The `DefectPolicy` class also creates new defects. In fact, the `DefectFactory` simply calls the `DefectPolicy`'s `createNewDefect()` method to create a new defect. This method enforces the rules for how a defect is created. In this implementation, the only rule that's enforced is that the new defect gets time stamped. Here's the code:

```
public businessmodel.DefectIntf createNewDefect(String uid)
    {
    businessmodel._DefectIntfTie base;

    // need to get assign a new uid to the defect
    PersistentDefect theDefect =    new PersistentDefect();
    theDefect.setDefectID(getNextDefectID());
    theDefect.setPolicy(this);

    Date rightNow = new Date();
    theDefect.setDateReported(rightNow.getTime());

    base = new businessmodel._DefectIntfTie(theDefect);
    implConnect(base);

    return base;

    }
```

A new `PersistentDefect` is created, and the `DefectPolicy`'s `getNextDefectID` method is called - this method generates a unique identifier for the defect object. A few members are set with accessor methods, and the new `Defect` object is connected to the ORB.

There are also methods implemented in the `DefectPolicy` object that aren't exposed through the `DefectPolicyIntf` interface. These are primarily concerned with performing checks to ensure that specifics are valid, and are called by the `businessmodel` objects when persisting their state. Let's take a look at one:

```
public void securityCheck(PersistentDefect defect, String username)
            throws AppSecurityException
{

    boolean stateChangedToVerified, stateChangedToResolved;
    boolean priorityChanged, assignmentChanged;

    // is this a new defect or already exists?
    PersistentDefect stored = new PersistentDefect();
    stored.setDefectID(defect.getDefectID());

    stateChangedToVerified = false;
    stateChangedToResolved = false;
    priorityChanged = false;
    assignmentChanged = false;

    if (stored.rowExists())
    {
        try
        {
            stored.fetch();
        }
        catch (SQLException sqle)
        {
            /* not the most elegant way to handle,
            but if you wind up here it's fairly
            nasty, so just bail out.
            */

            throw new AppSecurityException();

        }

        // check the fields that are secured
        if (!(stored.getAssignedTo().trim().equals(
                        defect.getAssignedTo().trim()
                        )))
        { assignmentChanged = true; }
        if (stored.getPriority() != defect.getPriority())
        { priorityChanged = true; }
        if (stored.getState() != defect.getState())
        {
            if (defect.getState() == DefectState.FIX_VERIFIED)
            { stateChangedToVerified = true; }
            else if (defect.getState() == DefectState.FIXED)
                { stateChangedToResolved = true; }
        }
    }
}
```

```
    else
    {
        if (defect.getAssignedTo().trim().length() > 0)
        {   assignmentChanged = true; }
        if (defect.getPriority() != DefectPriority.NULL)
        {   priorityChanged = true; }
        if (defect.getState() == DefectState.FIX_VERIFIED)
        {   stateChangedToVerified = true; }
        else if (defect.getState() == DefectState.FIXED)
        {   stateChangedToResolved = true; }
    }

    if ( assignmentChanged )
    {
        if ( !canAssign(username))
        {   throw new AppSecurityException(); }
    }
    if ( priorityChanged )
    {
        if ( !canPrioritize(username))
        {   throw new AppSecurityException(); }
    }
    if ( stateChangedToVerified )
    {
        if (!canVerify(username))
        {   throw new AppSecurityException(); }
    }
    else if ( stateChangedToResolved )
    {
        if (!canResolve(username))
        {   throw new AppSecurityException(); }
    }

}
```

This method is called by a `Defect` when it is being `committed`. The method above first determines if the defect already exists, and if so it reconstitutes a copy from the persistent store. It then determines which fields of the `Defect` have changed (it's only concerned with ones that are involved in enforcing business rules). Then, depending on whether the state of the object is legal - in terms of what has changed and the requesting user's privileges - it silently allows the operation or throws an `AppSecurityException`.

Constructing the User Interface Components

The Bug Tracker application user interface is a Swing-based application, with all of the user interface components placed in the `ui` package.

The visual structure for this user interface was described at the beginning of this chapter. The user interface consists of a main frame, with tabbed panels contained within. Each tabbed panel contains widgets that display the parts of the defect particular to that tab.

The logical structure of this user interface was described in the elaboration phase. The classes in the `ui` package implement that design.

The main class, `DefectForm`, extends `JFrame`. It provides the `main()` method that launches the user interface. The sequence for the `DefectForm` initialization was presented along with the logical structure, so let's take a look at the code that implements it. The sequence of events is pretty common for ORB clients. In fact, since you've already seen the initialization of the `DefectServer`, much of this code should look a bit familiar:

```
public static void main(String[] args)
    {
        apputil.AppConfig config;
        ui.DefectForm theForm;


        try
        {
            if (args.length == 0)
            { config = new apputil.AppConfig("BUGTRACKER.PROPS"); }
            else
            { config = new apputil.AppConfig(args[0]); }

            // create and initialize the ORB
            ORB orb = ORB.init(args, null);

            // get the root naming context
            org.omg.CORBA.Object objRef =
            orb.resolve_initial_references("NameService");
            NamingContext ncRef = NamingContextHelper.narrow(objRef);

            // resolve the Object Reference in Naming
            NameComponent nc = new
            NameComponent(config.getBugServerServiceName(), "");
            NameComponent path[] = {nc};

            //Get a reference to the bug server
            DefectServerIntf theBugServer;
            theBugServer =
            DefectServerIntfHelper.narrow(ncRef.resolve(path));

            //  if we've been able to get a reference to the bug
            //  server, go ahead and create the UI and pass the
            //  reference along to the UI object
            theForm = new DefectForm(orb, theBugServer);

        }
        catch (Exception e)
        {
            System.out.println("ERROR : " + e) ;
            e.printStackTrace(System.out);
        }
    }
```

There are just a handful of things going on in `main()`:

- The `AppConfig` object is created with the specified (or default) properties file
- The ORB is initialized
- A reference to the CORBA name service is obtained
- The name service is queried to get a reference to the `DefectServer`
- An instance of `DefectForm` is created. The constructor for the `DefectForm` is passed a reference to the ORB and the `DefectServer`

The constructor for the `DefectForm` sets up the form and does some more initialization:

```
public DefectForm(ORB orb, DefectServerIntf bugserver)
{
    super("BugTracker/J");
    m_DefectServer = bugserver;
    m_Orb = orb;

    // get the user id from the system properties
    String uid = System.getProperties().getProperty("user.name");
    setUserID(uid);

    m_DefectFactory = m_DefectServer.getDefectFactory();
    m_DefectPolicy = m_DefectServer.getPolicyObject();
    m_Model = new UIDefectModel();

    createEmptyDefect();

    initialize();

    m_Model.UpdateListeners();
}
```

First, the constructor for the `DefectForm` (`JFrame`) is called. Next, you may recall that several of the services that are provided by the `DefectPolicy` object rely on a user ID. The Bug Tracker application uses Java's system properties to retrieve the user ID from the operating system. That user ID is retrieved in the `DefectForm main()` method, and is stored as a member variable. The next two statements call the `DefectServer` to obtain references to the `DefectFactory` and `DefectPolicy` objects and store them in member variables.

The `UIDefectModel` that is created is part of the model-view architecture that was discussed earlier. This allows multiple user interface components to present consistent views of the same object. The `DefectForm` controls data flowing in and out of the panels that comprise the UI through the `UIDefectModel` object – it does not deal directly with the panels once they've been created.

The `initialize` method creates the user interface and adds the tab panels to the form. If you've done any Swing development, this will be very familiar – there's nothing really special about it, except perhaps when the panels are concerned.

Each of the panels has been designed as a separate class, and each implements the
DefectModelListener interface. That interface was briefly introduced earlier. That interface
identifies objects that will register with the UIDefectModel as listeners for changes to the current
defect. The collaboration diagram below illustrates:

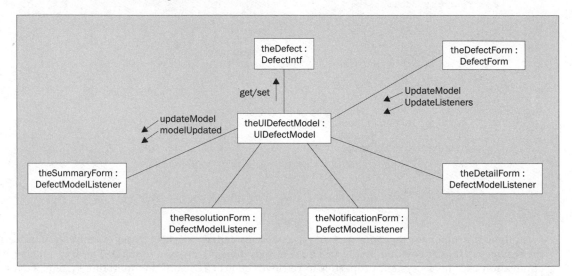

The UIDefectModel keeps a reference DefectIntf object to store the defect information. It also
retains a list of views - listeners that want to know when the defect has been changed or needs to be
updated from the listener.

The UIDefectModel provides two important methods for triggering data exchange between the
model and the views. The UpdateListeners() method is called when a new defect is plugged into
the interface. This method causes the UIDefectModel to iterate through the views that have
registered as listeners, and calls the modelUpdated() method of each. The DefectIntf reference
held by the UIDefectModel is passed as a parameter so that the view can update its presentation
based on the updated defect.

The updateModel() method of the UIDefectModel causes it to iterate through the registered
listeners and call the updateModel() method of each, passing the DefectIntf reference held by
the UIDefectModel as a parameter. Each listener then updates the DefectIntf object with its
data.

Constructing the BugTracker Servlet

We've decided to use a Java servlet to provide support for the browser-based client that was identified
as a project requirement. The servlet acts as kind of a client proxy that generates HTML to draw on
the screen. Because it's designed as a client proxy, the code will look very similar to the code in the
previous section, with a bit of servlet flair.

The init() method, called by the web server when the servlet is first loaded, performs the same
initialization as the main method and constructor of the DefectForm (the listing for the
BugTrackerServlet appears at the end of this section).

Since servlets don't have command lines, though, the servlet properties need to be set up to pass the appropriate information so the servlet can initialize. The servlet properties that can be defined include

Propsfile	filename of application properties file
ORBInitialHost	name of host that is running the CORBA name service (localhost by default)
ORBInitialPort	port of the naming service (900 by default)

The first value specifies the name of the file from which to create the `AppConfig` object. The next two allow the Bug Tracker to run on multiple machines. These values are assembled into a Properties object and used to initialize the ORB (See the "Distributed Bug Tracker" section later in this chapter).

Because it's not possible or desirable to create a user for each potential person that might create a defect report on the web, the `BugTrackerServlet` uses a user proxy (or pseudo-user) called "www" that will be used with the `DefectPolicy` object. Naturally, this user's privileges should be limited!

The `doPost()` method of the servlet handles Bug Tracker requests. This method looks for a parameter called `reqtype` to identify how the request should be handled. The request can be SUBMIT, in which case the incoming information is creating a new defect. If the request is QUERY, then the incoming request is passing a defect ID and wants the defect to be formatted and returned.

```java
public void doPost(HttpServletRequest req, HttpServletResponse resp)
{
    String reqType = req.getParameter("reqtype").toUpperCase();

    if (reqType.equals("SUBMIT"))
        handleSubmit(req, resp);
    else
    if (reqType.equals("QUERY"))
        handleQuery(req, resp);
    else
        handleBadRequest(req, resp);
}
```

The request handler methods are very similar to the routines in `DefectForm` that fetch and create defects, with the notable difference being that information is formatted as HTML instead of being displayed in Swing widgets.

Let's go through the `BugTrackerServlet`'s methods.

First off, we have to import the required packages. As well as the `io`, `servlet` and `servlet.http` packages we normally need in a servlet, we'll need the CORBA packages, and also the `businesslogic` and `businessmodel` packages from the Bug Tracker application.

```
import businesslogic.*;
import businessmodel.*;

import javax.servlet.*;
import javax.servlet.http.*;
import java.io.*;
import java.util.*;
import org.omg.CORBA.*;
import org.omg.CosNaming.*;

public class BugTrackerServlet extends HttpServlet
{

    .
    .
    .

}
```

We need to specify a couple of constants. The first is the userID of our generic web client, and the second is a string we'll use whenever a value is not submitted.

We'll also need to hold references to the defect server, factory and policy objects once we've obtained them from the ORB. While we're at it, we also need a placeholder for the ORB itself.

```
static final String WWWUSER = "www";
static final String NULLTEXT = "<not specified>";

DefectServerIntf m_DefectServer;
DefectFactoryIntf m_DefectFactory;
DefectPolicyIntf m_DefectPolicy;
ORB m_Orb;
```

The first method is the `init()` method. This version assumes a JSDK2.1 servlet engine, but it's easy to change the code to run on older containers. All this method does is initialize the ORB, get the application properties, and recover references to the objects we listed above.

```
public void init() throws ServletException
{
    System.out.println("trying to initialize orb...");
    try
    {
        String propsfile =
        config.getInitParameter("propsfile");

        apputil.AppConfig appcfg;
        if (propsfile == null)
        {   appcfg = new apputil.AppConfig("BUGTRACKER.PROPS"); }
        else
        {   appcfg = new apputil.AppConfig(propsfile); }

        Properties props = new Properties();

        String host = config.getInitParameter("ORBInitialHost");
        if (host != null)
        {   props.setProperty("ORBInitialHost", host); }
```

```
        String port = config.getInitParameter("ORBInitialPort");
        if (port != null)
        { props.setProperty("ORBInitialPort", port); }

        // create and initialize the ORB
        m_Orb = ORB.init((String[])null, props);

        // get the root naming context
        org.omg.CORBA.Object objRef =
                m_Orb.resolve_initial_references("NameService");

        NamingContext ncRef = NamingContextHelper.narrow(objRef);

        // resolve the Object Reference in Naming
        NameComponent nc = new
        NameComponent(appcfg.getBugServerServiceName(), "");
        NameComponent path[] = {nc};

        //Get a reference to the bug server
        m_DefectServer =
        DefectServerIntfHelper.narrow(ncRef.resolve(path));
        m_DefectFactory = m_DefectServer.getDefectFactory();
        m_DefectPolicy = m_DefectServer.getPolicyObject();

    }
    catch(Exception e)
    {
        System.out.println(e.toString());
        throw new ServletException(e.toString());
    }

}
```

We've looked at the doPost() method already, so let's see the three handlers which it calls, depending on the reqtype parameter. The first handles POST requests originating from the finddefect.html form, which has two user-completed fields: defectid, which is the code for the defect the user is interested in, and format, which is either "html", or "xml".

```
public void handleQuery(
            HttpServletRequest req, HttpServletResponse resp)
{

    try
    {
        String defectId = null;
        String xmlString;
        String[] defectIdList;
        String retBody;
        String format = new String("html");

        boolean gotDefectId = false;

        // get the writer object
        PrintWriter out = resp.getWriter();

        Enumeration enum;
        String parmName;
```

```
      enum = req.getParameterNames();
      while (enum.hasMoreElements())
      {
          parmName = (String)enum.nextElement();

          // is it the defect ids?
          if (parmName.trim().equals("defectid"))
          {
              // got a defect request
              defectId = req.getParameter(parmName);
              gotDefectId = true;

          }
          else if (parmName.trim().equals("format"))
          {
              format = req.getParameter(parmName);

              // make sure it's correct case
              format = format.toLowerCase();
          }
      }

      resp.setContentType("text/" + format);

      if (gotDefectId)
      {
          if (format.equals("xml"))
              retBody = OutputAsXML(defectId);
          else
              retBody = OutputAsHTML(defectId);
      }
      else
      {   retBody = "no defect specified"; }

      out.println(retBody);
      out.close();
  }

  catch(IOException ioe)
  {
      // oh well...
  }

}
```

The second method handles POST requests from the `submitdefectreport.html` form, which provides all of the following fields for the user to complete:

- `defectsummary`
- `defectdetails` - the user's description of the problem
- `name`, `fax`, `phone`, `company`, `email` - these are concatenated onto the defect details to provide a permanent record
- `productid`
- `notifyonresolve` - this value is submitted by a checkbox. If it comes back, we have to add the email address to the `resolvedMailList` of the defect.
- `product`
- `version`

```java
public void handleSubmit(
            HttpServletRequest req, HttpServletResponse resp)
{
    resp.setContentType("text/html");
    String retval = new String("");
    String errorText;
    int defectId;

    try
    {
        PrintWriter out = resp.getWriter();
        DefectIntf theDefect;

        try
        {
            String defectSummary = req.getParameter("defectsummary");
            if (defectSummary == null)
            {
                throw new BadInformationException(
                    "Defect summary is required");
            }

            String defectDetails = req.getParameter("defectdetails");
            if (defectDetails == null)
            {
                throw new BadInformationException(
                    "Defect detail is required");
            }

            String name    = req.getParameter("name");
            if (name == null)
                name = NULLTEXT;

            String phone = req.getParameter("phone");
            if (phone == null)
            {   phone = NULLTEXT; }

            String fax = req.getParameter("fax");
            if (fax == null)
            {   fax = NULLTEXT; }

            String company = req.getParameter("company");
            if (company == null)
            {   company = NULLTEXT; }

            boolean notifyonresolve = req.getParameter(
                "notifyonresolve").trim().equals("1"));

            String email = req.getParameter("email");
            if (email == null)
            {
                throw new BadInformationException(
                    "Email address is required");
            }

            String product = req.getParameter("product");
            if (product == null)
            {
                throw new BadInformationException(
                    "Product name is required");
            }
```

Continued on Following Page

431

```
        String version = req.getParameter("version");
        if (version == null)
        { version = NULLTEXT; }

        String productid = req.getParameter("productid");
        if (productid == null)
        { productid = NULLTEXT; }
...
```

If you had more validation rules, such as ensuring a valid serial number, etc., you could do so here. You would simply throw a `BadInformationException` to stop the defect submitting process if the information was invalid. The method has now gathered all of the information, and has to now fill in the fields on the `Defect` object.

```
...
        theDefect = m_DefectFactory.NewDefect(WWWUSER);
        defectId = theDefect.getDefectID();

        String appendText = new String("\nSubmitted by: " + name +
            "\nCompany: " + company +
            "\nPhone: " + phone +
            "\nFax: " + fax +
            "\nEmail: " + email +
            "\nProduct ID: " + productid);

        theDefect.setState(DefectState.NEW);
        theDefect.setReportedBy(WWWUSER);
        theDefect.setDefectSummary(defectSummary);
        theDefect.setDefectDetails(defectDetails + appendText);
        theDefect.setProduct(product);
        theDefect.setVersionReported(version);
        if (notifyonresolve)
        {   theDefect.setResolvedMailList(email); }

        theDefect.commit(WWWUSER);

        retval = retval.concat(
            "<head><title>Defect submitted</title></head>");
        retval = retval.concat(
            "<body><h1>Defect Submitted</h1>");
        retval = retval.concat(
            "<hr>Your report has been submitted as defect <b>" +
                    defectId);
        retval = retval.concat(
            "</b><p>Please refer to this number when inquiring " +
                    "on the status of ths defect");

    }
    catch(BadInformationException bie)
    {
        errorText = bie.toString();
        retval = retval.concat(
            "<head><title>Error submitting defect</title></head>");
        retval = retval.concat("<body><h1>Defect Not Submitted</h1>");
        retval = retval.concat(
            "<hr>The following error occurred:<p>" + errorText);
    }
```

```
        catch(UpdateException ue)
        {
           errorText = ue.toString();
           retval = retval.concat(
                   "<head><title>Error submitting defect</title></head>");
           retval = retval.concat("<body><h1>Defect Not Submitted</h1>");
           retval = retval.concat(
                   "<hr>The following error occurred:<p>" + errorText);
        }
        catch(AppSecurityException ase)
        {
           errorText = ase.toString();
           retval = retval.concat(
                   "<head><title>Error submitting defect</title></head>");
           retval = retval.concat("<body><h1>Defect Not Submitted</h1>");
           retval = retval.concat(
                   "<hr>The following error occurred:<p>" + errorText);
        }

        retval = retval.concat("</body></html>");
        out.println(retval);
        out.close();
     }
     catch (IOException ioe)
     { }
   }
```

The final handler routine deals with badly formatted POST requests, and simply returns a warning to the user.

```
     public void handleBadRequest(HttpServletRequest req,
             HttpServletResponse resp)
   {
      resp.setContentType("text/html");

      try
      {

         PrintWriter out = resp.getWriter();
         out.println(
                 "Bad request to servlet... see system administrator");
         out.close();
      }
      catch(IOException IOE)
      { }

   }
```

Now, we have to implement the two methods called in the handleQuery() method, which return the requested bug report as either HTML or XML. Getting XML is easy - we just get the defect and call its exportToXML() method.

```
String OutputAsXML(String defectId)
{
    DefectIntf theDefect;
    String retval;

    try
    {
        int id;
        id = Integer.parseInt(defectId);
        theDefect = m_DefectFactory.getDefect(id);
        retval = theDefect.exportToXML();
    }

    catch(NumberFormatException numfe)
    {
        retval = new String(defectId +
            " is not a properly formatted defect id.");
    }

    catch(NotFoundException nfe)
    {
        retval = new String(defectId +
            " is not a valid defect.");

    }

    return retval;

}
```

Formatting the defect into HTML is implemented internally. This is pretty much grunt work here, but there are better ways to do this - it would be a great place to get the defect as XML using the `DefectIntf.exportToXML()` method, and use XSL to format it to HTML. There are tools that are freely available to do this parsing and transformation - see IBM AlphaWorks (www.alphaworks.ibm.com) for some really effective tools.

```
String OutputAsHTML(String defectId)
{
    DefectIntf theDefect;
    int n;

    String retval = new String("");

    retval = retval.concat(
                "<html><head><title>Defect Report</title></head>");
    retval = retval.concat("<body><h1>BugTracker Defect Report</h1>");
    retval = retval.concat("<hr><p>");
    try
    {
        int id = Integer.parseInt(defectId);
        theDefect = m_DefectFactory.getDefect(id);

        retval = retval.concat("<b>Defect ID:</b>" +
            theDefect.getDefectID() + "<br>");

        retval = retval.concat("<b>Defect Status:</b> " +
            DefectState.stateNames[theDefect.getState()] + "<br>");
```

```
            retval = retval.concat("<b>Date Reported:</b> " +
                apputil.util.LongToDateString(theDefect.getDateReported())
                "<br>");

            retval = retval.concat("<b>Defect Summary:</b> " +
                theDefect.getDefectSummary() + "<br>");

            retval = retval.concat("<b>Defect Details:</b><pre> " +
                theDefect.getDefectDetails() + "</pre>");

            retval = retval.concat("<b>Date of last action:</b> " +
                apputil.util.LongToDateString(theDefect.getDateLastChanged())
                + "<br>");
        }
        catch(NumberFormatException numfe)
        {
            retval = retval.concat("<b>" + defectId +
                " is not a properly formatted defect id.<b>");
        }

        catch(NotFoundException nfe)
        {
            retval = retval.concat(defectId +
                " is not a valid defect.");
        }

        retval = retval.concat("</body></html>");
        return retval;
    }
}
```

All that's left is to define the `BadInformationException` class that we've been using all the way through, and we're done.

```
class BadInformationException extends Exception
{
    public BadInformationException()
    {
        super();
    }

    public BadInformationException(String s)
    {
        super(s);
    }
}
```

Building BugTracker

> Please note the requirements for building BugTracker at the start of the Construction section.

Make files are provided with the downloadable source for Bug Tracker. Remember to change directories to the code subdirectory under the directory in which you have installed the source.

Execute your make utility from that directory. The top level `Makefile` will iterate through the code directories, each of which contain a subordinate `Makefile`.

Note: the top level `Makefile` uses a Make macro to define the make utility name. That macro, as distributed with the source, uses Microsoft's `nmake`. If you want to use a different utility, simply edit the `Makefile` in the code directory and redefine the macro.

After the Bug Tracker components are built, you will need to set up the runtime options and the data source. The next section provides step-by-step instructions for completing the setup and running Bug Tracker.

Transition Phase

The objective of the transition phase is to deploy the software and provide the training necessary for the end user to effectively employ it. As such, the final step for the Bug Tracker is to go through the process of configuring and running the executable components of the application.

Configuring Runtime Options

The application code is in the `code/BugTrackerApp` subdirectory. In that directory, you'll find a file called `BUGTRACKER.PROPS`. This file contains the following properties that define how the Bug Tracker runs:

```
jdbcdriver = sun.jdbc.odbc.JdbcOdbcDriver
jdbcurl = jdbc:odbc:bug_tracker
jdbcuser = guest
jdbcpass = guest
smtphost = zorak.javasilo.com
servicename = BugTrackerService
agentemailaddress = bugtracker@javasilo.com
```

This file is loaded by the `AppConfig` class and used throughout the system to establish runtime properties, as discussed earlier. To change these settings, simply open the file in a text editor, alter the values, and save the file.

These settings are, for the most part, pretty universal and straightforward. You may want to change a few things, however, based on your system configuration. One thing that you will likely want to change is the `smtphost` property. This is the host name of an SMTP daemon that the bug tracker uses to send defect change notifications.

The `agentemailaddress` is a related field that identifies the mail user (or pseudouser) that will show up in automatically sent mail as the reply-to address. You might want to set this value to someone who is responsible for handling queries sent from people receiving defect update reports, or an appropriate mail alias.

Configuring and Building the Database

This properties file also provides fields for parameters specific to JDBC. These values are used to connect to a datasource to provide persistence for Bug Tracker data. If you will be using the Microsoft Access database provided with the Bug Tracker download, these values will work just fine. If you will be creating the Bug Tracker database on a different data source, you will need to make some changes to the properties file. Modify the first four fields in the properties file to correctly reflect the appropriate JDBC driver, the JDBC URL that points to the data source, and an appropriate user name and password for that data source.

> Note: This section describes setting up an ODBC data source and accessing a database through the JDBC/ODBC bridge. If you are running an operating system besides Windows, you will need to obtain the appropriate JDBC drivers for your database server, and create a database. The source code included with the Bug Tracker distribution includes scripts for populating both an Access database and an mSQL database; you can edit these scripts and adjust them as needed to work with your data source.

Assuming that you'll use the Access `.mdb` file that's included in the source archive and the JDBC/ODBC bridge, you'll want to set up an ODBC data source called "`bug_tracker`" (its name has to match the last part of the `jdbcurl` property in the properties file above). Open the **ODBC Data Source Administrator** window by selecting the **ODBC Data Sources** in the Windows Control Panel. Select the **System DNS** tab at the top of the dialog box and click on the **Add...** button on the right. In the list box that comes up, select **Microsoft Access Driver (*.mdb)** and click on **Finish**. The **ODBC Microsoft Access Setup** dialog box will appear. In the **Data Source Name** prompt, type in `bug_tracker`. Under the **Database** section, click on the **Select** button, and select the `bug_tracker.mdb` file in the data directory where you installed the Bug Tracker source. Click **OK** to close the file dialog, and then click **OK** to close the ODBC setup dialog. You should now see the `bug_tracker` data source listed in the **ODBC Data Source Administrator** window.

Next, use the `build_tables` utility to populate the database. This utility is located in the `code\build_tables` subdirectory where you installed the Bug Tracker source files. It is driven by scripts that contain the JDBC driver information and a sequence of SQL statements that create the tables and populate them. The `buildbugtracker_access.sql` script – no great surprise – contains the script for populating the Access database. There are a couple of other scripts for Sybase and mSQL; you may find these useful if you choose to host the Bug Tracker data on either of these databases. Thanks to JDBC, the Bug Tracker application doesn't mind which database is used for persistence.

From your command line, change directories to the `code\build_tables` subdirectory where you installed the Bug Tracker source files. Run the `build_tables` utility, specifying the script as the single command line parameter:

```
java build_tables buildbugtracker_access.sql
```

If all goes well, you'll see a series of dots march across the screen as each SQL statement is executed. Any errors will be displayed on the screen.

Running BugTracker

Because the Bug Tracker consists of separate components that can (but don't have to) run on separate computers, starting up the Bug Tracker is a bit more complicated than most desktop applications. There are three steps:

- ➤ Start the name service
- ➤ Start the defect server
- ➤ Start the client

The steps outlined below assume that the name service, the defect server and the defect client all reside on the same machine. Instructions for running Bug Tracker components on separate machines follow later.

Starting the Name Service

CORBA can pass object references across the network by creating a string of bytes called an "interoperable object reference," or IOR. The IOR is an encoded sequence that contains information about the type of object it references, where it is located, and additional information that allows the object's owning host to identify the object. A typical IOR will look something like this:

```
000000000000002849444c3a6f6d672e6f72672f436f734e616d696e672f4e616d696e6743f6e7465
78743a312e30000000000010000000000000034000100000000000b737061636567686f7370000043d0
00000000018afabcafe000000029a062ea100000008000000000000000
```

The IOR really is a magic cookie – it can be used by any ORB to identify and work with an object (assuming that the IOR is valid and the referenced object is still around). That power comes at a price, though. Clearly you can see that the IOR is not exactly user friendly. The name service, however, makes it easier to obtain object references without having to deal with long, ugly strings of bytes.

The name service is a standard CORBA service. It is essentially an online directory that associates CORBA object references with names. This allows the Bug Tracker components to create objects, register them by name with the name service, and to look up object references by commonly known names.

The JDK 1.2 ORB implementation provides a very simple naming service that will serve our needs quite nicely. Because the name service is used by the server and the clients alike, this component must be started first. To start the name service, run the `tnameserv` executable provided with the JDK:

```
tnameserv
```

When it's done initializing and is ready, you'll see a message displaying the name service's IOR and the message:

```
TransientNameServer: setting port for initial object references to: 900
```

Documentation on `tnameserv` is provided with the JavaIDL documentation.

Running the BugTracker Server

Now you're ready to run Bug Tracker. From the command line, change directories to the code\BugTrackerApp subdirectory where you installed the Bug Tracker source. Start the DefectServer in a new shell with the command:

```
start java businesslogic.DefectServer
```

The DefectServer will display diagnostic startup information as it initializes. It displays the IORs for its primary services, indicates that it is registering itself with the name service, and finally indicates when it is ready and listening:

```
java businesslogic.DefectServer {<configfile> <orb opt 1> .... <orb opt n>}
Created policy object as IOR:00000000000000002749444c3a627573696e6573736c6f6769632
f446566656374506f6c696379496e74663a312e30000000000000010000000000000034000100000000
0000b737061636567686f73740000043f000000000018afabcafe000000029a06d78b00000008000
0000000000000
Created defect factory object as IOR:00000000000000002849444c3a627573696e6573736c6
f6769632f446566656374466163746f7279496e74663a312e3000000000000010000000000000034000
100000000000b737061636567686f73740000043f000000000018afabcafe000000029a06d78b000
00000800000000100000000
Created user factory object as IOR:00000000000000002649444c3a627573696e6573736c6f6
769632f55736572466163746f7279496e74663a312e300000000000000001000000000000000034000100
0000000000b737061636567686f73740000043f000000000018afabcafe000000029a06d78b00000
0080000000200000000
Created server object as IOR:00000000000000002749444c3a627573696e6573736c6f6769632
f446566656374536572766572496e74663a312e30000000000000010000000000000034000100000000
0000b737061636567686f73740000043f000000000018afabcafe000000029a06d78b00000008000
0000300000000
Registering servers with naming service...
Ready.
```

Note: If you are experimenting with different databases and configurations, you may find it convenient to have multiple runtime properties configuration files. You can specify the properties file to use on the DefectServer command line:

```
java businesslogic.DefectServer mynewprops.prop
```

Running the BugTracker Client Application

Once the DefectServer has been started and is ready, you're ready to run the standalone UI. From the command line, change directories to the code\BugTrackerApp subdirectory where you installed the Bug Tracker source. Start the DefectForm application with the command:

```
java ui.DefectForm
```

If all goes well, you'll see the UI pop up (this can take a few seconds, or more than a few, depending on your machine):

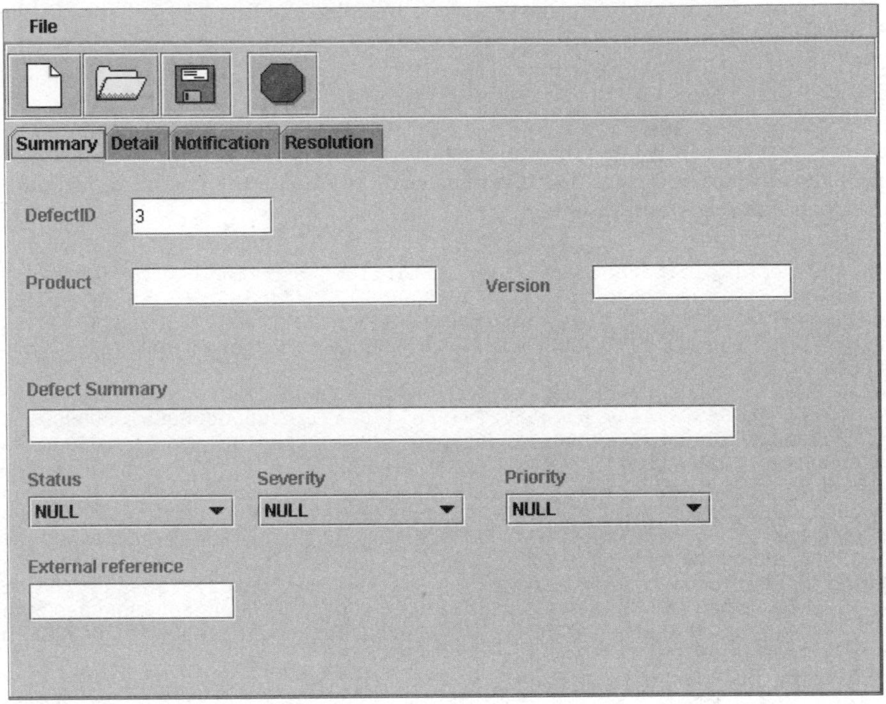

Test the application. Click on File/Open Defect (or click on the open folder button in the toolbar). An entry box will pop up and prompt you for a defect number. Enter "1" and click ok. You should see a defect read into the form.

Distributed BugTracker

It's a reasonably simple matter to run the Bug Tracker components on separate machines. The only requirement is to let the server and client components know where to find the name server.

By default, the client and server components assume that the name server is running on the local machine on the default port (port 900 for the JavaIDL name service). The command lines for both `DefectServer` and `DefectForm`, however, will accept command line parameters to identify where the Name Service can be found. The full command line format is:

```
java { DefectServer | DefectForm } ( [config file name]
        (-ORBInitialHost [name service hostname])
        (-ORBInitialPort [name service port]) )
```

where

`config file name`	identifies the properties file that specifies the runtime options bug tracker
`name service host`	identifies the host name where the name service is running; assumes localhost by default
`name service port`	identifies the port that the name service is listening on; assumes 900 by default

For example, suppose that the name service is running on the machine moltar.javasilo.com on port 4242.

To start `DefectServer`, type the following (all on a single command line):

```
java businesslogic.DefectServer BUGTRACKER.PROPS -ORBInitialHost
            moltar.javasilo.com -ORBInitialPort 4242
```

The `DefectForm` client application is started in a similar manner:

```
java ui.DefectForm BUGTRACKER.PROPS -ORBInitialHost
            moltar.javasilo.com -ORBInitialPort 4242
```

Note that if the command line parameters are used, the properties file must be specified as the first parameter.

Running the Web Client

The Bug Tracker provides a Web-based front end for the `DefectServer` that uses a Java servlet as a proxy. In order to use the Web client, first ensure that the name service and the `DefectServer` process are started as described in the previous section.

The simplest way to test the servlet and Web client is to use the `ServletRunner` utility. From the command line, change directories to the `code\BugTrackerApp\www` subdirectory where you installed the Bug Tracker source. In this directory, there is a file named `servlet.properties`. This contains the servlet registration information and the startup parameters. If you're not going to use ServletRunner and want to host the servlet on a servlet-compatible Web server such as JWS, you'll need to move the servlet and the `.html` files to the appropriate directories, register the servlet with the server and set up the startup parameters that are included in `servlet.properties` - see appendices F through H for details on how to do this with several popular web servers.

Start ServletRunner with the command line options for the port, servlet directory, servlet properties file, and document directory (all on a single command line):

```
ServletRunner -p 80 -d [installation dir]\code\bugtrackerapp\www
        -s [installation dir]\code\bugtrackerapp\www\servlet.properties
        -r [installation dir]\code\bugtrackerapp\www
```

In order to make testing a bit easier, there is a batch file called `servtest.bat` in the `code\bugtrackerapp\www` directory. Edit this file and change the working directory information to match your installation, and run servtest from the `code\BugTrackerApp\www` directory

Test the servlet with the browser-based "find a defect" form. From your web browser, open the file `code\BugTrackerApp\wwww\finddefect.html`. Type "1" at the Defect ID field, check the "HTML" box and click the "find it" button.

Conclusion

This has been a whirlwind tour of planning and building a distributed Java application. If you didn't download the code and examine it during the construction section, I'd encourage you to do so. With this quick of a survey, there have to be missing explanations, but you're bound to find the truth in the code.

The Bug Tracker app is a real, working application that you can continue to expand upon, or use the patterns and idioms of the Bug Tracker to build a different type of application. Some things you may care to add include

- Implementing a task list in the Defect Form that shows the defects that are assigned to the logged-in user.
- Providing a search interface to aid the Quality Engineers with matching duplicate bugs.
- Implementing XML/XSL or XML/CSS production of the HTML bug report.
- Building a statistics processing client to generate bug progress reports for different software projects.

Moving from CGI to Servlets

Overview

By now, you should have a pretty good idea of how easy it is to write a servlet and the benefits of servlets, but what are you going to do about all of those existing CGI scripts that you have? Can you do all of the same things in Java that you did in your CGI scripts? You bet. This chapter will address some of the common functions that exist in a large number of CGI scripts today. After getting through this chapter, you'll see that your task of converting your CGI scripts to Java shouldn't be that bad after all.

This chapter will cover the following:

> Discuss environment variables and show the methods used to access them.

> Revisit cookies and how to use them with your servlets.

> Develop a simple shopping cart servlet using cookies to track a customer's order.

> Give an overview of Perl-style 'regular expressions' and how they can be used in Java.

Retrieving Environment Variables

In CGI scripts, you were able to access information about the client by referencing CGI environment variables. Java is no different. In Java, this information is accessed through the request object using methods from the `HttpServletRequest` interface. For just about every CGI environment variable, there exists a corresponding method to access the same information from within a Java servlet (see table below).

CGI Variable	Java Method (`HttpServletRequest`)
SERVER_NAME	getServerName()
SERVER_PROTOCOL	getProtocol()
SERVER_PORT	getServerPort()
REQUEST_METHOD	getMethod()
PATH_INFO	getPathInfo()
PATH_TRANSLATED	getPathTranslated()
SCRIPT_NAME	getServletPath()
QUERY_STRING	getQueryString()
REMOTE_HOST	getRemoteHost()
REMOTE_ADDR	getRemoteAddr()
REMOTE_USER	getRemoteUser()
AUTH_TYPE	getAuthType()
CONTENT_TYPE	getContentType()
CONTENT_LENGTH	getContentLength()
HTTP_ACCEPT	getHeader("Accept")
HTTP_USER_AGENT	getHeader("User-Agent")
HTTP_REFERER	getHeader("Referer")

CGI variables NOT implemented in Java:

➤ SERVER_SOFTWARE
➤ GATEWAY_INTERFACE
➤ REMOTE_IDENT

Example – Environment Variables

This next example will simply display all of the CGI environment variable names and current values. It is important to note that the REMOTE_USER variable will contain valid data only when the user has authenticated himself or herself with the server. Also, some servlet environments may not maintain a valid set of environment variables. The figure following the code listing below is the result of running this example using the JSDK servlet runner. It doesn't report the REMOTE_USER environment variable since there was no user authentication involved.

```
import javax.servlet.*;
import javax.servlet.http.*;

import java.io.*;

import com.wrox.util.*;

/* Retrieves and echoes the available environment */
/* variables found in the request object.        */

public class Env extends HttpServlet
{

    public void doGet(HttpServletRequest req, HttpServletResponse res)
    throws ServletException, IOException
    {

    /* Set content type and create a new PrintWriter */
    res.setContentType("text/html");
    PrintWriter out = res.getWriter();

    /* Create a new HTML object to build response page */
    HTML h = new HTML("Environment Variables");
    h.add(HTML.HEADING, "Environment Variables", true);

    /* Add each individual element separately for efficiency */
    h.add(HTML.NORMAL, "SERVER_NAME: ", false);
    h.add(HTML.NORMAL, req.getServerName(), true);
    h.add(HTML.NORMAL, "SERVER_PROTOCOL: ", false);
    h.add(HTML.NORMAL, req.getProtocol(), true);
    h.add(HTML.NORMAL, "SERVER_PORT: ", false);
    h.add(HTML.NORMAL, Integer.toString(req.getServerPort()), true);
    h.add(HTML.NORMAL, "REQUEST_METHOD: ", false);
    h.add(HTML.NORMAL, req.getMethod(), true);
    h.add(HTML.NORMAL, "PATH_INFO: ", false);
    h.add(HTML.NORMAL, req.getPathInfo(), true);
    h.add(HTML.NORMAL, "PATH_TRANSLATED: ", false);
    h.add(HTML.NORMAL, req.getPathTranslated(), true);
    h.add(HTML.NORMAL, "SCRIPT_NAME: ", false);
    h.add(HTML.NORMAL, req.getServletPath(), true);
    h.add(HTML.NORMAL, "QUERY_STRING: ", false);
    h.add(HTML.NORMAL, req.getQueryString(), true);
    h.add(HTML.NORMAL, "REMOTE_HOST: ", false);
    h.add(HTML.NORMAL, req.getRemoteHost(), true);
    h.add(HTML.NORMAL, "REMOTE_ADDR: ", false);
    h.add(HTML.NORMAL, req.getRemoteAddr(), true);
    h.add(HTML.NORMAL, "REMOTE_USER: ", false);
    h.add(HTML.NORMAL, req.getRemoteUser(), true);
    h.add(HTML.NORMAL, "AUTH_TYPE: ", false);
```

Continued on Following Page

447

```
        h.add(HTML.NORMAL, req.getAuthType(), true);
        h.add(HTML.NORMAL, "CONTENT_TYPE: ", false);
        h.add(HTML.NORMAL, req.getContentType(), true);
        h.add(HTML.NORMAL, "CONTENT_LENGTH: ", false);
        h.add(HTML.NORMAL, Integer.toString(req.getContentLength()), true);
        h.add(HTML.NORMAL, "HTTP_ACCEPT: ", false);
        h.add(HTML.NORMAL, req.getHeader("Accept"), true);
        h.add(HTML.NORMAL, "HTTP_USER_AGENT: ", false);
        h.add(HTML.NORMAL, req.getHeader("User-Agent"), true);
        h.add(HTML.NORMAL, "HTTP_REFERER: ", false);
        h.add(HTML.NORMAL, req.getHeader("Referer"), true);

        /* Output page and close the PrintWriter */
        out.println(h.getPage());
        out.close();
    }

}
```

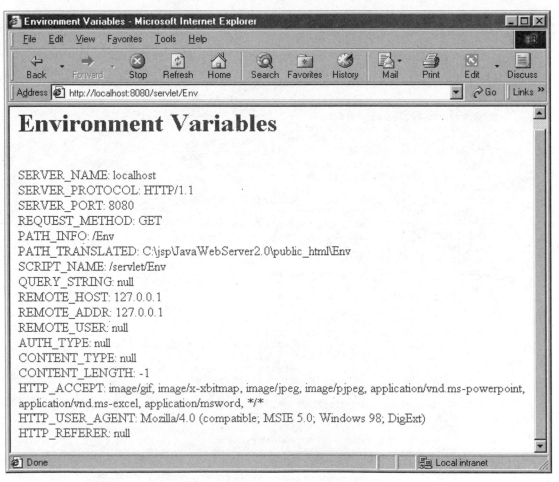

Using Cookies

Another common element of many CGI scripts is the cookie. A cookie is essentially a small text file that can be stored locally on a user's hard drive. Cookies originate from a program, or script, running on a web server. When the web browser starts up, these cookies are loaded into memory. Whenever the browser makes a request to a web server, it sends along all of its cookies with the request. A script on the web server can then search through the cookies that were sent with the request, find the one it needs, and proceed accordingly (See figure below).

Cookies are used for many different things. Web sites can make use of cookies to store user preferences for the site. Whenever a user comes back to a particular site, the web server processes the cookie and the appropriate personalized content is sent back to the user. Another common way that cookies are used is to keep track of items a user would like to purchase as part of a 'shopping cart' program. The user selects particular items to be purchased while browsing through an online catalog. When an item is selected, a cookie is placed on their machine. When it comes time for the user to 'check out' and pay for everything they are ordering, the cookies are collected and the entire order is processed.

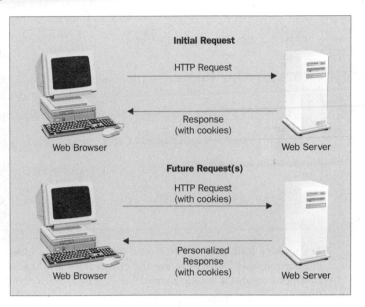

Processing Cookies with Java

To create a cookie in Java, you use the `javax.servlet.http.Cookie` class. This class is responsible for creating a cookie and setting its properties. The following table lists the methods that can be used with the `Cookie` class (as listed in the Java Servlet API 2.1 Specification).

Method Signature	Description
`public Cookie(String name, String value);`	Constructor. Creates a new Cookie object with the given name-value pair.
`public String getDomain();`	Returns the domain of the Cookie.
`public void setDomain(String _domain);`	Sets the domain of the Cookie.
`public int getMaxAge();`	Returns the maximum age of the Cookie.

Table Continued on Following Page

Method Signature	Description
`public void setMaxAge(int _expir);`	Sets the maximum age of the Cookie (in seconds).
`public String getName();`	Returns the name of the Cookie.
`public String getPath();`	Returns the prefix of all of the URL's for which the Cookie is valid.
`public void setPath(String _uri);`	Sets the path of the Cookie.
`public boolean getSecure();`	Returns true if the Cookie can only be transmitted over secure channels.
`public void setSecure(boolean _flag);`	Determines if the Cookie should be sent over secure channels only.
`public String getValue();`	Returns the value of the Cookie.
`public void setValue(String _val);`	Sets a new value for the Cookie.
`public int getVersion();`	Returns the version of the Cookie. New Cookies default to 0.
`Public void setVersion(int _ver);`	Sets the version to either 0 (default) or 1 (complies with RFC 2109).

Let's take a look at how you would use the `Cookie` class in your Java programs. The main things to concern yourself with here are the constructor and the `setMaxAge()` method. The following code fragment creates a cookie named "abc_pref" with a value of "frames=no" that is set to expire in 2 days.

```
Cookie x = new Cookie("abc_pref", "frames=no");
x.setMaxAge(2*60*60*24);  //2 days (expressed in seconds)
```

Once the cookie has been created, it has to be sent back to the browser. We do this by adding it to the response stream. Using the `HttpServletResponse` interface's `addCookie()` method, we attach the cookie to the response header that is sent back to the browser. The browser then writes the cookie to disk. The following code fragment adds our previously declared cookie to the response stream:

```
response.addCookie(x);
```

Example – Creating a Shopping Cart with Cookies

As previously mentioned, a shopping cart application is a popular use of cookies. The general idea is that the customer selects items to purchase from an online catalog. When customers have finished selecting items, they are ready to 'check out' and pay for their order. The following is a somewhat incomplete example of a shopping cart application, but it should give you a good idea about how to use cookies to exchange session information between a customer and the server. All of the processing takes place in a single servlet. The `doGet()` method returns a listing of the current contents of the cart while the `doPost()` method adds items to the cart.

Shopping Cart Interface

Our interface is going to consist of a list of catalog items and a button to add selected items to the cart. There is also a link for the customer to view the items currently in the cart. The button issues a POST request to the servlet while the link will simply issue a GET request by default. Normally, this online catalog would be dynamically generated from a database. For our purposes, we will simply hardcode the catalog items as a sku#, description, and price. The hidden field is used to pass the price on to our servlet.

```html
<HTML>
<HEAD>
     <TITLE>ACP Sporting Goods - Online Store</TITLE>
</HEAD>
<BODY>
<CENTER><H1>Catalog of Online Items</H1></CENTER>
<HR>
<FORM ACTION="http://localhost:8080/servlet/Cart" METHOD="POST">
<TABLE CELLSPACING="5" CELLPADDING="5">
<TR>
    <TD ALIGN="center"><B>Add to Cart</B></TD>
    <TD ALIGN="center"></TD>
    <TD ALIGN="center"></TD>
</TR>
<TR>
    <TD ALIGN="center"><INPUT TYPE="Checkbox" NAME="item_a" VALUE="sku_100"></TD>
    <TD ALIGN="left">Premium Graphite Tennis Raquet (Oversize)</TD>
    <TD ALIGN="left">$129.99<INPUT TYPE="Hidden"
           NAME="p_sku_100" VALUE="129.99"></TD>
</TR>
<TR>
    <TD ALIGN="center"><INPUT TYPE="Checkbox" NAME="item_b" VALUE="sku_200"></TD>
    <TD ALIGN="left">300lb Olympic Weightset</TD>
    <TD ALIGN="left">$119.99<INPUT TYPE="Hidden"
           NAME="p_sku_200" VALUE="119.99"></TD>
</TR>
<TR>
    <TD ALIGN="center"><INPUT TYPE="Checkbox" NAME="item_c" VALUE="sku_300"></TD>
    <TD ALIGN="left">10 - 12 Person Deluxe Cabin Tent</TD>
    <TD ALIGN="left">$239.99<INPUT TYPE="Hidden"
           NAME="p_sku_300" VALUE="239.99"></TD>
</TR>
</TABLE>
<HR><BR>
<CENTER>
<INPUT TYPE="Submit" NAME="btn_submit" VALUE="Submit"><BR><BR>
<A HREF="http://localhost:8080/servlet/Cart">View items currently in cart...</A>
</CENTER>
</FORM>
</BODY>
</HTML>
```

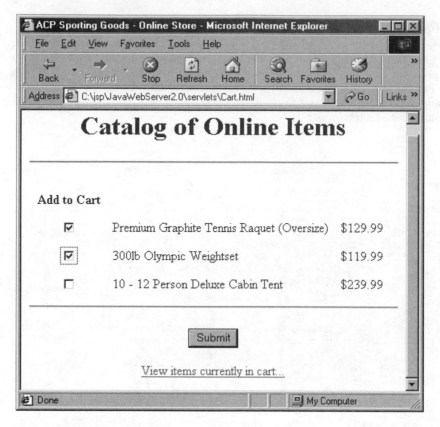

Adding Items to the Shopping Cart

When a user presses the 'Submit' button, the form data is sent to the servlet for processing. Its main job is to determine which items were selected, create a cookie for each one, and send them back to the browser via the response object. When we are finished, we send a redirect to the browser to issue a GET request to the servlet. This will display the items currently selected for purchase. We couldn't have simply called the doGet() method since the cookies were still part of the response object and have not yet been picked up in the request object. That is why we need to issue a redirect: So that the cookies can be dropped off and then picked up again for use in the doGet() method.

Here's what the doPost() method looks like:

```java
public void doPost(HttpServletRequest req, HttpServletResponse res)
    throws ServletException, IOException
    {

    res.setContentType("text/html");
    Cookie c = new Cookie("null", "null");

    /* Retrieve Form Data */
    Enumeration keys;
    String key, value;
    keys = req.getParameterNames();
      while (keys.hasMoreElements())
      {
      key = (String)keys.nextElement();
      value = req.getParameter(key);
        if (value.substring(0,3).equals("sku"))
        {
          if (value.equals("sku_100"))
          {
          c = new Cookie(value,
          "Premium Graphite Tennis Racquet (Oversize) - " +
          req.getParameter("p_sku_100"));
          }
          if (value.equals("sku_200"))
          {
          c = new Cookie(value, "300lb Olympic Weightset - " +
          req.getParameter("p_sku_200"));
          }
          if (value.equals("sku_300"))
          {
          c = new Cookie(value, "10 - 12 Person Deluxe Cabin Tent - " +
          req.getParameter("p_sku_300"));
          }
          c.setMaxAge(2*24*60*60);    //Expires in 2 days
        res.addCookie(c);
        }
      }

    /* Send a redirect to send the cookies and return
       a GET request to view the items in the cart */
    res.sendRedirect("http://localhost:8080/servlet/Cart");

    }
```

Viewing the Items in the Shopping Cart

When users click the hyperlink at the bottom to view the contents of the shopping cart, they are issuing a GET request that is processed in the doGet method of the servlet. To find the cookies relating to our shopping cart, we first execute the getCookies method of the request object. This will return an array of Cookie objects. All of the cookies that the browser has sent will be included in this array. To pick out our cookies from the bunch, we cycle through the array and check the first part of the cookie name. If it starts with "sku", then we go ahead and use the getName and getValue methods of the cookie to display the catalog item.

Here's what the `doGet()` method looks like:

```java
public void doGet(HttpServletRequest req, HttpServletResponse res)
   throws ServletException, IOException
   {

   res.setContentType("text/html");
   PrintWriter out = res.getWriter();

   HTML h = new HTML("Contents of your shopping cart");
   h.add(HTML.HEADING, "Your Shopping Cart Contains...", false);
   h.add(HTML.LINE, "", true);

   /* Read in Cookies */
   Cookie cookies[];

   cookies = req.getCookies();
      if (cookies != null)
      {
         for (int i = 0; i < cookies.length; i++)
         {
            if (cookies[i].getName().startsWith("sku"))
            {
            h.add(HTML.NORMAL, cookies[i].getName(), false);
            h.add(HTML.NORMAL, " : ", false);
            h.add(HTML.NORMAL, cookies[i].getValue(), true);
            h.add(HTML.NORMAL, "", true); //Extra Line Break
            }
         }
      }

   out.println(h.getPage());
   out.close();
   }
```

Here is the full listing for the cart class:

```java
import javax.servlet.*;
import javax.servlet.http.*;

import java.io.*;
import java.util.*;

import com.wrox.util.*;

public class Cart extends HttpServlet
{

  /* View items in shopping cart */
  public void doGet(HttpServletRequest req, HttpServletResponse res)
   throws ServletException, IOException
   {

   res.setContentType("text/html");
   PrintWriter out = res.getWriter();

   HTML h = new HTML("Contents of your shopping cart");
   h.add(HTML.HEADING, "Your Shopping Cart Contains...", false);
   h.add(HTML.LINE, "", true);
```

```
/* Read in Cookies */
Cookie cookies[];

cookies = req.getCookies();
   if (cookies != null)
   {
      for (int i = 0; i < cookies.length; i++)
      {
         if (cookies[i].getName().startsWith("sku"))
         {
         h.add(HTML.NORMAL, cookies[i].getName(), false);
         h.add(HTML.NORMAL, " : ", false);
         h.add(HTML.NORMAL, cookies[i].getValue(), true);
         h.add(HTML.NORMAL, "", true); //Extra Line Break
         }
      }
   }

  out.println(h.getPage());
  out.close();
  }

/* Edit items in shopping cart */
public void doPost(HttpServletRequest req, HttpServletResponse res)
 throws ServletException, IOException
 {

  res.setContentType("text/html");
  Cookie c = new Cookie("null", "null");

  /* Retrieve Form Data */
  Enumeration keys;
  String key, value;
  keys = req.getParameterNames();
  while (keys.hasMoreElements()) {
    key = (String)keys.nextElement();
    value = req.getParameter(key);
    if (value.substring(0,3).equals("sku"))
    {
       if (value.equals("sku_100"))
       {
        c = new Cookie(value,
           "Premium Graphite Tennis Raquet (Oversize) - " +
           req.getParameter("p_sku_100"));
       }
       if (value.equals("sku_200"))
       {
        c = new Cookie(value, "300lb Olympic Weightset - " +
        req.getParameter("p_sku_200"));
       }
       if (value.equals("sku_300"))
       {
    c = new Cookie(value, "10 - 12 Person Deluxe Cabin Tent - " +
    req.getParameter("p_sku_300"));
       }
     c.setMaxAge(2*24*60*60);    //Expires in 2 days
     res.addCookie(c);
    }
 }
```

Continued on Following Page

```
    /* Send a redirect to send the cookies and return
       a GET request to view the items in the cart */
    res.sendRedirect("http://localhost:8080/servlet/Cart");

  }
}
```

Contents of your shopping cart - Microsoft Internet Explorer

File Edit View Go Favorites Help

Back Forward Stop Refresh Home Search Favorites History Channels Fullscreen

Address http://localhost:8080/servlet/cart   Links

Your Shopping Cart Contains...

sku_200 : 300lb Olympic Weightset - 119.99

sku_100 : Premium Graphite Tennis Raquet (Oversize) - 129.99

Done   Local intranet zone

Note that this example allows you to "add" items to your shopping cart but not "remove" ones you have already added. This means that once you have checked one of the three items and submitted it, you cannot remove it from your shopping cart. The setting of the age of the cookies ensures that once checked and submitted, an item will stay in your shopping cart for two days.

Regular Expressions

One of the really useful things about the CGI scripting languages, particularly Perl, is the ability to parse text using something called 'regular expressions'. To the untrained eye, these regular expressions are sure to look like some kind of gibberish. To those of us who are more familiar with them, however, they present a very useful way to parse out and edit string expressions. To learn more about regular expressions, you can find some tutorials listed on the www.perl.com web site that are very good. If you have access to a Unix or Linux machine, try typing 'man perlre' to view the Perl manpage for regular expressions.

If you wish to carry this functionality over to Java, you have a few different options to consider. First, you could write your own regular expression compiler. This is what a few people have already done, and made available for the rest of us to download and use free of charge. Rather than reinventing the wheel, this is what I would suggest that you do. If you happen to be using Sun's Java Web Server, however, you have one more option. At the request of several developers, Sun has incorporated a regular expression package into the 1.1 release of the Java Web Server. You can find these classes in the `jws.jar` file in the `com.sun.server.util.regexp` package.

Using Regular Expressions in Java

For the purposes of this discussion, we'll be using the `com.sun.server.util.regexp` package that is included with the Java Web Server. These same techniques demonstrated here can be carried over to different regular expression packages with very little modification. The following examples were all created as command line applications but can also be used just the same within Java servlets as you'll see in the example following this section.

Creating a New Regular Expression Object

Before working with regular expressions, be sure to add the `com.sun.server.util.regexp` package (or `jws.jar`) to your classpath and add an import statement to your source file.

```
import com.sun.server.util.regexp.*;
```

The class you will need to perform regular expression operations is called RE. To create a new RE object, just create a new object of type RE and pass in a string containing a regular expression.

```
RE r = new RE("a(.*)b");
```

Now that you have a regular expression object created, you can proceed to use any one of the following methods. When creating and using regular expressions, you will need to enclose your code in a try-catch block and catch the RESyntaxException.

Setting Match Flags

When performing regular expression operations, there are a few flags that can be set that can affect the outcome of the operation. These flags are set using the setMatchFlags() method of the RE class. The possible flag values are MATCH_NORMAL(default), MATCH_CASEINDEPENDENT, or MATCH_MULTILINE. These values are actually just integer constants and translate into 0, 1, and 2 respectively. The following code causes the regular expression to be evaluated regardless of the case of the expression.

```
RE r = new RE("x(.*)b");
r.setMatchFlags(1);          // Case Independent
```

Performing Simple Pattern Matching

To find out if a particular string contains a particular string pattern, you can use the match() method of the RE class. Once you have your regular expression object created, you would simply call the match() method and pass into it the string you wish to have searched. The following example will successfully match the regular expression "wor" with the string "Hello World!".

```
import com.sun.server.util.regexp.*;

public class Re_match
{

    public static void main(String args[])
    {

        try
        {
        RE r = new RE("wor");
        r.setMatchFlags(1);
            if (r.match("HelloWorld!"))
            {
            System.out.println("Hello World!");
            }
        }
        catch (RESyntaxException e)
        {
        System.out.println("Error processing regular expression");
        }
    }
}
```

Using the Results of Parenthesized Expressions

Sometimes, when working with regular expressions, you need to extract a certain pattern of characters from a particular string. This is done by putting parentheses around a particular expression within a regular expression. For example, to get "nn" out of "xxannbcc", you would use a regular expression that looks like "a(.*)b". Now, the only thing left to figure out is how to access our newly derived substring. In Perl, you would simply reference it with $1. In Java, it's a little bit different.

To access a value that is the result of a regular expression, we use the getParen() method of the RE class. Each expression can return zero or more values depending on how many sets of parenthesis are included in the string. To obtain all of the values, we loop through and retrieve all of them based on the value of getParenCount(). This will tell us how many values exist.

The following code will produce 2 values – "annb" and "nn". Our desired result is "nn". So, an important lesson is learned here. The first value returned from an expression includes the outer characters while the second one gives us what we want.

```
import com.sun.server.util.regexp.*;

public class Paren
{
    public static void main(String args[])
    {

        try
        {
        RE r = new RE("a(.*)b");
        r.setMatchFlags(1);                          //Ignore Case
            if (r.match("xxannbcc"))
            {
            int i = r.getParenCount();
                for (int x = 0; x < i; x++)
                {
                System.out.println(r.getParen(x));
                }
            }
            else
            {
            System.out.println("No values returned.");
            }
        }
        catch (RESyntaxException e)
        {
        System.out.println("Syntax Error");
        System.out.println(e.toString());
        }
    }
}
```

Splitting Text Using the split() Method

There are many occurrences where it would make sense to break up a string based on a single delimiter and store the results in an array. For instance, you might be parsing a comma delimited input file and would like to be able to store each 'field' of the file into an array. The split() method allows you to do this using just a single line of code.

To use the `split()` method, first create your regular expression with the pattern you wish to split the string on. Then, call the `split()` method and pass it the input string as a parameter. The result will be in the form of a String array. The following code will produce a String array containing {"a","b","c","d"}.

```java
import com.sun.server.util.regexp.*;

public class Split
{
   public static void main(String args[])
   {
     try
     {
     RE r = new RE(",");
     r.setMatchFlags(1);                      //Ignore Case
     String elem[] = r.split("a,b,c,d");
         for (int i = 0; i < elem.length; i++)
         {
         System.out.println("Element: " + i + " - " + elem[i]);
         }
     }
     catch (RESyntaxException e)
     {
     System.out.println("Syntax Error");
     System.out.println(e.toString());
     }
   }
}
```

Substituting Characters With the subst() Method

The final regular expression operation we'll be discussing is that of substituting characters from one string with those of another string. To do this in Java, we first create a regular expression using the pattern that we will be matching and substituting. Then, we call the `subst()` method passing it our target string and a substitution string as parameters. The following code will replace all occurrences of "ab" in the string "xxabxxabxx" with "nn". Our resulting string should read "xxnnxxnnxx".

```java
import com.sun.server.util.regexp.*;

public class Subst
{
   public static void main(String args[])
   {
     try
     {
     RE r = new RE("ab");
     r.setMatchFlags(1);                      //Ignore Case
     String newString = r.subst("xxabxxabxx", "nn");
     System.out.println("New String: " + newString);
     }
     catch (RESyntaxException e)
     {
     System.out.println("Syntax Error");
     System.out.println(e.toString());
     }
   }
}
```

Example - Using Regular Expressions

In order to further enhance your understanding of regular expressions, the following is an example of doing simple pattern matching in an HTML form using a servlet to process the regular expression. The regular expression may or may not contain parenthesized expressions. The servlet will handle either accordingly. Take a look at the following source code and then the results.

```
<HTML>
<HEAD>
  <TITLE>Regular Expressions - Pattern Matching</TITLE>
</HEAD>
<BODY>
<CENTER><H1>Pattern Matching</H1></CENTER>
<HR>
<FORM ACTION="http://localhost:8080/servlet/Regexp" METHOD="GET">
<TABLE>
<TR>
  <TD>Expression (no quotes):</TD>
  <TD><INPUT TYPE="text" NAME="exp"></TD>
</TR>
<TR>
  <TD>String:</TD>
  <TD><INPUT TYPE="text" NAME="str"></TD>
</TR>
<TR>
  <TD>Ignore Case? <INPUT TYPE="Checkbox" NAME="caseFlag" VALUE="Y"></TD>
  <TD></TD>
</TR>
</TABLE>
<HR><BR>
<CENTER>
<INPUT TYPE="Submit" NAME="btn_submit" VALUE="Submit"><BR><BR>
</CENTER>
</FORM>
</BODY>
</HTML>
```

461

Here is the listing for the Regexp class

```java
import javax.servlet.*;
import javax.servlet.http.*;

import java.io.*;
import java.util.*;

import com.wrox.util.*;

import com.sun.server.util.regexp.*;

public class Regexp extends HttpServlet
{
    public void doGet(HttpServletRequest _req, HttpServletResponse _res)
    throws ServletException, IOException
    {

    _res.setContentType("text/html");
    PrintWriter out = _res.getWriter();

    HTML h = new HTML("Regular Expressions");
    h.add(HTML.HEADING, "Results of Regular Expression Operation", false);
    h.add(HTML.LINE, "", true);

    /* Read in the form values */
    String caseFlag = "N";
    String exp = _req.getParameter("exp");
    String str = _req.getParameter("str");
    Enumeration e = _req.getParameterNames();
    while(e.hasMoreElements()){
        if (e.nextElement().equals("caseFlag"))
        {
        caseFlag = _req.getParameter("caseFlag");
        }
    }

    /* Display original expression and string */
    h.add(HTML.NORMAL, "Expression: ", false);
    h.add(HTML.NORMAL, exp, true);
    h.add(HTML.NORMAL, "String: ", false);
    h.add(HTML.NORMAL, str, true);
    if (caseFlag.equals("Y"))
    {
    h.add(HTML.NORMAL, "Match Flags: Ignore Case", true);
    }
    else
    {
    h.add(HTML.NORMAL, "Match Flags: Normal", true);
    }

    /* Create and execute regular expression */
    try
    {
    RE r = new RE(exp);
        if (caseFlag.equals("Y"))
        {
        r.setMatchFlags(1);
        }
        else
        {
        r.setMatchFlags(0);
```

```
        }
    if (r.match(str))
    {
    /* Check for parenthesized results */
    int i = r.getParenCount();
        if (i > 1)
        {
        h.add(HTML.NORMAL, "Parenthesized Results:", true);
            for (int x = 0; x < i; x++)
            {
            h.add(HTML.NORMAL, r.getParen(x), true);
            }
        }
    else
    {
    h.add(HTML.NORMAL, "Match :)", true);
    }
    }
    else
    {
    h.add(HTML.NORMAL, "No Match :(", true);
    }
    }
    catch (RESyntaxException ex)
    {
    h.add(HTML.NORMAL, "Syntax error in expression.", true);
    }

     out.println(h.getPage());
     out.close();
     }
}
```

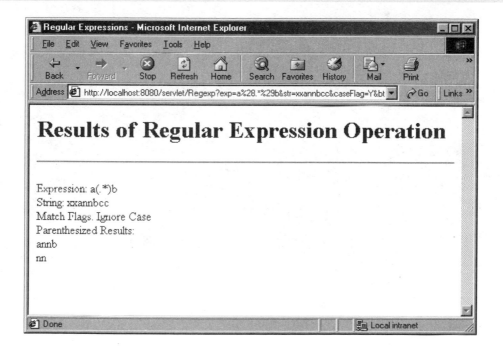

Summary

This chapter has given you some more tools to ease your transition from CGI to Java. You can now use the methods of the `HttpServletRequest` interface to access the environment variables as you may have done in your past CGI scripts. To process cookies, you can use the `javax.servlet.http.Cookie` class and for all of you Perl hackers, you can now use regular expressions in your servlets using either a third-party package or the `com.sun.server.util.regexp` package (Sun Java Web Server).

In this chapter, we learned the following:

> ➤ For almost every CGI environment variable, there is a corresponding Java method to access the same data. These methods exist in the `HttpServletRequest` interface.

> ➤ Cookies are small text files that can be sent to and from the web server to store persistent data.

> ➤ Using the `javax.servlet.http.Cookie` class, cookies can be created and manipulated through your Java servlets.

> ➤ Regular expressions can be used in Java in much the same way that they are used in a CGI script. To add this functionality to Java, either a third-party package needs to be added to the servlet, or the `com.sun.server.util.regexp` package from the Java Web Server libraries can be used.

Internationalizing Web Sites

Like many other software and networking projects the World Wide Web was first used by an English-speaking community. However, putting the 'World Wide' into the WWW demands ways to support other languages and writing systems that are used around the world.

In this chapter you will see how a Servlet can interact with users in different languages and character encodings. The following topics are covered in detail:

> Storing and sending text for different writing systems and character sets.
> Character encoding support in the Java core API.
> HTTP headers which show a user's preference for specific languages and character encodings.
> Internationalization support in the Servlet API.
> Performing content negotiation based on languages and character encodings and recoding documents as requested by a client.

Character Sets

In the USA, computers have mainly used the ASCII (American Standard Code for Information Interchange) and EBCDIC character sets in the past. Both character sets use 7 bit encodings where each 7 bit tuple represents one of 128 possible characters. These characters include the upper and lowercase Latin letters, Arabic numbers and punctuation marks.

The ASCII character set was later used as a starting point for extended character sets with 256 characters encoded in octets (tuples of 8 bits, nowadays usually referred to as "bytes"). Some of these extensions were of a proprietary nature, others are standardized by the ISO (International Standards Organization). One of the most common extended character sets is ISO-8859-1, also known as Latin-1, the first of the ISO-8859 family of 8 bit character sets. Latin-1 contains all characters required to write text in many western European languages. Specifically, the languages Afrikaans, Basque, Catalan, Danish, Dutch, English, Faeroese, Finnish, French, Galician, German, Icelandic, Irish, Italian, Norwegian, Portuguese, Scottish, Spanish, and Swedish are supported. Latin-1 is used as the primary character set for several Internet protocols, including HTTP.

There are many other character sets which include the same characters (often with different character codes) and many others which contain characters for languages not covered by Latin-1, for example the JIS (Japanese Industry Standard) character set for Japanese ideograms.

To solve the problem of having to work with many different character sets in an internationalized environment, the Unicode standard was created. In 1999 the standard is still evolving as support for more languages is being added. Unicode consists of 256 pages of 256 characters each, so each character can be represented by two bytes (a 16 bit tuple). The first page of Unicode is Latin-1, so all Latin-1 characters (including all ASCII characters, the lower half of Latin-1) have the same character codes in Unicode.

Character Encodings

When working only with simple 7 or 8 bit character sets like Latin-1, the distinction between character sets and character encodings does not usually come into play. Text files are written as a sequence of octets, each one being the code of a single character. If more than 256 different characters are required (e.g. for Asian languages like Chinese or Japanese) this simple scheme cannot be used any more. Even when writing raw Unicode characters there are two natural encodings for writing characters as 16 bit numbers: On *big endian* machines the high byte (the Unicode page number) would be written first, followed by the low byte (the cell number). On *little endian* machines that order would be reversed.

Java uses Unicode internally to represent text in all kinds of data types, including

> ➤ char, the 16 bit character type
> ➤ java.lang.String, the immutable string type
> ➤ java.lang.StringBuffer, the mutable string type
> ➤ java.io.Reader, the stream type for reading 16 bit characters
> ➤ java.io.Writer, the stream type for writing 16 bit characters

When exchanging data with other applications, characters have to be encoded with one of the standard Unicode encodings or an older encoding which supports a more limited set of characters. The following encodings are commonly used for Unicode:

> ➤ Raw Unicode data in network byte order (*big endian*)
> ➤ UTF-8: ASCII characters are written as is, higher characters are encoded with escape sequences. This allows the use of single Unicode characters in ASCII text and keeps the ASCII parts readable for applications that don't support UTF-8. The resulting files are also smaller than raw Unicode files if they contain a lot of ASCII characters.
> ➤ UTF-7: Like UTF-8 but only the low seven bits of each octet are used. The resulting files are longer than UTF-8 files but they can be transmitted over channels which are not eight bit clean which is required for sending e-mail and News messages. HTTP is eight bit clean, so it is not necessary to use UTF-7.

Character Encoding Support in the Java Core API

Some parts of the Java core API deal with character encodings. There are several ways to convert encoded text to the `char` and `java.lang.String` Unicode types and back:

> ➤ The `java.lang.String` constructors `String(byte[] bytes, int offset, int length, String encoding)` and `String(byte[] bytes, String encoding)` create a Unicode string from an array of bytes (or a part thereof) in the specified encoding.

> ➤ The `java.lang.String` method `getBytes(String encoding)` does the opposite of the previous methods. It returns a new byte array that represents a string in the specified encoding.

> ➤ `java.io.InputStreamReader` has a constructor that takes an "encoding" argument. An `InputStreamReader` can read text with the specified encoding from an underlying `InputStream`, e.g. a `FileInputStream` which has been constructed for a file on the local disk.

> ➤ `java.io.OutputStreamWriter` also has a constructor that takes an "encoding" argument. This class does the opposite of `InputStreamReader`, which is encoding and writing text data to an `OutputStream`.

The encoding names used by all Java methods dealing with character encodings are specific to Java. The following table lists some Java encoding names:

Name	Description
UnicodeBig	Raw Unicode data in *big endian* (network) byte order.
UnicodeLittle	Raw Unicode data in *little endian* byte order.
UTF8	The 8 bit Unicode Transport Format
UTF7	The 7 bit Unicode Transport Format
8859_1	ISO 8859-1, also known as Latin-1, for West European languages
8859_2	ISO 8859-2, also known as Latin-2, for East European languages
8859_3	ISO 8859-3, also known as Latin-3, for Southeast European languages
8859_4	ISO 8859-4, also known as Latin-4, for Scandinavian and Baltic languages
8859_9	ISO 8859-9, also known as Latin-5, for Turkish, a modified version of Latin-1
JIS	JIS, a Japanese encoding

IANA Charset Names

By default, HTTP requests and responses containing a body of a `text` sub-type are assumed to be encoded in Latin-1. Alternative encodings have to be specified explicitly by appending a `charset` tag to the `Content-Type` header as in the following example:

```
Content-Type: text/html; charset=UTF-8
```

An HTTP response with such a `Content-Type` header contains HTML text encoded with UTF-8. The `charset` names for MIME documents are not identical to the encoding names used by Java. For Internet protocols like HTTP only the official encoding names published by the Internet Assigned Numbers Authority (IANA) should be used. The following table shows Java encoding names and the corresponding IANA names:

Java Name	IANA Names
UTF8	UTF-8
UTF7	UTF-7
8859_1	ISO-8859-1 (preferred) ISO_8859-1:1987 iso-ir-100 ISO_8859-1 latin1 l1 IBM819 CP819 csISOLatin1

Note that unlike the official IANA names the Java encoding names are case-sensitive. They are actually parts of class names for byte to char and char to byte converter classes and as such bound to the naming rules for Java class names.

Content Negotiation

When a Web server offers a resource in different variants (which includes text documents in different languages and character encodings) there needs to be a way to select the variant which is most appropriate for the user (e.g. when selecting languages) and the web client (e.g. displayable character encodings). This is called "content negotiation" and can be implemented in two ways:

- Server-driven content negotiation: The server selects a variant based on information contained in the request. This can be one or more of the request headers, the requested URL or any other available information.

- Client-driven content negotiation: When multiple variants of a resource are available, the server offers a list of choices from which the user can select one directly.

There are several HTTP/1.1 request headers which support server-driven content negotiating by giving the server hints as to what the user prefers. One such header which is used for internationalization is `Accept-Charset`. It contains a list of character encodings which are acceptable to the client. The list entries are separated by commas and can optionally contain quality values which specify the relative quality of the choices. Here is an example of an `Accept-Charset` header:

```
Accept-Charset: UTF-8, ISO-8859-1, UTF-7;q=0.9
```

A client that sends this header indicates that it can display text encoded in UTF-8, UTF-7 and ISO-8859-1. The quality values which are appended as "q" tags to the list entries must be between 0 and 1 with higher values meaning more preferable choices. The default for entries without "q" tags is 1. For the example header this means that the UTF-7 encoding is acceptable to the client but it prefers UTF-8 and ISO-8859-1 if the server can create them.

The default character set ISO-8859-1 should be accepted by all clients, even if it is not explicitly listed in an `Accept-Charset` header.

A similar header exists for negotiating languages. The `Accept-Language` header contains a list of language names which are preferred by the user. The entries can also contain "q" tags for relative quality values. Language names consist of one or more parts separated by hyphens. Usually the first part is a two-letter ISO 639 language abbreviation code and the optional second (and final) part a two-letter ISO 3166 country code. Registration of language names is also administered by the IANA. Here is an example `Accept-Language` header:

```
Accept-Language: en-US;q=1.0, en;q=0.5
```

This header indicates that the user prefers American English (quality 1.0) but will take any form of English as an alternative (quality 0.5). Note that the absolute quality values are meaningless. They are only used to determine the order of the list entries. The following `Accept-Language` header has exactly the same meaning as the previous one:

```
Accept-Language: en-US;q=0.1, en;q=0.01
```

Below is an incomplete list of some IANA Language/Country codes.

Code	Language/Country Name	Code	Language/Country Name
af	Afrikaans	id	Indonesian
sq	Albanian	ga	Irish
eu	Basque	it	Italian
bg	Bulgarian	ja	Japanese
be	Byelorussian	ko	Korean
zh zh-CN zh-TW	Chinese Chinese/China Chinese/Taiwan	mk	Macedonian
hr	Croatian	no	Norwegian
cs	Czech	pl	Polish
da	Danish	pt pt-BR	Portuguese Portuguese/Brazil
nl nl-BE	Dutch Dutch/Belgium	ro	Romanian

Table Continued on Following Page

Code	Language/Country Name	Code	Language/Country Name
en	English	ru	Russian
en-GB	English/United Kingdom		
en-US	English/United States		
fo	Faeroese	gd	Scots Gaelic
fi	Finnish	sr	Serbian
fr	French	sk	Slovak
fr-BE	French/Belgium		
fr-CA	French/Canada		
fr-CH	French/Switzerland		
gl	Galician	sl	Slovenian
de	German	es	Spanish
de-AU	German/Austria	es-AR	Spanish/Argentina Spanish/Colombia
de-DE	German/Germany	es-CO	Spanish/Mexico
de-CH	German/Switzerland	es-MX	
el	Greek	es-ES	Spanish/Spain
hu	Hungarian	tr	Turkish
is	Icelandic	uk	Ukrainian

For a full list, see www.unicode.org/unicode/onlinedat/languages.html.

The I18NServlet ("I18N" means "Internationalization", "I" plus 18 letters plus "N") that we are going to develop needs to parse Accept-style headers to do the server-driven content negotiation. This functionality is best implemented in an auxiliary class which can be used for all headers with the same structure (Accept, Accept-Language, Accept-Charset, etc.).

The assorted "Accept" lists are managed by the AcceptList class which keeps arrays of list entries and their quality values in private variables.

```
private String[] names;
private double[] qualities;
```

Accessor methods similar to those of java.util.Vector make it possible to iterate through an AcceptList or find entries.

```
public int size() {

    return names.length;
}
```

returns the number of entries in the list.

```
public String nameAt(int i) {

   return names[i];
}

public double qualityAt(int i) {

   return qualities[i];
}
```

These methods return the name and quality at the specified position. They are used when iterating through the list.

```
public int indexOf(String name) {

   for (int i=0; i<names.length; i++) {
      if(names[i].equals(name)) {
         return i;
      }
      return -1;
   }
}

public int indexOf(double quality) {

   for (int i=0; i<qualities.length; i++) {
      if(qualities[i] == quality) {
         return i;
      }
   return -1;
   }
}
```

These return the index of an entry specified by its name or quality. If multiple entries have the same quality the first one is returned. Both methods return -1 if no matching entry was found.

```
public double qualityOf(String name) {

   int idx = indexOf(name);

   if(idx == -1) {
      return -1.0;
   } else {
      return qualities[idx];
   }
}
```

qualityOf() returns the quality associated with the given name, or a negative value if the name was not found. This is a convenience method which could also be implemented with the indexOf() and qualityAt() methods.

`AcceptList` has a constructor that takes a `String` argument which is the value of an `Accept`-style header. The constructor consists of four parts:

- ➢ Check for a `null` reference
- ➢ Split the string into tokens
- ➢ Parse the tokens
- ➢ Sort by quality

If a `null` reference is passed to the constructor, an empty `AcceptList` is created. This makes it easier to create `AcceptList` objects from HTTP headers because the constructor can be called without first having to check if the `getHeader()` method returned `null` because the header was not found.

```
public AcceptList(String s) {
    if(s == null) {
        names = new String[0];
        qualities = new double[0];
        return;
    }
```

If a non-null reference was supplied, the string is split into the single list entries, separated by commas, by using a `java.util.StringTokenizer`. The entries are added to a temporary `Vector` for further processing:

```
    Vector tokens = new Vector();
    StringTokenizer tok = new StringTokenizer(s, ",");
    while(tok.hasMoreTokens()) {
        tokens.addElement(tok.nextToken().trim());
    }
```

The `StringTokenizer` recognizes the comma-separated tokens and returns the next one on each call to the `nextToken()` method. Excessive whitespace at the beginning and end of each token is removed before adding it to the vector.

Now that the number of entries is known, the `names` and `qualities` arrays can be created and filled with the tokens. Each token is either only a name in which case it is added to the arrays with a quality of 1.0, or it is a name plus a quality value. In that case it is split into those two parts. The quality is converted from a string to a `double` value by creating a temporary `java.lang.Double` object with `Double.valueOf()`. If an illegal quality value is supplied that cannot be parsed as a number, the original value of 0.0 is retained.

```
    names = new String[tokens.size()];
    qualities = new double[tokens.size()];
    for(int i=0; i<names.length; i++) {
        String t = (String)tokens.elementAt(i);
        int sep = t.indexOf(";q=");
        if(sep == -1) {
            names[i] = t;
            qualities[i] = 1.0;
        } else {
            names[i] = t.substring(0,sep).trim();
            try {
```

```
                    qualities[i] = Double.valueOf(t.substring(sep+3)).doubleValue();
                } catch(NumberFormatException ignored) {
                }
            }
        }
        sort();
    }
```

Finally, the arrays are sorted with a bubble sort algorithm which is implemented in a separate method:

```
private void sort() {
    for (int i = 0; i < qualities.length; i++) {
        for (int j = i + 1; j < qualities.length; j++) {
            if (qualities[i] < qualities[j]) {
                double tmpq = qualities[i];
                qualities[i] = qualities[j];
                qualities[j] = tmpq;

                String tmpn = names[i];
                names[i] = names[j];
                names[j] = tmpn;
            }
        }
    }
}
```

The bubble sort algorithm is rather slow but straight-forward and easy to implement. Speed is not an issue because an `AcceptList` contains only a small number of entries. The algorithm does not change the order of equal elements, so entries with the same quality will appear in the sorted list in the same order in which they appeared in the header from which the list was constructed. This is important because there are web browsers which do not send correct `Accept-Language` headers with quality tags but instead list all acceptable language codes without quality tags in the order of preference. For example, if the user prefers `de-DE`, `de`, `en-US` and `en` in that order, the browser would send the following request header:

`Accept-Language: de-DE,de,en-US,en`

An HTTP/1.1 conforming version of this header would be:

`Accept-Language: de-DE;q=1.0,de;q=0.9,en-US;q=0.8,en;q=0.7`

By using a sorting algorithm which does not move elements which are already at a correct position in the list, both versions are equally acceptable to the `AcceptList` class.

Character Encoding Support in the Servlet API

When sending and receiving text data with a Servlet you usually do not have to worry about character encodings. When you get a `Reader` object for reading text from the `ServletRequest` `getReader()` method, the reader is automatically constructed with the character encoding that was supplied by the client in the `Content-Type` header, or the default encoding ISO-8859-1 if no other encoding was specified.

For writing a text response you can obtain a `PrintWriter` object with the `ServletResponse` `getWriter()` method. All text that gets written to this writer is automatically encoded with the character encoding that was specified in the `Content-Type` header. Note that all headers have to be set before getting a `PrintWriter` or `ServletOutputStream` to write the body of the response. If no encoding was specified the Servlet engine will find one automatically. In that case, all text written through the `PrintWriter` has to be cached. When the response has been completely written the servlet engine examines the text to find a suitable encoding for it which is also acceptable to the client. Then it modifies the `Content-Type` header that you supplied to include a proper `charset` tag and sends the cached text encoded with the selected `charset`.

All this is completely transparent to the servlet developer. You only have to take a few points into consideration:

Always use `Reader` and `Writer` objects which have been constructed by the Servlet engine (or are wrapped around such objects) to handle text data. `ServletInputStream` and `ServletOutputStream` should only be used for binary data which must not be modified by the Servlet engine or if you want to encode text data yourself instead of letting the Servlet engine do it for you.

The Servlet engine needs to cache the response if you don't explicitly specify a character encoding via the `charset` tag of the content type. This makes it impossible to send *streaming* responses to a client. Note that the response may need to be cached for other reasons as well, especially if you do not specify a content length before writing the response body.

The Internationalization Servlet

We can now move on to the actual `I18NServlet` class which should return localized documents in the user's preferred language. This servlet duplicates some of the core functionality of a web server: It returns documents from a directory tree on the local disk as requested by a virtual path. It does not have advanced features like file uploading or automatic creation of index pages but instead it can return documents with different variants which are selected dynamically. As usual, the `I18NServlet` extends `javax.servlet.http.HttpServlet`, the standard base class for HTTP Servlets. Most of the functionality is implemented directly in the `doGet()` method.

First, we need to define a format for storing the documents on disk. The Servlet API offers the `getPathTranslated()` method in the `HttpServletRequest` class to get the real path on disk for a document specified via a virtual path appended to the Servlet name in a URL. Let's say the servlet is installed as `/servlet/I18NServlet` on a local web server. The following URL could be used to access the file `test/hello.txt` relative to the server's document root:

http://localhost:8080/test/hello.txt

If you want to access the same file via the Servlet, you can use the following URL:

http://localhost:8080/servlet/I18NServlet/test/hello.txt

The `I18NServlet` should be able to return files such as `hello.txt` which are only available in a single variant. These files are simply stored under their real name. Files with variants must be stored with a language code and an encoding name. If the `test` directory contains localized versions of `hello.txt` for English, German, French and Japanese, these could be stored in the following files:

```
hello.txt--de
hello.txt--en.8859_1
hello.txt--fr.8859_1
hello.txt--ja.JIS
```

The file name is followed by a separator consisting of two dashes ("--"), then the language code in lower-case letters, followed by a dot and the Java encoding name. The encoding name can optionally be left out in which case the default encoding ISO-8859-1 will be used, as shown above for the German version of `hello.txt`.

The `I18NServlet` `getVariants()` method is used to compile a list of variants for a file which is specified in this way:

```
private String[] getVariants(File file) {

    File dir = new File(file.getParent());
    final String prefix = file.getName() + "--";
    int prefixLength = prefix.length();
    String[] variants = dir.list(new FilenameFilter() {

        public boolean accept(File dir, String name) {
            return name.startsWith(prefix);
        }
    });

    for(int i=0; i<variants.length; i++) {
        variants[i] = variants[i].substring(prefixLength);
    }
    return variants;
}
```

The method does its work in two steps. First, a list of file names for the variants is compiled by calling the `list()` method in `java.io.File`. This is then associated with the directory containing the file and its variants. An inner class which implements the `java.io.FilenameFilter` interface is used to restrict the files in the directory to only those which start with the right prefix, i.e. the original file name plus the two dashes. In the second step the entries in the array of file names are replaced with only the variant names, i.e. the file names without the prefix. When calling `getVariants()` for our `hello.txt` file it will return the following array of strings (but not necessarily in that order):

```
{"de", "en.8859_1", "fr.8859_1", "ja.JIS"}
```

A second auxiliary method, `findVariant()`, is used to select the most appropriate variant from such an array. It takes an `AcceptList` object as a second argument. This object should have been created from an `Accept-Language` HTTP request header.

```
private String findVariant(String[] variants, AcceptList langs) {
    for(int i=0; i<langs.size(); i++) {
        String lang = langs.nameAt(i).toLowerCase();
        for(int j=0; j<variants.length; j++) {
            if(variants[j].toLowerCase().startsWith(lang)) {
                return variants[j];
            }
        }
    }
    return null;
}
```

The method iterates through the entries of the AcceptList, starting with the most preferable one. If the variants array contains that entry or a longer name (for a more specialized language selection) which starts with that entry's name, it is returned. If all acceptable languages have been tried and there was no variant for any of them, null is returned to indicate the failure. Note that the language codes, both in the variants array and the langs list, are converted to lower case before being compared because they should be compared in a case-insensitive way.

By selecting an appropriate localized variant of the document, the I18NServlet can return different content for the same resource. A user who is using a web browser which is configured to prefer German-language text will see the following result when requesting the example resource hello.txt:

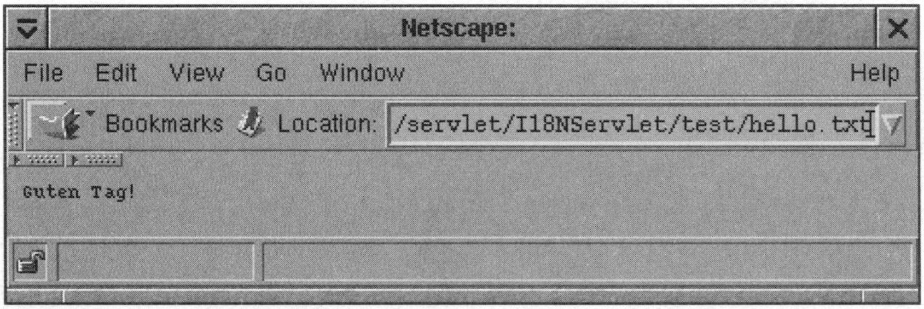

A user who prefers Japanese will see this instead:

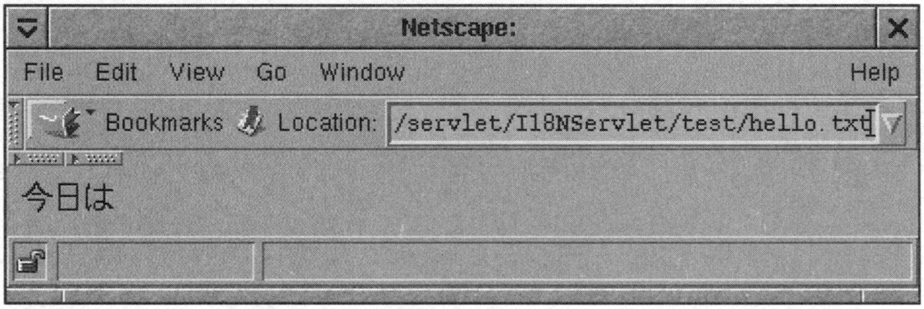

Note that the URL is the same in both cases.
The doGet() method which should return the localized documents starts by finding the file to be returned to the client:

```
public void doGet(HttpServletRequest req, HttpServletResponse res)
    throws ServletException, IOException {

    String ctype;

    String fname = req.getPathTranslated();
    if(fname == null) {
        res.sendError(res.SC_FORBIDDEN);
        return;
    }

    File file = new File(fname);
```

```
        if(file.isDirectory()) {
           StringBuffer url = HttpUtils.getRequestURL(req);
           if(!url.toString().endsWith("/")) {
             url.append('/');
             res.sendRedirect(url.toString());
             return;
           } else {
             file = new File(file, "index.html");
             ctype = "text/html";
           }
        } else {
           ctype = getServletContext().getMimeType(fname);
           if(ctype == null) {
             ctype = "text/plain"; }
           }
        }
        res.setContentType(ctype);
        [...]
```

If the virtual path cannot be mapped to a file name (in which case `getPathTranslated()` returns `null`) the Servlet replies with a "Forbidden" response code. This can happen, for example, if the user tries to request a Servlet or CGI script to be delivered through the `I18NServlet` instead of a regular file under the document root.

Another feature traditionally implemented in web servers is also implemented in the `I18NServlet` for compatibility reasons. When a URL maps to a directory for which an index file is retrieved or created on the fly, the URL path must end with a slash ("/"), otherwise relative links would use the wrong base directory. For example, take our `test` directory which could contain an index file `index.html` with a link to `hello.txt`:

```
<A href="hello.txt">A greeting in your language</A>
```

To follow that link, a browser would strip off the last component of the URL path of the document in which the link appeared to find the base path. The relative link would then be appended to that path. If the index file was requested as `/test/index.html` or as `/test/` the base path (everything up to the last slash) is `/test/` and the relative link becomes `/test/hello.txt`. However, if the server would return the index file when `/test` (without a trailing slash) is requested, the browser would see the base path as `/` and create the wrong URL path `/hello.txt` for the relative link. To make those wrong directory paths, without a trailing slash, work as expected the server redirects the client to the correct URL path, including the slash. This is transparent to the user who will only notice a slightly longer response time because an additional HTTP request has to be made.

To implement this behavior, the `I18NServlet` first checks if the requested path maps to a directory. If this is the case and the slash is missing, the client is redirected. The `javax.servlet.http.HttpUtils` class contains the static utility method `getRequestURL()` which can be used to create an absolute URL for a Servlet request. This is required because redirections may not use relative paths. A relative path would be rejected by the server. If the request maps to a directory and the URL path is already correct, The name `index.html` is appended and the content type set to `text/html`. If a file was requested instead of a directory, the `ServletContext` is queried for a MIME type for the file name with the `getMimeType()` method. If the server cannot provide a MIME type, `text/plain` is assumed.

It is important that the server is properly configured to return the right MIME types. If a server returns all files literally byte by byte a client could override a wrong content type and still handle that server's responses correctly (or at least it would seem to be correct), so that the wrong configuration does not even get noticed. This will fail when binary files are requested through the I18NServlet. If the server does not recognize them as binary files the default encoding "text/plain" is used and the files are copied as text data. Reading the files from disk is not a problem yet because the default character encoding ISO-8859-1 does not change the read data but the data can be destroyed when sending the response to the client because it may be encoded with a different charset which the client prefers over ISO-8859-1.

When the base file and its MIME type are determined there are three possibilities:

> The file to be returned is a text file (its content type starts with "text/")
> The file exists (and is not a text file)
> The file does not exist

These cases are handled by a big "if" clause that spans most of the doGet() method:

```
if(ctype.startsWith("text/")) {
   [...]
} else if(file.exists()) {
   [...]
} else res.sendError(res.SC_NOT_FOUND);
```

The case of a non-existent text file will be handled at a different place.
If a binary file does not exist, the Servlet responds with a "Not Found" status code. If a binary file should be sent (second branch of the "if" clause) it is simply copied literally byte by byte from a FileInputStream to the ServletOutputStream:

```
InputStream in = new FileInputStream(file);
OutputStream out = res.getOutputStream();
copy(in,out);

in.close();
out.close();
```

The actual copying is implemented in the copy() method. Reading and writing single bytes is inefficient, so we use an array with a size of one kilobyte which is read and written as a whole:

```
private void copy(InputStream in, OutputStream out) throws IOException {
   int num;
   byte[] ch = new byte[1024];
   while((num = in.read(ch,0,1024)) > 0) out.write(ch,0,num);
}
```

The method continuously tries to read blocks of 1024 bytes and writes the read data to the OutputStream. A call to read() may read less than the requested number of bytes which needs to be taken into account when writing the block (or a part of the block). The method returns when the end of the InputStream has been reached. In the case of a disk file this means that the entire file has been read.

We will later need a similar block-copy method which works on characters instead of bytes. It is almost identical to the previous method:

```
private void copy(Reader in, Writer out) throws IOException {
    int num;
    char[] ch = new char[1024];
    while((num = in.read(ch,0,1024)) > 0) out.write(ch,0,num);
}
```

Returning a Variant of a Text File

The core of the doGet() method deals with returning text files. There should be two ways to select a specific variant of a file:

Server-driven content negotiation

The Servlet reads the Accept-Language header and finds a language for which the requested document is available.

Client-driven content negotiation

If the client did not supply an Accept-Language header or there is no variant available for any of the acceptable languages, there needs to be a way for the client to explicitly request one of the available variants.

The client-driven content negotiation is handled with a lang parameter. A user who wants to see the French version of hello.txt would request the following URL:

```
http://localhost/servlet/I18NServlet/test/hello.txt?lang=fr
```

The auxiliary method getSelectedVariant() is used to find the first file that matches a selected base file and language:

```
private File getSelectedVariant(File file, String lang) {
    File dir = new File(file.getParent());
    final String prefix = file.getName() + "--" + lang.toLowerCase();
    String[] variants = dir.list(new FilenameFilter() {
        public boolean accept(File dir, String name) {
            return name.startsWith(prefix);
        }
    });

    if(variants.length >= 1) {
        return new File(dir, variants[0]);
    } else {
        return null;
    }
}
```

This method works similarly to the getVariant() method. It uses a custom file name filter that matches all files with the right base name and language code. If any such files were found, the first one is returned, otherwise the method returns null.

The method is used by doGet() in the following way:

```
        String selectedLang = req.getParameter("lang");
        File variant;
        String encoding = "8859_1";

        if(file.exists()) {
            variant = file;
        } else if(selectedLang != null) {
            variant = getSelectedVariant(file, selectedLang);
            if(variant == null) {
                res.sendError(res.SC_NOT_FOUND);
              return;
            } else {
              String s = variant.getName();
              s = s.substring(s.indexOf("--"));
              int sep = s.lastIndexOf('.');
              if(sep != -1) {
                  encoding = s.substring(sep+1);
              }
            }
        } else {
            [...]
```

First, the variables `variant` and `encoding` are declared and `encoding` is initialized with the default value. These variables are later filled with the right values. If the file exists under the requested name, it is assigned directly to the `variant` variable. The encoding is assumed to be the default encoding ISO-8859-1. Otherwise, if a variant has been selected with the `lang` parameter, the file for that variant is looked up with `getSelectedVariant()`. If the file name for the `variant` contains an encoding, it is extracted and assigned to the `encoding` variable.

If no variant could be determined up to this point, server-driven content negotiation is used to find one. A list of all variants is created with `getVariants()`. If no variants were found, the Servlet returns a "Not Found" status code. Otherwise an `AcceptList` is created for the `Accept-Language` header and the previously described `findVariant()` is used to select the best variant.

```
        [...]
    } else {
        String[] variants = getVariants(file);
        if(variants.length == 0) {
            res.sendError(res.SC_NOT_FOUND);
            return;
        }

        AcceptList langs = new AcceptList(req.getHeader("Accept-Language"));
            String variantName = findVariant(variants, langs);

            res.setHeader("Pragma", "no-cache");
            res.setHeader("Vary", "Accept-Language");
```

```
      if(variantName == null) {
        [...]
      } else {
        variant = new File(file.getParent(),
                  file.getName() + "--" + variantName);
        int sep = variantName.lastIndexOf('.');
        if(sep != -1) {
          encoding = variantName.substring(sep+1);
        }
      }
    }

    Reader in = new InputStreamReader(new FileInputStream(variant),
            encoding);
    Writer out = res.getWriter();
    copy(in,out);

    in.close();
    out.close();
```

If findVariant() was successful, the variant and encoding variables are filled.

Finally, the selected file can be sent to the client. The code is similar to that for sending a binary file, except that a Reader and Writer pair are used to handle text data instead of an InputStream and OutputStream. An InputStreamReader is constructed with the encoding of the input file. It reads the file and converts all characters to Unicode. The PrintWriter object returned by res.getWriter() method converts the Unicode characters to the encoding, which is determined automatically by the Servlet engine.

Note that two cache control headers are set if a variant is selected on the server side. Pragma: no-cache instructs HTTP/1.0 clients and proxy servers not to cache the response at all. HTTP/1.1 has more sophisticated cache control methods. The Vary: Accept-Language response header tells HTTP/1.1-enabled software that the response depends on the Accept-Language request header. It may be stored in a proxy cache and subsequent requests can be answered directly by the proxy server as long as they have an equivalent Accept-Language header. If the header is different, the request must be forwarded to the origin server.

User-Driven Content Negotiation

One essential part of the I18NServlet is still missing. What happens if the client sends an Accept-Language header and the requested resource exists but no variant matches? In that case, the selection of one of the available variants should be left to the user. The following code in doGet() creates an HTML page with links to all variants of the requested document:

```
      if(variantName == null) {
        res.setStatus(res.SC_MULTIPLE_CHOICES);
        res.setContentType("text/html");
        PrintWriter out = res.getWriter();
        out.println("<HTML><HEAD><TITLE>Select a language</TITLE>
                </HEAD>"+"<BODY><H1>Select a language</H1><UL>");
```

Continued on Following Page

```
            String url = URLEncoder.encode(file.getName());

            for(int i=0; i<variants.length; i++) {
                String v = variants[i];
                int sep = v.lastIndexOf('.');
                if(sep != -1) {
                    v = v.substring(0,sep);
                }
                out.println("<LI><A HREF=\""+url+"?lang="+v+"\">"+
                            languageNameFor(v)+"</A>");
            }
            out.println("</UL></BODY></HTML>");
            out.close();
            return;
    }
```

The HTTP status code "Multiple Choices" indicates that there is more than one variant of the requested resource. The details as to what a response with a "Multiple Choices" status should contain are not specified. If there is a default variant its absolute URL should be sent in a Location header, but this is not the case with our setup.

The variants are listed in the HTML page by iterating through the variants array and creating a link for each entry. The link leads back to the requested resource with an appended lang parameter to select that specific variant. Unlike a URL in a Location header (as used when redirecting a client), a link in an HTML page can be relative, so only the last component of the URL path (i.e. the file name) is used as a relative URL path. Note that the java.net.URLEncoder class is used to encode the file name in case it contains special characters (e.g. spaces) that may not be used as is in a URL. The reverse decoding process is implemented in the Servlet engine. When a virtual path is resolved with the getPathTranslated() method, it is automatically decoded prior to translating it into a file name.

The language codes are not very comprehensible to most users, so they are replaced by spelled out names in the list. These names are generated by the languageNameFor() method which looks them up in the languageNames hashtable:

```
private String languageNameFor(String code) {
    String name = (String)languageNames.get(code.toLowerCase());
    if(name != null) {
        return name;
    } else {
        return code;
    }
}
```

If no name was found for a language code, the code itself is returned as a makeshift solution. The language name table is filled in an init() block of the Servlet:

```
    private Hashtable languageNames = new Hashtable();

    public void init() throws ServletException {
        languageNames.put("af", "Afrikaans");
        languageNames.put("sq", "Albanian");
        languageNames.put("eu", "Basque");
        languageNames.put("bg", "Bulgarian");
        languageNames.put("be", "Byelorussian");
        languageNames.put("zh", "Chinese");
        languageNames.put("zh-cn", "Chinese/China");
        languageNames.put("zh-tw", "Chinese/Taiwan");
        [...]
        languageNames.put("tr", "Turkish");
        languageNames.put("uk", "Ukrainian");
    }
```

When the example resource `hello.txt` is requested and none of the available variants is acceptable to the user, the following list is returned:

```
<UL>
    <LI><A href="hello.txt?lang=fr">French</A>
    <LI><A href="hello.txt?lang=ja">Japanese</A>
    <LI><A href="hello.txt?lang=en">English</A>
    <LI><A href="hello.txt?lang=de">German</A>
</UL>
```

Below is the full source code for the I18NServlet servlet:

```
    import java.io.*;
    import java.net.URLEncoder;
    import java.util.*;

    import javax.servlet.*;
    import javax.servlet.http.*;

    public final class I18NServlet extends HttpServlet {

        private Hashtable languageNames = new Hashtable();

        public void init() throws ServletException {
            languageNames.put("af", "Afrikaans");
            languageNames.put("sq", "Albanian");
            languageNames.put("eu", "Basque");
            languageNames.put("bg", "Bulgarian");
            languageNames.put("be", "Byelorussian");
            languageNames.put("zh", "Chinese");
            languageNames.put("zh-cn", "Chinese/China");
            languageNames.put("zh-tw", "Chinese/Taiwan");
            languageNames.put("hr", "Croatian");
            languageNames.put("cs", "Czech");
            languageNames.put("da", "Danish");
            languageNames.put("nl", "Dutch");
            languageNames.put("nl-be", "Dutch/Belgium");
```

Continued on Following Page

```
            languageNames.put("en", "English");
            languageNames.put("en-bg", "English/United Kingdom");
            languageNames.put("en-us", "English/United States");
            languageNames.put("fo", "Faeroese");
            languageNames.put("fi", "Finnish");
            languageNames.put("fr", "French");
            languageNames.put("fr-be", "French/Belgium");
            languageNames.put("fr-ca", "French/Canada");
            languageNames.put("fr-ch", "French/Switzerland");
            languageNames.put("gl", "Galician");
            languageNames.put("de", "German");
            languageNames.put("de-au", "German/Austria");
            languageNames.put("de-de", "German/Germany");
            languageNames.put("de-ch", "German/Switzerland");
            languageNames.put("el", "Greek");
            languageNames.put("hu", "Hungarian");
            languageNames.put("is", "Icelandic");
            languageNames.put("id", "Indonesian");
            languageNames.put("ga", "Irish");
            languageNames.put("it", "Italian");
            languageNames.put("ja", "Japanese");
            languageNames.put("ko", "Korean");
            languageNames.put("mk", "Macedonian");
            languageNames.put("no", "Norwegian");
            languageNames.put("pl", "Polish");
            languageNames.put("pt", "Portuguese");
            languageNames.put("pt-br", "Portuguese/Brazil");
            languageNames.put("ro", "Romanian");
            languageNames.put("ru", "Russian");
            languageNames.put("gd", "Scots Gaelic");
            languageNames.put("sr", "Serbian");
            languageNames.put("sk", "Slovak");
            languageNames.put("sl", "Slovenian");
            languageNames.put("es", "Spanish");
            languageNames.put("es-ar", "Spanish/Argentina");
            languageNames.put("es-co", "Spanish/Colombia");
            languageNames.put("es-mx", "Spanish/Mexico");
            languageNames.put("es-es", "Spanish/Spain");
            languageNames.put("sv", "Swedish");
            languageNames.put("tr", "Turkish");
            languageNames.put("uk", "Ukrainian");
        }

    public void doGet(HttpServletRequest req, HttpServletResponse res)
        throws ServletException, IOException {

        String ctype;

        String fname = req.getPathTranslated();
        if(fname == null) {
            res.sendError(res.SC_FORBIDDEN);
            return;
        }
        File file = new File(fname);

        if(file.isDirectory()) {
            StringBuffer url = HttpUtils.getRequestURL(req);
            if(!url.toString().endsWith("/")) {
                url.append('/');
                res.sendRedirect(url.toString());
                return;
```

```
    } else {
     file = new File(file, "index.html");
     ctype = "text/html";
    }
} else {
   ctype = getServletContext().getMimeType(fname);
   if(ctype == null) {
      ctype = "text/plain";
   }
}

res.setContentType(ctype);

if(ctype.startsWith("text/")) {
   String selectedLang = req.getParameter("lang");
   File variant;
   String encoding = "8859_1";

   if(file.exists()) {
      variant = file;
   } else if(selectedLang != null) {
      variant = getSelectedVariant(file, selectedLang);

      if(variant == null) {
         res.sendError(res.SC_NOT_FOUND);
         return;
      } else {
         String s = variant.getName();
         s = s.substring(s.indexOf("--"));
         int sep = s.lastIndexOf('.');
         if(sep != -1) {
            encoding = s.substring(sep+1);
         }
      }
   } else {
      String[] variants = getVariants(file);
      if(variants.length == 0) {
         res.sendError(res.SC_NOT_FOUND);
         return;
      }

      AcceptList langs = new AcceptList(req.getHeader(
                                     "Accept-Language"));
      String variantName = findVariant(variants, langs);

      res.setHeader("Pragma", "no-cache");
      res.setHeader("Vary", "Accept-Language");

      if(variantName == null) {
         res.setStatus(res.SC_MULTIPLE_CHOICES);
         res.setContentType("text/html");
         PrintWriter out = res.getWriter();
         out.println("<HTML><HEAD><TITLE>Select a language</TITLE>
                     </HEAD>"+"<BODY><H1>Select a language</H1><UL>");

         String url = URLEncoder.encode(file.getName());
```

Continued on Following Page

487

```
                    for(int i=0; i<variants.length; i++) {
                        String v = variants[i];
                        int sep = v.lastIndexOf('.');
                        if(sep != -1) {
                            v = v.substring(0,sep);
                        }
                        out.println("<LI><A href=\""+url+"?lang="+v+"\">"+
                        languageNameFor(v)+"</A>");
                    }
                    out.println("</UL></BODY></HTML>");
                    out.close();
                    return;
                } else {
                    variant = new File(file.getParent(),
                                file.getName() + "--" + variantName);
                    int sep = variantName.lastIndexOf('.');
                    if(sep != -1) {
                        encoding = variantName.substring(sep+1);
                    }
                }
            }
            Reader in =
            new InputStreamReader(new FileInputStream(variant), encoding);
            Writer out = res.getWriter();
            copy(in,out);
            in.close();
            out.close();
        } else if(file.exists()) {
            InputStream in = new FileInputStream(file);
            OutputStream out = res.getOutputStream();
            copy(in,out);
            in.close();
            out.close();
        }
        else res.sendError(res.SC_NOT_FOUND);
    }

    private void copy(InputStream in, OutputStream out) throws IOException {
        int num;
        byte[] ch = new byte[1024];
        while((num = in.read(ch,0,1024)) > 0) out.write(ch,0,num);
    }

    private void copy(Reader in, Writer out) throws IOException {
        int num;
        char[] ch = new char[1024];
        while((num = in.read(ch,0,1024)) > 0) out.write(ch,0,num);
    }

    private String[] getVariants(File file) {
        File dir = new File(file.getParent());
        final String prefix = file.getName() + "--";
        int prefixLength = prefix.length();
        String[] variants = dir.list(new FilenameFilter(){
            public boolean accept(File dir, String name) {
                return name.startsWith(prefix);
            }
        });
        for(int i=0; i<variants.length; i++) {
            variants[i] = variants[i].substring(prefixLength);
```

```
        }
        return variants;
    }

    private String findVariant(String[] variants, AcceptList langs) {
        for(int i=0; i<langs.size(); i++) {
            String lang = langs.nameAt(i).toLowerCase();
            for(int j=0; j<variants.length; j++) {
                if(variants[j].toLowerCase().startsWith(lang)) {
                    return variants[j];
                }
            }
        }
        return null;
    }

    private File getSelectedVariant(File file, String lang) {
        File dir = new File(file.getParent());
        final String prefix = file.getName() + "--" + lang.toLowerCase();
        String[] variants = dir.list(new FilenameFilter() {
            public boolean accept(File dir, String name) {
                return name.startsWith(prefix);
            }
        });

        if(variants.length >= 1) {
            return new File(dir, variants[0]);
        } else {
            return null;
        }
    }

    private String languageNameFor(String code) {
        String name = (String)languageNames.get(code.toLowerCase());
        if(name != null) {
            return name;
        } else {
            return code;
        }
    }
}
```

The full code for the `AcceptList` class and all other source code can be downloaded from the Wrox website: http://www.wrox.com.

Summary

The essence of internationalizing web sites is to allow anyone the world over to be able to visit a web site and automatically view it in a language of their choice. The ability to choose the language to be displayed is available via the use of `Accept-Language` headers for content negotiation. The `I18NServlet` that we developed returns localized documents and other resources that are stored in the web server's document tree to a client. When receiving a request for the base name of such a file the `I18NServlet` goes through all variants to find the best match for the user's preferred languages and returns that variant with an acceptable character encoding. By making web sites totally international the numbers of people to which the Web is available increases significantly. This of course is perfect for any commercial website that is looking for an increase in their market coverage.

In this chapter we have looked at:

➤ The differing character encodings and languages available to Java

➤ Content negotiation, a feature which allows a servlet to return text in the user's preferred language.

➤ Character coding support in the API.

➤ An introduction to the concepts of character sets and character encodings.

➤ How text documents can have multiple variants, each in their own file.

Smart Servlets

Mixed Network Configurations

You've seen the common enterprise computing scenario: Various TCP/IP stacks, Novell IPX/SPX, Microsoft NetBEUI and IBM SNA/APC clutter an IT environment, requiring entertainingly conflicting client drivers, servers and various resources on both server and client workstations. These complexities cause technical and application support nightmares, yet interoperability of various systems is a necessary evil.

Keeping this environment in mind, consider all of software required to connect a workstation and servers to each of these servers and services, in terms of network drivers, stacks and so on, not to mention the different support libraries, configuration files, etc. that need to be installed and maintained.

For example, to install TCP/IP on a workstation or server, you need the proper TCP/IP "stack" running on both client and server. Additionally, you may require a telnet, ftp and http client executable on the client machine. To install IPX/SPX, you'll need the Netware server OS running on the server, with IPX/SPX drivers, as well as client network drivers on the client machine. Add in an SNA gateway to communicate with mainframe and TN3270 services on the client PC for terminal emulation. Finally, you'll need NetBEUI running on the client, if you plan on connecting to Windows NT.

Having fun yet? Most likely not! But the above quagmire clearly describes the average networked computing environment in the enterprise. Improvements in technology, technology management preferences and "best-of-breed" technology decisions are responsible for the rubbish that often clogs our networks. Traffic jams and collisions are imminent, but like any good urban planner knows, traffic control keeps things flowing and eliminates the network equivalent of a ten car pileup.

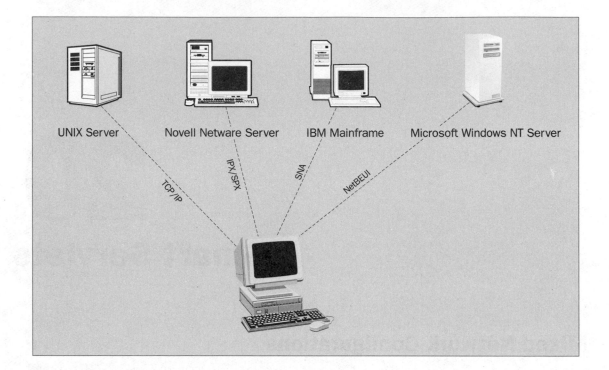

Mixed Database Platforms

With the same cluttered nature of networks, the same symptoms arise among the various database technologies. Oracle, Microsoft, Sybase, Informix and many other database software manufacturers each have their own custom means of communicating over the previously described networks. They too, require client drivers to be installed on server and client machines, adding to the pre–existing clutter of software and network traffic. Some of these drivers often conflict with the very network drivers they require to be installed to properly communicate with the server! The diagram exemplifies the next layer of complexity within the enterprise.

For example, setting up a Novell IPX/SPX Sybase database client not only requires an IPX/SPX client driver to be installed, but a Sybase Open Client driver as well. A specific version of the network client is required by the database client to operate and other database/network drivers may cause client operating system conflicts. This is only an example of what is faced when setting up a client workstation to communicate with a given network/database platform.

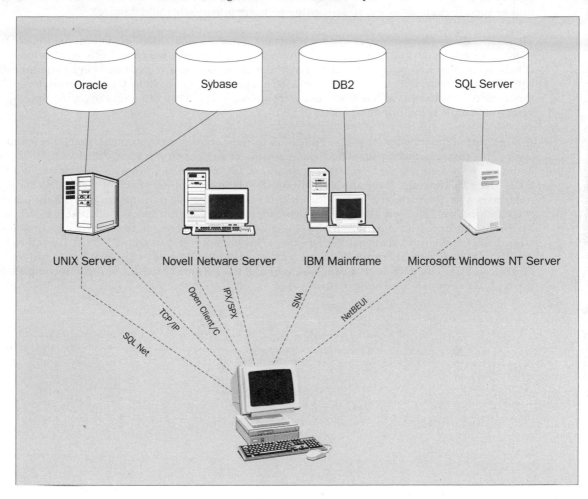

Mixed Processing and Operating System Platforms

Adding to the complexity, there's a slew of client and server operating systems (OSes) to contend with. NT, OS/2, VM, UNIX, Netware are just a handful of what the average I/T department needs to support and reliably build upon. The database operating system software resides on these OSes, as well as special application server/processing software (often called middleware).

These operating systems manage system resources, such as video, input (keyboard, mouse, etc.), sound, processing, memory, storage, etc. These operating systems are specifically written for a given combination of the above. Even in the case where the same operating system is available for different hardware platforms, they are indeed very different under the hood. In fact, no application or database server directly accesses the hardware and software resources. They often rely upon the operating system to handle those low-level tasks.

A large part of the uniqueness of an application infrastructure is what is known as the presentation layer. This comprises of the input and video portion of an operating system. A few of these that are found on the aforementioned operating systems are TN3270, Telnet, Motif (X-Windows), Windows GUI, Mac OS, Netscape Navigator and Microsoft Windows Explorer. Each of these presentation styles uses a keyboard/mouse and a video display to send/receive information to/from the client workstation. Also, it is very rare that the presentation layers are intrinsically adaptable to any given hardware platform. Third-party vendors emulate presentation layers in the "native" environment, to allow bridging the gap between differing OSes. This kind of software allows UNIX X-window applications to run on Microsoft Windows variants, as well as Windows applications to run on Macintosh PCs. The diagram is a conglomeration of the network, database and client complexities of the typical enterprise computing network.

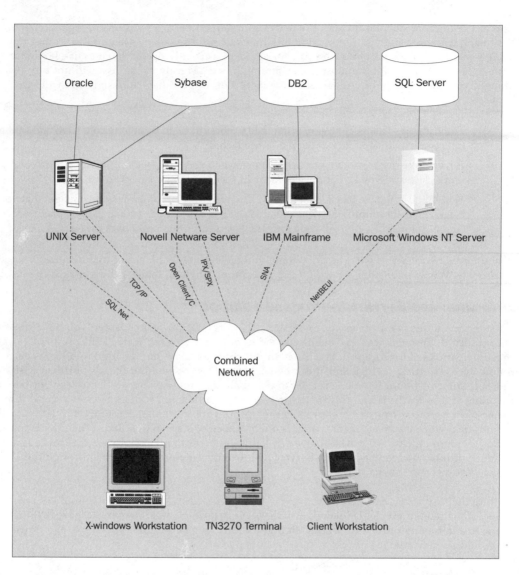

In summary, diverse networking topologies/protocols and database management servers, all running on various client and server operating systems wreak havoc within day–to–day system installations, operations and support of an enterprise client/server infrastructure. To resolve this, a centralized network, database and application solution is needed. This combines all of the network and database traffic and their associated drivers in a central repository. A thin–client approach is used on the presentation layer of each client, no matter what the operating system. This 'common desktop' approach lowers installation and support issues and keeps the maintenance costs of the system low.

If you are faced with a web development project that is like most development projects, several things are probably true.

You are doing new development. Very few e-commerce sites are revisions of legacy systems. That is not to say that your site will not need to talk to some of these legacy systems, but rather that you have a fairly free hand in the architecture of your site. You certainly do not have to use Java, but we believe Java will give you the most programming power. Merely using Java will not buy you much, though; you can write poor code in any language! You want to have a design that will have several features:

> Extensibility. That is, how easy is it to add features in to the system once it is up and running? Is the system maintainable without major headaches?

> Re-use. We don't want to start from scratch with every task we do. Inheriting from solidly built super-classes will make our development go faster and our changes easier.

> Flexibility. What we mean is that the system makes use of some of the advantages that your language of choice provides you with. In addition, avoid hard-coding like the plague! It is easier (and faster initially) to hard-code something, but this later comes back on you.

When implementing a servlet-based system, you have several choices of architecture to accomplish your goals. We will consider a few of these and present the one that we think makes the most sense.

One to One: the Servlet to Process solution

This design choice is fairly easy to understand. For each task in your system, you have one servlet to accomplish it. Suppose we have been retained to build a web site for the TallCoin bank, a rather prestigious financial institution, that after careful consideration, has decided to offer its customers online access to their savings and checking accounts, If we solved the Bank's problem with a one-to-one solution, we would have one servlet to do a balance inquiry, one servlet to transfer between accounts and so forth. While this is easy to code and implement, it does present several drawbacks. What if we need our transfer servlet to communicate with our balance inquiry servlet? Recall that the default behavior of servlets is that there is one instance of a servlet loaded. When the transfer servlet needs to communicate with the balance servlet, we need to first check to see that there is a valid instance of the balance servlet. The Servlet API provides methods to do this through the `ServletContext` object.

Calling the `ServletContext.getServlet(String servletName)` method will return a servlet object if the named servlet is loaded, or null if it is not. Once you have the servlet, Java still does not know this to be any particular servlet. In other words, to call methods specific to the transfer servlet, we would need to cast it as such:

```
BalanceServlet balServ = (BalanceServlet)ServletContext.getServlet
("BalanceServlet")

balServ.getAccountBalance();
```

What we have arrived at however, is a situation where every servlet on our site may need to know about every other servlet. In object oriented speak, this is tight coupling, where one class needs to know a lot about another class in order to do its job. Our transfer servlet needs to know about our balance servlet, down to the point of invoking methods on it. Therefore, any changes to the balance servlet may have a negative effect on the transfer servlet. For example if we were to add a parameter to the `getAccountBalance()` method above, we would not only have to recompile the balance servlet, but also the transfer servlet (after making the appropriate changes) and any other servlets that reference this method of the balance servlet. This is like a game of Twister, with too many arms and legs and they are all criss-crossed! Tight coupling should be avoided where possible.

There are also maintenance concerns. With each task you add to your site, you add another servlet. Suppose you have 20 tasks. If you implement the single-thread model of servlets, where there is not just one instance of a servlet, but rather each web site visitor gets his own instance of the servlet, you could have many instances of your servlets running if you have a high traffic site and if your hardware is not up to the chore, performance would take a nose-dive.

Even if you do not implement the single-thread model, your site still has a lot of servlets to manage and perhaps more importantly you, as a developer, are creating a maintenance quagmire for yourself.

For small sites that perform a minimal amount of simple tasks, the one-to-one model may be all right, but for anything beyond that, we do not recommend it.

Servlet Chaining Solution

Another design choice you have as a servlet developer is to chain your servlets. This is a process whereby the output of one servlet becomes the input to the next and so on. Servlet chaining has its place. For example, suppose in our banking example, we wanted to thank customers who used our site more than 5 times in a given 30 day period. When this condition was detected in our logon servlet, we could route the output of the logon servlet through another servlet that would record the users' information as someone to whom we want to extend the offer of a free toaster.

Servlet chaining can also be used in collaboration with your web server to process requests. The Java Web Server allows you to specify which servlet you want to handle certain content types.

Servlet chaining is a targeted solution that really does not offer much flexibility.

The Smart Servlet Solution

There are three basic tenets of object oriented programming: inheritance, encapsulation and polymorphism. Java supports inheritance very well, encapsulation is up to you to put into your design, but polymorphism gets a real shot in the arm from Java. The `Class` object (not to be confused with `class`, which is the keyword for identifying your source code file) has some methods that make runtime identification of class types easy and elegant and when we consider designing servlets for flexibility, these features of the `Class` object come in very handy.

Recall from our previous discussion of the one-to-one approach can get you into a situation where each servlet may need to know about every other servlet at *design time*. Under the smart servlet approach, it is not necessary for each servlet to be tightly coupled to any other servlet. Because of Javas' run time type identification, decisions about which class to load, or method to call are made at run time rather than when you write your code.

Request Processing

When a request comes in to a servlet, it can be the result of either a GET or a POST. The parameters coming into a servlet will be contained in the either the `QueryString`, or in the `HttpServletRequest` object. These requests are handled respectively by the `doGet()` and `doPost()` events. Consider the following code example, a snippet from our servlet for the TallCoin bank site:

```java
import java.io.*;
import javax.servlet.*;
import javax.servlet.http.*;

public class TallCoin extends HttpServlet {

    HttpSession session;
    PrintWriter out;

    public synchronized void doGet(HttpServletRequest req,HttpServletResponse res)
        throws ServletException, IOException {

        res.setContentType("text/html");
        out = res.getWriter();

        // If there is a parameter called, "Transaction", call doPost
        if (req.getQueryString() != null ||req.getParameter("Transaction")!= null){
          doPost(req,res);
        } else {
          out.println(Utilities.getHTMLfile(headFile));
          out.println(Utilities.getHTMLfile(bodyFile));
          out.println(Utilities.getHTMLfile(footFile));
        }
    }
}
```

When a servlet is first called, the doGet() method is executed. Our version of the doGet() method checks for a value in the QueryString, or whether there is a parameter called Transaction. If either of these conditions is met, we simply pass on any responsibilities to the doPost() method. If not, then we will serve up a page of HTML, using pre-fabricated text files to build the page. (More about that later).

This design allows the ultimate in flexibility. We are unconcerned with the contents of either the QueryString or the parameter. We simply delegate this to the doPost(), where it will be handled.

The doPost() code looks like this:

```java
public synchronized void doPost(HttpServletRequest req,HttpServletResponse res)
    throws ServletException, IOException {

    String command = req.getQueryString();
    Hashtable parms = new Hashtable(20);
    StringBuffer HTML = new StringBuffer();
    res.setContentType("text/html");
    out = res.getWriter();
    String parmName;
    String parmValue;

    session = req.getSession(true);

    HTML.append(Utilities.getHTMLfile(Utilities.getValue("
                        HTMLfilepath") + Utilities.getValue("headFile")));

    for (Enumeration e = req.getParameterNames(); e.hasMoreElements();) {
        parmName = (String)e.nextElement();
        parmValue = req.getParameter(parmName);
        parms.put(parmName, parmValue);
    }
```

```
      if (parms.get("Transaction")== null) {
         parms.put("Transaction",command);
      }

      try{
         Class c = Class.forName(req.getParameter("Transaction"));
         trans = (Transaction)c.newInstance();
         session.putValue("Transaction",trans);
      } catch(ClassNotFoundException cnfe) {
            HTML.append(cnfe.toString());
      } catch(InstantiationException ie) {
            HTML.append(ie.toString());
      } catch(IllegalAccessException iae) {
            HTML.append(iae.toString());
      }
      HTML.append(((Transaction)session.getValue("Transaction")).execute(
                  (Hashtable)parms.clone()));
      HTML.append(Utilities.getHTMLfile(Utilities.getValue("
                  HTMLfilepath") + Utilities.getValue("footFile")));
   }
}
```

The code in the `doPost()` will do several important things. At the top, we populate a variable with the contents of the `QueryString` (if one came in). We then instantiate a `Hashtable`, which will be used to hold any number of parameters that may come into the method. The loop that steps through an `Enumeration` of parameters will retrieve whatever variables were populated on the web page.

We have formulated our HTML to contain a parameter named "transaction." This variable contains the name of the class to instantiate. The following example shows a simple piece of HTML that might be used to authenticate a user of the TallCoin Bank web site:

```
<HTML>
  <HEAD>
    <TITLE>
      Welcome to the TallCoin Bank
    </TITLE>
  </HEAD>
  <BODY>
      <CENTER>
        <H3>
          Please Enter your Account Number:
        </H3>
      </CENTER>
        <FORM ACTION="/servlet/TallCoin" METHOD="POST">
          <CENTER>
            <INPUT TYPE="text" NAME="acctNum" SIZE="12" MAXLENGTH="12">
            <INPUT TYPE="hidden" NAME="Transaction" VALUE="Login">
            <P>
            <INPUT TYPE="submit" VALUE="     OK     ">
          </CENTER>
        </FORM>
  </BODY>
</HTML>
```

Here is what the page looks like:

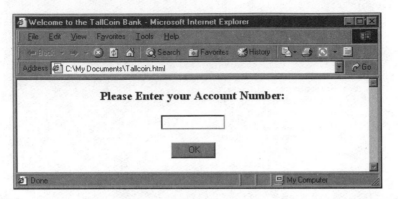

When the user clicks the OK button, the doPost() of the servlet will be called and the parameters will be extracted from the HttpServletRequest object. The value of the parameter named "Transaction" is "Login". The following line of code will populate a Class object with the name "Login":

```
Class c = Class.forName(req.getParameter("Transaction"));
```

After getting the name of the class, we call the newInstance() method of the Class object, which will give us a new instance of the Login class:

```
session.putValue("Transaction",Transaction)c.newInstance());
```

This is polymorphism at work. Here in the servlet, we are unconcerned with how the transaction actually accomplishes the Login procedure of a web site user. We do not know the name of the class, or what parameters it accepts. We simply know that we can instantiate the class that is the result of the forName() method, call its execute() method and it will work its magic.

(What we are doing in front of the newInstance() method is putting a reference to this class in the session object associated with this web site user. Session management is a complete topic in itself and we have deferred that to Chapter 5).

If there are any problems in the process of instantiating the class, we catch these exceptions and gently inform the user that their request cannot be processed. Assuming everything is alright, we go on to call the execute() method of the Login class. Everything we do in the doPost() with regard to calling functions is done through the session, which is an instance of HttpSession. As noted above, we put a reference to the Login class into the session after calling newInstance(). When we need to call a method of the Login class, we must get the reference from the session, cast it as a Transaction and then call the execute() method.

After all that, we put out whatever footer we want on our web page and serve the whole lot up to our customer!

```
HTML.append(((Transaction)session.getValue("Transaction")).
execute((Hashtable)parms.clone()));
  HTML.append(Utilities.getHTMLfile(footFile));
```

Process Delegation

At this point we need to explain a bit about the `Login` class (or whatever class comes in through the `Transaction` parameter in our HTML).

The TallCoin bank might want to give their customers a variety of services over this web site. Getting a balance, requesting a check be sent, transferring money between accounts are just a few examples. For the above code to work, every task we perform needs to inherit from a common ancestor. We have called this class `Transaction`:

```
import java.util.*;

public class Transaction {

    protected Hashtable parameters = new Hashtable(20);

    public String execute(Hashtable parms) {

        return "";
    }
}
```

Doesn't do much, does it? This is by design of course. It contains just the essentials. The `execute()` method will accept a `Hashtable` and return a `String`. The real work will be done in the descendant classes, which inherit from `Transaction`. Our login class might look like this:

```
import java.util.*;

public class Login extends Transaction {

    StringBuffer HTMLBuffer = new StringBuffer();
    String accountNum;

    public String execute(Hashtable parms) {

        accountNum = (String)parms.get("acctNum");

        // Do something here, such as execute some
        // SQL to verify that this is a valid acct.

        if (isValidAcct(acctNum)) {
            return HTMLBuffer.append(Utilities.getHTMLfile(
                                "promptForPin.txt")).toStirng;
        } else {
            return HTMLBuffer.append(Utilities.getHTMLfile(
                                "InvalidAcct.txt")).toString;
        }
    }
    public boolean isValidAcct(String acct) {

    // do some edit checking or validation to ensure that the number is valid
    return true;
    }
}
```

We would extract the account number from the `Hashtable` that comes in, then perhaps call a function to make sure that this is a valid account at the TallCoin bank. If so, we would probably want to put up some HTML to have the user enter their password or PIN number to gain access to the account.

Quite obviously, you would need to do a whole lot more than this to service online banking requests. However, what we want to stress with this design is that whatever processing you do, you should do it in these classes and not in the servlet itself. You could end up with a big and inefficient servlet by trying to do it all there. However, by keeping all your processing in classes that extend `Transaction`, you have an architecture that will allow you to add functionality with ease. It is quite possible to have one servlet that can do *anything*, since the actual processing is done in other classes entirely. What we have ended up with is our own application server!

Implementing the "Smart Servlet" in the Enterprise

Having in mind the complexity of the common enterprise, three very plausible system architecture scenarios and an in-depth view of how one of those options works under the hood, let's expand on how to solve the enterprise disparity with the features of the "Smart Servlet."

The Servlet as Task Master

As explained in an earlier section, the servlet architecture renders the servlet itself without much function, except for the ability to hand-off requests to another Java class. Conversely, if this technique was not used, a servlet would have a mammoth "switch-case" or "if-then-else-else if" statement to acquire not only the data to process, but also the type of processing to perform on that data. In addition, each individual process' code would also be in the servlet. This is seemingly a coding and debugging nightmare.

The Smart Servlet removes most of the processing from the servlet, except for the logic required to decide on which class to hand the parameterized data off to. This parameterized data can be seen as the details of a SQL SELECT statement, a date range, or whatever the processing "layer" requires as input to process. See a pictorial view of this concept in Figure 4.

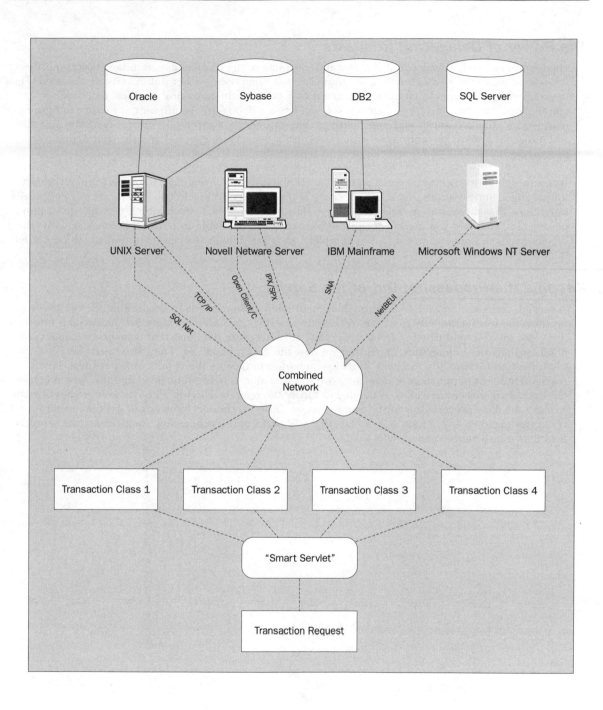

The Power of Delegating Requests

Have you ever wished you could simply hand–off some of the day–to–day mundane tasks your direct supervisor may give you, often to make room for that supervisor's other duties? Giving the servlet less to do gives it more time to complete the major task of properly managing sessions, database connections, transaction server connections, etc. From a debugging standpoint, it's easier to figure out if an "order" (i.e. a request) was improperly given, improperly carried out, or, not carried out at all when there is a manager/employee–type relationship between the servlet and the transaction processing layer. This eliminates the need to separate the duties within the servlet.

In short, delegating requests, much as in the workplace, allows processing to be performed without the manager understanding what is happening at the transaction level. The supervisor (servlet) needs only know that the resources needed for the task are available (data/formatting, network connections, parameters, etc.) and if someone (a capable transaction) is available to perform the task. Finally, the servlet needs to know when the task is complete, so it can deliver the results to that which requested it.

Keeping the Processing Out of the Servlet

A servlet, using the Smart Servlet model, as mentioned earlier, needs to ensure that the resources to perform the transaction are available. As certain raw materials are necessary for industrial production lines, the same is held true for servlets. Servlets need access to data and that is made available via a database/network connection, depending on how the data is acquired. They also need user identification information to check if the user qualifies to receive the results of the request. Finally, the servlet needs parameters to determine what transaction is being requested and just how much of the data source its connected to is needed to satisfy the request. Having all of these ingredients helps explain the data/process flow of the Smart Servlet. In short, the servlet needs to get the proper resources together, instantiate a Java class that will perform the processing, then release the resources, for other transactions to use.

Keeping Your Servlet and Ancestor Classes As Abstract as Possible

It has already been explained that a servlet needs to be free of larger processing tasks. Now let's take a step further into this design and explain how we can follow the Smart Servlet architecture into a robust design pattern.

The first step is to create an ancestor transaction class that can be extended suitably to handle specific details of a transaction, but only is defined with the rudiments of a transaction. These essentials are instantiation, resource gathering, processing and resource releasing. This carries over into the aforementioned Java classes, where these tasks are replicated in class methods. By keeping continuity between class methods and their signatures, the servlet can instantiate, gather resources, execute and release resources for a particular transaction class through reflection, Casting the result of a `Class.forName()` call to the name of the Transaction desired and calling class methods which are in the ancestor guarantees interface compatibility among descendant transactions. The only key rule here is to adhere to that interface when designing Transactions.

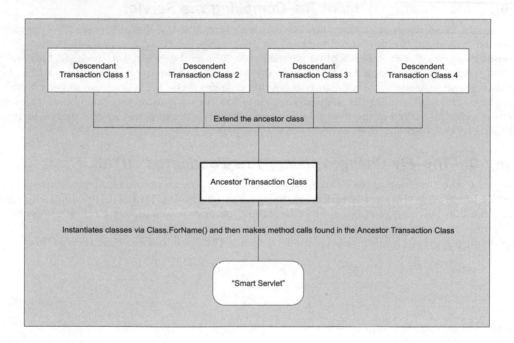

Smart Servlet Extensibility

Eliminating Method Parameters with Hashtables

One of our favorite objects in Java is the `Hashtable`. The reason we like it so much is its flexibility. `Hashtables` allow you to store key/value pairs and can grow dynamically. When we come into the `Login` class described above, we might only have one parameter, `acctNum`. However, if we were transferring funds from one account to another, we might well have parameters for the source account, target account and amount to transfer. Imagine if we implemented applying for a loan over the web site. We could well have 10 or 15 parameters coming into the `execute()` method of our class. If we had two `Strings`, three `Integers` and a `Vector` as parameters, the `Hashtable` would handle all of this, since it stores things as objects. Essentially, it allows you to have a method that can contain any number of parameters of any type, without changing the method signature at all. Now *that's* polymorphic!

Adding Functionality Without Re-Compiling the Servlet

How would these parameters affect how our `doPost()` method of the servlet handles the various requests? Not at all! We don't need to change a thing, since anything sent in through the `HttpServletRequest` object will be parsed in our loop and deposited in the `Hashtable`. In fact, we can even add new functionality to the site without bringing it down. If we add a class that extends `Transaction.java`, the only thing that changes is the HTML we use to get into the `doPost()` method. The servlet is already set up to handle any parameters that come in and to call whatever class is named in the `Transaction` variable. While this is not strictly design patterns in the Gang of Four sense, it does use inheritance in a patterns way.

Making On-The-Fly Changes Using "Pre-Fabricated" HTML Files

Our other favorite object is the `StringBuffer`. As most Java programmers know, Strings are actually immutable objects. If you change the contents of a String, Java actually allocates a new object under the hood. `StringBuffers`, however, allow you to concatenate any amount of text by using the `append()` method.

While you can certainly code your classes to output HTML one line at a time such as this,

```
HTMLBuffer.append("<TITLE>");
HTMLBuffer.append("Welcome to the TallCoin Bank");
HTMLBuffer.append("</TITLE>");
```

We think this is a rather inflexible way of doing things.

In both the servlet and the classes descended from `Transaction`, we refer to a class called `Utilities`. This is a class we use to do a variety of housekeeping jobs on behalf of the servlet and its helper classes. This class contains a series of static methods, so we never actually need an instance of it. One thing we do a lot of is reading text files to build our HTML that is put out to the browser. In the `Login` class, we read a file called `promptForPin.txt` that would contain everything we need to allow the user to enter their password and click OK. So the line

```
HTMLBuffer.append(Utilities.getHTMLfile("promptForPin.txt"));
```

will call a method `getHTMLfile()` which will read a text file and append its contents to the end of the `StringBuffer` called `HTMLBuffer`. The benefits of this should be obvious. If the way we want to present HTML changes, we simply edit this text file, without changing anything in our class. One other item to note is that the name of the file is hardcoded in this example. Under ideal circumstances, even this would be dynamic. What we like to do is store the names of these files in a `Hashtable`, along with the key to it. So, if we had a file that contained all the preformatted HTML to notify the user that the pin they entered is invalid, our key/value entry in the `Hashtable` might be something like `invalidPin/invalidPin.txt`. We serialize this `Hashtable` to disk and when our servlet loads, we "inflate" the `Hashtable` and have all of the names of the files at the ready. This would change the above call to look something like this:

```
HTMLBuffer.append(Utilities.getHTMLfile(
                    Utilities.getValue("promptForPin")));
```

Where `getValue()` would be a method to retrieve a value (`promptForPin.txt`) from the `Hashtable` based on the key (`promptForPin`). We maintain this `Hashtable` through a separate servlet, but this could also be done through a Java application. This works quite well and again makes our entire web site far more dynamic and extensible.

The code for the `Utilities` servlet follows:

```java
import java.util.*;
import java.io.*;
import java.text.*;

public class Utilities {

    public static Hashtable HelperFile;

    public static synchronized void getHelperFile(String filename) {

        HelperFile = new Hashtable();
        Object o = null;
        ObjectInputStream in;

        // Try to restore the object from the file.
        try {
            in = new ObjectInputStream(new FileInputStream(filename));
            o = in.readObject();

            if (o instanceof Hashtable) {
                HelperFile = (Hashtable)o;
            }
            in.close();
        } catch(Exception e) {
            HelperFile = null;
        }
    }

    public synchronized static String getValue(String name) {

        if (HelperFile.get(name) != null) {
            return (String)HelperFile.get(name);
        }
        return "";
```

Continued on Following Page

509

```
    }

    public static String getHTMLfile(String htmlSourceFile) {

        StringBuffer HTMLBuffer = new StringBuffer();
        String desc;
        char[] chars = null;
        int c;
        FileReader in;

        try {
            File inputFile = new File(htmlSourceFile);
            in = new FileReader(inputFile);

            while ((c = in.read()) != -1)
                HTMLBuffer.append((char) c);
            in.close();
        } catch (IOException ioe) {
            HTMLBuffer.append(ioe.toString());
        }

        return HTMLBuffer.toString();
    }
}
```

Below is the full code for the `Tallcoin` Servlet.

```
import java.io.*;
import java.util.*;
import javax.servlet.*;
import javax.servlet.http.*;

public class TallCoin extends HttpServlet {

    HttpSession session;
    PrintWriter out;

    public synchronized void init (ServletConfig config) {

        try {
            super.init(config);
        } catch(ServletException se) {
            System.out.println("Could not access Superclass.init.");
        }
        System.out.println("The config parameter is " +
                            config.getInitParameter("configParms"));
        Utilities.getHelperFile(config.getInitParameter("configParms"));
    }

    public synchronized void doGet (HttpServletRequest req,
                HttpServletResponse res)  throws ServletException, IOException {

        res.setContentType("text/html");
        out = res.getWriter();

        // if there is a parameter called, "Transaction", call doPost
        if (req.getQueryString() != null || req.getParameter("Transaction")!= null) {
            doPost(req,res);
        } else {
            out.println(Utilities.getHTMLfile(Utilities.getValue("HTMLfilepath") +
                            Utilities.getValue("headFile")));
```

```
          out.println(Utilities.getHTMLfile(Utilities.getValue("HTMLfilepath") +
                            Utilities.getValue("bodyFile")));
          out.println(Utilities.getHTMLfile(Utilities.getValue("HTMLfilepath") +
                            Utilities.getValue("footFile")));
     }
}

   public synchronized void doPost (HttpServletRequest req,
            HttpServletResponse res)  throws ServletException, IOException {

      String command = req.getQueryString();
      Hashtable parms = new Hashtable(20);
      StringBuffer HTML = new StringBuffer();
      res.setContentType("text/html");
      out = res.getWriter();
      String parmName;
      String parmValue;
      Transaction trans;

      session = req.getSession(true);

      HTML.append(Utilities.getHTMLfile(Utilities.getValue("HTMLfilepath") +
                            Utilities.getValue("headFile")));

      for (Enumeration e = req.getParameterNames() ; e.hasMoreElements() ;) {
         parmName = (String)e.nextElement();
         parmValue = req.getParameter(parmName);
         parms.put(parmName, parmValue);
      }

      // Determine which class to instantiate.

      if (parms.get("Transaction")== null) {
         parms.put("Transaction",command);
      }
      try{
         Class c = Class.forName(req.getParameter("Transaction"));
         trans =  (Transaction)c.newInstance();
         session.putValue("Transaction",trans);
      } catch(ClassNotFoundException cnfe) {
         HTML.append(cnfe.toString());
      } catch(InstantiationException ie) {
         HTML.append(ie.toString());
      } catch(IllegalAccessException iae) {
         HTML.append(iae.toString());
      }

      HTML.append(((Transaction)session.getValue("Transaction")).execute(
                            (Hashtable)parms.clone()));
      HTML.append(Utilities.getHTMLfile(Utilities.getValue("HTMLfilepath") +
                            Utilities.getValue("footFile")));
      }
   }
}
```

The full source code for the SiteAdmin class that controls and maintains the Hashtable can be downloaded from the Wrox website at: http://www.wrox.com.

Summary

Design decisions are a bit like a toothbrush: Someone else may have a very nice one, but that doesn't mean *you* want to use it! However, we feel that the ideas put forth here do represent sound design decisions in that they adhere to those three pillars of object–oriented programming, inheritance, polymorphism and encapsulation. In addition, they allow for extensibility in an easy and elegant manner. Our servlet (and we only need *one* servlet to manage our entire web site) is a master of generality. To cite our work for the TallCoin bank, details of account transfers or loan applications are kept entirely out of the servlet. These are handled by plain vanilla Java classes. This allows each component of our system to focus on what it does best. The servlet interacts with the web server – it doesn't need to worry about checking for insufficient funds. Classes that do data processing do just that – they do not need to be concerned with `HttpSession` objects or `ServletRequest` object or the like.

Finally, by moving as much HTML generation as possible out of the servlet and into text files, you provide yourself as a developer the most flexibility possible in managing the content of your site.

Java has many slick features that make it a programming tour-de-force and by carefully using it with the Servlet API, your web site can serve your users well, without becoming a maintenance headache for you.

Server Programming with JNDI

The Java Naming and Directory Interface (JNDI) is designed to simplify access to the directory infrastructure used in the development of advanced network applications. Directories are special types of databases that provide quick access to their data stores. Traditionally, you had to use different APIs to access different directory services such as LDAP (the Lightweight Directory Access Protocol) or Sun's NIS (Network Information Service). However, JNDI supplies a standard API to access any type of directory. JNDI also allows you to store and retrieve Java objects on the network. With the full SDK, you can even develop your own service providers for directory services that JNDI doesn't yet support (such as Banyan Vines).

In this chapter we are going to cover the following:

> What a directory service is

> What LDAP is

> What separates JNDI from a traditional directory SDK

> How to manage directory information with JNDI

> How to store and retrieve Java objects on the network

Finally, we're going to look at a real world case study, demonstrating the practical applications of JNDI & LDAP

Naming and Directory Services

The Network is the Computer

"The Network is the Computer" is a tag-line Sun Microsystems has used to sell quite a bit of Sun hardware and software. It is also the central tenet of successful Java programming. If you look at the areas where Java has had its greatest success (chat clients, servlets, middleware), they involve developing applications that communicate over the network.

In fact it is fairly safe to say that as we head into the post-Y2K era of computing, any application that is not able to communicate on a network is soon to be obsolete. In a weird twist of fate, the computing world has agreed upon a common network protocol suite, TCP/IP (e.g. the Internet protocols) while computing platforms have continued to diverge into a wider variety.

If the only computing you are consciously aware of is a personal computer, you might find this hard to believe. However, nearly every device you come into contact with from your refrigerator to your car to the gas pump where you fill up your car to your office's heating/cooling system has a microchip in it and increasingly these chips are networkable.

In many cases the purpose of putting these devices on the network is to make them easier to manage, in order to save time, which in turn saves money. For example in a multi-building office complex a networked heating/cooling system can "report" back to a central server that can display to the heating/cooling system team the status of all of the air conditioners and thermostats in the building complex. From this central screen the system's team can determine when a unit is potentially overheating, or when to schedule preventive maintenance (e.g. add more coolant to an air conditioner or when to replace air filters). Otherwise members of the team would have to manually go and check each device which could be an impossible task when dealing with a complex such as large university with nearly 100 buildings.

Unfortunately even if we have networkable devices and a great development language like Java, it becomes difficult to mesh the two together. Whenever you add a computer to the network, whether it's a PC, a server, a Palm Pilot or a toaster, there is a variety of configuration information that needs to be set. This includes things like an IP address, a domain name, the abilities of the networked device (e.g. print server, the ability to toast bread, etc.), who has rights to the device, etc. This information is usually available to the device itself, but not often to the outside world. For example, when you setup a new PC on the network you often need to setup a network printer for it. Currently there's not an easy way to "discover" what printer is available to you, nor its capabilities (e.g. color or black/white, laser or ink jet, etc.) unless you happen to ask your co-worker or network manager. By using a directory service and Java (using the JNDI API) you can put your networked device's capabilities and configuration information into a networked system that can then be queried by other networked devices that might want to use that device (e.g. PCs can query to discover printers available to them).

In this chapter we're going to discuss how the **Java Naming Directory Interfaces (JNDI) API** enables you to add these types of capabilities to your network applications.

Naming Services

A **naming service** is a service that provides for the creation of a standard name for a given set of data. For example, on the Internet, each host (each web server with a live Internet connection) has what is called a **Fully Qualified Domain Name (FQDN)**. www.wrox.com and www.coe.unt.edu are both FQDNs, and each FQDN is unique, so there is only one www.wrox.com and only one www.coe.unt.edu. A FQDN is constructed from a hostname (www), zero or more sub-domain names (coe) and a domain name (wrox.com or unt.edu).

The hostname and the sub-domain names are managed by the organization that owns the registered domain name (e.g. unt.edu which is owned by the University of North Texas). The domain name is provided to an organization by the InterNIC , which ensures that each domain name is unique. Through the use of sub-domains and domain names we can have systems that share the same hostname (e.g. www) yet are considered entirely separate entities. For example www.cs.wrox.com is different from www.wrox.com. In this case the sub-domain cs.wrox.com is actually "below" the root domain of wrox.com providing for its own unique namespace.

Directory Services

A directory service is a special type of database that is designed to be read very quickly through various indexing, caching and disk access techniques. They are also typically described using a hierarchical information model. This is in contrast to the Relational Database Management Systems such as Oracle or Microsoft SQL Server which are built to handle transaction based actions (e.g. an operation only succeeds if a series of steps are completed, otherwise it's "rolled back") and use a relational information model.

A directory service will always have a naming service (but a naming service doesn't necessarily have to have a directory service). An example of a directory service in the physical world is a telephone book. A telephone book allows us to look up the telephone number of a person or business very quickly, if we know the name of the person whose number we want.

There are a plethora of directory (and pseudo-directory) services in use on our networks today. One directory service we use every day on the Internet is the **Domain Naming Service** (DNS), which takes a FQDN and returns that FQDN's IP address. All Internet communication uses the Internet Protocol suite (consisting of TCP, UDP and IP). For successful communication between two computers, each system must know the IP address of the other. IP addresses consist of 32 bit numbers: 198.137.240.92, while hostnames take the form of something like www.yahoo.com. Computers are better at dealing with numbers, but humans (most humans anyway), are better at remembering names. Every time you try to connect to an Internet server using its name, your computer must first get the server's IP address via DNS.

Most likely your organization also uses one of the following directory services:

> Novell Directory Services (NDS)
> Network Information Services (NIS/NIS+)
> Windows NT Domains
> Active Directory Services (ADS)

Each of these directory services (although the NT Domains service isn't a true directory service, many people try to use it as one) provides more information than the simple name to IP mapping we get from DNS. Each one also allows us to store information about users (e.g. userid, passwords, names, etc.), user groups (e.g. for access control) and computers (e.g. their Ethernet and IP addresses). NDS and ADS allow more functions (such as the location of network printers, software, and so on) than either NIS or NT Domains.

Because there are so many directory services and we have so many systems on our networks, some larger problems have arisen. Essentially, it boils down to three issues: keeping track of users, network resources such as computers and printers, and keeping information consistent across all the various directory stores.

In many organizations you'll find that your users will need access to a Novell system (which uses NDS) for file and print sharing, an account on a Windows NT box for running Microsoft based applications and finally an account on a UNIX box (using NIS) for email & web page publication.

Unfortunately for network managers, none of these directory services interact with each other. As a result, users often end up with different ids and passwords on each system (which in turn leads to insecure passwords, because users have trouble remembering multiple passwords). As a further security risk, if a user leaves the organization, it's very difficult to make sure that all of the former user's accounts are removed.

Each directory service also has its own particular protocol, which makes it very difficult for the traditional application developer to interact with several different directory services.

Why LDAP?

The **Lightweight Directory Access Protocol (LDAP)** was developed in the early 1990s as standard directory protocol. Since LDAP is now the most popular directory protocol and JNDI can access LDAP, we'll be spending most of our time talking about how to harness LDAP to improve your Java applications with JNDI.

LDAP can trace its roots back to the X.500 protocol (AKA the "Heavy" Directory Access Protocol) which was originally based on the OSI networking protocols (an early "competitor" to the Internet protocols).

LDAP defines how clients should access data on the server. It does not specify how the data should be stored on the server. Most often you'll interact with a server that's been specifically built for LDAP such as the openLDAP or Netscape Directory server. However, LDAP can become a front-end to any type of data store. Because of this, most popular directory services now have an LDAP front-end of some type including NIS, NDS, Active Directory, and even Windows NT Domains.

LDAP Data

The data in LDAP is organized in a tree, called a **Directory Information Tree (DIT)**. Each "leaf" in the DIT is called an **entry**. The first entry in a DIT is called the **root entry**.

An entry is comprised of a **Distinguished Name** (DN) and any number of attribute/value pairs. The DN is the name of an entry and it must be unique. It's like the unique key of a relational database. A DN also shows the relation of the entry to the rest of the DIT, in a manner similar to the way the full path name of a file shows the relation of a particular file on your hard-drive to the rest of the files on your system. A path to a file on your system reads left to right when reading from root to file. A DN reads right to left when reading from root to entry.

Here is an example of a DN:

```
uid=scarter, ou=People, o=airius.com
```

The leftmost part of a DN is called a **Relative Distinguished Name (RDN)** and is made up of an attribute/value that is in the entry. The RDN in the example above would be `uid=scarter`.

LDAP attributes often use mnemonics as their names. Here are some of the more common LDAP attributes and what they define.

LDAP Attribute	Definition
cn	common name
sn	surname
givenname	first name
uid	userid
dn	Distinguished Name
mail	email address

Any attribute can have one or more values if defined by the schema. For example a user can have more than one email address so they could have more than one value for their `mail` attribute. Attribute values can be either text or binary data. Attributes are referred to in name/value pairs.

There is also a special attribute called `objectclass`. The `objectclass` attribute of an entry specifies what attributes are required and what attributes are allowed in a particular entry. Like objects in Java, object classes in LDAP can be extended. When an object class is extended, it keeps the existing attributes, but you can specify new attributes for a particular entry.

Here is an example LDAP entry represented in the **LDAP Data Interchange Format (LDIF),** This is a text-based format used to work on LDAP data, with both our applications and our end-users:

```
dn: uid=scarter, ou=People, o=fedup.com
cn: Sam Carter
sn: Carter
givenname: Sam
objectclass: top
objectclass: person
objectclass: organizationalPerson
objectclass: inetOrgPerson
ou: Accounting
ou: People
l: Sunnyvale
uid: scarter
mail: scarter@fedup.com
telephonenumber: +1 408 555 4798
facsimiletelephonenumber: +1 408 555 9751
roomnumber: 4612
```

Attributes also have **matching rules**. These rules tell the server how it should consider whether a particular entry is a "match" or not for a given query.

The possible matching rules are:

DN	Attribute is in the form of a Distinguished Name.
Case Insensitive String (CIS)	Attribute can match if values of the query equals the attribute's value, regardless of case.
Case Sensitive String (CSS)	Attribute can match if values of the query equals the attributes' value including the case.
Telephone	Is the same as CIS except that things like "+" and " " (space) are ignored when determining the match.
Integer	Attribute match is determined using only numbers.
Binary	Attribute matches if the value of the query and the value of the attribute are the same binary values (e.g. searching an LDAP database for a particular photo).

The definition of attributes, attribute matching rules and the relationship between `objectclasses` and attributes are defined in the server's schema. The server contains a predefined schema, "out of the box", but you can extend the schema (as long as the server supports the LDAP v3 protocol as defined in RFC 2251) to include your own attributes and object classes.

LDAP servers also support referrals (e.g. pointers to other LDAP directories where data resides), so a single LDAP server could search millions of entries from one client request. You can replicate LDAP data to improve reliability and speed. Finally LDAP has a very strong security model using ACLS to protect data inside the server and supporting the Secure Socket Layers (SSL)/Transport Layer Security (TLS) and Simple Authentication & Security Layer (SASL) protocols.

LDAP has growing momentum both as the standard protocol for electronic address books and as the central directory service for network services. For more information about LDAP see the book, *Implementing LDAP*, ISBN 1-861002-21-1, from Wrox press.

Introducing JNDI

While LDAP is growing in popularity and in usage, it's still a long way from being ubiquitous. Other directory services such as NIS (primarily developed by Sun) are still in widespread use. Another issue for the developers of Java was that for Java to succeed as an enterprise development language, it needed to support existing distributed computing standards such as the **Common Object Request Broker Architecture (CORBA)**, which is heavily used in large organizations that have many different types of applications interacting with each other. CORBA is a language and platform independent architecture for enabling distributed application programming (where an application on one machine can access a function of a different application located on a different machine as if it was calling an internal function). CORBA uses a naming service for defining the location of the available objects.

It was decided to make it easier on Java application developers by creating a standard API for interacting with naming and directory services, similar to what Java application developers have for databases in JDBC. This API is very important for the long-term development of Java, particularly the **Enterprise Javabeans** (EJB) initiative. A key component of the EJB initiative is the ability to store and retrieve Java objects on the network. A directory service (most likely LDAP), is going to be the primary data store for Java objects, in particular Java objects that are fairly stable (e.g. they are retrieved more often from the network than stored on the network). This is because when loading objects from the network, you want to be able to locate them quickly and a directory service enables very fast lookup & retrieval of data, which can be a person's record or binary data like a serialized Java object.

It would probably help to understand the relationships of directory services, JNDI and LDAP by looking at some diagrams.

Our first diagram shows the relationship between a client and a variety of directory services. Each directory service requires its own API which adds complexity and code bloat to our client application:

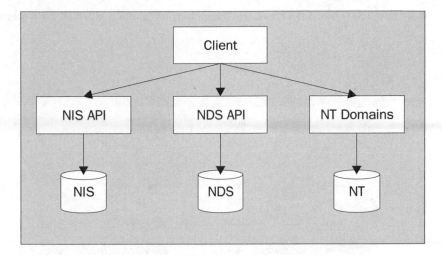

Our next example shows how we could simplify this with JNDI. With JNDI, we still have multiple servers and multiple APIs underneath, but to the application developer, it is effectively a single API.

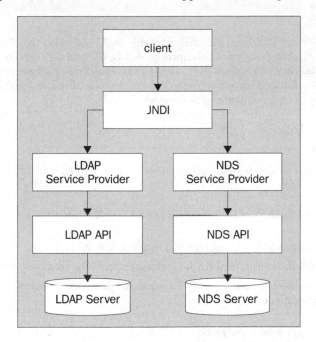

While the application developer now has an easier time developing network applications because they can concentrate on a single API, the developer still faces potential problems because not all **JNDI service providers** (JNDI terminology for the "drivers" that allow you to interact with different directory services) are created equal. Also each directory service is different (they name their entries differently, have different capabilities, and so on). Because of these differences, the developer builds an application that is larger in size and more prone to failure because of the number of different services in use.

Finally we show how JNDI and LDAP can work together, for a much more elegant solution:

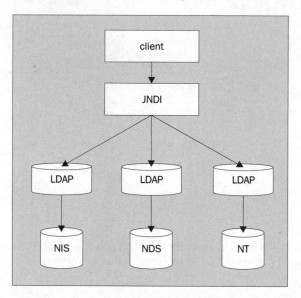

In this final example, we use JNDI to communicate with an LDAP server(s). To the developer, they are only having to worry about one particular protocol (LDAP) and API (JNDI). In this example we are relying on the availability of vendors providing LDAP interfaces to their respective protocols. And this is not such a far-fetched idea. For each of these popular directory services, there are products that allow you to communicate with them via LDAP.

Using JNDI

Now that you have a basic understanding of directory services, JNDI and LDAP, it's time to get our hands dirty doing some work.

To use JNDI as described in this chapter you will need the following:

> Sun's Java Development Kit 1.1 or higher (I'm using JDK 2.1)
> The JNDI Software Development Kit 1.2 (available from http://java.sun.com/jndi/)
> A LDAP v3 compliant directory server (I used Netscape's Directory server from http://home.netscape.com)

As a brief note before proceeding, the JNDI 1.2 SDK was still in beta when I wrote this, so some details may have changed slightly.

Installing JNDI

Here are the steps I followed to get things working on my system (Windows NT 4, Service Pack 3).

> Install Netscape Directory server (or your favorite LDAP v3 server)
> Install JDK 2.1

> ➢ Download JNDI 1.2
> ➢ Unzip JNDI 1.2 into a directory called `jndi2`
> ➢ Unzip the JNDI zip file into a directory called `jndi` inside of the `jndi2` directory
> ➢ Unzip the LDAP zip file into a directory called `ldap` inside the `jndi2` directory
> ➢ Make a directory called `jar` in your `jndi2` directory
> ➢ Copy all of the `*.jar` files in the `jndi/lib` and `ldap/lib` directories to the `jndi2/jar` directory (not really necessary but makes it easier to remember the paths to the JAR files when we do the next step)
> ➢ Create a system variable called `CLASSPATH` and set it to the paths to each of the JAR files (e.g. on a Windows system it might look like this: `CLASSPATH = d:\jndi2\jar\ldap.jar; d:\jndi2\jar\providerutil.jar; d:\jndi2\jar\jndi.jar;`)

Now you are ready to use JNDI and LDAP.

JNDI Packages

JNDI is made up of the following packages:

`javax.naming`	Allows applications to interact with naming services.
`javax.naming.directory`	Allows applications to interact with both directory and naming services, and is derived from the `javax.naming` package
`javax.naming.spi`	The package JNDI service providers use to interact with `javax.naming.*` packages, and allows for different providers to be plugged in, interchangeably with the overlying JNDI API
`javax.naming.ldap`	Allows your applications to use LDAP v3 extended operations and controls.

JNDI makes heavy use of interfaces. An interface is a type of abstract class that defines a set of methods that a particular class must implement in order for it to be concrete. They are often confused with abstract classes. The biggest difference to remember is that a class can only extend a single abstract class, while a class can implement many different interfaces. Interfaces enable the Java programmer to have access to something that resembles multiple inheritance.

The reason why JNDI uses interfaces so much is because most directory services have similar capabilities (e.g. to lookup entries via a unique name), but how they accomplish this is different between each directory service. So JNDI provides for a "lookup" method that each service provider must implement, so a Java programmer using JNDI knows to expect it, but how it's actually implemented is dependent upon the service provider and "black boxed" to the application programmer.

For a full list of packages available for the JNDI API see Appendix L.

JNDI Service Providers, AKA JNDI Drivers

You can't use JNDI without using a service provider so it's helpful to understand what they are.

A service provider is a set of Java classes that enable you to communicate with a directory service similarly to the way a JDBC driver enables you to communicate to a database. For a service provider to be available for use in JNDI it must implement the `Context` interface (actually most of the service providers you will use will likely implement the `DirectoryContext` interface which extends the `Context` interface to enable directory serivces).

What this means is that you only have to learn JNDI to know the API calls to connect to a naming or directory service, while the service provider worries about the ugly details (e.g. the actual network protocol, encoding/decoding values, etc).

Unfortunately service providers are not a magic bullet. You must know something about the underlying directory service so that you can correctly name your entries and build the correct search queries. Unlike relational databases, directory services do not share a common query language such as SQL.

In JNDI 1.2 service providers can support a concept of "federation" where a service provider can pass an operation to another service provider if it does not understand the naming or operation scheme. For example if you wanted to find out the MX record for a particular domain from DNS (the MX record contains the preferred destination email server for a domain), but your initial service provider was LDAP, it would not be able to answer the request. If federation was enabled it would be able to pass the request to the next service provider on the federation list, which if it was a DNS service provider would be able to handle the request for you.

Ideally this should be transparent to the application programmer. However, since this is a new feature, it has not been widely implemented/tested.

So to sum it up, a service provider enables your JNDI applications to communicate with a naming/directory service. The rest of the interfaces, classes and exceptions all revolve around your interaction with a service provider.

How to Obtain JNDI Service Providers

When you download the JNDI Software Development Kit (SDK), it will come with a number of existing service providers from Sun (an SDK comes with the API plus documentation and extras like service providers). These include providers for LDAP, NIS, COS (CORBA Object Service), RMI Registry and File System. Many different vendors also provide service providers for other directory services, or as replacements for the default providers Sun ships. For example Novell has a service provider for NDS, while both IBM and Netscape have written alternative service providers for LDAP.

It is easy to switch between service providers.

For example, to use the default Sun LDAP service provider you would make a call like this:

```
//Specify which class to use for our JNDI provider
env.put(Context.INITIAL_CONTEXT_FACTORY, "com.sun.jndi.ldap.LdapCtxFactory");
```

Now to switch to using IBM's LDAP service provider you would simply replace the
`"com.sun.jndi.ldap.LdapCtxFactory"` with the full package name of the IBM LDAP service
provider like this:

```
//Specify which class to use for our JNDI provider
env.put(Context.INITIAL_CONTEXT_FACTORY, "com.ibm.jndi.LDAPCtxFactory");
```

There is a list of existing service providers at:

http://java.sun.com/products/jndi/serviceproviders.html

Developing Your Own Service Provider

You may also need to implement your own service provider in particular if you need to use a
directory service (such as Windows NT domains or Banyan Vines) that doesn't already have an
existing service provider.

In the JNDI SDK Sun provides an example of how to write a service provider. The JNDI tutorial will
contain information on how to write a service provider and it's available at:
http://java.sun.com/products/jndi/tutorial/index.html.

Sun also provides a PDF document that describes the process of writing a service provider at
ftp://ftp.javasoft.com/docs/jndi/jndispi.pdf.

And Netscape's LDAP service provider is available as an open-source project at
http://www.mozilla.org/directory/.

Basic LDAP Operations

Before you can perform any type of operation on an LDAP sever, you must first obtain a reference
and a network connection to the LDAP server. You must also specify how you wish to be bound to
the server – either anonymously or as an authenticated user. Most LDAP servers allow some type of
anonymous access (generally read-only abilities for attributes like e-mail addresses & telephone
numbers), but LDAP also supports advanced security features via ACLs that are dependent upon who
the connection is authenticated as.

For example, an LDAP server may have several layers of rights for any given entry:

> Anonymous users can see an employee's email address and telephone number

> The employee can see their entire entry, but only modify certain attributes such as telephone
> number, password and office room number

> A user's manager can update an employee's telephone number and office room number, but
> nothing else. They can also see the employee's entire record

> A small group, the Directory Administrators, have full rights to the entire server including the
> ability to add or remove any entry

Standard LDAP Operations

There are a few standard operations in LDAP. They are:

> Connect to the LDAP server

> Bind to the LDAP server (you can think of this step as authenticating)

> Perform a series of LDAP operations:
>> Search the server
>> Add a new entry
>> Modify an entry
>> Delete an entry

> Disconnect from the LDAP server

In the rest of this chapter we will work through each of these steps.

Connecting to the LDAP Server with JNDI

In JNDI, you must first obtain a reference to an object that implements the `DirContext` interface. In most applications we will use an `InitialDirContext` object which takes a hash table as a parameter. This hash table can contain a number of different references – at the very least it should contain a reference to a field with the key `Context.INITIAL_CONTEXT_FACTORY` with a value of the fully qualified class name of the service provider and the hostname, port number to the LDAP server. You do this with the `Context.PROVIDER_URL` key. The value of this key should be the protocol, hostname and port number to the LDAP server like this: ldap://localhost:389.

Here is an example:

We first create a `Hashtable` to store our environmental variables that JNDI will use to connect to the directory service.

```
Hashtable env = new Hashtable();
```

Next we specify the fully qualified package name of our JNDI provider. We are using the standard Sun LDAP service provider that comes with the JNDI SDK.

```
//Specify which class to use for our JNDI provider
env.put(Context.INITIAL_CONTEXT_FACTORY, "com.sun.jndi.ldap.LdapCtxFactory");
```

Next we must specify the hostname and port number to our LDAP server.

```
// Specify host and port to use for directory service
env.put(Context.PROVIDER_URL, "ldap://localhost:389");
```

Finally we get a reference to our initial directory context with a call to the `InitialDirContext` constructor, giving it our `Hashtable` as its only parameter. A directory context tells JNDI what service provider we will be using, what naming/directory server we will be connecting to, at what location we will we be accessing the directory from initially (e.g. the search base) and any authentication information.

```
//Get a reference to a directory context
DirContext ctx = new InitialDirContext(env);
```

Binding

If you use the default values, the connection will be bound as anonymous. Many LDAP servers provide some type of read access to their directory data (e.g. for address book applications). Specifically the type of access an application has to the LDAP server is dependent upon the **Access Control Lists (ACLs)** of the LDAP server. Which ACLs apply to an operation are determined by how the application is "bound" or authenticated.

LDAP allows for an extremely flexible security model. ACLs determine what particular access is available to an entry by an application. Because an entry can have several ACLs defined, it is possible that an entry will have several different "views" to an application simply by changing the binding (e.g. who the application is authenticated as). LDAP also supports Transport Security Layer (TSL also still known as Secure Socket Layer/SSL) for protecting content "over the wire" or to improve authentication via client-certificates. Finally LDAP supports the Simple Authentication and Security Layer (SASL) protocol which enables you to use other authentication/encryption mechanisms such as Kerberos without "breaking" the protocol.

You can specify authentication by specifying the `Context.SECURITY_AUTHENTICATION`, `Context.SECURITY_PRINCIPAL`, and `Context.SECURITY_CREDENTIALS` in the hash table passed to the `InitialDirContext` object.

Here is an example of binding to a server:

```
Hashtable env = new Hashtable();
//This sends the id and password as plain text over the wire
env.put(Context.SECURITY_AUTHENTICATION, "simple");
env.put(Context.SECURITY_PRINCIPAL, MGR_DN);
env.put(Context.SECURITY_CREDENTIALS, MGR_PW);

//Get a reference to a directory context
DirContext ctx = new InitialDirContext(env);
```

To specifically bind to the server we must provide the environment with the method for our authentication (e.g. "simple", SSL , or SASL). Then we must specify the DN of the entry we wish to bind as and the entry's password.

What's the Difference Between "simple", "SSL/TLS", and "SASL"

The latest LDAP specification, LDAP v3, allows for three types of security:

> Simple
> SSL/TLS
> SASL

Simple

"Simple" security means that you will only authenticate to the server using standard plain-text userids and passwords without any encryption on the network. This is by far the most common, and least secure of the various authentication methods. It is insecure for two reasons, one of which is that userids and passwords are transmitted to the server over a public network, where anyone can steal the userids and passwords off the network. Secondly, there is nothing to guarantee that the person who types in the userid and password is the actual owner of that userid and password.

SSL/TLS

The Secure Socket Layer protocol was developed by Netscape Communications to improve the security of Web based transactions. It has become an official standard called Transport Layer Security (TLS), but is still often referred to as SSL.

SSL allows you to encrypt your entire transaction over the network, making it very hard for anyone to steal the information (such as your userids and passwords). Standard SSL does not verify the identity of the person who typed in the userid and password (however, it does ensure that the machine you are issuing your id and password to is "the real server"). Most servers that implement SSL also support client-certificates (certificates are text files that are used to vouch for the identity of the server and client) for user authentication. Instead of presenting a userid and password to the system, you can present a certificate to the server. If the certificate you present matches an allowed certificate, you are granted access.

Certificates are considered more secure because they are hard to fake. However, certificates are typically stored as a file on a local user's machine, which means that if the client machine is compromised, then a certificate can be used just like a stolen userid and password. If certificates are stored locally, then a mechanism must be developed to recover them if the machine they are stored on crashes or is upgraded. Certificates can be stored on smart cards instead of files on a local machine for more security and reliability. Finally the issuing and managing of client certificates is still in the early stages of development.

SASL

The **Simple Authentication and Security Layer** is an Internet standard for implementing authentication mechanisms besides simple or SSL.

There are two popular SASL mechanisms.

One is called MD5. In MD5, an MD5 hash is built of the password a user enters on the client. The userid and MD5-hashed password are sent to the server and are compared to see if they match. If the userid and MD-5-hashed password sent from the client match the userid and MD-5-hashed password stored on the server, then the client is allowed access. MD5 doesn't encrypt the transaction and it doesn't solve the problem of "who typed in the password". And if the MD5-hashed password is stolen while on its way to the server, a hacker could use that to gain access to the system, just as if it was a plain-text password. It does however, make it harder to guess what the password originally was, so if a hacker does steal the password, they won't be able to guess what the password was to try & use it to gain access to other systems.

The second popular SASL mechanism is called Kerberos. Kerberos encrypts the transaction, and in a Kerberos-aware network, it is very easy to implement a single-logon environment because of the way Kerberos works. However, managing a Kerberos network is very time- and resource-consuming, so many places haven't implemented Kerberos yet (though this may change if full Kerberos support does appear in Windows 2000 as is expected).

You can easily write your own SASL mechanisms, if your LDAP server supports them. Thus it would be possible to enable biometric authentication, once it becomes available (or if your organization has access to the technology already). Biometric authentication are systems that use parts of a person's body such as their thumbprint or iris for their userid and password. These systems are very secure.

LDAPv2 vs LDAPv3 Authentication

In LDAP v2 all clients had to authenticate themselves before performing any operations. In LDAP v3, if a client doesn't authenticate itself before performing an operation, the connection is assumed to be an anonymous authenticated connection.

Searching an LDAP Server

> **For the Search Examples in this section, I used the Airius.LDIF file that comes with the Netscape Directory Server**

The most used operation on any LDAP server is the search operation.

Any advanced LDAP applications use searching as their core functionality. Essentially, all search functions take an LDAP connection handle, the base to start the search from, the scope of the search and a search filter. A search filter is like a SQL query in that you tell the server the criteria to use to find matching entries. Searches always use an attribute name and a value to look for. Filters can use Boolean logic and wildcards. Some servers, such as the Netscape Directory server, support even more advanced query abilities such as "sounds like".

Example LDAP Filters

Find all users with the last name of Carter: `sn = Carter`
Find all users with last names that start with "Ca": `sn = Ca*`
Find all object classes of the type `GroupofUniqueNames` which have "Managers" in their Common Name: `(&(cn = * Managers * )(objectclass-groupofuniquenames))`

Searching with JNDI

In JNDI, we use the `search()` method of the `DirContext` interface. This will return a `NamingEnumeration` object if the search is successful.

Later in this section we will show you the various ways you can manipulate the values of this object to get back attributes and values of each returned entry.

Determining LDAP Scope

When you perform a search, you must specify the node (which we refer to as the base) of the tree you want to start at, as well as the scope of the search. The scope defines exactly how much of the tree you want to search. There are three levels of scope.

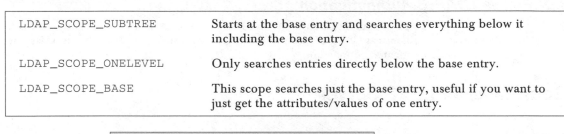

`LDAP_SCOPE_SUBTREE`	Starts at the base entry and searches everything below it including the base entry.
`LDAP_SCOPE_ONELEVEL`	Only searches entries directly below the base entry.
`LDAP_SCOPE_BASE`	This scope searches just the base entry, useful if you want to just get the attributes/values of one entry.

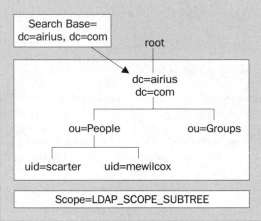

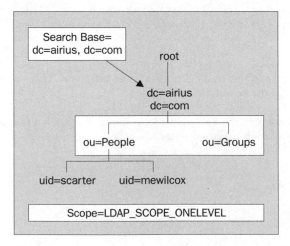

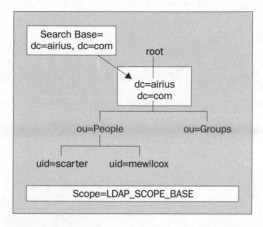

The Search Operation

We perform a search using the `search()` method of an object that implements the `DirContext` interface (such as the `InitialDirContext` class). The minimum requirement for this is the search base and a filter. There are other parameters we can use to help manage the results.

You should note that in most LDAP APIs, you must specify the scope as a parameter in the LDAP `search()` method. In JNDI, however, the scope is set in the `SearchControls` object, which is an optional parameter to the `search()` function of a `DirContext` interface (the `InitialDirContext` class provides an implementation of the `search()` function). By default it is set to `subtree`. The search is actually performed with whatever object you have that implements the `DirContext` interface such as the `InitialDirContext` class.

Our first example will show a very simple search example, where the search filter is `"sn=Carter"`. This will return all entries that have a surname (the attribute specified by the mnemonic `"sn"`) of Carter. This first example is an anonymous search.

Most of the examples here are non-GUI based. There is nothing to prevent them from being included in a GUI.

```
import java.util.Hashtable;
import java.util.Enumeration;

import javax.naming.*;
import javax.naming.directory.*;

public class JNDISearch {
    // initial context implementation
    public static String INITCTX = "com.sun.jndi.ldap.LdapCtxFactory";

    public static String MY_HOST = "ldap://localhost:389";

    public static String MY_SEARCHBASE = "o=Airius.com";

    public static String MY_FILTER = "(sn=Carter)";
```

Continued on Following Page

```java
    public static void main(String args[]) {
        try {
            //Hashtable for environmental information
            Hashtable env = new Hashtable();

            //Specify which class to use for our JNDI provider
            env.put(Context.INITIAL_CONTEXT_FACTORY, INITCTX);
            // Specify host and port to use for directory service
            env.put(Context.PROVIDER_URL, MY_HOST);

            //Get a reference to a directory context
            DirContext ctx = new InitialDirContext(env);

            //specify the scope of the search
            SearchControls constraints = new SearchControls();
            constraints.setSearchScope(SearchControls.SUBTREE_SCOPE);

            //peform the actual search
            //we give it a searchbase, a filter and a the constraints
            //containing the scope of the search
            NamingEnumeration results =
                            ctx.search(MY_SEARCHBASE,MY_FILTER,constraints);

            //now step through the search results
            while (results != null && results.hasMore()) {
                SearchResult sr = (SearchResult) results.next();

                String dn = sr.getName() + "," + MY_SEARCHBASE;
                System.out.println("Distinguished Name is "+dn);

                Attributes attrs = sr.getAttributes();

                for (NamingEnumeration ne = attrs.getAll();ne.hasMoreElements();) {
                    Attribute attr = (Attribute)ne.next();
                    String attrID = attr.getID();

                    System.out.println(attrID+":");
                    for (Enumeration vals = attr.getAll();vals.hasMoreElements();) {
                        System.out.println("\t"+vals.nextElement());
                    }
                }
                System.out.println("\n");
            }
        } catch(Exception e) {
            e.printStackTrace();
            System.exit(1);
        }
    }
}
```

The output from this code example is shown in the screenshot below:

How a JNDI Search is Performed

After we get initial context (which we set the variable `ctx` to), we next specify the scope of our search. If we don't specify a scope, JNDI will assume a scope of "subtree", so the next line is actually redundant but is useful to show you how to specify the scope.

Here is an example of how to set the scope to "subtree":

```
//specify the scope of the search
SearchControls constraints = new SearchControls();
constraints.setSearchScope(SearchControls.SUBTREE_SCOPE);
```

After we specify the scope we can perform the actual search like this:

```
//peform the actual search
NamingEnumeration results = ctx.search(MY_SEARCHBASE,MY_FILTER,constraints);
```

The `NamingEnumeration` class is equivalent to the `SearchResults` class in the Netscape Directory SDK for Java.

Each element in a `NamingEnumeration` object will contain a `SearchResult` object which we can retrieve like this:

```
SearchResult sr = (SearchResult) results.next();
```

We can get the DN of an entry like this:

```
String dn = sr.getName() + "," + MY_SEARCHBASE;
```

To get the attributes of an entry you use the `getAttributes()` method of the `SearchResult` class like this:

```
Attributes attrs = sr.getAttributes();
```

This will return back a concrete object that implements the `Attributes` interface (the `InitialDirContext` class returns back a `BasicAttributes` object)

After we have an `Attributes` object (remember this is a collection class), we can then step through them using a `NamingEnumeration` object like this:

```
for (NamingEnumeration ne = attrs.getAll();ne.hasMoreElements();) {
    Attribute attr = (Attribute)ne.next();
    String attrID = attr.getID();

    System.out.println(attrID+":");
    for (Enumeration vals = attr.getAll();vals.hasMoreElements();) {
        System.out.println("\t"+vals.nextElement());
    }
}
```

The `NamingEnumeration` class gives us methods that we can use to step through each attribute that was returned in our search. Each element in the `NamingEnumeration` object will contain an `Attribute` object that represents an attribute and its values.

Each element in the `Attribute` object is an object that has implemented the `Attribute` interface (the `InitialDirContext` class uses `BasicAttribute` objects). The `getID()` method of the `Attribute` interface returns the name of the attribute. The `getAll()` method of the `Attribute` interface will return back a standard Java Enumeration object, which we can then access to get the values of the individual attribute.

In every LDAP server, there are certain attributes that are not going to be available to anonymous users because of the access controls on the server. There are also certain attributes that may only be available to certain privileged users – pay scale, for example, may only be visible to human resources.

The code below shows how we can do an authenticated search:

```
    ...

    public static String MY_HOST = "ldap://localhost:389";
    public static String MGR_DN = "uid=kvaughan, ou=People, o=airius.com";
    public static String MGR_PW = "bribery";
    public static String MY_SEARCHBASE = "o=Airius.com";

    public static String MY_FILTER = "(sn=Carter)";

    public static void main(String[] args) {
        try {
            //Hashtable for environmental information
            Hashtable env = new Hashtable();

            //Specify which class to use for our JNDI provider
            env.put(Context.INITIAL_CONTEXT_FACTORY, INITCTX);

            //Security Information
            //authenticates us to the server
            env.put(Context.SECURITY_AUTHENTICATION,"simple");
            env.put(Context.SECURITY_PRINCIPAL,MGR_DN);
            env.put(Context.SECURITY_CREDENTIALS,MGR_PW);

            // Specify host and port to use for directory service
            env.put(Context.PROVIDER_URL, MY_HOST);
```

```
            //Get a reference to a directory context
            DirContext ctx = new InitialDirContext(env);

            SearchControls constraints = new SearchControls();
            constraints.setSearchScope(SearchControls.SUBTREE_SCOPE);
    ...
```

This second search example is exactly the same as the first one, except that we have authenticated ourselves to the server.

If you try compiling and running this example, you'll see that it produces the same output as before. Note that by default the LDAP server returns all of the attributes for a search. There may, however, be occasions when we don't want this, because we are only concerned with particular attributes.

In our third example, we ask to only be shown the common name (cn) and email address (mail) attributes:

```
import java.util.Hashtable;
import java.util.Enumeration;

import javax.naming.*;
import javax.naming.directory.*;

public class JNDISearch {

    // initial context implementation
    public static String INITCTX = "com.sun.jndi.ldap.LdapCtxFactory";

    public static String MY_HOST = "ldap://localhost:389";
    public static String MY_SEARCHBASE = "o=Airius.com";

    public static String MY_FILTER = "(sn=Carter)";

    //specify which attributes we are looking for
    public static String MY_ATTRS[] = {"cn","mail"};

    public static void main(String args[]) {
        try {
            //Hashtable for environmental information
            Hashtable env = new Hashtable();

            //Specify which class to use for our JNDI provider
            env.put(Context.INITIAL_CONTEXT_FACTORY, INITCTX);

            // Specify host and port to use for directory service
            env.put(Context.PROVIDER_URL,MY_HOST);

            //Get a reference to a directory context
            DirContext ctx = new InitialDirContext(env);

            //Specify the scope of the search
            SearchControls constraints = new SearchControls();
            constraints.setSearchScope(SearchControls.SUBTREE_SCOPE);

            NamingEnumeration results =
                        ctx.search(MY_SEARCHBASE,MY_FILTER,constraints);

            while (results != null && results.hasMore()) {
                SearchResult sr = (SearchResult) results.next();
```

Continued on Following Page

```
        String dn = sr.getName() + "," + MY_SEARCHBASE;

        System.out.println("Distinguised Name is "+dn);
        Attributes ar = ctx.getAttributes(dn, MY_ATTRS);

        if (ar == null) {
           System.out.println("Entry "+dn+" has
                             none of the specified attributes\n");
        } else {
           for (int i =0;i<MY_ATTRS.length;i++) {
              Attribute attr = ar.get(MY_ATTRS[i]);
              if (attr != null) {
                 System.out.println(MY_ATTRS[i]+":");
                 for (Enumeration vals =
                                attr.getAll();vals.hasMoreElements();)
                 {
                    System.out.println("\t"+vals.nextElement());
                 }
              }
           }
           System.out.println("\n");
        }
     }
  }
} catch(Exception e) {
  e.printStackTrace();
  System.exit(1);
}
  }
}
```

Because we have just specified the common name and mail attributes this time, the resulting output from the code should look like this:

The difference between this code and our earlier example searches is that we now limit the number of attributes we want retrieved.

First we created a `String` array that listed the attributes we wanted like this:

```
public static String MY_ATTRS[] = {"cn","mail"};
```

To retrieve this set of attributes we use the `getAttributes()` method of the `DirContext` interface, where we provide the DN of a specific entry and the array of attributes like this:

```
Attributes ar = ctx.getAttributes(dn,MY_ATTRS);
```

This will return back an `Attributes` object.

We can retrieve a particular `Attribute` object from an `Attributes` object like this:

```
Attribute attr = ar.get("cn");
```

I should point out that retrieving a specific set of attributes from an individual entry is very quick, but this is not very practical for general searching. In a general LDAP search, the end user is not going to know the existing Distinguished Names of the entries they are looking for, so we will have to search the LDAP server and retrieve a set of entries. In JNDI (as opposed to the Netscape Directory SDK for Java), this search will return all of the attributes associated with each individual entry. If we then make subsequent call to `getAttributes()`, (to retrieve a subset of attributes like in the previous example) this will require another call to the LDAP server and get back the set of attributes. This is inefficient because it requires us to use extra memory for all of the attributes and extra bandwidth for the extra communication. The extra memory is required because your application must hold the data of the LDAP search results for you to process. To improve performance in your Java applications you want to reduce the amount of extraneous memory you use because the JVM's garbage collector can be slow to react, or slow your application to a crawl as it reclaims memory.

LDAP Server Modifications

We can also use JNDI to add, delete and modify existing entries.

Adding Entries

Using JNDI to add entries to an LDAP server is in fact more difficult than it is with other LDAP SDKs. This is because JNDI's primary goal is to read/write Java objects to the network. A consequence of this is that a programmer must go through some extra hoops, such as creating a Java class for each type of entry you want to add to the LDAP server. Here we'll look at how to add and modify a simple entry in the LDAP server, but later in the chapter we'll learn how to use the LDAP server as an object store.

To store an entry in a LDAP server using JNDI, you must bind an object to a Distinguished Name (DN). This means that each object (whether this a simple person entry or a serialized Java class) we store in the server must have a DN associated with it. Remember a DN is the unique name that each entry in a LDAP server must posses. If you switch to a different directory service (such as NDS) you will still be required to have an unique name for each object. Now if you are bit overwhelmed by this, just remember that it will become second nature over time and that you do this (provide an unique name) each time you save a file to your hard disk. No file on the file system can share the same name. If you wish to have two files named `myfile.txt`, you must store them in separate directories in your file system otherwise one version will overwrite the other.

To store even a simple entry in the LDAP server, we must create a class that implements the `DirContext` interface. This interface defines how the object (whether a person or serialized Java class) should be stored into the directory server as well as retrieved from the server. For example if you have a person object, your class will specify how to build its DN, how to store the available attributes (e.g. full name, email address, telephone number, userid, password, etc) and provide various mechanisms to handle the retrieved data. The `DirContext` also provides for much more sophisticated data handling and is the basic interface for building a directory service provider.

As with any other LDAP SDK an 'ADD' can only be performed by an authenticated user who has rights to add a new entry into the server. LDAP ACLs can be setup so that users can only add entries into particular parts of the directory tree.

Our next code sample shows a very simple `Person` class that implements the `DirContext` interface. Most of the methods in the interface are not actually implemented (except to throw exceptions) because we don't need them for our very simple example here. I derived this class from the `Drink.java` example found in the JNDI tutorial (http://java.sun.com/products/jndi/tutorial).

The methods that we implement here, `getAttributes()` and the constructor, enable us to store/retrieve the data in a `Person` class as traditional LDAP entries. The rest of the methods that we don't fully implement are methods that are primarily used to build full service providers. Instead we simply throw exceptions that simply state we don't support the particular service.

> *New objects must also conform to the LDAP server's schema, or the entries will not be added.*

I think will be easier to explain how to add an Entry with JNDI if I explain the code as we go along. The complete source code for this example can be found on the Wrox Press Web site: http://www.wrox.com.

First is our class declaration, note that we state that we will implement the methods for the `DirContext` interface.

```
public class Person implements DirContext {
    String type;
    Attributes myAttrs;
```

Next we have our constructor. This constructor takes several strings that we will use to build an `inetOrgPerson` object class.

```
//Person("mewilcox","Mark","Wilcox","ou=Accounting","mewilcox@airius.com");
public Person(String uid,String givenname,String sn,String ou,String mail) {
    type = uid;
```

We will use the `BasicAttributes` class to store our attributes and their values. The `BasicAttributes` class stores attributes using the `BasicAttribute` class. By specifying true in the `BasicAttributes` constructor we are telling it to ignore the case of attribute names when doing attribute name lookups.

```
myAttrs = new BasicAttributes(true);
```

To add a multi-valued attribute we need to create a new `BasicAttribute` object which requires the name of the attribute in its constructor. We then add the values of the attribute with the `add()` method.

```
        Attribute oc = new BasicAttribute("objectclass");
        oc.add("inetOrgPerson");
        oc.add("organizationalPerson");
        oc.add("person");
        oc.add("top");

        Attribute ouSet = new BasicAttribute("ou");
        ouSet.add("People");
        ouSet.add(ou);

        String cn = givenname+" "+sn;
```

Finally we add all of our attributes to the `BasicAttributes` object.

```
        myAttrs.put(oc);
        myAttrs.put(ouSet);
        myAttrs.put("uid",uid);
        myAttrs.put("cn",cn);
        myAttrs.put("sn",sn);
        myAttrs.put("givenname",givenname);
        myAttrs.put("mail",mail);
    }
```

When `getAttributes()` is called it will return our `BasicAttributes` object when requested by a name in the form of a `String`. It is designed to only return the attributes of a specific entry, but since this class will only hold one entry, it's not going to be called. We're showing one way to implement it if it was.

```
    public Attributes getAttributes(String name) throws NamingException {
        if (! name.equals("")) {
            throw new NameNotFoundException();
        }
        return myAttrs;
    }
```

This method does the same thing as the first `getAttributes()` but is only called when the name is passed a `Name` object.

```
    public Attributes getAttributes(Name name) throws NamingException {
        return getAttributes(name.toString());
    }
```

The following method returns only the attributes listed in the `String` array `ids`. The `String name` should be a DN.

```
    public Attributes getAttributes(String name, String[] ids)
        throws NamingException {
        if (! name.equals("")) {
            throw new NameNotFoundException();
        }

        Attributes answer = new BasicAttributes(true);
        Attribute target;
```

Continued on Following Page

```
        for (int i = 0; i < ids.length; i++) {
            target = myAttrs.get(ids[i]);
            if (target != null) {
                answer.put(target);
            }
        }
    }
    return answer;
}
```

Same method as the other `getAttributes()`, except it takes a `Name` object.

```
public Attributes getAttributes(Name name, String[] ids)
    throws NamingException {
    return getAttributes(name.toString(), ids);
}
```

Used for serialization.

```
public String toString() {
    return type;
}
```

The following lines (complete set is in the full source code on this book's web site) are methods that are used to implement methods that a JNDI service provider (such as the `InitialDirContext` class) would use to provide an application with services such as reading entries from the directory or for authenticating to the server.

```
// not used for this example

public Object lookup(Name name) throws NamingException {
    throw new OperationNotSupportedException();
}

public Object lookup(String name) throws NamingException {
    throw new OperationNotSupportedException();
}

public void bind(Name name, Object obj) throws NamingException {
    throw new OperationNotSupportedException();
}
```

And here is the program that uses the `Person` class to add an entry for Mark Wilcox to the LDAP server:

```
import java.util.Hashtable;
import java.util.Enumeration;

import javax.naming.*;
import javax.naming.directory.*;

public class JNDIAdd {

    // initial context implementation
    public static String INITCTX = "com.sun.jndi.ldap.LdapCtxFactory";
```

```
        public static String MY_HOST = "ldap://localhost:389";
        public static String MGR_DN = "uid=kvaughan, ou=People, o=airius.com";
        public static String MGR_PW = "bribery";
        public static String MY_SEARCHBASE = "o=Airius.com";

        public static void main(String args[]) {

            try {
                //Hashtable for environmental information
                Hashtable env = new Hashtable();

                //Specify which class to use for our JNDI provider
                env.put(Context.INITIAL_CONTEXT_FACTORY, INITCTX);

                env.put(Context.PROVIDER_URL,MY_HOST);
                env.put(Context.SECURITY_AUTHENTICATION,"simple");
                env.put(Context.SECURITY_PRINCIPAL,MGR_DN);
                env.put(Context.SECURITY_CREDENTIALS,MGR_PW);

                //Get a reference to a directory context
                DirContext ctx = new InitialDirContext(env);

                Person p = new Person("mewilcox", "Mark", "Wilcox", "ou=Accounting",
                                    "mewilcox@airius.com");

                ctx.bind("uid=mewilcox,ou=People,o=airius.com", p);
            } catch(Exception e) {
                e.printStackTrace();
                System.exit(1);
            }
        }
    }
}
```

First we must create a new Java object that implements the `DirContext` interface such as our `Person` class like this:

```
    Person p = new Person("mewilcox", "Mark", "Wilcox", "ou=Accounting",
                        "mewilcox@airius.com");
```

Then we associate a name (specifically the DN of the entry) with this object in our current context with the `bind()` method of the `DirContext` interface like this:

```
        ctx.bind("uid=mewilcox,ou=People,o=airius.com", p);
```

The `InitialDirContext` interface will actually perform an LDAP 'ADD' operation. It will take all of the attributes we have placed into our Java class and then encode them for transfer into a LDAP server.

Because we used the `BasicAttribute` class to build our attributes, they will be stored/retrieved as standard LDAP data and not as pure Java objects. This means that if you store your LDAP data this way any other LDAP client regardless if it's written in C, Perl or Visual Basic will still be able to access it.

Modify an Entry

Just as soon as you add an entry to an LDAP server, you'll need to modify it. This could be for a variety of reasons including changing a user's password, updating an application's configuration, etc.

Modifications to an entry are made with the `ModificationItem` and `BasicAttribute` classes. When you make a modification, it can be one of ADD, REPLACE or DELETE. A REPLACE will add an attribute if it doesn't exist yet.

> **You should also be aware that if you perform a REPLACE on an attribute that has multiple values, if you don't send the extra values along with your replacement value, they will all be removed.**

Again, modifications must be performed by an authenticated user and those modifications that can be performed will be determined by the rights the bound entry has on a particular entry. For example, users can generally change their passwords but nothing else, while administrative assistants usually can change telephone numbers and mailing addresses. Finally, it usually takes a database administrator to do things like change a user's user ID.

The code shown below demonstrates how we can modify the attributes of the `Mark Wilcox` entry that we added in the previous example:

```
import java.util.Hashtable;
import java.util.Enumeration;

import javax.naming.*;
import javax.naming.directory.*;

public class JNDIMod {

    // initial context implementation
    public static String INITCTX = "com.sun.jndi.ldap.LdapCtxFactory";

    public static String MY_HOST = "ldap://localhost:389";
    public static String MGR_DN = "uid=kvaughan, ou=People, o=airius.com";
    public static String MGR_PW = "bribery";
    public static String MY_SEARCHBASE = "o=Airius.com";

    public static void main(String args[]) {

        try {
            //Hashtable for environmental information
            Hashtable env = new Hashtable();

            //Specify which class to use for our JNDI provider
            env.put(Context.INITIAL_CONTEXT_FACTORY, INITCTX);

            env.put(Context.PROVIDER_URL,MY_HOST);
            env.put(Context.SECURITY_AUTHENTICATION,"simple");
            env.put(Context.SECURITY_PRINCIPAL,MGR_DN);
            env.put(Context.SECURITY_CREDENTIALS,MGR_PW);

            //Get a reference to a directory context
            DirContext ctx = new InitialDirContext(env);
```

```
            ModificationItem[] mods = new ModificationItem[2];

            Attribute mod0 = new BasicAttribute("telephonenumber","940-555-2555");
            Attribute mod1 = new BasicAttribute("l", "Waco");

            mods[0] = new ModificationItem(DirContext.REPLACE_ATTRIBUTE,mod0);
            mods[1] = new ModificationItem(DirContext.ADD_ATTRIBUTE,mod1);

            //DirContext.DELETE_ATTRIBUTE not shown here
            ctx.modifyAttributes("uid=mewilcox,ou=People,o=airius.com", mods);
        } catch(Exception e) {
            e.printStackTrace();
            System.exit(1);
        }
    }
}
```

To modify an entry we use the `ModificationItem` class. The `ModificationItem` takes a modification type (e.g. add, replace or delete) and an `Attribute` object such as `BasicAttribute`. Here is a simple example that lets us add a new attribute, locality (the `l` attribute), with a new value of "Waco" to the entry:

```
Attribute mod1 = new BasicAttribute("l", "Waco");
        mods[1] = new ModificationItem(DirContext.ADD_ATTRIBUTE,mod1);
```

The actual modification is performed by the `DirContext` method, `modifyAttributes()`. Here is an example of this:

```
ctx.modifyAttributes("uid=mewilcox,ou=People,o=airius.com", mods);
```

Again this modifies the entry in the LDAP server using traditional LDAP and not as a Java object so that any other client can still access this data.

Delete Entry

Eventually, you will need to remove entries from your LDAP server. This is easily accomplished by calling the `destroySubContext()` method of the `DirContext` interface, with the distinguished name of the entry that needs to be removed. Normally, delete operations are restricted to the LDAP database administrators.

Here is an example of deleting an entry:

```
import java.util.Hashtable;
import java.util.Enumeration;

import javax.naming.*;
import javax.naming.directory.*;

public class JNDIDel {

    // initial context implementation
    public static String INITCTX = "com.sun.jndi.ldap.LdapCtxFactory";

    public static String MY_HOST = "ldap://localhost:389";
    public static String MGR_DN = "cn=Directory Manager";
    public static String MGR_PW = "jessica98";
```

```
    public static String MY_SEARCHBASE = "o=Airius.com";

    public static String MY_ENTRY = "uid=mewilcox, ou=People, o=airius.com";

    public static void main(String args[]) {

        try {
            //Hashtable for environmental information
            Hashtable env = new Hashtable();

            //Specify which class to use for our JNDI provider
            env.put(Context.INITIAL_CONTEXT_FACTORY, INITCTX);

            env.put(Context.PROVIDER_URL,MY_HOST);
            env.put(Context.SECURITY_AUTHENTICATION,"simple");
            env.put(Context.SECURITY_PRINCIPAL,MGR_DN);
            env.put(Context.SECURITY_CREDENTIALS,MGR_PW);

            //Get a reference to a directory context
            DirContext ctx = new InitialDirContext(env);

            ctx.destroySubcontext(MY_ENTRY);
        } catch(Exception e) {
            e.printStackTrace();
            System.exit(1);
        }
    }
}
```

The only real difference between the code in this example and the rest of our examples is this line:

```
ctx.destroySubcontext(MY_ENTRY);
```

This will remove the entry in the LDAP server.

More LDAP

I know this was a rush whirlwind tour through LDAP. If you want more information there are a number of resources you can check out.

For starters if you're a book kind of person (and since you're reading this one, I'll bet you are), then you should check out my book, "Implementing LDAP" also by Wrox.

I also maintain a Website with pointers on LDAP and an LDAP FAQ at http://www.mjwilcox.com/. You can also search http://www.deja.com/ which indexes most of the newsgroups on LDAP. Also check out the LDAP newsgroup on Mozilla.org at http://www.mozilla.org/directory/. If you want all the source code for the examples in this chapter go to http://www.wrox.com.

Summary

LDAP is fast becoming the standard for directory services communication on the Internet. There are several APIs available for Java to communicate with LDAP. JNDI is preferred in instances where you may need to interact with other directory services or you need to store/retrieve Java objects in a directory service.

We have covered in this chapter:

> The ideas and uses of naming and directory services.

> An introduction to LDAP and its uses.

> The benefits of using JNDI in mixed networks to ease the administrator's burden.

Using LDAP and Java

This chapter will show a short case study of how a fictitious package delivery company, FedUp Inc., uses Java, JNDI, LDAP, and the Web to improve customer service and streamline in-house operations. We assume you have worked though the previous chapter that introduces LDAP and JNDI, as we'll use the concepts and code from that chapter to build a servlet that interfaces to an LDAP server.

In this chapter we will:

> Look at the essential objects in business-oriented development
>
> Map business objects to Java
>
> Map business objects to LDAP
>
> Leverage LDAP for improved customer service
>
> Build an internal web-based ordering and tracking system

Storing and Retrieving Java Objects in LDAP

One of JNDI's strongest attributes is its ability to use LDAP as a network object store. What this means is that you can use LDAP to store Java objects that you need to either share between different applications or for later use.

There are several reasons why you would like to use LDAP as your data store:

- ➢ Leverage an existing centralized resource
- ➢ Use existing open standards
- ➢ LDAP is available on the network "out of the box"
- ➢ LDAP is designed for extremely quick read access
- ➢ LDAP has strong security built in

JNDI allows you to store several types of Java related objects into the LDAP server:

- ➢ **Standard LDAP directory entries** – This provides the ability to manipulate standard directory data (`inetOrgPerson`, `groupOfUniqueNames` classes, etc.). Standard directory data is smaller in size (that is, quicker to access and modify) and you can share it between different languages. Keeping directory data language neutral is of utmost importance in large enterprises, where several different languages maybe used for development.

- ➢ **Serialized Java objects** – This is the ability to store and retrieve Java objects that have been serialized (that is, the current object and all of its related classes, are stored in a binary format). This is probably the easiest format to use, but it requires the most bandwidth and storage space. Also, it is a format that is only understandable by Java programs.

- ➢ **Pointers to RMI Java objects** – Remote Method Invocation (RMI) is the Java-to-Java format for distributed computing. With RMI, a Java application can call a method in a remote class (that is, a class that has been loaded on a different JVM than the current Java application) just as if that class was available locally. You can store a reference (basically an RMI URL) to available RMI classes in your LDAP server instead of having to keep a registry of available methods on each computer with an RMI client application.

- ➢ **References to Java objects** – Sometimes you want to store a Java class using serialization, but you can't store the entire object either for security, size or other reasons. Java references allow you to store a subset of the object information in the directory server in a format that allows you to recreate the object using a Java factory class. See http://java.sun.com/jndi/ for more information.

So Many Options, Which One Do I Use?

How you store your objects will depend upon the application you are building and how you need to access the data.

Traditional LDAP

I think that at least half of the time you (or at least your organization) will want to access the data in the directory service from a variety of clients using a number of different languages. A popular use of a directory service is for user authentication. Obviously, storing user authentication data in a format that only Java can use is a poor solution.

A number of applications won't need authentication but could benefit from a directory service's address book features. For example your email program can use it to find the email address of co-workers, your marketing department can use it to build mail merges while your Web developers can use it to make a custom portal for each customer. Each of these applications could be built using Java as the development language, but they won't necessarily be. More importantly, your company reduces its overhead by maintaining consistent data about its people and clients in a central database.

One of the neat things about storing data in this fashion is that you can treat each entry like an object in Java, but other languages don't have to be object-oriented in order to access the data.

Serialized Java

If you have a growing number of Java applications that need access to a central repository of pre-built Java objects then use Java's serialization to store those objects into the LDAP server. Then, when an application needs a particular object (for example a 3D rendering engine), it can retrieve it from the LDAP server when it's needed. Another nice feature of this is that when you update the rendering engine, all of the applications that are using the engine will have access to the update without having to patch the end-application.

RMI Registery or CORBA Naming Services

If you have chosen to use RMI or CORBA as your distributed computing platform, then you probably realize the need for a central registry that maintains the location and capabilities of objects on the network. For example, if you need to use a matrix multiplication routine available on a supercomputer somewhere to offset the computational power, your application needs some way of knowing where such a routine exists.

Using LDAP enables you to store this information in a central repository which can be more easily managed and secured.

Java References

Finally, if you are in an all-Java environment you may wish to take advantage of Java References. References reduce the storage and bandwidth requirements of storing/retrieving entries because they don't store the entire object in the directory, instead only storing key components that are needed to rebuild the object in a factory class.

For example if you create a standard printer object, you can build a `PrinterFactory` that will take as parameters:

> ➢ Network location
>
> ➢ Color options (monochrome, color, etc.)
>
> ➢ Specialties (postscript, graphic plotter, etc.)
>
> ➢ Current status (out of paper, on-line, etc.)

These parameters can be passed to `PrinterFactory` which will return a `Printer` object that your application can use. This storage method reduces bandwidth/storage because only the above parameters need to be stored. It's also easier to deal with as an application programmer, because part of the reference is the fully-qualified package name of the actual factory so you don't have to include it with your application, just need to make sure the JVM can find the package.

In this chapter, we'll look at the first and second categories.

Duct Tape and Bailer Band

It's 1999 and your boss tells you that he wants to see the status of a package his mother just sent him, on the Web. Just as you get off the phone with him, the Director of Marketing calls you up and wants to send a mass mailing out to all customers who meet a certain profile. The Executive VP in charge of the FedUp web site decides he wants to make it into a portal like Yahoo! and let customers personalize the site to fit their needs. Finally, on your way back from the break room with a fresh cup of coffee, you overhear someone saying, "Wouldn't it be nice if you could look up customers' email addresses from the Web to ask them questions about their packages or to update customers on a package's status?"

What are you going to do?

You could continue to develop applications as you have been, writing custom client server applications for each request (using CORBA, DCOM or DCE, etc.). But what keeps nagging at you is the fact that you are taking precious developer time to create a mailing list for MS-Word using CORBA, which is a bit like using a fire-hose to put out a candle. You realize that you are forced to stick entirely with CORBA for the time being because the customer data is stored in a database on the mainframe. You can live with the applications that live on the mainframe because of their stability, but you wish that the data that fed those applications were more accessible. You also know that many departments are building their own databases and applications with the same data and logic (for example, to determine the shipping price of a package) that is contained in your mainframe. But you also know that their data and the mainframe are often out of sync and that their applications don't always contain work right (which everyone blames on you).

The figure below shows the situation in this company - with several copies of customer data in various stores for different applications:

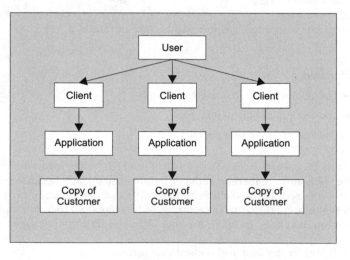

There has to be a better way.

The next figure shows how the same applications might share the same data through a central LDAP store.

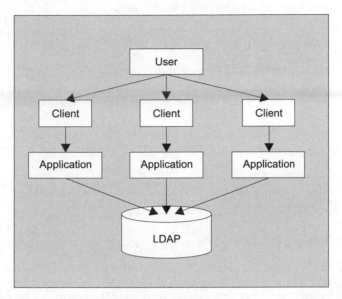

How we move the information from its current stores and how we interface the applications to the LDAP server are the next problems. There's the LDAP C API, various other extensions for specific languages and there's JNDI. We'll stick to JNDI here, but if you want more information on the full range of LDAP programming and data conversion, check out *Implementing LDAP* (ISBN 1-861002-21-1, Wrox Press) and *Understanding and Deploying LDAP Directory Services* (ISBN 1-578700-70-1, MTP).

Using Java and JNDI in the Middle Tier

As we've pointed out, after you have decided to use LDAP as the protocol to centrally manage your business data, you must figure out how to add LDAP capabilities to your existing applications. This is one area where Java can help. You have a couple of options. Either you change existing applications so that they talk to the LDAP store rather than the existing store, or you need to provide some way of centralizing and replicating the data between the LDAP store and existing stores.

Once you decide on a Java middleware application, you could even contemplate reducing the multitude of clients to a single web client that can interact with the Java middleware application. Our next figure shows an example of how this architecture could work.

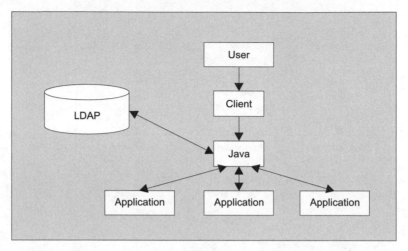

Once you have LDAP in place and you have developed a middle tier application or two using LDAP, you will probably want to begin to develop new applications that take advantage of this infrastructure or rewrite your legacy applications from scratch to better take advantage of LDAP. One benefit of using LDAP and JNDI is that you can have easy access to networked object persistence which enables you to exploit the benefits of a component architecture.

Let's get to grips with the case study.

Using JNDI/LDAP for Improved Customer Service

The management team at FedUp, Inc. believes that they offer the same great service as their competitors but at a better price. They feel that, because they are a relatively new company, they need to improve their brand awareness and provide even better customer service. They have decided that what they would like to do is to provide package tracking services over the Web and make partnerships with various portal providers so that links to FedUp's Package Tracking service would be on the top-level pages of major portals like Yahoo!.

They turn the project over to their IT department to make it happen. After a few meetings it is decided that the back-end processing would be done using Java servlets because they provided the scalability for web load and rapid-development time that is going to be needed to pull this project off successfully.

The key design issues are:

>   Data to be kept in a portable, accessible and language neutral format
>   Deployment of Java classes to be centralized

To share common data in a platform and language neutral format, you should use standard LDAP entries and attributes. Even if you don't care about sharing data between different development languages, you still want to use standard LDAP entries and attributes for storing common data because it will be smaller and quicker to access from the LDAP server. While there is no true limit on the amount of data you can store in an attribute in a LDAP server, common sense dictates that the more data you have to fetch from the directory over the network, the longer it will take. Also if you store all of your data in a binary format, you cannot easily search or index that data, which defeats the entire purpose of putting it into a directory in the first place. Remember if you can get a directory in place for one application, you'll probably find that it can be used for many different applications. Building a directory is like building a road - many different types of cars (that is, applications) should be able to use it.

One benefit of storing object data in an LDAP server is the ability to match an object's hierarchical relationship to its parent's class, because LDAP uses a hierarchical data relationship.

One problem with LDAP is its performance when you are writing more or less as often as reading data from the LDAP server. All of the LDAP server developers are working hard to improve write performance on a LDAP server, but currently write performance is still poor. On the other hand, you will be hard pressed to find something that is faster in read performance than an LDAP server. We'll see how, by using the LDAP data as a lookup to a database where the package location is written frequently, we can get round this problem.

Introducing our Basic Objects

Before we start the application, I want to break the application objects down into two types:

> Business Data Objects
> Business Rule Objects

What I call Business Data Objects (BDO) are objects that contain only data that correlates specifically with some part of the business. An example of a BDO would be a Customer or Package object. It's an abstraction of the 'physical' items the organization uses to do business. A BDO is made up of name and value pairs.

Business Rule Objects (BRO) are objects that define the computational logic of how the organization does business. This could be figuring out the price of an order, sending out a work order or checking on the status of a package.

Typically, a BRO uses one or more BDOs to complete its operations. For example if you are going to ship a package with FedUp Inc, a BRO that works out the price will use three objects, a sender (Customer object), a recipient (Customer object) and something to ship (Package object).

Getting at the Data

The next decision to be made is how to provide access to customer and package data to the servlets. There are three camps:

> One which wants to keep the data in the mainframe
> The second which wants to move the data to an Oracle database
> The third which wants to implement a solution that is both portable and Internet ready

553

After some more meetings the group decides to give LDAP a shot. The company is already using a system of Netscape Directory servers throughout the company's nationwide offices to provide single-logon authentication and address book directory services for employees.

They decide to use the JNDI API for Java because it is standardized, and enables them to use different directory services such as NDS if they need. They also want to store some common Java classes for use in various Java applications in the LDAP server.

What we will detail in the rest of this business case is the early beta version of this application, the `CustomerServlet` Java servlet.

Screenshots

Before we go into the code, let's take a look at the resulting application. The first thing a customer will do is log into the system with their customer id and password. If this matches a customer entry in the LDAP server, they will be granted access.

This first screenshot represents the screen a user sees after a successful authentication. It shows their name, customer id, and a listing of all packages that have been shipped by them or are on their way of being delivered to them.

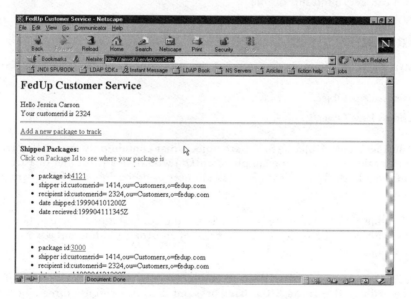

The next screenshot shows the resulting screen of when a user clicks on the package link in the first screen. In the fully functioning version, this would load a Java object from the LDAP server that would be able to query a system (either a mainframe application or database server) to determine the current location of the package. This gets round the write performance problem quite reasonably. For now, it just prints out a simple message, but the basic framework is in place – the Java class that generates this message is loaded from the LDAP server.

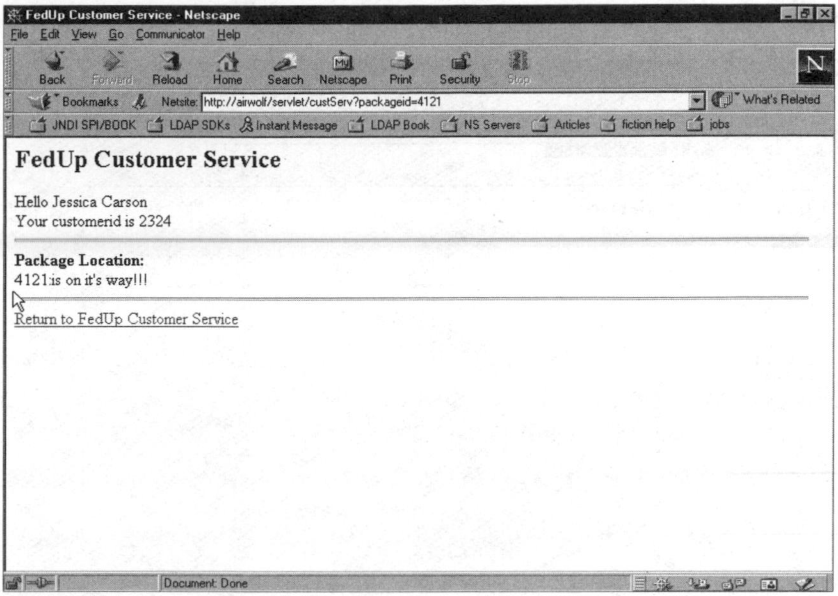

Our next screen shows how a customer can add a new package. All they have to do is provide the customer id for the recipient of the package. In the fully functioning version you'd probably want to provide a lookup mechanism for a customer's id and to add a new customer from scratch.

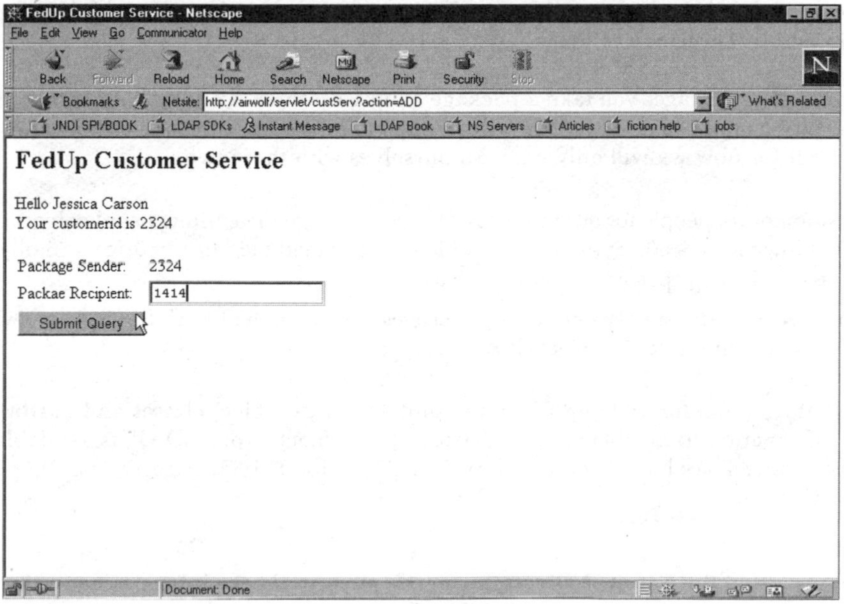

The final screen shows the resulting screen after adding a package.

The LDAP Directory Information Tree

Because this application relies so much on LDAP, it would be helpful to understand the setup of the LDAP server and its **Directory Information Tree (DIT)**.

When you deliver a package, you take a package from Customer A and deliver it to Customer B. We therefore have two major objects - a `Customer` object and a `Package` object. We may have auxiliary classes later, but for now we will only concern ourselves with these two.

> Customers are people for our purposes. We can leverage the existing people object classes in LDAP such as `inetOrgperson`. We will need to extend the `inetOrgperson` object to add some new FedUp specific attributes such as `customerid`.

> There is no `Package` class in the object classes defined in the LDAP RFCs, so we will have to create our own `Package` object class.

The schema information for adding `Customer` and `Package` object classes and attributes, as well as the schema information to be able to store/retrieve Java objects from LDAP, is available with the book's sample code. They have been developed for Netscape Directory server but they can be used with any LDAP server.

> If you are using the Netscape Directory server, simply add the information in the `user_oc.conf` and `user_at.conf` files from the Web site to the corresponding `user_oc.conf` and `user_at.conf` files in your Directory server's `config` directory. Restart your Directory server and you are ready to go.

The DIT, which is how we describe the way data is organized in LDAP, is fairly simple. We store all of our entries under a common root, `o=fedup.com`, with the following branches:

- `People` – Employee entries
- `Customers` – Customer entries
- `Package` – Package entries
- `Java` – Java entries
- `Groups` – Group entries
- `Directory Administrators` – Admin entries
- `Special Users` – Entries with extended privileges, but not as powerful as the Directory Administrators

Here is how the tree for a customer with a customer id of 2324 would look:

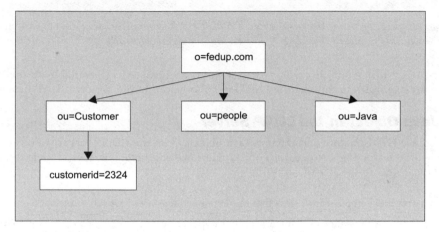

Customer LDAP Data Interchange Format File

Here is an example of `Customer` entry in the LDAP Data Interchange Format (LDIF) file which we use determine the structure we saw above:

```
dn: uid=timb,ou=Customers,o=fedup.com
objectclass: customer
objectclass: inetorgperson
objectclass: organizationalPerson
objectclass: person
objectclass: top
cn: Tim Briggs
uid: timb
givenname: Tim
customerid: timb
sn: Briggs
facsimiletelephonenumber: 4101
telephonenumber: 4145
creatorsname: uid=admin,ou-Administrators,ou=TopologyManagement,o-NetscapeRoot
createtimestamp: 19990715084016Z
aci: (target="ldap:///uid=timb,ou=Customers,o=fedup.com")(targetattr="*")
```

Continued on Following Page

```
(version 3.0; acl "unknown"; allow (all) userdn = "ldap:///anyone"; )
ou: Customers
mail:
userpassword: {SHA}eLNx8OoUEKvGLMubf0DDQoinLho=
modifiersname: uid=admin,ou=Administrators,ou=TopologyManagement,o=NetscapeRoot
modifytimestamp: 19990715185318Z
```

If you added a `postaladdress` attribute you should use the following format to make it easier to parse:

```
postaladdress:1234 Flamer ~ ~ Nowhere ~ OK ~ USA ~ 55557
```

While each attribute can have more than one value, the entire value of an attribute must not contain any carriage returns. So to keep all of the parts of a postal address (for example, house number and street) in one value, you separate them with a piece of data that you can use later to parse them apart. In our example here that data is the ~, but it could be anything.

> *Most examples use the $ because when X.500 (LDAP's big sister) was developed, many client terminals couldn't display a $ so parsing occurred naturally.*

The `fedup.ldif` with example employees, customers and packages is available on the Wrox web site. To use the examples in this chapter, you'll need to load that file as your LDAP data.

Storing a Java Object in the LDAP Server

You can also use JNDI to store and retrieve Java objects from the LDAP server. In our example servlet we will be retrieving a stored Java object. Here we will take a very brief look at how to store a serialized Java object to the LDAP server.

> ➤ First you must create a Java class that implements the `Serializable` interface
> ➤ Next create an instance of that class in your application
> ➤ Then you must create a connection to the LDAP server and authenticate to the server as an entry with 'write' permissions
> ➤ To store an entry to the server, you simply bind the entry to the server with the `bind()` method of the `DirContext` interface

Here's an example Java class that can be serialized:

```java
// Sample Java class to be stored in an LDAP server
// Had this been a real application it might have consulted with a database
// or a mainframe application to determine status. For now we just return a phrase

import java.io.*;

public class PackageLocation implements Serializable
{
    String message;
```

```
    public PackageLocation(String m) {
        message = m;
    }

    public String getLocation(String packageid) {
        return new String(packageid + ":" + message);
    }
}
```

Here's some sample code that stores an object of this class in the LDAP server:

```
import java.util.Hashtable;
import java.util.Enumeration;

import javax.naming.*;
import javax.naming.directory.*;

public class JNDIAdd {

    // Initial context implementation
    public static String INITCTX = "com.sun.jndi.ldap.LdapCtxFactory";
    public static String MY_HOST = "ldap://localhost:389";
    public static String MGR_DN = "cn=Directory Manager";
    public static String MGR_PW = "password";
    public static String MY_SEARCHBASE = "o=fedup.com";

    public static void main(String[] args)
    {
        try {
            // Hashtable for environmental information
            Hashtable env = new Hashtable();

            // Specify which class to use for our JNDI provider
            env.put(Context.INITIAL_CONTEXT_FACTORY, INITCTX);
            env.put(Context.PROVIDER_URL, MY_HOST);
            env.put(Context.SECURITY_AUTHENTICATION, "simple");
            env.put(Context.SECURITY_PRINCIPAL, MGR_DN);
            env.put(Context.SECURITY_CREDENTIALS, MGR_PW);

            // Get a reference to a directory context
            DirContext ctx = new InitialDirContext(env);

            PackageLocation wip = new PackageLocation("on its way!!!");

            // Add Java object
            ctx.bind("cn=PackageLocation,ou=Java,o=fedup.com", wip);
        }
        catch(Exception e) {
            e.printStackTrace();
            System.exit(1);
        }
    }
}
```

The LDAP server's schema must support storing Java objects. The necessary schema information is on the Web site for this book as well as being available with the JNDI 1.2 SDK from `java.sun.com`.

To specify a user schema with Netscape Directory Server, take the `slapd.user_at.conf` and `slapd.user_oc.conf` and put them in the `NetscapeServer/slapd-HostName/config` directory to replace the empty files that are there by default.

Customer Service Code

Now we are ready to move onto our application. We will be using four classes:

- `PackageLocation` - simulates a Java object that does sophisticated operations to determine a package's location. We retrieve the 'location' from the LDAP server
- `Customer` - a class that represents a `Customer` object and implements the `DirContext` interface so that we can store a `Customer` object in the LDAP server as a `Customer` object class entry
- `Package` - a class that represents a `Package` object and implements the `DirContext` interface so that we can store a `Package` object in the LDAP server as a `Package` object class entry
- `CustomerServlet` - our servlet class, where we spend most of our time

All of these class files must be put into the same servlet directory. You will also need to add the `ldap.jar`, `providerutil.jar`, and `jndi.jar` files from the JNDI SDK into your servlet engine's CLASSPATH, or into the `\jre\lib\ext` directory.

We have already looked at the `PackageLocation` class, so we won't discuss it here. The first class we will look at is the `Customer` class source.

The Customer Class

The second pair of `import` statements get the necessary classes so we can use JNDI to talk to the LDAP server.

```
import java.util.Hashtable;
import java.util.Enumeration;

import javax.naming.*;
import javax.naming.directory.*;

public class Customer implements DirContext {
    String type;
    Attributes myAttrs;
    String dn;

    public Customer(String dn, String cuid, String givenname, String sn,
                    String ou, String mail,
                    String telephone, String fax) {
        this.dn = dn;
        type = cuid;
```

The `BasicAttributes` class stores our attributes in a name/value format that can be used to store our data in LDAP form.

```
        myAttrs = new BasicAttributes(true);   // case ignore
```

The `Attribute` class is like a `Hashtable`, except that it can store many values associated with a single key.

```
        Attribute oc = new BasicAttribute("objectclass");
        oc.add("Customer");
        oc.add("inetOrgPerson");
        oc.add("organizationalPerson");
        oc.add("person");
        oc.add("top");

        Attribute ouSet = new BasicAttribute("ou");
        ouSet.add(ou);

        String cn = givenname+" "+sn;

        myAttrs.put(oc);
        myAttrs.put(ouSet);
        myAttrs.put("customerid",cuid);
        myAttrs.put("cn",cn);
        myAttrs.put("sn",sn);
        myAttrs.put("mail",mail);
        myAttrs.put("givenname",givenname);
        myAttrs.put("telephonenumber",telephone);
        myAttrs.put("facsimiletelephonenumber",fax);
    }

    public Attributes getAttributes() throws NamingException {
        return myAttrs;
    }

    public Attributes getAttributes(String name) throws NamingException {
        if (! name.equals("")) {
            throw new NameNotFoundException();
        }
        return myAttrs;
    }

    public Attributes getAttributes(Name name) throws NamingException {
        return getAttributes(name.toString());
    }

    public Attributes getAttributes(String name, String[] ids)
                                throws NamingException {
        if (! name.equals("")) {
            throw new NameNotFoundException();
        }

        Attributes answer = new BasicAttributes(true);
        Attribute target;
        for (int i = 0; i < ids.length; i++) {
            target = myAttrs.get(ids[i]);
            if (target != null) {
                answer.put(target);
            }
```

Continued on Following Page

```
        }
        return answer;
    }

    public Attributes getAttributes(Name name, String[] ids)
        throws NamingException {
        return getAttributes(name.toString(), ids);
    }

    public String getNameInNamespace() throws NamingException
    {
        return type;
    }

    public String toString() {
        return type;
    }
```

There are many methods of the `DirContext` interface that you have to implement. If you are only interested in storing an entry to the LDAP server, you don't have to implement most of them.

```
    // Not used for this example
    public Object lookup(Name name) throws NamingException {
        throw new OperationNotSupportedException();
    }

    public Object lookup(String name) throws NamingException {
        throw new OperationNotSupportedException();
    }

    public void bind(Name name, Object obj) throws NamingException {
        throw new OperationNotSupportedException();
    }
    ...
```

The Package Class

Next is our `Package` class. It's exactly the same as the `Customer` class except in the attributes it stores.

```
    ...

    public Package(String dn, String packageid, String receiverid,
                   String shipperid, String shipdate) {
        type = packageid;
        this.dn = dn;

        myAttrs = new BasicAttributes(true);   // case ignore

        Attribute oc = new BasicAttribute("objectclass");
        oc.add("package");
        oc.add("top");

        Attribute ouSet = new BasicAttribute("ou");
        ouSet.add("Packages");
```

```
        myAttrs.put(oc);
        myAttrs.put(ouSet);
        myAttrs.put("packageid",packageid);
        myAttrs.put("receiveid",receiverid);
        myAttrs.put("shipperid",shipperid);
        myAttrs.put("shipdate",shipdate);
    }
```

The CustomerServlet Class

Here is the real worker of our example, the `CustomerServlet` class.

```
import java.io.*;
import java.util.*;
import java.text.*;

import javax.servlet.*;
import javax.servlet.http.*;

import javax.naming.*;
import javax.naming.directory.*;

public class CustomerServlet extends HttpServlet {
```

Here are our global variables for our LDAP settings.

```
    public static String MY_PACKAGE_BASE = "ou=Packages,o=fedup.com";
    public static String MY_CUSTOMER_BASE = "ou=Customers,o=fedup.com";
    public static String INITCTX = "com.sun.jndi.ldap.LdapCtxFactory";
    public static int MY_PORT = 389;
    public static String MY_HOST = "ldap://localhost:" + MY_PORT;
    public static String MY_MGR = "cn=Directory Manager";
    public static String MY_PWD = "password";
    public static String MY_SEARCHBASE = "o=fedup.com";

    public static int nextPackageID = 5555;

    // In order to get the right starting package ID,
    // we need to read all existing packages.
    public void init() throws ServletException {
        String[] packaging = { "packageid" };
        Hashtable env = new Hashtable();

        env.put(Context.INITIAL_CONTEXT_FACTORY, INITCTX);
        env.put(Context.PROVIDER_URL, MY_HOST);

        try {
            // Get a reference to a directory context
            DirContext ctx = new InitialDirContext(env);

            // Perform the search
            NamingEnumeration results = ctx.search(MY_PACKAGE_BASE, null, packaging);

            while (results != null && results.hasMore()) {
                SearchResult sr = (SearchResult) results.next();
                Attributes attrs = sr.getAttributes();
```

Continued on Following Page

```
            Attribute attr = attrs.get("packageid");
            Integer packageNumber = new Integer((String) attr.get());
            if (nextPackageID <= packageNumber.intValue()) {
                nextPackageID = packageNumber.intValue() + 1;
            }
        }
    } catch (NamingException e) {
        log("Naming exception: " + e);
    }
}

public void doGet(HttpServletRequest req, HttpServletResponse res)
                        throws ServletException, IOException {
    res.setContentType("text/html");
    PrintWriter out = res.getWriter();
```

This checks to see if there is any data in the `"Authorization"` HTTP header from the browser. If not, it will prompt the browser for the username and password. Then we call the `allowedUser()` method giving it the data from the `"Authorization"` field.

```
    // Get Authorization header
    String auth = req.getHeader("Authorization");

    // Do we allow that user
    if (!allowedUser(auth)) {
        // Not Allowed, so report unauthorized
        res.setStatus(res.SC_UNAUTHORIZED);
        res.setHeader("WWW-Authenticate", "BASIC realm=\"users\"");
    } else {
        // User is allowed in
```

This means that we have authenticated successfully.

```
        out.println("<html><head><title>FedUp Customer " +
                    "Service</title></head><body>");
        out.println("<h2>FedUp Customer Service</h2>");
```

We parse the `"Authorization"` header information ourselves here to get the `customerid` which is the `userid` part of the `"Authorization"` header. The data will be BASE64-encoded, so we must decode it first.

```
        String userpassEncoded = auth.substring(6);
        sun.misc.BASE64Decoder dec = new sun.misc.BASE64Decoder();
        String userpassDecoded = new String(dec.decodeBuffer(userpassEncoded));
        StringTokenizer st = new StringTokenizer(userpassDecoded,":");
        String customerid = st.nextToken();
        String pwd = st.nextToken();

        try {
```

Now that we have the `customerid`, we want to get the `Customer` object of that id. We then print out the customer's name and customer ID.

```
        Customer c = getCustomer(customerid,out);
        Attributes attrs = c.getAttributes();
        Attribute attr = attrs.get("cn");
        out.println("Hello " + attr.get() + "<br>");
        out.println("Your customerid is " + customerid);
        String packageids[] = req.getParameterValues("packageid");
        String actions[] = req.getParameterValues("action");
```

If the request contained `"packageid=####"` in the query field of the URL, then we want to call the `packageLocation()` method, passing it the package id.

```
        if (packageids != null) {
            // If you've requested a package, go and list it
            packageLocation(packageids[0],out);
        }
```

If the query parameter contains an `action` parameter, then we want to print out a form to add a new `Package` to the system.

```
        else if (actions != null) {
            // Print out the form to add a package
            printAddPackageForm(customerid,out);
        } else {
```

Or we can just print out all packages that relate to this `customerid`. The `PrintWriter` should be the same one that you use to display HTML to the browser.

```
            // Print off end of welcome page and get all tracked packages
            out.println("<hr><a href=\"CustomerServlet?action=ADD\">" +
                    "Add a new package to track</a>");
            printCustomerPackages(c,out);
        }
    } catch(NamingException x) {
        log("ERROR:Try to Get Customer object for user " + customerid +
            ": " + x.toString());
        out.println("No customer matching " + customerid);
    } catch(NullPointerException n) {
        log("ERROR:Trying to get Customer object for user " + customerid +
            ": " + n.toString());
        out.println("NullPointer for Customer " + customerid);
    }

        out.println("</body></html>");
    }
}
```

Here's where we handle `POST` requests. The only one we should expect to receive would be to add a new package to the system.

```
    // Handle POST request
    public void doPost(HttpServletRequest req, HttpServletResponse res)
                                    throws ServletException, IOException
    {
        res.setContentType("text/html");
        PrintWriter out = res.getWriter();
```

Continued on Following Page

```
        // Get Authorization header
        String auth = req.getHeader("Authorization");

    // Do we allow that user
    if (!allowedUser(auth)) {
        // Not Allowed, so report he's unauthorized
        res.setStatus(res.SC_UNAUTHORIZED);
        res.setHeader("WWW-Authenticate", "BASIC realm=\"users\"");
    } else {
        // User is allowed in
        out.println("<html><head><title>FedUp Add Package
Service</title></head><body>");
        out.println("<h2>FedUp Add Package Service</h2>");

        String userpassEncoded = auth.substring(6);
        sun.misc.BASE64Decoder dec = new sun.misc.BASE64Decoder();
        String userpassDecoded = new String(dec.decodeBuffer(userpassEncoded));
        StringTokenizer st = new StringTokenizer(userpassDecoded,":");
        String customerid = st.nextToken();

        String shipperids[] = req.getParameterValues("sender");
        String receiverids[] = req.getParameterValues("receiver");

        try {
            out.println("Shipper is " + shipperids[0] + "<br>");
            out.println("Receiver is " + receiverids[0] + "<br>");
```

Here we call the method that adds a new package to the system, passing it the shipper customer id, the recipient's customer id and a stream to display the results on the Web browser.

```
            addNewPackage(shipperids[0], receiverids[0],out);
        } catch(NullPointerException ne) {
            out.println("Shipper or Receiver not set!<br>");
            out.println("<pre>" + ne.toString() + "</pre>");
        } catch(NamingException nx) {
            out.println("Package couldn't be added<br>");
            out.println(nx.toString());
        } catch(ParseException pe) {
            out.println("Package couldn't be added<br>");
            out.println(pe.toString());
        }
    }
}

    // This method checks to see if the user is in the LDAP database
    protected boolean allowedUser(String auth) throws IOException {

        Hashtable env = new Hashtable();
        boolean status = false;

        try {
            if (auth == null) return false; // no auth
```

We can only handle `"BASIC"` authentication which is the traditional Web authentication. Other possibilities could be MD5 hash or SSL certificates.

```
            if (!auth.toUpperCase().startsWith("BASIC ")) {
                return false; //only do BASIC
            }
```

```
// Get encoded user and password, comes after BASIC
String userpassEncoded = auth.substring(6);

// Decode it, using any base 64 decoder
sun.misc.BASE64Decoder dec = new sun.misc.BASE64Decoder();
String userpassDecoded = new String(dec.decodeBuffer(userpassEncoded));
StringTokenizer st = new StringTokenizer(userpassDecoded,":");
String customerid = st.nextToken();
String pwd = st.nextToken();
```

Now the way LDAP authentication works is by attempting to bind to the server with a DN and a password. Of course, no user in their right mind will remember their DN so we use some other attribute such as a user-id. Then we search in the LDAP server to find an entry that contains the attribute. For a secure system, you should use an attribute that will be unique per entry such as uid or in our case the customerid attribute.

Then we create a new LDAP connection and bind with the DN of the found entry and the password we got from the browser.

If that doesn't throw an exception, we consider this to be a successful authentication.

```
// Prepare for context
env.put(Context.INITIAL_CONTEXT_FACTORY, INITCTX);
env.put(Context.PROVIDER_URL, MY_HOST);

// Get a reference to a directory context
DirContext ctx = new InitialDirContext(env);

// Specify the scope of the search
SearchControls constraints = new SearchControls();
constraints.setSearchScope(SearchControls.SUBTREE_SCOPE);

// Perform the actual search
// We give it a searchbase, a filter and the constraints
// containing the scope of the search
NamingEnumeration results =
         ctx.search(MY_CUSTOMER_BASE, "(customerid=" + customerid +
                                     ")", constraints);

String dn = null;

// Now step through the search results
while (results != null && results.hasMore()) {
   SearchResult sr = (SearchResult) results.next();
   dn = sr.getName() + "," + MY_CUSTOMER_BASE;
}

env.put(Context.SECURITY_AUTHENTICATION, "simple");
env.put(Context.SECURITY_PRINCIPAL, dn);
env.put(Context.SECURITY_CREDENTIALS, pwd);

try {
   DirContext ctx2 = new InitialDirContext(env);
   status = true;
} catch (AuthenticationException e) {
   log(e.toString());
}
```

Continued on Following Page

```
    } catch (NamingException x) {
        log(x.toString());
    }
    return status;
}
```

In this method we retrieve an customer entry from the LDAP server matching the `customerid`. I've included the `PrintWriter` for debugging purposes.

```java
protected Customer getCustomer(String customerid, PrintWriter out)
                    throws NamingException   {
    Hashtable env = new Hashtable();

    env.put(Context.INITIAL_CONTEXT_FACTORY, INITCTX);
    env.put(Context.PROVIDER_URL, MY_HOST);

    // Get a reference to a directory context
    DirContext ctx = new InitialDirContext(env);

    SearchControls constraints = new SearchControls();
    constraints.setSearchScope(SearchControls.SUBTREE_SCOPE);

    // Perform the search
    NamingEnumeration results =
                ctx.search(MY_CUSTOMER_BASE, "customerid=" + customerid,
                            constraints);

    Customer c = null;

    // Now step through the search results
    while (results != null && results.hasMore()) {
        SearchResult sr = (SearchResult) results.next();
        String dn = sr.getName();

        Attributes attrs = sr.getAttributes();
        Attribute attr = attrs.get("givenname");
        String givenname = (String) attr.get();

        attr = attrs.get("sn");
        String sn = (String) attr.get();

        attr = attrs.get("ou");
        String ou = (String) attr.get();

        attr = attrs.get("mail");
        String mail = (String) attr.get();

        attr = attrs.get("telephonenumber");
        String telephone = (String) attr.get();

        attr = attrs.get("facsimiletelephonenumber");
        String fax = (String)attr.get();

        // Build a new Customer object with the retrieved attributes
        c = new Customer(dn, customerid, givenname, sn, ou, mail,
                        telephone, fax);
    }
    return c;
}
```

This next method prints out all of the packages that relate to a particular customer. We search all of the entries that have a `shipperid` or `receiveid` attribute that matches the DN of the `Customer` object.

```java
protected void printCustomerPackages (Customer c,PrintWriter out)
                        throws NamingException {
     out.println("<hr>");
     out.println("<b>Shipped Packages:</b><br>");
     out.println("<font color=#FF0000>" +
               "Click on Package Id to see where your package is</font>");

     Hashtable env = new Hashtable();

     env.put(Context.INITIAL_CONTEXT_FACTORY, INITCTX);
     env.put(Context.PROVIDER_URL, MY_HOST);

     // Get a reference to a directory context
     DirContext ctx = new InitialDirContext(env);

     SearchControls constraints = new SearchControls();
     constraints.setSearchScope(SearchControls.SUBTREE_SCOPE);
     log("Customer Name " + c.getNameInNamespace());

     NamingEnumeration results = ctx.search(MY_PACKAGE_BASE,
          "(|(receiveid=customerid=" + c.getNameInNamespace() + "," +
          MY_CUSTOMER_BASE + ")(shipperid=customerid=" +
          c.getNameInNamespace() + "," + MY_CUSTOMER_BASE + "))", constraints);

     while (results != null && results.hasMore()) {
        SearchResult sr = (SearchResult) results.next();
        String dn = sr.getName();
        Attributes attrs = sr.getAttributes();

        out.println("<ul>");

        Attribute attr = attrs.get("packageid");
        String packageid = (String) attr.get();
        out.println("<li>package id:<a href=\"CustomerServlet?packageid=" +
                   packageid + "\">" + packageid + "</a>");

        attr = attrs.get("shipperid");
        String shipperid = (String) attr.get();
        out.println("<li>shipper id:"+shipperid);

        attr = attrs.get("receiveid");
        String receiveid = (String) attr.get();
        out.println("<li>recipient id:"+receiveid);

        attr = attrs.get("shipdate");
        String shipdate = (String) attr.get();
        out.println("<li>date shipped:"+shipdate);

        try {
           // Not all packages will have a receivedate
           attr = attrs.get("receivedate");
           String receivedate = (String) attr.get();
           out.println("<li>date recieved:"+receivedate);
        } catch(NullPointerException n) { }
```

Continued on Following Page

```
            out.println("</ul><hr>");
        }
    }
```

This class prints out the location of a particular package. It takes a `packageid` and a `PrintWriter` to display the results.

This method locates the `PackageLocation` object stored in the LDAP server and passes it the package id to the `getLocation()` method. It's pretty simple code for something that is probably one of the most exciting uses of JNDI.

```
    protected void packageLocation(String packageid, PrintWriter out)
                            throws NamingException {
        Hashtable env = new Hashtable();

        // Get Java object
        env.put(Context.INITIAL_CONTEXT_FACTORY, INITCTX);
        env.put(Context.PROVIDER_URL, MY_HOST);

        // Get a reference to a directory context
        DirContext ctx = new InitialDirContext(env);

        out.println("<hr><b>Package Location:</b><br>");

        // Now get Java object
        PackageLocation wip = (PackageLocation) ctx.lookup("cn=PackageLocation," +
                                                "ou=Java,o=fedup.com");

        out.println(wip.getLocation(packageid)+"<br>");
        out.println("<hr>");
        out.println("<a href=\"CustomerServlet\">" +
                "Return to FedUp Customer Service</a>");
    }

    protected void printAddPackageForm(String customerid,PrintWriter out) {
        out.println("<form name=\"addpackage\" method=\"POST\"" +
                "action=\"CustomerServlet\">");
        out.println("<table border=0>");
        out.println("<tr><td>Package Sender:</td><td>" + customerid +
                "<input type=\"hidden\" name=\"sender\" value=\"" + customerid +
                "\"></td></tr>");
        out.println("<tr><td>Package Recipient:</td>" +
                "<td><input name=\"receiver\"></td></tr>");
        out.println("<tr><td><input type=\"submit\"></td><td></td></tr>");
        out.println("</table></form>");
    }
```

This final method is how we add a new Package entry to the LDAP server. It takes a `shipperid`, `receiverid` and a `PrintWriter` for display. We must bind to the LDAP server as a user with "write" rights. This user will act on behalf of the customer because customer's don't have write rights except on their own entries.

```
    protected void addNewPackage(String shipperid, String receiverid,
            PrintWriter out) throws NamingException, ParseException {
        Hashtable env = new Hashtable();
```

```
env.put(Context.INITIAL_CONTEXT_FACTORY, INITCTX);
env.put(Context.PROVIDER_URL, MY_HOST);
env.put(Context.SECURITY_AUTHENTICATION,"simple");
env.put(Context.SECURITY_PRINCIPAL,MY_MGR);
env.put(Context.SECURITY_CREDENTIALS,MY_PWD);

// We must be authenticated as a user with "write" privileges.
// We'll logon as an account on behalf of the customer.

// Get a reference to a directory context
DirContext ctx = new InitialDirContext(env);

// Now Create a Package object so that we can store in the LDAP server
// Get package id
String packageid = new String(new Integer(nextPackageID++).toString());

String dn = "packageid="+packageid + "," + MY_PACKAGE_BASE;

String shipperdn = "customerid=" + shipperid + "," + MY_CUSTOMER_BASE;
String receiverdn = "customerid=" + receiverid + "," + MY_CUSTOMER_BASE;
```

We store the `dateshipped` and `datereceived` as timestamp using GMT time. The format we use is the same format that is used by Netscape Directory server as their timestamp format for the `createtimestamp` attribute just because if we build search filters for one of these attributes, it can be used for all of them. We store in GMT timezone because people using this system will be in different timezones.

```
// Get timestamp in LDAP time format:
// 19990501024738Z
DateFormat format = new SimpleDateFormat("yyyyMMddHHmmss");
TimeZone tz = TimeZone.getTimeZone("GMT");
format.setTimeZone(tz);
Calendar cal = Calendar.getInstance();
Date now = new Date();
cal.setTimeZone(tz);
cal.setTime(now);

String shipdate = format.format(cal.getTime())+"Z";

out.println("<hr><b>Package Information:</b><br>");
out.println("<ul>");
out.println("<li>shipperid: " + shipperid);
out.println("<li>receiverid: " + receiverid);
out.println("<li>packageid: " + packageid);
out.println("<li>shipdate is " + shipdate);
out.println("</ul>");

Package p = new Package (dn, packageid, receiverdn, shipperdn, shipdate);

//now add Package to the LDAP server
ctx.bind(dn,p);
out.println("<font color=\"#FF0000\"><b>Package Shipped!</b></font><hr>");
out.println("<a href=\"CustomerServlet\">" +
            "Back to Fedup Customer Service</a>");
    }
  }
```

Summary

In this business case we have shown how you can utilize Java, LDAP and JNDI to improve service to your customers and build an infrastructure that can be used by many different applications.

We have learned how it is important to separate your Business Data Objects from your Business Rule Objects, which implement your business logic. By storing your BDO in LDAP, you can provide a common access protocol to your data over the network using a standard open protocol.

Java and JNDI give you cross-platform and cross-directory capability for providing access to your network directory infrastructure. The most functional system will still be based on LDAP because you can concentrate on a single standard protocol and that JNDI is best suited for utilizing Java objects on the network through LDAP.

Finally we showed how simply you can abstract your data out and develop a server-side Java application to take advantage of your directory infrastructure to improve customer service.

Enterprise JavaBeans

In this chapter we will look at Enterprise Java Beans and how they integrate with the other Java 2 Enterprise Edition APIs we've seen in this book so far.

The chapter is quite theoretical, but that allows us to discuss the different types of EJB and why and where you should use them in a short space. It doesn't assume any prior knowledge of EJBs, just a basic understanding of client-server systems and database transactions.

We'll cover:

- ➢ The Java platform as a Web Operating System - how Java provides the portability at system, application and service levels necessary for it to be a contender for the WebOS crown
- ➢ Web applications as services
- ➢ Roles in the EJB specification - deployer, developer and container creator
- ➢ The EJB container as a level of indirection to your EJB component
- ➢ Contract programming - keeping users, containers and sys-admins happy
- ➢ Session beans - representing the client on the web server
- ➢ Beans with and without state
- ➢ Entity beans representing the back end data on the web server
- ➢ Bean-managed persistence and container-managed persistence and their ramifications
- ➢ Activating pooled entity beans
- ➢ Querying data through entity beans
- ➢ Transaction management - when to take charge and when to let it happen for you
- ➢ Deployment descriptors

The Web Needs Portability

When we talk about server-side Java, we are really talking about a specific implementation of the **web operating system**. It's a term that is by no means an accepted, or even a widely used one, but I hope it will become clear over the next few pages that the body of software that is coming together on modern web servers is, in effect, a WebOS.

Java and the Web

Since the introduction of the web, many people have tried to offer application server platforms that in one way or another tie legacy and software services into the Web. At the time of this writing (July 1999) the market for web application servers is saturated, with almost 30 different implementations. A standard for web application servers has not yet been established nor has a dominant player emerged.

Developers therefore need to learn a specific product and its interface and usage before they can code. And they probably have had to deal with several different web application servers. Since we're waiting for a 'big shake-out', it can be a daunting choice for software professionals to settle on a platform they will learn to operate, use for development and specialize in. In the pre-web days the answer was easy: you could always default to the Microsoft platform. Now, however, the choice is more difficult.

Several factors are keeping the web platform open:

> The protocols for communication over the Internet are open.

> The emergence of the Linux and *BSD platforms as serious platforms for web deployment has prevented any one OS dominating, the way Windows dominates the PC market. Most importantly, the free Unices have won the loyalty of ISP system administrators. And if anyone has the real power to shape the future of the web it is the system administrators, and not the developers.

> Apache, with a commanding 60% share of the market, is the leading web server platform, and is open source.

But, while the web was born an open platform, is, and most likely will remain so, there is no such agreement for the applications that interface to the web.

How Java fits into this picture is a matter of some importance. From the standards point of view, Java is very much a vendor-defined standard. But, so far, in its definition of APIs it has managed to walk the tightrope between being a single vendor solution and committee fudge. By involving interested parties, Sun has been able to achieve a high level of consensus. Seeing EJB servers at JavaONE from five companies running identical EJB applications has proved that point.

Today, Java's server APIs (soon to be repackaged as the Enterprise Edition) is a maturing set of technologies, most of which are presented in this book. It is their adoption by web professionals to form the standard Internet server platform that will determine the success of server-side Java. There is much evidence that as an industry, server-side Java is a booming field, proving itself the platform of choice for robust web deployment.

The real shake out is happening now, as standards are defined, and we believe the web operating system is what will remain once the dust settles and it will have Java at its core.

This is not to say that more traditional client/server applications for EJB and the Java Enterprise APIs aren't common - just that we think web interfaces to all applications will become ubiquitous.

Server-Side Portability

Working with application server platforms is inherently based on the adoption of standards. By that, I mean that if you are going to standardize your development or gain a new set of skills, you'll ensure you use a platform that is unlikely to disappear in a year.

Web standards are free and open - you're not constrained by machine, OS or application. Now take those ideas and apply them to application servers. Freedom of platform requires portability. The favored way to get software portability is through Java. Therefore stick to Java. Portability is the one key feature that Java has, and the reason for its success as a web technology despite being under vendor control. Neat logic, huh?

Let's investigate a little bit more what "portability" means on the Web.

I believe there are four layers of portability that define the Web as we know it.

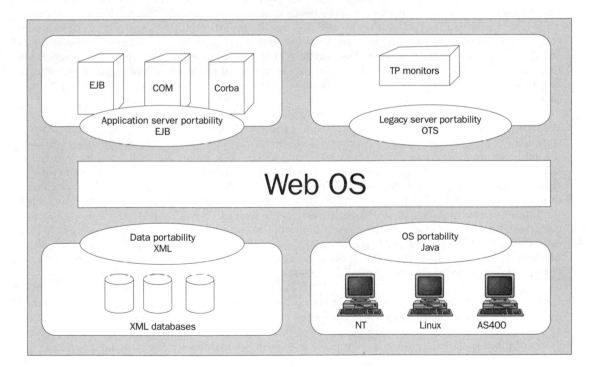

The first layer of portability is in the **data** itself. The Web allows us to ship data around easily and with great portability, but we are limited in what we can do with the data except present it. The promise of XML is that it ensures that the sea of data that exists in every system today can be exposed with a shape that is readily *understandable* by other machines. The XML file is distributed with its own description, so that data has attached meaning. In effect, XML is the best serialization engine currently in existence. The link between stored data and data that can live in applications (such as a Word document and the Word application, a PDF document and the PDF reader) is today mostly proprietary. XML/XSL and the associated parsers promise to unlink the executables from the data, a necessary step before that data freely moves around the web.

The second layer of portability is **systems portability**. It is an obvious statement to say that today's web servers are a hodgepodge of platforms. To address this platform called 'web servers' means that a developer needs to abstract the underlying system platform as much as possible. There is no web development without an abstracted system platform. To some extent the best effort in this direction, for a while, has been the Apache server, which exists on virtually every platform. But programmatically, the `cgi-bin` solution is not fully portable. Neither is it very powerful. CGI is more an extension of a web server than a full-blown software platform on which to build applications. Enter Java. The Java virtual machine and bytecode achieve the portability at this system layer, a necessary step before we can really claim we are coding to the web.

The third layer of portability is **application server portability**. Think about servlets. What is good about the servlet API is not the fact that it runs in-thread, in-process whereas CGI does not. In fact, `mod-perl` does that in Apache already and the "cgi-bin is slow out of process" is a lot of baloney. No, the real advantage is that if you want to move from Apache on NT to Netscape on Solaris, you can do it without recompiling code. The servlet API is a guarantee that a compliant web server will run your classes. The services offered by the web server to an application (such as making calls, building input and output streams, and parsing the session data) have been encapsulated in a standard object-oriented way.

We can now talk about **services** offered by application servers to objects living on the web. As your service needs grow more complex, say to include threading, persistence and transactions, you probably want to move to a still higher abstraction where these issues are addressed for you. This is the essential difference between a web server and an application server, and is where Enterprise Java Beans come in. As we will detail, the EJB specification standardizes the API the applications server offers to the business objects. If you deploy your bean on a specific EJB server, you can later move the same bean to another EJB compliant server, say in order to redeploy the bean in another part of a company, on different systems. The person doing the bean development in both cases does not need to bother with these 'details', and can concentrate on coding web applications that target the web platform through the EJB APIs. The application server and the system platforms are secondary. To summarize, the third layer is the portability across EJB application servers or web servers.

Finally the fourth layer of portability is in **legacy integration**. Imagine a legacy system that offers its own API and that is platform specific. It's a core part of your business, and you need all new applications to integrate with it. Any application you create will only integrate with that legacy system in that specific environment. To make a generic, standalone service which is platform independent, you have two options.

In the first scenario, in order to continue programming at the application server level, you have to use COM or CORBA as your conduit to the legacy system (which you hope can be an application server for its own objects). You then use a bridge (JIntegra and RMI-IIOP respectively) to access those applications through Java. Although wrapping existing objects as Java objects is a possibility, COM/CORBA offer the flexibility of working at a systems level and offering the application to Java code rather than a set of objects.

The second option is to create services in the legacy system that can talk to the Web. A mail server offering mail services through standard web protocols is one such service. The naming servers, the white pages of the Web, can be largely be seen as services offered to the application that need it (including web browsers).

The Java 2 Enterprise Edition APIs aim to help you standardize your applications interfaces to allow web application portability.

Services for Web Applications

Distributed client/server development, using CORBA or COM, has already demonstrated the use of interfaces to specify services. This gives you location transparency for objects - in that they can reside on any machine, any platform even, and the client need not worry about finding them. However both deal with a fairly static view of the world in the sense that the executables still need to be deployed to their target systems, and objects by and large are stuck where they're put. As a result, the management of distributed libraries and objects in CORBA and COM can be somewhat complicated. With the web and URLs, though, we have the ability to find any named resource on the web.

It's not a new idea that a network, rather than a system, should supply an application with the software services it needs. However in the world of Java it takes on a new twist. The web, from the point of view of Java, is a collection of collaborating virtual machines. To an object born in a given virtual machine, the boundaries of its visibility and scope are not limited to the walls of its native virtual machine, and therefore not even confined to the walls of its native physical machine. A Java object in the context of its virtual machine, and using the `initialContext` object, can ask to look for an object by name, using a directory service. For EJB, this is standardized on the Java Naming and Directory Interface (JNDI). It provides the capacity for any object in any VM to identify and locate any object built and deployed as an EJB in any VM by a string.

Consider the following:

```
Context initialContext = ... // obtain reference initial context - see Ch21
InterfaceA aRemoteObject = (InterfaceA) initialContext.lookup(beanRus/InterfaceA);
```

This returns a live reference in the present VM, even though the initial context can look up this object anywhere listed in the directory.

Furthermore, in the case of the Remote Method Invocation (RMI) libraries the Java programming model goes one step further. The code that implements a given `Serializable` class can travel with the serialized object, so that not even the class libraries are bound to live in a given virtual machine's classpath. In other words the code travels with the values. EJB builds heavily upon the distributed foundation supplied by the RMI programming model. Arguments and return values must be valid RMI types (that is `Remote` or `Serializable`).

All distributed objects also need to automatically generate remote invocation classes. Fortunately, EJB servers will generate the classes needed to execute the distributed calls. Developers will not need to code these distributed interfaces, extend `Java.rmi.server.UnicastRemoteObject` or even understand what the technology is all about, since the server will generate the code needed to have those classes available on the web. An EJB server will also take on the responsibilities of threading access to these classes, and offers transactional services and context propagation for these beans and calls.

Following the same services pattern, it happens that sending an email is something that web applications do quite often. On any e-commerce site you will find the mandatory confirmation email that needs to be fired to the purchasing client. In some ways, this is a service offered to applications, just like the "printing" services are offered by the Win32 APIs to Windows applications. As you develop an application, it's good to know that you can always rely on the printing API of a given system's operating system to offer printing capability in your application. In very much the same sense, modern web applications can call upon a set of services that should be offered to them, and it's simply a different set of services, appropriate for Internet applications. Just as Windows offers printing services, web applications will have access to email services through the JavaMail API.

What we are touching upon here is not new, but is only now becoming practicable: a true web operating system must offer applications access to all necessary web services.

Let's consider the following code, where the servlet session tracking API is used to keep track of the current EJB session associated with the class:

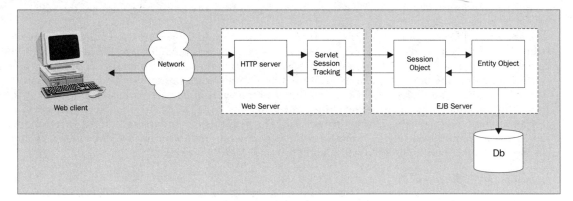

```
import java.io.*;
import javax.servlet.*;

/*
 * The EJBServlet enables a web-based client to access an EJB through http
 * We use the session tracking properties of the servlet to keep a live EJB
session
 */
public synchronized class EJBServlet extends HttpServlet {

    /*
     * We use the post method to retrieve the data
     * We also use the session tracking mechanism of the servlet to keep
     * the association with an EJB
```

```
      */
  public void doPost(HttpServletRequest request, HttpServletResponse response)
              throws ServletException, IOException {

      response.setContentType("text/plain");
      PrintWriter printWriter = response.getWriter();

      // Get the http session, create it if necessary
      HttpSession httpSession = request.getSession(true);

      // Now get the EJB session. Create it if necessary
      Teller accountTeller = (Teller) httpSession.getValue("EJBSession");

      if (accountTeller == null) {
          Context initialContext = ... //obtain initial context from EJB server

          // Obtain the home interface to the accounts
          BankTellerHome bankTellerHome = (BankTellerHome)
                          javax.rmi.PortableRemoteObject.narrow
                            (initialContext.lookup(bankOfEJB/bankTellerBean),
                              BankTellerHome.class);
          int accountNumberId = 12345678;

          // Create a teller session to my account number
          // Note that it is an EJBObject ready to use
          accountTeller = bankTellerHome.create(accountNumberId);

          // Store it in the servlet session for future use
          httpSession.putValue("EJBSession", accountTeller);
      }

      // We passed the method argument as a method parameter to the servlet
      String method = request.getParameter("method").trim();

      if (method.equals("getBalance")) {
          // How to further use the parameters, is it a savings or checking
account?
          String accountType = request.getParameter("accountType");

          // The method is getBalance(), exists on the teller machine and
          // returns a formatted String
          printWriter.println(myTeller.getBalance(accountType));
      }
  }
}
```

The important part of this servlet is that the EJB's client is the servlet itself.

It's now widely accepted that servlets, JSPs and EJBs form the web equivalent of the Model View Controller (MVC) pattern. This pattern occurs in many places, but has a clear implementation in the web platform.

> Servlets build a first layer to integrate HTTP invocations with state and thread them as individual client requests. The servlet API is the **controller layer**. As we can see in the example, it controls which beans are called and what work they do. In our case, the actual method to be called is taken from the parameters passed to the POST method. In other words, the client uses URL encoding to pass the actual name of the method to use.

581

> EJBs with their solid transactional nature and their capacity to access back end representations constitute the **model** part of the MVC pattern. In short, the main body of logic can be coded in these beans.

Whereas servlet chaining, can offer a fast way to deliver some elaborate logic, the API, with its `doPost(request, response)` parameters suffers from the same problem that piped commands in Unix suffer from - namely, that input needs to match the output of the previous body of code, an unnecessary restriction in chaining that Perl dealt with.

It is rather obvious that a real object implementation of the model offers much more flexibility in design and implementation. Furthermore, the transactional nature of some beans is a must.

> Finally, the capacity to generate dynamic content using JSP constitutes the **view** part of the MVC pattern.

I must say I'm not a great fan of talking about software in terms of patterns, believing rather in "may the source be with you", but sometimes a little pattern here and there does not hurt. So there it is, the web operating system, in its first primitive incarnation, is made of servlets talking to beans responding to clients through JSP. A nice MVC pattern, and it works.

Enterprise Java Beans and the WebOS

JavaSoft is now working towards defining the APIs of this web operating system: everything from JSP through Java Messaging Service to the forthcoming connector specification. But the cornerstone of this scheme, as it is implemented in the Java API, is definitely the EJB specification.

We are about to look in some detail at the programming model that EJBs offer but before we do that let's finish off the webOS puzzle. The scope of the EJB specification is broad enough to cover the ground between the client session, as we will see naturally embodied in the notion of Session beans, and in the back-end persistent representation, built with Entity beans. In short the EJB specification mixes state from clients and back-ends on a middle-tier server. In our example we can further break down the model by saying that the teller session accesses an account entity bean in the bank database. EJB also includes a robust transactional mechanism in its model, and security with bells and whistles such as access control entries that can discriminate down to the method level.

Lastly, the EJB specification brings system administration to the center of our web puzzle. By and large, with the web we are still in the Jurassic period, where the dominant species is still the developer. Many people claim that open source software is a success because of a close understanding of system administration issues, and in fact the free Unices are where they are today largely thanks to the system administration crowd. Ease of administration as much as ease of development makes or breaks web projects. If an application is hard to maintain, and if it is not easily distributed across networks and systems, it becomes an administrative burden. One can read the EJB spec and realize that the deployer role defined in the spec is really that of a super system administrator, and that tools such as the Deployment Descriptor (in its XML incarnation) are really geared towards system administration and deployment problems. Of which, more later.

The EJB Specification

It's difficult to talk about the EJB specification. It is 300 pages long and is intended for four audiences. To users of EJBs, only a few pages are useful or even relevant. Actually using EJBs is a trivial task, because the server hides so much complexity from the end user. As we will see, a developer using EJBs only needs to understand how to find and call methods on a bean, and maybe manage state (in case of server crash).

To bean developers, more of the spec is relevant and this will be our main focus (I will assume most of you are in the business of building beans), but even then not all of it is relevant. A bean developer, unlike a bean user, needs to understand fully the state management operations, since they define the interfaces to the container and needs to code the callbacks for the container in the bean. Many bean developers will also need to be familiar with the transaction management and the declaration of management type.

The rest of the specification is squarely targeted at server developers and all the complexities of the server implementation should be screened from the bean developer and most certainly from the bean user.

Roles in the EJB Specification

The EJB specification defines the various types of IT professionals involved in running the platform. Just like the database world clearly defines the role of a Database Administrator or DBA, the EJB spec deals with the various roles a component-based world requires. Each role works on different products, and they all come together on the EJB server.

The first role defined is that of a bean provider (called "Aardvark Inc" in the EJB 1.1 specification). The Aardvark company is a highly specialized shop. Their main competence is in writing components, or beans in the Java world, that do one task and do it well. Let's say that the Aardvark company knows everything there is to know about carts for modern e-commerce sites. The user interaction is the result of years of market behavior research and the resulting bean is sold. In other words, they are **bean producers**.

The following diagram shows the various parts and views of an EJB application, with the relevant bits indicated by a solid line.

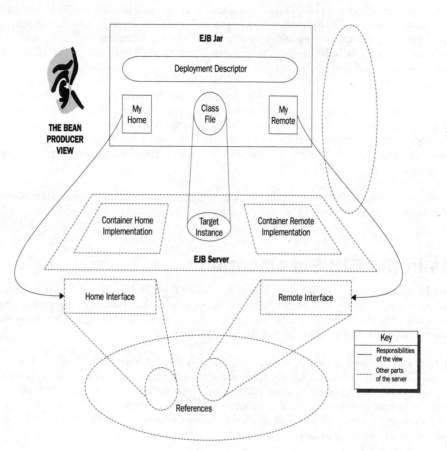

The second role is that of the **application assembler**. An application assembler from the "Wombat company" (in the 1.1 specification) is a high level consultant who knows a functional domain pretty well, say the e-commerce domain. He is a bean user and can assemble, on demand, an application for a given client. This role shares similarities to that of an IT developer doing in-house development for a large shop. There is very little he needs to know about the EJB programming model, he just uses the beans to stitch together custom applications.

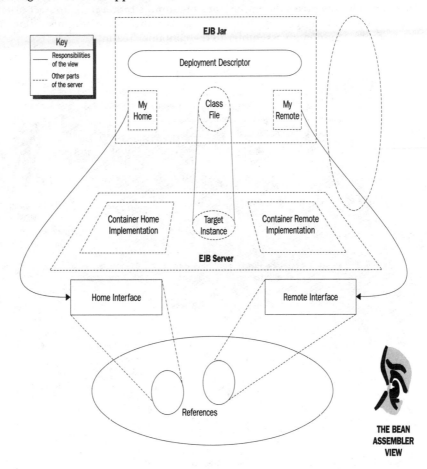

The third role, and perhaps the most important role, is that of the **system administrator** (from the ABC enterprise IT staff). This role, also known as the deployer, is the closest to the DBA of the RDBMS world. He is in charge of the actual production system, and oversees deployment and administration of the beans. This role, though familiar in the database world, is somewhat new in the object world. Like it or not, the object world has, for a long time, been the private playground of developers, while in the real world the operational side of things has mostly been owned by DBAs. The EJB specification recognizes the importance of administration in the object-oriented world of the web. The EJB spec acknowledges this and tries to standardize some administration issues such as the deployment from the component assembler to the container realm.

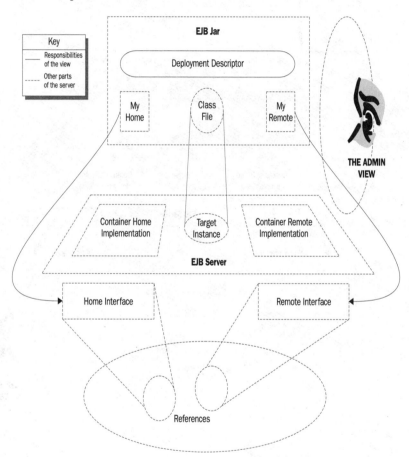

The fourth and final role the specification defines is, of course, that of the **server implementer**. The EJBoss organization (http://www.ejboss.org) is such an implementer. This is the world of container and server providers (ACME corporation in the spec).

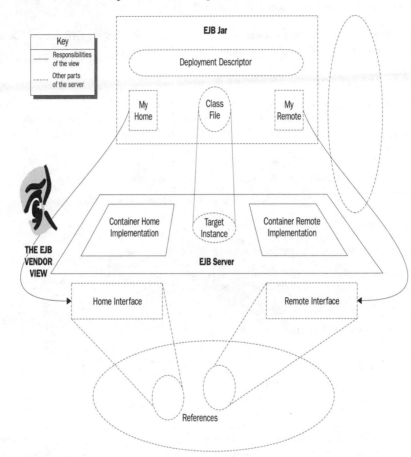

I will guide you through some of the specification, focussing on issues of interest to EJB users and EJB developers. In particular, we'll focus on the parts that shed light on the development model and on administration.

The Idea of Indirection

Having said that we are ignoring the complexities of containers, we do need to look at one important container concept.

Even though it is implemented by the container providers, the notion of **indirection**, once clearly understood, opens a lot of doors to understanding how EJBs work, how to code them and how to use them. By examining indirection now, we will shed some light on the contracts defined by the EJB specification between the container and the client as well as the container and the bean implementation.

Probably the best way to go about this is to understand how a container deploys a bean.

Let's imagine you are in the role of a bean developer for a second. In a run-time scenario, a user will call your object through its interface. What the container will do is intercept that call, do all the things it needs to do (such as security checks, if the deployer defined ACLs on your bean), and then finally pass the call to your bean implementation.

As a bean developer you have to provide a `jar` for deployment to an EJB server, and in it you have to include a bean and two views of it – a bean and two interfaces.

The EJBHome Interface

The first interface is a **home interface** extending `javax.ejb.EJBHome`. It defines the factory methods for your bean, that is, those that are not associated with a specific instance of the bean nor a given state, but which look after things like finding the bean and controlling its lifecycle. The `EJBHome` interface is defined as:

```
public interface javax.ejb.EJBHome extends java.rmi.Remote {

    // Obtain metaData about the object in a EJB format
    public abstract EJBMetaData getEJBMetaData();

    // Remove the live EJBObject identified with this handle
    public abstract void remove(Handle handle);

    // Remove the EJBObject identified by the primary key
    public abstract void remove(Object primaryKey);
}
```

Our interface will extend it to include:

```
public interface BankTellerHome extends Javax.ejb.EJBHome {

    public BankTeller create(int bankAccountNumber)
                            throws javax.ejb.ObjectNotFoundException ;
}
```

As complicated as the first interface might look to the bean developer, we will not concern ourselves with it for now. A bean developer is responsible for supplying an implementation of the second interface (we'll see below, why he does *not* need to declare `implements` and implement all the methods defined in these interfaces), but isn't responsible for implementing the first interface.

The EJBObject Interface

The second interface, the **remote interface**, needs to extend `javax.ejb.EJBObject`. This interface really describes the business methods of your beans, that is, its logic. These are instance methods (as opposed to the static methods of the factory).

The `EJBObject` interface is defined by:

```
public interface javax.ejb.EJBObject extends java.rmi.Remote {

    // Obtain an EJBHome for this object
    public abstract EJBHome getEJBHome();
```

```
    // This is a live object, get its handle
    public abstract Handle getHandle();

    // If this comes with a persistent representation, get its key
    public abstract Object getPrimaryKey();

    // The notion of "identity" is somewhat new in EJB, redefine equals
    public abstract boolean isIdentical(EJBObject obj);

    // Same as the home, but on the "this" instance
    public abstract void remove();
}
```

Again, the developer should not concern himself with the implementation of these methods as they are provided by the container. However the bean developer should define the business methods that go in the `EJBObject` interface, as in:

```
public interface BankTeller extends javax.ejb.EJBObject {

    // The method from the servlet example
    public String getStatement();

    // The bank teller session is created with a bank account number
    // We can get it in the session.
    public int getBankAccountIdNumber();
}
```

These methods need an implementation in the final bean.

You need to provide a bean implementation along with the two interfaces. Note that the bean gives implementations of both your interfaces. In that sense the interfaces are really views of your beans methods. For now, just bear in mind this interesting bit of information: a bean should not declare that it `implements` any of the two interfaces you just defined along with it. By implements we mean that the actual signature of your bean should not define `public class BankTellerBean implements BankTellerHome, BankTeller`. Why? Well, because as we will see that is where the magic of the indirection happens. You should implement without declaring `implements`. Confused yet?

Once you have provided these three classes in a compiled form (as in `.class`) you can package this in a jar and send it off to a server for deployment. What will the server do? Well, the server will look at your declared interfaces and introspect to get all the methods declared in both your interfaces. What it will then do is generate two bodies of code that actually implement the two interfaces. In that code, a server can use CORBA or RMI (as is the case with EJBoss) to make these interfaces available to the network in a distributed fashion. Here is the first service the EJB server brings to the developer - the developer never has to code distributed classes, the server will generate them from the interface description.

Another thing that generated code can do is include a few calls to a security manager and when these calls return the code can also make sure that the transactional context propagated through the interface is associated with all interested parties in this call.

Of course, the most interesting 'interested party' in this case is the final bean, your bean, that the body of code is going to call eventually. At the end of all the generated code behind the interface, the real fun can begin and the code will now call your corresponding method on the bean. In between the call on the client interface class to the bean, the server has done a lot of work, in an indirect fashion.

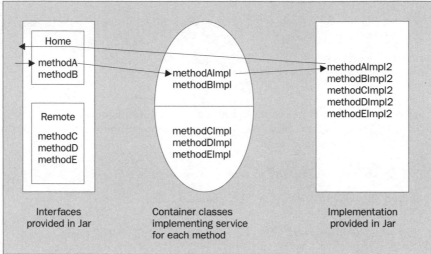

The bean implementation should then contain at least the following methods

```
public class BankTellerBean implements javax.ejb.EnterpriseBean,
                                       javax.ejb.SessionBean {

    // Let's define the entity bean Account (we will see it in more detail later)
    private BankAccount bankAccount;
    private int bankAccountNumber;

    // The equivalent of the create() method
    public void ejbCreate(int bankAccountNumber) throws
                                        javax.ejb.NoSuchObjectException{
        this.bankAccountNumber = bankAccountNumber;

        // Obtain a reference to the entity account (entity EJB hookup)
        bankAccount = ...;

        // Note the void return
        return;
    }

    // The business methods
    public String getStatement() {
        // Get the statement from the entity bean, bank Account is the entity
        String statement = bankAccount.getStatement();

        // Return the string statement to the calling servlet
        return statement;
    }
```

```
    public int getBankAccountIdNumber() {
        return bankAccountIdNumber;
    }

    // The callback method from the SessionBean

    /*
     * We skip all the methods from the SessionBean (state management methods)
     * These are unnecessary for now, we will see them later
     * among them setSessionContext(javax.ejb.SessionContext)
     *
     * EnterpriseBean only defines Serializable ... nothing to do for this one
     */
}
```

If you were to define

```
public class BankTellerBean implements BankTellerHome, BankTeller {}
```

then your code would *not* compile since we have defined, as the specification requires, that the `create()` method be renamed `ejbCreate()` and return `null`.

When the client calls `bankTellerHome.create(1322)`, the container really implements that method and does some checks before firing the corresponding `bankTellerBean.ejbCreate(1322)` on your bean implementation.

Thanks to indirection the container can accept your call on the remote interface as in `bankTeller.getBankAccountNumber()`, and the server will behave as if everything is normal even though it removed your actual target `bankTellerBean` to save memory. When the call comes in, the server will busy itself rebuilding the same object by bringing that instance up and firing a few callbacks on the bean, such an `ejbActivate()` to make sure the state is loaded in that bean before actually firing the call to the bean. To the user of the bean it looks as if nothing has changed and that the `EJBObject` he has been using was on the server all the time, even though behind the scenes it was really another instance of your bean that answered the call.

By now you should see the value of indirection. It can provide software services both to the client and beans, as well as juggling server responsibilities like high availability and load balancing and the life cycle of beans, without ever requiring extra work from the software developer. To be a part of this, all your code must do is provide the right hooks and callbacks for the container to plug into.

It should also be clear why a bean should in fact *not* implement, as in `implements`, the interfaces it declares. If it did, the indirection model could fail. A bean could return a reference to itself, that is, return `this` in a method call, allowing a client to use that reference to access the bean directly. Some of the EJB lifecycle methods even bear different names, for example `create()` and `ejbCreate()`, respectively in the remote interface and bean class, to make sure that such a case would raise an exception (`NoSuchMethodException`). In these ways, the EJB specification ensures that the bean can only be accessed through the container.

Basically the whole EJB magic is built into this code indirection. And if this concept is clear, you've understood the most important design pattern behind EJB, that indirection defines the container contracts with the clients and beans.

Indirection is a deployment and run time consideration. At development time, the interfaces to this container are known and are detailed in the specification. They fall into three categories.

Three Contracts define a Container

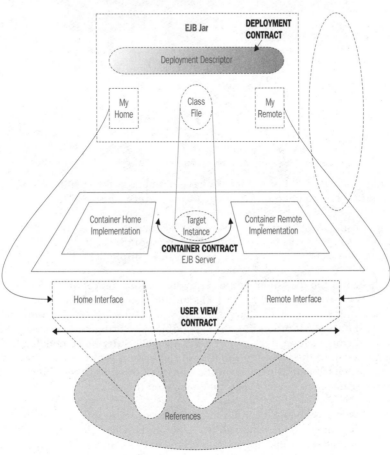

The first category is the **client view**. It defines how a client is to interface with the objects living in a container. We will see that the notion of a live `EJBObject` is an abstraction not linked to any particular object but to an association of them. However the client does not need to know about these details. All it needs to know is:

> ➤ How to find an object's factory, that is, the object home through the JNDI mechanism
>
> ➤ How to create and destroy an object
>
> ➤ How and what methods to call on the remote object
>
> ➤ How to get a handle to that live `EJBObject` for later reuse

The second category is the **bean view**. It defines the callbacks that a bean implementation must have. These really provide the hooks for the container to manage the bean lifecycle and pass information as needed (such as context information). If a bean provider implements these methods, any EJB-compliant container will be able to deploy it. The target bean's interaction with the outside world is restricted by the container since all calls, even business logic, are filtered by the container. That container contract is what hooks beans together.

The last contract used to be an interface but is now an XML file. It is the **deployment descriptor**. Once you have written your bean implementation and the two interfaces that go with it, you might wonder how you package this so that an assembler and the bean deployer's tools will automatically work with your code. Well the short answer is that you need to describe your package a little bit before the EJB platform can really take over. That is done by creating a `.jar` that includes your bean classes and the interfaces. Since the implementation does not implement the interfaces (indirection, remember?), it is necessary for you to declare that this particular class in your package is the implementation bean and these particular interfaces are the home class and the remote class. You also do other things in there:

> ➢ Baptize your bean with its JNDI name, the name under which it will be deployed and known to the outside world

> ➢ Declare what type of bean (as session or entity, and if session, what type)

> ➢ Define certain properties of your bean methods such as execution identity and what type of transaction management they require

> ➢ Specify what ACL you want associated with the runtime environment of the bean

> ➢ Make environment properties available to the target instance

Here we touch upon another potentially confusing notion, since "you" refers both to the bean developer (for the class names for example) and the bean deployer (for the JNDI name and the ACLs).

What makes the deployment descriptor special is that it is supposed to be edited by the bean developer for some basic things such as the bean class name and the type of transaction management it implements or requires. Other issues like the ACL are system administration business, since there is simply no way that a third party developer can know the particulars of a security policy as implemented in operations by a company (unless that developer is an IT developer working directly for the company).

The only software notion that needs to be clearly understood at this point is the fact that this is done declaratively. It is, in fact, called declarative programming. For those familiar with Unix command line it is akin to the options one would pass the server program as it is invoked from the command line, that is, a series of declaration that the server's `main()` method will parse and keep as declarative variables. This comparison is a bit weak, given the massive volume of information deployers and developers pass to the system through this file. The one point to bear in mind is that in our case, the declarative management is really a mix of declarations from the developer (this is my transactional model, that is my EJB type and this is my implementation) along with declarations from the system administrator (this is my time out for this bean, these are the ACLs I want for this bean, these are the sizes of my pools).

Session Beans

The first type of bean the EJB specification defines is the **session bean**. Its name is well chosen since it is really a client representation on the web server. As we showed in our servlet example, web servers can nowadays keep track of state over an inherently stateless HTTP connection. The servlet engine has a built-in mechanism to track calls that belong to the same session - the `HttpSession` object modern servlet engines provide through URL encoding. Even if one uses this to keep some state associated with the call, an EJB application would rather associate a session bean with the servlet so as to keep the state of the calls in this session bean. This is a cleaner object-oriented approach.

Session beans are representation of clients on EJB servers. In fact, the execution of a session bean is always on behalf of a single client; for example the bean instance keeps the reference to the bank account of this client (represented by another bean in the system), as well as `bankAccountNumberId` variable. It is illegal for the container to allow two clients to call the same session bean, or for two different clients to have the same view of the `bankAccountBean`. Session beans can be transaction aware. A session bean can participate in a web transaction as well as register call backs that will permit synchronization with a transaction manager. A final property of session beans is that they can access any back end they wish but they do so outside the context of the container. This might change in the near future since offering data source access is something that may be standardized in a future EJB release.

There are two types of session beans that the bean developer can deal with - **stateful** and **stateless** sessions. A stateless bean is a bean that does not keep state between invocations. The decision to make a bean stateless is made by the bean developer. If the bean does not keep state from its conversation with a client, then the stateless bean model is probably a good choice, though servlets are also an option here. The developer declares through the deployment descriptor that a bean is coded in a stateless fashion. Of course, knowing whether a bean keeps state or not rests solely with the developer; there is no way at run time for a container to know that a particular bean is stateless. Therefore this knowledge must be passed declaratively with the deployment descriptor.

What a container can do in case of a stateless bean is reuse the instances across many invocations. Obviously a stateful bean needs to stay with a particular client, and setting aside the case where it is passivatedmoved to secondary storage and removed from active memory), a bean instance needs to live in between invocations in memory. That implies that the machine requirements for a given number of users on the system are that much higher than the equivalent number of stateless users. In the case of stateless users, most implementations will maintain pools of equivalent beans already pre-instantiated. Again to the user of these stateless beans, this is mostly transparent - they need only remember that the instance of the bean that does the work may change from call to call. The bean developer needs to worry about this basic design choice and declare it to the container with the declarative deployment descriptor.

Let's look in some more detail at the home interface for a session bean. This is the interface that a client can look up by name. Unlike entity beans that we will meet later, session beans cannot be found directly by clients – they do not have an identity that they expose to the outside world, although they do have one inside the container. They only live in the client session and are created as needed through the home interface. The lookup for this interface is done through the JNDI lookup mechanism. Given a JNDI name, a client can obtain a reference to the home interface through the following calls:

```
Context initialContext = ... ;
BankTellerHome bankTellerHome = (BankTellerHome)
                    javax.rmi.PortableRemoteObject.narrow(
                        initialContext.lookup(bankOfEJB/bankTellerBean),
                        BankTellerHome.class);
```

There are a few important things to look at in these lines of code. First, the actual lookup code is done through the initial context. The initial context offers a naming context to any object in any VM. It is in this `Context` implementation that a client can call the `lookup()` method and that lookup must in turn return a reference to a possibly remote object. The other thing is that the naming of the bean, its JNDI name, is absolutely independent of the class name. The bindings between the object and its JNDI string representation are defined in the deployment descriptor, and not hardcoded in any way. The object name is given by the bean developer, while the JNDI name will follow any installation naming conventions defined by the deployer.

Finally, what is returned to the client is a reference to the home interface of the bean, not necessarily to a live `EJBObject`. This distinction is a departure from the standard RMI programming model where a client can expect to find an instance ready for calls on it. Instead of maintaining references whether they're in use or not, EJB opts for a "just-in-time" approach to handling requests. In the case of EJB, establishing a live session for the client is achieved by first going to the home interface. From this interface the client can call `create()`.

```
Teller accountTeller = bankTellerHome.create(accountNumberId);
```

What happens then is that the EJB server will busy itself establishing a session for this client. Note that we assume the bean is going to be stateful. We pass it unique user information at creation time, in this case, the account number that this client has with this particular e-commerce site. What this returns is the second interface we are interested in. This interface is the remote interface. The remote interface, as we saw, is the one that holds the real instance methods for the client to access. Now remember that this is all smoke and mirrors, since the actual `ejbCreate()` implementation has a `void` return type. You now believe you're talking to a live EJB object, but behind the scenes, the server could be doing all kinds of optimizations. In fact, even the code that implements the interfaces does not need to live in separate bodies of code (and we played with this idea for a while in EJBoss). All that matters to the user of this bean is that he asked for a reference to the home by name, got one and could call the `create()` method on it to obtain a reference to a live EJB object. We will go back to this 'live' concept, but for now all that really matters is that we can call,

```
teller.getStatement();
```

and have the session bean keep all that information in the body of this session bean. Note that all the information that is in this bean not only pertains to you by functional design (you are the proprietor of the account) but also by technology, in the sense that the session bean is not accessible to others, nor is the servlet. It is not a shared entity and it exists as long as the client interface is alive, or until it is timed out by the server.

Being Alive – References and Handles

At this point let's look at what a 'live' bean means. It is a central concept in EJB since it hints at the larger notion of the identity of a live object on the web. One thing that is interesting in the remote interface is that you can get a handle to the `EJBObject` you're using in the following fashion:

```
Handle tellerHandle = teller.getHandle();
```

What is remarkable about this handle is that a client can at any moment say,

```
Teller reconstitutedTeller = tellerHandle.getEJBObject();
```

This might not look like much now, but we hope you will understand the implications of this simple call. What this says in effect is that you can reconstruct your object from a simple client representation. By the way, but this is not so important at the moment, the handle can be persisted, it can be stored to disk or sent on the network for usage in another virtual machine. In other words, from any virtual machine, the handle, even a serialized handle, can conjure up a live session. Even in the case of a passivated session on the server, the handle can reconstruct a live reference with that simple `getEJBObject()` call.

From a client view this is rather straightforward, but the notion needs to be seen from the point of view of the container implementation. Remember that a server really puts together three pieces of code to really service a client. What a client perceives as a live `EJBObject` is in fact the loose congregation of its distributed server implementation, the indirection code generated and operated on the server and all the services it calls, and finally the actual bean implementation provided by the developer. The bean identity that is so simple for the client user is far more diffuse on the server side.

Although identity is one of the more interesting problems in EJB, understanding it in-depth is not necessary to bean users and developers. From 'does not exist and is not referenced', one can use the `home.create()` to go to the 'exists and is referenced' as in exists on the server side and is referenced in the client VM. The `object.remove()` and `home.remove(object)` calls, as well as a server crash or timeout, will move the session bean to 'does not exist and is referenced' – the bean instance no longer exists on the server but the client still holds a reference to it. Note that there is no real way for the server to automatically reach out and invalidate the client reference. If a client calls `remove()` on an object and at the next line decides to call a business method on the same object, there is not much that the container can do but throw an exception. In that sense the reference still lives in the client VM, until it is released, but the `EJBobject` is no longer on the server.

What's of most interest to us is the 'exists and is not referenced' state. Suppose that for some reason the client lets go of its reference to the object but keeps a handle to it (for example, decides to close his/her current session to go have lunch but wants to restart it in the afternoon). Then the server still holds a live object in memory, one that it might passivate in the future, but that is still alive, at least according to the handle. The way back to the 'exists and is referenced state' is through that same handle.

Session Bean Lifecycle

Now that we have looked at the client view of the bean, we need to look at the container contract and how it demarcates the lifecycle of the bean as well as transaction notification to the target bean.

When the client calls a `create()` the container will go through the steps of creating a live `EJBObject` for this client. In the case of a stateless client this is pretty simple since the container maintains a pool of objects already instantiated. However, in the case of a stateful bean, there is no such pool, at least for bean instances. Also there is no way for the specification to require the bean developer to code something that would in effect 'clean up' beans for reuse, so the only option a container has is to call a `new()` on the target bean The recommendation in the specification is to use `newInstance()` on the class.

This new instance is first associated with the `EJBObject` through the `SessionContext` that is passed to it with the `setSessionContext()` call from the container. With this `SessionContext`, the target bean is able to do several things – namely get information about the caller as well as the transaction context associated with the calls. This is the way for the container to tell the bean, 'this is the environment (user and transaction) in which you will do your work'. A bean implementation can always use this interface to obtain information about who is calling you by getting a `User` object. After this first interface has been set, the container can finally call the `ejbCreate()` method corresponding to the `create()` method that was called on the home interface.

This means that as a bean developer you need to provide a method declaring:

```
public void setSessionContext(SessionContext sessionContext) {
...
}
```

The simplest way to implement this is to keep a private reference to the `SessionContext`:

```
private SessionContext sessionContext;

public void setSessionContext(SessionContext sessionContext) {
    this.sessionContext = sessionContext;
}
```

What you do with the session context is entirely up to you. It might be the case that the identity of the caller or his transactional context, as well as the other services the interface offers are entirely irrelevant to the logic in your bean, in which case you might even provide an empty implementation of the `setSessionContext()` method. This is valid since the container can at least call your method. Ain't contract programming great?

However, if you want to use the information provided, say to use the transaction in which a user is already participating, your code might look something like this

```
public void setSessionContext(SessionContext sessionContext) {
    this.sessionContext = sessionContext;
}

public String getStatement() {

    // Get the caller by the sessionContext
    Identity caller = sessionContext.getCallerIdentity();

    // Verify that the account is OK
    if (!bankAccount.gettingStatementIsOK(caller)) {
        Transaction userTransaction = sessionContext.getUserTransaction();
```

```
         // Invalidate the transaction we are part of
      userTransaction.setRollbackOnly();
      return null;
   } else {
      String statement = bankAccount.getStatement();

      // Return the string statement to the calling servlet
      retun statement;
   }
}
```

Here we make use of the transaction to invalidate the full operation through the
`setRollbackOnly()` which ensures that this transaction will be rolled back by the transaction
monitor. We also made use of the caller identity, something that is propagated by the server through
the `SessionContext`.

As a bean developer you also need to code the appropriate `ejbCreate()` method. What you do
with this method is entirely up to you – for our bank teller program, we pass account information. All
you need to understand is that the container will notify your bean, through this callback mechanism,
that a user requested a creation and will pass the necessary parameters. Once the `ejbCreate()`
method has been called on your bean it is considered to be in a state ready to accept method calls. At
this point the client can also get the handle we discussed in the user view.

Transactional and Non-transactional Methods

From this state, the client can invoke any of the business methods you declared in your remote
interface. The methods can be transactional or non-transactional. Non-transactional methods do not
require any synchronization mechanism on the part of the bean, so there is no extra communication
going on with the container when the client calls non-transactional methods on the remote interface.
They are merely forwarded to the target bean.

In the case of transactional methods however, the container needs to notify the bean of the
transaction demarcation. The lifecycle of the transaction impacts the flow of methods in the bean. A
container will issue an `afterBegin()` call on the target bean to notify it that the transaction
associated with the client issuing the call is already in progress. The target bean, as we saw, can make
use of the `SessionContext` to access the transactional information and context. The bean is now in
transactional mode and all transactional methods can be called on it, until one commits.

We need to consider two issues, one where the transaction commits, and one where the transaction
aborts and rolls back. In case the transaction commits the container will issue a
`beforeCompletion()` and an `afterCompletion(true)` (if the commitment was succesful),
mainly to allow two-phase commit protocols to work. If the transaction is rolled back in some
component, the container will issue an `afterCompletion(false)` call to all interested parties.

Passivation and Activation

Finally the only other callback defined by the specification on containers is not one that directly concerns the client users at all, but that needs to be coded for management and optimization of the container. Stateful session beans are more demanding in terms of resources than stateless beans (that do not need to be associated with any particular client more than the time it takes to actually field the request). However, in the case of stateful beans, we can be sure that we have a one-to-one mapping from client to bean instance. The way the specification makes room for some optimization in a standard way is to require the `passivate()` and `activate()` call on all its beans.

Over the course of its lifetime, a bean, while it is associated with a given client, will be asked by the container to prepare itself to be **passivated**. The container notifies the bean and the bean can take necessary actions, such as releasing resources it is using (such as file locks or JDBC connections). This is really a pure callback method, almost a gentleman's agreement between the container and the bean. Even though it is really the container that takes care of the persistence of the bean's state (the bean is not required to save itself), it is notified of the event. The reverse `activate()` call, is really the same notification. These calls, even though secondary in the sense that they are just callbacks and require no real implementation, need to be coded by the bean implementer, since they will be called by the container. However if there are no resources held by the bean, these implementations can be left empty.

Stateless session beans are specific session beans that do not store any client state between invocations. A very simple consequence of this lack of state is that these beans need only concern themselves with the present. They can however participate in an ongoing transaction. For example, they can start local transactions, and, if they fail, can call `setRollBackOnly()` on the global transaction of which they are a part.

However a stateless bean is aware of its immediate environment, that is, the environment variables that define the context of the execution. This is equivalent to saying that the session context information is passed and used by the bean during the execution of a call. However, unlike stateful session beans, which are associated with a unique `EJBObject` and client over the course of their lifetime, stateless sessions are reused across invocations in as many environment contexts as are needed. In the case where the container fully reuses the instances at every call (something EJBoss does) then the container needs to make the new context available only for the duration of the call. What is interesting about these beans is the scalability they offer to the application server. Since the container will deploy a pool of pre-instantiated beans, the server can then dispatch stateless calls to these beans requiring that they come back to the resource pool as soon as the call is fielded. In terms of the number of beans per client, it is not a one-to-one but a one-to-many relationship. In fact, the specification explicitly talks about the pooled state, suggesting that implementation containers should provide for this type of bean.

It's worth noting that the lifecycle interface required of stateful session beans is suitable for the stateless beans as well. In fact, the initialization of a bean state is akin to the ones of stateful sessions in the sense that the container will instantiate beans and pass a generic session context object. It is not absolutely clear at least to this writer why the passing of the `SessionContext` interface is absolutely necessary at this point of the lifecycle of the stateless bean, in the sense that only execution time needs to have this interface active. Of course the specification writers do mention that this is 'just an interface' and that the actual implementation is available during call execution. If a bean gets created and thrown into the pool, it will be picked up during call execution, and before servicing a call, it will be passed a `SessionContext` describing the environment for that single call. It will be stripped of that context before being returned to the pool. This is a pretty standard and straightforward way to implement stateless objects, and is about the only time that the specification delves into the real details of container implementation.

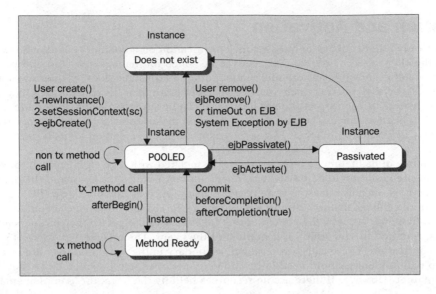

Entity Beans

Entity beans offer little difference in their programming model. Even though there are a few subtleties that one needs to understand about entity beans, from a programming standpoint, their interfaces look deceptively familiar.

By design and philosophy, entity beans are transactional representations of back end data. Put simply, just as session beans represent data from the client and its state on a EJB server, entity beans represent legacy object and data state on this middle tier server. If an object 'lives' in a relational database, it is natural to wrap its behavior in Java methods and have this object now live on the web through its entity bean avatar. Think of entity beans as solid transactional representations of back end data.

Unlike session beans that, by definition, live for one client only, entity beans have a life of their own. Because entity beans are tightly coupled to their back end representation and not one particular user, they can be seen by many users on the web. Entity beans are shared, so subsequent calls on the methods of an entity bean are not necessarily issued by the same client.

Persistence of Entity Beans

Because they hold the state of a back end persistent object (say, the bank account status in our BankTeller application), entity beans are responsible for handling that persistent representation and synchronizing their state with the storage used. In fact, the way the entity bean deals with persistence is the defining characteristic of entity beans. By persistence we mean the mechanism by which the different states, that is, the one in the object and the one in back end storage, are synchronized.

If one takes the point of view of the bean being deployed, one can imagine that ideally a bean could ask the container to save its state on its behalf. Simply put, an object service a container can offer its hosts is persistence, or the capacity to store the state under a unique key on that container for later retrieval (possibly from another virtual machine). We are again touching upon the notion of object services being offered to the web and the persistence is a clear case of a service that non-persistence capable objects will require of their environment. The specification defines how a bean is supposed to ask for that service from the server it is being deployed on. Some beans will require that the container takes care of their back end representation and declare themselves as **container managed persistence** beans (CMP beans) as they register with the server. More autonomous beans that take care of their own persistent representation can declare themselves as **bean managed persistence** beans (BMP beans). We will now see these in some more detail.

To the end user of these beans, or the application assembler, BMP or CMP is absolutely transparent. All the assembler cares about is that the bean he is dealing with is transactional and that the state he accesses in the back end is being manipulated in a controlled environment. In other words, if you are an application assembler, you do not really need to understand how a bean deals with its persistence and you probably do not need to bother reading this section.

Bean Managed Persistence

There are really two cases. The first case is where the developer is extending an existing database and pre-existing data lives independently of the application design under consideration. In that case, the objects that will be born on the web really come from a given data structure and let's say for discussion purposes that it is an RDBMS. The actual object structure and the tables that define it are only known to the developer, in fact he starts from these tables to populate his Java objects. The state of the web object needs, when persistence is needed, to map exactly to these tables.

There is little room to automate a priori this operation. By that, I mean that an object-relational mapping cannot guess what tables and what fields, or even what database is associated with the current live Java object. Since that structural understanding of the bean's state is a direct map to the back end storage, only the developer will be able to say, "This is how I should store myself, let me do it."

Some EJB servers like Persistence PowerTier and IBM Websphere Advanced\Enterprise, offer mapping tools that allow the deployer to tell the container how to look after persistence at deployment time for those shops who already have standard ways they map their objects to databases. So, for bottom-up design of entity beans from existing tables, you have a choice, based on the tools you use, of container or bean management.

I am certain that some of you are saying, "What if we declaratively expose this persistence knowledge to the container," at which point I would encourage you to join EJBoss and help us figure it out, since you obviously like running ahead of the pack. There is work going on in the UML and XML world to do just that.

The point is that you might want to do it differently, in different contexts. Some bean developers want to specify everything, some will want to give the deployer/container the choice.

Let's say, for example, that the account we are talking about exists in a specific database on a specific system as a set of specific tables. You would need to build an entity bean and implement the `ejbLoad()` method that actually reads the fields from the database in an ad-hoc fashion. This is what this bean would look like:

```
public class BankAccount extends javax.ejb.EntityBean {

    private int bankAccountNumber;
    private int balance;

    public void ejbLoad() {
        // Get connection to the database
        // Prepare statement to retrieve the data
        // Assign balance value from the statement
        // Commit transaction
    }

    public void ejbStore() {
        // Get connection to the database
        // Prepare statement with balance information
        // Store data to the database
        // Commit transaction
    }

    ... Other API methods

    ... Business methods

    public string getStatement() {
        return ("The balance for account " + bankAccountNumber + " is " + balance);
    }
}
```

The natural question that arises is why code these methods as `ejbLoad()` and `ejbStore()` at all. After all if the bean is going to take care of its persistence implementation and manage its persistent structure, why code the callback methods under standard calls such as `ejbLoad()` and `ejbStore()`. Well the answer is pretty simple. The container still has the knowledge of *when* these methods should be called on the entity bean. Synchronization of the 'synchronizing' operation still rests with the container. Therefore the container needs standard callbacks on the target beans. One can declaratively request that the state be reloaded after each method invocation and as a result the container would issue an `ejbLoad()` and `ejbStore()` each time. In other words, what the container provides the developer is the lifecycle of these calls, not the call implementations themselves. The developer has the assurance that the synchronization calls for storage will be triggered and issued by the container in a manner that is consistent with the transactions encapsulating these distributed method calls. The main advantage of this is that one relies on the transaction abstraction to manage the demarcation of the persistence calls.

Container Managed Persistence

Let's now look at the second case, container managed persistence. Let's imagine a web object for a second. The web object's state exists in and primarily comes from the web world, as opposed to some table in some RDBMS. The fact that it lives on the web does not preclude the possibility that the object requires a 'place to stay' from the host container. We might require at some point that the object state be saved to persistent storage. Since the object come from the web it isn't necessarily tied to a pre-existing back end representation, nor does it really care about the relative merits of one persistence mechanism or another or one place or the other. All the object really requires is that someone somewhere somehow takes its state and persists it. Oh, and we also want to be able to access that state and re-invoke the object by name, providing a primary key.

What we really want from our environment is a persistence service coupled with a naming service. Ideally we would like to say, "this is my state, I don't really care how you persist it, just persist it." This is where CMP comes in handy - if you have no legacy back end to integrate or if your container is itself aware of the back end structures (which might be the case for some highly specialized datasources) then you can rely on the container to provide persistence services. What the container will do for you in this case is take your object, extract the relevant values (those that are declared `public`) and save those values under a moniker you can later use to retrieve them from whatever storage the container uses. Note that even the retrieval is done through the container - the instance does not have direct access to the back end representation. The actual technology used is transparent to the user (assembler) of the beans and to the bean developer as well. This is where object-relational mapping technology is useful for container implementers.

The way to use this feature is to declare your bean as container-managed. Since we've already seen that the persistence callbacks are issued by the container, which is to say that the specification defines clearly when such commits are supposed to happen, you do not need to worry at all about the actual implementation or even the timing of the persistence calls.

This was a rather long introduction to the following pattern for entity bean developers.

If you need to deal with the object's structure in any persistent representation *and* you want your code to be completely portable between EJB containers, then you need to design your bean as a BMP. This will be the case for people extending preexisting RDBMS structures to the web world, or people that need a tight control on the tables being addressed by the object. The need for absolute portability would apply to third-party component developers. But be aware that this involves more code, making the bean less business logic and more component.

If all you care about is the web world, and the first incarnation of your object will be on the web, that is its state is built for the first time in an EJB server, then you can safely choose the CMP route. Also, if your entity bean is designed for a specific container which supports deployment time specification of the persistent store, then you should use CMP. Such containers will probably let you determine/control/implement things like transaction isolation at deployment or even runtime.

This will save you a lot of headaches since the state will be managed and saved by the container. You may not have access to the underlying representation of the object but then again you probably do not care either. This is the low effort and more usual solution and a very web-oriented one, since you will be making good use of the persistence and naming services in the EJB server.

Identity of Entity Beans

Persistence requirements really determine the type of bean you code. In other words, it is the defining API of the container/component contract. There is another concept central to the entity contract and that is identity. We will see that it is somewhat more complex than the notion of identity of session beans.

Session bean identity is exposed to the outside world through a handle. The identity of a session is an illusion. The handle is just a trick so that clients believe they have a permanent reference to a live object on the server, when in fact it is just a mechanism to invoke a live session. In the case of entity beans the notion of the handle is still present and does map to the illusion of a live bean achieved by the server. However there is a more pervasive definition of identity – using the `PrimaryKeyClass`.

As we saw, entity beans have their representation in back end storage. This representation must be named, through the primary key. The primary key is usually linked to the identity of the object as it exists in the database. It is the way users can find a specific instance of an entity bean in a database or persistent storage. In fact, a primary key is what your bean implementation is supposed to return to the container upon being asked to look for specific instances in persistent storage. The EJB server will then map these primary keys to a set of remote objects that the client can call, just as in the case of session beans. The keys are used internally by the server to identify which entity is being mapped from storage to the web.

The common link in this three-stage export is the identity:

> The first stage is the key as the identity of the entity living in storage, for example the unique key of a table.

> The second layer of identity is when this key is passed by specific bean implementations back to the containers that call them. This signifies a real persistent object whose identity and state they are ready to take on.

> The final stage is the getPrimaryKey() method a user can call on a remote interface. This, in effect, exports this newly assumed middle tier identity, originally the back end identity, to the web user.

Let's look in some more detail at the home for an entity bean. Just like session beans their home is located through JNDI.

```
Context initialContext = ... ;
BankAccountHome bankAccountHome = (BankAccountHome)
                        javax.rmi.PortableRemoteObject.narrow(
                            initialContext.lookup(bankOfEJB/bankAccountBean),
                            BankAccountHome.class);
```

From this home the user of an entity bean is capable of calling:

```
BankAccount bankAccount = bankAccountHome.create(accountNumberId);
```

It's likely that this operation would not be permitted for end-users. But let's imagine that this method comes with an ACL in the deployment descriptor that says that the create() *method is only accessible to the manager of a retail bank branch. In this, we can see the advantage of having the home interface and the policy that defines access to it written at separate times. A bean producer can write the* AccountBean *and the* create() *method that comes with it without worrying about the security policy that will be defined by the end user in actual deployment.*

The container will actually intercept and implement the create() call. On the target bean, the container will issue a ejbCreate(accountNumberId) that matches the signature of the public method. What is interesting about the signature of the bean that takes the final call is that it returns the primary key. On the remote interface, we call,

```
public EJBObject create(accountNumberId);
```

whereas on the home interface:

```
public PrimaryKeyClass ejbCreate(accountNumberId);
```

Here we can begin to understand how containers manufacture identity and remote objects in the case of entity beans. To the final user or assembler, the contract is exactly the same as for session beans in the sense that the `create()` method returns an `EJBObject`. The contract to look at is the container/component contract, which specifies that the return of the `ejbCreate()` method is a `PrimaryKeyClass` object. As will become clear, the container deals differently with BMP and CMP.

Implementing a Primary Key

In the case of BMP, the bean manages the database access needed to store itself. It is only natural that the knowledge of what the primary key is, and its actual value, come from the bean. In other words it is up to the bean developer to provide the primary key that will identify the persisted entity as well as code the valid key creation in the `ejbCreate()` method they provide for the bean. With this primary key, the target bean signifies that an `ejbLoad()` issued on it will populate the bean with the right values from the back end. By returning a primary key, the entity bean contractually says that the identity of this entity is assumed. The container then maps the key and the identity it represents to the remote interface, which provides access to the public methods of this underlying object. The mix-and-match of generated classes in the container here is very similar to that of the session beans but the primary identity assumed by the bean is not the handle anymore, even though it still exists in this case, but the primary key. The primary key is the link between the back end, the bean implementation, the container wrappers, and the scope of the remote interface (that is, the interface only accesses this bean).

Finally a container will issue `ejbPostCreate()` on the bean. This is a callback to notify to the bean implementation that the identity of the entity bean is now assumed by all parties and it also gives the bean implementation a chance to use its newly minted web identity. Among other things, the bean implementation has access to the `EJBObject` through the `EntityContext` interface and can pass this reference to other enterprise beans. The whole stack of code, including the implementation, can now present a remote face to the outside world through the remote `EJBObject` and the methods it offers. The `ejbPostCreate()` method call issued by the container on the implementation is just a notification that bean creation is now complete, all parties share one key and that the shiny new remote object with the correct identity is now available to anyone that wishes to access it. The remote interface is now available in a solid transactional manner - more on this later.

In the case of CMP the whole scenario is played a bit differently due to the primary key creation. In case of CMP, it is obvious that the bean implementation has little say in what (as in what class) or who (as in what instance) represent its state in back end storage. Since the back end is fully managed by the container, it is only natural that the container should generate the value of the key. The EJB 1.1 specification requires that the return value of the `ejbCreate()` method be `null`. In other words, it requires that the implementer specifies:

```
public PrimaryKeyClass ejbCreate(...) {
    // set the values up from the parameters;
    ...
    // but do nothing about it
    return null;
}

// The EJB 1.0 specification had a slightly different requirement
public void ejbCreate(...) {
    // set the values up from the parameters;
    return;
}
```

After issuing the `ejbCreate()` call on the target CMP bean, the container knows that the target bean is ripe for harvesting. This is not just a figure of speech; after the `ejbCreate()` call your bean is supposedly populated with the right values given the input to the `ejbCreate()` method and ready to be persisted for the first time in the database by the container. This is a specification requirement. The container will then create its identity through the primary key. The primary key of course comes from the container that alone can really manage the persistent representation. This is the only real distinction from the BMP case.

The primary key and the remote interface to the newly created entity bean are again made available to the bean implementation through the `EntityContext` interface. An `ejbPostCreate()` call notifies the bean implementation that all the values are now available to the bean implementation through that interface. In other words, if you are a bean implementer using CMP, be aware that, in the `ejbPostCreate()` call you need to implement, you can use this context call mechanism to access all the EJB layers created for your implementation and its clients. In the case of BMP you have access to this information first hand, since you provide it.

We can sum up what we just discussed in the following lines:

> For BMP beans, the `ejbCreate()` creates the bean state and the representation in the database. It returns the primary key to the container. The container will create a remote `EJBObject` and assign it the key. The container will make this remote reference available to the implementation through the `EntityContext` interface (as well as the key, but the bean already has that since it created it) and notify the bean that the creation lifecycle is complete to give the bean a chance to own the flow of execution in a `ejbPostCreate()` call.

> For CMP, the `ejbCreate()` creates the bean state but not the representation in the database. It returns `null` to the container. The container knows to extract the newly created fields from the instance and insert them in the database as well as create a key for it. It will make the key and remote implementation available to the instance through the `EntityContext` interface and issue a call to `ejbPostCreate()` to notify the instance that it has finished the creation cycle.

Finders

The final contract that differs from the session contract is the finders on the home interface. An entity bean home must at least define the public `EJBObject findByPrimaryKey(Object primaryKey)` method by default. This enables clients to locate entities ab-initio (or invoke entities from thin air as an EJBoss participant put it). As the name indicates it locates entity beans by their primary key.

Unlike session beans, entity beans exist beyond the scope of the client interaction. For session beans, the concept of a live bean was embodied in the handle abstraction. A handle lives as long as the session lives; it identifies the session. A live entity bean, as we saw, is also expressed by a handle, signifying a particular session or interaction with the entity bean, but really it is the primary key that represents an entity to the container. Whereas a session still holds a reference to a live object for an entity (as with session beans, you can just say `getHandle()` and `handle.getEJBObject()`) it presupposes that you created the object and that you already have a session with a working entity bean. In other words there is no way to bootstrap an `EJBObject` through the handle, since the handle requires a previous session and you need to establish a first session.

The way to establish a session in the case of session beans is rather limited. It involves the `create()` call on the home interface. And the `handle.getEJBObject()` does not count since we are looking for a way to establish that first session. There are two ways to bootstrap an entity bean. You have your usual `create()` method, which we have detailed to some extent, but there is also a mechanism that goes through the key of an existing entity. An implementation, or the user of a server, can ask to look for a given, pre-existing instance of an entity bean and establish a first session (that is, obtain a remote interface to it). This is different from the lookup mechanism of JNDI, which enables you to look a class by the name of the class. At least for EJBs (other JNDI implementations may enable you to look up an instance by name) the only thing you get back is the home interface to the bean. JNDI looks up the class, the bean home class to be more precise, the finder calls on the home interface of entity beans look up the instances.

So how does this fit with BMP and CMP? Well in case of CMP it is pretty simple. The finder must be provided on the container/user contract, but cannot be on the container/component contract. The finders on the user contract do not result in a call being issued to the implementation. Nothing to do for you the coder. Pretty simple huh?

In case of BMP, things get a little bit more hairy. Of course the container still does not have any knowledge of your particular database server and much less about your primary key mappings. In short, the container must rely on your implementation to find a particular instance in your database since your bean implementation, and only your bean implementation, is aware of the underlying mapping scheme. For the container to delegate, you must provide a corresponding `ejbFindByPrimaryKey()` in your bean for the container to call following a `findByPrimaryKey()` call on its public interfaces. The container handling a BMP bean will pass the `primaryKey` parameter from the first call to the second. In `ejbFindByPrimaryKey()` you must be able to validate that the bean does indeed exist in the database and return the key or throw the appropriate exception accordingly.

Of more interest in the case of BMP are the criteria-based finders. The specification allows for more complex finders. These advanced beasts basically specify a method to find the corresponding instance matching certain criteria. These are exposed through `find<METHOD>()` calls on the home interface, and are mapped to `ejbFind<METHOD>()` calls on the target instance. For example, the same interface that defined the calls for the creation of new accounts by a bank manager can define an `ejbFindClosedAccounts()` method to expose the primary key of those accounts that were closed recently, audit the reasons for closure and double check that the balance is indeed zero.

In the case of CMP, the container knows about fields of the bean it persists, and should be in a position to retrieve instances or collections of instances based on a query. Some containers provide tools to enable the interactive building of such finder queries in the container. Both of which reduce the work for you as a bean developer.

Activation and Passivation

We have looked at persistence, we have looked at identity and we have looked at creation and finders for entity beans. There is one more API that we need to look at in order to round out our presentation of the component/container contract, and that is `ejbActivate()` and `ejbPassivate()`.

Remember that for session beans, these are pure administrative calls to squeeze some performance. Because entity beans have their state in a back end representation, and, unlike session beans, they are not associated with one particular instance or one particular client, entity beans have the luxury of acting out multiple personalities on behalf of clients and back end entities. Remember that the session hardwires the connection between the client, the container and the target bean implementation because the latter holds state on behalf of everyone else. Since entities store their state, the entity bean can divorce itself from its state, a trick sessions can't perform. The container and the bean instance can now load and store the values of several entities to service multiple requests.

Reusing the various parts of the server (the container classes, as well as the target instance) now becomes feasible. The EJB specification discusses a pooled state for entity target beans. This is very close to the stateless model where target beans can field any request due to their inherent lack of state. In our case, the entity can behave in pretty much the same way since it can load its state in an ad-hoc fashion from the back end. Even though they are radically more complex, entity beans behave just like stateless beans with respect to keeping their state in between invocations (sessions don't care, entities are flexible). Naturally the primary key is what enables a bean to identify the back end representation it is supposed to assume, and in the case of BMP this information is available, and must be used, through the `SessionContext`.

Let's focus some more on the pooling entity beans. Just like the stateless session beans, entity beans in the pooled state do not hold the state of any particular back end representation. The way to activate an entity bean is through the `ejbActivate()` call that has the effect of telling the instance that it is being associated with a back end representation and that subsequent business method calls are on their way. In theory entity beans are not supposed to load their state during this call, since only the `ejbLoad()` call issued by the container should initiate these operations. In other words, bean code *never* explicitly calls the `ejbLoad()` and `ejbStore()` methods. This is all done by the container in between calls, according to the transaction model. However the identity of the back end object this bean implementation will assume is available from the primary key in the entity context.

The `activate()` and `passivate()` methods are utility calls that enable the creation of scalable server by standardizing the hooks necessary for bean life cycle manipulation as a server moves a specific bean from memory to the pool, but in the case of entities it is a rather clever standard optimization. Goes to prove 'standard optimization' is not an oxymoron.

Finally, it should be now clear that the result of the `passivate()` call on a session and an entity bean are somewhat different. In case of a session bean, the server will move the instance, as in the actual physical object, to secondary storage, and the identity of the session remains completely imprinted in the state of the session. Furthermore, the live object in memory will be garbage-collected. In the case of an entity bean, that identity means little to the instance since `ejbStore()` and `ejbLoad()` in effect flush and set state values on demand. These instances are not moved to secondary storage, merely their values (maybe in relational tables). The physical object can be reused, as opposed to being only good for GC, and is put back in the pool.

Now we can look at the life cycle of the enterprise bean. Just as for session beans, the lifecycle is only important for the bean developer. For bean users, the model is almost identical to the session model, excepting the finder methods.

The Lifecycle of Entity Beans

After instantiation, the EJB instance can go to the pooled state. Basically this amounts to:

> ➤ Creating that object with the `new()` call (`newInstance()` on the class in the specification)
>
> ➤ Setting an empty entity context is also done at this stage

Note that in the pooled stage the information on the entity context is useless, as there is no key or remote object associated with it. However, during a finder call that leaves the entity in the known pooled state, the identity of the caller is available to the instance. The instance might choose to make use of that identity even in the pooled state.

In case a client calls a `find<METHOD>()` on the home interface of this entity bean, a container can use any instance in the pool to do the finding work for it. Again this delegation only makes real sense in the case of BMP, since CMP cannot rely on the implementation to do anything. Once an instance has done its finding it still needs to be associated with an identity, for the simple reason that an `ejbFindMethod()` can return many entity primary keys to the container. A container will use the `ejbActivate()` method to notify to a bean instance that it will be moved to the ready state and that business methods will be issued on it. At that stage, going from the pooled state to ready, the identity is available to the bean through the `EntityContext` set earlier.

In the ready state, the container can tell the instance that the state is being loaded and stored with `ejbLoad()` and `ejbStore()` calls. The ready state is the state where business methods can be issued on the target implementation. `ejbCreate()` is another way to reach the ready state. The big difference is of course that `ejbActivate()` works with a pre-existing back end representation whereas `ejbCreate()` also creates the aforementioned back end representation. In effect what the specification says is that the instance that fields the `create()` method, unlike the one that fields the find methods, ends up with the identity of the back end object it just helped create. This is not absolutely necessary (one could require that the state be associated with the classic `ejbActivate()` or `ejbLoad()` calls and by that mechanism only) but letting `ejbCreate()` move instances makes sense, given that the state for the bean is by definition valid at the end of the create call, and that saves a few steps for the container.

Deactivating an instance means removing the particular association between the target instance and an entity in the back end representation. What that achieves of course is moving the instance back to the pooled state. An `ejbRemove()` call will move a particular instance to the pooled state. Note that this is specific to the entities, as a session would discard the instance because there is no standard way to cleanse and reuse one (in a session bean equivalent to `ejbLoad()`). Also the whole concept does not mean anything to stateless sessions (the `remove()` merely removing an identity association) since stateless sessions do not have identity. The `ejbPassivate()` achieves the same result, namely an instance in the pooled state, but just as `activate()` does not create records in the DB whereas `create()` does, so `passivate()` does not touch the back end representation. `ejbRemove()` will also permanently remove the back end representation whereas `passivate()` will just suspend the association between the instance and the back end.

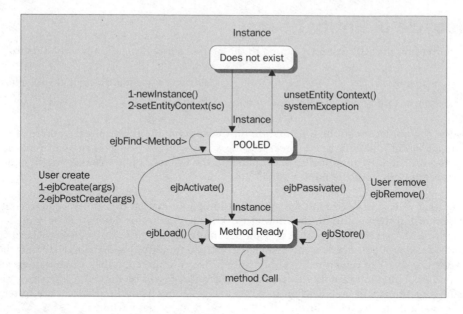

Transaction Management

We have just seen that entities extend pre-existing back end data to the web. However we have not addressed an important feature, namely that the EJB platform offers transactional services to these extensions. As we are moving to the object web we are really laying the foundation for distributed application to cooperate through transactions.

A distributed application needs to synchronize the different parties involved in the processing taking place. More precisely, either the flow of calls on the web covers all the parties involved or there is a third party tool that notifies everyone of the boundaries of cooperation (when it starts and when it is supposed to end). Transactions are the programmatic abstraction used to delimit space/time cooperation for software components. A bean participating in a more global computing engine can register itself with a central party in order to create an **association** with other beans. That association is pure software and it says, "These other beans and I are all participating in the same computation, so we all need to know what happens to each other." This central point can then notify all the involved components when the cooperation is supposed to end.

There are several computing paradigms that can benefit from this centralized management of messaging. The first one that comes to mind is the database transaction. A transaction on the web is somewhat more complex than a database transaction, but still has a lot in common - namely the capacity to commit or roll back several participating components.

Transactions should be ACID (atomic, consistent, isolated, durable). This means that they should appear to happen in one call, that they should leave the system in a consistent state, that each transaction should be isolated from others, and that the changes made by the transactions should be irrevocable once the transaction has been committed.

A simple way to achieve this commitment is to require participating beans to implement the **two-phase commit protocol**. A transaction monitor notifies all the participating components of the lifecycle of the transaction, namely that the transaction is about to begin or about to end. When it ends, the first phase of the two-phase commit will check that all the components are happy. This may involve polling datasources to check that they can commit to any changes they've made. If the response is OK from all components, the transaction moves to the second phase and commits all parts. If one part says that its work failed, the transaction asks all the components to roll their state back to what they had before the transaction began. The calls specified by the container on the session bean with bean managed transaction are `beforeCompletion()` and `afterCompletion(boolean)` where the Boolean indicates the success or failure of the first pass. This is not a radical departure from the traditional database transaction, it's just applied in a more generic fashion.

The specification defines two types of transactions, **local** and **global**. The local transactions are the ones associated with the local **resource managers**. This can be a JDBC driver and the underlying database it supports. One must keep in mind that the EJB specification is written for the web. The word local makes sense when one has the web but it is of course an empty word to the driver implementer who is supposed to take care of any distributed tables involved in the process. The global transaction is the real web transaction. It is a distributed transaction that can span several EJB servers and therefore several VMs. The distinction between the local and global is somewhat superfluous. At a certain level, a transaction is a transaction is a transaction and there are just so many ways to provide ACID properties to a piece of distributed code.

That said, this distinction comes in handy when talking about some EJB-specific rules such as what happens when local resources are used by an EJB enlisted in a global transaction. It is also pretty obvious, given the changes in transaction between 1.0 and 1.1 (where the global versus local distinction was introduced) that the concept of a web transaction is still a moving target. Everyone is trying to come up with the right infrastructure for when mainstream computing discovers OC3 lines and fast connections when the transactional web will be ubiquitous. EJB is one attempt, a courageous one, but the specification is still a work in progress and feels very much like one.

Global Transactions

The specification defines two possible behaviors for the beans themselves. Just like persistence, transaction management is a service performed by the container for the bean. And as with persistence, a bean can choose to use this service or not. Again, as with the persistence, it is up to the bean developer to make this choice. A bean developer can decide to access the global transactions himself or to let the container do it for him. Letting the container manage the transaction means that local resources accessed through the EJB server will be enlisted in the global transaction by the container and that the container will issue the right synchronization calls to target resources at transaction demarcation time.

The specification states that only session beans are allowed to declare that they manage their own transaction demarcation on global transactions. In other words, entity beans are not allowed to access the `javax.jts.UserTransaction` interface. It is part of the programming model that entity beans must let the container manage the transaction demarcation. Of course, you can start transactions locally on, for example, a JDBC connection that implements the persistence of a bean, but the actual commit should only be performed by the container. For the container to be able to perform this commit with the transaction resources means that they need to be registered with it. The simplest way to do this is to require that containers offer the lookup mechanism for the connections to resources. If a container offers such services then it can keep track of component association within one given global transaction, including resource managers.

To summarize, entity beans can only be container managed when it comes to transaction demarcation, whereas session beans can manage their own transaction demarcation. Telling the container what type of transaction management your bean requires is naturally done with the deployment descriptor.

We will now investigate some of the transaction attributes defined for container-managed transactions. These define how the container must behave with respect to the implementation being deployed. The deployment descriptor can specify six different types of transaction handling by the container prior to the handling of the transaction by the bean.

Attribute	Description
SUPPORTS	This declares to the container that the implementation can deal with calls that are associated with transactional context as well as those that are not. If a call to the container has a previous transactional context, it will be propagated. Where there is no context associated with the call, none will be created and the implementation call will be executed without any context.
REQUIRED	This declares to the container that the implementation always needs transaction context to execute. If the bean passes a transaction context with its call, the container will propagate this transaction to the implementation. If the call is made without any context, the container will create a new one and begin() it as well as commit it upon return.
REQUIRES NEW	This attributes sets the container so that no matter what calls comes in, it will create a new transaction, pass it to the bean implementation and commit the transaction upon return
MANDATORY	This is the REQUIRED case with teeth. In a MANDATORY-declared transaction, a container will throw a javax.ejb.TransactionRequiredException if a call arrives without a context.
NOT SUPPORTED	Declares to the container that the bean being deployed does not support transactional features. This can be a bean-managed transaction. In the case that the incoming call is associated with a transaction from the invoker, the container will not propagate this context to the implementation. The transactional context will not be available through the EntityContext.
NEVER	NOT SUPPORTED with bite, this will cause the container to throw an exception (java.rmi.RemoteException, the lack of symmetry with MANDATORY is annoying) to the client if a call comes with a context.

Entities must declare their transaction management as belonging to the container. Even in the case of bean-managed persistence, it rests upon the container to issue the right synchronization calls. Entity beans use container-supplied transaction demarcation and the ensuing `ejbLoad()` and `ejbStore()` calls to synchronize their state. In effect, the entity beans are never notified when their transaction demarcation happens. Since ensuring the ACID properties in the case of entities can be achieved through a combination of load and store procedures and since these are initiated by the container there is little the bean needs to know about its transaction demarcation. Given that an entity bean cannot call upon the methods of the `javax.jts.UserTransaction` interface, what happens if a bean decides that a transaction must be rolled back because it is in an invalid state? The entity can access the global transaction and mark it with `setRollBackOnly()`. Giving the bean the possibility to `setRollBackOnly()` means that all the participating beans can veto the transaction. An entity bean does not directly rollback a transaction but can mark it so that when the time comes to actually commit the transaction the transaction manager and the container rollback all participating beans (that is, they do not issue `ejbStore()` calls on entities and instead return them all to the pool).

Sessions beans are somewhat more interesting. The state in the bean needs to be managed somehow. In the case of entity beans this is easy since the `ejbLoad()` in fact refreshes the state of the bean. However in case of stateful beans, one must rely on the bean to manage its own state. In other words, the bean must be notified that something went wrong or that the transaction commited. For comparison, entities are not even notified when a transaction commits, since load and store do all the work. The session bean must therefore implement the `javax.ejb.SessionSynchronization` interface to explicitly perform the two-phase commit through the `beforeCompletion()` and `afterCompletion(boolean)` methods. This provides the bean with an opportunity to cast its vote on the transaction commit and the chance to roll back if a bean vetoed the transaction. A session bean that implements the `SessionSynchronization` interface is relying on third parties to commit the transaction and explicitly ask for notification from the container. These beans therefore fall in the container-managed category since they rely on the container to hook them up and notify them.

The transaction attributes for session beans must be of type MANDATORY, REQUIRES NEW, or REQUIRED. The explanation given by the specification is somewhat obscure, although strictly speaking it is logically correct (check for yourselves after this explanation). Here is how we understand it. If a session bean coder decided to implement the `SessionSynchronization` interface, chances are they coded their beans to rely on the notification of the wrapping up of the global transaction to do some other things (say, commit or roll back local database transactions not enlisted with the container). In this case, if the call was issued without a transaction context, no such wrap-up would happen on the target bean thereby potentially leaving the session bean in an undecided state. Since the transaction attribute is set later than coding time, the bean deployer can forget that this bean implements `SessionSynchronization` and in fact relies on the notification to move between valid states.

This is probably not an uncommon scenario since neither the deployer nor the assembler are supposed to know about the implementation of the bean. It would be a understandable mistake for an assembler to say for example that the bean SUPPORTS transactions thereby potentially breaking the state of the bean or omitting important local commits. Saying MANDATORY, REQUIRES NEW, or REQUIRED ensures that a global transaction is always associated with the implementation and that it always behaves as the original implementer intended. Of course, the load falls on the container implementer to not allow other declarative tags in case it detects that the implementation of the bean declares `implements SessionSynchronization`. Also, do not declare this interface lightly, just for the sake of being notified, since you restrict valid transactional choices and should only do so if you have a functional requirement or a justification for doing so.

As an aside here's the original sentence from the specification:

> *"The above restriction is necessary to ensure that the enterprise bean is invoked only in a global transaction. If the bean were invoked without a global transaction, the container would not be able to send the transaction synchronization calls because the container does not have control of the local transactions."*

Deployment Descriptors

As we have seen, the deployment descriptor offers a text-based way of declaring things to the container as well as other interested parties. Some information needs to flow between the bean developer, the bean assembler and the person responsible for deployment. The deployment descriptor offers a standard way of passing this information. There are two new things in the EJB 1.1 deployment descriptor.

First of all, it was realized that a Java-based deployment descriptor was not enough to enforce portability among vendors. All the EJB suppliers (including EJBoss) took it upon themselves to extend the `javax.ejb.deployment.DeploymentDescriptor` to add in proprietary information and serialized the beast as is. The end result was that another EJB vendor could not read the deployment descriptor thereby breaking the promise of portability before we even got started. The serialized deployment descriptor contains two types of information (as does any serialized class) - the values (fields) of the deployment descriptor and the class description for the extended `DeploymentDescriptor` class.

It was therefore agreed that the new serialized form of the `DeploymentDescriptor` would use XML and that the actual class definition would be defined in the DTD to enforce some coherence among the different deployment descriptor. In other words, the XML file is the serialization of the values and the DTD for the class description is defined by Sun. Then any XML parser can reconstruct the deployment descriptor from its serialized (maybe stored as a file) form. The main advantage of this is that the information contained in these files is not lost when the version of the class changes. In fact the information in the XML file is pretty much self-sufficient. Where previously the right class for the right serialized deployment descriptor was necessary we can now send a standalone XML file and assume that the server will parse our XML file correctly.

The second thing the EJB 1.1 specification acknowledges is the different roles involved in producing the document. As we saw earlier, the information contained in the deployment descriptor really comes from all the parties involved in the process of making the distributed application a reality.

Though most EJB servers will provide tools to read and manipulate the XML, we will walk through the deployment descriptor example given in the specification to show what information the descriptor can contain.

Consider the following declaration of a session bean:

```
<!DOCTYPE ejb-jar
  PUBLIC  -//Sun Microsystems Inc.//DTD Enterprise JavaBeans 1.1//EN >
<ejb-jar>
   <description>
   This ejb-jar file contains assembled enterprise beans that are part of employee
   self-service application.
   </description>
```

The `description` tag is a tag that enables the different parties to communicate verbally. A developer can put descriptions of the bean for an assembler to read and understand.

```
<enterprise-beans>
    <session>
        <description>
        The EmployeeService session bean implements a session between an employee
        and the employee self-service application.
        </description>
        <ejb-name>EmployeeService</ejb-name>
```

The first thing about an enterprise bean is the name under which it will be known, in our case `EmployeeService`. Note that this is a logical name given by the developer of the bean, it is not the JNDI name that will be used at run-time.

```
<home>com.wombat.empl.EmployeeServiceHome</home>
<remote>com.wombat.empl.EmployeeService</remote>
<ejb-class>com.wombat.empl.EmployeeServiceBean</ejb-class>
```

These declarations tell the container the actual classes to be used. The first two tags declare the home and the remote interface by giving a fully qualified package name. Remember that there is no declaration in the implementation class that these particular interfaces are being implemented. The `ejb-class` tag effectively declares the implementation class.

One thing the container can guess from the `ejb-class` tag is the type of bean being used (whether it is session or entity). However, it cannot guess the exact type within a given category. For example, one needs to specify if a session bean is stateful or stateless:

```
<session-type>Stateful</session-type>
```

Also, the transaction management the bean requires must be declared at this point. In our example the session bean declares that it manages its own transactions:

```
<transaction-type>Bean</transaction-type>
```

The deployment descriptor can also set up the environment for a bean in a specific environment. The XML lists the various entries, their type and the actual value:

```
<env-entry>
    <env-entry-name>envvar1</env-entry-name>
    <env-entry-type>String</env-entry-type>
    <env-entry-value>String</env-entry-value>
</env-entry>
```

If a bean accesses other beans, you need to say so. Since the JNDI name of a bean is a run-time notion, you need to reference the other beans. The `ejb-ref-name` name is the bean name used in your code, with other tags holding its expected type, fully qualified home and remote interfaces and an optional `ejb-link` names the referenced EJB. Typically this forms part of the application and is within the same JAR file.

```
                <ejb-ref>
                    <ejb-ref-name>ejb/EmplRecords</ejb-ref-name>
                    <ejb-ref-type>Entity</ejb-ref-type>
                    <home>com.wombat.empl.EmployeeRecordHome</home>
                    <remote>com.wombat.empl.EmployeeRecord</remote>
                    <ejb-link>EmployeeRecord</ejb-link>
                </ejb-ref>
        </session>
```

Next we see the declaration of an entity bean. The class declaration is of course the same:

```
        <entity>
            <description>
            The Payroll entity bean encapsulates access to the payroll system.The
            deployer will use container-managed persistence to integrate the entity
            bean with the back-end system managing payroll information.
            </description>
            <ejb-name>AaardvarkPayroll</ejb-name>
            <home>com.aardvark.payroll.PayrollHome</home>
            <remote>com.aardvark.payroll.Payroll</remote>
            <ejb-class>com.aardvark.payroll.PayrollBean</ejb-class>
```

Just as session beans declare their type, so entity beans must declare their persistence type (whether they're bean or container managed):

```
            <persistence-type>Container</persistence-type>

            <cmp-field>
                <field-name>employeeID</field-name>
            </cmp-field>
```

A bean deployer can define security roles associated with bean methods. The `role-link` tag will be linked to the actual definitions of security roles defined in the assembly descriptor:

```
            <security-role-ref>
                <role-name>payroll-org</role-name>
                <role-link>payroll-department</role-link>
            </security-role-ref>
        </entity>
    </enterprise-beans>
```

Next we look at the **assembly descriptor**. These take declarative input from the application assembler.

Of primary concern is the security mapping. This is supposed to happen and be defined at deployment time since this is when the knowledge of the internal security policies is available. The assembly descriptor will define many security roles. The security roles first define the name of the role as defined previously. These only include the description and the name at first.

```
    <assembly-descriptor>
        <security-role>
            <description>
            This role includes the employees of the enterprise who are allowed to
            access the employee self-service application. This role is allowed only
```

```
          to access his/her own information.
        </description>
        <role-name>employee</role-name>
    </security-role>
    <security-role>
        <description>
        This role includes the employees of the human resources department. The
        role is allowed to view and update all employee records.
        </description>
        <role-name>hr-department</role-name>
    </security-role>
    ...
```

The assembly descriptor then goes on to grant access to specific methods in the bean. You can define default method access and override this default as needed. First we will see that we can declare that the `employee role-name` has access to all the methods in the `EmployeeService` bean:

```
<method-permission>
    <role-name>employee</role-name>
    <method>
        <ejb-name>EmployeeService</ejb-name>
        <method-name>*</method-name>
    </method>
</method-permission>
```

Next we say that the `employee` role can use the `findByPrimaryKey()` method on the bean as well as `getDetail()` and `updateDetail()` on their record.

```
<method-permission>
    <role-name>employee</role-name>
    <method>
        <ejb-name>EmployeeRecord</ejb-name>
        <method-name>findByPrimaryKey</method-name>
    </method>
    <method>
        <ejb-name>EmployeeRecord</ejb-name>
        <method-name>getDetail</method-name>
    </method>
    <method>
        <ejb-name>EmployeeRecord</ejb-name>
        <method-name>updateDetail</method-name>
    </method>
</method-permission>
```

Now we will look at how an XML file defines the transaction management that a container is supposed to adopt for a container-managed declared method. The following snippet of XML basically says that all the methods in the `EmployeeRecord` are to be accessed in a transaction context by declaring that all the methods use the `REQUIRED` transactional attribute.

Remember that the `Required` tag means that if the method is accessed by a client already associated with a transaction then the method on the bean will be called with this transaction context. If, on the other hand, the method is accessed without a transaction context, the container will start a new transaction and associate with the calling flow so that the method on the bean executes within this new transaction.

```
        <container-transaction>
            <method>
                <ejb-name>EmployeeRecord</ejb-name>
                <method-name>*</method-name>
            </method>
            <trans-attribute>Required</trans-attribute>
        </container-transaction>

    </assembly-descriptor>
</ejb-jar>
```

Summary

In this chapter, we have looked in some detail at how the EJB programming model defines the user interaction with beans hosted in an EJB container and server. Because EJB is a standard, rather than just an implementation, we are seeing massive adoption by multiple vendors. At the forefront of the adoption are existing transaction monitor and database vendors.

Specifically, we have discussed:

> Roles in the EJB specification - bean developer, bean assembler, system administrator and container writer

> Indirection - how the EJB container acts as a go-between for clients and beans

> Contracts for clients, containers and components

> Session beans which represent web sessions, and can be stateful or stateless

> Entity beans which represent back end data

> Container- and bean-managed persistence of entity beans

> The lifecycle of beans - creating, finding, reusing and saving beans

> Transaction management by beans and containers

> The deployment descriptor and its constituent parts

We have also seen how EJBs and the Java platform constitute a first crude incarnation of what a WebOS will look like. Just like the PC architecture and the Windows platform consolidated a fragmented PC world back in the 80s, the EJB specification has the potential to consolidate server-side APIs for application development and deployment. The result in the PC world is well known - there was a violent period of competition among the PC vendors and that drove prices down significantly, leading to an explosion in personal computing. At the same time, the advantage of one unifying platform was obvious to application developers who were quick to standardize on the Windows platform.

Java and the WebOS now strive at creating a similar layer of abstraction in between the physical layer of application deployment and runtime and the world of application APIs. It is easy to proclaim that Java on the server is already a well-established field but it remains to be seen if the greater picture, the WebOS, will indeed crystallize around the framework offered by servlets, JSP and the EJB specification and the implementations available on the market.

Indexing and Searching

A system for cataloguing and indexing data has three main constituents – a method of collecting information about the data, a database for storing the information and a method of selectively accessing data using the information. There has been phenomenal growth in recent years in the use of hyperlinked documents for information storage with the development of the World Wide Web and Intranets. The lingua franca of these electronic libraries is the Hypertext Markup Language HTML, using the hypertext protocol HTTP. The main tool to have emerged for getting at the information in this environment is the *search engine*.

Contrary to popular belief, when one queries most Web search engines the search engine goes nowhere near the list of sites it returns. The query is simply passed over to a pre-compiled database and this database supplies the site information. The manner in which the database is compiled divides search engines into two categories: catalogue-based and spider-based. Catalogue-based search engines, such as Yahoo, rely on manual submission of links to pages (complete with descriptions) for the index. Spider-based systems on the other hand need minimal human intervention, usually just the submission of one of the URLs (Universal Resource Locator) in the site to be indexed. Hyperlinks on the page of the submitted URL point the engine to other pages in the site and further hyperlinks. Indexing information and descriptions of pages are picked up automatically from the HTML tags and text of the page.

In practice the complicated part of creating a Web based cataloguing and indexing system is getting the information into the database. Once the information has been stored, it is relatively straightforward to search and manipulate using standard database techniques. With servlets and browsers available, the user interface design is also straightforward.

To demonstrate the operation of such a system, there now follows the complete code for a search engine. The prerequisites for this are a Java compiler and virtual machine, access to a SQL conformant database with a JDBC driver and access to a Web server capable of running servlets. Naturally, access is also needed to the server containing the documents to be indexed. In a Windows environment this can be achieved on a standalone machine running MS Access and Personal Web Server with the JDK and JSDK. For live use of the search engine a more likely set up would include a Linux machine running the Apache Web Server, Jserv and PostgreSQL.

The Spider

To keep things simple, the area to crawl is determined from the address of the start page. Any page that is in the same directory as, or subdirectory of, the one in the URL will be scanned. Status messages are periodically passed to the console screen (System.out) giving the current page, the number of pages crawled and the size of the Queue. The basic functional blocks of the Spider are shown in the figure below.

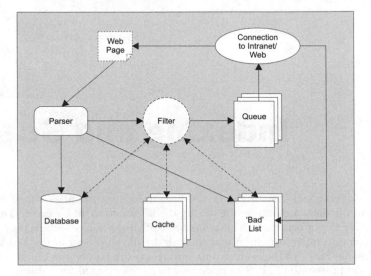

The operation is described here. The system is initialized and a starting URL is put in the Queue. The spider is then set crawling. A connection is made with the top URL in the Queue, and the corresponding page is read into the system. If there is a problem getting the page (e.g. it might not exist), the URL is put on the 'Bad' List. The page obtained is then passed to a Parser, which dissects and analyses the HTML on the page. The URL is added to the Database, together with significant parts of the page. Any hyperlinks found on the page are filtered and resolved to absolute URLs. These are then checked against the Cache to make sure they haven't already been filed. If the URLs are valid they are then put in the Queue, and the cycle restarted. Periodically the URLs of the most frequently encountered pages are copied from the database into the Cache.

The code of the Spider compiles into two packages: **spider** which holds the classes largely concerned with processing and **data** which holds the classes dealing with the information obtained. The code compiles to the following individual classes:

- ➢ spider.Index – the main servlet and user interface
- ➢ spider.Spider – acts as central control and accesses Web pages
- ➢ spider.Hparser – extracts indexing information from Web pages

- ➢ data.Dbaccess – opens and closes the JDBC connection
- ➢ data.Dbspider – handles the database operations
- ➢ data.Cache – holds the most popular links
- ➢ data.Queue – holds the queue of links to be visited

Information Gathering

To keep things simple, the program only handles standard HTML files. No provision is made for accessing extensions of this such as Javascript, which may contain links. The information the Spider gathers can be best shown in relation to an HTML page. Suppose we have the page `http://myserver/test.htm` as shown below.

```
<HTML>
<HEAD>
<META NAME="Description" CONTENT="A Test Page">
<META NAME="Keywords" CONTENT="testing, testing, one, two, three">
<TITLE>A Sample Page</TITLE>
</HEAD>
<BODY>
This is the text of the page.
<A HREF= "http://myserver/java/tutorial/index.htm>Java Tutorial</A>
</BODY>
</HTML>
```

The first thing of interest is the URL of the page, `http://myserver/test.htm`, which will be unique and is stored in our database as the primary index. Next come the `<META>` tags, which are not visible in browsers and primarily serve to give information to search engines. Many different `<META>` tags may be encountered, but two of the most common are the only ones stored in our database – 'Description' and 'Keywords'. The 'Keywords' tag acts as a kind of "File Under..." heading for search engines, and the 'Description' should be a summary of the contents of the page. The content of the `<TITLE>` tags is normally shown on the title bar of browsers. This, together with the 'Description' data, can form a natural language report of the contents of the page. In the real world, page authors often leave out the `<META>` tags and so it is left to the search engine to derive its own keywords and description. Thus the program described here, like many commercial search engines, takes a sample of the text of the page with the assumption that the text itself will contain key words and that the first few lines should give a good indication of what is to follow.

Additional Information

Analysts of the structure of the World Wide Web have noted two particular types of page known as *authorities* and *hubs,* both of which are useful resources and have significance in terms of indexing. On a given subject there will be pages that act as a valuable source of information, and are thus cited on many other pages. An authority is thus a page to which a great number of pages link. There are also pages that are compiled as list of useful sites on a given subject. These are known as hubs, and contain a great number of outbound hyperlinks. It is with this in mind that two more pieces of information about every page are gathered – the number of incoming links and the number of outward links.

Another key to the content of a page is the anchor text of a link that points to that page, for example `<A HREF=" http://myserver/test.htm">An example</A>`. Despite being on another page, this gives useful information about the `test.htm` page. Our Spider will also gather this information.

One final item that is collected is the date and time a page is visited. This is of limited use here, except as an aid to debugging. If the Spider is developed further, this data can be used to make sure records are up to date. For every page we wish to index we will store the following information: URL, Title, Description, Keywords, Page text, Incoming links, Link text, Outward links, and Date/Time.

Parser

The parsing of HTML can be achieved with the aid of a finite state machine. The characters on a page are read in turn and the state of the machine changed to represent the significance of the current position in the page. For instance, upon receiving a '<' character, the state would be 'inside tag'. If the next character was an 'A' the state would change to 'inside anchor tag'. By the use of structured case statements it is possible to extract the required information. The coding for such a parser can get very complicated indeed, especially when one remembers that not only do HTML tags have many variants, but pages may not even contain valid HTML and yet such pages must still be handled.

Fortunately, with Java 2 much of the work has been done for us, and it is only now necessary to attach the required actions to particular sections of HTML code. The key classes are in the standard package javax.swing.text.html. This is currently rather poorly documented, but seeing these classes in action should make their operation more clear. There is a class called parser in the API, but we do not deal with this directly. The Web page data is streamed through a delegator which co-ordinates the parsing for us. When the parse method of ParserDelegator is called, we have to supply it with a ParserCallback, which contains the actions we require when particular tags and data are encountered. In this application we have extended ParserCallback with a subclass of our own, Hparser, in which we have overridden the parent class's methods to perform our actions.

The class definition for the Hparser class is as follows:

```
package spider;
import javax.swing.text.html.HTMLEditorKit.*;
import javax.swing.text.*;
import javax.swing.text.html.*;
import java.util.*;

public class Hparser extends ParserCallback
{
    String title, description, keywords, pagetext, linktext;
    Vector links;
    char state;
    static final char NONE = 0;
    static final char TITLE = 1;
    static final char HREF = 2;
    // insert other methods in here

}
```

The methods to be inserted into this class are described below. The information about the page is kept in strings, with the vector links holding a series of strings made of link and linktext pairs. For example, <A HREF=" http://myserver/test.htm ">An example</A> would be stored as …[http://myserver/test.htm],[An example]…
The current state of the parser is stored in state, and for our purposes this may only have three values; TITLE, when it is reading between the <TITLE> and </TITLE> tags, HREF when it is between anchor tags and NONE at any other time. The actual values 0, 1 and 2 are arbitrary, though they allow us to use switch statements later on.

In the constructor we simply have the initialization of the variables that will hold the information we want about the page:

```
public Hparser()
{
    title = new String();
    description = new String();
    keywords = new String();
    pagetext = new String();
    linktext = new String();
    links = new Vector();
}
```

The `ParserCallback` has four methods we will override. These are `handleSimpleTag`, `handleStartTag`, `handleEndTag` and `handleText`. The first of these is called when the parser encounters a simple tag (a standalone tag like <P> or <HR>). The only simple tag of interest here is <META>. When this tag is encountered we will call a method of our own, passing on the attributes (name and content) found in the tag:

```
public void handleSimpleTag(HTML.Tag tag, MutableAttributeSet
        attribs, int pos)
{
    if(tag.equals(HTML.Tag.META))
    {
        handleMeta(attribs);
    }
}
```

The extraction of the description and keywords is straightforward, and these are passed down to the class variables:

```
public void handleMeta(MutableAttributeSet attribs)
{
    String name = new String();
    String content = new String();
    name = (String)attribs.getAttribute(HTML.Attribute.NAME);
    content = (String)attribs.getAttribute(HTML.Attribute.CONTENT);
    if(name==null||content==null) return;
    name = name.toUpperCase();
    if(name.equals("DESCRIPTION"))
    {
        description = content;
        return;
    }
    if(name.equals("KEYWORDS"))
    {
        keywords = content;
        return;
    }
}
```

The start tag and end tag, as seems natural, are found in pairs. The pairs we are interested in start with `<TITLE>` and `<A HREF="...">`. The `<TITLE>` start tag is dealt with here by setting our state variable appropriately. The anchor start tag is treated in the same way as the META tag above, having its attributes passed to another custom method:

```java
public void handleStartTag(HTML.Tag tag, MutableAttributeSet
       attribs, int pos)
{
  if(tag.equals(HTML.Tag.TITLE))
  {
     state  = TITLE;
  }
  if(tag.equals(HTML.Tag.A))
  {
     handleAnchor(attribs);
  }
}

public void handleAnchor(MutableAttributeSet attribs)
{
   String href = new String();
   href = (String)attribs.getAttribute(HTML.Attribute.HREF);
   if(href==null) return;
   links.add(href);
   state = HREF;
}
```

Whenever the parser is not actually inside a tag, it will respond to any plain text it finds by calling the `handleText()` method. Here we have a simple handler to deliver the data to the appropriate class variable, depending on the current state:

```java
public void handleText(char[] text, int pos)
{
   switch(state)
   {
     case NONE:
     pagetext += new String(text)+" ";
     break;
     case TITLE:
     title = new String(text);
     break;
     case HREF:
     linktext = new String(text);
     break;
   }
}
```

Whenever the parser encounters an end tag, one of the form </...>, the following method is called:

```java
public void handleEndTag(HTML.Tag tag, int pos)
{
   if(state == NONE) return;
   // In order of precedence == > &&
   if(state == TITLE && tag.equals(HTML.Tag.TITLE))
   {
      state  = NONE;
   }
   if(state == HREF && tag.equals(HTML.Tag.A))
   {
      links.add(linktext);
      state = NONE;
   }
}
```

This method resets the state variable when a balancing tag is met, and where the tag was an anchor, the displayed link text is sent to the class variable. The remaining methods in the class Hparser allow access to the class variables:

```java
// Returns page title
public String getTitle()
{
   return title.length()<100 ? title : title.substring(0,100);
}

// Returns description (from META tags)
public String getDescription()
{
   return description.length()<100 ? description :
          description.substring(0,100);
}

// Returns keywords (from META tags)
public String getKeywords()
{
   return keywords.length()<100 ? keywords :
          keywords.substring(0,100);
}

// Return pagetext
public String getPagetext()
{
   return pagetext.length()<200 ? pagetext :
          pagetext.substring(0,200);
}

// Return links
public Vector getLinks()
{
   int size = links.size();
   if(size%2 != 0) links.add("filler");
   return links;
}
```

To avoid gathering excessive amounts of information the strings have their sizes checked and are truncated if necessary. Note the use of the ? : operator. The statement

```
expression ? op1 : op2
```

evaluates *expression* and returns `op1` if true and `op2` if false. The last method above ensures the vector links contains an even number of elements to prevent errors elsewhere in the code. Any good HTML will have links and linktext matched, but there is no guarantee this will be the case. The handling of this is crude, but it is an exceptional circumstance and probably isn't worth the overheads of anything more sophisticated.

Database

It would be fairly straightforward to create a custom database for our indexing system using Java, and provide data persistence by saving files. This approach would, however, have several potential disadvantages, notably limited platform independence and scalability. Although generally Java written for one platform will run on another, when one wishes to take advantage of the native file system this independence can go out of the window. The database we require will need to have efficient random access facilities, something which may not be a problem for a file-based system when handling a couple of hundred records, but when scaled to several thousand may grind to a halt. We can sidestep all these issues by using a standard SQL-compliant database. Chances are such a database is already in use within the target system, all we have to do is gain access using JDBC and piggyback a few of our own tables on top of it. If necessary we can just pick a new database off the shelf, such as Access or SQL Server for a Microsoft environment or one of the powerful (and free) open source databases such as MySQL and PostgreSQL for a Linux environment.

To use the Spider, it is necessary to create a table to receive the data. This could all be done from Java, but it is easiest to use whatever tools are available with the database. The following fields are required:

Field	Type	Size
URL	Text	100
TITLE	Text	100
DESCRIPTION	Text	100
KEYWORDS	Text	100
PAGETEXT	Text	200
INLINKS	Long	-
LINKTEXT	Text	100
OUTLINKS	Long	-
STAMP	Date/Time	-

The size of the fields is fairly arbitrary, and we have made the assumption that a URL is highly unlikely to be longer than 100 characters, that a page of text will include key words in the first 200 characters and so on. The types above are given for MS Access, with ANSI equivalents as follows:

MS Access	ANSI SQL Data Type	Synonym
Text	CHARACTER, CHARACTER VARYING	ALPHANUMERIC, CHAR, CHARACTER, STRING, VARCHAR
Date/Time	DATE, TIME, TIMESTAMP	DATE, TIME, TIMESTAMP
Long	INTEGER	INT, INTEGER, INTEGER4

To allow for reuse, the basic code required to handle a JDBC connection is defined in the `Dbaccess` class:

```
package data;
import java.sql.*;
import java.util.*;

public class Dbaccess
{
    Connection connection;

    public Dbaccess()
    {
        try
        {
            Class.forName("sun.jdbc.odbc.JdbcOdbcDriver");
            Properties prop = new Properties();
            prop.setProperty("user","wrox");
            prop.setProperty("password","press");
            connection =
                DriverManager.getConnection("jdbc:odbc:Indexdb",prop);
        }
        catch(SQLException sqle)
        {
            System.out.println(sqle.toString());
        }
        catch(ClassNotFoundException cnfe)
        {
            System.out.println(cnfe.toString());
        }
    }

    public void closeConnection()
    {
        if(connection != null)
        try
```

Continued on Following Page

```
          {
            connection.close();
            connection = null;
          }
        catch(SQLException sqle)
          {
            System.out.println(sqle.toString());
          }
      }
  }
```

The constructor for this class creates the connection, and the `closeConnection()` method destroys it. In the code above the driver used is the JDBC-ODBC bridge driver, which is suitable for virtually any database on a MS Windows system. The class will attempt to connect to a database *Indexdb* with a user name of *wrox* and password *press* (if the database is not password protected, these terms will usually be ignored). Using this driver, the database will normally be specified in the System DSN of the ODBC setup in the Control Panel. If another operating system and database is used then the appropriate JDBC driver should be substituted.

The second class that handles database communication is `Dbspider`. This has more specific database methods, inheriting the basic connection functions of `Dbaccess`. This class makes use of SQL statements to query the database:

```
package data;
import java.sql.*;
import java.util.*;
import spider.Index;

public class Dbspider extends Dbaccess
{
    PreparedStatement addSiteSQL;
    PreparedStatement incinlinksSQL;
    PreparedStatement updatelinktextSQL;
    Statement containsSQL;
    Statement getTopsSQL;

    public void prepareSQL()
    {
        try
        {
            addSiteSQL = connection.prepareStatement
                    ("INSERT INTO SITES VALUES (?,?,?,?,?,?,?,?,?)");

            incinlinksSQL= connection.prepareStatement("UPDATE SITES SET "+
                "SITES.INLINKS = [SITES].[INLINKS]+? WHERE SITES.URL = ?

            updatelinktextSQL = connection.prepareStatement("UPDATE SITES
                SET "+ "SITES.LINKTEXT = [SITES].[LINKTEXT]+? WHERE SITES.URL
                = ? ");
```

```
        getTopsSQL = connection.createStatement();
        containsSQL = connection.createStatement();
        containsSQL.setMaxRows(1);
    }
    catch(SQLException sqle)
    {
        System.out.println(sqle.toString());
    }
}

//insert other methods in here

}
```

The statement in the `prepareSQL` method that adds the details of a visited page to the database is

```
addSiteSQL = connection.prepareStatement
                ("INSERT INTO SITES VALUES (?,?,?,?,?,?,?,?,?)");
```

with the markers corresponding to the following fields: URL, Title, Description, Keywords, Pagetext, Inlinks, Linktext, Outlinks, and Timestamp. Next we have a SQL statement that will increment the incoming link counter of a particular URL by a given amount.

```
incinlinksSQL = connection.prepareStatement("UPDATE SITES SET  " +
        "SITES.INLINKS = [SITES].[INLINKS]+? WHERE SITES.URL = ? ");
```

The next statement, associated with the last, will append the incoming link text to its field in the record.

```
updatelinktextSQL = connection.prepareStatement("UPDATE SITES SET "+
        "SITES.LINKTEXT = [SITES].[LINKTEXT]+? WHERE SITES.URL = ? ");
```

The following statement will pull off the most linked-to URLs, ready for the Cache.

```
getTopsSQL = connection.createStatement();
```

This statement, and the one below, are only created here: the actual SQL is elsewhere. The JDBC driver used for the prototype would not properly support SELECT queries as `PreparedStatements`. Some degree of customization is likely to be needed whichever database and driver are used, either to downgrade the code within the limitations of the driver, or to take advantage of optimizing facilities available in more advanced databases.

The final statements will be used to check whether a given URL has already been filed.

```
containsSQL - connection.createStatement();
containsSQL.setMaxRows(1);
```

The `PreparedStatements` are applied with calls to the following methods (which should be included in the `Dbspider` class). This fills in the blanks of the precompiled `addSiteSQL` above with data sent to the method, the current time being placed in the last field. The `addSite()` method sends the details of a page to the database as a single record:

```
public void addSite(String url, String title, String description,
            String keywords, String pagetext, Integer inlinks, String
            linktext, int outlinks)
{
    Timestamp now = new Timestamp(System.currentTimeMillis());
    try
    {
    // Defined in PreparedStatement
        addSiteSQL.setString(1, url);
        addSiteSQL.setString(2, " "+title);
        addSiteSQL.setString(3, " "+description);
        addSiteSQL.setString(4, " "+keywords);
        addSiteSQL.setString(5, " "+pagetext);
        addSiteSQL.setInt(6, inlinks.intValue());
        addSiteSQL.setString(7, " "+linktext);
        addSiteSQL.setInt(8, outlinks);
        addSiteSQL.setTimestamp(9, now);
        addSiteSQL.executeUpdate();
    }
    catch (SQLException sqle)
    {
        System.out.println(sqle.toString());
    }
}
```

The `checkRecord()` method queries the database for to see if a URL has already been visited. If such a record is found, that record's INLINKS value is incremented, and any additional LINKTEXT is appended to that field:

```
public boolean checkRecord(String urlstring, String linktext, int
        increment)
{
    boolean contains = false;
    try
    {
        ResultSet rs = containsSQL.executeQuery("SELECT SITES.URL FROM
                SITES WHERE SITES.URL = '"+urlstring+"'");
        contains = rs.next();
        if(contains)
        {
            incinlinksSQL.setInt(1, increment);
            incinlinksSQL.setString(2, urlstring);
            incinlinksSQL.executeUpdate();
            updatelinktextSQL.setString(1, " "+linktext);
            updatelinktextSQL.setString(2, urlstring);
            updatelinktextSQL.executeUpdate();
        }
```

```
        }
        catch(SQLException sqle)
        {
            System.out.println(sqle.toString());
        }
        return contains;
    }
```

The Cache is a local store of the most linked-to pages, to avoid making unnecessary trips to the database. When a link is found that points to a page that has already been scanned and is popular enough to be in the Cache, it is still necessary to update the INLINKS and LINKTEXT fields, and so any extra data for these is held in the Cache. The following method uses an SQL query to select the most popular URLs, with their associated INLINKS and LINKTEXT.

```
    public Vector getTopURLs()
    {
        Vector tops = new Vector();
        try
        {
            ResultSet results = getTopsSQL.executeQuery("SELECT TOP " +
                    Index.CACHESIZE+" SITES.URL, " + "SITES.INLINKS FROM
                    SITES ORDER BY SITES.INLINKS DESC");
            while(results.next())
            {
                tops.add(results.getString("URL"));
            }
        }
        catch(SQLException sqle)
        {
            System.out.println(sqle.toString());
        }
        return tops;
    }
```

The Cache itself is housed in another class, imaginatively called Cache. As mentioned above, it is necessary to keep a record of the INLINKs and LINKTEXT in addition to the URLs. Each of these fields is given its own Vector, and the three Vectors are accessed in parallel, that is to say that element x of Vector URLCache will always correspond to element x of inlinkCache and linktextCache. The code begins by creating these Vectors and with an empty constructor. The two methods to be included in this class are described afterwards.

```
package data;
import java.util.*;
import spider.*;

public class Cache
{
    static Vector URLCache = new Vector();
    static Vector inlinkCache = new Vector();
    static Vector linktextCache = new Vector();
```

Continued on Following Page

```
    public void Cache()
    {
    }

    //insert methods here

}
```

The `contains` method checks the URL vector for occurrences of the received URL. In this Spider the check is made when new links are discovered, and the text of the link is passed to `contains` along with the URL. If the URL is not found `Vector.indexOf()` returns -1 and the caller is notified. If the URL is already in the Cache, the `Vector.indexOf()` method will return the index of the URL in the Vector. In this case, the value in the Cache corresponding to the number of links to the URL is incremented, and the link text is appended. Note that as the Cache is simply a copy of some of the data in the database, it is not necessary to retain the total INLINKS and whole of the LINKTEXT data, only any extra added since the URL was put in the Cache. The `Vector.set()` allows the elements of a Vector to be addressed directly by an index, in this case the value of `check`.

```
    public static boolean contains(String urlstring, String linktext)
    {
        Integer count;
        int check = URLCache.indexOf(urlstring);
        if(check != -1)
        {
        // already visited, increment inlinks & add linktext
            count = (Integer)inlinkCache.elementAt(check);
            count = new Integer(count.intValue()+1);
            inlinkCache.set(check,count);
            linktext = (String)linktextCache.elementAt(check)+" "
                    +linktext;
            linktextCache.set(check, linktext);
            return true;
        }
        else
            return false;
    }
```

Whenever the number of pages scanned is divisible by the value REFRESH (defined in `spider.Index`) the next method is called. If the Cache is full (as it is when the Spider has scanned CACHESIZE pages), the elements of the Cache are submitted in turn to the database `checkRecord` method. As all the elements in the Cache are already in the database, the `checkRecord` method will update the back-end record with the new INLINKS and LINKTEXT data. Once the current Cache data has been pushed into the database, the database `getTopURLs` method retrieves the most popular URLs and these are placed in the Cache Vectors.

```
    public void refresh()
    {
        System.out.println("*** Cache Refresh ***");
        Vector tops = new Vector();
        // push cache into db
        if(URLCache.size()>0)
        {
```

```
                for(int i = 0;i<Index.CACHESIZE;i++)
                    Index.db.checkRecord((String)URLCache.elementAt(i),
                        (String)linktextCache.elementAt(i),
                        ((Integer)inlinkCache.elementAt(i)).intValue());
            }

            // load new cache values
            tops = Index.db.getTopURLs();
            URLCache.clear();
            linktextCache.clear();
            inlinkCache.clear();
            for(Enumeration e = tops.elements(); e.hasMoreElements();)
        {
                URLCache.add((String)e.nextElement());
                linktextCache.add(new String(" "));
                inlinkCache.add(new Integer(0));
            }
        }
    }
```

The next part of the Spider to consider is the Queue. The Spider finds the next page to scan from the Queue. Initially the program operator will have supplied a 'seed' URL that will be in the Queue, and from that time on whenever a hyperlink is found on a page the link is placed on the Queue. The lists of data in the Cache above could arguably have been better handled by different objects than Vectors (e.g. traditional arrays), as the number of elements is predetermined. The Queue on the other hand can be of any length, and to avoid going into any advanced design issues it is easiest to let Java do the hard work and opt for Vectors here.

As in the Cache, we begin by setting up the Vectors. There is one addition here, a Vector `badlist` that will hold links that are known to be dead or malformed.

```
package data;
import java.sql.*;
import java.io.*;
import java.net.*;
import java.util.*;
import data.*;
import spider.Index;

public class Queue
{
    static Vector badList = new Vector();
    static Vector URLQueue = new Vector();
    static Vector inlinkQueue = new Vector();
    static Vector linktextQueue = new Vector();
    int qnext = 0;

    public Queue()
    {
    }
```

Continued on Following Page

```
      public static int getSize()
      {
         return URLQueue.size();
      }


      // insert other methods here

   }
```

The `getSize` method does exactly what you'd expect; it retrieves the number of URLs in the Queue. This value is a useful indicator of the progress of the Spider, and would be invaluable for checking any modifications to the Spider. The other methods of the `Queue` class are described below.

The `addLink` method also does what you'd expect, but looks remarkably ugly for what one might have thought a simple operation. The reason for this is that the link as taken from a Web page is unlikely to be in a simple URL format. The original link as submitted is kept as `rawlink`, whereas the `link` variable is shaped into our required absolute URL format. If it turns out after processing that the link is invalid, then the `rawlink` value is put in the `badlink` Vector, for quick recognition if encountered in the future. After checking the link is not on the 'bad' list, subsequent processing sorts out links that point to particular anchors in Web pages. These links contain the hash symbol, and if the anchor is on the same page the link will begin with a #. There is no point in requeing a link, and the part of a page pointed to is relatively unimportant. Thus no link beginning with # is queued, and where the link contains a #, only the text to the left of this symbol (i.e. the page reference) is queued. Next, links that do not end with `.htm` or `.html` are filtered out. It is not written in stone that a valid HTML file has this extension, but problems are less likely if other extensions are avoided. The only exception made is for links that end with a '/' character. Despite being bad practice, it is common to find these links in use when the intended target is the `index.html` file in that directory. A check is then made to see if the link is relative or absolute, and if relative the base reference (extracted from the current page) is prepended. Use is made of the `java.net.URL` constructor to check for malformed URLs, and to resolve relative moves such as '../' that might be embedded in the link. When the link is in the normalized form we require, it is compared with our list of valid domains. If the link is wanted and not already in the Queue it gets pushed in line. If it is in the Queue, the INLINKS value for this item is incremented in advance of the page being visited.

```
      public static boolean addLink(String URLbase, String rawlink, String
           linktext)
      {
         if(badList.contains(rawlink)) return false;
         URL url;
         Integer count;
         String link, filename;
         int index, hash;
         boolean inadomain;
         link = rawlink;
         hash = link.indexOf("#");
         if(hash == 0) return false;
         if(hash != -1) link = link.substring(0, hash);
         if(!link.endsWith(".htm") && !link.endsWith(".html") &&
            !link.endsWith("/")) return false;
```

```
        if(link.endsWith("/")) link = link+"index.html";
        if(!link.startsWith("http:")) link = URLbase+link;
        try
        {
            url = new URL(link);
            link = url.toString();
        }
        catch(MalformedURLException mue)
        {
            addBad(rawlink);
            return false;
        }
        inadomain = true;
        for(Enumeration e=Index.domains.elements(); e.hasMoreElements();)
        {
            if(link.indexOf((String)e.nextElement()) != -1) break;
            inadomain = false;
        }
        if(!inadomain) return false;
        if(data.Cache.contains(link, linktext)) return false;
        if(URLQueue.isEmpty())
        {       // to stop null inlink exception
            index = -1;
        }
        else
        {
            index = URLQueue.indexOf(link);
        }
        if(index != -1)
        {
            // already queued, increment inlinks variable in queue
            count = (Integer)inlinkQueue.elementAt(index);
            count = new Integer(count.intValue()+1);
            inlinkQueue.set(index,count);
            return false;
        }
        // add it to the queue
        URLQueue.addElement(link);
        linktextQueue.addElement(linktext);
        count = new Integer(1);
        inlinkQueue.addElement(count);
        return true;
    }
```

Once we have addresses of pages piled up in the Queue, we need a way of pulling off a link for the next page to scan. This is achieved by the getNextURL() method which uses the same rule of thumb as the Cache; that pages which have been pointed to a lot already are likely to be pointed at a lot again. The Vector holding the INLINKS values is scanned to find the highest value. The index of this value is held as a static variable and used to address the required inlink and linktext in the subsequent methods, getNextInlink() and getNextLinktext(). This way of doing things will make Object-Oriented purists squirm, but it works and is not so complicated that it could hide bugs.

```
public String getNextURL()
{
   int currentscore, topscore = 0;
   for (int i = 0;i<URLQueue.size();i++)
   {
      currentscore = ((Integer)inlinkQueue.get(i)).intValue();
      if(currentscore > topscore)
      {
         topscore = currentscore;
         qnext = i;
      }
   }
      String urlstring = (String)URLQueue.get(qnext);
      URLQueue.remove(qnext);
      return urlstring;
}

public int getNextInlink()
{
   int inlink = ((Integer)inlinkQueue.get(qnext)).intValue();
   inlinkQueue.remove(qnext);
   return inlink;
}

public String getNextLinktext()
{
   String linktext = (String)linktextQueue.get(qnext);
   linktextQueue.remove(qnext);
   return linktext;
}
```

The final method keeps tabs on bad links. For convenience a message is passed to the standard output stream. If the Spider is extended this could be passed to a table in the database, for debugging the code and detecting HTML errors on the spidered sites.

```
public static void addBad(String badlink)
{
   System.out.println("** Bad list size = "+badList.size()+"     added
                     : "+badlink);
   if(badList.contains(badlink)) return;
   badList.add(badlink);
   return;
}
```

GUI

The user interface for the Spider is provided by an HTML start page (`index.htm`) and then subsequent pages are dynamically generated by the class `spider.Index`. The communication from operator to Spider is limited to starting the servlet (which is carried out automatically), the specification of 'seed' URLs from which to start crawling and a 'Pause' command. The information given back to the operator by the Spider is a simple set of status details – the number of pages scanned, the size of the queue, etc. This process is illustrated below.

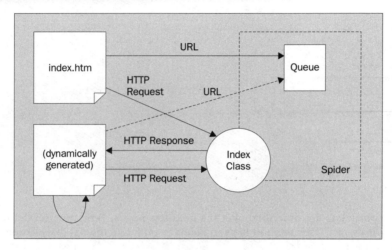

The little piece of HTML that starts the system rolling (index.htm) is:

```
<HTML>
<HEAD>
<TITLE>INDEX</TITLE>
</HEAD>
<BODY>
<CENTER><H2>Indexer</H2></CENTER>
<FORM ACTION="http://localhost:8080/servlet/spider.Index" METHOD="POST">
<B>Start URL : </B>
<INPUT TYPE="text" SIZE="20" NAME="query">
<INPUT TYPE="submit">
</FORM>
</BODY>
</HTML>
```

This shows an edit field into which the operator should put the URL of the page the Spider will start from. Note that the full URL should be used, including the filename, for example `http://www.wrox.com/index.htm`. When the 'Submit' button is clicked, the contents of the edit box are passed to the `doPost` method of class `spider.Index`. This class handles the user interface of the Spider and contains global variables.

```
package spider;
import javax.servlet.*;
import javax.servlet.http.*;
import java.util.*;
import java.io.*;
import data.*;

public class Index extends HttpServlet implements Runnable
{
   public static int sitecount = 0;
   public static int CACHESIZE = 25;
   public static int REFRESH = 100;
   public static Vector domains = new Vector();
   public static Dbspider db;
   public static Spider spider;
   public static boolean running;
   public static int qsize;
   public static long starttime = System.currentTimeMillis();
   public static long threadtime;
   private Thread indexThread = null;


   // insert other methods here

}
```

The methods of this class are described over the next few pages. When the servlet is first called, its `init` method will be run. This method is overridden to initialise the database communications and to create a Spider object.

```
public void init(ServletConfig config) throws ServletException
{
   // Store the ServletConfig object and log the initialization
   super.init(config);
   // Load the database to prepare for requests
   db = new Dbspider();
   db.prepareSQL();
   spider = new Spider();
}
```

Generally, servlets are used where a request is made from a browser or other client, the process carried out and the results returned to the client within seconds. Given that the Spider will be running for hours at a time, it could be argued that it would be more appropriate to build the Spider as a standard Java application. This is certainly one option, and in fact prototyping for this Spider was done that way. It is however possible to create a servlet that will give an immediate response by the use of threads. When the `start()` method below is called, a new thread is created and the program flow returns to the caller.

```
public void start()
{
   indexThread = new Thread(this, "Index");
   indexThread.start();
}
```

This Spider does not make sophisticated use of threads, in fact under normal circumstances only one thread of the main code will be running at a time. To ensure this is the case, the first thing a thread does upon starting is to set a global variable to announce that a thread is running.

```
public void run()
{
    running = true;
    threadtime =  System.currentTimeMillis();
    while(running)
    {
        qsize =Queue.getSize();
        if(qsize>0)
        {
            System.out.println("Queue size = "+qsize);
            spider.Crawl();
        }
        else
        {
            try
            {
                Thread.sleep(2000);
            }
            catch(InterruptedException e)
            {
                System.out.println("Thread woken");
            }
        }
    }
    System.out.println("Paused");
}
```

The time the thread is started is noted and while there are pages in the queue they are accessed and crawled using the `Crawl()` method in the Spider class. If the queue is empty, rather than waste processor cycles in a pointless loop, the thread is sent to sleep for a couple of seconds.

The keys to user interaction with the Spider are the `doPost` and `doGet` methods. The code in `doPost` below extracts the URL provided by the operator to the browser using `getParameterNames` and `getParameterValues`. Note that the `Enumeration` is only used to pull off the first name-value pair. If the Spider is not currently running then a thread for this is started. The URL supplied by the operator is passed to the queue as a 'seed'. The success or failure of this is passed to the browser via the `outputPage` method described later.

```
public void doPost(HttpServletRequest req, HttpServletResponse res)
            throws ServletException, IOException
{
    String urlstatus;

    // set header field
    res.setContentType("text/html");
```

Continued on Following Page

```
            //Get the response's PrintWriter to return text to the client.
            PrintWriter toClient = res.getWriter();

            // Get client data
            Enumeration values = req.getParameterNames();
            String name = (String)values.nextElement();
            String value = req.getParameterValues(name)[0];

            if(!running)
            {
                start();
                System.out.println("\nStarted Indexer");
            }
            urlstatus = spider.addSeed(value);
            outputPage(res, urlstatus, value);
    }
```

To keep things simple, the communication between the browser and this servlet has (somewhat artificially) been split into two types: data and command. The data (the seed URLs submitted) is handled by the doPost method above. Commands, of which we have the grand total of one, are handled by the doGet method below. This command is 'Pause', and when delivered by a browser will reset the running flag and cause the current thread (in the run method above) to break out of its loop and run to completion. It should be remembered that although this will release a lot of resources, the servlet will remain loaded. This method also calls outputPage to give the operator some feedback.

```
    public void doGet(HttpServletRequest req, HttpServletResponse res)
            throws ServletException, IOException
    {
        // set header field first
        res.setContentType("text/html");

        //Get the response's PrintWriter to return text to the client.
        PrintWriter toClient = res.getWriter();

        // Get client's query data
        Enumeration values = req.getParameterNames();
        String name = (String)values.nextElement();
        String value = req.getParameterValues(name)[0];
        if(value.equals("pause")) running = false;
        outputPage(res, "Command", value);
    }
```

The information provided to the operator is fairly short and so is hardcoded as a simple http response. The page generated by this method depends in part on whether or not the Spider is running, and if the Spider is running a link back to the servlet is provided to allow it to be paused using the doGet method. A form section is again provided to add further 'seed' URLs. If the data submitted here is not a valid URL or left blank then the data is ignored and the page is refreshed with the current status information.

```
public void outputPage(HttpServletResponse res, String string1,
      String string2) throws IOException
{
    PrintWriter out = res.getWriter();
    out.println("<HEAD><TITLE> Index</TITLE></HEAD><BODY>");
    out.println("<CENTER><H2>Indexer</H2></CENTER>");
    out.println("<P><UL>");
    out.println("<LI>Time on this run : "+(new
        Long((System.currentTimeMillis()-threadtime)/60000)+"
        mins").toString());
    out.println("<LI>Total runtime : "+(new
        Long((System.currentTimeMillis()-starttime)/60000)+"
        mins").toString());
    out.println("<LI>Total pages = "+sitecount);
    out.println("<LI>Queue size = "+qsize);
    out.println("<LI>Cache size = "+CACHESIZE+" URLS (fixed)");
    out.println("<LI>Cache refresh after "+REFRESH+" pages (fixed)");
    out.println("<LI>Domains being scanned : "+domains);
    out.println("</UL><P>");
    out.print("<P><FONT COLOR=red><B>");
    if(running)
    {
        out.print("Running</B></FONT>  ");
        out.println("<A HREF=http://localhost:8080/servlet/spider.Index
            ?command=pause><B>Pause</B></A>");
    }
    else
    {
        out.print("Paused</B></FONT>");
    }
    out.println("<P>"+string1+"         "+string2);
    out.println("<P><FORM
        ACTION=http://localhost:8080/servlet/spider.Index
        METHOD=POST>");
    out.println("<B>Seed URL :<B>");
    out.println("<INPUT TYPE=text NAME=query SIZE=50><BR><BR> <INPUT
        TYPE=submit>");
    out.println("</FORM>");
    out.println("</BODY>");
    out.close();
}
```

We provide a little etiquette by way of the last method of this class.

```
public String getServletInfo()
{
    return "Index Servlet";
}
```

At the heart of the Spider is (not surprisingly) the class Spider. The code begins by setting up a few variables and initialising the Queue, Cache and Hparser.

```
package spider;
import java.net.*;
import java.io.*;
import java.util.*;
import javax.swing.text.html.parser.ParserDelegator;
import data.*;

public class Spider
{
    static Queue queue;
    static Cache cache;
    int qsize;
    Hparser hparse;
    URL currenturl;

    public Spider()
    {
        queue = new Queue();
        cache = new Cache();
        hparse = new Hparser();
    }


    // insert other methods here

}
```

Once again, the methods of this class are described below. To give the Spider somewhere to start, a 'seed' URL is passed as a `String`. Simple checks as described in the `Queue` class above are made on this string, before it is forwarded to the Queue.

```
public String addSeed(String urlstring)
{
    if(urlstring.equals("")) return "";
    if(Index.db.checkRecord(urlstring, "", 0)) return "Already
        Scanned";
    String scanres = scanPage(urlstring);
    if(scanres.equals("bad")) return "Bad URL";
    String domain = urlstring.substring(0,
                    urlstring.lastIndexOf('/'));
    if(Index.domains.isEmpty()) Index.domains.add(domain);
    if(!Index.domains.contains(domain)) Index.domains.add(domain);
    if(queue.addLink("",urlstring,""))
    {
        return "URL Added";
    }
    else
        return "Already in Queue";
}
```

Any good Spider should be able to crawl, and that's what the next method does.

```java
public int Crawl()
{
    String file = new String();
    String URLbase = new String();
    String urlstring = new String(queue.getNextURL());
    int currentinlinks = queue.getNextInlink();
    String currentlinktext = new String(queue.getNextLinktext());
    hparse = new Hparser();
    System.out.println("\nLookup : "+urlstring);
    if(!Index.db.checkRecord(urlstring, currentlinktext,1))
    {
        System.out.println("New page = "+urlstring);
        urlstring = scanPage(urlstring);
        if(!urlstring.equals("bad"))
        {
            // Get the URL base
            URLbase = currenturl.getProtocol()+"://";
            URLbase += currenturl.getHost();
            file = currenturl.getFile();
            int dirend = file.lastIndexOf("/") > file.lastIndexOf("\\")
                ? file.lastIndexOf("/") : file.lastIndexOf("\\");

            URLbase += file.substring(0,dirend)+"/";
                    //http://www.host.com/THIS/PART/filename.htm

            Vector links = hparse.getLinks();
            int outlinks;
            if(!links.isEmpty())
            {
                outlinks = links.size()/2;
                for (Enumeration e = hparse.getLinks().elements() ;
                    e.hasMoreElements();)
                {
                    queue.addLink(URLbase, (String)e.nextElement(),
                                (String)e.nextElement());
                }
            }
            else
                outlinks = 0;

            Index.db.addSite(urlstring, hparse.getTitle(),
                    hparse.getDescription(), hparse.getKeywords(),
                    hparse.getPagetext(), new Integer(currentinlinks),
                    currentlinktext, outlinks);
            System.out.println("Added : "+hparse.getTitle());
            Index.sitecount++;
            System.out.println("Total Pages = "+Index.sitecount);
```

Continued on Following Page

```
                if(Index.sitecount%Index.REFRESH == 0)
                {
                    cache.refresh();
                    System.gc(); // Garbage Collection
                }
            }
        }
        return queue.getSize();
    }
```

The `Crawl` method works as follows. After making sure the page hasn't already been visited by querying the database, the page is passed to the method `scanPage`, described later, which will visit the page and parse it. If the page was scanned successfully, various methods from the `java.net.URL` class are called and after a bit of juggling the `URLbase` string is constructed. This allows the location of the current page to be expressed in terms of host and directory, and gives the point to which relative URLs found in the page may be resolved.

The `Hparser` instance created above has been filled with data in the `scanPage` method, and the links found on the page may be got as a Vector. This Vector contains link-linktext pairs, and so the number of links on the page is half the size of this Vector. The links are then placed on the Queue.

We are then finally in a position to add a record to the database, with most of the fields being provided by the `Hparser` object. After a couple of informative message to the standard output, if the number of pages has reached a suitable value the Cache is refreshed.

This Spider hasn't been built with a lot of attention to use of resources, but one small effort is made above with `System.gc()`. Under normal circumstances garbage collection is left to the Virtual Machine to schedule, but as we have a place in the program that is periodically visited after a reasonable number of operations a garbage collection cycle is forced. This may or may not make a difference to resources, but we do it anyway.

The tangled mess that is the `scanPage` method is really a simple extension of a basic connection as described in the Java Tutorial and elsewhere. The difference here is that we have started with a `URLConnection`, which has features specific to URLs, and then cast it to a `HttpURLConnection`. A browse through the library for this class will reveal the advantages of this. The main one used here is the `getResponseCode()` method, which informs us the http connection is ok by returning `HTTP_OK`. There are a whole range of http response codes that could be of use if this Spider were modified, for example the terse `HTTP_GONE` and the verbose `HTTP_ENTITY_TOO_LARGE`. When the connection is all set up, a `BufferedReader` streams the characters of the Web page to the parser. Most of the rest of this block is concerned with ensuring that the data we receive is valid text-format HTML.

```
    public String scanPage(String urlstring)
    {
        String httpresp = new String();
        String status = new String("good");
        ParserDelegator pd = new ParserDelegator();
        try
        {
            currenturl = new URL(urlstring);
```

```
        urlstring = currenturl.toString();  // removes /../ from URL
        if(!currenturl.getProtocol().equals("http"))
        {
            status = currenturl.getProtocol()+" protocol";
        }
        else
        {
            URLConnection conn = currenturl.openConnection();
            HttpURLConnection httpconn = (HttpURLConnection)conn;
            if(httpconn.getResponseCode() == HttpURLConnection.HTTP_OK)
            {
                if(httpconn.getContentType().equals("text/html"))
                {
                    System.out.println("OK, parsing...");
                    InputStreamReader isr = new
                        InputStreamReader(conn.getInputStream());
                    BufferedReader in = new BufferedReader(isr);
                    pd.parse(in, hparse, true);
                    in.close();
                    isr.close();
                    httpconn.disconnect();
                }
                else
                    status = "Not text/html";
            }
            else
                status = "bad"; // Mark as a bad URL
        }
    }
    catch(MalformedURLException mue)
    {
        status = mue.toString();
    }
    catch(java.net.UnknownHostException uh)
    {
        status = uh.toString();
    }
    catch(java.io.IOException ioe)
    {
        status = ioe.toString();
    }
    if(status.equals("good"))
    {
        return urlstring;
    }
    else
    {
        System.out.println("Bad URL = "+urlstring);
        return "bad";
    }
}
```

That pretty much covers the code for the Spider servlet.

Get Crawling!

The following instructions are given for a MS Windows environment, and the procedures should be modified as appropriate for other platforms.

To compile the Spider make sure the source files are in the following directories (the 'root' can be anywhere on your machine):

> ➤ root\spider\Index.java
> ➤ root\spider\Spider.java
> ➤ root\spider\Hparser.java
> ➤ root\data\Dbaccess.java
> ➤ root\data\Dbspider.java
> ➤ root\data\Cache.java
> ➤ root\data\Queue.java
> ➤ root\index.htm

The index.htm file is only placed here for convenience. Add the root directory to your CLASSPATH. The JDK and JSDK libraries should already be in your CLASSPATH (if in doubt try compiling the JSDK 'HelloWorld' servlet). Then, at a command prompt type:

```
javac spider\Index.java
```

To set the Spider crawling, create the table described in the Database section above, and set up the ODBC. Start the servletrunner, and open a browser at the page root\index.htm. Enter a valid fully qualified URL, including the filename and click 'Submit Query'. If everything is working, after a small delay, the browser should look like this:

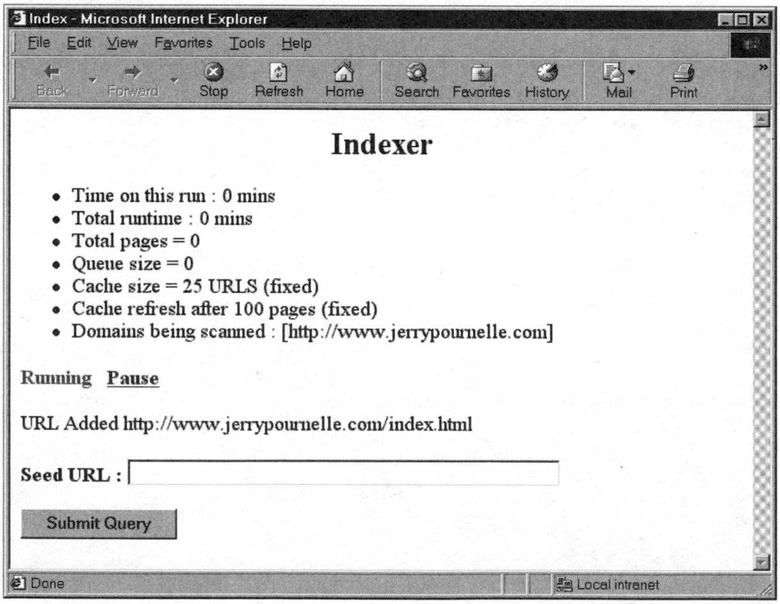

Not very interesting, it has to be admitted. Wait a few moments and click the 'Submit Query' button. The first four values should have changed. It's still not that interesting, so take a look at the servletrunner window. Chugging up the screen should be text blocks that look like this:

```
Lookup : http://www.jerrypournelle.com/VIEW/view26.html
New page = http://www.jerrypournelle.com/VIEW/view26.html
OK, parsing...
Added : View 26
Total Pages = 15
Queue size = 212
```

Amazing! Well not quite, but at least there is some activity on this window. If you then open your database at the relevant table, there should already be a considerable list of pages, complete with details. Don't be worried if the 'Keywords' and 'Description' columns are blank – these rely on conscientious page designers.

I, Robot

A Web Spider acts autonomously by deciding where to crawl as it goes along, and so it can be classified as a robot, or, to be trendy, an *agent*. Whereas a human using a browser may jump from page to page in an erratic manner for no good reason, a robot can do this a whole lot faster. A robot can swamp a Web server with requests, slowing the server and hogging precious bandwidth. In addition, a robot might stumble into an active element where its requests can mess things up, for instance in a voting system. To reduce this problem a **'Standard for Robot Exclusion'** was developed around 1994 where a file, called `robots.txt`, holding a list of restrictions for robots was placed on the Web server. The number of robots in use has escalated tremendously since those days, including widespread use of applications that allow an individual to download whole sites. It is unlikely that all these robots take the trouble to check for such restrictions, though sensible programming should have minimised the potential damage they could cause. If a spider is set loose in the wild, it is strongly recommended that some thought be given to this issue. Even if the robot does not look for a `robot.txt` file, there is often relevant information to be found in META tags. Although not covered here, HTTP does support 'User-agent' and 'From' fields to identify the browser or robot and the identity of the robot master. In practice the limitation of this Spider to text `.htm` and `.html` files will avoid a huge proportion of potential problems.

The Client

Once the Spider has had a good crawl, we need to provide a way of using the information it has acquired. This function is achieved through a servlet to handle the user interface, with a class to communicate queries through JDBC to the database. The source code compiles to three classes:

> ➢ Wquery – the main servlet and user interface

> ➢ data.Dbquery – handles the database operations

> ➢ data.Dbaccess – opens and closes the JDBC connection

The client system is independent of the Spider, but as we already have a class with methods to make a connection with the database, data.Dbaccess, we might as well recycle it. In this simple client the user will enter a keyword into an HTML form and submit this to the servlet. A SQL query is constructed and this copies records of interest from the main table into a second buffer table, HITLIST, and then a scoring system using additional SQL statements is applied to these hits. This information is passed back to the user's browser by the servlet, giving a list of the hits in order of merit.

The HITLIST table has the same structure as the SITES table, with the addition of a SCORE field, type Long. The three methods in the Dbquery class prepare the SQL statements (PrepareSQL), retrieve the records which have the keyword in their PAGETEXT (findHits) and pass these result back to the user interface (getHits).
Again we extend Dbaccess:

```
package data;
import java.sql.*;
import java.util.*;

public class Dbquery extends Dbaccess
{
    PreparedStatement clearHitlistSQL;
    PreparedStatement query0SQL;
    PreparedStatement query1SQL;
    PreparedStatement query2SQL;
    PreparedStatement query3SQL;
    PreparedStatement query4SQL;
    PreparedStatement getHitsSQL

    // insert methods here

}
```

After initializing our variables we have the method that is first called by the user interface. The clearHitlistSQL statement empties the temporary table that will contain our results. The technique we use for matching records to keywords is given courtesy of SQL, in the form of the Like operator. The action of this operator is that suggested intuitively by the word, and it is normally used in conjunction with wildcard characters. For instance "fish%" is like "fish", "fishing" and "fish and chips". To find a key word in a string of text, we look for the word preceded by a single space (to make sure it is a discrete word) with anything before or after. The keyword passed to this method is wrapped in these wildcards and the resultant string pushed into the SQL statements, which are subsequently applied to the database:

```
public void findHits(String key)
{
    try
    {
        clearHitlistSQL.executeUpdate();
        key = "% "+key+"%"; // SQL wildcards, note space
        query0SQL.setString(1, key);
        query0SQL.executeUpdate();
        query0SQL.close();
```

```
        query1SQL.setString(1, key);
        query1SQL.executeUpdate();
        query1SQL.close();
        query2SQL.setString(1, key);
        query2SQL.executeUpdate();
        query2SQL.close();
        query3SQL.setString(1, key);
        query3SQL.executeUpdate();
        query3SQL.close();
        query4SQL.setString(1, key);
        query4SQL.executeUpdate();
        query4SQL.close();
    }
    catch(SQLException sqle)
    {
        System.out.println(sqle.toString());
    }
}
```

What these statements do can be seen in the next method, `prepareSQL()`:

```
public void prepareSQL()
{
    try
    {
        clearHitlistSQL = connection.prepareStatement("DELETE FROM
                        HITLIST");

        query0SQL = connection.prepareStatement("INSERT INTO HITLIST "+
                "SELECT SITES.*,1 AS SCORE FROM SITES WHERE
                (SITES.PAGETEXT LIKE ?)");

        query1SQL = connection.prepareStatement("UPDATE HITLIST SET
                HITLIST.SCORE = [HITLIST].[SCORE] + 5 "+"WHERE
                HITLIST.TITLE LIKE ?");

        query2SQL = connection.prepareStatement("UPDATE HITLIST SET
                HITLIST.SCORE = [HITLIST].[SCORE] + 2 "+"WHERE
                HITLIST.DESCRIPTION LIKE ?");

        query3SQL = connection.prepareStatement("UPDATE HITLIST SET
                HITLIST.SCORE = [HITLIST].[SCORE] + 3 "+"WHERE
                HITLIST.KEYWORDS LIKE ?");

        query4SQL = connection.prepareStatement("UPDATE HITLIST SET
                HITLIST.SCORE = [HITLIST].[SCORE] + 4 "+"WHERE
                HITLIST.LINKTEXT LIKE ?");
```

Continued on Following Page

```
            getHitsSQL = connection.prepareStatement("SELECT HITLIST.* FROM
                    HITLIST ORDER BY HITLIST.SCORE DESC");
    }
    catch(SQLException sqle)
    {
        System.out.println(sqle.toString());
    }
}
```

We begin with the statement to clear the buffer table:

```
            clearHitlistSQL = connection.prepareStatement("DELETE FROM
                    HITLIST");
```

Then we want to extract the records which contain the keyword in their main text.
The conditional ...WHERE (SITES.PAGETEXT LIKE ?) receives our keyword/wildcard combination,
and using the pattern matching of Like pulls out the records which have the keyword somewhere in
the text. INSERT puts these records into the HITLIST table. The '...1 AS SCORE...' bit puts the value
1 into the SCORE field of HITLIST for all records, just as a starting value:

```
            query0SQL = connection.prepareStatement("INSERT INTO HITLIST "+
                    "SELECT SITES.*,1 AS SCORE FROM SITES WHERE
                    (SITES.PAGETEXT LIKE ?)");
```

Then we have a list of all pages that mention the keyword at least once in their body text in a
separate table (HITLIST), all with a ranking score of 1. To make the ranking meaningful, the next
statement checks the HITLIST records to see if the title of the page includes the keyword. It is fair to
assume that such a page would be highly relevant to the query, so we add 5 to SCORE:

```
            query1SQL = connection.prepareStatement("UPDATE HITLIST SET
                    HITLIST.SCORE = [HITLIST].[SCORE] + 5 "+"WHERE
                    HITLIST.TITLE LIKE ?");
```

The rest of the fields are checked in the same manner, and SCORE increased with a value estimated
to correspond to the relevance of the page. These queries could be neatly prepared as a single
PreparedStatement, with a '?' in place for each field and score, but for clarity they have been
expanded here. The last PreparedStatement of this method will just return all the records (complete
with SCORE fields) in the HITLIST table:

```
            getHitsSQL = connection.prepareStatement("SELECT HITLIST.* FROM
                    HITLIST ORDER BY HITLIST.SCORE DESC");
```

The next method uses the getHitsSQL statement to query the database, and puts all the results into a
Vector. So that we don't have to worry about huge lists being returned to the user, we limit the
number of results to 10. As these results are going to be displayed as strings, we don't have to deal
with the type of each individual field and can extract these as Object classes, and use the generic
toString method.

```
   public Vector getHits()
   {
      String hit = new String();
      Vector hits = new Vector();
      int hitcount;
      try
      {
         ResultSet results = getHitsSQL.executeQuery();
         hitcount = 0;
         while (results.next() && hitcount != 10)
         {
            for(int i=1; i<11; i++)
            {
               hits.add(results.getObject(i).toString());
            }
            hitcount++;
         }
      }
      catch(SQLException sqle)
      {
         System.out.println(sqle.toString());
      }
      return hits;
   }
```

Now we have a way of looking up queries in the database, we need to give the user access. All the browser stuff is dealt with by the `Wquery` class, which is another textbook servlet. The familiar code of a `doPost` method sets the header field.

```
import javax.servlet.*;
import javax.servlet.http.*;
import java.util.*;
import java.io.*;
import data.*;

public class Wquery extends HttpServlet
{
   public void doPost(HttpServletRequest req, HttpServletResponse res)
         throws ServletException, IOException
   {
      res.setContentType("text/html");
      Dbquery db = new Dbquery();
      Vector results = new Vector();
      db.prepareSQL();

      Enumeration values = req.getParameterNames();
      String name = (String)values.nextElement();
      String value = req.getParameterValues(name)[0];

      db.findHits(value);
```

Continued on Following Page

```
        PrintWriter out = res.getWriter();
        out.println("<HEAD><TITLE> Search</TITLE></HEAD><BODY>");
        out.println("<H2> Search Results </H2>");
        out.println("<P>");

        results = db.getHits();
        db.closeConnection();

        if(results.isEmpty()) out.println("<B>No matches found</B>");
        for (Enumeration e = results.elements() ; e.hasMoreElements() ;)
        {
            out.println("<A HREF=");
            out.println(e.nextElement()); // URL
            out.println(">");
            out.println(e.nextElement()); // TITLE
            out.println("</A><BR><B>Description :</B>  ");
            out.println(e.nextElement()); // DESCRIPTION
            out.println("<BR><B>Keywords :  </B>");
            out.println(e.nextElement()); // KEYWORDS
            out.println("<BR><B>Text :</B>  ");
            out.println(e.nextElement()); // PAGETEXT
            out.println("<BR><B>Citations :</B> ");
            out.println(e.nextElement()); // INLINKS
            out.println("     ");
            out.println(e.nextElement()); // LINKTEXT
            out.println("<BR><B>Links :</B> ");
            out.println(e.nextElement()); // OUTLINKS
            out.println("       
                        <B>Last Crawled :</B>  ");
            out.println(e.nextElement()); // STAMP
            out.println("</A><BR><B>Score :</B>  ");
            out.println(e.nextElement()); // SCORE
            out.println("<P>");
        }

        out.println("</BODY>");
        out.println("<P>");
        out.println("<FORM ACTION=http://localhost:8080/servlet/Wquery
                    METHOD=POST>");
        out.println("<B><P>New Search :<B>");
        out.println("<INPUT TYPE=text NAME=query SIZE=50> <INPUT
                    TYPE=submit>");
        out.println("</P></FORM>");
        out.println("</BODY>");
        out.close();
    }

    public String getServletInfo()
    {
        return "Wquery Servlet";
    }
}
```

We set up our database connection and a Vector to receive the results data. All the `prepareStatement` methods are then called:

```
Dbquery db = new Dbquery();
Vector results = new Vector();
db.prepareSQL();
```

We then need the query string provided by the user. As in `spider.Index`, only the first parameter sent by the browser is of interest:

```
Enumeration values = req.getParameterNames();
String name = (String)values.nextElement();
String value = req.getParameterValues(name)[0];
```

Then we have our string with which to build the HITLIST table:

```
db.findHits(value);
```

We get the response's `PrintWriter` to return text to the client browser, and start building the HTML:

```
PrintWriter out = res.getWriter();
out.println("<HEAD><TITLE> Search</TITLE></HEAD><BODY>");
out.println("<H2> Search Results </H2>");
out.println("<P>");
```

Then we are ready for the results:

```
results = db.getHits();
db.closeConnection();
```

The result Vector will then be enumerated, and the strings inserted into a suitable position in the HTML. It is very easy to handle the case where there are no hits, as the Enumeration will not have more elements:

```
if(results.isEmpty()) out.println("<B>No matches found</B>");
for (Enumeration e = results.elements() ; e.hasMoreElements() ;)
{
    out.println("<A HREF=");
    out.println(e.nextElement()); // URL
    out.println(">");
    out.println(e.nextElement()); // TITLE
    out.println("</A><BR><B>Description :</B>  ");
```

Note the formatting that is used here – the HTML will come out as
`<A HREF=result.url>Title of the Page</A>`, a standard hyperlink. The following few lines
generate more HTML. It is safe to assume that our user will not be satisfied on the first query, so we
finish the HTML by providing another form field for more attempts:

```
out.println("<FORM ACTION=http://localhost:8080/servlet/Wquery
          METHOD=POST>");
out.println("<b><p>New Search :<b>");
out.println("<INPUT TYPE=text NAME=query SIZE=50> <INPUT
          TYPE=submit>");
out.println("</p></form>");
out.println("</BODY>");
```

And that's it. The HTML document for the users query (`search.htm`) is:

```
<HTML>
<HEAD>
<TITLE>Search</TITLE>
</HEAD>
<BODY>
<FORM ACTION="http://localhost:8080/servlet/Wquery" METHOD="POST">
<B>Search for : </B>
<INPUT TYPE="text" size="20" NAME="query">
<INPUT TYPE="submit">
</FORM>
</BODY>
</HTML>
```

The classes are compiled as usual (remembering to change the Dbaccess database properties if
necessary), and the class should be put on the classpath. The HITLIST table should also have been
created. If used, `servletrunner.exe` should then be started. The HTML above will appear in a
browser more or less like this:

When the query is submitted, the browser reveals:

This may not be aesthetically pleasing, but it is functional. You may have noticed that to some extent the code that does the presentation has been kept separate from data processing code, and this is the reason.

Optimization & Extension

Although this code will work, it is by no means suggested as a release version. In fact, it should be classed around v0.1 alpha. There is work to be done on tidying up the code as it stands, and there are a lot of additional feature that could be added to improve efficiency. If you've read the other chapters in this book, then you should be able to make significant improvement in this code straight away. In any case, if you feel like getting your hands dirty, then here are a few suggestions.

Threading should be addressed. Although the Spider shouldn't present any problems in normal use, it is not properly thread safe. For example, a lot of clients could send URLs to the Queue simultaneously, with unpredictable results. Similarly, the client has only been built to properly handle multiple requests. If the Spider was to be extended to trawl huge sites, then it would make sense to run multiple threads (remember that the JDBC may have limitations here). Time to revise the *synchronized* keyword.

Other details of the code that could do with work include the use of the `String` class – many of these could be profitably replaced with `StringBuffers`. There are also quite a few unnecessary static variables, which are convenient for debugging but wouldn't be so numerous in a release version.

The use of `Vectors` in the Cache and Queue could be tidied up considerably, perhaps by making a generic 'record' class with a field for URL, LINKTEXT etc, and making this the element of the lists.

The database is used here in a very 'flat' manner, and more efficient access could be achieved by using several relationally linked tables possibly in the crawling phase but most certainly in the lookup phase.

Speaking of the lookup phase, the kind of query that can be given is severely limited. Possible extensions include phrase and boolean queries, and if you fancy some hard but interesting work, consider adding natural language and expert queries (perhaps using JESS, the Java Expert System Shell). It would be a start just to improve the handling of punctuation.

If the search facilities were required for a huge site, then aspects of existing search engines should be added to speed queries up. Probably the most significant addition would be to use reverse indexing to match keyword patterns. In other words, build a database with records corresponding to words, each pointing to the URLs where the word can be found.

It would be impossible in this day and age not to mention XML, so here goes: there is a class `javax.swing.text.html.parser.DTD` so work with XML is viable. The classes in this section may find use in other areas. For example, with minor modifications they could make sense of those forgotten Web bookmarks.

Links

Search Engine and Bot Related:
> http://www.searchbots.net/
> http://www.botspot.com/
> http://info.webcrawler.com/mak/projecs/robots/guidelines.html

Newsgroups:
> comp.infosystems.search

Jini and JavaSpaces:
Servers of the Future

Warning: Imminent Changes Ahead

If you want to change your entire outlook of how a server application should be designed and written under the Java Platform then you should read this chapter and the next two. What is going to be said will be 'against the grain' of everything you have read so far in this entire book. Beware: *resistance is futile*; do not read this if you would never want to change your current way of doing things!!

There are lots of comments and claims made in this initial chapter, for example, of which you may be skeptical, but stick with both the claims and the code, especially that in the third chapter, and you will realize that a revolution is afoot. Reading these three chapters will change the way you envision and design complex server systems once and forever.

No new programming concept can be conveyed without first examining at a high level how it fits into the existing environment and how it works within the environment, *especially* when that concept is different or anti-establishment. So, we'll spend most of the first chapter introducing these new concepts, thus setting the stage for all the coding and system design that will happen in the chapters following.

In the interest of the 'clear illustration of concepts', many excellent performance and optimization tips introduced in the earlier chapters will **not** be used in this chapter. While these techniques do work wonders in real production life, they do complicate the code somewhat and hinder the conveyance of concepts and information. When and if you put some of our infrastructure code introduced in the later chapters into production, please practice all the excellent performance enhancing tips introduced in earlier chapters – this is said without reservation.

In the meantime, optimized code or no, you will need at least **three** networked 'heavy duty' machines running either Windows, Linux, or Solaris to try out the grand-finale distributed configuration. A good spec would involve at least a 300 MHz processor and 128 MB+ of RAM on each one. If you have access to **five** or more 'heavy duty' machines to play with, so much the better. Hopefully, being the technology collectors that most of us are, this should not present too much of a problem.

Looking Ahead: A Jini Case Study

Even though we will not take on the actual design and coding of our case study system until the next chapter, for the benefit of those readers who can carry on two threads of thoughts simultaneously (pun intended), we will describe the system infrastructure to be implemented in the final stretch of this book. In fact, you are encouraged to think about how **you** would implement it using the server and servlet technologies covered so far. Imagine the complexity involved, and the coding and administration that would be necessary. Then, we will show you how this **new way** of system design will propose to solve this same problem – in the simplest way we know how today.

An OnLine Loan Approval Website

The system in question here is an Online Loan Approval Website. Here is the major use-case scenario:

Users arrive at the website, filling in their names and membership IDs to make a request for the approval of a loan. The system then :

> verifies their name and membership ID via an in-house, internal mainframe database, pulling out their business history with the company, and

> makes a credit check, fetching a credit report from an on-line credit agency over a virtual private network (on a secured, encrypted channel) via the Internet

The results of both the above queries are routed to one of the national credit centers (the North American one works from 8 AM to 8 PM EST, and the South Pacific one works from 8 PM to 8 AM EST), and displayed to a bank of live, human credit officers for approval veto and/or final acceptance.

Meanwhile, our end-users are still online, awaiting approval while this is happening. When a decision is made, they will each receive a loan approval (or rejection) page, detailing the amount approved (or the reasons for rejection). In graphical form, the component and operation of the required system looks like this:

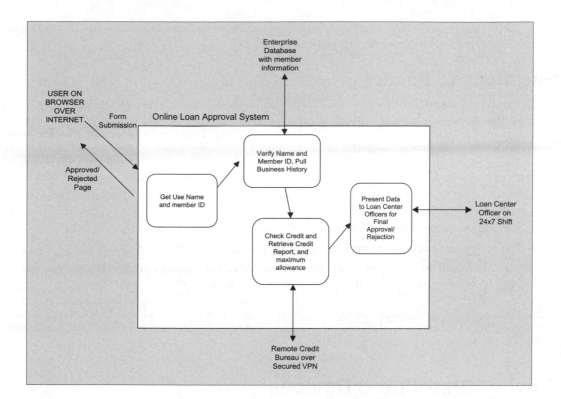

Initially, the system is required to take a relatively low volume of traffic per day – up to 1,000 loan approvals/rejections per day. However, due to the unpredictability of how popular some of the promotions may be, we need to design the system so that it can approve up to 100,000 applications per day. Roughly, that's 100,000 divided by 24 divided by 60 equals 69 approvals/rejections per minute, assuming traffic is constant. Ideally, the system should also be able to handle yet another order of magnitude increase in traffic without major re-design time and costs.

Needless to say, while the current requirements are not difficult to meet using any system design methodologies available today, the ultimate requirement – and beyond – will dictate some careful considerations at initial design time.

Design Objectives

Goals for the system, obviously, are:

> **Availability** – The system should be up and running 24 hours a day, 7 days a week. The staffed credit approval centers worldwide run 24 hours a day, as does the Internet and therefore so should it.

> **Scalability** – As the traffic increases, we should be able to add resources (things money can buy immediately) to handle the increased volume without re-design or additional implementation; the system must not hit a brick wall upon some ceiling traffic level.

> **Timely response** – The average waiting time for the end user waiting for loan approval must be under 1 minute at the low watermark (1000 approvals/rejections per day) and under 3 minutes for the high watermark (100,000 per day)

> ➤ **Throughput** – The system must meet the specified watermarks, and offer us the option to grow it by yet another order of magnitude

Questions to Ponder

The above, in a nutshell, forms a showcase for the problems that the new technology we introduce in this chapter will help us solve. For now, keep the problem in mind, and think about how **you** would design such a system today. Do not concentrate on the details of 'credit approvals through a secure network', 'in-house database verification', or 'a user interface for final human approval'; these are **easy** side issues, and having gone through the chapters in this book so far, you are well equipped to implement them. Concentrate instead on the **hard** issues – the ones related to system architecture:

> ➤ How will the server or servers work together on the system?
>
> ➤ How can you ensure availability?
>
> ➤ How can you contain response time explosion against increasing traffic volume?
>
> ➤ How will the system scale without re-design and without hitting a brick-wall when the SMP processors limit is reached on your beloved enterprise server?

So then, with the problem specified, and placed onto one of your background processing threads, let us start the introduction to this 'new' applied technology area: affordable and attainable, network based, distributed and parallel processing.

Driving Distributed Devices

Now that the high level stuff is out of the way, let's turn our attention to writing device drivers.

"What?!!", you may instinctively ask.

Having just talked about distributed, highly available server systems, what on earth do they have to do with the lowest of the low in programming – device drivers? Engineers who have had the pleasure of working with the latest cluster computing and other bleeding-edge distributed computing technologies will tell you quite succinctly – a lot! A truly distributed computing environment has its very own unique set of requirements and its own view of 'devices'. In fact, this view is quite different from that of a standalone operating system. Drawing from this analogy, we will finally commence our description of the two elusive new technologies from Sun: **Jini** and **JavaSpaces**.

Distributed Computing

While JavaSpaces, as a "distributed computing substratum", will eventually help us solve our On-line Loan Approval Website problem, Jini is the very fundamental 'low level' technology that will make all the magic possible. Trying to understand (and therefore program or code for) JavaSpaces without understanding Jini first is not a recommended avenue.

History has shown that shoving a new non-conventional operating system down developers' throats doesn't work. Shortly after the highly successful launch and licensing of the ever-popular UNIX operating system, the gurus at AT&T released a distributed OS called **Plan 9**. Judging from how many people have actually heard of this OS, one can see that the concepts were too far ahead of its time. So, with Jini and JavaSpaces, Sun is breaking up the bulky revolutionary chunk into smaller, easier to swallow, pieces for your consumption.

A Natural Dissonance

One major reason why Plan 9 was hard to swallow, and why Jini and JavaSpaces may also encounter difficulties is what I call the classic "natural dissonance". It has to do with the very same uneasy feeling that you have encountered when we switched from high level distributed system design discussions to device driver writing.

Most professional software engineers, analysts, and programmers fall into one of the categories on the classic programmer's spectrum – as illustrated below.

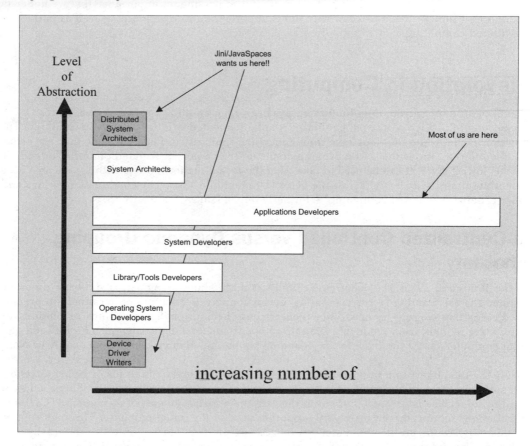

We can see clearly that the group of engineers that write and design device drivers, and who therefore understand intimately the concern and issues involved are in the minority. They often have to deal with imperfection in hardware specifications, and often code in Assembler to get the performance they need for a particular operating system. At the other extreme end of the spectrum, also a minority, are the distributed system architects, many of whom do not do any coding at all. It is their responsibility to create the actual design and simulation of a complex (frequently multi-machine or even multi-network) system.

The majority of us as application developers are caught in the middle of these two extremes and yet while an understanding of Jini requires us to put on the device driver writer's hat for a moment, the application of JavaSpaces requires us to play the distributed system architect role in contrast. One immediately senses a re-vibrating internal 'natural dissonance'.

It's not difficult to find evidence of this uneasy dissonance either. Simply visit some of the Jini and JavaSpaces newsgroups and public lists on the Internet today and on one hand you'll see the device driver specialists screaming for more rigid and precise specifications (something obtainable in the hardware filled worlds that they originate from), while the distributed systems architects clamor for abstract-level niceties, industrial-grade implementation and performance/operational guarantees on the other.

The irony is that while these specialists will contribute to the early development of Jini and JavaSpaces, it will be us – the bulk of the generalists – that will best be able to deploy and exploit the resulting technology in the near future. As such, it is of paramount importance that we understand the operation of Jini. We need to know why Jini is important on its own merit, as well as in the distributed computing context supported by JavaSpaces.

A Revolution in Computing

The popular hype surrounding Jini has always been spun around its role as a rival and/or replacement for Microsoft's well publicized – and often hated – 'Plug and Play' technology. The truth however is that while Jini does have some functional similarity to Plug and Play, they are actually totally different. Jini is the lowest programmable layer of a new distributed platform for computing. As this lowest layer, it can be used to take what the Java 2 platform offers within a single VM, and extend it (almost seamlessly) across the network to multiple VMs. The combination of Java and Jini makes "networked based computing" – formerly only a fantasy – a reality.

The Centralized Controlled versus Dynamic Grouping Dichotomy

In the 1960s and 1970s, the mainframe computers that we now recognize as 'die-hard' dinosaurs roamed the earth and the term 'computing' meant connecting teletypes or 'terminals' to prepare work for feeding these legacy systems. Since then, we have been through two distinct 'revolutions' of computing models, from the highly centralized mainframe to a departmental centralization offered by mini-computers and from there to the 'island of computing' of microcomputer Local Area Networks.

While the final microcomputer revolution was the most democratic in terms of giving the end users the computing power and autonomy they need, it also created several major problems, all extremely hard to solve. The latest such problem is the extremely high total cost of ownership (TCO) for such 'democratic' set-ups, driven mainly by support costs after the initial purchase. This high support cost is illustrative of the problem of a non-centralized environment where control cannot easily be exerted. The end user is free to install, service and upgrade software on their own computer (with or without the employer's consent), the result is a support nightmare.

The only solution to this problem must be centralized control. This time however, it must be built on top of the existing 'island of computing' created by the microcomputer revolution. In place of 'patch of the day' solutions come ever-expanding directory services, providing a mammoth chart of the sea of computers as a centralized 'navigable' entity, along with other ad-hoc technologies that provide piece-meal control over the chaos.

Similarly in the real world, management and organizational structures have moved from centralized hierarchical through tiered regional/departmental to individual empowerment and are now swinging back to a centralized structure once again. It is interesting to observe the high correlation between organizational and computing architecture and then rather unsurprising when you realize that computing resources (and therefore the architecture) are purchased to support (or match) the organization's own structure.

With the arrival of the Internet, a dynamic 'virtual workgroup' phenomenon has started to take center stage. Unlike any of the previous discussed organizational structures, this new style prescribes the formation of dynamic workgroups or teams to solve problem as needed. These task teams transcend all regular management hierarchy, departmental, and often even geographical boundaries. It leverages and taxes the communications infrastructure within an organization, and it allows quick reaction to problems with the best resources available to solve them. It comes the closest to organizational nirvana so far with one oddity – the computing infrastructure today is ill equipped to reflect this change in organizational working methods. That is, until Jini!

Jini – It is How We Work Together!

The premise of Jini is a dynamic and ever changing word of clients and available computing resources, the snapshot of which is never the same at any constant in time. This is a perfect mirror of the 'virtual workgroups' described in the last section. It is also precisely how we work together on this Internet-enabled world. Chat rooms, newsgroups and discussion forums are all examples of these ephemeral unions that we form in cyberspace thanks to a common interest or a common cause.

Jini allows us to work naturally in these environments. The Jini model provides for the ephemeral union of resources and services over the network on an as-needed basis – service provider and service user 'bond together' in the Jini world only for as long as is required to get the job done. These temporary unions are called **federations**.

Mirroring the Internet, An Uncontrolled Dynamic Federation of Birds-of-a-Feather Unions

As individuals, we surf the Internet and visit newsgroups, chat rooms, BBS, etc. In the Jini world, individual **clients** can find and use **services** that are available over the network. This grouping of client and services forms a distributed Jini system called a **djinn**. (distributed **Jini n**etwork – also another type of genie in the mythical sense)

When we surf the web, we rely on search engines (e.g. AltaVista) and listings sites (e.g. Yahoo) to point us to the resource of interest. Jini defines standard interfaces for **lookup services** that a client can use to locate services of interest. Furthermore, it also defines a **discovery protocol** for clients to get in contact with a lookup service – much like how we remember AltaVista and Yahoo as our starting points. Once the client discovers a lookup service, it can join the djinn and start using the services available via the **join protocol**. The act of a client or a service joining up to a djinn is called **federating**, and the djinn itself is also called a **federation**.

Back on the web, search engines are unlikely to help people find your site unless you have already registered with them. Likewise in the Jini world, when a service first starts up, it must use the discovery and join protocols to join a djinn and then **register** its availability with one or more lookup services. This is the only way to let clients know about their existence.

Some sites may take others further, amalgamating and consolidating others' contents into their own. Take for example the meta-search engine AskJeeves or one of the many portal-cum-linksites out there. In Jini too, there are services which make use of and consolidate the work of other services within a djinn and, just like those websites, they need not say which other services they make use of. To the client, these are just individual services (providing the consolidated functionality) that it can make use of.

The figure below puts many of these terms into perspective.

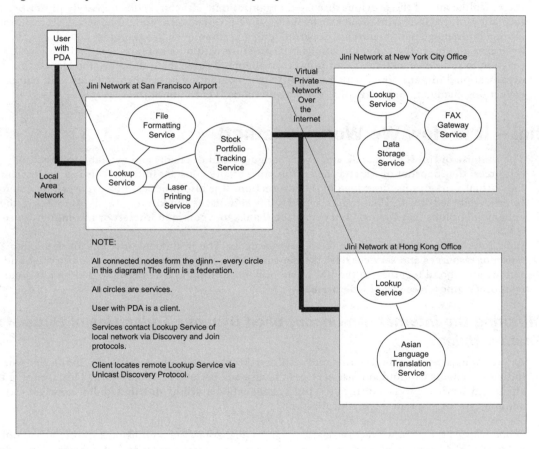

Every **federation** of **client** and **service**(s) is unique and independent. They are formed in an ephemeral (for a brief moment in time and e-space) fashion. There needs to be no obligation or history for this union. When the union is completed, the connection with the **federation** is dissolved, work is usually done and the **client** typically satisfied. It is the electronic equivalent of a highly popular 1970's concept: the one night stand.

Now if you can grasp these concepts and think they are cool, then you've absorbed the very essence of Jini itself. Congratulations!! On the other hand, if you find such a world/system unwieldy and out of control, you may consider buying the very next Microsoft technology book and maw over that instead.

A Total and Complete Lack of Centralized Control

One important thing to note about the world of Jini, as described above, is the lack of a centralized control system. There isn't one. Just as there is no way to track on an Internet-wide basis who has connected to whom for how long, the Jini world likewise does not encourage such centralized control behavior. In fact, there is no easy way to know and track all the federations that may occur in a Jini enabled world. Individually, and on a per-service basis, one can imagine writing tracking schemes to count accesses and audit resource usage. On a system wide basis, however, Jini neither specifies nor requires any centralized administration of available services, and it doesn't enforce any policies that restrict federation between client and services.

There exists no centralized directory service that keeps tracks of all namespaces in the system, there is no centralized repository of interfaces and/or code modules for perusal, no single lookup service that is more important than another, etc. Jini is the basis for a truly distributed world, potentially a completely democratized one – if we so choose.

Relinquishing Control of Jini

It would be completely hypocritical of Sun, to invent and provide such a democratized technology, one that preaches a model of 'no centralized control', and then quickly turn around and control the definition and growth of the technology itself. In order to be able to sleep restfully at night, the folks at Sun have placed the future and evolution of the Jini technology in the hands of the Jini Community at http://www.jini.org/.

The complete source code of the Jini technology (currently at the 1.0 release level at the time of writing) is available to members who have completed a SCSA (Sun Community Source Agreement), a modified version of the Open Source agreement, specifically fostering 'friendly competition' and rights to maintain intellectual properties outside of the basic infrastructure. It is infinitely more acceptable to the commercial interest, and Sun is hoping to attract them to the table with jini.org.

Enforcing Order in a World with No Centralized Control

Turning the previous point about on its head however, without laying down some ground rules, the community will descend into disorganization and chaos. So, just as the Internet has net etiquette and local legislation that ensure a certain level of order, with Jini, several standard mechanisms have been established to ensure order and interoperability:

> * the required **discovery and join protocols** for clients and services to find one another
> * the Jini specified `ServiceRegistrar` interface for the lookup service
> * the Jini specified `Entry` interface enforcing what a lookup entry should look like

To a lesser degree, there are some other fundamental components of Jini which also add to this 'law and order' in the Jini world:

> * Jini specified distributed **Events** interface and mechanism for providing distributed notifications between djinn participants
> * A distributed **lease** mechanism to reduce the impact of partial system failure, and ease the long-term cleanup situation
> * **Transaction** and **TransactionManager** interfaces to provide for Jini services that can guarantee transaction semantics across the distributed environment

We'll see later on how each of these mechanisms enable orderly operation without dictating specific implementation or design policies for Jini services.

A Jini System In Action – Remote PDA Printing

Imagine this scenario, one that can be implemented today using Jini 1.0 technology. You are on your way across the country to meet an important client. Working on your pocket PDA at a strange airport due to a delayed connecting flight, you receive a cellular phone call from your trusted assistant in the office, stating that a very important large document has arrived for you at the office in electronic form.

You must give a hard copy of this document to your client to rescue the sale from another competitor. Looking around the airport business center, you are ecstatic to find a Jini-enabled RJ-45 jack! You plug your Jini-enabled PDA into the RJ-45 jack via a supplied cable and almost instantly a selection of printers available at the business center pops up on the PDA screen. Also on the screen is an icon representing your filing system back in the office.

You click on the filing system icon, and see that your able assistant has already placed the large document there. Smiling, you configure one of the high-resolution laser printers, and then drag the document icon over the printer icon. Several seconds later, the document starts to print out on the business center's laser printer. You gladly paid the business center for the document, board the delayed flight, and have a successful business meeting.

Let's take a look again at the technologies involved here. But first, notice the following:

> Your Jini enabled PDA couldn't possibly know about the printers in the business center ahead of time.

> The document, being large and bulky, was never transferred to the PDA; it was fetched directly from the office to the business center's high speed Internet connection, and printed on the laser printer.

> You have full control of the printer options selection right from your PDA, through a graphical user interface.

Here's what is happening behind the scenes:

1. When you connect the PDA to the RJ-45 jack, the PDA immediately uses the discovery and join protocol to find all the lookup service(s) available at the business center. In this case, there is only one.

2. Shortly after connection, your PDA discovered the lookup service available and obtained an RMI interface to the service.

3. Since your office's lookup service is pre-configured into your PDA, your PDA also connects directly to the lookup service back in your home office over the business center's Internet connection.

4. The PDA performs a lookup for services available at the business center and finds the printer devices (represented by printing services).

5. The lookup service sends a proxy object (in Java), supplied by each printing service, to the PDA.

6. The PDA uses this proxy object to display the selected printer's config panel on the screen.

7. The PDA performs a lookup for services available at your remote office, and finds the file
    system service.

8. The remote lookup service also sends a proxy object (Java) from the file system.

9. Using the user interface provided by the printing service proxy object, you configure and set
    the printer for printing your document.

10. When you drag and drop your document to the configured printing service, the file system
    proxy object co-ordinates the transfer and printing of the document from your remote office to
    the printer without going through the PDA.

The diagram below shows this sequence of operations.

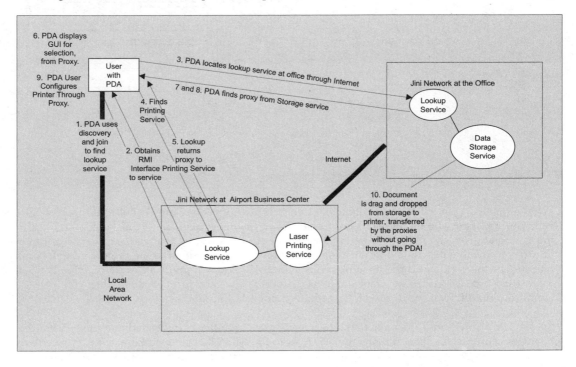

The thing to note here is the extensive leveraging of Java's ability to transmit behavior (code) through
the wire. Without this capability, it would be very difficult for the lookup service to provide the PDA
with a proxy object of the printer (an intelligent driver, if you will). Thanks to the Java platform, a
GUI 'applet' can be supplied by the proxy to actually display a configuration user interface on the
PDA. Once configured, the proxy object can use whatever method it wants to communicate back to
the printer and perform the actual configuration. Since the proxy object is supplied by the printer
itself, it would know intimately how to configure the printer. The figure below depicts this
transmission of proxy objects. All proxy objects are 100% Java objects that are downloaded
automatically (via the class loader) and executed in the Java VM on the PDA. All of this is made
possible by RMI.

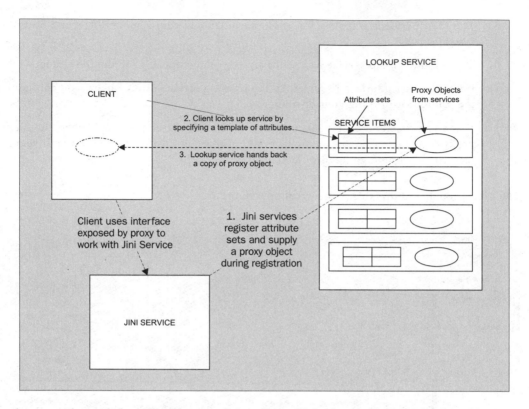

What happens if you click on the file icon of the remote file system and do not find the file? You then call your assistant who immediately copies the file to the file system. In this instance, the implementation of the file system proxy object on your PDA can be written to make use of Jini events in order to receive distributed notification of whenever a file is added to the remote system. Going one step further, the basic Jini lookup service actually provides support for notifying clients whenever a specified type of service registers and joins the djinn. Thus any printer added after you have connected the PDA to the djinn can immediately show up on the display.

So, having printed your document, you hear your plane number being called and hurry from the business center to the gate, pulling your PDA from the RJ-45 jack and walking away. How will the business center's Jini system know that you are through with the printer? Furthermore, how will the remote file system know it is okay to allow removal of the large file? The solution lies in the use of **leases** throughout the Jini system. When resources are granted to the client, like the printer was to the PDA, they are granted on a time-limited lease. If the client wishes to continue using the resource after the lease is due to expire, it must renew the lease before this happens. If it does expire, all the resources associated with it will be released back to the djinn, providing a long-lived, self-healing system.

Peeling Back The Layers Of Jini

The momentum now behind the Jini effort is such that it is bound to change shape and form as it evolves. Jini 1.0, meanwhile, importantly provides a basic yet workable foundation of interfaces and reference implementations that we can experiment and code with today.

In this next section, we'll drill down a few levels into a Jini implementation looking at the various key protocols, interfaces and classes that every Jini programmer needs to be aware of. We'll start with a proper look at the Discovery and Join Protocols.

The Discovery and Join Protocols

There is no single protocol which a Jini implementation uses as its discovery and join protocol. In fact, during the course of discovering and joining a djinn, a service may actually use three:

> ➢ Unicast discovery protocol
> ➢ Multicast announcement protocol
> ➢ Multicast discovery protocol

All three protocols are designed for clients and services to discover (and connect to) lookup services within a djinn but since their default implementations are provided within the Jini libraries, there's no reason not to use them for other (service implementation) purposes.

During the discovery and join process, services find lookup servers and register with them according to the groups that are specified by owners/administrators. **Groups** are on-the-wire text based names for djinns advertised by the discovery protocols, allowing services to federate together. A default group, called **public**, but signified internally with an empty string is always available in any Jini system.

The Unicast Discovery Protocol

The simplest protocol of the bunch is the **Unicast Discovery Protocol**. This is typically used by a client/service to connect to a lookup service that it already knows the IP address of and also to connect disjoint Jini systems across a wide-area-network (i.e. the Internet). All the other discovery protocols rely on UDP multicast to function properly. In order to reach systems that are out of the coverage of UDP multicast, this protocol must be used.

> **UDP (User Datagram Protocol) is one of the three core Internet protocols (The others are TCP and IP). Unlike TCP, which only allows one-to-one (unicast) connections, UDP allows multicast (one-to-many) networking.**

In UDP, the lookup service monitors requests (playing the part of a unicast discovery service) at a well known port by setting up a TCP server. The port listened to is at **CAFÉ-BABE**, which when translated to decimal is **4160**.

Any client wishing to talk to this lookup service (and have its IP ready), can connect to the lookup service through port 4160 and submit a **discovery request**. This discovery request contains the names of the groups that the client is interested in. If the lookup service supports one of the groups requested, it will respond to the request and pass a reference (RMI stub) to an object supporting its `net.jini.core.lookup.ServiceRegistrar` implementation. The client can make use of the lookup service through this Java RMI stub.

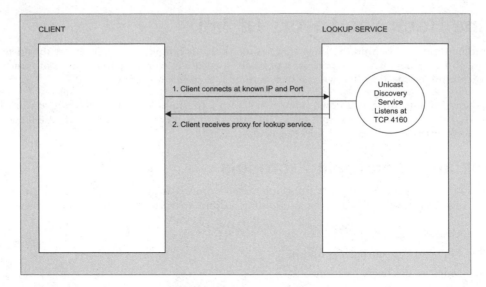

The Multicast Announcement Protocol

This protocol is used by lookup services to multicast their existence at regular intervals. These multicasts are made via multicast UDP packets to **IP 224.0.1.84** and **port 4160**. Indeed, all lookup services are obliged to do this.

A client/service wishing to locate a lookup service will use the Multicast Request Protocol at first (see description in the next section). If this fails, it then falls back to listening for the announcement multicast made by the lookup service(s).

Services or clients that wish to discover the lookup service will bind to UDP port 4160 and listen explicitly for these UDP multicasts. By comparing the groups found in the announcement against the group that it seeks, the client/service can then use the Unicast Discovery Protocol described earlier to connect to the lookup server, and obtain the RMI stub to an object with the `net.jini.core.lookup.ServiceRegistrar` implementation as required.

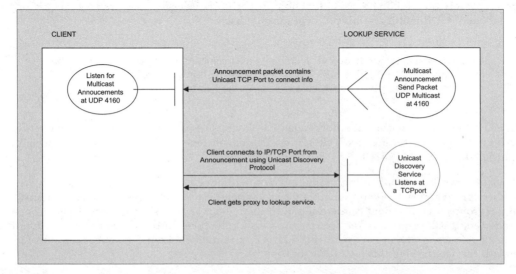

The Multicast Discovery Protocol

The Multicast Discovery Protocol builds upon the previous protocol, and is actually one of the most complex in the Jini suite.

The client/service wanting to locate a lookup service sets up a TCP server to listen for connection to support the Unicast Discovery Protocol as detailed above (but not necessarily at the well known port). It then uses UDP multicast over **224.0.1.84 port 4160** to let listening lookup services (they are obliged to listen at this port) know about the request. The request multicast packet will contain information on the client/service's own IP and port for the TCP server, the groups wanted, and the services already heard from.

The lookup services are required to be set up to listen for multicast discovery. They will examine the multicast message, make sure the client/service has not already heard from it, and then check the groups requested against their own list. If a match is found, the lookup service will respond by connecting to the listening TCP server on the client/service via the Unicast Discovery Protocol and supply an RMI stub to an object with its net.jini.core.lookup.ServiceRegistrar implementation.

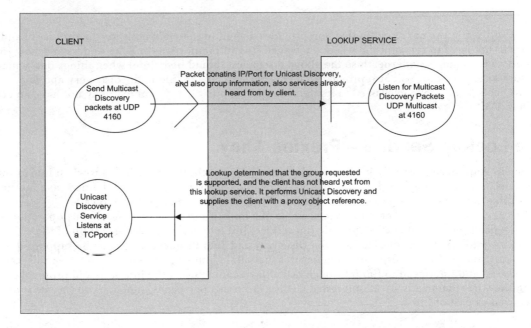

No matter which protocol is used, the net result is that the client/service within the **djinn** will receive an RMI reference to the ServiceRegistrar (actually an object supporting the net.jini.core.lookup.ServiceRegistrar interface). Once this reference is obtained, the client/service can then use it to perform lookups or export its services.

The Join Protocol

The join protocol describes how a service object should behave in order to export its services to one or more lookup services in one or more djinns. Most of the specifying conditions are quite straightforward:

> ➤ For each group/djinn that a service belongs to, it should register itself with every lookup service supporting that group – located via the discovery protocols.

> ➤ During registration, the service must use the same service ID (described shortly) and register the same set of attributes with all lookup services.

> ➤ The service must manage its lease with the lookup services.

> ➤ If an attribute associated with a service is changed, the change must be made on all lookup services it has registered with.

> ➤ The service should maintain a persistent list of lookup services which should be connected to via the unicast discovery protocol at startup.

> ➤ The service should maintain a persistent list of groups to join which should be used during discovery

We will see in the next section that Sun provides default implementations for the protocol handlers so we do not have to reinvent the wheel. However, it is still important for us to understand how Jini performs its magic underneath so the above discussion should be helpful when things don't quite work as expected. It will also provide some insight into how to mimic the discovery and join protocols, should one ever need to implement a Jini compatible system that may not have an actual Java VM!

The Lookup Service – Proxies Ahoy

The lookup service is really just another Jini service. As such, it can decide to work in one or more djinns. On an abstract level, it provides a service to its client through a well defined Java interface just like any other Jini service. In this case, the interface is defined by Jini and called `ServiceRegistrar`. The only special status of a lookup service is that fact that its operation and existence is fundamental to a dynamic Jini service. Jini fully specifies the operation of the `ServiceRegistrar` interface and the **Discovery and Join Protocols** that must be supported by a lookup service. This full specification ensures that all the implementations of such a service can be accessed and interfaced to (both through actual Java coding using the interface and protocol coding on-the-wire) identically by all interested clients. From this perspective, the lookup service is often viewed as part of Jini.

Peer Lookup

In fact, if the clients and services in a Jini system have advanced knowledge of each other and the djinns that they belong to, a lookup service is not strictly mandatory. In a system without a lookup service, all the members of a djinn locate each other via direct lookup using only the Unicast Discovery Protocol. However, the chief advantage of dynamic unions may be lost on a system that uses this **peer lookup** behavior exclusively.

Basic Requirements for A Lookup Service

We have talked a lot about the lookup service so far, without really knowing how it works in detail. A Jini lookup service must be able to:

> implement the discovery and join protocol to allow clients/services to locate it.

> allow service registration based on a set of attributes.

> generate and provide services with globally unique **service IDs**.

> maintain the mapping of service and attributes in a persistent manner.

> lookup services based on a template supplied.

Internally, the lookup service keeps track of a collection of **service items**, each of which is a mapping between **attribute sets** and a **proxy** object to the service. The `ServiceItem` class is defined as:

```
public class ServiceItem implements Serializable
{
    public ServiceItem (ServiceID serviceID, Object service,
                        Entry[] attributeSets);
    public ServiceID serviceID;
    public Object service;
    public Entry[] attributeSets;
};
```

The attribute sets associated with a service can be modified. Since each attribute can contain a Java object, it is possible to use them to provide other interface objects for the service. In most cases, however, attribute sets are used for **template matching**, when a client looks for a specific service. The **ServiceID** type contains a 128-bit globally unique identifier (often called a **UUID** or a **GUID**) generated by the lookup service when it first registers a service. This then becomes the service's identity across all djinns and should be persisted by the service accordingly. Note that `attributeSets` is an array of `Entry` types – we will see what an Entry is in the next section.

Lookup by Type and Templates

The quintessential function for a lookup service is to search for services available within a djinn based on some criterion. With the Jini lookup service specification, this criterion can be:

> an interface (type) supported by the service proxy

> a template consisting of a set of specified attributes

A primary use of the first criterion is for locating industry standard support. For example, we could look for services supporting the `com.wrox.WroxJiniServices.IWroxJiniService` interface and the end result will be all services that implement this interface (as well as interfaces extending this interface). More realistically, when the printer and storage working groups complete their work, we can look up printers and service devices by looking up the specific interfaces that they end up agreeing upon.

In the second case, a set of attributes is specified as an instance of a Java class, where each public member field is an attribute. In this way, each attribute will carry with it a Java type (class), as well as a specific instance value. The general form that a set of attributes must conform to is specified in the `net.jini.core.entry.Entry` interface, which you can find in Appendix N.

Definition of an Entry

The `net.jini.core.entry.Entry` interface is a simple marker interface that all attributes sets (sometimes called **lookup entries**) in a lookup service must support. It has no methods or fields of its own. However, all of its descendents can have fields and methods, but they must ensure that all public fields are serializable object references.

A helper class, `net.jini.entry.AbstractEntry`, is provided to give a base class when you implement your own lookup entry (attribute sets) as you'll see later on when we start coding.

In practice, there are already several pre-implemented Jini lookup entries that you may use, each of which inherit from `net.jini.entry.AbstractEntry`. They contain the most commonly used lookup attributes so, most of the time, you will not need to define your own custom lookup entry.

Entry Class	Fields	Description
`net.jini.lookup.entry.ServiceInfo`	*java.lang.String* manufacturer; *java.lang.String* model; *java.lang.String* name; *java.lang.String* serialNumber; *java.lang.String* vendor; *java.lang.String* version;	
`net.jini.lookup.entry.ServiceType`	*java.lang.String* DisplayName; *java.awt.Image* Icon; *java.lang.String* ShortDescription;	This class is read-only. It also implements the `net.jini.lookup.entry.ServiceControlled` marker interface, meaning that the field values cannot be changed by the client.
`net.jini.lookup.entry.Name`	*java.lang.String* name;	Used in naming a service for searches. This entry is frequently used.
`net.jini.lookup.entry.Address`	*java.lang.String* country; *java.lang.String* locality; *java.lang.String* organization; *java.lang.String* organizationalUnit; *java.lang.String* postalCode; *java.lang.String* stateOrProvince; *java.lang.String* street;	Used in specifying the address of a device and or service.
`net.jini.lookup.entry.Location`	*java.lang.String* building: *java.lang.String* floor; *java.lang.String* room;	Used in specifying the location of a device or service.

Entry Class	Fields	Description
net.jini.lookup.entry.Comment	*java.lang.String* comment;	Used to add comments to a service/device. Useful if the client provide user interface for selecting service/devices.
net.jini.lookup.entry.Status	*net.jini.lookup.entry.StatusType* Severity;	This class is read-only. It also implements the net.jini.lookup.entry.ServiceControlled marker interface, meaning that the field values cannot be changed by the client. In operation, it may be modified by the service itself to indicate status.

To use one of these pre-defined entries, the coding can be as simple as:

```
import net.jini.lookup.entry.*;
...
Entry [] myAttributeSets = new Entry[] { new Name("WroxService") };
```

In this code, we have created myAttributeSets with only one set of attributes. The set contains the pre-defined Name entry.

When you create a new custom entry (as we shall do later), you should also create a JavaBean associated with the Entry to store its attributes and make them available to browsers and editors. It could even provide a custom editing user interface for these tools if you want. There's more on the creation of JavaBeans in Chapter 23 and if you look into the Extended Jini API documentation online, you will find a JavaBean class for each of the pre-defined Entries.

The ServiceRegistrar Interface

The main interface to the lookup service, net.jini.core.lookup.ServiceRegistrar, is defined as follows:

```
public abstract interface  ServiceRegistrar
{
    public final static int TRANSITION_MATCH_MATCH;
    public final static int TRANSITION_MATCH_NOMATCH;
    public final static int TRANSITION_NOMATCH_MATCH;

    public String[ ]           getGroups( )
                                    throws RemoteException;
    public LookupLocator       getLocator( )
                                    throws RemoteException;
    public ServiceID           getServiceID( );
    public Class[ ]            getEntryClasses( ServiceTemplate tmpl)
                                    throws RemoteException;
```

Continued on Following Page

```
        public Object[ ]          getFieldValues( ServiceTemplate tmpl,
                                                  int setIndex,
                                                  String field)
                                          throws NoSuchFieldException,
                                                 RemoteException;
        public Class[ ]           getServiceTypes( ServiceTemplate tmpl,
                                                   String prefix)
                                          throws RemoteException;
        public Object                 lookup( ServiceTemplate tmpl)
                                          throws RemoteException;
        public ServiceMatches         lookup( ServiceTemplate tmpl,
                                              int maxMatches)
                                          throws RemoteException;
        public EventRegistration      notify( ServiceTemplate tmpl,
                                              int transitions,
                                              RemoteEventListener listener,
                                              MarshalledObject handback,
                                              long leaseDuration)
                                          throws RemoteException;
        public ServiceRegistration register( ServiceItem item,
                                             long leaseDuration)
                                          throws RemoteException;
    }
```

The most frequently used method of these is `register()`, which lets a service register with a lookup service. Notice that a service item (containing the service proxy object and an `Entry[]` array of attribute sets) must be created and passed as a parameter, as well as a desired lease duration. The service ID field will not be available (null) if the service is registering for the first time in which case the service should also examine the `ServiceRegistration` object for the assigned ID. It is quite important to persist and reuse this assigned ID every time the service startup because the lookup service will replace entries based on this ID alone. If you use a new service ID each time you register, the lookup service may end up with stale references to your service.

The two forms of the `lookup()` method can find either one or more matching services for a given template as specified in `net.jini.core.lookup.ServiceTemplate`.

```
    public class ServiceTemplate implements Serializable
    {
      public ServiceID serviceID;
      public Class[]    serviceTypes;
      public Entry[]    attributeSetTemplates;
      public           ServiceTemplate    (ServiceID serviceID,
                                            Class[] serviceTypes,
                                            Entry[] attrSetTemplates)
    };
```

Any fields that are not filled in (i.e. left to be null) are considered wild cards. So then, filling in a `ServiceID` will match only a unique service and completing the `serviceTypes` array will match all services supporting the specified interfaces and/or (super) classes with the specified type. Meanwhile, by specifying the `attributeSetTemplates` field, one can match services based on any of the attributes associated with a service.

The multiple match form of `lookup()` returns an object of type `ServiceMatches`. Here is how it is defined:

```
public class ServiceMatches implements Serializable
{
    public ServiceItem[] items;
    public int          totalMatches;
    public              ServiceMatches (ServiceItem[] items,
                                        int totalMatches);
};
```

Once an object of this class has been returned from the search, we can use it to determine the number of matches, and examine each `ServiceItem` that has matched. Our actual goal – the proxy object for the service we want to use – is easily extracted from the `ServiceItem` field.

Here's a quick rundown of the remaining methods in the `ServiceRegistrar` interface:

> The `notify()` method is used by the client to register for notification when a service matching the template specified registers.

> The `getEntryClasses()`, `getFieldValues()` and `getServiceTypes()` methods are used to match subsets of the services registered in a lookup service. These methods are typically used by browser tools to display a hierarchical view of the service attributes.

> `getServiceID()` returns the service ID of the lookup service itself. A persistent ID (as long as you do not destroy the storage of the lookup service), the lookup service always registers with itself using this ID.

> `getLocator()` retrieves a `LookupLocator` class that can be used with the Unicast Discovery Protocol to directly connect to this lookup service (**peer lookup**).

> `getGroups()` returns the name of the groups (djinns) that this lookup service belongs to.

This concludes our brief discussion of the lookup service.

Three Ways to Implement a Proxy Object

When one gets down to implementing a proxy object, there are basically three ways this can be handled. First, we'll take a brief look at each of them and then later, we'll write some code to illustrate how to implement each of these proxy objects.

Completely Local Proxy

A completely local proxy object implements its entire interface via local code and once it is received by the client, it is executed only within the client VM. In effect, the proxy never connects back to the network in any way, and cannot control anything outside of its new host VM.

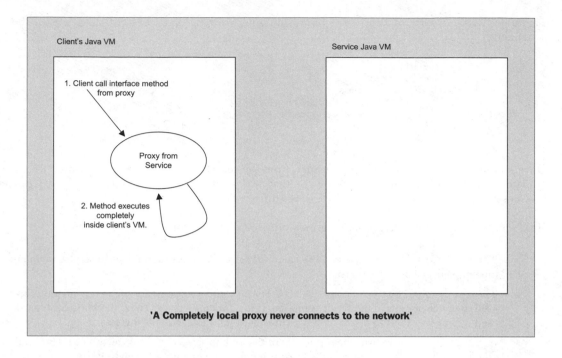

This may sound a little stupid and look like nothing more than simple remote class loading, but in the real world, there are many scenarios where a completely local proxy may be a viable implementation alternative. Here are just a few examples:

> Code for rent service – for example, a highly proprietary encryption system available on lease as a Jini service. In this case, the encrypting and decrypting proxies are hosted on the client machine and both have a built-in timed self-destruct. The client is billed for usage each time the encryption and decryption is used.

> Specialist calculator service – for example, a complex mortgage/mutual funds analyzer. This service can include all the required analysis data with the proxy object, thus eliminating any network traffic back to the actual server and allowing it to service a very large user base.

> A debugger or probing service for another service – in this case, the debugger/probe is code that the client needs to 'x-ray' the other service with. The client has no interest in keeping the complex proxy code around after the debugging session, so the debugger/probe proxy works locally, investigating the proxy of the target service currently executing in the client.

RMI stub as a Proxy

If the interface supported by your proxy is an actual remote (RMI) interface, it is possible to use the RMI stub (a Java object on its own) as the proxy object. In this case, all calls that the client makes through the interface will be remoted. Typically, this will be a very expensive operation, requiring multiple network round trips on each and every call. Using the RMI stub as a proxy should be the very last option one considers where designing a Jini service, but, to prove the exception to the rule, there are two scenarios where this option is justified:

Bootstrapping – as the very first service that a client encounters. In this case, there really is no alternative to multiple trips to and from the client as it doesn't have any data or code that the remote service can work on yet. The first `ServiceRegistrar` interface obtained for a lookup service could be implemented as a RMI stub proxy, but for added flexibility and efficiency, even this interface is not defined to be remote! Of course, your own Jini implementation has the option one way or another and it should be considered, especially if it uses peer lookup.

Instant legacy code to Jini translation – Thanks to the significant lead RMI technology had before the arrival of Jini, there exist large bodies of RMI code that can be converted to Jini services simply by wrapping these RMI interfaces up with the support for lookup registration. The many 'RMI wraps' of mainframe and legacy systems such as CICS and AS/400 can thus be rapidly made available as Jini gateway services!

While this is not the recommended way to design a Jini system, it is a totally viable alternative that will be used in real life. The idea here is that any standalone, tested and operational RMI interface that you have today can instantly become a Jini service.

The figure below illustrates the operation of an RMI stub acting as the proxy object for a service.

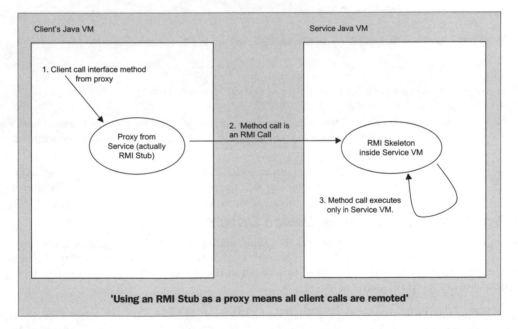

'Using an RMI Stub as a proxy means all client calls are remoted'

Smart Proxy

The third kind of proxy is the most usual. In fact, most proxies you find on Jini services will be of this variety. The '**smart proxy**' is smart because it performs work both locally (in the client's VM) and also remotely (anywhere else, not necessarily in a Java VM at all). Electing to implement your proxy object in this way will give you maximum flexibility in design. The proxy can choose to wrap an RMI stub object (that it will call internally only as needed) for communications back to the server, or it could use another socket based protocol to talk to machines over the network as shown below. It can even use other proprietary means to perform its work over the network.

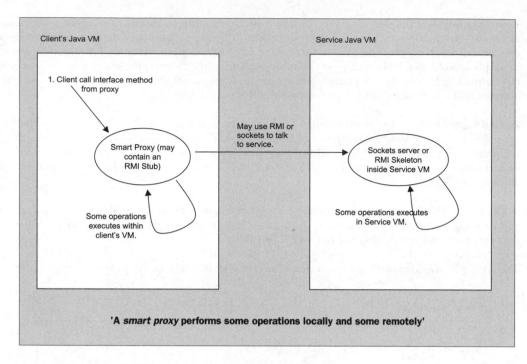

'A *smart proxy* performs some operations locally and some remotely'

There are many, many examples of this type of proxy. Here are two:

> **A printer service proxy** – Does some formatting and processing locally in the client's host VM, as well as talking to and controlling the remote printer to configure it and print the document.

> **A storage service proxy** – Performs path translations and data compression and/or encoding in the client's host VM, and then communicates with the remote storage device to actually store the data.

Why Proxies are Mistaken for Device Drivers

As you can see, each type of proxy results in a small and dedicated piece of code controlling a significantly larger system – a database, name service, filtering agent, etc – or a device (printer, storage subsystem, etc). In the prior case, this situation is not a classical concept, except perhaps in the database realm (JDBC, anyone?).

On the other hand, the idea of using a small and dedicated piece of code to control a device is classic – dating back to the very first dinosaur OS! It is called a device driver. It is no wonder that Jini service proxies are often called device drivers.

About Device Implementations

Let's carry on with the Jini service/device driver analogy where the proxy object in the client VM talks only to a physical device. How do you implement a device that can participate in a Jini network? Depending on cost, there are three basic ways to create such a device. Other implementations are possible, but they will be similar to one of the three listed below.

Devices that run a Java VM

This is the ideal situation where the device actually runs a Java VM. RMI or socket based technology can easily be used to communicate between the device itself and proxy objects that may be running in client VM(s). The only down side is that 'low end' devices typically do not have enough processing power and/or memory to run a complete Java VM. When cost is an issue, this may not be an alternative.

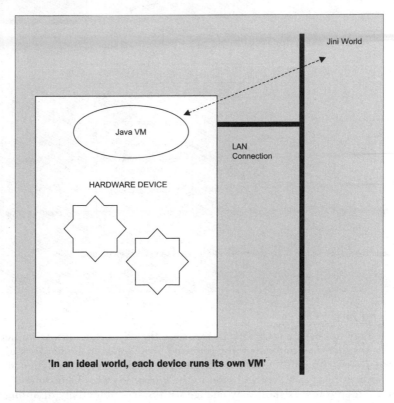

Devices that share a Java VM

In the case where a docking station or a bus may be connecting multiple devices (e.g., USB can connect up to 256 devices), it is possible for the devices to share the intelligence of a single Java VM to communicate with the proxy object in the client space. In this scenario, the proxy object sends commands via RMI or socket level protocol to the controller VM. The controlling VM then addresses the appropriate device via the proprietary native protocol over the bus. In this case, the Java VM on the device side must perform the necessary enumeration and must know the devices on the bus intimately. The cost saving can be significant in this case. In fact, in the case of a PC or workstation, the host PC can run the shared Java VM required for operations.

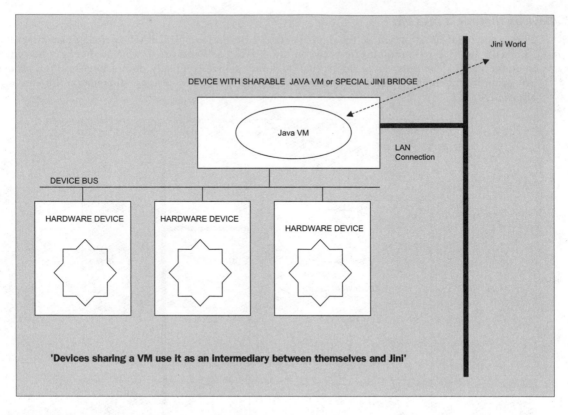

DEVICE WITH SHARABLE JAVA VM or SPECIAL JINI BRIDGE

Jini World

Java VM

LAN
Connection

DEVICE BUS

HARDWARE DEVICE

HARDWARE DEVICE

HARDWARE DEVICE

'Devices sharing a VM use it as an intermediary between themselves and Jini'

Devices that have no Java VM

Low cost devices may not have a Java VM. In this case, they'll work within a Jini network only over-the-wire. This means that they implement the required protocol over the network using their own means – assembler or C code in ROM, for example. They will also store a byte code representation of the required proxy object that they will send to the lookup service. Unfortunately, since Jini is an evolving standard, the protocol details may change with time – potentially disabling these devices from participating in the near future.

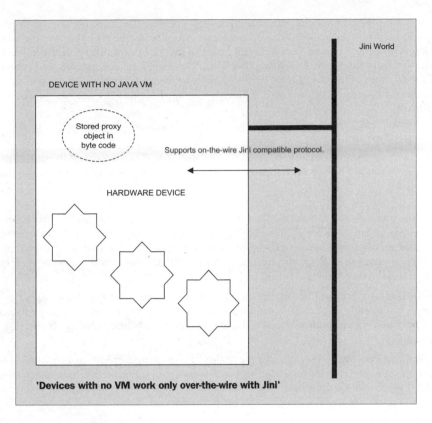

Jini World

DEVICE WITH NO JAVA VM

Stored proxy
object in
byte code

Supports on-the-wire Jini compatible protocol.

HARDWARE DEVICE

'Devices with no VM work only over-the-wire with Jini'

Printing and Storage – Areas of Initial Interest

Before we can arrive at the utopian Jini world, device and service providers must arrive at a consensus on some minimal operable interface for any particular device groups. For example, defining a base "printer" interface would enable a basic client to be written making use of this class of devices. Manufacturers adhering to the base standard could then add value with their own proprietary implementation on top of it.

This is pretty much the current focus of the Jini Community. The first two working groups turning out interface specifications will be the printing and storage groups, representing most of the "Java friendly" printer and storage manufacturers. Community members (that's you) are encouraged to form their own working groups and start mapping out the other hundreds of standard interfaces required for Jini interoperation with every other device we care about.

That said, let's turn our minds from this avenue of thought.

Proxies are Not Just Device Drivers

The proxy returned from the lookup service is an object reference that typically refers to a local object; i.e., it exists in the client's VM. In the case of a proxy implemented directly via an RMI interface, it is an RMI stub object that is passed back to the client. How this proxy ends up implementing the actual service interface for the client is left wide open.

With this variety of implementation, you should come to realize that proxies are much more than just device drivers. It is important to keep this in mind, so as not to stereotype the possibilities offered by the Jini architecture. I urge you to play an active part in the Jini community. If there has ever been a time where opportunity has been knocking, this is it. The headroom for growth and innovation in exploiting the non-device possibilities of Jini is enough to foster a healthy industry of new startup companies. Take for example, the following (inevitable) applications for proxies (and therefore services) in Jini.

Proxies for Software Systems

Existing software systems are ideal candidates for Jini services. This is especially true if the client of the service is already using the service through a TCP/IP network. Some examples that immediately come to mind are:

> **Database services**: A plain old database service, even if it is front-ending a JDBC source, can be a valuable generic service for a Jini network. With dynamic connectivity and RMI, the possibility of extending an object oriented database for use as a general purpose persistent store over a Jini network is quite exciting. Obviously, content specific databases can also expose their query facility as specialized data retrieval service in a Jini network.

> **Credit Checking Service**: The ability for clients to check credit on-line, based on a pay-as-you-go scheme, has already appeared on the Internet. With Jini, this same service can be federated into a djinn and be used in situation specific contexts to enforce business rules for financial service companies.

> **Credit Card Processing Service**: The possibility of federating a credit card processing service to complete an e-commerce transaction will enable complex transaction to take place over the Jini enabled portion of the Internet.

Proxies for Legacy Systems

As was mentioned earlier, systems that are currently running on legacy mainframe computers or minicomputers can be 'wrapped' and encapsulated in a Java object which then exposes its interface to a Jini system. This done, Jini clients can then get at both the huge store of historical data available in an enterprise and sometimes the transactioned operations of some legacy systems as well.

Proxies for Bridging to the Non-Jini World

Many Jini services could be created simply to bridge existing protocols and services, "bringing the outside world" into a Jini service. Examples include:

> **Directory Services** – Bridging large and small directory services, wrapping LDAP lookups, translating DNS lookups, etc. Effectively, this type of project could provide a 'larger' or 'wide-area' lookup service by mapping a global directory into the Jini space.

> **Middleware Services** – Bridging CORBA\COM systems and exposing them to Jini systems, bridging existing Transaction Monitors with Jini or bridging existing Queuing services to JavaSpaces, to name but three.

> **Tunneling Services** – allowing two physically disjoint Jini systems to logically federate together. For example, two TCP/IP based networks separated by a non-TCP/IP network in between.

Proxies Anywhere for Value Added Services

Taking our blue-skying one step further, it is not difficult to see that all the protocols we use daily on the Internet are subject to proxying in the Jini world. They include, but are not limited to:

> ➢ HTTP for web surfing
> ➢ FTP for file transfer
> ➢ NNTP for newsgroup reading
> ➢ SMTP/POP for mail

Why would anyone want to write a Jini service to do something that one can already get from a free browser? How will a company profit from it? Simple – by angling towards a scenario where no browsers are available. A sizable number of users – those with PDAs – are already at this point, implying that several value added Jini services would be well received even now:

> ➢ **An HTTP filtering and reformatting service** that intelligently reduces HTML pages for display on a Jini-compliant PDA. This service will allow users to surf the web while on the go, without being restricted to custom design sites.

> ➢ **A third party FTP service** for use between a source and destination on the Internet, supplying the PDA with the necessarily user interface proxy, but never involving the PDA in actual file transfer. In fact, this service was used in our 'airport document printing' scenario described earlier.

> ➢ **An NNTP data extracting and filtering service** that creates summarized information from newsgroups and presents the end result to the PDA user.

> ➢ **A mail checking and forwarding service**. This service takes requests from PDA users to check mail from several sources and gathers all the headers for presentation via a GUI proxy. The user can then select the mail they want forwarded to a POP account that the PDA can access directly.

All of the above services add value to the basic operation afforded by the underlying protocols. Many of them border on an 'Internet Agent' style of service.

Sun Provided Implementations

While the discovery and join protocols are understandable and not overly complex, and working with a lookup service is not rocket science, implementing this code in raw Java can take some heavy-duty coding and extensive testing. Thankfully, the Jini extended API provides well behaved and guaranteed compliant protocol handler implementations for both Jini services and Jini clients as follows.

> ➢ `com.Sun.jini.lookup.JoinManager` – Implements all the protocol handling requirements of a service, including the complete discovery and join protocol handling. This class will find the lookup services in the group(s) specified by you and register with all of them. It will also handle the assignment of a new ServiceID to a new service registering with the group, the renewal of leases and the keeping up to date of attributes as required by the Jini specification.

> ➢ `net.jini.discovery.LookupDiscovery` – Implements all the protocol handling requirements for a client, including the discovery of all the lookup services in the group(s) you specify, and the subsequent acquisition of the object that supports the `ServiceRegistrar` interface from each one found.

> ➢ `net.jini.core.discovery.LookupLocator` – Implements the complete Unicast Discovery Protocol for directly connecting to Jini lookup services with a known IP and port number. This is used in peer lookup scenarios, as well as bridging Jini systems across wide-area networks.

The following is a more in-depth look at each of these classes. We will be using them extensively in our coding effort throughout this and the next two chapters.

com.Sun.jini.lookup.JoinManager for Services

This is the current definition of the class:

```
public class JoinManager
{
    public                      JoinManager  (Object obj,
                                              Entry[] attrSets,
                                              ServiceIDListener callback,
                                              LeaseRenewalManager leaseMgr)
                                          throws IOException;
    public                      JoinManager  (Object obj,
                                              Entry[] attrSets,
                                              String[] groups,
                                              LookupLocator[] locators,
                                              ServiceIDListener callback,
                                              LeaseRenewalManager leaseMgr)
                                          throws IOException;
    public                      JoinManager  (ServiceID serviceID,
                                              Object obj,
                                              Entry[] attrSets,
                                              String[] groups,
                                              LookupLocator[] locators,
                                              LeaseRenewalManager leaseMgr)
                                          throws IOException;
    public ServiceRegistrar[]   getJoinSet   ();
    public LookupLocator[]      getLocators  ();
    public void                 addLocators  (LookupLocator[] locators);
    public void                 removeLocators  (LookupLocator[] locators);
    public void                 setLocators  (LookupLocator[] locators);
    public String[]             getGroups    ();
    public void                 addGroups    (String[] groups)
                                          throws IOException;
    public void                 removeGroups  (String[] groups)
                                          throws IOException;
    public void                 setGroups    (String[] groups)
                                          throws IOException;
    public Entry[]              getAttributes  ();
    public void                 addAttributes  (Entry[] attrSets);
    public void                 modifyAttributes  (Entry[] attrSetTemplates,
                                              Entry[] attrSets);
    public void                 setAttributes  (Entry[] attrSets);
    public void                 addAttributes  (Entry[] attrSets,
                                              boolean checkSC);
    public void                 modifyAttributes  (Entry[] attrSetTemplates,
                                              Entry[] attrSets,
                                              boolean checkSC);
    public void                 terminate    ();
};
```

There are three constructors for this class.

The first is used when the service registers for the first time, and doesn't yet have a service ID: the callback object in the parameter list will implement the ServiceIDListener interface and be notified with the assigned service ID as soon as it becomes available.

The second constructor is similar to the first one, but should be used only when you want to configure specific groups to join and Jini lookup services to find. The additional `groups` and `locators` arguments allow you to specify these.

The third constructor is used in the case where your service ID is known already (and the specification says you should persist it). Passing `null` for the `leaseMgr` argument will cause `JoinManager` to use the default `com.Sun.jini.lease.LeaseRenewalManager` implementation. This will keep all leases current and renewed with all active lookup services as long as the `JoinManager` instance exists.

The `callback` object passed as an argument in the first two constructors implements the `ServiceIDListener` interface, which is defined as:

```
public abstract interface ServiceIDListener extends java.util.EventListener
{
    public void serviceIDNotify (ServiceID serviceID);
};
```

The new service ID assigned to the service is returned via `serviceIDNotify()`. This is the same ID registered with all lookup service(s) in the djinn(s) by the `JoinManager`.

If you are interested in the set of lookup services that the `JoinManager` has registered your service with, you can get to them via the `getJoinSet()` method. Each member in the array returned is a lookup service that you can access immediately via the `ServiceRegistrar` interface.

The `getLocators()` method returns a set of `LookupLocators`, one for each lookup service. Each locator holds a location to connect to the lookup services directly through the Unicast Discovery Protocol. The `addLocators()`, `removeLocators()`, and `setLocators()` methods allow the programmatic management of the set of lookup services being connected to. If a lookup service is removed from the set, all existing registrations with the removed lookup service will be cancelled.

The `getGroups()`, `addGroups()`, `removeGroups()` and `setGroups()` methods manage the djinns (groups) that the service belongs to. If a group is removed from the list, the `JoinManager` implementation will ensure that registrations in all affected lookups are updated appropriately.

Similarly, the `getAttributes()`, `addAttributes()`, `modifyAttributes()` and `setAttributes()` methods manage the attribute sets associated with the service held on every lookup service within the participating djinns. Once again, the `JoinManager` takes care of notifying all the lookup services when something in an attribute set is changed.

The second form of `modifyAttributes()` checks attributes against their 'write protect' property as specified in the `ServiceControlled` marking interface. If an attempt is made to alter one of these logically read-only attributes, a `SecurityException` will be thrown.

Finally, the `terminate()` method provides a 'clean' way of terminating `JoinManager` activities. All leases with lookup services will be cancelled (implying that all unregistration is already done) before it shuts down all the threads working inside `JoinManager`. This is a somewhat cleaner way for a service to exit, instead of leaving entries in lookup services waiting to expire.

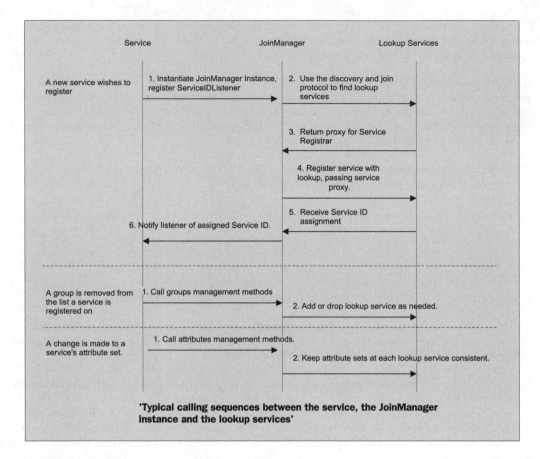

'Typical calling sequences between the service, the JoinManager
instance and the lookup services'

net.jini.discovery.LookupDiscovery for Clients

The `JoinManager` class takes all the hard work out of implementing a Jini service. The
`net.jini.discovery.LookupDiscovery` class does about the same for any Jini client. Here is
its definition:

```
public final class LookupDiscovery
{
   public static final String[] ALL_GROUPS;
   public static final String[] NO_GROUPS;
   public                    LookupDiscovery (String[] groups)
                                    throws IOException;
   public void        addDiscoveryListener (DiscoveryListener l);
   public void     removeDiscoveryListener (DiscoveryListener l);
   public void                     discard (ServiceRegistrar reg);
   public void                    finalize ();
   public String[]                getGroups ();
   public void                    setGroups (String[] groups)
                                    throws IOException;
   public void                    addGroups (String[] groups)
                                    throws IOException;
   public void                 removeGroups (String[] groups);
   public void                    terminate ();
};
```

The single constructor takes a set of group names as parameters. It will immediately proceed to discover the lookup services in the set of groups specified. The special constant, `LookupDiscovery.ALL_GROUPS`, is often used to find all lookup services within a Local Area Network, regardless of groups.

After instantiating the `LookupDiscovery` object, the client should immediately add a listening object using the `addDiscoveryListener()` method. The listening object, which could be the client class itself, must implement the `DiscoveryListener` interface. Here is the `DiscoveryListener` interface:

```
public interface DiscoveryListener extends EventListener
{
    public void discovered (DiscoveryEvent e);
    public void discarded  (DiscoveryEvent e);
};
```

The listening object will be alerted via the `discovered()` callback regarding the lookup services discovered. After the initial discovery session, any new lookup services discovered will cause another callback to the `discovered()`. The `discarded()` callback is made when an existing lookup service is discarded – we'll come back to this later.

Within the `discovered()` callback, a `DiscoveryEvent` object is passed as a parameter. This class is defined as:

```
public class DiscoveryEvent extends EventObject
{
    public                  DiscoveryEvent(Object source,
                                           ServiceRegistrar[] regs);
    public ServiceRegistrar[] getRegistrars ();
};
```

The method of interest here is `getRegistrars()`. The listener object can call this method to get an array of all the lookup services discovered. It can then proceed to use the `ServiceRegistrar` interface to perform templated searches for the desired Jini service.

Back in the `LookupDiscovery` class, the remaining methods include

- ➤ `removeDiscoveryListener()` to unregister an object for discovery notifications,
- ➤ `discard()` to discard an existing (stale) lookup service from the discovered set,
- ➤ `getgroups()`, `addgroups()`, `removeGroups()` and `setGroups()` in ,
- ➤ a 'clean' shutdown called `terminate()` as in `JoinManager`.

At the time of writing, `LookupDiscovery` has a known bug that prevents the location of lookup services supporting a specific lookup for the public group on Windows 98/NT systems. This is not a major problem, and for all experimentation, it's OK to simply use the `LookupDiscovery.ALL_GROUPS` constant and then check with the server if a particular group is supported after location.

'Typical Calling Sequences between the client and the LookupDiscovery class'

net.jini.core.discovery.LookupLocator for Peer Lookup Clients

The final helper class in this section is the `net.jini.core.discovery.LookupLocator` class. This class is useful for **peer lookup**, directly connecting to a known Jini lookup service. Here is the definition of the class:

```
public class LookupLocator implements Serializable
{
   protected String              host;
   protected int                 port;
   public                 LookupLocator (String url)
                                 throws MalformedURLException;
   public                 LookupLocator (String host,
                                     int port);
   public String          getHost ();
   public int             getPort ();
   public ServiceRegistrar getRegistrar ()
                       throws IOException, ClassNotFoundException
   public ServiceRegistrar getRegistrar (int timeout)
                       throws IOException, ClassNotFoundException;
   public String          toString ();
   public boolean           equals (Object o);
   public int             hashCode ();
};
```

Unlike its cousins, `LookupLocator` does not start discovery upon instantiation; its constructors simply set the host and port of the lookup service to be discovered. If you use the first constructor, the URL passed should be in the form `jini://<hostname>:port/`. For example:

```
LookupLocator myRemoteLookup = new LookupLocator("jini://jini.wrox.com:4232/");
```

With the second form of the constructor, you can pass in the host name and port directly. The `getHost()` and `getPort()` methods allow you access to the host name and port number which is useful if you have obtained the `LookupLocator` somewhere else – e.g. from a `JoinManager` or `LookupDiscovery` instance.

The next method, `getRegistrar()`, is the method that actually causes the Unicast Discovery Protocol to start. There are two forms of this method with the second one allowing the specification of a timeout value in milliseconds after which the discovery attempt is stopped if the lookup service has not been located.

Finally, we have three methods which override those in `java.lang.Object`:

> the `toString()` method will retrieve the URL that the locator represents

> the `equals()` method ensures that `LookupLocator` instances with the same host and port are considered equal

> the `hashCode()` method generates a hash value for serialization that is unique based on host and port number.

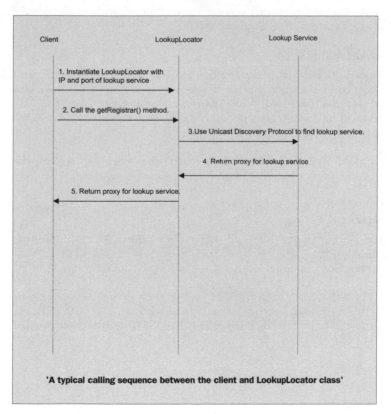

'A typical calling sequence between the client and LookupLocator class'

Plunging into the Jini Sea

Unlikely as it may sound, we have now covered everything we need to know prior to beginning the coding a complete Jini system. But before we do so, let us play with Sun's implementation of a reference lookup service. This will also give us a chance to try and set up a working Jini system on our own machines.

Prepping Your System for Exploration

As we mentioned at the top of the chapter, the rest of this chapter and the next two will assume your computer matches or betters the following specification:

> ➤ Windows NT (with SP5), Windows 98 or Windows 95 (at least OSR2 with Winsock 2 installed)
> ➤ 128 MB of memory at least
> ➤ 300 MHz Pentium II or faster

This is not a minimum spec, so if you have lesser machines, you may still want to try the examples (we did - *Ed*). In truth, your code performance will vary on more than just these recommendations. **But**, if you do not have the OS software level specified above, upgrade it! Earlier socket and TCP/IP implementation may not support all the required network functionality correctly.

JDK 1.2.1 Or Greater

Make sure too that your JDK is at least version 1.2.1. If not, download and upgrade your JVM from http://java.sun.com/products/jdk/1.2/index.html

Hotspot Optimizing VM Installation

Download and install the Hotspot performance engine as well. This VM will actually instrument and profile all your Java code execution, and then optimize and compile to native code only those segments that are executed repeatedly. In any case, make sure you have this VM installed on all the machines that you will be testing the supplied code on. You can find Hotspot at http://java.sun.com/products/hotspot/index.html

This is a warning: do not mix and match VM levels on the networked systems that you will be testing on. It only adds to the already long list of problems you may encounter when setting up a distributed system.

The Jini and JavaSpaces Kit

Download the Jini Core Platform (JCP), Jini Extended Platform (JXP), Jini Software Kit (JSK), and JavaSpaces Technology Kit (JSTK). You can find them all on one page at http://developer.java.Sun.com/developer/products/jini/product.offerings.html

Please note that you will need to sign an SCSL and join the Java Developer's Connection before you can get access to this download (current at the time of writing). The JCP, JXP, and JSK are all bundled together as the Jini Starter Kit download. The JSTK must be downloaded separately and installed on top of the Jini Starter Kit.

Verifying Connectivity Between Systems

Once you have the above downloads and installed them on all your test systems, it would be a good idea to verify that they can all see one another over the network. Use the following command:

```
PING <hostname>
```

The output should be similar to:

```
C:\WIN98>ping win98p300

Pinging win98p300.wrox.com [192.168.23.30] with 32 bytes of data:

Reply from 192.168.23.30: bytes=32 time=1ms TTL=128
Reply from 192.168.23.30: bytes=32 time<10ms TTL=128
Reply from 192.168.23.30: bytes=32 time<10ms TTL=128
Reply from 192.168.23.30: bytes=32 time<10ms TTL=128

Ping statistics for 192.168.23.30:
    Packets: Sent = 4, Received = 4, Lost = 0 (0% loss),
Approximate round trip times in milli-seconds:
    Minimum = 0ms, Maximum =  1ms, Average =  0ms
```

The important statistic to notice here is the average round trip time. If it is more than 10 ms, you may have a network problem that you should resolve before proceeding any further. Do this from every station you will be using. Make sure as well that every machine can reach every other machine using their hostnames and **not** their IP addresses. Finally, check the HOSTS file to ensure that:

➤ localhost is mapped to 127.0.0.1

➤ your own host name is mapped to its IP address

➤ all other hosts reachable from this machine have their hostname mapped

On Windows 98 and Windows 95 systems, you will find the HOSTS file in the Windows directory. On Windows NT system, you will find the HOSTS file under `<windows directory>/system32/drivers/etc`.

To compare with your own HOSTS file, ours looked like this with three test machines configured correctly:

```
127.0.0.1              localhost
192.168.23.30          win98p300
192.168.23.38          PENT166
192.168.23.34          PENT200
```

> **IMPORTANT: A warning message concerning multi-homed machines. If you have more than one network card on your machine; or if you are connected to the Internet via dial-up networking, DO NOT try the examples! This also applies to people with ADSL or cable modem connections in addition to the LAN. On Windows 98 you can disable the additional network card from the control panel, but on other OSes you may need to physically remove the network card. Trying the tests on multi-homed systems will cause untold evenings of agony fighting intermittent 'lost packets' problems. We would not wish this even on our worst enemy.**

Meet Reggie – the Reference Lookup Service

Okay, we are now almost ready to start experimenting with a Jini system. Our first **djinn** will consist of a single lookup service – the reference implementation from Sun. Its code name is **REGGIE**. You can find all its classes at \<jini installation directory>\lib\reggie.jar and \<jini installation directory>\lib\reggie-dl.jar.

The `reggie-dl.jar` file contains stubs and interfaces definition that a client will need to access the function of the lookup service. In fact, to make sure things work across the network (for example, because the remote machine has no local copy of `reggie-dl.jar`), an HTTP server must be started to serve this JAR file to the client whenever the classes are needed.

Starting the Minimal HTTP Server

Thankfully, a minimal version of an HTTP server is provided and can be found at \<jini installation directory>\lib\tools.jar. This JAR file has been configured (via the MANIFEST file) to start the HTTP server daemon if the `-jar` option is used when starting a Java VM. Thus the syntax for starting the HTTP server at port 8080 and with root directory at the Jini **Lib** directory would be:

```
java -jar <jini installation directory>\lib\tools.jar
    -port 8080 -dir <jini installdir>\lib -trees -verbose
```

The `-trees` option ask the server to scan all JAR files while the `-verbose` option will show us every single class or file that the server has served. Note that this command should all be on one line.

In fact, we will be performing this task so frequently that we have created a `.BAT` file, called `RunHTTPD.BAT` for this purpose. On our machines, this file looks like

```
set JiniPATH=D:\Jini1_0

start java -jar %JiniPATH%\lib\tools.jar -port 8080
          -dir %JiniPATH%\lib -trees -verbose
```

but the batch file is easily modified to work on your system by changing the `JiniPATH` variable to reflect where your Jini installation is located. Note that the use of `start` will cause Windows to use a new task to run the Java VM, leaving us conveniently at the command prompt to do more work. If you run this batch file now, you should see a list of JAR files displayed by the HTTP server as it scans the directory, something similar to:

```
d:\jini1_0\lib\Sun-util.jar
d:\jini1_0\lib\tools.jar
d:\jini1_0\lib\jini-examples.jar
d:\jini1_0\lib\jini-ext.jar
d:\jini1_0\lib\jini-core.jar
d:\jini1_0\lib\jini-examples-dl.jar
d:\jini1_0\lib\outrigger.jar
d:\jini1_0\lib\transient-outrigger.jar
d:\jini1_0\lib\pro.zip
d:\jini1_0\lib\outrigger-dl.jar
d:\jini1_0\lib\transient-outrigger.jar
d:\jini1_0\lib\pro.zip
d:\jini1_0\lib\space-examples.jar
d:\jini1_0\lib\jini-examples.jar
d:\jini1_0\lib\jini-ext.jar
d:\jini1_0\lib\jini-core.jar
d:\jini1_0\lib\space-examples-dl.jar
```

Now, if instead of the above, you are seeing a stack trace or exception report, you have a network problem that you will need to fix before proceeding.

> **IMPORTANT: Many developers have all sort of web servers, ICQ, custom servers, all running on their experimental systems. Stop all servers before trying these examples! The use of port 8080 on a machine is quite common on many servers, and our examples use it.**

Quickly, before we start REGGIE, we must side-track and recap some RMI fundamentals. This is aimed primarily at those who have seen and used RMI before, but for those who haven't, it's hoped that you can pick up the ideas we point out. A basic understanding of RMI is required simply for the next steps in our Jini coding to make sense.

A Quick RMI Recap

RMI stands for **Remote Method Invocation**. It is a basic technology enabled by the Java 2 Platform. When RMI is used,

> ➢ Method invocations may cross VM boundaries and/or be transmitted over a network.

> ➢ Parameters passed in method invocations can be remote object references

> ➢ All the parameters passed to a remote method call must be serializable – they must implement `java.io.Serializable`

> ➢ Call by copy is possible when making RMI calls, causing both data and behavior to be transmitted to the callee

This last point is the most interesting. In reality, the parameter object is serialized over the wire – thanks to `java.io.Serializable` – and is then re-constituted at the receiving end. The two objects that perform this tunneling (called marshaling in RMI-speak), are the stub and skeleton objects for the interface. The object at the caller is the stub, and the object at the callee is the skeleton. A basic RMI operation thus looks like this diagrammatically.

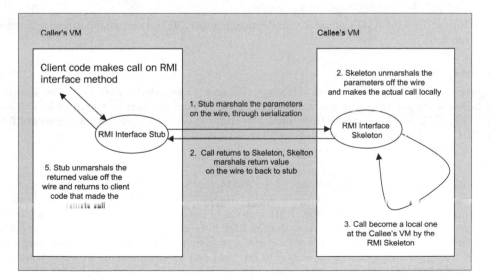

Note that the remote VM fielding the call must somehow have:

> the class definition of the skeleton object, and
> the class definition for any parameters that the skeleton needs to re-constitute at the other end.

These class files are loaded as and when they are needed, just like any other Java class in a program. However, in this case, they must be loaded from across the network. This is where the HTTPD server comes in. A system property called `java.rmi.codebase` can be set for a RMI server. It should be set to a URL pointing to the server that can serve the required class files, for example:

```
java.rmi.codebase=http://win98p300.wrox.com:8080/
```

Once this property is set, any remote object reference exported from the server will have the `codebase` embedded in its serialized form (called annotation in RMI-speak). This will tell the receiving end how and where to find the corresponding class definition file.

Client Transparency

The fact that a particular interface is remote is relatively transparent to the client. The client simply makes a call on a method of an interface. The only tell-tale sign is the existence of `RemoteException` on any remote method call (or local calls that are in turn composed of one or more remote calls). This is necessary due to the fact that the network can fail at any time during the method invocation or passing of return value.

Steps to Create RMI Callable Remote Interfaces

The steps to creating an RMI callable remote server object are:

> Define an interface that extends the `java.rmi.Remote` marker interface. This is called the remote interface.
> Implement the object that in turn will implement the remote interface. We call this the remote server object.
> Compile the remote server using `javac`.
> Run `rmic` – the RMI Compiler – on the resulting class file to generate the stub and skeleton required.

RMIC Binary Parsing

Note that `rmic` in the last step above actually works on the compiled binary class file. This is what distinguishes a 'native' remoting mechanism such as RMI from an alien one such as CORBA and/or COM. With RMI, interfaces are defined normally and stub/skeleton generation comes not from special IDL files, but from the compiled binaries.

RMIregistry

Before Jini, the most popular way to start up an RMI based system was via a bootstrap name service known infamously as the **rmiregistry**. This utility, originally intended for demonstration purposes, had become the de facto way to start up RMI systems because it gave us an answer to a question faced by any RMI based system – how to get the initial object reference. When using the RMI registry, the solution is simply to have a TCP server always listening to a well known port – in this case, **1099**. Remote clients can then connect to this port and obtain a remote object reference via a name mapping. Effectively, rmiregistry acted (and still acts) as a port mapper.

Jini, then, introduces two big differences to the RMI system equation, the first being that while rmiregistry can only map local services, the Jini lookup service can be running anywhere on a djinn and all RMI based services within the djinn can make use of it. The second is the facility with which a remote server can be written thanks to the friendly default implementation of `JoinManager`. Furthermore, the code factoring of a Jini service hides very well the support requirement for a bootstrap service.

There still remains one problem, however. Even in Jini. How do you start up the required services of a Jini system? One by one, by hand is certainly one answer: with rmiregistry in fact, it is the only answer.

RMID

With the arrival of Java 2, RMI has gained a new 'activation' executable called RMID, or **the RMI Daemon**, which supports 'activation on demand'. In a nutshell, RMID implements a reference to remote objects not yet activated until a method of the object is invoked by the client, as shown.

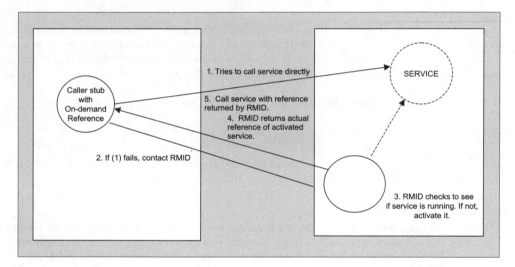

RMID is the key to enabling 'activation on demand' and creating 'activation on demand' references. Services trying to acquire such a reference must first create or setup an activation group that the service object will run in. In reality, each of these groups is a separate Java VM started and managed by RMID. Calls to create a group then must be fully qualified with codebase, classpath, location of security policy file and so on. In addition, they also need to hold specific information about starting the server object itself – an Activation Description – which will be submitted to RMID for registration. Once registered with RMID, an 'activation on demand' reference to the object will be returned. This reference can then be submitted to the Jini lookup service, etc.

What this all means is that the only process that must run all the time on a server is RMID. It also means that RMID is the parent process to all VMs (Activation Groups) running RMI activated objects.

The Need for Persistence

In fact, the new RMI activation system provides an easy way, finally, to implement the semantics of a persistent service – one that always runs and maintains its state between reboots/failure. This is obviously vital if we need to be able to build high availability and robust systems.

When the setup application registers the Activation Description for a service object with RMID, it has an option to set the 'restart mode' of the service object. One restart mode is to always start the service when the RMID restarts. Combining this restart mode with the service object's own implementation of persistent state, one can design a persistent service that can survive crashes and reboots.

Steps in Bringing Reggie to Life

With an understanding of RMI and RMI Activation, we are ready to tackle REGGIE – the Jini lookup service. Now that we have already started the HTTPD to serve up the required codebase downloads, we are ready to startup the almighty RMID.

Always Run RMID First

The startup syntax for RMID is:

```
rmid [-J<Java VM options for RMID>] [-C<Java VM options for child VMs>]
     -log <logfile location>
```

RMID uses the logfile to keep track of the on-demand activation and persistent service registrations so that once a service has registered with RMID, it does not have to re-register after each reboot. Instead, RMID will restart it upon startup (if its restart mode is to start with RMID) or when the reference is used in a method call (if its restart mode is on-demand).

We have created a startup batch file, called `RunRMID.BAT`, and it contains:

```
start rmid -J-Xms2m -log %JiniPath%\tmp\rmid.log
```

In this case, we use the Java option -Xms2m to start the Java heap of the RMID VM at 2 MB initially. If you run this, a blank Command Prompt box will startup with RMID running.

Dealing with RMID's Log Files

Since RMID maintains its registrations in the log files, we should not be deleting them. However, during testing and experimentation, it is often necessary to delete the log files in order to force RMID to start from a blank slate. To do so, the following command works under Windows 98/95:

```
deltree <jini directory>\tmp\rmid.log
```

On Windows NT, the deltree command will not work. You need to delete the log directory using the explorer.

Getting Acquainted with Reggie

Finally, after starting both the HTTP daemon and RMID, we can now start REGGIE. The command line for starting REGGIE is:

```
java [VM options for the 'set up']
     -jar  <jini directory>\lib\reggie.jar  <codebase> <security policy file>
     <log dir>  <group list> [VM options for actual service]
```

Just like RMID, REGGIE uses log files to persist its own service ID and service registrations across restarts. Note the two different sets of VM options: one set for the initial setup program that registers with RMID, and the second set for the actual VM that will be started by RMID to run REGGIE.

We have created a `RunREGGIE.BAT` file to start REGGIE:

```
set JiniPATH=D:\jini1_0

java -Xmx8m -jar %JiniPATH%\lib\reggie.jar http://localhost:8080/reggie-dl.jar
policy.all %JiniPATH%\tmp\reggie.log public -Xmx8m
```

As you can see from the script

> The `codebase` for all the REGGIE stub classes and interfaces points to `http://localhost:8080/reggie-dl.jar`

> For testing purposes, we are using a `policy.all` file to give us unconditional access to the system.

> The REGGIE log file will be in the same directory as the RMID logs.

> REGGIE is initialized to service the `public` (default) group.

> Both the setup VM and the final service VM are started with a maximal heap size of up to 8 MB (via the `-Xmx8m` option).

REGGIE is a quiet beast. If it runs successfully, you will see a Command Prompt box pop up, stay around for a while and then goes away. This should happen with no error and or exception messages. What you are observing is the startup of the 'setup VM' that registers REGGIE with RMID. This 'setup VM' starts up REGGIE before it disappears. Once it 'goes away', you know that registration is completed, and RMID has already started REGGIE.

Running the Lookup Service Browser

With REGGIE running properly, we are ready to try a client and see Jini in action. One special client that we can run is a lookup service browser supplied as part the Jini Starter Kit. It is a class called `com.Sun.jini.example.browser.Browser`, which is contained in `<jini install directory>\lib\jini-examples.jar`.

We have created a batch file called `RunJiniBrowser.bat` that contains:

```
java -cp .;d:\jini1_0\lib\jini-examples.jar -Djava.security.policy=policy.all
    -Djava.rmi.server.codebase=http://PENT200:8080/jini-examples-dl.jar
    com.sun.jini.example.browser.Browser
```

Don't forget to modify both the Jini install directory and the codebase to reflect your locations.

In fact, if you have more than one machine setup, you should try and run the browser on another machine of the Jini network. Remember to run the HTTPD server to serve your codebase using `RunHTTPD.Bat` on this new machine. If everything is working okay, the browser's GUI should be displayed on your screen, like so.

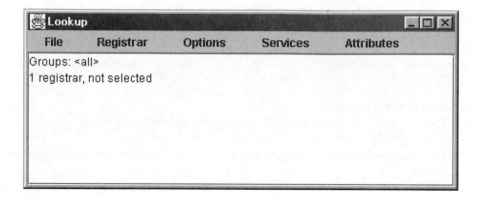

Exploring with the Lookup Service Browser

Notice that the browser is indicating one registrar has been located. Since REGGIE is currently the only service in the djinn, this is the registrar. Select the lookup service via the Registrar menu. REGGIE always registers itself after startup and you can see this by selecting the Services menu. Here, you see the three interfaces that the service supports:

> ➢ net.jini.core.lookup.ServiceRegistrar
> ➢ net.jini.admin.Administrable
> ➢ java.io.Serializable

The Attributes menu, meanwhile, allows you to select any pre-defined ServiceInfo attribute by checking the radio box set next to it. You can also view the name/value pairs for each of the attributes in the ServiceInfo attribute set. For example:

You can continue to experiment with the browsing feature of the tool. If you take a peek back in the HTTPD window, you should see a request to serve reggie-dl.jar from the browser machine. You will also see a request to serve jini-examples.jar from the REGGIE machine. This is the codebase at work here – the browser requires the stubs and interfaces to work with REGGIE, and REGGIE requires the browser's stub and classes to make call backs.

Other Basic Jini Pieces

Now we've set that up, we need to get acquainted with a few more pieces of the Jini puzzle before we go on to our own Jini service coding. We will not go into details for these pieces due to time and space constraints. However, the interested reader can consult the reference specifications at the Sun website for more details. We will also have an opportunity to examine and work with a transaction service in the next chapter.

Leases

A lease in Jini is a finite duration agreement between two Jini entities. For example, when a service submits a registration with a lookup service, a lease is granted. By designing the system in this way, resources claimed in a lease can be automatically released after a period of time. Thanks to this, a long-running Jini system

> ➢ can effectively recover from disconnections and/or partial system failure
> ➢ has the equivalent of a garbage collection process for stale and unreferenced entries and resources

A lease is negotiated between the entity requesting (by asking for a duration) and the entity granting the lease (by replying with a duration). The requesting entity is also responsible for renewing the lease before it expires if it would like to retain the resources leased. Alternatively, it can also cancel a lease before expiry.

A lease is an object that supports the `net.jini.core.lease.Lease` interface. Jini also provides a default implementation of the `com.Sun.jini.lease.LeaseRenewalManager` class, which can be instantiated and easily used by applications to maintain the automatic renewal of an arbitrary number of leases.

Transaction Service

A distributed transaction service ensures that multiple operations, across components and/or systems, are either all performed successfully as a whole (atomically) or that the components/systems will be reset to a state as if the operation has not taken place. Various levels of Atomicity, Consistency, Isolation, and Durability (ACID) can be implemented and guaranteed when working with the Jini transaction service.

The transaction service specification itself describes a set of interfaces that support the co-ordination of a two-phase commit protocol. It is up to the participants, or enlisting resource managers, to co-operatively define the exact guarantees and/or transaction semantics. If the managers are implemented using existing transaction process (TP) monitors and/or transactional database systems, industrial grade ACID operations can be achieved. There are three key interfaces of which you should be aware.

> ➢ `net.core.jini.transaction.Transaction` interface defines a transaction, with its usual `commit()` and `abort()` methods.
> ➢ `net.core.jini.transaction.server.TransactionManager` and `net.core.jini.transaction.server.NestedTransactionManager` define the interface to a transaction manager.

The implementation of the `net.core.jini.transaction.TransactionFactory` class meanwhile can be used to create a transaction associated with a particular transaction manger.

Jini provides a reference implementation of a transaction manger, code name **mahalo**, which we will be working with in the next chapter when we code our JavaSpaces system.

Events

Distributed event notification is handled via registration to event generating entities and providing objects that implement the appropriate listener interface. In this way, it can be viewed as a distributed extension of the existing JDK 1.2 JavaBean event model. In practice, the `net.jini.core.event.RemoteEvent` interface defines a remote event, while the `net.jini.core.event.RemoteEventListener` interface defines the role of a listener.

These interfaces are specially designed to cater for the less predictable event propagation characteristic over a distributed system. Specifically, it caters for having agents or middlemen that will manage and handle event registration and notification on behalf of client objects. Various flavors of event services, event managers and event filtering agents can be created readily through the current distributed events specification.

Coding Three Jini Services

Time to put the theory and concepts to work and write our own Jini Services. And, in the tradition of diving in at the deep end, we're going to write not one, but three Jini Services. Each of these will perform a very trivial task, almost like a "Hello World" program, but each of them will be doing it slightly differently. The difference will be the way in which the proxy object operates. Here is the breakdown of the three services:

Source File Name of Service	Proxy Object Operation
`LocalProxyJiniServiceImpl.java`	Proxy executes completely local to the client's Java VM. In production, we may use this architecture for complex calculator, code for rent, etc.
`RMIBasedJiniServiceImpl.java`	Proxy uses RMI stub to provide a remote interface. In production, we may use this architecture for bootstrapping a service or the quick conversion of RMI projects to Jini.
`ProxyRemoteJiniServiceImpl.java`	Smart proxy that does some processing local to the client's Java VM and some processing remotely. In production, this architecture will be frequently used for different purposes. The communication back to the 'server' or 'device' is not limited to RMI, but can use raw socket level calls instead.

The source tree can be found in your source distribution in the `com\wrox\WroxJiniServices` directory. In fact, the classes are actually

```
com.wrox.WroxJiniServices.LocalProxyJiniServiceImpl.java
com.wrox.WroxJiniServices.RMIBasedJiniServiceImpl.java
com.wrox.WroxJiniServices.ProxyRemoteJiniServiceImpl.java
```

respectively.

Defining the Standard Service Interface

All three of the services will support the `IWroxJiniService` interface. This implementing of the same interface is analogous to what the Jini Community is attempting to do, as we saw earlier.

to specify standard interfaces in vertical application areas (and for device classes), and encourage many implementations of that standard from a healthy competitive industry.

Here is `IWroxJiniService.java`:

```java
package com.wrox.WroxJiniServices;

import net.jini.core.entry.*;
import java.io.*;
import java.rmi.*;

public interface IWroxJiniService extends java.io.Serializable {
    public String grabData() throws RemoteException;
    public Entry[] getEntries() throws RemoteException;
}
```

There are a couple of things to note here. First up, `IWroxJiniService` is not a remote interface. This will ensure that implementations are not forced to use RMI Stub implementations only. Second, notice that both methods throws `RemoteException`. This is necessary for the implementation that will be using direct RMI stubs, at which instance these methods will be remote. Even in the smart proxy architecture, these methods are implemented in terms of a combination of remote methods. Note also that the interface must extend Serializable for proper marshaling.

Service Implementation with a Completely Local Proxy

Here is the local proxy service implementation found in `LocalProxyJiniServiceImpl.java`. We start with some initial declarations:

```java
package com.wrox.WroxJiniServices;

import net.jini.core.entry.*;
import net.jini.lookup.entry.*;
import java.net.*;

public class LocalProxyJiniServiceImpl implements IWroxJiniService {

    static final String SERVICE_NAME = "Jini Service - Local Proxy";
    static final String SERVICE_MFR = "Sing Li";
    static final String SERVICE_VENDOR = "Wrox";
    static final String SERVICE_VERSION = "1.0";
    static final String SERVICE_COMMENT =
                              "This is a local proxy implementation.";
    static final String LOCATION_FLOOR = "first";
    static final String LOCATION_ROOM = "computer";
    static final String LOCATION_BUILDING = "8C";
    static final String CLASS_NAME = "wroxCallable";

    public LocalProxyJiniServiceImpl() {
    }
```

With the prelims out of the way, we now need to implement the methods required for the IWroxJiniService interface. Notice that the execution of these methods is completely local to the client's VM. The InetAddress.getLocalHost() call should return the hostname/IP address of the machine where this code will be executed on.

```
public String grabData() {
    try {
        return "Executed on " + InetAddress.getLocalHost()
                + ". Data Returned locally from within the client.";
    } catch (java.net.UnknownHostException e) {
        return "Data returned locally from within the client.";
    }
}
```

getEntries() is called by the service registration class (described later) to obtain attribute sets for the service. Note our use of the pre-defined ServiceInfo, Name, Comment, and Location entries. Using these makes creating attribute sets for the lookup service straightforward and simple.

```
public Entry[] getEntries() {
    Entry myEntry[] = new Entry[4];
    myEntry[0] = new ServiceInfo(
            SERVICE_NAME,
            SERVICE_MFR,
            SERVICE_VENDOR,
            SERVICE_VERSION,
            "",                                 //    Model goes here
            ""                                  //    Serial Number goes here
            );
    myEntry[1] = new Name(
            CLASS_NAME
            );
    myEntry[2] = new Comment(
            SERVICE_COMMENT
            );
    myEntry[3] = new Location(
            LOCATION_FLOOR,
            LOCATION_ROOM,
            LOCATION_BUILDING
            );
    return myEntry;
}
```

Service Implementation with an RMI Stub

The second service we will look at uses an RMI stub to implement the service interface. In order to do this, we must define a remote interface in terms of IWroxJiniService.

Deriving the Remote Interface

This new remote interface definition is found in IRMIBasedJiniService.java:

```
package com.wrox.WroxJiniServices;

import java.rmi.*;

public interface IRMIBasedJiniService extends IWroxJiniService, Remote {
}
```

Note that this child interface of IWroxJiniService has no methods of its own. It relies on the methods of the parent interface.

Subtype Matching for Implementing Proprietary Extensions

This derivation of the IRMIBasedJiniService interface from IWroxJiniService effectively makes the standard interface remote. Imagine if this interface also contained its own methods. In this case, the new interface would still be a subtype of IWroxJiniService – and would match all lookups for IWroxJiniService – but could also add special value (or proprietary features) to distinguish itself for all clients. This feature of the lookup service is very, very important for successful commercial adoption of Jini.

Implementing the Remote Interface

The source for RMIBasedJiniServceImpl.java is as follows:

```
package com.wrox.WroxJiniServices;

import java.rmi.*;
import java.net.*;
import java.rmi.server.*;
import net.jini.lookup.entry.*;
import com.sun.jini.lookup.*;
import com.sun.jini.lease.*;
import net.jini.core.entry.*;
import net.jini.core.lookup.*;
import net.jini.discovery.*;

public class RMIBasedJiniServiceImpl extends UnicastRemoteObject
        implements IRMIBasedJiniService, IWroxJiniService {

    static final String SERVICE_NAME = "Jini Service - RMI";
    static final String SERVICE_MFR = "Sing Li";
    static final String SERVICE_VENDOR = "Wrox";
    static final String SERVICE_VERSION = "1.0";
    static final String SERVICE_COMMENT = "This is an RMI implementation.";
    static final String LOCATION_FLOOR = "second";
    static final String LOCATION_ROOM = "computer";
    static final String LOCATION_BUILDING = "8C";
    static final String CLASS_NAME = "wroxCallable";

    public RMIBasedJiniServiceImpl() throws RemoteException {
    }
```

The implementation of grabData() is identical to that in the local proxy version of this service. This time, however, stub and skeleton will be available (via compilation through RMIC.EXE) to remote this call. Now the InetAddress.getLocalHost() should return the hostname/IP address of the **remote** server host!

```
    public String grabData() {
        try {
            return "Executed on " + InetAddress.getLocalHost()
                    + ". Data Returned remotely via RMI from server.";
        } catch (java.net.UnknownHostException e) {
            return "Data transmitted remotely via RMI from server.";
        }
    }
```

This implementation of getEntries() is almost identical to that in the local proxy implementation. The astute reader will recognize a new attribute set in myEntry index 4 called WroxServiceAttributes. We will have much more to say about this custom attribute in the next section.

```
public Entry[] getEntries() {
    Entry myEntry[] = new Entry[5];
    myEntry[0] = new ServiceInfo(
            SERVICE_NAME,
            SERVICE_MFR,
            SERVICE_VENDOR,
            SERVICE_VERSION,
            "",                         //   Model goes here
            ""                          //   Serial Number goes here
            );
    myEntry[1] = new Name(
            CLASS_NAME
            );
    myEntry[2] = new Comment(
            SERVICE_COMMENT
            );
    myEntry[3] = new Location(
            LOCATION_FLOOR,
            LOCATION_ROOM,
            LOCATION_BUILDING
            );
    myEntry[4] = new WroxServiceAttributes(
            "Professional Java Server Programming"
            );
    return myEntry;
    }
}
```

Service Implementation with a Smart Proxy

Our third and final service implementation uses a smart proxy. We also demonstrate here how one can define attribute sets other than the pre-defined ones from Jini. Creating our own attribute sets gives us better control over the way clients use the lookup service to locate us.

Creating Our Own Custom Attribute Sets

The attribute set we will define is called WroxServiceAttributes, found in WroxServiceAttributes.java:

```
package com.wrox.WroxJiniServices;

import net.jini.lookup.entry.*;
import net.jini.entry.AbstractEntry;

public class WroxServiceAttributes extends AbstractEntry
        implements ServiceControlled {

    public String bookName;

    public WroxServiceAttributes() {
    }

    public WroxServiceAttributes(String name) {
        bookName = name;
    }
}
```

Note that we are deriving from `AbstractEntry` (described earlier) to make our implementation simple and that we have marked this class with the `ServiceControlled` interface, indicating that clients should never modify our new attribute – a `String` called `bookName`.

Creating a JavaBean to Support Browsing

To support browsers, like the Jini lookup service browser that we tried earlier, we will define a JavaBean for editing the attribute set. This bean is called, by convention, `WroxServiceAttributesBean`:

```
package com.wrox.WroxJiniServices;

import net.jini.entry.AbstractEntry;
import net.jini.core.entry.*;
import java.io.*;
import net.jini.lookup.entry.*;
```

An 'attribute sets bean' must implement the `EntryBean` interface, and be serializable.

```
public class WroxServiceAttributesBean implements EntryBean, Serializable {
```

The bean contains an instance of our custom attribute sets, called `assoc`.

```
    protected WroxServiceAttributes assoc;

    public WroxServiceAttributesBean() {
        super();
        assoc = new WroxServiceAttributes();
    }
```

JavaBean writing conventions impose a standard way to expose a read/write property for a bean and so we have `getBookName()` and `setBookName()`.

```
    public String getBookName() {
        return assoc.bookName;
    }

    public void setBookName(String a) {
        assoc.bookName=a;
    }
```

The final methods in this bean, `makeLink()` and `followLink()`, are required by the `EntryBean` interface, and cater for linking an instance of `WroxServiceAttributes` into the bean, displaying or modifying its value using the bean, and extracting the modified instance out again. This is especially useful if the bean actually offers custom GUI editing of the attributes.

```
    public void makeLink(Entry obj) {
        assoc = (WroxServiceAttributes) obj;
    }

    public Entry followLink() {
        return assoc;
    }
}
```

Smart Proxy Implementation with a Custom Attribute Set

The actual service implementation is found in `ProxyRemoteJiniServiceImpl.java`:

```
package com.wrox.WroxJiniServices;

import net.jini.core.entry.*;
import net.jini.lookup.entry.*;
import java.net.*;
```

Since the service will be doing some work local to the client's VM, we must not implement a remote interface. Instead, we implement the standard – local – `IWroxJiniService` interface.

```
public class ProxyRemoteJiniServiceImpl implements IWroxJiniService {
```

To communicate easily back to the server, we make use of the already defined RMI remote interface! In practice, we are also free to use socket level calls and any other proprietary means to communicate back to the server.

```
        IRMIBasedJiniService myRemoteService;

    static final String SERVICE_NAME = "Jini Service - Remote Proxy";
    static final String SERVICE_MFR = "Sing Li";
    static final String SERVICE_VENDOR = "Wrox";
    static final String SERVICE_VERSION = "1.0";
    static final String SERVICE_COMMENT =
                                "This is a remote proxy implementation.";
    static final String LOCATION_FLOOR = "third";
    static final String LOCATION_ROOM = "computer";
    static final String LOCATION_BUILDING = "8C";
    static final String CLASS_NAME = "wroxCallable";

    public ProxyRemoteJiniServiceImpl() {
    }
```

We define an additional constructor that takes a remote object reference as its parameter.

```
    public ProxyRemoteJiniServiceImpl(IRMIBasedJiniService inRMIProxy) {
        myRemoteService = inRMIProxy;
    }
```

The smart proxy implementation of `grabData()` will execute locally and this time we call (indirectly) `InetAddress.getLocalHost()` three times. The first and third calls are executed locally and should print out the hostname/IP address of the client's VM. The second, called indirectly by `myRemoteService.grabData()` on the server's VM, returns the server's hostname/IP address.

```
    public String grabData() {
        try {
            return "First Local: " + InetAddress.getLocalHost()
                    + ". Then... " + myRemoteService.grabData()
                    + " ... then local: " + InetAddress.getLocalHost()
                    + " again!";
        } catch (Exception e) {
            return "Data returned locally from within the client.";
        }
    }
```

Finally, we introduce our custom attribute set `WroxServiceAttributes` in the `getEntries()` call. It has no immediate effect until you actually browse the lookup service using a browser tool.

```
public Entry[] getEntries() {
    Entry myEntry[] = new Entry[5];
    myEntry[0] = new ServiceInfo(
            SERVICE_NAME,
            SERVICE_MFR,
            SERVICE_VENDOR,
            SERVICE_VERSION,
            "",                       //   Model goes here
            ""                        //   Serial Number goes here
            );
    myEntry[1] = new Name(
            CLASS_NAME
            );
    myEntry[2] = new Comment(
            SERVICE_COMMENT
            );
    myEntry[3] = new Location(
            LOCATION_FLOOR,
            LOCATION_ROOM,
            LOCATION_BUILDING
            );
    myEntry[4] = new WroxServiceAttributes(
            "Beginning Java 2"
            );
    return myEntry;
}

}
```

This wraps up our discussion on the proxy object implementation for our three services. Now, we need to see how we manage discovery and join protocol to locate and register with the lookup service(s).

Discovery and Join Implementation

The `JoinManager` implementation that we covered at length earlier is going to help us out big time here. You can find the source file for this `main()` class in `GenericServices.java`

```
package com.wrox.WroxJiniServices;

import java.rmi.*;
import java.net.*;
import java.util.*;
import java.rmi.server.*;
import com.sun.jini.lookup.*;
import com.sun.jini.lease.*;
import net.jini.core.entry.*;
import net.jini.core.lookup.*;
import net.jini.lookup.entry.*;
import net.jini.discovery.*;
```

A local class is defined here to catch the notification from `JoinManager` once the lookup service assigns us a Service ID. Keeping it simple, we'll just print out the Service ID when we do get it. As it is obliged to, our class implements the `ServiceIDListener` interface.

```
class NotifyCatcher implements ServiceIDListener {
    public void serviceIDNotify (ServiceID id) {
        System.out.println("Registered with Service ID: " + id);
    }
}
```

Here is the actual code to use the `JoinManager` to perform discovery and join. All the logic is in the simple `main()` method.

```
public class GenericServices {
    static GenericServices myInstance;

    public static void main(String args[]) throws Exception {

        Vector servicesToRegister = new Vector(3);
        myInstance = new GenericServices();
```

We need to install an RMI security manager, if one is not already available.

```
        if (System.getSecurityManager() == null)
                System.setSecurityManager(new RMISecurityManager());
```

Next, we instantiate and store the proxies for the services that we want to register in a vector we've created called `servicesToRegister`, Notice that for the smart proxy, we also create a remote object reference for it to "call back" into the server on an as-needed basis.

```
        servicesToRegister.add(new LocalProxyJiniServiceImpl());
        servicesToRegister.add(new ProxyRemoteJiniServiceImpl
                                (new RMIBasedJiniServiceImpl()));
        servicesToRegister.add(new RMIBasedJiniServiceImpl());

        System.out.println("Registering servers with lookup service...");
```

Finally, we iterate through the vector and, for each service within, create a new `JoinManager` instance. We use this `JoinManager` to start the discovery and join protocol by passing it the attribute sets to be associated with the service by the lookup service. In turn, these are obtained by calling the `getEntries()` method of the `IWroxJiniService` interface – one that we know all our services must implement.

```
        try {
            Iterator it = servicesToRegister.iterator();

            while (it.hasNext()) {
                IWroxJiniService me = (IWroxJiniService) it.next();
                new JoinManager(
                            me,
                            me.getEntries(),
                            new NotifyCatcher(),
                            null
                            );
            System.out.println("Registered a service");
            }
```

After instantiating the `JoinManager` instances, we need to hang around for the notification of registration from the lookup service(s). Since the client may be making remote calls back to our server, we also hang around to field these calls.

```
                synchronized (servicesToRegister) {
                    servicesToRegister.wait(0);
                }

        } catch (Exception e) {
            System.out.println("Caught exception " +e);
        }
    }
}
```

That is all the code for the three Jini services that we will experiment with. Let us turn our attention now to the code for a simple client.

Coding a Jini Client

We created our Jini client in its own package, `com.wrox.WroxJiniClients`. This is more realistic in practice since most clients will not have source code level access to their services. Recalling our discussion earlier, the magical helper class for Jini clients is the `LookupDiscovery` implementation class and the code in our client must:

> ➤ create an instance of the `LookupDiscovery` helper class
> ➤ start discovery and join and find the lookup service (accessed via its `ServiceRegistrar` interface)
> ➤ use the lookup service to find our remote Jini services
> ➤ call the three different implementations of `grabData()` from the three proxies and display the result

```
package com.wrox.WroxJiniClients;

import net.jini.core.entry.*;
import net.jini.lookup.entry.*;
import net.jini.entry.*;
import net.jini.discovery.*;
import net.jini.core.lookup.*;
import java.rmi.*;
import com.wrox.WroxJiniServices.*;
```

Instead of using a local class, we will make the client class itself handle the discovery callback from `LookupDiscovery`. This is done by implementing the `DiscoveryListener` interface.

```
public class JiniUser implements DiscoveryListener {
```

The major method in the `DiscoveryListener` interface is called `discovered()`. Run after the first discovery cycle, you can get from it a list of lookup services discovered using the `DiscoveryEvent` object passed into it as a Parameter.

```
public void discovered(DiscoveryEvent e) {

    try {
```

Inside the `discovered()` callback, we know that one or more lookup service(s) have been located. `getRegistrars()` returns the array of lookup service proxies.

```
            ServiceRegistrar regs[] = e.getRegistrars();
```

Unless you've started multiple copies of REGGIE on different machines, there should only be one `discovered()` lookup service(s) but we've defined a loop to look at them all in case.

```
        for (int i = 0; i < regs.length; i++) {
            System.out.println("Registrar " +
                              regs[i].getLocator().toString());
            System.out.println();
            System.out.println("Searching for Entries I can call: ");
```

To prepare for the template used in the lookup, we create an instance of the pre-defined `Name` attribute set.

```
            Entry entries[] = new Entry[] {new Name("wroxCallable")};
```

`regs[i]` is the current lookup service's `ServiceRegistrar` interface. We call its `lookup` method and create a `ServiceTemplate` that will use the attribute set with the `Name` attribute. In this case, we search for `Name=wroxCallable`. All of our Jini services were coded to have this attribute set.

```
            ServiceMatches sm = regs[i].lookup(
                new ServiceTemplate(null, null, entries), 10
                );
```

The `ServiceMatched` instance returned from `lookup()` should contain all three of the services. We iterate through this array, cast the contents to the `IWroxJiniService` interface that they all implement, and then call the `grabData()` method and print out the result.

```
            if (sm.totalMatches > 0) {
                for (int j=0; j<sm.totalMatches; j++) {
                    IWroxJiniService myServ =
                        (IWroxJiniService) sm.items[j].service;
                    System.out.println("Service Number: " + j + " found!");
                    System.out.println("Grabbed Data: " +
                        myServ.grabData());
                }
            }
        }
    } catch (Exception err) {
        System.out.println("Exception: " + err.getMessage());
        err.printStackTrace();
    }
}

public void discarded(DiscoveryEvent e) {
}
}
```

The `main()` method is where we instantiate the `LookupDiscovery` instance and start the discovery and join protocol.

```
        static JiniUser aClient;

    public static void main(String args[]) throws Exception {
        aClient = new JiniUser();
        System.out.println("A Simple Jini Client");
        System.out.println("Getting security manager");
        System.setSecurityManager(new RMISecurityManager());
```

The instance of `LookupDiscovery` used here – `ld` – searches for every group in this djinn. In practice, a complete search is unlikely to be necessary and a more selective list of groups will be used. We simply register this instance of `JiniUser` to receive discovery notification and we finish by pausing and waiting around for discover to complete.

```
        System.out.println("Starting Lookup Discovery ...");
        LookupDiscovery ld = new LookupDiscovery(LookupDiscovery.ALL_GROUPS);
        System.out.println("... and join");
        ld.addDiscoveryListener(aClient);

        System.out.println("Waiting to hear from REGGIE");
        synchronized(aClient) {
            aClient.wait();
        }
    }
```

Testing Your Very Own Djinn

To compile and build the code for services and client, we have provided two batch files, `BuildJiniClient.bat` and `BuildJiniServices.bat`, to make it all simple and repeatable. `BuildJiniClient.bat` reads like this

```
set JiniPATH=D:\jini1_0

set CLASSPATH=%JiniPATH%\lib\jini-core.jar;%JiniPATH%\lib\jini-ext.jar;
            %JiniPATH%\lib\sun-util.jar;%JiniPATH%;.

javac com\wrox\WroxJiniClients\*.java
```

while `BuildJiniServices.bat` is a little more complex.

```
set JiniPATH=D:\jini1_0

set CLASSPATH=%JiniPATH%\lib\jini-core.jar;%JiniPATH%\lib\jini-ext.jar;
            %JiniPATH%\lib\sun-util.jar;%JiniPATH%;.

javac com\wrox\WroxJiniServices\*.java

rmic -d . com.wrox.WroxJiniServices.RMIBasedJiniServiceImpl

jar cvf %JiniPATH%\lib\WroxJiniServices-dl.jar
        com\wrox\WroxJiniServices\IWroxJiniService.class
        com\wrox\WroxJiniServices\LocalProxyJiniServiceImpl.class
        com\wrox\WroxJiniServices\ProxyRemoteJiniServiceImpl.class
        com\wrox\WroxJiniServices\IRMIBasedJiniService.class
        com\wrox\WroxJiniServices\RMIBasedJiniServiceImpl_Stub.class
        com\wrox\WroxJiniServices\WroxServiceAttributes.class
        com\wrox\WroxJiniServices\WroxServiceAttributesBean.class
```

Between them, the two batch files:

> ➢ Set the class path for compilation
> ➢ Compile all the service and client source files
> ➢ Use `RMIC` to generate the stub and skeletons for the remote interface
> ➢ Use the JAR tool to create a JAR file including all the stub, interfaces, and class definition required by a remote client of the services; the resulting file is called `WroxJiniServices-dl.jar`

Once more, don't forget to adjust the path assignments in both batch files to match your own environment. Once you have run them successfully, you are ready to test out your new djinn.

Setting Up the Machines for Testing

All being well, you can now have your very own djinn with one client and four services (including the lookup service). That is a healthy five participants in your djinn. By adding the Jini lookup browser tool that we have covered earlier, you can actually get a total of six participants.

As one last convenience, we've made up one more pair of batch files for you to modify and use. `RunJiniServices.bat` starts the Jini server that we wrote.

```
set JiniPATH=D:\jini1_0
set CLASSPATH=.;%JiniPATH%;%JiniPATH%\lib\jini-core.jar;
            %JiniPATH%\lib\jini-ext.jar;%JiniPATH%\lib\sun-util.jar
java -Djava.rmi.server.codebase=http://jamesh:8080/WroxJiniServices-dl.jar
     -Djava.security.policy=policy.all com.wrox.WroxJiniServices.GenericServices
```

Before you run this, you will need to copy the `WroxJiniService-dl.jar` file created from `BuildJini.bat` to the `HTTPD` root directory.

The other batch file in the pair is `RunJiniClient.bat`:

```
set JiniPATH=D:\jini1_0
set CLASSPATH=.;%JiniPATH%;%JiniPATH%\lib\jini-core.jar;
            %JiniPATH%\lib\jini-ext.jar;%JiniPATH%\lib\sun-util.jar
java -Djava.security.policy=policy.all com.wrox.WroxJiniClients.JiniUser
```

Using three networked machines, you can run the following configuration:

Machine	Files to run
Machine A	RunHTTPD
	RunRMID
	RunREGGIE
Machine B	RunHTTPD
	RunJiniServ
Machine C	RunJiniClient

If everything is setup correctly, you should see output similar to this after running `RunJiniServ.bat`:

```
Registering servers with lookup service...
registered 1!
registered 1!
registered 1!
Registered with service ID: c0dbffe4-8de5-4b7e-bbbb-d4c6c586b8f3
Registered with service ID: 5e7e0e4a-6337-4938-9899-bfc6acfac29a
Registered with service ID: cbf5663b-ad46-4f22-8d9b-d8607cc6264a
```

We get a first look here at what a Service ID actually looks like in String form. Readers who have worked with DCE RPC and/or Microsoft DCOM should recognize this UUID/GUID format readily.

The output of `RunJiniClient.bat` should show the difference between the three different implementation of proxy as expected.

If you want to really impress yourself, run `RunJiniBrowser.bat` either from Machine B or a new machine that has `HTTPD` running. Connect to your instance of the REGGIE registrar, and check out the **Attributes** available. Lo and behold, thanks to the JavaBean, we see that our custom attribute set (`WroxServiceAttributes`) is available from two of the three services:

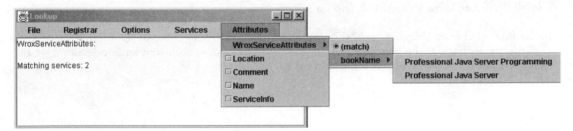

Moving Forward with Jini Technology

Before we move on, let's pause for breath and recap what we have seen so far in our exploration of Jini. We know that computing architecture mirrors organizational changes and that the Internet has caused major changes the way we work together and the way we communicate. However, the speed with which these changes have occurred has meant that the available computing architecture has not had time to catch up to these changes. The major movement to de-centralize and democratize on a large scale is but an empty cry falling on deaf ears.

Jini has the potential to change all of this. We saw how Jini works by building ephemeral federations of computing resources over a network. These federations can be formed in an on-demand basis, for long enough just to complete useful work. We learnt that these federations are called djinns. Jini leverages Java's ability to ship both data and code through the wire, and extends the notion of a Java system beyond the simple peer machine model. Based on the Jini model, we envisioned many kinds of new services that could be created. We noted that these services would also include migrations of legacy non-Jini services, as well as many new and exciting value added services brought about by the Jini Community.

We know that Sun has relinquished control of Jini to the Jini Community, with an almost OpenSource effort called Community Licensing that still provides for individual innovation and proprietary rights protection. We cleared up some widespread misunderstandings that label Jini as a device driver technology. Exploring the device possibilities, we found out why Jini is indeed a natural technology for enabling the widespread dynamic use of device based services. We even looked at three ways to create such device based services.

Going deeper into the technology, we learnt about the discovery and join protocol that gives Jini its dynamic nature, the vital lookup service, the `ServiceRegistrar` interface that it supports and how it allows the lookup of server proxy objects based on attribute sets. We saw three different ways of implementing proxy objects and studied the way to build attribute sets used by lookup services by way of looking at the pre-defined one that can readily be used. Looking at the structure of a Jini service, we found out how to create one using the `JoinManager` support class and, similarly, looked at the structure of a Jini client and found out how to create one using the `LookupDiscovery` support class.

Finally, we got our hands wet and coded three Jini services from scratch, with each one using a different strategy in its proxy operation, and a Jini client to test them out. In testing our new djinn, we set-up Jini in a small network of several machines, and used a browser tool to see our services' interaction with the lookup service.

Hopefully, it had been a rewarding trip for you.

In the next couple of chapters, we'll turn our attention back to the poser of the Online Loan Approval Website we set back at the beginning of this discussion. If you've followed and understood what we've learnt here, it will truly be a piece of cake.

Working With JavaSpaces

What is JavaSpaces?

Now that we've had a fairly long look at Jini, what it can do and how it all works, it's time to turn our attention to the second nascent technology that we've alluded to – JavaSpaces. It is based on Jini, yet conceptually, it is at the other extreme of the "Natural Dissonance" spectrum. Where Jini resides in the hidden valleys of device driver dell, JavaSpaces exists on the sprawling plains of distributed systems design.

Developing with this technology will allow us to build workflow into our distributed systems, and to leverage the inexpensive PCs available today to perform cost-effective parallel processing. Amazingly though, while JavaSpaces is all of these complex sounding things, it remains at heart a simple and intuitive way to build distributed computing systems. If you're skeptical, I don't blame you, but in reality, JavaSpaces is a single Java interface.

JavaSpaces is a Single Java Interface!

Are you ready? Here it is:

```java
public abstract interface JavaSpace {

    public static final long NO_WAIT;

    public Lease            write (Entry entry,
                                   Transaction txn,
                                   long lease)
                            throws TransactionException,
                                   SecurityException,
                                   RemoteException;

    public Entry            read (Entry tmpl,
                                  Transaction txn,
                                  long timeout)
                            throws UnusableEntryException,
                                   TransactionException,
                                   SecurityException,
                                   InterruptedException,
                                   RemoteException;

    public Entry        readIfExists (Entry tmpl,
                                      Transaction txn,
                                      long timeout)
                            throws UnusableEntryException,
                                   TransactionException,
                                   SecurityException,
                                   InterruptedException,
                                   RemoteException;

    public Entry            take (Entry tmpl,
                                  Transaction txn,
                                  long timeout)
                            throws UnusableEntryException,
                                   TransactionException,
                                   SecurityException,
                                   InterruptedException,
                                   RemoteException;

    public Entry        takeIfExists (Entry tmpl,
                                      Transaction txn,
                                      long timeout)
                            throws UnusableEntryException,
                                   TransactionException,
                                   SecurityException,
                                   InterruptedException,
                                   RemoteException;

    public EventRegistration notify (Entry tmpl,
                                     Transaction txn,
                                     RemoteEventListener listener,
                                     long lease,
                                     MarshalledObject handback)
                            throws TransactionException,
                                   SecurityException,
                                   RemoteException;
```

```
        public Entry           snapshot (Entry e)
                                   throws RemoteException;
    };
```

Not that daunting really, is it?! At the current level of release (version 1.0), this is the precise machine-readable definition of what JavaSpaces is!

JavaSpaces is a Jini Service!

The service that implements the JavaSpaces interface takes the form of a Jini service. Indeed, you can use a lookup service to find your JavaSpaces service in exactly the same way you found the `wroxCallable` services in the previous chapter. In this case, the service codename for the JavaSpaces service is **OUTRIGGER**.

The OUTRIGGER service is started up just like any other Jini service – REGGIE, for example. The slight difference however, is that it actually comes in two different 'flavors', one transient and the other persistent. Fortunately, code that uses OUTRIGGER does not have to distinguish between the two.

The persistent OUTRIGGER service preserves its state just like RMID and REGGIE. We however will be working exclusively with the transient version. It is less of a memory hog and it is significantly simpler to setup and administer. It will allow us to concentrate more on other important aspects of JavaSpaces system design.

JavaSpaces is a like a Lookup Service!

So what will the OUTRIGGER Jini service do for us through the JavaSpaces standard interface? Well, it can be viewed as a glorified version of a lookup service. Instead of keeping track of `serviceItems` like REGGIE, however, the item of interest in a JavaSpaces implementation are `Entry`s.

Conveniently, the interface `net.jini.core.entry.Entry` is the same root for both JavaSpaces entries and Jini lookup service attribute sets. In fact, even the matching mechanism is quite similar between the two services.

It should be made clear now though that a JavaSpace service is not a genuine lookup service – it is not obliged to support the discovery and join protocols as others would. What it can do is **write** entries into the space, and then have other clients **read** the entries back using a template matching mechanism.

JavaSpaces is a True Object Database!

Entries that you write into a JavaSpace can exist indefinitely. This is true of any persistent JavaSpaces implementation. At any moment in time, your application and/or another client can search that space, find the entry you wrote into the space by using a template to match it and then **take** that entry from the database. This ability to store entries, which can contain object references, gives JavaSpaces an object database-like quality.

JavaSpaces is your MOM!

Probably the closest approximation to JavaSpaces is MOM – **Message Oriented Middleware** – which some will recognize as a synonym for Message Queue Services. Most software engineers with over a decade of industry exposure will have worked with some form of queuing engine and/or services. The most famous of the bunch comes from Big Blue – IBM – and is called the IBM MQ*Series. For the slightly younger of you who have not encountered these legacy beasties before, you may have recently read about or worked with Microsoft MSMQ (or DCOM Queued Components). This is the microcomputer evolution of those legacy systems – fossilized bones in a brand new body.

A Quick Introduction to Traditional Queuing Services

A queuing service works by sending messages between clients and server components. On a single machine, one can see how a trivial non-robust queuing system can be implemented using internal data structures (such as a Java 2 stack used as a queue). However, most queuing systems are robust and work over a networked group of computers making their implementation considerably more complex.

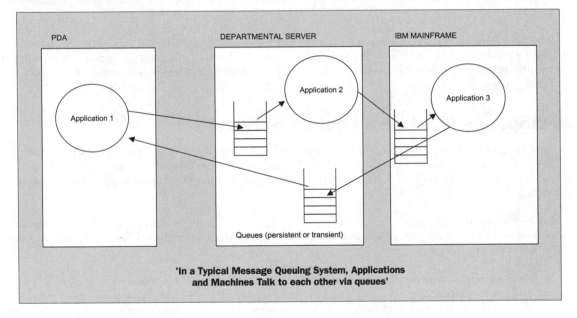

'In a Typical Message Queuing System, Applications
and Machines Talk to each other via queues'

There are one or two interesting things to bear in mind regarding queuing systems:

> The system passes messages between applications. It is an *application to application* communication conduit, not a user to application, or user to user one. It is definitely not email, even though it is sometimes referred to as a message queuing system.

> For a mainframe computer to interoperate with a PDA, the only requirement is for the PDA to be able to write a message into a queue that the mainframe will scan. This is one of the strengths of queuing systems, allowing many diverse systems to work with one another.

➢ The systems do not have to be connected to each other all the time in order to work together. In fact, the network connecting the systems together can be intermittent. This will even allow, for example, applications on a computer with dial-up network access to participate in the system – another strength of a queuing system.

➢ The queues themselves can be hosted on a variety of platforms. Depending on the need, one can get durable queues that guarantee it will never lose a message. On the other hand, for the fastest possible performance, one may want to use in-memory queues if message loss is not an issue.

➢ In its very classic sense, a queue acts as a buffer between a producer and consumer process. It enables the processing resources to be utilized in the most efficient possible way given a specific network configuration.

➢ From a distributed system perspective, queuing systems can convert a predominately "push" style of operation into one that "pulls" info as needed. Without a queuing system, for example, incoming online order must be processed as they are "pushed" into the system. By adding a queue in between the web server taking the order and the order processing system, the order processing system can now "pull" orders out of the queue and process them one by one at the fastest possible speed.

One thing not obvious from the observations above is that a queuing system typically provides various degrees of guarantee for the messages written to and read from its queues. Typically, some of the queues will have their operations executed as transactions, guaranteeing for example that a successful write into a durable queue will not lose the message regardless of partial or complete network crash.

In most programming environments, the queuing system exists as a middleware layer (hence the name Message Oriented **Middleware**) that guarantees the robust delivery of these messages to and from the queues between the communicating components. While in most cases, an application will have to program an explicit API to access queuing functions, there have been implementations where the queuing mechanism is used to map traditional procedure calls into messages. Before this can happen however, new semantics such as "call and forget" for procedures and "fire and forget" for event notification must be introduced into the programming model.

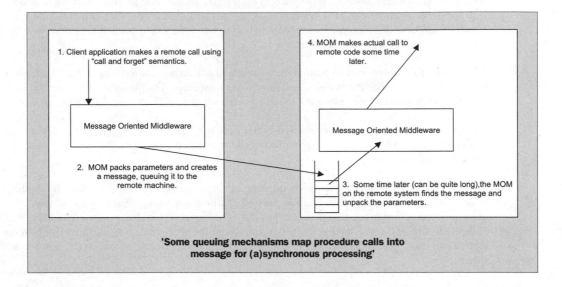

'Some queuing mechanisms map procedure calls into
message for (a)synchronous processing'

JavaSpaces is a Queuing Service on Steroids

So, is JavaSpaces simply a queuing service for Jini? The straightforward answer is **NO**. The interesting answer is "*Well, kinda...*" Let us take a look at the typical topology of a very simple JavaSpaces system.

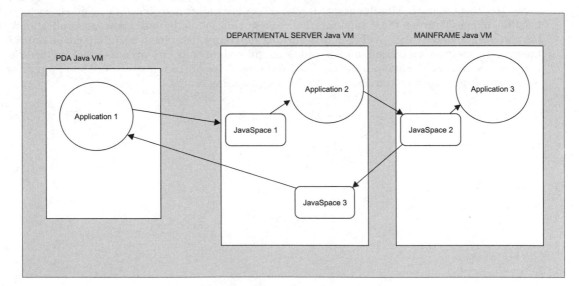

Does this look familiar? *Well, kinda...*

Despite the fact that each of the six statements previously made about queues can equally be made about JavaSpaces, you should keep in mind that they are not just a queuing service for Java! No, no! As a Jini enthusiast (such as yours truly) will insist, the differences are many.

> ➤ For starters, I said "Spaces." That's "S-P-A-C-E-S"! Spaces are, by definition, not queues.

> ➤ JavaSpaces can transmit more than just lame text, mime-types, or simple binary streams. They are also capable of sending meaningful, raw-iron, system behavior – code that will be run later by the receiver and custom work to be done by the receiver that only the sender can direct! Nice.

> ➤ JavaSpaces are defined to work only over a homogeneous world of Java systems, and even more specifically over Jini djinns. But since we already knew that any processor that supports a NOP instruction can run Java, and that a Jini djinn can span the Internet, this practically means JavaSpaces can work anywhere.

> ➤ There are no production quality, commercial implementations of JavaSpaces, as yet.

Looking at Clouds Floating Over a Blue Sky

Hopefully, now that you've read over what JavaSpaces is and what it can do, you've found something in its operation which has perked up your interest. Bear in mind that the definition of exactly what JavaSpaces **is,** is still very much up in the air. It's up to you and everyone else who develops and experiments with this great technology to derive its exact purpose in the weeks and months to come!

Your Personal JavaSpaces Construction Set

Just because we cannot decide on exactly what something is, does not imply that we cannot make productive use of it. If that was the case, most middle management types will be immediately out of a job. In any case, we are determined to forge ahead with JavaSpaces. After all, it is based on Jini, so it must be good.

As Many Spaces As You Want

In the previous figure, we saw a sample topology of a JavaSpaces system. One thing that should be obvious is that we can create as many instances of JavaSpaces as we need in a typical working system. We can also run them on any machine (that supports a Java VM) within the system.

For any particular project, however, the number of JavaSpaces to use and their physical location will be a very specific engineering design decision. One must judge this from the architecture of the overall system and the connection topology bearing in mind the throughput and response time requirements. Another typical design decision in a JavaSpaces project is when and where to use persistent spaces versus non-persistent spaces and, again, the optimal answer will be very situation specific.

Both these decisions will be helped by knowing how the various elements of the JavaSpaces API work. Our next task then is to drill down into the API and look at each of these 'very simple' operations.

An Entry in JavaSpaces

Everything we learnt about creating Jini attribute sets is also true for `Entry`s in JavaSpaces, notably that:

> ➤ An Entry must implement the `net.jini.core.entry.Entry` interface (which extends `java.io.Serializable`).

> ➤ An Entry can be a subclass of `net.jini.entry.AbstractEntry` to facilitate their implementation.

> ➤ Every public field is an attribute of the entry. Each attribute must be a serializable object reference – no primitive types allowed.

> ➤ A JavaBean should be created for each new entry type you define to assist browsers and editors in displaying your entry.

> ➤ There are predefined `Entry`s like `net.jini.lookup.entry.Name` that can be used immediately without further custom coding. These predefined entries already have JavaBeans defined for their display and editing.

Template matching in JavaSpaces is done by passing in an instance of an Entry. Any unspecified attribute in an Entry (i.e. null, since they must be all object references) acts as a wildcard, while any attribute that is specified within the entry must be matched in the search. Attributes are deemed equal if their types are the same and their states (values) are identical.

The write() Method

```
public Lease                        write (Entry entry,
                                           Transaction txn,
                                           long lease)
                                    throws TransactionException,
                                           SecurityException,
                                           RemoteException;
```

A call to `write()` results in a copy of the specified `Entry` being written into the JavaSpace and is always transacted with respect to any other operation. This means a successful write always implies that the entry has been deposited into the JavaSpace – regardless of how many others are trying to write to or what else is happening in the space.

If you include a transaction in the parameter list (i.e. a non-null value for `txn`), `write()` will be incorporated into it. So, if the transaction aborts later on, the effect of the write will be reversed.

Finally, the `lease` parameter allows you to request a specific lease duration. The actual duration granted by the JavaSpaces implementation can be found in the returned `Lease` object – usually the same or less time than what you asked for.

The read() Method

```
public Entry                        read (Entry tmpl,
                                          Transaction txn,
                                          long timeout)
                                    throws UnusableEntryException,
```

```
                                          TransactionException,
                                          SecurityException,
                                          InterruptedException,
                                          RemoteException;
```

Performs a search in the JavaSpace, and returns a copy of an entry (no guarantee which one if there are multiple matches) that matches the template entry passed in. This operation will block until a match is made or until a time limit, specified in the `timeout` parameter in milliseconds, is exceeded.

If a transaction is passed in to `read()` as a parameter, any entries written within that transaction will be visible to the method. Entries written within an uncommitted transaction are not visible outside that transaction.

The readIfExists() Method

```
        public Entry        readIfExists (Entry tmpl,
                                          Transaction txn,
                                          long timeout)
                            throws UnusableEntryException,
                                   TransactionException,
                                   SecurityException,
                                   InterruptedException,
                                   RemoteException;
```

`readIfExists()` works in exactly the same way to `read()` but will not block and returns null if an entry cannot be matched immediately. It will, however, wait for unsettled transactions: if there exists an entry that matches the template in the space but is not available because of an uncommitted transaction (see the write operation described above). In this case, it will wait up to `timeout` milliseconds for the entry's release before giving up and returning null.

The take() Method

```
        public Entry                take (Entry tmpl,
                                          Transaction txn,
                                          long timeout)
                            throws UnusableEntryException,
                                   TransactionException,
                                   SecurityException,
                                   InterruptedException,
                                   RemoteException;
```

`take()` performs a search of the space against the template, returns a copy of a matched entry (any one if more than one matches), and removes the entry from the space.

`take()` is always transacted with respect to any other operation. If a transaction is passed as a parameter, this take operation will become part of the transaction. Entries taken from the space within a transaction will not be visible to subsequent reads in the same transaction. If an entry cannot be matched, this operation will block until one is available or, again, until `timeout` milliseconds have passed.

The takeIfExists() Method

```
public Entry        takeIfExists (Entry tmpl,
                                  Transaction txn,
                                  long timeout)
                          throws UnusableEntryException,
                                 TransactionException,
                                 SecurityException,
                                 InterruptedException,
                                 RemoteException;
```

takeIfExists() works in exactly the same way with respect to take() as readIfExists() works with respect to read().

Registering for Notification: Jini Distributed Events

```
public EventRegistration  notify (Entry tmpl,
                                  Transaction txn,
                                  RemoteEventListener listener,
                                  long lease,
                                  MarshalledObject handback)
                          throws TransactionException,
                                 SecurityException,
                                 RemoteException;
```

If an entry cannot be matched, and the application does not want to block waiting for a matched entry, it is possible to register one's interest in any template-matching entries, and to be notified by the JavaSpace when a matching entry becomes available. To set this up, you must supply an object that supports the RemoteEventListener interface for callback as a parameter for notify, the method designed for this operation.

The template to be matched is passed in tmpl. Note that registering for a notification is equivalent to doing an automatic re-match each and every time a new entry is written to the space. The notification can be part of a transaction if the txn parameter is specified. In this case, entries written subsequently within the transaction that matches a notify() template will trigger notification. The event registration will be leased, and you can request a lease period in milliseconds via the lease parameter.

The handback parameter is a MarshalledObject type, and is an object that will be passed along to the recipient of the notification without modification. MarshalledObject allows the JavaSpace implementation to temporarily store an object of unknown type or composition and then *hand back* the object to the event handler without ever examining what is inside. This turns out to be an extremely powerful concept in distributed event handling. Imagine that the object we register to receive the notification is actually an event management service. This would allow a client of the service to associate arbitrary behavior for handling the event – even if the client is no longer running by the time the event fires!

The `EventRegistration` object returned has the following definition:

```
public class EventRegistration implements java.io.Serializable {

    protected long          eventID;
    protected Lease         lease;
    protected long          seqNum;
    protected Object        source;

    public      EventRegistration (long eventID,
                                   Object Source,
                                   Lease Lease,
                                   long seqNum);
    public long              getID ();
    public Object       getSource ();
    public Lease         getLease ();
    public long getSequenceNumber ();
}
```

The actual lease granted by the JavaSpace can be found through the `getLease()` method. The ID assigned to this event, which can be used by a general purpose handler to distinguish between multiple events is obtained via `getID()`. `getSource()` will return the JavaSpace that registered the event. Finally, a call to `getSequenceNumber()` will return the current event sequence number associated with this event type. An **event sequence number** is a monotonically increasing number incremented when events are fired. This is useful in a distributed environment where events may be lost or delivered out-of-order.

The object to receive the notification implements the `RemoteEventListener` interface which is detailed below:

```
public interface RemoteEventListener extends Remote, EventListener {

    public void notify (RemoteEvent theEvent)
            throws UnknownEventException, RemoteException;
}
```

The only method here is the `notify()` method. When this callback occurs, the object receiving the notification will get the reference to an instance of a `RemoteEvent` object. This object is defined as:

```
public class RemoteEvent extends EventObject {

    protected Object                source;
    protected long                  eventID;
    protected long                  seqNum;
    protected MarshalledObject      handback;

    public                      RemoteEvent (Object source,
                                             long eventID,
                                             long seqNum,
                                             MarshalledObject handback)
    public long                 getID ();
    public long       getSequenceNumber ();
    public MarshalledObject getRegistrationObject ();
}
```

Therefore, upon notification, the event handler can identify the source of the event (i.e. the JavaSpace) via a call to `getSource()`. It can also get the assigned event ID using `getID()`, the actual sequence number of this specific notification via `getSequenceNumber()` and the `MarshalledObject` that was given to the JavaSpace upon event registration by calling `getRegistrationObject()`.

In fact, the sequence of interactions for event registration described above is the exact mechanism specified by Jini for handling distributed events as we saw briefly in the last chapter.

Optimization of Entry Submission

```
public Entry          snapshot (Entry e)
                         throws RemoteException;
```

The very last method in the `net.jini.Space` interface is called `snapshot()`. Its sole purpose is to optimize the actual `Entry` submission process when one of the methods involving a template entry is called. If a snapshot is not used, every call to one of the methods (i.e. `read()`, `take()`, etc.) involving a template will re-serialize the template entry into the JavaSpace. This is necessary since there is no easy way for the JavaSpace to know that an entry that you may be repeatedly submitting as a template is the same entry.

If you do submit the same valued template quite frequently, and you are interested in this optimization, then you can make a call to `snapshot`. By passing in the entry that you will be using repeatedly, the JavaSpace will return a special snapshot entry for you to use in your repeated operations.

By using this special snapshot entry, the JavaSpace will know not to re-serialize the entry and thus save some processing time when performing the operation. This snapshot entry is specific to the instance of JavaSpace you called the `snapshot()` method on. You cannot pass it to another instance or out of your VM.

Implementing Workflow with JavaSpaces

Using JavaSpaces, one can easily implement solutions using an object flow model. Since an object encompasses both state and behavior (data and code), we are hitting both the data flow and workflow birds with one stone. Consider the following workflow scenario:

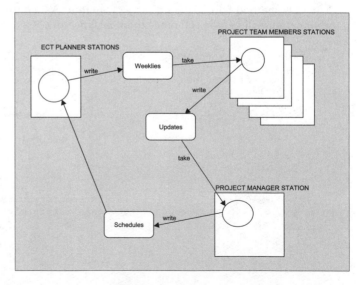

This is a project management scenario. The Project Planners' stations churn out weekly schedules for a project. Each member of the project team runs a service on their machine that retrieves these schedules from the Weeklies JavaSpace and monitors the progress of the member against the schedule. Once their performance level is determined, the team member's system writes the status to the Updates JavaSpace which in turn is monitored by a service on the project manager's station. In fact this service monitors the progress levels of all the project members and presents the big picture to the project manager.

The Project Manager then resolves issues, adjusts and merges the changes, and approves the schedule. At the moment of approval, the system will write the revised project schedule to the Schedules JavaSpace. Back to the start of this circle, the project planners monitor this space and update the weekly schedules accordingly and so the workflow cycle begins again.

Note how the JavaSpaces are used to connect each stage of the workflow, and act as a reliable store and forward buffer between each segment. As long as the servers along the workflow chain support state persistence and recovery, we can combine them with persistent JavaSpaces and a transaction service to create robust workflow systems.

Adding Parallelism into JavaSpaces Systems

Let us take a scenario more similar to our Online Loan Approval System. It is a simple online order processing system. The sequence of events that occur in the system is as follows.

> The customer fills a shopping cart and completes the order by providing credit card information.

> The front end servlet collects the information, creates an order object and writes it as an entry into the `Pending` JavaSpace. The type of credit card is stored as one of the attributes on the entry.

> The `CreditCardProcessing` Server takes an entry containing credit card information from the `Pending` JavaSpace, processes the credit card, and if successful, writes the order object into the `PendingFulfillment` JavaSpace. If unsuccessful, an entry is written to the `PaymentProblem` JavaSpace.

> The `EmailNotification` Server periodically scans the `PaymentProblem` JavaSpace using `takeIfExists` and collects bad credit verification entries. It emails a notification back to the customer.

> The `Fullfillment` Server uses a `take` to block up the `PendingFullfillment` JavaSpace, and goes to work on fulfilling the order whenever one is written into the JavaSpace.

The system looks like this schematically:

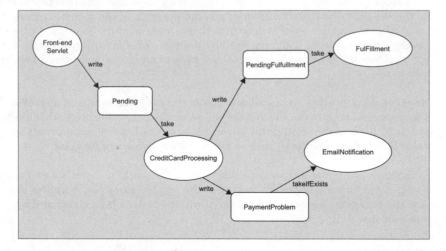

Notice that we have specifically isolated each service function onto its own server. This allows us to configure the server machine specifically for its requirement (i.e. in the case of the CreditCardProcessing Servers: synchronous communications link for encrypted connection to credit card approval agencies). This way, we do not have to provide all the exotic hardware and external connectivity to every node. In addition, it also allows us to add parallelism into the system simply by adding hardware!!

This system works in a linear pipeline fashion. Now, if we determine after a while, that at the current traffic level the CreditCardProcessing Server is holding up the entire pipeline, what can we do?

The solution is to configure and add another CreditCardProcessing Server into the system. Notice that, thanks to JavaSpaces, this server can be added at anytime without affecting the on-going operation of the system. The 'connection' into the system at both the input and output end are both JavaSpaces. This is where the Jini dynamism underneath really pays off. You simply "plug in" the new server alleviating the bottleneck and the system throughput goes up. The new system, after adding in one more CreditCardProcessing server, looks like this:

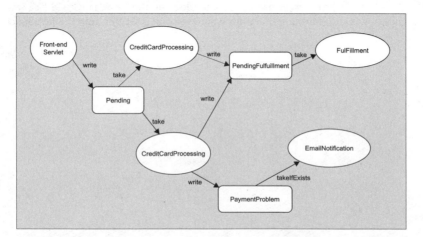

Since we have specifically designed our system to have server functions isolated onto individual server machines, we can use the same technique in adding parallelism into any stage of our processing pipeline. Our only limitation will be the overall LAN bandwidth if there are many stages and there is a lot of traffic.

Adding JavaSpaces To Our Case Study

Unlike Jini, there are relatively few details that we need to know in order to work with JavaSpaces. Most issues we have encountered so far, as expected, relate to system design and distributed system architecture rather than programming details of JavaSpaces. Let us apply these newfound concepts to the design of our original Online Loan Approval Website.

Services in the System

Here are the services/systems that we will need:

Services/Systems Name	Purpose
SpaceServlet	The front-end servlet that processes the Loan System's form submission. It should also monitor the output JavaSpaces and report the approval/rejection to the end-user as soon as it is available.
NameVerifierNode	This node/service takes output entries from the SpaceServlet and verifies the names and member IDs with an in-house database. It also retrieves the member's business history and attaches it to the application entry.
CreditCheckerNode	This node/service takes entries from the output JavaSpace of the SpaceServlet, and then performs a credit check over a secure virtual private network. A credit report on the individual is also obtained from the credit bureau and attached to the application entry.
HumanVerificationNode	This node/service takes entries from the output JavaSpace of the CreditCheckerNode, and then presents it to a member of staff at the loan approval center for final approval. The officer can examine the results from the two automated systems (the attached business history plus credit report) if necessary, and then make a final approval decision.

JavaSpaces in the System

Here are the JavaSpaces that we will need:

JavaSpace Name	Description
VerifySpace	Space holding loan application and user details which must be verified. VerifySpace is written to by SpaceServlet and read by NameVerifierNode.

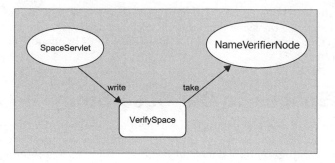

JavaSpace Name	Description
CreditSpace	Holds validated user details written there by NameVerifierNode. CreditCheckerNode takes these user details to run credit checks on users applying for a loan.

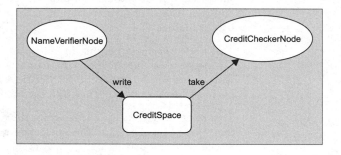

JavaSpace Name	Descripiton
ConfirmedSpace	Contains credit reports for users applying for loans written there by CreditCheckerNode. These reports are taken by HumanVerificationNode for final approval from a human member of staff.

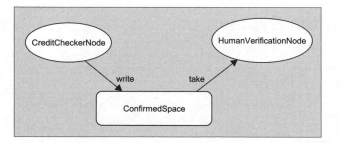

JavaSpace Name	Description
SuccessSpace	This space contains approved loan entries. The `HumanVerificationNode` writes to this space. The `SpaceServlet` takes from this space and presents the status to the user who applied for the loan.

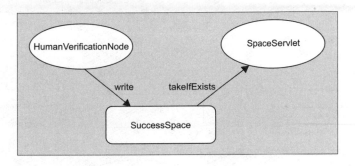

JavaSpace Name	Description
FailureSpace	This space contains rejected loan entries. The `NameVerifierNode`, `CreditCheckerNode` and `HumanVerificationNode` can all write to this space. The `SpaceServlet` then takes from this space when a rejection appears and presents the bad news to the user who made the application.

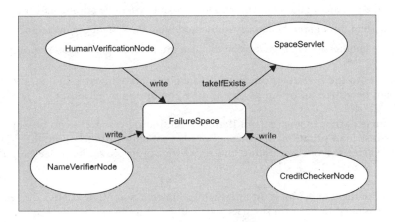

The System's Schematics

Putting it altogether, we have the schematic for our design.

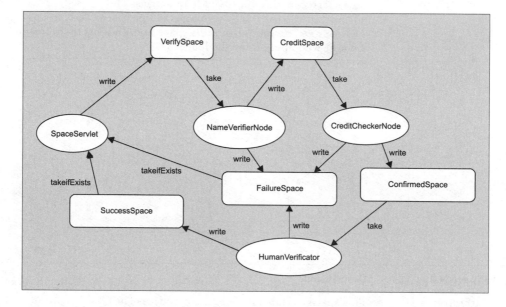

Refining Our Design

Currently, our system is designed as a completely linear pipeline. While this is the easiest way to design a JavaSpaces system, it is frequently not the optimal solution for the problem. Three questions that we need to ask are:

> ➢ Does the system organization allow us to scale our system by adding hardware?
> ➢ Can system throughput be improved by modifying the system organization?
> ➢ Is there another system organization that can improve the per session response time?

The answer is **yes** to the first question. Since it is a completely linear pipeline, the processing resource at any stage can be scaled up by simply by adding configured machines.

The second one is harder to answer, but if all the computing resources can be kept at a high level of use during a stress load situation, our throughput is probably close to optimal. We need to look at each server at each stage of the pipeline and see if we can improve the processing performance individually.

The answer to the third question is one that will point to a potentially better design and is itself a question: "Do we need to perform the user verification and the credit check in sequence?" In fact, we can get a better per session response time by running them in parallel. This will break the linear pipeline design, however, so we must rethink the system topology.

Parallel Execution of Two Different Activities

The new schematics that we want will now look like this:

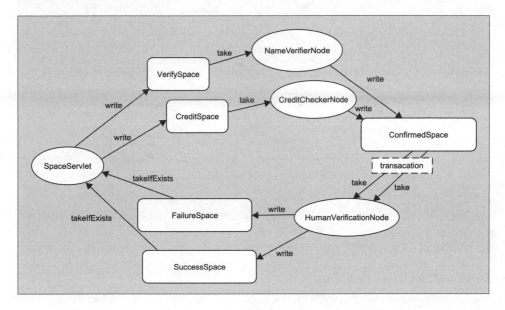

Notice the changes:

> ➤ `SpaceServlet` must now write the same application to two JavaSpaces - both `CreditSpace` and `VerifySpace`.

> ➤ Both `NameVerifierNode` and `CreditCheckerNode` can no longer write directly to `FailureSpace`. If they continue to do so, we may end up with multiple spurious entries which will be hard for `SpaceServlet` to decipher.

> ➤ `NameVerifierNode` now writes its output to `ConfirmedSpace` as well. This means that there can be up to two entries from the same loan application in the `ConfirmedSpace` at any time.

> ➤ `HumanVerificationNode` must now perform an aggregation function, as well as its original job to combine the completed entries from both `NameVerifierNode` and `CreditCheckerNode` into one, and write only one entry to either `SuccessSpace` or `FailureSpace`.

Secondary Problems to Consider

The changes above create some additional secondary design problems. They include:

> ➤ We need to ensure that adding more hardware can still allow us to scale the system.

> ➤ We need to describe the consolidation function that HumanVerificationNode must now perform in more detail.

Ensuring Scalability

In the old design, we can just add servers at each stage of the pipeline to scale the system. It is still true in the new design. For example, if we need more throughput for the `CreditCheckerNode` stage of processing, we can add one more `CreditCheckerNode` machine:

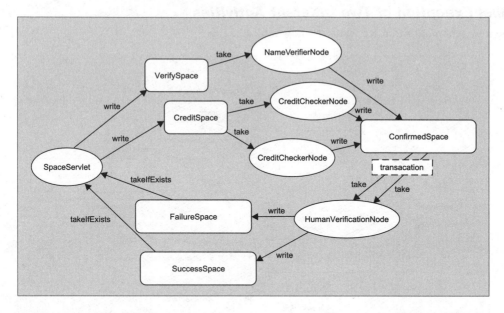

Avoiding Deadlock and Other Problems

The consolidation that we need to do with the `HumanVerificationNode` has the following pseudocode:

```
take two matching entries from the Confirmed Space
if (both entries has been verified by earlier servers in the pipeline) {

    send to human officer for final approval

    if (human officier approves) {
       write a single entry to SucessSpace
    } else {
       write a single entry to FailureSpace
    }
} else {
    write a single entry to FailureSpace
}
```

All that remains for us to do is to figure out how to take two matching entries from `ConfirmedSpace` and check if both entries have been verified by earlier servers.

The first half of this task turns out to be fairly tricky – the `take` operation for a JavaSpace can only match one entry at a time. We could perform a second `take` looking for the same user name and member ID but the second entry may not have reached `ConfirmedSpace` yet, or another instance of the `HumanVerificationNode` (or even another thread in one of the instances) may have taken the other entry. In this second case, we can reach a **deadlock** situation if

> ➤ one instance of `HumanVerificationNode` has performed a `take` of the entry for the user name *U* from `ConfirmedSpace`, written by **NameVerifierNode**, and is waiting for the second entry to be written by `CreditCheckerNode`.

while

> another instance of `HumanVerificationNode` has performed a take of the entry for the user name *U* from `ConfirmedSpace`, written by **`CreditCheckerNode`**, and is waiting for the second entry to be written by `NameVerifierNode`.

This is a classic **hold and wait** situation. We must resolve this, and can do so by enforcing the order of the `take` operation by all the instances of `HumanVerificationNode`. One solution is to make the rule that

> all instances of `HumanVerificationNode` must attempt to take an entry written by `NameVerifierNode` first, and then wait for the second entry to be written from `CreditCheckerNode`.

By imposing this order, we have eliminated the deadlock situation. On the other hand, we have introduced a new problem – we must now know how to identify entries written by `NameVerifierNode`s.

Before we look at how this can be solved, let us think about another more important problem. In order to avoid potentially long hang-ups if we experience partial system failure, `HumanVerificationNode` should not wait too long for the second entry to be written from `CreditCheckerNode`. This means that we should:

> Take an entry written by the `NameVerifierNode`, noting the user name.
> Try to take an entry by the same user name (written by the `CreditCheckerNode`), but don't wait too long for it.
> Repeat.

This will work, but there's a problem (surprise, surprise). As we repeat the first instruction and take another arbitrary entry, we end up with orphaned entries in the JavaSpace when the `CreditCheckerNode` comes through. One solution is to write the first entry with no pair back into the JavaSpace. A much better solution is to **use a transaction**.

By using a transaction, we can abort the transaction to implicitly write the first entry back into the JavaSpace should the second one not come through in time. This means that our three steps have now become five.

> Create a new transaction.
> Take an entry written by the `NameVerifierNode` using the transaction, noting the user name.
> Try to take an entry by the same user name (written by `CreditCheckerNode`) using the same transaction, but don't wait too long for it.
> If the second entry is located before the timeout, commit the transaction. If it's not available, abort the transaction.
> Repeat.

The only remaining unsolved mystery is how we are going to identify entries in the `ConfirmedSpace` as ones being written by the `NameVerifierNode`. This we'll solve by adding a flag to the entry's custom attribute set, which we had better define next.

Mapping out Our Custom Entry

The custom entry that we define will be called `UserEntry`, and these are the attributes in the entry:

Attribute Name	Type	Description
userName	String	The name of the web site user.
memberID	String	The membership ID of the user. Used in conjunction with the name for verification against the membership database by `NameVerifierNode`.
amountOfLoan	Double	Indicates the loan amount desired.
verified	Boolean	A flag to indicate if name verification has been passed.
creditLimit	Double	The credit limit granted after the `CreditCheckerNode` has finished checking credit.
verifyFlag	Boolean	Indicating that the entry is one processed by `NameVerifierNode`.

By matching on `verifyFlag = true` in the `ConfirmedSpace` for a `UserEntry`, `HumanVerificationNode` can find entries that have been processed by `NameVerifierNode`.

Ready for Implementation

Let us quickly revisit some of the design goals we set back in the last chapter to make sure we have not missed out anything. Here they are again:

> - **Availability** – The system should be up and running 24 hours a day, 7 days a week. The staffed credit approval centers worldwide run 24 hours a day, as does the Internet and so should it therefore.

> - **Scalability** – As the traffic increases, we should be able to add resources (things money can buy immediately) to handle the increased volume without re-design or additional implementation; the system must not hit a brick wall upon some ceiling traffic level.

> - **Timely response** – The average waiting time for the end user waiting for loan approval must be under 1 minute at the low watermark (1000 approvals/rejections per day) and under 3 minutes for the high watermark (100,000 per day).

> - **Throughput** – The system must meet the specified watermarks, and offer us the option to increase it by yet another order of magnitude.

And here's how our design meets/fits in with those goals.

Availability – Through the judicial use of RMID, persistent services, and redundant standby servers, one can see how we can design an overall system that will never completely fail. As long as we have at least one instance of each server in the pipeline, the system will continue to run – albeit potentially at a reduced capacity if there is partial system failure. In any case, high availability is an achievable goal through a careful design and deployment plan.

Scalability – The system is designed with this in mind. Increased volume can be addressed by adding hardware servers at each stage of the processing pipeline. Our limit is the interconnect bandwidth (LAN).

Timely Response – Through the refinement of our design, the response time is now bounded by:

```
Response time = max(time to verify name, time to check credit) +
                time for human verification +
                JavaSpaces Overhead
```

We can tune the system for better response time by improving the completion time for each of the elements listed above.

Throughput – Adding more hardware servers allow us to achieve better throughput.

At last, our design for the Online Loan Application Website has been mapped out. We are now ready to proceed and code the various service nodes, and try out the distributed system!

JavaSpaces In Summary

In this chapter, we have had a brief encounter with JavaSpaces. We now know that it is a Jini service, exposing service proxies that support the well-defined JavaSpace interface. We have discovered that Sun's reference implementation is code-named OUTRIGGER and that there exist both transient and persistent versions of it.

While we do not have a precise definition of what a JavaSpace is, we do know that it has characteristics of a lookup service, an object database, and most importantly that it resembles today's queuing services. However, being completely Java based, JavaSpaces goes beyond most queuing services by providing a means to propagate behaviors as well as data.

In the latter part of the chapter, we looked at every method of the JavaSpaces interface individually. The programming model is both simple to understand and highly functional. We then visited some design scenarios and saw how we can implement workflow and parallel systems readily using JavaSpaces. We finished up the chapter by revisiting our Online Loan Approval Website, and actually designed the complete distributed system using JavaSpaces.

Coding a Jini-based Website

Taking the design and specifications we laid down in the last chapter, we can now proceed to code and test our Online Loan Approval Website. We'll start off by building the basic elements of our djinn, and then we'll code some test tools which will enable us to put the system through its paces. At the end, we'll have a scalable, robust, distributed system.

Simulating Business Logic

In order to focus on the JavaSpaces interconnecting the code, and the distributed system aspect of the setup, we are not going to code actual business logic into the pipeline nodes. Instead, the `NameVerifierNode`, `CreditCheckerNode`, and `HumanVerificationNode` will all have an "approval simulator" built using a random number generator and a pre-programmed probability. The service nodes will use this to generate an approval or rejection accordingly.

Local Optimizations

Unlike other case studies you have encountered thus far in this book, we will not be coding the individual modules to optimize performance. The purpose here is to illustrate how to code a JavaSpaces based distributed application, how to design systems using this technology, and how to get the system up and running. All the tips and tricks mentioned in the earlier chapters are applicable here as well, but they become simple local optimization in a distributed JavaSpaces network. In production, you should write optimized code from the start, of course. However, in order to illustrate clearly the important concepts, we won't include them here.

A major example of this is the use of single threaded servers throughout. We are not using a thread pool on any of our servers. This will keep the code uncluttered, make the diagnostic output easy to understand, and will avoid us spending too much time figuring out service-node specific problems that may arise because of this code, rather than because of our JavaSpaces implementation. We will need that extra time to resolve setup and architectural issues.

Additional Modules

In addition to the service nodes we already covered, we also need to code some general-purpose classes for both internal service use, and testing.

`ServerNode` is a general purpose class that all of our services use for:

> ➤ discovery and join with lookup services
> ➤ locate instances of JavaSpaces service
> ➤ locate an instance of a Transaction server

Other tools we will code include a `SpaceWriter` to write a specific `UserEntry` into a JavaSpace, a traffic generator to simulate the action of the `SpaceServlet`, but in high volume, and a `SpaceDumper` to dump out contents of a particular JavaSpace.

We will examine the coding of the elements and services in the following order:

> ➤ `UserEntry`
> ➤ `ServerNode`
> ➤ `JSpaceServlet`
> ➤ `NameVerifierNode`
> ➤ `CreditCheckerNode`
> ➤ `HumanVerificationNode`
> ➤ Other Tools

Coding the Custom Entry

As per our design, all JavaSpaces template searches will be via a custom entry called `UserEntry`. We will be creating `UserEntry` here in the same fashion as `WroxServiceAttributes` in chapter 25.

UserEntry

First of all, let's get the preliminaries out of the way. To make creating our `UserEntry` really simple, we derive the class from `AbstractEntry`.

```
package com.wrox.javaSpaces;
import net.jini.core.entry.*;
import net.jini.entry.AbstractEntry;
public class UserEntry extends AbstractEntry
{
.
.
.
}
```

All public members become an attribute of the entry, which will be used for template matching later on. They must be `serializable` object references, therefore numeric values must be represented by their object equivalent and not the primitive type (i.e. `Double` instead of `double`, and `Boolean` instead of `boolean`). We also include two constructors – one which takes no arguments, and is empty, and a second which takes a series of parameters and uses them to fill in the public fields.

```
   public String userName;
   public String memberID;
   public Double amountOfLoan;
   public Boolean verified;
   public Double creditLimit;
   public Boolean verifyFlag;
   public UserEntry()
   { }

   public UserEntry(String inName, String inID, Double inLoan,
              Boolean inVerified, Double inLimit, Boolean verFlag)
   {
      userName=inName;
      memberID = inID;
      amountOfLoan = inLoan;
      verified = inVerified;
      creditLimit = inLimit;
      verifyFlag = verFlag;
   }
```

UserEntryBean

To be friendly to browsers and editors that may want to decode and work with our `UserEntry`
custom type, we provide a JavaBean for display and editing of the values. This bean must implement
the `EntryBean` interface.

```
package com.wrox.javaSpaces;
import net.jini.core.entry.*;
import java.io.*;
import net.jini.lookup.entry.*;
public class UserEntryBean implements EntryBean, Serializable
{
   protected UserEntry internalInst;
   .
   .
   .
}
```

We keep an internal instance here for field value access and/or modifications. For each field, we
provide both a `setxxx()` and a `getxxx()` method, as per JavaBean specifications.

```
   public String getuserName()
   {
      return internalInst.userName;
   }
   public void setuserName(String a)
   {
      internalInst.userName = a;
   }

   public String getmemberID()
   {
      return internalInst.memberID;
   }
   public void setmemberID(String a)
   {
      internalInst.memberID = a;
   }
```

Continued on Following Page

```
public Double getamountOfLoan()
{
   return internalInst.amountOfLoan;
}
public void setamountOfLoan(Double a)
{
   internalInst.amountOfLoan = a;
}

public Boolean getverified()
{
   return internalInst.verified;
}
public void setverified(Boolean a)
{
   internalInst.verified = a;
}

public Double getcreditLimit()
{
   return internalInst.creditLimit;
}
public void setcreditLimit(Double a)
{
   internalInst.creditLimit = a;
}

public Boolean getverifyFlag()
{
   return internalInst.verifyFlag;
}
   public void setverifyFlag(Boolean a)
{
   internalInst.verifyFlag = a;
}

// constructor
public UserEntryBean()
{
   internalInst = new UserEntry();
}
```

The default constructor simply creates the internal instance as a new UserEntry object.

Here, we implement the EntryBean interface by providing methods to link an instance of UserEntry to the bean, display or modify its properties, and then extract the modified instance.

```
public void makeLink(Entry obj)
{
   internalInst = (UserEntry) obj;
}

public Entry followLink()
{
   return internalInst;
}
```

Coding ServerNode

ServerNode is a utility class that all of our services extend. It handles all the liaisons with lookup services. It will also locate instances of JavaSpaces services and the transaction service.

```
package com.wrox.javaSpaces;

import net.jini.core.lease.*;
import net.jini.space.JavaSpace;
import net.jini.core.transaction.Transaction;

import java.rmi.Naming;
import java.rmi.RMISecurityManager;
import net.jini.discovery.*;
import net.jini.core.lookup.*;

import com.sun.jini.mahout.binder.RefHolder;

import net.jini.lookup.entry.*;
import net.jini.core.entry.*;
import net.jini.core.transaction.server.*;
```

Not surprisingly, this class uses a LookupDiscovery instance to find lookup services. Since LookupDiscovery fires DiscoveryEvent, we have the ServerNode itself implement the DiscoveryListener interface to catch these events. We'll also set up some internal instance variables, the name of our transaction service, and create an empty default constructor so the class is instantiable.

```
public class ServerNode implements DiscoveryListener
{
    static final String TX_MANAGER_NAME = "TransactionManager";

    private JavaSpace tpSpace;
    private String spaceToFind;
    private ServiceRegistrar myReg = null;
    private TransactionManager myTxMgr = null;

    public ServerNode()
    { }

        .
        .
        .
}
```

This is the locateSpace() method, the most frequently called method for ServerNode. Its sole purpose is to locate a JavaSpaces service instance and find a transaction service. It operates by creating a LookupDiscovery instance and using it to find lookup services. Once it has instantiated an instance of LookupDiscovery, ld in this case, it will wait for DiscoveryEvent notification. This notification will have to be handled by a discovered() method. We'll use synchronization to wait for the discovered() method to complete before allowing this method to end and return the JavaSpace located.

```
public JavaSpace locateSpace(String spaceToLocate)
{
   spaceToFind = spaceToLocate;
   tpSpace = null;

   try
   {
      LookupDiscovery ld = new LookupDiscovery(LookupDiscovery.ALL_GROUPS);
      ld.addDiscoveryListener(this);
      synchronized (this)
      {
         wait();
      }
   }
   catch (Exception err)
   {
      System.out.println("Error: " + err.getMessage());
      err.printStackTrace();
   }
   return tpSpace;
}
```

This method, `discovered()`, is the event notification method. It will be called once the `LookupDiscovery` instance has completed the discovery and join process and located the lookup service(s). We are going to iterate through the list of lookup services found, and check each one for the specific JavaSpace service that we want to locate. It is assumed that the name of the JavaSpace service is stored in the `spaceToFind` member. We'll see how this is accomplished later.

```
public void discovered(DiscoveryEvent e)
{
   try
   {
      ServiceRegistrar[] regs = e.getRegistrars();
      for (int i = 0; i < regs.length; i++)
      {
         System.out.println("Registrar " + regs[i].getLocator().toString());
         System.out.println();
         System.out.println("Searching for a JavaSpace called " +
                                   spaceToFind + ": ");
         Entry[] entries = new Entry[] {new Name(spaceToFind)};
         tpSpace = (JavaSpace) regs[i].lookup(new ServiceTemplate(
                                             null, null, entries)
                          );
```

If the JavaSpace is located, we also save a reference to the registrar in `myReg`. We will use it to locate the transacation manager service if required later.

```
         if (tpSpace != null)
         {
            System.out.println("... Space located!");
            myReg = regs[i];
            break;
         }
         else
         {
            System.out.println("... Not found in " +
                                 regs[i].getLocator().toString());
         }
      }
```

Now we've located a lookup service, it's okay to wake up the `locateSpace()` method, and then our work here is done.

```
        synchronized (this)
        {
            notifyAll();
        }
    }
    catch (Exception err)
    {
        System.out.println("Error: " + err.getMessage());
        err.printStackTrace();
    }
}
```

The next method, `findTxManager()` will locate a transaction manager service. It should be called only after JavaSpaces location has completed (i.e. a call to `locateSpace()` has been made), because it reuses the `ServiceRegistrar` found then. It uses the name of the transaction manager we declared at the start of the class in its template lookup to locate a transaction manager instance.

```
protected TransactionManager findTxManager()
{
    try
    {
        if (myReg != null)
        {
            System.out.println("Looking for a transaction manager on " +
            myReg.getLocator().toString());
            if (myTxMgr == null)
            {
                myTxMgr = (TransactionManager) myReg.lookup(
                            new ServiceTemplate(null, null,
                                new Entry[] {new Name(TX_MANAGER_NAME)}
                            )
                         );
                System.out.println(myTxMgr == null
                            ? "Transaction Manager Found!"
                            : "No Transaction manager found");
            }
        }
    }
    catch (Exception err)
    {
        System.out.println("Error: " + err.getMessage());
        err.printStackTrace();
    }
    return myTxMgr;
}
```

Finally, we'll code a test routine inside `main()` that verifies proper operation of the class, and specifically the `locateSpace()` method. It locates a JavaSpace called "ServletSpace", and writes an instance of `UserEntry` into it. After the write, it will read the entry back from the JavaSpace and print out the value.

```
static final String INPUT_SPACE = "ServletSpace";
static final String TEST_USER = "me";
static final String TEST_ID = "12345";
static final Double TEST_AMOUNT = new Double(12.45);
```

Continued on Following Page

```
public static void main(String[] args)
{
    String seekSpace = INPUT_SPACE;
    if (args.length > 0)
    {   seekSpace = args[0]; }

    if (System.getSecurityManager() == null)
    {   System.setSecurityManager(new RMISecurityManager()); }

    JavaSpace space = (new ServerNode()).locateSpace(seekSpace);

    if (space != null)
    {   System.out.println("Got a remote reference to the JavaSpace " +
                                        seekSpace); }
    else
    {
        System.out.println("JavaSpace " + seekSpace + " not found. Exiting...");
        System.exit(1);
    }

    UserEntry msg = new UserEntry(TEST_USER, TEST_ID, TEST_AMOUNT,
                                        null, null, null);
    Transaction txn = null;
    long timeToLive = Lease.FOREVER;

    try
    {
        space.write(msg, txn, timeToLive);
        System.out.println("Wrote an entry to the space");
        UserEntry template = new UserEntry();
        System.out.println("Created a template");
        long timeToWait = 0L;
        Transaction sotxn = null;
        UserEntry result = (UserEntry) space.read(template, sotxn, timeToWait);
        System.out.println("Read an entry from the space");

        String valueToPrint = "";

        valueToPrint = result.memberID;

        System.out.println("and the result was: " + valueToPrint);
    }
    catch (Exception err)
    {
        System.out.println("Error: " + err.getMessage());
        err.printStackTrace();
    }

    System.exit(0);

}
```

The next coding module we will look at is the front-end servlet.

Coding the JSpaceServlet

The JSpaceServlet class is the front-end servlet that will accept form input from the end-user. The form that collects the user information is in the loan.html file and contains:

```
<HTML>
  <HEAD>
    <TITLE>JavaSpaces Distributed Parallel Loan Approval System</TITLE>
  </HEAD>
  <BODY>
    <H1>Apply for your Loan here instantly!</H1>
    <FORM ACTION="servlet/loan" METHOD="GET" >
      Username:<INPUT NAME="username" TYPE="TEXT">
      <P>Member ID:<INPUT NAME="memberid" TYPE="TEXT">
      <P><INPUT TYPE="submit"><INPUT TYPE="reset">
      <INPUT TYPE="hidden" NAME="forminp" VALUE="abc">
    </FORM>
  </BODY>
</HTML>
```

It displays this very simple user interface:

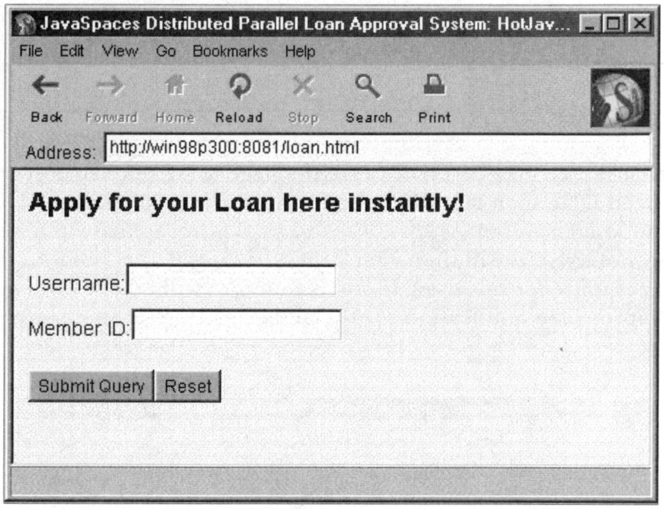

When this form is submitted, the JSpaceServlet will go to work. Notice the submission is a GET method, and will contain a hidden field called forminp with value abc. JSpaceServlet depends on this to recognize that it is an initial form submission, and not a request for refresh.

Upon this initial submission, JSpaceServlet will extract the userName and memberID values from the form, create an instance of UserEntry containing them, and write a copy each to both the CreditSpace and VerifySpace. It then generates the following page dynamically in return:

```
<HTML>
  <HEAD>
    <META HTTP-EQUIV="REFRESH" CONTENT="30;
              URL=loan?username=bob&memberid=22233&dummy=a">
  <HEAD>
  <BODY>
    <H2>Loan Approval in Progress</H2>
    <H3>Please wait...</H3>
  </BODY>
</HTML>
```

The page simply looks like:

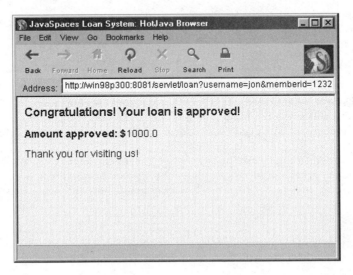

The key here is the <META> tag. This will cause the page to be refreshed every 30 seconds, but using a *different* synthesized URL than the original one. Note that this is still a GET method used, but the forminp field is no longer present. JSpaceServlet will recognize a refresh request by checking that forminp does not exist, it will then check the SuccessSpace and FailureSpace in turn for any loan approval response for this user. If one is found, it will take it from the JavaSpaces, decode it, and generate the appropriate notification for the end user. Here is an example of a final response page:

The code for `JSpaceServlet` follows the structure for any servlet – by now, this should be old news.

```
package com.wrox.javaSpaces;

import javax.servlet.*;
import javax.servlet.http.*;
import java.io.*;
import java.util.*;

import java.net.*;

import net.jini.space.JavaSpace;
import net.jini.core.lease.*;

import net.jini.discovery.*;
import net.jini.core.discovery.*;
import net.jini.core.entry.*;
import net.jini.core.lookup.*;
import net.jini.lookup.entry.*;

public class JSpaceServlet extends HttpServlet
{
    .
    .
    .
}
```

These are the input and output JavaSpaces that this servlet will use during its operations. We also set up HTML headers and footers as constants.

```
static final String IN_SPACE1 = "SuccessSpace";
static final String IN_SPACE2 = "FailureSpace";
static final String OUT_SPACE1 = "CreditSpace";
static final String OUT_SPACE2 = "VerifySpace";

static final String HTML_HEADER =
    "<HTML><HEAD><TITLE>JavaSpaces Loan Approval System</TITLE></HEAD><BODY>";
static final String HTML_FOOTER = "</BODY></HTML>";
```

The instances of JavaSpaces can be shared amongst all the threads of this servlet. JavaSpaces operations are all thread-safe.

```
static JavaSpace outSpace1,
                 outSpace2,
                 inSpace1,
                 inSpace2;
```

Recall that the servlet engine will guarantee that the `init()` method of a servlet is called only once, before any requests are processed. Here, we will set the system `codebase` property, and locate all the JavaSpaces that we need for the servlet.

```
    public void init() throws ServletException
    {
        System.setProperty("java.rmi.server.codebase",
                           "http://win98p300:8080/wroxjs-dl.jar");
        if (outSpace1 == null)
        {
            log("Initializing...");
            ServerNode sn = new ServerNode();
            outSpace1 = sn.locateSpace(OUT_SPACE1);
            outSpace2 = sn.locateSpace(OUT_SPACE2);
            inSpace1 = sn.locateSpace(IN_SPACE1);
            inSpace2 = sn.locateSpace(IN_SPACE2);
        }
    }
```

Note that we have hard-coded the `codebase` in the servlet above. This is not necessary if you have a servlet engine that takes an external specification of `codebase` and `classpaths` (the Apache JServ, for example, will allow you to do this). With the simple ServletRunner supplied in the JSDK, this is necessary because there is no way to specify the `codebase` otherwise. You will need to change the URL above to point to your own HTTPD, running on the same machine as the servlet engine. You could also make it a startup argument to the servlet by modifying the `servlet.properties` file. Watch out for port clashes, and make sure that the web server's port is different from the one you use for the RMI HTTPD server.

The next method, `generateRefreshPage()`, will generate and write to the `OutputStream` the HTML page for performing repeated GET requests. Note the way we include the `userName` and `memberID` back into the page, but not the hidden `forminp` field.

```
    public void generateRefreshPage(PrintWriter out, String url,
                                    String userName, String memberID)
    {
        out.print("<HTML><HEAD><META HTTP-EQUIV=\"REFRESH\" CONTENT=\"30; URL=" +
url);
        out.print("?username=");
        out.print(userName);
        out.print("&memberid=");
        out.print(memberID);
        out.println("&dummy=a\"></HEAD><BODY>");
        out.println("<H2>Loan Approval in Progress</H2>");
        out.println("<H3>Please Wait...</H3></BODY></HTML>");
    }
```

Most of the logic in this servlet is implemented in the `doGet()` method. First, we must distinguish a form submission of the `loan.html` file from a refresh request. We do this by checking for the existence of the hidden `forminp` field.

```
    protected UserEntry sucEntry;
    protected UserEntry failEntry;

    public void doGet(HttpServletRequest req, HttpServletResponse res)
            throws ServletException, IOException
    {
        String formFirst[] = req.getParameterValues("forminp");
        String userName = req.getParameter("username");
        String memberID = req.getParameter("memberid");
```

```
            if (formFirst != null)
            {

                //  Code to handle initial form input

                return;
            }

            //  Code to handle refresh requests

        }
```

If the `formFirst` array is not `null`, then we are taking the initial form submission. In this case, we use the `userName` and `memberID` information from the request to create a `UserEntry` containing these values, and write a copy of the same entry into both the `VerifySpace` and the `CreditSpace`. Finally, we generate the refresh page and return it to the user.

```
        UserEntry myEnt = new UserEntry(userName, memberID,
                            null, null, null, null);
        try
        {
            outSpace1.write(myEnt, null, Lease.FOREVER);
            outSpace2.write(myEnt, null, Lease.FOREVER);
        }
        catch (Exception err)
        {
            log("Error writing to output JavaSpaces", err);
        }
        log("wrote two entries...");

        res.setContentType("text/html");
        PrintWriter out = new PrintWriter(res.getOutputStream());
        generateRefreshPage(out,req.getRequestURI(),userName, memberID);
        out.close();
```

Otherwise, we are taking a refresh request. Here, we must first check the `SuccessSpace` and `FailureSpace` for entries matching our `userName` and `memberID`. Note the on-the-fly creation of templates for the `takeIfExist()` operation. We want the refresh operation to be as fast as possible, so we are not waiting for any transactions to settle, just passing in `JavaSpace.NO_WAIT` as the timeout parameter.

```
        try
        {
            sucEntry = null;
            failEntry = null;
            sucEntry = (UserEntry) inSpace1.takeIfExists(
                            new UserEntry(userName, memberID,
                                    null, null, null, null),
                            null, JavaSpace.NO_WAIT
                        );

            failEntry = (UserEntry) inSpace2.takeIfExists(
                            new UserEntry(userName, memberID,
                                    null, null, null, null),
                            null, JavaSpace.NO_WAIT
                        );
        }
```

Continued on Following Page

```
    catch (Exception err)
    {
        log("Error reading from input JavaSpaces", err);
    }
```

We now check to see if any entry has been successfully retrieved from the JavaSpaces. If we matched no entries, the system is still processing our request, therefore we simply generate the refresh page again and return to the user.

```
    res.setContentType("text/html");
    PrintWriter out = new PrintWriter(res.getOutputStream());
    if ((sucEntry == null) && (failEntry == null))
    { generateRefreshPage(out, req.getRequestURI(), userName, memberID); }
    else
    {
        .
        .
        .
    }

    out.close();
```

Otherwise, we have either a loan approval (if entry is pulled from SuccessSpace) or a loan rejection (if entry is pulled from FailureSpace). On a loan approval, we generate a page to congratulate the user and let him know the amount he has qualified for. On a rejection, we generate a status page and report to the user the reason(s) for rejection by decoding the UserEntry.

```
    else
    {
        out.println(HTML_HEADER);
        if (sucEntry != null)
        {
            out.print("<H2>Congratulations! Your loan is approved.</H2>");
            out.print("<B>Amount approved: $</B>");
            if(sucEntry.creditLimit != null)
            { out.println(sucEntry.creditLimit.toString()); }
        }
        else
        {
            out.print("<H2>Sorry, your loan has been rejected.</H2>");
            out.print("<B>Reasons:</B>");
            if (failEntry.verified != null)
            {
                if (!failEntry.verified.booleanValue())
                { out.print("Membership not found<BR>"); }
            }
            if (failEntry.creditLimit != null)
            {
                if (failEntry.creditLimit.doubleValue() == 0.0)
                { out.print("credit not approved<BR>"); }
            }
            if (failEntry.verifyFlag != null)
            {
                if (!failEntry.verifyFlag.booleanValue())
                { out.print("loan center officer rejection<BR>"); }
            }
        }
        out.print("<P><H3>Thankyou for visiting!</H3>" + HTML_FOOTER);
    }
```

This is all the code for the servlet. It connects to the rest of the system only through the four JavaSpaces: `VerifySpace`, `CreditSpace`, `SuccessSpace`, and `FailureSpace`. One can see that we can even scale the system on the servlet level (ie. we can add more web servers and servlet engines to take more hits from the Internet) if required.

Coding the Service Nodes

Each service node has a similar structure, but their interactions with the JavaSpaces are slightly different (as specified in our design). We will examine the coding of the service nodes in this order:

- ➤ NameVerifierNode
- ➤ CreditCheckerNode
- ➤ HumanVerificationNode

NameVerifierNode

This node takes entries from the `VerifySpace` and writes entries to the `ConfirmedSpace`. It does not implement any actual verification logic, instead it uses an approval simulator that has an 80% probability of verifying an entry (and therefore 20% probability of failing it). Implementing real business functionality is simply a matter of replacing the relevant method.

```
package com.wrox.javaSpaces;

import com.sun.jini.mahout.binder.RefHolder;
import net.jini.core.lease.*;
import net.jini.space.JavaSpace;
import net.jini.core.transaction.Transaction;
import java.rmi.Naming;
import java.rmi.RMISecurityManager;
import java.util.*;
import net.jini.core.entry.*;
```

All our service nodes inherit from `ServerNode` to get its JavaSpaces and transaction server locating capability. The constructor simply calls the superclass constructor. We also need to set up constants for the JavaSpaces we'll be using and the probability of a verification succeeding.

```
public class NameVerifierNode extends ServerNode
{

    static final String IN_SPACE = "VerifySpace";
    static final String OUT_SPACE = "ConfirmedSpace";
    static final double CHANCE_OF_VERIFICATION = 0.8;
    private JavaSpace inSpace;
    private JavaSpace outSpace;
    private Random myRand = new Random();

    public NameVerifierNode()
    {
        super();
    }

        .
        .
        .

}
```

The generalized structure for all our service nodes is:

➤ instantiate a service node
➤ call its Initialize() method
➤ call its doWork() method

We will see how this lifecycle is managed in the main() method later.

The Initialize() method locates all the required JavaSpaces using the inherited locateSpace() capability.

```
public void Initialize()
    {
        if (System.getSecurityManager() == null)
        { System.setSecurityManager(new RMISecurityManager()); }

        System.out.println("Name verifier server running...");
        inSpace = locateSpace(IN_SPACE);
        outSpace = locateSpace(OUT_SPACE);
    }
```

In doWork(), NameVerifierNode will block with a take() operation on VerifySpace waiting for an entry to be deposited. Once an entry is found (matching anything), it will:

➤ take the entry from the space
➤ perform name verification (using the simulator in our case)
➤ modify the attributes in the entry indicating success/failure in verification
➤ mark up the entry to indicate that NameVerifierNode has processed this entry (by setting the attribute verifyFlag to true)
➤ write the modified entry to the ConfirmedSpace

```
public void doWork()
{
    while (true)
    {
        try
        {
            UserEntry workEntry = (UserEntry) inSpace.take(
                new UserEntry(null,null,null,null,null,null), // Template
                null,                                         // Transaction
                Lease.FOREVER                                 // Time to wait
                    );
            System.out.println("Took an entry for Name: " +
                                        workEntry.userName + "...");
            workEntry.verified = verifyName(workEntry.userName,
                                        workEntry.memberID);
            System.out.println("Checked for authenticity... result is " +
                    (workEntry.verified.booleanValue()
                            ? "positive"
                            : "negative"
                    ));
            //  Mark entry as from NameVerifier
            workEntry.verifyFlag = new Boolean(true);
            outSpace.write(workEntry, null, Lease.FOREVER);
        }
```

```
        catch (Exception err)
        {
            System.out.println(err.getMessage());
            err.printStackTrace();
        }
    }
}
```

For our purpose, we ask that the entries written to the `ConfirmedSpace` last forever. In production, you will likely want to set an expiry time to keep the system clean – in case of partial system failure.

Here is the code for the simulator. It uses `java.util.Random` to generate a random number between 0 and 1. The number is then used to determine a pass or fail for the verification. In a real system, this method could easily be replaced with code to perform a real name check.

```
Boolean verifyName(String userName, String memberID)
{
    boolean tpBool = (myRand.nextDouble() < CHANCE_OF_VERIFICATION);
    return new Boolean(tpBool);
}
```

The `main()` method simply instantiates the service node, initializes it, and call its `doWork()` method.

```
public static void main(String[] args)
{
    NameVerifierNode myNode = new NameVerifierNode();
    myNode.Initialize();
    myNode.doWork();      // forever
    System.exit(0);
}
```

CreditCheckerNode

The `CreditCheckerNode` reads from the `CreditSpace`, and writes to the `ConfirmedSpace`. It has a simulator that will approve a credit check 80% of the time. When credit is approved, the average amount approved is $10,000. Credit not approved is indicated by a `creditLimit` value of $0 after processing. The implementation is very similar to `NameVerifierNode` above.

```
package com.wrox.javaSpaces;

import com.sun.jini.mahout.binder.RefHolder;
import net.jini.core.lease.*;
import import net.jini.space.JavaSpace;
import net.jini.core.transaction.Transaction;
import java.rmi.Naming;
import java.rmi.RMISecurityManager;
import java.util.*;
import net.jini.core.entry.*;
```

Like all other service nodes, `CreditCheckerNode` inherits from `ServerNode`.

```
public class CreditCheckerNode extends ServerNode
{

    static final String IN_SPACE = "CreditSpace";
    static final String OUT_SPACE = "ConfirmedSpace";
    static final double CHANCE_OF_NO_CREDIT = 0.2;
    static final double AVERAGE_CREDIT = 10000.0;
    private JavaSpace inSpace;
    private JavaSpace outSpace;
    private Random myRand = new Random();

    public CreditCheckerNode()
    {
        super();
    }
```

We locate references to the JavaSpaces in the `Initialize()` method.

```
public void Initialize()
{
    if (System.getSecurityManager() == null)
    {  System.setSecurityManager(new RMISecurityManager()); }

    System.out.println("Credit Checker server running...");
    inSpace = locateSpace(IN_SPACE);
    outSpace = locateSpace(OUT_SPACE);
}
```

In `doWork()`, the `CreditCheckerNode` will block on a take operation in `CreditSpace` waiting for a `UserEntry` to be deposited. Once a `UserEntry` is located, it will:

➢   take the `UserEntry` from `CreditSpace`

➢   perform `DetermineCredit()` method for the `userName`, in our case we use a simulator to generate the credit granted

➢   modify the `UserEntry` to reflect the new `creditLimit`

➢   write the modified `UserEntry` to the `ConfirmedSpace`

```
public void doWork()
{
    while (true)
    {
        try
        {
            UserEntry workEntry = (UserEntry) inSpace.take(
                    new UserEntry(null,null,null,null,null,null), // Template
                    null,                                         // Transaction
                    Lease.FOREVER                                 // Time to wait
                    );
            System.out.println("Took an entry for Name: " +
                                    workEntry.userName + "...");
            workEntry.creditLimit = determineCredit(workEntry.userName,
                                    workEntry.memberID);
            System.out.println("Checked for credit... credit granted is $" +
                                    workEntry.creditLimit);
```

```
                outSpace.write(workEntry, null, Lease.FOREVER);
            }
            catch (Exception err)
            {
                System.out.println(err.getMessage());
                err.printStackTrace();
            }
        }
    }
```

determineCredit() contains our simulator. It will approve credit with a probability of (1 – CHANCE_OF_NO_CREDIT). The amount approved will be equally distributed between (0.5 * AVERAGE_CREDIT) and (1.5*AVERAGE_CREDIT).

```
    Double determineCredit(String userName, String memberID)
    {
        if (myRand.nextDouble() < CHANCE_OF_NO_CREDIT)
        { return new Double(0.0); }
        else
        { return new Double((AVERAGE_CREDIT / 2.0) +
                            (myRand.nextDouble() * AVERAGE_CREDIT)); }
    }
```

The main() method simply starts an instance of the service node.

```
    public static void main(String[] args)
    {
        CreditCheckerNode myNode = new CreditCheckerNode();
        myNode.Initialize();
        myNode.doWork(); // forever
        System.exit(0);
    }
```

HumanVerificationNode

The HumanVerificationNode reads from the ConfirmedSpace and writes to both the SuccessSpace and the FailureSpace. It requires an instance of the transaction manager for its operation. The simulator it uses will approve loans with an 80% probability, given that both name verification and credit check has been successful.

```
    package com.wrox.javaSpaces;

    import com.sun.jini.mahout.binder.RefHolder;
    import net.jini.core.lease.*;
    import net.jini.space.JavaSpace;
    import net.jini.core.transaction.*;
    import java.rmi.Naming;
    import java.rmi.RMISecurityManager;
    import net.jini.core.transaction.server.*;
    import java.util.*;
    import net.jini.core.entry.*;
```

This service node also inherits from ServerNode.

```
public class HumanVerificationNode extends ServerNode
{

    static final String IN_SPACE = "ConfirmedSpace";
    static final String OUT_GOODSPACE = "SuccessSpace";
    static final String OUT_BADSPACE = "FailureSpace";
    static final double CHANCE_OF_HUMAN_APPROVAL = 0.8;
    static final int MAX_PROCESS_TIME = 10000;

    private JavaSpace inSpace;
    private JavaSpace successSpace;
    private JavaSpace failSpace;
    private Random myRand = new Random();

    public HumanVerificationNode()
    {
        super();
    }
```

MAX_PROCESS_TIME controls how long a HumanVerificationNode will wait for the second entry from a CreditCheckerNode when it is performing the consolidation task (i.e. combining the output entries from NameVerificationNode and CreditCheckerNode into one resulting entry). It really should never be longer than the maximum known time to perform a credit check. In our case, we have set it to 10000 milliseconds or 10 seconds.

Initialize finds all the JavaSpaces as usual, but we do not want to locate the transaction server here yet.

```
public void Initialize()
{
    if (System.getSecurityManager() == null)
    {  System.setSecurityManager(new RMISecurityManager());  }

    System.out.println("Human Verification server running...");
    inSpace = locateSpace(IN_SPACE);
    successSpace = locateSpace(OUT_GOODSPACE);
    failSpace = locateSpace(OUT_BADSPACE);
}
```

In doWork(), HumanVerificationNode must locate the transaction service and perform work only if one can be located. The internal logic is a little more involved because it must perform the consolidation task as well as performing the final human approval. Once a transaction service is located, it will:

> Create a new transaction using the static create() method of the TransactionFactory class and the transaction service proxy. We set the lease of the transaction to a reasonable multiple of the MAX_PROCESS_TIME*6 in our case.

> Perform a take() (with transaction) from the ConfirmedSpace for any entry processed by the NameVerifierNode (i.e. with verifyFlag=true in the UserEntry); block waiting at the ConfirmedSpace if necessary

> Perform a take() (with transaction) again from the ConfirmedSpace, looking for another entry with the same userName and memberID as the first one; block up to MAX_PROCESS_TIME while waiting for one

> If the second take() times out, abort the transaction and go back to the start

> If the second take() succeeds, commit the transaction

➢ Combine the two entries by using the entry from `NameVerifierNode` as base and copying the `creditLimit` from the other entry into the base one

➢ Check the combined entry, if either name verification has failed (i.e. `verified=false`) or credit check has failed (i.e. `creditLimit=0`), write the entry into `FailureSpace` and return

➢ Otherwise, run `PerformHumanCheck()` on the entry. In an actual implementation, this method can take the data and present it to the live officer for approval via a GUI. In our case, it will trigger the simulator with an 80% probability of approval

➢ Write the approval status into the combined entry (reusing the `verifyFlag` attribute)

➢ If the loan was approved, write the entry into the `SuccessSpace`; otherwise, write it into the `FailureSpace`

Here is the code that performs the ten steps above:

```
public void doWork()
{

    TransactionManager txMgr = findTxManager();
    UserEntry workEntry, secondEntry;
    Transaction.Created mycr;
    Transaction mytx;

    if (txMgr != null)
    {
        while (true)
        {
            try
            {
                while (true)
                {
                    mycr = TransactionFactory.create(txMgr, 6 * MAX_PROCESS_TIME);
                    mytx = mycr.transaction;
                    workEntry = null;
                    secondEntry = null;
                    try
                    {
                        workEntry = (UserEntry) inSpace.take(
                            new UserEntry(null, null, null, null,
                                            null, new Boolean(true)),
                            mytx,
                            Lease.FOREVER
                            );
                        System.out.println(
                                "Took an entry for Name: " + workEntry.userName +
                                "... Waiting for second.");
                        secondEntry = (UserEntry) inSpace.take(
                            new UserEntry(workEntry.userName, workEntry.memberID,
                                            null, null,null, null),
                            mytx,
                            MAX_PROCESS_TIME
                            );
                    }
                    catch (TransactionException err)
                    {
                        System.out.println("Timeout waiting for item... Resetting.");
                        continue;
                    }
```

Continued on Following Page

```
                   if (secondEntry == null)
                   {
                      System.out.println("Waited too long. Aborting...");
                      mytx.abort();
                      continue;
                   }
                   else
                   {
                      System.out.println("Got the other one!");
                      mytx.commit();
                      break;
                   }
               }

               workEntry.creditLimit = secondEntry.creditLimit;

               if (!(workEntry.verified.booleanValue())
                    || (workEntry.creditLimit.doubleValue()
                          == 0.0))
               {
                   System.out.println("Rejected without need for human
approval...");
                   failSpace.write(workEntry, null, Lease.FOREVER);
               }
               else
               {
                   System.out.println("Performing human check...");
                   if (performHumanCheck(workEntry))
                   {
                      System.out.println("Approved!");
                      successSpace.write(workEntry, null, Lease.FOREVER);
                   }
                   else
                   {
                      System.out.println("Rejected.");
                      workEntry.verifyFlag = new Boolean(false);
                      failSpace.write(workEntry, null, Lease.FOREVER);
                   }
               }
           }
           catch (Exception err)
           {
               System.out.println(err.getMessage());
               err.printStackTrace();
               System.exit(1);
           }
       }
   }
   else
   { System.out.println("Transaction manager not available!"); }
}
```

PerformHumanCheck() is our wrapper for the approval simulator.

```
boolean performHumanCheck(UserEntry myEntry)
{
   return (myRand.nextDouble() < CHANCE_OF_HUMAN_APPROVAL);
}
```

As in other service nodes, the `main()` method starts an instance, initializes it and runs the core logic.

```
public static void main(String[] args)
{
    HumanVerificationNode myNode = new HumanVerificationNode();
    myNode.Initialize();
    myNode.doWork(); // forever
    System.exit(0);
}
```

Coding Test Tools

We need to create some simple tools to test our system effectively. It may be tempting to use the form and servlet as the testing vehicle initially. They are limited, however, to testing the entire system, and then only at relatively slow rate – as fast as one can type and submit a form. In order to be able to test individual service nodes independently, and to create a large flow of traffic through the system without using the form repeatedly, we will create several utilities.

Utility Name	Purpose
DataPut	Place an `UserEntry` into a JavaSpace, taking the value for the attributes from the command line. This utility is coded for the `SuccessSpace` and `FailureSpace`, and can be used to test the servlet without running the entire system.
TrafficGenerator	Generate a specified number of random entries into the `VerifySpace` and `CreditSpace`, using randomly generated `userNames` and `memberIDs`. This tool can be used to load test the system without using the servlet.
DumpSpace	This utility will take all entries from a specified JavaSpace and print the `userName` and `memberID` values. This is useful for testing the system without re-activating the form each and every time. It also allows you to empty a JavaSpace of entries if the system breaks down!

DataPut - A Space Writer

This utility writes a specified `UserEntry` into the `SuccessSpace` or `FailureSpace`. The command line arguments specifies the values for the attributes in the `UserEntry`. The command line syntax is:

```
java com.wrox.pssjp.Javaspaces.Dataput [username] [memberid] [loan amount]
                    [verified 1 or 0] [credit limit] [verFlag 1 or 0]
```

The two boolean values, `verified` and `verFlag`, should be specified by using a 1 for `true`, and 0 for `false`.

```
package com.wrox.javaSpaces;

import com.sun.jini.mahout.binder.RefHolder;
import net.jini.core.lease.*;
import net.jini.space.JavaSpace;
import net.jini.core.transaction.*;
import java.rmi.Naming;
import java.rmi.RMISecurityManager;
import net.jini.core.transaction.server.*;
import java.util.*;
import net.jini.core.entry.*;
```

We inherit from `ServerNode` in order to get at JavaSpaces services easily.

```
public class DataPut extends ServerNode
{

    static final String OUT_SPACE1 = "SuccessSpace";
    static final String OUT_SPACE2 = "FailureSpace";

    private JavaSpace outSpace1;
    private JavaSpace outSpace2;

    private Random myRand = new Random();

    public DataPut()
    {
        super();
    }

    .
    .
    .

}
```

The structure follows that of a service node. We obtain references to the JavaSpaces in the `Initialize()` method.

```
public void initialize()
{
    if (System.getSecurityManager() == null)
    {   System.setSecurityManager(new RMISecurityManager()); }

    System.out.println("Data Injecter running...");

    outSpace1 = locateSpace(OUT_SPACE1);
    outSpace2 = locateSpace(OUT_SPACE2);
}
```

This `doWork()` method, unlike a regular service node, takes parameters for constructing the `UserEntry`. The parameter values are obtained from the command line. We create a new `UserEntry` instance based on these values. Next, we test the attributes to decide whether to deposit the entry into `SuccessSpace` or `FailureSpace`. Finally, we write the `UserEntry` into one of these spaces.

```
    public void doWork(String name, String mid, double loan,
                boolean verified, double credit, boolean verFlag)
{
    System.out.print("Injecting data...");
    try
    {
        UserEntry myEnt = new UserEntry(name, mid, new Double(loan),
                                    new Boolean(verified),
                                    new Double(credit),
                                    new Boolean(verFlag));

        if ((credit != 0.0) && (verified) && (verFlag)) //success
        {
            outSpace1.write( myEnt,
                            null,
                            Lease.FOREVER);
            System.out.print("writing to SuccessSpace");
        }
        else   // failed
        {
            outSpace2.write(myEnt,
                            null,
                            Lease.FOREVER);
            System.out.print("writing to FailureSpace");
        }

        System.out.print("...Done!");

    }
    catch (Exception e)
    {
        System.err.println(e.getMessage());
        e.printStackTrace(System.err);
    }
}
```

The `main()` method parses the input arguments, initializes the utility, and then calls `doWork()` with all the parsed parameters.

```
    public static void main(String [] args)  {
        int maxItr = 200;
        String userName = "";
        String memberID ="";
        double credit = 0.0;
        double loan = 0.0;
        boolean verified = false;
        boolean verFlag = false;

        if (args.length == 6)
        {
            userName = args[0];
            memberID = args[1];
            loan = Double.parseDouble(args[2]);
            verified = (Integer.parseInt(args[3]) != 0);
            credit = Double.parseDouble(args[4]);
            verFlag = (Integer.parseInt(args[5]) != 0);
        }
        else
        { System.exit(1);, }
```

Continued on Following Page

```
        DataPut myNode = new DataPut();
        myNode.Initialize();
        myNode.doWork(userName, memberID, loan, verified, credit, verFlag);
        System.exit(0);
    }
```

A Traffic Generator

The `TrafficGenerator` class generates a specified number of random requests into the system. Like `JSpaceServlet`, it writes into `VerifySpace` and `CreditSpace`. The command line invocation syntax is:

```
java com.wrox.pssjp.Javaspaces.TrafficGenerator ([number of requests])
```

If you do not specify the number of requests you want, it will generate 200 requests by default.

```
package com.wrox.javaSpaces;

import com.sun.jini.mahout.binder.RefHolder;
import net.jini.core.lease.*;
import net.jini.space.JavaSpace;
import net.jini.core.transaction.*;
import java.rmi.Naming;
import java.rmi.RMISecurityManager;
import net.jini.core.transaction.server.*;
import java.util.*;
import net.jini.core.entry.*;
```

It inherits from `ServerNode`, as expected.

```
public class TrafficGenerator extends ServerNode
{
    static final String OUT_SPACE1 = "VerifySpace";
    static final String OUT_SPACE2 = "CreditSpace";

    private JavaSpace outSpace1;
    private JavaSpace outSpace2;

    private Random myRand = new Random();

    public TrafficGenerator()
    {
        super();
    }

    public void initialize()
    {
        if (System.getSecurityManager() == null)
        {  System.setSecurityManager(new RMISecurityManager()); }

        System.out.println("Traffic Generator running...");
        outSpace1 = locateSpace(OUT_SPACE1);
        outSpace2 = locateSpace(OUT_SPACE2);
    }
```

doWork() uses the `java.util.Random` class to generate random `userNames` and `memberIDs`, and then creates the corresponding `UserEntry`. It will repeat as many times as specified by `maxIterations`, the command line parameter parsed by `main()`.

```
public void doWork(int maxIterations)
{
    System.out.print("Generating...");
    try
    {
        for (int i=0; i<maxIterations; i++)
        {
            UserEntry myEnt = new UserEntry("test user " + myRand.nextInt(), "" +
myRand.nextInt(),
                        null, null, null, null);
            outSpace1.write(myEnt, null, Lease.FOREVER);
            outSpace2.write(myEnt, null, Lease.FOREVER);
            System.out.println("..."+ (i+1));
        }
        System.out.println("...Done!");
    }
    catch (Exception err)
    {
        System.out.println(err.getMessage());
        err.printStackTrace();
    }
}
```

The `main()` method initializes the utility, parses the command line argument, and calls `doWork()` with the count.

```
public static void main(String[] args)
{
    int maxItr = 200;

    if (args.length > 0)
    {maxItr = Integer.parseInt(args[0]); }

    TrafficGenerator myNode = new TrafficGenerator();
    myNode.Initialize();
    myNode.doWork(maxItr);
    System.exit(0);
}
```

DumpSpace - A Space Dumper

The DumpSpace utility takes entries one by one out of a specified space, and prints out their `userName` and `memberID` attributes. It takes as a parameter the name of the JavaSpace to dump. The syntax to invoke this utility is:

```
java com.wrox.pssjp.Javaspaces.DumpSpace ([JavaSpace name])
```

The default JavaSpace name is "nospace" and will most likely result in a failed lookup.

```
package com.wrox.pssjp.Javaspaces;

import com.sun.jini.mahout.binder.RefHolder;

import net.jini.core.lease.*;
import net.jini.space.JavaSpace;
import net.jini.core.transaction.*;
import java.rmi.Naming;
import java.rmi.RMISecurityManager;
import net.jini.core.transaction.server.*;
import java.util.*;
import net.jini.core.entry.*;
```

DumpSpace inherits from ServerNode as usual.

```
public class DumpSpace extends ServerNode {

    private JavaSpace spaceToDump;

    public DumpSpace()
    {
        super();
    }

    .
    .
    .

}
```

Note that this time, it is initialize() that is parameterized. The parameter is expected to be the name of the JavaSpace to dump.

```
public void initialize(String mainSpace)
{
    if (System.getSecurityManager() == null)
    {  System.setSecurityManager(new RMISecurityManager()); }

    System.out.println("Space Dumper running...");

    spaceToDump = locateSpace(mainSpace);
}
```

The doWork() method simply keeps taking entries (matching anything) out of the space and prints them, blocking after the last available one has been taken.

```
public void doWork()
{
    UserEntry myEnt;
    int count = 0;

    try
    {
```

```
        while (true)
        {
            myEnt = (UserEntry) spaceToDump.take(
                        new UserEntry(null,null,null,null,null,null),
                        null,
                        Lease.FOREVER
                        );
            count++;
            System.out.println("(" + count +") Got one with name=" +
                        myEnt.userName + " id=" + myEnt.memberID);
            if (myEnt.creditLimit != null)
            System.out.println("... and"  +
                        " credit=" + myEnt.creditLimit + " verify=" +
                        ((myEnt.verified.booleanValue())
                        ? "POSITIVE"
                        : "NEGATIVE")
                );
        }
    }
    catch (Exception e)
    {
        System.err.println(e.getMessage());
        e.printStackTrace(System.err);
    }
}
```

The `main()` method parses the command line and calls the `initialize()` method with the desired JavaSpace name.

```
public static void main(String[] args)
    {

        int maxItr = 200;

        if (args.length > 0)
        {maxItr = Integer.parseInt(args[0]); }

        TrafficGenerator myNode = new TrafficGenerator();
        myNode.Initialize();
        myNode.doWork(maxItr);
        System.exit(0);
    }
```

This completes our coverage of all the code that we will be using to run and test the system. We will now turn our attention to compiling the code, setting up the environment, configuring the systems, and finally running the entire system.

> You can download the complete source code for the loan approval application from the Wrox Press website: www.wrox.com, including batch files for compiling and running the code on Windows.

Compiling the Code

A batch file, called BUILDJSPACES.BAT, is included with the source-code download, for you to re-compile all the JavaSpaces support source code. Here is what it contains:

```
set JINIPATH=d:\jini1_0
set CLASSPATH=.;%JINIPATH%\lib\jini-core.jar;
                   %JINIPATH%\lib\jini-ext.jar;
                   %JINIPATH%\lib\sun-util.jar;
                   %JINIPATH%\lib\pro.zip;
                   %JINIPATH%\lib\tools.jar;
                   %JINIPATH%\lib\space-examples.jar
javac com\wrox\javaSpaces\*.java
```

You will want to modify the JINIPATH variable to reflect the location of your Jini installation.

If you are only testing and compiling the JSpaceServlet, which runs independently of any service nodes, you can use the BUILDSERVLET.BAT file:

```
set JINIPATH=d:\jini1_0
set CLASSPATH=.;%JINIPATH%\lib\jini-core.jar;
                   %JINIPATH%\lib\jini-ext.jar;
                   %JINIPATH%\lib\sun-util.jar;
                   %JINIPATH%\lib\pro.zip;
                   %JINIPATH%\lib\tools.jar;
                   %JINIPATH%\lib\space-examples.jar
javac com\wrox\javaSpaces\JSpaceServlet.java
```

To create a downloadable codebase for browsers of JavaSpace services, you may want to run the batch file MAKEJAR.BAT. It contains the following lines:

```
set JINIPATH=d:\jini1_0
jar cvf %JINIPATH%\lib\wroxjs-dl.jar com\*
```

It creates a JAR file with all the classes in the library in the root of the HTTPD directory serving the codebase. You will need to edit the file to reflect your root directory.

Creating JavaSpaces

In the Jini chapter, we learnt about the basic requirements for setting up a Jini system. This included:

> HTTPD – to serve codebase of servers on a node
> RMID – to provide support for persistent activation, and activation on demand for services
> REGGIE – the basic lookup service

In order to run JavaSpaces, we must first run an instance of a transaction service. Recall that most operations on a JavaSpace are transacted with respect to other concurrent operations; Sun's JavaSpaces implementation makes use of a transaction service to carry this out. Therefore, outrigger has a dependency on mahalo, Sun's implementation of the transaction manager service.

mahalo – The Sun Transaction Service

`mahalo` is Sun supplied implementation of a Jini transaction manager. It persists its state between reboots, therefore it also uses a log file just like RMID and REGGIE. The command level invocation syntax for `mahalo` is:

```
java  ([setup VM options]) -jar
             -Dcom.sun.jini.mahalo.managerName=[name of manager]
             [jini install dir]\lib\mahalo.jar [codebase URL]
             [security policy file] [path to log files]
             ([lookup service group])
```

`RUNMAHALO.BAT` starts up the transaction service:

```
set JINIPATH=d:\jini1_0
start java -Djava.security.policy=policy.all -jar
                  -Dcom.sun.jini.mahalo.managerName=TransactionManager
                  %JINIPATH%\lib\mahalo.jar
                  http://win98p300:8080/mahalo-dl.jar
                  policy.all d:\tmp\txn_log
                  public
```

You can edit the file to reflect your path. Remember to point the `codebase` to the HTTP server on the machine where you will be running `mahalo`.

As with REGGIE, this service will first run a setup VM. The setup VM registers with RMID, activates the `mahalo` server, and then dies. Therefore, the VM runnng `mahalo` will be a child of RMID, and you will see `mahalo`'s output inside the RMID command prompt box.

If things stop working for some reason you cannot figure out, you may want to run the batch file `RUNCLEAN.BAT` to allow a fresh start for the entire system. This batch file deletes all the log files used by the persistent services:

```
deltree d:\tmp\rmid.log
deltree d:\tmp\txn_log
deltree d:\tmp\reggie_log
```

Unfortunately, the `deltree` command only works in Windows 98/95, you will need to perform the cleanup manually from the explorer under Windows NT.

outrigger – The Sun JavaSpaces Service

Sun supplies two separate implementation of JavaSpaces with the JSTK. One is a transient service (entries are not persistent, and do not survive reboots), the other one is persistent. The persistent space has a significantly larger memory requirement, and it also maintains a set of log files for persisting its state. For convenience and conservation of memory resources, we will use the transient service in our examples. The persistent service is available as `<jini install directory>\lib\outrigger.jar`, while the transient one is available as `<jini install directory>\lib\transient-outrigger.jar`.

The invocation syntax for starting an instance of a `transient outrigger` is:

```
java ([VM options]) -jar
     -Dcom.sun.jini.outrigger.spaceName=[name of space]
     [Jini install directory]\jini1_0\lib\transient-outrigger.jar
     [groups]
```

`RUNSPACE.BAT` is the batch file to start `outrigger`. It passes a command line parameter on to the java command which starts the JavaSpace up.

```
set JINIPATH=d:\jini1_0
start java -Xmx4m -jar -Djava.security.policy=policy.all
        -Djava.rmi.server.codebase=http://win98p300:8080/outrigger-dl.jar
        -Dcom.sun.jini.outrigger.spaceName=%1
        %JINIPATH%\lib\transient-outrigger.jar public
```

So, to start a JavaSpace called `VerifySpace`, we would type:

```
RUNSPACE VerifySpace
```

Note again the requirement to set the codebase pointing to an HTTPD on the machine where outrigger is being run. Remember to adjust the paths and URL to match your system before running it.

Conducting The JavaSpaces Symphony

We can now illustrate the dependencies between the Jini services that are provided by the Jini Starter Kit, and JSTK.

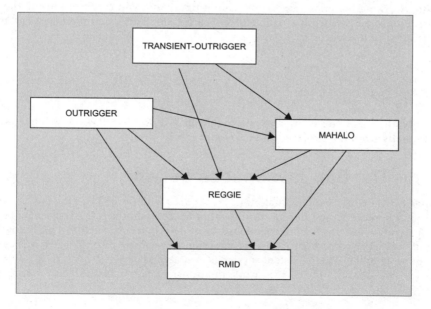

In order to successfully start a JavaSpace, we must make sure that all the servers it depends upon are started up, and the servers they depend on, etcetera, etcetera. This means that a batch file to start HTTPD, RMID, REGGIE, MAHALO, and OUTRIGGER altogether will not work. This is because each service takes a significant amount of time to come up. So, it looks like we'll have to start them up manually.

Therefore, from the HTTPD to starting JavaSpaces, here is the procedure that you must follow in order to obtain a stable running Jini/JavaSpaces system. This scenario assumes that you have cleaned all the log files out.

> Start HTTPD, wait until it has finished printing out all the JAR files.
> Test your HTTPD with a web browser. The verbose mode will print served files.
> Start RMID, wait until the disk stops running. You will have to wait much longer if you did not remove the log files first.
> Start REGGIE, wait until the setup VM goes away.
> Start MAHALO, wait until the setup VM goes away.
> Start one or more OUTRIGGER instances.

Remember that you will need an HTTPD serving your `codebase` on every node that runs a server. You should also consider running another instance of the HTTPD (at another port number) on the node that runs REGGIE, just to serve REGGIE's stub and interfaces. This will keep the server `codebase` different to avoid confusion.

Setting Up the Systems

Okay, I can hear the engines roaring in your giant systems, ready to test out our wonderful JavaSpaces creation. The next step is to plan carefully where you are going to run which services before proceeding.

I will assume you have at least 3 large machines to run this application. If you have 4 or 5, so much the better. Our staging notes will be based on 3 machines, and you can adjust accordingly.

Before we proceed any further, check again:

> each machine can ping all the others using only the machine name
> there are no other servers running on any of the machines
> any multi-homed (multiple network adapters) machine has their non-LAN connection removed or disabled
> you have installed JDK 1.2.1 (or better) and HotSpot on every one of the machines
> you have installed and tested Jini Starter Kit and JSTK on every one of the machines
> you have started and tried out the Jini samples and they worked across this network

Running through this checklist will enable you to avoid most puzzling network problems that have nothing to do with JavaSpaces directly.

Staging on a Network of Three Machines

Now, it is time to copy the required class files and libraries to each and every machine in the configuration. To give a point of reference, here is how I set up my network of 3 machines to test the system:

Machine	RUNNING
Machine A	HTTPD #1 servicing `REGGIE`
	HTTPD #2 servicing `MAHALO`
	`RMID`
	`REGGIE`
	`MAHALO`
	`ServletRunner` **serving** `JSpaceServlet` **and** `loan.html`
Machine B	HTTPD **servicing** `OUTRIGGER`
	`OUTRIGGER` **as** `VerifySpace`
	`OUTRIGGER` **as** `CreditSpace`
	`OUTRIGGER` **as** `SuccessSpace`
	`OUTRIGGER` **as** `FailureSpace`
	`OUTRIGGER` **as** `ConfirmedSpace`
Machine C	HTTPD **servicing** `wroxjs-dl.jar`
	`NameVerifierNode`
	`CreditCheckerNode`
	`HumanVerificationNode`

If you have more than three machines to work with, the logical split would be to run the service nodes on Machine C independently on separate machines. If you have enough machines to experiment with, you can try running parallel instances of multiple service nodes as well.

On Machine A, we have purposely run everything that has a dependency on `RMID`. This server, then, should theoretically restart clean if it ever crashes.

On Machine B, we run all the spaces. If you ever want to run persistent spaces, you can simply start an instance of `RMID` on this server, and then start the persistent version of `OUTRIGGER` instead.

Machine C is where we run our service nodes (or Machine D & E as well if you have more). You should make sure their consoles are visible so you can see the entries flowing through the system.

The servlet requires a `servlet.properties` file to start. We should have the following entry in our file:

```
servlet.loan.code=com.wrox.Javaspaces.JSpaceServlet
```

The batch file we we'll create to start the servlet is called RUNSERVLET.BAT, and contains:

```
set JINIPATH=d:\jini1_0
set CLASSPATH=.;%JINIPATH%\lib\jini-core.jar;
            %JINIPATH%\lib\jini-ext.jar;
            %JINIPATH%\lib\sun-util.jar;
            %JINIPATH%\lib\pro.zip;
            %JINIPATH%\lib\tools.jar;
            %JINIPATH%\lib\reggie-dl.jar;
            %JINIPATH%\lib\wroxjs-dl.jar;
            %JINIPATH%\lib\outrigger.jar;
            %JINIPATH%\lib\outrigger-dl.jar;
            %JINIPATH%\lib\mahalo.jar;
            %JINIPATH%\lib\mahalo-dl.jar
            servletrunner -v -p 8082 -r %JINIPATH%\wroxcode\
            -d %JINIPATH%\wroxcode -s %JINIPATH%\wroxcode\servlet.properties
```

You will need to adjust the paths as usual. Note that we have started this HTTP server (ServletRunner) at port 8082. This means that on Machine A, we have 3 different instances of HTTP servers running:

Port Number	Instance of	Purpose
8080	lib\tools.jar	Serves reggie stubs and interfaces to remote clients
8081	lib\tools.jar	Serves mahalo stubs and interfaces to remote clients
8082	servletrunner	Servlet engine for our system, serves loan.html and handles submission of loan.html form

Many Java Virtual Machines

The reason why we need machines with a large amount of memory is now evident. There are many Java VMs that we need to run at the same time when staging this system. In fact, here is the count of Java VMs:

Machine	Number of Java VMs
Machine A	6, but up to 7 when starting up reggie and mahalo
Machine B	6
Machine C	4

Whenever you start to run one of the utilities or browser on one of the machines, you will need to add another VM to the count. With the current (relatively large) Java VM overhead, starting 6-7 VMs on a limited memory system can immediately bring it to its knees.

Step by Step Startup Procedure

For my network of three machines, here is the step-by-step startup procedure. You will need to modify this if you are running with more (or even less, if you're brave) machines in your system.

Machine A Startup

This machine runs many servers with interdependencies. The first thing is to check and make sure:

➤ All `codebase` in `RUNREGGIE.BAT` and `RUNTX.BAT` are pointing to the correct servers on port 8080 and port 8081 of this machine. `Localhost` won't do – it has to be the correct hostname for the machine

➤ Ensure that the hardcoded `codebase` in the `JSpaceServlet.java` points to the server on port 8080 of this machine. Recompile the servlet if you need to

➤ You know where `loan.html` is stored

➤ Clean off all log files, either using `RUNCLEAN.BAT` or manually

➤ Check `loan.html` manually, make sure the URL for the servlet (`ACTION`) is correctly pointing to port 8082 of this server

The startup steps for this node are:

➤ execute `RUNHTTPD` and wait for a display of the JAR files to complete

➤ execute `RUNRMID` and wait until `RMID` has started completely (ie. no more disk activity – about 20 seconds)

➤ execute `RUNREGGIE` and wait until the setup VM (the additional console) disappears

➤ execute `RUNTX` and wait until the setup VM (the additional console) disappears

➤ run the servlet engine by executing `RUNSERVLET`

Machine B Startup

On this machine we run all our JavaSpaces. We can use the `RUNSPACE.BAT` file that we created earlier to start the spaces. Before you do, make sure that:

➤ the codebase in the RUNSPACE.BAT file is a URL pointing to the HTTPD server on this machine – once again, using its full hostname.

The step-by-step setup for this machine is:

➤ execute `RUNHTTPD` and wait for a display of the JAR files to complete

➤ execute `RUNSPACE` `VerifySpace`

➤ execute `RUNSPACE` `CreditSpace`

➤ execute `RUNSPACE` `ConfirmSpace`

➤ execute `RUNSPACE` `SuccessSpace`

➤ execute `RUNSPACE` `FailureSpace`

Machine C Startup

This machine runs most of the service nodes. You will be using a batch file called `RUNJSPACES.BAT` to start these services one by one. The batch file should contain:

```
set JINIPATH=d:\jini1_0
set CLASSPATH=.;%JINIPATH%\lib\jini-core.jar;
        %JINIPATH%\lib\jini-ext.jar;
        %JINIPATH%\lib\sun-util.jar;
        %JINIPATH%\lib\pro.zip;
        %JINIPATH%\lib\tools.jar;
        %JINIPATH%\lib\outrigger.jar;
        %JINIPATH%\lib\outrigger-dl.jar;
        %JINIPATH%\lib\mahalo.jar;
        %JINIPATH%\lib\mahalo-dl.jar
java -Djava.security.policy=policy.all
        -Djava.rmi.server.codebase=http://win98p300:8080/wroxjs-dl.jar
        com.wrox.pssjp.Javaspaces.%1 %2 %3 %4 %5 %6 %7
```

You will need to adjust the path and URL for your own use. Make sure you adjust the codebase to point to the HTTP server on this machine. Using this batch file to start `NameVerifierNode`, you would type:

```
RUNJSPACES NameVerifierNode
```

The step-by-step startup for this machine is:

> ➢ execute `RUNHTTPD` and wait for a display of the JAR files to complete

> ➢ execute `RUNJSPACES NameVerifierNode`, and watch the console until all the required JavaSpaces have been discovered

> ➢ execute `RUNJSPACES CreditCheckerNode`, and watch the console until all the required JavaSpaces have been discovered

> ➢ exeucte `RUNJSPACES HumanVerificationNode`, and watch the console until all the required JavaSpaces have been discovered

That's it. If everything has proceeded smoothly, you have the entire Online Loan Approval Website system setup and ready to go.

A Problem You May Encounter: Paging of Protocol Implementation Code

There is one common problem that you may encounter trying to start up the system. Anyone trying to run the entire system shown above on a single machine will almost always encounter this problem.

This problem only occurs on highly loaded systems (for example, running 4 or more Java 2 VMs on a 32 MB system). What you may find here are intermittent failures that are very hard to track down. Because the system is overloaded and the virtual memory on the operating system is severely over-committed, once in a while the system will swap memory pages to and from disk. The timing and duration is completely non-deterministic. If this happens while the Java VM is executing application code, the pause is normally acceptable. However, if the Java VM is in the middle of executing timing sensitive protocol implementation code (as it does frequently in a Jini system), this can present a problem. Native implementations of the protocol stacks (such as Microsoft's TCP/IP stack WinSock) are not subjected to this effect. This is not only because they are typically implemented in assembler and C, but also that system programming calls to lock down sensitive code pages and prevent swapping are available at this level. The solution to this problem is to design your system so that heavy swapping never occurs. We have done that by using 3 machines with at least 128 MB of memory each. With the upcoming availability of Java OS and other Java friendly environments, this problem may totally disappear in the near future.

Testing Out Our Distributed System

To test our system, start a browser anywhere on the network. If you only have 3 machines, machine A or B may be better choice than Machine C. You may want to watch the console of Machine C to see the entry flow through the system. From the browser, type in the URL:

```
http://<machine A>:8082/loan.html
```

The loan form should be displayed. Now, enter in a member name and any member ID. Try "jon" and "12345" for example. If everything is running okay, the form submission should bring back the "please wait" page, and you will see some activities on the consoles on Machine C. Thirty seconds later, your HTML page should be refreshed with either an approval or a rejection of your loan application.

Now, if you want to really see a lot of traffic flowing through your system, try using the TrafficGenerator tool to generate 100 requests. This command line should do it:

```
RUNJSPACES TrafficGenerator 100
```

Watch the Machine C console as the service nodes crank through the processing and display the trace. After the system has gone through the motions, you may want to clear `SuccessSpace` and `FailureSpace`. You can do this with the `DumpSpace` utility. These command lines will clear up the two spaces:

```
RUNJSPACES DumpSpace SuccessSpace
RUNJSPACES DumpSpace FailureSpace
```

The JavaSpaces Browser

One useful tool for you to examine the JavaSpaces in a system, and the entries in a JavaSpace, is the JavaSpaces Browser supplied by Sun. It is contained in the `com.sun.jini.example.spaceBrowser.Browser` class in the `<jini install directory>\lib\space-examples.jar` file.

We'll set up a batch file to make running it easier. It is called `RUNJSBROWSER.BAT`, and it contains:

```
java -cp d:\jini1_0\lib\space-examples.jar -Djava.security.policy=policy.all
        -Djava.rmi.server.codebase=http://win98p300:8080/space-examples-dl.jar
        com.sun.jini.example.spaceBrowser.Browser -admin
```

The user interface is almost exactly the same as the Jini browser we saw earlier. However, if you now highlight a service that is a JavaSpace, and right click on the item, you can select a browse entry option. Here is how it might look like if we look into `VerifySpace` with many instances of `UserEntry` present:

What We Have Accomplished

With relatively few lines of Java coding, we have created a distributed processing system that solves a business problem using an object flow. This system can be configured to be a high availability system. The system itself is also highly scalable, allowing us to "just add servers" as the volume of processing increases.

We have taken a technology whose precise definition we can not quite pin down, and created a system that can do very useful work. We have taken a binary, preview technology from Sun, and created an infrastructure that a production system can one day rest upon.

We have seen how Java gives life to Jini, allowing it to be dynamic, allowing it to preach a completely decentralized way of looking at computing systems. We have also seen how Jini gives life to JavaSpaces, giving it a foundation upon which to build robust, scalable, distributed systems.

Jini is at release level one point zero, and JavaSpaces is a brand new version one technology as we go to press. This is only the very tip of the iceberg. If you are interested in becoming part of history, steering and shaping how these exciting technologies may evolve in the near future, join the Jini community today.

HTTP

The Hypertext Transfer Protocol (HTTP) is an application-level protocol for distributed hypermedia information systems. It is a generic, stateless protocol, which can be used for many tasks beyond its use for hypertext. A feature of HTTP is the typing and negotiation of data representation, allowing systems to be built independently of the data being transferred.

The first version of HTTP, referred to as HTTP/0.9, was a simple protocol for raw data transfer across the Internet. HTTP/1.0, as defined by RFC 1945 improved the protocol by allowing messages to be in a MIME-like format, containing meta-information about the data transferred and modifiers on the request/response semantics. The current version HTTP/1.1, made performance improvements by making all connections persistent and supporting absolute URLs in requests.

HTTP communication usually takes place over TCP/IP connections. The default port is TCP 80, but other ports can be used. This does not preclude HTTP from being implemented on top of any other protocol on the Internet, or on other networks. HTTP only presumes a reliable transport; any protocol that provides such guarantees can be used.

URIs, URLs, and URNs

A Uniform Resource Identifier (URI) is a means of unambiguously locating a resource on the Internet. The resources can be files, email addresses, programs, services, or something else. There are two types of URIs; Uniform Resource Locators (URLs), and Uniform Resource Names (URNs).

A URL is a pointer to a particular resource on the internet at a particular location, for example http://www.wrox.com and ftp://ftp.wrox.com/pub/examples. A URL specifies the protocol used to access the server, the name of the server and the location of the resource on the server. For example, the URL http://www.wrox.com/index.html specifies http as the protocol, www.wrox.com as the server location and /index.html as that path of the resource.

Uniform Resource Names (URNs) are intended to serve as persistent, location-independent, resource identifiers. So given a URN a client will be able to retrieve it from any server that has the resource. HTTP exclusively deals with URLs.

Overall Operation

The HTTP protocol is a request/response protocol. A client sends a request to the server in the form of a request method, URI, and protocol version, followed by a MIME-like message containing request modifiers, client information, and possible body content over a connection with a server. The server responds with a status line, including the message's protocol version and a success or error code, followed by a MIME-like message containing server information, entity meta-information, and possible entity-body content.

Most HTTP communications are initiated by a **user agent**, which is the client which initiates a request. User agents are typically browsers, editors, spiders or other end-user tools. The communication consists of a request to be applied to a resource on a server. In the simplest case, this may be accomplished via a single connection between the user agent and the HTTP server as shown in the figure below.

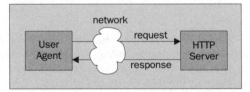

A more complicated situation occurs when one or more intermediaries are present in the request/response chain. There are three common forms of intermediary: **proxy**, **gateway**, and **tunnel**. A proxy is a forwarding agent, receiving requests for a URI in its absolute form, rewriting all or part of the message, and forwarding the reformatted request toward the server identified by the URI. A gateway is a receiving agent, acting as a layer above some other server(s) and, if necessary, translating the requests to the underlying server's protocol. A tunnel acts as a relay point between two connections without changing the messages; tunnels are used when the communication needs to pass through an intermediary (such as a firewall) even when the intermediary cannot understand the contents of the messages. The server where the actual request URI resides is called the **origin server**. The figure below illustrates a HTTP communication when intermediaries are present.

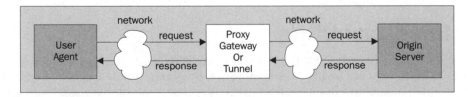

Any party to the communication that is not acting as a tunnel may employ an internal cache for handling requests. The effect of a **cache** is that the request/response chain is shortened if one of the participants along the chain has a cached response applicable to that request. Not all responses are usefully cacheable, and some requests may contain modifiers that place special requirements on cache behavior

HTTP Basics

Each HTTP client request and server response has three parts: the request or response line, a header section and the entity body.

Client Request

The client initiates the transaction as follows.

The client connects to a HTTP based server at a designated port (by default, 80) and sends a request by specifying an HTTP command called a method, followed by a document address, and an HTTP version number. The format of the request line is

```
Method        Request-URI    Protocol
```

For example,

```
GET   /index.html      HTTP/1.0
```

uses the `GET` method to request the document `/index.html` using version 1.0 of the protocol.

Next, the client sends optional header information to the server about its configuration and the document formats it will accept. All header information is sent line by line, each with a header name and value in the form

```
Keyword: Value
```

For example,

```
User-Agent:      Lynx/2.4 libwww/5.1k
Accept:          image/gif, image/x-xbitmap, image/jpeg, */*
```

The `User-Agent` keyword lets the server determine what browser is being used. This allows the server to send files optimized for the particular browser type. The `Accept` keyword will inform the server what kinds of data the client can handle. The request line and the subsequent header lines are all terminated by a carriage return/linefeed (\r\n) sequence. The client sends a blank line to end the headers.

Finally, after sending the request and headers the client may send additional data. This data is mostly used by CGI programs using the `POST` method. This additional information is called the request entity. Finally a blank line (\r\n\r\n) terminates the request. A complete request might look like the following:

```
GET /index.html HTTP/1.0
Accept: */*
Connection: Keep-Alive
Host: www.w3.org
User-Agent: Generic
```

Server Response

The HTTP response also contains 3 parts.

Firstly, the server replies with status line containing three fields: the HTTP version, status code, and description of status code in the following format.

```
Protocol    Status-code      Description
```

For example, the status line

```
HTTP/1.0   200    OK
```

indicates that the server uses version 1.0 of the HTTP in its response. A status code of 200 means that the client request was successful.

After the response line, the server sends header information to the client about itself and the requested document. All header information is sent line by line, each with a header name and value in the form

```
Keyword: Value
```

For example,

```
HTTP/1.1 200 OK
Date: Wed, 19 May 1999 18:20:56 GMT
Server: Apache/1.3.6 (Unix) PHP/3.0.7
Last-Modified: Mon, 17 May 1999 15:46:21 GMT
ETag: "2da0dc-2870-374039cd"
Accept-Ranges: bytes
Content-Length: 10352
Connection: close
Content-Type: text/html; charset=iso-8859-1
```

The Server keyword lets the browser know what server is being used. The date header will inform the client the time of the response (in terms of server time zone). The Last-Modified header will let the browser know the last time this document was modified and finally the Content-type and Content-length will inform the browser the properties of the document that is being sent. The response line and the subsequent header lines are all terminated by a carriage return/linefeed (\r\n) sequence. The server sends a blank line to end the headers.

If the client's request if successful, the requested data is sent. This data may be a copy of a file, or the response from a CGI program. This result is called a response entity. If the client's request could not be fulfilled, additional data sent may be a human-readable explanation of why the server could not fulfill the request. The properties (type and length) of this data are sent in the headers. Finally a blank line (\r\n\r\n) terminates the response. A complete response might look like the following:

```
HTTP/1.1 200 OK
Date: Wed, 19 May 1999 18:20:56 GMT
Server: Apache/1.3.6 (Unix) PHP/3.0.7
Last-Modified: Mon, 17 May 1999 15:46:21 GMT
ETag: "2da0dc-2870-374039cd"
Accept-Ranges: bytes
```

```
Content-Length: 10352
Connection: close
Content-Type: text/html; charset=iso-8859-1

<!DOCTYPE HTML PUBLIC "-//W3C//DTD HTML 4.0 Transitional//EN"
"http://www.w3.org/TR/REC-html140/loose.dtd">
<HTML>
 ....
</BODY>
</HTML>
```

In HTTP/1.0, after the server has finished sending the response, it disconnects from the client and the transaction is over unless the client sends a `Connection: KeepAlive` header. In HTTP/1.1, however the connection is maintained so that the client can make additional requests unless the client had sent and explicit `Connection: Close` header. Since many HTML documents embed other documents as inline images, applets, and frames for example, this persistent connection feature of HTTP/1.1 protocol will save the overhead of the client having to repeatedly connect to the same server just to retrieve a single page.

Entity

Request and response messages may transfer an entity if not otherwise restricted by the request method or response status code. An entity consists of entity-header fields and an entity-body, although some responses will only include the entity-headers. For example, in the above server response the following are the entity-headers:

```
Last-Modified: Mon, 17 May 1999 15:46:21 GMT
ETag: "2da0dc-2870-374039cd"
Content-Length: 10352
Content-Type: text/html; charset=iso-8859-1
```

Request Methods

The first line of a request contains command, request-URI, and protocol components. The HTTP command is called the method. The method tells the server the purpose of the client's request. There are many methods defined for HTTP, but three of them, GET, HEAD, and POST, are widely used.

GET

```
GET        Request-URI    Protocol
```

The GET method is used to retrieve whatever information (in the form of an entity) is identified by the Request-URI. GET is the most commonly used method by browsers. When you type http://www.w3.org in your browser, the browser sends the following GET command to the server www.w3.org:

```
GET / HTTP/1.0
Accept: */*
Connection: Keep-Alive
Host: www.w3.org
User-Agent: Generic
```

If the Request-URI refers to a data-producing process such as a CGI program, it is the produced data that will be returned as the entity in the response rather than the source text of the process, unless that text is the output of the process. The entity body portion of the **GET** request is always empty. The GET method can also be used to send limited amount of input to programs like CGI through form tags. When a HTML form tag specifies the method=GET attribute, the key-value pairs representing the form input are appended to the URL following a question mark (?). Pairs are separated by ampersand. For example

```
GET /cgi/sendGreeting.pl?name=krishna&email=krishnav@valicert.com HTTP/1.0
```

The length of the GET Request-URI will be limited to the input-buffer sizes on various machines. This limits the amount of data that can be sent to the server through HTML form tags. To send large amounts of data usually POST method is used.

The GET method may also have two other meanings. If the request message contains a Range header field then only part of the entity is transferred. This allows partially retrieved entities to be fully retrieved without the transfer of data already held by the client, and so is known as a "partial GET". If the request message contains an If-Modified-Since, If-Unmodified-Since, If-Match, If-None-Match, or If-Range header field, then the request is a "conditional GET" and the entity will only be transferred if the conditions in these header fields are fulfilled. Both the partial GET and conditional GET methods are intended to reduce unnecessary network usage by making sure data already held by the client is not transferred again.

HEAD

```
HEAD       Request-URI    Protocol
```

The HEAD and GET methods are identical except that the server will not return a message-body in the response to the HEAD method. The information contained in the HTTP headers in the response to a HEAD request will be identical to that sent in response to a GET request, and so the method can be used to obtain information about the entity implied by the request without actually transferring the entity-body itself. This method is often used to check that a hypertext link is valid, or when a link was last modified. For example the following HEAD request for the same GET Request-URI,

```
HEAD / HTTP/1.0
Accept: */*
Connection: Keep-Alive
Host: www.w3.org
User-Agent: Generic
```

Produces the same response without the entity body.

```
HTTP/1.1 200 OK
Date: Thu, 20 May 1999 16:21:35 GMT
Server: Apache/1.3.6 (Unix) PHP/3.0.7
Last-Modified: Mon, 17 May 1999 15:46:21 GMT
ETag: "2da0dc-2870-374039cd"
Accept-Ranges: bytes
Content-Length: 10352
Keep-Alive: timeout=15
Connection: Keep-Alive
Content-Type: text/html; charset=iso-8859-1
```

POST

```
POST        Request-URI     Protocol
Headers
...
<newline>
<entitydata>
```

The Request-URI in POST methods usually refers to a data-producing process like a CGI program, it is the produced data that will be returned as the entity in the response and not the source text of the process, unless that text happens to be the output of the process. The entity body portion of the POST request is always non-empty. The POST method is used to send any amount of input to programs like CGI through form tags. When an HTML form tag specifies the method=POST attribute, the key-value pairs representing the form are sent in the entity body of the POST request, with pairs separated by an ampersand. For example

```
POST /cgi/sendGreetins.pl HTTP/1.0
Accept: */*
Connection: Keep-Alive
Host: tcl.ooha.com
User-Agent: Generic

name=krishna&email=krishnav@valicert.com
```

Since GET can only send limited amount of data to the server, the POST method is used to send any amount of data to the server in a client request. POST is designed to cover functions such as posting a message to a newsgroup or mailing list, submitting forms to a data-handling process or adding entries to a database.

The function performed by the POST method is determined by the server and usually depends on the Request-URI. The posted entity is subordinate to that URI, just as a file is subordinate to the directory it is in, and a news article is subordinate to the newsgroup it is posted to. The action that the POST method performs may result in a resource that cannot be identified by a URI, in which case the response from the server should be 200 (OK) if the response includes an entity describing the result or 204 (No Content) otherwise. If a resource has been created on the origin server, the response will be 201 (Created) and will contain an entity describing the status of the request and referring to the new resource.

PUT

```
PUT        Request-URI    Protocol
```

The PUT method requests that the origin server stores the entity enclosed with the request under the supplied Request-URI. If the Request-URI refers to an already existing resource, then the enclosed entity is considered to be a modified version of this resource. If it refers to a resource that doesn't exist, then the origin server will create a resource with that URI if the requesting user agent is able to define that URI as a new resource. If the origin server creates a new resource, it will inform the user agent with a 201 (Created) response. If an existing resource is modified, the origin server should respond with a 200 (OK) or 204 (No Content) response to indicate that the request was successfully completed. If the resource referred to by the supplied URI could not be created or modified, an appropriate error response should be returned.

OPTIONS

```
OPTIONS      *      Protocol
```

The OPTIONS method allows a client to request information about the communication options available on a server for the Request-URI. It allows the client to determine what options and requirements are associated with a resource without retrieving the resource or performing an action upon it. It also allows the client to examine the capabilities of the server. For example, the following request

```
OPTIONS / HTTP/1.0
Accept: */*
Connection: Keep-Alive
Host: www.w3.org
User-Agent: Generic
```

will result in the response given below, giving the operations allowed by the destination server.

```
HTTP/1.1 200 OK
Date: Wed, 19 May 1999 19:38:46 GMT
Server: Apache/1.3.6 (Unix) PHP/3.0.7
Content-Length: 0
Allow: GET, HEAD, POST, PUT, DELETE, CONNECT, OPTIONS, PATCH, PROPFIND,
    PROPPATCH, MKCOL, COPY, MOVE, LOCK, UNLOCK, TRACE
Keep-Alive: timeout=15
Connection: Keep-Alive
```

DELETE

```
DELETE          Request-URI      Protocol
```

The DELETE method requests that the server deletes the resource that is identified by the supplied Request-URI. This request for deletion may be overridden on the origin server, either by human intervention or by some other means. The client has no guarantee that the deletion has been carried out, even if the status code returned from the origin server indicates that the action has been completed successfully. However, the server should not indicate a successful deletion to the client unless it intends to carry out the request.

TRACE

```
TRACE           Request-URI      Protocol
```

The TRACE method is used to invoke a server loop-back of the request message. The final recipient of the request will reflect the received message back to the client as the entity-body of a 200 (OK) response. A TRACE request will not include an entity. Using the TRACE method allows the client to see what is being received at the other end of the request chain and then use that data for either testing or diagnostic purposes. For example, the following trace request

```
TRACE / HTTP/1.0
Accept: /
Connection: Kccp Alive
Host: www.w3.org
UserAgent: Generic
X_Fwd_IP_Addr: 63.65.221.2
```

will result in the response

```
HTTP/1.1 200 OK
Date: Wed, 19 May 1999 19:31:35 GMT
Server: Apache/1.3.6 (Unix) PHP/3.0.7
Connection: close
Content-Type: message/http
```

CONNECT

This is a method name reserved for future use. CONNECT will be used with a proxy that can dynamically switch to being a tunnel.

Server Response Codes

The HTTP server reply status line contains three fields: HTTP version, status code, and description in the following format. Status is given with a three-digit server response code. Status codes are grouped as follows:

Code Range	Meaning
100-199	Informational
200-299	Client request successful
300-399	Client request redirected, further action necessary
400-499	Client request incomplete
500-599	Server errors

Informational 1XX

This class of status code consists only of the Status-Line and optional headers, terminated by an empty line. HTTP/1.0 did not define any 1xx status codes.

100 Continue

The client should continue with its request. This is an interim response that is used to inform the client that the initial part of the request has been received and has not yet been rejected by the server. The client should send the rest of the request or ignore this response if the request has already completed. The server sends a final response when the request is fully completed.

101 Switching Protocols

The server understands the client's request for a change in the application protocol being used on this connection, and is willing to comply with it.

Client Request Successful 2XX

These status codes indicate that the client's request was successfully received, understood, and accepted.

200 OK

The request has succeeded. The server's response contains the requested data.

201 Created

The request has been carried out and a new resource has been created. The URI(s) returned in the entity of the response can be used to reference the newly created resource.

202 Accepted

The request has been accepted but not yet fully processed. The request may or may not eventually be acted upon, since it might be disallowed when the processing actually takes place.

203 Non-Authoritative Information

The returned information in the entity-header is not the definitive set coming from the origin server, but instead comes from a local or a third-party copy.

204 No Content

The server has carried out the request but does not need to return an entity-body. Browsers should not update their document view upon receiving this response. This is useful code for an image-map handler to return when the user clicks on the useless or blank areas of the image.

205 Reset Content

The browser should clear the form that caused the request to be sent. This response is intended to allow the user to input actions via a form, followed by the form being cleared so the user can input further actions.

206 Partial Content

The server has carried out a partial GET request for the resource. This is used in response to a request specifying a `Range` header. The server must specify the range included in the response with the `Content-Range` header.

Redirection 3XX

These codes indicate that the user agent needs to take further actions for the request to be successfully carried out.

300 Multiple Choices

The requested URI corresponds to any one of a set of representations; for example, the URI could refer to a document that has been translated into many languages. Agent-driven negotiation information is provided to the user agent so that the preferred representation can be selected and the user agent's request redirected to that location.

301 Moved Permanently

The requested resource has been assigned a new permanent URI, and any future references to this resource should use one of the returned URIs in the `Location` header.

302 Found

The requested resource resides temporarily under a different URI. The `Location` header points to the new location. The client should use the new URI to resolve the request but the old URI should be used for future requests, since the redirection may not be permanent.

303 See Other

The response to the request can be found at a different URI that is specified in the `Location` header, and should be retrieved using a GET method on that resource.

304 *Not Modified*

The client has performed a conditional `GET` request using `If-Modified-Since` header, but the document has not been modified. The entity body is not sent and the client should use its local copy.

305 *Use Proxy*

The requested resource must be accessed through a proxy whose URI is given in the `Location` field.

Client Request Incomplete   4xx

The 4xx class of status code is intended for cases where the client seems to have made an error.

400 *Bad Request*

The request could not be understood by the server due to badly formed syntax.

401 *Unauthorized*

The result code is given along with the `WWW-Authenticate` header to indicate that the request lacked proper authorization, and the client should supply proper authentication when the requesting the same URI again.

402 *Payment Required*

This code is reserved for future use.

403 *Forbidden*

The server understood the request, but is refusing to fulfill it. The request should not be repeated.

404 *Not Found*

The server has not found anything matching the `Request-URI`. If the server knows that this condition is permanent then code 410 (Gone) should be used instead.

405 *Method Not Allowed*

The method specified in the `Request-Line` is not allowed for the resource identified by the `Request-URI`.

406 *Not Acceptable*

The resource identified by the request can only generate response entities which have content characteristics incompatible with the accept headers sent in the request.

407 *Proxy Authentication Required*

This code indicates that the client must first authenticate itself with the proxy, using the `Proxy-Authenticate` header.

408 *Request Timeout*

The client did not produce a request within the time that the server was prepared to wait.

409 *Conflict*

The request could not be completed because of a conflict with the current state of the resource.

410 *Gone*

The requested resource is no longer available at the server and no forwarding address is known.

800

411 Length Required

The server is refusing to accept the request without a defined `Content-Length` from the client.

412 Precondition Failed

The precondition given in one or more of the `IF` request-header fields evaluated to false when it was tested on the server.

413 Request Entity Too Large

The request entity is larger than the server is willing or able to process.

414 Request-URI Too Long

The `Request-URI` is longer than the server is willing to interpret

415 Unsupported Media Type

The entity body of the request is in a format not supported.

Server Error   5xx

These response status codes indicate cases in which the server is aware that it has made an error or cannot perform the request.

500 Internal Server Error

The server encountered an unexpected condition, which prevented it from fulfilling the request.

501 Not Implemented

The server does not support the functionality required to fulfill the request.

502 Bad Gateway

The server, while acting as a gateway or a proxy, received an invalid response from the upstream server it accessed while trying to carry out the request.

503 Service Unavailable

The server is unable to handle the request at the present time due to a temporary overloading or maintenance of the server.

504 Gateway Timeout

The server, while acting as a gateway or proxy, did not receive a response from the upstream server within the time it was prepared to wait.

505 HTTP Version Not Supported

The server does not (or refuses to) support the HTTP protocol version that was used in the request message.

HTTP Headers

HTTP headers are used to transfer information between the client and server. There are four categories of headers:

General	Information that is not related to the client, server or HTTP protocol
Request	Preferred document formats and server parameters
Response	Information about the server
Entity	Information on the data that is being sent between the client and server.

General and Entity headers are same for both client and servers. All headers follow the `"Name:value"` format. Header names are case insensitive. In HTTP/1.1, the value of headers can extend over multiple lines by preceding each extra line with at least one space or tab. All headers are terminated by a carriage-return newline sequence (`\r\n`).

General Headers

These header fields have general applicability for both request and response messages, but do not apply to the entity being transferred. These header fields apply only to the message being transmitted.

Cache-Control: Directives

Caching directives are specified in a comma-separated list. They fall into 2 categories, request-based and response-based. The following tables list the allowed directives.

Request directives

`no-cache`	Do not cache the information.
`no-store`	Remove the information from volatile storage as soon as possible after forwarding it.
`Max-age = seconds`	The client is willing to accept a response whose age is no greater than the specified time in seconds.
`Max-stale [= seconds]`	If max-stale is assigned a value, then the client is willing to accept a response that has exceeded its expiration time by no more than the specified number of seconds. The client will accept a stale response of any age if no value is assigned.
`Min-fresh = seconds`	Indicates that the client is willing to accept a response that will still be fresh for the specified time in seconds.
`only-if-cached`	This directive is used if a client wants a cache to return only those responses that it currently has stored, and not to reload or revalidate with the origin server.

Response directives

No-transform	Caches that convert data to different formats to save space or reduce traffic should not do so if they see this directive.
cache-extension	Cache extension tokens are interpreted by individual applications and ignored by the applications that don't understand them.
Public	Indicates that the response may be cached by any cache.
Private	Indicates that all or part of the response message is intended for a single user and must not be cached by a shared cache.
must-revalidate	A cache must not use an entry after it becomes stale to respond to a subsequent request, without first revalidating it with the origin server.
proxy-revalidate	The proxy-revalidate directive has the same meaning as the must-revalidate directive, except for private client caches.
Max-age = seconds	This directive may be used by an origin server to specify the expiry time of an entity.

Connection: options

The header allows the sender to specify options that are to be used for a particular connection and must not be communicated by proxies over further connections. HTTP/1.1 defines the "close" connection option to allow the sender to signal that the connection will be closed after the response has been completed.

Date: date-in-rfc1123-format

Represents the date and time at which the message was originated. The field value is sent in RFC 1123 date format. An example is
```
Date: Tue, 15 Nov 1994 08:12:31 GMT
```

Pragma: no-cache

When a request message contains the no-cache directive, an application should forward the request to the origin server even if it has a cached copy of what is being requested.

Trailer: header-fields

This header indicates that the given set of header fields is present in the trailer of a message encoded with chunked transfer-coding.

Transfer-Encoding: encoding-type

Transfer-coding values are used to indicate an encoding transformation that has been, can be, or may need to be applied to an entity-body in order to ensure "safe transport" through the network.

Upgrade: protocol/version

This header allows the client to specify to the server what additional communication protocols it supports and would like to use. If the server finds it appropriate to switch protocols, it will use this header within a 101 (Switching Protocols) response.

Via: protocol receiver-by-host [comment]

This header must be used by gateways and proxies to indicate the intermediate protocols and recipients between both the user agent and the server on requests, and the origin server and the client on responses.

Warning: warn-code warn-agent warn-text

This header carries extra information about the status or transformation of a message that might not be present in the message.

Request Headers

These header fields allow the client to pass additional information about the request, and about the client itself, to the server.

Accept: type/subtype [; q=value]

This header specifies which media types are acceptable for the response. Accept headers can be used to indicate that the request is limited to a small set of specific types, as in the case of a request for an in-line image. The q=value parameter ranges from 0 to 1 (with 1 being the default) and is used to indicate a relative preference for that type. For example,
Accept: text/plain; q=0.5, text/html; q=0.8

Accept-Charset: charset [; q=value]

This header is used to indicate which character sets are acceptable for the response. The q=value parameter represents the user's preference for that particular character set.

Accept-Encoding: encoding-types [; q=value]

This header restricts the content-codings that are acceptable in the response. The q=value parameter allows the user to express a preference for a particular type of encoding.

Accept-Language: language [; q=value]

This header restricts the set of natural languages that are preferred as a response to the request. Each language may be given an associated preference with the q=value parameter.

Authorization: credentials

This provides the client's authorization to access the URI. When a requested URI requires authorization, the server responds with a WWW-Authenticate header describing the type of authorization required. The client then repeats the request with proper authorization information.

Expect: 100-continue | expectation

This header indicates that particular server behaviors are required by the client. A server that cannot understand or comply with any of the expectation values in the Expect field of a request will respond with an appropriate error status.

From: email

This header contains an Internet e-mail address for the human controlling the requesting user agent.

Host: host [: port]

This header specifies the Internet host and port number of the resource being requested.

If-Match:

A client that has previously obtained one or more entities from the resource can include a list of their associated entity tags in this header field to verify that one of those entities is current.

If-Modified-Since: datein-rfc1123-format

This header specifies that the URI data should be sent only if it has been modified since the date given.

If-None-Match: entity-tags

This header is similar to the If-Match header, but is used to verify that none of those entities previously obtained by the client is current.

If-Range: entity-tag | date

If a client has a partial copy of an entity in its cache, it can use this header to retrieve the rest of the entity if it is unmodified, or the whole entity if it has changed.

If-Unmodified-Since: date-in-rfc1123-format

This specifies that the URI data should only be sent if it has not been modified since the given date.

Max-Forwards: number

This header limits the number of proxies and gateways that can forward the request.

Proxy-Authorization: credentials

The Proxy-Authorization request-header field allows the client to identify itself (or its user) to a proxy that requires authentication.

Range: bytes= n-m

Using this header with a conditional or unconditional GET allows the retrieval of one or more sub-ranges of an entity, rather than the entire entity.

Referer: url

The `Referer` request-header field allows the client to specify the URI of the resource from which the `Request-URI` was obtained.

TE: transfer-encoding [; q = val]

The `TE` request-header field indicates which extension transfer-codings the client is willing to accept in the response. If the keyword "`trailers`" is present then the client is willing to accept trailer fields in a chunked transfer-coding.

User-Agent: product | comment

This header contains information about the user agent originating the request. This allows the server to automatically recognize user agents and tailoring its responses to avoid particular user agent limitations.

Response Headers

The response-header fields allow the server to pass additional information about the response that cannot be placed in the `Status-Line`. These header fields give information about the server and about further access to the resource identified by the `Request-URI`.

`Accept-Ranges:    range-unit | none`

This header allows the server to indicate its acceptance of range requests for a resource.

`Age:      seconds`

This header contains the sender's estimate of the amount of time since the response was generated at the origin server.

`Etag:   entity-tag`

This header provides the current value of the requested entity tag.

`Location: URI`

This is used to redirect the recipient to a location other than the `Request-URI` to complete the request.

`Proxy-Authenticate: scheme realm`

This header indicates the authentication scheme and parameters applicable to the proxy for this `Request-URI`.

`Retry-After:   date | seconds`

This is used by the server to indicate how long the service is expected to be unavailable to the requesting client.

`Server   string`

The `Server` header contains information about the software that the origin server used to handle the request.

`Vary: * | headers`

This header specifies that the entity has multiple sources and may therefore vary according to specified list of request headers. Multiple headers can be listed separated by commas. An asterisk means another factor other than the request headers may affect the response that is returned.

`WWW-Authenticate:   scheme realm`

This header is used with the 401 response code to indicate to the client that the requested URI needs authentication . The value specifies the authorization scheme and the realm of authority required from the client.

Entity Headers

Entity-header fields define meta-information about the entity-body or, if no body is present, about the resource identified by the request.

`Allow:    methods`

This header is used to inform the recipient of valid methods associated with the resource.

`Content-Encoding:    encoding`

This header indicates what additional content codings have been applied to the entity-body, and hence what decoding must be carried out in order to obtain the media-type referenced by the `Content-Type` header field.

`Content-Language:    languages`

The `Content-Language` header describes the natural language(s) of the intended audience for the enclosed entity.

`Content-Length: n`

This header indicates the size of the entity-body. Due to the dynamic nature of some requests, the content-length is sometimes unknown and this header is omitted.

`Content-Location: uri`

The `Content-Location` header supplies the resource location for the entity enclosed in the message when that entity may be accessed from a different location to the requested resource's URI.

`Content-MD5: digest`

This header contains an MD5 digest of the entity-body that is used to provide an end-to-end message integrity check (MIC) of the entity-body. See RFC 1864 for more details.

`Content-Range: bytes n-m/length`

The `Content-Range` header is sent with a partial entity-body to specify where in the full entity-body the partial body should come from.

`Content-Type: type/subtype`

This header describes the media type of the entity-body sent to the recipient. In the case of the HEAD method, it describes the media type that would have been sent had the request been a GET.

`Expires: RFC-1123-date`

The `Expires` header gives the date and time after which the response is considered stale.

`Last-Modified:    RFC-1123-date`

This header indicates the date and time at which the origin server believes the variant was last modified.

References

> "Hypertext Transfer Protocol - HTTP/1.1" specification: (http://www.w3.org/Protocols/HTTP/1.1/draft-ietf-http-v11-spec-rev-06.txt)

> MIME (Multipurpose Internet Mail Extensions): (http://www.faqs.org/rfcs/rfc1341.html)

> Date and Time specifications: RFC 1123:(http://www.faqs.org/rfcs/rfc1123.html)

> The Content-MD5 header field: RFC 1864: (http://www.faqs.org/rfcs/rfc1864.html)

> Standard for Interchange of USENET Messages: (http://www.faqs.org/rfcs/rfc850.html)

> World Wide Web Consortium: (http://www.w3.org)

Java Object Streams and Serialization

In order for any program to manipulate data, it must be able to read and write information. Java streams provide a consistent mechanism for input/output operations across different devices and for various data types. In this appendix, we cover the basics of I/O streams and provide various examples. Your servlets may very well need to read and write data to sources other than the browser and therefore a good understanding of Java streams is helpful in implementing servlets with sophisticated functionality.

Another topic that is discussed in this appendix is object serialization. Serialization is a mechanism for storing and retrieving "live" objects. In other words, serialization allows you to add persistence behavior to your objects (when needed). This feature is useful in servlet-to-servlet communication and for using servlets to create objects that are later used by other programs.

I/O in Java

Java provides an extensive set of APIs for data input and output. Being dubbed as the network programming language, Java must be able to provide a consistent interface to various data sources. Pretty much everything, including files, directories, etc., is wrapped in a class. This way, as a developer, you don't have to deal with the platform-specific details of I/O. For example, on Windows-based machines, the character for separating directories is '\' but on Unix platforms it is '/'. As long as you stay within the confines of the Java I/O API, your applications will run on any Java-supported platform.

The basis for all of Java I/O operations, including file and network operations, is a stream. Data is represented as a stream that is then either written out or read in. Primitive data types, complex data types, and objects can all be written or read from a stream. In fact, object serialization uses streams to read and write data. In this section, we provide an overview of Java I/O support and its various flavors. We also provide simple examples to demonstrate the API.

The most basic elements in file operations are the files and directories themselves. The File class contains information about the properties of a file or directory. There are three ways to construct a File object. They are:

```
File(String path)
File(String directoryPath, String filename)
File(File directory, String filename)
```

The File class has two interesting fields. The first is the separatorChar defined like this:

```
public static final char separatorChar
```

This field contains the character used to separate directories and files in a given path. On UNIX systems the value of this field is '/', whereas on Win32 systems it is '\'. The other field is pathSeparatorChar. As its name indicates, this is the character used to separate different path entries. On UNIX systems, this character is ':', on Win32 systems it is ';'.

Each of the fields mentioned above has a corresponding field containing the String corresponding to the character field. These fields are called separator and pathSeparator respectively.

Before going on, take a few moments to familiarize yourself with the File class. It is part of the java.io package. There are a number of methods in this class that you should be familiar with. These methods provide you with access permissions and other information about the file. They also allow you to perform file operations such as renaming and deleting a file. A common mistake for beginning Java programmers is that they try to perform such operations by executing a shell command, which may work, but it makes the code system dependent.

The following listing shows some simple code that renames a file.

```java
import java.io.*;

class fileRename
{
    public static void main (String args[])
    {
        File foo = new File ("C:\\temp\\foo.txt");
        File foo2 = new File ("C:\\temp\\foo2.txt");
        foo.renameTo (foo2);
        System.out.println("done.");
    }
}
```

Streams

When you think of I/O, different devices come to mind. Input to a program may come from a keyboard, a file stored on disk, or a buffer in memory. Output of a program may be directed to the console, a physical file or some memory buffer. Regardless of the source or destination of I/O operations, the end effect is the same. That is, we want to read/write a series of bytes. In Java, streams are used to create a uniform interface to I/O operations. A stream is an abstraction for a source or destination of data. Once that abstraction is created, then the same methods could be used to read/write to a variety of streams (which are themselves abstractions of a variety of different I/O devices).

Java utilizes two main types of streams. The first are character streams that are used for reading/writing characters and strings. Although Java represents characters according to the 16-bit Unicode encoding, this may not be the desired encoding for a particular device. Character streams allow you to translate between various encoding formats.

The other type of streams are byte streams. These streams are used for reading/writing raw bytes. Depending on the encoding, a character may be represented by one or more bytes so you could say the character streams are built on top of byte streams, but for the purposes of our discussion, we keep them separate. Anytime you need to read/write binary data you would use a byte stream. In the remainder of this section, we take a look at various character and byte streams.

Reading Character Streams

We start our discussion with the Reader class. This is an abstract class for reading character data. A subclass of Reader is required to at least implement the read(char[],int, int) and close() methods. The subclass, however, is free to override other methods as well. Here are the method listings for Reader:

Method	Description
abstract void close()	Close the stream.
Void mark(int readAheadLimit)	Mark the present position in the stream.
boolean markSupported()	Tell whether this stream supports the mark() operation.
int read()	Read a single character.
int read(char[] cbuf)	Read characters into an array.
abstract int read(char[] cbuf, int off, int len)	Read characters into a portion of an array.
boolean ready()	Tell whether this stream is ready to be read.
Void reset()	Reset the stream.
Long skip(long n)	Skip characters.

The following are subclasses of `Reader` that are part of the Java API. Classes in bold typeface are discussed in this section.

```
class java.io.Reader
```
> **`class java.io.BufferedReader`**
> `class java.io.LineNumberReader`
> `class java.io.CharArrayReader`
> `class java.io.FilterReader`
> `class java.io.PushbackReader`
> **`class java.io.InputStreamReader`**
> **`class java.io.FileReader`**
> `class java.io.PipedReader`
> `class java.io.StringReader`

One of the most common classes used is the `InputStreamReader`. This class is a bridge between bytes and characters. It translates a stream of bytes into a stream of characters based on the specified encoding scheme. If no encoding is specified, then the default character encoding for the platform is used. The two constructors are:

```
InputStreamReader(InputStream instream)
InputStreamReader(InputStream instream, String encoding)
```

The following listing shows a simple program where `InputStreamReader` is used. We use the `System.in` as an argument to the constructor (which in this case means the input is coming from the keyboard). Note that we are also printing the default encoding using the `getEncoding()` method. We then read characters from the console and write them out. We close the stream at the end.

```java
import java.io.*;

class InputStreamReaderDemo
{
    public static void main(String args[])
    {
        try
        {
          // create an InputStreamReader
            InputStreamReader instream = new InputStreamReader(System.in);
            System.out.println("Character Encoding is: " +
                               instream.getEncoding());

          // Echo everything that is read
            int i;
```

```
            while ((i = instream.read()) != -1)
            {
                System.out.print((char) i);
            }
            instream.close();
        }
        catch (Exception e)
        {
            System.out.println("Exception: " + e);
        }
    }
}
```

Taking this a step further, the `FileReader` class inherits from `InputStreamReader`, but gets its input from a file. There are three constructors for the `FileReader` class:

```
FileReader(String filename)
FileReader(File f)
FileReader (FileDescriptor fd)
```

The next listing is similar to the code above, but we use a `FileReader` to read the input from a file. We have hard-coded the name of the file, but we could change the code so the filename is specified as a command-line argument.

```
import java.io.*;

class FileReaderDemo
{
    public static void main(String args[])
    {
        try
        {
            // create an InputStreamReader
            FileReader freader = new FileReader("read_input.txt");
            System.out.println("Character Encoding is: " +
                        freader.getEncoding());

            // Echo everything that is read
            int i;
            while ((i = freader.read()) != -1)
            {
                System.out.print((char) i);
            }
            freader.close();
        }
        catch (Exception e)
        {
            System.out.println("Exception: " + e);
        }
    }
}
```

To run the program, create a text file in the same directory as the `.class` file and call it `read_input.txt`. You can then run the program by typing

```
java FileReaderDemo
```

To increase efficiency and performance, you can use the `BufferedReader` class for inputting characters. There are two constructors for `BufferedReader` as follows:

```
BufferedReader(Reader r)
BufferedReader(Reader r, int size)
```

With the second constructor, you specify the size of the buffer to be used. Since buffers reduce the number of times a device has to be accessed, they increase performance. For this reason, it is often advised that you wrap other subclasses of `Reader` such as `FileReaders` and `InputStreamReaders` inside `BufferedReader`. Here is an example where `FileReader` is wrapped inside `BufferedReader`:

```
BufferedReader in = new BufferedReader(new FileReader("foo.in"));
```

The next listing is an example of how the `BufferedReader` class can be used. This time, instead of hard coding the filename, we specify it at the command line. Also, notice that we are using the `readLine()` method to go through each line in the file. The `readLine()` method discards the newline character it reads, so we probably want to use a `System.out.println()` method instead of the `System.out.print()` method to compensate for the discarded newline character.

```java
import java.io.*;

class BufferedReaderDemo
{
    public static void main(String args[])
    {
        try
        {
            //create a file reader
            FileReader freader = new FileReader(args[0]);

            // attach a buffered reader to it
            BufferedReader breader = new BufferedReader(freader);
            String str = null;
            while ((str = breader.readLine()) != null)
            {
                System.out.print(str);
            }
            freader.close();
        }
        catch (Exception e)
        {
            System.out.println("Exception: " + e);
        }
    }
}
```

Writing Character Streams

If we can read streams, we must be able to write to a stream. For the most part, writing to a stream is the exact opposite of reading from it and the methods and classes closely mirror the ones we have learned so far. The `Writer` class is an abstract class for writing character data. A subclass of `Writer` is required to at least implement the `write(char[],int, int)`, `flush()` and `close()` methods. The subclass, however, is free to override other methods as well. Here are the method listings for `Writer`:

Method	Description
abstract void close()	Close the stream, flushing it first.
abstract void flush()	Flush the stream.
Void write(char[] cbuf)	Read a single character.
abstract void write(char[], int off, int len)	Write a portion of an array of characters.
Void write(int c)	Write a single character.
Void write(String str)	Write a string.
void write(String str, int off, int len)	Write a portion of a string.

As you can see, there are a few different methods for writing characters. Next is a listing of subclasses of `Writer`. Classes in bold typeface are discussed in this section.

class java.io.Writer
>   **class java.io.BufferedWriter**
>   class java.io.CharArrayWriter
>   class java.io.FilterWriter
>   **class java.io.OutputStreamWriter**
>   **class java.io.FileWriter**
>   class java.io.PipedWriter
>   **class java.io.PrintWriter**
>   class java.io.StringWriter

One of the most basic classes for writing out characters is `OutputStreamWriter`. This class is used to translate characters into a stream of bytes to be written out. This means that the class must be aware of the encoding used so it can perform its translation correctly. The two constructors are:

```
OutputStreamWriter(OutputStream ostream)
OutputStreamWriter(OutputStream ostream, String encoding)
```

The following listing shows a simple program where `OutputStreamWriter` is used. We use the `System.out` as an argument to the constructor (which in this case means the output is going to the console). Note that we are also printing the default encoding using the `getEncoding()` method. We use a loop to write out a few characters (nothing fancy, but it does show how the class is used).

```
import java.io.*;

class OutputStreamWriterDemo
{
    public static void main(String args[])
    {
        try
        {
            OutputStreamWriter outstream = new
                            OutputStreamWriter(System.out);
            System.out.println("Character Encoding is: " +
                            outstream.getEncoding());

            for (int i=65; i< 75; i++)
            {
                outstream.write(i);
                outstream.write("\n");
            }
            outstream.close();
        }
        catch (Exception e)
        {
            System.out.println("Exception: " + e);
        }
    }
}
```

The `FileWriter` class allows you to perform write operations on a file. There are three constructors for the `FileWriter` class:

```
FileWriter(String filename)
FileWriter(File f)
FileWriter(File f, boolean append)
FileWriter (FileDescriptor fd)
```

The listing below is similar to the one above, but we use a `FileWriter` to write the characters to a file. We have hard-coded the name of the file. Again, we could change it so the filename is specified as a command-line argument.

```
import java.io.*;

class FileWriterDemo
{
    public static void main(String args[])
    {
        try
        {
            FileWriter fwriter = new FileWriter("write_output.txt");
            for (int i=100; i< 110; i++)
            {
                fwriter.write("Price going up: " + i + "\n");
            }
            fwriter.close();
```

```
        }
        catch (Exception e)
        {
            System.out.println("Exception: " + e);
        }
    }
}
```

To increase efficiency and performance, you can use the `BufferedWriter` class. There are two constructors for `BufferedWriter` as follows:

```
BufferedWriter(Writer r)
BufferedWriter(Writer r, int size)
```

With the second constructor, you specify the size of the buffer to be used. As mentioned earlier, buffers reduce the number of times a device has to be accessed and so they increase performance. It is often advised that you wrap other subclasses of `Writer` such as `FileWriter` and `OutputStreamWriter` inside `BufferedWriter`. Here is an example where `FileWriter` is wrapped inside `BufferedWriter`:

```
BufferedWriter out = new BufferedWriter(new FileWriter("foo.in"));
```

The following code shows an example of how the `BufferedWriter` class can be used.

```
import java.io.*;

class BufferedWriterDemo
{
    public static void main(String args[])
    {
        try
        {
            //create a file Writer
            FileWriter fwriter = new FileWriter(args[0]);

            // attach a buffered Writer to it
            BufferedWriter bwriter = new BufferedWriter(fwriter);
            String str = null;

            for (int i=0; i< 15; i++)
            {
                fwriter.write("Now serving " + i + "\n");
            }
            fwriter.close();
        }
        catch (Exception e)
        {
            System.out.println("Exception: " + e);
        }
    }
}
```

There are many different data types available in Java such as `int`, `long`, `float`, `char`, etc. You also have an unlimited number of classes. Some are defined within the various Java specification and some are application-dependent. It would be nice to have a class that lets you write out any type of data without knowing what the type is. That class is `PrintWriter`. The key methods are `print()` and `println()` which take both primitive data types and object data type. For primitive data types, the argument is converted to a string and written out. For object data types, the methods will call the object's `toString()` method and display the returned value. You can initialize `PrintWriter` like this:

```
PrintWriter pw = new PrintWriter(System.out);
```

Now, you can call `pw.println()` with different argument types and they'll all get printed out to the console.

Byte Streams

What you have learned about streaming characters can easily be applied to streaming bytes. The main thing you have to be concerned with is that the methods and classes are used to read/write raw bytes, and every byte counts. You may be used to ignoring a white space when outputting a character or string and since an extra space among other extra spaces is not going to show, the end result is satisfactory. This is not the case with binary data and byte streams. Again, every byte counts.

The two main classes for reading and writing bytes are `InputStream` and `OutputStream`. Here is the class hierarchy for each one. Note the similarity to the character streaming classes.

```
class java.io.InputStream
```
- ➤ class java.io.ByteArrayInputStream
- ➤ class java.io.FileInputStream
- ➤ class java.io.FilterInputStream
- ➤ class java.io.BufferedInputStream
- ➤ class java.io.DataInputStream (implements java.io.DataInput)
- ➤ class java.io.LineNumberInputStream
- ➤ class java.io.PushbackInputStream
- ➤ class java.io.ObjectInputStream (implements java.io.ObjectInput, java.io.ObjectStreamConstants)
- ➤ class java.io.PipedInputStream
- ➤ class java.io.SequenceInputStream
- ➤ class java.io.StringBufferInputStream

```
class java.io.OutputStream
    ➤   class java.io.ByteArrayOutputStream
    ➤   class java.io.FileOutputStream
    ➤   class java.io.FilterOutputStream
    ➤   class java.io.BufferedOutputStream
    ➤   class java.io.DataOutputStream (implements java.io.DataOutput)
    ➤   class java.io.PrintStream
    ➤   class java.io.ObjectOutputStream (implements java.io.ObjectOutput,
        java.io.ObjectStreamConstants)
    ➤   class java.io.PipedOutputStream
```

The following code uses `FileOutputStream` to write out a few bytes to a file. The code looks similar to what we wrote for `FileWriter`, but it is using `OutputStream`.

```java
import java.io.*;

class FileOutputStreamDemo
{
    public static void main(String args[])
    {
        try
        {
            FileOutputStream foutstream = new
                    FileOutputStream("write_output_byte.txt");
            for (int i=10; i< 20; i++)
            {
                foutstream.write(i);
            }
            foutstream.close();
        }
        catch (Exception e)
        {
            System.out.println("Exception: " + e);
        }
    }
}
```

If you try to print out the content of `write_output_byte.txt`, it is garbled characters. We need to write another program that uses `FileInputStream` to read the binary files and display them in "text" format. One such program is shown below.

```java
import java.io.*;

class FileInputStreamDemo
{
    public static void main(String args[])
    {
        try
        {
            FileInputStream finstream = new
                    FileInputStream("write_output_byte.txt");
            int i;
            while ((i = finstream.read()) != -1)
            {
                System.out.print(i + " ");
            }
            finstream.close();
        }
        catch (Exception e)
        {
            System.out.println("Exception: " + e);
        }
    }
}
```

The program reads each byte and prints it out. Subsequent bytes are separated by a space.

What is serialization?

A Java class can be instantiated into an object. A Java program is then a collection of various objects, interacting and communicating with each other to accomplish the goals of the program. It is possible to follow an object from the time it is created until it is destroyed. This can be considered as the life span of an object. Some objects don't change much during their life span, but some do. Let's assume that you had a camera that could capture the state of an object at any given time. The state of an object would be determined by the value of its properties. While typically, we may think of an object having a continuous life span, that may not necessarily be the case. It is conceivable that we capture the state of an object at a given time, disregard the object, and then use it again at a later time. We could create the object from scratch again (there is nothing new here), or we could recreate the object based on its last saved state (now that would be cool). Object serialization is a mechanism in Java to do just this.

A given object can be serialized into a persistent form (e.g., a file) thus saving its current state. The same object can be recreated at a later time from the file it was saved in. For example, through serialization it is possible for you to save an object to a file, send it to your friend, and your friend can then recreate the object exactly as you saved it and start working on it.

The Java documentation describes Object Serialization as follows:

> "Object Serialization extends the core Java Input/Output classes with support for objects. Object Serialization supports the encoding of objects, and the objects reachable from them, into a stream of bytes; and it supports the complementary reconstruction of the object graph from the stream. Serialization is used for lightweight persistence and for communication via sockets or Remote Method Invocation (RMI). The default encoding of objects protects private and transient data, and supports the evolution of the classes. A class may implement its own external encoding and is then solely responsible for the external format."

To demonstrate serialization, let's propose and solve a problem first without using serialization and then with serialization. Suppose we have a simple class representing a Pizza as shown below.

```java
class Pizza
{

    String topping;
    String size;
    float price;

    Pizza(String t, String s, float p)
    {

        this.topping = t;
        this.size = s;
        this.price = p;
    }

    void showValue()
    {
        System.out.println("Topping: " + topping);
        System.out.println("Size: " + size);
        System.out.println("Price: " + price);
    }
}
```

The class has three simple properties representing the topping, size and price of the pizza. The constructor, simply assigns the given property values to the current instance of the Pizza class. We also have a utility method that prints out the values of the pizza's properties.

We want to create a Pizza object and then save it to a file. We will use that file to recreate the Pizza object again with the same properties as when it was saved. For a simple class like our Pizza class, this type of operation is relatively simple. The next listing shows one way to create the Pizza object and write it out to a file.

```java
import java.io.*;
import java.util.*;

class writePizza
{

    static public void main(String[] args)
    {

        float f = Float.parseFloat(args[2]);
        Pizza pizza = new Pizza (args[0], args[1], f);
        pizza.showValue();

        System.out.println ("Now writing Pizza to pizza.txt");

        try
        {
            FileWriter fw = new FileWriter("pizza.txt");

            fw.write(args[0] + "\n");
            fw.write(args[1] + "\n");
            fw.write(args[2] + "\n");

            fw.close();
        }
        catch(Exception e)
        {
            System.out.println("Exception: " + e);
        }

    }
}
```

The program accepts three arguments at the command line each representing the topping, size and price respectively. Notice that no error checking is done on the arguments. A new instance of `Pizza` is created and we call its `showValue()` method to see that it is properly initialized. We then open a file called `pizza.txt` and write each property value in a line in that file.

After compiling, we run the program with

```
java writePizza chicken L 12.89
```

and get the output

```
Topping: chicken
Size: L
Price: 12.89
Now writing Pizza to pizza.txt
```

Here is the content of `pizza.txt` after the above run:

```
chicken
L
12.89
```

As you can see, we have the values for all the properties of the object right before we saved it. This should be sufficient to recreate the object. The next listing shows some code that reads the `pizza.txt` file and recreates the object. We know we have recreated the object with the correct state after we call the `showValue()` method of the recently created object.

```java
import java.io.*;
import java.util.*;

class readPizza
{

    static public void main(String[] args)
    {

        String s=null;
        String t = null;
        float f=0;

        System.out.println ("Now reading Pizza from pizza.txt");

        try
        {
            FileReader fr = new FileReader("pizza.txt");
            BufferedReader br = new BufferedReader(fr);

            t = br.readLine();
            s = br.readLine();
            f = Float.parseFloat(br.readLine());
            fr.close();
        }
        catch(Exception e)
        {
            System.out.println("Exception: " + e);
        }

        System.out.println ("Creating pizza object...");

        Pizza pizza = new Pizza(t, s, f);
        pizza.showValue();

    }
}
```

When we run the program, we get the output

```
Now reading Pizza from pizza.txt
Creating pizza object...
Topping: chicken
Size: L
Price: 12.89
```

What we have shown here is the basic idea behind object serialization, but we have done everything manually. Object serialization support in Java makes our life much easier, and the end result is the same. We have created an object, saved it to a file and then recreated the exact object at a later time. If you consider the life span of an object against a timeline, we have been able to successfully create a break in that life span. This concept is shown below.

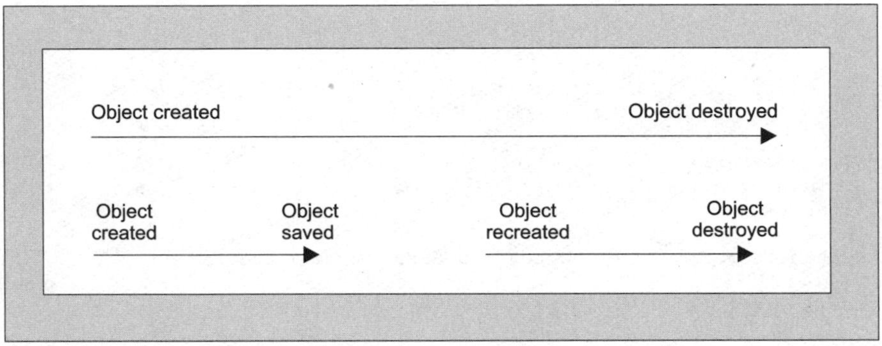

Objects that wish to take advantage of the serialization capabilities of Java, must implement the `Serializable` interface. `Serializable` is an interesting interface. Here is its definition:

```
package java.io;
public interface Serializable
{
     // there's nothing in here!
};
```

As you can see, there are no methods! The interface is merely used to identify classes that can be serialized. For a class to be serializable, its properties should also be serializable. Since we want the `Pizza` class to be serializable, we create a serializable version of the class and call it `Pizza2` as shown in the listing below.

```
import java.io.*;

class Pizza2 implements Serializable
{
```

```
      String topping;
      String size;
      float price;

      Pizza2(String t, String s, float p)
      {
         this.topping = t;
         this.size = s;
         this.price = p;
      }

      void showValue()
      {
         System.out.println("Topping: " + topping);
         System.out.println("Size: " + size);
         System.out.println("Price: " + price);
      }
   }
```

Writing an object

Now that we have a class that is serializable, we need to write some code to instantiate the class and serialize it. This will store the object in a file that we call `pizza.ser`. The process is not very difficult. Again, we read the arguments necessary to create the `Pizza` object from the command-line. We use the `showValue()` method to make sure the object was indeed created properly.

Next, we create a `FileOutputStream` to store our object. We hard code the filename to be `pizza.ser`. The next step is perhaps the most crucial one where we create an `ObjectOutputStream` on top of the `FileOutputStream`. The `ObjectOutputStream` knows how to write out objects to a stream that is then stored in a file. After all, this is what we wanted to do. Once we have an `ObjectOutputStream`, we can then use the `writeObject` method to write various objects to it. We write out two objects. The first is simply a string (remember strings are objects in Java). The next is the current instance of our `Pizza` class. Notice that in our code, there is no reference to the properties of `Pizza`. Java takes care of the details of finding out what properties `Pizza` has and how to write them out.

Actually the method used to write the objects is `defaultWriteObject`. This method automatically writes out everything required to reconstruct an instance of the class, including the following:

  ➢ Class of the object
  ➢ Class signature
  ➢ Values of all non-transient and non-static members, including members that refer to other objects

For many cases, this default behavior is sufficient. If there is a need, the class itself can implement the `writeObject` method to provide additional functionality as shown below:

```
private void writeObject(ObjectOutputStream s)
          throws IOException
{
   s.defaultWriteObject();
   // customized serialization code
}
```

This technique is typically used when the application requires additional data about the class or the application to be appended to the serialized object. Note that even when a class implements the `writeObject` method directly, it must still call the `defaultWriteObject()` method as the first action. The customized code for writing additional data would come later.

For our simple case, the default behavior is sufficient. The next listing shows how the `Pizza` object can be serialized.

```
import java.io.*;
import java.util.*;

class writePizza2
{

   static public void main(String[] args)
   {

      float f = Float.parseFloat(args[2]);

      Pizza2 pizza2 = new Pizza2 (args[0], args[1], f);
      pizza2.showValue();

      System.out.println ("Now serializing pizza...");

      try
      {
         FileOutputStream fout = new FileOutputStream("pizza.ser");
         ObjectOutputStream outStream = new ObjectOutputStream(fout);
         outStream.writeObject("Pizza is: \n");
         outStream.writeObject(pizza2);
         outStream.flush();
         outStream.close();
      }
      catch(IOException e)
      {
         System.out.println("Exception: " + e);
      }
   }
}
```

The two most important lines from the above code are the following:

```
ObjectOutputStream  outStream  =  new  ObjectOutputStream(fout);
outStream.writeObject(pizza2);
```

They open the `ObjectOutputStream` and write out the object to it. You can run the program with

```
java writePizza2 chicken L 12.89
```

and should see the output

```
Topping: chicken
Size: L
Price: 12.89
Now serializing pizza...
```

Note that after running the program, there is a new file created called `pizza.ser`. Its content is not human-readable, but all the information necessary to reconstruct the pizza object is in that file. There are some efforts under way to change the format of serialized objects to an XML-based standard. This would allow for greater ease in exchanging serialized objects across the network and gaining information about the object without fully deserializing it.

We have now successfully used Java serialization to convert the Pizza object to a persistent form and store it in a file. Note that during the entire process, we did not have to specify anything about the class itself. Java automatically determines what fields the class has and what fields need to be serialized to recreate the object at a later time. Now that we know how to serialize an object, let's see how we can do the reverse. That is how we can deserialize an object.

Reading an object

Reading a serialized object is basically the reverse process to writing out an object. A `FileInputStream` is created to point to the file containing the serialized object(s). Next, an `ObjectInputStream` is created and associated with the `FileInputStream`. An `ObjectInputStream` knows how to read various object types from a stream (which in this case is coming from a file). An object can be read using the `readObject()` method and cast to its original data type.

Again, the default behavior which is implemented in the `defaultReadObject()` method is sufficient for most applications. If you need to, you can write your own implementation of `readObject()`. This must correspond to the `writeObject()` method that you used for writing out an object. Note that the first method called in the `ReadObject()` is the `defaultReadObject()`.

```
private void readObject(ObjectInputStream s)
            throws IOException
{
    s.defaultReadObject();
    //customized deserialization code
```

Continued on Following Page

```
        //followed by code to update the object (if necessary)
    }
```

The following listing shows one way to recreate the `Pizza` object.

```
import java.io.*;
import java.util.*;

class readPizza2
{

    static public void main(String[] args)
    {

        String s=null;
        String t = null;
        float f=0;

        System.out.println ("Deserializing pizza from pizza.ser");

        try
        {
            FileInputStream fin = new FileInputStream("pizza.ser");
            ObjectInputStream inStream = new ObjectInputStream(fin);
            String stringObj = (String)inStream.readObject();
            System.out.print(stringObj);

            Pizza2 mypizza = (Pizza2)inStream.readObject();
            mypizza.showValue();

            inStream.close();
        }
        catch(ClassNotFoundException e)
        {
            System.out.println("Exception: " + e);
        }
        catch(IOException e)
        {
            System.out.println("Exception: " + e);
        }
    }
}
```

We have again hard coded the filename where the serialized object exists. Recall that before writing out the `Pizza` object, we wrote out a string to the serialization stream. Therefore, when we try reading from the file, we must first read a `String` object and then the `Pizza` object.

The `defaultReadObject()` method can only be called from the `readObject()` method of the class being serialized. Otherwise, you would get a `NotActiveException`. We don't catch that exception since it doesn't apply to this example. We are, however, catching the `IOException` and the `ClassNotFoundException`.

When we run the program, we get the following output.

```
Deserializing pizza from pizza.ser
Pizza is:
Topping: chicken
Size: L
Price: 12.89
```

Versioning and security considerations

Object serialization is easy. So easy that one may forget the security implications of serializing and deserializing an object. There may be a field in a class that should not be serialized. For example, a user object may contain a password field in addition to other fields. Although it makes sense to serialize a user object, you probably don't want the password field serialized. Also, you should not serialize fields that are used to hold system-dependent values such as a file descriptor.

When you define a class to implement `Serializable`, you should spend a few minutes looking at all the fields. If there are fields that should not be serialized (for one reason or another), then you should use the keyword transient to identify such fields. Java will not serialize any field marked as transient. Also, Java does not serialize static fields.

Another area that you should be concerned with is class hierarchy. In our example, we were dealing with only one class, but in more complex situations, it is very likely that multiple interconnected objects (forming an object tree) are needed to save the current state of an object and recreate it later. Fortunately, the Java serialization mechanism traverses the object tree until it satisfies all the required fields. However, it is possible that one of the classes in the tree has not implemented the `Serializable` interface. In this case the `NotSerializableException` will be thrown and will identify the class of the non-serializable object. Keep this in mind as you design multiple classes. If one of your classes needs to be serialized and it depends on other classes, then make sure others also implement `Serializable`.

Anytime you serialize an object, some information about the class from which the object was instantiated is also stored along with the object information. This is necessary so the correct class file can be loaded when the object is deserialized. This information is captured by the `java.io.ObjectStreamClass` class. Among the information it contains are the class name and a version number. The version number is necessary because an earlier version of a class may not be able to successfully deserialize an object that was created by a later version of the same class. The version number is stored in a field called `serialVersionUID`. You can use the `serialver` command (which comes as part of the JDK) to determine what the version number for a serialized object is. Here is what we get for the Pizza2 class:

```
static final long serialVersionUID = 3984636534014755227L;
```

Unless the class explicitly defines the `serialVersionUID`, it is automatically calculated by applying a hash algorithm to the class name and its fields and methods. Therefore any changes to the class will result in a new version number. If you don't want this to happen for minor changes, then declare a `serialVersionUID` constant and only change it when major changes are made to the class. That may cause incompatibility with previous serialized versions. You can use the `serialver` command to calculate updated version numbers.

Cryptography and Servlets

Overview

Suppose you are connecting to your bank securely to do an e-commerce transaction. How does your bank ensure that your communication is not being spoofed? How do you make sure that you are talking to the bank and not to some intermediate rogue agent pretending to be your bank? If you are downloading a document from your bank, how can you be sure that your bank is the author of that document? The answers to all of these questions lie in the understanding and usage of cryptography.

In this chapter we will discuss topics such as:

> What is cryptography?

> The need for cryptography

> Basic concepts of cryptography like message digests, message authentication codes, etc.

> Encryption and decryption of messages

> How to use cryptography to secure communications

> How to create servlets with message signing and verification capabilities

Cryptography Overview

Essentially, cryptography is the science of secret writing. Cryptanalysis is the study of how to compromise (defeat) cryptographic mechanisms, and cryptology (from the Greek *kryptós lógos*, meaning "hidden word") is the discipline of cryptography and cryptanalysis combined. To most people, cryptography is concerned with keeping communications private. Indeed, the protection of sensitive communications has been the emphasis of cryptography throughout much of its history.

Encryption and Decryption

Encryption is the transformation of data into a form that is as close as possible to being impossible to read without the appropriate knowledge (a key). Its purpose is to ensure privacy by keeping information hidden from anyone for whom it is not intended; even from those who have access to the encrypted data. Decryption is the reverse of encryption; it is the transformation of encrypted data back into an intelligible form. Encryption and decryption generally require the use of some secret information, referred to as a key. For some encryption mechanisms, the same key is used for both encryption and decryption; for other mechanisms, the keys used for encryption and decryption are different. The mathematical formula that performs the encryption and decryption is called a cipher. A key (private or public) is a special number of a few special numbers that are used in the formula called cipher. The easiest way to think of key is conceptually. First, visualize a cipher as a machine. To start the machine you need to use a key. Once the machine is started, the input for the machine could be plain text while the output from the machine is encrypted text.

Symmetric/Secret-Key Ciphers

In the olden days, when two people wanted to communicate secretly with each other, they would somehow share a secret code. The sender would encrypt the message with the shared key and the recipient would decrypt the message with the same key. This kind of system is called secret-key crypto system. The ciphers used in secret-key crypto systems are called symmetric ciphers, because the same key is used for both encryption and decryption. The main challenge is getting the sender and receiver to agree on the secret key without anyone else finding out. If they are in separate physical locations, they must trust a courier, a phone system, or some other transmission medium to prevent the disclosure of the secret key. Anyone who overhears or intercepts the key in transit can later read, modify, and forge all messages encrypted or authenticated using that key. The process of generation, transmission and storage of keys is called key management; all crypto-systems must deal with key management issues. Because all keys in a secret-key cryptosystem must remain secret, secret-key cryptography often has difficulty providing secure key management, especially in open systems with a large number of users. This requires a method by which the two parties can communicate without fear of eavesdropping. With Internet usage exploding, the boundaries between nations are essentially fading; it will be very difficult for every person to share a known secret key with every other person/system she interacts with.

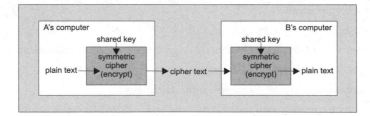

Stream and Block Ciphers

Symmetric key ciphers come in two flavors. Block ciphers encrypt and decrypt fixed-size blocks of data, usually 64 bits long. Stream ciphers operate on a stream of bits or bytes. The distinction is blurry, however. A block cipher can be made to work like a stream cipher. When would you choose a block or stream cipher? It depends on the application. In a secure mail client, you might use a block cipher. In a cryptographically-enabled talk application, you will use a stream cipher. Block cipher algorithms are much more prevalent than stream ciphers. The table below shows commonly used symmetric ciphers.

Symmetric cipher	Description
Data Encryption Standard (DES)	Block cipher with 64-bit key sizes
RC2	Block cipher
RC4	Stream cipher
RC5	Block cipher
IDEA	Block cipher with 128-bit keys
Skipjack	Stream cipher with 80-bit keys

Asymmetric/Public-Key Ciphers

Public-key cryptography solves the issue of secret key sharing and key distribution problems. In order to solve the key management problem, Whitfield Diffie and Martin Hellman introduced the concept of public-key cryptography in 1976. Public-key crypto systems have two primary uses, encryption and digital signatures. In this system, each person gets a pair of keys, a public key and a private key. The public key is published, while the private key is kept secret. The need for the sender and receiver to share secret information is eliminated; all communications involve only public keys, and no private key is ever transmitted or shared. In this system, it is no longer necessary to trust the security of some means of communications. The only requirement is that public keys be associated with their users in a trusted (authenticated) manner (for instance, in a trusted directory). Anyone can send a confidential message by just using public information, but the message can only be decrypted with a private key, which is in the sole possession of the intended recipient.

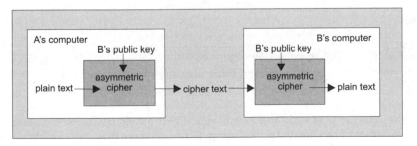

Public-key cryptography can be used not only for privacy (encryption), but also for authentication (digital signatures) and other various techniques. The ciphers used in public-key crypto systems are called asymmetric ciphers, because they use different keys for encryption and decryption purposes. The table shows commonly used asymmetric ciphers.

Asymmetric Cipher	Description
RSA	Public key encryption and digital signatures
ElGamal	Public key encryption and digital signatures
DSA	Digital signatures only
Diffie-Hellman	Key exchange protocol based on public key algorithm

Hybrid Systems

Asymmetric ciphers are much slower than symmetric ciphers, so they are not usually used to encrypt long messages. This has led to the invention of hybrid crypto systems. Hybrid systems combine symmetric and asymmetric ciphers. In these systems, when two parties want to communicate with each other, they will agree upon a secret key or session key. The session key itself will be negotiated using an asymmetric cipher. The session key is used with a symmetric cipher to encrypt the remainder of the conversation. The session key's life is over when the two participants finish their conversation. Nearly all public-key crypto systems in use today are hybrid systems.

Terminology

The terms used in crypto-systems can be quite confusing. An asymmetric cipher uses public/private key pairs. A symmetric cipher uses a private key or a secret key or a session key. Symmetric ciphers are also called secret key ciphers.

Message Digests and Digital Signatures

When you download a file over the Internet, you would like to be sure that the file you are downloading is the one you wanted and that it has not changed. Many people make the assumption that the file they have downloaded is not a malicious program, and has not been changed in the transit. But this is not always the case. For example, there could be a separate computer in between you and the server, which is sending you a malicious program. This is called the "man-in-the-middle" attack. A message digest (also known as cryptographic checksum or cryptographic hash code) can be used to verify the data integrity. A message digest is a special number that is effectively a hash code produced by a function that is very difficult to reverse.

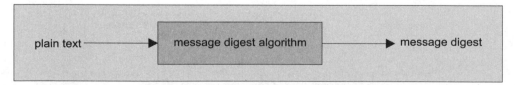

If a server on the Internet puts a file and its message digest online, after downloading both the file and the message digest of the file, users can compute the message digest of the file to ensure that the document is not modified. Pure message digests will not eliminate the man-in-the-middle attacks, because a rogue computer between the user and the server can replace both the file and a valid message digest. When paired with other cryptographic techniques, however, a message digest may become useful. See the table for commonly used message digest algorithms.

Digest Algorithm	Description
MD2, MD4, MD5	All produce 128 bit number
SHA	Produces a 160 bit number
Haval	Modified MD5, produces digests of length ranging from 92 to 256 bits
SNEFRU	Produces 128 or 256 bit hash codes

A Message Authentication Code (MAC), for example, is a message digest with an associated key. It produces a value based both on input and a key. In theory, only someone with the same key can produce the same MAC from the same input data.

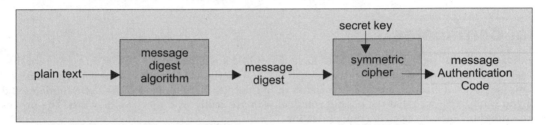

Another approach to message integrity is to use digital signatures. A digital signature is a message digest encrypted with someone's private key to certify contents. The process of encrypting the message digest is called signing. The encrypted message digest is called a signature.

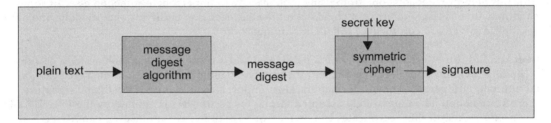

Digital signatures can perform three important functions, all very important to the security of your system.

> Integrity: A digital signature indicates whether a file or a message has been modified.

> Authentication: A digital signature makes it possible to mathematically verify the name of the person who signed the message.

> Non-repudiation: Non-repudiation makes it impossible to deny sending a message after you have signed and sent it. You cannot repudiate your signature, because the message was signed with your private key.

To verify a digital signature of a document, you need to have the public key of the person who signed the document so that you can decrypt the signature to find out the digest at signature time. Separately, you can compute the digest of the message and compare it with the decrypted digest. If they match, you can be guaranteed that the document was signed by the person who holds the private key to the public key you have used to decrypt the digest.

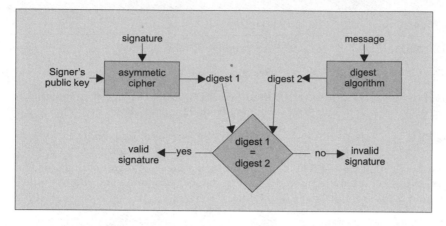

Digital Certificates

To validate a digital signature, we need to have the public key of the signer. How do we obtain the public key of the signer? The signer can publish her key on the Internet. But what is the guarantee that another person masquerading as the signer didn't publish the public key? At some fundamental level you want to be sure that the people you deal with are really who they say they are. The process of providing this identity is called authentication.

Digital certificates provide this kind of authentication for a signer's public key. Certificates are digital documents attesting to the binding of a public key to an individual or other entity. They allow verification of the claim that a specific public key does, in fact, belong to a specific individual. Certificates help prevent someone from using a phony key to impersonate someone else. In some cases, it may be necessary to create a chain of certificates, each one certifying the previous one until the parties involved are confident of the identity in question.

In their simplest form, certificates contain a public key and a name. As commonly used, a certificate also contains an expiration date, the name of the certifying authority that issued the certificate, a serial number, and perhaps other information. Most importantly, it contains the digital signature of the certificate issuer. The most widely accepted format for certificates is defined by the ITU-T X.509 international standard; thus, certificates can be read or written by any application complying with the X.509 standard.

Digital Certificate Authorities

Certificates are issued by a certifying authority (CA), which can be any trusted central administration willing to vouch for the identities of those to whom it issues certificates and their association with a given key. A company may issue certificates to its employees, or a university to its students, or a town to its citizens. In order to prevent forged certificates, the CA's public key must be trustworthy: a CA must either publicize its public key or provide a certificate from a higher-level CA attesting to the validity of its public key. The latter solution gives rise to hierarchies of CAs. An example of certificate issuance proceeds as follows: JoAnne generates a key pair and sends the public key to an appropriate CA with some proof of her identification. The CA checks the identification and makes sure that the request really did come from JoAnne and that the public key is not modified in transit. The CA then sends JoAnne a certificate attesting to the binding between JoAnne and her public key, along with a hierarchy of certificates verifying the CA's public key. JoAnne can present this certificate chain whenever desired in order to demonstrate the legitimacy of her public key.

Since the CA must check for proper identification, organizations find it convenient to act as a CA for their own members and employees. There are also CAs that issue certificates to unaffiliated individuals. For example, the Thawte certificate authority (www.thawte.com) issues free email certificates to individuals who are not associated with Thawte. While issuing these certificates, Thawte performs certain minimal checks, like cross-referencing Social Security Numbers; however, it does not perform extensive background checks for free email certificates.

Different CAs may issue certificates with varying levels of identification requirements. One CA may insist on seeing a driver's license, another may want the certificate request form to be notarized; yet another may want fingerprints of anyone requesting a certificate. Each CA should publish its own identification requirements and standards, so verifiers can attach the appropriate level of confidence to the certified name-key bindings. CAs with lower levels of identification requirements produce certificates with lower "assurance." CAs can thus be considered to be of high, medium, and low assurance. One type of CA is the persona CA. This type of CA creates certificates that bind only e-mail addresses and their corresponding public keys. It is designed for users who wish to remain anonymous, yet want to be able to participate in secure electronic services. For more information about certificate-related products, visit the VeriSign, Inc. (www.verisign.com), or Thawte (www.thawte.com) websites.

Since CAs sign the public keys of users, who signs the keys of the CAs themselves? Most of the CA keys are self-signed, indicating a supreme level of trust. Most of the modern browsers embed CAs' self-signed root certificates. Also, some browsers embed some of the CA certificates that chain up to the self-signed root. For example, in Internet Explorer 5.0, Tools → Internet Options → Content → Certificates → Trusted Root Certification Authorities menu will display the self-signed roots of all the trusted CAs that Internet Explorer trusts.

If you double-click on one of the self-signed roots, IE will display a certificate details tab. You can find that the issuer and the subject are the same for root certificates.

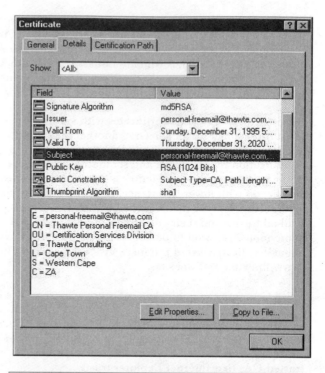

If you look at any other certificate that is not self-signed, IE will show the complete path up to the root. This is called certificate chaining. In the picture shown below, Microsoft Authenticode Root signs Code Signing Authority #1's public key.

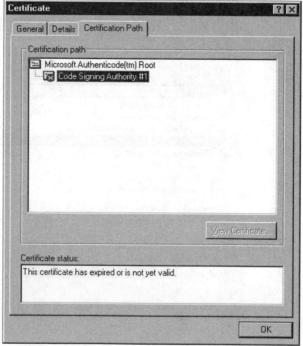

Certificate Revocation Lists

There are two ways in which a certificate issued by a CA can become invalid. The certificate will expire at the end of its validation period. The private key associated with the certificate could also become compromised, in which case the certificate should no longer be valid. Certificates can be cancelled, or revoked, by the person who owns it or by a higher authority that has issued it. After the certificate has been revoked, it will be placed in a list called Certificate Revocation List (CRL). A CRL is issued by a CA against the certificates it has issued. Each entry in a CRL consists of the serial number of the certificate, when the certificate was revoked and the reason for its revocation. CRLs have also validity periods. Once the CRL is expired, a new one will be issued by the CA. Essentially, during a transaction that involves certificates, it is not only necessary to ensure that the certificate is not expired, but also that it has not been revoked. For example, if Adam receives a signed message from Eve, Adam can verify the signature. He can also check the validity period of the certificate. But, how does Adam know whether or not Eve cancelled the certificate because her private key got compromised? Adam should download the CRL from the CA that issued Eve's certificate and make sure that Eve's certificate is not present on the list. Currently, this is the only way to ensure transactional validity. This is the reason why CRLs play a very important role in the public key infrastructure. For more information on CRLs, visit ValiCert Inc. at http://www.valicert.com

Java Cryptography Overview

We have now described the basic concepts of cryptography. It is interesting to note how Java goes about implementing these concepts. Java cryptography software comes in two parts: One part is Java Cryptography Architecture (JCA), which is a part of JDK; the second part is Java Cryptography Extension (JCE). JCE is used for strong cryptography.

The overall design of the cryptography classes is governed by JCA. The concepts are encapsulated by classes in `java.security` and `javax.crypto` packages. "Cryptographic providers" supply implementations of these concepts. The Java Development Kit (JDK) 1.2 comes with a default provider, named `SUN`, that implements a few cryptographic algorithms such as DSA digital signatures and message digests.

JCE 1.2 provides a framework and implementations for encryption, key generation and key agreement, and Message Authentication Code (MAC) algorithms. Support for encryption includes symmetric, asymmetric, block, and stream ciphers. The software also supports secure streams and sealed objects. JCE 1.2 is designed so that other cryptography libraries can be plugged in as a service provider, and new algorithms can be added seamlessly.

JCE 1.2 comes with a default provider called `SunJCE`. Because of export restrictions, `SunJCE` is not available for export outside of the United States. `SunJCE` does not include implementations for RSA algorithm-based public key encryption, because RSA Data Security Corporation has patented RSA algorithms.

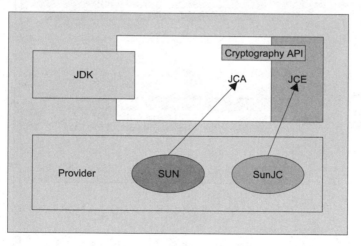

Java Cryptography Architecture

JCA is designed to separate cryptographic concepts from implementations. The first release of JDK Security in JDK 1.1 introduced the "Java Cryptography Architecture", which refers to a framework for accessing and developing cryptographic functionality for the Java platform. In JDK 1.1, the JCA included APIs for digital signatures and message digests.

JDK 1.2 significantly extends the JCA. It also upgrades the certificate management infrastructure to support X.509 v3 certificates, and introduces a new Java Security Architecture for fine-grain, highly configurable, flexible, and extensible access control.

JCA was designed around the following:

➤   Implementation independence and interoperability

➤   Algorithm independence and extensibility

Implementation independence and algorithm independence are complementary: their aim is to let users of the API utilize cryptographic *concepts*, such as digital signatures and message digests, without concern for the implementations or even the algorithms being used to implement these concepts. When complete algorithm-independence is not possible, the JCA provides developers with standardized algorithm-specific APIs. When implementation-independence is not desirable, the JCA lets developers indicate the specific implementations they require.

Implementation independence is achieved using a "provider"-based architecture. The term Cryptographic Service Provider refers to a package or set of packages that implement one or more cryptography services, such as digital signature algorithms, message digest algorithms, and key conversion services. A program may simply request a particular type of object (such as a `Signature` object) implementing a particular service (such as the DSA signature algorithm) and get an implementation from one of the installed providers. If desired, a program may instead request an implementation from a specific provider (each provider uses a specific name to refer to it). Providers may be updated transparently to the application, for example when faster or more secure versions are available.

Implementation interoperability means that various implementations can work with each other, use each other's keys, or verify each other's signatures. This would mean, for example, that for the same algorithms, a key generated by one provider would be usable by another, and a signature generated by one provider would be verifiable by another.

Algorithm independence is achieved by defining types of cryptographic "engines" (services), and defining classes that provide the functionality of these cryptographic engines. These classes are called *engine classes*, and examples are the `MessageDigest` (`java.security.MessageDigest`), `Signature` (`java.security.Signature`), and `KeyFactory` (`java.security.KeyFactory`) classes.

Algorithm extensibility means that new algorithms that fit in one of the supported engine classes can easily be added.

In JDK 1.1 a provider could, for example, contain an implementation of one or more digital signature algorithms, message digest algorithms, and key generation algorithms. JDK 1.2 adds five additional types of services: key factories, keystore creation and management, algorithm parameter management, algorithm parameter generation, and certificate factories. It also enables a provider to supply a random number generation (RNG) algorithm. Previously, RNGs were not provider-based; a particular algorithm was hard-coded in the JDK.

Sun's version of the Java runtime environment comes standard with a default provider, named SUN for JCA. The SUN provider package includes:

> An implementation of the Digital Signature Algorithm (DSA).

> An implementation of the MD5 (RFC 1321) and SHA-1 message digest algorithms.

> A DSA key pair generator for generating a pair of public and private keys suitable for the DSA algorithm.

> A DSA algorithm parameter generator.

> A DSA algorithm parameter manager.

> A DSA "key factory" providing bi-directional conversions between (opaque) DSA private and public key objects and their underlying key material.

> An implementation of the proprietary "SHA1PRNG" pseudo-random number generation algorithm, following the recommendations in the IEEE P1363 standard.

> A "certificate factory" for X.509 certificates and Certificate Revocation Lists (CRLs).

> A keystore implementation for the proprietary keystore type named "JKS".

As an example to demonstrate how MessageDigests work in Java, the following code segment creates message digest from the given input:

```java
import java.io.*;
import java.security.*;

// sun.misc.*  package defines BASE64 Encoder/Decoder  classes

import sun.misc.*;

public class Md5Input
{
    public static void main (String[] args) throws Exception
    {

        if (args.length < 1)
        {
         System.out.println("Usage: javac Md5Input input");
         return;
        }

        // collect input string into one big string
        String input = args[0];
        for (int i =1;  i < args.length; i++)
        {
        input += " " + args[i];
        }

        // Convert the string to UTF8 bytes for md5 input
        byte[] inputBytes = input.getBytes("UTF8");

        // Obtain md5 message digest through factory method
        MessageDigest  md5 =  MessageDigest.getInstance("MD5");

        // Update the message digest with input
        md5.update(inputBytes);
```

```
      // generate digest
      byte[] digest = md5.digest();

      // Print out the digest in base64.
      BASE64Encoder encoder = new BASE64Encoder();
      String base64 = encoder.encode(digest);
      System.out.println(base64);
   }
}
```

To execute the program, save the code into `Md5Input.java` file and compile it under JDK 1.2 using the command javac Md5Input.java. You can then run the program as follows:

```
d:\krishna\code>java Md5Input hello world
XrY7u+Ae7tCTyyK7j1rNww==
```

```
d:\krishna\code>java Md5Input hello world!
/D/5joxqDTCH1RXARz+Gdw==
```

As you can see from the above output, if you change the input by a single character, the message digest looks completely different. Given a message digest, it is very hard to figure out what input produced that digest. It is extremely rare that two different inputs can ever produce the same digest. Some message digest algorithms, like SHA-1, actually guarantee that no two inputs can produce the same digest value. Here is how the program works:

> Checks to make sure that program is invoked properly by checking the number of arguments.

> Concatenates all the input into one string, multiple spaces between different words of the input are replaced by a single space.

> Converts the input string to byte array (since the `MessageDigest` object operates only on bytes, instead of characters).

> Obtains a `MessageDigest` object. Uses a factory method `MessageDigest.getInstance("MD5")` which is a special static method that returns an instance of `MessageDigest`. The factory method accepts the name of an algorithm as input. In this case we use an algorithm called MD5.

```
MessageDigest  md5 =  MessageDigest.getInstance("MD5");
```

> Updates the `MessageDigest` object with the input data.

> Calculates the message digest. Note that the value of the message digest is always in a byte array form, which is not readable by humans, so we use `BASE64Encoder` class from `sun.misc.*` package to convert the digest into base64 encoded form.

> Outputs the base64-encoded digest.

In step 4, we asked for a Message Digest factory method from Java Runtime Environment (JRE). By default, JRE looks into its list of MD5 algorithm-based message digest providers and gives an instance of object from the first providers. The list of security providers in JRE is statically specified in the file JAVA_HOME/jre/lib/security/java.security. Here is an excerpt from that file:

```
# In this file, various security properties are set for use by
# java.security classes. This is where users can statically register
# Cryptography Package Providers ("providers" for short). The term
# "provider" refers to a package or set of packages that supply a
# concrete implementation of a subset of the cryptography aspects of
# the Java Security API. A provider may, for example, implement one or
# more digital signature algorithms or message digest algorithms.
#
# Each provider must implement a subclass of the Provider class.
# To register a provider in this master security properties file,
# specify the Provider subclass name and priority in the format
#
#     security.provider.<n>=<className>
#
# This declares a provider, and specifies its preference
# order n. The preference order is the order in which providers are
# searched for requested algorithms (when no specific provider is
# requested). The order is 1-based; 1 is the most preferred, followed
# by 2, and so on.
#
# <className> must specify the subclass of the Provider class whose
# constructor sets the values of various properties that are required
# for the Java Security API to look up the algorithms or other
# facilities implemented by the provider.
#
# There must be at least one provider specification in java.security.
# There is a default provider that comes standard with the JDK. It
# is called the "SUN" provider, and its Provider subclass
# named Sun appears in the sun.security.provider package. Thus, the
# "SUN" provider is registered via the following:
#
#     security.provider.1=sun.security.provider.Sun
#
# (The number 1 is used for the default provider.)
#
# Note: Statically registered Provider subclasses are instantiated
# when the system is initialized. Providers can be dynamically
# registered instead by calls to either the addProvider or
# insertProviderAt method in the Security class.
```

So, for example, in the above code we could have requested an explicit provider for MD5 message digest (MD5Provider) by asking for a factory method:

```
MessageDigest md5 = MessageDigest.getInstance("MD5","MD5Provider");
```

This is possible provided that MD5Provider is registered (either statically using java.security file or dynamically by addProvider methods) in Security class.

So how do we know what each provider's capabilities are? There are two ways to find out. One way is to go through the documentation and the second way is programmatically, as shown below. Programmatically, you can only find out the list of algorithms a provider supports.

```
import java.io.*;
import java.util.*;
import java.security.*;

import sun.misc.*;

public class Providers
{
    public static void main (String[] args) throws Exception
    {

    // Get a list of all the loaded providers.
    Provider[] providers = Security.getProviders();

    // query each provider for the services (algorithms)
    // that it provides

        for (int i=0; i < providers.length; i++)
        {
            System.out.println(providers[i]);
            for (Enumeration e = providers[i].keys(); e.hasMoreElements();)
            System.out.println("\t" + e.nextElement());
        }
    }
}
```

When I compile and run the above program on my computer, I get the following result:

```
d:\krishna\code>java Providers
SUN version 1.2
        KeyStore.JKS
    MessageDigest.SHA
    CertificateFactory.X509
    Signature.SHA1withDSA
    AlgorithmParameters.DSA
    KeyFactory.DSA
    AlgorithmParameterGenerator.DSA
    SecureRandom.SHA1PRNG
    MessageDigest.MD5
    KeyPairGenerator.DSA
            Deleted aliases…
SunJCE version 1.2
    KeyAgreement.DiffieHellman
    Cipher.Blowfish
    Cipher.DES
    Cipher.PBEWithMD5AndDES
    SecretKeyFactory.PBE
    AlgorithmParameters.Blowfish
    SecretKeyFactory.DES
    AlgorithmParameters.DiffieHellman
    KeyGenerator.DES
    KeyPairGenerator.DiffieHellman
    KeyFactory.DiffieHellman
    AlgorithmParameters.PBE
    AlgorithmParameters.DESede
    AlgorithmParameters.DES
```

```
AlgorithmParameterGenerator.DiffieHellman
KeyGenerator.DESede
KeyGenerator.Blowfish
Mac.HmacMD5
Cipher.DESede
KeyStore.JCEKS
SecretKeyFactory.DESede
Mac.HmacSHA1
        Deleted aliases...
```

From the above output you can clearly see the capabilities of each of the providers.

Since keys (both secret and public) are essential ingredients for most of the cryptographic algorithms, how does one goes about creating these keys. Lets look at a simple example to generate a key pair for DSA signing algorithm:

```java
import java.io.*;
import java.security.*;

import sun.misc.*;

public class GenKeys
{
    public static void main (String[] args) throws Exception
    {

        SecureRandom sr = new SecureRandom();
        byte[] pseudoRandom = new byte[100];
        sr.nextBytes(pseudoRandom);

        KeyPairGenerator kpg = KeyPairGenerator.getInstance("DSA");

        System.out.println("Initializing the DSA key pair generator...");
        kpg.initialize(512, sr);

        System.out.println("Generating DSA key pair...");
        System.out.println("This may take a while...");

        KeyPair kp = kpg.genKeyPair();

        System.out.println("DSA Public Key:");

        Key pubKey = kp.getPublic();

        // save the public key to DSApublic.der file for later decoding
        try
        {
            ObjectOutputStream out = new ObjectOutputStream(
            new FileOutputStream("DSApublic.key"));
            out.writeObject(pubKey);
            out.close();
        }

        catch(Exception e)
        {
            System.out.println("Could not save public key...");
            System.out.println(e);
        }
```

```
        byte[] pubkeyBytes = pubKey.getEncoded();
        System.out.println("Public key format is: " + pubKey.getFormat());
        BASE64Encoder encoder = new BASE64Encoder();
        String base64 = encoder.encode(pubkeyBytes);
        System.out.println(base64);


        System.out.println("DSA Private Key:");
        Key privKey = kp.getPrivate();

            // save the private key to DSAprivkey.der file for later decoding
            try
            {
                ObjectOutputStream out = new ObjectOutputStream(
                new FileOutputStream("DSAprivate.key"));
                out.writeObject(privKey);
                out.close();
            }

            catch(Exception e)
            {
                System.out.println("Could not save private key...");
                System.out.println(e);
            }

        byte[] privkeyBytes = privKey.getEncoded();
        System.out.println("Private key format is: " + privKey.getFormat());
        BASE64Encoder encoder2 = new BASE64Encoder();
        base64 = encoder2.encode(privkeyBytes);
        System.out.println(base64);
        }
}
```

Save the program in a file named `GenKeys.java`; compile the program under JDK 1.2 and execute the program. The program should generate output something similar to the one below. Every time this program is executed, a new set of keys will be generated.

```
d:\krishna\code>java GenKeys
Initializing the DSA key pair generator...
Generating DSA key pair...
This may take a while...
DSA Public Key:
Public key format is: X.509
MIHxMIGoBgcqhkjOOAQBMIGcAkEA/KaCzo4Syrom78z3EQ5SbbB4sF7ey80etKII864WF64B81uRpH5t9j
QTxeEu0ImbzRMqzVDZkVG9xD7nN1kuFwIVAJYu3cw2nLqOuyYO5rahJtk0bjjFAkBnhHGyepz0TukaScUU
fbGpqvJE8FpDTWSGkx0tFCcbnjUDC3H9c9oXkGmzLik1Yw4cIGI1TQ2iCmxBblC+eUykA0QAAkEAiOtdFV
J+F2AedbFKb6zNwXxKLBpcjrVa6/ABKl2XQ6jVY6MW1A0AfmFW7ZTA2V2q34oX6T31AR6St9Kmr0xG0w==
DSA Private Key:
Private key format is: PKCS#8
MIHGAgEAMIGoBgcqhkjOOAQBMIGcAkEA/KaCzo4Syrom78z3EQ5SbbB4sF7ey80etKII864WF64B81uRpH
5l9jQTxeEu0ImbzRMqzVDZkVG9xD7nNlkuFwlVAJYu3cw2nLqOuyYO5rahJtk0bjjFAkBnhHGyepz0Tuka
ScUUfbGpqvJE8FpDTWSGkx0tFCcbnjUDC3H9c9oXkGmzLik1Yw4cIGI1TQ2iCmxBblC+eUykBBYCFFr7YU
Yri0tBPlhrURUkq7Af1Of9
```

This is how the above program works:

> Creates a new Pseudo Random Generator object and generates 100-byte pseudo random number. This number will be used as a seed for DSA key pair generation.

> Obtains a `KeyPairGenerator` object through one of `Java.Security.KeyPairGenerator`'s factory methods.

> Initializes the `KeyPairGenerator` object with a keysize of 512 bits and a seed random number.

> Generates the `KeyPair` object form `KeyPairGenerator` object.

> Obtains the private and public keys from the `KeyPair` object and saves them into `DSApublic.key` and `DSAprivate.key` files, respectively.

> In addition to saving the public and private keys, their format and BASE64 encodes values are printed to standard output.

Now that we have generated a DSA `KeyPair`, we can use these keys to sign a message and verify the signature. The following program illustrates these concepts:

```java
import java.io.*;
import java.security.*;

import sun.misc.*;

public class Signer
{
    public static void main (String[] args) throws Exception
    {

    // Check program usage.
        if (args.length < 1)
        {
            System.out.println("Usage: java input");
            return;
        }
    // collect all the input into in big string
    String msg  = args[0];
        for (int i =1;  i < args.length; i++)
        {
            msg += " " + args[i];
        }

    Signature dsaSig = Signature.getInstance("SHA1withDSA");

    PublicKey pubKey;
    PrivateKey privKey;

    System.out.println("Reading private key from file DSAprivate.key...");
        try
        {
            ObjectInputStream in = new ObjectInputStream(
            new FileInputStream("DSAprivate.key"));
            privKey = (PrivateKey)in.readObject();
            in.close();
        }
        catch (Exception e)
        {
```

```
          System.out.println("Could not read the private key from DSAprivate.key");
          return;
      }

   System.out.println("Reading public key from file DSApublic.key...");

      try
      {
          ObjectInputStream in = new ObjectInputStream(
          new FileInputStream("DSApublic.key"));
          pubKey = (PublicKey)in.readObject();
          in.close();
      }
      catch (Exception e)
      {
          System.out.println("Could not read the public key from DSApublic.key");
          return;
      }

   System.out.println("Signing the message with the private key...");

   dsaSig.initSign(privKey);
   byte[] msgBytes = msg.getBytes("UTF8");
   dsaSig.update(msgBytes);
   byte[] sigBytes = dsaSig.sign();

   System.out.println("Verifying the signed message with the public key...");

   dsaSig.initVerify(pubKey);
   dsaSig.update(msgBytes);
   boolean verifies = dsaSig.verify(sigBytes);
   System.out.println("signature verifies: " + verifies);

   }
}
```

If you save the above program into a file named `Signer.java`, compile it and run under JDK 1.2, the output of the program will be as follows:

```
d:\krishna\code>java Signer Hello World!
Reading private key from file DSAprivate.key...
Reading public key from file DSApublic.key...
Signing the message with the private key...
Verifying the signed message with the public key...
signature verifies: true
```

Since DSA algorithm is used only for the signing operation, we can't use these keys for general-purpose asymmetric key encryption and decryption. The above program works as follows:

> Checks for command line usage.

> Collects the input that needs to be signed into one big string.

> Creates a signature object.

> Reads private and public key objects from `DSApublic.key` and `DSAprivate.key` files respectively.

> ➢ Retrieves the bytes from the string that is being signed and places them into a data buffer.
> ➢ Signs the data buffer with the private key.
> ➢ Verifies the signed message with the public key.

JDK 1.2 also comes bundled with classes to deal with certificates and Certificate Revocation Lists. Lets develop an example to see how to parse and see what a X509 Version 3 certificate actually looks like. Here is the code to read and display a certificate information:

```java
import java.io.*;
import java.util.*;
import java.security.*;
import java.security.cert.*;

import sun.misc.*;

public class ParseCert
{
    public static void main (String[] args) throws Exception
    {

        if (args.length < 1)
        {
            System.out.println("Usage java ParseCert \"certfile\"");
            return;
        }

        FileInputStream fis = new FileInputStream(args[0]);
        DataInputStream dis = new DataInputStream(fis);

        CertificateFactory cf = CertificateFactory.getInstance("x.509");

        Collection c = cf.generateCertificates(fis);
        Iterator i = c.iterator();
        while (i.hasNext())
        {
            java.security.cert.Certificate cert =
(java.security.cert.Certificate)i.next();
            System.out.println(cert);
        }
    }
}
```

The above program works in the following way:

> ➢ Checks the input arguments.
> ➢ Creates a `DataInputStream` to read the certificate object from input file.
> ➢ Obtains an instance of `CertificateFactory` object from a Factory method of `java.security.CerificateFactory` class. `CertificateFactory` class defines the functionality of a certificate factory, which is used to generate certificate and certificate revocation list (CRL) objects from their encoding.
> ➢ Initializes the `CertificateFactory` class with the data in the input file.
> ➢ Generates the certificates from the `CertificateFactory` class.
> ➢ Iterates through all the certificates and prints them.

When you compile and run the above program, it will produce output something similar to the following:

```
d:\krishna\code>java ParseCert labrador-x509.cer
[
[
  Version: V3
  Subject: CN=Labrador MS Test CA2, OU=Administration, O=Acme Co, L=San Jose,
ST=CA, C=US
  Signature Algorithm: MD5withRSA, OID = 1.2.840.113549.1.1.4

  Key:  algorithm = RSA, unparsed keybits =
0000: 30 47 02 40 7F DE EE 29   C7 A3 5B 55 DA 5C D4 99  0G.@...)..[U.\..
0010: D5 93 30 D6 2D 47 A1 D4   87 22 45 79 A5 DF C2 25  ..0.-G..."Ey...%
0020: 4A DC AC C4 A9 AC E6 C5   4A 86 1F 75 EB 34 82 B9  J.......J..u.4..
0030: F7 40 64 7F 94 DB 56 50   83 FA 21 5D C2 6E BA 14  .@d...VP..!].n..
0040: A7 47 DF ED 02 03 01 00   01                       .G......

  Validity: [From: Wed Dec 16 15:46:51 PST 1998,
             To: Tue Dec 16 15:46:51 PST 2003]
  Issuer: CN=Labrador MS Test CA2, OU=Administration, O=Acme Co, L=San Jose,
ST=CA, C=US
  SerialNumber: [    17c9d14b 10007fb4 11d29541 1107a2a4 ]
Certificate Extensions: 3
[1]: ObjectId: 2.5.29.14 Criticality=false
SubjectKeyIdentifier [
KeyIdentifier [
0000: 20 9C 47 14 8F 8D F2 22   B1 F3 67 D2 8A DE 0D 16  .G...."..g.....
0010: D2 16 70 74                                        ..pt
]
]

[2]: ObjectId: 2.5.29.15 Criticality=false
KeyUsage [
  DigitalSignature
  Non_repudiation
  Key_CertSign
]

[3]: ObjectId: 2.5.29.19 Criticality=false
BasicConstraints:[
CA:true
PathLen: undefined ]

]
  Algorithm: [MD5withRSA]
  Signature:
0000: 7D FD 5C 3C 80 E4 0C C7   8B B6 30 4F AF FC 34 D2  ..\<......0O..4.
0010: 66 6F 25 CB 47 AC 93 EB   8A 93 76 00 03 37 B3 FB  fo%.G.....v..7..
0020: 16 73 28 A4 85 7A 85 44   8D A0 91 94 11 12 A9 E3  .s(..z.D........
0030: D8 10 30 7C 25 EE F9 49   79 AC C5 46 C5 58 01 92  ..0.%..Iy..F.X..

]
```

So from the above input, you can see that an X509 Version 3 certificate essentially contains these elements:

> Certificate version

> Subject description

> Signature algorithm used to sign the subject's public key

> Subject's public key

> Validity period

> Issuer's identity

> Certificate Serial number, Certificate extensions

> Signature

JCA also contains facilities to analyze Certificate Revocation Lists. The following program parses and prints the contents of a given CRL:

```java
import java.io.*;
import java.util.*;
import java.security.*;
import java.security.cert.*;

import sun.misc.*;

public class ParseCrl
{
    public static void main (String[] args) throws Exception
    {

        if (args.length < 1)
        {
            System.out.println("Usage java ParseCert \"crlfile\"");
            return;
        }
        FileInputStream fis = new FileInputStream(args[0]);
        DataInputStream dis = new DataInputStream(fis);

        CertificateFactory cf = CertificateFactory.getInstance("x.509");

        X509CRL crl = (X509CRL) cf.generateCRL(fis);
        System.out.println(crl);

        // Retrieve each entry in the CRL and print it.

        Set s = crl.getRevokedCertificates();
        Iterator i = s.iterator();
        while (i.hasNext()) {
        java.security.cert.X509CRLEntry entry =
(java.security.cert.X509CRLEntry)i.next();
        System.out.println(entry);
        }
    }
}
```

The program above works just like the `ParseCert` program. It creates a `CertificateFactory` object and reads the CRL file through it and then prints the contents of the CRL. When run with a CRL as input, the output will be something similar to this:

```
d:\krishna\code>java ParseCrl testcva.crl
X.509 CRL v2
Signature Algorithm: MD5withRSA, OID=1.2.840.113549.1.1.4
Issuer: CN=Test CVA, OU=Test CVA - Inappropriate Usage Prohibited, O=Valicert
Inc., L=Mountain View, ST=CA, C=US

This Update: Wed Mar 17 11:36:37 PST 1999
Next Update: Thu Mar 18 12:46:37 PST 1999

Revoked Certificates: 2
[1] SerialNumber: [     01bee400 000004]  On: Wed Mar 17 11:46:22 PST 1999

[2] SerialNumber: [     0350e000 000001]  On: Wed Mar 17 10:42:15 PST 1999
Signature:
0000: 72 9E 8E 4B A8 B9 27 AD   18 B1 6B 7B 51 67 EA 21   r..K..'...k.Qg.!
0010: 2F 6D 04 20 5C 19 55 F6   71 56 51 2F CB 11 E8 00   /m. \.U.qVQ/....
0020: 0C 5F 93 77 49 50 F1 0C   6E 1E 65 E0 95 25 26 E9   ._.wIP..n.e..%&.
0030: D1 05 DE 37 29 D3 EE 0C   18 B5 B0 AC 36 23 9B 39   ...7).......6#.9
```

As you can see from the output, the CRL contains the version, issuer, signature algorithm used to sign the CRL, validity period, list of revoked certificates and signature by the issuing authority. Each revoked entry in the CRL contains the serial number of the certificate and the date it was revoked.

Java Cryptography Extension

We have seen how the basic framework JDK 1.2 provides for cryptography operations like message digests, signatures, classes to deal with certificates, and CRLs. We have not seen any encryption and decryption operations. JCE provides a framework for some of these strong crypto operations.

Due to U.S government cryptographic export restrictions, Sun split its cryptography classes into two groups. The first is `java.security.*` packages that are part of JDK 1.2. These classes can be exported without any restrictions. The second group, the Java Cryptography Extension, is for U.S and Canadian distribution only. The JCE is an extension to JCA and includes a cryptographic provider, called `SunJCE`.

JCE 1.2 supplements JDK 1.2, which already includes interfaces and implementations of message digests and digital signatures. JCE 1.2 is provided as an extension to the Java platform. The architecture of the JCE follows the same design principles found elsewhere in the JCA: implementation independence and, whenever possible, algorithm independence. It uses the same "provider" architecture.

JCE 1.2 comes with a provider named SunJCE, which supplies the following services:

> An implementation of the DES (FIPS PUB 46-1), Triple DES, and Blowfish encryption algorithms in the Electronic CodeBook (ECB), Cipher Block Chaining (CBC), Cipher Feedback (CFB), Output Feedback (OFB), and Propagating Cipher Block Chaining (PCBC) modes.

> Key generators for generating keys suitable for the DES, Triple DES, and Blowfish algorithms.

> An implementation of the MD5 with DES-CBC password-based encryption (PBE) algorithm defined in PKCS #5.

> "Secret-key factories" providing bi-directional conversions between opaque DES, Triple DES and PBE key objects and transparent representations of their underlying key material.

> An implementation of the Diffie-Hellman key agreement algorithm between two or more parties.

> A Diffie-Hellman key pair generator for generating a pair of public and private values suitable for the Diffie-Hellman algorithm.

> A Diffie-Hellman algorithm parameter generator.

> A Diffie-Hellman "key factory" providing bi-directional conversions between opaque Diffie-Hellman key objects and transparent representations of their underlying key material.

> Algorithm parameter managers for Diffie-Hellman, DES, Triple DES, Blowfish, and PBE parameters.

> An implementation of the HMAC-MD5 and HMAC-SHA1 keyed-hashing algorithms defined in RFC 2104.

> An implementation of the padding scheme described in PKCS#5.

> A keystore implementation for the proprietary keystore type named "JCEKS".

For most of the encryption and decryption operations using symmetric key algorithms, the essential requirement is the secret key. The following example generates a 64-bit DES key:

```java
import java.io.*;
import java.security.*;
import javax.crypto.*;

import sun.misc.*;

public class GenPrivKey
{
    public static void main (String[] args) throws Exception
    {

        if (args.length < 1)
        {
            System.out.println("Usage java GenPrivKey filename");
            return;
        }
        // Generate and save a DES key to file args[0]

        System.out.println("Generating a DES key...");
        KeyGenerator generator = KeyGenerator.getInstance("DES");

        // DES keys can be either 56 or 64 bits long

        generator.init(64, new SecureRandom());
        Key key = generator.generateKey();
        System.out.println("Generating DES key... done");
```

```
    try
    {
        ObjectOutputStream out = new ObjectOutputStream(
        new FileOutputStream(args[0]));
        out.writeObject(key);
        out.close();
        System.out.println("DES key is saved to file " + args[0]);
    }
    catch(Exception e)
    {
        System.out.println("Could not save DES key to file " + args[0]);
        System.out.println(e);
    }
}
}
```

When you run the program it will generate a 64-bit DES key to a given file.

```
d:\krishna\code>java GenPrivKey des.key
Generating a DES key...
Generating DES key... done
DES key is saved to file des.key
```

Here is how the key generation program works:

> Checks the input arguments.

> Creates DES `KeyGenerator` object.

> Initializes the `KeyGenerator` object with key strength (64) and a random number object for source or random data for secret key.

> Generates the key from `KeyGenerator` object.

> Saves the key to the specified file.

Now that we know how to generate a secret key, how will we go about using this key to encrypt and decrypt messages and files? The following example shows how to encrypt a given string on the command line using the specified key:

```
import java.io.*;
import java.security.*;
import javax.crypto.*;

import sun.misc.*;

public class Encrypt
{
    public static void main (String[] args) throws Exception
    {

    // check arguments
```

Continued on Following Page

```
   if (args.length < 2)
   {
      System.out.println("Usage: java Encrypt keyfile text");
      return;
   }

// you can dynamically add the extension if needed
// Security.addProvider(new com.sun.crypto.provider.SunJCE());

// read the key from the keyfile

Key key;

   try
   {
      ObjectInputStream in = new ObjectInputStream(
      new FileInputStream(args[0]));
      key  = (Key)in.readObject();
      in.close();
   }
   catch (Exception e)
   {
      System.out.println("Could not read private key from file " + args[0]);
      System.out.println(e);
      return;
   }

// Create a cipher

Cipher cipher = Cipher.getInstance("DES/ECB/PKCS5Padding");

// Initialize the cipher to encryption mode

cipher.init(Cipher.ENCRYPT_MODE, key);

// collect input string
String input = args[1];
   for (int i =2;  i < args.length; i++)
   {
      input += " " + args[i];
   }

// convert the input the UTF8 format

byte[] inputBytes = input.getBytes("UTF8");

// Encode

byte[] outputBytes = cipher.doFinal(inputBytes);

// Print out the digest in base64.

BASE64Encoder encoder = new BASE64Encoder();
String base64 = encoder.encode(outputBytes);
System.out.print(base64);
   }
}
```

When you compile and run the program with some input text as argument, it will produce BASE64 encoded version of encrypted text. For example:

```
d:\krishna\code>java Encrypt des.key "Secret Message!"
Zp5tacxvk6uB3FS4qEjZlw==
```

The above program works as follows:

> ➢ Checks the input arguments.
> ➢ Reads the secret key from the key file and generates a key object.
> ➢ Creates a symmetric cipher object.
> ➢ Sets the cipher object in encrypt mode.
> ➢ Converts the input text that needs to be encrypted into a byte array.
> ➢ Updates the cipher object with input data.
> ➢ Calls the `doFinal` method of the cipher object to encrypt the data.
> ➢ Encodes the encrypted data into BASE64 format for readability.

One thing to note in the above example is that it statically loads the `javax.crypto.*` package, which contains classes for DES based encryption. If users wish to load the classes dynamically, they can do so by uncommenting the line:

```
// Security.addProvider(new com.sun.crypto.provider.SunJCE());
```

Cipher Objects

In the above example, one very important object is the `Cipher` object. Like other engine classes in the API, `Cipher` objects are created using the `getInstance` factory methods of the `Cipher` class. A factory method is a static method that returns an instance of a class, in this case, an instance of `Cipher`, which provides the requested transformation. A transformation is a string that describes the operation (or set of operations) to be performed on the given input, to produce some output. A transformation always includes the name of a cryptographic algorithm (e.g., DES), and may be followed by a feedback mode and padding scheme. A transformation is of the form:

> ➢ "algorithm/mode/padding" or
> ➢ "algorithm"

(in the latter case, provider-specific default values for the mode and padding scheme are used). For example, the following is a valid transformation:

```
Cipher c = Cipher.getInstance("DES/CBC/PKCS5Padding");
```

When requesting a block cipher in stream cipher mode (e.g., DES in CFB or OFB mode), you may optionally specify the number of bits to be processed at a time, by appending this number to the mode name as shown in the "DES/CFB8/NoPadding" and "DES/OFB32/PKCS5Padding" transformations. If no such number is specified, a provider-specific default is used. (For example, the SunJCE provider uses a default of 64 bits). The objects returned by factory methods are uninitialized, and must be initialized before they become usable.

Initializing a Cipher Object

A cipher object obtained from getInstance must be initialized for one of two modes (encryption or decryption), which are defined as final integer constants in the Cipher class. The two modes can be referenced by their symbolic names:

> ➤ ENCRYPT_MODE
> ➤ DECRYPT_MODE

Each of the Cipher initialization methods takes a mode parameter (opmode), and initializes the Cipher object for that mode.

To initialize a Cipher object, call one of the init methods:

```
public void init(int opmode, Key key);
```

Encrypting and Decrypting Data

Data can be encrypted/decrypted in one step (*single-part operation*) or in multiple steps (*multiple-part operation*). A multiple-part operation is useful if you do not know in advance how long the data is going to be, or if the data is too long to be stored in memory all at once.

To encrypt or decrypt data in a single step, call one of the doFinal methods:

```
public byte[] doFinal(byte[] input);
```

To encrypt or decrypt data in multiple steps, call one of the update methods:

```
public byte[] update(byte[] input);
```

A multiple-part operation must be terminated by one of the above doFinal methods of the Cipher.

The following example will show how to use the Cipher objects to decrypt the encrypted text.

```
import java.io.*;
import java.security.*;

import javax.crypto.*;
import sun.misc.*;

public class Decrypt
{
    public static void main (String[] args) throws Exception
    {

    // check arguments
```

```
      if (args.length < 2)
      {
      System.out.println("Usage: java Decrypt keyfile text");
      return;
      }


   // you can dynamically add the extension if needed
   // Security.addProvider(new com.sun.crypto.provider.SunJCE());


   // Read the key from private key file privkey.der

   Key key;
      try
      {
       ObjectInputStream in = new ObjectInputStream(
      new FileInputStream(args[0]));
       key = (Key)in.readObject();
       in.close();
      }
      catch (Exception e)
      {
       System.out.println("Could not read the key from file " + args[0]);
       System.out.println(e);
       return;
      }

   // Create a cipher with the key

   Cipher cipher = Cipher.getInstance("DES/ECB/PKCS5Padding");
   cipher.init(Cipher.DECRYPT_MODE, key);

   // BASE64 decode the input buffer
   BASE64Decoder decoder = new BASE64Decoder();
   System.out.println(args[0]);

     // Decode the actual encrypted string
   byte[] inputBytes = decoder.decodeBuffer(args[1]);
   byte[] outputBytes = cipher.doFinal(inputBytes);

   // Convert the output bytes to string

   String result = new String (outputBytes, "UTF8");
   System.out.println(result);
   }
 }
```

The program is the same as the encryption example, except that the Cipher object's mode is set to DECRYPT. Also, the BASE64-encoded encrypted text is first decoded before feeding it to the cipher object. If we run the above program against the output generated by our encrypt program, it will produce the actual string:

```
d:\krishna\code>java Decrypt des.key Zp5tacxvk6uB3FS4qEjZlw==
des.key
Secret Message!
```

Servlets that Sign

Now that we have seen how to use cryptographic APIs in JDK 1.2 , JCA and JCE, we shall use those APIs to develop servlets that perform cryptographic operations. Before we dwell into developing these servlets, there are a couple of points to be noted. The standard Java Servlet Development Kit (JSDK 2.1) and Java Web Server 2.0 do not come with a complete JDK 1.2 compliant cryptography API. So all the servlet examples use Java Web Server 2.0 with JDK 1.2 Java Run Time environment. To enable this feature the user should set JAVA_HOME environment variable to point to the JDK 1.2 Java install directory and invoke the Java Web Server 2.0 with -nojre command line flag. For example:

On the Windows NT platform, using command shell:

```
D:\local\jws2.0\bin>set JAVA_HOME=c:\local\jdk1.2.1
D:\local\jws2.0\bin>httpdnojre -verbose
```

Also, for some of the examples we need a secure web server. Java Web Server 2.0, by default will not start a secure web server, unless a self-signed certificate is created for the site. Authstore executable that comes with the Java Web Server 2.0 can be used to create a self-signed certificate for the secure site.

Authstore command line tool can also be used to import other CA certificates, so that your web server can trust the certificates issued by that CA. Please refer to the Authstore tool documentation for more information.

Once the Java Web Server 2.0 is set up with JDK 1.2 JRE, we can use Java Crypto API in the servlets we develop. Let us first develop a simple servlet, `ParseCert`, which parses the certificate posted by the user and displays the contents of the certificate in a human-readable form. The user interface to the servlet is illustrated below:

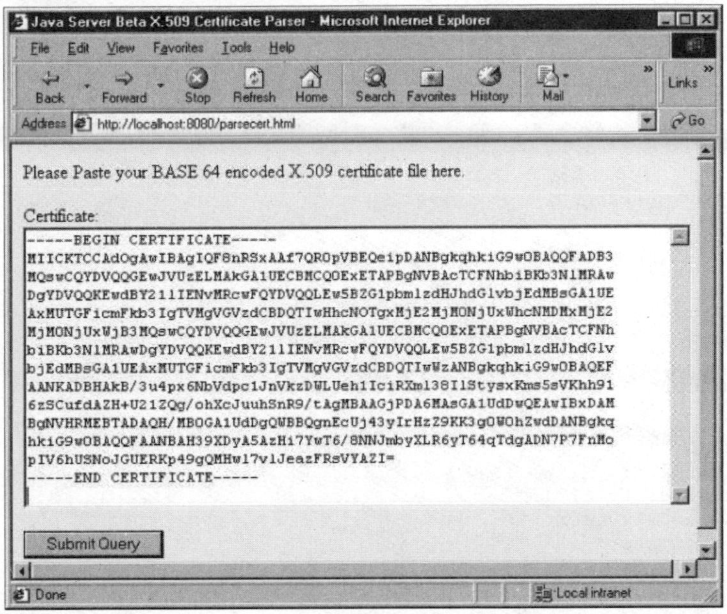

If the user pastes the certificate file and clicks on the 'Submit Query' button, the servlet will parse the certificate file and displays the results as shown below:

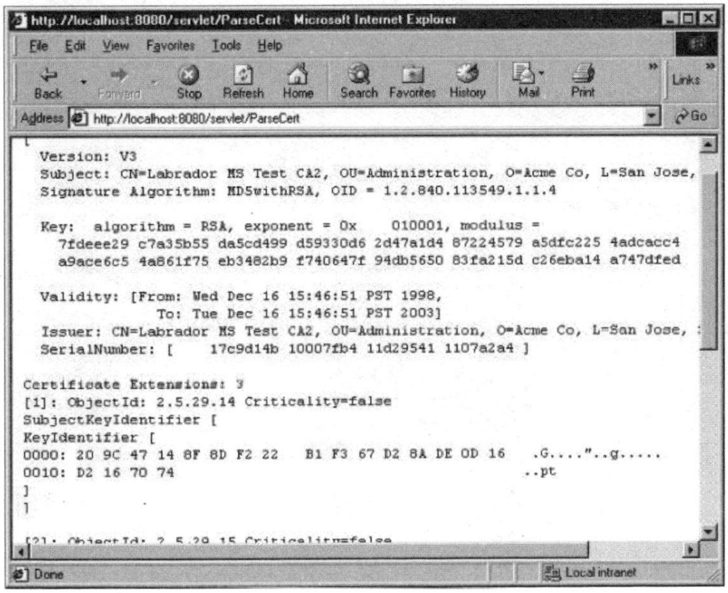

The following html file will produce the user interface for the `ParseCert` servlet:

```
<!DOCTYPE HTML PUBLIC "-//IETF//DTD HTML//EN">
<HTML><A NAME="top">
<HEAD>
<TITLE>
Java Server 2.0 X.509 Certificate Parser
</TITLE>
</HEAD>
<BODY BGCOLOR="#eeeeff">
    Please Paste your BASE 64 encoded X.509 certificate file here.
<FORM METHOD=POST ACTION="/servlet/ParseCert">
Certificate:
<TEXTAREA NAME=cert ROWS=15 COLS=70 >
</TEXTAREA>
<P>
<INPUT TYPE=submit NAME=parse>
</BODY>
</HTML>
```

The code that implements the `ParseCert` servlet is as follows:

```
import java.io.*;
import java.util.*;
import java.security.*;
import java.security.cert.*;
import javax.crypto.*;
import javax.servlet.*;
import javax.servlet.http.*;

public class ParseCert extends HttpServlet
{
   public void   doPost(HttpServletRequest req, HttpServletResponse res) throws
ServletException, IOException
    {
        res. setContentType("text/html");
        PrintWriter out = res.getWriter();
        String certData = req.getParameter ("cert");
        byte[] data = certData.getBytes("UTF8");
        ByteArrayInputStream bais = new ByteArrayInputStream(data);
        java.security.cert.CertificateFactory cf;

        out.println("<HTML>");
        out.println("<PRE>");

        try
        {
        cf  = CertificateFactory.getInstance("x.509");
           while (bais.available() > 0)
            {
             java.security.cert.Certificate cert = cf.generateCertificate(bais);
             out.println(cert.toString());
            }
        }
```

```
            catch (Exception e)
            {
            out.println("Exception is thrown....");
            out.println(e);
            }
            out.println("</PRE>");
            out.println("</BODY></HTML>");
      }

      public void  doGet(HttpServletRequest req, HttpServletResponse res) throws
ServletException, IOException
      {
      res. setContentType("text/html");
      PrintWriter out = res.getWriter();
      out.println("<HTML>");
      out.println("<H3>");
      out.println("GET method is not supported");
      out.println("</H3>");
      out.println("</BODY></HTML>");
      }
}
```

The servlet works as follows:

> If it receives a GET request, then it will output an error message.

> On a post request, reads the posted data into a string and obtains the actual bytes of the posted data.

> Creates a factory instance of CertificateFactory object for X.509-based certificates.

> Calls the generateCertificate method of the CertificateFactory object with the input data.

> Prints the generated certificates' string representation to the response object's write stream.

If you look at the core of the functionality of the ParseCert servlet, you can see that it is the same as the ParseCertificate application we have described above.

Let's look at another example, this time using a secure web server. When a client (browser) connects to a secure web server over https, both client and server negotiate and agree upon what cipher suite to use. The following servlet will display the cipher suite information in such a case.

```
public class SSLInfo extends HttpServlet
{
    public void
    doGet(HttpServletRequest req, HttpServletResponse res) throws ServletException,
IOException
    {
        res. setContentType("text/html");
        PrintWriter out - res.getWriter();

        out.println("<HTML><BODY>");
        out.println("<PRE>");
```

Continued on Following Page

```
    String cipherSuite = (String) req.getAttribute("javax.net.ssl.cipher_suite");
    out.println("Cipher Suite: " + cipherSuite);

        if (cipherSuite != null)
        {
            java.security.cert.Certificate [] certChain =
            (java.security.cert.Certificate [])
    req.getAttribute("javax.net.ssl.peer_certificates");
            if (certChain != null)
            {
                for (int i =0; i < certChain.length; i++)
                {
                    out.println("Client Certificate [" + i + "] ="
                    + certChain[i].toString());
                }
            }
        }
    out.println("</PRE>");
    out.println("</BODY></HTML>");
    }
     public void
    doPost(HttpServletRequest req, HttpServletResponse res) throws
    ServletException, IOException {
    res. setContentType("text/html");
    PrintWriter out = res.getWriter();
    out.println("<HTML>");
    out.println("<H3>");
    out.println("POST method is not supported");
    out.println("</H3>");
    out.println("</BODY></HTML>");
    }
}
```

In this case, when the client connects to the server securely and presuming the server is set up to do client authentication, the client has to authenticate to server by presenting a digital certificate in order for the connection to take place. This is done in the Cipher suite negotiation of the SSL connect. In the above example, the servlet requests the javax.net.ssl.ciper_suite attribute of the request object and parses the Cipher suite for client certificates (if any are present) and displays the certificate information as the response:

References

> Java[R] 2 SDK Documentation (http://www.javasoft.com/products/jdk/1.2/docs/index.html)
> Java[TM] Security Architecture (http://java.sun.com/products/jdk/1.2/docs/guide/security/spec/security-spec.doc.html)
> Java[TM] Cryptography Extension 1.2 (http://java.sun.com/products/jce/)
> Java Servlet Specification V 2.1 (http://java.sun.com/products/servlet/2.1/index.html)
> Java Web Server (http://wwwwswest2.sun.com/software/jwebserver/index.html)
> Java[R] 2 Platform API Specification (http://java.sun.com/products/jdk/1.2/docs/api/index.html)

The LogWriter class

This appendix describes the `LogWriter` class used by some of the applications in this book. It's a utility class that you can also use in your own applications.

Usage

The `LogWriter` simplifies printing log messages to a `PrintWriter`. It adds a timestamp and the owner's name to each message to make it easier to interpret a large log file with messages from many different parts of an application.

It also supports severity-level based logging. A `LogWriter` has a log level property that can be set to a value representing the severity level to log, e.g. log only error messages or log error messages and information messages. The `log` methods take a severity level parameter and the log message is only written if the severity level is lower than or the same as the `LogWriter`'s log level.

You can use the `LogWriter` in your application like this:

```
import java.io.PrintWriter;
import com.wrox.util.LogWriter;

public class MyApp {
    private LogWriter logWriter;

    public MyApp() {
        PrintWriter pw = new PrintWriter(System.err, true);
        logWriter = new LogWriter("MyApp", LogWriter.INFO, pw);
    }

    public void myMethod() {
        logWriter.log("An error message", LogWriter.ERROR);
        logWriter.log("An info message", LogWriter.INFO);
        logWriter.log("A debug message", LogWriter.DEBUG);
    }
}
```

> If you create many instances of the LogWriter that are writing to the same file, make sure you just create one instance of the PrintWriter for the file and use it in all LogWriter instances. Otherwise the messages may interfere with each other.

Variables

```
public static final int NONE = 0;
```

Use as log level if no messages should be logged.

```
public static final int ERROR = 1;
```

Use as log level and severity level for error messages.

```
public static final int INFO = 2;
```

Use as log level and severity level for information messages.

```
public static final int DEBUG = 3;
```

Use as log level and severity level for debug messages.

Constructors

```
public LogWriter(String owner, int logLevel, PrintWriter pw)
```

Creates new LogWriter.

- ➢ owner - A string to use for all log messages
- ➢ logLevel - The highest severity level to log
- ➢ pw - The PrintWriter to write log messages to

```
public LogWriter(String owner, int logLevel)
```

Creates new LogWriter.

> owner - A string to use for all log messages
> logLevel - The highest severity level to log

Methods

```
public int getLogLevel()
```

Returns the current log level.

```
public PrintWriter getPrintWriter()
```

Returns the current PrintWriter.

```
public void log(String msg, int severityLevel)
```

Writes the message to the current PrintWriter if the severity level is lower than or equal to the current log level.

> msg - The message
> severityLevel - The severity level for the message

```
public void log(Throwable t, String msg, int severityLevel)
```

Writes the message to the current PrintWriter if the severity level is lower than or equal to the current log level. If so, the stack trace for the Throwable is also logged.

> t - The Throwable to include in the message
> msg - The message
> severityLevel - The severity level for the message

```
public void setLogLevel(int logLevel)
```

Sets the current log level

> logLevel - The highest severity level to log

```
public void setPrintWriter(PrintWriter pw)
```

Sets the current PrintWriter.

> pw - The current PrintWriter

UML Notation

Classes and Objects

A class is represented in the UML like this:

Class
attribute1
attribute2
MethodA()
MethodB()

The rectangle representing the class is divided into three compartments, the top one showing the class name, the second showing the attributes and the third showing the methods.

An object looks very similar to a class, except that its name is underlined:

<u>AnObject</u>
attribute1
attribute2
MethodA()
MethodB()

Relationships

Relationships between classes are generally represented in class diagrams by a line or an arrow joining the two classes. UML can represent the following, different sorts of object relationships.

Dependency

If **A** depends on **B**, then this is shown by a dashed arrow between **A** and **B**, with the arrowhead pointing at **B**:

Association

An association between **A** and **B** is shown by a line joining the two classes:

If there is no arrow on the line, the association is taken to be bidirectional. A unidirectional association is indicated like this:

Aggregation

An aggregation relationship is indicated by placing a white diamond at the end of the association next to the aggregate class. If **B** aggregates **A**, then **A** is a part of **B**, but their lifetimes are independent:

Composition

Composition, on the other hand, is shown by a black diamond on the end of association next to the composite class. If **B** is composed of **A**, then **B** controls the lifetime of **A**.

Multiplicity

The multiplicity of a relationship is indicated by a number (or *) placed at the end of an association.

The following diagram indicates a one-to-one relationship between **A** and **B**:

This next diagram indicates a one-to-many relationship:

A multiplicity can also be a range of values. Some examples are shown below:

1	One and only one
*	Any number from 0 to infinity
0..1	Either 0 or 1
n..m	Any number in the range *n* to *m* inclusive
1..*	Any positive integer

Naming an Association

To improve the clarity of a class diagram, the association between two objects may be named:

Inheritance

An inheritance (generalization/specialization) relationship is indicated in the UML by an arrow with a triangular arrowhead pointing towards the generalized class.

If **A** is a base class, and **B** and **C** are classes derived from **A**, then this would be represented by the following class diagram:

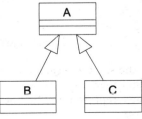

Multiple Inheritance

The next diagram represents the case where class **C** is derived from classes **A** and **B**:

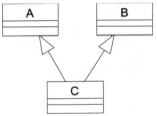

States

States of objects are represented as rectangles with rounded corners. The *transition* between different states is represented as an arrow between states, and a *condition* of that transition occurring may be added between square braces. This condition is called a guard.

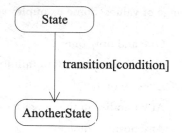

Object Interactions

Interactions between objects are represented by interaction diagrams – both sequence and collaboration diagrams. An example of a collaboration diagram is shown below. Objects are drawn as rectangles and the lines between them indicate links – a link is an instance of an association. The order of the messages along the links between the objects is indicated by the number at the head of the message:

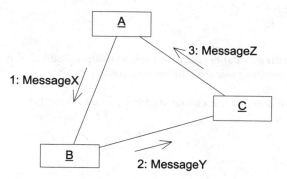

Sequence diagrams show essentially the same information, but concentrate on the time-ordered communication between objects, rather than their relationships. An example of a sequence diagram is shown below. The dashed vertical lines represent the lifeline of the object:

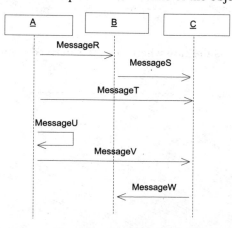

JServ Configuration

Apache JServ (or simply JServ) is a module for the popular Apache web server that implements Sun's Java Servlet API for running server-side Java code. Both the Apache web server and the Apache JServ module are freely downloadable as is their complete source code. You can find these at http://www.apache.org/dist/ and at http://java.apache.org/jserv/dist/ respectively.

At the time of writing, JServ 1.0 had just been made available from the Java Apache project. This release implements version 2.0 of Sun's Java Servlet API only, though work is actively proceeding on the next version which—among other things—will support version 2.1 of the Servlet API which is also currently available.

This appendix covers the following aspects of JServ, its configuration and set-up, on both Linux\Unix and on Windows:

- ➢ The Apache JServ Architecture
- ➢ Basic Installation
- ➢ Configuration Files
- ➢ Adding and Running Servlets
- ➢ Adding Servlet Zones
- ➢ Classpaths and Class Reloading
- ➢ Mapping URLs
- ➢ Virtual Hosts
- ➢ Automatic vs Manual Mode
- ➢ Troubleshooting

> ➤ Supporting Multiple developers
> ➤ Security
> ➤ Debugging
> ➤ Tuning Performance
> ➤ Add-on Functionality

This appendix covers both the Windows and the Linux/Unix installations of Apache / Apache JServ. There are several differences between the set-ups of which you should be aware.

> ➤ **Pathnames**
> The syntax for pathnames differs between Linux/Unix and Windows. For example, , the Apache configuration file has the default pathname `/usr/local/apache/conf/httpd.conf`. In Windows, the equivalent might be `d:\apache\conf\httpd.conf`.

> ➤ **Scripts**
> The scripts and calls demonstrated in this appendix are written for a Unix installation. The majority can be easily translated into Windows equivalents by adding in correct paths to the same file on a Windows box. Where not easily convertible, a Windows equivalent script has been explicitly given.

> ➤ **Configuration Files**
> The majority of this appendix deals with manipulating the Apache and ApacheJServ configuration files which will be covered in the next few pages. While a Windows installation comes with only one set of these files, the Linux/Unix installation comes with a default set and an example set in different directories. This appendix deals with this latter set for L/U installations. The location and names of these files will be given in the relevant sections of this appendix. Where possible, references to these files have been given by their OS-neutral name.

The Apache JServ Architecture

When Apache JServ was designed, it was apparent that JServ would need access to a Java Virtual Machine (JVM) - Java servlets must be executed from within a JVM, and hence any servlet execution environment (like Apache JServ) must include a JVM. However, simply adding a JVM to the Apache server was not a viable option. The complexity and overhead associated with a JVM are prohibitive and would have degraded the architecture of the server. The solution adopted instead was to separate the JVM from the Apache server completely.

Separating the JVM from the Apache server has several advantages:

> ➤ Any compatible JVM can be used in conjunction with Apache.
> ➤ No alterations need be made to Apache when a user upgrades their JVM.
> ➤ Stability is also improved by separating the server and JVM processes, thus allowing process-level protections by the operating system. If the JVM should crash or be misconfigured the web server will still operate normally.
> ➤ It also allows for some advanced functionality, including automatic versus manual start-up, separate JVMs for different configurations, and the ability to support load balancing on high traffic sites.

The Apache web server incorporates a modular architecture through which additional functionality can be added to the web server. Modules may be linked statically to the web server or may be loaded dynamically at run-time using Dynamic Shared Object (DSO) support on Unix or Dynamically Linked Libraries (DLLs) on Windows. The API for these modular components is based on the C programming language.

Apache JServ is implemented as two separate components, one written in C and the other in Java. The C and Java sides communicate using a special protocol, called **Apache JServ Protocol (AJP)**. The current version of this protocol is 1.1, and hence the protocol is designated **ajpv11**.

The C side of Apache JServ, called **mod_jserv**, provides an interface between the Apache web server and the Java side. The module passes requests and information between the web server and the Java side and can also be used to automatically start and stop the JVM in which the Java side is executed.

The Java side of Apache JServ, called the **Servlet Engine**, implements the servlet API, and is where most of the functionality of Apache JServ resides. The Java side is, in fact, completely separate from the C side, the only link between them being the AJP. It is possible to attach the Java side to any web server, provided an appropriate communication module using AJP is written for the web server.

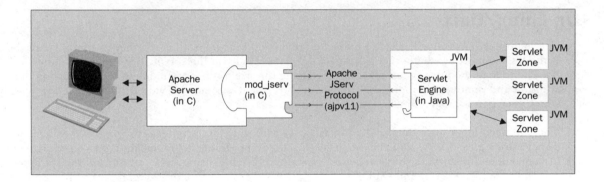

Mod_jserv can be thought of as a client of the Java side of Apache JServ. Similarly, the Java side can be thought of as a server that handles requests from the client. This is essentially a three-tier model, in which the web browser acts as a front end, the web server is the middle layer, and the Java side of Apache JServ is the backend. This three-tier model can be extended to an N-tier model if additional services, such as databases or application servers, are accessed via Apache JServ. In this model, the layer comprised of the Apache web server and mod_jserv can be replaced with any program that can use the AJP protocol to communicate with Apache JServ.

Apache JServ also introduces the concepts of servlet repositories and servlet zones. **Servlet repositories** are locations from which Java class files are loaded, including Java ARchive (JAR) files and directories containing Java class file hierarchies. **Servlet zones** are analogous to virtual directories in a web server. Each zone can have its own set of servlets and can even use a dedicated JVM. Later sections will go into further detail on how to use servlet zones and repositories.

Basic Installation

While the end goal is the same, the procedures for installing Apache JServ on Linux/Unix and on Windows are quite different. For your reference, the comparable install points are as follows:

	On Linux/Unix	On Windows
Apache Install Directory	`/usr/local/apache`	`C:\Program Files\Apache Group\Apache`
Apache Config File	`/usr/local/apache/conf/httpd.conf`	`C:\Program Files\Apache Group\Apache\conf\httpd.conf`
JServ Install Directory	`/usr/local/src/ApacheJServ-1.0`	`C:\Program Files\Apache Group\Apache JServ`

On Linux/Unix

The main decision you will need to make before attempting an install is whether to compile Apache with DSO support or whether to link Apache JServ statically to the server. DSO support allows Apache to load modules at run time, thus reducing the size of the executable as well as making the addition and removal of modules more convenient. Not all systems provide DSO support however, in which case you will need to use static compilation.

You will need to perform the installation as a user with sufficient privileges to write to the affected directories, e.g., as `root`. You can, however, install the programs in any location on your disk, even in your home directory, as the installation location is specified using the `--prefix` directive to Apache's configure script and with the `--with-apache-install` or `--with-apache-src` directives to Apache JServ's configure script.

With this in mind, the basic installation consists of three steps:

> Disabling or uninstalling previous versions of the software.
> Installation of the Apache web server
> Installation of Apache JServ

Requirements

To get version 1.0 of Apache JServ running, you will need a working copy of the JDK v1.1 or v1.2 and the JSDK version 2.0 already installed on your machine. Your Java runtime must be compatible with JDK 1.1. NB. Apache JServ 1.0 is compatible **only** with version 2.0 of the JSDK and will not work with any other version of the JSDK including 2.1.

You will also need a C compiler and **make** utility, such as the GNU project's **gcc** and **gmake**, available via the Free Software Foundation's web site at http://www.fsf.org. Nearly every Unix system already includes appropriate versions or equivalents of these programs in its standard installation. In the sample installation, I have also used the GNU project's free **wget** utility to download the applications. If you do not have wget on your system then you can download the files using any web browser.

Disk requirements are pretty nominal. A complete installation of Apache and Apache JServ on my Intel Pentium Linux system is about 3MB, with an additional 10MB needed to compile and build both programs. Memory requirements depend to a great extent on your operating system and JVM. Since the JVM uses the lion's share of memory resources you should consult your JVM's documentation, though a good rule of thumb is to have at least 32MB to 64MB available.

To simplify the development of servlets you should add the JSDK to your classpath. This will also allow the installation script supplied with Apache JServ to automatically locate the JSDK. Otherwise, you will need to specify the path to the JSDK each time you compile a servlet. For instance, on Unix you could add the lines

```
CLASSPATH=$CLASSPATH:/usr/local/java/jsdk/lib/jsdk.jar
export CLASSPATH
```

to your .profile file, where /usr/local/java/jsdk is the location where you installed Sun's JSDK package.

Uninstalling Previous Versions of Apache and Apache JServ

Depending on what variant and version of Linux/Unix you are running, Apache JServ will run on only certain versions of Apache. You can find the compatibility list at http://java.apache.org/faq/index.cgi?file=38. The latest version is 1.3.6 and will run Apache JServ happily on all platforms. The final release of Apache JServ 1.0 should also replace any previous betas on your machine.

Note that if you are uninstalling Apache previously installed as a .rpm file, you will need to uninstall both the apache and apache-devel packages.

Installing Apache Web Server

Depending on whether or not you have chosen to install Apache with DSO support, you should run one of the following two sample scripts. The target download file remains the same however - apache_1.3.6.tar.gz. Feel free to change the script to a local server or to download it first from www.apache.org/dist or a local mirror. The script assumes that it has been downloaded into /usr/local/src.

With DSO Support

Sample script for installing the Apache web server with DSO support.

```
cd /usr/local/src
wget http://www.apache.org/dist/apache_1.3.6.tar.gz
gunzip -c apache_1.3.6.tar.gz | tar x
cd apache_1.3.6
./configure --prefix=/usr/local/apache --enable-module=most--enable-shared=max
make
make install
```

Without DSO Support

Sample script for installing the Apache web server without DSO support.

```
cd /usr/local/src
wget http://www.apache.org/dist/apache_1.3.6.tar.gz
gunzip -c apache_1.3.6.tar.gz | tar x
cd apache_1.3.6
./configure --prefix=/usr/local/apache
make
make install
```

Finishing The Installation

Before Apache is up and running, you need to tell it what server name it should give itself. The usual one is 'localhost'. Open up the file httpd.conf. You'll find this in /usr/local/apache/conf/httpd.conf. Locate the ServerName directive within and change it to your server's name or IP address. For example,

```
ServerName http://localhost
```

At this point, assuming installation proceeded without any errors, you should be able to start Apache and confirm that it is working by accessing the default home page, like so.

```
/usr/local/apache/bin/apachectl start
lynx http://localhost
```

If you are not able to access the default homepage then please refer to the Apache web site at http://www.apache.org and the online documentation for further assistance.

The above procedure will provide you with a very rudimentary installation and you should refer to the online Apache documentation, available via the default home page, for further configuration and installation instructions. For instance, you may want to enable automatic start-up of Apache on system reboot.

Installing Apache JServ

Again, depending on whether or not you have chosen to install Apache with DSO support, you should run one of the following two sample scripts to install Apache JServ as either a statically or a dynamically linked module. For those wishing to download from java.apache.org/jserv/dist or a local mirror first instead of within the script, the target file is called Apache-JServ-1.0.tar.gz. Again, the script assumes that it has been downloaded into /usr/local/src.

With DSO Support

Sample script for installing Apache JServ with DSO support.

```
cd /usr/local/src
wget http://java.apache.org/jserv/dist/Apache-JServ-1.0b5.tar.gz
gunzip -c Apache-JServ-1.0b5.tar.gz | tar x
cd ApacheJServ-1.0b5
./configure --with-apache-install=/usr/local/apache
make
make install
```

Without DSO Support

Sample script for installing Apache JServ as a statically linked module. This script rebuilds and reinstalls Apache after building and installing Apache JServ.

```
cd /usr/local/src
wget http://java.apache.org/jserv/dist/Apache-JServ-1.0b5.tar.gz
gunzip -c Apache-JServ-1.0b5.tar.gz | tar x
cd ApacheJServ-1.0b5
./configure --with-apache-src=/usr/local/src/apache_1.3.6--enable-apache-conf
make
make install
/usr/local/apache/bin/apachectl stop
cd /usr/local/src/apache_1.3.6
make
make install
```

Finishing The Installation

Once you have installed Apache JServ you still need to configure the Apache server to communicate with Apache JServ. You can do this by adding the following line to the end of your Apache config file, httpd.conf:

```
Include /usr/local/src/ApacheJServ-1.0/example/jserv.conf
```

Assuming installation proceeded without any errors you should be able to restart Apache, wait several seconds to give Apache JServ time to start-up, and then access the example Hello servlet to confirm that your installation was successful.

```
/usr/local/apache/bin/apachectl restart
lynx http://localhost/example/Hello
```

If you're not able to access the servlet then you may want to refer to the section on troubleshooting later on in this appendix. You might also try accessing the URL a few times as it can take several seconds for Apache JServ to be loaded and start accepting requests.

On Windows

Running Apache and Apache JServ instead of Microsoft's own Internet Information Server couldn't be simpler. The installation is very simple as detailed here and both server and add-on are very configurable as will be demonstrated later.

The basic installation consists of three steps:

> ➤ Disabling or uninstalling IIS
> ➤ Installation of the Apache web server
> ➤ Installation of the Apache JServ servlet runner.

You can add Apache JServ to an existing Apache server by skipping the basic Apache installation and performing just the Apache JServ installation. Similarly, if IIS has not been installed on your machine then you can skip the first stage also.

Requirements

Like the Linux installation, to get version 1.0 of Apache JServ running, Windows users need working copies of the JDK 1.1 or 1.2 and the JSDK version 2.0 already installed on their machine. Servlet development can also be made easier by adding the path to the `jsdk.jar` file to the classpath in your `autoexec.bat` file, to look something like this:

```
set classpath=D:\javelin\jdk1.2.1;D:\javelin\jsdk2.0\lib\jsdk.jar
```

While slightly larger than their Unix counterparts, a complete installation needs only a little over 6Mb free space on your hard drive. Memory resources will depend on which JVM you are using and it is best to consult your JVM's documentation for that information.

Disabling Internet Information Server

Internet Information Server is Microsoft's own web server and is often present on Windows NT systems. It will clash with Apache for control of port 80 - the default port for HTTP 'conversations' - if it is still running when Apache is installed, so the neatest thing to do is disable it. This is done simply by opening the Services Control Panel in Windows NT, stopping and then disabling the following services:

> - World Wide Web Publishing Service
> - STMP Publishing Service
> - NNTP Publishing Service
> - FTP Publishing Service
> - IIS Admin Service

Another alternative is to completely uninstall IIS. It's really your choice.

Installing Apache Web Server

Installing Apache is very simple:

> - Download the Apache installer for Windows from http://www.apache.org/dist/. For Apache 1.3.6 the installer is in the file `apache_1_3_6_win32.exe`.
> - Run the installer by double clicking on the `.exe` file.

Before Apache is up and running, you need to tell it what server name it should give itself. The usual one is 'localhost'. Open up the file `httpd.conf`. You'll find this in your install directory's `conf` subdirectory. Locate the ServerName directive within, uncomment it and change it to your server's name or IP address. For example,

```
ServerName http://localhost
```

Now launch Apache from the **Apache Web Server** group under the **Start** menu or from a command prompt. Then use your web browser to access the default home page at `http://localhost`. You should get an Apache "Congratulations!" screen if everything is working fine. If this does not work then consult the Apache documentation and the Apache web site.

Installing Apache JServ

The procedure for installing Apache JServ on Windows is very similar to that for installing Apache web server:

> ➤ Download the Apache JServ installer for Windows from http://java.apache.org/jserv/dist/. For Apache JServ 1.0, the installer is in the file `Apache_JServ_1.0.exe`.

> ➤ Run the installer by double clicking on the `.exe` file

> ➤ Select integrated installation so that Apache JServ is started and stopped automatically by the web server.

> ➤ Restart the web server after installation (i.e., stop and then start the server).

Note that the Windows JServ installer automatically edits Apache's `httpd.conf` file with the lines

```
# Include the configuration files needed for mod_jserv
include "c:\Program Files\Apache Group\Apache JServ\conf\mod_jserv.conf"
```

so that JServ can talk to Apache and vice versa.

To test your installation access the URL http://localhost/servlets/IsItWorking, which should run the sample servlet and display a simple page. If you are not able to access the servlet then you may want to refer to the section on troubleshooting. You might also try accessing the URL a few times as it can take several seconds for Apache JServ to be loaded and start accepting requests.

Configuration Files and Directives

There are several configuration files used by Apache and Apache JServ. On the Apache side, of interest is the Apache configuration file, **httpd.conf**, which we've already met. This contains (amongst other things) directives for loading modules and an `Include` statement to the mod_jserv configuration file.

The main configuration file for the servlet engine is called the **Engine Properties File** and is usually named **jserv.properties**. This file contains properties passed to the JVM, various options and security preferences, and a list of all servlet zones and their respective property files.

Each servlet zone also uses its own **Zone Properties File**. This contains properties that specify the repositories from which servlets are loaded for the zone, whether the classes are automatically reloaded when they are changed, and other settings specific to a single servlet zone.

Before we look more closely at each of these files, you should be aware that depending on which operating system you are using, these files have different names. Further to that, the Linux\Unix installation comes with an example set of config files and a set of 'clean' files, again, named differently. For your reference, the synonymous filenames are:

	Linux/Unix 'Example' Configuration	Linux/Unix 'Clean' Configuration	Windows Default Configuration
Default directory	/usr/local/src/ ApacheJServ-1.0/ example/	/usr/local/src/ ApacheJServ- 1.0/conf/	C:\Program Files\ Apache Group\ Apache JServ\ conf\
Mod_jserv configuration file	jserv.conf	httpd.conf	mod_jserv. conf
(Servlet) Engine Properties file	jserv.properties	jserv.properties	jserv.prop erties
Zone Properties file	example.properties	zone.properties	zone.prope rties

The remainder of the appendix uses the Linux\Unix example filenames as a reference.

mod_jserv Configuration

The directives within the mod_jserv configuration file jserv.conf are used to configure mod_jserv so that it can communicate with the servlet engine. If you are using Apache JServ as a DSO module, then you must include a LoadModule directive in httpd.conf to load mod_jserv. On Unix, this would look like the following:

```
LoadModule jserv_module libexec/mod_jserv.so
```

The LoadModule directive is part of mod_so and should not be used if you statically linked mod_jserv when you built Apache.

In Windows, mod_jserv is loaded into Apache dynamically as a .dll file with the following line.

```
LoadModule jserv_module modules/ApacheModuleJServ.dll
```

The directives that are specific to mod_jserv are best wrapped in an IfModule directive so that the web server can be started even if mod_jserv is temporarily removed. For example,

```
<IfModule mod_jserv.c>
  ApJServProperties /usr/local/apache/conf/jserv.properties
  ApJServLogFile /usr/local/apache/logs/mod_jserv.log
  ApJServSecretKey DISABLED
  ApJServMount /servlets /servlets
```

```
    <Location /jserv/>
      SetHandler jserv-status
      order deny, allow
      deny from all
      allow from localhost
    </Location>

  </IfModule>
```

Descriptions of all the available configuration directives can be found as comments in `jserv.conf` which can be found in JServ's `conf` subdirectory. This file is actually included in `httpd.conf` (as mentioned earlier) following the successful installation of Apache JServ, so **you can also configure mod_jserv by adding the appropriate directives directly to httpd.conf**.

NB: `httpd.conf` is only loaded when the web server starts up, so you will need to restart the server after any modifications to either it or `jserv.conf`.

The Engine Properties File

The engine properties file, `jserv.properties`, is read by both mod_jserv and the servlet engine. This file contains the properties needed to launch a JVM, communication and security settings for internal communication with the Apache web server, and properties for enabling logging. There is a single engine properties file for each JVM used by Apache JServ and each is loaded once at start-up, so changes are available only after a restart of the web server and of the JVM.

The following is an example of a minimal engine properties file with one servlet zone:

```
wrapper.bin=/usr/local/java/jdk/bin/java
wrapper.class=org.apache.jserv.JServ
wrapper.classpath=/usr/local/jserv/lib/ApacheJServ.jar
wrapper.classpath=/usr/local/java/jsdk/lib/jsdk.jar
port=8007
security.allowedAddresses=127.0.0.1
security.authentication=false
zones=servlets
servlets.properties=/usr/local/apache/conf/servlets.properties
```

There are six basic types of configuration properties to be found in `jserv.properties`:

> The `wrapper` properties are used by mod_jserv to automatically start the servlet engine.

> The `port` property tells the servlet engine which port to use for communicating with mod_jserv.

> The `zones` property lists the servlet zones that are available.

> The property starting with the name of a servlet zone followed by the text "`.properties`" specifies the location of the zone properties file for the corresponding servlet zone.

> The security properties specify what security measures the server should take

> The log properties (not seen here) configure the server log

Zone Properties

Each servlet zone uses a zone properties file. The zone properties file contains a list of repositories containing class files and Java servlets. It also contains aliases and initialization arguments for the servlets in the zone.

Following is an example of a minimal zone properties file:

```
repositories=/usr/local/apache/servlets
```

This properties file just specifies a directory which may contain servlets.

Adding and Running Servlets

Servlets are added to a servlet zone by placing the compiled class files for the servlet in one of the zone's repositories (as specified in the zone's property file). For instance, you can add a servlet to the example servlet zone which is set up during the Apache JServ installation by placing the servlet's compiled .class file into the (repository) directory specified in example.properties. By default, this is JServ's example subdirectory.

You might like to try this yourself. A good sample servlet to try it with is **SnoopServlet,** which is included with Sun's JSDK in the examples directory. Compile SnoopServlet if you haven't already and then copy SnoopServlet.class into your repository directory (jserv_directory\example).

To run SnoopServlet, enter its URL in your web browser. For example:

```
http://localhost/example/SnoopServlet
```

The general form of a URL for accessing a servlet is

```
protocol://host:port/zone/name
```

Where protocol is usually http, host is your web server's host name or IP number, port is the port to which to connect to the web server, zone is a servlet zone's mount point, and name is the full class name or alias of a servlet in the specified servlet zone.

A mistake commonly made by novices is to attempt to access a servlet using the AJP. The AJP is only for internal communication between the web server and Apache JServ; it is never used to access the web server. Thus, do not try a URL such as ajpv11://yourdomain:8007/example/SnoopServlet, as this will not work. Always access your servlets using a standard protocol like HTTP.

Aliasing Servlets

Servlets whose classes are in a package are accessed using their fully qualified class name. For instance, if you add a servlet named FooServlet in the package com.domain.foo to a servlet zone whose mount point is /servlets then you would access the servlet using the URL

```
http://domain.com/servlets/com.domain.foo.FooServlet
```

You can hide the actual servlet and package name from URLs by defining an **alias** to your servlet. You define an alias in your servlet repository using the

```
servlet.alias.code=class name
```

syntax, where alias is the name you want to assign to your servlet. For instance, to define an alias foo for the class com.yourdomain.foo.FooServlet you would add the following property to your servlet's zone properties file:

```
servlet.foo.code=com.domain.foo.FooServlet
```

You can then access the servlet using the URL `http://domain.com/servlets/foo`. Note that foo remains case-sensitive. Calling `http://domain.com/servlets/Foo` would result in a 404: Not Found error from Apache.

Passing Additional Information to Servlets

Some servlets may need additional information passed to them at start-up. You can pass any number of arguments to a servlet using `initArgs` properties in the zone properties file. You can access the arguments using the `getInitParameter` method of `javax.servlet.ServletConfig`. For instance, to pass initialization arguments to `FooServlet`, you might write.

```
servlet.foo.initArgs=name=This is foo servlet
servlet.foo.initArgs=purpose=Nothing in particular
```

Note that you could replace foo with any servlet class name or alias to add start-up parameters to the servlet of your choice.

If you have many initialization arguments for a servlet you may want to store the arguments in a separate file. You can do this by omitting any `initArgs` directives in the zone properties file and instead providing a file `<name>.initArgs` in the same directory containing the servlet's class.

The special property **servlets.default.initArgs** lets you define initialization arguments that are passed to all servlets. For instance, you could pass the email address of your webmaster to all of your servlets so that the address can be included in error messages generated by the servlets.

Normally, servlets are loaded into memory the first time they are accessed; if no one ever accesses a servlet then it will never get loaded into memory. You may want, however, to have certain servlets executed when the web server (or JVM) is started up. You can use the `servlets.startup` directive to provide a list of servlets that are loaded when the JVM is started. You may want to add servlets to the startup list if you have a servlet that performs background processing, or if you have a servlet that takes several seconds to start-up and you would rather not subject your users to a lengthy delay.

Classpath and Class Reloading

The classpath is where the JVM looks for definitions of classes and is maintained by Apache JServ as:

> ➢ A system classpath, and
> ➢ Any number of servlet zone classpaths.

The system classpath is shared by all servlets, while each servlet zone's classpath is available only within that zone.

The system classpath is defined in one of two ways depending on whether the `ApJServManual` setting in `jserv.conf` is set to `off` or `on`. In automatic mode (`off`), the system classpath is defined using the `wrapper.classpath` directives in the engine properties file (`jserv.properties`). In manual mode (`on`), the system classpath is whatever classpath was specified to the Java runtime via the `CLASSPATH` environment variable or the `-classpath` option.

Class Loading and Reloading

Each servlet zone is assigned its own class loader. The zone's class loader is responsible for loading class definitions from class repositories into the JVM and for detecting modifications to class repositories. For instance, if you have two zones, A and B, and each of them uses class C from repository R, then there will be two copies of class C, each of which is inaccessible to the other. Likewise, any objects that are instances of class C are inaccessible to other zones. It does not matter that the repository is the same file or directory, since each zone has a separate class loader.

A useful feature when developing servlets is the ability to automatically reload classes when they are modified. Apache JServ will automatically reload classes in a zone if a repository containing a class has been modified. A servlet zone will also be reloaded if its properties file is modified. This allows you to install and test new versions of your servlets without having to restart your web server, unlike `httpd.conf` or `jserv.conf`.

Classes in a servlet zone's repositories list are available only to that zone. Also, only classes loaded from a servlet zone's repositories are subject to automatic reloading if the servlet zone's repositories or properties file are modified. In effect, you can use a zone as an isolated testing ground for your servlet code.

In contrast, classes in the system classpath **are not** automatically reloaded and it is recommended that you place only commonly used or stable classes and libraries like those found in the JDK or JSDK here. Those classes and libraries placed in the system classpath are accessible to all processes, thus improving overall performance by sharing code.

Automatic class reloading, which is **enabled by default**, reduces performance because every repository must be checked on each and every execution of a servlet. You can disable class reloading for a particular zone by setting the auto reload properties in the zone's property file to false with the following call:

```
autoreload.classes=false
```

This can lead to significant performance improvements at the cost of a more cumbersome development cycle requiring a server restart if a class file is modified.

Another performance drawback of class reloading is that even a small change to a single class file will force the entire zone to be reloaded. This is usually not a problem if you have only a few small class files, but it can be a significant performance problem if you have several large repositories. However, you can get around this problem by moving large repositories into your system classpath. Though you will lose the benefits of automatic class reloading for the large repositories, you will benefit from a quicker update and test cycle on the classes on which you are working.

When a servlet zone is reloaded, all of the objects created in that zone are destroyed. With automatic reloading enabled, even the smallest change to the servlet zone's properties file or to one of the repositories in a zone will cause the affected zone to be reloaded. This can be a problem if you are maintaining state between executions of a servlet. For instance, if you keep track of a user's session in memory, then that session will be lost when the zone is reloaded. In this instance, automatic reloading is just a special case of the more general problem of maintaining persistent state in a servlet.

The best solution to maintaining session data is to provide a persistence mechanism. Before Apache JServ destroys a servlet zone, it calls each loaded servlet's `destroy` method. Your servlets can then store the session data to a persistent store, such as a file or a database. When your servlets are reloaded, their `init` methods can load the stored session data. Notice that you might also want to store sessions whenever the session is updated to avoid loss of data due to an unexpected failure (JVM crash, power outage, etc.)

Access to methods implemented via the Java Native Interface (JNI) must be provided by classes loaded via the system class loader in the system classpath. This is a limitation imposed by the way Java class loaders are implemented and which allows only the system class loader to load JNI methods. In other words, you cannot access JNI methods in classes listed in a servlet zone's classpath, but must instead list the classes in the system classpath.

Adding Servlet Zones

Apache JServ can be configured to run with one or more servlet zones and every servlet you design is run within one of these zones. Each one is assigned a unique mount point and name. The mount point corresponds to a virtual directory, such that a request for a servlet in that virtual directory is handled by one in that zone. The default Windows installation, for example, includes a single zone named `root` mapped to the virtual directory `/servlets`. In this default installation then, the call to `http://localhost/servlets/IsItWorking` implies that the `IsItWorking` servlet is hosted in the zone called `root`.

Multiple servlet zones provide several advantages. They allow you to segregate servlets for security purposes, to run multiple JVMs, to support multiple virtual hosts, etc. Each servlet zone requires an `ApJServMount` directive in Apache's `httpd.conf` file (via `jserv.conf`), an entry in the engine properties file, and a corresponding zone properties file.

The `ApJServMount` directive tells mod_jserv how to map URLs to servlet zones. The syntax of the directive is

```
ApJServMount path protocol://host:port/zone
```

where

> ➤ `path` is the leading path portion of the URL that is mapped to the zone,
> ➤ `protocol` is the internal AJP communications protocol,
> ➤ `host` is the host name or IP number of the host on which the JVM is running,
> ➤ `port` is the port with which to communicate internally with Apache JServ, and
> ➤ `zone` is the name of a servlet zone.

`Path` and `zone` are both required. If `protocol` is omitted, it assumes the value of the `ApJServDefaultProtocol` directive, `ajpv11` by default. If `host` is omitted, it assumes the value of the `ApJServDefaultHost` directive, or `localhost` if not specified. If `port` is omitted it defaults to the value of `ApJServDefaultPort`, or its default `8007`.

For instance, to map requests for the path `/dev/servlets` to the zone `devservlets` on the local machine, you could use the directive

```
ApJServMount /dev/servlets /devservlets
```

Requests to a URL starting with `/dev/servlets` will be handled by the servlets in the zone `devservlets`. In the engine properties file, you need to add an entry for a zone by adding it to the `zones` property and by providing the path to its zone properties file. For instance,

```
zones=devservlets
devservlets.properties=/usr/local/apache/conf/devservlets.properties
```

The properties file for the `devservlets` zone must contain at least one `repositories` entry specifying a repository from which servlets are loaded, for instance:

```
repositories=/usr/local/apache/devservlets
```

Once you have finished configuring the zone you can restart the web server. For the above example, you might use a URL such as `http://yourdomain/dev/servlets/MyServlet` which will run the servlet `MyServlet` in the zone `devservlets`.

Mapping URLs

There are a couple of ways in which you can map URLs in addition to servlet zones and servlet aliases. The mod_jserv module can map files ending in a particular suffix to a servlet so that when the servlet is run, the path to the file is passed as extra path info to the servlet. The other way to map URLs is to use the very flexible mod_rewrite module, which is provided with Apache.

Using ApJServAction

The ApJServAction directive lets you specify a servlet that is executed for files ending in a particular suffix. The path to the requested file is passed along to the servlet, and the servlet can access it using the getPathInfo or getPathTranslated methods of javax.servlet.HttpServletRequest. For instance, the Java Apache project provides the Apache JSSI servlet. This servlet can incorporate the output of another servlet in an HTML file. So, to map files ending in the suffix .jhtml to the Apache JSSI servlet, you would add the following line to your jserv.conf (or directly to your httpd.conf) file:

```
ApJServAction .jhtml /servlets/org.apache.servlet.ssi.SSI
```

Following a server restart, and assuming you installed the Apache JSSI servlet, any files ending in .jhtml will be parsed by the Apache JSSI servlet.

Working with mod_rewrite

Sometimes you do not want users to see a path such as /dev/servlets/MyServlet when accessing your site. Alternatively, you may want to wrap existing files in a servlet to provide authentication or dynamic content. Apache is supplied with a very flexible module called mod_rewrite that you can use to modify URLs in almost any conceivable manner.

The only important thing to remember is that the AddModule directive (in Linux - LoadModule in Windows) for mod_jserv must come before the AddModule directive for mod_rewrite in httpd.conf,

```
ClearModuleList
...
AddModule mod_jserv.c
AddModule mod_rewrite.c
```

This is because modules are executed in the reverse order to which they are specified using the AddModule directive, and mod_rewrite must be executed before mod_jserv.

The remainder of this section includes some simple recipes for using mod_rewrite with mod_jserv.

Our first code snippet rewrites any URL starting with /auth to /servlets/AuthServlet. The [PT] option instructs mod_rewrite to pass the rewritten URL along for further processing within Apache.

```
<IfModule mod_rewrite.c>
  RewriteEngine on
  RewriteRule ^/auth(.*)  /servlets/AuthServlet$1 [PT]
</IfModule>
```

Now let's consider the scenario where we're looking to add some dynamic content into our static pages with the use of server-side includes. As we demonstrated above, an `ApJServAction` directive has already been added to `jserv.conf` so that any files whose suffix is `.jhtml` go through the Apache JSSI module. The main problem is that you cannot simply rename the files as that would break existing URLs. You also would rather not maintain a list of mappings from existing html files to new jhtml files. The solution is to use `mod_rewrite`'s `RewriteMap` directive and a little Perl program.

```
<IfModule mod_rewrite.c>
  RewriteEngine on
  RewriteMap suffixmap prg:/usr/local/apache/conf/suffixmap
  RewriteRule ^(.*)\.html$ $1.${suffixmap:$1|html}
</IfModule>
```

The code works by passing any URL ending in `.html` to the program `/usr/local/bin/suffixmap`. (Simply change the address accordingly for Windows compatibility.) The suffix-mapping program then returns either a new suffix or the string `NULL` to use the default suffix.

The source code for the suffix map program is:

```
#!/usr/bin/perl
# Used for mapping urls with mod_rewrite
$| = 1;
$root = "/usr/local/apache/htdocs";
@suffixes = ("jhtml");
MATCH:
while (<>) {
  chop;
  $file = $root . $_;
  foreach $suffix (@suffixes) {
    if (-f "$file.$suffix") {
      print "$suffix\n";
      next MATCH;
    }
  }
  print "NULL\n";
}
```

This script concatenates the server's document root to the supplied URL and then tests for the existence of a file with one of the desired suffixes (additional suffixes can easily be added). If a match is found the script returns the matching suffix to `mod_rewrite` by writing it to standard output, otherwise it writes `NULL` to indicate that the default suffix should be used. This solution is not the most efficient approach since it requires a lookup on each and every URL ending in `.html`. It would be more efficient to manually or automatically generate a text or DBM file that maps specific URLs. The above script, though, is convenient during development and does demonstrate some of the power and flexibility available with `mod_rewrite`. Note that in order for this and other perl programs to run under Windows, you will need to install mod_perl–available at www.cpan.org–or some other perl engine.

A full and comprehensive set of documentation and samples written by the author of `mod_rewrite`, Ralf S. Engelschall can be found at `http://www.engelschall.com/pw/apache/rewriteguide`. Some docs are also installed with Apache web server.

Virtual Hosts

Virtual hosts are a convenient way for a single web server to handle requests for multiple domains. Each virtual host can have separate Apache JServ configurations, while several shared directives must be placed outside of any virtual host configuration. The shared directives include the directives for the properties and log files and the status URL. Other directives, such as servlet mount points and zones, can be specified separately for each virtual host.

The following example shows a sample mod_jserv configuration file for two virtual hosts named `vhost1` and `vhost2`. Substituting in Windows pathnames for the Linux ones will produce the equivalent Windows config file.

```
# shared directives
LoadModule jserv_module libexec/mod_jserv.so
<IfModule mod_jserv.c>
  ApJServProperties /usr/local/apache/conf/jserv.properties
  ApJServLogFile /usr/local/apache/logs/mod_jserv_log
  ApJServSecretKey DISABLED
  <Location /status/jserv/>
     SetHandler jserv-status
     order deny,allow
     deny from all
     allow from localhost
  </Location>
</IfModule>

# directives for vhost1
NameVirtualHost 192.168.1.1
<VirtualHost 192.168.1.1>
  ServerName vhost1.com
  DocumentRoot /usr/local/hosts/vhost1/htdocs
  <Directory /usr/local/hosts/vhost1/htdocs>
    order allow,deny
    allow from all
  </Directory>
  <IfModule mod_jserv.c>
    ApJServDefaultHost vhost1.com
    ApJServMount /servlets ajpv11://vhost1.com/vhost1
  </IfModule>
</VirtualHost>

# directives for vhost2
<VirtualHost 192.168.1.1>
  ServerName vhost2.com
  DocumentRoot /usr/local/hosts/vhost2/htdocs
  <Directory /usr/local/hosts/vhost2/htdocs>
    order allow,deny
    allow from all
  </Directory>
  <IfModule mod_jserv.c>
    ApJServDefaultHost vhost2.com
    ApJServMount /servlets ajpv11://vhost2.com/vhost2
  </IfModule>
</VirtualHost>
```

For this example I have used a dummy IP number. The `ApJServDefaultHost` directive is required since both virtual hosts share the same IP number; using the directive allows Apache JServ to match the request to the correct servlet zone.

You will need to create `htdocs` directories for each virtual host, and you should also create the directories in which to store servlets:

```
mkdir -p /usr/local/hosts/vhost1/htdocs
mkdir -p /usr/local/hosts/vhost2/htdocs
mkdir -p /usr/local/hosts/vhost1/servlets
mkdir -p /usr/local/hosts/vhost2/servlets
```

The engine properties file should contain properties for both `vhost1` and `vhost2`, and must allow access from the virtual host's IP address:

```
wrapper.bin=/usr/local/java/jdk/bin/java
wrapper.class=org.apache.jserv.JServ
wrapper.classpath=/usr/local/jserv/lib/ApacheJServ.jar
wrapper.classpath=/usr/local/java/jsdk/lib/jsdk.jar
port=8007
security.allowedAddresses=192.168.1.1
security.authentication=false
zones=vhost1,vhost2
vhost1.properties=/usr/local/apache/conf/vhost1.properties
vhost2.properties=/usr/local/apache/conf/vhost2.properties
```

Each zone also needs a corresponding servlet zone property file, `vhost1.properties` and `vhost2.properties`, which are just like any other servlet zone properties file. The file `vhost1.properties` might look like the following:

```
repositories=/usr/local/hosts/vhost1/servlets
```

Additional repositories and settings can be added, just like for any other servlet zone. A similar file can be created for `vhost2`.

Following the above configuration, requests via URLs such as `http://vhost1.com/servlets/...` would be handled by servlet zone `vhost1`, while requests via URLs such as `http://vhost2.com/servlets/...` would be handled by servlet zone `vhost2`.

With the `ApJServMountCopy` directive you can make shared servlet zones available to each virtual host. You can use this directive to provide a common set of basic servlets to each virtual host. With mount copy enabled, zones defined outside of any virtual host section are automatically accessible to each virtual host. If the following directives were added to the shared portion of the sample virtual host configuration, then both `vhost1` and `vhost2` would have access to the zone `/share`.

```
ApJServMountCopy on
ApJServMount /share/servlets /share
```

You will also need to add a zone properties file and an entry in the engine properties file for the shared servlet zone (just follow the same procedure as for any other servlet zone). Then, given a servlet `MailServlet` in zone share, URLs such as `http://vhost1.com/share/servlets/MailServlet` and `http://vhost2.com/share/servlets/MailServlet` would both execute the same instance of `MailServlet`.

Automatic vs Manual Mode

Apache JServ can be used in one of two modes, known as automatic and manual modes.

Automatic mode is the most convenient way to run Apache JServ as this lets the mod_jserv module both launch and shut down the JVM automatically. The module also monitors the JVM and relaunches it if it exits unexpectedly. When the Apache server is restarted or shutdown the module restarts or shuts down the JVM. All you need to configure automatic mode is to set `ApJServManual` to `off` in your mod_jserv config file and to properly configure the wrapper properties in your engine properties file. Automatic mode is suitable for basic installations using a single JVM

Manual mode, on the other hand, takes a bit more work to configure correctly, but is much more powerful, giving you the onus to launch a JVM separately using an external program, such as a shell script or batch file, or from the command prompt. The advantage here comes in that you can then launch more than one JVM at a time, giving you the ability to isolate a client's data and Java executables from another - useful for multiple site hosting and isolating test material. Manual mode is also required for site administrators wishing to take advantage of the load balancing features in Apache JServ 1.0.

The following is a sample Unix shell script that you can use to launch Apache JServ in manual mode. Before you can use this script you will need to adjust the paths for the locations of the files on your system.

```
#!/bin/sh
properties=/usr/local/apache/conf/jserv.properties
log=/usr/local/apache/logs/jserv_manual.log
CLASSPATH=$CLASSPATH:/usr/local/jsdk/lib/jsdk.jar
CLASSPATH=$CLASSPATH:/usr/local/jserv/lib/ApacheJServ.jar
java org.apache.jserv.JServ $properties $1 2>> $log
```

In Windows, having added `ApacheJServ.jar` to your classpath, an equivalent windows shell command would be

```
java org.apache.jserv.JServ D:\Javelin\jserv10\conf\jserv.properties >>
d:\jserv.log
```

When run in manual mode the standard error and standard output of the JVM (`System.err` and `System.out`) go, by default, to the regular output device, typically the local terminal window. You will probably want to redirect the output to a log file, both so that the terminal is not awash in output and so that you can retain output for future reference.

One of the drawbacks of manual mode is that there is no built-in monitoring of the JVM. If the JVM crashes you will need to manually restart it. An external monitoring package, such as **mon** (available from `http://www.kernel.org/software/mon/`), is therefore a necessity for any site using manual mode.

Another drawback of manual mode is that the JVM is not notified when the web server is restarted or shutdown. As a rule, you should never terminate an Apache JServ process using Unix's kill command or Windows NT's task manager. Terminating a JVM in this manner prevents it from cleanly destroying all servlets. To cleanly restart or terminate Apache JServ you should use the appropriate option to Apache JServ, i.e.,

Option	Action
-v	Echo server version
-V	Echo server version and details
-r	Restart server
-s	Stop server

For instance, if the preceding Unix shell script were saved in a file called `jserv` then you could restart the server using the command `jserv -r`

Working With Multiple JVMs

Apache JServ allows you to have any number of JVMs. This feature can be used to support enhanced security, load balancing, and fault tolerance. The drawback is that each JVM may require a significant amount of memory and processor resources, which can be a factor in deciding how many JVMs to allow and what hardware to purchase.

The Java side of Apache JServ listens on a specific port number for requests from the web server. If you are running multiple copies of Apache JServ on the same virtual host you need to assign each instance a separate port number. The port number is specified in the engine properties file, so each instance also requires a separate engine properties file. The engine properties files can be identical except for the port number, or they may even be completely different since each JVM is independent of other JVMs.

On The Same Server

To run multiple JVMs you need to run Apache JServ in manual mode. The previous section on running Apache JServ explains the difference between automatic and manual modes and shows how to launch a JVM in manual mode. The following sample configuration shows how you can configure Apache JServ to use a different JVM for each servlet zone.

```
<IfModule mod_jserv.c>
  ApJServManual on
  ApJServMount /servlets1 ajpv11://localhost:9001/jvm1
  ApJServMount /servlets2 ajpv11://localhost:9002/jvm2
  ApJServLogFile /usr/local/apache/logs/mod_jserv.log

  <Location /status/jserv/>
    SetHandler jserv-status
    order deny,allow
    deny from all
    allow from localhost
  </Location>

</IfModule>
```

Requests starting with /servlets1 will be handled by the zone jvm1 listening on port 9001, while requests starting with /servlets2 will be handled by the zone jvm2 listening on port 9002. You will need to start two instances of the JVM, one listening on port 9001 and the other on port 9002, for instance, with the commands:

```
java org.apache.jserv.JServ /usr/local/apache/conf/jvm1.properties
java org.apache.jserv.JServ /usr/local/apache/conf/jvm2.properties
```

On Different Servers

You can also offload the work of running the JVM to other computers. Furthermore, because Java is available for many platforms, you can run your code unchanged on various set-ups with no need to recompile, allowing you to take advantage of almost any capable hardware at your disposal. You could, for instance, mix and match servers running Windows NT, Solaris, Linux, and HP/UX on various hardware platforms.

With minor modifications, the preceding configuration can be used to dispatch requests to two different machines:

```
<IfModule mod_jserv.c>
  ApJServManual on
  ApJServLogFile /usr/local/apache/logs/mod_jserv.log
  ApJServMount /servlets1 ajpv11://server1/zone1
  ApJServMount /servlets2 ajpv11://server2/zone2

  <Location /status/jserv/>
      SetHandler jserv-status
      order deny,allow
      deny from all
      allow from localhost
  </Location>

</IfModule>
```

With this example, requests starting with /servlets1 will be handled by the instance of Apache JServ running on server1, while requests starting with /servlets2 will be handled by the instance of Apache JServ running on server2. You will, of course, need to install the Java side of Apache JServ on each server, as well as configure appropriate engine and zone property files for each server. You may also need to list the web server's IP address in the security.allowedAddresses property in each server's engine properties file. Furthermore, when using the ApJServSecretKey directive, you will need to keep the secret key file available to each server (either by copying the file or via a shared file system).

For Reliability

Load balancing and fault tolerance functionality was added to Apache JServ in version 1.0b4. An overview with instructions on configuration are available in **How to: Scalability - Load-Balancing - Fault tolerance** by Bernard Bernstein and Jean-Luc Rochat which is available online at http://java.apache.org/jserv/howto.load-balancing.html. This functionality is suitable for sites that experience significant demand and which require reliability even in the event of the failure of a JVM.

For Security

Another reason to use separate JVMs is to provide greater security. While separating virtual hosts into separate zones is sufficient when you can trust the people writing servlets, it may not be appropriate if you need to provide a higher level of security.

Say for example you need to ensure that code written by developers for one virtual host cannot access files maintained by another virtual host. Given the example mod_jserv config file in the 'Virtual Hosts' section, both `vhost1` and `vhost2` share a single JVM running with the same permissions as the user who started Apache. In order to completely isolate the two virtual hosts you need to use manual mode to launch two separate JVMs. The changes to the sample virtual host configuration are outlined below:

```
# shared directives
LoadModule jserv_module libexec/mod_jserv.so
<IfModule mod_jserv.c>
  ApJServManual on
  ApJServLogFile /usr/local/apache/logs/mod_jserv_log
  ApJServSecretKey DISABLED
  <Location /status/jserv/>
     SetHandler jserv-status
     order deny,allow
     deny from all
     allow from localhost
  </Location>
</IfModule>
NameVirtualHost 192.168.1.1

# directives for vhost1
<VirtualHost 192.168.1.1>
  ServerName vhost1.com
  DocumentRoot /usr/local/hosts/vhost1/htdocs
  <Directory /usr/local/hosts/vhost1/htdocs>
    order allow,deny
    allow from all
  </Directory>
  <IfModule mod_jserv.c>
    ApJServDefaultHost vhost1.com
    ApJServMount /servlets ajpv11://vhost1.com:9001/vhost1
  </IfModule>
</VirtualHost>

# directives for vhost2
<VirtualHost 192.168.1.1>
  ServerName vhost2.com
  DocumentRoot /usr/local/hosts/vhost2/htdocs
  <Directory /usr/local/hosts/vhost2/htdocs>
    order allow,deny
    allow from all
  </Directory>
  <IfModule mod_jserv.c>
    ApJServDefaultHost vhost2.com
    ApJServMount /servlets ajpv11://vhost2.com:9002/vhost2
  </IfModule>
</VirtualHost>
```

You will also need an engine properties file for each virtual machine. The files can be identical except for the port property, which must have the appropriate value for each JVM. For instance, following is a very simple properties file for `vhost1`.

```
security.allowedAddresses=192.168.1.1
security.authentication=false
port=9001
zones=vhost1
vhost1.properties=/usr/local/apache/conf/vhost1.zone.properties
```

The properties file for `vhost2` is nearly identical:

```
security.allowedAddresses=192.168.1.1
security.authentication=false
port=9002
zones=vhost2
vhost2.properties=/usr/local/apache/conf/vhost2.zone.properties
```

To complete this example, each JVM may also be launched as a separate user. Under Unix, you can use the `su` command to launch the JVM as the desired user. For instance,

```
su - user1 -c
"java -classpath _
  $CLASSPATH:/usr/local/jsdk/lib/jsdk.jar:/usr/local/jserv/lib/ApacheJServ.jar _
  org.apache.jserv.JServ /usr/local/apache/conf/vhost1.engine.properties"

su - user2 -c
"java -classpath
  $CLASSPATH:/usr/local/jsdk/lib/jsdk.jar:/usr/local/jserv/lib/ApacheJServ.jar _
  org.apache.jserv.JServ /usr/local/apache/conf/vhost2.engine.properties"
```

You may also want to redirect output from each instance to an appropriate log file, and/or use the log properties in each engine's properties file to route log messages to appropriate files. Note that under Windows, this 'user-switching' on the fly is not possible.

Troubleshooting

Apache JServ is a complex application. Successful installation and configuration requires that both the Apache web server, the Apache JServ module, and a JVM are properly installed and configured. Each of these tasks involves many subsystems, including your system's networking code, file and other access permissions, several configuration files, and many configuration directives. Even experienced users can be confused by the multitude of interacting factors.

The Java Apache project includes a community of experienced developers and users. The project's home site—http://java.apache.org—includes (among other things) a significant amount of information about Apache JServ. The online user-maintained FAQ, accessible from the home page, is an excellent resource. There are configuration and set-up issues that I have not had an opportunity to tackle, but a quick check of the constantly growing FAQ often reveals an answer. The mailing lists (for details see the web site) are also excellent resources.

Log Files

The main sources of information when tracking down configuration problems are the status URL (described in the previous section) and the server log files. Before you can make any sense of what is broken you will need to enable logging and examine the resulting entries in the log files. Between Apache and ApacheJServ there are quite a few log files. I will do my best to summarize what each of them contains. Recommended names for each file are shown in parentheses.

> - **Access log** (access.log)–A record of the URLs requested from your server.
> - **Error log** (error.log)–A record of errors encountered by the Apache server. This includes things like file not found errors.
> - **mod_jserv log** (mod_jserv.log)–A record of messages and errors encountered by the C side of ApacheJServ (the mod_jserv module). This includes messages relating to communication via AJP with the Java side of ApacheJServ and problems launching the JVM in automatic mode. This log can be disabled, in which case the messages are redirected to the Apache error log.
> - **JServ log** (jserv.log)–A record of messages and errors encountered by the Java side of ApacheJServ. This can be configured to include exception stack traces, requestand response headers, and various internal debugging information.

You may need to look in all of the above files to track down the source of a problem.
To enable logging in Apache you need to have a few directives enabled in its configuration file, httpd.conf as follows. These directives are enabled with the default installation on both Linux\Unix and Windows.

```
LogLevel warn
LogFormat "%h %l %u %t \"%r\" %>s %b" common
CustomLog /usr/local/apache/logs/access.log common
ErrorLog /usr/local/apache/logs/error.log
```

To enable the mod_jserv log file you need to have enabled the ApJServLogFile directive in your mod_jserv config file.

```
ApJServLogFile /usr/local/apache/logs/mod_jserv.log
```

If you use the tag DISABLED instead of a file name the messages are redirected to the Apache error log. This can make tracking errors a bit easier since there is one less log file to monitor.

To enable the jserv.log file you need to enable the log directives in your engine properties file, for instance:

```
log=true
log.file=/usr/local/apache/logs/jserv.log
log.timestamp=true
log.dateFormat=yyyyMMdd.HHmmss.SSS:
log.channel.init=true
log.channel.terminate=true
log.channel.serviceRequest=true
log.channel.authentication=true
log.channel.requestData=true
```

```
log.channel.responseHeaders=true
log.channel.signal=true
log.channel.exceptionTracing=true
log.channel.servletManager=true
log.channel.singleThreadModel=true
```

One common problem is restricted access permissions to the log files that do not allow the Java side of Apache JServ to write to its log file. The `jserv.log` file must be writable by the user as whom the JVM is executed. In automatic mode this means the file must be writable by the user or group as whom the Apache server is run, typically user 'nobody' (In Windows, Apache is executable by the Everyone group). If you are running on Unix, and the Apache User and Group directives are set to user and group nobody, then you may need to do the following before trying to generate the `jserv.log` file:

```
mkdir /usr/local/apache/logs
chgrp nobody /usr/local/apache/logs
chmod ug+rwx /usr/local/apache/logs
```

Log files can grow quite large and may contain much information that is not relevant to the task at hand. A good way to ensure that you are viewing only essential information is to clear out your log files and then perform a single test to regenerate the logs with relevant information. You do this by stopping Apache, deleting your old log files, and then restarting Apache. Now you are ready to execute a single request that will generate an error. For instance, say your problem URL is `http://localhost/servlets/HelloWorldServlet`. You enter this URL into your web browser and try to access it. Now you have log files containing just the absolutely relevant information. Before doing anything else you can examine and/or make copies of your log files.

An excellent method to analyze problems is to continually monitor your log files. In Unix, you can use the `tail -f` command to display entries as they are written to the logs. Additionally, if you are using X Windows, then you can open multiple terminal windows, each one of which may be used to monitor a separate log file. The following is a sample script you can use to monitor the log files with:

```perl
#!/usr/bin/perl
$loc=10;
$logdir="/usr/local/apache/logs";
$options="-bg black -fg green -font fixed -e tail -f";
for each $file ("access.log", "error.log", "mod_jserv.log", "jserv.log")
{
    system "xterm -geometry \"100x10+5+$loc\" -T $logdir/$file
$options$logdir/$file &";
    $loc += 180;
}
```

MS Windows does not have a `tail` command. The best I have managed to do under Windows is to load the log files into the Notepad application. Unfortunately, this requires reloading the log files each time you want to check for new data. It also stops loading data past some arbitrary file size limit after which you have to manually truncate the log files. You may be able to use Cygnus' Cygwin utilities (find them at `http://sourceware.cygnus.com/cygwin`), which includes a `tail` command for Windows.

If you cannot tell what the log files are telling you or how to fix things, you can look at the source code for Apache JServ. If you can read Java code then you can probably figure out what it expects you to type into its configuration files. You can also look at the C code for mod_jserv, especially the sources for the wrapper (`jserv_wrapper.c`, `jserv_wrapper_unix.c`, and `jserv_wrapper_win.c`) that handle launching the JVM in automatic mode.

Status URL

Apache JServ includes a special handler and an internal servlet that can be used to monitor the server via a web browser. If you are using the example configuration supplied with Apache JServ then the URL to display the status page is `http://localhost/status/jserv/`. NB The trailing slash is required. In your engine properties file you may also enable the complete status functionality by adding the following property

```
security.selfservlet=true
```

which will enable access to information about mapped servlet zones.

The status URL will bring up a page listing the configured hosts and servlet engines. Each configured host corresponds to either the default host for the web server or to a virtual host. Each mapped servlet engine corresponds to a distinct servlet engine as specified with `ApJServMount` directives in the mod_jserv config file.

Clicking on one of the configured hosts displays configuration information about that host, including configuration directives, mount points, and file extensions. Clicking on one of the mapped servlet engines lets you review the JVM, the class path and various parameters as well as the configuration for each individual zone.

To enable the Apache JServ status handler you need to add a `Location` directive in your mod_jserv config file with a nested `SetHandler` directive specifying the JServ-status handler. You might like to maintain a uniform style for all status URLs (e.g., for Apache JServ, mod_perl, etc.) such that all such URLs start with `/status/`, in which case you can use a `Location` directive like the following

```
<Location /status/jserv/>
  SetHandler jserv-status
  order deny,allow
  deny from all
  allow from localhost
</Location>
```

Note that this text is already inserted into mod_jserv.conf in the default Windows installation of Apache JServ.

Start-up problems

If you are experiencing problems with starting up JServ, try running it in manual mode. By running in manual mode you isolate the scope of a problem. If you can start the JVM in manual mode then you know the problem is in the configuration or set-up of mod_jserv, e.g., the mod_jserv module is not loaded or the settings in the mod_jserv config file are incorrect. If you cannot run in manual mode then you know that the problem is in the engine properties file, one of the zone properties or repositories, or in your Java set-up.

Port Conflicts

A common start-up problem is caused by a port conflict. If you try to start Apache JServ while an existing process, typically another instance of Apache JServ, is already bound to the same port then you will see the following error message in the mod_jserv log file (or as the output from the Java runtime if running in manual mode):

ApacheJServ/1.0: Exception creating the serversocket: java.net.BindException: Address already in use

To solve this port conflict you can try running Apache JServ on a different port by changing the port setting in the `ApJServMount` directive in `jserv.conf` and in the port property in the engine properties file. You should also check the process list to see if another instance of Apache JServ may be bound to the same port.

File Permissions

Another common source of problems is caused by file permissions that do not allow access to required resources. You should make sure that the user as whom Apache JServ is run has read access to the `ApacheJServ.jar` file and to the engine property and zone property files. The user should also have write access to the `jserv.log` file. For instance, if the user does not have read access to the `ApacheJServ.jar` file then the `error.log` file will contain entries such as the following:

/usr/local/jserv/lib/ApacheJServ.jar: Permission denied
Can't find class org.apache.jserv.JServ

If the directory containing the `jserv.log` file is not writable then the `error.log` file may contain entries such as:

ApacheJServ/1.0: Error opening log file:java.io.IOException: Directory not writable: /usr/local/apache/logs

at the same time, the `mod_jserv.log` file contains generic entries such as:

[20/05/1999 13:04:00:044] (INFO) wrapper: Java VM restarting (PID=1690)
[20/05/1999 13:04:00:046] (INFO) wrapper: Java VM spawned (PID=1953,PPID=1690)
[20/05/1999 13:04:01:054] (INFO) wrapper: Java VM exited (PID=1690)

Supporting Multiple Developers

The requirements for supporting multiple developers working on a single project using Apache JServ are similar to the requirements for supporting multiple clients as an ISP, except that you probably will not be overly concerned with security between developers.

Each developer should have his or her own servlet zone. This lets each developer install and test changes without impacting the activities of other developers. In a basic installation you might use a single Apache web server and no virtual hosts, with Apache JServ running in automatic mode. Each developer would be assigned his or her own servlet zone named in some logical manner, such as

```
ApJServMount /alice/servlets /alice
ApJServMount /bob/servlets /bob
```

Another way to provide this functionality is to assign each developer a separate virtual host. This offers no specific advantages over simply having separate zones, but it may provide additional flexibility for each developer to tailor their own environments.

An alternative configuration could have each developer given access to their own private Apache installation. If the servers are located and maintained on a single main server (e.g., for access to shared data or configuration files) then each server should be run with a separate port number, e.g., 8080, 8081, 8082, etc. The developer can then start and stop the Apache server without impacting other users and without requiring assistance from a system administrator. Alternatively, the servers could be run on each developer's local machine, allowing each developer full control over the server.

Security

The security facilities provided with Apache and Apache JServ are available at several levels. These can be roughly divided into **communication security measures** and **internal Java protections**.

Communication Security

At the communications level, you can filter access to the Apache and Apache JServ servers by using a firewall or other external facilities. At the next level, the Apache web server includes features for limiting access to specific URLs. You can use `Location` directives and access control using htaccess files to limit access to the URLs that run servlets. For instance, to protect a set of servlets for access only from a particular domain and user you can use a `Location` directive like this in your mod_jserv config file:

```
<Location /private-servlets>
      order deny,allow
      deny from all
      allow from .domain.com
      require user foo
      AuthType Basic
      AuthName private
      AuthUserFile /usr/local/apache/conf/users
</Location>
```

This example restricts access to URLs starting with `/private-servlets`, which should correspond to the mount point for the servlet zone to which you want to restrict access. Only the user `foo` accessing the site from a machine in the domain `.domain.com` may access the protected location. The Apache documentation has much more information about protecting a URL, for instance, by specifying privileged users or groups or by enabling a specific authentication method.

Further in from the web server is the level of communication between the web server and Apache JServ. Even if you fully protect access to the web server you still need to protect access to the servlet engine. You can limit access to the servlet engine by specifying IP addresses from which it will accept connections and by using a secret key file known only to the servlet engine and to trusted clients.

To limit IP addresses, you use the `security.allowedAddresses` property in your engine properties file. For instance, adding the following line

```
security.allowedAddresses=192.168.1.2,196.168.1.3
```

would allow access to the servlet engine only from those listed IP addresses.

You can add further security by using a secret key file and a randomly generated challenge string. Both of these features are enabled in the engine properties file:

```
security.authentication=true
security.challengeSize=5
security.secretKey=/usr/local/apache/conf/jserv.secret.key
```

The secret key file must also be known to the Apache JServ client (mod_jserv), so you need to add an ApJServSecretKey file directive to your mod_jserv config file:

```
ApJServSecretKey /usr/local/apache/conf/jserv.secret.key
```

The secret key file can contain any random data and should be readable only by mod_jserv and the servlet engine. One limitation of the secret key file approach is that any Java code run by the servlet engine can read the secret key file, so only trusted people can be allowed to install servlets.

Within Apache JServ, you can manage security by using multiple servlet zones to segregate code and objects. Code executing within one servlet zone does not have access to code executed within any other servlet zone as we have shown. You can also use servlet zones to partition class paths, since classes included in one servlet zone's repository are not accessible to another servlet zone(unless the classes are explicitly added to that zone).

Complementing the use of multiple servlet zones, extra security can be provided by running multiple copies of Apache JServ in completely separate JVMs. Each JVM would be executed within its own process space and could be run with a unique user ID, thus allowing the use of operating-system level file and process protections. The sections on adding servlet zones and running multiple JVMs go into more detail on these features.

Internal Java Security

Java is designed to be a safe language, incorporating a safe type system and byte-code verifiers that ensure that only valid code is executed. It is also more difficult to accidentally create careless security holes in Java than in other popular languages (for instance, through accidental meta-evaluation of user input or by a buffer overrun error). Of course, it is still possible to write insecure software in Java, it is just that the language itself is less likely to be the source of the problem.

It also includes built-in methods for preventing unauthorized operations. The client machines which execute Java applets have always been protected by these security features. However, a server executing Java servlets does not mandate this protection level and therefore both Java servlets and any other Java code being executed on the server are not constrained by strict security policies. It is possible, at least theoretically, to add a security manager (JDK1.1) or to customize a security policy (JDK1.2) for Apache JServ. In JDK1.2, it is possible to specify a custom security policy to be loaded by the JVM. Anyone could develop a policy appropriate to their environment, though the documentation available from Sun is not as easy to follow as one might have hoped. To date, no custom security manager or policy is available with Apache JServ, though there are plans to add such functionality in future releases.

Debugging

The Java side of Apache JServ is executed as a regular Java application with a static `main` method in class `org.apache.jserv.JServ`. Servlets are run within this application. This means that you can use pretty much any Java debugger to debug Apache JServ and your servlets.

A quick way to debug at first would be to use the log methods in `javax.servlet.ServletContext` to pass messages to Apache JServ's log file (e.g., `jserv.log`), or even just write directly to `System.err` or `System.out`. You can do a lot of debugging with log statements, though eventually it will become tedious and you may want to use a real debugger.

Sun's JDK includes the **jdb** debugger. To invoke jdb and debug a servlet, you should start Apache JServ in manual mode. Not forgetting to set `ApJServManual` to on in `jserv.conf`, we can use a shell script similar to one we saw earlier to launch Apache JServ in manual mode using jdb.

```
#!/bin/sh
properties=/usr/local/apache/conf/jserv.properties
log=/usr/local/apache/logs/jserv_manual.log
CLASSPATH=$CLASSPATH:/usr/local/jsdk/lib/jsdk.jar
CLASSPATH=$CLASSPATH:/usr/local/jserv/lib/ApacheJServ.jar
jdb org.apache.jserv.JServ $properties
```

Similarly in Windows, after making sure `ApacheJServ.jar` and `jsdk.jar` are in the classpath, we can use the following command from the shell to the same effect

```
jdb org.apache.jserv.JServ D:\Javelin\jserv10\conf\jserv.properties
```

Optimizing Performance

There are two options for creating performance gains in Apache JServ—optimizing the settings within Apache JServ and optimizing the platform and software that interacts with it.

Optimizing ApacheJServ

The two primary performance losses in Apache JServ are due to **logging** and **automatic class reloading**. Most of the delay in logging is due to the large number of objects created and managed for logging. Automatic class reloading can be particularly slow if there are many separate class files. To disable logging on the Java side set the `log` property to false in the engine properties file. To disable automatic class reloading set the `autoreload.classes` and `autoreload.file` properties in the servlet zone property files to `false`.

Another performance drain is the small initial and maximum process sizes allocated by default by some JVMs. This results in excessive garbage collection and/or heap resizing. In automatic mode you can use the `wrapper.bin` properties in the engine properties file to pass values for the `-ms` and `-mx` options to the Java runtime. For instance,

```
wrapper.bin.parameters=-ms32m
wrapper.bin.parameters=-mx128m
```

Consult your Java runtime's documentation for further options.

You can also disable some of the security authentication features in ApacheJServ. By removing the `security.secretKey` property and setting `security.authentication` to false you can eliminate the time spent authenticating connections between the Apache JServ client and server. You should only remove this authentication, however, if you are certain that you can protect your installation by other means and/or if the performance gain is justified by the decrease in security.

Optimizing The System

You can gain additional performance by optimizing your own Java code. Two useful tools for profiling Java code are Intuitive System's **OptimizeIt!** detailed at `http://www.optimizeit.com` and IBM's **JInsight** at `http://alphaworks.ibm.com/tech/jinsight`. OptimizeIt works best with JDK1.2 which provides more advanced instrumentation than JDK1.1.

If tuning Apache JServ and optimizing your own code have not provided the performance gains you require then you might investigate using a different JVM. Any JVM compatible with JDK 1.1 can be used with Apache JServ. Sun, IBM, and Microsoft all make competitive JVMs. Vendors are steadily improving the performance of JVMs. For instance, Sun released HotSpot in April 1999. This offers performance improvements over the regular Sun JVM and is primarily targeted at server-side Java.

You could also explore compilation to native code, which compiles Java source or byte codes into native machine instructions rather than Java byte codes. The current leading product for native compilation is Tower Technology's **TowerJ** (`http://www.towerj.com`). Native compilation, however, can be cumbersome and less flexible than portable Java byte codes.

For servers with a heavy load, you could try to split the load across multiple servers with the load balancing features in Apache JServ. An overview, with instructions on configuration, is available online in **How to: Scalability - Load-Balancing -Fault tolerance** by Bernard Bernstein and Jean-Luc Rochat at `http://java.apache.org/jserv/howto.load-balancing.html`. This approach, however, introduces various administrative issues that are not present in a single server. Purchasing upgraded hardware is probably a simpler solution than trying to maintain multiple servers.

Add-on Functionality

By installing Apache JServ on your server you have increased your options for server-side software. A growing number of Java servlets and generic Java libraries are being developed. You can write your own servlets from scratch, or you can integrate existing servlets into your environment.

Page Compilation Servlets

A very useful category of servlets, known as **page compilation servlets**, can be used to add dynamic content to a site. These servlets parse a source file, extract and interpret special tags, and generate output that is a combination of the original file and the interpreted tags.

A typical page compilation servlet is Apache JSSI, which allows you to include the output of a servlet within an HTML page as a server-side include. Adding dynamic content to your HTML pages then is a simple matter of embedding special `<servlet>` tags in your documents. Apache JSSI then executes the servlets specified by the tags and replaces them with the output of the servlets.

To demonstrate, let's assume you have installed Apache JSSI and also a servlet called `DateServlet` that returns the current date. The following code

```
<HTML>
  <HEAD>
    <TITLE>Date</TITLE>
  </HEAD>
  <BODY>
    <H1>Date</H1>
    <SERVLET NAME="DateServlet"></SERVLET>
  </BODY>
</HTML>
```

would result in the following output from the server.

```
<HTML>
  <HEAD>
    <TITLE>Date</TITLE>
  </HEAD>
  <BODY>
    <H1>Date</H1>
    July 9, 1999
  </BODY>
</HTML>
```

Page compilation servlets get the location of the file to parse from the extra path information passed in the URL. When you request a file that is to be served via a page compilation servlet, the URL looks something like the following:

```
http://domain/zone/servlet/path
```

where `zone` is your servlet zone's mount point, `servlet` is the name of the page compilation servlet, and `path` is the relative path to the file to compile. For instance, using Apache JSSI, `http://domain/servlets/org.apache.servlet.ssi.SSI/products/file.html` would pass the path `/products/file.html` along to the Apache JSSI servlet, which would then output any plain HTML in the file as well as execute any embedded servlet tags.

If you want your page compilation servlet to handle files in any arbitrary location on your web server then you need to add an action handler so that Apache JServ will pass any file ending in a particular suffix along to the page compilation servlet. To do this, as we saw earlier, you add an `ApJServAction` directive to your `jserv.conf` file. For instance, you could add

```
ApJServAction .jhtml /servlets/org.apache.servlet.ssi.SSI
```

Now, every time a document ending in `.jhtml` is requested, Apache JServ will invoke the Apache JSSI servlet.

Once you have documents with a particular suffix served via your page compilation servlet you may want to add an entry to the `DirectoryIndex` directive in the Apache configuration file `httpd.conf` so that you can use such a file as the default file served from a directory. For instance,

```
DirectoryIndex index.html index.jhtml
```

In general, using a special suffix is the preferred way to invoke a page compilation servlet. Using a suffix is better than using URLs that contain a servlet zone and the name of the servlet because it hides internal web server details from your users. If you would rather not use a special suffix (perhaps you are adding dynamic content to an existing site) then you can use mod_rewrite to rewrite URLs that contain a plain .html suffix to URLs that will invoke the desired servlet. See the section on using mod_rewrite with Apache JServ for an example of such an application.

Java Server Pages

With Java Server Pages (JSP) you can embed Java code directly in an HTML document. The Java code is automatically compiled whenever its containing file is modified. The compiled byte codes are then run through the JVM and their output is served up by the web server along with any surrounding HTML. JSP provides integration between Java code and HTML. The JSP specification and reference implementation are available from Sun's Java web site at http://java.sun.com/products/jsp.

There are at least two publicly available and free implementations of programs that let you embed Java code in HTML documents: **GNU Server Pages (GSP)** and **GNU Java Server Pages (GNUJSP)**. These products are independent development efforts. Since version 1.0 of Sun's specification of JSP was only recently released, neither product conforms yet to the latest specification, though you can already use these programs to develop web pages. Both GSP and GNUJSP are written as regular Java servlets, which means that they should work with any compatible servlet engine on any operating system. In addition to these free programs there are commercial implementations of JSP.

GSP

This section shows how you can add GSP to an Apache JServ installation. The following directions refer to GSP v0.86, which was the most current version available at the time of writing. You can download this from the Bit mechanic website at http://www.bitmechanic.com.

Configuring GSP consists of:

> Creating a directory in which GSP can store dynamically compiled class files.
> Adding several properties to your servlet zone's properties file.
> Creating a GSP properties file.
> Optionally adding an ApJServAction directive to jserv.conf.
> Testing your installation.

These steps are expanded below.

1. Create a classes directory
GSP needs a directory in which it can write dynamically compiled class files, for instance /usr/local/apache/gsp-classes, but you could place this directory anywhere you want. For instance, if you were configuring multiple virtual hosts you would want to set this so that each virtual host gets its own directory. This directory needs to be writable by the user as whom Apache JServ runs (e.g., user nobody).

2. Add properties to the zone properties file

The necessary servlet configuration can be done by adding the following lines to your servlet zone's properties file. You will need, of course, to adjust the paths to correspond to the locations of the files on your system.

```
repositories=/usr/local/java/gsp-0.86/gsp-0.86.jar
repositories=/usr/local/apache/gsp-classes
servlet.gsp.code=com.bitmechanic.gsp.GspServlet
servlet.gsp.initArgs=propfile=/usr/local/apache/conf/gsp.properties
```

3. Create GSP properties file

GSP uses its own properties file. The example supplied with GSP by default includes comments that explain the directives. The following is a sample `gsp.properties` file.

```
logger.filename=/usr/local/apache/logs/gsp.log
parser.classdir=/usr/local/apache/gsp-classes
parser.javac=/usr/local/java/jdk/bin/javac
parser.extraclasspath=/usr/local/java/gsp/ _
      gsp-0.86.jar:/usr/local/apache/gsp-classes
parser.classreloader=com.bitmechanic.gsp.GspClassLoader
```

4. Add `ApJServAction` directive to `httpd.conf`

To have any document ending in `.gsp` processed by GSP add the following directive to jserv.conf:

```
ApJServAction .gsp /servlets/gsp
```

To also allow directory indexes using `.gsp` files add the following entry for `.jsp` to the `DirectoryIndex` directive in `httpd.conf`:

```
DirectoryIndex index.html index.gsp
```

5. Test

Restart Apache, then test your GSP installation by copying the `.gsp` files from the GSP distribution's test directory to your document root and then access the documents. For instance,

```
cp /usr/local/java/gsp/examples/date_test.gsp/usr/local/apache/htdocs
lynx http://localhost/date_test.gsp
```

This may not run correctly the first time around and you will have to work through errors in each of the configuration files (httpd.conf, engine properties, zone properties, and GSP properties). While tracking down errors, do not forget to look in all of the log files, including the GSP log file specified with the `logger.filename` property in the GSP properties file.

Conclusion

Apache JServ is a flexible open-source servlet engine suitable for many types of sites. The large user base of the Apache web server and the growing popularity of Java servlets practically ensures sustained interest in Apache JServ. As an open source project you have full access to the source code and can make fixes and submit patches directly to the group, or, if you demonstrate interest and reasonable ability, directly to the source archives. The Java Apache project itself has evolved beyond its initial goal to create the Apache JServ servlet engine and now acts as an umbrella for several open source Java projects. An enthusiastic and informed group of developers and users keep the projects moving forward and provide valuable assistance.

Resources

Apache Project	`http://www.apache.org`
Java Apache Project	`http://java.apache.org`
Sun's JSDK	`http://java.sun.com/products/servlet/index.html`
Sun's Java Server Pages	`http://java.sun.com/products/jsp`
GNU Server Pages (GSP)	`http://www.bitmechanic.com`
GNU Java Server Pages (GNUJSP)	`http://www.klomp.org/gnujsp`
Intuitive System's OptimizeIt!	`http://www.optimizeit.com`
IBM's JInsight	`http://alphaworks.ibm.com/tech/jinsight`
Service monitoring daemon	`http://www.kernel.org/software/mon`
Cygnus' Cygwin utilities	`http://sourceware.cygnus.com/cygwin`
TowerJ	`http://www.towerj.com`

ServletRunner and Java Web Server Configuration

The Java Servlet Development Kit

When first learning how to develop servlets, chances are pretty good that you'll be doing it using the Java Servlet Development Kit (JSDK) from Sun. The JSDK contains the actual servlet packages as well as a servlet engine that can be used to test your servlets. While the JSDK is not intended to be a production quality servlet engine, it does perform quite well and is very functional. The latest release now includes support for Java Server Pages 1.0.

Obtaining the JSDK

The JSDK can be downloaded free of charge from `java.sun.com/products`. The latest releases are usually made available through the Java Developer Connection (`java.sun.com/jdc`) before they appear on the Java web site. Recently, the JSDK was rolled in with the Java Server Pages (JSP) reference implementation and is now available under the name 'Java Web Server Development Kit' as an early-access developer release. This includes the servlet packages, a mini web server, and support for Java Server Pages.

Installation

To install the JSDK, double-click on the downloaded file to unzip the included files. A good place to install this directory hierarchy would be underneath your java-root directory. That's all there is to installing the JSDK. Since it operates as a stand alone servlet engine and web server, there is no need to configure anything else.

Administration

To start the servlet engine, from a command prompt, run the startserver batch file. Similarly, to stop the server, run the stopserver batch file. The stopserver batch file may not work correctly every time. If this is the case, select the other open DOS window and press *CTRL-C* to close the server down.

Before you can run any of your servlets, two things have to happen first. The servlet class files have to be copied into the `jsp1.0\webpages\WEB-INF\servlets` directory and they need to be listed in the servlet.properties file located in the `jsp1.0\webpages\WEB-INF` directory. The format of this file is as follows:

```
<servletname>.code=<servletclass>
<servletname>.initparams=<name=value>,<name=value>
```

It is important to note that even if your servlet does not have any initialization parameters, you must always include the initparams line, even if it is just 'servletname.initparams=dummy=null'. Without this line, the servlet engine will not recognize it.

The Java Web Server

The large majority of servlet engines available today are simply servlet engines that are meant to work in conjunction with one of the popular web servers. The Java Web Server from Sun combines both the web server and the servlet engine. As a result, every one of the web server's functions is carried out by a servlet. For instance, if the user requests a CGI program written in Perl, the web server invokes the CGIServlet to handle the request (how's that for irony!).

Obtaining the Java Web Server

A trial version of the Java Web Server can be obtained from `java.sun.com`. This trial version will expire in 90-days if not purchased within that timeframe.

Installation

To install the Java Web Server, double click the downloaded file to begin. The install process simply copies the files to a directory that you specify and gives you the option of having the web server start every time the system starts. Since the Java Web Server is both a web server and a servlet engine, there is no need to configure anything else at this point.

Administration

To start the Java Web Server, from a command prompt, run the httpd executable located in the \bin directory underneath the JWS root directory. This will, by default, run the web server on port 8080. The administrative interface to the web server runs on port 9090 and can be accessed by typing http://localhost:9090 in the URL window of any web browser. On some Windows installations of Java Web Server, you may find it necessary to type http://<Server_Host_Name>:9090 where <Server_Host_Name> is the name assigned to your computer. To find this name, click on the Identification tab in the Network control panel. This will load a Java applet that first asks you to login (see figure below).

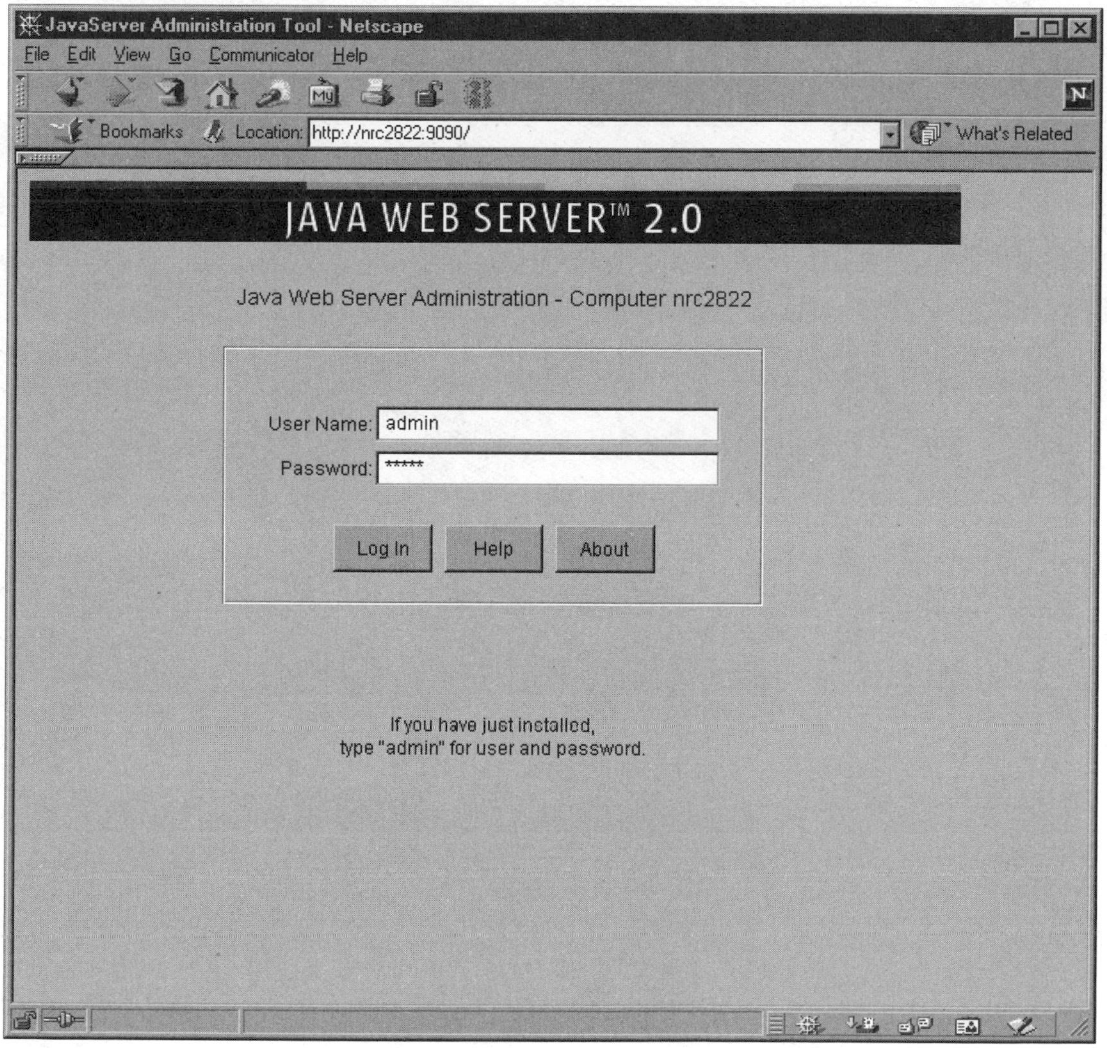

Once logged in, the user is presented with the services screen (see figure below). From this screen, general server properties can be changed, services can be stopped and started, and services can be individually configured. The web server itself can also be shut down from this screen.

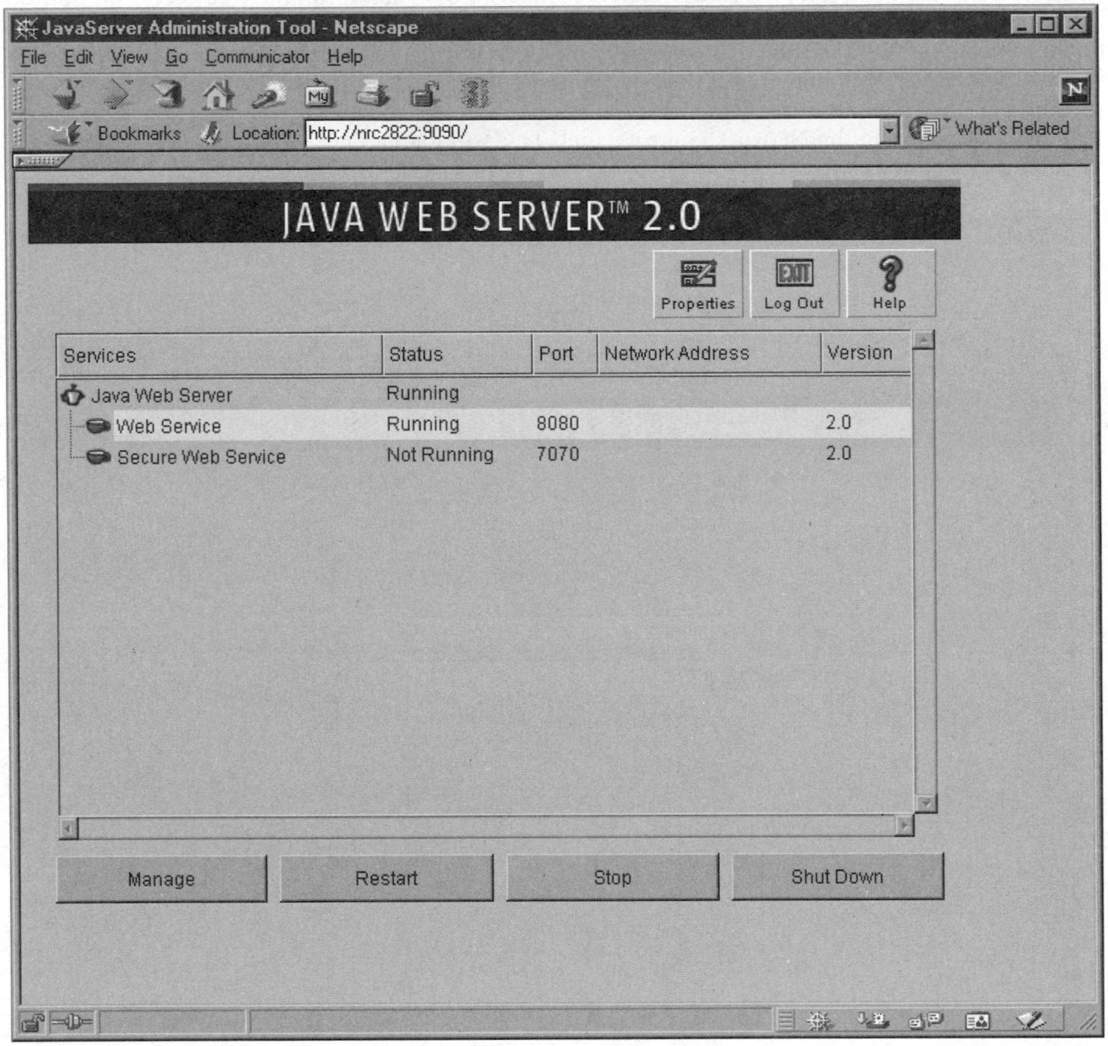

From the services screen, if you were to select the 'Web Service' and click on the 'Manage' button, you would open up a new browser window with all of the configuration options for that particular service (see figure below). To get you started we'll walk through adding a servlet to the Java Web Server (servlets must be added to the server explicitly).

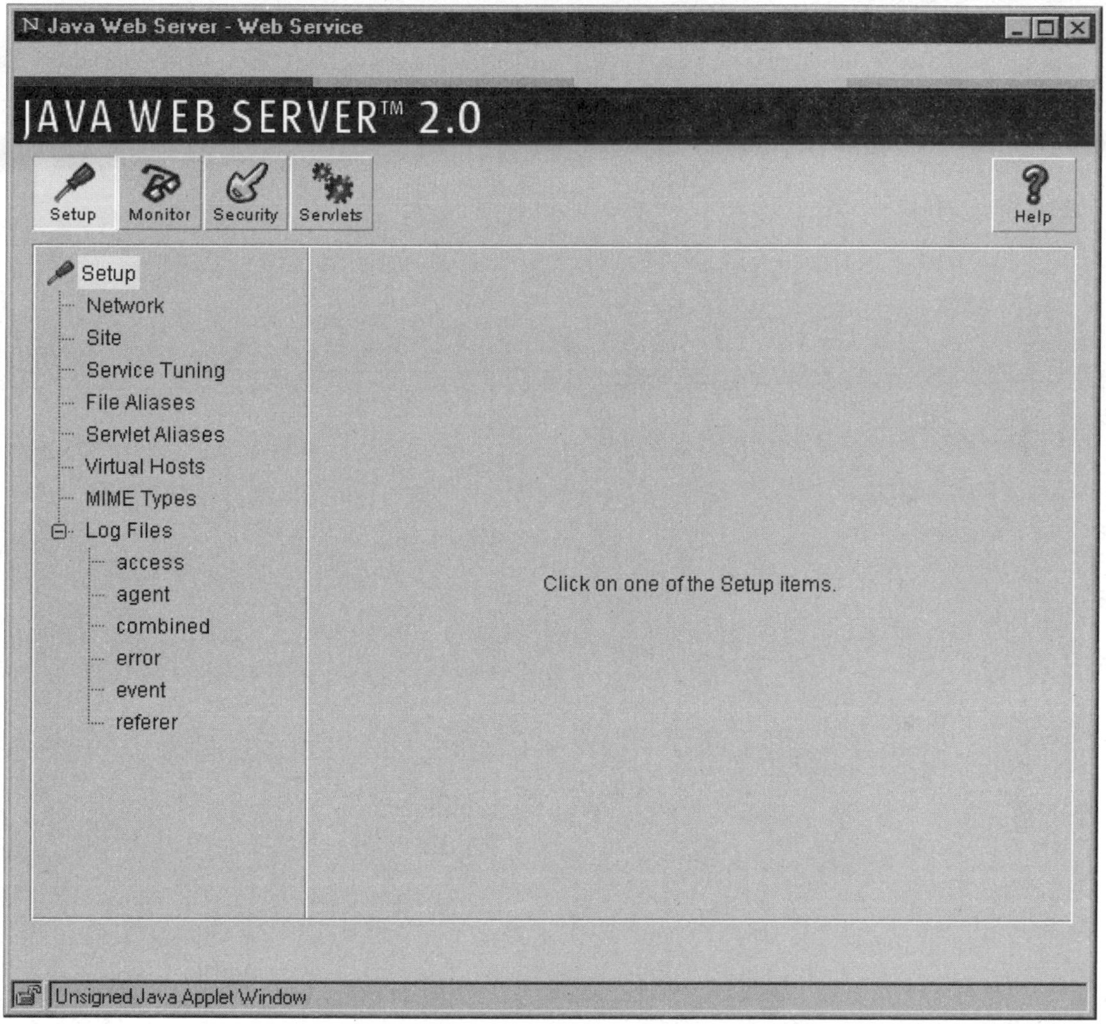

To add a servlet to the Java Web Server, click on the 'Servlets' button located across the top row of buttons. Click the 'Add' item along the left-hand side of the screen. In the right-hand portion of the screen, you can fill in the servlet name and associated class file. At this point, click the 'Add' button (don't worry about the bean servlet section right now, that's a specialized topic that doesn't concern us).

Once the servlet has been added, it is time to configure it (see figures below). You can add a description, specify if it should be loaded at startup, and also if it resides on a remote machine, you can identify that it should be loaded remotely.

Once this information has been filled in, click on the 'Properties' tab to add initialization parameters.

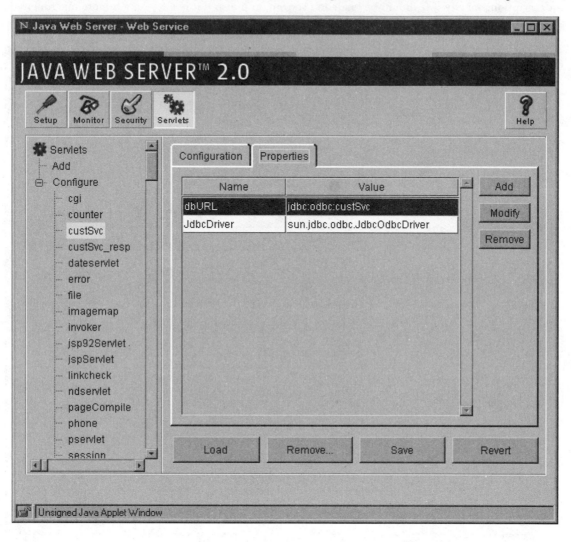

JRun Configuration

JRun

JRun from Live Software is a Java server with various capabilities. It has one of the most popular servlet engines in use today. It currently supports all industry-standard web servers and platforms. JRun also includes a basic Java web server. The current release (version 2.3), supports Java Server Pages 0.92 (JSP 1.0 to be supported in the next release) and the Java Servlet API 2.1.

Obtaining JRun

JRun comes in two different flavors, JRun and JRun Pro. JRun Pro is essentially the same as JRun standard with a few exceptions. JRun Pro can run up to 5 JVM's at once whereas JRun standard can only run a single JVM. JRun standard allows for up to 5 concurrent user requests. JRun Pro allows an unlimited number of concurrent requests. JRun Pro also adds the ability to perform remote administration.

Both versions of JRun can be obtained at www.livesoftware.com. The standard edition is available free of charge. The JRun Pro edition can be downloaded on a 30-day trial basis.

Installation

To install JRun, simply double-click the downloaded file to begin. After walking through the basic screens that will determine where to copy the files to, you'll be presented with a series of screens to select a connector for the external web server that you are using (see figures below). This will install the necessary files to your web server so that when a request is made that JRun should handle, your web server will know where to send it.

Note that changing the default host and port may be necessary when running more than one JRun Servlet Engine on the same machine. JRun Service Manger (JSM) is the main component of JRun with responsibility for loading and initializing services or protocol-independent components that have certain functionality. It is possible to have multiple JSM instances, which is why it is necessary to determine which JSM the connector is to communicate with. JRun will initially have only one JSM named 'default'.

In the case we have considered, Apache is the external web server for which we installed a connector. Note that Apache 1.2.* does not support Dynamic Shared Objects (DSO) modules. Since Apache 1.3.4. started using a different DSO module format, in the next screen we need to tell JRun what version of Apache is installed on the system.

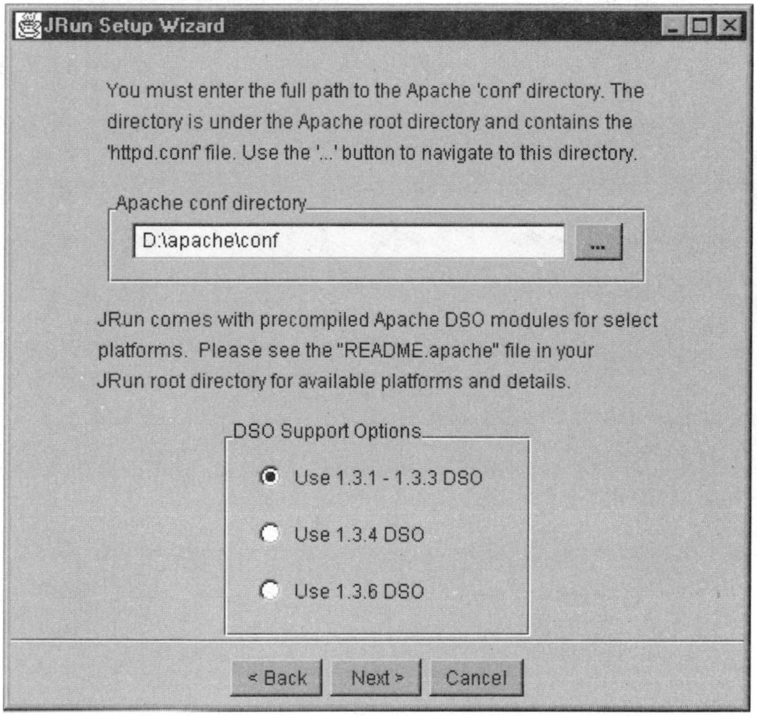

Administration

To administer the JRun servlet engine, begin by double-clicking on the 'JRun Administrator' icon in your JRun folder. You will be presented with a screen showing the available JSM instances.

Select the required JSM and click on 'Configure'. Choosing to edit 'jsm-default' presents you with a screen listing the four JRun default java services.

By clicking on the 'General' tab at the top of the screen, you can view the current settings for that particular JSM. From there you can change JSM administration port number and redirect error messages from System.out and System.err to log files in the directory of that JSM, which is 'jsm-default' in the above example.

The 'Services' tab gives you access to 'General Config' and 'Service Config'. Click on 'General Config' to set network settings for the service. 'Service Config' is for changing various settings of the selected service. For instance, to administer the servlet engine, select the 'jse' service and click on 'Service Config'. This will take you to this screen:

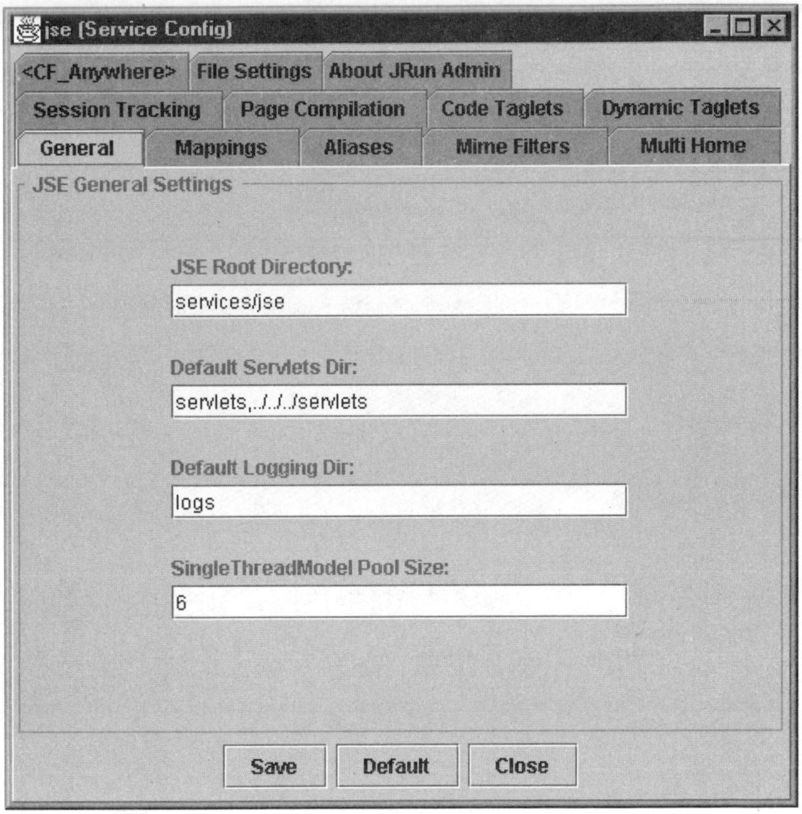

The 'General' tab is for setting the basic configuration of JRun, including JRun Survlet Engine (JSE) root directory and the default servlets and logging directories.

Under the 'Mappings' tab, prefix and suffix mappings for the servlets can be defined. When a prefix mapping is defined, it is possible to specify that any HTTP request containing that particular prefix should be treated as a servlet request. Suffix mappings are used to associate file extensions with servlets, so that when a file with a mapped extension is requested, JRun invokes the respective servlet to process that file.

With JRun, servlets are loaded automatically and do not require an entry in the configuration files, as they do with most other servlet engines. However, with the 'Aliases' tab, JRun gives you the ability to define an alias for a servlet, along with initialization parameters, as well as an option to load it at startup.

Using 'Mime Filters' you can specify the mime-type that should trigger a servlet to run. The 'Multi Home' tab allows you to have alternate servlet and logging directories for virtual hosts. With 'File Settings' you can specify the sequence of default document names that JRun uses when a document name is not specified in an URL. The 'Session Tracking' tab is used for saving and reloading user session information when the server is stopped and restarted. Under 'Page Compilation' you can specify JSP compilation options. 'Code Taglets' and 'Dynamic Taglets' are used for specifying user defined server-side tags known as taglets. Taglets are implemented in Java using Live Software's Taglet API.

JSDK API Reference

Key

Within this API Reference, the following conventions are used:

➤ Interface, Class and Exception names within the APIs listed are all written in **bold**.
➤ Interface, Class and Exception names not within the APIs listed are all written in *italics*.
➤ Method names are all written in `Courier Bold`.

Package javax.servlet

javax.servlet is found in the Java Servlet Development Kit. This package contains classes and interfaces for developing generic servlets.

Interfaces

public abstract interface	**RequestDispatcher**
public abstract interface	**Servlet**
public abstract interface	**ServletConfig**
public abstract interface	**ServletContext**
public abstract interface	**ServletRequest**
public abstract interface	**ServletResponse**
public abstract interface	**SingleThreadModel**

Classes

public abstract class	**GenericServlet**	implements	*javax.servlet.***Servlet,** *javax.servlet.***ServletConfig,** *java.io.Serializable*
public abstract class	**ServletInputStream**	extends	java.io.InputStream
public abstract class	**ServletOutputStream**	extends	java.io.OutputStream

Exceptions

public class	**ServletException**	extends	*java.lang.exception*
public class	**UnavailableException**	extends	javax.servlet.**ServletException**

Interface javax.servlet.RequestDispatcher

```
public abstract interface RequestDispatcher
```

Appears in JSDK 2.1 only. RequestDispatcher defines an object that receives requests from a client and `forwards` them to any resource (such as a servlet, HTML file, or JSP file) on the server.

Methods in JSDK 2.1

public void	`forward`	(**ServletRequest** request, **ServletResponse** response)
	throws	*javax.servlet.***ServletException**, *java.io.IOException*;
public void	`include`	(**ServletRequest** request, **ServletResponse** response)
	throws	*javax.servlet.***ServletException**, *java.io.IOException*;

Interface javax.servlet.Servlet

```
public abstract interface Servlet
```

Appears in JSDK 2.0, 2.1. Is implemented by *javax.servlet*. `GenericServlet`. Servlet defines the methods that all servers must implement. In its life-cycle, a servlet is created and `init`ialized, `service`s any requests it receives and is then **destroy**ed.

Methods in JSDK 2.0 and 2.1

public void	`init`	(**ServletConfig** config)
	throws	*javax.servlet.***ServletException***;
public void	`service`	(**ServletRequest** request, **ServletResponse** response)
	throws	*javax.servlet.***ServletException**, *java.io.IOException*;
public void	`destroy`	();
public **ServletConfig**	`getServletConfig`	();
public *java.lang.String*	`getServletInfo`	();

Interface javax.servlet.ServletConfig

```
public abstract interface ServletConfig
```

Appears in JSDK 2.0, 2.1. Is implemented by javax.servlet.GenericServlet. ServletConfig defines an object holding the configuration information necessary to initialize a servlet.

Methods in JSDK 2.0 and 2.1

public *java.lang.String*	`getInitParameter`	(*java.lang.String* name);
public *java.util.Enumeration*	`getInitParameterNames`	();
public **ServletContext**	`getServletContext`	();

Interface javax.servlet.ServletContext

```
public abstract interface ServletContext
```

Appears in JSDK 2.0, 2.1 though the method set varies between the two. Some methods have been deprecated. ServletContext defines a set of methods that servlet uses to find out about the server that it is running on and other servlets that are also running on the server besides itself.

Methods new in JSDK 2.1

public *java.util.Enumeration*	`getAttributeNames`	();
public **ServletContext**	`getContext`	(*java.lang.String* name);
public int	`getMajorVersion`	();
public int	`getMinorVersion`	();
public **RequestDispatcher**	`getRequestDispatcher`	(*java.lang.String* urlPath);
public *java.net.URL*	`getResource`	(*java.lang.String* path);
public *java.io.InputStream*	`getResourceAsStream`	(*java.lang.String* path);
public void	`log`	(*java.lang.String* message, *java.lang.Throwable* throwable);
public void	`removeAttribute`	(*java.lang.String* name);
public void	`setAttribute`	(*java.lang.String* name, *java.lang.Object* object);

Methods in JSDK 2.0 and 2.1

public *java.lang.Object*	`getAttribute`	(*java.lang.String* name);
public *java.lang.String*	`getMimeType`	(*java.lang.String* file);
public *java.lang.String*	`getRealPath`	(*java.lang.String* path);
public *java.lang.String*	`getServerInfo`	();
public *void*	`log`	(*java.lang.String* msg);

Deprecated Methods

public **Servlet**	`getServlet` throws	(*java.lang.String* name) *javax.servlet.***ServletException**;
public *java.util.Enumeration*	`getServletNames`	();
public *java.util.Enumeration*	`getServlets`	();
public void	`log`	(*java.lang.Exception* exception, *java.lang.String* msg);

Interface javax.servlet.ServletRequest

```
public abstract interface ServletRequest
```

Appears in JSDK 2.0, 2.1 though the method set varies between the two. Some methods have been deprecated. **Is extended by**: *javax.servlet.http.***HttpServletRequest**. ServletRequest defines the object that servlet engines use to pass (information about) client requests onto servlets.

Methods new in JSDK 2.1

public *java.util.Enumeration*	`getAttributeNames`	();
public void	`setAttribute`	(*java.lang.String* key, *java.lang.Object* o);

Methods in JSDK 2.0 and 2.1

public *java.lang.Object*	`getAttribute`	(*java.lang.String* name);
public *java.lang.string*	`getCharacterEncoding`	();
public int	`getContentLength`	();
public *java.lang.String*	`getContentType`	();
public **ServletInputStream**	`getInputStream`	()
	throws	*java.io.IOException*;
public *java.lang.String*	`getParameter`	(*java.lang.String* name);
public *java.util.Enumeration*	`getParameterNames`	();
public *java.lang.String[]*	`getParameterValues`	(*java.lang.String* name);
public *java.lang.String*	`getProtocol`	();
public *java.io.BufferedReader*	`getReader`	()
	throws	*java.io.IOException*;
public *java.lang.String*	`getRemoteAddr`	();
public *java.lang.String*	`getRemoteHost`	();
public *java.lang.String*	`getScheme`	();
public *java.lang.String*	`getServerName`	();
public int	`getServerPort`	();

Deprecated Methods

public *java.lang.String*	`getRealPath`	(*java.lang.String* path);

Interface javax.servlet.ServletResponse

```
public abstract interface ServletResponse
```

Appears in JSDK 2.0, 2.1. Is extended by: *javax.servlet.http*.HttpServletResponse. ServletResponse objects are passed by servlet engines as arguments to a servlet's `service` method. The servlet uses it to send MIME-encoded data back to the client.

Methods in JSDK 2.0 and 2.1

public *java.lang.String*	`getCharacterEncoding`	();
public **ServletOutputStream**	`getOutputStream`	()
	throws	*java.io.IOException*;
public *java.io.PrintWriter*	`getWriter`	()
	throws	*java.io.IOException*;
public void	`setContentLength`	(int len);
public void	`setContentType`	(*java.lang.String* type);

Interface javax.servlet.SingleThreadModel

```
public abstract interface SingleThreadModel
```

Appears in JSDK 2.0, 2.1. SingleThreadModel is used to ensure that servlets handle only one request at a time. If a servlet implements this interface, you are guaranteed that no two threads will execute concurrently in the servlet's `service` method.

SingleThreadModel has no methods.

Class javax.servlet.GenericServlet

```
public abstract class GenericServlet
```

implements *javax.servlet.***Servlet,** *javax.servlet.***ServletConfig,** *java.io.Serializable*

Appears in JSDK 2.0, 2.1 though the method set varies between the two. Is extended by *javax.servlet.http.*HttpServlet. GenericServlet defines a generic, protocol-independent servlet. To write an HTTP servlet to use with a Web site, you must extend HttpServlet. To write a generic servlet, you need only override the `service` method.

Constructor Method

public	`GenericServlet`	();

Methods new in JSDK 2.1

public void	`init`	()
	throws	*javax.servlet.***ServletException**;
public void	`log`	(*java.lang.String* message,
		java.lang.Throwable t)

Methods in JSDK 2.0 and 2.1

public void	`log`	(*java.lang.String* message);

Specified by *javax.servlet.***Servlet**
`init, service, destroy, getServletConfig, getServletInfo`

Specified by *javax.servlet.***ServletConfig**
`getInitParameter, getInitParameternames, getServletContext`

Inherited from *java.lang.object*
`clone, equals, finalize, getClass, hashCode, notify, notifyAll, toString, wait, wait, wait`

Class javax.servlet.ServletInputStream

```
public abstract class ServletInputStream
```

extends *java.io.InputStream*

Appears in JSDK 2.0, 2.1. ServletInputStream must be implemented by all servlet engines as it provides an input stream for reading binary data from a client request. Any subclasses of this class must implement the *java.io.InputStream.*`read` method.

Constructor Method

protected	`ServletInputStream`	();

Methods in JSDK 2.0 and 2.1

public int	`readLine`	(byte[] b,
		int off, int len)
	throws	*java.io.IOException*;

Inherited from *java.io.InputStream*
`available, close, mark, markSupported, read, read, read, reset, skip`

Inherited from *java.lang.object*
```
clone, equals, finalize, getClass, hashCode, notify, notifyAll, toString, wait,
wait, wait
```

Class javax.servlet.ServletOutputStream

```
public abstract class ServletOutputStream
```

extends *java.io.OutputStream*

Appears in JSDK 2.0, 2.1. ServletOutputStream provides servlet engines with an output stream to send binary data back to the client. Therefore engines usually extend and define it. Any subclasses of this class must implement the java.io.OutputStream.`write(int)` method.

Constructor Method

protected	`ServletOutputStream`	();

Methods in JSDK 2.0 and 2.1

public void	`print`	(long l)
	throws	*java.io.IOException*;
public void	`print`	(float f)
	throws	*java.io.IOException*;
public void	`print`	(double d)
	throws	*java.io.IOException*;
public void	`print`	(int i)
	throws	java.*io.IOException*;
public void	`print`	(*java.lang.String* s)
	throws	java.*io.IOException*;
public void	`print`	(boolean b)
	throws	java.*io.IOException*;
public void	`print`	(char c)
	throws	*java.io.IOException*;
public void	`println`	()
	throws	*java.io.IOException*;
public void	`println`	(long l)
	throws	*java.io.IOException*;
public void	`println`	(float f)
	throws	*java.io.IOException*;
public void	`println`	(double d)
	throws	*java.io.IOException*;
public void	`println`	(int i)
	throws	*java.io.IOException*;
public void	`println`	(*java.lang.String* s)
	throws	*java.io.IOException*;
public void	`println`	(boolean b)
	throws	*java.io.IOException*;
public void	`println`	(char c)
	throws	*java.io.IOException*;

Inherited from *java.io.OutputStream*
```
close, flush, write, write, write
```

Inherited from *java.lang.object*
```
clone, equals, finalize, getClass, hashCode, notify, notifyAll, toString, wait,
wait, wait
```

Class javax.servlet.ServletException

```
public class ServletException
```

extends *java.lang.Exception*

Appears in JSDK 2.0, 2.1 though the method set varies between the two. Is extended by *javax.servlet*.UnavailableException. ServletException defines the general exception a servlet throws when it encounters difficulty.

Constructor Methods (JSDK 2.1 only)

public	`ServletException`	(*java.lang.Throwable* rootCause);
public	`ServletException`	(*java.lang.String* message, *java.lang.Throwable* rootCause);

Constructor Methods (JSDK 2.0 and 2.1)

public	`ServletException`	();
public	`ServletException`	(*java.lang.String* message);

Methods in JSDK 2.1 only

public *java.lang.Throwable*	`getRootCause`	();

Methods in JSDK 2.0 and 2.1

Inherited from *java.lang.Throwable*
`fillInStackTrace, getLocalizedMessage, getMessage, printStackTrace, printStackTrace, printStackTrace, toString`

Inherited from *java.lang.object*
`clone, equals, finalize, getClass, hashCode, notify, notifyAll, toString, wait, wait, wait`

Class javax.servlet.UnavailableException

```
public class UnavailableException
```

extends *javax.servlet*.**ServletException**

Appears in JSDK 2.0, 2.1. UnavailableException defines the specific exception a servlet throws to indicate that it is either temporarily or permanently available.

Constructor Method

public	`UnavailableException`	(*javax.servlet*.**Servlet** servlet, *java.lang.String* msg);
public	`UnavailableException`	(int seconds, *javax.servlet*.**Servlet** servlet, *java.lang.String* msg);

Methods in JSDK 2.1 only

Inherited from javax.servlet.**ServletException**
`getRootCause`

Methods in JSDK 2.0 and 2.1

public boolean	`isPermanent`	`();`
public **Servlet**	`getServlet`	`();`
public int	`getUnavailableSeconds`	`();`

Inherited from *java.lang.Throwable*
`fillInStackTrace, getLocalizedMessage, getMessage, printStackTrace, printStackTrace, printStackTrace, toString`

Inherited from *java.lang.object*
`clone, equals, finalize, getClass, hashCode, notify, notifyAll, toString, wait, wait, wait`

Package javax.servlet.http

javax.servlet is found in the Java Servlet Development Kit. This package contains classes and interfaces for writing servlets that work with the HTTP protocol used by web servers.

Interfaces

public abstract interface	**HttpServletRequest**	extends	*javax.servlet.***ServletRequest**
public abstract interface	**HttpServletResponse**	extends	*javax.servlet.***ServletResponse**
public abstract interface	**HttpSession**		
public abstract interface	**HttpSessionBindingListener**	extends	*java.util.EventListener*

Classes

public class	**Cookie**	implements	*java.lang.Cloneable*
public abstract class	**HttpServlet**	extends	*javax.servlet.***GenericServlet**
		implements	*java.io.Serializable*
public class	**HttpSessionBindingEvent**	extends	*java.util.EventObject*
public class	**HttpUtils**		

Deprecated

public abstract interface	**HttpSessionContext**

Interface javax.servlet.http.HttpServletRequest

`public abstract interface HttpServletRequest`

`extends` *javax.servlet.***ServletRequest**

Appears in JSDK 2.0, 2.1 though the method set varies between the two. Some methods have been deprecated. HttpServletRequest is a specialization of *javax.servlet.*ServletRequest providing additional functionality for the request object that is passed to an HTTP servlet.

Methods new in JSDK 2.1

public boolean	`isRequestedSessionIdFromURL`	`();`
public **HttpSession**	`getSession`	`();`

Inherited from *javax.servlet.***ServletRequest**
`getAttributeNames, setAttribute`

940

Methods in JSDK 2.0 and 2.1

public *java.lang.String*	getAuthType	();
public **Cookie**[ ]	getCookies	();
public long	getDateHeader	(*java.lang.String* name);
public *java.lang.String*	getHeader	(*java.lang.String* name);
public *java.lang.Enumeration*	getHeaderNames	();
public int	getIntHeader	(*java.lang.String* name);
public *java.lang.String*	getMethod	();
public *java.lang.String*	getPathInfo	();
public *java.lang.String*	getPathTranslated	();
public *java.lang.String*	getQueryString	();
public *java.lang.String*	getRemoteUser	();
public *java.lang.String*	getRequestedSessionId	();
public *java.lang.String*	getRequestURI	();
public *java.lang.String*	getServletPath	();
public **HttpSession**	getSession	(boolean create);
public boolean	isRequestedSessionIdFromCookie	();
public boolean	isRequestedSessionIdValid	();

Inherited from *javax.servlet.***ServletRequest**
getAttribute, getCharacterEncoding, getContentLength, getContentType,
getInputStream, getParameter, getParameterNames, getParameterValues,
getProtocol, getReader, getRemoteAddr, getRemoteHost, getScheme, getServerName,
getServerPort

Deprecated Methods

public boolean	isRequestedSessionIdFromUrl	();

Interface javax.servlet.http.HttpServletResponse

```
public abstract interface HttpServletResponse
```

extends *javax.servlet.***ServletResponse**

Appears in JSDK 2.0, 2.1 though the method set varies between the two. Some
methods have been deprecated. HttpServletResponse is implemented by an HTTP
servlet engine to allow a servlet's service method to access HTTP headers and
return data to its client.

Methods new in JSDK 2.1

public *java.lang.String*	encodeRedirectURL	(*java.lang.String* url);
public *java.lang.String*	encodeURL	(*java.lang.String* url);

Methods in JSDK 2.0 and 2.1

public void	addCookie	(*javax.servlet.http.***Cookie** cookie);
public boolean	containsHeader	(*java.lang.String* name);
public void	sendError	(int sc)
	throws	java.*io.IOException*;
public void	sendError	(int sc,
		java.lang.String msg)
	throws	java.*io.IOException*;
public void	sendRedirect	(*java.lang.String* location)
	throws	java.*io.IOException*;

public void	setDateHeader	(*java.lang.String* name, long date);
public void	setHeader	(*java.lang.String* name, *java.lang.String* value);
public void	setIntHeader	*java.lang.String* name, int value);
public void	setStatus	(int sc);

Inherited from *javax.servlet.***ServletResponse**
getCharacterEncoding, getOutputStream, getWriter, setContentLength,
setContentType

Deprecated Methods

public *java.lang.String*	encodeRedirectUrl	(*java.lang.String* url);
public *java.lang.String*	encodeUrl	(*java.lang.String* url);
public void	setStatus	(int sc, *java.lang.String* sm);

Field Constants

public final static int	SC_ACCEPTED;
public final static int	SC_BAD_GATEWAY;
public final static int	SC_BAD_REQUEST;
public final static int	SC_CONFLICT;
public final static int	SC_CONTINUE;
public final static int	SC_CREATED;
public final static int	SC_FORBIDDEN;
public final static int	SC_GATEWAY_TIMEOUT;
public final static int	SC_GONE;
public final static int	SC_HTTP_VERSION_NOT_SUPPORTED;
public final static int	SC_INTERNAL_SERVER_ERROR;
public final static int	SC_LENGTH_REQUIRED;
public final static int	SC_METHOD_NOT_ALLOWED;
public final static int	SC_MOVED_PERMANENTLY;
public final static int	SC_MOVED_TEMPORARILY;
public final static int	SC_MULTIPLE_CHOICES;
public final static int	SC_NO_CONTENT;
public final static int	SC_NON_AUTHORITATIVE_INFORMATION;
public final static int	SC_NOT_ACCEPTABLE;
public final static int	SC_NOT_FOUND;
public final static int	SC_NOT_IMPLEMENTED;
public final static int	SC_NOT_MODIFIED;
public final static int	SC_OK;
public final static int	SC_PARTIAL_CONTENT;
public final static int	SC_PAYMENT_REQUIRED;
public final static int	SC_PRECONDITION_FAILED;
public final static int	SC_PROXY_AUTHENTICATION_REQUIRED;
public final static int	SC_REQUEST_ENTITY_TOO_LARGE;
public final static int	SC_REQUEST_TIMEOUT;
public final static int	SC_REQUEST_URI_TOO_LONG;
public final static int	SC_RESET_CONTENT;
public final static int	SC_SEE_OTHER;
public final static int	SC_SERVICE_UNAVAILABLE;
public final static int	SC_SWITCHING_PROTOCOLS;
public final static int	SC_UNAUTHORIZED;
public final static int	SC_UNSUPPORTED_MEDIA_TYPE;
public final static int	SC_USE_PROXY;

Interface javax.servlet.http.HttpSession

```
public abstract interface HttpSession
```

Appears in JSDK 2.0, 2.1 though the method set varies between the two. Some methods have been deprecated. HttpSession provides a concept of state and user identification across more than one page request or visit to a web site.

Methods new in JSDK 2.1

public int	getMaxInactiveInterval	();
public void	setMaxInactiveInterval	(int interval);

Methods in JSDK 2.1 and 2.0

public long	getCreationTime	();
public *java.lang.String*	getId	();
public long	getLastAccessedTime	();
public *java.lang.String*[ ]	getValueNames	();
public *java.lang.Object*	getValue	(*java.lang.String* name);
public void	invalidate	();
public boolean	isNew	();
public void	putValue	(*java.lang.String* name, *java.lang.Object* value);
public void	removeValue	(*java.lang.String* name);

Deprecated Methods

public **HttpSessionContext**	getSessionContext	();

Interface javax.servlet.http.HttpSessionBindingListener

```
public abstract interface HttpSessionBindingListener
```

extends *java.util.EventListener*

Appears in JSDK 2.0, 2.1. Causes an object to be notified when it is bound to or unbound from a session. The object is notified by an HttpSessionBindingEvent object.

Methods in JSDK 2.1 and 2.0

public void	valueBound	(*javax.servlet.http.***HttpSessionBindingEvent** event);
public void	valueUnbound	(*javax.servlet.http.***HttpSessionBindingEvent** event);

Class javax.servlet.http.Cookie

```
public class Cookie
```

implements *java.lang.Cloneable*

Appears in JSDK 2.0, 2.1. Represents a cookie which is used to store information on a client's computer.

Constructor Method

public	Cookie	(*java.lang.String* name, *java.lang..String* value);

Methods in JSDK 2.0 and 2.1

public *java.lang.Object*	clone	();
public *java.lang.String*	getComment	();
public *java.lang.String*	getDomain	();
public int	getMaxAge	();
public *java.lang.String*	getName	();
public *java.lang.String*	getPath	();
public boolean	getSecure	();
public *java.lang.String*	getValue	();
public int	getVersion	();
public void	setComment	(*java.lang.String* purpose);
public void	setDomain	(*java.lang.String* pattern);
public void	setMaxAge	(int expiry);
public void	setPath	(*java.lang.String* uri);
public void	setSecure	(boolean flag);
public void	setValue	(*java.lang.String* newValue);
public void	setVersion	(int v);

Class *javax.servlet.http.HttpServlet*

```
public abstract class HttpServlet
```

extends   *javax.servlet.*GenericServlet
implements *java.io.Serializable*

Appears in JSDK 2.0, 2.1 though the method set varies between the two. Provides an abstract class to create an HTTP servlet which then responds to and receives information from a web site.

Constructor Method

public	HttpServlet	();

Methods new in JSDK 2.1

Inherited from *javax.servlet.*GenericServlet
init, log

Methods in JSDK 2.0 and 2.1

protected void	doDelete	(**HttpServletRequest** req, **HttpServletResponse** resp)
	throws	java.*servlet.*ServletException, *java.io.IOException*;
protected void	doGet	(**HttpServletRequest** req, **HttpServletResponse** resp)
	throws	java.*servlet.*ServletException, *java.io.IOException*;
protected void	doOptions	(**HttpServletRequest** req, **HttpServletResponse** resp)
	throws	java.*servlet.*ServletException, *java.io.IOException*;
protected void	doPost	(**HttpServletRequest** req, **HttpServletResponse** resp)
	throws	java.*servlet.*ServletException, *java.io.IOException*;
protected void	doPut	(**HttpServletRequest** req, **HttpServletResponse** resp)
	throws	java.*servlet.*ServletException, *java.io.IOException*;
protected void	doTrace	(**HttpServletRequest** req, **HttpServletResponse** resp)
	throws	java.*servlet.*ServletException, *java.io.IOException*;

protected long	getLastModified	(**HttpServletRequest** req);
protected void	service	(**HttpServletRequest** req,
		HttpServletResponse resp)
	throws	java.*servlet*.**ServletException**,
		java.io.IOException;
public void	service	(*javax.servlet*.**ServletRequest** req,
		javax.servlet.**ServletResponse** resp)
	throws	java.*servlet*.**ServletException**,
		java.io.IOException;

Inherited from *javax.servlet*.**GenericServlet**
init, service, destroy, getServletConfig, getServletInfo, log

Inherited from *java.lang.Object*
clone, equals, finalize, getClass, hashCode, notify, notifyAll, toString, wait, wait, wait

Class javax.servlet.http.HttpSessionBindingEvent

public class HttpSessionBindingEvent

extends *java.util.EventObject*

Appears in JSDK 2.0, 2.1. Represents the message to an object telling it that it has been bound to or unbound from the session.

Constructor Method

public	HttpSessionBindingEvent	(**HttpSession** session,
		java.lang.String name)

Methods in JSDK 2.0 and 2.1

public *java.lang.String*	getName	();
public **HttpSession**	getSession	();

Inherited from *java.util.EventObject*
getSource, toString

Inherited from *java.lang.Object*
clone, equals, finalize, getClass, hashCode, notify, notifyAll, toString, wait, wait, wait

Class javax.servlet.http.HttpUtils

public class HttpUtils

Appears in JSDK 2.0, 2.1. Adds a few methods useful for writing servlets with.

Constructor Method

public	HttpUtils	();

Methods in JSDK 2.0 and 2.1

public static *java.lang.StringBuffer*	getRequestURL	(**HttpServletRequest** req);
public static *java.util.Hashtable*	parsePostData	(int len,
		ServletInputStream in);
public static *java.util.Hashtable*	parseQueryString	(*java.lang.String* s)

Inherited from *java.lang.object*
clone, equals, finalize, getClass, hashCode, notify, notifyAll, toString, wait, wait, wait

JavaServer Pages API Reference

Key

Within this API Reference, the following conventions are used:

> ➢ Interface, Class and Exception names within the APIs listed are all written in **bold**.
> ➢ Interface, Class and Exception names not within the APIs listed are all written in *italics*.
> ➢ Method names are all written in `Courier Bold`.

Package javax.servlet.jsp

javax.servlet.jsp is the only package in the Java Server Pages API. At the time of writing, version 1.0 had just been put into final release. This appendix is correct for version 1.0.

Interfaces

public abstract interface	**JspPage**	extends	*javax.servlet.Servlet*
public abstract interface	**HttpJspPage**	extends	*javax.servlet.jsp.***JspPage**

Classes

public abstract class	**JspEngineInfo**		
public abstract class	**JspFactory**		
public abstract class	**JspWriter**	extends	*java.io.Writer*
public abstract class	**PageContext**		

Interface javax.servlet.jsp.JspPage

```
public abstract interface JspPage
```

extends *javax.servlet.Servlet*

JspPage defines a protocol which every Java Server Page must adhere to. Note that `jspInit` and `jspDestroy` are defined by the author but `_jspService` (is not listed here as it) is defined automatically by the JSP processor based on the contents of the JSP page. **JspPage** is extended by *javax.servlet.jsp.***HttpJspPage**

Methods

```
public void                    jspDestroy                    ();
public void                    jspInit                       ();
```

Inherited from *javax.servlet.Servlet*
`destroy, getServletConfig, getServletInfo, init, service`

Interface javax.servlet.jsp.HttpJspPage

```
public abstract interface HttpJspPage
```

extends *javax.servlet.jsp.***JspPage**

HttpJspPage is the interface that a JSP processor-generated class for the HTTP protocol must satisfy. Note that its one method **_jspService** is defined automatically by the JSP processor and should never be defined by the JSP author.

Methods

```
public void                    _jspService
                               (javax.servlet.http.HttpServletRequest request,
```

javax.servlet.http.HttpServletResponse response)
```
                               throws                        javax.servlet.ServletException,
                                                             java.io.IOException
```

Inherited from *javax.servlet.jsp.***JspPage**
`jspDestroy, jspInit`

Inherited from *javax.servlet.Servlet*
`destroy, getServletConfig, getServletInfo, init, service`

Class javax.servlet.jsp.JspEngineInfo

```
public abstract class JspEngineInfo
```

JspEngineInfo is a class that allows an author to access information on the current JSP engine.

Constructor Method

```
public                         JspEngineInfo                 ();
```

Methods

```
public abstract java.lang.String    getImplementationVersion    ();
```

Inherited from *java.lang.object*
`clone, equals, finalize, getClass, hashCode, notify, notifyAll, toString, wait, wait, wait`

Class javax.servlet.jsp.JspFactory

```
public abstract class JspFactory
```

JspFactory makes available to JSP pages a number of methods for the creation of various classes and interfaces used to support the JSP implementation. Standard JSP engines will create a subclass of JspFactory on initialization and make it globally available using the static **setDefaultFactory** method.

Constructor Method

| public | JspFactory | (); |

Methods

public static **JSPFactory**	getDefaultFactory	();
public abstract **JspEngineInfo**	getEngineInfo	();
public abstract **PageContext**	getPageContext	(*javax.servlet.Servlet* servlet, *javax.servlet.ServletRequest* request, *javax.servlet.ServletResponse* response, *java.lang.String* errorPageURL, boolean needsSession, int buffer, boolean autoFlush);
public abstract void	releasePageContext	(*javax.servlet.jsp.***PageContext** pc);
public static void	setDefaultfactory	(*javax.servlet.jsp.***JspFactory** deflt);

Inherited from *java.lang.object*

```
clone, equals, finalize, getClass, hashCode, notify, notifyAll, toString, wait,
wait, wait
```

Class javax.servlet.jsp.JspWriter

```
public abstract class JspWriter
```

extends *java.io.Writer*

JspWriter emulates some of the functionality found in *java.io.BufferedWriter* and *java.io.PrintWriter*.
However it also throws
java.io.IOException from the print methods which *java.io.PrintWriter* does not.

Constructor Method

| protected | JspWriter | (int buffersize, boolean autoFlush); |

Methods

public abstract void	clear	()
	throws	*java.io.IOException*;
public abstract void	clearBuffer	()
	throws	*java.io.IOException*;
public abstract void	close	()
	throws	*java.io.IOException*;
public abstract void	flush	()
	throws	*java.io.IOException*;
public int	getBufferSize	();
public abstract int	getRemaining	();
public boolean	isAutoFlush	();
public abstract void	newLine	()
	throws	*java.io.IOException*;
public abstract void	print	(boolean b)
	throws	*java.io.IOException*;
public abstract void	print	(char c)
	throws	*java.io.IOException*;
public abstract void	print	(char[] s)
	throws	*java.io.IOException*;
public abstract void	print	(double d)
	throws	*java.io.IOException*;
public abstract void	print	(float f)
	throws	*java.io.IOException*;
public abstract void	print	(int i)
	throws	*java.io.IOException*;

949

public abstract void	print	(long l)
	throws	*java.io.IOException*;
public abstract void	print	(*java.lang.Object* obj)
	throws	*java.io.IOException*;
public abstract void	print	(*java.lang.String* s)
	throws	*java.io.IOException*;
public abstract void	println	()
	throws	*java.io.IOException*;
public abstract void	println	(boolean b)
	throws	*java.io.IOException*;
public abstract void	println	(char c)
	throws	*java.io.IOException*;
public abstract void	println	(char[] s)
	throws	*java.io.IOException*;
public abstract void	println	(double d)
	throws	*java.io.IOException*;
public abstract void	println	(float f)
	throws	*java.io.IOException*;
public abstract void	println	(int i)
	throws	*java.io.IOException*;
public abstract void	println	(long l)
	throws	*java.io.IOException*;
public abstract void	println	(*java.lang.Object* obj)
	throws	*java.io.IOException*;
public abstract void	println	(*java.lang.String* s)
	throws	*java.io.IOException*;

Inherited from *java.io.Writer*

```
write, write, write, write, write
```

Inherited from *java.lang.object*

```
clone, equals, finalize, getClass, hashCode, notify, notifyAll, toString, wait,
wait, wait
```

Fields

protected boolean	`autoFlush`
protected int	`bufferSize`
public static int	`DEFAULT_BUFFER`
public static int	`NO_BUFFER`

Class javax.servlet.jsp.PageContext

```
public abstract class PageContext
```

A **PageContext** instance provides access to all the namespaces associated with a JSP page, provides access to several page attributes, as well as a layer above the implementation details.

Constructor Method

public	`PageContext`	();

Methods

public abstract *java.lang.Object*	`findAttribute`	(*java.lang.String* name);
public abstract void	`forward`	(*java.lang.String* relativeUrlPath)
	throws	*javax.servlet.ServletException*,
		java.io.IOException;
public abstract *java.lang.Object*	`getAttribute`	(*java.lang.String* name);
public abstract *java.lang.Object*	`getAttribute`	(*java.lang.String* name, int scope);
public abstract *java.util.Enumeration*	`getAttributeNamesInScope`	(int scope);
public abstract int	`getAttributesScope`	(*java.lang.String* name);
public abstract *java.lang.Exception*	`getException`	();
public abstract **JspWriter**	`getOut`	();

public abstract *java.lang.Object*	`getPage`	();
public abstract *javax.servlet.ServletRequest*		
	`getRequest`	();
public abstract *javax.servlet.ServletResponse*		
	`getResponse`	();
public abstract *javax.servlet.ServletConfig*		
	`getServletConfig`	();
public abstract *javax.servlet.ServletContext*		
	`getServletContext`	();
public abstract *javax.servlet.http.HttpSession*		
	`getSession`	();
public abstract void	`handlePageException`	(*java.lang.Exception* e)
	throws	*javax.servlet.ServletException,*
		java.io.IOException;
public abstract void	`include`	(*java.lang.String* relativeUrlPath)
	throws	*javax.servlet.ServletException,*
		java.io.IOException;
public abstract void	`initialize`	(*javax.servlet.Servlet* servlet,
		javax.servlet.ServletRequest request,
		javax.servlet.ServletResponse response,
		java.lang.String errorPageURL,
		boolean needsSession,
		int bufferSize,
		boolean autoFlush)
	throws	*java.io.IOException,*
		java.lang.IllegalStateException,
		java.lang.IllegalArgumentException;
public abstract void	`release`	();
public abstract void	`removeAttribute`	(*java.lang.String* name);
public abstract void	`removeAttribute`	(*java.lang.String* name,
		int scope);
public abstract void	`setAttribute`	(*java.lang.String* name,
		java.lang.Object attribute);
public abstract void	`setAttribute`	(*java.lang.String* name,
		java.lang.Object attribute,
		int scope);

Inherited from *java.lang.object*
`clone, equals, finalize, getClass, hashCode, notify, notifyAll, toString, wait, wait, wait`

Fields

public static final	*java.lang.String*	`APPLICATION`
public static final	int	`APPLICATION_SCOPE`
public static final	*java.lang.String*	`CONFIG`
public static final	*java.lang.String*	`EXCEPTION`
public static final	*java.lang.String*	`OUT`
public static final	*java.lang.String*	`PAGE`
public static final	int	`PAGE_SCOPE`
public static final	*java.lang.String*	`PAGECONTEXT`
public static final	*java.lang.String*	`REQUEST`
public static final	int	`REQUEST_SCOPE`
public static final	*java.lang.String*	`RESPONSE`
public static final	*java.lang.String*	`SESSION`
public static final	int	`SESSION_SCOPE`

951

JNDI API Reference

Key

Within this API Reference, the following conventions are used:
- ➤ Interface, Class and Exception names within the APIs listed are all written in **bold**.
- ➤ Interface, Class and Exception names not within the APIs listed are all written in *italics*.
- ➤ Method and Class names are written in `Courier Bold`.

Package javax.naming

Interfaces

public abstract interface	**Context**		
public abstract interface	**Name**	extends	*java.lang.Cloneable, java.io.Serializable*
public abstract interface	**NameParser**		
public abstract interface	**NamingEnumeration**	extends	*java.util.Enumeration*
public abstract interface	**Referenceable**		

Classes

public class	**BinaryRefAddr**	extends	*javax.naming.*RefAddr
public class	**Binding**	extends	javax.naming.NameClassPair
public class	**CompositeName**	implements	javax.naming.Name
public class	**CompoundName**	implements	javax.naming.Name
public class	**InitialContext**	implements	javax.naming.Context
public class	**LinkRef**	extends	javax.naming.Reference
public class	**NameClassPair**	implements	java.io.Serializable
public abstract class	**RefAddr**	implements	java.io.Serializable
public class	**Reference**	implements	java.lang.Clonable, java.io.Serializable
public class	**StringRefAddr**	extends	javax.naming.RefAddr

Exceptions

public class	AuthenticationException	extends	*javax.naming*.NamingSecurityException
public class	**AuthenticationNotSupportedException**		
		extends	javax.naming.NamingSecurityException
public class	**CannotProceedException**	extends	javax.naming.NamingException
public class	**CommunicationException**	extends	javax.naming.NamingException
public class	**ConfigurationException**	extends	javax.naming.NamingException
public class	**ContextNotEmptyException**	extends	javax.naming.NamingException
public class	**InsufficientResourcesException**	extends	javax.naming.NamingException
public class	**InterruptedNamingException**	extends	javax.naming.NamingException
public class	**InvalidNameException**	extends	javax.naming.NamingException
public class	LimitExceeded**Exception**	extends	javax.naming.NamingException
public class	Link**Exception**	extends	javax.naming.NamingException
public class	LinkLoop**Exception**	extends	javax.naming.LinkException
public class	MalformedLink**Exception**	extends	javax.naming.LinkException
public class	NameAlreadyBound**Exception**	extends	javax.naming.NamingException
public class	NameNotFound**Exception**	extends	javax.naming.NamingException
public class	Naming**Exception**	extends	java.lang.Exception
public abstract class	NamingSecurity**Exception**	extends	javax.naming.NamingException
public class	NoInitialContext**Exception**	extends	javax.naming.NamingException
public class	NoPermission**Exception**	extends	javax.naming.NamingSecurityException
public class	NotContext**Exception**	extends	javax.naming.NamingException
public class	OperationNotSupported**Exception**	extends	javax.naming.NamingException
public class	PartialResult**Exception**	extends	javax.naming.NamingException
public abstract class	Referral**Exception**	extends	javax.naming.NamingException
public class	ServiceUnavailable**Exception**	extends	javax.naming.NamingException
public class	SizeLimitExceeded**Exception**	extends	javax.naming.LimitExceededException
public class	TimeLimitExceeded**Exception**	extends	javax.naming.LimitExceededException

Interface javax.naming.Context

```
public abstract interface Context
```

Is extended by *javax.naming*.DirContext. Is implemented by *javax.naming*.**InitialContext**. Represents a naming context - a way in which to associate names to objects.

Methods

Any method in this interface can throw a *javax.naming*.NamingException (or any of its subclasses)

public *java.lang.Object*	**addToEnvironment**	(*java.lang.String* propName, *java.lang.Object* propVal);
public void	**bind**	(*javax.naming*.**Name** name, *java.lang.Object* obj);
public void	**bind**	(*java.lang.String* name, *java.lang.Object* obj);
public void	**close**	();
public Name	**composeName**	(*javax.naming*.**Name** name, *javax.naming*.Name prefix);
public *java.lang.String*	**composeName**	(*java.lang.String* name, *java.lang.String* prefix);
public Context	**createSubcontext**	(*javax.naming*.**Name** name);
public Context	**createSubcontext**	(*java.lang.String* name);
public void	**destroySubcontext**	(*javax.naming*.**Name** name);
public void	**destroySubcontext**	(*javax.naming*.**Name** name);
public *java.util.Hashtable*	**getEnvironment**	();
public NameParser	**getNameParser**	(*javax.naming*.**Name** name);
public NameParser	**getNameParser**	(*java.lang.String* name);
public NamingEnumeration	**list**	(*javax.naming*.**Name** name);
public NamingEnumeration	**list**	(*java.lang.String* name);
public NamingEnumeration	**listBindings**	(*javax.naming*.**Name** name);

public NamingEnumeration	`listBindings`	*(java.lang.String* name);
public *java.lang.Object*	`lookup`	*(javax.naming.***Name** name);
public *java.lang.Object*	`lookup`	*(java.lang.String* name);
public *java.lang.Object*	`lookupLink`	*(javax.naming.***Name** name);
public *java.lang.Object*	`lookupLink`	*(java.lang.String* name);
public void	`rebind`	*(javax.naming.***Name** name, *java.lang.Object* obj);
public void	`rebind`	*(java.lang.String* name, *java.lang.Object* obj);
public *java.lang.Object*	`removeFromEnvironment`	*(java.lang.String* propName);
public void	`rename`	*(javax.naming.***Name** oldName, *javax.naming.***Name** newName)
	throws	*javax.naming.***NameAlreadyBoundException;**
public void	`rename`	*(java.lang.String* oldName, *java.lang.String* newName)
	throws	*javax.naming.***NameAlreadyBoundException;**
public void	`unbind`	*(javax.naming.***Name** name);
public void	`unbind`	*(java.lang.String* name);

Field Constants

public final static *java.lang.String*	`AUTHORITATIVE`
public final static *java.lang.String*	`BATCHSIZE`
public final static *java.lang.String*	`DNS_URL`
public final static *java.lang.String*	`INITIAL_CONTEXT_FACTORY`
public final static *java.lang.String*	`LANGUAGE`
public final static *java.lang.String*	`OBJECT_FACTORIES`
public final static *java.lang.String*	`PROVIDER_URL`
public final static *java.lang.String*	`REFERRAL`
public final static *java.lang.String*	`SECURITY_AUTHENTICATION`
public final static *java.lang.String*	`SECURITY_CREDENTIALS`
public final static *java.lang.String*	`SECURITY_PRINCIPAL`
public final static *java.lang.String*	`SECURITY_PROTOCOL`
public final static *java.lang.String*	`URL_PKG_PREFIXES`

Interface javax.naming.Name

```
public abstract interface Name
```

`extends` *java.lang.Cloneable, java.io.Serializable*

Is implemented by *javax.naming.*CompoundName, *javax.naming.*CompositeName. Makes available the basic lifecycle methods for a generic naming convention and (multipart) name.

Methods

public Name	add	(int posn, *java.lang.String* comp)
	throws	*javax.naming.*InvalidNameException;
public Name	`add`	*(java.lang.String* comp)
	throws	*javax.naming.*InvalidNameException;
public Name	`addAll`	*(javax.naming.***Name** suffix)
	throws	*javax.naming.*InvalidNameException;
public Name	`addAll`	(int posn, *javax.naming.*Name n)
	throws	*javax.naming.*InvalidNameException,
		java.lang.ArrayIndexOutOfBoundsException
public *java.lang.Object*	`clone`	()
public int	`compareTo`	*(java.lang.Object* obj)
	throws	*java.lang.ClassCastException.*
public boolean	`endsWith`	*(javax.naming.***Name** n)

public *java.lang.String*	**get**	(int posn)
	throws	*java.lang.ArrayIndexOutOfBoundsException*
public *java.util.Enumeration*	**getAll**	();
public Name	**getPrefix**	(int posn)
	throws	*java.lang.ArrayIndexOutOfBoundsException*
public Name	**getSuffix**	(int posn)
	throws	*java.lang.ArrayIndexOutOfBoundsException*
public boolean	**isEmpty**	()
public *java.lang.Object*	**remove**	(int posn)
	throws	*javax.naming*.InvalidNameException
		java.lang.ArrayIndexOutOfBoundsException
public int	**size**	()
public boolean	**startsWith**	(*javax.naming*.**Name** n)

Fields

Inherited from *java.io.Serializable*:
serialVersionUID

Interface javax.naming.NameParser

```
public abstract interface NameParser
```

Used to translate a hierarchical name into a 'location' within the namespace for which it parses names.

Methods

public Name	**parse**	(*java.lang.String* name)
	throws	*javax.naming*.InvalidNameException,
		javax.naming.NamingException.

Interface javax.naming.NamingEnumeration

```
public abstract interface NamingEnumeration
```

```
extends java.util.Enumeration
```

Provides an implementor with a couple of methods for enumerating lists returned by other JNDI methods.

Methods

public boolean	**hasMore**	()
	throws	*javax.naming*.NamingException.
public *java.lang.Object*	**next**	()
	throws	*javax.naming*.NamingException.

Inherited from *java.util.Enumeration*:
HasMoreElements, nextElement

Interface javax.naming.Referenceable

```
public abstract interface Referenceable
```

For use with objects which are to be made accessible outside of the current naming system.
getReference can be used as a 'beacon' for binding to the object.

Methods

public Reference	getReference throws	() *javax.naming*.NamingException.

Class *javax.naming.BinaryRefAddr*

`public class BinaryRefAddr`

`extends` *javax.naming*.RefAddr

Represents the binary form of the address of a communications end-point, e.g. the client or server machine.

Constructor Method

public	`BinaryRefAddr`	(*java.lang.String* addrType, byte[] src)
public	`BinaryRefAddr`	(*java.lang.String* addrType, byte[] src, int offset, int count)

Methods

public boolean	`equals`	(*java.lang.Object* obj)
public *java.lang.Object*	`getContent`	()
public int	`hashcode`	()
public *java.lang.String*	`toString`	()

Inherited from *javax.naming*.**RefAddr**
`getType`

Inherited from *java.lang.Object*
`clone, finalize, getClass, notify, notifyAll, wait, wait, wait`

Field Constants

Inherited from *javax.naming*.RefAddr.
`AddrType`

Class *javax.naming.Binding*

`public class Binding`

`extends` *javax.naming*.NameClassPair

Is extended by *javax.naming*.**SearchResult**. Represents the way an object is bound to its name within a naming system (context).

Constructor Method

public	`Binding`	(*java.lang.String* name, *java.lang.Object* obj)
public	`Binding`	(*java.lang.String* name, *java.lang.Object* obj, boolean isRelative)
public	`Binding`	(*java.lang.String* name, *java.lang.String* classname, *java.lang.Object* obj)
public	`Binding`	(*java.lang.String* name, *java.lang.String* classname, *java.lang.Object* obj, boolean isRelative)

Methods

public *java.lang.String*	getClassName	()
public *java.lang.Object*	getObject	()
public void	setObject	(*java.lang.Object* obj)
public *java.lang.String*	toString	()

Inherited from *javax.naming*.NameClassPair:
getName, isRelative, setClassName, setName, setRelative

Inherited from *java.lang.Object*:
clone, equals, finalize, getClass, hashCode, notify, notifyAll, wait, wait, wait

Class *javax.naming.CompositeName*

```
public class CompositeName
```

extends *javax.naming.*Name

Represents a string of names from different namespaces making up one composite name. Each of these names on the whole is a component name.

Constructor Method

public	CompositeName	()
public	CompositeName	(*java.lang.String* n)
	throws	*javax.naming*.InvalidNameException.
protected	CompositeName	(*java.util.Enumeration* comps)

Methods

public Name	add	(*java.lang.String* comp)
	throws	*javax.naming*.InvalidNameException
public Name	add	(int posn,
		java.lang.String comp)
	throws	*javax.naming*.InvalidNameException,
public Name	addall	(*javax.naming*.Name suffix)
	throws	*javax.naming*.InvalidNameException.
public Name	addall	(int posn,
		javax.naming.Name n)
	throws	*javax.naming*.InvalidNameException,
public *java.lang.Object*	clone	()
public int	compareTo	(*java.lang.Object* obj)
	throws	*java.lang.ClassCastException*.
public boolean	endsWith	(*javax.naming*.Name n)
public boolean	equals	(*java.lang.Object* obj)
public *java.lang.String*	get	(int posn)
public *java.util.Enumeration*	getall	()
public Name	getPrefix	(int posn)
public Name	getSuffix	(int posn)
public int	hashCode	()
public boolean	isempty	()
public *java.lang.Object*	remove	(int posn)
	throws	*javax.naming*.InvalidNameException,
public int	size	()
public boolean	startsWith	(*javax.naming*.Name n)
public *java.lang.String*	toString	()

Inherited from *java.lang.Object*
finalize, getClass, notify, notifyAll, wait, wait, wait

Class javax.naming.CompoundName

```
public class CompoundName
```

implements *javax.naming*.Name

Represents a single name from a hierarchical namespace - a compound name.

Constructor Method

public	**CompoundName**	(*java.lang.String* n, *java.util.Properties* syntax)
	throws	*javax.naming*.InvalidNameException,
protected	**CompoundName**	(*java.util.Enumeration* comps, *java.util.Properties* syntax)

Methods

public Name	**add**	(int posn, *java.lang.String* comp)
	throws	*javax.naming*.InvalidNameException
public Name	**add**	(*java.lang.String* comp)
	throws	*javax.naming*.InvalidNameException
public Name	**addall**	(int posn, *javax.naming*.Name n)
	throws	*javax.naming*.InvalidNameException,
public Name	**addall**	(*javax.naming*.Name suffix)
	throws	*javax.naming*.InvalidNameException
public *java.lang.Object*	**clone**	()
public int	**compareTo**	(*java.lang.Object* obj)
public boolean	**endsWith**	(*javax.naming*.Name n)
public boolean	**equals**	(*java.lang.Object* obj)
public *java.lang.String*	**get**	(int posn)
public *java.util.Enumeration*	**getAll**	()
public Name	**getPrefix**	(int posn)
public Name	**getSuffix**	(int posn)
public int	**hashCode**	()
public boolean	**isEmpty**	()
public *java.lang.Object*	**remove**	(int posn)
	throws	*javax.naming*.InvalidNameException
public int	**size**	()
public boolean	**startsWith**	(*javax.naming*.Name n)
public *java.lang.String*	**toString**	()

Inherited from *java.lang.Object*

```
finalize, getClass, notify, notifyAll, wait, wait, wait
```

Field Constants

protected transient NameImpl **impl**
protected transient *java.util.Properties* **mySyntax**

Class javax.naming.InitialContext

```
public class InitialContext
```
implements *javax.naming*.Context

Is extended by **InitialContext**. Represents the naming system that the implementor uses initially (by default) to name objects.

Constructor Method

public	`InitialContext`	()
	throws	*javax.naming*.NamingException
public	`InitialContext`	(*java.util.Hashtable* environment)
	throws	*javax.naming*.NamingException

Methods

public *java.lang.Object*	`addToEnvironment`	(*java.lang.String* propName, *java.lang.Object* propVal)
	throws	*javax.naming*.NamingException
public void	`bind`	(*javax.naming*.Name name, *java.lang.Object* obj)
	throws	*javax.naming*.NamingException
public void	`bind`	(*java.lang.String* name, *java.lang.Object* obj)
	throws	*javax.naming*.NamingException
public void	`close`	()
	throws	*javax.naming*.NamingException
public Name	`composeName`	(*javax.naming*.Name name, *javax.naming*.Name prefix)
	throws	*javax.naming*.NamingException
public *java.lang.String*	`composeName`	(*java.lang.String* name, *java.lang.String* prefix)
	throws	*javax.naming*.NamingException
public Context	`createSubcontext`	(*javax.naming*.Name name)
	throws	*javax.naming*.NamingException
public Context	`createSubcontext`	(*java.lang.String* name)
	throws	*javax.naming*.NamingException
public void	`destroySubcontext`	(*java.lang.String* name)
	throws	*javax.naming*.NamingException
public void	`destroySubcontext`	(*javax.naming*.Name name)
	throws	*javax.naming*.NamingException
protected Context	`getDefaultInitCtx`	()
	throws	*javax.naming*.NamingException
public *java.util.Hashtable*	`getEnvironment`	()
	throws	*javax.naming*.NamingException
public NameParser	`getNameParser`	(*javax.naming*.Name name)
	throws	*javax.naming*.NamingException
public NameParser	`getNameParser`	(*java.lang.String* name)
	throws	*javax.naming*.NamingException
protected Context	`getURLOrDefaultInitCtx`	(*javax.naming*.Name name)
	throws	*javax.naming*.NamingException
protected Context	`getURLOrDefaultInitCtx`	(*java.lang.String* name)
	throws	*javax.naming*.NamingException
public NamingEnumeration	`list`	(*java.lang.String* name)
	throws	*javax.naming*.NamingException
public NamingEnumeration	`list`	(*javax.naming*.Name name)
	throws	*javax.naming*.NamingException
public NamingEnumeration	`listBindings`	(*java.lang.String* name)
	throws	*javax.naming*.NamingException
public NamingEnumeration	`listBindings`	(*javax.naming*.Name name)
	throws	*javax.naming*.NamingException
public *java.lang.Object*	`lookup`	(*java.lang.String* name)
	throws	*javax.naming*.NamingException
public *java.lang.Object*	`lookup`	(*javax.naming*.Name name)
	throws	*javax.naming*.NamingException
public *java.lang.Object*	`lookupLink`	(*java.lang.String* name)
	throws	*javax.naming*.NamingException
public *java.lang.Object*	`lookupLink`	(*javax.naming*.Name name)
	throws	*javax.naming*.NamingException
public *java.lang.String*	`rebind`	(*java.lang.String* name, *java.lang.Object* obj)
	throws	*javax.naming*.NamingException

public *java.lang.String*	rebind	(*javax.naming*.name name, *java.lang.Object* obj)
	throws	*javax.naming*.NamingException
public *java.lang.Object*	removeFromEnvironment	(*java.lang.String* propName)
	throws	*javax.naming*.NamingException
public void	rename	(*java.lang.String* oldName, *java.lang.String* newName)
	throws	*javax.naming*.NamingException
public void	rename	(*javax.naming*.Name oldName, *javax.naming*.Name newName)
	throws	*javax.naming*.NamingException
public void	unbind	(*java.lang.String* name)
	throws	*javax.naming*.NamingException
public void	unbind	(*javax.naming*.Name name)
	throws	*javax.naming*.NamingException

Inherited from *java.lang.Object*
```
clone, equals, finalize, getClass, hashCode, notify, notifyall, toString, wait,
wait, wait
```

Field Constants

protected Context	defaultInitCtx
protected boolean	gotDefault
protected *java.util.Hashtable*	myProps

Class javax.naming.LinkRef

```
public class LinkRef
```

extends *javax.naming*.**Reference**

Represents a link (reference) to an object in a naming system.

Constructor Method

public	LinkRef	(*javax.naming*.Name linkName)
public	LinkRef	(*java.lang.String* linkName)

Methods

public *java.lang.String*	getLinkName	()
	throws	*javax.naming*.NamingException

Inherited from *javax.naming*.Reference: `add, add, clear, clone, equals, get, get, getAll, getClassName, getFactoryClassLocation, getFactoryClassName, hashCode, remove, size, toString`

Inherited from *java.lang.Object*:
```
finalize, getClass, notify, notifyAll, wait, wait, wait
```

Fields

Inherited from *javax.naming*.**Reference**:
```
addrs, classFactory, classFactoryLocation, className
```

Class javax.naming.NameClassPair

```
public class NameClassPair
```

implements *java.io.Serializable*

Is extended by *javax.naming.***Binding**. Represents the name and class pair of an object (which has been bound).

Constructor Method

public	NameClassPair	(*java.lang.String* name, *java.lang.String* className)
public	NameClassPair	(*java.lang.String* name, *java.lang.String* className, boolean isRelative)

Methods

public *java.lang.String*	getClassName	()
public *java.lang.String*	getName	()
public boolean	isRelative	()
public void	setClassName	(*java.lang.String* name)
public void	setName	(*java.lang.String* name)
public void	setRelative	(boolean r)
public *java.lang.String*	toString	()

Inherited from *java.lang.Object*
clone, equals, finalize, getClass, hashCode, notify, notifyall, wait, wait, wait

Class javax.naming.RefAddr

```
public abstract class RefAddr
```

implements *java.io.Serializable*

Is extended by *javax.naming.***BinaryRefAddr**, *javax.naming.***StringRefAddr**. Base class for representing the address of a communications end-point.

Constructor Method

protected	RefAddr	(*java.lang.String* addrType)

Methods

public boolean	equals	(*java.lang.Object* obj)
public abstract *java.lang.object*	getContent	()
public *java.lang.String*	getType	()
public int	hashCode	()
public *java.lang.String*	toString	()

Inherited from *java.lang.Object*:
clone, finalize, getClass, notify, notifyall, wait, wait, wait

Fields

protected *java.lang.String*	addrType

Class javax.naming.Reference

```
public class Reference
```

implements *java.lang.Cloneable, java.io.Serializable*

Is extended by *javax.naming.***LinkRef**. Provides a way to refer to objects that are not within the naming system being used.

Constructor Method

public	Reference	(*java.lang.String* className)
public	Reference	(*java.lang.String* className, *javax.naming.*RefAddr addr)
public	Reference	(*java.lang.String* className, java.lang.String factory, *java.lang.String* factoryLocation)
public	Reference	(*java.lang.String* className, *javax.naming.*RefAddr addr, java.lang.String factory, *java.lang.String* factoryLocation)

Methods

public void	add	(int posn, *javax.naming.*RefAddr addr)
public void	add	(*javax.naming.*RefAddr addr)
public void	clear	()
public *java.lang.Object*	clone	()
public boolean	equals	(*java.lang.Object* obj)
public RefAddr	get	(*java.lang.String* addrType)
public RefAddr	get	(int posn)
public *java.util.Enumeration*	getAll	()
public *java.lang.String*	getClassName	()
public *java.lang.String*	getFactoryClassLocation	()
public *java.lang.String*	getFactoryClassName	()
public int	hashCode	()
public *java.lang.Object*	remove	(int posn)
public int	size	()
public *java.lang.String*	toString	()

Inherited from *java.lang.Object*:
finalize, getClass, notify, notifyAll, wait, wait, wait

Fields

protected *java.util.Vector*	addrs
protected *java.lang.String*	classFactory
protected *java.lang.String*	classFactoryLocation
protected *java.lang.String*	className

Class javax.naming.StringRefAddr

```
public class StringRefAddr
```

extends *javax.naming.*RefAddr

Represents the string form of the address of a communications end-point, e.g. the client or server machine.

Constructor Method

public   **StringRefAddr**   (*java.lang.String* addrType, *java.lang.String* addr)

Methods

public *java.lang.Object*   **getContent**   ()

Inherited from *javax.naming.*RefAddr
equals, getType, hashCode, toString

Inherited from *java.lang.Object*
clone, finalize, getClass, notify, notifyAll, wait, wait, wait

Fields

Inherited from *javax.naming.*RefAddr
     AddrType

Class javax.naming.AuthenticationException

```
public class AuthenticationException
extends javax.naming.NamingSecurityException
```

Thrown when an authentication error is reported while accessing a naming or directory service.

Constructor Method

public   **AuthenticationException**   (*java.lang.String* explanation)
public   **AuthenticationException**   ()

Methods

Inherited from *javax.naming.*NamingException
appendRemainingComponent, appendRemainingName, getExplanation, getRemainingName, getResolvedName, getResolvedObj, getRootCause, setRemainingName, setResolvedName, setResolvedObj, setRootCause, toString, toString

Inherited from javax.lang.Throwable
fillInStackTrace, getLocalizedMessage, getMessage, printStackTrace, printStackTrace, printStackTrace

Inherited from *java.lang.Object*
clone, equals, finalize, getClass, hashCode, notify, notifyall, wait, wait, wait

Fields

Inherited from *javax.naming.*NamingException:
remainingName, resolvedName, resolvedObj, rootException

Class javax.naming.AuthenticationNotSupportedException

```
public class AuthenticationNotSupportedException
extends javax.naming.NamingSecurityException
```

Thrown when the required form of authentication is not supported.

Constructor Method

public	`AuthenticationNotSupportedException`	`()`
public	`AuthenticationNotSupportedException`	(*java.lang.String* explanation)

Methods

Inherited from *javax.naming.*NamingException
```
appendRemainingComponent, appendRemainingName, getExplanation,
getRemainingName, getResolvedName,getResolvedObj, getRootCause,
setRemainingName, setResolvedName, setResolvedObj, setRootCause, toString,
toString
```

Inherited from javax.lang.Throwable
```
fillInStackTrace, getLocalizedMessage, getMessage, printStackTrace,
printStackTrace, printStackTrace
```

Inherited from *java.lang.Object*
```
clone, equals, finalize, getClass, hashCode, notify, notifyall, wait, wait, wait
```

Fields

Inherited from *javax.naming.*NamingException:
```
remainingName, resolvedName, resolvedObj, rootException
```

Class javax.naming.CannotProceedException

```
public class CannotProceedException
extends javax.naming.NamingException
```

Thrown when an operation cannot proceed any further.

Constructor Method

public	`CannotProceedException`	`()`
public	`CannotProceedException`	(*java.lang.String* explanation)

Methods

public *javax.naming.*Name	`getAltName`	`()`
public *javax.naming.*Context	`getAltNameCtx`	`()`
public *java.util.Hashtable*	`getEnvironment`	`()`
public *javax.naming.*Name	`getRemainingNewName`	`()`
public void	`setAltName`	(*javax.naming.*Name altName)
public void	`setAltNameCtx`	(*javax.naming.*Context altNameCtx)
public void	`setEnvironment`	(*java.util.Hashtable* environment)
public void	`setRemainingNewName`	(*javax.naming.*Name newname)

Inherited from *javax.naming.*NamingException
```
appendRemainingComponent, appendRemainingName, getExplanation,
getRemainingName, getResolvedName,getResolvedObj, getRootCause,
setRemainingName, setResolvedName, setResolvedObj, setRootCause, toString,
toString
```

Inherited from *javax.lang.Throwable*
`fillInStackTrace, getLocalizedMessage, getMessage, printStackTrace,`
`printStackTrace, printStackTrace`

Inherited from *java.lang.Object*
`clone, equals, finalize, getClass, hashCode, notify, notifyall, wait, wait, wait`

Fields

protected *javax.naming.***Name**	`altName`	
protected *javax.naming.***Context**	`altNameCtx`	
protected *java.util.Hashtable*	`environment`	
protected *javax.naming.***Name**	`remainingNewName`	

Inherited from *javax.naming.*NamingException:
`remainingName, resolvedName, resolvedObj, rootException`

Class javax.naming.CommunicationException

`public class CommunicationException`
`extends` *javax.naming.*NamingException

Thrown when communication between the client and directory or naming service fails.

Constructor Method

public	`CommunicationException`	`()`
public	`CommunicationException`	(*java.lang.String* explanation)

Methods

Inherited from *javax.naming.*NamingException
`appendRemainingComponent, appendRemainingName, getExplanation,`
`getRemainingName, getResolvedName, getResolvedObj, getRootCause,`
`setRemainingName, setResolvedName, setResolvedObj, setRootCause, toString,`
`toString`

Inherited from javax.lang.Throwable
`fillInStackTrace, getLocalizedMessage, getMessage, printStackTrace,`
`printStackTrace, printStackTrace`

Inherited from *java.lang.Object*
`clone, equals, finalize, getClass, hashCode, notify, notifyall, wait, wait, wait`

Fields

Inherited from *javax.naming.*NamingException:
`remainingName, resolvedName, resolvedObj, rootException`

Class javax.naming.ConfigurationException

`public class ConfigurationException`
`extends` *javax.naming.*NamingException

Thrown when a problem arises in the server/client configuration.

966

Constructor Method

public	ConfigurationException	()	
public	ConfigurationException	(*java.lang.String* explanation)	

Methods

Inherited from *javax.naming*.NamingException
`appendRemainingComponent, appendRemainingName, getExplanation, getRemainingName, getResolvedName, getResolvedObj, getRootCause, setRemainingName, setResolvedName, setResolvedObj, setRootCause, toString, toString`

Inherited from javax.lang.Throwable
`fillInStackTrace, getLocalizedMessage, getMessage, printStackTrace, printStackTrace, printStackTrace`

Inherited from *java.lang.Object*
`clone, equals, finalize, getClass, hashCode, notify, notifyall, wait, wait, wait`

Fields

Inherited from *javax.naming*.NamingException:
`remainingName, resolvedName, resolvedObj, rootException`

Class javax.naming.ContextNotEmptyException

`public class ContextNotEmptyException`
`extends` *javax.naming*.NamingException

Thrown when an attempt is made to destroy a context which is not empty.

Constructor Method

public	ContextNotEmptyException	()	
public	ContextNotEmptyException	(*java.lang.String* explanation)	

Methods

Inherited from *javax.naming*.NamingException
`appendRemainingComponent, appendRemainingName, getExplanation, getRemainingName, getResolvedName, getResolvedObj, getRootCause, setRemainingName, setResolvedName, setResolvedObj, setRootCause, toString, toString`

Inherited from javax.lang.Throwable
`fillInStackTrace, getLocalizedMessage, getMessage, printStackTrace, printStackTrace, printStackTrace`

Inherited from *java.lang.Object*
`clone, equals, finalize, getClass, hashCode, notify, notifyall, wait, wait, wait`

Fields

Inherited from *javax.naming*.NamingException:
`remainingName, resolvedName, resolvedObj, rootException`

Class javax.naming.InsufficientResourcesException

```
public class InsufficientResourcesException
extends javax.naming.NamingException
```

Thrown when an operation fails due to insufficient resources on the server, client or connection.

Constructor Method

public	`InsufficientResourcesException`	(*java.lang.String* explanation)
public	`InsufficientResourcesException`	()

Methods

Inherited from *javax.naming*.NamingException
`appendRemainingComponent, appendRemainingName, getExplanation, getRemainingName, getResolvedName, getResolvedObj, getRootCause, setRemainingName, setResolvedName, setResolvedObj, setRootCause, toString, toString`

Inherited from java.lang.Throwable
`fillInStackTrace, getLocalizedMessage, getMessage, printStackTrace, printStackTrace, printStackTrace`

Inherited from *java.lang.Object*
`clone, equals, finalize, getClass, hashCode, notify, notifyall, wait, wait, wait`

Fields

Inherited from *javax.naming*.NamingException:
`remainingName, resolvedName, resolvedObj, rootException`

Class javax.naming.InterruptedNamingException

```
public class InterruptedNamingException
extends javax.naming.NamingException
```

Thrown when a naming operation (which supports interruption) is disrupted by another application.

Constructor Method

public	`CommunicationException`	()
public	`CommunicationException`	(*java.lang.String* explanation)

Methods

Inherited from *javax.naming*.NamingException
`appendRemainingComponent, appendRemainingName, getExplanation, getRemainingName, getResolvedName, getResolvedObj, getRootCause, setRemainingName, setResolvedName, setResolvedObj, setRootCause, toString, toString`

Inherited from javax.lang.Throwable
`fillInStackTrace, getLocalizedMessage, getMessage, printStackTrace, printStackTrace, printStackTrace`

Inherited from *java.lang.Object*
`clone, equals, finalize, getClass, hashCode, notify, notifyall, wait, wait, wait`

Fields

Inherited from *javax.naming.*NamingException:
`remainingName, resolvedName, resolvedObj, rootException`

Class javax.naming.InvalidNameException

`public class InvalidNameException`
`extends` *javax.naming.*NamingException

Thrown when a name fails to meet the naming syntax of a system.

Constructor Method

public	`CommunicationException`	()
public	`CommunicationException`	(*java.lang.String* explanation)

Methods

Inherited from *javax.naming.*NamingException
`appendRemainingComponent, appendRemainingName, getExplanation, getRemainingName, getResolvedName, getResolvedObj, getRootCause, setRemainingName, setResolvedName, setResolvedObj, setRootCause, toString, toString`

Inherited from javax.lang.Throwable
`fillInStackTrace, getLocalizedMessage, getMessage, printStackTrace, printStackTrace, printStackTrace`

Inherited from *java.lang.Object*
`clone, equals, finalize, getClass, hashCode, notify, notifyall, wait, wait, wait`

Fields

Inherited from *javax.naming.*NamingException:
`remainingName, resolvedName, resolvedObj, rootException`

Class javax.naming.LimitExceededException

`public class LimitExceededException`
`extends` *javax.naming.*NamingException

Thrown when exceeding a user or system specified limit causes a method to terminate.

Constructor Method

public	`LimitExceededException`	()
public	`LimitExceededException`	(*java.lang.String* explanation)

Methods

Inherited from *javax.naming*.NamingException
```
appendRemainingComponent, appendRemainingName, getExplanation,
getRemainingName, getResolvedName,getResolvedObj, getRootCause,
setRemainingName, setResolvedName, setResolvedObj, setRootCause, toString,
toString
```

Inherited from javax.lang.Throwable
```
fillInStackTrace, getLocalizedMessage, getMessage, printStackTrace,
printStackTrace, printStackTrace
```

Inherited from *java.lang.Object*
```
clone, equals, finalize, getClass, hashCode, notify, notifyall, wait, wait, wait
```

Fields

Inherited from *javax.naming*.NamingException:
```
remainingName, resolvedName, resolvedObj, rootException
```

Class javax.naming.LinkException

```
public class LinkLoopException
extends javax.naming.NamingException
```

LinkException carries information about problems encountered resolving links.

Constructor Method

| public | LinkException | () |
| public | LinkException | (*java.lang.String* explanation) |

Methods

public *java.lang.String*	getLinkExplanation	()
public *javax.naming*.**Name**	getLinkRemainingName	()
public *javax.naming*.**Name**	getLinkResolvedName	()
public *java.lang.Object*	getLinkResolvedObj	()
public void	setLinkExplanation	(*java.lang.String* msg)
public void	setLinkRemainingName	(*javax.naming*.**Name** name)
public void	setLinkResolvedName	(*javax.naming*.**Name** name)
public void	setLinkResolvedObj	(*java.lang.Object* obj)
public *java.lang.String*	toString	()
public *java.lang.String*	toString	(boolean detail)

Inherited from *javax.naming*.NamingException
```
appendRemainingComponent, appendRemainingName, getExplanation,
getRemainingName, getResolvedName,getResolvedObj, getRootCause,
setRemainingName, setResolvedName, setResolvedObj, setRootCause
```

Inherited from *javax.lang.Throwable*
```
fillInStackTrace, getLocalizedMessage, getMessage, printStackTrace,
printStackTrace, printStackTrace
```

Inherited from *java.lang.Object*
```
clone, equals, finalize, getClass, hashCode, notify, notifyall, wait, wait, wait
```

Fields

protected *java.lang.String*	`linkExplanation`
protected *javax.naming.*Name	`linkRemainingName`
protected *javax.naming.*Name	`linkResolvedName`
protected *java.lang.Object*	`linkResolvedObj`

Inherited from *javax.naming.*NamingException:
`remainingName, resolvedName, resolvedObj, rootException`

Class javax.naming.LinkLoopException

```
public class LinkLoopException
extends javax.naming.LinkException
```

Thrown if while resolving a link, a loop is formed or the number of links used exceeds an implementation-defined limit.

Constructor Method

public	`LinkLoopException`	()
public	`LinkLoopException`	(*java.lang.String* explanation)

Methods

Inherited from *javax.naming.*LinkException
`getLinkExplanation, getLinkRemainingName, getLinkResolvedName, getLinkResolvedObj, setLinkExplanation, setLinkRemainingName, setLinkResolvedName, setLinkResolvedObj, toString, toString`

Inherited from *javax.naming.*NamingException
`appendRemainingComponent, appendRemainingName, getExplanation, getRemainingName, getResolvedName, getResolvedObj, getRootCause, setRemainingName, setResolvedName, setResolvedObj, setRootCause`

Inherited from *java.lang.Throwable*
`fillInStackTrace, getLocalizedMessage, getMessage, printStackTrace, printStackTrace, printStackTrace`

Inherited from *java.lang.Object*
`clone, equals, finalize, getClass, hashCode, notify, notifyall, wait, wait, wait`

Fields

Inherited from *javax.naming.*LinkException:
`linkExplanation, linkRemainingName, linkResolvedName, linkResolvedObj`

Inherited from *javax.naming.*NamingException:
`remainingName, resolvedName, resolvedObj, rootException`

Class *javax.naming.*MalformedLinkException

```
public class MalformedLinkException
extends javax.naming.LinkException
```

Thrown when attempting to resolve or construct a link results in a malformed link being encountered.

Constructor Method

public	`MalformedLinkException`	()
public	`MalformedLinkException`	(*java.lang.String* explanation)

Methods

Inherited from *javax.naming.*LinkException
`getLinkExplanation, getLinkRemainingName, getLinkResolvedName, getLinkResolvedObj, setLinkExplanation, setLinkRemainingName, setLinkResolvedName, setLinkResolvedObj, toString, toString`

Inherited from *javax.naming.*NamingException
`appendRemainingComponent, appendRemainingName, getExplanation, getRemainingName, getResolvedName, getResolvedObj, getRootCause, setRemainingName, setResolvedName, setResolvedObj, setRootCause`

Inherited from *javax.lang.Throwable*
`fillInStackTrace, getLocalizedMessage, getMessage, printStackTrace, printStackTrace, printStackTrace`

Inherited from *java.lang.Object*
`clone, equals, finalize, getClass, hashCode, notify, notifyall, wait, wait, wait`

Fields

Inherited from *javax.naming.*LinkException:
`linkExplanation, linkRemainingName, linkResolvedName, linkResolvedObj`

Inherited from *javax.naming.*NamingException:
`remainingName, resolvedName, resolvedObj, rootException`

Class *javax.naming.*NameAlreadyBoundException

```
public class NameAlreadyBoundException
extends javax.naming.NamingException
```

Thrown when an attempt is made to add a binding when the name is already bound to another object.

Constructor Method

public	`NameAlreadyBoundException`	()
public	`NameAlreadyBoundException`	(*java.lang.String* explanation)

Methods

Inherited from *javax.naming.*NamingException
`appendRemainingComponent, appendRemainingName, getExplanation, getRemainingName, getResolvedName, getResolvedObj, getRootCause, setRemainingName, setResolvedName, setResolvedObj, setRootCause, toString, toString`

Inherited from javax.lang.Throwable
`fillInStackTrace, getLocalizedMessage, getMessage, printStackTrace, printStackTrace, printStackTrace`

Inherited from *java.lang.Object*
`clone, equals, finalize, getClass, hashCode, notify, notifyall, wait, wait, wait`

Fields

Inherited from *javax.naming.*NamingException:
`remainingName, resolvedName, resolvedObj, rootException`

Class javax.naming.NameNotFoundException

```
public class NameNotFoundException
extends javax.naming.NamingException
```

Thrown when an attempt is made to resolve a component of a name which is not bound.

Constructor Method

public	`NameNotFoundException`	()	
public	`NameNotFoundException`	*(java.lang.String* explanation)	

Methods

Inherited from *javax.naming.*NamingException
`appendRemainingComponent, appendRemainingName, getExplanation, getRemainingName, getResolvedName, getResolvedObj, getRootCause, setRemainingName, setResolvedName, setResolvedObj, setRootCause, toString, toString`

Inherited from javax.lang.Throwable
`fillInStackTrace, getLocalizedMessage, getMessage, printStackTrace, printStackTrace, printStackTrace`

Inherited from *java.lang.Object*
`clone, equals, finalize, getClass, hashCode, notify, notifyall, wait, wait, wait`

Fields

Inherited from *javax.naming.*NamingException:
`remainingName, resolvedName, resolvedObj, rootException`

Class javax.naming.NamingException

```
public class NamingException
extends java.lang.Exception
```

Stores information about the failure of operations in *javax.naming.*Context and *javax.naming.*DirContext.

Constructor Method

public	`NamingException`	*(java.lang.String* explanation)
public	`NamingException`	()

973

Methods

public void	`appendRemainingComponent`	(*java.lang.String* name)
public void	`appendRemainingName`	(*javax.naming*.Name name)
public *java.lang.String*	`getExplanation`	()
public *javax.naming*.**Name**	`getRemainingName`	()
public *javax.naming*.**Name**	`getResolvedName`	()
public *java.lang.Object*	`getResolvedObj`	()
public *java.lang.Throwable*	`getRootCause`	()
public void	`setRemainingName`	(*javax.naming*.Name name)
public void	`setResolvedName`	(*javax.naming*.Name name)
public void	`setResolvedObj`	(*java.lang.Object* obj)
public void	`setRootCause`	(*java.lang.Throwable* e)
public *java.lang.String*	`toString`	()
public *java.lang.String*	`toString`	(boolean detail)

Inherited from *javax.lang.Throwable*
fillInStackTrace, getLocalizedMessage, getMessage, printStackTrace, printStackTrace, printStackTrace

Inherited from *java.lang.Object*
`clone, equals, finalize, getClass, hashCode, notify, notifyall, wait, wait, wait`

Fields

protected *javax.naming*.Name	`remainingName`
protected *javax.naming*.Name	resolvedName
protected *java.lang.Object*	resolvedObj
protected *java.lang.Throwable*	rootException

Class javax.naming.NamingSecurityException

```
public class NamingSecurityException
extends javax.naming.NamingException
```

NamingSecurityException captures details of security related exceptions thrown by operations in the *javax.naming*.Context and *javax.naming*.DirContext interfaces.

Constructor Method

public	`NamingSecurityException`	()
public	`NamingSecurityException`	(*java.lang.String* explanation)

Methods

Inherited from *javax.naming*.NamingException
`appendRemainingComponent, appendRemainingName, getExplanation, getRemainingName, getResolvedName, getResolvedObj, getRootCause, setRemainingName, setResolvedName, setResolvedObj, setRootCause, toString, toString`

Inherited from javax.lang.Throwable
`fillInStackTrace, getLocalizedMessage, getMessage, printStackTrace, printStackTrace, printStackTrace`

Inherited from *java.lang.Object*
`clone, equals, finalize, getClass, hashCode, notify, notifyall, wait, wait, wait`

Fields

Inherited from *javax.naming*.NamingException:
`remainingName, resolvedName, resolvedObj, rootException`

Class javax.naming.NoInitialContextException

```
public class NoInitialContextException
extends javax.naming.NamingException
```

Thrown when no initial context implementation can be created.

Constructor Method

| public | `NoInitialContextException` | (*java.lang.String* explanation) |
| public | `NoInitialContextException` | () |

Methods

Inherited from *javax.naming*.NamingException
`appendRemainingComponent, appendRemainingName, getExplanation, getRemainingName, getResolvedName, getResolvedObj, getRootCause, setRemainingName, setResolvedName, setResolvedObj, setRootCause, toString, toString`

Inherited from javax.lang.Throwable
`fillInStackTrace, getLocalizedMessage, getMessage, printStackTrace, printStackTrace, printStackTrace`

Inherited from *java.lang.Object*
`clone, equals, finalize, getClass, hashCode, notify, notifyall, wait, wait, wait`

Fields

Inherited from *javax.naming*.NamingException:
`remainingName, resolvedName, resolvedObj, rootException`

Class javax.naming.NoPermissionException

```
public class NoPermissionException
extends javax.naming.NamingSecurityException
```

Thrown when a client attempts an operation it does not have permission to perform.

Constructor Method

| public | `NoPermissionException` | (*java.lang.String* explanation) |
| public | `NoPermissionException` | () |

Methods

Inherited from *javax.naming*.NamingException
`appendRemainingComponent, appendRemainingName, getExplanation, getRemainingName, getResolvedName, getResolvedObj, getRootCause, setRemainingName, setResolvedName, setResolvedObj, setRootCause, toString, toString`

Inherited from javax.lang.Throwable
`fillInStackTrace, getLocalizedMessage, getMessage, printStackTrace, printStackTrace, printStackTrace`

Inherited from *java.lang.Object*
`clone, equals, finalize, getClass, hashCode, notify, notifyall, wait, wait, wait`

Fields

Inherited from *javax.naming.*NamingException:
`remainingName, resolvedName, resolvedObj, rootException`

Class javax.naming.NotContextException

```
public class NotContextException
extends javax.naming.NamingException
```

Thrown when a naming operation requires a context, but the resolved object is not a context.

Constructor Method

public	`NotContextException`	(*java.lang.String* explanation)
public	`NotContextException`	()

Methods

Inherited from *javax.naming.*NamingException
`appendRemainingComponent, appendRemainingName, getExplanation, getRemainingName, getResolvedName, getResolvedObj, getRootCause, setRemainingName, setResolvedName, setResolvedObj, setRootCause, toString, toString`

Inherited from javax.lang.Throwable
`fillInStackTrace, getLocalizedMessage, getMessage, printStackTrace, printStackTrace, printStackTrace`

Inherited from *java.lang.Object*
`clone, equals, finalize, getClass, hashCode, notify, notifyall, wait, wait, wait`

Fields

Inherited from *javax.naming.*NamingException:
`remainingName, resolvedName, resolvedObj, rootException`

Class javax.naming.OperationNotSupportedException

```
public class OperationNotSupportedException
extends javax.naming.NamingException
```

Thrown when an operation is invoked which the context implementation does not support.

Constructor Method

public	`OperationNotSupportedException`	()
public	`OperationNotSupportedException`	(*java.lang.String* explanation)

Methods

Inherited from *javax.naming*.NamingException
```
appendRemainingComponent, appendRemainingName, getExplanation,
getRemainingName, getResolvedName,getResolvedObj, getRootCause,
setRemainingName, setResolvedName, setResolvedObj, setRootCause, toString,
toString
```

Inherited from javax.lang.Throwable
```
fillInStackTrace, getLocalizedMessage, getMessage, printStackTrace,
printStackTrace, printStackTrace
```

Inherited from *java.lang.Object*
```
clone, equals, finalize, getClass, hashCode, notify, notifyall, wait, wait, wait
```

Fields

Inherited from *javax.naming*.NamingException:
```
remainingName, resolvedName, resolvedObj, rootException
```

Class javax.naming. *PartialResultException*

```
public class PartialResultException
extends javax.naming.NamingException
```

Thrown when an operation cannot be completed, and only partial data is returned.

Constructor Method

| public | PartialResultException | () |
| public | PartialResultException | (*java.lang.String* explanation) |

Methods

Inherited from *javax.naming*.NamingException
```
appendRemainingComponent, appendRemainingName, getExplanation,
getRemainingName, getResolvedName,getResolvedObj, getRootCause,
setRemainingName, setResolvedName, setResolvedObj, setRootCause, toString,
toString
```

Inherited from javax.lang.Throwable
```
fillInStackTrace, getLocalizedMessage, getMessage, printStackTrace,
printStackTrace, printStackTrace
```

Inherited from *java.lang.Object*
```
clone, equals, finalize, getClass, hashCode, notify, notifyall, wait, wait, wait
```

Fields

Inherited from *javax.naming*.NamingException:
```
remainingName, resolvedName, resolvedObj, rootException
```

Class *javax.naming.ReferralException*

```
public abstract class ReferralException
extends javax.naming.NamingException
```

ReferralException represents an exception occuring in response to a referral.

Constructor Method

public	`ReferralException`	()
public	`ReferralException`	(*java.lang.String* explanation)

Methods

public abstract Context	`getReferralContext`	()
public abstract *java.lang.Object*	`getReferralInfo`	()
public abstract boolean	`skipReferral`	()

Inherited from *javax.naming.*NamingException
`appendRemainingComponent, appendRemainingName, getExplanation, getRemainingName, getResolvedName,getResolvedObj, getRootCause, setRemainingName, setResolvedName, setResolvedObj, setRootCause, toString, toString`

Inherited from *javax.lang.Throwable*
fillInStackTrace, getLocalizedMessage, getMessage, printStackTrace, printStackTrace, printStackTrace

Inherited from *java.lang.Object*
`clone, equals, finalize, getClass, hashCode, notify, notifyall, wait, wait, wait`

Fields

Inherited from *javax.naming.*NamingException:
`remainingName, resolvedName, resolvedObj, rootException`

Class *javax.naming.ServiceUnavailableException*

```
public class ServiceUnavailableException
extends javax.naming.NamingException
```

Thrown when an attempt is made to access a directory or naming service which is unavailable.

Constructor Method

public	`ServiceUnavailableException`	()
public	`ServiceUnavailableException`	(*java.lang.String* explanation)

Methods

Inherited from *javax.naming.*NamingException
`appendRemainingComponent, appendRemainingName, getExplanation, getRemainingName, getResolvedName,getResolvedObj, getRootCause, setRemainingName, setResolvedName, setResolvedObj, setRootCause, toString, toString`

Inherited from javax.lang.Throwable
`fillInStackTrace, getLocalizedMessage, getMessage, printStackTrace, printStackTrace, printStackTrace`

Inherited from *java.lang.Object*
`clone, equals, finalize, getClass, hashCode, notify, notifyall, wait, wait, wait`

Fields

Inherited from *javax.naming.*NamingException:
`remainingName, resolvedName, resolvedObj, rootException`

Class javax.naming.*SizeLimitExceededException*

```
public class SizeLimitExceededException
extends javax.naming.LimitExceededException
```

Thrown when the size of a result exceeds a limit.

Constructor Method

public	`SizeLimitExceededException`	()
public	`SizeLimitExceededException`	(*java.lang.String* explanation)

Methods

Inherited from *javax.naming.*NamingException
`appendRemainingComponent, appendRemainingName, getExplanation, getRemainingName, getResolvedName, getResolvedObj, getRootCause, setRemainingName, setResolvedName, setResolvedObj, setRootCause, toString, toString`

Inherited from javax.lang.Throwable
`fillInStackTrace, getLocalizedMessage, getMessage, printStackTrace, printStackTrace, printStackTrace`

Inherited from *java.lang.Object*
`clone, equals, finalize, getClass, hashCode, notify, notifyall, wait, wait, wait`

Fields

Inherited from *javax.naming.*NamingException:
`remainingName, resolvedName, resolvedObj, rootException`

Class javax.naming. *TimeLimitExceededException*

```
public class TimeLimitExceededException
extends javax.naming.LimitExceededException
```

Thrown when a method continues executing past a pre-defined time limit.

Constructor Method

public	`TimeLimitExceededException`	()
public	`TimeLimitExceededException`	(*java.lang.String* explanation)

Methods

Inherited from *javax.naming.*NamingException
```
appendRemainingComponent, appendRemainingName, getExplanation,
getRemainingName, getResolvedName,getResolvedObj, getRootCause,
setRemainingName, setResolvedName, setResolvedObj, setRootCause, toString,
toString
```

Inherited from javax.lang.Throwable
```
fillInStackTrace, getLocalizedMessage, getMessage, printStackTrace,
printStackTrace, printStackTrace
```

Inherited from *java.lang.Object*
```
clone, equals, finalize, getClass, hashCode, notify, notifyall, wait, wait, wait
```

Fields

Inherited from *javax.naming.*NamingException:
```
remainingName, resolvedName, resolvedObj, rootException
```

Package javax.naming.directory

Interfaces

public abstract interface	**Attribute**	extends	*java.lang.Cloneable, java.io.Serializable*
public abstract interface	**Attributes**	extends	*java.lang.Cloneable, java.io.Serializable*
public abstract interface	**DirContext**	extends	*javax.naming.***Context**

Classes

public class	**BasicAttribute**	implements	*javax.naming.directory.*Attribute
public class	**BasicAttributes**	implements	*javax.naming.directory.*Attributes
public class	**InitialDirContext**	implements	
	*javax.naming.directory.*DirContext		
		extends	*javax.naming.*InitialContext
public class	**ModificationItem**	implements	*java.io.Serializable*
public class	**SearchControls**	implements	*java.io.Serializable*
public class	**SearchResult**	extends	*javax.naming.*Binding

Exceptions

public class	AttributeInUseException	extends	*javax.naming.*NamingException
public class	**AttributeModificationException**	extends	*javax.naming.*NamingException
public class	InvalidAttributeIdentifierException	extends	*javax.naming.*NamingException
public class	**InvalidAttributesException**	extends	*javax.naming.*NamingException
public class	**InvalidAttributeValueException**	extends	*javax.naming.*NamingException
public class	**InvalidSearchControlsException**	extends	*javax.naming.*NamingException
public class	**InvalidSearchFilterException**	extends	*javax.naming.*NamingException
public class	**NoSuchAttributeException**	extends	*javax.naming.*NamingException
public class	**SchemaViolationException**	extends	*javax.naming.*NamingException

Interface javax.naming.directory.Attribute

```
public abstract interface Attribute
```

extends *java.lang.Cloneable, java.io.Serializable*

Is implemented by *javax.naming.directory.*BasicAttribute, Represents an attribute associated with a named object.

Methods

public boolean	`add`	(*java.lang.Object* attrVal)
public void	`clear`	()
public *java.lang.Object*	`clone`	()
public boolean	`contains`	(*java.lang.Object* attrVal)
public *java.lang.Object*	`get`	()
	throws	*javax.naming.*NamingException
public NamingEnumeration	`getAll`	()
	throws	*javax.naming.*NamingException
public DirContext	`getAttributeDefinition`	()
	throws	*javax.naming.*NamingException
public DirContext	`getAttributeSyntaxDefinition`	
		()
	throws	*javax.naming.*NamingException
public *java.lang.String*	`getID`	()
public boolean	`remove`	(*java.lang.Object* attrVal)
public int	`size`	()

Fields

Inherited from *java.io.Serializable*:
`serialVersionUID`

Interface javax.naming.directory.Attributes

```
public abstract interface Attributes
```

extends *java.lang.Cloneable, java.io.Serializable*

Is implemented by *javax.naming.directory.*BasicAttributes. Represents a collection of attributes.

Methods

public *java.lang.Object*	`clone`	()
public Attribute	`get`	(*java.lang.String* attrID)
public NamingEnumeration	`getAll`	()
public NamingEnumeration	`getIDs`	()
public boolean	`isCaseIgnored`	()
public Attribute	`put`	(*java.lang.String* attrID, *java.lang.Object* val)
public Attribute	`put`	(*javax.naming.directory.*Attribute attr)
public Attribute	`remove`	(*java.lang.String* attrID)
public int	`size`	()

Field Constants

Inherited from *java.io.Serializable:*
`serialVersionUID`

Interface *javax.naming.directory.DirContext*

```
public abstract interface DirContext
```

extends *javax.naming.*Context

Is implemented by *javax.naming.*InitialDirContext. Represents a directory service and its basic methods.

Methods

public void	**bind**	(*javax.naming.*Name name, *java.lang.Object* obj)
	throws	*javax.naming.*NamingException
public void	**bind**	(*java.lang.String* name, *java.lang.Object* obj, *javax.naming.directory.*Attributes attrs)
	throws	*javax.naming.*NamingException
public DirContext	**createSubcontext**	(*javax.naming.*Name name, *javax.naming.directory.*Attributes attrs)
	throws	*javax.naming.*NamingException
public DirContext	**createSubcontext**	(*java.lang.String* name, *javax.naming.directory.*Attributes attrs)
	throws	*javax.naming.*NamingException
public Attributes	**getAttributes**	(*javax.naming.*Name name)
	throws	*javax.naming.*NamingException
public Attributes	**getAttributes**	(*java.lang.String* name)
	throws	*javax.naming.*NamingException
public Attributes	**getAttributes**	(*javax.naming.*Name name, *java.lang.String*[] attrIds)
	throws	*javax.naming.*NamingException
public Attributes	**getAttributes**	(*java.lang.String* name, *java.lang.String*[] attrIds)
	throws	*javax.naming.*NamingException
public DirContext	**getSchema**	(*java.lang.String* name)
	throws	*javax.naming.*NamingException
public DirContext	**getSchema**	(*javax.naming.*Name name)
	throws	*javax.naming.*NamingException
public DirContext	**getSchemaClassDefinition**	(*java.lang.String* name)
	throws	*javax.naming.*NamingException
public DirContext	**getSchemaClassDefinition**	(*javax.naming.*Name name)
	throws	*javax.naming.*NamingException
public void	**modifyAttributes**	(*java.lang.String* name, int mod_op, *javax.naming.directory.*Attributes attrs)
	throws	*javax.naming.*NamingException
public void	**modifyAttributes**	(*javax.naming.*Name name, int mod_op, *javax.naming.directory.*Attributes attrs)
	throws	*javax.naming.*NamingException
public void	**modifyAttributes**	(*javax.naming.*Name name, *javax.naming.directory.*ModificationItem[] mods)
	throws	*javax.naming.*NamingException
public void	**modifyAttributes**	(*java.lang.String* name, *javax.naming.directory.*ModificationItem[] mods)
	throws	*javax.naming.*NamingException
public void	**rebind**	(*java.lang.String* name, *java.lang.Object* obj, *javax.naming.directory.*Attributes attrs)
	throws	*javax.naming.*NamingException
public void	**rebind**	(*javax.naming.*Name name, *java.lang.Object* obj, *javax.naming.directory.*Attributes attrs)
	throws	*javax.naming.*NamingException

public NamingEnumeration	**search**	(*javax.naming*.Name name,
		javax.naming.directory.Attributes matchingAttributes,
		java.lang.String[] attributesToReturn)
	throws	*javax.naming*.NamingException
public NamingEnumeration	**search**	(*java.lang.String* name,
		javax.naming.directory.Attributes matchingAttributes,
		java.lang.String[] attributesToReturn)
	throws	*javax.naming*.NamingException
public NamingEnumeration	**search**	(*javax.naming*.Name name,
		javax.naming.directory.Attributes matchingAttributes)
	throws	*javax.naming*.NamingException
public NamingEnumeration	**search**	(*java.lang.String* name,
		javax.naming.directory.Attributes matchingAttributes)
	throws	*javax.naming*.NamingException
public NamingEnumeration	**search**	(*javax.naming*.Name name,
		java.lang.String filter
		javax.naming.directory.SearchControls cons)
	throws	*javax.naming*.NamingException
public NamingEnumeration	**search**	(*java.lang.String* name,
		java.lang.String filter
		javax.naming.directory.SearchControls cons)
	throws	*javax.naming*.NamingException
public NamingEnumeration	**search**	(*javax.naming*.Name name,
		javax.naming.directory.Attributes matchingAttributes,
		java.lang.String filterExpr,
		java.lang.Object[] filterArgs,
		javax.naming.directory.SearchControls cons)
	throws	*javax.naming*.NamingException
public NamingEnumeration	**search**	(*java.lang.String* name,
		javax.naming.directory.Attributes matchingAttributes,
		java.lang.String filterExpr,
		java.lang.Object[] filterArgs,
		javax.naming.directory.SearchControls cons)
	throws	*javax.naming*.NamingException

Field Constants

public static final int	**ADD_ATTRIBUTE**
public static final int	**REMOVE_ATTRIBUTE**
public static final int	**REPLACE_ATTRIBUTE**

Inherited from *javax.naming*.Context:

AUTHORITATIVE, BATCHSIZE, DNS_URL, INTIAL_CONTEXT_FACTORY, LANGUAGE, OBJECT_FACTORIES, PROVIDER_URL, REFERRAL, SECURITY_AUTHENTICATION, SECURITY_CREDENTIALS, SECURITY_PRINCIPAL, SECURITY_PROTOCOL, URL_PKG_PREFIXES

Class javax.naming.directory.BasicAttribute

public class BasicAttribute

implements *javax.naming.directory*.Attribute

Represents simple attributes (name/value pairs) and the methods associated with them.

Field Constants

protected *java.lang.String*	**attrID**
protected transient *java.util.Vector*	**values**

Constructor Method

public	BasicAttribute	(*java.lang.String* id)
public	BasicAttribute	(*java.lang.String* id, *java.lang.Object* value)

Methods

public boolean	add	(*java.lang.Object* attrVal).
public void	clear	()
public *java.lang.Object*	clone	()
public boolean	contains	(*java.lang.Object* attrVal)
public boolean	equals	(*java.lang.Object* obj)
public *java.lang.Object*	get	()
	throws	*javax.naming*.NamingException
public NamingEnumeration	getAll	()
	throws	*javax.naming*.NamingException
public DirContext	getAttributeDefinition	()
	throws	*javax.naming*.NamingException
public DirContext	getAttributeSyntaxDefinition	()
	throws	*javax.naming*.NamingException
public *java.lang.String*	getID	()
public int	hashCode	()
public boolean	remove	(*java.lang.Object* attrVal).
public int	size	()
public *java.lang.String*	toString	()

Inherited from *java.lang.Object*:
`finalize, getClass, notify, notifyAll, wait, wait, wait`

Class javax.naming.directory.BasicAttributes

```
public class BasicAttributes
```

implements *javax.naming.directory*.Attributes

A simple implementation of a collection of attributes.

Constructor Method

public	BasicAttributes	()
public	BasicAttributes	(boolean ignoreCase)
public	BasicAttributes	(*java.lang.String* attrID, *java.lang.Object* val)
public	BasicAttributes	(*java.lang.String* attrID, *java.lang.Object* val, boolean ignoreCase)

Methods

public *java.lang.Object*	clone	()
public Attribute	get	(*java.lang.String* attrID)
public NamingEnumeration	getAll	()
public NamingEnumeration	getIDs	()
public boolean	isCaseIgnored	()
public Attribute	put	(*java.lang.String* attrID, *java.lang.Object* val)
public Attribute	put	(*javax.naming.directory*.Attribute attr)
public Attribute	remove	(*java.lang.String* attrID)
public int	size	()
public *java.lang.String*	toString	()

Inherited from *java.lang.Object*
`equals, finalize, getClass, hashCode, notify, notifyAll, wait, wait, wait`

Class javax.naming.directory.InitialDirContext

```
public class InitialDirContext
```

extends *javax.naming.*InitialContext
implements *javax.naming.directory.*DirContext

Represents the initial context (naming system) for directory operations.

Constructor Method

public	**InitialDirContext**	()
	throws	*javax.naming.*NamingException
public	**InitialDirContext**	(*java.util.Hashtable* environment)
	throws	*javax.naming.*NamingException

Methods

public void	**bind**	(*javax.naming.*Name name, *java.lang.Object* obj, *javax.naming.directory.*Attributes attrs)
	throws	*javax.naming.*NamingException
public void	**bind**	(*java.lang.String* name, *java.lang.Object* obj, *javax.naming.directory.*Attributes attrs)
	throws	*javax.naming.*NamingException
public DirContext	**createSubcontext**	(*javax.naming.*Name name, *javax.naming.directory.*Attributes attrs)
	throws	*javax.naming.*NamingException
public Context	**createSubcontext**	(*java.lang.String* name, *javax.naming.directory.*Attributes attrs)
	throws	*javax.naming.*NamingException
public Attributes	**getAttributes**	(*java.lang.String* name, *java.lang.String*[] attrIds)
	throws	*javax.naming.*NamingException
public Attributes	**getAttributes**	(*javax.naming.*Name name)
	throws	*javax.naming.*NamingException
public Attributes	**getAttributes**	(*java.lang.String* name)
	throws	*javax.naming.*NamingException
public Attributes	**getAttributes**	(*javax.naming.*Name name, *java.lang.String*[] attrIds)
	throws	*javax.naming.*NamingException
public DirContext	**getSchema**	(*javax.naming.*Name name)
	throws	*javax.naming.*NamingException
public DirContext	**getSchema**	(*java.lang.String* name)
	throws	*javax.naming.*NamingException
public DirContext	**getSchemaClassDefinition**	(*javax.naming.*Name name)
	throws	*javax.naming.*NamingException
public DirContext	**getSchemaClassDefinition**	(*java.lang.String* name)
	throws	*javax.naming.*NamingException
public void	**modifyAttributes**	(*java.lang.String* name, int mod_op, *javax.naming.directory.*Attributes attrs)
	throws	*javax.naming.*NamingException
public void	**modifyAttributes**	(*javax.naming.*Name name, int mod_op, *javax.naming.directory.*Attributes attrs)
	throws	*javax.naming.*NamingException
public void	**modifyAttributes**	(*java.lang.String* name, *javax.naming.directory.*ModificationItem[] mods)
	throws	*javax.naming.*NamingException

985

public void	**modifyAttributes**	(*javax.naming*.Name name *javax.naming.directory*.ModificationItem[] mods)
	throws	*javax.naming*.NamingException
public void	**rebind**	(*java.lang.String* name, *java.lang.Object* obj, *javax.naming.directory*.Attributes attrs)
	throws	*javax.naming*.NamingException
public void	**rebind**	(*javax.naming*.Name name, *java.lang.Object* obj, *javax.naming.directory*.Attributes attrs)
	throws	*javax.naming*.NamingException
public NamingEnumeration	**search**	(*java.lang.String* name, *javax.naming.directory*.Attributes matchingAttributes)
	throws	*javax.naming*.NamingException
public NamingEnumeration	**search**	(*javax.naming*.Name name, *javax.naming.directory*.Attributes matchingAttributes)
	throws	*javax.naming*.NamingException
public NamingEnumeration	**search**	(*java.lang.String* name, *javax.naming.directory*.Attributes matchingAttributes, *java.lang.String*[] attributesToReturn)
	throws	*javax.naming*.NamingException
public NamingEnumeration	**search**	(*javax.naming*.Name name, *javax.naming.directory*.Attributes matchingAttributes, *java.lang.String*[] attributesToReturn)
	throws	*javax.naming*.NamingException
public NamingEnumeration	**search**	(*java.lang.String* name, *java.lang.String* filter, *javax.naming.directory*.SearchControls cons)
	throws	*javax.naming*.NamingException
public NamingEnumeration	**search**	(*javax.naming*.Name name, *java.lang.String* filter, *javax.naming.directory*.SearchControls cons)
	throws	*javax.naming*.NamingException
public NamingEnumeration	**search**	(*java.lang.String* name, *java.lang.String* filterExpr, *java.lang.Object*[] filterArgs, *javax.naming.directory*.SearchControls cons)
	throws	*javax.naming*.NamingException
public NamingEnumeration	**search**	(*javax.naming*.Name name, *java.lang.String* filterExpr, *java.lang.Object*[] filterArgs, *javax.naming.directory*.SearchControls cons)
	throws	*javax.naming*.NamingException

Inherited from *javax.naming*.InitialContext:
addToEnvironment, bind, bind, close, composeName, composeName, createSubcontext, createSubcontext, destroySubcontext, destroySubcontext, getDefaultInitCtx, getEnvironment, getNameParser, getNameParser, getURLOrDefaultInitCtx, getURLOrDefaultInitCtx, list, list, listBindings, listBindings, lookup, lookup, lookupLink, lookupLink, rebind, rebind, removeFromEnvironment, rename, rename, unbind, unbind

Inherited from *java.lang.Object*
clone, equals, finalize, getClass, hashCode, notify, notifyall, toString, wait, wait, wait

Fields

Inherited from *javax.naming*.InitialContext:
defaultInitCtx, gotDefault, myProps

Class *javax.naming.directory.ModificationItem*

```
public class ModificationItem
```

implements *java.io.Serializable*

Represents a modification to an item, holding the type of modification and the target object.

Constructor Method

public	`ModificationItem`	(int mod_op, *javax.naming.directory.*Attribute attr)

Methods

public Attribute	`getAttribute`	()
public int	`getModificationOp`	()
public *java.lang.String*	`toString`	()

Inherited from *java.lang.Object*

clone, equals, finalize, getClass, hashCode, notify, notifyall, toString, wait, wait, wait

Class *javax.naming.directory.SearchControls*

```
public class SearchControls
```

implements *java.io.Serializable*

Represents the variants in a search, namely its scope and the result format.

Constructor Method

public	`SearchControls`	()
public	`SearchControls`	(int scope, long countlim, int timelim, *java.lang.String*[] attrs, boolean retobj, boolean deref)

Methods

public long	`getCountLimit`	()
public boolean	`getDerefLinkFlag`	()
public *java.lang.String*[]	`getReturningAttributes`	()
public boolean	`getReturningObjFlag`	()
public int	`getSearchScope`	()
public int	`getTimeLimit`	()
public void	`setCountLimit`	(long limit)
public void	`setDerefLinkFlag`	(boolean on)
public void	`setReturningAttributes`	(*java.lang.String[]* attrs)
public void	`setReturningObjFlag`	(boolean on)
public void	`setSearchScope`	(int scope)
public void	`setTimeLimit`	(int ms)

Inherited from *java.lang.Object*

clone, equals, finalize, getClass, hashCode, notify, notifyall, toString, wait, wait, wait

Fields

public static final int	`OBJECT_SCOPE`
public static final int	`ONELEVEL_SCOPE`
public static final int	`SUBTREE_SCOPE`

Class javax.naming.directory.SearchResult

```
public class SearchResult
```

extends *javax.naming*.Binding

Represents an object in a list of objects found to have matched a search.

Constructor Method

public	`SearchResult`	(*java.lang.String* name, *java.lang.Object* obj, *javax.naming.directory*.Attributes attrs)
public	`SearchResult`	(*java.lang.String* name, *java.lang.Object* obj, *javax.naming.directory*.Attributes attrs, boolean isRelative)
public	`SearchResult`	(*java.lang.String* name, *java.lang.String* className, *java.lang.Object* obj, *javax.naming.directory*.Attributes attrs)
public	`SearchResult`	(*java.lang.String* name, *java.lang.String* className, *java.lang.Object* obj, *javax.naming.directory*.Attributes attrs, boolean isRelative)

Methods

public Attributes	`getAttributes`	()
public void	`setAttributes`	(*javax.naming.directory*.Attributes attrs)
public *java.lang.String*	`toString`	()

Inherited from *javax.naming*.Binding
`getClassName, getObject, setObject`

Inherited from *javax.naming*.NameClassPair
`getName, isRelative, setClassName, setName, setRelative`

Inherited from *java.lang.Object*
`clone, equals, finalize, getClass, hashCode, notify, notifyall, wait, wait, wait`

Class javax.naming.directory.AttributeInUseException

```
public class AttributeInUseException
extends javax.naming.NamingException
```

Thrown when an attempt is made to add an attribute which is already present.

Constructor Method

public	`AttributeInUseException`	()
public	`AttributeInUseException`	(*java.lang.String* explanation)

Methods

Inherited from *javax.naming*.NamingException
appendRemainingComponent, appendRemainingName, getExplanation, getRemainingName, getResolvedName, getResolvedObj, getRootCause, setRemainingName, setResolvedName, setResolvedObj, setRootCause, toString, toString

Inherited from javax.lang.Throwable
fillInStackTrace, getLocalizedMessage, getMessage, printStackTrace, printStackTrace, printStackTrace

Inherited from *java.lang.Object*
clone, equals, finalize, getClass, hashCode, notify, notifyall, wait, wait, wait

Fields

Inherited from *javax.naming*.NamingException:
remainingName, resolvedName, resolvedObj, rootException

Class javax.naming. *AttributeModificationException*

```
public class AttributeModificationException
extends javax.naming.NamingException
```

Thrown when a method continues executing past a pre-defined time limit.

Constructor Method

public	**AttributeModificationException**	()
public	**AttributeModificationException**	(*java.lang.String* explanation)

Methods

public ModificationItem[]	**getUnexecutedModifications**	()
public void	**setUnexecutedModifications**	(*java.naming.directory*.ModificationItem[] e)
public *java.lang.String*	**toString**	()

Inherited from *javax.naming*.NamingException
appendRemainingComponent, appendRemainingName, getExplanation, getRemainingName, getResolvedName, getResolvedObj, getRootCause, setRemainingName, setResolvedName, setResolvedObj, setRootCause, toString

Inherited from *javax.lang.Throwable*
fillInStackTrace, getLocalizedMessage, getMessage, printStackTrace, printStackTrace, printStackTrace

Inherited from *java.lang.Object*
clone, equals, finalize, getClass, hashCode, notify, notifyall, wait, wait, wait

Fields

Inherited from *javax.naming*.NamingException:
remainingName, resolvedName, resolvedObj, rootException

Class javax.naming.directory.InvalidAttributeIdentifierException

```
public class InvalidAttributeIdentifierException
extends javax.naming.NamingException
```

Thrown when an attempt is made to create an attribute with an invalid name.

Constructor Method

```
public                    InvalidAttributeIdentifierException    ()
public                    InvalidAttributeIdentifierException    (java.lang.String explanation)
```

Methods

Inherited from *javax.naming.*NamingException
```
appendRemainingComponent, appendRemainingName, getExplanation,
getRemainingName, getResolvedName, getResolvedObj, getRootCause,
setRemainingName, setResolvedName, setResolvedObj, setRootCause, toString,
toString
```

Inherited from javax.lang.Throwable
```
fillInStackTrace, getLocalizedMessage, getMessage, printStackTrace,
printStackTrace, printStackTrace
```

Inherited from *java.lang.Object*
```
clone, equals, finalize, getClass, hashCode, notify, notifyall, wait, wait, wait
```

Fields

Inherited from *javax.naming.*NamingException:
```
remainingName, resolvedName, resolvedObj, rootException
```

Class javax.naming.directory.InvalidAttributesException

```
public class InvalidAttributesException
extends javax.naming.NamingException
```

Thrown when an attempt is made to alter a set of attributes that has been specified incorrectly.

Constructor Method

```
public                    InvalidAttributesException    ()
public                    InvalidAttributesException    (java.lang.String explanation)
```

Methods

Inherited from *javax.naming.*NamingException
```
appendRemainingComponent, appendRemainingName, getExplanation,
getRemainingName, getResolvedName, getResolvedObj, getRootCause,
setRemainingName, setResolvedName, setResolvedObj, setRootCause, toString,
toString
```

Inherited from javax.lang.Throwable
`fillInStackTrace, getLocalizedMessage, getMessage, printStackTrace, printStackTrace, printStackTrace`

Inherited from *java.lang.Object*
`clone, equals, finalize, getClass, hashCode, notify, notifyall, wait, wait, wait`

Fields

Inherited from *javax.naming.*NamingException:
`remainingName, resolvedName, resolvedObj, rootException`

Class javax.naming.directory.InvalidAttributeValueException

`public class InvalidAttributeValueException`
extends *javax.naming.*NamingException

Thrown when an attempt is made to give an attribute a value which conflicts with the range of values it may have. (Its schema)

Constructor Method

public	`InvalidAttributeValueException`	()
public	`InvalidAttributeValueException`	(*java.lang.String* explanation)

Methods

Inherited from *javax.naming.*NamingException
`appendRemainingComponent, appendRemainingName, getExplanation, getRemainingName, getResolvedName, getResolvedObj, getRootCause, setRemainingName, setResolvedName, setResolvedObj, setRootCause, toString, toString`

Inherited from javax.lang.Throwable
`fillInStackTrace, getLocalizedMessage, getMessage, printStackTrace, printStackTrace, printStackTrace`

Inherited from *java.lang.Object*
`clone, equals, finalize, getClass, hashCode, notify, notifyall, wait, wait, wait`

Fields

Inherited from *javax.naming.*NamingException:
`remainingName, resolvedName, resolvedObj, rootException`

Class javax.naming.directory.InvalidSearchControlsException

`public class InvalidSearchControlsException`
extends *javax.naming.*NamingException

Thrown when the control attributes for a search are incorrectly specified when the search is run.

Constructor Method

public	`InvalidSearchControlsException`	()
public	`InvalidSearchControlsException`	(*java.lang.String* explanation)

991

Methods

Inherited from *javax.naming*.NamingException
`appendRemainingComponent, appendRemainingName, getExplanation, getRemainingName, getResolvedName,getResolvedObj, getRootCause, setRemainingName, setResolvedName, setResolvedObj, setRootCause, toString, toString`

Inherited from javax.lang.Throwable
`fillInStackTrace, getLocalizedMessage, getMessage, printStackTrace, printStackTrace, printStackTrace`

Inherited from *java.lang.Object*
`clone, equals, finalize, getClass, hashCode, notify, notifyall, wait, wait, wait`

Fields

Inherited from *javax.naming*.NamingException:
`remainingName, resolvedName, resolvedObj, rootException`

Class javax.naming.directory.InvalidSearchFilterException

`public class InvalidSearchFilterException`
extends *javax.naming*.NamingException

Thrown when a search filter is incorrectly specified.

Constructor Method

public	`InvalidSearchFilterException`	()
public	`InvalidSearchFilterException`	(*java.lang.String* explanation)

Methods

Inherited from *javax.naming*.NamingException
`appendRemainingComponent, appendRemainingName, getExplanation, getRemainingName, getResolvedName,getResolvedObj, getRootCause, setRemainingName, setResolvedName, setResolvedObj, setRootCause, toString, toString`

Inherited from javax.lang.Throwable
`fillInStackTrace, getLocalizedMessage, getMessage, printStackTrace, printStackTrace, printStackTrace`

Inherited from *java.lang.Object*
`clone, equals, finalize, getClass, hashCode, notify, notifyall, wait, wait, wait`

Fields

Inherited from *javax.naming*.NamingException:
`remainingName, resolvedName, resolvedObj, rootException`

Class javax.naming.directory.NoSuchAttributeException

`public class NoSuchAttributeException`
extends *javax.naming*.NamingException

Thrown when trying to access an attribute that does not exist.

Constructor Method

```
public            NoSuchAttributeException         ()
public            NoSuchAttributeException         (java.lang.String explanation)
```

Methods

Inherited from *javax.naming*.NamingException
```
appendRemainingComponent, appendRemainingName, getExplanation,
getRemainingName, getResolvedName,getResolvedObj, getRootCause,
setRemainingName, setResolvedName, setResolvedObj, setRootCause, toString,
toString
```

Inherited from javax.lang.Throwable
```
fillInStackTrace, getLocalizedMessage, getMessage, printStackTrace,
printStackTrace, printStackTrace
```

Inherited from *java.lang.Object*
```
clone, equals, finalize, getClass, hashCode, notify, notifyall, wait, wait, wait
```

Fields

Inherited from *javax.naming*.NamingException:
```
remainingName, resolvedName, resolvedObj, rootException
```

Class javax.naming.directory.SchemaViolationException

```
public class SchemaViolationException
extends javax.naming.NamingException
```

Thrown when a method being called violates the current schema.

Constructor Method

```
public            SchemaViolationException          ()
public            SchemaViolationException          (java.lang.String explanation)
```

Methods

Inherited from *javax.naming*.NamingException
```
appendRemainingComponent, appendRemainingName, getExplanation,
getRemainingName, getResolvedName,getResolvedObj, getRootCause,
setRemainingName, setResolvedName, setResolvedObj, setRootCause, toString,
toString
```

Inherited from javax.lang.Throwable
```
fillInStackTrace, getLocalizedMessage, getMessage, printStackTrace,
printStackTrace, printStackTrace
```

Inherited from *java.lang.Object*
```
clone, equals, finalize, getClass, hashCode, notify, notifyall, wait, wait, wait
```

Fields

Inherited from *javax.naming*.NamingException:
```
remainingName, resolvedName, resolvedObj, rootException
```

Core JavaMail / JAF API Reference

Key

Within this API Reference, the following conventions are used:

> ➤ Interface, Class and Exception names within the APIs listed are all written in **bold**.
> ➤ Interface, Class and Exception names not within the APIs listed are all written in *italics*.
> ➤ Method names are all written in `Courier Bold`.

The core JavaMail API package, **javax.mail,** provides a set of classes and interfaces that model a mail system and is implemented as a Java platform standard extension. The current version of the JavaMail API at time of going to press is 1.1.2.

In order for JavaMail to run correctly, you also need the JavaBeans Activation Framework which is currently at version 1.0.1. Thus the JAF API (**javax.activation**) is detailed first.

Package javax.activation

javax.activation is the single package that contains the Java Activation Framework (JAF) standard extension. The JAF is a component registry that maintains a list of JavaBeans that can perform named actions (such as "edit" and "print") on specified MIME data types.

Interfaces

public abstract interface	**CommandObject;**
public abstract interface	**DataContentHandler;**
public abstract interface	**DataContentHandlerFactory;**
public abstract interface	**DataSource;**

Classes

public class	**ActivationDataFlavor**	extends	*java.awt.datatransfer.DataFlavor*;
public class	**CommandInfo**;		
public abstract class	**CommandMap**;		
public class	**DataHandler**	implements	
	java.awt.datatransfer.Transferable;		
public class	**FileDataSource**	implements	*javax.activation.**DataSource**;
public abstract class	**FileTypeMap**;		
public class	**MailcapCommandMap**	extends	*javax.activation.**CommandMap**;
public class	**MimeType**	implements	*java.io.Externalizable*;
public class	**MimeTypeParameterList**;		
public class	**MimetypesFileTypeMap**	extends	*javax.activation.**FileTypeMap**;
public class	**URLDataSource**	implements	*javax.activation.**DataSource**;

Exceptions

public class	**MimeTypeParseException**	extends	*java.lang.Exception*;
public class	**UnsupportedDataTypeException**	extends	*java.io.IOException*;

Interface javax.activation.CommandObject

```
public abstract interface CommandObject
```

CommandObject provides JavaBeans with what they're being asked to do and where to find the data they should be operating on.

Methods

public abstract void	setCommandContext	(*java.lang.String* verb,
		javax.activation.**DataHandler** dh)
	throws	*java.io.IOException*;

Interface javax.activation.DataContentHandler

```
public abstract interface DataContentHandler
```

Generally called indirectly through the equivalent methods in *javax.activation.**DataHandler**, **DataContentHandler** is used to extend the JAF to convert streams into objects and write objects to streams.

Methods

public java.lang.Object	getContent	(javax.activation.DataSource ds)
	throws	*java.io.IOException*;
public java.lang.Object	getTransferData	(java.awt.datatransfer.DataFlavor df,
		javax.activation.DataSource ds)
	throws	java.awt.datatransfer.UnsupportedFlavorException,
		java.io.IOException;
public java.awt.datatransfer.DataFlavor[ ]		
	getTransferDataFlavors	();
public void	writeTo	(*java.lang.Object* obj,
		java.lang.string mimeType,
		java.io.OutputStream os)
	throws	*java.io.IOException*;

Interface javax.activation.DataContentHandlerFactory

```
public abstract interface DataContentHandlerFactory
```

DataContentHandlerFactory defines a factory for **DataContentHandlers**. Authors writing implementations of this interface should map a MIME type into an instance of **DataContentHandler**.

Methods

public **DataContentHandler**	createDataContentHandler	(*java.lang.String* mimeType);

Interface javax.activation.DataSource

```
public abstract interface DataSource
```

Is implemented by *javax.activation.***FileDataSource** and *javax.activation.***URLDataSource**. DataSource acts as a locator and descriptor of an arbitrary collection of data, giving it a type and access routes through *InputStream*s and *Outputstream*s.

Methods

public *java.lang.String*	getContentType	();
public *java.io.InputStream*	getInputStream	()
	throws	*java.io.IOException*;
public *java.lang.String*	getName	();
public *java.io.OutputStream*	getOutputStream	()
	throws	*java.io.IOException*;

Class javax.activation.ActivationDataFlavor

```
public class ActivationDataFlavor
```

extends java.awt.datatransfer.DataFlavor

ActivationDataFlavor is a special subclass of *java.awt.datatransfer.DataFlavor* with the exception that it can also set the three values used in the *DataFlavor* class with its methods which override those in *DataFlavor*.

Constructor Methods

public **ActivationDataFlavor**	(*java.lang.String* mimeType, *java.lang.String* humanPresentableName);
public **ActivationDataFlavor**	(*java.lang.Class* representationClass, *java.lang.String* humanPresentableName);
public **ActivationDataFlavor**	(*java.lang.Class* representationClass, *java.lang.string* mimeType, *java.lang.String* humanPresentableName);

Methods

public boolean	equals	(*java.awt.datatransfer.DataFlavor* dataFlavor);
public *java.lang.String*	getHumanPresentableName	();
public *java.lang.String*	getMimeType	();
public *java.lang.Class*	getRepresentationClass	();
public boolean	isMimeTypeEqual	(*java.lang.String* mimeType);
protected *java.lang.String*	normalizeMimeType	(*java.lang.String* mimeType);
protected *java.lang.String*	normalizeMimeTypeParameter	(*java.lang.String* parameterName, *java.lang.String* parameterValue);
public void	setHumanPresentableName	(*java.lang.String* humanPresentableName);

Inherited from java.awt.datatransfer.DataFlavor
```
clone, equals, equals, getParameter, getPrimaryType, getSubType,
isFlavorJavaFileListType,
isFlavorRemoteObjectType, isFlavorSerializedObjectType, isMimeTypeEqual,
isMimeTypeSerializedObject,
isRepresentationClassInputStream, isRepresentationClassRemote,
isRepresentationClassSerializable,
readExternal, tryToLoadClass, writeExternal
```

Inherited from java.lang.object

```
clone, equals, finalize, getClass, hashCode, notify, notifyAll, toString, wait,
wait, wait
```

Fields

Inherited from java.awt.datatransfer.DataFlavor

```
javaFileListFlavor, javaJVMLocalObjectMimeType, javaRemoteObjectMimeType,
javaSerializedObjectMimeType,
plainTextFlavor, stringFlavor
```

Class javax.activation.CommandInfo

```
public class CommandInfo
```

CommandInfo is used by (*javax.activation.*)**CommandMap** implementations to describe the results of command requests. NB. The `getCommandClass` method may return NULL depending on how it was called. Do not depend on this method returning a valid value.

Constructor Method

public	CommandInfo	(*java.lang.String* verb, *java.lang.String* className);

Methods

public *java.lang.String*	getCommandClass	();
public *java.lang.String*	getCommandName	();
public *java.lang.Object*	getCommandObject	(*javax.activation.***DataHandler** dh, *javax.lang.ClassLoader* loader)
	throws	*java.io.IOException*, *java.lang.ClassNotFoundException*;

Inherited from java.lang.object

```
clone, equals, finalize, getClass, hashCode, notify, notifyAll, toString, wait,
wait, wait
```

Class javax.activation.CommandMap

```
public abstract class CommandMap
```

Is extended by *javax.activation.***MailcapCommandMap**. **CommandMap** provides a way to access a registry of command objects available in the system.

Constructor Method

public	CommandMap	();

Methods

public abstract **DataContentHandler**	createDataContentHandler	(*java.lang.String* mimeType);
public abstract **CommandInfo**[ ]	getAllCommands	(*java.lang.String* mimeType);
public abstract **CommandInfo**	getCommand	(*java.lang.String* mimeType, *java.lang.String* cmdName);
public static **CommandMap**	getDefaultCommandMap	();
public abstract **CommandInfo**[ ]	getPreferredCommands	(*java.lang.String* mimeType);
public static void	setDefaultCommandMap	(*javax.activation.***CommandMap** commandMap);

Inherited from java.lang.object
```
clone, equals, finalize, getClass, hashCode, notify, notifyAll, toString, wait,
wait, wait
```

Class javax.activation.DataHandler

```
public class DataHandler
```

implements *java.awt.datatransfer.Transferable*

DataHandler acts as a consistent interface to any set of data, whichever format it is in. It implements *java.awt.datatransfer.Transferable* to be able to handle operations like cut, paste and drag and drop.

Constructor Methods

public	`DataHandler`	(*javax.activation.***DataSource** ds);
public	`DataHandler`	(*java.net.URL* url);
public	`DataHandler`	(*java.lang.Object* obj,
		java.lang.String mimeType);

Methods

public **CommandInfo**[ ]	`getAllCommands`	();
public *java.lang.Object*	`getBean`	(*javax.activation.***CommandInfo** cmdinfo);
public **CommandInfo**	`getCommand`	(*java.lang.String* cmdName);
public *java.lang.Object*	`getContent`	()
	throws	*java.io.IOException*;
public *java.lang.String*	`getContentType`	();
public **DataSource**	`getDataSource`	();
public *java.io.InputStream*	`getInputStream`	()
	throws	*java.io.IOException*;
public *java.lang.String*	`getName`	();
public *java.io.OutputStream*	`getOutputStream`	()
	throws	*java.io.IOException*;
public **CommandInfo**[ ]	`getPreferredCommands`	();
public *java.lang.Object*	`getTransferData`	(*java.awt.datatransfer.DataFlavor* flavor)
	throws	*java.awt.datatransfer.UnsupportedFlavorException*,
		java.io.IOException;
public *java.awt.datatransfer.DataFlavor*[ ]	`getTransferDataFlavors`	();
public boolean	`isDataFlavorSupported`	(*java.awt.datatransfer.DataFlavor* flavor);
public void	`setCommandMap`	(*javax.activation.***CommandMap** commandMap);
public static void	`setDataContentHandlerFactory`	
		(*javax.activation.***DataContentHandlerFactory**
		java.lang.String
newFactory);		
public void	`writeTo`	(*java.io.OutputStream* os)
	throws	*java.io.IOException*;

Inherited from java.lang.object
```
clone, equals, finalize, getClass, hashCode, notify, notifyAll, toString, wait,
wait, wait
```

Class javax.activation.FileDataSource

```
public class FileDataSource
```

implements *javax.activation.***DataSource**

FileDataSource implements *javax.activation.***DataSource** to represent a file. Of those methods in FileDataSource, four methods are actually specified in *javax.activation.***DataSource**: `getContentType`, `getName`, `getInputStream`, `getOutputStream`.

Constructor Methods

public	FileDataSource	(*java.lang.String* name);
public	FileDataSource	(*java.io.File* File);

Methods

public *java.lang.String*	getContentType	();
public *java.io.File*	getFile	();
public *java.lang.String*	getName	();
public void	setFileTypeMap	(*javax.activation.*FileTypeMap map);
public *java.io.InputStream*	getInputStream	()
	throws	*java.io.IOException*;
public *java.io.OutputStream*	getOutputStream	()
	throws	*java.io.IOException*;

Inherited from java.lang.object
`clone, equals, finalize, getClass, hashCode, notify, notifyAll, toString, wait, wait, wait`

Class javax.activation.FileTypeMap

`public abstract class FileTypeMap`

Is extended by *javax.activation.***MimetypesFileMap**. **FileTypeMap** is an abstract class that provides a data typing interface for files.

Constructor Method

public	FileTypeMap	();

Methods

public abstract *java.lang.String*	getContentType	(*java.io.File* file);
public abstract *java.lang.String*	getContentType	(*java.lang.String* filename);
public static **FileTypeMap**	getDefaultFileTypeMap	();
public static void	setDefaultFileTypeMap	(*javax.activation.*FileTypeMap map);

Inherited from java.lang.object
`clone, equals, finalize, getClass, hashCode, notify, notifyAll, toString, wait, wait, wait`

Class javax.activation.MailcapCommandMap

`public class MailcapCommandMap`

extends *javax.activation.***CommandMap**

MailcapCommandMap extends the *javax.activation.***CommandMap** class to create a map that conforms to the mailcap specification as laid down in RFC 1524. All the non-constructor methods except **addMailcap** override those laid out in **CommandMap**.

Constructor Methods

public	MailcapCommandMap	();
public	MailcapCommandMap	(*java.io.InputStream* is);
public	MailcapCommandMap	(*java.lang.String* fileName)
throws	*java.io.IOException*;	

Methods

public void	addMailcap	(*java.lang.String* mail_cap);
public **DataContentHandler**	createDataContentHandler	(*java.lang.String* mimeType);
public **CommandInfo[ ]**	getAllCommands	(*java.lang.String* mimeType);
public **CommandInfo**	getCommand	(*java.lang.String* mimeType, *java.lang.String* cmdName);
public **CommandInfo[ ]**	getPreferredCommands	(*java.lang.String* mimeType);

Class javax.activation.MimeType

```
public class MimeType
```

implements java.io.*Externalizable*

MimeType represents a Multipurpose Internet Mail Extension (MIME) type, as defined in RFCs 2045 and 2046.

Constructor Methods

public	MimeType	();
public	MimeType	(*java.lang.String* rawdata)
	throws	*javax.activation.***MimeTypeParseException**;
public	MimeType	(*java.lang.String* primary, *java.lang.String* sub)
	throws	*javax.activation.***MimeTypeParseException**;

Methods

public *java.lang.String*	getBaseType	();
public *java.lang.string*	getParameter	(*java.lang.String* name);
public **MimeTypeParameterList**	getParameters	();
public *java.lang.String*	getPrimaryType	();
public *java.lang.String*	getSubType	();
public boolean	match	(*java.lang.String* rawdata)
	throws	*javax.activation.***MimeTypeParseException**;
public boolean	match	(*javax.activation.***MimeType** type);
public void	readExternal	(*java.io.ObjectInput* in)
	throws	*java.io.IOException*, *java.lang.ClassNotFoundException*;
public void	removeParameter	(*java.lang.String* name);
public void	setParameter	(*java.lang.String* name, *java.lang.String* value);
public void	setPrimaryType	(*java.lang.String* primary)
	throws	*javax.activation.***MimeTypeParseException**;
public void	setSubType	(*java.lang.String* sub)
	throws	*javax.activation.***MimeTypeParseException**;
public *java.lang.String*	toString	();
public void	writeExternal	(*java.io.ObjectOutput* out)
	throws	*java.io.IOException*;

Inherited from java.lang.object
clone, equals, finalize, getClass, hashCode, notify, notifyAll, wait, wait, wait

Class javax.activation.MimeTypeParameterList

```
public class MimeTypeParameterList
```

Represents the parameter list of a Mime type as specified in RFCs 2045 and 2046. The Primary type of the object must already be stripped off.

Constructor Methods

public	`MimeTypeParameterList`	`();`
public	`MimeTypeParameterList`	*(java.lang.String* parameterList)
	throws	*javax.activation.***MimeTypeParseException**;

Methods

public boolean	`isEmpty`	`();`
public *java.util.Enumeration*	`getNames`	`();`
public *java.lang.string*	`get`	*(java.lang.String* name);
public void	`remove`	*(java.lang.String* name);
public void	`set`	*(java.lang.String* name,
		java.lang.String value);
public int	`size`	`();`
protected void	`parse`	*(java.lang.String* parameterList)
	throws	*javax.activation.***MimeTypeParseException**;
public *java.lang.String*	`toString`	`();`

Inherited from *java.lang.object*
`clone, equals, finalize, getClass, hashCode, notify, notifyAll, wait, wait, wait`

Class javax.activation.MimetypesFileTypeMap

`public class MimetypesFileTypeMap`

`extends` *javax.activation.***FileTypeMap**

MimetypesFileTypeMap provides a file typing system by checking a file's extension against available Mime type lists. It uses the **.mime.types** format.

Constructor Methods

public	`MimetypesFileTypeMap`	`();`
public	`MimetypesFileTypeMap`	*(java.lang.String* mimeTypeFileName)
	throws	*java.io.IOException*;
public	`MimetypesFileTypeMap`	*(java.io.InputStream* is);

Methods

public void	`addMimeTypes`	*(java.lang.String* mime_types);
public *java.lang.String*	`getContentType`	*(java.io.File* f);
public *java.lang.String*	`getContentType`	*(java.lang.String* filename);

Inherited from *javax.activation.***FileTypeMap**
`getDefaultFileTypeMap, setDefaultFileTypeMap`

Inherited from *java.lang.object*
`clone, equals, finalize, getClass, hashCode, notify, notifyAll, toString, wait,`
`wait, wait`

Class javax.activation.URLDataSource

`public class URLDataSource`

`implements` *javax.activation.***DataSource**

If a data source is specified by a URL, **URLDataSource** provides an object to wrap that URL in a **DataSource** interface. NB: The **DataHandler** object creates a **URLDataSource** internally, when it is constructed with a URL.

Constructor Method

public	URLDataSource	(*java.net.URL* url);

Methods

public *java.lang.String*	getContentType	();
public *java.io.InputStream*	getInputStream	()
throws	*java.io.IOException*;	
public *java.lang.String*	getName	();
public *java.io.OutputStream*	getOutputStream	()
throws	*java.io.IOException*;	
public *java.net.URL*	getURL	();

Inherited from *java.lang.object*
clone, equals, finalize, getClass, hashCode, notify, notifyAll, toString, wait, wait, wait

Class javax.activation.MimeTypeParseException

`public class MimeTypeParseException`

`extends` *java.lang.Exception*

An exception class to cover MimeType parsing related exceptions.

Constructor Methods

public	MimeTypeParseException	();
public	MimeTypeParseException	(*java.lang.String* s);

Methods

Inherited from java.lang.Throwable
fillInStackTrace, getLocalizedMessage, getMessage, printStackTrace, printStackTrace, printStackTrace, toString

Inherited from *java.lang.object*
clone, equals, finalize, getClass, hashCode, notify, notifyAll, wait, wait, wait

Class javax.activation.UnsupportedDataTypeException

`public class UnsupportedDataTypeException`

`extends` *java.io.IOException*

An exception class signalling that the requested operation does not support the requested data type.

Constructor Methods

public	UnsupportedDataTypeException	();
public	UnsupportedDataTypeException	(*java.lang.String* s);

Methods

Inherited from java.lang.Throwable
fillInStackTrace, getLocalizedMessage, getMessage, printStackTrace, printStackTrace, printStackTrace, toString

Inherited from *java.lang.object*
clone, equals, finalize, getClass, hashCode, notify, notifyAll, wait, wait, wait

Package javax.mail

javax.mail implements the JavaMail standard extension and contains the high-level classes and interfaces necessary for working with electronic mail.

Interfaces

public abstract interface	**MessageAware**;		
public abstract interface	**MultipartDataSource**	extends	*javax.activation.***DataSource**;
public abstract interface	**Part**;		
public abstract interface	**UIDFolder**;		

Classes

public abstract class	**Address** ;		
public abstract class	**Authenticator** ;		
public abstract class	**BodyPart**	implements	*javax.mail.***Part**;
public class	**FetchProfile**;		
public static class	**FetchProfile.Item**;		
public class	**Flags**	implements	*java.lang.Cloneable*;
public static final class	**Flags.Flag**;		
public abstract class	**Folder**;		
public class	**Header**;		
public abstract class	**Message**	implements	*javax.mail.***Part**;
public static class	**Message.RecipientType**;		
public class	**MessageContext**;		
public abstract class	**Multipart**;		
public final class	**PasswordAuthentication**;		
public class	**Provider**;		
public static class	**Provider.Type**;		
public abstract class	**Service**;		
public abstract class	**Store**	extends	*javax.mail.***Service**;
public abstract class	**Transport**	extends	*javax.mail.***Service**;
public final class	**Session**;		
public static class	**UIDFolder.FetchProfileItem**	extends	*javax.mail.***FetchProfile.Item**;
public class	**URLName**;		

Exceptions

public class	**AuthenticationFailedException**	extends	*javax.mail.***MessagingException** ;
public class	**FolderClosedException**	extends	*javax.mail.***MessagingException** ;
public class	**FolderNotFoundException**	extends	*javax.mail.***MessagingException** ;
public class	**IllegalWriteException**	extends	*javax.mail.***MessagingException** ;
public class	**MessageRemovedException**	extends	*javax.mail.***MessagingException** ;
public class	**MessagingException**	extends	*java.lang.Exception*;
public class	**MethodNotSupportedException**	extends	*javax.mail.***MessagingException** ;
public class	**NoSuchProviderException**	extends	*javax.mail.***MessagingException** ;
public class	**SendFailedException**	extends	*javax.mail.***MessagingException** ;
public class	**StoreClosedException**	extends	*javax.mail.***MessagingException** ;

Interface javax.mail.MessageAware

```
public abstract interface MessageAware
```

Is implemented by javax.mail.**MimePartDataSource**. Supplies information to a
(*javax.activation.*)**DataContentHandler** about the message context in which the data content object is
running.

Methods

public abstract **MessageContext**   getMessageContext   ();

Interface javax.mail.MultipartDataSource

public abstract interface MultipartDataSource

extends *javax.activation.*DataSource

MultipartDataSource acts as the interface to data sources such as mail messages which have multiple body parts to them. It contains the appropriate methods to access the individual body parts.

Methods

public **BodyPart**	getBodyPart throws	(int index) *javax.mail.*MessagingException;
public int	getCount	();

Inherited from *javax.activation.*DataSource
getContentType, getInputStream, getName, getOutputStream

Interface javax.mail.Part

public abstract interface Part

Is extended by *javax.mail.internet.MimePart*. Is implemented by *javax.mail.*BodyPart and *javax.mail.*Message. Part is the common base interface for Messages and BodyParts.

Methods

public void	addHeader	(*java.lang.* header_name, *java.lang.String* header_value)
	throws	*javax.mail.*MessagingException;
public *java.util.Enumeration*	getAllHeaders	()
	throws	*javax.mail.*MessagingException;
public *java.lang.*Object	getContent	()
	throws	*java.io.IOException*, *javax.mail.*MessagingException;
public *java.lang.String*	getContentType	()
	throws	*javax.mail.*MessagingException;
public **DataHandler**	getDataHandler	()
	throws	*javax.mail.*MessagingException;
public *java.lang.String*	getDescription	()
	throws	*javax.mail.*MessagingException;
public *java.lang.String*	getDisposition	()
	throws	*javax.mail.*MessagingException;
public *java.lang.String*	getFileName	()
	throws	*javax.mail.*MessagingException;
public *java.io.InputStream*	getInputStream	()
	throws	*java.io.IOException*, *javax.mail.*MessagingException;
public int	getLineCount	()
	throws	*javax.mail.*MessagingException;
public *java.lang.String*[ ]	getHeader	(*java.lang.String* header_name)
	throws	*javax.mail.*MessagingException;
public *java.util.Enumeration*	getMatchingHeaders	(*java.lang.String*[ ] header_names)
	throws	*javax.mail.*MessagingException;
public *java.util.Enumeration*	getNonMatchingHeaders	(*java.lang.String*[ ] header_names)
	throws	*javax.mail.*MessagingException;

public int	`getSize`	()
	throws	*javax.mail.***MessagingException**;
public boolean	`isMimeType`	(*java.lang.String* mimeType)
	throws	*javax.mail.***MessagingException**;
public void	`removeHeader`	(*java.lang.String* header_name)
	throws	*javax.mail.***MessagingException**;
public void	`setContent`	(*javax.mail.*Multipart mp)
	throws	*javax.mail.***MessagingException**;
public void	`setContent`	(*java.lang.Object* obj,
		java.lang.String type)
	throws	*javax.mail.***MessagingException**;
public void	`setDataHandler`	(*javax.activation.***DataHandler** dh)
	throws	*javax.mail.***MessagingException**;
public void	`setDescription`	(*java.lang.String* description)
	throws	*javax.mail.***MessagingException**;
public void	`setDisposition`	(*java.lang.String* disposition)
	throws	*javax.mail.***MessagingException**;
public void	`setFileName`	(*java.lang.String* filename)
	throws	*javax.mail.***MessagingException**;
public void	`setHeader`	(*java.lang.String* header_name,
		java.lang.String header_value)
	throws	*javax.mail.***MessagingException**;
public void	`setText`	(*java.lang.String* text)
	throws	*javax.mail.***MessagingException**;
public void	`writeTo`	(java.io.OutputStream os)
	throws	java.io.*IOException*,
		*javax.mail.***MessagingException**;

Fields

public static final *java.lang.String*	`ATTACHMENT`;
public static final *java.lang.String*	`INLINE`;

Interface javax.mail.UIDFolder

```
public abstract interface UIDFolder
```

UIDFolder is implemented by (mail) folders that can operate 'offline' - disconnected from the mail server. It does this by providing unique IDs for messages in the folder.

Inner Class

public static class	**UIDFolder.FetchProfileItem**	extends	**FetchProfile.Item** ;

Methods

public **Message**	`getMessageByUID`	(long uid)
	throws	*javax.mail.***MessagingException**;
public **Message**[ ]	`getMessagesByUID`	(long[ ] uids)
	throws	*javax.mail.***MessagingException**;
public **Message**[ ]	`getMessagesByUID`	(long start,
		long end)
	throws	*javax.mail.***MessagingException**;
public long	`getUID`	(*javax.mail.***Message** message)
	throws	*javax.mail.***MessagingException**;
public long	`getUIDValidity`	()
	throws	*javax.mail.***MessagingException**;

Field

public static final long	`LASTUID`;

Class javax.mail.Address

```
public abstract class Address
```

Is extended by *javax.mail.internet.InternetAddress* and *javax.mail.internet.NewsAddress*. Represents the addresses in the message. Its subclasses provide specific implementations.

Constructor Method

public	Address	();

Methods

public abstract *java.lang.String*	getType	();
public abstract boolean	equals	(*java.lang.Object* address);
public abstract *java.lang.String*	toString	();

Inherited from *java.lang.object*
```
clone, finalize, getClass, hashCode, notify, notifyAll, wait, wait, wait
```

Class javax.mail.Authenticator

Represents the (method of obtaining) authentication required for a network connection.

Constructor Method

public	Authenticator	();

Methods

protected final *java.lang.String*	getDefaultUserName	();
protected **PasswordAuthentication**	getPasswordAuthentication	();
protected final int	getRequestingPort	();
protected final *java.lang.String*	getRequestingPrompt	();
protected final *java.lang.String*	getRequestingProtocol	();
protected final *java.net.InetAddress*	getRequestingSite	();

Inherited from *java.lang.object*
```
clone, equals, finalize, getClass, hashCode, notify, notifyAll, toString, wait,
wait, wait
```

Class javax.mail.BodyPart

```
public abstract class BodyPart
```

```
implements javax.mail.Part
```

Is extended by *javax.mail.internet.MimeBodyPart*. This class models a message part within a MultiPart message. Subclasses of this abstract class provide the actual implementations.

Constructor Method

public	BodyPart	();

Methods

public **Multipart**	getParent	();

Inherited from *java.lang.object*
```
clone, equals, finalize, getClass, hashCode, notify, notifyAll, toString, wait,
wait, wait
```

Fields

protected **Multipart**	parent;	

Class javax.mail.FetchProfile

```
public class FetchProfile
```

Used to list the (*javax.mail.*)**Message** attributes that clients wish to prefetch before downloading the full message.

Inner Class

public static class	**FetchProfile.Item**;

Constructor Method

public	FetchProfile	();

Methods

public void	add	(*java.lang.String* headerName);
public void	add	(*javax.mail.***FetchProfile.Item** item);
public boolean	contains	(*java.lang.String* headerName);
public boolean	contains	(*javax.mail.***FetchProfile.Item** item);
public *java.lang.String*[ ]	getHeaderNames	();
public **FetchProfile.Item**[ ]	getItems	();

Inherited from *java.lang.object*
```
clone, equals, finalize, getClass, hashCode, notify, notifyAll, toString, wait,
wait, wait
```

Class javax.mail.FetchProfile.Item

```
public static class FetchProfile.Item
```

This inner class is the base class of all items that can be requested in a **FetchProfile**. The items currently defined here are **ENVELOPE**, **CONTENT_INFO** and **FLAGS**. The **UIDFolder** interface defines the UID Item as well. Note that this class only has a protected constructor, thereby restricting new Item types to either this class or subclasses. This effectively implements an enumeration of allowed Item types.

Constructor Method

protected	FetchProfile.Item	(*java.lang.String* name);

Methods

Inherited from *java.lang.object*
```
clone, equals, finalize, getClass, hashCode, notify, notifyAll, toString, wait,
wait, wait
```

Fields

public final static **FetchProfile.Item**	CONTENT_INFO;
public final static **FetchProfile.Item**	ENVELOPE;
public final static **FetchProfile.Item**	FLAGS;

Class javax.mail.Flags

```
public class Flags
```

implements *java.lang.Cloneable*

Represents the set of flags on a Message.

Inner Class

public static final class	**Flags.Flag**

Constructor Methods

public	Flags	();
public	Flags	(*javax.mail.***Flags.Flag** flag);
public	Flags	(*java.lang.String* flag);
public	Flags	(*javax.mail.***Flags** flags);

Methods

public void	add	(*javax.mail.***Flags.Flag** flag);
public void	add	(*java.lang.String* flag);
public void	add	(*javax.mail.***Flags** flags);
public *java.lang.Object*	clone	();
public boolean	contains	(*javax.mail.***Flags.Flag** flag);
public boolean	contains	(*java.lang.String* flag);
public boolean	contains	(*javax.mail.***Flags** flags);
public boolean	equals	(*java.lang.Object* obj);
public **Flags.Flag**[ ]	getSystemFlags	();
public *java.lang.String*[ ]	getUserFlags	();
public int	hashCode	();
public void	remove	(*javax.mail.***Flags.Flag** flag);
public void	remove	(*java.lang.String* flag);
public void	remove	(*javax.mail.***Flags** flags);

Inherited from *java.lang.object*
```
finalize, getClass, notify, notifyAll, toString, wait, wait, wait
```

Class javax.mail.Flags.Flag

```
public static final class Flags.Flag
```

This inner class represents the set of predefined standard system flags.

Methods

Inherited from *java.lang.object*
```
clone, equals, finalize, getClass, hashCode, notify, notifyAll, toString, wait,
wait, wait
```

Fields

public final static **Flags.Flag**	ANSWERED;
public final static **Flags.Flag**	DELETED;
public final static **Flags.Flag**	DRAFT;
public final static **Flags.Flag**	FLAGGED;
public final static **Flags.Flag**	RECENT;
public final static **Flags.Flag**	SEEN;
public final static **Flags.Flag**	USER;

Class javax.mail.Folder

```
public abstract class Folder
```

Represents a mail folder (in an information store). Subclasses of Folder represent protocol specific folders.

Constructor Method

protected	Folder	(*javax.mail*.**Store** store);

Methods

public void	addConnectionListener	(*javax.mail.event.ConnectionListener* l);
public void	addFolderListener	(*javax.mail.event.FolderListener* l);
public void	addMessageChangedListener	(*javax.mail.event.MessageChangedListener* l);
public void	addMessageCountListener	(*javax.mail.event.MessageCountListener* l);
public abstract void	appendMessages	(*javax.mail*.**Message**[ ] msgs)
	throws	*javax.mail*.**MessagingException**;
public abstract void	close	(boolean expunge)
	throws	*javax.mail*.**MessagingException**;
public void	copyMessages	(*javax.mail*.**Message**[ ] msgs, *javax.mail*.**Folder** folder)
	throws	*javax.mail*.**MessagingException**;
public abstract boolean	create	(int type)
	throws	*javax.mail*.**MessagingException**;
public abstract boolean	delete	(boolean recurse)
	throws	*javax.mail*.**MessagingException**;
public abstract boolean	exists	()
	throws	*javax.mail*.**MessagingException**;
public abstract **Message**[ ]	expunge	()
	throws	*javax.mail*.**MessagingException**;
public void	fetch	(*javax.mail*. **Message**[ ] msgs, *javax.mail*.**FetchProfile** fp)
	throws	*javax.mail*.**MessagingException**;
protected void	finalize	()
	throws	*java.lang.Throwable*;
public abstract **Folder**	getFolder	(*java.lang.String* name)
	throws	*javax.mail*.**MessagingException**;
public abstract *java.lang.String*	getFullName	();
public abstract Message	getMessage	(int msgnum)
	throws	*javax.mail*.**MessagingException**;
public abstract int	getMessageCount	()
	throws	*javax.mail*.**MessagingException**;
public **Message**[ ]	getMessages	()
	throws	*javax.mail*.**MessagingException**;
public **Message**[ ]	getMessages	(int[ ] msgnums)
	throws	*javax.mail*.**MessagingException**;
public **Message**[ ]	getMessages	(int start, int end)
	throws	*javax.mail*.**MessagingException**;
public int	getMode	();
public abstract *java.lang.String*	getName	();
public int	getNewMessageCount	()
	throws	*javax.mail*.**MessagingException**;
public abstract **Folder**	getParent	()
	throws	*javax.mail*.**MessagingException**;

public abstract **Flags**	getPermanentFlags	();
public abstract char	getSeparator	()
	throws	*javax.mail*.**MessagingException**;
public **Store**	getStore	();
public abstract int	getType	()
	throws	*javax.mail*.**MessagingException**;
public int	getUnreadMessageCount	()
	throws	*javax.mail*.**MessagingException**;
public **URLName**	getURLName	()
	throws	*javax.mail*.**MessagingException**;
public abstract boolean	hasNewMessages	()
	throws	*javax.mail*.**MessagingException**;
public abstract boolean	isOpen	();
public boolean	isSubscribed	();
public **Folder**[ ]	list	()
	throws	*javax.mail*.**MessagingException**;
public abstract **Folder**[ ]	list	(*java.lang.String* pattern)
	throws	*javax.mail*.**MessagingException**;
public **Folder**[ ]	listSubscribed	()
	throws	*javax.mail*.**MessagingException**;
public **Folder**[ ]	listSubscribed	(*java.lang.String* pattern)
	throws	*javax.mail*.**MessagingException**;
protected void	notifyConnectionListeners	(int type);
protected void	notifyFolderListeners	(int type);
protected void	notifyFolderRenamedListeners	(*javax.mail*.**Folder** folder);
protected void	notifyMessageAddedListeners	(*javax.mail*.**Message**[ ] msgs);
protected void	notifyMessageChangedListeners	(int type,
		javax.mail.**Message** msg);
protected void	notifyMessageRemovedListeners	(boolean removed,
		javax.mail.**Message**[ ] msgs);
public abstract void	open	(int mode)
	throws	*javax.mail*.**MessagingException**;
public void	removeConnectionListener	(*javax.mail.event.ConnectionListener* l);
public void	removeFolderListener	(*javax.mail.event.FolderListener* l);
public void	removeMessageChangedListener	(*javax.mail.event.MessageChangedListener*
l);		
public void	removeMessageCountListener	(*javax.mail.event.MessageCountListener* l);
public abstract boolean	renameTo	(*javax.mail*.**Folder** f)
	throws	*javax.mail*.**MessagingException**;
public **Message**[ ]	search	(*javax.mail.search.SearchTerm* term)
throws	*javax.mail*.**MessagingException**;	
public **Message**[ ]	search	(*javax.mail.search.SearchTerm* term,
		javax.mail.**Message**[ ] msgs)
	throws	*javax.mail*.**MessagingException**;
public void	setFlags	(*javax.mail*.**Message**[ ] msgs,
		javax.mail.**Flags** flag,
		boolean value)
	throws	*javax.mail*.**MessagingException**;
public void	setFlags	(int[ ] msgnums,
		javax.mail.**Flags** flag,
		boolean value)
	throws	*javax.mail*.**MessagingException**;
public void	setFlags	(int start,
		int end,
		javax.mail.**Flags** flag,
		boolean value)
	throws	*javax.mail*.**MessagingException**;
public void	setSubscribed	(boolean subscribe)
	throws	*javax.mail*.**MessagingException**;
public *java.lang.String*	toString	();

Inherited from *java.lang.object*
clone, equals, getClass, hashCode, notify, notifyAll, wait, wait, wait

Fields

public final static int	HOLDS_FOLDERS;
public final static int	HOLDS_MESSAGES;
public final static int	READ_ONLY;
public final static int	READ_WRITE;
protected int	mode;
protected **Store**	store;

Class javax.mail.Header

```
public class Header
```

Represents a mail header as a name - value pair.

Constructor Method

public	**Header**	(*java.lang.string* name, *java.lang.string* value);

Methods

public *java.lang.String*	getName	();
public *java.lang.String*	getValue	();

Inherited from *java.lang.object*
```
clone, equals, finalize, getClass, hashCode, notify, notifyAll, toString, wait,
wait, wait
```

Class javax.mail.Message

```
public abstract class Message
```

```
implements javax.mail.Part
```

Is extended by *javax.mail*.**MimeMessage**. This abstract class represents an email message. Its subclasses represent actual types of message.

Inner Class

public static final class	**Message.RecipientType**

Constructor Methods

protected	**Message**	();
protected	**Message**	(*javax.mail*.**Session** session);
protected	**Message**	(*javax.mail*.**Folder** folder, int msgnum);

Methods

public abstract void	addFrom	(*javax.mail.Address*[ ] addresses)
	throws	*javax.mail*.**MessagingException**;
public void	addRecipient	(*javax.mail*.**Message.RecipientType** type, *javax.mail*.**Address** addresses)
	throws	*javax.mail*.**MessagingException**;
public abstract void	addRecipients	(*javax.mail*.**Message.RecipientType** type, *javax.mail*.**Address**[ ] addresses)
	throws	*javax.mail*.**MessagingException**;
public **Address**[ ]	getAllRecipients	()
	throws	*javax.mail*.**MessagingException**;
public abstract **Flags**	getFlags	()

public **Folder**	getFolder	();
public abstract **Address**[ ]	getFrom	()
	throws	*javax.mail*.**MessagingException**;
public int	getMessageNumber	();
public abstract *java.util.Date*	getReceivedDate	()
	throws	*javax.mail*.**MessagingException**;
public abstract **Address**[ ]	getRecipients	(*javax.mail*.**Message.RecipientType** type)
	throws	*javax.mail*.**MessagingException**;
public **Address**[ ]	getReplyTo	()
	throws	*javax.mail*.**MessagingException**;
public abstract *java.util.Date*	getSentDate	()
	throws	*javax.mail*.**MessagingException**;
public abstract *java.lang.String*	getSubject	()
	throws	*javax.mail*.**MessagingException**;
public boolean	isExpunged	();
public boolean	isSet	(*javax.mail*.**Flags.Flag** flag)
	throws	*javax.mail*.**MessagingException**;
public boolean	match	(*javax.mail.search.SearchTerm* term)
	throws	*javax.mail*.**MessagingException**;
public abstract **Message**	reply	(boolean replyToAll)
	throws	*javax.mail*.**MessagingException**;
public abstract void	saveChanges	()
	throws	*javax.mail*.**MessagingException**;
protected void	setExpunged	(boolean expunged);
public void	setFlag	(*javax.mail*.**Flags.Flag** flag, boolean set)
	throws	*javax.mail*.**MessagingException**;
public abstract void	setFlags	(*javax.mail*.**Flags** flag, boolean set)
	throws	*javax.mail*.**MessagingException**;
public abstract void	setFrom	()
	throws	*javax.mail*.**MessagingException**;
public abstract void	setFrom	(*javax.mail*.**Address** address)
	throws	*javax.mail*.**MessagingException**;
protected void	setMessageNumber	(int msgnum);
public void	setReplyTo	(*javax.mail*.**Address**[ ] addresses)
	throws	*javax.mail*.**MessagingException**;
public abstract void	setSentDate	(*java.util.Date* date)
	throws	*javax.mail*.**MessagingException**;
public abstract void	setSubject	(*java.lang.String* subject)
	throws	*javax.mail*.**MessagingException**;
public void	setRecipient	(*javax.mail*.**Message.RecipientType** type, *javax.mail*.**Address** addresses)
	throws	*javax.mail*.**MessagingException**;
public abstract void	setRecipients	(*javax.mail*.**Message.RecipientType** type, *javax.mail*.**Address**[ ] addresses)
	throws	*javax.mail*.**MessagingException**;

Inherited from *java.lang.object*
clone, equals, finalize, getClass, hashCode, notify, notifyAll, toString, wait, wait, wait

Fields

protected boolean	expunged;
protected **Folder**	folder;
protected int	msgnum;
protected **Session**	session;

Class javax.mail.Message.RecipientType

```
public abstract class Message.RecipientType
```

Is extended by javax.mail.internet.*MimeMessage.RecipientType*. Defines the recipient fields allowed by the Message class.

Constructor Methods

protected	`Message.RecipientType`	(*java.lang.String* type);

Methods

Inherited from *java.lang.object*
`clone, equals, finalize, getClass, hashCode, notify, notifyAll, toString, wait, wait, wait`

Fields

public final static **Message.RecipientType**	BCC;
public final static **Message.RecipientType**	CC;
public final static **Message.RecipientType**	TO;
protected *java.lang.String*	type;

Class javax.mail.MessageContext

```
public class MessageContext
```

Represents the context under which a piece of Message content, regarded as a data source, is being kept. For example, which part of the message, which session, etc.

Constructor Methods

public	`MessageContext`	(*javax.mail.*Part part);

Methods

public **Message**	`getMessage`	();
public **Part**	`getPart`	();
public **Session**	`getSession`	();

Inherited from *java.lang.object*
`clone, equals, finalize, getClass, hashCode, notify, notifyAll, toString, wait, wait, wait`

Class javax.mail.Multipart

```
public abstract class Multipart
```

Is extended by javax.mail.internet.*MimeMultipart*. Represents a many-parted body of a message.

Constructor Method

protected	`Multipart`	();

Methods

public void	addBodyPart	(*javax.mail.***BodyPart** part)
	throws	*javax.mail.***MessagingException**;
public void	addBodyPart	(*javax.mail.***BodyPart** part,
		int index)
	throws	*javax.mail.***MessagingException**;
public **BodyPart**	getBodyPart	(int index)
	throws	*javax.mail.***MessagingException**;
public *java.lang.String*	getContentType	();
public int	getCount	()
	throws	*javax.mail.***MessagingException**;
public **Part**	getParent	();
public boolean	removeBodyPart	(*javax.mail.***BodyPart** part)
	throws	*javax.mail.***MessagingException**;
public void	removeBodyPart	(int index)
	throws	*javax.mail.***MessagingException**;
protected void	setMultipartDataSource	(*javax.mail.***MultipartDataSource** mp)
	throws	*javax.mail.***MessagingException**;
public void	setParent	(*javax.mail.***Part** parent);
public abstract void	writeTo	(*java.io.OutputStream* os)
	throws	*java.io.IOException*,
		*javax.mail.***MessagingException**;

Inherited from *java.lang.object*
```
clone, equals, finalize, getClass, hashCode, notify, notifyAll, toString, wait,
wait, wait
```

Fields

protected *java.lang.String*	contentType;
protected **Part**	parent;
protected java.util.Vector	parts;

Class javax.mail.PasswordAuthentication

```
public final class PasswordAuthentication
```

Holds for a password and user id for use by *javax.mail.***Authenticator**

Constructor Method

public	PasswordAuthentication	(*java.lang.String* userName,
		java.lang.String password);

Methods

public *java.lang.String*	getPassword	();
public *java.lang.String*	getUserName	();

Inherited from *java.lang.object*
```
clone, equals, finalize, getClass, hashCode, notify, notifyAll, toString, wait,
wait, wait
```

Class javax.mail.Provider

```
public class Provider
```

Describes the implementation of a protocol. It uses the values given in the *javamail.providers* and *javamail.default.providers* resource files.

Inner Class

public static class	Provider.Type	

Methods

public *java.lang.String*	`getClassName`	();
public *java.lang.String*	`getProtocol`	();
public **Provider.Type**	`getType`	();
public *java.lang.String*	`getVendor`	();
public *java.lang.String*	`getVersion`	();
public *java.lang.String*	`toString`	();

Class javax.mail.Provider.Type

```
public static class Provider.Type
```

Defines the type of protocol being implemented. Currently, this is limited to either **STORE** or **TRANSPORT**.

Methods

Inherited from *java.lang.object*
`clone, equals, finalize, getClass, hashCode, notify, notifyAll, toString, wait, wait, wait`

Fields

public static final **Provider.Type**	STORE;
public static final **Provider.Type**	TRANSPORT;

Class javax.mail.Service

```
public abstract class Service
```

Is extended by *javax.mail*.**Store** and *javax.mail*.**Transport**. Abstract class holding the standard functionality common to messaging systems.

Constructor Method

protected	`Service`	(*javax.mail*.**Session**, *javax.mail*.**URLName** urlname);

Methods

public void	`addConnectionListener`	(*javax.mail.event.ConnectionListener* l);
public void	`close`	()
	throws	*javax.mail*.**MessagingException**;
public void	`connect`	()
	throws	*javax.mail*.**MessagingException**;
public void	`connect`	(*java.lang.String* host, *java.lang.string* user, *java.lang.string* password)
	throws	*javax.mail*.**MessagingException**;
public void	`connect`	(*java.lang.String* host, int port, *java.lang.string* user, *java.lang.string* password)
	throws	*javax.mail*.**MessagingException**;
protected void	`finalize`	()
	throws	*java.lang.Throwable*;

public **URLName**	getURLName	();
public boolean	isConnected	();
protected void	notifyConnectionListeners	(int type);
protected boolean	protocolConnect	(*java.lang.String* host,
		int port,
		java.lang.string user,
		java.lang.string password)
	throws	*javax.mail*.**MessagingException**;
protected void	queueEvent	(*javax.mail.event.MailEvent* event,
		java.util.Vector vector);
public void	removeConnectionListener	(*javax.mail.event.ConnectionListener* l);
protected void	setConnected	(boolean connected);
protected void	setURLName	(*javax.mail*.**URLName** url);
public *java.lang.String*	toString	();

Inherited from *java.lang.object*

clone, equals, getClass, hashCode, notify, notifyAll, wait, wait, wait

Fields

protected boolean	debug;
protected **Session**	session;
protected **URLName**	url;

Class javax.mail.Session

```
public final class Session
```

Represents a mail session which can be shared among many applications. Holds settings and defaults as used by the mail APIs.

Methods

public boolean	getDebug	();
public static **Session**	getDefaultInstance	(*java.util.Properties* props,
		javax.mail.**Authenticator** authenticator);
public static **Session**	getInstance	(*java.util.Properties* props,
		javax.mail.**Authenticator** authenticator);
public **Folder**	getFolder	(*javax.mail*.**URLName** url)
	throws	*javax.mail*.**MessagingException**;
public **PasswordAuthentication**	getPasswordAuthentication	(*javax.mail*.**URLName** url);
public *java.util.Properties*	getProperties	();
public *java.lang.string*	getProperty	(*java.lang.string* name);
public **Provider**	getProvider	(*java.lang.String* protocol)
	throws	*javax.mail*.**NoSuchProviderException**;
public **Provider**[ ]	getProviders	();
public **Store**	getStore	()
	throws	*javax.mail*.**NoSuchProviderException**;
public **Store**	getStore	(*java.lang.String* protocol)
	throws	*javax.mail*.**NoSuchProviderException**;
public **Store**	getStore	(*java.lang.String* protocol)
	throws	*javax.mail*.**NoSuchProviderException**;
public **Store**	getStore	(*javax.mail*.**URLName** url)
	throws	*javax.mail*.**NoSuchProviderException**;
public **Transport**	getTransport	()
	throws	*javax.mail*.**NoSuchProviderException**;
public **Transport**	getTransport	(*javax.mail*.**Provider** provider)
	throws	*javax.mail*.**NoSuchProviderException**;
public **Transport**	getTransport	(*javax.mail*.**Address** address)
	throws	*javax.mail*.**NoSuchProviderException**;
public **Transport**	getTransport	(*javax.mail*.**URLName** url)
	throws	*javax.mail*.**NoSuchProviderException**;

public **Transport**	getTransport	(*java.lang.String* protocol)
	throws	*java.mail.***NoSuchProviderException**;
public **PasswordAuthentication**	requestPasswordAuthentication	(*java.net.InetAddress* addr,
		int port,
		java.lang.string protocol,
		java.lang.string prompt,
		java.lang.String defaultUserName);
public void	setDebug	(boolean debug);
public void	setProvider	(*javax.mail.***Provider** provider)
	throws	*javax.mail.***NoSuchProviderException**;
public void	setPasswordAuthentication	(*javax.mail.***URLName** url,
		*javax.mail.***PasswordAuthentication** pw);

Inherited from *java.lang.object*
```
clone, equals, finalize, getClass, hashCode, notify, notifyAll, toString, wait,
wait, wait
```

Class javax.mail.Store

```
public abstract class Store
```

```
extends javax.mail.Service
```

Abstract class representing a message store. Actual implementations are covered by subclasses.

Constructor Method

protected	Store	(*javax.mail.***Session** session,
		*javax.mail.***URLName** urlname);

Methods

public void	addFolderListener	(*javax.mail.event.FolderListener* l);
public void	addStoreListener	(*javax.mail.event.StoreListener* l);
public abstract **Folder**	getDefaultFolder	()
	throws	*javax.mail.***MessagingException**;
public abstract **Folder**	getFolder	(*javax.mail.***URLName** url)
	throws	*javax.mail.***MessagingException**;
public abstract **Folder**	getFolder	(*java.lang.String* name)
	throws	*javax.mail.***MessagingException**;
protected void	notifyFolderListeners	(int type,
		*javax.mail.***Folder** folder);
protected void	notifyFolderRenamedListeners	(*javax.mail.***Folder** oldF,
		*javax.mail.***Folder** newF);
protected void	notifyStoreListeners	(int type,
		java.lang.string message);
public void	removeFolderListener	(*javax.mail.event.FolderListener* l);
public void	removeStoreListener	(*javax.mail.event.StoreListener* l);

Inherited from *java.mail.***Service**
```
addConnectionListener, close, connect, connect, connect, finalize, getURLName,
isConnected, notifyConnectionListeners, protocolConnect, queueEvent,
removeConnectionListener, setConnected, setURLName, toString
```

Inherited from *java.lang.object*
```
clone, equals, getClass, hashCode, notify, notifyAll, wait, wait, wait
```

Fields

Inherited from *javax.mail.***Service**
```
debug, session, url
```

Class *javax.mail.Transport*

```
public abstract class Transport
```

extends *javax.mail.***Service**

Abstract class representing a message transport mechanism. Actual implementations are covered by subclasses.

Constructor Method

public	`Transport`	(*javax.mail.***Session** session, *javax.mail.***URLName** urlname);

Methods

public void	`addTransportListener`	(*javax.mail.event.TransportListener* l);
protected void	`notifyTransportListeners`	(int type, *javax.mail.***Address**[ ] validSent, *javax.mail.***Address**[ ] validUnsent, *javax.mail.***Address**[ ] invalid, *javax.mail.***Message** msg);
public static void	`send`	(*javax.mail.***Message** msg)
public static void	`send`	(*javax.mail.***Message** msg, *javax.mail.***Address**[ ] addresses)
	throws	*javax.mail.***MessagingException**;
public abstract void	`sendMessage`	(*javax.mail.***Message** msg, *javax.mail.***Address**[ ] addresses)
	throws	*javax.mail.***MessagingException**;
public void	`removeTransportListener`	(*javax.mail.event.TransportListener* l);

Inherited from *javax.mail.***Service**
`addConnectionListener, close, connect, connect, connect, finalize, getURLName, isConnected, notifyConnectionListeners, protocolConnect, queueEvent, removeConnectionListener, setConnected, setURLName, toString`

Inherited from *java.lang.object*
`clone, equals, getClass, hashCode, notify, notifyAll, wait, wait, wait`

Fields

Inherited from *javax.mail.*Service
`debug, session, url`

Class *javax.mail.UIDFolder.FetchProfileItem*

```
public static class UIDFolder.FetchProfileItem
```

extends *javax.mail.***FetchProfile.Item**

An inner class of *javax.mail.***FetchProfile.Item,** this represents a way to add new FetchProfile.Item types specific to UIDFolders.

Constructor Method

protected	`UIDFolder.FetchProfileItem`	(*java.lang.String* name);

Methods

Inherited from *java.lang.object*

clone, equals, finalize, getClass, hashCode, notify, notifyAll, toString, wait, wait, wait

Fields

public final static **UIDFolder.FetchProfileItem**
                               UID;

Inherited from *javax.mail.***FetchProfile.Item**
CONTENT_INFO, ENVELOPE, FLAGS

Class javax.mail.URLName

`public class URLName`

Represents a URL name and also provides the basic parsing functionality to parse most internet standard URL schemes.

Constructor Methods

public	**URLName**	(*java.net.URL* url);
public	**URLName**	(*java.lang.String* url);
public	**URLName**	(*java.lang.String* protocol,
		java.lang.string host,
		int port,
		java.lang.string file,
		java.lang.string username,
		java.lang.string password);

Methods

public boolean	**equals**	(*java.lang.Object* obj);
public *java.lang.String*	**getFile**	();
public *java.lang.String*	**getHost**	();
public *java.lang.String*	**getPassword**	();
public int	**getPort**	();
public *java.lang.String*	**getProtocol**	();
public *java.lang.String*	**getRef**	();
public *java.net.URL*	**getURL**	()
	throws	*java.net.MalformedURLException*;
public *java.lang.String*	**getUsername**	();
public int	**hashCode**	();
protected void	**parseString**	(*java.lang.String* url);
public *java.lang.String*	**toString**	();

Inherited from *java.lang.object*

clone, finalize, getClass, notify, notifyAll, wait, wait, wait

Fields

protected *java.lang.String*   **fullURL;**

Class javax.mail.AuthenticationFailedException

`public class AuthenticationFailedException`

extends *javax.mail.***MessagingException**

Represents the exception thrown when a user is not authenticated when connecting to a (*javax.mail.*)**Store** or (*javax.mail.*)**Transport** object.

Constructor Methods

```
public                          AuthenticationFailedException   ( );
public                          AuthenticationFailedException   (java.lang.String message);
```

Methods

Inherited from *javax.mail.*MessagingException
`getMessage, getNextException, setNextException`

Inherited from *java.lang.Throwable*
`fillInStackTrace, getLocalizedMessage, printStackTrace, printStackTrace,`
`printStackTrace, toString`

Inherited from *java.lang.object*
`clone, equals, finalize, getClass, hashCode, notify, notifyAll, wait, wait, wait`

Class javax.mail.FolderClosedException

```
public class FolderClosedException
```

extends *javax.mail.*MessagingException

Represents the exception thrown when a method is run on a messaging object in a folder that has 'died' for some reason.

Constructor Methods

```
public                          FolderClosedException           (javax.mail.Folder folder);
public                          FolderClosedException           (javax.mail.Folder folder,
                                                                java.lang.String message);
```

Methods

```
public Folder                   getFolder                       ();
```

Inherited from *javax.mail.*MessagingException
`getMessage, getNextException, setNextException`

Inherited from *java.lang.Throwable*
`fillInStackTrace, getLocalizedMessage, printStackTrace, printStackTrace,`
`printStackTrace, toString`

Inherited from *java.lang.object*
`clone, equals, finalize, getClass, hashCode, notify, notifyAll, wait, wait, wait`

Class javax.mail.FolderNotFoundException

```
public class FolderNotFoundException
```

extends *javax.mail.*MessagingException

Represents the exception thrown when a method is run on a messaging object in a folder that does not exist.

Constructor Methods

public	`FolderNotFoundException`	`();`
public	`FolderNotFoundException`	`(java.lang.String s,` `javax.mail.Folder folder);`

Methods

public **Folder**	`getFolder`	`();`

Inherited from *javax.mail.***MessagingException**
`getMessage, getNextException, setNextException`

Inherited from *java.lang.Throwable*
`fillInStackTrace, getLocalizedMessage, printStackTrace, printStackTrace,`
`printStackTrace, toString`

Inherited from *java.lang.object*
`clone, equals, finalize, getClass, hashCode, notify, notifyAll, wait, wait, wait`

Class javax.mail.IllegalWriteException

`public class IllegalWriteException`

extends *javax.mail.***MessagingException**

Represents the exception thrown when a write method is called upon a read-only object.

Constructor Methods

public	`IllegalWriteException`	`();`
public	`IllegalWriteException`	`(java.lang.String s);`

Methods

Inherited from *javax.mail.***MessagingException**
`getMessage, getNextException, setNextException`

Inherited from *java.lang.Throwable*
`fillInStackTrace, getLocalizedMessage, printStackTrace, printStackTrace,`
`printStackTrace, toString`

Inherited from *java.lang.object*
`clone, equals, finalize, getClass, hashCode, notify, notifyAll, wait, wait, wait`

Class javax.mail.MessageRemovedException

`public class MessageRemovedException`

extends *javax.mail.***MessagingException**

Represents the exception thrown when an invalid method is called upon a message that has been removed.

Constructor Methods

public	`MessageRemovedException`	`();`
public	`MessageRemovedException`	`(java.lang.String s);`

Methods

Inherited from *javax.mail.***MessagingException**
```
getMessage, getNextException, setNextException
```

Inherited from *java.lang.Throwable*
```
fillInStackTrace, getLocalizedMessage, printStackTrace, printStackTrace,
printStackTrace, toString
```

Inherited from *java.lang.object*
```
clone, equals, finalize, getClass, hashCode, notify, notifyAll, wait, wait, wait
```

Class javax.mail.MessagingException

```
public class MessagingException
```

Is extended by **AuthenticationFailedException, FolderClosedException, FolderNotFoundException, IllegalWriteException, MessageRemovedException, MethodNotSupportedException, NoSuchProviderException, ParseException, SearchException, SendFailedException, StoreClosedException.** This is the base class for all the other messaging exception classes in the **javax.mail** package.

Constructor Methods

public	MessagingException	();
public	MessagingException	(*java.lang.String* s);
public	MessagingException	(*java.lang.string* s, java.lang.Exception e);

Methods

public *java.lang.String*	getMessage	();
public *java.lang.Exception*	getNextException	();
public boolean	setNextException	(*java.lang.Exception* ex);

Inherited from *java.lang.Throwable*
```
fillInStackTrace, getLocalizedMessage, printStackTrace, printStackTrace,
printStackTrace, toString
```

Inherited from *java.lang.object*
```
clone, equals, finalize, getClass, hashCode, notify, notifyAll, wait, wait, wait
```

Class javax.mail.MethodNotSupportedException

```
public class MethodNotSupportedException
```

```
extends javax.mail.MessagingException
```

Represents the exception thrown when a method is called that is not incorporated into the implementation.

Constructor Methods

public	MethodNotSupportedException	();
public	MethodNotSupportedException	(*java.lang.String* s);

Methods

Inherited from *javax.mail.*MessagingException
`getMessage, getNextException, setNextException`

Inherited from *java.lang.Throwable*
`fillInStackTrace, getLocalizedMessage, printStackTrace, printStackTrace, printStackTrace, toString`

Inherited from *java.lang.object*
`clone, equals, finalize, getClass, hashCode, notify, notifyAll, wait, wait, wait`

Class javax.mail.NoSuchProviderException

`public class NoSuchProviderException`

extends *javax.mail.*MessagingException

Represents the exception thrown when a mail Session attempts to instantiate a Provider that has not been defined.

Constructor Methods

| public | `NoSuchProviderException` | (); |
| public | `NoSuchProviderException` | (*java.lang.String* message); |

Methods

Inherited from *javax.mail.*MessagingException
`getMessage, getNextException, setNextException`

Inherited from *java.lang.Throwable*
`fillInStackTrace, getLocalizedMessage, printStackTrace, printStackTrace, printStackTrace, toString`

Inherited from *java.lang.object*
`clone, equals, finalize, getClass, hashCode, notify, notifyAll, wait, wait, wait`

Class javax.mail.SendFailedException

`public class SendFailedException`

extends *javax.mail.*MessagingException

Represents the exception thrown when a mail message cannot be sent.

Constructor Methods

public	`SendFailedException`	();
public	`SendFailedException`	(*java.lang.String* s);
public	`SendFailedException`	(*java.lang.String* s, *java.lang.Exception* e);
public	`SendFailedException`	(*java.lang.String* s, *java.lang.Exception* e, *javax.mail.*Address[ ] validSent, *javax.mail.*Address[ ] validUnsent, *javax.mail.*Address[ ] invalid);

Methods

public **Address**[ ]	getInvalidAddresses	();
public **Address**[ ]	getValidSentAddresses	();
public **Address**[ ]	getValidUnsentAddresses	();

Inherited from *javax.mail.***MessagingException**
`getMessage, getNextException, setNextException`

Inherited from *java.lang.Throwable*
`fillInStackTrace, getLocalizedMessage, printStackTrace, printStackTrace, printStackTrace, toString`

Inherited from *java.lang.object*
`clone, equals, finalize, getClass, hashCode, notify, notifyAll, wait, wait, wait`

Fields

protected transient **Address**[ ]	invalid;
protected transient **Address**[ ]	validSent;
protected transient **Address**[ ]	validUnsent;

Class javax.mail.StoreClosedException

`public class StoreClosedException`

extends *javax.mail.***MessagingException**

Represents the exception thrown when a method is run on a messaging object in a store that has 'died' for some reason. This should be treated as a fatal error.

Constructor Methods

public	StoreClosedException	(*javax.mail.***Store** store);
public	StoreClosedException	(*javax.mail.***Store** store, *java.lang.String* message);

Methods

public **Store**	getStore	();

Inherited from *javax.mail.***MessagingException**
`getMessage, getNextException, setNextException`

Inherited from *java.lang.Throwable*
`fillInStackTrace, getLocalizedMessage, printStackTrace, printStackTrace, printStackTrace, toString`

Inherited from *java.lang.object*
`clone, equals, finalize, getClass, hashCode, notify, notifyAll, wait, wait, wait`

Core Jini API Reference

Key

Within this API Reference, the following conventions are used:

- ➤ Interface, Class and Exception names within the APIs listed are all written in **bold**.
- ➤ Interface, Class and Exception names not within the APIs listed are all written in *italics*.
- ➤ Method names are all written in `Courier Bold`.

Package net.jini.core.discovery

The Jini Discovery API is used by previously unconnected services (devices) that wish to join a Jini federation.

Classes

public class	*LookupLocator*	*implements* java.io.Serializable

Class net.jini.core.discovery.LookupLocator

```
public class LookupDiscovery
```

implements java.io.Serializable

A utility class that performs unicast discovery.

Constructor Methods

public	*LookupLocator* *throws*	*(java.lang.String url)* *java.net.MalformedURLException;*
public	*LookupLocator*	*(java.lang.String host,* *int port);*

Methods

public java.lang.String	**getHost**	*();*
public int	**getPort**	*();*
public ServiceRegistrar	**getRegistrar**	*()*
	throws	java.io.IOException, java.lang.ClassNotFoundException;
public ServiceRegistrar	**getRegistrar**	*(int timeout)*
	throws	java.io.IOException, java.lang.ClassNotFoundException;
public boolean	**equals**	*(java.lang.Object o);*
public int	**hashCode**	*();*
public java.lang.String	**toString**	*();*

Fields

protected java.lang.String	**host;**	
protected int	**port;**	

Package net.jini.core.entry

Holds the supertype definition of an Entry marker that all Jini objects must have to be seen within a Jini federation. Contrast with net.jini.entry which holds an abstract implementation of this marker and net.jini.lookup.entry which holds several specific implementations.

Interfaces

public abstract interface	**Entry**	*extends*	java.io.Serializable

Exceptions

public class	**UnusableEntryException**	*extends*	java.lang.Exception

Interface net.jini.core.entry.Entry

```
public abstract interface Entry
```

extends java.io.Serializable

The supertype of all entry markers that are used within Jini lookup services.

Fields

Inherited from java.io.Serializable
serialVersionUID

Class net.jini.core.UnusableEntryException

```
public class UnusableEntryException
```

extends java.lang.Exception

Thrown when an Entry found in a Jini lookup service is deemed unusable.

Constructor Methods

public	**UnusableEntryException**	*(java.lang.Throwable e);*
public	**UnusableEntryException**	*(net.jini.core.entry.Entry partial,* java.lang.String[ ] badFields, java.lang.Throwable[ ] exceptions);

Methods

Inherited from java.lang.Throwable
`fillInStackTrace, getLocalizedMessage, getMessage, printStackTrace, printStackTrace, printStackTrace, toString`

Inherited from *java.lang.Object*
`clone, equals, finalize, getClass, hashCode, notify, notifyAll, wait, wait, wait`

Fields

public java.lang.Throwable*[ ]*	`nestedExceptions;`
public Entry	`partialEntry;`
public java.lang.String*[ ]*	`unusableFields;`

Package net.jini.core.event

Defines the core support for remote events in a Jini environment.

Interfaces

public abstract interface	*RemoteEventListener*	*extends*	java.rmi.Remote, java.util.EventListener;

Classes

public class	*EventRegistration*	*implements*	java.io.Serializable;
public class	*RemoteEvent*	*extends*	java.util.EventObject;
public class	*UnknownEventException*	*extends*	java.lang.Exception ;

Interface net.jini.core.event.RemoteEventListener

`public abstract interface RemoteEventListener`

extends java.rmi.Remote, java.util.EventListener

Allows the object implementing it to be aware of remote events and their occurence.

Method

public abstract void	*notify*	*(*net.jini.core.event.*RemoteEvent theEvent)*
	throws	net.jini.core.event.*UnknownEventException*, java.rmi.*RemoteException*;

Class net.jini.core.event.EventRegistration

`public class EventRegistration`

implements java.io.Serializable

Represents the information needed by a client to note an event occurring in response to a registration request.

Constructor Method

public	*EventRegistration*	*(long eventID,* java.lang.Object *source,* net.jini.core.lease.*Lease lease,* long seqNum);

Methods

public long	`getID`	`();`
public **Lease**	`getLease`	`();`
public long	`getSequenceNumber`	`();`
public java.lang.Object	`getSource`	`();`

Fields

protected long	`eventID;`
protected **Lease**	`lease;`
protected long	`seqNum;`
protected java.lang.Object	`source;`

Class net.jini.core.event.RemoteEvent

```
public class RemoteEvent
```

extends java.util.EventObject

Is extended by net.jini.core.lookup.**ServiceEvent**. The base class for remote events.

Constructor Method

public	`RemoteEvent`	(java.lang.Object *source*, *long eventID*, *long seqNum*, java.rmi.MarshalledObject *handback*);

Methods

public long	`getID`	`();`
public java.rmi.MarshalledObject	`getRegistrationObject`	`();`
public long	`getSequenceNumber`	`();`

Inherited from java.util.EventObject
`getSource, toString`

Inherited from *java.lang.Object*
`clone, equals, finalize, getClass, hashCode, notify, notifyAll, wait, wait, wait`

Fields

protected long	`eventID;`
protected java.rmi.MarshalledObject	`handback;`
protected long	`seqNum;`
protected java.lang.Object	`source;`

Inherited from java.util.EventObject
`Source`

Class net.jini.core.event.UnknownEventException

```
public class UnknownEventException
```

extends java.lang.Exception

Thrown when an object is given notice of a remote event in which it is not interested.

Constructor Methods

public	**UnknownEventException**	*();*
public	**UnknownEventException**	*(*java.lang.String *reason);*

Methods

Inherited from java.lang.Throwable
`fillInStackTrace, getLocalizedMessage, getMessage, printStackTrace, printStackTrace, printStackTrace, toString`

Inherited from *java.lang.Object*
`clone, equals, finalize, getClass, hashCode, notify, notifyAll, wait, wait, wait`

Package net.jini.core.lease

Defines the core Leasing API for Jini. Every client that uses a Jini lookup service has a lease during which it may using the resources or services available.

Interfaces

public abstract interface	*Lease*		
public abstract interface	*LeaseMap*	*extends*	java.util.Map

Exceptions

public class	*LeaseDeniedException*	*extends*	net.jini.core.lease.*LeaseException;*
public class	*LeaseException*	*extends*	java.lang.Exception;
public class	*LeaseMapException*	*extends*	net.jini.core.lease.*LeaseException;*
public class	*UnknownLeaseException*	*extends*	net.jini.core.lease.*LeaseException;*

Interface net.jini.core.lease.Lease

`public abstract interface Lease`

Represents the lookup service lease that clients hold and its properties.

Methods

public boolean	*canBatch*	*(*net.jini.core.lease.*Lease lease);*
public void	*cancel*	*()*
	throws	net.jini.core.lease.*UnknownLeaseException,* java.rmi.RemoteException
public LeaseMap	*createLeaseMap*	*(long duration);*
public long	*getExpiration*	*();*
public int	*getSerialFormat*	*();*
public void	*renew*	*(long duration)*
	throws	net.jini.core.lease.*LeaseDeniedException,* net.jini.core.lease.*UnknownLeaseException,* java.rmi.RemoteException
public void	*setSerialFormat*	*(int format);*

Field Constants

public static final int	*ABSOLUTE*
public static final long	*ANY*
public static final int	*DURATION*
public static final long	*FOREVER*

1031

Interface net.jini.core.lease.LeaseMap

```
public abstract interface LeaseMap
```

```
extends java.util.Map
```

Represents the connection (unsynchronized) between a lease and its duration.

Methods

public void	*cancelAll*	*()*
	throws	net.jini.core.lease.*LeaseMapException*, java.rmi.RemoteException;
public boolean	*canContainKey*	*(java.lang.Object key)*;
public void	*renewAll*	*()*
	throws	net.jini.core.lease.*LeaseMapException*, java.rmi.RemoteException;

Inherited from java.util.Map
clear, containsKey, containsValue, entrySet, equals, get, hashCode, isEmpty, keySet, put, putAll, remove, size, values

Class net.jini.core.lease.LeaseDeniedException

```
public class LeaseDeniedException
```

```
extends net.jini.core.lease.LeaseException
```

Thrown when a lease request or renewal is refused.

Constructor Methods

public	*LeaseDeniedException*	*()*;
public	*LeaseDeniedException*	*(java.lang.String reason)*;

Methods

Inherited from java.lang.Throwable
fillInStackTrace, getLocalizedMessage, getMessage, printStackTrace, printStackTrace, printStackTrace, toString

Inherited from *java.lang.Object*
clone, equals, finalize, getClass, hashCode, notify, notifyAll, wait, wait, wait

Class net.jini.core.lease.LeaseException

```
public class LeaseException
```

```
extends java.lang.Exception
```

Is extended by net.jini.core.lease.**LeaseDeniedException**, net.jini.core.lease.**LeaseMapException**, net.jini.core.lease.**UnknownLeaseException.**
The base class for all lease related exceptions.

Constructor Methods

public	*LeaseException*	*()*;
public	*LeaseException*	*(java.lang.String reason)*;

Methods

Inherited from java.lang.Throwable
`fillInStackTrace, getLocalizedMessage, getMessage, printStackTrace, printStackTrace, printStackTrace, toString`

Inherited from *java.lang.Object*
`clone, equals, finalize, getClass, hashCode, notify, notifyAll, wait, wait, wait`

Class net.jini.core.lease.LeaseMapException

`public class LeaseMapException`

extends net.jini.core.lease.**LeaseException**

Thrown when one or more leases throw an exception during a LeaseMap renewAll or cancelAll operation is called.

Constructor Methods

public	`LeaseMapException`	*(*java.lang.String *s,* java.util.Map *exceptionMap);*

Methods

Inherited from java.lang.Throwable
`fillInStackTrace, getLocalizedMessage, getMessage, printStackTrace, printStackTrace, printStackTrace, toString`

Inherited from *java.lang.Object*
`clone, equals, finalize, getClass, hashCode, notify, notifyAll, wait, wait, wait`

Fields

public java.util.Map	`exceptionMap`

Class net.jini.core.lease.UnknownLeaseException

`public class UnknownLeaseException`

extends net.jini.core.lease.**LeaseException**

Thrown when a lease is not known to the executor of the lease, due to deletion or cancellation, for example.

Constructor Methods

public	`UnknownLeaseException`	*();*
public	`UnknownLeaseException`	*(*java.lang.String *reason);*

Methods

Inherited from java.lang.Throwable
`fillInStackTrace, getLocalizedMessage, getMessage, printStackTrace, printStackTrace, printStackTrace, toString`

Inherited from *java.lang.Object*
`clone, equals, finalize, getClass, hashCode, notify, notifyAll, wait, wait, wait`

Package net.jini.core.lookup

Interfaces

public abstract interface	*ServiceRegistrar*
public abstract interface	*ServiceRegistration*

Classes

public abstract class	*ServiceEvent*	*extends*	net.jini.core.event.*RemoteEvent*
public final class	*ServiceID*	*implements*	java.io.Serializable
public class	*ServiceItem*	*implements*	java.io.Serializable
public class	*ServiceMatches*	*implements*	java.io.Serializable
public class	*ServiceTemplate*	*implements*	java.io.Serializable

Interface net.jini.core.lookup.ServiceRegistrar

```
public abstract interface ServiceRegistrar
```

Defines the client-server interface for a Jini lookup service

Methods

public java.lang.Class[]	`getEntryClasses`	(net.jini.core.lookup.*ServiceTemplate tmp1*)
	throws	java.rmi.RemoteException;
public java.lang.Object[]	`getFieldValues`	(net.jini.core.lookup.*ServiceTemplate tmp1*,
	int setIndex)	
	throws	java.lang.NoSuchFieldException,
		java.rmi.RemoteException;
public java.lang.String[]	`getGroups`	()
	throws	java.rmi.RemoteException;
public *LookupLocator*	`getLocator`	()
	throws	java.rmi.RemoteException;
public *ServiceID*	`getServiceID`	();
public java.lang.Class	`getServiceTypes`	(net.jini.core.lookup.*ServiceTemplate tmpl*,
		java.lang.String *prefix)*
	throws	java.rmi.RemoteException;
public java.lang.Object	`lookup`	(net.jini.core.lookup.*ServiceTemplate tmp1*)
	throws	java.rmi.RemoteException;
public ServiceMatches	`lookup`	(net.jini.core.lookup.*ServiceTemplate tmp1*,
		int maxMatches)
	throws	java.rmi.RemoteException;
public *EventRegistration*	`notify`	(net.jini.core.lookup.*ServiceTemplate tmp1*,
		int transitions,
		net.jini.core.event.*RemoteEventListener listener,*
		java.rmi.MarshalledObject *handback,*
		long leaseDuration)
	throws	java.rmi.RemoteException;
public *ServiceRegistration*	`register`	(net.jini.core.lookup.*ServiceItem item,*
		long leaseDuration)
	throws	java.rmi.RemoteException;

Fields

public final static int	`TRANSITION_MATCH_MATCH;`
public final static int	`TRANSITION_MATCH_NOMATCH;`
public final static int	`TRANSITION_NOMATCH_MATCH;`

Interface net.jini.core.lookup.ServiceRegistration

```
public abstract interface ServiceRegistration
```

Used to change the registration details of a service item.

Methods

public void	**setAttributes**	*(*net.jini.core.entry.***Entry**[] *attrSets)*
	throws	net.jini.core.lease.***UnknownLeaseException**, java.rmi.RemoteException*;*
*public **Lease***	**getLease**	*();*
*public **ServiceID***	**getServiceID**	*();*
public void	**addAttributes**	*(*net.jini.core.entry.***Entry**[] *attrSets)*
	throws	net.jini.core.lease.***UnknownLeaseException**, java.rmi.RemoteException;
public void	**modifyAttributes**	*(*net.jini.core.entry.***Entry**[] *attrSetTemplates,* net.jini.core.entry.***Entry**[] *attrSets)*
	throws	net.jini.core.lease.***UnknownLeaseException**, java.rmi.RemoteException;

Class net.jini.core.lookup.ServiceEvent

```
public abstract class ServiceEvent
```

extends net.jini.core.event.**RemoteEvent**

Represents any remote event that the lookup service might have sent.

Constructor Method

public	**ServiceEvent**	*(*java.lang.Object *source,* long eventID, long seqNo, java.rmi.MarshalledObject *handback,* net.jini.core.lookup.***ServiceID** serviceID, int transition);*

Methods

*public **ServiceID***	**getServiceID**	*();*
*public abstract **ServiceItem***	**getServiceItem**	*();*
public int	**getTransition**	*();*

Inherited from net.jini.core.event.**RemoteEvent**
getID, getRegistrationObject, getSequenceNumber

Inherited from java.util.EventObject
getSource, toString

Inherited from *java.lang.Object*
clone, equals, finalize, getClass, hashCode, notify, notifyAll, wait, wait, wait

Fields

*protected **ServiceID***	**serviceID;**
protected int	**transition;**

Inherited from net.jini.core.event.**RemoteEvent**
eventID, handback, seqNum, source

Inherited from java.util.EventObject
source

Class net.jini.core.lookup.ServiceID

```
public final class ServiceID
```

implements java.io.Serializable

Represents the UID given to all services registered in the Jini federation.

Constructor Methods

public	*ServiceID*	*(java.io.DataInput in)*
	throws	java.io.IOException;
public	*ServiceID*	*(long mostSig,*
		long leastSig);

Methods

public boolean	*equals*	*(java.lang.Object obj);*
public long	*getLeastSignificantBits*	*();*
public long	*getMostSignificantBits*	*();*
public int	*hashCode*	*();*
public java.lang.String	*toString*	*();*
public void	*writeBytes*	*(java.io.DataOutput out)*
	throws	java.io.IOException;

Inherited from *java.lang.Object*
`clone, finalize, getClass, notify, notifyAll, wait, wait, wait`

Class net.jini.core.lookup.ServiceItem

```
public class ServiceItem
```

implements java.io.Serializable

Items are stored in and retrieved from the lookup service using instances of this class.

Constructor Method

public	*ServiceItem*	*(net.jini.core.lookup.ServiceID serviceID,*
		java.lang.Object *service,*
		net.jini.core.entry.*Entry[ ] attrSets);*

Methods

Inherited from *java.lang.Object*
`clone, equals, finalize, getClass, hashCode, notify, notifyAll, wait, wait, wait`

Fields

public Entry[ ]	*attributeSets;*
public java.lang.Object	*service;*
public ServiceID	*serviceID;*

Class net.jini.core.lookup.ServiceMatches

```
public class ServiceMatches
```

implements java.io.Serializable

Represents the value returned after searching for more than one item in the lookup service.

Constructor Method

public	*ServiceMatches*	(net.jini.core.lookup.*ServiceItem[ ] items,* *int totalMatches);*

Methods

Inherited from *java.lang.Object*
`clone, equals, finalize, getClass, hashCode, notify, notifyAll, wait, wait, wait`

Fields

public ServiceItem[ ]	`items;`
public int	`totalMatches;`

Class net.jini.core.lookup.ServiceTemplate

`public class ServiceTemplate`

`implements java.io.Serializable`

Represents the templates used by searches to match items in the lookup table.

Constructor Method

public	*ServiceTemplate*	(net.jini.core.lookup.*ServiceID serviceID,* java.lang.Class*[ ] serviceTypes,* net.jini.core.entry.*Entry[ ] attrSetTemplates);*

Methods

Inherited from *java.lang.Object*
`clone, equals, finalize, getClass, hashCode, notify, notifyAll, wait, wait, wait`

Fields

public Entry[ ]	`attributeSetTemplates;`
public ServiceID	`serviceID;`
public Class[ ]	`serviceTypes;`

Package net.jini.core.transaction

As the name implies, this package provides the basic building blocks for supporting (two phase) transacted services.

Interfaces

public abstract interface	*NestableTransaction*	*extends*	net.jini.core.transaction.*Transaction*
public abstract interface	*Transaction*		

Classes

public static class	*NestableTransaction.Created*	*implements*	java.io.Serializable
public static class	*Transaction.Created*	*implements*	java.io.Serializable
public class	*TransactionFactory*		

Exceptions

public class	*CannotAbortException*	*extends*	net.jini.core.transaction.*TransactionException*
public class	*CannotCommitException*	*extends*	net.jini.core.transaction.*TransactionException*
public class	*CannotJoinException*	*extends*	net.jini.core.transaction.*TransactionException*
public class	*CannotNestException*	*extends*	net.jini.core.transaction.*TransactionException*
public class	*TimeoutExpiredException*	*extends*	net.jini.core.transaction.*TransactionException*
public class	*TransactionException*	*extends*	java.lang.Exception
public class	*UnknownTransactionException*	*extends*	net.jini.core.transaction.*TransactionException*

Interface net.jini.core.transaction.NestableTransaction

```
public abstract interface NestableTransaction
```

extends net.jini.core.transaction.**Transaction**

Is extended by net.jini.core.server.transaction.server.**NestableServerTransaction**.
Interface for classes representing nested transactions.

Inner Classes

public static class	*NestableTransaction.Created*	*implements*	java.io.Serializable;

Inherited from net.jini.core.transaction.**Transaction**
> `Transaction.Created`

Methods

public NestableTransaction.Created	**create**	*(long leaseTime)*
	throws	net.jini.core.transaction.*UnknownTransactionException*,
		net.jini.core.transaction.*CannotJoinException*,
		net.jini.core.lease.*LeaseDeniedException*,
		java.rmi.RemoteException;
public NestableTransaction.Created	**create**	*(net.jini.core.transaction.server.NestableTransactionManager mgr,*
		long leaseTime)
	throws	net.jini.core.transaction.*UnknownTransactionException*,
		net.jini.core.transaction.*CannotJoinException*,
		net.jini.core.lease.*LeaseDeniedException*,
		java.rmi.RemoteException;

Interface net.jini.core.transaction.Transaction

```
public abstract interface Transaction
```

Is extended by net.jini.core.transaction.**NestedTransaction**. Is implemented by
net.jini.core.transaction.server.**ServerTransaction**. Interface for classes
representing transactions.

Inner Classes

public static class	*Transaction.Created implements*	java.io.Serializable;

Methods

public void	**commit**	*()*
	throws	net.jini.core.transaction.*UnknownTransactionException*,
		net.jini.core.transaction.*CannotCommitException*,
		java.rmi.RemoteException;
public void	**commit**	*(long waitFor)*
	throws	net.jini.core.transaction.*UnknownTransactionException*,
		net.jini.core.transaction.*CannotCommitException*,
		net.jini.core.transacton.*TimeoutExpiredException*,
		java.rmi.RemoteException;
public void	**abort**	*()*
	throws	net.jini.core.transaction.*UnknownTransactionException*,
		net.jini.core.transaction.*CannotAbortException*,
		java.rmi.RemoteException;
public void	**abort**	*(long waitFor)*
	throws	net.jini.core.transaction.*UnknownTransactionException*,
		net.jini.core.transaction.*CannotAbortException*,
		net.jini.core.transacton.*TimeoutExpiredException*,
		java.rmi.RemoteException;

Class net.jini.core.transaction.NestableTransaction.Created

```
public static class NestableTransaction.Created
```

implements java.io.Serializable

Inner class that holds return values from create methods stored in
net.jini.core.transaction.**NestableTransaction**.

Constructor Method

public   `NestableTransaction.Created`
    (net.jini.core.transaction.NestableTransaction transaction,
net.jini.core.lease.Lease lease);

Methods

Inherited from *java.lang.Object*
```
clone, equals, finalize, getClass, hashCode, notify, notifyAll, toString, wait,
wait, wait
```

Fields

public final **Lease**   `lease;`
public final **NestableTransaction**   `transaction;`

Class net.jini.core.transaction.Transaction.Created

```
public static class Transaction.Created
```

implements java.io.Serializable

Inner class that holds return values from create methods stored in net.jini.core.transaction.
Transaction.

Constructor Method

public   `Transaction.Created`   *(net.jini.core.transaction.Transaction transaction,*
net.jini.core.lease.Lease lease);

Methods

Inherited from *java.lang.Object*
```
clone, equals, finalize, getClass, hashCode, notify, notifyAll, toString, wait,
wait, wait
```

Fields

public final **Lease**   `lease;`
public final **Transaction**   `transaction;`

Class net.jini.core.transaction.TransactionFactory

```
public class TransactionFactory
```

Factory methods for creating top-level transactions.

Methods

*public static **Transaction.Created***	`create`	
	(net.jini.core.transaction.server.***TransactionManager*** *mgr,*	
		long leaseTime)
	throws	net.jini.core.lease.***LeaseDeniedException***,
		java.rmi.RemoteException;
*public static **NestableTransaction.Created***	`create`	
	(net.jini.core.transaction.server.***NestableTransactionManager*** *mgr,*	
		long leaseTime)
	throws	net.jini.core.lease.***LeaseDeniedException***,
		java.rmi.RemoteException;

Inherited from *java.lang.Object*
```
clone, equals, finalize, getClass, hashCode, notify, notifyAll, toString, wait,
wait, wait
```

Class net.jini.core.transaction.CannotAbortException

```
public class CannotAbortException
```

extends net.jini.core.transaction.**TransactionException**

Thrown when a transaction cannot abort as it has already been committed.

Constructor Methods

public	`CannotAbortException`	*()*;
public	`CannotAbortException`	(java.lang.String *desc)*;

Methods

Inherited from java.lang.Throwable
```
fillInStackTrace, getLocalizedMessage, getMessage, printStackTrace,
printStackTrace, printStackTrace, toString
```

Inherited from *java.lang.Object*
```
clone, equals, finalize, getClass, hashCode, notify, notifyAll, wait, wait, wait
```

Class net.jini.core.transaction.CannotCommitException

```
public class CannotCommitException
```

extends net.jini.core.transaction.**TransactionException**

Thrown when a transaction cannot commit as it has already been aborted or must be aborted.

Constructor Methods

public	`CannotCommitException`	*()*;
public	`CannotCommitException`	(java.lang.String *desc)*;

Methods

Inherited from java.lang.Throwable
```
fillInStackTrace, getLocalizedMessage, getMessage, printStackTrace,
printStackTrace, printStackTrace, toString
```

Inherited from *java.lang.Object*
```
clone, equals, finalize, getClass, hashCode, notify, notifyAll, wait, wait, wait
```

Class net.jini.core.transaction.CannotJoinException

```
public class CannotJoinException
```

extends net.jini.core.transaction.**TransactionException**

Thrown when a transaction can no longer be added to (joined) as it has already finished.

Constructor Methods

public	`CannotJoinException`	*();*
public	`CannotJoinException`	*(*java.lang.String *desc);*

Methods

Inherited from java.lang.Throwable
`fillInStackTrace, getLocalizedMessage, getMessage, printStackTrace, printStackTrace, printStackTrace, toString`

Inherited from *java.lang.Object*
`clone, equals, finalize, getClass, hashCode, notify, notifyAll, wait, wait, wait`

Class net.jini.core.transaction.CannotNestException

```
public class CannotNestException
```

extends net.jini.core.transaction.**TransactionException**

Thrown when nested transactions are not supported by the active object.

Constructor Methods

public	`CannotNestException`	*();*
public	`CannotNestException`	*(*java.lang.String *desc);*

Methods

Inherited from java.lang.Throwable
`fillInStackTrace, getLocalizedMessage, getMessage, printStackTrace, printStackTrace, printStackTrace, toString`

Inherited from *java.lang.Object*
`clone, equals, finalize, getClass, hashCode, notify, notifyAll, wait, wait, wait`

Class net.jini.core.transaction.TimeoutExpiredException

```
public class TimeoutExpiredException
```

extends net.jini.core.transaction.**TransactionException**

Thrown when the timeout value set for the transaction has passed.

Constructor Methods

public	`TimeoutExpiredException`	*(boolean committed);*
public	`TimeoutExpiredException`	*(*java.lang.String *desc, boolean committed);*

Methods

Inherited from java.lang.Throwable
`fillInStackTrace, getLocalizedMessage, getMessage, printStackTrace,`
`printStackTrace, printStackTrace, toString`

Inherited from *java.lang.Object*
`clone, equals, finalize, getClass, hashCode, notify, notifyAll, wait, wait, wait`

Fields

public boolean	`committed;`

Class net.jini.core.transaction.TransactionException

`public class CannotNestException`

`extends` java.lang.Exception

This is the base class for all exceptions thrown during a transaction. Is extended by all other exception classes in net.jini.core.transaction and also by net.jini.core.transaction.server.**CrashCountException.**

Constructor Methods

public	`TransactionException`	`();`
public	`TransactionException`	(java.lang.String *desc);*

Methods

Inherited from java.lang.Throwable
`fillInStackTrace, getLocalizedMessage, getMessage, printStackTrace,`
`printStackTrace, printStackTrace, toString`

Inherited from *java.lang.Object*
`clone, equals, finalize, getClass, hashCode, notify, notifyAll, wait, wait, wait`

Class net.jini.core.transaction.UnknownTransactionException

`public class UnknownTransactionException`

`extends` net.jini.core.transaction.**TransactionException**

Thrown when a target transaction is either not known or not valid.

Constructor Methods

public	`UnknownTransactionException`	`();`
public	`UnknownTransactionException`	(java.lang.String *desc);*

Methods

Inherited from java.lang.Throwable
`fillInStackTrace, getLocalizedMessage, getMessage, printStackTrace,`
`printStackTrace, printStackTrace, toString`

Inherited from *java.lang.Object*
`clone, equals, finalize, getClass, hashCode, notify, notifyAll, wait, wait, wait`

Package net.jini.core.transaction.server

Provides the server-side support for supporting (two phase) transacted services.

Interfaces

public abstract interface	*NestableTransactionManager*	*extends* net.jini.core.transaction.server.*TransactionManager*
public abstract interface	*TransactionConstants*	
public abstract interface	*TransactionManager*	*extends* java.rmi.Remote, net.jini.core.transaction.server.*TransactionConstants*
public abstract interface	*TransactionParticipant*	*extends* java.rmi.Remote, net.jini.core.transaction.server.*TransactionConstants*

Classes

public class	*NestableServerTransaction*	*extends* net.jini.core.transaction.server.*ServerTransaction* *implements* net.jini.core.transaction.*NestableTransaction*
public class	*ServerTransaction*	*implements* net.jini.core.transaction.*Transaction*, java.io.Serializable
public static class	*TransactionManager.Created*	*implements* java.io.Serializable

Exceptions

public class	*CrashCountException*	*extends* net.jini.core.transaction.*TransactionException*

Interface net.jini.core.transaction.server.NestableTransactionManager

```
public abstract interface NestableTransactionManager
```

extends net.jini.core.transaction.server.**TransactionManager**

Base class for transaction managers that can deal with nestable transactions. Applications that use nestable transactions must 'attach' them to this class.

Inner Class

Inherited from net.jini.core.transaction.server.**TransactionManager**
```
    TransactionManager.Created
```

Methods

*public **TransactionManager.Created***	`create`	(net.jini.core.transaction.server.*NestableTransactionManager* parentMgr, long parentID, long lease)
	throws	net.jini.core.transaction.*UnknownTransactionException*, net.jini.core.transaction.*CannotJoinException*, net.jini.core.lease.*LeaseDeniedException*, java.rmi.RemoteException;
public void	`promote`	(long id, net.jini.core.transaction.server.*TransactionParticipant[]* parts, long[] crashCounts, net.jini.core.transaction.server.*TransactionParticipant*
drop)		
throws		net.jini.core.transaction.*UnknownTransactionException*, net.jini.core.transaction.*CannotJoinException*, net.jini.core.transaction.server.*CrashCountException*, java.rmi.RemoteException;

Inherited from net.jini.core.transaction.server.**TransactionManager**
```
abort, abort, commit, commit, create, getstate, join
```

Fields

Inherited from net.jini.core.transaction.server.**TransactionConstants**
```
ABORTED, ACTIVE, COMMITTED, NOTCHANGED, PREPARED, VOTING
```

Interface net.jini.core.transaction.server.TransactionConstants

```
public abstract interface TransactionConstants
```

Is extended by the other three interfaces in this package. This interface contains some constants common to transactions and transaction managers.

Fields

public static final int	**ABORTED;**
public static final int	**ACTIVE;**
public static final int	**COMMITTED;**
public static final int	**NOTCHANGED;**
public static final int	**PREPARED;**
public static final int	**VOTING;**

Interface net.jini.core.transaction.server.TransactionManager

```
public abstract interface TransactionManager
```

extends java.rmi.Remote, net.jini.core.transaction.server.**TransactionConstants**

Is extended by net.jini.core.transaction.server.**NestedTransactionManager**. Base interface for top-level transaction managers.

Inner Class

public static class	*TransactionManager.Created*	*implements*	java.io.Serializable;

Methods

public void	**abort**	*(long id)*
	throws	net.jini.core.transaction.*UnknownTransactionException*,
		net.jini.core.transaction.*CannotAborttException*,
		java.rmi.RemoteException;
public void	**abort**	*(long id,*
		long waitFor
	throws	net.jini.core.transaction.*UnknownTransactionException*,
		net.jini.core.transaction.*CannotAbortException*,
		net.jini.core.transaction.*TimeoutExpiredException*,
		java.rmi.RemoteException;
public void	**commit**	*(long id)*
	throws	net.jini.core.transaction.*UnknownTransactionException*,
		net.jini.core.transaction.*CannotCommitException*,
		java.rmi.RemoteException;
public void	**commit**	*(long id,*
		long waitFor
	throws	net.jini.core.transaction.*UnknownTransactionException*,
		net.jini.core.transaction.*CannotCommitException*,
		net.jini.core.transaction.*TimeoutExpiredException*,
		java.rmi.RemoteException;
public TransactionManager.Created	**create**	*(long lease)*
	throws	net.jini.core.lease.*LeaseDeniedException*,
		java.rmi.RemoteException;
public int	**getState**	*(long id)*
	throws	net.jini.core.transaction.*UnknownTransactionException*,
		java.rmi.RemoteException;
public void	**join**	*(long id,*
		net.jini.core.transaction.server.*TransactionParticipant part)*
	throws	net.jini.core.transaction.*UnknownTransactionException*,
		net.jini.core.transaction.*CannotJoinException*,
		net.jini.core.transaction.server.*CrashCountException*,
		java.rmi.RemoteException;

Fields

Inherited from net.jini.core.transaction.server.**TransactionConstants**
ABORTED, ACTIVE, COMMITTED, NOTCHANGED, PREPARED, VOTING

Interface net.jini.core.transaction.server.TransactionParticipant

`public abstract interface TransactionParticipant`

extends java.rmi.Remote, net.jini.core.transaction.server.**TransactionConstants**

Base interface for top-level transaction participants containing methods called by the transaction's manager object.

Methods

public void	**abort**	(net.jini.core.transaction.*TransactionManager* mgr, *long id)*
	throws	net.jini.core.transaction.*UnknownTransactionException*, java.rmi.RemoteException;
public void	**commit**	(net.jini.core.transaction.*TransactionManager* mgr, *long id)*
	throws	net.jini.core.transaction.*UnknownTransactionException*, java.rmi.RemoteException;
public int	**prepare**	(net.jini.core.transaction.*TransactionManager* mgr, *long id)*
	throws	net.jini.core.transaction.*UnknownTransactionException*, java.rmi.RemoteException;
public void	**prepareAndCommit**	(net.jini.core.transaction.*TransactionManager* mgr, *long id)*
	throws	net.jini.core.transaction.*UnknownTransactionException*, java.rmi.RemoteException ;

Fields

Inherited from net.jini.core.transaction.server.**TransactionConstants**
ABORTED, ACTIVE, COMMITTED, NOTCHANGED, PREPARED, VOTING

Class net.jini.core.transaction.server.NestableServerTransaction

`public class NestableServerTransaction`

extends net.jini.core.transaction.server.**ServerTransaction**
implements net.jini.core.transaction.**NestableTransaction**

Class for nestable transactions that implement the default transaction methods in **NestableTransaction**.

Constructor Method

public	**NestableServerTransaction**	(net.jini.core.transaction.*NestableTransaction* mgr, *long id,* net.jini.core.transaction.*NestableTransaction*
parent);		

Methods

public NestableTransaction.Created	**create**	*(long leaseTime)*
	throws	net.jini.core.transaction.*UnknownTransactionException*, net.jini.core.transaction.*CannotJoinException*, net.jini.core.lease.*LeaseDeniedException*, java.rmi.RemoteException;
public NestableTransaction.Created	**create**	(net.jini.core.transaction.*NestableTransaction* mgr, *long leaseTime)*
	throws	net.jini.core.transaction.*UnknownTransactionException*, net.jini.core.transaction.*CannotJoinException*, net.jini.core.lease.*LeaseDeniedException*, java.rmi.RemoteException;
public boolean	**enclosedBy**	(net.jini.core.transaction.*NestableTransaction* enclosing);
public boolean	**isNested**	();

public void	**promote**	net.jini.core.transaction.server.*TransactionParticipant[]* parts,
		long[] crashCounts,
		net.jini.core.transaction.server.*TransactionParticipant*
drop)		
	throws	net.jini.core.transaction.*UnknownTransactionException*,
		net.jini.core.transaction.*CannotJoinException*,
		net.jini.core.transaction.server.*CrashCountException*,
		java.rmi.RemoteException;

Inherited from net.jini.core.transaction.server.**ServerTransaction**
```
abort, abort, commit, commit, equals, getState, hashCode, join
```

Inherited from *java.lang.Object*
```
clone, finalize, getClass, notify, notifyAll, toString, wait, wait, wait
```

Fields

public final **NestableServerTransaction**   `parent`;

Inherited from net.jini.core.transaction.server.**ServerTransaction**
```
id, mgr
```

Class net.jini.core.transaction.server.ServerTransaction

```
public class ServerTransaction
```

```
implements net.jini.core.transaction.Transaction, java.io.Serializable
```

Class for transactions that implement the default transaction methods in **Transaction**.

Constructor Method

public	**ServerTransaction**	(net.jini.core.transaction.*NestableTransaction* mgr,
		long id);

Methods

public void	**abort**	()
	throws	net.jini.core.transaction.*UnknownTransactionException*,
		net.jini.core.transaction.*CannotAbortException*,
		java.rmi.RemoteException;
public void	**abort**	(long waitFor)
	throws	net.jini.core.transaction.*UnknownTransactionException*,
		net.jini.core.transaction.*CannotAbortException*,
		net.jini.core.transaction.*TimeoutExpiredException*,
		java.rmi.RemoteException;
public void	**commit**	()
	throws	net.jini.core.transaction.*UnknownTransactionException*,
		net.jini.core.transaction.*CannotCommitException*,
		java.rmi.RemoteException;
public void	**commit**	(long waitFor)
	throws	net.jini.core.transaction.*UnknownTransactionException*,
		net.jini.core.transaction.*CannotCommitException*,
		net.jini.core.transaction.*TimeoutExpiredException*,
		java.rmi.RemoteException;
public boolean	**equals**	(java.lang.Object *other);*
public int	**hashCode**	();
public boolean	**isNested**	();
public int	**getState**	();
	throws	net.jini.core.transaction.*UnknownTransactionException*,
		java.rmi.RemoteException;
public void	**join**	(net.jini.core.transaction.server.*TransactionParticipant* part,
		long crashCount)
	throws	net.jini.core.transaction.*UnknownTransactionException*,
		net.jini.core.transaction.*CannotJoinException*,
		net.jini.core.transaction.server.*CrashCountException*,
		java.rmi.RemoteException;

Inherited from *java.lang.Object*
clone, finalize, getClass, notify, notifyAll, toString, wait, wait, wait

Fields

public final long	**id**;
public final TransactionManager	**mgr**;

Class net.jini.core.transaction.server.TransactionManager.Created

```
public static class TransactionManager.Created
```

implements java.io.Serializable

Class that holds values made by **create** methods in **TransactionManager**.

Constructor Method

public	**Transaction.Created**	(net.jini.core.transaction.*Transaction transaction,* net.jini.core.lease.*Lease lease);*

Inherited from *java.lang.Object*
clone, equals, finalize, getClass, hashCode, notify, notifyAll, toString, wait, wait, wait

Fields

public final Lease	**lease**;
public final Transaction	**transaction**;

Class net.jini.core.transaction.server.CrashCountException

```
public class CrashCountException
```

extends net.jini.core.transaction.**TransactionException**

Thrown when a transaction cannot be joined because there is a difference between the crash counts the transaction participant currently has and the one kept by the transaction manager which the participant gave on joining the transaction.

Constructor Methods

public	**CrashCountException**	();
public	**CrashCountException**	(java.lang.String *reason);*

Methods

Inherited from java.lang.throwable
fillInStackTrace, getLocalizedMessage, getMessage, printStackTrace, printStackTrace, printStackTrace, toString

Inherited from class *java.lang.Object*
clone, equals, finalize, getClass, hashCode, notify, notifyAll, wait, wait, wait

JavaSpaces API Reference

The JavaSpaces API is contained in one small package in the standard extension to the core Jini API reference: **net.jini.space**.

Key

Within this API Reference, the following conventions are used:

➤ Interface, Class and Exception names within the APIs listed are all written in **bold**.

➤ Interface, Class and Exception names not within the APIs listed are all written in *italics*.

➤ Method and Class names are written in `Courier Bold`.

Package net.jini.space

Interface

public abstract interface   **JavaSpace**

Exception

public class   **InternalSpaceException**   extends *java.lang.RuntimeException*

Interface net.jini.space.JavaSpace

```
public abstract interface JavaSpace
```

Interface that supports the JavaSpaces technology. Provides the base methods that all JavaSpaces support.

Methods

public abstract *net.jini.core.event.EventRegistration*		
	notify	(net.jini.core.entry.Entry tmpl,
		net.jini.core.transaction.Transaction txn,
		net.jini.core.event.RemoteEventListener listener,
		long lease,
		java.rmi.MarshalledObject handback)
	throws	net.jini.core.transaction.TransactionException,
		java.lang.SecurityException,
		java.rmi.RemoteException;
public abstract *net.jini.core.entry.*Entry	read	(net.jini.core.entry.Entry entry,
		net.jini.core.transaction.Transaction txn,
		long timeout)
	throws	net.jini.core.entry.UnusableEntryException,
		net.jini.core.transaction.TransactionException,
		java.lang.SecurityException,
		java.lang.InterruptedException,
		java.rmi.RemoteException;
public abstract *net.jini.core.entry.*Entry	readIfExists	(net.jini.core.entry.Entry entry,
		net.jini.core.transaction.Transaction txn,
		long timeout)
	throws	net.jini.core.entry.UnusableEntryException,
		net.jini.core.transaction.TransactionException,
		java.lang.SecurityException,
		java.lang.InterruptedException,
		java.rmi.RemoteException;
public abstract *net.jini.core.entry.*Entry	snapshot	(net.jini.core.entry.Entry e)
	throws	java.rmi.RemoteException;
public abstract *net.jini.core.entry.*Entry	take	(net.jini.core.entry.Entry tmpl,
		net.jini.core.transaction.Transaction txn,
		long timeout)
	throws	net.jini.core.entry.UnusableEntryException,
		net.jini.core.transaction.TransactionException,
		java.lang.SecurityException,
		java.lang.InterruptedException,
		java.rmi.RemoteException;
public abstract *net.jini.core.entry.*Entry	takeIfExists	(net.jini.core.entry.Entry tmpl,
		net.jini.core.transaction.Transaction txn,
		long timeout)
	throws	net.jini.core.entry.UnusableEntryException,
		net.jini.core.transaction.TransactionException,
		java.lang.SecurityException,
		java.lang.InterruptedException,
		java.rmi.RemoteException;
public abstract *net.jini.core.lease.*Lease	write	(net.jini.core.entry.Entry entry,
		net.jini.core.transaction.Transaction txn,
		long lease)
	throws	net.jini.core.transaction.TransactionException,
		java.lang.SecurityException,
		java.rmi.RemoteException;

Field

public static final long	NO_WAIT	

Class net.jini.space.InternalSpaceException

```
public class InternalSpaceException
```

extends *java.lang.RuntimeException*

Thrown when a problem is detected with the local implementation of a JavaSpace.

Constructor Methods

public	`InternalSpaceException`	(*java.lang.String* str)
public	`InternalSpaceException`	(*java.lang.String* str, *java.lang.Throwable* ex)

Methods

public void	`printStackTrace`	()
public void	`printStackTrace`	(*java.io.PrintStream* out)
public void	`printStackTrace`	(*java.io.PrintWriter* out)

Inherited from *java.lang.Throwable*
`fillInStackTrace, getLocalizedMessage, getMessage, toString`

Inherited from *java.lang.Object*
`clone, equals, finalize, getClass, hashCode, notify, notifyAll, wait, wait, wait`

Field

public final *java.lang.Throwable*	`nestedException`

Enterprise JavaBeans API Reference

Key

Within this API Reference, the following conventions are used:

> Interface, Class and Exception names within the APIs listed are all written in **bold**.

> Interface, Class and Exception names not within the APIs listed are all written in *italics*.

> Method names are all written in `Courier Bold`.

The Enterprise JavaBeans API is part of Java 2, Enterprise Edition within its API set. This reference details version 1.1 of the EJB API. It contains one package, **javax.ejb**.

Package javax.ejb

The contents of **javax.ejb** have changed between versions 1.0 and 1.1 and the differences have been noted accordingly.

Interfaces new in EJB 1.1

public abstract interface	**HomeHandle**	extends	*java.io.Serializable*;

Interfaces

public abstract interface	**EJBContext**;		
public abstract interface	**EJBHome**	extends	*java.rmi.Remote*;
public abstract interface	**EJBMetaData**;		
public abstract interface	**EJBObject**	extends	*java.rmi.Remote*;
public abstract interface	**EnterpriseBean**	extends	*java.io.Serializable*;
public abstract interface	**EntityBean**	extends	*javax.ejb.EnterpriseBean*;

public abstract interface	**EntityContext**	extends	*javax.ejb.***EJBContext**;
public abstract interface	**Handle**	extends	*java.io.Serializable*;
public abstract interface	**SessionBean**	extends	*javax.ejb.***EnterpriseBean**;
public abstract interface	**SessionContext**	extends	*javax.ejb.***EJBContext**;
public abstract interface	**SessionSynchronization**;		

Exceptions new in EJB 1.1

public class	**NoSuchEntityException**	extends	*javax.ejb.***EJBException**;

Exceptions

public class	**CreateException**	extends	*java.lang.Exception*;
public class	**DuplicateKeyException**	extends	*javax.ejb.***CreateException**;
public class	**EJBException**	extends	*java.lang.RuntimeException*;
public class	**FinderException**	extends	*java.lang.Exception*;
public class	**ObjectNotFoundException**	extends	*javax.ejb.***FinderException**;
public class	**RemoveException**	extends	*java.lang.Exception*;

Interface javax.ejb.EJBContext

```
public abstract interface EJBContext
```

Provides the implementor with access methods to the runtime context of an Enterprise bean.

Methods new in EJB 1.1

public *java.security.Principal*	`getCallerPrincipal`	();
public boolean	`isCallerInRole`	(*java.lang.String* roleName);

Methods

public **EJBHome**	`getEJBHome`	();	
public boolean	`getRollbackOnly`	()	
	throws		*java.lang.IllegalStateException*;
public *javax.transaction.UserTransaction*		`getUserTransaction`	()
	throws		*java.lang.IllegalStateException*;
public void	`setRollbackOnly`	()	
	throws		*java.lang.IllegalStateException*;

Methods Deprecated in EJB 1.1

public *java.security.Identity*	`getCallerIdentity`	();
public *java.util.Properties*	`getEnvironment`	();
public boolean	`isCallerInRole`	(*java.securityIdentity* role);

Interface javax.ejb.EJBHome

```
public abstract interface EJBHome
```

extends *java.rmi.Remote*

Apparent in all EJBs, **EJBHome** is the base interface defining some of a bean's lifecycle methods.

Methods new in EJB 1.1

public **HomeHandle**	`getHomeHandle`	();

Methods

public **EJBMetaData**	getEJBMetaData	()
	throws	*java.rmi.RemoteException*;
public void	remove	(*java.lang.Object* primaryKey)
	throws	*java.rmi.RemoteException*,
		*javax.ejb.***RemoveException**;
public void	remove	(*javax.ejb.***Handle** handle)
	throws	*java.rmi.RemoteException*,
		*javax.ejb.***RemoveException**;

Interface javax.ejb.EJBMetaData

```
public abstract interface EJBMetaData
```

Every EJB has some metadata associated with it for use in applications and interaction with uncompiled scripts. **EJBMetaData** allows access to this.

Methods new in EJB 1.1

public boolean	isStatelessSession	();

Methods

public **EJBHome**	getEJBHome	();
public *java.lang.Class*	getHomeInterfaceClass	();
public *java.lang.Class*	getPrimaryKeyClass	();
public *java.lang.Class*	getRemoteInterfaceClass	();
public boolean	isSession	();

Interface javax.ejb.EJBObject

```
public abstract interface EJBObject
```

extends *java.rmi.Remote*

EJBObject is the base interface for every EJB's remote interface which in turn provides clients with a view of the EJB.

Methods

public **EJBHome**	getEJBHome	()
	throws	*java.rmi.RemoteException*;
public **Handle**	getHandle	()
	throws	*java.rmi.RemoteException*;
public *java.lang.Object*	getPrimaryKey	()
	throws	*java.rmi.RemoteException*;
public boolean	isIdentical	(*javax.ejb.***EJBObject** obj)
	throws	*java.rmi.RemoteException*;
public void	remove	()
	throws	*java.rmi.RemoteException*,
		*javax.ejb.***RemoveException**;

Interface Javax.ejb.EnterpriseBean

```
public abstract interface EnterpriseBean
```

extends *java.io.Serializable*

Is extended by *javax.ejb.***EntityBean** and *javax.ejb.***SessionBean**. Used as a marker interface to indicate that both EntityBeans and SessionBeans are EJBs. This interface **must** be implemented by every EJB.

Fields

Inherited from *java.io.Serializable*
`serialVersionUID`

Interface *javax.ejb.EntityBean*

`public abstract interface EntityBean`

extends *javax.ejb.***EnterpriseBean**

Implemeted by all entity EJBs to define their lifecycle events.

Methods

public void	`ejbActivate`	()
	throws	*javax.ejb.***EJBException**, *java.rmi.RemoteException*;
public void	`ejbLoad`	()
	throws	*javax.ejb.***EJBException**, *java.rmi.RemoteException*;
public void	`ejbPassivate`	()
	throws	*javax.ejb.***EJBException**, *java.rmi.RemoteException*;
public void	`ejbRemove`	()
	throws	*javax.ejb.***RemoveException**, *javax.ejb.***EJBException**, *java.rmi.RemoteException*;
public void	`ejbStore`	()
	throws	*javax.ejb.***EJBException**, *java.rmi.RemoteException*;
public void	`setEntityContext`	(*javax.ejb.***EntityContext** ctx)
	throws	*javax.ejb.***EJBException**, *java.rmi.RemoteException*;
public void	`unsetEntityContext`	()
	throws	*javax.ejb.***EJBException**, *java.rmi.RemoteException*;

Fields

Inherited from *java.io.Serializable*
`serialVersionUID`

Interface *javax.ejb.EntityContext*

`public abstract interface EntityContext`

extends *javax.ejb.***EJBContext**

Provides the implementor with access methods to the runtime context of an entity Enterprise bean.

Methods

public **EJBObject**	`getEJBObject`	()
	throws	*java.lang.IllegalStateException*;
public *java.lang.Object*	`getPrimaryKey`	()
	throws	*java.lang.IllegalStateException*;

Inherited from *javax.ejb.***EJBContext**
`getCallerIdentity, getCallerPrincipal, getEJBHome, getEnvironment,`
`getRollbackOnly, getUserTransaction, isCallerInRole, isCallerInRole,`
`setRollbackOnly`

Interface javax.ejb.Handle

```
public abstract interface Handle
```

extends *java.io.Serializable*

The base interface for all handles to EJBs, where a handle is a "robust persistent reference" to an EJB object. Eg. A network reference.

Methods

public **EJBObject**	`getEJBObject`	()
	throws	*java.rmi.RemoteException*;

Fields

Inherited from *java.io.Serializable*
`serialVersionUID`

Interface javax.ejb.HomeHandle

```
public abstract interface HomeHandle
```

extends *java.io.Serializable*

This is a new interface in EJB 1.1. This is the base interface for all handles to home objects, where a handle is a "robust persistent reference" to a home object. Eg. A network reference.

Methods

public **EJBHome**	`getEJBHome`	()
	throws	*java.rmi.RemoteException*;

Fields

Inherited from *java.io.Serializable*
`serialVersionUID`

Interface javax.ejb.SessionBean

```
public abstract interface SessionBean
```

extends *javax.ejb.***EnterpriseBean**

Implemeted by all session EJBs to define their lifecycle events.

Methods

public void	`ejbActivate`	()
	throws	*javax.ejb.***EJBException**, *java.rmi.RemoteException*;
public void	`ejbPassivate`	()
	throws	*javax.ejb.***EJBException**, *java.rmi.RemoteException*;
public void	`ejbRemove`	()
	throws	*javax.ejb.***RemoveException**, *javax.ejb.***EJBException**, *java.rmi.RemoteException*;
public void	`setSessionContext`	(*javax.ejb.***SessionContext** ctx)
	throws	*javax.ejb.***EJBException**, *java.rmi.RemoteException*;

Fields

Inherited from *java.io.Serializable*
`serialVersionUID`

Interface javax.ejb.SessionContext

```
public abstract interface SessionContext
```

extends *javax.ejb.***EJBContext**

Provides the implementor with access methods to the runtime session context of a session Enterprise bean.

Methods

public **EJBObject**	**getEJBObject**	()
	throws	*java.lang.IllegalStateException*;

Inherited from *javax.ejb.***EJBContext**
`getCallerIdentity, getCallerPrincipal, getEJBHome, getEnvironment,`
`getRollbackOnly, getUserTransaction, isCallerInRole, isCallerInRole,`
`setRollbackOnly`

Interface javax.ejb.SessionSynchronization

```
public abstract interface SessionSynchronization
```

Used if the implementor wishes his session EJB state to be in synchronization with ongoing transactions.

Methods

public void	**afterBegin**	()
	throws	*javax.ejb.***EJBException**,
		java.rmi.RemoteException;
public void	**afterCompletion**	(boolean committed)
	throws	*javax.ejb.***EJBException**,
		java.rmi.RemoteException;
public void	**beforeCompletion**	()
	throws	*javax.ejb.***EJBException**,
		java.rmi.RemoteException;

Class javax.ejb.CreateException

```
public class CreateException
```

extends *java.lang.Exception*

Is extended by *javax.ejb.***DuplicateMailException**. Universal error thrown when a call to create an EJB object fails. Should be present in the throw clause of all relevant `create` methods.

Constructor Methods

public	**CreateException**	();
public	**CreateException**	(*java.lang.String* message);

Methods

Inherited from *java.lang.throwable*
`fillInStackTrace, getLocalizedMessage, getMessage, printStackTrace, printStackTrace, printStackTrace, toString`

Inherited from class *java.lang.Object*
`clone, equals, finalize, getClass, hashCode, notify, notifyAll, wait, wait, wait`

Class *javax.ejb.DuplicateKeyException*

`public class DuplicateKeyException`

extends *javax.ejb.***CreateException**

Thrown when an entity EJB cannot be created because another has already been instantiated with the same key.

Constructor Methods

public	`DuplicateKeyException`	();
public	`DuplicateKeyException`	(*java.lang.String* message);

Methods

Inherited from *java.lang.throwable*
`fillInStackTrace, getLocalizedMessage, getMessage, printStackTrace, printStackTrace, printStackTrace, toString`

Inherited from class *java.lang.Object*
`clone, equals, finalize, getClass, hashCode, notify, notifyAll, wait, wait, wait`

Class *javax.ejb.EJBException*

`public class EJBException`

extends *java.lang.RuntimeException*

Is extended by *javax.ejb.***NoSuchEntityException**. Thrown by an EJB object to report that one of its methods failed unexpectedly.

Constructor Methods

public	`EJBException`	();
public	`EJBException`	(*java.lang.Exception* ex);
public	`EJBException`	(*java.lang.String* message);

Methods

public *java.lang.Exception*	`getCausedByException`	();

Inherited from *java.lang.throwable*
`fillInStackTrace, getLocalizedMessage, getMessage, printStackTrace, printStackTrace, printStackTrace, toString`

Inherited from class *java.lang.Object*
`clone, equals, finalize, getClass, hashCode, notify, notifyAll, wait, wait, wait`

Class *javax.ejb.FinderException*

```
public class FinderException
```

extends *java.lang.Exception*

Is extended by *javax.ejb.***ObjectNotFoundException**. Thrown when a call to find an EJB object fails to do so. Should be present in the throw clause of all relevant `find` methods.

Constructor Methods

```
public                    FinderException            ();
public                    FinderException            (java.lang.String message);
```

Methods

Inherited from *java.lang.throwable*
```
fillInStackTrace, getLocalizedMessage, getMessage, printStackTrace,
printStackTrace, printStackTrace, toString
```

Inherited from class *java.lang.Object*
```
clone, equals, finalize, getClass, hashCode, notify, notifyAll, wait, wait, wait
```

Class *javax.ejb.NoSuchEntityException*

```
public class NoSuchEntityException
```

extends *javax.ejb.***EJBException**

Is a new exception class in EJB 1.1. Thrown by an EJB object to report that one of its methods failed because the database no longer has an entry for the entity underlying the method.

Constructor Methods

```
public                    NoSuchEntityException      ();
public                    NoSuchEntityException      (java.lang.Exception ex);
public                    NoSuchEntityException      (java.lang.String message);
```

Methods

Inherited from *java.lang.Exception*
```
getCausedByException
```

Inherited from *java.lang.throwable*
```
fillInStackTrace, getLocalizedMessage, getMessage, printStackTrace,
printStackTrace, printStackTrace, toString
```

Inherited from class *java.lang.Object*
```
clone, equals, finalize, getClass, hashCode, notify, notifyAll, wait, wait, wait
```

Class *javax.ejb.ObjectNotFoundException*

```
public class ObjectNotFoundException
```

extends *javax.ejb.***FinderException**

Thrown when a call to find a single (and not a collection of) EJB object(s) fails to do so.

Constructor Methods

| public | `ObjectNotFoundException` | `()`; |
| public | `ObjectNotFoundException` | (*java.lang.String* message); |

Methods

Inherited from *java.lang.throwable*
`fillInStackTrace, getLocalizedMessage, getMessage, printStackTrace, printStackTrace, printStackTrace, toString`

Inherited from class *java.lang.Object*
`clone, equals, finalize, getClass, hashCode, notify, notifyAll, wait, wait, wait`

Class *javax.ejb.RemoveException*

```
public class RemoveException
```

extends *java.lang.Exception*

Thrown when a call to remove an EJB object is made upon an object that it cannot or may not remove.

Constructor Methods

| public | `RemoveException` | `()`; |
| public | `RemoveException` | (*java.lang.String* message); |

Methods

Inherited from *java.lang.throwable*
`fillInStackTrace, getLocalizedMessage, getMessage, printStackTrace, printStackTrace, printStackTrace, toString`

Inherited from class *java.lang.Object*
`clone, equals, finalize, getClass, hashCode, notify, notifyAll, wait, wait, wait`

JDBC API Reference

Key

Within this API Reference, the following conventions are used:

> Interface, Class and Exception names within the APIs listed are all written in **bold**.

> Interface, Class and Exception names not within the APIs listed are all written in *italics*.

> Method and Class names are written in `Courier Bold`.

Package java.sql

The Java Data Base Connectivity API contains one core package, **java.sql**, and one extension package, **javax.sql**, which is not covered in this appendix. The core package enables the use and execution of SQL queries and operations within Java applications. It also provides support for the retrieval of results and their manipulation. Note that this appendix covers version 2.0 of the JDBC API which became available with the release of Java 2.

Interfaces

public abstract interface	**Array**		
public abstract interface	**Blob**		
public abstract interface	**CallableStatement**	extends	*java.sql.***PreparedStatement**
public abstract interface	**Clob**		
public abstract interface	**Connection**		
public abstract interface	**DatabaseMetaData**		
public abstract interface	**Driver**		
public abstract interface	**PreparedStatement**	extends	*java.sql.***Statement**
public abstract interface	**Ref**		
public abstract interface	**ResultSet**		
public abstract interface	**ResultSetMetaData**		
public abstract interface	**SQLData**		
public abstract interface	**SQLInput**		
public abstract interface	**SQLOutput**		
public abstract interface	**Statement**		
public abstract interface	**Struct**		

Classes

public class	**Date**	extends	*java.util.***Date**
public class	**DriverManager**		
public class	**DriverPropertyInfo**		
public class	**Time**	extends	java.util.**Date**
public class	**TimeStamp**	extends	java.util.**Date**
public class	**Types**		

Exceptions

public class	**BatchUpdateException**	extends	*java.sql.***SQLException**
public class	**DataTruncation**	extends	*java.sql.***SQLWarning**
public class	**SQLException**	extends	*java.lang.Exception*
public class	**SQLWarningException**	extends	*java.sql.***SQLException**

Interface java.sql.Array

```
public abstract interface Array
```

Corresponds to the SQL **Array** type.

Methods

public *java.lang.Object*	**getArray**	()
	throws	*java.sql.***SQLException**
public *java.lang.Object*	**getArray**	(*java.util.Map* map)
	throws	*java.sql.***SQLException**
public *java.lang.Object*	**getArray**	(long index, int count)
	throws	*java.sql.***SQLException**
public *java.lang.Object*	**getArray**	(long index, int count, java.util.Map map)
	throws	*java.sql.***SQLException**
public int	**getBaseType**	()
	throws	*java.sql.***SQLException**
public *java.lang.String*	**getBaseTypeName**	()
	throws	*java.sql.***SQLException**
public *java.sql.***ResultSet**	**getResultSet**	()
	throws	*java.sql.***SQLException**
public *java.sql.***ResultSet**	**getResultSet**	(*java.util.Map*)
	throws	*java.sql.***SQLException**
public *java.sql.***ResultSet**	**getResultSet**	(long index, int count)
	throws	*java.sql.***SQLException**
public *java.sql.***ResultSet**	**getResultSet**	(long index, int count, *java.util.Map* map)
	throws	*java.sql.***SQLException**

Interface java.sql.Blob

```
public abstract interface Blob
```

Corresponds to the SQL **Blob** type.

Methods

public *java.io.InputStream*	**getBinaryStream**	()
	throws	*java.sql.***SQLException**
public *java.lang.Byte[]*	**getBytes**	(long pos, int length)
	throws	*java.sql.***SQLException**
public long	**length**	()
	throws	*java.sql.***SQLException**

public long	position	(*java.lang.Byte*[] pattern, long start)
	throws	*java.sql*.**SQLException**
public long	position	(*java.sql*.Blob pattern, long start)
	throws	*java.sql*.**SQLException**

Interface *java.sql.CallableStatement*

```
public abstract interface CallableStatement
```

Extends *java.sql*.**PreparedStatement**. **CallableStatement** executes stored SQL procedures. Some methods have been deprecated.

Methods

public *java.sql*.Array	getArray	(int i)
	throws	*java.sql*.**SQLException**
public *java.math.BigDecimal*	getBigDecimal	(int parameterIndex)
	throws	*java.sql*.**SQLException**
public *java.sql*.Blob	getBlob	(int i)
	throws	*java.sql*.**SQLException**
public boolean	getBoolean	(int parameterIndex,)
	throws	*java.sql*.**SQLException**
public *java.lang.Byte*	getByte	(int parameterIndex)
	throws	*java.sql*.**SQLException**
public *java.lang.Byte*[]	getBytes	(int parameterIndex)
	throws	*java.sql*.**SQLException**
public *java.sql*.Clob	getClob	(int i)
	throws	*java.sql*.**SQLException**
public *java.sql*.Date	getDate	(int parameterIndex, *java.util.Calendar* cal)
	throws	*java.sql*.**SQLException**
public double	getDouble	(int parameterIndex)
	throws	*java.sql*.**SQLException**
public float	getFloat	(int parameterIndex)
	throws	*java.sql*.**SQLException**
public int	getInt	(int parameterIndex)
	throws	*java.sql*.**SQLException**
public long	getLong	(int parameterIndex)
	throws	*java.sql*.**SQLException**
public *java.lang.Object*	getObject	(int parameterIndex)
	throws	*java.sql*.**SQLException**
public *java.lang.Object*	getObject	(int i, *java.util.Map* map)
	throws	*java.sql*.**SQLException**
public *java.sql*.Ref	getRef	(int i)
	throws	*java.sql*.**SQLException**
public short	getShort	(int parameterIndex)
	throws	*java.sql*.**SQLException**
public *java.lang.String*	getString	(int parameterIndex)
	throws	*java.sql*.**SQLException**
public *java.sql*.Time	getTime	(int parameterIndex)
	throws	*java.sql*.**SQLException**
public *java.sql*.Time	getTime	(int parameterIndex, *java.util.Calendar* cal)
	throws	*java.sql*.**SQLException**
public *java.sql*.Timestamp	getTimeStamp	(int parameterIndex)
	throws	*java.sql*.**SQLException**
public *java.sql*.Timestamp	getTimeStamp	(int parameterIndex, *java.util.Calendar* cal)
	throws	*java.sql*.**SQLException**
public void	registerOutParameter	(int parameterIndex, int sqlType)
	throws	*java.sql*.**SQLException**

public void	registerOutParameter	(int parameterIndex, int sqlType, int scale)
	throws	java.sql.**SQLException**
public void	registerOutParameter	(int paramIndex, int sqlType, java.lang.String typeName)
	throws	java.sql.**SQLException**
public boolean	wasNull	()
	throws	java.sql.**SQLException**

Inherited from *java.sql.***PreparedStatement**:
```
addBatch, clearParameters, execute, executeQuery,
executeUpdate,getMetaData, setArray, setAsciiStream, setBigDecimal,
setBinaryStream,setBlob, setBoolean, setByte, setBytes,
setCharacterStream, setClob, setDate, setDate, setDouble, setFloat,
setInt, setLong, setNull, setNull, setObject, setObject, setObject,
setRef, setShort, setString, setTime, setTime, setTimestamp,
setTimestamp, setUnicodeStream
```

Inherited from *java.sql.***Statement**:
```
addBatch, cancel, clearBatch, clearWarnings, close,
execute,executeBatch, executeQuery, executeUpdate,
getConnection, getFetchDirection, getFetchSize,
getMaxFieldSize, getMaxRows, getMoreResults,
getQueryTimeout, getResultSet, getResultSetConcurrency,
getResultSetType, getUpdateCount, getWarnings,
setCursorName, setEscapeProcessing, setFetchDirection,
setFetchSize, setMaxFieldSize, setMaxRows,
setQueryTimeout
```

Deprecated Methods

| public *java.math.BigDecimal* | getBigDecimal | (int parameterIndex,
int scale) |
| | throws | java.sql.**SQLException** |

Interface java.sql.Clob

```
public abstract interface Clob
```

Corresponds to the SQL **Clob** type.

Methods

public *java.io.InputStream*	getAsciiStream	()
	throws	java.sql.**SQLException**
public *java.io.Reader*	getCharacterString	()
	throws	java.sql.**SQLException**
public *java.lang.String*	getSubString	(long pos, int length)
	throws	java.sql.**SQLException**
public long	length	()
	throws	java.sql.**SQLException**
public long	position	(java.lang.String searchstr, long start)
	throws	java.sql.**SQLException**
public long	position	(java.sql.Clob searchstr, long start)
	throws	java.sql.**SQLException**

Interface *java.sql.Connection*

```
public abstract interface Connection
```

Connection provides a connection(session) with a database, within which SQL statements may be executed and the results read.

Field Constants

public final static int	`TRANSACTION_NONE`
public final static int	`TRANSACTION_READ_COMMITTED`
public final static int	`TRANSACTION_READ_UNCOMMITTED`
public final static int	`TRANSACTION_REPEATABLE_READ`
public final static int	`TRANSACTION_SERIALIZABLE`

Methods

public void	`clearWarnings`	()
	throws	*java.sql.*SQLException
public void	`close`	()
	throws	*java.sql.*SQLException
public void	`commi`	()
	throws	*java.sql.*SQLException
public *java.sql.*Statement	`createStatement`	()
	throws	*java.sql.*SQLException
public *java.sql.*Statement	`createStatement`	(int resultSetType, int resultSetConcurrency)
	throws	*java.sql.*SQLException
public boolean	`getAutoCommit`	()
	throws	*java.sql.*SQLException
public *java.lang.String*	`getCatalog`	()
	throws	*java.sql.*SQLException
public *java.sql.*DatabaseMetaData	`getMetaData`	()
	throws	*java.sql.*SQLException
public int	`getTransactionIsolation`	()
	throws	*java.sql.*SQLException
public *java.util.Map*	`getTypeMap`	()
	throws	*java.sql.*SQLException
public *java.sql.*SQLWarning	`getWarnings`	()
	throws	*java.sql.*SQLException
public boolean	`isClosed`	()
	throws	*java.sql.*SQLException
public boolean	`isReadOnly`	()
	throws	*java.sql.*SQLException
public *java.lang.String*	`nativeSQL`	(*java.lang.String* sql)
	throws	*java.sql.*SQLException
public *java.sql.*CallableStatement	`prepareCall`	(*java.lang.string* sql, int resultSetType, int resultSetConcurrency)
	throws	*java.sql.*SQLException
public *java.sql.*CallableStatement	`prepareCall`	(*java.lang.string* sql)
	throws	*java.sql.*SQLException
public *java.sql.*PreparedStatement	`prepareStatement`	(*java.lang.string* sql, int resultSetType, int resultSetConcurrency)
	throws	*java.sql.*SQLException
public *java.sql.*PreparedStatement	`prepareStatement`	(*java.lang.string* sql)
	throws	*java.sql.*SQLException
public void	`rollback`	()
	throws	*java.sql.*SQLException
public void	`setAutoCommit`	(boolean autoCommit)
	throws	*java.sql.*SQLException
public void	`setCatalog`	(*java.lang.String* catalog)
	throws	*java.sql.*SQLException
public void	`setReadOnly`	(boolean readOnly)
	throws	*java.sql.*SQLException

public void	setTransactionIsolation	(int level)
	throws	*java.sql.*SQLException
public void	setTypeMap	(*java.util.Map* map)
	throws	*java.sql.*SQLException

Interface java.sql.DatabaseMetaData

```
public abstract interface DatabaseMetaData
```

DatabaseMetaData provides information about the full database.

Field Constants

public static final int	bestRowNotPseudo
public static final int	bestRowPseudo
public static final int	bestRowSession
public static final int	bestRowTemporary
public static final int	bestRowTransaction
public static final int	bestRowUnknown
public static final int	columnNoNulls
public static final int	columnNullable
public static final int	columnNullableUnknown
public static final int	importedKeyCascade
public static final int	importedKeyInitiallyDeferred
public static final int	importedKeyInitiallyImmediate
public static final int	importedKeyNoAction
public static final int	importedKeyNotDeferrable
public static final int	importedKeyRestrict
public static final int	importedKeySetDefault
public static final int	importedKeySetNull
public static final int	procedureColumnIn
public static final int	procedureColumnInOut
public static final int	procedureColumnOut
public static final int	procedureColumnResult
public static final int	procedureColumnReturn
public static final int	procedureColumnUnknown
public static final int	procedureNoNulls
public static final int	procedureNoResult
public static final int	procedureNullable
public static final int	procedureNullableUnknown
public static final int	procedureResultUnknown
public static final int	procedureReturnsResult
public static final short	tableIndexClustered
public static final short	tableIndexHashed
public static final short	tableIndexOther
public static final short	tableIndexStatistic
public static final int	typeNoNulls
public static final int	typeNullable
public static final int	typeNullableUnknown
public static final int	typePredBasic
public static final int	typePredChar
public static final int	typePredNone
public static final int	typeSearchable
public static final int	versionColumnNotPseudo
public static final int	versionColumnPseudo
public static final int	versionColumnUnknown

Methods

public boolean	allProceduresAreCallable	()
	throws	*java.sql.*SQLException
public boolean	allTablesAreSelectable	()
	throws	*java.sql.*SQLException
public boolean	dataDefinitionCausesTransactionCommit	()
	throws	*java.sql.*SQLException
public boolean	dataDefinitionIgnoredInTransactions	()
	throws	*java.sql.*SQLException
public boolean	deletesAreDetected	(int type)
	throws	*java.sql.*SQLException

public boolean	**doesMaxRowSizeIncludeBlobs**	()
	throws	*java.sql.*SQLException
public *java.sql.*ResultSet	**getBestRowIdentifier**	(*java.lang.String* catalog,
		java.lang.String schema,
		java.lang.String table,
		int scope,
		boolean nullable)
	throws	*java.sql.*SQLException
public *java.sql.*ResultSet	**getCatalogs**	()
	throws	*java.sql.*SQLException
public *java.lang.String*	**getCatalogSeparator**	()
	throws	*java.sql.*SQLException
public *java.lang.String*	**getCatalogTerm**	()
	throws	*java.sql.*SQLException
public *java.sql.*ResultSet	**getColumnPrivileges**	(*java.lang.String* catalog,
		java.lang.String schema,
		java.lang.String table,
		java.lang.String columnNamePattern)
	throws	*java.sql.*SQLException
public *java.sql.*ResultSet	**getColumns**	(*java.lang.String* catalog,
		java.lang.String schemaPattern,
		java.lang.String tableNamePattern,
		java.lang.String columnNamePattern)
	throws	*java.sql.*SQLException
public *java.sql.*Connection	**getConnection**	()
	throws	*java.sql.*SQLException
public *java.sql.*ResultSet	**getCrossReference**	(*java.lang.String* primaryCatalog,
		java.lang.String primarySchema,
		java.lang.String primaryTable,
		java.lang.String foreignCatalog,
		java.lang.String foreignSchema,
		java.lang.String foreignTable)
	throws	*java.sql.*SQLException
public *java.lang.String*	**getDatabaseProductName**	()
	throws	*java.sql.*SQLException
public *java.lang.String*	**getDatabaseProductVersion**()	
	throws	*java.sql.*SQLException
public int	**getDefaultTransactionIsolation**	()
	throws	*java.sql.*SQLException
public int	**getDriverMajorVersion**	()
	throws	*java.sql.*SQLException
public int	**getDriverMinorVersion**	()
	throws	*java.sql.*SQLException
public *java.lang.String*	**getDriverName**	()
	throws	*java.sql.*SQLException
public *java.lang.String*	**getDriverVersion**	()
	throws	*java.sql.*SQLException
public *java.sql.*ResultSet	**getExportedKeys**	(*java.lang.String* catalog,
		java.lang.String schema,
		java.lang.String table)
	throws	*java.sql.*SQLException
public *java.lang.String*	**getExtraNameCharacters**	()
	throws	*java.sql.*SQLException
public *java.lang.String*	**getIdentifierQuoteString**	()
	throws	*java.sql.*SQLException
public *java.sql.*ResultSet	**getImportedKeys**	(*java.lang.String* catalog,
		java.lang.String schema,
		java.lang.String table)
	throws	*java.sql.*SQLException
public *java.sql.*ResultSet	**getIndexInfo**	(*java.lang.String* catalog,
		java.lang.String schema,
		java.lang.String table,
		boolean unique,
		boolean approximate)
	throws	*java.sql.*SQLException

public int	getMaxBinaryLiteralLength()	
	throws	*java.sql*.**SQLException**
public int	getMaxCatalogNameLength	()
	throws	*java.sql*.**SQLException**
public int	getMaxCharLiteralLength	()
	throws	*java.sql*.**SQLException**
public int	getMaxColumnNameLength	()
	throws	*java.sql*.**SQLException**
public int	getMaxColumnsInGroupBy	()
	throws	*java.sql*.**SQLException**
public int	getMaxColumnsInIndex	()
	throws	*java.sql*.**SQLException**
public int	getMaxColumnsInOrderBy	()
	throws	*java.sql*.**SQLException**
public int	getMaxColumnsInSelect	()
	throws	*java.sql*.**SQLException**
public int	getMaxColumnsInTable	()
	throws	*java.sql*.**SQLException**
public int	getMaxConnections	()
	throws	*java.sql*.**SQLException**
public int	getMaxCursorNameLength	()
	throws	*java.sql*.**SQLException**
public int	getMaxIndexLength	()
	throws	*java.sql*.**SQLException**
public int	getMaxProcedureNameLength	()
	throws	*java.sql*.**SQLException**
public int	getMaxRowSize	()
	throws	*java.sql*.**SQLException**
public int	getMaxSchemaNameLength	()
	throws	*java.sql*.**SQLException**
public int	getMaxStatementLength	()
	throws	*java.sql*.**SQLException**
public int	getMaxStatements	()
	throws	*java.sql*.**SQLException**
public int	getMaxTableNameLength	()
	throws	*java.sql*.**SQLException**
public int	getMaxTablesInSelect	()
	throws	*java.sql*.**SQLException**
public int	getMaxUserNameLength	()
	throws	*java.sql*.**SQLException**
public *java.lang.String*	getNumericFunctions	()
	throws	*java.sql*.**SQLException**
public *java.sql*.ResultSet	getPrimaryKeys	(*java.lang.String* catalog,
		java.lang.String schema,
		java.lang.String table)
	throws	*java.sql*.**SQLException**
public *java.sql*.ResultSet	getProcedureColumns	(*java.lang.String* catalog,
		java.lang.String schemaPattern,
		java.lang.String procedureNamePattern,
		java.lang.String columnNamePattern)
	throws	*java.sql*.**SQLException**
public *java.sql*.ResultSet	getProcedures	(*java.lang.String* catalog,
		java.lang.String schemaPattern,
		java.lang.String procedureNamePattern)
	throws	*java.sql*.**SQLException**
public *java.lang.String*	getProcedureTerm	()
	throws	*java.sql*.**SQLException**
public *java.sql*.ResultSet	getSchemas	()
	throws	*java.sql*.**SQLException**
public *java.lang.String*	getSchemaTerm	()
	throws	*java.sql*.**SQLException**
public *java.lang.String*	getSearchStringEscape	()
	throws	*java.sql*.**SQLException**
public *java.lang.String*	getSQLKeywords	()
	throws	*java.sql*.**SQLException**

public *java.lang.String*	**getStringFunctions**	()
	throws	*java.sql*.**SQLException**
public *java.lang.String*	**getSystemFunctions**	()
	throws	*java.sql*.**SQLException**
public *java.sql*.ResultSet	**getTablePrivileges**	(*java.lang.String* catalog,
		java.lang.String schemaPattern,
		java.lang.String
tableNamePattern)		
	throws	*java.sql*.**SQLException**
public *java.sql*.ResultSet	**getTables**	(*java.lang.String* catalog,
		java.lang.String schemaPattern,
		java.lang.String
tableNamePattern,		
		java.lang.String[] types)
	throws	*java.sql*.**SQLException**
public *java.sql*.ResultSet	**getTableTypes**	()
	throws	*java.sql*.**SQLException**
public *java.lang.String*	**getTimeDateFunctions**	()
	throws	*java.sql*.**SQLException**
public *java.sql*.ResultSet	**getTypeInfo**	()
	throws	*java.sql*.**SQLException**
public *java.sql*.ResultSet	**getUDTs**	(*java.lang.String* catalog,
		java.lang.String schemaPattern,
		java.lang.String typeNamePattern,
		int[] types)
	throws	*java.sql*.**SQLException**
public *java.lang.String*	**getURL**	()
	throws	*java.sql*.**SQLException**
public *java.lang.String*	**getUserName**	()
	throws	*java.sql*.**SQLException**
public *java.sql*.ResultSet	**getVersionColumns**	(*java.lang.String* catalog,
		java.lang.String schema,
		java.lang.String table)
	throws	*java.sql*.**SQLException**
public boolean	**insertsAreDetected**	(int type)
	throws	*java.sql*.**SQLException**
public boolean	**isCatalogAtStart**	()
	throws	*java.sql*.**SQLException**
public boolean	**isReadOnly**	()
	throws	*java.sql*.**SQLException**
public boolean	**nullPlusNonNullIsNull**	()
	throws	*java.sql*.**SQLException**
public boolean	**nullsAreSortedAtEnd**	()
	throws	*java.sql*.**SQLException**
public boolean	**nullsAreSortedAtStart**	()
	throws	*java.sql*.**SQLException**
public boolean	**nullsAreSortedHigh**	()
	throws	*java.sql*.**SQLException**
public boolean	**nullsAreSortedLow**	()
	throws	*java.sql*.**SQLException**
public boolean	**othersDeletesAreVisible**	(int type)
	throws	*java.sql*.**SQLException**
public boolean	**othersInsertsAreVisible**	(int type)
	throws	*java.sql*.**SQLException**
public boolean	**othersUpdatesAreVisible**	(int type)
	throws	*java.sql*.**SQLException**
public boolean	**ownDeletesAreVisible**	(int type)
	throws	*java.sql*.**SQLException**
public boolean	**ownInsertsAreVisible**	(int type)
	throws	*java.sql*.**SQLException**
public boolean	**ownUpdatesAreVisible**	(int type)
	throws	*java.sql*.**SQLException**
public boolean	**storesLowerCaseIdentifiers**	()
	throws	*java.sql*.**SQLException**
public boolean	**storesLowerCaseQuotedIdentifiers**	()
	throws	*java.sql*.**SQLException**
public boolean	**storesMixedCaseIdentifiers**	()
	throws	*java.sql*.**SQLException**

public boolean	storesMixedCaseQuotedIdentifiers	()
	throws	*java.sql*.**SQLException**
public boolean	storesUpperCaseIdentifiers	()
	throws	*java.sql*.**SQLException**
public boolean	storesUpperCaseQuotedIdentifiers	()
	throws	*java.sql*.**SQLException**
public boolean	supportsAlterTableWithAddColumn	()
	throws	*java.sql*.**SQLException**
public boolean	supportsAlterTableWithDropColumn	()
	throws	*java.sql*.**SQLException**
public boolean	supportsANSI92EntryLevelSQL	()
	throws	*java.sql*.**SQLException**
public boolean	supportsANSI92FullSQL	()
	throws	*java.sql*.**SQLException**
public boolean	supportsANSI92IntermediateSQL	()
	throws	*java.sql*.**SQLException**
public boolean	supportsBatchUpdates	()
	throws	*java.sql*.**SQLException**
public boolean	supportsCatalogsInDataManipulation	()
	throws	*java.sql*.**SQLException**
public boolean	supportsCatalogsInIndexDefinitions	()
	throws	*java.sql*.**SQLException**
public boolean	supportsCatalogsInPrivilegeDefinitions	()
	throws	*java.sql*.**SQLException**
public boolean	supportsCatalogsInProcedureCalls	()
	throws	*java.sql*.**SQLException**
public boolean	supportsCatalogsInTableDefinitions	()
	throws	*java.sql*.**SQLException**
public boolean	supportsColumnAliasing	()
	throws	*java.sql*.**SQLException**
public boolean	supportsConvert	()
	throws	*java.sql*.**SQLException**
public boolean	supportsConvert	(int fromType, int toType)
	throws	*java.sql*.**SQLException**
public boolean	supportsCoreSQLGrammar	()
	throws	*java.sql*.**SQLException**
public boolean	supportsCorrelatedSubqueries	()
	throws	*java.sql*.**SQLException**
public boolean	supportsDataDefinitionAndDataManipulationTransactions	()
	throws	*java.sql*.**SQLException**
public boolean	supportsDataManipulationTransactionsOnly	()
	throws	*java.sql*.**SQLException**
public boolean	supportsDifferentTableCorrelationNames	()
	throws	*java.sql*.**SQLException**
public boolean	supportsExpressionsInOrderBy	()
	throws	*java.sql*.**SQLException**
public boolean	supportsExtendedSQLGrammar	()
	throws	*java.sql*.**SQLException**
public boolean	supportsFullOuterJoins	()
	throws	*java.sql*.**SQLException**
public boolean	supportsGroupBy	()
	throws	*java.sql*.**SQLException**
public boolean	supportsGroupByBeyondSelect	()
	throws	*java.sql*.**SQLException**
public boolean	supportsGroupByUnrelated	()
	throws	*java.sql*.**SQLException**
public boolean	supportsIntegrityEnhancementFacility	()
	throws	*java.sql*.**SQLException**
public boolean	supportsLikeEscapeClause	()
	throws	*java.sql*.**SQLException**

public boolean	supportsLimitedOuterJoins()	
	throws	*java.sql*.**SQLException**
public boolean	supportsMinimumSQLGrammar()	
	throws	*java.sql*.**SQLException**
public boolean	supportsMixedCaseIdentifiers	
		()
	throws	*java.sql*.**SQLException**
public boolean	supportsMixedCaseQuotedIdentifiers	
		()
	throws	*java.sql*.**SQLException**
public boolean	supportsMultipleResultSets	
		()
	throws	*java.sql*.**SQLException**
public boolean	supportsMultipleTransactions	
		()
	throws	*java.sql*.**SQLException**
public boolean	supportsNonNullableColumns	
		()
	throws	*java.sql*.**SQLException**
public boolean	supportsOpenCursorsAcrossCommit	
		()
	throws	*java.sql*.**SQLException**
public boolean	supportsOpenCursorsAcrossRollback	
		()
	throws	*java.sql*.**SQLException**
public boolean	supportsOpenStatementsAcrossCommit	
		()
	throws	*java.sql*.**SQLException**
public boolean	supportsOpenStatementsAcrossRollback	
		()
	throws	*java.sql*.**SQLException**
public boolean	supportsOrderByUnrelated	
		()
	throws	*java.sql*.**SQLException**
public boolean	supportsOuterJoins	
		()
	throws	*java.sql*.**SQLException**
public boolean	supportsPositionedDelete	
		()
	throws	*java.sql*.**SQLException**
public boolean	supportsPositionedUpdate	
		()
	throws	*java.sql*.**SQLException**
public boolean	supportsResultSetConcurrency	(int type,
		int concurrency)
	throws	*java.sql*.**SQLException**
public boolean	supportsResultSetType	(int type)
	throws	*java.sql*.**SQLException**
public boolean	supportsSchemasInDataManipulation	
		()
	throws	*java.sql*.**SQLException**
public boolean	supportsSchemasInIndexDefinitions	
		()
	throws	*java.sql*.**SQLException**
public boolean	supportsSchemasInPrivilegeDefinitions	
		()
	throws	*java.sql*.**SQLException**
public boolean	supportsSchemasInProcedureCalls	
		()
	throws	*java.sql*.**SQLException**
public boolean	supportsSchemasInTableDefinitions	
		()
	throws	*java.sql*.**SQLException**
public boolean	supportsSelectForUpdate	
		()
	throws	*java.sql*.**SQLException**
public boolean	supportsStoredProcedures	
		()
	throws	*java.sql*.**SQLException**
public boolean	supportsSubqueriesInComparisons	
		()
	throws	*java.sql*.**SQLException**
public boolean	supportsSubqueriesInExists	
		()
	throws	*java.sql*.**SQLException**
public boolean	supportsSubqueriesInIns	
		()
	throws	*java.sql*.**SQLException**
public boolean	supportsSubqueriesInQuantifieds	
		()
	throws	*java.sql*.**SQLException**
public boolean	supportsTableCorrelationNames	
		()
	throws	*java.sql*.**SQLException**
public boolean	supportsTransactionIsolationLevel	(int level)
	throws	*java.sql*.**SQLException**
public boolean	supportsTransactions	
		()
	throws	*java.sql*.**SQLException**
public boolean	supportsUnion	
		()
	throws	*java.sql*.**SQLException**

public boolean	**supportsUnionAll**	()	
	throws	*java.sql.***SQLException**	
public boolean	**updatesAreDetected**	(int type)	
	throws	*java.sql.***SQLException**	
public boolean	**usesLocalFilePerTable**	()	
	throws	*java.sql.***SQLException**	
public boolean	**usesLocalFiles**	()	
	throws	*java.sql.***SQLException**	

Interface java.sql.Driver

```
public abstract interface Driver
```

Driver is the basic interface which must be implemented by every driver class.

Methods

public boolean	**acceptsURL**	(*java.lang.String* url)	
	throws	*java.sql.***SQLException**	
public *java.sql.*Connection	**connect**	(*java.lang.String* url, *java.util.Properties* info)	
	throws	*java.sql.***SQLException**	
public int	**getMajorVersion**	()	
public int	**getMinorVersion**	()	
public *java.sql.*DriverPropertyInfo[]	**getPropertyInfo**	(*java.lang.String* url, *java.util.Properties* info)	
	throws	*java.sql.***SQLException**	
public boolean	**jdbcCompliant**	()	

Interface java.sql.PreparedStatement

```
public abstract interface PreparedStatement
```

Extends *java.sql.***Statement**
PreparedStatement represents a compiled SQL statement. Some methods are deprecated.

Methods

public void	**addBatch**	()
	throws	*java.sql.***SQLException**
public void	**clearParameters**	()
	throws	*java.sql.***SQLException**
public boolean	**execute**	()
	throws	*java.sql.***SQLException**
public *java.sql.*ResultSet	**executeQuery**	()
	throws	*java.sql.***SQLException**
public int	**executeUpdate**	()
	throws	*java.sql.***SQLException**
public *java.sql.*ResultSetMetaData	**getMetaData**	()
	throws	*java.sql.***SQLException**
public void	**setArray**	(int i *java.sql.*Array x)
	throws	*java.sql.***SQLException**
public void	**setAsciiStream**	(int parameterIndex, *java.io.InputStream* x, int length)
	throws	*java.sql.***SQLException**
public void	**setBigDecimal**	(int parameterIndex, *java.math.BigDecimal* x)
	throws	*java.sql.***SQLException**
public void	**setBinaryStream**	(int parameterIndex, *java.io.InputStream* x, int length)
	throws	*java.sql.***SQLException**

public void	setBlob	(int i
		java.sql.Blob x)
	throws	java.sql.**SQLException**
public void	setBoolean	(int parameterIndex,
		boolean x)
	throws	java.sql.**SQLException**
public void	setByte	(int parameterIndex,
		byte x)
	throws	java.sql.**SQLException**
public void	setBytes	(int parameterIndex, byte[] x)
	throws	java.sql.**SQLException**
public void	setCharacterStream	(int parameterIndex,
		java.io.Reader reader,
		int length)
	throws	java.sql.**SQLException**
public void	setClob	(int i,
		java.sql.Clob x)
	throws	java.sql.**SQLException**
public void	setDate	(int parameterIndex,
		java.sql.Date x)
	throws	java.sql.**SQLException**
public void	setDate	(int parameterIndex,
		java.sql.Date x,
		java.util.Calendar cal)
	throws	java.sql.**SQLException**
public void	setDouble	(int parameterIndex,
		double x)
	throws	java.sql.**SQLException**
public void	setFloat	(int parameterIndex,
		float x)
	throws	java.sql.**SQLException**
public void	setInt	(int parameterIndex,
		int x)
	throws	java.sql.**SQLException**
public void	setLong	(int parameterIndex,
		long x)
	throws	java.sql.**SQLException**
public void	setNull	(int parameterIndex,
		int sqlType)
	throws	java.sql.**SQLException**
public void	setNull	(int paramIndex,
		int sqlType,
		java.lang.String typeName)
	throws	java.sql.**SQLException**
public void	setObject	(int parameterIndex,
		java.lang.Object x,
		int targetSqlType,
		int scale)
	throws	java.sql.**SQLException**
public void	setObject	(int parameterIndex,
		java.lang.Object x,
		int targetSqlType)
	throws	java.sql.**SQLException**
public void	setObject	(int parameterIndex,
		java.lang.Object x)
	throws	java.sql.**SQLException**
public void	setRef	(int i
		java.sql.Ref x)
	throws	java.sql.**SQLException**
public void	setShort	(int parameterIndex,
		short x)
	throws	java.sql.**SQLException**
public void	setString	(int parameterIndex,
		java.lang.String x)
	throws	java.sql.**SQLException**

public void	setTime	(int parameterIndex, *java.sql.*Time x)
	throws	*java.sql.***SQLException**
public void	setTime	(int parameterIndex, *java.sql.*Time x, *java.util.*Calendar cal)
	throws	*java.sql.***SQLException**
public void	setTimestamp	(int parameterIndex, *java.sql.*TimeStamp x)
	throws	*java.sql.***SQLException**
public void	setTimestamp	(int parameterIndex, *java.sql.*TimeStamp x, *java.util.Calendar* cal)
	throws	*java.sql.***SQLException**

Inherited from *java.sql.*Statement:
addBatch, cancel, clearBatch, clearWarnings, close, execute, executeBatch, executeQuery, executeUpdate, getConnection, getFetchDirection, getFetchSize, getMaxFieldSize, getMaxRows, getMoreResults, getQueryTimeout, getResultSet, getResultSetConcurrency, getResultSetType, getUpdateCount, getWarnings, setCursorName, setEscapeProcessing, setFetchDirection, setFetchSize, setMaxFieldSize, setMaxRows, setQueryTimeout

Deprecated Methods

| public void | setUnicodeStream | (int parameterIndex, *java.io.InputStream* x, int length) |

Interface java.sql.Ref

```
public abstract interface Ref
```

Ref is a reference to an SQL structured type value.

Methods

| public *java.lang.String* | getBaseTypeName | () |
| | throws | *java.sql.***SQLException** |

Interface java.sql.ResultSet

```
public abstract interface ResultSet
```

ResultSet allows access to a table of data. Some methods are deprecated.

Methods

public boolean	absolute	(int row)
	throws	*java.sql.***SQLException**
public void	afterLast	()
	throws	*java.sql.***SQLException**
public void	beforeFirst	()
	throws	*java.sql.***SQLException**
public void	cancelRowUpdates	()
	throws	*java.sql.***SQLException**
public void	clearWarnings	()
	throws	*java.sql.***SQLException**
public void	close	()
	throws	*java.sql.***SQLException**
public void	deleteRow	()
	throws	*java.sql.***SQLException**

public int	findColumn	(*java.lang.String* columnName)
	throws	*java.sql*.**SQLException**
public boolean	first	()
	throws	*java.sql*.**SQLException**
public *java.sql*.Array	getArray	(int i)
	throws	*java.sql*.**SQLException**
public *java.sql*.Array	getArray	(*java.lang.String* colName)
	throws	*java.sql*.**SQLException**
public *java.io.InputStream*	getAsciiStream	(int columnIndex)
	throws	*java.sql*.**SQLException**
public *java.io.InputStream*	getAsciiStream	(*java.lang.String* columnIndex)
	throws	*java.sql*.**SQLException**
public *java.math.BigDecimal*	getBigDecimal	(int columnIndex)
	throws	*java.sql*.**SQLException**
public *java.math.BigDecimal*	getBigDecimal	(*java.lang.String* columnName)
	throws	*java.sql*.**SQLException**
public *java.io.InputStream*	getBinaryStream	(int columnIndex)
	throws	*java.sql*.**SQLException**
public *java.io.InputStream*	getBinaryStream	(*java.lang.String* columnIndex)
	throws	*java.sql*.**SQLException**
public *java.sql*.Blob	getBlob	(int i)
	throws	*java.sql*.**SQLException**
public *java.sql*.Blob	getBlob	(*java.lang.String* colName)
	throws	*java.sql*.**SQLException**
public boolean	getBoolean	(int columnIndex)
	throws	*java.sql*.**SQLException**
public boolean	getBoolean	(*java.lang.String* columnIndex)
	throws	*java.sql*.**SQLException**
public byte	getByte	(int columnIndex)
	throws	*java.sql*.**SQLException**
public byte	getByte	(*java.lang.String* columnIndex)
	throws	*java.sql*.**SQLException**
public byte[]	getBytes	(int columnIndex)
	throws	*java.sql*.**SQLException**
public byte[]	getBytes	(*java.lang.String* columnIndex)
	throws	*java.sql*.**SQLException**
public *java.io.Reader*	getCharacterStream	(int columnIndex)
	throws	*java.sql*.**SQLException**
public *java.io.Reader*	getCharacterStream	(*java.lang.String* columnName)
	throws	*java.sql*.**SQLException**
public *java.sql*.Clob	getClob	(int i)
	throws	*java.sql*.**SQLException**
public *java.sql*.Clob	getClob	(*java.lang.String* colName)
	throws	*java.sql*.**SQLException**
public int	getConcurrency	()
	throws	*java.sql*.**SQLException**
public *java.lang.String*	getCursorName	()
	throws	*java.sql*.**SQLException**
public *java.sql*.Date	getDate	(int columnIndex)
	throws	*java.sql*.**SQLException**
public *java.sql*.Date	getDate	(*java.lang.String* columnIndex)
	throws	*java.sql*.**SQLException**
public *java.sql*.Date	getDate	(int columnIndex, *java.util.Calendar* cal)
	throws	*java.sql*.**SQLException**
public *java.sql*.Date	getDate	(*java.lang.String* columnName *java.util.Calendar* cal)
	throws	*java.sql*.**SQLException**
public double	getDouble	(int columnIndex)
	throws	*java.sql*.**SQLException**
public double	getDouble	(*java.lang.String* columnIndex)
	throws	*java.sql*.**SQLException**
public int	getFetchDirection	()
	throws	*java.sql*.**SQLException**
public int	getFetchSize	()
	throws	*java.sql*.**SQLException**

public float	**getFloat**	(int columnIndex)
	throws	*java.sql*.**SQLException**
public float	**getFloat**	(*java.lang.String* columnIndex)
	throws	*java.sql*.**SQLException**
public int	**getInt**	(int columnIndex)
	throws	*java.sql*.**SQLException**
public int	**getInt**	(*java.lang.String* columnIndex)
	throws	*java.sql*.**SQLException**
public long	**getLong**	(int columnIndex)
	throws	*java.sql*.**SQLException**
public long	**getLong**	(*java.lang.String* columnIndex)
	throws	*java.sql*.**SQLException**
public *java.sql*.ResultSetMetaData	**getMetaData**	()
	throws	*java.sql*.**SQLException**
public *java.lang.Object*	**getObject**	(int columnIndex)
	throws	*java.sql*.**SQLException**
public *java.lang.Object*	**getObject**	(*java.lang.String* columnName)
	throws	*java.sql*.**SQLException**
public *java.lang.Object*	**getObject**	(*java.lang.String* colName, *java.util.Map* map)
	throws	*java.sql*.**SQLException**
public *java.lang.Object*	**getObject**	(int i *java.util.Map* map)
	throws	*java.sql*.**SQLException**
public *java.sql*.Ref	**getRef**	(*java.lang.String* colName)
	throws	*java.sql*.**SQLException**
public *java.sql*.Ref	**getRef**	(int i)
	throws	*java.sql*.**SQLException**
public int	**getRow**	()
	throws	*java.sql*.**SQLException**
public short	**getShort**	(int columnIndex)
	throws	*java.sql*.**SQLException**
public short	**getShort**	(*java.lang.String* columnIndex)
	throws	*java.sql*.**SQLException**
public *java.sql*.Statement	**getStatement**	()
	throws	*java.sql*.**SQLException**
public *java.lang.String*	**getString**	(int columnIndex)
	throws	*java.sql*.**SQLException**
public *java.lang.String*	**getString**	(*java.lang.String* columnIndex)
	throws	*java.sql*.**SQLException**
public *java.sql*.Time	**getTime**	(int columnIndex)
	throws	*java.sql*.**SQLException**
public *java.sql*.Time	**getTime**	(*java.lang.String* columnIndex)
	throws	*java.sql*.**SQLException**
public *java.sql*.Time	**getTime**	(int columnIndex *java.util.Calendar* cal)
	throws	*java.sql*.**SQLException**
public *java.sql*.Time	**getTime**	(*java.lang.String* columnName, *java.util.Calendar* cal)
	throws	*java.sql*.**SQLException**
public *java.sql*.Timestamp	**getTimestamp**	(int columnIndex)
	throws	*java.sql*.**SQLException**
public *java.sql*.Timestamp	**getTimestamp**	(*java.lang.String* columnIndex)
	throws	*java.sql*.**SQLException**
public *java.sql*.Timestamp	**getTimestamp**	(int columnIndex *java.util.Calendar* cal)
	throws	*java.sql*.**SQLException**
public *java.sql*.Timestamp	**getTimestamp**	(*java.lang.String* columnName, *java.util.Calendar* cal)
	throws	*java.sql*.**SQLException**
public int	**getType**	()
	throws	*java.sql*.**SQLException**
public *java.sql*.SQLWarning	**getWarnings**	()
	throws	*java.sql*.**SQLException**

public void	insertRow	()
	throws	*java.sql*.**SQLException**
public boolean	isAfterLast	()
	throws	*java.sql*.**SQLException**
public boolean	isBeforeFirst	()
	throws	*java.sql*.**SQLException**
public boolean	isFirst	()
	throws	*java.sql*.**SQLException**
public boolean	isLast	()
	throws	*java.sql*.**SQLException**
public boolean	last	()
	throws	*java.sql*.**SQLException**
public void	moveToInsertRow	()
	throws	*java.sql*.**SQLException**
public void	moveToCurrentRow	()
	throws	*java.sql*.**SQLException**
public boolean	next	()
	throws	*java.sql*.**SQLException**
public boolean	previous	()
	throws	*java.sql*.**SQLException**
public void	refreshRow	()
	throws	*java.sql*.**SQLException**
public boolean	relative	(int rows)
	throws	*java.sql*.**SQLException**
public boolean	rowDeleted	()
	throws	*java.sql*.**SQLException**
public boolean	rowInserted	()
	throws	*java.sql*.**SQLException**
public boolean	rowUpdated	()
	throws	*java.sql*.**SQLException**
public void	setFetchDirection	(int direction)
	throws	*java.sql*.**SQLException**
public void	setFetchSize	(int rows)
	throws	*java.sql*.**SQLException**
public void	updateAsciiStream	(int columnIndex, *java.io.InputStream* x, int length)
	throws	*java.sql*.**SQLException**
public void	updateAsciiStream	(*java.lang.String* columnName, *java.io.InputStream* x, int length)
	throws	*java.sql*.**SQLException**
public void	updateBigDecimal	(int columnIndex, *java.math.BigDecimal* x)
	throws	*java.sql*.**SQLException**
public void	updateBigDecimal	(*java.lang.String* columnName, *java.math.BigDecimal* x)
	throws	*java.sql*.**SQLException**
public void	updateBinaryStream	(int columnIndex, *java.io.InputStream* x, int length)
	throws	*java.sql*.**SQLException**
public void	updateBinaryStream	(*java.lang.String* columnName, *java.io.InputStream* x, int length)
	throws	*java.sql*.**SQLException**
public void	updateBoolean	(int columnIndex, boolean x)
	throws	*java.sql*.**SQLException**
public void	updateBoolean	(*java.lang.String* columnName, boolean x)
	throws	*java.sql*.**SQLException**
public void	updateByte	(int columnIndex, byte x)
	throws	*java.sql*.**SQLException**

public void	**updateByte**	(*java.lang.String* columnName, byte x)
	throws	*java.sql.***SQLException**
public void	**updateBytes**	(int columnIndex, byte[] x)
	throws	*java.sql.***SQLException**
public void	**updateBytes**	(*java.lang.String* columnName, byte[] x)
	throws	*java.sql.***SQLException**
public void	**updateCharacterStream**	(int columnIndex, *java.io.Reader* x, int length)
	throws	*java.sql.***SQLException**
public void	**updateCharacterStream**	(*java.lang.String* columnName, *java.io.Reader* reader, int length)
	throws	*java.sql.***SQLException**
public void	**updateDate**	(int columnIndex, *java.sql.*Date x)
	throws	*java.sql.***SQLException**
public void	**updateDate**	(*java.lang.String* columnName, *java.sql.*Date date)
	throws	*java.sql.***SQLException**
public void	**updateDouble**	(int columnIndex, double x)
	throws	*java.sql.***SQLException**
public void	**updateDouble**	(*java.lang.String* columnName, double x)
	throws	*java.sql.***SQLException**
public void	**updateFloat**	(int columnIndex, float x)
	throws	*java.sql.***SQLException**
public void	**updateFloat**	(*java.lang.String* columnName, float x)
	throws	*java.sql.***SQLException**
public void	**updateInt**	(int columnIndex, int x)
	throws	*java.sql.***SQLException**
public void	**updateInt**	(*java.lang.String* columnName, int x)
	throws	*java.sql.***SQLException**
public void	**updateLong**	(int columnIndex, long x)
	throws	*java.sql.***SQLException**
public void	**updateLong**	(*java.lang.String* columnName, long x)
	throws	*java.sql.***SQLException**
public void	**updateNull**	(int columnIndex) (*java.lang.String* columnName)
	throws	*java.sql.***SQLException**
public void	**updateObject**	(int columnIndex, *java.lang.Object* x, int scale)
	throws	*java.sql.***SQLException**
public void	**updateObject**	(int columnIndex, *java.lang.Object* x)
	throws	*java.sql.***SQLException**
public void	**updateObject**	(*java.lang.String* columnName, *java.lang.Object* x, int scale)
	throws	*java.sql.***SQLException**
public void	**updateObject**	(*java.lang.String* columnName, *java.lang.Object* x)
	throws	*java.sql.***SQLException**

public void	**updateRow**	()
	throws	*java.sql.***SQLException**
public void	**updateShort**	(int columnIndex, short x)
	throws	*java.sql.***SQLException**
public void	**updateShort**	(*java.lang.String* columnName, short x)
	throws	*java.sql.***SQLException**
public void	**updateString**	(int columnIndex, *java.lang.String* x)
	throws	*java.sql.***SQLException**
public void	**updateString**	(*java.lang.String* columnName, *java.lang.String* x)
	throws	*java.sql.***SQLException**
public void	**updateTime**	(int columnIndex, *java.sql.*Time x)
	throws	*java.sql.***SQLException**
public void	**updateTime**	(*java.lang.String* columnName, *java.sql.*Time time)
	throws	*java.sql.***SQLException**
public void	**updateTimestamp**	(int columnIndex, *java.sql.*Timestamp x)
	throws	*java.sql.***SQLException**
public void	**updateTimestamp**	(*java.lang.String* columnName, *java.sql.*Timestamp x)
	throws	*java.sql.***SQLException**
public boolean	**wasNull**	()
	throws	*java.sql.***SQLException**

Deprecated Methods

public *java.math.BigDecimal*	**getBigDecimal**	(int columnIndex, int scale)
public *java. math.BigDecimal*	**getBigDecimal**	(*java.lang.String* columnName, int scale)
public *java.io.InputStream*	**getUnicodeStream**	(int columnIndex)
public *java.io.InputStream*	**getUnicodeStream**	(*java.lang.String* columnName)

Fields

public static final int	**CONCUR_READ_ONLY**
public static final int	**CONCUR_UPDATABLE**
public static final int	**FETCH_FORWARD**
public static final int	**FETCH_REVERSE**
public static final int	**FETCH_UNKNOWN**
public static final int	**TYPE_FORWARD_ONLY**
public static final int	**TYPE_SCROLL_INSENSITIVE**
public static final int	**TYPE_SCROLL_SENSITIVE**

Interface java.sql.ResultSetMetaData

```
public abstract interface ResultSetMetaData
```

ResultSetMetaData allows access to types and properties of ResultSet columns.

Methods

public *java.lang.String*	**getCatalogName**	(int column)
	throws	*java.sql.***SQLException**
public *java.lang.String*	**getColumnClassName**	(int column)
	throws	*java.sql.***SQLException**
public int	**getColumnCount**	()
	throws	*java.sql.***SQLException**

public int	getColumnDisplaySize	(int column)
	throws	java.sql.**SQLException**
public java.lang.String	getColumnLabel	(int column)
	throws	java.sql.**SQLException**
public java.lang.String	getColumnName	(int column)
	throws	java.sql.**SQLException**
public int	getColumnType	(int column)
	throws	java.sql.**SQLException**
public java.lang.String	getColumnTypeName	(int column)
	throws	java.sql.**SQLException**
public int	getPrecision	(int column)
	throws	java.sql.**SQLException**
public int	getScale	(int column)
	throws	java.sql.**SQLException**
public java.lang.String	getSchemaName	(int column)
	throws	java.sql.**SQLException**
public java.lang.String	getTableName	(int column)
	throws	java.sql.**SQLException**
public boolean	isAutoIncrement	(int column)
	throws	java.sql.**SQLException**
public boolean	isCaseSensitive	(int column)
	throws	java.sql.**SQLException**
public boolean	isCurrency	(int column)
	throws	java.sql.**SQLException**
public boolean	isDefinitelyWritable	(int column)
	throws	java.sql.**SQLException**
public int	isNullable	(int column)
	throws	java.sql.**SQLException**
public boolean	isSearchable	(int column)
	throws	java.sql.**SQLException**
public boolean	isSigned	(int column)
	throws	java.sql.**SQLException**
public boolean	isReadOnly	(int column)
	throws	java.sql.**SQLException**
public boolean	isWritable	(int column)
	throws	java.sql.**SQLException**

Fields

public static final int	columnNoNulls
public static final int	columnNullable
public static final int	columnNullableUnknown

Interface java.sql.SQLData

```
public abstract interface SQLData
```

SQLData provides customizable mapping in Java for SQL user-defined types.

Methods

public java.lang.String	getSQLTypeName	()
	throws	java.sql.**SQLException**
public void	readSQL	(java.sql.SQLInputstream, java.lang.String typeName)
	throws	java.sql.**SQLException**
public long	writeSQL	(java.sql.SQLOutputstream)
	throws	java.sql.**SQLException**

Interface java.sql.SQLInput

```
public abstract interface SQLInput
```

SQLInput represents an instance of an SQL structured or distinct type as a stream of values.

Methods

public *java.sql*.Array	**readArray**	()
	throws	*java.sql*.**SQLException**
public *java.io.InputStream*	**readAsciiStream**	()
	throws	*java.sql*.**SQLException**
public *java.math.BigDecimal*	**readBigDecimal**	()
	throws	*java.sql*.**SQLException**
public *java.io.InputStream*	**readBinaryStream**	()
	throws	*java.sql*.**SQLException**
public *java.sql*.Blob	**readBlob**	()
	throws	*java.sql*.**SQLException**
public boolean	**readBoolean**	()
	throws	*java.sql*.**SQLException**
public byte	**readByte**	()
	throws	*java.sql*.**SQLException**
public byte[]	**readBytes**	()
	throws	*java.sql*.**SQLException**
public *java.io.Reader*	**readCharacterStream**	()
	throws	*java.sql*.**SQLException**
public *java.sql*.Clob	**readClob**	()
	throws	*java.sql*.**SQLException**
public *java.sql*.Date	**readDate**	()
	throws	*java.sql*.**SQLException**
public double	**readDouble**	()
	throws	*java.sql*.**SQLException**
public float	**readFloat**	()
	throws	*java.sql*.**SQLException**
public int	**readInt**	()
	throws	*java.sql*.**SQLException**
public long	**readLong**	()
	throws	*java.sql*.**SQLException**
public *java.lang.Object*	**readObject**	()
	throws	*java.sql*.**SQLException**
public *java.sql*.Ref	**readRef**	()
	throws	*java.sql*.**SQLException**
public short	**readShort**	()
	throws	*java.sql*.**SQLException**
public *java.lang.String*	**readString**	()
	throws	*java.sql*.**SQLException**
public *java.sql*.Time	**readTime**	()
	throws	*java.sql*.**SQLException**
public *java.sql*.TimeStamp	**readTimeStamp**	()
	throws	*java.sql*.**SQLException**
public boolean	**wasNull**	()
	throws	*java.sql*.**SQLException**

Interface java.sql.SQLOutput

```
public abstract interface SQLOutput
```

SQLOutput represents an instance of an SQL structured or distinct type as a stream of values.

Methods

public void	**writeArray**	(*java.sql*.**Array** x)
	throws	*java.sql*.**SQLException**
public void	**writeAsciiStream**	(*java.io.InputStream* x)
	throws	*java.sql*.**SQLException**
public void	**writeBigDecimal**	(*java.math.BigDecimal* x)
	throws	*java.sql*.**SQLException**
public void	**writeBinaryStream**	(*java.io.InputStream* x)
	throws	*java.sql*.**SQLException**
public void	**writeBlob**	(*java.sql*.**Blob** x)
	throws	*java.sql*.**SQLException**

public void	writeBoolean	(boolean x)
	throws	*java.sql.*SQLException
public void	writeByte	(byte x)
	throws	*java.sql.*SQLException
public void	writeBytes	(byte[] x)
	throws	*java.sql.*SQLException
public void	writeCharacterStream	(*java.io.Reader* x)
	throws	*java.sql.*SQLException
public void	writeClob	(*java.sql.*Clob x)
	throws	*java.sql.*SQLException
public void	writeDate	(*java.sql.*Date x)
	throws	*java.sql.*SQLException
public void	writeDouble	(double x)
	throws	*java.sql.*SQLException
public void	writeFloat	(float x)
	throws	*java.sql.*SQLException
public void	writeInt	(int x)
	throws	*java.sql.*SQLException
public void	writeLong	(long x)
	throws	*java.sql.*SQLException
public void	writeObject	(*java.sql.*SQLData x)
	throws	*java.sql.*SQLException
public void	writeRef	(*java.sql.*Ref x)
	throws	*java.sql.*SQLException
public void	writeShort	(short x)
	throws	*java.sql.*SQLException
public void	writeString	(*java.lang.String* x)
	throws	*java.sql.*SQLException
public void	writeStruct	(*java.sql.*Struct x)
	throws	*java.sql.*SQLException
public void	writeTime	(*java.sql.*Time x)
	throws	*java.sql.*SQLException
public void	writeTimeStamp	(*java.sql.*TimeStamp x)
	throws	*java.sql.*SQLException

Interface java.sql.Statement

```
public abstract interface Statement
```

Statement executes a static SQL statement and reads the results (given in a resultset).

Methods

public void	addBatch	(*java.lang.String* sql)
	throws	*java.sql.*SQLException
public void	cancel	()
	throws	*java.sql.*SQLException
public void	clearBatch	()
	throws	*java.sql.*SQLException
public void	clearWarnings	()
	throws	*java.sql.*SQLException
public void	close	()
	throws	*java.sql.*SQLException
public boolean	execute	(*java.lang.String* sql)
	throws	*java.sql.*SQLException
public int[]	executeBatch	()
	throws	*java.sql.*SQLException
public *java.sql.*ResultSet	executeQuery	(*java.lang.String* sql)
	throws	*java.sql.*SQLException
public int	executeUpdate	(*java.lang.String* sql)
	throws	*java.sql.*SQLException
public *java.sql.*Connection	getConnection	()
	throws	*java.sql.*SQLException
public int	getFetchDirection	()
	throws	*java.sql.*SQLException

public int	getFetchSize	()
	throws	*java.sql*.**SQLException**
public int	getMaxFieldSize	()
	throws	*java.sql*.**SQLException**
public int	getMaxRows	()
	throws	*java.sql*.**SQLException**
public boolean	getMoreResults	()
	throws	*java.sql*.**SQLException**
public int	getQueryTimeout	()
	throws	*java.sql*.**SQLException**
public *java.sql*.ResultSet	getResultSet	()
	throws	*java.sql*.**SQLException**
public int	getResultSetConcurrency	()
	throws	*java.sql*.**SQLException**
public int	getResultSetType	()
	throws	*java.sql*.**SQLException**
public int	getUpdateCount	()
	throws	*java.sql*.**SQLException**
public *java.sql*.SQLWarning	getWarnings	()
	throws	*java.sql*.**SQLException**
public void	setCursorName	(*java.lang.String* name)
	throws	*java.sql*.**SQLException**
public void	setEscapeProcessing	(boolean enable)
	throws	*java.sql*.**SQLException**
public void	setFetchDirection	(int direction)
	throws	*java.sql*.**SQLException**
public void	setFetchSize	(int rows)
	throws	*java.sql*.**SQLException**
public void	setMaxFieldSize	(int max)
	throws	*java.sql*.**SQLException**
public void	setMaxRows	(int max)
	throws	*java.sql*.**SQLException**
public void	setQueryTimeout	(int seconds)
	throws	*java.sql*.**SQLException**

Interface java.sql.Struct

```
public abstract interface Struct
```

Struct represents standard mapping for an SQL structured type.

Methods

public *java.lang.Object*[]	getAttributes	()
	throws	*java.sql*.**SQLException**
public *java.lang.Object*[]	getAttributes	(*java.util*.Map map)
	throws	*java.sql*.**SQLException**
public *java.lang.String*	getSQLTypeName	()
	throws	*java.sql*.**SQLException**

Class java.sql.Date

```
public class Date
extends java.util.Date
```

Date represents a date in milliseconds since 1/1/1970:00:00:00 GMT, stored as a long. Some methods and constructors have been deprecated.

Constructor Method

public	Date	(long date)

Deprecated Constructor Method

public	**Date**	(int year, int month, int day)

Methods

public void	**setTime**	(long date)
public static *java.sql.*Date	**valueOf**	(*java.lang.String* s)
public *java.lang.String*	**toString**	()

Inherited from *java.util.*Date:
```
after, before, clone, compareTo, compareTo, equals, getDate, getDay,
getMonth, getTime, getTimezoneOffset, getYear, hashCode, parse,
setDate, setMonth, setYear, toGMTString, toLocaleString, UTC
```

Inherited from *java.lang.Object*:
```
finalize, getClass, notify, notifyAll, wait, wait, wait
```

DeprecatedMethods

public int	**getHours**	()
public int	**getMinutes**	()
public int	**getSeconds**	()
public void	**setHours**	()
public void	**setMinutes**	()
public void	**setSeconds**	()

Class java.sql. DriverManager

```
public class DriverManager
```

DriverManager manages a set of JDBC drivers. Some methods have been deprecated.

Methods

public static void	**deregisterDriver** throws	(*java.sql.*Driver driver) *java.sql.*SQLException
public static *java.sql.*Connection	**getConnection** throws	(*java.lang.String* url, *java.util.Properties* info) *java.sql.*SQLException
public static *java.sql.*Connection	**getConnection** throws	(*java.lang.String* url, *java.lang.String* user, *java.lang.String* password) *java.sql.*SQLException
public static *java.sql.*Connection	**getConnection** throws	(*java.lang.String* url) *java.sql.*SQLException
public static *java.sql.*Driver	**getDriver** throws	(*java.lang.String* url) *java.sql.*SQLException
public static *java.util.*Enumeration	**getDrivers**	()
public static int	**getLoginTimeout**	()
public static *java.io.PrintWriter*	**getLogWriter**	()
public static void	**println**	(*java.lang.String* message)
public static void	**registerDriver** throws	(*java.sql.*Driver driver) *java.sql.*SQLException
public static void	**setLoginTimeout**	(int seconds)
public static void	**setLogWriter**	(*java.io.PrintStream* out)

Inherited from *java.lang.Object*:
```
clone, equals, finalize, getClass, hashCode, notify, notifyAll, toString, wait,
wait, wait
```

Deprecated Methods

public static *java.io.PrintStream*	getLogStream	()
public static int	setLogStream	(*java.lang.String* url)

Class java.sql.DriverPropertyInfo

```
public class DriverPropertyInfo
```

DriverPropertiesInfo contains the driver properties used in creating connections.

Constructor Method

public	DriverPropertyInfo	(*java.lang.String* name, *java.lang.String* value)

Methods

Inherited from *java.lang.Object*:
```
clone, equals, finalize, getClass, hashCode, notify, notifyAll, toString, wait,
wait, wait
```

Fields

public *java.lang.String*[]	choices
public *java.lang.String*	description
public *java.lang.String*	name
public boolean	required
public *java.lang.String*	value

Class java.sql.Time

```
public class Time
extends java.sql.Date
```

Adds to the *java.util.Date* class the ability to parse and work with the JDBC escape syntax for time values. Also equates *java.util.Date* with SQL TIME values.

Constructor Methods

public	Time	(int hour, int minute, int second)
public	Time	(long time)

Methods

public void	setTime	(long time)
public *java.lang.String*	toString	()
public static *java.sql*.Time	valueOf	(*java.lang.String* s)

Inherited from *java.util.*Date:
```
after, before, clone, compareTo, compareTo, equals, getHours,
getMinutes, getSeconds, getTime, getTimezoneOffset, hashCode, parse,
setHours, setMinutes, setSeconds, toGMTString, toLocaleString, UTC
```

Inherited from *java.lang.Object*:
```
finalize, getClass, notify, notifyAll, wait, wait, wait
```

Deprecated Methods

public int	getDate	()
public int	getDay	()
public int	getMonth	()
public int	getYear	()
public void	setDate	(int i)
public void	setMonth	(int i)
public void	setYear	(int i)

Class java.sql.Timestamp

```
public class Timestamp
extends java.util.Date
```

Timestamp represents an SQL TIMESTAMP value. Some methods and constructors have been deprecated.

Constructor Methods

public	Timestamp	(long time)

Deprecated Constructor Methods

public	Time	(int year,
		int month,
		int date,
		int hour,
		int minute,
		int second,
		int nano)

Methods

public boolean	after	(java.sql.Timestamp ts)
public boolean	before	(java.sql.Timestamp ts)
public boolean	equals	(java.sql.Timestamp ts)
public boolean	equals	(java.lang.Object ts)
public int	getNanos	()
public void	setNanos	(int n)
public java.lang.String	toString	()
public static Timestamp	valueOf	(java.lang.String s)

Inherited from *java.util.*Date:

```
after, before, clone, compareTo, compareTo, getDate, getDay, getHours,
getMinutes, getMonth, getSeconds, getYear, hashCode, parse, setDate,
setHours, setMinutes, setMonth, setSeconds, setTime, setYear, toGMTString,
toLocaleString, UTC
```

Inherited from *java.lang.Object*:

```
finalize, getClass, notify, notifyAll, wait, wait, wait
```

Class java.sql.Types

```
public class Types
```

Types defines the constants used to identify generic SQL types.

Methods

Inherited from *java.lang.Object*:

```
clone, equals, finalize, getClass, hashCode, notify, notifyAll, toString,
wait, wait, wait
```

Fields

public static final int	ARRAY
public static final int	BIGINT
public static final int	BINARY
public static final int	BIT
public static final int	BLOB
public static final int	CHAR
public static final int	CLOB
public static final int	DATE
public static final int	DECIMAL
public static final int	DISTINCT
public static final int	DOUBLE
public static final int	FLOAT
public static final int	INTEGER
public static final int	JAVA_OBJECT
public static final int	LONGVARBINARY
public static final int	LONGVARCHAR
public static final int	NULL
public static final int	NUMERIC
public static final int	OTHER
public static final int	REAL
public static final int	REF
public static final int	SMALLINT
public static final int	STRUCT
public static final int	TIME
public static final int	TIMESTAMP
public static final int	TINYINT
public static final int	VARBINARY
public static final int	VARCHAR

Class java.sql.BatchUpdateException

```
public class BatchUpdate
extends java.sql.SQLException
```

Thrown when an error occurs during a batch update operation.

Constructor Methods

public	BatchUpdateException	()
public	BatchUpdateException	(int[] updateCounts)
public	BatchUpdateException	(*java.lang.String* reason, int[] updateCounts)
public	BatchUpdateException	(*java.lang.String* reason, *java.lang.String* SQLState, int[] updateCounts)
public	BatchUpdateException	(*java.lang.String* reason, *java.lang.String* SQLState, int vendorCode, int[] updateCounts)

Methods

public int[]	getUpdateCounts	()

Inherited from *java.sql.***SQLException**:
getErrorCode, getNextException, getSQLState, setNextException

Inherited from *java.lang.Throwable*:
fillInStackTrace, getLocalizedMessage, getMessage, printStackTrace,
printStackTrace, printStackTrace, toString

Inherited from *java.lang.Object*:
clone, equals, finalize, getClass, hashCode, notify, notifyAll, wait, wait,
wait

Class *java.sql.DataTruncation*

```
public class DataTruncation
extends java.sql.SQLWarning
```

DataTruncation is thrown when JDBC truncates a data value during a write, or reports a warning when JDBC truncates a data value during a read.

Constructor Methods

public	`DataTruncation`	(int index, boolean parameter, boolean read, int dataSize, int transferSize)

Methods

public int	`getDataSize`	()
public int	`getIndex`	()
public boolean	`getParameter`	()
public boolean	`getRead`	()
public int	`getTransferSize`	()

Inherited from *java.sql.*SQLWarning:
   `getNextWarning, setNextWarning`

Inherited from *java.sql.*SQLException:
   `getErrorCode, getNextException, getSQLState, setNextException`

Inherited from *java.lang.Throwable*:
   `fillInStackTrace, getLocalizedMessage, getMessage, printStackTrace,`
   `printStackTrace, printStackTrace, toString`

Inherited from *java.lang.Object*:
   `clone, equals, finalize, getClass, hashCode, notify, notifyAll, wait, wait,`
   `wait`

Class *java.sql.SQLException*

```
public class DataTruncation
extends java.lang.SQLException
```

SQLException is thrown following a database access error, returning information about it.

Constructor Methods

public	`SQLException`	()
public	`SQLException`	(*java.lang.String* reason)
public	`SQLException`	(*java.lang.String* reason, *java.lang.String* SQLState)
public	`SQLException`	(*java.lang.String* reason, *java.lang.String* SQLState, int vendorCode)

Methods

public int	getErrorCode	()
public *java.sql.*SQLException	getNextException	()
public *java.lang.String*	getSQLState	()
public void	setNextException	(*java.lang.*SQLException)

Inherited from *java.lang.Throwable*:
> fillInStackTrace, getLocalizedMessage, getMessage, printStackTrace, printStackTrace, printStackTrace, toString

Inherited from *java.lang.Object*:
> clone, equals, finalize, getClass, hashCode, notify, notifyAll, wait, wait, wait

Class java.sql. SQLWarning

```
public class SQLWarning
                 extends                         java.sql.SQLException
```

SQLWarning returns information about database access warnings, attached to the object invoking the warning.

Constructor Methods

public	SQLWarning	()
public	SQLWarning	(*java.lang.String* reason)
public	SQLWarning	(*java.lang.String* reason, *java.lang.String* SQLState)
public	SQLWarning	(*java.lang.String* reason, *java.lang.String* SQLState, int vendorCode)

Methods

public *java.sql.*SQLWarning	getNextWarning	()
public void	setNextWarning	(*java.sql.*SQLWarning w)

Inherited from *java.sql.*SQLException:
> getErrorCode, getNextException, getSQLState, setNextException

Inherited from *java.lang.Throwable*:
> fillInStackTrace, getLocalizedMessage, getMessage, printStackTrace, printStackTrace, printStackTrace, toString

Inherited from *java.lang.Object*:
> clone, equals, finalize, getClass, hashCode, notify, notifyAll, wait, wait, wait

Support and Errata

One of the most irritating things about any programming book is when you find that bit of code you've just spent an hour typing simply doesn't work. You check it a hundred times to see if you've set it up correctly and then you notice the spelling mistake in the variable name on the book page. Of course, you can blame the authors for not taking enough care and testing the code, the editors for not doing their job properly, or the proofreaders for not being eagle-eyed enough, but this doesn't get around the fact that mistakes do happen.

We try hard to ensure no mistakes sneak out into the real world, but we can't promise that this book is 100% error free. What we can do is offer the next best thing by providing you with immediate support and feedback from experts who have worked on the book and try to ensure that future editions eliminate these gremlins. The following section will take you step by step through the process of posting errata to our web site to get that help. The sections that follow, therefore, are:

- ➤ Wrox Developer Membership
- ➤ Finding a list of existing errata on the web site
- ➤ Adding your own errata to the existing list
- ➤ What happens to your errata once you've posted it (why doesn't it appear immediately)?

There is also a section covering how to e-mail a question for technical support. This comprises:

- ➤ What your e-mail should include
- ➤ What happens to your e-mail once it has been received by us

So that you only need view information relevant to yourself, we ask that you register as a Wrox Developer Member. This is a quick and easy process that will save you time in the long-run. If you are already a member, just update membership to include this book.

Wrox Developer Membership

To get your *free* Wrox Developer Membership click on Membership in the navigation bar of our home site – http://www.wrox.com. This is shown in the following screenshot:

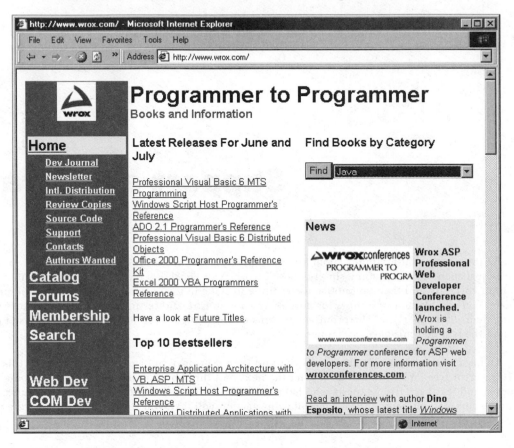

Then, on the next screen (not shown), click on New User. This will display a form. Fill in the details on the form and submit the details using the Send Form button at the bottom. Before you can say 'The best read books come in Wrox Red' you will get the following screen:

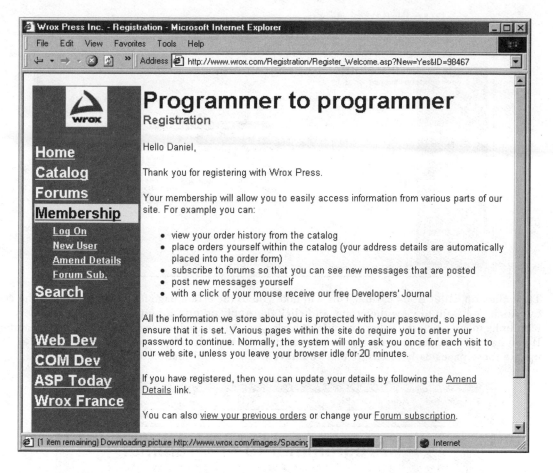

Finding an Errata on the Web Site

Before you send in a query, you might be able to save time by finding the answer to your problem on our web site – http:\\www.wrox.com.

Each book we publish has its own page and its own errata sheet. You can get to any book's page by clicking on Support from the left hand side navigation bar.

From this page you can locate any book's errata page on our site. Select your book from the pop-up menu and click on it.

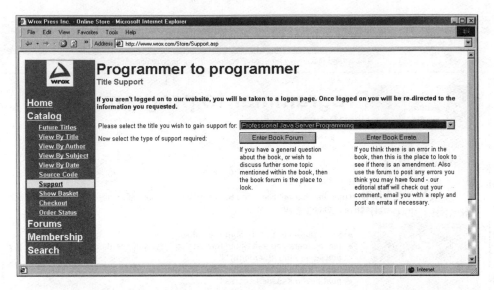

Then click on Enter Book Errata. This will take you to the errata page for the book. Select the criteria by which you want to view the errata, and click the Apply criteria... button. This will provide you with links to specific errata. For an initial search, you are advised to view the errata by page numbers. If you have looked for an error previously, then you may wish to limit your search using dates. We update these pages daily to ensure that you have the latest information on bugs and errors.

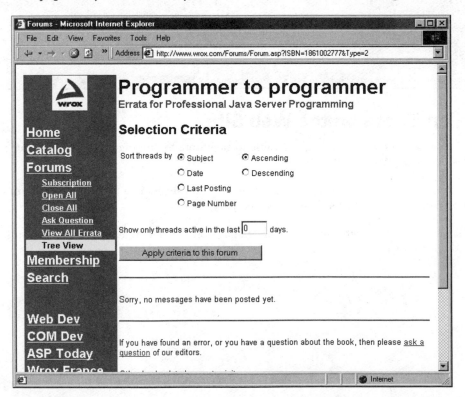

Adding an Errata to the Sheet Yourself

It's always possible that you may find your error is not listed, in which case you can enter details of the fault yourself. It might be anything from a spelling mistake to a faulty piece of code in the book. Sometimes you'll find useful hints that aren't really errors on the listing. By entering errata you may save another reader hours of frustration, and of course, you will be helping us provide even higher quality information. We're very grateful for this sort of advice and feedback. You can enter errata using the 'ask a question of our editors' link at the bottom of the errata page. Click on this link and you will get a form on which to post your message.

Fill in the subject box, and then type your message in the space provided on the form. Once you have done this, click on the Post Now button at the bottom of the page. The message will be forwarded to our editors. They'll then test your submission and check that the error exists, and that the suggestions you make are valid. Then your submission, together with a solution, is posted on the site for public consumption. Obviously this stage of the process can take a day or two, but we will endeavor to get a fix up sooner than that.

E-mail Support

If you wish to directly query a problem in the book with an expert who knows the book in detail then e-mail support@wrox.com, with the title of the book and the last four numbers of the ISBN in the subject field of the e-mail. A typical email should include the following things:

We won't send you junk mail. We need the details to save your time and ours. If we need to replace a disk or CD we'll be able to get it to you straight away. When you send an e-mail it will go through the following chain of support:

Customer Support

Your message is delivered to one of our customer support staff who are the first people to read it. They have files on most frequently asked questions and will answer anything general immediately. They answer general questions about the book and the web site.

Editorial

Deeper queries are forwarded to the technical editor responsible for that book. They have experience with the programming language or particular product and are able to answer detailed technical questions on the subject. Once an issue has been resolved, the editor can post the errata to the web site.

The Authors

Finally, in the unlikely event that the editor can't answer your problem, s/he will forward the request to the author. We try to protect the author from any distractions from writing. However, we are quite happy to forward specific requests to them. All Wrox authors help with the support on their books. They'll mail the customer and the editor with their response, and again all readers should benefit.

What We Can't Answer

Obviously with an ever-growing range of books and an ever-changing technology base, there is an increasing volume of data requiring support. While we endeavor to answer all questions about the book, we can't answer bugs in your own programs that you've adapted from our code. So, while you might have loved the help desk systems in our Active Server Pages book, don't expect too much sympathy if you cripple your company with a live adaptation you customized from Chapter 12. But do tell us if you're especially pleased with the routine you developed with our help.

How to Tell Us Exactly What You Think

We understand that errors can destroy the enjoyment of a book and can cause many wasted and frustrated hours, so we seek to minimize the distress that they can cause.

You might just wish to tell us how much you liked or loathed the book in question. Or you might have ideas about how this whole process could be improved. In which case you should e-mail feedback@wrox.com. You'll always find a sympathetic ear, no matter what the problem is. Above all you should remember that we do care about what you have to say and we will do our utmost to act upon it.

Index

A

Abstract Windowing Toolkit
  see AWT
AbstractEntry class (net.jini.core.entry
package), 678
access control list
  see ACL
Access log, 902
accessing data, 553
ACLs (access control lists), 527
ActionListener interface, 229
ActivationDataFlavor class (javax.activation
package), 997
Active Server Pages
  see ASP
AddModule directive (JServ, Linux), 893
addNotify method
  AWT toolkit, 104
add-on functionality
  JServ, 909
  JSP, 911
  page compilation servlets, 909
Address class (javax.mail package), 1007
AJP (Apache JServ Protocol), 879
aliases, 213, 217
aliasing servlets
  JServ, 888
AlreadyExistsException class (businesslogic
package), 398
Apache JServ
  see JServ
Apache JServ Protocol
  see AJP
ApJServAction directive, 893
ApJServMountCopy directive, 896
applets, 227
  communication with servlets, 228
  event handling, 230
  servlets invoked from, 227
  user interfaces, 153, 229
application architecture, 387
  logical partitioning, 389

physical partitioning, 388
application assembler, 585
application implicit object (JSP), 129
application server portability, 578
Array interface (java.sql package), 1064
ASP (Active Server Pages), 17
assembly descriptors, 616
asymmetric/public-key ciphers, 834
Attribute interface (javax.naming.directory
package), 981
AttributeInUseException interface
(javax.naming.directory package), 988
AttributeModificationException interface
(javax.naming.directory package), 989
Attributes interface (javax.naming.directory
package), 981
AuthenticationException class
(javax.naming package), 964
AuthenticationFailedException class
(javax.mail package), 1020
AuthenticationNotSupportedException class
(javax.naming package), 964
Authenticator class (javax.mail package),
1007
automatic mode (JServ), 897
AWT (Abstract Windowing Toolkit), 103

B

bar charts, 115
BasicAttribute interface
(javax.naming.directory package), 983
BasicAttributes interface
(javax.naming.directory package), 984
BDOs (Business Data Objects), 553
bean managed persistence, 601
bean producers, 583
binary data, 103
BinaryRefAddr class (javax.naming
package), 957
Binding class (javax.naming package), 957